THE INSIDER'S GUIDE
TO CLASSICAL RECORDINGS

THE INSIDER'S GUIDE TO CLASSICAL RECORDINGS

From the Host of *The Record Shelf*, a Highly Opinionated, Irreverent, and Selective Guide to What's Good and What's Not

Sixth Revised and Expanded Edition

Jim Svejda

PRIMA PUBLISHING

PRIMA PUBLISHING and colophon are registered trademarks of Prima Communications, Inc.

Library of Congress Cataloging-in-Publication Data

Svejda, Jim.
    The insider's guide to classical recordings: from the host of The Record Shelf, a highly opinionated, irreverent, and selective guide to what's good and what's not / Jim Svejda.—[6th ed.]
      p. cm.
    Previous ed. published under title: The Record Shelf guide to classical CDs and audiocassettes. 5th rev. and expanded ed. c1996.
    Includes index.
    ISBN 0-7615-1711-1
    1. Sound recordings—Reviews. 2. Audiocassettes—Reviews. 3. Compact discs—reviews. 4. Music—Discography. I. Svejda, Jim. Record shelf guide to classical CDs and audiocassettes. II. Record shelf. III. Title. IV. Title: Irreverent guide to classical recordings.
ML156.9.S86 1998
780.26'6—dc21   98-41694
                                                            CIP
                                                            MN

99 00 01 02 03 04 BB 10 9 8 7 6 5 4 3 2 1
Printed in the United Stated of America

How to Order

Single copies may be ordered from Prima Publishing, P.O. Box 1260BK, Rocklin, CA 95677; telephone (916) 632-4400. Quantity discounts are also available. On your letterhead, include information concerning the intended use of the books and the number of books you wish to purchase.

Visit us online at www.primalife.com

For Ben, who made me do it;
Kevin, who should have done it;
and Cathy, for all the rest.

Foreword

I admit that I am not impartial when it comes to Jim Svejda. Long before I met him, I was an ardent fan of his radio program, *The Record Shelf.* His musical taste, his sardonic wit, his urbanity, and his unique connection with his listeners I find unequaled. And I am not alone. I have since learned—not from him—that of some three thousand letters received each month by KUSC, fifteen hundred are for Jim.

Some years ago, after conducting the Minnesota Orchestra, I had made dinner reservations with some musician friends. I couldn't budge them. They refused to go until they finished listening to that week's *Record Shelf.* To my surprise and ensuing delight, Jim began the program with a lusty Teutonic male choir, developed a comparison with my Sing-A-Longs, and concluded by featuring my oboe and English horn recordings from 1947 to 1951. Over the air, Jim anointed me his favorite oboe–English horn player of all time. The compliment was better than dessert.

When we finally did meet, my impressions were more than confirmed and we became instant friends. He truly loves music, being a former oboe player himself. The breadth of his knowledge is extraordinary. He thoroughly understands every kind of music and every conductor, composition, and nuance of performance, from early jazz through the entire classical repertoire. His taste is consummate; his integrity, unswayed by today's musical hype.

Sure, I am prejudiced, but so will you be after referring to this book for your recording needs. You may not always agree, but believe me, you'll *never be wrong* listening to Jim Svejda.

MITCH MILLER

Acknowledgments

This book grew out of the comparative survey programs that are a regular feature of my weekly radio program, *The Record Shelf,* a production of KUSC, the radio station of the University of Southern California. I would like to thank Brenda Pennell and my friends and colleagues at KUSC for their many kindnesses and indulgences. To my closest musical friends, Kevin Mostyn, Robert Goldfarb, and Henry Fogel, no amount of thanks can adequately repay what I owe them. I also owe a special debt of gratitude to Dr. Christian Rutland, without whose encouragement this book might never have been undertaken, and to Dr. Karl-Heinrich Vogelbach, without whose timely intervention it might never have been completed. I am singularly lucky in having such a tolerant, music-loving publisher as Ben Dominitz, whose enthusiasm seems to know no bounds. I'm grateful for my tennis partners Ed and Pat Self, Cathy Crockett, and Bill Kraft for keeping me in such excellent shape, for my friends at the Pacific Jewish Center (especially the Altschulers, the Genuths, the Magilnicks, the Medveds, the Schechters, and Harry Medved) for their warmth and hospitality, and for Kate Zeng for prodigious feats of Duck-sitting.

A Note on the Sixth Edition

Since the publication of the fifth edition two years ago, it has become even clearer than before that sooner or later, *everything* is going to be released on CD. In addition to landmark series like the Testament reissues of all the recordings by the legendary Hollywood String Quartet (see page 354), other adventurous companies like Pearl, Biddulph, and Preiser are constantly unearthing buried treasures from the past. Moreover, wonderful bargains continue to be found on those two-for-one sets from Philips, London, Deutsche Grammophon, and the other major labels; in fact, the recycled recordings tend to be far more interesting and musically worthy than the newer mainline releases. In which regard, two labels continue to set new standards for the industry: Chandos, for its superlative recordings of generally unusual repertoire, and Naxos, for making an astonishing amount of material available in good-to-superior performances at an extremely reasonable price. If this edition of the *Guide* continues to look, at times, like a Chandos/Naxos catalogue, then that's because they're consistently delivering the goods *and long may they wave*. Dire—and largely preposterous—predictions continue to be made about the health of the classical recording industry. A stroll through the isles of any well-stocked store will reveal that in terms of volume and quality of selection, things have never been better.

Introduction

Along with those of Dr. Johnson ("Were it not for imagination, Sir, a man would be as happy in the arms of a chambermaid as of a Duchess"), Georg Chrisoph Lichtenberg ("Reading means borrowing"), and François, Duc La Rochefoucauld ("Love diminishes the lesser passions and augments the great, as the wind snuffs out the candle and ignites the flame"), the aphorisms that did the most to shape my youthful character were those that came from my paternal grandmother. My grandmother was a God-fearing woman—and the feeling was undoubtedly mutual. Of all the many maxims I imbibed at her flinty knee—including the great Czech beatitude "Blessed are they who expect nothing, for they shall not be disappointed"—the one that made the most lasting impression was the rueful suggestion that "There's no such thing as a bargain and *everything* costs more than it's worth." A quick browse through the bins of any well-stocked CD store will suggest that she may have had a point. Although they are actually cheaper to produce than the late (and, in some quarters, still greatly lamented) LP, CDs, for all their convenience and durability, are becoming a frightfully expensive investment. While some stores have a no-questions-asked return policy, young or inexperienced listeners can have their views permanently distorted by a feeble or senselessly perverse interpretation. Moreover, there are so many choices (in a recent edition of *Opus,* over eighty available versions of Beethoven's Fifth alone), how do you know that you've gotten the best possible return on that hard-earned investment, unless you've sampled a fair number of the alternatives beforehand?

That is what this book was intended to help you do.

Unlike the invaluable *Penguin Guide, The Insider's Guide to Classical Recordings* does not pretend to be all-inclusive or objective. (Not that *they're* all that objective, either. For instance, in their one- to three-asterisk rating system, you can safely deduct from one-half to a full asterisk for any recording featuring a British composer, conductor, performer, or recording company, or any recording featuring liner notes by anyone associated with that admittedly finest of all music magazines, *The Gramophone.*) Although *The Insider's Guide to Classical Recordings* has grown with each edition, many things continue to slip through the cracks, while as many others have been *shoved* through them. Except for its indisputable giants, the Baroque still remains sparsely represented, as does the music of our time: The former, because of my unshakable conviction that life is too short for the virtually interchangeable sewing-machine music of the Torelli-Corelli-Nardini-Spumoni-Linguini school; the latter, because what, in all the baffling variety of music being written today, is actually worth hearing remains anybody's guess. In others words, the bulk of the book is devoted to music that people actually tend to *listen* to, which is to say, music produced from the middle of the eighteenth century to roughly the midway point of our own.

Following the pattern of the comparative survey programs that have been a regular feature of *The Record Shelf* from its beginning, the *Guide* attempts to say something cogent, enlightening, or amusing about the works themselves, and then blithely tell you which of the many available recordings you should actually go out and buy. Needless to say, this involves a measure of arrogance on my part—for which I make no apology—and an element of risk on the part of the reader. Actually, since the book itself isn't *all* that much more expensive than one full-priced CD, you'd still be well ahead of the game if it did nothing more than warn you off a single Nikolaus Harnoncourt recording or any of the several versions of the Gorecki *Third Symphony*. Besides, it can always be put to other uses. (As the German composer Max Reger wrote in a famous blast to a critic: "I am seated in the smallest room in my house. Your review is in front of me. Shortly, it will be behind me.")

As to the criteria that were used in arriving at the final choices, they were surprisingly simple. In the first place, what *didn't* count was the reputation of the performer. Young, unknown musicians have made some astonishing recordings over the years, just as famous—yea, verily, *legendary*—musicians can on occasion perform like pigs. Nor was recorded sound much of a consideration. Never having been an audiophile, I will automatically opt for a bad-sounding recording of a great performance over a brilliant recording of a very good one. (People listening to the sound of their play-back system instead of what's being *played* should seriously begin thinking about finding another hobby.)

What *was* taken into consideration and what would seem to bind most of these recommendations together was the presence, in one way or another, of something that is becoming all too rare in the musical world: an instantly recognizable musical personality. Increasingly, as the late twentieth-century obsession with mechanical perfection continues—aided and abetted by the wonders of editable recording tape—commercial recordings have had less and less to say in musical and human terms. With a few notable exceptions, the world's major orchestras are losing their individuality (jet-set Maestros have turned them into something with all the character of airport terminals), while the conductors themselves—again with a few notable exceptions—are becoming ever more bland and faceless, like the Swiss characters in a spy novel.

For better or worse then, this *Guide* has become a celebration of musical individuality. Fortunately, the reissue of many recordings from the 1950s and '60s, when such wonderfully individual musicians as Beecham, Björling, Furtwängler, Klemperer, Reiner, Rubinstein, and Walter were still active, is a bittersweet reminder—as Mrs. Fisher put it in *Enchanted April*—"of better times, and better men," while the emergence of younger musicians with real personalities offers some reason for hope. The *Guide* constantly strives to sift the personal, the unique, and the truly memorable from the dull, the routine, and the mundane, selecting, wherever possible, the *one* recording of a given work that seems the most exciting and individual currently available. On occasion, this has meant recommending two possible choices for a given work, not because I have any trouble making up my mind, but because there may more than one equally exciting and individual interpretation that belongs in everyone's library.

More than any other edition of the *Guide,* this one reflects those two inevitable by-products of the coming of age of the compact disc: the disheartening, increasingly profligate use of the deletions ax and the heartening emergence of the bargain-basement label. Although every effort has been made to keep the *Guide* as current as possible, favorite recordings continue to vanish without warning—often to turn up in some other form. That other form, more often than not, is the second exploitation label—EMI Encore, RCA Silver Seal, Philips Concert Classics, DG Galleria—which frequently offers superb performances in perfectly adequate sound at something less than half the cost of a full-priced CD. Even more encouraging is the arrival of labels such as Naxos, which present new digital recordings by lesser-known orchestras and artists at an equally reasonable price. Wherever warranted, these recordings have been enthusiastically recommended throughout the *Guide*—needless to say, for their *musical* as opposed to their economic virtues, since there are, *pace* Grandma, some bargains that no one can afford.

I continue to hope that you will find what follows useful in putting your recording library together, that it will help save you some money and make some for me (Dr. Johnson did say that "No man but a blockhead ever wrote except for money"), and that you will pardon its errors and excesses, which are wholly my own.

Adam, Adolphe-Charles

(1803–1856)

Giselle (complete ballet)

Orchestra of the Royal Opera House, Covent Garden, Bonynge.
  London 433007-2 [CD].

The fame of the French composer Adolphe Adam continues to hang on a dangerously slender thread. Apparently, though, the thread is made of something with the tensile strength of piano wire, since *Giselle,* the oldest Romantic ballet to retain a place in the standard repertoire, shows no sign of losing any of its gooey appeal. (I once saw a performance of this tenacious warhorse at the Bolshoi in Moscow. The dancing, costumes, and scenery were beautiful, but the auditorium was badly overheated, the audience fetid, and somewhere in the middle of the first act I managed to fall asleep.)

If this innocent, slightly oversweetened bonbon is to your taste—although, at well over two hours, "bonbon" is hardly the appropriate metaphor—then you can't possibly do better than Richard Bonynge's sumptuous London recording. Over the years, Bonynge has taken a good deal of undeserved heat from critics who have suggested that he has gotten where he is *solely* because of his wife. (Many still refer to him, churlishly, as "Mr. Joan Sutherland.") A recording like this one should wring the neck of that honking canard. The performance is both warm and richly detailed, with superb playing from the Covent Garden Orchestra. But even more to the point, this is an engagingly *theatrical* interpretation: so much so that, for the first time ever, listening to old *Giselle,* I didn't nod off once.

While not as consistently inspired as *Giselle, Le Corsaire* has many fine and memorable moments and is also brilliantly served by Bonynge, who this time conducts the English Chamber Orchestra (London 430286 [CD]).

Adams, John   (1947–)

The Chairman Dances; Two Fanfares, and so forth

**San Francisco Symphony, De Waart. Nonesuch 79144-2 [CD],
79144-4 [T].**

For anyone who finds Minimalism to be the dim-witted musical rip-off that
it probably is, the music of John Adams presents a problem. Unlike Philip Glass,
Steve Reich, Terry Riley, and the rest, Adams is a composer of demonstrable abilities and considerable charm, and this attractive Nonesuch recording will provide
an excellent introduction to his humane and refreshingly *human* Minimalist
idiom.

While the controversial opera *Nixon in China* (Nonesuch 79177-2 [CD],
79177-4 [T]), his most celebrated work to date, may be too much of a not-so-
good thing, the *Chairman Dances* are pert, lively, and never wear out their welcome, and the five-minute "Short Ride in a Fast Machine" may be the most
amusing and immediately appealing Minimalist composition written thus far.

De Waart and the San Franciscans are consistently alert and committed, and
the recorded sound is close to ideal.

Addinsell, Richard   (1904–1977)

*M*usic of Addinsell

**Martin, Elms, pianos; BBC Concert Orchestra, Alwyn. Marco Polo
8.223732 [CD].**

Along with the superbly mushy *Warsaw Concerto* from the World War II
tear-jerker *Dangerous Moonlight*—handsomely served these days by Mischa
Dichter and Sir Neville Marriner on Philips (411123-2 [CD])—Richard Addinsell
was the composer of much memorable film music, from the unforgettable 1939
version of *Goodbye, Mr. Chips* to the classic Marilyn Monroe–Laurence Olivier
costume comedy, *The Prince and the Showgirl.*

The lovely Addinsell installment of Marco Polo's British Light Music
Series combines some of the finest of the composer's screen inspirations with
concert items like the three-movement *Smokey Mountains Concerto,* a work of
considerable imagination and charm. The performances by the BBC Concert

Orchestra, led by Kenneth Alwyn, are among the most accomplished in the series thus far, making this yet another indispensable release.

Admirers of the Oscar-winning score that Addinsell's near contemporary Brian Easdale wrote for *The Red Shoes* will enjoy Alwyn's spirited, colorful version of *The Red Shoes Ballet*—conducted in the film by Sir Thomas Beecham—on a Silva America CD (SIL 1028) that also features suites from other British scores, including *Conquest of the Air* by Sir Arthur Bliss, *Attack on the Iron Coast* and *The Two-Headed Spy* by Gerard Schurmann (who supplied the magnificent orchestrations for *Lawrence of Arabia*), and Vaughan Williams's *Coastal Command*.

Albéniz, Isaac   (1860–1909)

*I*béria (Suite for Piano, 4 books)

De Larrocha, piano. London 417887-2 [CD].

Every so often, a work becomes so completely identified with a specific performer that the interpreter and the thing being interpreted become all but indissoluble. A half century ago, Fritz Kreisler's version of the Brahms Violin Concerto, Wanda Landowska's *Goldberg Variations,* and the Furtwängler *Eroica* all existed on that remote Olympian summit; so, too, for more than three decades now, has Alicia de Larrocha's continuously growing version of that lexicon of modern Spanish music, Isaac Albéniz's *Iberia.*

In her latest and finest recording of the Suite, De Larrocha probes more deeply, finds more color and drama, and somehow infuses *Iberia* with a rhythmic subtlety and life that even her earlier versions lacked. London's warmly detailed recorded sound is a worthy frame for a performance that will probably never lose its bloom and spontaneity.

The best available recording of the skillful orchestral suite arranged by the composer's friend Enrique Arbós—Ravel was contemplating an arrangement of his own; when he learned of Arbós's project, he abandoned the idea and wrote *Bolero* instead—is the highly colored, meticulously performed version by the Philharmonia Orchestra conducted by Yan-Pascal Tortelier on Chandos (CHAN 8904 [CD]).

Music for Guitar

Bream, Guitar. RCA 09026-61608-2 [CD],
09026-61608-4 [T].

Williams, guitar. CBS Sony Classical MK 36679 [CD].

Here are two of the most enjoyable recordings of Albéniz's music, played on the archetypal Spanish instrument. While John Williams is at his flawless best in his *Echoes of Spain* album, projecting the individual character of each of these vivid miniatures with uncanny grace and sensitivity, Julian Bream has never been better than in his *Music of Spain* album, his own favorite of the many recordings he has made. The playing is bewitching, while the recorded sound is almost unbelievably lifelike. ·

Albert, Eugen d' (1864–1932)

Piano Concertos (2)

Lane, piano; BBC Scottish Symphony, Francis. Hyperion CDA 66747 [CD].

Born in Glasgow of a French father and a German (though some historians claim, English) mother—"Unfortunately, I studied for a considerable period in that land of fogs, but during that time I learned absolutely nothing"—the diminutive, largely self-taught Eugen d'Albert, the "Little Giant" of European concert halls, recreated himself in Germany, where in the early 1880s he became a pupil of Franz Liszt. "Albertus Magnus," as Liszt called him, would become the most celebrated pianist of his generation, especially famous for his interpretations of Beethoven, Liszt, and Bach. By the turn of the century he allowed his technique to collapse, preferring to devote himself to composition. While he considered himself an operatic composer—the powerful and engrossing *Tiefland,* the seventh of his twenty operas, is occasionally revived in Germany and has been recorded several times, most successfully by Eurodisc (7797-2-RG [CD]) in a production starring the late Rudolf Schock—d'Albert is best remembered for his piano music, including many character and genre pieces and a pair of predictably daunting concertos.

Released as the ninth volume of Hyperion's Romantic Piano Concerto Series, d'Albert's B Minor Piano Concerto is an impressive forty-five-minute fusion of lyric grace and barnstorming virtuosity, made all the more impressive by the fact that its composer was barely twenty years old. The E Major Concerto from 1893 is more compact and controlled, though memorable themes and excitement abound. On the basis of this, Piers Lane is a virtuoso of considerable stature, either thundering or poetic as the music demands. As in every installment of this series, the recorded sound is wonderfully lifelike and the documentation is first rate.

Albinoni, Tommaso (1671–1750)

Adagio for Strings and Organ

I Musici. Philips 410606-2 [CD], 410606-4 [T].

One of the minor tragedies of musical history is that Tommaso Albinoni had more money than he knew what to do with. The son of a wealthy Venetian paper merchant who described himself proudly as a "dilettante Veneto," Albinoni was never forced to earn his living as a musician, and more's the pity. Had he been made to work a bit harder at the craft for which he was so perfectly suited, he might well have become one of the giants of the Italian Baroque, instead of the tantalizing "What If?" curiosity he remains today.

Although he was the composer of numerous instrumental concertos and nearly fifty operas, Albinoni is known primarily through the arrangements of his music made by his German admirer Johann Sebastian Bach and through the well-known *Adagio for Strings and Organ,* skillfully concocted by the modern Italian musicologist Remo Giazotto.

As Baroque confections go, the Albinoni *Adagio* is very nearly as popular as Pachelbel's equally high-cholesterol *Kanon* and has been recorded almost as frequently. I Musici gives the piece one of those typically aristocratic yet meltingly lyrical performances that neither cheapens the music nor robs it of emotional impact. The twenty-year-old recorded sound remains impressive on both the CD and the tape, and the Bach and Handel concertos (to say nothing of the Pachelbel *Kanon*) that fill out the collection make this one of the more attractive Baroque albums on the market.

Concertos cinque (12) for 1 or 2 oboes and strings, Op. 9

Holliger, oboe; Ayo, violin; I Musici. Philips 456333-2 [CD].

When the thought of hearing yet another Vivaldi concerto fills you with an irresistible urge to strangle the cat, turn to any one of these enchanting works, release the beast, and relax. Many Baroque aficionados rate the best Albinoni concertos with the best of Vivaldi's, and this generously packed two-disc set will help explain why. These are warm, generous, open-throated works, bursting with lyrical inventiveness and the sheer joy of creation. Heinz Holliger has never made a finer recording, and with I Musici in top form and the modest Philips Duo price tag, the set is a genuine bargain.

Albrechtsberger, Johann Georg (1736–1809)

Concertos (2) for Jew's Harp, Mandora, and Orchestra

Mayr, Jew's harp; Munich Chamber Orchestra, Stadlmair. Orfeo C-035821.

Walk into any bar in the world at any time of the day or night and suggest that *anyone* is the world's greatest conductor, pianist, violinist, or cellist and you're bound to get an argument. On the other hand, among devotees of the oft-misunderstood and much-maligned Jew's harp, only one name need do: the redoubtable Fritz Mayr, who is the Heifetz, Casals, Horowitz—take your pick—of his chosen instrument. I have never had the pleasure of hearing Herr Mayr in person or even of seeing a photograph of the man; I would dearly love to see what his dedication to his art has done to his bicuspids. Listening to Mayr perform, one is painfully reminded of David Niven's description of the dental malformations of the producer Darryl Zanuck, who, the actor alleged, "could eat an apple through a tennis racket."

These two Jew's harp concertos by Beethoven's principal teacher are all the loonier because they were written as more or less serious works. Mayr twangs and doinks magnificently through both, and one can only hope that he and the admirable Munich Chamber Orchestra will soon get around to the five or six *other* such works that Albrechtsberger is alleged to have composed.

Alfvén, Hugo (1872–1960)

Midsommarvaka; Symphony No. 2.

Stockholm Philharmonic, Järvi. BIS CD 385 [CD].

Any investigation of the still strangely unexplored riches of modern Swedish music should begin with the major works of Hugo Alfvén, whose *Midsommarvaka*—an utterly delectable Swedish meatball variously known as the "Midsummer Vigil" and the "Swedish Rhapsody No. 1"—made its composer an international celebrity in the years immediately before the First World War. While Alfvén never managed to duplicate the popular success of this enchanting trifle, his five symphonies, written between 1896 and 1952, are all important and appealing works, especially the Second Symphony of 1899.

Predictably, Neeme Järvi proves to be an ideal advocate of this warm and instantly approachable music. This version of *Midsommarvaka* is easily the finest that is currently available, while the performance of the Symphony is even more impressive still, sounding for much of the time like early Sibelius without the static basses or rough edges.

The CD has superb performances and strikingly lifelike recorded sound.

Alkan, Charles-Henri Valentin (1813–1888)

Piano Music

Hamelin, piano. Hyperion CDA 66794 [CD].

Ringeissen, piano. Harmonia Mundi HMA 190927 [CD].

Mustonen, piano. London 433055-2 [CD].

The eldest of the five musical brothers Morhange, who all went by the same assumed name, Charles-Henri Valentin Alkan was one of the most colorful of the early Romantic musicians. A friend of Chopin and Liszt, both of whom admired his darkly flamboyant, harmonically adventurous music, he was a Jew who remained strictly observant until his death (there is no evidence to support the legend that he was fatally crushed by a bookcase that contained the heavy volumes of the *Talmud*). Alkan became increasingly misanthropic with the passage of years, rarely leaving the Paris apartment where he maintained a large menagerie of exotic animals, including a chimpanzee and an emotionally disturbed nephew. As he frequently disappeared for long periods—nothing is known of his activities from 1838 to 1844, and the entire decade of the 1860s is a virtual blank—and published his work on a very sporadic basis, his startling originality would not be fully appreciated until the latter decades of the twentieth century.

Until Sony Classical reissues Raymond Lewenthal's pathbreaking (and vastly entertaining) Alkan series, including the bizarre, wonderfully morbid *Marcia funebre sulla morta d'un papagallo*—an 1859 funeral march for a pet parrot that contains astonishing pre-echoes of Mahler's *Das Lied von der Erde*—the three albums listed here will provide an eye-opening entrée into Alkan's peculiar and fascinating world. The best place to begin is with the brilliant Marc-André Hamelin's second Hyperion album, which includes the *Grande sonata* of 1847. Subtitled *Les Quatre Ages,* this incredible four-movement work is structured to represent four successive decades in a man's life—his twenties, thirties, forties, and fifties—each movement becoming gradually slower. Bernard Ringeissen's Harmonia Mundi album surveys some of the most demonically difficult Alkan pieces, including the aptly named *Scherzo diabolico,* while Olli Mustonen's version of the poetic, generally introspective Op. 25 *Preludes* is one of the loveliest Alkan albums yet made.

Marco Polo, which has promised a complete survey of the composer's equally provocative chamber music, has launched its series handsomely with a well-played, well-recorded album (8.223383 [CD]) devoted to three important, highly individual works: the Piano Trio in G Minor, the *Sonata de concert* for cello and piano, and the hair-raising *Grand duo concertante* for piano and violin.

Allegri, Gregorio   (1582–1652)

Miserere

(see Palestrina)

Alwyn, William (1905–1985)

Autumn Legend for English Horn and Orchestra; *Lyra Angelica* (concerto) for Harp and Orchestra; *Pastoral Fantasia* for Viola and Orchestra; *Tragic Interlude* for Two Horns, Timpani, and Strings

> Soloists, City of London Sinfonia, Hickox. Chandos CHAN 9065 [CD].

> Symphony No. 4; *Elizabethan Dances; Festival March.* Chandos CHAN 8902 [CD].

For anyone with even a passing interest in twentieth-century English music, Chandos's brilliant and courageous series devoted to the major works of William Alwyn must be counted among the most exciting recording projects of the last decade. A near contemporary of Britten, Walton, and Tippett, Alwyn never achieved anything like their celebrity, for reasons that aren't that difficult to explain. On the surface, his music seems to have less in the way of a readily recognizable personality (to say nothing of instantly memorable tunes), and his preference for established forms—the symphony, the concerto, the string quartet—and traditional harmonic language might create the impression of a composer with nothing new or original to say.

On closer examination—and his music absolutely *requires* repeated hearings to make its points—Alwyn emerges as one of the most rewarding modern English composers. The music is passionate, dramatic, and uncompromising, with a craggy power and an awesome sense of scale. It is also among the most intensely virile music produced in this century: forthright, unaffected, and unabashedly romantic.

Perhaps the best place to begin dipping into this epic project is the album of concerted pieces that includes the darkly beautiful *Lyra Angelica,* the composer's own favorite of all his works and possibly the finest harp concerto ever written. The other works are no less memorable—*Autumn Legend* is a kind of English *Swan of Tuonela*—and all are thrillingly played.

The symphonies are probably Alwyn's finest achievement, and none is more powerfully argued or richly orchestrated than the Fourth. Each of its three movements is brimming with mystery and character, especially the wonderful finale, a ravishing *passacaglia* concluding in a blaze of glorious brass. The colorful *Elizabethan Dances* and the stirring *Festival March* make for extremely attractive filler.

Although the playing of the London Symphony—like that of the City of London Sinfonia—is exemplary (as is the work of the Chandos engineers), the real secret of the series' success is the consistently inspired work of Richard Hickox. Alwyn has never had a more probing or persuasive interpreter, including

Alwyn himself. While the composer's own recordings from the 1970s are now available on a series of extremely expensive Lyrita reissues, the Hickox versions are preferable in almost every way. Four stars and three cheers to all concerned.

Anderson, Leroy (1908–1975)

Music of Leroy Anderson

> Orchestra, Anderson. 2-MCA Classics MCAD2-98156 [CD], MCAC 531 [T].
>
> Boston Pops, Fiedler. RCA O9026-61237-2 [CD], 09026-61237-4 [T].

Leroy Anderson once described the kind of music he wrote as "concert music with a pop quality" and let it go at that. It has also been described as "light music," "semiclassical" music, as well as a number of other less flattering things by those who simply fail to get the point. And the point is that he was a hugely gifted, highly original composer whose music came to epitomize the 1950s as unmistakably as Eisenhower, fallout shelters, and the hula hoop. By the time of Anderson's death, many of his best-known works had long since become a part of the national consciousness, as indelibly ingrained in the American ear as the paintings of his near contemporary Norman Rockwell had been imprinted on the American eye. While Anderson's music never plumbed the depths, stormed the heights, inflamed the passions, or stirred the soul, he had a knack for making people feel a little better. Given what life can be, that might well prove the greater gift.

The most numerous and popular of Anderson's works were those witty novelty items that became favorite Boston Pops encores and have remained pops concert staples ever since. Yet whatever the central gimmick—from the sounds of some actual office equipment to those of a musical cat, an old time vaudeville soft-shoe dancer, or a horse-drawn sleigh—it was never the sound effects or the high-concept central idea that animated the piece. Rather, Anderson's melodic genius and impeccable craftsmanship, coupled with an unwillingness to wear out his welcome and a genuine eagerness to please, were what made him one of the most popular of all American composers.

As this indispensable MCA collection of virtually his entire output proves, Anderson was a splendid interpreter of his own music. Recorded between 1950 and 1962, the forty-seven items are all invested with an irresistible freshness and sense of life, especially the more familiar pieces that here sound newly minted.

Arthur Fiedler hired Anderson as the Boston Pops's chief arranger and introduced most of his music to the world. His interpretations also are incomparable, though they tend to be a bit more literal and roughshod. Still, their energy and feeling of fun make them irresistible, and the recorded sound is marginally more up to date.

Finally, Leonard Slatkin leads the St. Louis Symphony in an immensely enjoyable program for RCA (09026-68046-2 [CD]) that mixes old favorites with rarities like "Clarinet Candy" and "Home Stretch." What a thrill it is to hear Anderson played by a major American orchestra in state-of-the-art recorded sound.

Antheil, George (1900–1959)

Piano Music

Verbit, piano. Albany. TROY 146-2 [CD].

Throughout the 1920s, the American composer George Antheil reveled in his self-appointed role as "The Bad Boy of Music," whose ultra-modern *Ballet mécanique*—scored for eight pianos, airplane propellers, and an enormous percussion battery—caused a sensation at its Paris premiere in 1926. As can now be heard from the MusicMasters recording of this famous work (01612-67094-2 [CD]), Antheil was less a revolutionary visionary than an entertaining iconoclast, a musical H. L. Mencken of the Jazz Age. Although he was extravagantly praised by figures as diverse as Aaron Copland and Ezra Pound—who in 1927 authored the virtually incomprehensible *Antheil and the Treatise on Harmony, with Supplementary Notes*—as the Roaring Twenties roared on, Antheil's reputation began to fade. He ended his career forgotten and ignored, writing conventionally neo-Romantic music, as well as scores for television and film.

In her well-planned and generous Albany anthology, Marthanne Verbit offers much of the composer's best and most characteristic piano music, from the noisy *Airplane Sonata* and *Sonata sauvage* to the jazzy *Little Shimmy* and *Transatlantic Tango*. Best of all are the twenty engaging miniatures from a set of forty-five called *La femme 100 têtes* (whose real-life model—if she existed—one would dearly love to have met). The sheer enthusiasm of the performances is completely infectious, making us hope that more are on the way.

One of Antheil's most colorful scores, the ballet after Hemingway, *The Capital of the World*, is now available on EMI (CDM 66548 [CD]); this is a reissue of the celebrated Capitol album from the early 1950s by Joseph Levine and the Ballet Theater Orchestra, coupled with Raffaello de Banfield's *The Combat* and a suite from William Schuman's 1945 ballet *Undertow.*

Arensky, Anton (1861–1906)

Piano Trios (2)

Beaux Arts Trio. Philips 442127-2 [CD].

Anton Stephanovich Arensky was one of those classic self-destructive Russian wild men who managed to drink themselves into early graves. Yet unlike the frequently disturbing music of his dipsomaniacal near contemporary Modest Mussorgsky, Arensky's art rarely reflects the darker side of his personality. His music is elegantly crafted and generally well mannered, with a Slavic soulfulness lurking just beneath the surface—to say nothing of an engaging rhythmic quirkiness *on* the surface—that reveals him to be a far more distinctive talent than his detractors (including his teacher Rimsky-Korsakov) were willing to admit.

The First Piano Trio has always been Arensky's most popular work, and it is given an impeccable reading by the latest incarnation of the Beaux Arts Trio. The players make it seem the equal of similar works by Tchaikovsky and Smetana, and, coupled with an equally compelling version of the more ambitious F Minor Trio, this is a recording that no lover of Romantic chamber music can afford to be without.

Arensky's youthful Piano Concerto is given exceptionally handsome treatment as part of Hyperion's Romantic Piano Concerto series (CDA 66624 [CD]), while the once popular *Variations on a Theme of Tchaikovsky* comes off splendidly on an album of Russian string music by Johannes Somary and the English Chamber Orchestra (Vanguard Classics SVC-37 [CD]).

Violin Concerto in A Minor, Op. 54

> **Trostiansky, violin; I Musici de Montréal, Turovsky. Chandos CHAN 9528 [CD].**

Given the world's seemingly inexhaustible appetite for big Romantic violin concertos, it's frankly amazing that Anton Arensky's only work in the form isn't better known. Full of the lyric grace and openhearted expressiveness that so endeared the composer's music to his pupil Sergei Rachmaninoff, Arensky's A Minor Concerto is easily the equal of Alexander Glazunov's and, with enough performances like this one, might become just as popular. The young Russian violinist Alexander Trostiansky is a seductive, yet eminently musical, advocate of the piece, with Yuli Turovsky's finely drilled chamber orchestra lending their typically adroit support. To fill out the album, the producers wisely opted for a pair of Glazunov rarities (as opposed to the predictable Violin Concerto): the exceedingly ripe and romantic Piano Concerto No. 1 from 1910, and the lush—and arguably *overripe*—*Concerto balletta for Cello and Orchestra,* dating from the composer's final years as a Parisian.

Arne, Thomas Augustine

(1710–1778)

Favorite Concertos (8) for Keyboard and Orchestra

> **Nicholson, keyboards; Parley of Instruments, Holman. Hyperion CDA 66509 [CD].**

This prolific Englishman has achieved a curiously anonymous immortality as the composer of Britain's second national anthem, "Rule Britannia," the hit tune of his 1740 masque *Alfred.* Alas, in none of Arne's dozens of other stage works would the lightning strike again. Published a decade after his death, the eight concertos featured on this Hyperion recording reveal him to be a charming and resourceful composer who, while lacking the power and personality of his older contemporary Handel, shared much of his buoyant energy. With either the organ, harpsichord, or pianoforte, Paul Nicholson is a stylish and sympathetic exponent of these engaging works, with the Parley of Instruments lending admirable support.

Nearly as appealing is a Chandos collection (CHAN 8403 [CD]) of Arne's surviving symphonies, featuring enthusiastic performances by Cantilena led by Adrian Shepherd, and a diverting Hyperion anthology of songs (CDA 66237 [CD]) called "Dr. Arne at Vauxhall Gardens," in which the Parley of Instruments is joined by the marvelous Emma Kirkby.

Arnold, Sir Malcolm (1921–)

Four Cornish Dances; Four English Dances; Four Irish Dances; Four Scottish Dances

London Philharmonic, Arnold. Lyrita SRCD 201 [CD].

With nine numbered symphonies to date, memorable scores for films like *The Bridge on the River Kwai,* and even a zany contribution or two to the Hoffnung Festivals, Malcolm Arnold has been one of the most prolific and versatile of all British composers. This Lyrita compilation of his four sets of British dances provides an ideal introduction to Arnold's eclectic, colorful, instantly digestible idiom: from the sassy *Scottish Dances,* with their vivid evocation of the skirl of highland pipes and the jaunty rhythms of the strathspey and reel, to the somber, often surprisingly substantial *Irish Dances,* written as recently as 1986. The interpretations, needless to say, are definitive, as is the swaggering playing of the London Philharmonic.

In the wake of Sir Malcolm's richly deserved and long-overdue knighthood, a relative flood of new Arnold recordings has been issued in the last few years. Easily the most entertaining of all is a Chandos album (CHAN 9100 [CD]) of suites from some of the finest of the composer's film scores, including *The Bridge on the River Kwai, The Inn of the Sixth Happiness,* and *Hobson's Choice.* Although copyright restrictions prevented using Arnold's inspired arrangement of Kenneth Alford's "Colonel Bogey March"—for the sake of continuity, the piece is played in its original version—the *Inn of the Sixth Happiness* excerpts include as much of "This Old Man" as anyone could wish. The performances by the London Symphony led by Richard Hickox are even more vivid than those heard in the actual films.

Two Hyperion albums (CDA 66172 [CD], CDA 66173 [CD]) offer some of the best of Arnold's consistently imaginative, superbly crafted chamber music, while the composer himself leads a delightful program of his overtures for Reference (RR 48 [CD]), including the irrepressible *Beckus the Dandipratt* and the shockingly unknown *A Sussex Overture.*

Best of all, two new Arnold symphony cycles are now under way: one from Hickox, the other from Andrew Penny and the National Symphony of Ireland. Predictably, the Hickox versions of the Third and Fourth (Chandos CHAN 9290) are superlative, especially in the conductor's projection of the '50s pop music elements that dominate the Fourth. Yet Penny is no less impressive in the First and Second (Naxos 8.553406 [CD]), both recorded in the composer's presence. The rather gnarly First Symphony has plenty of clarity and bite—especially in the finale's impressive fugue—while the far more jovial Second bubbles over with high spirits and goodwill. While both cycles should prove most distinguished when complete, the Naxos price tag will make the Penny difficult to ignore.

Arriaga, Juan Crisostómo

(1806–1826)

String Quartets (3)

Chilingirian Quartet. CRD 3312/13 [CD].

Few musical careers began with more promise than that of the Spanish composer Juan Crisostómo Jacomo Antonio de Arriaga y Balzola. Born in Bilboa on January 27th, 1806—the date that marked the fiftieth anniversary of Mozart's birth—and called the "Spanish Mozart" by his contemporaries, Arriaga's youthful achievements were extraordinary. After acquiring a complete knowledge of harmony within three months, he began composing before his tenth birthday and produced the opera *Los esclavos felices* when he was only fifteen. He entered the Paris Conservatory in 1821, was appointed répétiteur in harmony and composition in 1824, and shortly thereafter published the three string quartets upon which the bulk of his reputation continues to rest. Over the next two years, he devoted himself so assiduously to composing, teaching, and performing that his health broke; he died of what was then called "galloping consumption" on January 17, 1826, ten days before what would have been his twentieth birthday.

Arriaga's string quartets not only demonstrate the teenage composer's firm grasp of voicing and counterpoint but also suggest something of the wit and imaginative power of the middle-period quartets of Haydn. These are graceful, inventive, surprisingly distinctive works full of youthful exuberance and melodic charm. The Chilingirian String Quartet makes the strongest possible case for all three, with playing that is as polished as it is enthusiastic. The analogue sound remains completely serviceable.

Atterburg, Kurt (1887–1974)

Symphony No. 6; *Ballad without Words; A Värmland Rhapsody*

Norrköping Symphony, Hirokami. BIS CD 553 [CD].

The most important of the modern Swedish symphonists, Kurt Atterburg continues to be best known for *A Värmland Rhapsody,* which he wrote in 1933 to celebrate the seventy-fifth birthday of the Nobel Prize–winning novelist Selma Lagerlöf, and the sixth of his nine symphonies, which launched—and nearly ruined—his career in 1928. After winning the ten-thousand-dollar first prize offered by Columbia Records to commemorate the centenary of Schubert's death, the Sixth Symphony was taken up by a diverse and important collection of champions that included Beecham and Toscanini. At the height of its popularity, a group of critics—led by Ernest Newman in the *Sunday Times*—suggested that Atterburg had "borrowed" many of the Symphony's ideas, though they stopped short of making an actual charge of plagiarism. In an eloquent rebuttal in the *Musical Digest,* the composer hotly denied he had borrowed from anyone, with the exception of a single deliberate quotation from Schubert.

Like *A Värmland Rhapsody,* which is based on a series of folk songs identified with the setting of Lagerlöf's *Gösta Berlings Saga,* the Sixth Symphony is a colorful and restlessly imaginative work that owes little to anyone. If the Bis recording might not be the last word in technical legerdemain and individuality—memories of Beecham's classic interpretation will be difficult to efface—then it still gives a fair indication of the quality and importance of a work that deserves to be far better known.

Auber, Daniel-François-Esprit (1782–1871)

Le Domino noir

Soloists, London Voices, English Chamber Orchestra, Bonynge.
London 440646-2 [CD].

So few of the innumerable comic operas of this important rival of Rossini are heard today that the sheer quality of *Le Domino noir* comes as something of a shock. First staged in Paris in 1837, the opera concerns of a pair novices in a convent who contrive to secretly attend a masked ball (this is a *French* opera, after all!). The libretto by his frequent collaborator, the much-maligned Eugène Scribe, drew from Auber a tuneful, fizzing score, brimming with charm, wit, and unfailing imagination, and all of it as light and delectable as a puff pastry dredged in confectioners' sugar.

Once again, the indefatigable Richard Bonynge is responsible for this enchanting discovery, and he also managed to unearth some recitatives that Tchaikovsky wrote for a production intended for St. Petersburg. The conducting sparkles with an infectious enthusiasm from first note to last, while the cast—headed by the spellbinding Korean soprano Sumi Jo—seems ideal.

EMI has reissued the 1984 recording (CDCB 54810 [CD]) of Auber's best-known opera, *Fra Diavolo*, in a performance that is nearly as fine as the London *Le Domino noir*. Nicolai Gedda's rather hard-pressed hero is the only serious drawback in a recording that mixes music and spoken dialogue in the seamless style of *opéra comique*.

Recordings of Auber's delightful and once hugely popular overtures have become inexplicably rare. Three of the best—*Fra Diavolo*, *The Bronze Horse*, and *Masaniello*—are currently available in the classic 1959 Mercury recording (434309-2 [CD]) by the Detroit Symphony conducted by Paul Paray.

Avinson, Charles (1709–1770)

Concerti Grossi (12) after Scarlatti

> **Academy of St. Martin-in-the-Fields, Marriner.**
> **Philips 438806-2 [CD].**

Organist, composer, and impresario, whose series of subscription concerts in his native Newcastle were among the first ever organized in England, Charles Avinson seems destined to be remembered for those dozen concertos he skillfully arranged from keyboard sonatas of Domenico Scarlatti. These enchanting works will offer the baroque junkie a refreshing break from Corelli and Vivaldi, and all are played with their usual grace by Sir Neville Marriner and the Academy.

Babbitt, Milton (1916–)

Piano Works

> **Taub, piano. Harmonia Mundi HMC 905160 [CD].**

I first encountered Milton Babbitt when I was conducting interviews for a documentary series on the music of Arnold Schoenberg. After greeting me as though I might have been a long-lost illegitimate son, he proceeded to give the single most astonishing interview I've ever heard (or heard about): four hours of nonstop, rapid-fire brilliance (he talks very quickly when he gets excited, which is most of the time) from one of the great minds of our time. There is apparently nothing that Milton Babbitt doesn't know—except how to compromise. For six decades, he has been one of the most tenaciously provocative of composers, expanding the twelve-tone system in ways that Schoenberg could scarcely have imagined and becoming the first major American composer to work in the various electronic media.

Robert Taub's adventurous recital, recorded in the composer's presence in 1985, covers roughly forty years of Babbitt's increasingly challenging output, from the early *Three Compositions for Piano* of 1948, his first mature application of Schoenbergian principals, to *Lagniappe* from 1985, a work composed specifically for the album. One is struck throughout not only by the intellectual depth of Babbitt's music, but also by its charm, antic wit, and physical beauty.

In short, this is a perfect introduction to a giant of the avant-garde.

Bach, Carl Philipp Emanuel

(1714–1788)

Symphonies (6) "Hamburg sinfonias"

C. P. E. Bach Orchestra, Haenchen. Capriccio 10106 [CD].

The most prolific and long-suffering of Johann Sebastian's sons—and you'd suffer, too, if you had to spend twenty-seven years in the employ of Frederick the Great—C. P. E. Bach is finally being seen with some of the awe with which his near-contemporaries always viewed him. For Haydn, his influence was decisive— "For what I know, I have to thank Philipp Emanuel Bach"—and for Mozart, a pupil of his brother Johann Christian, the "Berlin Bach" was an even more important figure. "He is the father," Mozart said, "and we the children."

While he is still best known for his keyboard music and the innumerable works he was forced to compose for his flute-loving employer—Frederick *was* a fair musician but a complete musical reactionary—the so-called "Hamburg sinfonias," composed for the Baron von Swieten in 1773, are a superb showcase for his robust talent. Hartmut Haenchen and the C. P. E. Bach Chamber Orchestra, playing on modern—that is, non-period—instruments, offer alert and loving interpretations of these exhilarating works, and Capriccio's recorded sound is flawless.

Another unusually attractive Capriccio release (10 101 [CD]) brings together a flock of the composer's Flute Sonatas in performances that are equally stirring.

Bach, Johann Christian

(1735–1782)

Sinfonias (6), Op. 6

Camerata Budapest, Gmür. Naxos 8.553083 [CD].

Known as the "London Bach" because of his long stay in the English capital, Johann Christian was the youngest surviving son of Johann Sebastian and Anna Magdalena Bach. When his father died in 1750, Johann Christian went to Berlin to live with his brother Carl Philipp Emanuel, who completed his education in clavier performance and composition. After six years in Italy, Bach was invited to England by the director of London's Haymarket Theatre, for which he wrote a successful series of Italian operas. In 1764, he met the young Mozart, who would later write, "I love him, as you know, and respect him with all my heart." Although most celebrated during his lifetime for his thirteen operas, he is best remembered today for his many concertos and symphonies, which had a decisive influence on the emerging sonata form.

The six Sinfonias of Opus 6 are a superb collection, with warmly expressive slow movements and strikingly dramatic outer movements that clearly point the way to middle-period Haydn. Under Hanspeter Gmür's stylish direction, the Camerata Budapest plays them all with spirited enthusiasm, captured in first-rate recorded sound.

A second album (8.553085 [CD]) devoted to the slightly less captivating but still rewarding Opus 9 Sinfonias is perhaps even more desirable because of the excellent performances of two of the composer's finest works: the Sinfonia Concertante in A for Violin and Cello, and the Sinfonia Concertante in E-Flat for Two Violins and Oboe, which includes a striking reference to "Che farò senza Euridice" from Gluck's *Orfeo ed Euridice*.

Bach, Johann Sebastian

(1685–1750)

*A*nna Magdalena Notebook

> Blegen, soprano; Luxon, baritone; Kipnis, harpsichord; Meinis, violin.
> Nonesuch/Elektra 79020-2 [CD].

With Wagner's *Siegfried Idyll* and all the music that Robert Schumann composed with Clara in mind, few acts of husbandly devotion are more touching than this series of short works, arrangements, and exercises that Bach compiled for his youthful second wife in 1725. The *Anna Magdalena Notebook* represents the composer at his most intimate and domestic, with a quiet charm rarely encountered in his more obviously serious works. The performances on this Nonesuch recording are warm and lively, radiating an affection that matches that of the music itself.

*T*he Art of Fugue, S. 1080

Juilliard Quartet. Sony Classical S2K 45937 [CD].

Prior to my first experience with the composer's final monumental essay in the art of counterpoint, I had been blissfully unaware that Bach had never intended *Die Kunst der Fuge* to actually be *performed*. Someone forgot to tell the music director of the small station where I broke in as an announcer. One night, early in my first week on the air, I had to introduce and then sit through the whole of *The Art of Fugue*. I've never been the same.

Although with its seemingly interminable variations on the same dreary subject, *Die Kunst der Fuge* can make for a life-altering experience, those with a taste for it will find the recording by the Juilliard Quartet both valuable and revealing, provided it's ingested in the proper doses and *not* experienced while operating heavy equipment. The playing is clear and direct, admirably disentangling the most hopelessly tangled lines.

The wackiest—and by far the most entertaining—version is easily the arrangement made by the late William Malloch called "The Art of Fugueing" (Sheffield Lab SLS-502 [CD]), in which brisk tempos and an orchestral palette that owes much to Schoenberg produce an alternately amusing and hypnotic effect.

*B*randenburg Concertos (6), S. 1046/51

English Chamber Orchestra, Britten. London 443847-2 [CD].

English Concert, Pinnock. Deutsche Grammophon 410500-2 [CD], 410500-4 [T]; 410501-2 [CD], 410501-4 [T].

Just as Johann Sebastian Bach was the final summation of all that the baroque era gave to music, the *Brandenburg Concertos* are the apotheosis of the concerti grossi, the most diverse and important of all baroque instrumental forms.

For years, the standard recordings of the *Brandenburg Concertos* were those wonderfully musical performances from the 1930s by the Adolf Busch Chamber Orchestra, an interpretation that can now be found, along with Busch's equally memorable versions of the Orchestral Suites, on a brilliantly remastered set from EMI Classics (64047-2 [CD]). While not for baroque purists (the *continuo* is realized on a piano by a very young Rudolf Serkin), the playing is marvelously virile and delightfully old-fashioned: a memorable souvenir of the days when Bach was generally considered a stylistic contemporary of Robert Schumann.

Another persuasively modern interpretation—and my favorite modern recording of the *Brandenburgs*—is that lush and stylish account turned in by the English Chamber Orchestra conducted by Benjamin Britten. The playing projects an aura of ease, freshness, and authority, together with that sense of instantly responsive give-and-take characteristic of chamber music making at its best. The warmth of the playing is greatly enhanced by the perfect acoustics of the Maltings, Snape—the converted brewery that became the principal concert venue of Britten's Aldeburgh Festival.

If baroque "authenticity" is an absolute necessity, then the best choice is the version by the English Concert and Trevor Pinnock on Deutsche Grammophon. Although the recording has drawn extravagant praise from both the English and American press, I find much of it rather prissy and effete. Nevertheless, the English Concert version is an enterprise that deserves to be taken seriously, unlike that inept and embarrassing scandal perpetrated by Nikolaus Harnoncourt and his abysmal Concentus Musicus of Vienna.

Cantatas (212)

The two-hundred-plus cantatas that he ground out like so many Holy sausages contain much of what is most ethereal and inspired, and a great deal of what is most gloomy and depressing, in Bach's music. Some literally seem to have been produced with the aid of divine intervention, while others reveal one of the giants of music dutifully and ponderously marking time. A generation ago, perhaps twenty or thirty of the most enduring of them were available to the record-buying public; today, all of them have been recorded, some more than once.

While it is impossible to make specific recommendations for all of these works—I won't pretend I've heard each and every recording: life, as we know, is *much* too short for that—I can offer a few words of warning and encouragement to the prospective Bach Cantata Collector, beginning with the heartfelt injunction to avoid any of the Teldec recordings as though they were (to quote Baudelaire) "the breeches of a man with the itch."

The Teldec series is divided up between Nikolaus Harnoncourt and Gustav Leonhardt, who gleefully take turns mauling the luckless pieces beyond recognition. The Harnoncourts are packed with the usual belly laughs, and the Leonhardts aren't much better. It is almost as if these two clowns were engaged in some sort of bizarre contest as to who can conjure up the most screechy and etiolated instrumental sound and the most feeble choral outbursts. (I hate to sound like some sort of reverse sexist, but why give us a gaggle of struggling boys when a group of accomplished female singers would do even better?)

On the other hand, virtually all of the recordings made by Sir John Eliot Gardiner, Helmut Rilling, or Joshua Rifkin have lovely and important things to say, as do the performances in a new series from the bargain-basement label

Naxos. While the names of the performers won't ring any bells, the interpretations are pointed, large-scaled, and endearingly dramatic. Besides, at six bucks a pop, how can you possibly go wrong?

Christmas Oratorio, S. 248

Argenta, von Otter, Blochwitz, Bär, Monteverdi Choir, English Baroque Soloists, Gardiner. Deutsche Grammophon 423332-2 [CD], 423332-4 [T].

The reason that the *Christmas Oratorio* doesn't hang together as well in actual performance as that other seasonal staple, Handel's *Messiah,* is that its composer never intended it to be downed in one gulp. The six separate and discrete cantatas were meant to be heard over a half dozen days of the Christmas period, and taken in that dosage the *Oratorio* constitutes one of the most rewarding and affecting of all of Bach's works.

As in his festive recording of the Bach *Magnificat* (Philips 411458-2 [CD]), which is also wholeheartedly recommended, Sir John Eliot Gardiner here reaffirms his position as the foremost antiquarian of our time. From the exiting, brilliantly articulated opening with trumpets and timpani, through the witty, briskly paced choruses, Gardiner infuses the music with an incomparable zest and vigor, without overlooking its gentle warmth and tenderness.

The soloists, the choir, and the always impeccable English Baroque Soloists are all at the top of their forms, and if you're in the market for something to wash down the inevitable *Messiahs* and *Nutcrackers* during the holidays, search no further than this.

Chromatic Fantasy and Fugue in D Minor, S. 903; Italian Concerto in F, S. 971

Rousset, harpsichord. L'Oiseau-Lyre 433054-2 [CD].

The Chromatic Fantasy and Fugue and the Italian Concerto are among the most understandably popular and frequently recorded of all baroque keyboard works. The Fantasy's often dizzying chromatic modulations can still sound strikingly modern, while the Concerto's extroverted exuberance makes it one of the most heroic and exciting of Bach's creations.

The brilliant harpsichordist Christophe Rousset makes a very strong case for both works on his superb L'Oiseau-Lyre recital. There is nothing remotely stuffy or pedantic in these refreshing interpretations that seem to flow out of the instrument with the utmost naturalness and ease.

Clavier Concertos (7), S. 1052-1058

**Kipnis, harpsichord; London Strings, Marriner. CBS Odyssey MB2K
45616 [CD], MGT-39801-4 [T].**

Of Bach's seven surviving keyboard concertos—the first such works written
by a major composer—most are transcriptions of other concertos, primarily for
the violin. As in all of the music that he so transformed, Bach has the uncanny
knack of making the music seem as if it couldn't possibly have been written for
any other instrument: each of these glowing entertainments cry out "keyboard"
as clearly as their original versions say "violin."

Igor Kipnis is one of those rare early-music specialists who is able to combine those usually mutually exclusive qualities of scholarship and showmanship
without compromising either: the interpretations are as thoughtful as they are
impetuous, and he receives the usual imaginative help from Sir Neville and the
gang.

Among recordings by pianists, none is finer than the London set (425676-2
[CD]) with András Schiff leading members of the Chamber Orchestra of Europe
from the keyboard. These are lithe, beautifully proportioned performances that
never call attention to themselves. From first to last, the playing has the alert give-
and-take of the best chamber music performances—which is precisely what the
composer intended.

Concerto in A Minor for Violin, S. 1041; Concerto in E Major for Violin, S. 1042; Concerto in D Minor for 2 violins, S. 1043

**Mutter, Accardo, English Chamber Orchestra, Accardo. Angel CDC
47005-2 [CD].**

It's hardly surprising that of all his innumerable instrumental concertos,
these three works for the violin should remain among Bach's most popular works
in the form. Lyrical, dramatic, and overflowing with rich and memorable melody,
these concertos were often taken up as vehicles by Fritz Kreisler, Eugène Ysaÿe,
and other important turn-of-the-century violinists whose performances of any
baroque music tended to be as scarce as hockey players' teeth. Another sure sign
of their enduring popular appeal was the enlistment of a cantata for a key dramatic role in the hit film *Children of a Lesser God*.

For years, the most completely satisfying recording of all three concertos
was that unabashedly Romantic account by David and Igor Oistrakh, which is
still available on Deutsche Grammophon. Those achingly beautiful performances
would have remained my first choice in a very crowded field had it not been for
the release of an even more lush and lovely interpretation by the young German
violinist Anne-Sophie Mutter.

When Mutter first arrived on the scene a few short years ago, I must admit I took little, if any, notice. I simply assumed that as the latest in a long line of Herbert von Karajan protégés, she would inevitably develop along the same cold, impersonal lines. Fortunately—if this marvelous Angel recording is any indication—she has shed all vestiges of Karajan's reptilian influence to become one of the most magnetic young musicians before the public today.

Stylistically, her performances of the Bach concertos are throwbacks. Cast on a large scale and full of late-Romantic gestures—has anyone since Kreisler made the slow movement of the E Major Concerto sound as languorously sexy as this?—the interpretations are a perfect complement to her immense tone and seamless technique. As usual, Salvatore Accardo, as conductor and second violinist in the Double Concerto, brings a wealth of warmth and experience to what I suspect may become *the* indispensable Bach concerto recording.

Of the many fine recordings of the Concerto for Violin, Oboe, and Strings, the most impressive in terms of the oboist's contribution is Harold Gomberg's recording with Isaac Stern, the New York Philharmonic, and Leonard Bernstein, now available on CBS (MK-42258 [CD]; MGT-39798). As always, this great artist's command of tone color, phrasing, dynamics, and breath control is little short of amazing: indeed, his physical sound is so rich and large it frequently threatens to overwhelm the violinist's.

A more evenly matched contest can be found on a fine EMI recording with Itzhak Perlman and Ray Still (CDC 47073-2 [CD]).

English Suites (6), S. 806-811

Schiff, piano. London 421640-2 [CD].

Even for those who, like Sir Thomas Beecham, are not especially enthralled by Bach's music—"Too much counterpoint," Sir Thomas breezily insisted, "and what is worse, *Protestant* counterpoint"—the English Suites are very hard to resist. With their catchy tunes, engaging rhythms, and transparent textures, they represent Bach at his most joyously unbuttoned: the light-footed secular flip side of the often turgid sacred composer.

The formidably accomplished András Schiff is a nearly perfect advocate of these alluring works. While admittedly not as individual as Glenn Gould in his revelatory CBS recording (M2K-42268 [CD]), Schiff is neither as controversial nor as perverse. Like Gould, Schiff proves that the resources of the modern piano will do no serious injury to the composer's intentions, and he does so with playing that is as luxuriant as it is natural and unforced.

Schiff is equally compelling in his version of the composer's French Suites (London 433313-2 [CD]). In addition to clear textures and lightly sprung rhythms, there is nothing remotely forced or calculated in the pianist's playing, only the obvious joy in bringing these engaging works to life.

Goldberg Variations, S. 988

Gould, piano. CBS MYK-38479 [CD], MYT-38479 [T] (1955 version).

CBS MK-37779 [CD], IMT-37779 [T] (1981 version).

Pinnock, harpsichord. Deutsche Grammophon 415130-2 [CD].

The most cogent thing that anyone has ever said about that mystery wrapped in an enigma, Glenn Gould, was an offhand wisecrack dropped by the conductor George Szell shortly after he had performed with the late Canadian pianist for the first time. "That nut is a genius," Szell was heard to mumble, and history should probably let it go at that. Willful, unpredictable, eccentric, reclusive, and maddeningly brilliant, Glenn Gould was easily the most provocative pianist of his generation and one of the great musical originals of modern times.

The 1955 recording of the *Goldberg Variations* introduced Glenn Gould to an unsuspecting world and began an entirely new chapter in the history of Bach interpretation. Legend has it that the *Goldberg Variations* were originally written as a soporific for a music-loving nobleman who was a chronic insomniac. In most recordings of the work—which as a rule do tend to be rather stultifying—the legend can certainly be believed. Gould changed all that with driving tempos, a bracing rhythmic vitality, and an ability to clarify and untangle the dense contrapuntal lines that was, and remains, amazing.

After twenty-five years of further study, Gould rerecorded the work in 1981 and the result was every bit as controversial as his original recording. While sacrificing none of the razor clarity of the earlier performance, the interpretation became more profound and reflective with tempos that not only were dramatically slower, but also had been chosen—according to the pianist—to help each of the variations fit into a more homogeneous, integrated whole.

For a many years, I've been trying to choose between the two recordings without very much success. But then, too, the choice boils down to either the youthful brashness of the original, or the mature, studied brashness of the Revised Standard Version. Although only the 1981 recording is available on a compact disc, CBS has conveniently packaged both performances, together with a typically zany and illuminating interview with the pianist, in a handsome three-record boxed set.

For those who insist on a harpsichord, try the alert, intelligent recording by Trevor Pinnock.

Keyboard Music

Tureck, piano. VAI Audio VAIA 1029; 1041; 1051 [CD].

These are the famous recordings made at William F. Buckley Jr.'s home in Connecticut in that series of concerts that began as a birthday surprise from his wife. A highly knowledgeable music lover with a passion for the music of Bach, Buckley was understandably moved and promptly resolved to share the experience with others. One evening eventually expanded to five, spread out over a four-and-a-half-year period from November 1979 to May of 1984.

With Pablo Casals, Wanda Landowska, and Glenn Gould, Rosalyn Tureck is one of the century's most distinctive Bach interpreters and each of these performances—from the slightest prelude to the magisterial *Goldberg Variations*—has what Stravinsky called "the instant imprint of personality." In addition to the depth, imagination, and technical finish of the performances, the sense of occasion only adds to the excitement. There are few more compelling Bach recordings—or recordings of *anyone's* keyboard music, for that matter—currently available.

For another intensely personal, deeply satisfying view of Bach's keyboard music, investigate the two-disc, medium-priced collection from Deutsche Grammophon (439672-2 [CD]) that the octogenarian Wilhelm Kempff made toward the end of his distinguished career. Few Bach recordings seem so refreshing and youthful, with beloved miniatures like *Jesu, Joy of Man's Desiring, Nun komm' der Heiden Heiland,* and the *Capriccio on the Departure of His Most Beloved Brother* invested with a simple, heartrending eloquence.

Mass in B Minor, S. 232

Monteverdi Choir, English Baroque Soloists, Gardiner. Deutsche Grammophon Archiv 415514-2 [CD].

Nelson, Baird, Dooley, Hoffmeister, Opalach, Schultze, Bach Ensemble, Rifkin. Nonesuch 79036-2 [CD], 79036-4 [T].

The baroque revival of the 1960s was a very shrewd marketing ploy of the recording industry. Compared to operas or Mahler symphonies, baroque music was far easier, and, more important (at least from *their* point of view), far *cheaper* to record. Thus we were inundated not only by torrents of music by composers who for centuries had been little more than names in a book but also by well-intentioned and generally lamentable recordings by organizations like the Telemann Society and such stellar European ensembles as the Pforzheim Chamber Orchestra of Heilbronn.

Next, the Baroque Boom was further complicated by the emergence of the Baroque Authenticity Movement, whose exponents argued—at times persuasively—that for baroque music to make the points the composer intended, it had to be presented on instruments of the period. Like all such upheavals, the Period Instrument Revolution spawned its fair share of frauds and fanatics: untalented, uninspired charlatans who forgot that making music *does not* consist entirely of making physically repellent noises and arcane musicological points.

In the work of three English musicians, Christopher Hogwood, Trevor Pinnock, and, preeminently, Sir John Eliot Gardiner, we finally have convincing evidence that the Authenticity–Period Instrument Movement has at last grown up: for each of the three finest antiquarians before the public today is a musician first, a musicologist second. Gardiner's recording of the Bach Mass in B Minor is as stirring and compassionate as his exhilarating recordings of the Handel Oratorios. He mixes grace, finesse, and dramatic grandeur into an immensely satisfying amalgam, while managing to coax more physical beauty from those old instruments than any other conductor ever has before or since.

For an interesting companion piece to Gardiner, try Joshua Rifkin—a versatile and vastly gifted musician who did as much as anyone to make the musical establishment take the music of Scott Joplin seriously—and his controversial Nonesuch recording with the Bach Ensemble. Rifkin's recording of the Mass in B Minor is a radical experiment that audaciously assigns only a single voice to each of the choral parts. From a musician of lesser stature, the project might easily have degenerated into yet another Baroque Authenticity gimmick. But Rifkin, in a brilliantly argued essay and an even more convincingly argued performance, proves that "authenticity" has to do far less with editions and instrumentation than with the authentic gifts of the performers.

Motets (6) for Chorus, S. 225-230

Monteverdi Choir, Gardiner. Erato 2292-45979-2 [CD].

The six Motets are among the most imposing of all Bach's choral works. Moving, musically intricate, deeply serious, their appeal is more to the confirmed Bach specialist than to the casual listener, who might be forgiven for finding them almost *oppressively* serious, if not downright gloomy.

Both sorts will find much to admire in Sir John Eliot Gardiner's splendid 1980 recording, which, in addition to refreshingly direct and unfailingly imaginative performances of the Motets, offers stylish performances of a pair of motet-like cantatas—*Nun ist das Heil und die Kraft* (No. 50) and *O Jesu Christ, mein's Lebens Licht* (No. 118)—and the rarely recorded (and possibly spurious) seventh motet, *Sei Lob und Preis mit Ehren*, S. 231.

A Musical Offering, S. 1079

Leipzig Bach Collegium. Capriccio CDC 10032 [CD].

In addition to forging Prussia into a modern military state—with all the pleasant consequences that this would have for the world over the next two centuries—Frederick the Great was an accomplished amateur flutist and composer who early in his reign maintained one of the most musical courts in northern Europe. In 1747, he invited the aging father of his Kapellmeister, Carl Phillip Emanuel Bach, to Potsdam and was amazed when "old Bach" improvised a six-part fugue on a melody of the king's devising. Back in Leipzig, Bach expanded the idea into a work consisting of two *ricercares,* several canons, and a concluding trio and dispatched *A Musical Offering* to Frederick as a way of saying thanks.

With Karl Münchinger's fine recording with the Stuttgart Chamber Orchestra and Sir Neville Marriner's adroit, enormously musical Philips recording temporarily out of print, the best alternative is the stylish Capriccio recording by the Leipzig Bach Collegium. Tempos are brisk, textures transparent, and all is beautifully recorded.

Organ Music

Hurford, organ. London 444410-2 [CD].

In his organ music Bach is at his most personal and reactionary. This windy, glorious monstrosity was his favorite instrument, and the music he composed for it—largely during the Weimar period—all looked back into the past. In the forms he inherited from Buxtehude and Frescobaldi—from the brilliant, finger-twisting *toccatas* to those *fantasias* in which the finest keyboard composer of the baroque era allowed his imagination free reign—Bach wove some of his most intricate and imposing inspirations. For many, the organ works represented not only his first great creative phase but also the summit of his art.

If you're one of those Bach lovers who can't seem to get enough of this stuff, then Peter Hurford's six-volume, seventeen-CD set on London's medium-priced Jubilee label should very nearly satisfy you. The performances are invariably fresh, imaginative, and hugely accomplished, and the fact that the project was spread out over several years and numerous venues goes a long way to preventing any serious listener fatigue. Wisely, London has gathered together some of the best-known works on a "Greatest Hits" sampler (443485-2 [CD]), which is not only a revealing introduction to the series, but also one of the best collections on the market.

For the vandals among us, Pearl has also reissued Leopold Stokowski's famous Philadelphia Orchestra recordings of some of his gooey orchestral transcriptions (PEA 9488 [CD]). This breathtaking exercise in shameless self-indulgence easily ranks with the most enjoyable Bach recordings of all time.

Partitas (6) for harpsichord, S. 825-830

Hewitt, piano. Hyperion CDA 67191/2 [CD].

There is a freshness and disarming simplicity in this fine Canadian pianist's approach to Bach that makes this one of the most satisfying recordings of any of the keyboard works currently available. In Angela Hewitt's nimble hands, the Partitas unfold with all their grace, charm, and expressive variety; nothing is overdone (or done for show); tempos seem ideally judged, the phrasing is elegant but natural, and throughout there is an almost innocent joy in the act of music making that proves irresistible. Hyperion's warm, unfussy recorded sound is in every way worthy of the performances.

For those needing a version with harpsichord, Christophe Rousset's splendid L'Oiseau-Lyre recording (440217-2 [CD] has many of the same unaffected qualities, together with wit and energy in abundance.

Saint John Passion, S. 245

Harper, Hill, Hodgson, Burgess, Pears, Tear, Thompson, Tobin, Shirley-Quirk, Howell, Wandsworth School Boys' Choir, English Chamber Orchestra, Britten. London 443859-2 [CD].

Even the most devoted admirers of the *Saint Matthew Passion* readily concede that the earlier, less familiar *Saint John Passion* of 1724 is the swifter and more dramatically involving work. The choruses are among the most stirring in Bach's output, with many rising to climaxes that seem almost operatic in their intensity. And while the recitatives are also tremendously expressive, memorable arias also abound, especially the contralto's moving "Es ist vollbracht" and the magnificent "Betrachte meine Seel'" for the bass.

Recorded following a series of live performances at the 1971 Aldeburgh Festival, Benjamin Britten's revelatory interpretation is one of his finest achievements as a conductor, a worthy companion to his magnificent version of the *Brandenburg Concertos* (see page 21). Paying no attention whatever to scholarly matters or period instrument concerns, Britten approaches the music with only his instincts, experience, and native musicality to guide him. The result is a powerfully dynamic, warmly lyrical performance that manages to be devout *and* theatrical, in the best possible sense of each term. Responding to the obvious sense of occasion, the singers, musicians, and recording engineers all give their absolute best.

Saint Matthew Passion, S. 244

Soloists, Monteverdi Choir, English Baroque Soloists, Gardiner. Deutsche Grammophon 427648-2 [CD].

There are several ways to view this towering masterpiece, the most common of which is to regard it as the greatest single sacred work—and quite possibly the greatest single *musical* work—yet devised by the human mind.

As a naive yet ridiculously hypercritical youth, I once took part in a performance of the *Saint Matthew Passion* and the experience nearly killed me. Later, as a somewhat less demanding adult, I attended a production that Sir Georg Solti gave early in his tenure as music director of the Chicago Symphony. Sir Georg presented his Easter-tide version of the *Passion*, Bayreuth-style, which is to say, it began early in the afternoon and—after a break for dinner—continued later that night. To my shame, I must admit that I and my wife (as she then was) availed ourselves of the opportunity to make a hasty getaway and take in a movie—which I still remember was the splashy, gory, well-intentioned *Waterloo*, with Rod Steiger and Christopher Plummer.

With its numberless arias, countless chorales, and interminable recitatives with the Savior speaking over an aureole of shimmering strings, the *Saint Matthew Passion* has always been a severe test of concentration and patience that I have never been fully able to pass. And if that makes me a clod and a philistine, so be it; I remain firmly convinced that the thing has done more than any musical work in history to keep the mosques and synagogues filled.

For those who disagree—and they are certainly in the vast majority—the eloquence and physical beauty of Sir John Eliot Gardiner's set will prove impossible to resist. Aided by a topflight cast of singers, he invests the familiar story with a gripping sense of urgency—so much so, in fact, that infidels will be kept on the edge of their seats, anxious to learn how it all comes out.

An excellent budget-priced alternative from Naxos (8.550832/34) offers a fresh and imaginative interpretation from Hungary that features modern instruments and very crisp tempos from a first-rate choral conductor named Géza Oberfrank. No allowances need be made for either the performance or the recorded sound.

Sonatas (3) and Partitas (3) for Unaccompanied Violin, S. 1001-1006

Grumiaux, violin. Philips 438736-2 [CD].

More than any other important violinist since Fritz Kreisler, the late Arthur Grumiaux created the impression of a very great musician who only happened to play the violin. Although far more technically reliable than Kreisler—who never really cared for practicing and after a certain point in his career all but gave it up—Grumiaux was completely indifferent to virtuosity for its own sake. His mission in life was to illuminate great music rather than dazzle an audience.

Recorded in the early 1960s, Grumiaux's versions of the solo Partitas and Sonatas are *very* dazzling from both a musical and technical point of view. No other recordings reveal the music's structural bones quite so clearly or do it with such an easy, natural grace.

Except for those of Mark Kaplan. If this extraordinary musician dressed as preposterously as Nigel Kennedy or indulged in the stage antics of a Joshua Bell or Nadja Salerno-Sonnenberg, then he would probably be far better known, since he plays circles around all of them. His recordings of the Sonatas and Partitas (Mitch Miller Music 14630) are the most musical since Grumiaux's and are marginally better played.

Grumiaux's versions of the Sonatas for Violin and Continuo with Christiane Jaccottet (Philips 454011-2 [CD]) are no less stylish than his famous recordings of the Sonatas and Partitas. While no detail of phrasing and dynamics seems left to chance, there is also a flowing spontaneity in the music making that creates the illusion that everything is being made up on the spot.

Sonatas (6) for Flute and Continuo, S. 1030-1035

Galway, flute; Moll, harpsichord; Cunningham, viola da gamba. RCA 09026-62555-2 [CD].

For many baroque purists, the sound will be too large, the tone too liquid and various, the playing too irrevocably modern. Poor them. Galway's recording of the Bach Flute Sonatas is one of his best in years: colorful, dramatic, lively, fabulously played. For those who insist on a period instrument, Stephen Preston plays with consummate finesse on a CRD album (3314/15 [CD]), stylishly accompanied by Simon Preston and Jordi Savall.

Sonatas (3) for Viola da gamba, S. 1027-29

Maisky, cello; Argerich, piano. Deutsche Grammophon 415471-2 [CD].

Whether one prefers the dry, pure sound of the viola da gamba—so named because it was held on or between the player's legs—or the richer, more expressive voice of the modern cello, Mischa Maisky proves an exciting guide to these warmly thoughtful works, with Martha Argerich an unusually able and imaginative partner. His only real competition comes from Yo-Yo Ma, whose Sony recording is severely compromised by his decision to use harpsichord accompaniment, which—despite Kenneth Cooper's intelligent contribution—makes for a rather jarring clash of styles.

For industrial-strength authenticity, the Virgin Classics recording (CDM 61291 [CD]) with Jordi Savall and Ton Koopman offers all the desiccated wanness that the most extreme baroque purist could wish but with playing that is always lively, vivid, and intensely musical.

Suites (6) for Cello, S. 1007/12

Starker, cello. Mercury Living Presence 432756-2 [CD].

Ma, cello. CBS M2K-37867 [CD], IMT-39508/9 [T].

In the right hands, Bach's six Suites for Solo Cello can be an ennobling, thoroughly rewarding experience; in the wrong hands, they can be a crashing, unmitigated bore. There is certainly nothing boring about Pablo Casals's legendary recordings from the 1930s, which are still available on two Angel CDs (CDH 61028/9-2). While professional musicians tend to admire them without reservation (Mitch Miller once told me that he developed his wonderful singing style on the oboe by trying to emulate the long lines that the cellist achieved on those famous old discs), my reaction to Casals's playing has always been similar to Igor Stravinsky's: "Of course, he is a very great man. He is in favor of Peace, against General Franco, and plays Bach in the manner of Brahms."

My own introduction to the Solo Cello Suites were those superb and now recently resuscitated Mercury Living Presence recordings by the always provocative Janos Starker. Like his great Galician predecessor Emanuel Feuermann, Starker has always been a welcome tonic to Casals's Rough-and-Tumble School of modern cello playing. His interpretations of the Bach Suites capture the essence of his unmannered, but always virile and distinctive, art with playing that mixes polish and control with fire and daring. Like all of the Mercury Living Presence recordings of the late '50s and early '60s, the sound on this one is astonishingly fresh and alive.

The eagerly anticipated account by Yo-Yo Ma, the most accomplished cellist of his generation, was a considerable disappointment. While the playing itself is thrillingly beautiful, there is a certain sameness in the performances that leaves one flat, as though we'd overheard a youthful run-through of what undoubtedly will be a great interpretation a few years down the road. Nevertheless, Ma's is still the preferred version in the tape format.

Suites (4) for Lute, S. 995/7 and 1006a

Williams, guitar. London 433022-2 [CD].

Given that Bob Dylan and the Beatles were its principal exponents in my youth, it's not surprising I never took the guitar all that seriously as a medium for

Serious Music. In the 1960s, it was something that any idiot could (and frequently did) play, especially in my college dorm, which was so riddled with scruffy, smelly Dylan clones that anyone who didn't have one was immediately suspected of being a secret supporter of Lyndon Johnson, napalm, and apartheid.

John Williams is such a fabulously accomplished musician that it scarcely matters what he plays. His versions of the Lute Suites are among the most musical and enjoyable of all Bach recordings, with playing that is lively, witty, and phenomenally precise. In the London transfer, the recorded sound is a bit bright and forward—the only minor drawback to an otherwise flawless release.

Suites (4) for Orchestra, S. 1066/69

**Academy of St. Martin-in-the-Fields, Marriner. London 430378-2
[CD].**

Nikolaus Harnoncourt's pioneering period instrument recording in the late 1960s established his reputation as an interpreter of Bach's music. I remember buying this work and being moderately enthusiastic at the time. Listening to it again, after nearly three decades, demonstrates what a woefully uncritical listener I was twenty years ago. It still seems to me the best of Harnoncourt's recordings, but that's a bit like trying to determine which of one's root-canal procedures bothered one the least. By no means should you waste your money buying this recording, but the next time you hear it on the radio, notice how crude and lifeless the playing is. In fact, in his driven, humorless approach to everything, Harnoncourt suggests nothing so much as a kind of technically inept Toscanini of the baroque.

The first of Marriner's three separate recordings to date, the London version is a reissue of that dazzling Argo edition prepared with the help of the late English musicologist Thurston Dart. As in Marriner's interpretation of the *Brandenburg Concertos*, the playing is brisk and ingratiating, with memorable contributions by every solo voice.

Unaccountably, Sir John Eliot Gardiner's wonderful period instrument recording for Erato has been withdrawn, demonstrating once again that an alarming number of children who tear the wings off butterflies and push little old ladies into manure spreaders eventually grow up to become recording executives. Until those silly people come to their senses, the best of the "authentic" versions is the warm and bracing Pinnock recording for Deutsche Grammophon (423492-2 [CD]), which comes with equally satisfying period accounts of the *Brandenburg Concertos*.

The Well-Tempered Clavier, S. 846/93

Gould, piano. Sony Classical SM2K 52600 [CD]; SM2K 52603 [CD].

Gilbert, harpsichord. Deutsche Grammophon Archiv ARC-413439-2 [CD].

In a charming little one-page essay called "Masters of Tone," the great American newspaperman, iconoclast, and linguistics scholar H. L. Mencken summed up the music of Johann Sebastian Bach as "Genesis I:1." Nowhere is Bach's seminal importance to the development of Western Music more obvious than in that most significant of all baroque keyboard collections, *The Well-Tempered Clavier.* Beginning with a disarmingly simple C Major Prelude that makes Beethoven's *Für Elise* seem like the Third Rachmaninoff Concerto, *The Well-Tempered Clavier* moves triumphantly through all the major and minor keys with forty-eight masterworks that not only encapsulate the entire scope of baroque contrapuntal thinking but also epitomize the essential greatness of Bach's mature keyboard style.

Like *The Art of Fugue, The Well-Tempered Clavier* was probably never intended for public performance and is in fact dedicated to the "musical youth, desirous of learning." Be that as it may, some of the major keyboard artists of the twentieth century, beginning with Wanda Landowska and Edwin Fischer, have left immensely personal visions of this towering monument that continues to exert an irresistible fascination for performers today.

As a *performance,* the most staggering modern interpretation could be heard on a Melodiya/Angel recording by Sviatoslav Richter, now long out of print. Like Serge Koussevitzky's Beethoven, Richter's conception of *The Well-Tempered Clavier* may have had very little to do with the music of Bach, but as a lesson in the art of piano playing given by the most fabulously complete pianist of the last forty years, it has never been approached.

As in his recording of the *Goldberg Variations,* Glenn Gould's performance remains a model of imaginative musical brinkmanship. In spite of all the eccentricities—which include some of the fastest and slowest performances the individual preludes have ever received—the playing is a triumph of Gouldian textural clarity and pizzazz: the way he manages to make the most complicated fugues sound so trivially easy will leave the jaws of the ten-fingered dragging on the floor.

For a less personal, though by no means anonymous, vision supplied by one of today's preeminent harpsichordists, the Deutsche Grammophon recording by Kenneth Gilbert offers many quiet and unexpected revelations. With playing that is alternately relaxed and pointed, Gilbert—without ever letting us forget that we are in the presence of a major artist—allows us to focus our entire attention where it properly belongs: on the music itself.

Bach, Wilhelm Friedemann (1710–1784)

Keyboard Music

Rousset, harpsichord. Harmonia Mundi HMA 1901305 [CD].

Often called the "Halle Bach" after the post that brought him his greatest fame, Wilhelm Friedemann Bach received his earliest musical training from his father, who wrote the first part of the *Well-Tempered Clavier* and the *Inventions* for his eldest son. In 1733, he was appointed organist of the Sophienkirche in Dresden and in 1746 took up a similar post at the Liebfrauenkirke in Halle, where he remained for eighteen years. Feeling that his gifts and achievements were insufficiently appreciated, he suddenly resigned his post in 1764 and, for the remaining twenty years of his life, was forced to eke out a tenuous living teaching and dedicating works to wealthy patrons. Lazy, hot-tempered, dissolute, and boorish, Wilhelm Friedemann was nonetheless a hero to his younger brothers, including Carl Philipp Emanuel, who insisted, "he could replace our father better than all the rest of us put together."

Christophe Rousset's stunning recital—recorded when that *wunderkind* harpsichordist was only nineteen—confirms C. P. E.'s glowing assessment, bringing together several of Wilhelm Friedemann's most exceptional keyboard works, including the powerfully dramatic Fantasia in C Minor with its obvious references to his father's Chromatic Fantasy and Fugue.

The playing throughout is pretty fabulous, as is the music itself.

Balakirev, Mily (1837–1910)

Symphony No. 1 in C Major; *Rus* (Second Overture on Russian Themes)

Philharmonia, Svetlanov. Hyperion CDA 66493 [CD].

After César Cui, whose music has slipped into an oblivion from which it seems unlikely ever to emerge, Mily Balakirev—accent on the second, not the penultimate, syllable—remains the most obscure member of that group of Russian composers that the critic Vladimir Stasov dubbed "The Mighty Five." As a conductor, composer, teacher, and propagandist, Balakirev probably did more

for the cause of Russian national music than anyone, including his more celebrated colleagues Borodin, Mussorgsky, and Rimsky-Korsakov.

With the glistening Oriental Fantasy *Islamey*—fabulously played by Andrei
Gavrilov as an encore to his electrifying recordings of the first piano concertos of
Tchaikovsky and Prokofiev on EMI Classics (CDM 64329-2 [CD]—the
Symphony in C Major is the most enjoyable and representative of Balakirev's
works. Until Sir Thomas Beecham's classic 1955 interpretation returns to general
circulation, Yevgeny Svetlanov's Hyperion recording makes for a sumptuous alternative. If the performance lacks the bite and character of Beecham's, then the
playing of the Philharmonia is as richly overripe as Hyperion's recorded sound is
richly resonant. A companion album (CDA 66586 [CD]) makes a similar case for
the composer's Second Symphony, the symphonic poem *Tamara,* and the delightful *Overture on Three Russian Themes.*

Balakirev's two piano concertos are available on another Hyperion album
(CDA 66640 [CD]) in committed, authoritative-sounding performances by pianist Malcolm Binns with the English Northern Philharmonia conducted by
David Lloyd-Jones. If the youthful F-sharp Minor Concerto is largely a passionate homage to the piano concertos of Balakirev's idol, Chopin, then the unfinished E-flat Major from 1861 is something altogether more individual and
important, even in the performing version prepared after its composer's death by
his pupil Sergei Lyapunov. The album is generously (and appropriately) rounded
out by the colorful and appealing Piano Concerto by Rimsky-Korsakov.

Bantock, Sir Granville

(1868–1946)

Sappho

Bickley, mezzo-soprano; Royal Philharmonic, Handley. Hyperion CDA
66899 [CD].

Apart from the tone poem *Fifine at the Fair* that his contemporary Sir
Thomas Beecham kept in his active repertoire for years, the music of this kindly
and prolific Englishman remains largely unknown. An accomplished conductor,
Bantock was unusually generous to his fellow composers; the Scotsman William
Wallace owed much of his early success to Bantock, who was also one of the first
foreign musicians to recognize the importance of Jean Sibelius. (In gratitude,

Sibelius dedicated his Third Symphony to his staunch English friend.) Bantock's own music contains obvious echoes of Wagner and Richard Strauss but is far better behaved, harmonically and emotionally; he also tended to think in very grand and frequently exotic terms, with his three-part setting of Edward Fitzgerald's translation of *The Rubáiyát of Omar Khayyám* running to more than two-and-a-half hours.

The orchestral song-cycle *Sappho,* a "Prelude and Nine Fragments," composed between 1898 and 1905 and lasting nearly an hour, is one of Bantock's most arresting works: a complex, richly varied series of responses to the erotic fragments of the most famous poet of Lesbos. A deeply satisfying high-Victorian decadence permeates the cycle, evoking images of faded tuberoses and the ink drawings of Aubrey Beardsley. Susan Bickley sings with subtlety and ardor throughout, while Vernon Handley inspires the Royal Philharmonic to prodigious feats of virtuosity. As an attractive bonus, the delicate *Sapphic Poem* for cello and orchestra is beautifully played by Julian Lloyd Webber.

Barber, Samuel   (1910–1981)

Adagio for Strings *(from String Quartet, Op. 11)*

> Los Angeles Philharmonic, Bernstein. Deutsche Grammophon 427806-2 [CD].

Even before achieving its current celebrity as "The Love Theme from *Platoon,*" Barber's moltenly beautiful *Adagio for Strings* had acquired many powerful nonmusical associations. In fact, the case can be made that it was the moving use to which the work was put during Franklin Delano Roosevelt's funeral that established Samuel Barber's popular reputation.

Of all the many recordings that the *Adagio* has thus far been given, none can come within hailing distance of the live performance—preserved superbly by Deutsche Grammophon—that Leonard Bernstein gave a few years ago with the Los Angeles Philharmonic. Adopting a tempo that is so measured that the music is almost guaranteed to fall apart, Bernstein, with vast dignity and deliberation, wrenches the last ounce of pain and pathos from the *Adagio,* while building one of the most devastating climaxes any piece has received in recent memory. While the Barber is clearly the principal selling point, there are also equally thrilling interpretations of Bernstein's *Candide Overture,* William Schuman's *American*

Festival Overture, and Aaron Copland's *Appalachian Spring,* making this one of the most exciting recordings of American music released in a decade.

For those interested in the ravishing String Quartet from which the *Adagio* was taken, the finest recorded performance the work has yet received can now be heard on a Deutsche Grammophon recording (435864-2 [CD]) by the Emerson String Quartet.

A further, rapturous version from 1967 features the words of the Latin *Agnus Dei* attached to the famous melody, a setting that fits so perfectly it's difficult to believe the composer didn't have the words in mind when he was originally writing the music. Matthew Best leads a seamless, intensely felt performance on a Hyperion collection of American music (CDA 66219 [CD]) that also includes excellent performances of Leonard Bernstein's *Chichester Psalms* and some Copland rarities, including the motet *In the Beginning.*

*A*dagio for Strings; Overture to *The School for Scandal*; Essay No. 2 for Orchestra; *Medea's Meditation and Dance of Vengeance*

New York Philharmonic, Schippers. Sony Classical MHK 62837 [CD];
   Odysey YT 33230 [T].

*A*dagio for Strings; Overture to *The School for Scandal*; Essays for Orchestra Nos. 1-3; *Medea's Meditation and Dance of Vengeance*

St. Louis Symphony, Slatkin. Angel CDC-49463 [CD], 4DS-49463 [T].

Except for the powerful and powerfully original Symphony No. 1, these two treasurable releases contain most of the works upon which Samuel Barber's reputation as a composer of orchestral music will probably rest.

The late Thomas Schippers's credentials as a Barber conductor were unassailable. An intimate friend of the composer, Schippers was responsible for perhaps the finest of all Barber recordings: an ineffably tender account of the composer's masterpiece, *Knoxville: Summer of 1915.* That luminescent RCA recording with Leontyne Price appears on CD (09026-61983-2) with its original companion piece, two scenes from Barber's unjustly maligned opera *Anthony and Cleopatra,* together with material from a 1953 Library of Congress recital that includes the composer accompanying Price in the *Hermit Songs.* No singer, not even the wonderful Eleanor Steber for whom it was written, can approach Price in *Knoxville* (or, indeed, in any of these lovely works) for sheer vocal beauty or musical acuity: it is one of the principal glories in a career strewn with glory, one of the classic interpretations upon which her enormous reputation will rest.

In the Sony Classical recording, the New York Philharmonic is on its best behavior—Harold Gomberg's oboe solo in the Overture is dumbfoundingly beautiful—and Schippers has never been better in the recording studio. The *Adagio* is the only one that compares favorably with Bernstein's, the Overture crackles with gaiety and wit, and *Medea's Meditation and Dance of Vengeance* is unleashed with such horrifying fury that it almost persuades you that Mother's Day ought to be canceled. The gem of the collection, however, is the Second Essay for Orchestra, in which lyricism, passion, and architectural integrity are kept in nearly perfect equilibrium by one of the most strangely underrated conductors of his time. For the CD transfer—part of the thus far indispensable "Masterworks Heritage" series—Sony Classical has wisely added as a bonus Martina Arroyo's withering reading of *Andromache's Farewell*.

Leonard Slatkin's recent Angel recording of the same repertoire confirms *his* position as the foremost Barber conductor before the public today. The St. Louis Symphony—which is now second to no orchestra in the country—romps through the music as though it were part of its standard repertoire, and Slatkin's interpretations are both refreshing and insightful. Especially valuable are the performances of the two "unknown" Essays: the First, for a change, sounds neither as monotonous nor as grim as it frequently can, and the Third—Barber's last major work—is imbued with all the richness and dignity of a genuine valedictory. The recorded sound, like the playing, is state-of-the-art.

Chamber Music

Canzone for Flute and Piano; Cello Sonata; *Excursions,* Op. 20; *Nocturne* (Homage to John Field); *Souvenirs: Pas de deux* and *Two-Step; Summer Music,* Op. 31

> Chamber Ensemble. EMI CDC 55400 [CD]
>
> Dover Beach, Op. 3; Serenade for String Quartet, Op. 1; String Quartet, Op. 11; Songs.
>
> Allen, baritone; Vignoles, piano; Endellion String Quartet. Virgin Classics CDC 45033 [CD].

Contained on these two discs is the bulk of Barber's chamber music output, from engaging miniatures like the haunting *Canzone* for flute and piano, to important works like the Cello Sonata, String Quartet, and *Summer Music,* the latter the result of a commission from Karl Haas's Detroit radio audience and a prime candidate—along with Irving Fine's *Partita*—for the distinction of being the finest American woodwind quintet. Not one performance on either disc is anything less than exemplary, including a darkly mature reading of *Dover Beach* from Thomas Allen that gives Thomas Hampson his only serious competition; for those reluctant to invest in the Deutsche Grammophon recording of the complete Barber songs (see page 43), this is an obvious first choice. (As splendid as both recordings are, one can only hope that some enterprising label will reissue the debut recording from the late '40s featuring the composer himself as the excellent baritone soloist.)

Concerto for Violin and Orchestra, Op. 14

Shaham, violin; London Symphony, Previn. Deutsche Grammophon 439886-2 [CD].

Barber's Violin Concerto was written on a commission from a wealthy American businessman who intended it for a young protégé. When the first two movements were eventually delivered, the young violinist dismissed them as being insufficiently virtuosic, whereupon a painful comedy of errors ensued. Barber promised to make amends in the Concerto's *Finale,* which the violinist then pronounced unplayable. The businessman demanded his money back, but alas, it had already been spent. To avoid litigation, Barber arranged for his friend Oscar Shumsky to play the work at a private concert, thus proving that it was anything but unperformable. As a final compromise, Barber agreed to relinquish half his fee, while the young violinist agreed to forgo his right to the first performance, which was finally given by the English violinist Albert Spalding at a Philadelphia Orchestra concert on February 7, 1941.

Gil Shaham's inspired recording is the finest the work has had since the pioneering stereo version made by Isaac Stern and Leonard Bernstein in 1964. Whatever Stern did, Shaham does better, bringing even more romance, subtlety, drama, and insight to the score. His ferocious articulation makes the *moto perpetuo* finale the nail-biter it needs to be, with Sir André Previn and the London Symphony lending exhilarating support. As though the CD could have been any more attractive, it comes with one of most successful versions of Erich Wolfgang Korngold's swashbuckling Violin Concerto, together with a suite—with Previn at the piano—from the incidental music to Shakespeare's *Much Ado About Nothing.*

Barber's wartime Cello Concerto is one of the most conspicuously neglected of all his works, for reasons that are difficult to explain. A lush, eloquent, elegiac score, it is given a thoughtful and impassioned reading by Steven Isserlis and the St. Louis Symphony conducted by Leonard Slatkin (RCA 09026-68283-2 [CD]). Although this brings a duplicate version of the Violin Concerto—in an excellent performance with Kyoko Takezawa—a delightful bonus is the witty *Capricorn Concerto* for flute, oboe, trumpet, and orchestra, one of the most successful of all American attempts to revive the spirit of the Classical *sinfonia concertante.*

The Lovers; Prayers of Kierkegaard

Soloists, Chicago Symphony Chorus and Orchestra, Schenck. Koch 7125-2 [CD]; KIC 7125 [T].

Major works by this maddeningly reticent composer are sufficiently scarce that the world premiere recording of one and the first really adequate version of another are events of some significance. Composed in 1953 on a commission from Serge Koussevitzky, the *Prayers of Kierkegaard* is an alternately grave and rapturous setting of the Danish philosopher's ruminations, while *The Lovers,* a 1971 setting of nine poems of Pablo Neruda in the splendid translations by Christopher Logue and W. S. Merwin, was Barber's only major work after the crushing disaster of *Antony and Cleopatra* in 1966. Less powerfully concentrated than the *Prayers,* it is nonetheless a lovely and sensual work, containing some of the most frankly erotic music Barber would ever compose.

Recorded at a Chicago Symphony concert in 1991, the carefully prepared interpretations have the added excitement of a live performance with none of the usual drawbacks: both the orchestra and Margaret Hillis's Chicago Symphony Chorus are predictably flawless and the audience forgets to breathe.

Obviously, no one with even a passing interest in Barber's music can afford to pass this one up.

Piano Music

McCawley, piano. Virgin Classics VC5 45270-2 [CD].

Here on one convenient disc is Barber's entire output for solo piano, including the four *Excursions,* Op. 20; the two-hand version of *Souvenirs;* and the Sonata he wrote for Vladimir Horowitz—which, along with the sonatas of Griffes, Ives, Copland, and Carter, is surely one of the finest such works written by an American. If the 1950 Horowitz recording of the Sonata (RCA 60377-2-RG [CD]) remains in a very special class, then Leon McCawley nonetheless offers it some serious competition, with an even more warmly expressive approach to the opening movement and an electrifying account of the thorny *Fuga.* The other performances are no less gripping, including a suitably valedictory account of the posthumous *Interlude.*

*S*ongs *(complete)*

Studer, soprano; Hampson, baritone; Browning, piano; Emerson String Quartet. Deutsche Grammophon 435867-2 [CD].

This is the most beautiful and important album of American music released in a decade, the first integral recording of a key facet of Barber's output featuring two of America's finest singers accompanied by a pianist with a profound and special insight into the composer's work. John Browning, who also supplied the illuminating notes for this two-CD set of Barber's entire output of songs, was a friend of the composer and thus a uniquely qualified guide to this material, which from the earliest to the latest items shows an astonishing consistency of melodic and dramatic inspiration. Nor is it possible to imagine a better choice of singers for the project than Cheryl Studer and Thomas Hampson. Although Studer's delivery is not ideally effortless throughout, she sings with perception and taste; if her version of the *Hermit Songs* doesn't completely efface the memory of Price and Steber, then it can still be mentioned in the same breath with theirs: the singing is lush and feminine, the word-painting both subtle and shrewd. Hampson's contributions, on the other hand, only add further fuel to the argument that he is now America's finest singer. Nothing now seems beyond his vocal, musical, or expressive grasp, with the *Mélodies passagères* and *Dover Beach* receiving their most haunting recorded performances ever.

All in all, this is a milestone in the recording history of American music.

*S*ymphony No. 1 in One Movement; Piano Concerto, Op. 38; *Souvenirs*

Browning, piano; St. Louis Symphony, Slatkin. RCA 60732-2-RC [CD].

Given that along with the Third Symphony of Roy Harris it may well be the finest work in the form ever written by an American, Samuel Barber's Symphony No. 1 has not been all that well served by the recording industry. Apart from Bruno Walter's blazing account from the 78 era, there has never been a completely satisfying commercial recording of this taut and turbulent masterpiece—at least, until now.

Along with the excellent Argo recording by the Baltimore Symphony under David Zinman and a fine version from Neemi Järvi and the Detroit Symphony that served as a makeweight for their performance of Amy Beach's *Gaelic* Symphony, the recording by the St. Louis Symphony under Leonard Slatkin is the one that finally does something like complete justice to the piece. On balance, the Slatkin is not only the most dramatically searching and impressively played of the three, but it also comes with a superb performance of the Barber Piano Concerto, featuring the pianist Barber personally chose to give the world premiere. If not quite as electric as John Browning's earlier, long-out-of-print recording with the Cleveland Orchestra and George Szell, then the new one still towers above all the current competition. With Slatkin joining Browning for a charming two-piano version of *Souvenirs* as an encore, this is another indispensable Barber album from St. Louis.

Vanessa, Op. 32

Steber, Elias, Resnik, Gedda, Tozzi, Metropolitan Opera Chorus and Orchestra, Mitropoulos. RCA Victor 7899-2-RG [CD].

If there was ever a contemporary opera for people who think they hate contemporary operas, then it is Samuel Barber's *Vanessa*. The reason, of course, is obvious: *Vanessa* is a full-fledged nineteenth-century grand opera, even though it may have had its world premiere in 1958.

From the mid-1930s until his death, Barber was something of an anomaly among the major twentieth-century American composers. Recognition came early, his first musical champions included figures as diverse and powerful as Arturo Toscanini and Serge Koussevitzky and Bruno Walter, and for the next half century he enjoyed the kind of popular and critical acclaim that might have ruined the career of a lesser man.

To the very end, his expressive idiom remained stubbornly and unashamedly Romantic, though it was a Romanticism guided by a commanding modern intellect, coupled with extraordinary elegance and finesse. After George Gershwin, he was also the most gifted melodist of his generation, the American composer whose art was most firmly grounded in the natural grace of song.

While *Vanessa* may not be universally regarded as a *great* opera—though I, for one, am inclined to think that it is—there has been little argument that it is a haunted and haunting work, with moments of rare and voluptuous beauty. For instance, Erika's tiny throwaway "aria," "Why must the winter come so soon?" is in itself nearly worth the price of admission.

It was extremely decent of RCA to reissue this historic recording, made with the original cast in 1958. Eleanor Steber, for whom the *Hermit Songs* and *Knoxville: Summer of 1915* were written, more than lives up to the legend in the title role. The supporting cast is uniformly excellent (Rosalind Elias and Nicolai Gedda especially so) and that largely unsung hero of modern music, Dimitri Mitropoulos, leads a performance in which the unearthly lyricism and dramatic tension of the piece are given free and equal reign. For lovers of Barber, opera (modern or otherwise), glorious melody, and lovely singing, this one cannot be passed up.

For those who have always suspected that the failure of *Antony and Cleopatra* at the opening of the new Metropolitan Opera House in 1966 had to do with something other than Barber's music—Franco Zeffirelli's fussy, overblown staging, for instance, or that expensive machinery that stubbornly refused to work—a live performance recorded at the 1983 Spoleto Festival (New World NW 80322/24-2 [CD]), featuring a fine if hardly stellar cast, proves that the score abounds in the riveting set pieces and memorable tunes that New York critics accused it of lacking. If nothing else, the recording demonstrates how badly *Antony and Cleopatra* deserves a second chance.

Bartók, Béla (1881–1945)

Bluebeard's Castle

> Martón, Ramey, Hungarian State Opera Orchestra, Fischer. CBS MK-44523 [CD].

Bartók's greatest stage work is certainly not for children or sissies. And this has nothing to do with the gruesome violence of the piece, since there is none. What makes *Bluebeard's Castle* so taxing for most people is that it has only two extremely talkative characters and practically no action. Yet because it is a work about a man who values his privacy, the pathologically private composer threw his entire being into the project, producing a score of unsurpassed richness, subtlety, and depth. It is not only prime early Bartók, but also—since so little actually takes place on stage—an ideal opera for home listening.

While the brilliant London recording (414167-2 [CD]) has much to recommend it, especially the conducting of the young Istvàn Kertèsz, who turns in the most powerful realization of the orchestral part, it is the singing on the more recent CBS version that sets it apart and will probably keep it streets ahead of the competition for decades. With its inky, resonant lower register and brilliant baritonal top end, the voice of Samuel Ramey is perfect for the hero. Eva Martón, vocally phenomenal as always, here seems capable of shattering flowerpots, much less wineglasses. Adam Fischer is an able accomplice, keeping the tension at an almost uncomfortably high level from beginning to end.

Concerto for Orchestra

> **Chicago Symphony, Reiner. RCA 09026-61504-2 [CD]; 09026-61504-4 [T].**
>
> **City of Birmingham Symphony, Rattle. EMI Classics CDC 55094 [CD].**

Like his near contemporary George Szell, Fritz Reiner was one of the consummate orchestral technicians of the twentieth century. There was nothing that his minuscule, but infinitely various, beat could not express and even less that escaped his hooded, hawk-like eye. He was also a humorless despot who terrorized orchestras for more than fifty years. Once, at a Reiner rehearsal, a jovial bass player whipped out a huge brass telescope and shouted, "I'm looking for the beat." The man was fired on the spot.

Like Szell—of whom one frequently hears the same nonsense—Reiner was frequently accused of being rather chilly and aloof in his performances: a kind of radioactive ice cube who sacrificed depth and emotion in favor of brilliantly polished surface details. There are dozens of Reiner recordings that ably refute this preposterous contention, none more convincingly than his stupendous version of Bartók's Concerto for Orchestra.

In its new compact disc format, this ageless performance sounds as if it might have been recorded a few years ago, instead of at the very dawn of the stereo era. Reiner's characteristic combination of complete flexibility and cast-iron control can be heard in every bar of the interpretation, from the dark melancholy of the opening movement to the giddy reaffirmation of life in the *Finale*.

If Sir Georg Solti's more recent Chicago Symphony performance on a London compact disc offers clearer sound and slightly better orchestral execution, then the brusque and intermittently vulgar reading is no match for Reiner's. And since the Reiner CD offers, as a bonus, the most hair-raising of all recordings of the *Music for Strings, Percussion, and Celesta* and a splendidly atmospheric *Hungarian Sketches,* it constitutes—at something over sixty-five minutes—one of the few authentic bargains on the market today.

Sir Simon Rattle's EMI Classics recording is the first to mount a serious challenge to Reiner's in a generation. In addition to playing that nearly matches Reiner's in its polish and intensity, the recording has the further advantages of the excitement generated by a live performance and state-of-the-art digital sound. Coupled with an exhilarating *Miraculous Mandarin,* this is a Bartók album that should be added to every collection without delay.

Concertos for Piano and Orchestra (3)

Schiff, piano; Budapest Festival Orchestra, Fischer. Teldec 13158-2.

Sándor, Hungarian State Orchestra, Fischer. Sony Classical SK 45835 [CD].

The three concertos that Bartók composed primarily for his own use are so central to the language of twentieth-century piano music that one wonders why they aren't performed and recorded more frequently. While the percussive First Concerto is still a fairly difficult pill for most people to swallow, and the fiendish Second Concerto is all but unplayable, the lyrical, sweet-spirited Third should have entered the standard repertoire years ago. A deceptively simple, often child-ish piece, it should pose no problem for anyone who enjoys Rachmaninoff or Tchaikovsky and, further, becomes an ideal invitation to explore the more complex pleasures of the two masterworks that precede it.

Given the warmth and clarity of his many outstanding Bach recordings, it should come as no surprise that András Schiff brings an abundance of both qualities to his countryman's piano concertos. Along with being among the most humane and meticulous recordings these challenging works have yet received, they are also bursting with wit, passion, and an innate understanding of their intensely Hungarian idiom: in other words, the most thrillingly *complete* interpretations on the market today. The accompaniments are comparably brilliant and natural, as is the Teldec recorded sound.

For the last word in absolute authenticity, the recordings by the composer's friend György Sándor remain in a class by themselves. Not only did he study the music with Bartók himeslf, but he was also chosen by the Bartók family to give the Third Concerto's world premiere after the composer's death. As in his earlier cycle for Vox (now available on CDX2 5506), Sándor brings a fire and authority to the music that no other living pianist can match.

Concerto No. 2 in B Minor for Violin and Orchestra

Chung, violin; Chicago Symphony, Solti. London 425015-2 [CD].

Like the life-affirming Concerto for Orchestra that was written while the composer was dying of leukemia, the exuberant B Minor Violin Concerto was produced during an unusually harrowing period of Bartók's life. Begun during the dark months of 1938, when the composer was fearing the spread of Nazism throughout central Europe and worrying, correctly, about "the imminent danger that Hungary, too, will surrender to this system of robbers and murderers," the Second Violin Concerto is one of his most optimistic and proudly nationalistic statements. Folk-like melodies permeate the entire fabric of the score, as does a giddy virtuosity that makes it one of the more challenging and rewarding works in the violinist's repertoire.

Kyung-Wha Chung brings a towering technique to the music and a sharp objectivity that many might find distant or cold. The approach works exceptionally well in the often uncompromising outer movements of the Concerto, and Solti's equally cool yet idiomatic accompaniment clearly places the piece in the mainstream of twentieth-century violin concertos.

Dance Suite; *Divertimento; Hungarian Sketches; Two Pictures*

Chicago Symphony, Boulez. Deutsche Grammophon 445825-2 [CD].

Since in order to get one or more of these richly colorful pieces you usually have to buy yet another recording of the Concerto for Orchestra, it's especially rewarding to see them all gathered together on a single compact disc. Released to coincide with Pierre Boulez's seventy-fifth birthday in 1995, this is one of the most worthwhile of the conductor's recent recordings: the rhythms of the Dance Suite are projected with enormous bite and clarity, the *Divertimento* emerges with all its neo-Classical elegance and humor intact, while the *Hungarian Sketches* are as distinctively Hungarian as anyone could wish. The prize of the collection, though, is Boulez's version of the early *Two Pictures for Orchestra*, which here for once sounds like something considerably more than a series of intriguing promises of what was to come.

Given its long Bartók tradition, it comes as no surprise that the Chicago Symphony plays the music as if they owned it, while the DG engineers respond with their most beautifully natural recorded sound.

Mikrokosmos (selections); *Contrasts*

Bartók, piano. Sony Classical MPK 47676 [CD].

Consisting of 153 tiny pieces in six volumes, Bartók's *Mikrokosmos* was written to teach children the logic and meaning of contemporary music. From simple studies in dotted notes, syncopation, and parallel motion to more elaborate examinations of polytonality and poly-rhythms, *Mikrokosmos* represents precisely that: a series of "little worlds" in which the composer's inventive genius was at its purest and most disarming.

As these famous recordings made in 1940 clearly prove, Bartók himself was an ideal guide to these enchanting microcosms: the playing is simple and unaffected, a paradigm of that art that conceals art. With the equally famous recording of *Contrasts* made with Benny Goodman and Joseph Szigeti, this is a thrillingly immediate reminder of a great musician and a great soul.

The Miraculous Mandarin (complete ballet)

New York Philharmonic, Boulez. Sony Classical SMK 45837 [CD].

I had a close friend who had an extremely effective method of getting rid of visitors who overstayed their welcomes. Rather than yawn ostentatiously or consult his watch every five minutes, he would put on a recording of the *Miraculous Mandarin* and within minutes would find himself alone.

Though written as long ago as 1919, Bartók's savage, sensational, frequently sickening ballet remains a startlingly modern work. Emotionally—if not necessarily musically—it often seems more advanced than Stravinsky's *Rite of Spring;* at the very least, it is one of the first important musical works that seems to have completely digested the horrific implications of the then recently concluded First World War.

Early in his unhappy stay in Chicago, the late Jean Martinon made a recording of the *Miraculous Mandarin* Suite for RCA Victor that may always be the last word in orchestral ferocity; coupled with an equally memorable version of Hindemith's ballet on the life of St. Francis of Assisi, *Nobilissima Visione,* it was one of the best of Victor's Chicago Symphony recordings and certainly deserves a CD reissue.

Pierre Boulez's stunning New York Philharmonic recording not only underscores the *Miraculous Mandarin's* link to Stravinsky but also invests it with a lyric grace that will surprise many admirers of the ballet. Which is not to say that the performance soft-pedals the more savage elements: when the finale begins grunting and snarling in earnest, wimps will make for the nearest door.

Bartók's vastly different fairy-tale ballet, the warm and cuddly *Wooden Prince,* is now best represented by a sumptuous Chandos recording (CHAN 8895 [CD]) by the Philharmonia Orchestra led by the ubiquitous Neeme Järvi. In addition to being the only note-complete version now available, it is also one of the most vividly graphic recordings of *any* ballet. Järvi's gifts as a musical storyteller are such that one can easily follow the dramatic argument without the slightest hint of what's going on. The performance of the *Hungarian Pictures* that comes as a filler is no less splendid.

Piano Music

Kocsis, piano. Hungariton HCD 12304 [CD]; Philips 434104-2 [CD].

Szokolay, piano. Naxos 8.550451-2 [CD].

The inexplicable withdrawal of both of György Sándor's classic recordings of Bartók's complete piano music leaves a serious gap in the catalogue that can be filled—at least in part—by a number of fine recent recordings.

Zoltán Kocsis's Hungariton recording of *For Children* is both subtle and exciting, while his generously packed Philips anthology—announced as "Volume 1" of what will presumably become a complete cycle—is even more vivid and imaginative, with thrillingly realistic recorded sound.

If, as a pianist, Balázs Szokolay is not a quite in Kocsis's league, then his Naxos collection is still tremendously enjoyable, with the same intelligence and natural ease that make his recordings of Grieg's *Lyric Pieces* so affecting (see page 301).

Of course, for the *absolute* last word on the subject, one should consult the massive six-CD collection from Hungariton (HCD 12326/31 [CD]) called "Bartók at the Piano," which contains virtually every recording that the composer made between 1920 and 1945. Naturally, the recorded sound is variable, especially in the off-the-air transcriptions and unpublished test pressings. Nonetheless, for the thrill and honor of hearing one of giants of music in action, it could be a whole lot worse.

String Quartets (6)

Emerson String Quartet. Deutsche Grammophon 423657-2 [CD].

With the possible exceptions of the quartets of Dmitri Shostakovich, Arnold Schoenberg, and Leoš Janáček, those of Béla Bartók are the most significant contribution that a twentieth-century composer has yet made to the form. Each of these adventurous masterworks is an important signpost in the evolution of Bartók's stylistic development: from the folk-like elements that pervade the early works, to the astringent flirtation with atonality in the middle two, to a more direct and simple mode of communication in the last two works of the series.

For more than three decades, the cycle has very nearly been the private property of the Juilliard String Quartet. When their most recent recording was withdrawn—possibly to be reissued as a CBS compact disc—many of us despaired of ever hearing its like again, at least until the arrival of the new Deutsche Grammophon recording by the Emerson String Quartet.

There are many who insist that the Emerson is the finest young American string quartet now before the public. I would agree with that assessment, if one were to drop the modifiers "young" and "American." Judging from the series of "Great Romantic Quartets" they recorded for the Book-of-the-Month Club and this hair-raising version of the Bartók Quartets, there seems to be nothing that the Emersons cannot do. They play with the all the fire and polish of the old Juilliard, yet still produce a sinuous beauty of tone reminiscent of the Guarneri Quartet in its prime. It is also the only quartet in living memory that literally has no second fiddle: the two violinists change roles from concert to concert and often from piece to piece.

This is easily one of the finest Bartók cycles yet recorded, with interpretations that are large, audacious, brooding, risky, colorful, and richly "histrionic" in the best possible sense of the word. The hell-bent performance of the Second Quartet may be the most frighteningly exciting ever, and the Fifth has never seemed more amusing or profound.

Among other recordings of Bartók's chamber music, Gidon Kremer's versions of the two Violin Sonatas for Hungariton (HCD 11655-2 [CD]) represent some of his finest work in the recording studio to date: the performances have a scale and intensity unlike any other, including the pioneering interpretations of the composer's friend Joseph Szigeti.

The astonishing Sonata for Solo Violin has never been better served than in Mark Kaplan's recent Arabesque recording, which combines musical insight, breathtaking virtuosity, and flawless recorded sound (Z6649 [CD]). A program of Bartòk's shorter works for violin and piano rounds out a most desirable disc.

Bax, Sir Arnold   (1883–1953)

The Garden of Fand; The Happy Forest; November Woods; Summer Music

Ulster Orchestra, Thomson. Chandos CHAN-8307 [CD].

After Ralph Vaughan Williams, Sir Arnold Bax, late the Master of the King's Musick and composer of the score for David Lean's immortal movie version of *Oliver Twist,* was the major English symphonist of the twentieth century. While his gentlemanly yet deeply Romantic music contains occasional echoes of Vaughan Williams and Sibelius, there is a strong, highly individual personality that informs the best of it, especially the four masterful tone poems with which the late Bryden Thomson and the Ulster Orchestra began their complete cycle of Bax's music for Chandos. In all of them, the composer's obsession with Celtic legend and his fascination with French Impressionism are clearly evident: these are darkly chromatic, vividly evocative scores that become all the more fascinating on repeated hearings.

For those who find themselves drawn to Bax—and I treasure him almost as much as I do Walton and Tippett—the next logical step is to explore the seven symphonies, all of which have now been recorded by Thomson and his excellent band. While the quality tends to vary, at least four of them rank with the finest symphonies ever written by an Englishman. The Second, composed for Serge Koussevitzky, is a sweeping, deeply spiritual work, with an almost baroque opulence of ornamental detail (CHAN-8493 [CD]). The mystical Third—first recorded in 1943 by Sir John Barbirolli—is perhaps the most accomplished and original of the cycle (CHAN-8454 [CD]), while the Fifth (CHAN-8669 [CD] and Sixth (CHAN-8586 [CD]) are clearly the works of an independent master who owes nothing to anyone or to any school.

Thomson and his orchestra cannot be praised too vigorously for either their meticulous execution or their ability to immerse themselves so completely in the composer's unique idiom. As with that other great Nature poet, Frederick Delius, Bax is decidedly an acquired taste; yet like many acquired tastes, he can quickly turn into an acquired passion.

Finally, in what may well be the loveliest Bax album yet released (Hyperion CDA 66807 [CD]), the Nash Ensemble give typically wise and sympathetic performances of five of the composer's most important chamber works, including the Nonet of 1930, the *Elegiac Trio* from 1916, and the Clarinet Sonata of 1934. Best of all, though, are the amiably folksy Oboe Quintet of 1922 and the Harp Quintet of 1919, in which one can almost hear the strumming of the Celtic bards. Everything about the album is flawless, from the glowing performances to the cover art, a haunting landscape with cows called *Pastures at Malahide* by Nathaniel Hone the Younger (1831–1917).

Beach, Mrs. H. H. A. (Amy Marcy Cheny) (1867–1944)

Symphony in E Minor, Op. 64, "Gaelic Symphony"

Detroit Symphony, Järvi. Chandos CHAN 8958 [CD].

Mrs. H. H. A. Beach, to use the designation that this hugely proper and very gifted Bostonian preferred, wrote what has the distinction of being only the second symphony ever published by an American composer, the "Gaelic Symphony" of 1896. As with virtually all of the serious American music written at the time, the spirit of Dvořák hangs heavily over Mrs. Beach's major orchestral score, as do the shades of Schubert, Brahms, and Liszt. Still, the "Gaelic" is a skillful manipulation of a series of familiar Irish folk tunes and a work of considerable power and charm.

The new Chandos recording—the first since the game but not especially inspired outing released by the long-defunct Society for the Preservation of the American Musical Heritage—features the resurgent Detroit Symphony, sounding better than it has in years, with Järvi providing his predictable blend of insight and enthusiasm. The versions of Barber's First Symphony and Overture to *The School for Scandal,* if not the first choice for either piece, make for an attractive and generous filler.

Mrs. Beach's attractive piano music can be heard on a pair of CDs from Northeastern (NR 223; NR 9004). Although the music is largely of the *fin-de-siècle,* potted-palm variety, it has considerable freshness and period charm, particularly in the definitive-sounding interpretations of the wonderful Virginia Eskin. Two of the composer's more important larger works—the Piano Concerto in C-sharp Minor and the Piano Quintet in F-sharp Minor, which many Beacheans have long argued is her masterpiece—are available in fine recent ASV recording (ASV 932 [CD]) by Martin Roscoe and the Endellion Quartet.

Beethoven, Ludwig van

(1770–1827)

*B*agatelles (24), Op. 33, 119, 126

Jandó, piano, Naxos 8.550474 [CD].

There are few works that make this crusty, often forbidding, giant seem more endearingly human than the three sparkling sets of *Bagatelles:* rarely is Beethoven this consistently charming, humorous, and relaxed.

As in the wondrous and inexplicably withdrawn Philips recording by Stephen Kovacevich (né Bishop, latterly Bishop-Kovacevich), Jenö Jandó is an ideal exponent of these attractive miniatures. The playing is both imaginative and wholly unaffected, allowing the natural charm of the pieces to emerge.

*C*antata on the Death of Emperor Joseph II; Cantata on the Accession of Emperor Leopold II; Meerstille und glückliche Fahrt (Calm Sea and Prosperous Voyage); *Opferlied*

Soloists, Corydon Singers and Orchestra, Best. Hyperion CDA 66880 [CD].

Although the forty-minute *Cantata on the Death of Emperor Joseph II* is an early work, written when the nineteen-year-old composer was still living in Bonn, it offers music of astonishing confidence and quality, as the mature Beethoven came to realize all too well: he would eventually cannibalize one of the soprano's arias for Leonore's "O Gott! Welch ein Augenblick" from the finale of *Fidelio*. The three shorter works that fill out the album are no less fascinating, especially the late *Opferlied* (Song of Sacrifice), which glances backward to *Fidelio*'s "Prisoners' Chorus" and forward to the "Casta Diva" from Bellini's *Norma*.

Matthew Best leads alert and glowing performances of all of these inexplicably neglected works, receiving dedicated support from all the soloists, especially the fetching Janice Watson. Predictably, Hyperion's recorded sound, notes, and packaging are all superb.

Choral Fantasy (Fantasia in C Minor for Piano, Chorus, and Orchestra, Op. 80)

> **Serkin, piano; Westminster Choir, New York Philharmonic, Bernstein.**
>   **CBS MYK-38526 [CD], MYT-38526 [T].**

This odd, hybrid piece—and no one would again write for this combination of forces until Ferruccio Busoni unveiled his mammoth Piano Concerto (albeit for Piano, Orchestra, and *Male* Chorus) more than a century later—owes much of its popularity to the fact that it is usually viewed as a kind of dry run for the *Finale* of the Ninth Symphony. It isn't, really, but the *Fantasia*'s choral theme *is* a close cousin of the "Ode to Joy," and in the right hands, it can make for an intriguing, uplifting experience.

In my experience, only one recording has ever made this peculiar hodgepodge come off, and that is the version taped in the early 1960s by Rudolf Serkin and Leonard Bernstein. As usual, Serkin's seriousness of purpose imbues the music with a dignity and significance that no other interpretation does, while Bernstein's enthusiasm proves a perfect foil to the high-mindedness (though never high-*handedness*) of his partner.

A vintage Serkin interpretation of the Third Piano Concerto fills out both the compact disc and tape.

Concertos (5) for Piano and Orchestra

> **Fleisher, Cleveland Orchestra, Szell. CBS M3K-42445 [CD].**

> **Schnabel, London Symphony, Sargent. Pearl PEA 9063 [CD].**

Since the extravagantly gifted William Kapell died in a plane crash near San Francisco in 1953, the careers of America's finest pianists have been the cause of great sadness, consternation, and alarm. The mercurial, highly strung Byron Janis began canceling appearances on such a regular basis that his brief but brilliant career was over almost before it began; similarly, the unjustly maligned Van

Cliburn, after years of abuse from the critics, lapsed into a stony silence from which he has only recently emerged. Gary Graffman has been plagued in the last decade by a crippling neurological disorder, as has the most accomplished American pianist since William Kapell, Leon Fleisher.

The recent CBS compact disc reissue of Fleisher's classic account of the Beethoven Concertos with George Szell and the Cleveland Orchestra is a major cause for rejoicing. Rarely, if ever, have a pianist and conductor shown more unanimity of purpose and execution in this music. The rhythms are consistently crisp and vibrant. The phrasing is meticulous almost to a fault, and the hair-trigger reflexes of the Cleveland Orchestra are a perfect complement to Fleisher's once fabulous technique. Although some listeners might find the approach uncomfortably patrician, Fleisher and Szell manage to scrape off so many layers of accumulated interpretive treacle that we are able, in effect, to hear these familiar and frequently hackneyed works as if for the very first time.

If state-of-the-art recorded sound and mechanical perfection are not absolute necessities, the recordings made in the 1930s by Fleisher's great teacher, Artur Schnabel, are still the standard by which all other recordings must be judged. Never a pianist's pianist, Schnabel's technical imperfections were the butt of countless jokes among his colleagues. When told that Schnabel had been exempted from military service for physical reasons during the First World War, that mordant turn-of-the-century virtuoso Moritz Rosenthal quipped, "Naturally, the man has no fingers." Nevertheless, it was the force of Schnabel's personality that virtually rediscovered Beethoven's piano music in the 1920s and '30s, and in Arabesque's immaculate transfers, these impetuous, headstrong, and always deeply personal interpretations emerge as touchstones of twentieth-century keyboard art.

Concerto for Violin and Orchestra in D Major, Op. 61

Menuhin, Philharmonia Orchestra, Furtwängler. Angel CDH-69799 [CD].

Perlman, Philharmonia Orchestra, Giulini. Angel CDC-56210 [CD].

It has been argued—and argued persuasively—that Yehudi Menuhin has yet to make a finer recording than the 1932 version of the Elgar Violin Concerto, made when that extraordinary child prodigy was only sixteen years old. And in the last couple of decades, Menuhin's Olympian technique has eroded alarmingly. Although the warmth and musicianship are still there in ample supply, the digital dexterity is now a mere shadow of its former self.

With the Elgar, this famous recording of the Beethoven Concerto ranks with the violinist's greatest achievements. In it, the high-minded nobility and melting tenderness of this unique musician are conspicuously on display. Add to that the surging yet impeccably disciplined accompaniment that Wilhelm Furtwängler provided in one of his final commercial recordings, and we are left with something very close to a Beethoven Violin Concerto for the ages.

For those who require more up-to-date sound—although in EMI's compact disc transfer, the 1954 acoustics sound remarkably detailed and warm—the best modern version comes from Itzhak Perlman and Carlo Maria Giulini. The violinist offers his usual blend of exuberance and arching lyricism, while the conductor's elegant yet probing support confirms his reputation as one of the great modern accompanists.

Concerto for Violin, Cello, Piano, and Orchestra in C Major, Op. 56 ("Triple Concerto")

Kalichstein, piano; Laredo, violin; Robinson, cello; English Chamber Orchestra, Gibson. Chandos CHAN 6501 [CD].

Although it doesn't exactly bear the same relationship to Beethoven's other concertos that *Wellington's Victory* does to the symphonies, the "Triple Concerto" can be a lame, long-winded thing, even when given the most committed kind of performance. For the already converted—I myself will remain a naysaying heretic to the end—the Kalichstein-Laredo-Robinson Trio with Sir Alexander Gibson and the English Chamber Orchestra (like the Bernard Haitink and the Beaux Arts Trio in their now deleted Philips recording) give the thing every opportunity to sound important and interesting. Everyone—including Philips's engineers—works together beautifully. Only the Concerto itself refuses to cooperate.

On a more positive note, the performance comes with a fascinating bonus: the sketches for the first movement of the Tenth Symphony, in the reconstruction by Dr. Barry Cooper. While this is less an actual Beethoven symphonic movement than a series of scholarly speculations, the actual musical materials are distinctive and memorable, as is the performance by the City of Birmingham Symphony conducted by Walter Weller.

The creatures of Prometheus (complete ballet)

Orpheus Chamber Orchestra. Deutsche Grammophon 419608-2 [CD].

Once again, the Orpheus Chamber Orchestra seems to prove that the cheapest instrument of the orchestra is the conductor's baton. This is easily the most alert and vivid recording ever made of Beethoven's youthful ballet, which, apart from the overture and the famous tune that would turn up in the finale of the "Eroica" Symphony, is very little known. Although clearly not top-drawer Beethoven, *The Creatures of Prometheus* makes for some extremely agreeable listening, especially in so fine a performance as this.

Sir Thomas Beecham's crackling account of the *Ruins of Athens* music has finally been reissued as the filler for his extremely individual recording of Beethoven's Mass in C (EMI Classics CDM 64385 [CD]), and Michael Tilson Thomas's spirited recording of the *King Stephen* incidental music (CBS MK-33509 [CD]) really is a must for the Beethoven freak who has to have everything. For in addition to that splendid performance—which includes the best version of the Overture since the Victor recording by Pierre Monteux—the album offers first-rate versions of *Calm Sea and Prosperous Voyage* and those *genuine* choral rarities, the *Opferlied, Bundeslied,* and *Elegischer Gesang.*

*E*gmont (complete incidental music)

Lorengar, soprano; Wussow, narrator; Vienna Philharmonic, Szell.
London 448 593-2 [CD].

When Beethoven was first approached to write the incidental music for a production of Johann Wolfgang von Goethe's *Egmont* by Vienna's Burgtheater in 1809, the composer jumped at the chance. Like everyone else, he revered Goethe as the central figure of German cultural life. Moreover, the theme of the play, which concerns the Dutch struggle for independence from Spain in the late 1560s, greatly appealed to Beethoven's egalitarian instincts: a similar story formed the plot of his one and only opera, *Fidelio.* Beethoven wrote to the poet about "This glorious *Egmont,* which I read so ardently, thought over and experienced again and gave out in music," while, for his part, Goethe answered with measured deliberation that while he hadn't yet in fact *heard* the music, he had heard it "spoken of with praise by several."

When the two great men met for the first time at Teplitz in July of 1812, relations between them seem to have been strained from the beginning. The older Goethe found the composer rather impertinent and uncouth while, for his part, Beethoven found his hero to be somewhat stuffy and pretentious. A famous anecdote finds them strolling through the wooded grounds of the Bohemian spa, drawing smiles and bows from the numerous passers-by. The poet, pretending to be put out by all the attention, says: "It is annoying, but I can't help getting these compliments." At which point Beethoven is alleged to have replied, "Don't let them bother you, your Excellency. Perhaps they are meant for me."

This famous recording was one of the highlights of the Beethoven Bicentennial in 1970, a performance so dramatically gripping and full of life that one can easily overlook the necessarily patchwork nature of the score. To help glue things together, the producers wisely opted for a linking narration by the Austrian poet Franz Grillparzer. Though when listening, do follow along with the English translation: non-German listeners might find Klaus-Jürgen Wussow's delivery of the hero's gallows speech somewhat unsettling, sounding—as it does—like one of Hitler's Nuremberg rally harangues. Rarely has the Vienna Philharmonic sounded so taut and electric, while the late Pilar Lorengar never sang more beautifully.

Fidelio, Op. 72

Ludwig, Vickers, Berry, Unger, Crass, Frick, Philharmonia Chorus and Orchestra, Klemperer. EMI Classics CDMB 56211 [CD].

Nearly two centuries after *Fidelio*'s first successful production—and none of the composer's works would ever cost him as much time, pain, and backbreaking labor—Beethoven's one and only opera still provokes heated debates. Is the rickety rescue melodrama worthy of the magnificent music that fleshes it out? Is *Fidelio* a successful *opera* at all or simply a breathtaking collection of musical essays in the composer's mature middle-period style?

No one ever made a stronger case for *Fidelio* both as music and as musical theater than Otto Klemperer, whose legendary recording from the early 1960s features some of the noblest conducting ever captured on records. With a monumentality and scope that literally dwarfs the competition, the Klemperer *Fidelio* is also a gripping dramatic experience. Leonore's *Abscheulicher!* Florestan's second-act aria, the Dungeon Scene, and the exultant *Finale* all crackle and pop with an immediate and vivid realism, beside which almost all other recorded performances seem flaccid and pale.

Obviously, Klemperer was aided and abetted by an exemplary cast of singers: the ink-black Pizzaro of Gottlob Frick, the intensely moving and musical Leonore of Christa Ludwig, and the incomparable Florestan of Jon Vickers, who thoroughly sounds like what he so obviously was for forty years—the greatest dramatic tenor of his time.

Lieder

Bär, baritone; Parsons, piano. EMI Classics CDC 548790 [CD].

Bartoli, mezzo-soprano; Schiff, piano. London 440297-2 [CD].

Fischer-Dieskau, baritone; Klust, piano. Testament SBT 1057 [CD].

Schreier, tenor; Olbertz, piano. Berlin Classics BER 2082 [CD]; BER 2083 [CD]; BER 2084 [CD].

Wunderlich, tenor; Giesen, piano. Deutsche Grammophon 449747-2 [CD].

As anyone who has ever sung in the chorus of the Ninth Symphony has probably come to suspect, Beethoven was not at his most comfortable or idiomatic writing for the human voice. Which is not to say that he didn't write some of the most inspired pages ever conceived for that instrument: the simple fact is that his vocal writing is often awkward, ungrateful, or both, and singers have been paying the price for years. While Beethoven's output of seventy-odd songs pales in comparison with that of his younger contemporary Schubert, they still form an important link in the evolution of the Mozartean aria into the Schubert *lied.*

Olaf Bär's splendid EMI Classics recital only confirms his stature as one of the preeminent lieder specialists of his generation. Suave, intelligent, and unfailingly musical, these are among the most completely satisfying Beethoven song recordings currently available.

Cecilia Bartoli's interpretations of the Italian songs—including *In questa tomba oscura*—are all one might have expected from this lovely singer; the performances are unfailingly charming, perceptive, and musical, as are the accompaniments by András Schiff.

Dietrich Fischer-Dieskau's 1965 Salzburg recital has been withdrawn by Orfeo, to be replaced by an even finer Testament anthology that finds the voice at its freshest and the singer at his most perceptive.

Though the recitals for Berlin Classics may not capture Peter Schreier at his vocal peak, the experience and sensitivity behind the singing never cease to instruct and delight. The version of *An die ferne Geliebte*—that moving little cycle addressed "to the distant Beloved"—is as tender and perceptive as one could possibly wish.

The recordings that Fritz Wunderlich made in the year before his death are all very special, especially the soaring reading of *Adelaide,* the best-known Beethoven song. The voice is almost heartbreakingly beautiful throughout and one cannot listen to *Ich liebe Dich* or *Resignation* without an involuntary shudder at the thought of what might have been.

Mass in C Major, Op. 86

Soloists, Monteverdi Choir, Orchestre Révolutionnaire et Romantique, Gardiner. Deutsche Grammophon 435391-2 [CD].

The standard reaction among people hearing this extraordinary sacred work for the first time is to wonder why they've never heard it before. The Mass in C is prime middle-period Beethoven: grand, heroic, frequently sublime, with a unique power and authority that makes its neglect in the concert hall and recording studio all the more perplexing. Had there never been a *Missa Solemnis,* this would rightly be considered Beethoven's choral masterpiece.

Sir John Eliot Gardiner's thrilling interpretation invests the music with a sense of new-minted freshness through an interpretation that remains wonderfully sensitive to the work's lyrical warmth while constantly suggesting the rippling muscles underneath. The soloists—particularly Charlotte Margiono and Catherine Robbin—contribute substantially to this winning performance, as does the superbly focused recorded sound.

Missa Solemnis in D, Op. 123

> **Soloists, Monteverdi Choir, English Baroque Soloists, Gardiner.**
> **Deutsche Grammophon 429779-2 [CD].**
>
> **Soloists, Leipzig Radio Chorus, Eric Ericson Chamber Chorus, Vienna**
> **Philharmonic, Levine. Deutsche Grammophon 435770-2 [CD].**

With Leonard Bernstein's transcendent live performance on Deutsche Grammophon currently withdrawn, first choice among available versions of Beethoven's greatest choral work now falls to one of two spectacularly successful recordings from the same company.

As in his recording of the Mass in C, Sir John Eliot Gardiner is a new broom that not only sweeps all the interpretive cobwebs clean but also infuses the music with a searing intensity that even the most romantic interpreters—Bernstein included—might envy. For instance, not since Carlo Maria Giulini's EMI Classics recording—now also deleted—have the opening pages of the *Gloria* erupted with such open-throated power. Curiously, the actual number of singers the performance employs is one of the smallest on record; this is the recording's only and, as it turns out, barely noticeable concession to period authenticity.

James Levine's live recording from the 1991 Salzburg Festival is also extremely powerful. Given in memory of the Festival's long-time director, Herbert von Karajan, the performance is so heartfelt and exultant it makes one wonder whether the occasion was intended as a memorial or a celebration. (Noting the massive turn-out at the funeral of the detested head of Columbia Pictures, Harry Cohn, the late Red Skelton remarked, "It proves what they always say: give the public what they want to see, and they'll come out for it.")

Overtures

> **Leipzig Gewandhaus Orchestra, Masur. Philips 438706-2 [CD].**
>
> **Bavarian Radio Symphony, Davis. CBS MDK 44790 [CD].**
>
> **Nicolaus Esterházy Sinfonia, Drahos. Naxos 8.553431 [CD].**

Kurt Masur's cycle remains one of the most completely successful of his Leipzig recordings, with interpretations that are clear-cut and unaffected and with playing of the very highest order. Combined in a two-CD set with Sir Neville Marriner's delightful recordings of the composer's dances, this makes for a very attractive bargain.

Sir Colin Davis's superbly played and brilliantly recorded collection of Beethoven's most popular overtures very nearly takes the sting out of CBS's senseless decision to withdraw its brilliant set with the Cleveland Orchestra and George Szell. (A few of the Szell recordings have returned as filler for his Beethoven cycle on Sony Classical.) The Davis interpretations are taut and dramatic when the music demands (*Coriolan, Egmont, Leonore* Nos. 1 and 3), yet are easygoing and flexible in the more lightweight fare *(The Ruins of Athens, The Creatures of Prometheus).*

Béla Drahos leads the finely honed Nicolaus Esterházy Sinfonia in an imaginative program that combines the lesser-known overtures (*Consecration of the House, King Stephan, Leonore* Nos. 1 and 2) with some *real* rarities: the *Namensfeier* (Name-Day Celebration); the *Musik zu einem Ritterballett* (Music for a Knightly Ballet), an orchestral version of the funeral march from the Opus 26 Sonata adapted for Duncker's inexplicably forgotten drama *Leonore Prohaska* (rumor has it that Sylvester Stallone is negotiating the movie rights); and the *Triumphal March* for the play *Tarpeja* by Christoph Kuffner.

Piano Music

> **Brendel, piano. Vox 3017 [CD].**

Here is an excellent and inexpensive way to acquire most of Beethoven's shorter piano works, from the childhood torture device *Für Elise* to the stirring variations on "Rule Britannia" and "God Save the King." (The composer became a devout Anglophile after the Duke of Wellington thrashed his personal boogey man, Napoleon.) Brendel's approach is direct and unaffected, with ample reserves of brilliance and tenderness as the situation demands. Although the aging recorded sound is at times a bit brittle and forward, the bargain-basement price tag lets you ignore a lot.

Piano Sonatas (32)

> **Schnabel, piano. EMI Classics CDHH-63765 [CD].**
>
> **Kempff, piano. Deutsche Grammophon 429306-2 [CD].**
>
> **Jandó, piano. Deutsche Grammophon 429306-2 [CD].**

Even more than in his pioneering recordings of the five Beethoven Piano Concertos, Artur Schnabel's great recorded cycle of the Piano Sonatas sparked the modern revival of interest in Beethoven's keyboard music and ensured (as much as mere recordings ever can) this extraordinary pianist's immortality. Originally recorded by the Beethoven Piano Sonata Society on a subscription basis between 1932 and 1935—the idea of recording so many completely unknown works commercially was unthinkable—the Schnabel interpretations have lost none of their originality or wisdom over the years. Even the technical flaws, with time, have acquired an aura of quaintness, like the dings on a beloved jalopy or the chips in your grandmother's china. This is one of the supreme accomplishments in the history of recording and is still the place where any journey into the heart of this music must begin.

The modern cycle that most closely rivals Schnabel's in terms of depth of insight is Wilhelm Kempff's second complete recording from the mid-1960s. Although markedly less individual than Schnabel, Kempff is also less willful. The interpretations have a distinct, intellectually probing personality all their own and a stature that consistently dwarfs all the cycles by Kempff's younger contemporaries. Moreover, the bargain price makes the set all but irresistible. Although temporarily withdrawn from American circulation, the set can be readily imported from England through any of the record stores listed in *Gramophone*.

Jenö Jandó's recent cycle for the super-budget Naxos label is one of the most exciting in years. Virtually every performance is full of life and a sense of discovery, and the fine digital recording captures an unusually realistic piano sound. If state-of-the-art recording is a necessity, then the Jandó is to be preferred to any other modern cycle, including those by far more famous names.

Piano Sonata No. 8 in C Minor, Op. 13, "Pathétique"; Sonata No. 14 in C-sharp Minor, Op. 27, No. 2, "Moonlight"; Sonata No. 23 in F Minor, Op. 57, "Appassionata"

Rudolf Serkin, piano. CBS MYK-37219 [CD].

Rudolf Serkin often told an amusing story about his Berlin debut in the 1920s, when he performed Bach's *Fifth Brandenburg Concerto* with the man who would eventually become his father-in-law, Adolf Busch. Following the audience's warm reception, Busch invited the young pianist to favor them with an encore. Serkin responded with the whole of Bach's *Goldberg Variations*. As Serkin later recalled the scene, "At the end of the evening there were only four people left in the hall: Adolf Busch, Artur Schnabel, (the musicologist) Alfred Einstein, and me." Throughout his career, there was an endearing, almost boyish, earnestness in Serkin's playing, and to the music of Beethoven, Mozart, Schubert, and Brahms he always brought a special authority and integrity that few other pianists could match.

In this attractive collection of three of the most popular Beethoven piano sonatas, Serkin's lofty, thoroughly committed approach serves this familiar music extremely well. The performances are vastly intelligent without ever becoming pedantic, selfless though never self-effacing, impassioned yet never overblown.

Piano Sonata No. 21 in C Major, Op. 53, "Waldstein"; Sonata No. 23 in F Minor, Op. 57, "Appassionata"; Sonata No. 26 in E-flat Major, Op. 81a, "Les Adieux"

Gilels, piano. Deutsche Grammophon 419162-2 [CD].

The popular "Waldstein" and "Les Adieux" Sonatas have never been given more distinguished performances than in these recordings made in the mid-1970s by Emil Gilels. Toward the end of his life, Gilels—always a searching and dynamic Beethoven interpreter—began to find a subtlety and depth in the composer's music that was unique even for him. The "Waldstein" has a mechanical perfection that few recordings can begin to match, while "Les Adieux" has a wistful poignancy that recalls the historic version made by Artur Schnabel in the 1930s. With a two-fisted, heaven-storming "Appassionata" to fill it out, this is one of the most desirable Beethoven sonata recordings now in the catalog.

Piano Sonata No. 28 in A Major, Op. 101; Piano Sonata No. 29 in B-flat Major, Op. 106, "Hammerklavier"; Sonata No. 30 in E Major, Op. 109; Sonata No. 31 in A-flat Major, Op. 110; Sonata No. 32 in C Minor, Op. 11

Pollini, piano. Deutsche Grammophon 419199-2 [CD].

Solomon, piano. EMI Classics ZDBH 64708 [CD].

There are many—and for years, I had to include myself among them—who never fully recovered from the Beethoven Bicentennial of 1970. Virtually everything was so over-played, over-broadcast, over-recorded, and over-packaged that more than one sensitive sensibility snapped. It's only been in the last five years that I have again been able to sit through the Fifth Symphony or the *Egmont* Overture without feeling an uncontrollable urge to run amok with a meat cleaver, and my best friend—who knows every note of the man's music—has flatly refused to listen to Beethoven for the rest of his natural life, except as penance or on salary or as the only alternative to root canal work.

Fortunately, a handful of works remained unsullied in that shameless marketing orgy, primarily the last handful of piano sonatas, which will *never* be transformed into popular commodities. Except for the "Hammerklavier," to which only the bravest musicians sometimes turn during their most masochistic moments, these sublimely imponderable creations remain as mysterious and unfathomable to us as they must have been to audiences of the early nineteenth century. They represent Beethoven at his most private, withdrawn, and mystical: a voice that hardly seems to be speaking to anyone at all, except, perhaps, to himself or to God.

While more impressive individual performances of some of these pieces can certainly be found—Gilels, for instance, turns in a "Hammerklavier" of titanic strength and immeasurable scale (Deutsche Grammophon 410527-2 [CD]) and Rudolf Serkin, in the slow movements of the last three sonatas, finds a shattering stillness that no other pianist can seem to hear (Sony Classical SM3K 64490 [CD])—Maurizio Pollini's integral set from the late 1970s is one of the great modern Beethoven recordings and probably this gifted pianist's finest outing to date. Like Gilels, Pollini brings ample amounts of power and poetry to the music: each of the interpretations is full of character and individuality, yet each seems utterly natural, devoid of any pointless originality or excess. The restored recorded sound is for the most part warm and spacious, if a touch muddy when the going gets rough.

If recorded sound is not a consideration, then that series of astonishing recordings made by the English pianist Solomon remain in a category by themselves. Recorded between 1951 and 1956, the year he suffered the crippling stroke that ended his career, the performances delve as deeply into the mysteries of the music as Schnabel's did but with a far finer technique. Indeed, as examples of transcendent piano playing and profoundly moving human communication, they are among the greatest Beethoven recordings ever made. As EMI Classics tends to withdraw its historical reissues without warning, snap this one up at once.

Quintet in E-flat for Piano and Winds, Op. 16

Perahia, piano. English Chamber Orchestra Winds. CBS MK 42099 [CD].

In an otherwise chatty letter written to his father in the spring of 1784 about a recent subscription concert, Mozart made the following rather startling statement: "I composed two grand concertos and then a quintet which called forth the very greatest applause. I myself consider it the best work I have ever composed." Along with Mozart himself, one of the most passionate admirers of the E-flat Major Quintet for Piano and Winds was the young Beethoven, who in 1795 composed his own work for the same combination of instruments in the same exact key, which also *happened* to begin with a slow introduction *(Grave* to Mozart's *Largo)* and conclude with a moderately paced rondo finale (Beethoven's tempo indication is *Allegro ma non troppo,* while Mozart's is *Allegro moderato).* While clearly not the equal of one of Mozart's greatest chamber works, the Beethoven Quintet was nonetheless the finest work *he* had written up to that time.

Of all the many recordings that offer the two quintets in tandem, none is more satisfying than the version by Murray Perahia and the English Chamber Orchestra Winds. Unlike so many other couplings in which the Beethoven comes off sounding like the decidedly lesser work, Perahia and company almost suggest that the exact opposite is true: the interpretation has a scale and power unlike any other, with many tantalizing hints of the composer Beethoven would soon become.

Sonatas (5) for Cello and Piano

Rostropovich, cello; Richter, piano. Philips 442565-2 [CD].

These five alluring works have never achieved the popularity of the composer's violin or piano sonatas for reasons that are not so easy to explain. While the first two are ingratiating early pieces that contain echoes of both Haydn and Mozart, the Opus 69 is from the heart of Beethoven's heaven-storming middle period, and the pair of Opus 102 sonatas are among the most forward-looking of his final works.

Although several recent releases have offered it serious competition, this Philips recording with Mstislav Rostropovich and Sviatoslav Richter from the early 1960s continues to mop up the field, especially in the fine sonic face-lift as part of Philips's medium-priced "Duo" series. The pianist is as gracious and powerful as ever, while the cellist has never been more probing or refined.

Sonatas for Violin and Piano (10)

Kremer, violin; Argerich, piano. Deutsche Grammophon 415138 [CD]; 419787 [CD]; 445652 [CD]; 447054 [CD].

With two of the most individual cycles of the violin and piano sonatas currently out of circulation—David Oistrakh's elegant and insightful Philips recording with Lev Oborin and those endearingly idiosyncratic versions with Zino Francescatti and Robert Casadesus—the series with Gidon Kremer and Martha Argerich is the one that combines personality and perceptiveness in the most satisfying mix. These are big, exhilarating interpretations by musicians for whom "character" and "individuality" are not dirty words; nowhere is the endless resourcefulness of the composer's invention more obvious than it is here, nor are there any rival recordings in which the participants seem to be having quite so much fun. Itzhak Perlman and Vladimir Ashkenazy offer equally beautiful playing on four medium-priced London CDs (421453-2 [CD]), but for sheer seat-of-the-pants spontaneous combustion, this pair is difficult to beat.

Sonata No. 9 in A Major for Violin and Piano, Op. 47, "Kreutzer"

Huberman, violin; Friedman, piano. Angel CDH-62194 [CD].

Perlman, violin; Ashkenazy, piano. London 410554-2 [CD].

I have had countless heated arguments with violinist friends over the years whenever I made so bold as to suggest that Jascha Heifetz was not, as far as I was concerned, the great violinist of the twentieth century. Granted, his was probably the most phenomenal technique since Paganini's, but, with a handful of recorded exceptions—the Second Prokofiev Concerto and the D Major Concerto of Erich Wolfgang Korngold—I have always found his playing heartless, distant, and cold. When challenged to name a finer violinist, I typically supply a list of at least a half dozen possibilities—a list that invariably begins with the name of Bronislaw Huberman.

Like Fritz Kreisler, Jacques Thibaud, Joseph Szigeti, and the other giants of the era, Huberman was never a note-perfect player. Nor was he a paragon of consistency: more often than not, his performances were flawed by the most elementary kind of mistakes, even though his technical finish could be nearly as impressive as Heifetz's whenever the occasion arose. For Huberman was of that generation of violinists for whom technique was never an end in itself: always a great musician who only *happened* to play the violin, he was far more deeply concerned with what lay between and beneath the notes.

Compare this justly celebrated 1930 recording of the "Kreutzer" Sonata with any of the several versions that Heifetz left, and you'll begin to understand the difference between flesh and blood music making and mere superhuman facility. In spite of some minor slips and the errant sour note, Huberman invests every bar of the piece with passion, profundity, and an instantly recognizable musical personality. It is an interpretation riddled with rubato, *portamenti,* and other Romantic liberties, yet a performance of such conviction that everything sounds utterly natural, inevitable, and right. The playing of pianist Ignaz Friedman more than lives up to its almost mythic proportions. In addition, this priceless six-record collection preserves virtually all the commercial recordings that the legendary Polish pianist ever made.

The most completely satisfying modern version of the "Kreutzer" is the London compact disc by Itzhak Perlman and Vladimir Ashkenazy, who also turn in a delectably verdant account of the composer's "Spring" Sonata.

String Quartets (16)

> **Alban Berg Quartet. Angel CDC-47126 (Op. 18); CDC-47130 (Op. 59, 74, 95); DC-3973 or CDC-47134 (Op. 127, 130, 131, 132, 135, Grosse Fugee).**

If in the nine Symphonies Beethoven became the composer who had the most seismic impact on the development of nineteenth-century music, then with that astonishing series of sixteen string quartets we are introduced—more revealingly than anywhere else—to the man inside the public figure. Beethoven reserved the most personal and intimate of his musical thoughts for his chamber music, and in his chamber works, the most restlessly original composer in the history of music became his most consistently adventurous.

Since the days of those pioneering, and still magically effective, recordings made by the Lener Quartet during the 78 era, virtually every important ensemble has come to terms with the cycle, and none more successfully in recent years than Vienna's Alban Berg Quartet. Named after the great Viennese composer, the Alban Berg Quartet is probably without equal in the world today. They play with a finesse and finish that only the Guarneri Quartet, at the height of its fame, could begin to match. The Berg Quartet's technical prowess is reminiscent of the young Juilliard, and the engaging warmth and mellowness of its physical sound has probably not been heard since the disbandment of the great—and greatly lamented—Quartetto Italiano.

For the audiophile or the novice listener, the Berg Quartet's complete recording of the Beethoven quartets is a nearly perfect introduction to the cycle, and even the most jaded collector will find much here that seems startlingly fresh, original, and new. The Opus 18 collection sparkles with a suitably Haydn-esque wit and charm; the middle-period quartets are appropriately tempestuous and heroic. If in those final mysterious master-works the Quartet is unable to probe quite as deeply as the Busch Quartet did a half century ago, its perfor-mance is still more than adequate to leave most of the current competition far behind.

String Trios (complete)

> Perlman, violin; Zukerman, viola; Harrell, cello. EMI Classics ZDCB-54198 [CD].

Not even the most passionate Beethoven admirer would ever suggest that the string trios are great or even very significant works. Composed between 1796 and 1798, when the brash young Rhinelander was still trying to ingratiate him-self with Vienna's upper crust, the trios are far closer in spirit and execution to the late-eighteenth-century serenades and divertimenti, then enjoying the final flush of their European vogue.

Except for a lovely recording of the Opus 8 Serenade from the 78 era that featured the extraordinary team of Szymon Goldberg (then concertmaster of the Berlin Philharmonic), *violist* Paul Hindemith, and the great Galician cellist Emanuel Feuermann, Beethoven's charming early works have never been given recorded performances quite as fine as these. Indeed, they seem less performances than convenient excuses for three close friends to kick back and have a good time. Which is not to say that the playing is in any way slack or slaggard; the whirlwind finale of the G Major Trio, for instance, rushes by with a precise fero-ciousness that takes the breath away. The recorded sound of these concert perfor-mances is more than adequate, and most of the time the audience forgets to breathe.

Symphonies (9)

Vienna Philharmonic, Bernstein. Deutsche Grammophon 423481-2 [CD].

Cleveland Orchestra, Szell. Sony SB5K 48396 [CD].

Orchestre Révolutionnaire et Romantique, Gardiner. Deutsche Grammophon 436900-2 [CD].

For those who prefer a single interpretive vision in these nine cornerstones of Western musical thought—to say nothing of the convenience and economic advantages of having them all together in a single box—one of the indispensable sets listed here should satisfy practically every taste and budget.

Leonard Bernstein's Vienna cycle from the late 1970s offers exciting, deeply personal, often visionary utterances that come closest in depth and stature to the classic interpretations of Wilhelm Furtwängler (EMI CDHE 63606 [CD]). Yet it is not the eccentricities in the performances that stand out—they are, in fact, few and far between—so much as their enthralling sense of adventure. This is music making at its most spontaneous-sounding and creative, bursting with energy and life—an enduring tribute to the conductor who was to the second half of the century what Furtwängler was to the first.

George Szell was the most compelling modern exponent of the more direct, "objective" style expounded by Furtwängler's principal rival, Arturo Toscanini. Yet in place of the often joyless precision and manic intensity that infested the Maestro's later Beethoven recordings, Szell's are driven by passions that smolder just beneath the elegantly polished surface. In terms of sheer orchestral execution, there are no more thrillingly perfect recordings on the market today or—on five budget-priced CDs—any that offer greater value on the dollar.

The final measure of the success of Sir John Eliot Gardiner's superlative period-instrument cycle is that it scarcely seems a period-instrument cycle at all. As in the pioneering recordings by Sir Roger Norrington, Gardiner generally follows Beethoven's brisk—often *uncomfortably* brisk—metronome indications, but he also has an uncanny knack for making them seem perfectly natural, if not downright inevitable. The interpretations themselves are all vivid and emotionally rewarding, with the phenomenal Orchestre Révolutionnaire et Romantique handling those unwieldy contraptions as skillfully as any of their modern-instrument counterparts.

Symphony No. 1 in C Major, Op. 21

Chicago Symphony, Reiner. RCA 60002-2-RG [CD].

The gleaming version of Beethoven's most youthful symphony was the original companion piece on that series of subscription concerts that also led to the conductor's celebrated recording of the Ninth Symphony (see page 72). Along with the hair-trigger precision that always characterized the work of this famous collaboration, there is an ease and amiability in the interpretation that is unique among Reiner's Chicago Symphony recordings. In the concert hall, it was the perfect relaxed foil to the heaven-storming Ninth, and after all these years its geniality and gentle boisterousness remain undimmed. The CD reissue couples it with Reiner's generally underrated version of the "Pastoral" Symphony, which shares many of the same qualities of his glowing First.

Symphony No. 2 in D Major, Op. 36; Symphony No. 8 in F Major, Op. 93

> London Classical Players, Norrington. Virgin Classics CDM 61375 [CD].

The thought of a group of musicians actually going out of their way to wrestle with those treacherous and invariably vile-sounding antiques has always reminded me of my quasi-hippie, back-to-the-basics friends of the 1960s, who took such inexplicable pride in outdoor plumbing, home-ground grain, and miserably inefficient—to say nothing of vastly malodorous—wood-burning stoves. Thank goodness, times have changed. It's now possible to dismiss such nonsense for what it was without people suspecting you of having been a secret supporter of the Vietnam War.

Imagine, then, my dumbfounded amazement at being so thoroughly swept away by this electrifying period instrument recording, further heartening proof that the Authenticity Movement has finally moved out of the finger-painting stage. The London Classical Players are obviously crackerjack musicians one and all, as opposed to the hacks and second-raters that the phrase "period instrument" always seemed to imply. They play with genuine polish and fire and, urged on by Roger Norrington, deliver two of the most ferociously exciting Beethoven Symphony recordings released in years. Had such recordings been available when the period-instrument revival began, I might have given up eating Wonderbread years ago.

Pearl has reissued on a two-disc set (PEA 9185 [CD]) one of the most incandescent of all Beethoven symphony recordings, Serge Koussevitzky's 1928 version with the Boston Symphony. In its stunning virtuosity, flashing wit, lyrical warmth, and elfin lightness, Koussevitzky's version of the Second Symphony has a fair claim to being the most completely satisfying ever made: this from a conductor who was alleged to have been uncomfortable walking down the center of *any* well-worn path. The recordings of the Eighth Symphony, Haydn's "Surprise" and 102nd Symphonies and Nos. 29 and 34 by Mozart are no less exceptional and the 78 transfers are as impeccable as always from this source.

Symphony No. 3 in F-flat Major, Op. 55, "Eroica"

Vienna Philharmonic, Furtwängler. Arkadia CDWFE 363 [CD].

Cleveland Orchestra, Szell. Sony Classical SBK 46328 [CD], SBT 46328 [T].

From 1922, the year he succeeded Arthur Nikisch as music director of both the Berlin Philharmonic and Leipzig Gewandhaus Orchestra, to his death in 1954, Wilhelm Furtwängler was the most potent and eloquent spokesman for a style of interpretation that could trace its roots to the work of Richard Wagner, the major conducting force of nineteenth-century music. In Furtwängler, Wagner's radical theories about phrasing, tempo modification, and the idealized image of the interpreter as an artist on equal footing with the composer were given—depending on one's point of view—their final grotesque or glorious expression.

For those who grew up under the spell of Arturo Toscanini's new Objectivism, Furtwängler was an anachronism: an unpleasant reminder of a time when Romantic excesses practically made a composer's intentions unintelligible. For those who were unpersuaded by the Italian conductor's manic, though essentially simpleminded, approach, Furtwängler was one of the last of the heroically subjective individualists: a man whose mystic, almost messianic, faith in his own ideas transfigured all he touched with the sheer force of his personality alone.

If any other interpretation of Beethoven's "Eroica" does more to justify the Symphony's subtitle, I have yet to hear it. Only Otto Klemperer found a comparable grandeur in this music; however, along with the titanic *scale* of Furtwängler's performance comes a dramatic power and an animal magnetism that remain unique. No one has ever transformed the funeral march into the stuff of such inconsolable tragedy, nor has any other conductor found such individuality in each of the final movement's variations or galvanized that movement into such a unified, indissoluble whole. In short, this is one of the great interpretations of the century.

For a more brilliant modern version of this popular work, George Szell's recording with the Cleveland Orchestra—like all the performances from his memorable Beethoven cycle—has stood the test of time magnificently, with sound that steadfastly refuses to show its age.

Symphony No. 4 in B-flat Major, Op. 60

Columbia Symphony, Walter. Sony Classical SMK 64462 [CD].

Robert Schumann inadvertently invited posterity to think of the Fourth as something of a weak sister among the Beethoven symphonies when, in one of his poetic moments, he described it as a Greek maiden standing between two Norse gods. If so, then the volcanic live performance that Carlos Kleiber led on a now deleted Orfeo recording suggested that the maiden was one hell of a girl. With his customary flair, Kleiber virtually rethought this essentially light and graceful symphony. The outer movements—especially the finale—rushed by at a breakneck clip, while the slow movement and Scherzo were invested with an uncommon significance and weight. Although it is the only music on a full-priced CD, the performance was very nearly worth it; perhaps in a future medium-priced reissue it could be coupled with something else.

Until the Kleiber reappears, the field now belongs almost entirely to Bruno Walter. His performance has incredibly vitality and expressive warmth and is coupled with his legendary "Pastoral" (see below).

Symphony No. 5 in C Minor, Op. 67

Vienna Philharmonic, Carlos Kleiber. Deutsche Grammophon 447400-2 [CD].

Dozens of recorded versions of this popular symphony have come and gone since the mid-1970s, when this withering recording introduced many of us to one of the most electric musical personalities of our time. For more than fifteen years, only one other version—that majestic and tremendously adult interpretation by Carlo Maria Giulini and the Los Angeles Philharmonic, also on Deutsche Grammophon (410028-2 [CD])—has seriously challenged what may well be the single most exciting Beethoven recording of the stereo era.

The first movement is a triumph of cataclysmic energy and hushed mystery, while the ensuing *Andante con moto* has never seemed more poetic and refined. Yet in the Symphony's final movements, Kleiber leaves the competition panting in the dust. The Scherzo is transformed into a diabolically grotesque witches' sabbath, and the finale, with the incomparable Vienna Philharmonic in full cry, sweeps all before it in a flood of C Major sunshine.

I suppose one should applaud Deutsche Grammophon's decision to finally repackage the recording with the conductor's version of the Seventh Symphony (see page 72) on a medium-priced CD. But as they were charging *full* bloody price for a thirty-four-minute album for *fifteen years* (twenty, if you include the LP), you'll pardon me if I don't drop dead with gratitude.

Symphony No. 6 in F Major, Op. 68, "Pastoral"

Columbia Symphony, Walter. Sony Classical SMK 64463 [CD].

Like dogcatchers, truant officers, old-time side-show geeks, and syndicate hit men, recording company executives have always had a rather unsavory reputation: cost-conscious bureaucrats whose artistic standards—such as they are—

have always taken a distant backseat to the pursuit of the almighty bottom line. In fact, with a slight change of gender, their behavior has reminded many musicians and music lovers of Dr. Samuel Johnson's pronouncement on Lady Diana Beauclerk: "The woman's a whore, and there's an end on't."

And yet the recording executive at Columbia Records—now Sony Classical—who in the late 1950s turned the eighty-year-old Bruno Walter loose on the heart of his repertoire deserves some sort of medal or, at very least, our undying gratitude and admiration. For like the Homeric series of recordings that Otto Klemperer made in London during the final years of his career, Walter's protracted recording swan song is an enduring monument to one of the greatest twentieth-century conductors.

For more than six decades—and Walter had been conducting professionally for three years *before* the death of Johannes Brahms—the "Pastoral" Symphony was one of his most famous house specialties, and this beautiful recording, so full of freshness, wide-eyed innocence, and vivid nature-painting, has never been approached.

Symphony No. 7 in A Major, Op. 92

Royal Philharmonic, Davis. EMI Classics CDFB 69364 [CD].

Originally released in 1961 and now available in the medium-priced EMI Classics "Doubleforte" series, coupled with George Szell's final recording of Schubert's "Great C Major" Symphony, Sir Colin Davis's first recording of the Beethoven Seventh is arguably the most electrifying ever made. With the possible exception of Berlioz's *Les Troyens* (see page 90), this is the conductor's finest achievement on records: a performance so fresh in outlook and breathtaking in its execution that the microphones seem to disappear. The irresistibly sprung rhythms of the opening movement and the high jinks of the Scherzo constantly remind us why Wagner called the Symphony "the apotheosis of the dance"; the slow movement is both dignified and impassioned, while the finale becomes an inexorable but joyous bacchanal. The Royal Philharmonic play like those stoned on Olympian ambrosia and the recorded sound has been spruced up magnificently. Be warned, though: EMI Classics is typically so irresponsible with its deletions ax that one or more copies of the set should be snatched up without delay.

Symphony No. 9 in D Minor, Op. 125, "Choral"

Curtin, Kopleff, McCollum, Gramm, Chicago Symphony Chorus and Orchestra, Reiner. RCA 09026-61795-2 [CD].

Shortly after the beginning of his final season as music director of the Chicago Symphony, Fritz Reiner became so seriously ill that many feared he would never lead the orchestra again. (My father and I actually had tickets for the concert where Erich Leinsdorf stepped in at the last moment to officiate at Sviatoslav Richter's American debut.) Reiner recovered sufficiently to return for the final subscription concerts of the season, programs that were devoted to Beethoven's First and Ninth Symphonies, both of which were recorded in the following week.

Perhaps it is simply my vivid memory of those concerts—and for the first five years of my career as a concertgoer, Fritz Reiner's Chicago Symphony was the only professional orchestra I ever heard—but this recording has always seemed to me something breathlessly close to the ideal realization of Beethoven's Ninth. Brilliantly played and beautifully sung, it is a suave, rugged, polished, explosive, and inspiring performance that captures Reiner's special gifts at, or very near, their absolute peak. In its original 1963 incarnation, the sound—like that of most of the recordings made in pre-renovation Orchestra Hall—was a wonder of clarity, warmth, and detail. In RCA's elegant compact disc transfer, it still rivals all but the very best on the market today.

Trios (11) for Violin, Cello, and Piano

Barenboim, piano; Zukerman, violin; DuPré, cello. EMI ZDMC 63124 [CD].

This is precisely what chamber music was intended to be: a series of intimate, fascinating conversations among some very close friends who are willing to share the experience with others. Beethoven's piano trios are second only to the string quartets in terms of the depth and quality; while Barenboim, Zukerman, and DuPré clearly realize this, they never let the music's importance stand in the way of their—or our—enjoyment. These are warm, pointed, beautifully shaped performances that both challenge and console—and make us miss this irreplaceable cellist all the more.

Trio for Piano, Violin, and Cello in D Major, Op. 70, No. 1, "Ghost"; Trio in B-flat Major, Op. 97, "Archduke"

Beaux Arts Trio. Philips 412891-2 [CD].

More than any other ensemble of the last quarter century, the Beaux Arts Trio is almost as much fun to *watch* as it is to hear. Much of the fun comes from the contrast between the rather stoic-looking cellist, Bernard Greenhouse, and the Trio's nervous, restless, hyperkinetic Ewok of a pianist. On stage, Menahem Pressler is alert to the point of distraction. Hunched over the keyboard like a watchmaker over a priceless heirloom, fingers flashing, eyes darting everywhere at once, he *is* quite a sight. Watching him, one is reminded of what the Pittsburgh

Pirate great Willie Stargell once said of the twitchy mannerisms of the pitcher Luis Tiant: "That guy would make a cup of coffee nervous."

The recordings of Beethoven's two most popular trios are vintage Beaux Arts performances, full of energy, wit, pith, and vinegar. While the Suk Trio on Supraphon (11 0707-2 [CD]) gives them a run for their money in the "Archduke," the diaphanous playing in the "Ghost" is unapproachable, and the two trios offered together on a single CD represent a major bargain.

Variations (33) on a Waltz by Anton Diabelli, Op. 120

Kinderman, piano. Hyperion CDA 66763 [CD].

In 1821, the Viennese music publisher Anton Diabelli asked a number of his composer friends to write a variation on a banal little waltz of his own devising. Dozens of the leading figures of the period responded, including Schubert, Hummel, Moscheles, Mozart's son, and the eleven-year-old Franz Liszt. Beethoven, whose passion for banal tunes was obvious from all the mileage he got out of the "Eroica" theme, produced a set of thirty-three variations that ranks with the "Hammerklavier" Sonata as his most important work for the instrument. With Bach's *Goldberg Variations*, it is also the greatest single series of variations ever written, a masterpiece that Hans von Bülow characterized as "the microcosmos of Beethoven's genius."

With Rudolf Serkin's classic 1957 recording shamefully withdrawn, the recent version by William Kinderman provides a surprisingly satisfying alternative. While hardly in the same household-word category as Serkin, the young pianist-scholar nonetheless offers an interpretation of comparable stature and insight, plus a lively—even willful—sense of adventure that the Serkin occasionally lacks. His accompanying essay makes for very fascinating reading, making one wish he'll soon turn his attention to the sonatas and concertos.

Wellington's Victory

Cincinnati Symphony, Kunzel. Telarc CD-80079 [CD].

As if it weren't bad enough losing most of his army to the Russian winter and then getting mauled at Waterloo, poor Napoleon—and what else could actually make one feel *sorry* for that miserable little cretin?—also had to have his nose rubbed in it by two of history's supreme masterpieces of musical schlock: Tchaikovsky's refined and tasteful *1812 Overture* and this embarrassing garbage by Beethoven. Even with the historic recording led by Antal Dorati reissued on Mercury—remember the miniature French and English flags you could put on your speakers so as to tell who was shooting at whom?—this generally impressive effort from Telarc should keep most people happy. The performance itself is excellent, though the musketry sounds a trifle anemic, almost as if no one was really all that angry.

Bellini, Vincenzo (1801–1835)

Norma

Callas, Stignani, Filippeschi, Rossi-Lemeni, La Scala Chorus and
Orchestra, Serafin. Angel CDCC 56271 [CD].

There are few words that get the true opera lover's juices flowing more effusively than the title of Vincenzo Bellini's masterpiece, *Norma*. In one of his rare bouts of genuine humility, a celebrated opera lover named Richard Wagner said that he hoped *Tristan und Isolde* would some day been seen as the German equivalent of the opera he loved more than any other. The celebrated Wagnerian soprano, Lilli Lehmann, insisted that a half dozen Isoldes were far less physically and emotionally exhausting than *one* encounter with Bellini's Druid priestess.

In this century, the great exponents of what is widely regarded as the most brutally demanding of all soprano roles can be counted easily on the fingers of one hand. Seventy years ago, the matchless American soprano Rosa Ponselle began the modern *Norma* revival with an interpretation whose sheer vocal splendor has never been equaled. In more recent times, the Norma of Dame Joan Sutherland was a technical wonder, if something of a dramatic joke. And then, of course, for a few brief seasons in the 1950s, there was the Norma of Maria Callas, which, both as a vocal and theatrical experience, ranks with Lotte Lehmann's Marschallin and the Boris Godunov of Feodor Chaliapin as one of the supreme operatic experiences of the twentieth century.

Angel was extremely wise to choose this 1954 recording for reissue as a compact disc. Unlike her performance on the much less successful, but still overwhelming, stereo remake—easily the first choice among available tapes—Callas's voice in the 1954 *Norma* had yet to acquire many of the hooty, wobbling eccentricities for which her admirers are always needlessly apologizing and upon which her detractors fasten like barnacles on a once-majestic ship. Here, the voice is heard at its youthful best: from the velvety grace of the "Casta Diva" to the spine-tingling fireworks of "Mira, o Norma." Even though the Pollione and Oroveso might just as well have phoned their performances in, the choice of the indestructible Ebe Stignani as Adalgisa was an inspired one. Although well past her prime at the time the recording was made, this greatest Italian mezzo of the 1930s and '40s was still a worthy foil for perhaps the finest Norma that history has so far known.

Run, don't walk, to buy this one.

I *Puritani*

Sutherland, Pavarotti, Ghiaurov, Cappuccilli, Luccardi, Chorus and
   Orchestra of the Royal Opera House, Covent Garden, Bonynge.
London 417588-2 [CD].

There are at least two overwhelming pieces of evidence that Vincenzo Bellini was not, like Ponchielli, Leoncavallo, and Mascagni, a one-opera composer. The first is the delightfully coquettish *La Sonnambula*—best represented by the 1957 Angel recording featuring Maria Callas and the usual suspects (CDCB-47377 [CD]; the second is his final stage work, *I Puritani*.

While the wooden, intermittently goofy story about English Roundheads and Cavaliers lacks the weight and dramatic thrust of *Norma* (although the same might be said of virtually any bel canto opera), there are some glorious things in this hugely underrated score. The aria "Qui la voce" is cut from the same radiant cloth as *Norma*'s great hit tune, "Casta Diva"; for once in a Bellini opera, the tenor has as much important music to sing as the half-mad heroine, and the hectoring duet "Suoni la tromba" that closes Act II is as fine a bit of martial drum-thumping as exists in Italian opera.

The London recording achieved something close to legendary stature on the day it was first released, and it has only improved with age. Joan Sutherland can't really be touched in a role like this one, perhaps because all—all!—Elvira really needs to do is sing magnificently without paying any special attention to the words or the dramatic context in which they appear. Dame Joan has not fluttered and warbled more thrillingly since her first recording of *Lucia di Lammermoor,* made in the late 1950s.

Yet the real stars of the show are Richard Bonynge, who tightens the often flaccid action into something as lean and mean as middle-period Verdi, and Luciano Pavarotti, who here gives the performance of his life. The singing has a suppleness and taste that recalls the feats of Fernando de Lucia, Allesandro Bonci, and other late-nineteenth-century giants, and the high F-sharp above high C that he uncorks in the final scene will curl the hair on a steel brush.

The supporting cast is uniformly excellent—in fact, the Cappuccilli-Ghiaurov delivery of "Suoni la tromba" very nearly hijacks the show.

Ben Haim, Paul (1897–1984)

Violin Concerto

Perlman, Israel Philharmonic, Mehta. EMI CDC 54296 [CD].

The Sweet Psalmist of Israel

New York Philharmonic, Bernstein. SMK 47533 [CD].

Israel's most celebrated composer was born Paul Frankenburger in Munich and emigrated to Palestine shortly after the Nazis came to power in 1933. He worked first as an arranger and accompanist for several folk singers, becoming immersed in the wealth of Jewish folk material that would become increasingly important in his own work. Scores like the *Variations on a Palestinian Tune,* the suite *From Israel,* and the cantata *Vision of a Prophet* suggest the depth of the composer's feeling for the Jewish homeland and the folk music of the Middle East.

Written for the Israeli violinist Zvi Zeitlin in 1960, Ben Haim's Violin Concerto is one of his most succinct and brilliantly argued works, featuring a tersely energetic opening movement and vigorous finale, with a moving central *Andante* whose mood hovers between synagogue and folk song. Recorded in concert at Tel Aviv's Mann Auditorium, Itzhak Perlman's performance is a commanding and thrilling one, with the Israel Philharmonic on its best behavior.

The Sweet Psalmist of Israel was commissioned by Serge Koussevitzky to help mark Jerusalem's three-thousandth anniversary. A portrait of King David the musician, Ben Haim's masterpiece is by turns lyrical, brooding, and brilliant and is given its definitive performance by Bernstein and the Philharmonic.

Bennett, Richard Rodney

(1936–)

Diversions; Violin Concerto; Symphony No. 3

> Gluzman, violin; Monte Carlo Philharmonic, DePreist. Koch 3-7431-2
> [CD].

One of the most versatile, accomplished, and cheerfully unfashionable composers of his generation, Richard Rodney Bennett was born in Broadstairs, Kent, on March 29, 1936. His father was an author of children's books, his mother a gifted pianist who once studied composition with Gustav Holst. While still a child, Bennett studied composition with Elizabeth Lutyens, then at the Royal Academy of Music with Howard Ferguson and Sir Lennox Berkeley. As a composer, he is probably best known in America for his many distinguished film scores, from *Far from the Madding Crowd* (1967), *Nicholas and Alexandra* (1973), and *Murder on the Orient Express*—all of which received Academy Award nominations—to the 1994 hit *Four Weddings and a Funeral*.

Bennett has also produced an impressive body of concert music, including the Violin Concerto of 1975, the Third Symphony of 1987, and the elegantly crafted, hugely entertaining *Diversions* of 1990. While the Concerto and Symphony are ambitious and important, the *Diversions*—a sequence of highly diverting variations on an Irish jig—may be Bennett's most thoroughly appealing work to date, an effective fusion of serious symphonic thinking with the direct emotional appeal of his film music. DePreist and his fine French orchestra are poised and enthusiastic in all three works, with the Ukrainian violinist Vadim Gluzman unusually commanding in the Concerto. It also has excellent recorded sound.

Berg, Alban (1885–1935)

Altenberg Lieder; Songs

> Norman, soprano; London Symphony, Boulez. Sony Classical SK
> 66826 [CD].

Peter Altenberg, the flamboyant coffeehouse poet whose verses jotted down on picture postcards served as the basis for Alban Berg's great orchestral song cycle *Fünf Orchesterlieder nach Ansichtskartentexten von Peter Altenberg,* was one of the most colorful bohemian figures in an era known for its bohemian colorful figures. For instance, he used to brag, regularly, that he slept with all the windows open on the coldest night of the year. Calling his bluff one winter evening, a group of his friends—including Berg and Schoenberg's son-in-law Felix Greissle—went over to check up. As all the windows were tightly shut, they began berating Altenberg from the street. When reminded of his boast, the undaunted poet said, "But it isn't the *coldest* night."

Rarely has Jessye Norman's sumptuous voice been put to better use than in this indispensable album of Berg songs. In addition to a performance of the *Altenberg Lieder* that makes them seem as sinuously beautiful as Puccini arias (which, of course, they *are*), the soprano offers gorgeous readings of the *Jugenlieder* (Youthful Songs) and the Seven Early Songs of 1905–1908, all of which have the appropriate hints of lost (or rapidly vanishing) innocence and *fin-de-siècle* decadence. In his best Berg recording yet, Boulez coaxes colors from the orchestra that are straight out of a Gustav Klimt painting, and the recorded sound is superb.

In one of the most valuable reissues in its "The Originals" series, which not only reproduces the original cover art but actually paints the CDs to look like old LPs, Deutsche Grammophon has restored the conductor's version, with violinist Pinchas Zukerman, pianist Daniel Barenboim, and the Ensemble Inter-Contemporain of the thorny *Chamber Concerto,* which has never been made to seem quite this approachable or clear.

Concerto for Violin and Orchestra

> Krasner, violin; Stockholm Philharmonic, F. Busch. GM Recordings
> 2006 [CD].

> Perlman, violin; Boston Symphony, Ozawa. Deutsche Grammophon
> 447445 [CD].

If a single work establishes Alban Berg's credentials as one of the giants of twentieth-century music, then it is his moving and powerful Violin Concerto, finished only a few weeks before his death. While written to "the memory of an Angel"—the young Manon Gropius, the daughter of Alma Mahler—the Concerto was obviously Berg's own Requiem as well. According to Louis Krasner, the American violinist who commissioned the work (and for whom Berg's teacher, Arnold Schoenberg, would also write *his* Violin Concerto), Berg was fully aware that the Concerto would be his final work. "It was not written with ink," Krasner would later insist, "but with his own blood."

The small Massachusetts-based company GM Recordings, a labor of love of the American composer Gunther Schuller, has released two live Krasner performances of those two extraordinary works that he helped create. Although the performances themselves are less than perfect, and the recorded sound is of the early-'30s and late-'50s air check variety, the living history it represents makes the recording an absolute necessity for anyone interested in the music of the twentieth century.

Among modern recordings of the Concerto, none underscores its essentially Romantic nature more tellingly than Itzhak Perlman's sumptuous Deutsche Grammophon recording, reissued as part of DG's "The Originals" series. Perlman brings a Brahmsian grandeur and romance to Berg's great score, while never ignoring its almost impressionistic delicacy and shattering violence. Ozawa and the Boston Symphony are alert and sympathetic accomplices, while the re-mastered analogue sound remains superb.

Lyric Suite for String Quartet

LaSalle Quartet. Deutsche Grammophon 419994-2 [CD].

This great work was already clearly established as one of the cornerstones of modern chamber music when a series of sensational discoveries proved what many listeners had long suspected: there was a bit more to the *Lyric Suite* than met the eye. The composer himself offered a key to the *Lyric Suite*'s mystery, with that cryptic and, until recently, inexplicable quotation of the "Love Potion" motif from Wagner's *Tristan und Isolde* embedded in the work's final movement.

The brilliant American composer and Berg authority, George Perle, finally discovered what the piece was really *about*. A score, annotated by Berg himself, came into Perle's possession, which contained the startling revelation that the *Lyric Suite* had in fact been written to a secret program.

Called by the composer "A small monument to a Great Love," the work traces the events of a lengthy and passionate love affair that the composer conducted with a lady who was not his wife. The final movement is, in fact, a wordless setting of "De profundus clamavi," a tortured poem about doomed, impossible love from Charles Baudelaire's *Fleurs du Mal*.

Needless to say, while the fact that the cat, after a half century, is finally out of the bag does much to add to our understanding of Berg's motives and emotional state when he composed the *Lyric Suite*, nothing could seriously add or detract to what has been, in all that time, one of the most profound and profoundly moving of all twentieth-century chamber works.

The famous recording by the LaSalle Quartet is only available as part of a larger release that includes most of the major chamber works of Berg, Webern, and their teacher, Arnold Schoenberg. Although a considerable investment, the set is more than worth the expense. The performance of the *Lyric Suite* is especially warm and lyrical. And unlike so many performances that make the music seem far more complex and forbidding than it needs to be, the LaSalle Quartet's fluent, natural grasp of its language and vocabulary make this piece as lucid and approachable as one of the late Beethoven quartets.

*W*ozzeck

Silja, Wächter, Jahn, Laubenthal, Zednik, Vienna Philharmonic, Dohnányi. London 417348-2 [CD].

With Puccini's *Turandot,* which had its world premiere only four months later, *Wozzeck* was the last great opera to enter the standard repertoire. From the perspective of three-quarters of a century, it is now obvious that these two wildly disparate works have far more in common than was once supposed. In spite of its once radical, atonal musical language—to say nothing of its lurid subject matter—*Wozzeck*, like *Turandot,* is an old-fashioned, intensely Romantic opera that creates a darkly lyrical universe all its own. Anyone who tells you that the opera has no singable arias or memorable tunes, invite them over to hear this lovely London recording; if it isn't *precisely* late Puccini, then it is certainly something that isn't that far removed.

Much of the credit for the success of the recording must go to Christoph von Dohnányi, whose approach to *Wozzeck* might be loosely described as treating it as though it were a Mahler symphony with words. His eye for the larger structures is as keenly developed as is his ear for the minor details: the music unfolds with all the sweep and power that anyone could wish, yet in its textures and inner voices, it has the character of fine chamber music. In short, by the time Marie's orphaned child delivers his final "hop-hop" at the end of the performance, we feel as annihilated as we always should; yet it is a subtle, enthralling feeling of annihilation, as at the end of Debussy's *Pelléas et Mélisande.*

While Dohnányi and—in this music—the incomparable Vienna Philharmonic are the principal selling points of the recording, the cast is also excellent. Vocally, the title role is something of a struggle for Eberhard Wächter, although the rough-and-ready raggedness somehow suits the character very well. Anna Silja is superb as Marie, as she is in the blistering performance of Schoenberg's monodrama *Erwartung*, which comes as a generous bonus.

For those who respond to *Lulu*, Berg's repulsive, alluring, hypnotic final masterpiece, the complete opera—with the unfinished final act put into performing shape by Friedrich Cerha—is presently available in the staggering Paris Opera production led by Pierre Boulez (Deutsche Grammophon 415489-2 [CD]).

Berkeley, Sir Lennox (1903–1989)

Orchestral Works

London Philharmonic, Berkeley. Lyrita SRCD 226 [CD].

Sir Lennox Berkeley would have been happier as a man, no doubt—and far more respected as a composer—had he actually lived in the eighteenth century where he properly belonged. A disciple of Mozart born more than a century too late, Berkeley wrote some of the most urbane and civilized music of the twentieth century: polished, intelligent, translucent, profoundly entertaining modern music that is never pretentious, abrasive, or impossible to understand. No wonder Berkeley is currently out of fashion.

This Lyrita album collects most of those delectable performances the composer recorded with the London Philharmonic in the early 1970s. From the early *Mont Juic*, a suite of Catalan dances that Berkeley arranged in collaboration with Benjamin Britten in 1937, to the enchanting Partita for Orchestra from 1965, this is serious, healthy, eminently *adult* music that might just save you several trips to the psychiatrist's.

Berio, Luciano (1925–)

Folk Songs; Laborintus II; Points on the Curve to Find . . . ; Sequenza VII

Berberian, mezzo-soprano; Holliger, oboe; RTSI Orchestra, Berio.
    Ermitage ERC 12014 [CD].

While best known as one of the leading voices of today's avant-garde—his *Sinfonia* of 1968 had a surprising popular vogue, thanks to its inspired send-up of a movement from Mahler's "Resurrection" Symphony and its other-worldly meditation (by the Swingle Singers) on the name of Dr. Martin Luther King—Luciano Berio has also produced an impressive body of work that has a direct appeal to more conservative musical tastes: from the witty and tender *Folk Songs* of 1964, written for his then wife, Cathy Berberian, to that captivating little piece with the jaw-breaking title, *Quattro versioni originali della "Ritirata notturna di Madrid" di L. Boccherini sovrapposte e trascritte per orchestra* (Four original versions of Luigi Boccherini's "Ritirata Notturna di Madrid" superimposed and transcribed for orchestra).

This Ermitage CD provides an excellent introduction to several sides of Berio's complex musical personality. Berberian brings great sensitivity and a bewitching vocal beauty to the *Folk Songs* and is equally meticulous as the speaker in the astonishing "theatrical speech on Dante," *Laborintus II*, a hodge-podge of quotations from Dante, Pound, and Eliot that likens the horrors of the *Inferno* to the excesses of modern capitalist society. (Oh, these Italian leftists!) "Astonishing" is also the only word to describe oboist Heinz Holliger's performance of *Sequenza VII*, one of a series of such works that push the expressive capabilities of various instruments—flute, harp, solo voice, viola, soprano saxophone, violin, clarinet, alto saxophone, guitar—far beyond any previously recognizable limits.

Berlioz, Hector (1803–1869)

Béatrice et Bénédict

> Cantelo, Veasey, Watts, Mitchinson, Cameron, Shilling, Shirley-Quirk,
>   St. Anthony Singers, London Symphony, Davis. London 448113-2
>   [CD].

Given that it is so unmistakably one of the finest of all Shakespearean operatic settings, the neglect of this enchanting comedy—both in the theater and in the recording studio—is all but impossible to fathom. Although the more "serious" elements in *Much Ado About Nothing* have been eliminated, the opera remains remarkably faithful to the spirit of its source. Berlioz never produced a more brilliantly witty score nor one that throbs with more warmly sensual music.

While Sir Colin Davis's superb Philips recording with Dame Janet Baker and Robert Tear has yet to appear in this country (it can be found in Europe on 416952-2 [CD]), the conductor's earlier Oiseau-Lyre recording is, if anything, even finer, with even more *joie de vivre* in the conducting and a group of voices—especially those of the lovely April Cantelo and Josephine Veasey—that seem consistently younger, fresher, and far more full of fun. The 1962 recorded sound has been given a renewed scrubbing, with everything coming up bright, vivid, and alive.

La Damnation de Faust, Op. 24 (complete oratorio)

> Von Stade, Riegel, Van Dam, Chicago Symphony Chorus and
>   Orchestra, Solti. London 414680-2 [CD].

Hector Berlioz could never quite make up his mind about *The Damnation of Faust,* so it's hardly surprising that posterity hasn't either. He hedged his bets by calling it "A Dramatic Legend," and while it can—and has—been staged as both an opera and an oratorio, for most people the piece consists of that trio of familiar excerpts, "Minuet of the Will-o'-the-Wisps," "Dance of the Sylphs," and the "Rákóczy March," based on a Hungarian tune the composer learned from his friend Franz Liszt. *The Damnation of Faust* can be unbearably tedious, as any of a half dozen previous recordings clearly prove. The late Sir Georg Solti's ripe, mysterious, ripsnorting interpretation almost makes you believe that the *Damnation*'s historic problems are more attributable to the performers than to the piece. Wisely, the conductor treats it like a full-blown grand opera, with compellingly theatrical results. All of the famous set pieces crackle with new life, and even the typically less-than-inspired moments seem abnormally engrossing. The soloists and the late Margaret Hillis's chorus sing superbly, while the Chicago Symphony plays the orchestral part to within an inch of its life.

L'*Enfance du Christ,* Op. 25

> Von Otter, Johnson, Cachemaille, Van Dam, Bastin, Monterverdi Choir, Lyon Opera Orchestra, Gardiner. Erato 2292-45275-2 [CD].

Like marriage, Christmas is essentially an invention of English literature: for just as the poet Edmund Spenser made wedded love both fashionable *and* respectable, a great Victorian propagandist named Charles Dickens transformed a lovely sacred holiday into the red-blooded, two-fisted, multibillion-dollar secular orgy we enjoy and endure today. If there *is* any universal justice, the author of "The Chimes," "The Cricket on the Hearth," and "A Christmas Carol" is standing right now in some cosmic Macy's or Bloomingdales, being prodded, gouged, and jostled by large, rude women, sneered and snapped at by snotty adolescent clerks, screamed at by whining children—in short, going through what we *all* go through at that wretched time of the whirling year.

Whenever I feel the milk of human kindness congealing into rancid crankcase oil, a dose of Berlioz's eternally fresh and innocent *L'Enfance du Christ* is usually all it takes to get me back on track, for there is as much of the real spirit of the season in this gentlest of the great Christmas classics as in any work I know.

While nothing could persuade me to give up my beloved old Victor recording with the Boston Symphony led by Charles Munch—especially since it's been reissued on a pair of medium-priced Gold Seal CDs (RCA 09026-61234-2)—Sir John Eliot Gardiner has better soloists, a better and more idiomatic chorus, and far finer recorded sound. Next time the holiday crush leaves you feeling like a piece of chewed string, give this eternal charmer a try.

H*arold in Italy,* for Viola and Orchestra, Op. 16

> Imai, viola; London Symphony, Davis. Philips 416431-2 [CD].

Ironically, the foremost champions of the music of France's major nineteenth-century composer have tended to be British. It was Sir Hamilton Harty—an Ulsterman by birth, and proud of it, thank you—who began the modern Berlioz revival through his revelatory performances with the Hallé Orchestra of Manchester in the 1920s, and Sir Thomas Beecham's zany, scintillating interpretations in the middle decades of the century finally helped make the music of this strange and original composer a bona fide box office draw. From the mid-1960s onward, this long and fruitful tradition has been ably continued by Sir Colin

Davis: in the opinion of many, the finest Berlioz conductor the century has so far produced.

A comparison of his two recorded versions of *Harold in Italy* provides a fascinating glimpse at Sir Colin's growth as a Berlioz conductor. In the first, made with Sir Yehudi Menuhin, Davis was much too deferential to a far more famous colleague. It was as if both the soloist and the conductor had forgotten that whatever else *Harold in Italy* may be, it is certainly *not* a viola concerto. (After all, Niccoló Paganini, who commissioned the work to show off his new Stradivarius viola, actually refused to play it in public, complaining that he had far too little to do.)

On the other hand, Sir Colin's second recording is clearly the conductor's show. As in all of his Berlioz performances, the image of the composer that Davis tries to project is that of an arch-Romantic whose roots were firmly planted in the Classical past. While the interpretation has an appealing sweep and impulsiveness, it is also meticulously controlled. The Japanese violist Nabuko Imai plays her pivotal role with great zest and distinction, offering an unusually urbane and sensitive approach to phrasing and a physical sound whose size and beauty will make you want to check the record jacket to make certain she really *does* play a viola, not a cello.

If recorded sound is not a primary consideration, then the *only* recording—now and probably forever—is that smoldering 1944 powder keg with William Primrose and the Boston Symphony conducted by Serge Koussevitzky (Dutton Laboratories CDEA 5013 [CD]). In none of his subsequent recordings was the great Scottish violist quite so focused or eloquent, nor has any performance of the orchestral part even *begun* to match the searing intensity of this one, from the coiled menace of the opening bars to the riotous eruption of the Brigands' Orgy.

As a bonus, the CD offers that equally stunning version of Strauss's *Till Eulenspiegel's Merry Pranks* from April of 1945, a performance whose wit and jaw-dropping virtuosity remain equally undimmed. As always, Dutton's transfers from the 78 originals are models of sensitivity and skill.

Messe solennelle (1824; rediscovered 1991)

Soloists, Monteverdi Choir, Orchestre Révolutionnaire et Romantique,
Gardiner. Philips 442137-2 [CD]; 442137-4 [T].

For those who could never quite believe that the *Symphonie fantastique* sprang completely without warning from Berlioz's brain like Minerva from the head of Zeus, this mammoth, endlessly fascinating early work suggests the kind of thing that had been percolating in that extraordinary mind for at least a half dozen years. Completed in 1824 when the struggling, virtually self-taught composer was only twenty, the *Messe solennelle* is a sprawling, inconsistent work in which youthful clumsiness constantly vies with genuine inspiration. While Berlioz would eventually lay the *Mass* aside, he thought well enough of it to use it as a kind of musical organ bank for other works; he detached and revised the powerful *Resurrexit* as a free-standing choral piece and cannibalized other themes for the *Roman Carnival Overture, Te Deum,* and *Symphonie fantastique.*

Sir John Eliot Gardiner leads the kind of carefully planned, intensely committed performance that smoothes over most of the jagged edges and youthful indiscretions, while allowing the many wonderful—and in some cases, startlingly forward-looking—moments to speak for themselves. Like the singing of the Monteverdi Choir, the playing of Gardiner's period-instrument orchestra is exceptional, all of it enhanced by warm and vivid recorded sound.

Les Nuits d'été (song cycle)

Baker, mezzo-soprano; New Philharmonia Orchestra, Barbirolli. EMI Classics 69544 [CD].

Even though he never actually composed any chamber music—and what could you expect from a man whose ideal ensemble included a total of 465 musicians, playing everything from 120 violins and five saxophones to an ophicleide in C *and* an ophicleide in B?—the delicate song cycle *Les Nuits d'été* has a hushed intimacy that almost suggests what a Berlioz string quartet might have been.

Dame Janet Baker never made a lovelier recording than this one, whose reissue helps take the sting out of London's brutal decision to delete—temporarily, one hopes—the ecstatic recording by Régine Crespin. If anything, Dame Janet sings with an even greater degree of sensuality, with Sir John Barbirolli providing a backdrop of incomparable tactile variety and depth.

As a bonus, the repackaging offers her equally molten versions—with Sir Alexander Gibson and the London Symphony—of the ravishing *La Mort de Cléopâtre* and the final scene of *Les Troyens,* both long out of print.

Overtures

Boston Symphony, Munch. RCA 09026-61400-2 [CD]

Scottish National Orchestra, Gibson. Chandos CHAN 8316 [CD].

San Diego Symphony, Talmi. Naxos 8.553034 [CD].

Munch's recording of the four most popular Berlioz overtures—*Roman Carnival, Benvenuto Cellini, Le Corsaire,* and *Béatrice et Bénédict*—is one of the most thrilling the mercurial Alsatian ever made. The performances have that exciting, scatterbrained quality that Munch's best performances always had, coupled with the hair-raising virtuosity of what was still very much Serge Koussevitzky's Boston Symphony. The "Queen Mab Scherzo" from *Roméo et*

Juliette is the most ethereal since Toscanini's, while in its poetry and explosive drama this version of the *Royal Hunt and Storm* from *Les Troyens* is the greatest ever recorded.

Sir Alexander Gibson's Chandos anthology makes an ideal supplement, especially since the strongest individual performances are of the rarely heard *Rob Roy* and *King Lear,* both of which fairly leap out of the speakers.

The Naxos recording with Yoav Talmi and the San Diego Symphony makes for a fine budget alternative, with sensible—though by no means impersonal—interpretations, solid orchestral execution, and warmly natural recorded sound.

*R*equiem (Grande Messe des morts), Op. 5

> Pavarotti, tenor; Ernst Senff Chorus, Berlin Philharmonic, Levine.
> Deutsche Grammophon 429724-2 [CD].

Of all his major compositions, including the sprawling *La Damnation de Faust,* the *Requiem* is probably Hector Berlioz's most problematic work. For just as that other great Requiem by Giuseppe Verdi is a thinly veiled opera disguised as a sacred service, the *Grande Messe des morts* is a dramatic symphony that, almost incidentally, takes as its point of departure one of the most moving texts of the Roman Catholic liturgy.

With virtually all of Sir Colin Davis's Berlioz cycle currently out of circulation, including his imposing Westminster Cathedral version of the *Requiem*—the good people at Philips are certainly nobody's fools: all of these revelatory readings will undoubtedly be showing up again at medium price—Levine's excellent Berlin recording is the best in a surprisingly uncrowded field. (Charles Munch's inspired 1959 recording is now only available as part of RCA's eight-CD "Munch conducts Berlioz" set (0902-668444-2 [CD]), which is certainly worth having if you can spare the cash.) Along with an excellent tenor soloist, the Levine benefits greatly from the Berlin Philharmonic at the top of its game and the lease-breaking recorded sound. For those who absolutely must have a Berlioz *Requiem now,* this is clearly the one to get.

*R*oméo et Juliette, Op. 17

> Roggero, Chabay, Sze, Harvard Glee Club, and Radcliffe Choral
> Society, Boston Symphony, Munch. RCA 09026-60681-2 [CD].

In the last decade or so, Charles Dutoit has worked a minor miracle in Montreal by transforming a fine regional ensemble into an orchestra of international importance. On a good day—and to hear their recordings or broadcast concerts, they seem to have nothing but *very* good days—the Montreal Symphony must now be considered one of the great orchestras of the world.

Beginning with their intoxicating version of Ravel's *Daphnis and Chloé*, they have had such an unbroken string of recording triumphs that their gifted music director has become the first superstar conductor of the digital age.

Dutoit's recording of Berlioz's *Roméo et Juliette*—the most far-reaching and startlingly modern of all that composer's scores—has much in common with Sir Colin Davis's famous London Symphony recording for Philips. All of the famous set pieces have tremendous character and individuality, while the connecting episodes refuse to sound, as they so often do, alas, like patchwork filler in which both the composer and the performers are merely marking time. While the Dutoit performance benefits from a chorus that sings with marvelously idiomatic French inflection and feeling, to say nothing of state-of-the-art recorded sound, the real surprise is the ease with which the orchestra outplays even the great London Symphony, which on records is an all but impossible feat.

Although it's temporarily out of print, look for the recording to reappear on London's midpriced Jubilee label. Until it does, Charles Munch's impassioned—if occasionally wayward—Boston Symphony performance is a perfectly adequate stopgap.

Symphonie fantastique, Op. 14

> Concertgebouw Orchestra of Amsterdam, Davis. Philips 411425-2 [CD].
>
> Boston Symphony, Munch. RCA Victor 09026-61721 [CD]; 09026-61721-4 [T].

In many ways, this odd and perplexing masterpiece remains the most daringly original large-scale orchestral work produced during the entire Romantic Era. Completed barely eight years after the premiere of Beethoven's Ninth, the *Symphonie fantastique* helped to define an entirely new compositional aesthetic that would have an incalculable effect on the subsequent development of nineteenth-century orchestral music. For unlike the modest nature-painting that Beethoven had employed in his "Pastoral" Symphony, the *Symphonie fantastique* was one of the first important orchestral works that attempted to tell a distinct and detailed story. Thus, it became one of the seminal works in the development of Program Music, which would be further expanded in the tone poems of composers from Liszt and Smetana to Richard Strauss. And in his use of the *idée fixe*—a recurrent melody associated in the composer's mind with the heartthrob of the symphony's hero—Berlioz anticipated the use of leitmotif technique, the structural glue that would bind the gargantuan music dramas of Richard Wagner together.

Since the invention of electrical recording in the mid-1920s, Berlioz's bizarre, colorful, and outrageously flamboyant score has been handsomely served on records. Bruno Walter and Felix Weingartner made famous early recordings, though perhaps the greatest single recording ever made—a 1929 version by Pierre Monteux and a Parisian pickup orchestra, long treasured by 78 collectors—has never, to the best of my knowledge, surfaced as an LP.

Sir Colin Davis has so far recorded the *Symphonie* three times: initially with the London Symphony, most recently with the Vienna Philharmonic, and in between as the first work he chose to record with Amsterdam's great Concertgebouw Orchestra. It is Davis's second recording that continues to offer the most balanced and exciting view of the *Symphonie fantastique* presented in the last half century. It goes without saying that the playing of the Concertgebouw Orchestra is a model of modern orchestral execution, and the conception, while beautifully organized, is also wonderfully detailed. Except for the late Jean Martinon, whose Angel recording is only a hairsbreadth less effective, Davis is the only conductor on records to make use of the haunting cornet part in the "Scene at the Ball." Similarly, he is the only conductor who sees fit to observe the all-important repeat in the opening section of the "March to the Scaffold." While the first three movements are superbly disciplined and extravagantly expressive, the final two are as exciting as any Berlioz recording on the market today.

For a delightfully scatterbrained and thoroughly exhausting second opinion, consult Charles Munch's first Boston Symphony recording, recently reissued, with his equally madcap performance of the *Requiem,* on a pair of RCA Victor compact discs. Never one of the century's great disciplinarians—at his very first session with the orchestra, Munch cut the rehearsal short and invited such members of the orchestra who were so inclined to join him for a round of golf—Munch, like Beecham before him, believed that *under*-rehearsal was the key to excitement and spontaneity. If the menacing, insanely driven performance of the "Witches' Sabbath" is any indication, he certainly had a point.

Les Troyens

> Lindholm, Veasey, Vickers, Glossop, Soyer, Chorus and Orchestra of
> the Royal Opera House, Covent Garden, Davis. Philips 416432-2
> [CD].

Even though it has had its fair share of enthusiastic advocates—Sir Thomas Beecham was preparing a new production of it at the time of his death—Berlioz's elephantine opera in two parts, *The Trojans,* has always seemed to me to suffer from one of two possible flaws: it is either an hour too long or two hours too short. Part I is simply too brief to do justice to an event as fraught with possibilities as the Trojan War. The role of Cassandra, one of the most rewarding in the show, could stand to be twice again as long, as could the scenes involving Troy's Royal Family, who are given very short shrift. Perhaps Berlioz simply couldn't wait to get to Carthage and on with the *real* business of the opera, the romance of Dido and Aeneas, which did indeed yield some of the most inspired passages the composer would ever produce.

This quibble aside, the triumphant Philips recording ranks among the dozen or so supreme achievements in the history of the gramophone. With his uncanny, instinctive grasp of Berlioz's intentions, Sir Colin Davis tightens and clarifies the sprawling action to the point where we are almost persuaded we are listening to something as succinct and economical as *Salome* or *La Bohème*.

The cast, which could have included the incomparable Dido of Dame Janet Baker but didn't, is more than equal to the opera's formidable challenges, except, perhaps, for the Cassandra of Birgit Lindholm, who sounds hard-pressed and uncomfortable much of the time. Josephine Veasey is a warm and winning Dido, and Jon Vickers's Aeneas is the stuff of legend, a worthy addition to his already storied Otello, Tristan, and Peter Grimes.

Originally released in the early 1970s, the recording was widely regarded as the outstanding entry in that flood of releases that accompanied the hundredth anniversary of the composer's death in 1969. Three decades later, it seems even more clearly the most significant Berlioz recording yet made.

Berners, Lord (Gerald Hugh Tyrehitt-Wilson, Baronet) (1883–1950)

The Triumph of Neptune (ballet); *Nicholas Nickleby* (film music); *Fantaisie espagnol; Three Pieces for Orchestra*

> Royal Liverpool Philharmonic, Wordsworth. EMI Classics CDM 65098 [CD].

Often described as "The English Satie," Gerald, Lord Berners was a balmy British eccentric with a passion for outlandish costumes and elaborate practical jokes. He was also a gifted painter who had successful exhibitions in London in 1931 and 1936, an accomplished writer who published six novels and two engaging volumes of autobiography (*First Childhood*, 1934, and *A Distant Prospect*, 1945) and the composer of some of wittiest and most original English music of the era between the World Wars.

In 1914, he published the *Trois petites marches funèbres* (funeral marches for a statesman, a canary, and a rich aunt) and in 1926 became the first English composer to write a ballet (*The Triumph of Neptune*, wherein—among other oddities—a baritone is heard singing "The Last Rose of Summer," off key, in the shower) for Sergei Diaghilev's *Ballets Russes*. His work was admired by Shaw, Stravinsky, H. G. Wells, and Walton, who dedicated *Belshazzar's Feast* to him.

This EMI Classics anthology is a splendid introduction to Berners at his goofiest, beginning with a performance of the suite from *The Triumph of Neptune* that can actually be mentioned in the same breath with Sir Thomas Beecham's classic recording. While Barry Wordsworth is acutely sensitive to the highly strung quirkiness of the music, he also responds to its endearing lyricism and rhythmic vitality. The miniatures that round out the album are similarly delectable and the playing, like the recorded sound, is superb.

An equally delectable Marco Polo CD (8.223780) offers the complete 1946 ballet *Les Sirènes,* together with a suite from *Cupid and Psyche* and the *Caprice Péruvien* from the one-act opera *La Carrosse du Saint-Sacrement.* While the latter works are completely engaging, *Les Sirènes* represents Berners at close to his best, with a piquant art deco elegance reminiscent of Walton's music for *Façade.* The RTE Sinfonietta performs so enthusiastically for David Lloyd-Jones that one only hopes this will be the first in a series.

Bernstein, Leonard (1918–1990)

Candide

> Anderson, Ludwig, Jones, Hadley, Gedda, Green, Ollman, London Symphony Orchestra and Chorus, Bernstein. Deutsche Grammophon 429734-2 [CD]; 429734-4 [T].

Although *West Side Story* is the one Bernstein work that everybody knows and loves, *Candide* may well be the finer score. From a purely musical point of view it's a far more interesting show, not only its brilliantly sophisticated parodies of everything from bel canto opera to Gilbert and Sullivan but also in its deeply affecting serious moments, from "Candide's Lament" to one of Bernstein's signature tunes, "Make Our Garden Grow." Because of the relative failure of its initial 1956 Broadway run, *Candide* has acquired the status of a fascinating, noble flop over the years, a myth that this stunning production of the final revised version of the score blows to smithereens.

Based on a series of performances at the Barbican in London that Bernstein led about a year before his death, this *Candide* is—if anything—even more impressive than the composer's version of *West Side Story.* The cast is uniformly better, with June Anderson a vocally dazzling Cunegonde and Jerry Hadley a moving Candide; the decision to cast Lenny's old friend and collaborator Adolph Green as Dr. Pangloss was positively inspired, as are the cameo star turns of Christa Ludwig and Nicolai Gedda. Bernstein conducts with an effortless grace and wit, while the London Symphony Chorus and Orchestra perform with prodigious panache and precision.

In sum, this is one of the most important and enjoyable recordings in a decade.

Chichester Psalms

**London Symphony Chorus and Orchestra, Hickox. MCA Classics
MCAD 6166 [CD].**

The late Leonard Bernstein made no secret of the fact that he was rather embittered over the reception that most of his music received. Apart from the apparently imperishable *Candide* Overture—heard to best advantage in the composer's New York Philharmonic recording for Sony Classical (SMK 47529 [CD])—none of his pieces have established a serious foothold in the concert hall, and aside from the composer himself and a few of his friends, conductors seem reluctant to program Bernstein's music, however fine that music might be.

The *Chichester Psalms* from 1965 is among the most instantly affecting of Bernstein's compositions: jazzy, colorful, unaffected, and devout, it may well be the most important choral work yet written by an American. With both of the composer's recordings currently out of print—the earlier, and marginally more exciting, CBS recording is undoubtedly scheduled for imminent reissue as part of Sony Classical's "Bernstein Century" series—the Hickox recording has many of the same bracing, energetic qualities that make his version of Walton's *Belshazzar's Feast* so memorable. Along with predictably incisive contributions from the fabulous London Symphony Chorus, Aled Jones makes a memorable solo contribution to the ravishing setting of the 23rd Psalm.

The inspired, astonishingly inventive *Serenade* after Plato's *Symposium* has a fair claim to being the finest American violin concerto, in every way a match for those of Samuel Barber and William Schuman. The passion and authority of Itzhak Perlman's richly complex interpretation (EMI Classics CDC 55360 [CD]) would make it the preferred recording, even if either of the composer's own versions were currently available. Ozawa and the Boston Symphony are ideal partners, alternately brash and sensitive as the occasion warrants. With equally memorable versions of the Barber Concerto and the rarely heard but thoroughly engaging *American Pieces* by Lukas Foss, this is an essential recording for any collection of American music.

Bernstein's three symphonies—the *Jeremiah, The Age of Anxiety,* and *Kaddish* (Deutsche Grammophon 445245-2 [CD])—are also among the most daring, original, and moving that any American has ever produced. The performances, it goes without saying, are definitive.

Fancy Free; On the Town (ballet music); *On the Waterfront*

New York Philharmonic, Bernstein. Sony Classical SMK 47530 [CD].

The ballet *Fancy Free* and the dances from *On the Town* contain some of the composer's most brilliantly infectious music, while there are many—myself included—who believe that there is no finer Bernstein score than the symphonic suite from *On the Waterfront*. Unfortunately, his music for Elia Kazan's classic 1954 film was Bernstein's only brush with the movies, although there was actually talk at one time about giving him a screen test for the starring role in a screen biography of Tchaikovsky! It's a pity that Bernstein never again worked in a medium that suited his talents so perfectly.

All the recordings are from Bernstein's vintage New York Philharmonic days, and if the sound on the later versions for Deutsche Grammophon is marginally better, the performances are not.

Mass

Titus, baritone; various ensembles, Bernstein. Sony SMK 63089 [CD].

On July 12, 1971, FBI Director J. Edgar Hoover issued a stern warning to then Attorney General John Mitchell and presidential advisor Robert Haldeman that "important governmental officials, perhaps even the President, are expected to attend this ceremony and it is anticipated that they will applaud the composition without recognizing the true meaning of the words." Not only would President Nixon miss the world premiere of the work commissioned to open the Kennedy Center for the Performing Arts in Washington, D.C., but so, too, would the widow of the man for whom the Center was named: although Jacqueline Onassis announced she would attend, she later decided against it "for strong private reasons." Thus, appropriately enough, Leonard Bernstein's most daring and audacious work, *Mass: A Theater Piece for Singers, Players, and Dancers*, managed to stir up a storm of controversy even before a single note of the piece was heard.

Like the *War Requiem* of his friend Benjamin Britten, Bernstein's score takes the Latin liturgy as its point of departure, around which the composer weaves a series of songs and choruses giving vent to two of his favorite themes: the problem of sustaining faith in God in an apparently godless universe—a central concern of the *Kaddish* Symphony—and man's inhumanity to man, given most recent expression in the Vietnam War. In a program note written in the following year, Bernstein described the novel formal structure of *Mass* and gave a few hints about its philosophical implications:

> It has all the qualities of a dramatic work, catastrophe and climax, all those terms
> out of Aristotle. The ritual is conducted by a young man of mysterious simplicity

(called the Celebrant) who throughout the drama is invested by his acolytes with increasingly ornate robes and symbols which connote both an increase in the superficial formalism of his obligation and of the burden that he bears. There is a parallel increase in the resistance of his Congregation—in the sharpness and bitterness of their reactions—and in the deterioration of his own faith. At the climax of Communion, all ceremony breaks down and the Mass is shattered. It then remains for each individual on the stage to find a new seed of faith within himself through painful Meditation, enabling each individual to pass on the embrace of peace (Pax) to his neighbor, ultimately with the audience and hopefully into the world outside.

It is undoubtedly a measure of the success of this vivid, exasperating, and moving work—finally making its long-delayed debut on CD as part of Sony's "Bernstein Century" series—that most of its intensity, daring, tastelessness, and staggering originality remain intact after all these years, and that after the passions of period have long since cooled, *Mass* still has the power to inspire and inflame. The composer conducts the piece as though it were the most desperately important thing he ever had to say, and in the face of such conviction it would be impertinent to disagree.

West Side Story

Te Kanawa, Carreras, Troyanos, Ollman, Horne, Chorus, and
   Orchestra, Bernstein. Deutsche Grammophon 415253-2 [CD],
   415253-4 [T].

If there are any lingering doubts that *West Side Story* ranks with Gershwin's *Porgy and Bess* as one of the two greatest works of the American musical theater, this indispensable Deutsche Grammophon recording should go a long way to dispelling them. While Bernstein may have written more important or more obviously "serious" works—the endlessly inventive *Serenade for Violin, Strings, and Percussion* and the deeply moving *Chichester Psalms*—this inspired transformation of Shakespeare's *Romeo and Juliet* will probably outlast anything that any American composer, except for Gershwin, has ever written before or since.

The controversial choice of José Carreras as Tony—and one quickly gets used to the dramatic incongruity of a Jet singing with a heavy Spanish accent—is far less problematic than the Maria of Dame Kiri Te Kanawa. As always, listening to that gorgeous instrument is an unalloyed pleasure, and, as always, she does little with it other than make an admittedly beautiful collection of sounds. (Compare her performance to that of the brilliant Marni Nixon—Natalie Wood's voice in the Robert Wise film—and you'll begin to hear just how emotionally and theatrically deficient Te Kanawa's interpretation is.)

The rest of the performances, especially the sly yet earthy Anita of the late Tatiana Troyanos, are uniformly excellent, yet the composer's conducting is the real revelation. Each of the numbers is infused with the last degree of depth, tenderness, and animal excitement: from the inspired poetry of the love music to the jazzy bravado of "Cool" and the great *Quintet*.

Even if you don't normally respond to Broadway musicals, don't worry: *West Side Story* is no more a Broadway musical than the Grand Canyon is merely a large hole in the ground.

Berwald, Franz (1796–1868)

Symphony No. 1 in G Minor, "Sérieuse"; Symphony No. 2 in D, "Capricieuse"; Symphony No. 3 in C, "Singulière; Symphony No. 4 in E-flat

Swedish Radio Symphony, Goodman. Hyperion CDA 67081/2 [CD].

The next time you're in the mood for a Romantic symphony but can't bear the thought of yet another dose of the Sibelius Second, Tchaikovsky's "Pathétique," or anything else too well-known or serious, the pleasant, unassuming symphonies of Franz Berwald might just do the trick. The first Scandinavian symphonist of any consequence, Berwald was a fine craftsman whose music owed much to that of his hero, Felix Mendelssohn. And while echoes of the other voices—primarily those of Beethoven and Weber—can also be heard throughout his work, Berwald could often be modestly original, in a limited but altogether charming way.

The release of Roy Goodman's exhilarating cycle could not have been more timely, given Deutsche Grammophon's decision to drop Neeme Järvi's Gothenberg Symphony recording from the domestic catalogue. While the Goodman interpretations tend to be cooler and quicker, there is no want of feeling for Berwald's unique voice or the innocent purity of his early-Romantic vision. In addition to the four symphonies and the overtures *Estrella di Soria* and *The Queen of Golconda*, the set contains the recording debut of the fragmentary Symphony in A from 1820, in the skillful performing version by Duncan Druce.

As a gift for the music lover who has practically everything, you can't go wrong with this—even if the gift is for yourself.

Biber, Heinrich Ignaz Franz von (1644–1703)

Sonatas for Violin and Continuo (8)

Romanesca. Harmonia Mundi HMU 907134.35 [CD].

The Bohemian-born Heinrich Ignaz Franz von Biber was universally acknowledged as the great violinist of the seventeenth century. The music he composed for the instrument is among "the most difficult and most fanciful of any I have seen of the period"—to quote the eighteenth-century English musical historian Charles Burney—and it remains so to the present day. The eight sonatas of 1681 are astonishing and unpredictable works, full of wild flights of improvisatory fancy and an unruly formlessness quite unlike anything else from the high Baroque. These are mad, dangerous-sounding pieces that both fascinate and disconcert.

Even those who cordially dislike the Baroque Authenticity Movement and its works and pomps, will be thoroughly swept away by the passion and dizzying virtuosity of Romanesca's recording. Brilliantly aided and abetted by Nigel North (lute and theorbo) and John Toll (harpsichord and organ), Andrew Manze demonstrates why he is the reigning master of the baroque violin: his range of effects and expression, like his command of color and dynamics, prove every bit as astonishing as the works themselves.

Billings, William (1746–1800)

Anthems, Hymns, and Fuguing Tunes

Gregg Smith Singers, Adirondack Symphony, Smith. Premier PRCD 1008 [CD].

Best known for the three hymns "Be Glad Then America," "When Jesus Wept," and "Chester," which the late William Schuman used as the thematic basis for his popular *New England Triptych,* the Colonial composer and tanner William Billings was an authentic American original, one of those ruggedly individual genius-cranks whose later manifestations included Charles Ives and John Cage.

Billings was entirely self-taught as a composer, developed the "fuguing tune"—which in an early advertisement he claimed was "more than twenty times more powerful than the old slow tunes"—and died in abject poverty at the age of forty-five, leaving behind a wife and numerous hungry children.

In addition to the three memorable *New England Triptych* hymns in their original versions, this wonderful collection runs the entire dizzying gamut of Billingsian invention, from the wacky "Jargon," which is harmonized entirely in dissonances, to the lithely beautiful "I Am the Rose of Sharon," the composer's most famous work after "Chester," which would become the unofficial marching song of the Continental Army.

The performances by the Gregg Smith Singers are wonders of poise, enthusiasm, and almost superhuman accuracy, while Premier's remastered sound is cleaner and sharper than the CBS originals. Gregg Smith's *The Continental Harmonist Ballet,* arranged from Billings themes, makes for a very attractive bonus.

Bizet, Georges (1838–1875)

L'Arlésienne (incidental music); Symphony in C

Royal Philharmonic; French National Radio Orchestra, Beecham.
Angel CDC-47794 [CD].

After *Carmen* and the sadly neglected *Pearl Fishers*—one of the most hauntingly lovely of all French operas that, alas, is hamstrung by its relentlessly vapid and dippy text—the incidental music that Georges Bizet wrote for Alphonse Daudet's play *L'Arlésienne* is the most attractive and justly popular of all his theatrical scores.

No recording has ever made the *L'Arlésienne* music seem as colorful, original, or utterly fresh as that luminous miracle that Sir Thomas Beecham taped with the Royal Philharmonic in the 1950s. As in his celebrated versions of Grieg's *Peer Gynt* and Rimsky-Korsakov's *Scheherazade,* Beecham's ability to rejuvenate and revitalize a familiar warhorse remains uncanny. Each of the individual sections of the *L'Arlésienne* Suites emerges like a freshly restored painting: the rhythms are consistently infectious, the phrasing is pointed and always original, and, as is so often the case in a Beecham recording, the solo winds are given a degree of interpretive freedom that no other major conductor would ever dare allow.

The same qualities dominate Beecham's performance of the composer's youthful C Major Symphony. While the playing of the French National Radio Orchestra is not quite up to the standard of the Royal Philharmonic, the octogenarian conductor's obvious affection and boyish enthusiasm easily make this the preferred recording of the piece.

Carmen

Horne, Maliponte, McCracken, Krause, Metropolitan Opera Chorus and Orchestra, Bernstein. Deutsche Grammophon 427440-2 [CD].

Recorded in 1973 around the time of the conductor's controversial production at the Metropolitan Opera, Bernstein's *Carmen* is obviously not going to be everybody's *Carmen*. For anyone who needs the recitatives composed by Ernest Guiraud—competent bridgework by a fine journeyman composer, to be sure, but *not* the work of Georges Bizet—Bernstein's decision to return to the spoken dialogue of the original 1875 production will pose some problems, for this is *not* the way that *Carmen* usually goes. There will also be those who'll take exception to some of the conductor's eccentric tempos, to say nothing of Marilyn Horne's elemental characterization and occasionally coarse delivery and the late James McCracken's barking and bellowing.

On the other hand, if you like to leave a performance of *Carmen* feeling like you've been hit by a freight train, then this is the one. For all of its many flaws, Bernstein's *Carmen* packs a tremendous emotional wallop. Not only does spoken dialogue intensify the drama, but you also get the feeling that the occasional rough vocal edge is simply the result of an excess of uncontrollable passion. This is old-fashioned, big time, go-for-the-glands grand opera. Long may it grunt and groan.

Carmen Suites

Montreal Symphony, Dutoit. London 417839-2 [CD], 417839-4 [T].

For those who prefer *Carmen*'s greatest hits without the singing—and who defined opera as "That thing fat foreigners do until you get a headache"?—Dutoit's suave and slinky performances of the Suites are easily the best around, with a very honorable mention going to the overripe but completely winning CBS recording that Leopold Stokowski made while in his nineties (MYK-37260 [CD], MYT-37260 [T]). The Dutoit also comes with a superlative account of the *L'Arlésienne* music, possibly the best since Beecham's.

Jeux d'enfants, Op. 72

Paris Conservatory Orchestra, Martinon. London 443033-2 [CD].

Ogdon, Lucas, pianos. EMI Classics CDFB 69386 [CD].

The only time that my old boss at WONO Syracuse, Henry Fogel (now the executive director of the Chicago Symphony), ever vetoed a piece of my programming was when I scheduled Bizet's delectable suite immediately prior to a performance of Mahler's *Kindertotenlieder.* Like all enthusiastic but inexperienced classic radio types, I went in for that kind of thematic programming in those days: morning programs devoted to music by composers who had died of syphilis (Beethoven probably, but *definitely* Schubert, Schumann, Smetana, Delius, and Wolf), plus evening shows in which the first letters of the last names of the performers spelled out dirty messages to various girl friends.

Jean Martinon's affectionate 1960 recording comes from one of the great periods of the conductor's career, the period that also saw his memorable recordings of the Shostakovich First Symphony and the Borodin Second. His *Jeux d'enfants* bursts with charm and character, as do the rest of the items in this delectable French anthology—especially the sassiest version of the Ibert *Divertissement* ever recorded.

The original version of the suite for piano four-hands is given a sumptuous, note-complete performance by John Ogdon and Brenda Lucas on a two-CD anthology that also contains both of the Rachmaninoff two-piano suites and a genuine rarity: the Second Suite for Two Pianos by Anton Arensky.

Les Pêcheurs de perles

Hendricks, Aler, Quilico, Toulouse Capitole Orchestra and Chorus,
Plasson. Angel CDCB-49837 [CD].

Except for the ravishing duet "Au Fond du temple saint," which many of the greatest tenor-baritone combos of the century recorded in every language except Esperanto, neither history nor the recording studio has been very kind to *The Pearl Fishers.* In 1916, the Metropolitan mounted it with a dream cast headed by Frieda Hempel, Giuseppe de Luca, and Enrico Caruso. The production was a resounding failure and, with a couple of exceptions, international Big Time Opera ignored it ever since.

Several years ago, the New York City Opera unveiled a new production that proved beyond question that, given half a chance, *The Pearl Fishers* will not only work but can also make for a very rewarding evening. The performances featured City Opera's characteristically earnest but bargain-basement vocal talent and some conducting from the late and greatly lamented Calvin Simmons that ranks with the finest I have ever heard in an opera house.

If this recent EMI recording won't convince everyone that *The Pearl Fishers* is a forgotten masterpiece, then at the very least it will win it some surprised and delighted friends. The best things in the production are the Leïla of Barbara Hendricks and the conducting of Michel Plasson. The soprano makes more than almost anyone could out of what may be the dizziest role since Pamina in Mozart's *The Magic Flute,* and Plasson contributes an interpretation that is full of quiet insight while maintaining the long, uninterrupted line. If John Aler and Louis Quilico don't exactly efface the memory of Caruso and De Luca, Björling and Merrill, Domingo and Milnes, and the countless others who have recorded *the* duet, both sing admirably throughout.

Carmen-lovers and/or the only slightly adventurous really should give this lovely little ball of fluff a try.

Bliss, Sir Arthur (1891–1975)

A *Colour Symphony; Metamorphic Variations*

> BBC Welsh Symphony, Wordsworth. Nimbus NI 5294 [CD].

Pastoral: *Lie Strewn the White Flocks*

> Minton, Holst Singers and Orchestra, Wetton. Hyperion CDA-66175
> [CD]; KA-66175 [T].

Best known for his score for Alexander Korda's 1936 screen version of H. G. Wells's *Things to Come*—whose beguiling Suite with its famous march in three-quarter time really *does* need to appear on compact disc very soon—Sir Arthur Bliss succeeded another vastly underrated English composer, Sir Arnold Bax, as Master of the Queen's Musick in 1953. After study with Stanford, Vaughan Williams, and Holst, Bliss established himself as one of the leading figures of modern English music with some of the most ambitious British scores of the 1920s, '30s, and '40s: the fascinating *Colour Symphony;* the moving *Mourning Heroes,* written to the memory of his brother and other friends killed during the First World War (Bliss himself was wounded in 1916 and gassed two years later); the ballet *Checkmate;* and the opera *The Olympians.* There is also a civilized tenderness in Bliss's music that makes it unlike that of any other modern English composer—a tenderness heard to special advantage in the haunting pastoral *Lie Strewn the White Flocks.* His music was aptly described by the critic Alec Robertson as "aristocratic"; he added, "Physically, it is healthy and sane;

mentally, it is distinguished without being aloof; spiritually, it is undenominational. It displays unvaryingly fine craftsmanship, a wit that has mellowed with the years, and a note of almost Mediterranean passion and liveliness."

An ideal way to meet this brilliant and urbane composer is with the superb Nimbus recording of *The Colour Symphony* and the *Metamorphic Variations*—Bliss's first important work and his last—both of which demonstrate an extraordinary facility and inventiveness that remained intact for half a century. *Lie Strewn the White Flocks* is one of the most serenely beautiful English choral works ever written, especially in the ravishing performance that Hilary Davan Wetton coaxes out of his small group of performers.

While the composer's first recording of *Things to Come* is most welcome in a typically handsome transfer from Dutton Laboratories (DUT 2501 [CD]), John Mauceri's Philips recording with the Hollywood Bowl Orchestra (446403-2 [CD]) contains the first really adequate modern performance this vital, colorful work has ever received. Listen to the tingling menace of the opening "War Montage" and you'll understand why David Raksin—who knows whereof he speaks—considers Mauceri the finest living conductor of film music. The album also contains superlative versions of excerpts from Franz Waxman's *The Bride of Frankenstein* and Bernard Herrmann's *The Day the Earth Stood Still*.

Now, would that some enterprising record company produce one of the joys of my youth: the throat-lumping march that Sir Arthur composed as the title music for the BBC Shakespeare series *An Age of Kings*.

Bloch, Ernest (1880–1959)

Schelomo—Rhapsody for Cello and Orchestra

Harnoy, cello; London Philharmonic, Mackerras. RCA 60757-2-RG [CD]; 60757-4-RC [T].

While Ernest Bloch's creative life spanned more than six decades, it is for that music the Swiss-born composer produced from about 1915 through the mid-1920s that he remains best remembered, and rightly so. For the major works of Bloch's so-called "Jewish Period"—when he made a conscious attempt to give musical expression to "the complex, glowing, agitated Jewish soul"—contain some of the most expressive and individual music written by a twentieth-century composer.

Schelomo, the Hebraic Rhapsody for Cello and Orchestra, has long remained Bloch's most popular and frequently recorded work.

Gregor Piatigorsky left an impassioned account of this brooding, exotic piece in the 1950s, a recording that was joined by equally distinguished interpretations by Janos Starker and Mstislav Rostropovich.

With Lynn Harrell's richly operatic London recording currently out of circulation, the version by Ofra Harnoy and Sir Charles Mackerras is clearly the one to own. The soloist is suitably impassioned and rhapsodic, while Mackerras—always a first-rate accompanist—responds in kind.

Fortunately, Arabesque has begun reissuing the Portland String Quartet's versions of the five quartets that Bloch composed between 1916 and 1956. The recording of the somewhat Brahmsian First Quartet (Arabesque Z-6543 [CD]) is a good introduction to a group of works that not only follows the composer's development over a forty-year period but also constitutes one of the undiscovered silver mines of twentieth-century chamber music. For those who become hooked, the versions of the Second and Third Quartets (6626 [CD]) and the Fourth and Fifth (6627 [CD]) are every bit as good.

Finally, the reissue of Leonard Bernstein's 1958 New York Philharmonic recording of the *Sacred Service (Avodath Hakodesh)* (Sony Classical SMK 47533 [CD]) is a major cause for rejoicing. With deeply committed support from the various choirs and a performance from Robert Merrill that ranks with the finest of his distinguished career, Bernstein makes a virtually airtight case that this is not only Ernest Bloch's masterpiece but also one of the great choral works of the century. The remastered sound is shockingly good.

Blomdahl, Karl-Birger (1916–1968)

Sisyfos (choreographic suite); Symphony No. 3

Stockholm Philharmonic, Dorati; Ehrling. Caprice CAP 21365 [CD].

This deeply pessimistic Swedish composer, who refused to have children because "I can't see the meaning of having any," enjoyed his greatest international success with the first-ever science fiction opera, initially mounted at the Royal Opera in Stockholm in May of 1959. The story of *Aniara* concerns a group of refugees from a nuclear holocaust bound for Mars on the spaceship of that name. A day before they reach their destination, a glitch in the navigational system throws them off course; for the next twenty years, they drift aimlessly through the solar system, eventually succumbing to utter hopelessness before dying off one by one.

(Not exactly *The Barber of Seville,* is it?) *Aniara* was promptly recorded, played to sold-out audiences in Hamburg, and was performed with great success at Expo '67 in Montreal. Blomdahl did not live to finish a second, even darker sci-fi opera, *The Saga of the Super Computer,* designed, in the composer's words, "to shake people, to awaken them to the reality of catastrophes that are closer than they think."

It's hardly surprising that Blomdahl should have been so attracted to that figure from Greek mythology whose very name has become a byword for futility. Yet Blomdahl's 1954 ballet *Sisyfos* is a lively, acerbic work whose final, irresistibly energetic *Dance of Life* is one of the most exhilarating moments ever produced by a Swedish composer. Antal Dorati leads the Stockholm Philharmonic in what sounds like a definitive performance, as does Sixten Ehrling in the powerful, darkly rugged Third Symphony of 1951.

Blow, John (1649–1708)

Ode on the Death of Mr. Henry Purcell

Bowman, Chance, countertenors; King's Consort, King. Hyperion CDA 66253 [CD].

Those who insist that serious English music died with Henry Purcell forget the remarkable John Blow, who survived his famous pupil by more than thirteen years. The composer of the most important English church music of the second half of the seventeenth century, Blow also had a key role in the emergence of English opera: his 1685 masque *Venus and Adonis* clearly paved the way for Purcell's *Dido and Aeneas.* Moreover, his odes, anthems, and ceremonial music— including the three he wrote for the coronation of the detested James II and a fourth for the coronations of William and Mary—are the most accomplished and stirring prior to those of Handel.

Written to a moving text by John Dryden, Blow's *Ode on the Death of Mr. Henry Purcell* is perhaps his most heartfelt and personal work, here given a freshly eloquent performance by countertenors James Bowman and Michael Chance with the King's Consort. "Ah, Heaven! What Is't I Hear?" from the 1691 St. Cecilia's Day Ode *The Glorious Day Is Come* is also exquisitely done, as are the Purcell songs that round out the collection.

Another rewarding Hyperion anthology (CDA 66658 [CD]) features a wide-ranging and well-chosen collection of shorter works, including "Awake My Lyre," "Musick's the Cordial of the Troubled Breast" (who would argue with that?), and "Chloe Found Amyntas Lying All in Tears" (as she usually does).

Boccherini, Luigi (1743–1805)

Quintets (3) for Guitar and Strings

P. Romero, guitar; Academy Chamber Ensemble. Philips 420385-2 [CD].

The Italian cellist and composer Luigi Boccherini, who spent his most productive years as court composer to the Infante Don Luis and later King Carlos III of Spain, was in many ways the Classical era's answer to Georg Philipp Telemann: a greatly respected, fabulously prolific composer—he wrote 102 quartets alone—whose civilized, well-made music all sounds pretty much the same.

There are a few exceptions. His wildly popular "Ritirata notturna di Madrid"—a series of variations on the nightly retreat that the city's military bands would play to call the soldiers back to the barracks—was the eighteenth-century equivalent of "Stardust," and the minuet from his E Major String Quintet contains one of the most famous tunes in musical history. (This is the music that Alec Guinness and his band of desperadoes "played" in Mrs. Wilberforce's upstairs room throughout the imperishable Ealing comedy *The Ladykillers*.) Rather unbelievably, Boccherini's one lasting contribution to Western civilization is now represented by only a couple of recordings, the best of which is an excellent Vanguard CD (OVC 8006).

Among the more attractive and individual of Boccherini's works are those several quintets he wrote for guitar and strings. In them, the local color that the traditional Spanish instrument evokes is handled with enormous skill and tact—don't expect any flamenco fireworks or shouts of *Olé!*—and the three that Pepe Romero and members of the Academy Chamber Ensemble present are among the composer's most appealing pieces.

The performances are flawless, as is the recorded sound.

Symphonies

London Festival Orchestra, Pople. Hyperion CDA 66903 [CD]; CDA 66904 [CD].

If Boccherini is best remembered for his chamber music, then his thirty-odd symphonies contain much that is attractive and memorable, with the best of them reaching a level of quality not far removed from middle-period Haydn. (Witness the wildly entertaining *La casa del diavolo*, whose finale *does* go like the devil.) While there is little here that is either original or profound, the themes are appealing, the invention unfailing, the craftsmanship of a very high order.

The performances on these two Hyperion albums are as full of life and character as anyone could wish. Instead of treating Boccherini like a Rococo fuddy-duddy, Ross Pople makes the persuasive case that much here clearly points the way to Beethoven. The London Festival Orchestra plays with both finesse and élan and the recorded sound is superb.

Jacqueline DuPré's fondly remembered recording of Boccherini's B-flat Major Cello Concerto sounds as elegantly passionate as ever in its latest transfer (EMI CDC 47840 [CD]), while cellist Christophe Coin leads the excellent Limoges Baroque Ensemble (Astrée E 8517 [CD]) in an ingratiating period instrument performance, coupled with two more of the composer's dozen cello concertos.

Boito, Arrigo (1842–1918)

Mefistofele

> Treigle, Caballé, Domingo, Ambrosian Singers, London Symphony,
> Rudel. Angel CDCB-49522 [CD].

It is rare that a single performer, through the force of his or her personality, will provoke a drastic reevaluation of a work that had always been dismissed as unimportant or uninteresting. *Boris Godunov* never made much of an impression outside of Russia until a lunatic named Chaliapin began terrifying audiences with it shortly after the turn of the century; by that same token, most people were probably persuaded that Boito's *Mefistofele* was little more than souped-up, cut-rate Verdi until they saw and heard Norman Treigle in the title role. And it was something to hear *and* to see: the lithe, slight, almost painfully emaciated body of a consummate actor from which that unimaginably cavernous, ink-black instrument would rumble forth. On stage, the Treigle Mefistofele was one of the great operatic experiences since the end of the War; on record, this indispensable Angel recording captures much of the Treigle miracle intact.

This is also, by several light-years, the most persuasive recorded performance the opera has ever received. Another New York City Opera alumnus, Placido Domingo, is nearly perfect as Faust, and Caballé is both alluring and dignified, keeping the scooping and drooping to a bare minimum. Julius Rudel's contribution is only slightly less distinguished than Treigle's.

The action flows more easily than it ever has, giving the lie to the nonsense that *Mefistofele* is a fatally episodic work, and in the thrilling choral passages—

the celebrated *Prologue in Heaven* and in the opera's *Finale*—Rudel musters a collection of sounds that Verdi would have been proud to have included in the *Requiem*.

Boito's other opera, *Nerone*, is clearly worth investigating, if for no other reason than to hear what occupied the composer for virtually his entire adult life. Begun in 1877 and finished in 1915—on the last page of the final revision, the composer wrote: "The End: Arrigo Boito and Kronos"—the opera is a complex examination of good and evil in Nero's Rome. While the libretto is predictably brilliant and perceptive, the music is often tentative and forced. Nonetheless, there are moments of genuine power and beauty that clearly deserve to be heard. A well-intentioned live performance from 1975, recorded by RAI Turin and available on Italian Opera Rarities (IOR 7704 [CD]), while neither as skillful nor persuasive as the long-deleted Hungariton recording, is nonetheless worth considering—if only as a gift for the opera lover who seems to have everything.

Borodin, Alexander (1833–1887)

Prince Igor

> Evstatieva, Mitcheva, Martinovich, Ghiaurov, Ghiuselev, Sofia
> National Opera Chorus and Festival Orchestra, Tchakarov. Sony
> Classical S3K-44878 [CD].

Alexander Borodin was without question the greatest composer in history who was, by profession, a chemist. After his dipsomaniacal, atrabilious friend Modest Mussorgsky, he was the most original of that group of Russian composers who came to be known as "The Mighty Five," and like Mussorgsky, he left much important music unfinished at the time of his death. A true weekend composer, Borodin spent decades putzing around with his masterpiece, *Prince Igor,* which had to be wrestled into performing shape by Rimsky-Korsakov. (He never bothered to write the Overture down; fortunately, Rimsky's pupil Alexander Glazunov had heard him play it so often that he was able to reconstruct it from memory.) As Borodin once ruefully confessed: "In winter I can only compose when I am too unwell to give my lectures. So my friends, reversing the usual custom, never say to me, 'I hope you are well' but 'I do hope you are ill.'"

The exceptional Sony Classical recording is the first really adequate recorded performance that Borodin's opera has ever received. The singing ranges from the very good to the truly memorable—Nicolai Ghiaurov is tremendously imposing as the Polovtsian Khan, Kontchak—while the conductor's canny pacing tends to minimize the episodic nature of the work while revealing the peculiar color and character of every scene. Add spectacular contributions from the brilliantly drilled chorus and orchestra and recorded sound that is both sumptuous and realistic, and the result is an exciting, invaluable release.

Prince Igor: Overture, *Polovtsian Dances*

London Symphony, Solti. London 417689-2 [CD].

Boston Pops, Fiedler. RCA 7813-4 [T].

The most ecstatic of all recordings of the familiar *Prince Igor* Overture and *Polovtsian Dances,* an Angel recording from the early 1960s by the Philharmonia Orchestra conducted by Lovro von Matačič (available for a time on the Quintessence label), is, alas, no longer in print. Should the performance ever resurface again, or should you come across it in the LP cut-out bins, buy at least a half-dozen copies: three for yourself, and three to lend out to friends. (If your friends are like mine, you'll never see the records again.)

Nearly as arresting as the Matačič were those versions that Sir Georg Solti recorded with the London Symphony that are out now on one of those hyper-cheap London Weekend Classics CDs. With a hell-bent-for-leather dash through Glinka's *Russlan and Ludmilla* Overture and a bone-chilling run-through of Mussorgsky's *Night on Bald Mountain,* this is one of the finest of all Solti recordings.

Among available tapes, the performances by Arthur Fiedler and the Boston Pops, in a handsome package of Russian orchestral showpieces, are more than competitive with the best on the market today.

*S*tring Quartet No. 1 in A Major; Quartet No. 2 in D Major

Borodin Quartet. Angel CDC-47795 [CD].

Among that pathetically small handful of works that Borodin managed to complete, the String Quartets rank very high in his canon; the lesser-known A Major Quartet is full of energy and invention, and the familiar D Major Quartet is one of the most justly popular of all Russian chamber works—made all the more so by the famous "Nocturne," which has enjoyed a life of its own as a free-standing concert piece, and by a couple of tunes that eventually found their way into the Broadway musical *Kismet.*

In their most recent recording, the Borodin Quartet gives both works unusually thoughtful, natural-sounding interpretations, as though their eponym had actually written the music specifically for them. The playing is relaxed and efficient, with results that are deeply Romantic without ever becoming self-indulgent.

A tape of the two quartets together cannot currently be had for love or money, but an equally fine performance of the D Major by the Emerson String Quartet is available from Book-of-the-Month Club Records (21-7526 [CD], 11-7525 [T]). The good news is that the recording is every bit the equal of the Borodin's. The bad news is that it can only be had as part of a four-CD or three-tape set called "The Great Romantic Quartets." The *best* news is that their versions of the popular quartets of Ravel, Debussy, Smetana, Schumann, Tchaikovsky, and Brahms are among the finest ever recorded. The situation would have been far less complicated had the Emerson's second recording for Deutsche Grammophon (427618-2 [CD]) been as fresh and vital as their first. Unfortunately, a note of calculation has crept into the interpretation, making it somewhat less enjoyable than it once was.

Symphony No. 2 in B Minor

> National Philharmonic, Tjeknavorian. RCA 60535-2-RV [CD]; 60535-4-RV [T].

Once one of the most understandably popular of all Russian symphonies, the Borodin Second has inexplicably fallen on hard times. Incorporating many ideas that Borodin planned to include in *Prince Igor,* the Symphony is therefore—not surprisingly—an unusually tuneful and pleasantly exotic work whose powerful first movement, the composer's friend Vladimir Stasov revealed, was intended to evoke the gathering of the ancient Russian tribes, while the cheerfully orgiastic finale depicts a hero's banquet not unlike the Polovtsian blowout that concludes *Prince Igor*'s second act. Why conductors don't program the work more frequently remains a mystery: the piece is a certified crowd-pleaser, in addition to being one of the finest of all Romantic symphonies.

With the budget reissue of Loris Tjeknavorian's vivid 1977 interpretation, the classic but rather shrill-sounding recording by Ernest Ansermet may now be honorably retired. The Armenian conductor finds nearly as much drama and poetry as his great predecessor did, but he has a finer orchestra to work with and dramatically superior recorded sound. Coupled with equally bracing versions of the Overture, *Polovtsian Dances,* and *Polovtsian March* from *Prince Igor*—not *quite* as bracing as Solti's, but close—and one of the finest versions of *In the Steppes of Central Asia* ever recorded, this is a completely irresistible bargain.

The charming *Petite Suite,* a series of six piano miniatures arranged by Borodin's friend Rimsky-Korsakov, is handsomely served by the Philharmonia Orchestra conducted by Geoffrey Simon on a Cala recording (CALA 1011 [CD]) that also includes *In the Steppes of Central Asia,* the *Prince Igor* excerpts, plus a couple of genuine rarities: an arrangement for violin and orchestra (again by Rimsky-Korsakov) of the wistful *Nocturne* from the Second String Quartet, and a five-minute hoot called *Requiem* (arrangement by the ever-tasteful Leopold Stokowski), which consists of a crescendo—thundering climax—decrescendo on "chopsticks" (the European version, not the one Marilyn Monroe and Tom Ewell play in lieu of Rachmaninoff in *The Seven Year Itch*), decked out with tenor and male chorus.

Bottesini, Giovanni

(1821–1889)

Gran Concerto in F-sharp Minor for Double Bass and Orchestra; Gran Duo Concertante for Violin, Double Bass, and String Orchestra

> **Martin, double bass; English Chamber Orchestra, Litton. ASV 563 [CD].**

Called the "Paganini of the double-bass" by his contemporaries, Giovanni Bottesini learned the rudiments of music from his father and entered the Milan Conservatory in 1835 when the only remaining scholarships were for bassoon and double-bass. Four years later, he graduated with a three-hundred-franc prize for solo playing and soon embarked on a long and distinguished solo career, preferring to perform on a three-stringed instrument tuned a tone higher than usual. Bottesini was also a gifted conductor who in 1871 led the world premiere of Verdi's *Aida* and held the posts of music director of London's Covent Garden and the Italian Opera in Paris. In addition to ten operas, Bottesini also composed numerous works for double-bass, which, because of their enormous difficulty, are seldom performed today.

Thomas Martin is a formidable virtuoso who dispatches these horrifically challenging works with abandon, bringing the same technical facility and lyric grace to his unwieldy instrument that others bring to the cello. Andrew Litton provides his usual stylish accompaniments and the recorded sound is excellent. Here is yet another example of a party record with genuine musical virtues.

Boulanger, Lili (1893–1918)

Choral Works

Soloists, Elisabeth Brasseur Chorale, Lamoureux Orchestra, Markevitch. Everest EVC 9034 [CD].

Along with being the fairy godmother to virtually every important American composer from Aaron Copland to Ned Rorem, Nadia Boulanger was also the teacher of her younger sister Lili, the perpetually ill, prodigiously gifted French composer who became the first woman to win the *Prix de Rome* and who finally succumbed to Crohn's Disease at the age of twenty-four.

Recorded under Mlle. Boulanger's supervision during March of 1960, this famous Everest album remains the best single-volume introduction to Lili Boulanger's music ever: from the brief, starkly powerful *Psaume 24* to the ethereal, otherworldly *Pie Jesu,* which the failing composer was forced to dictate line by line from her deathbed. Best of all is the version of the *Du Fond de l'abîme,* a setting of Psalm 130 whose majestic, almost medieval grandeur completely belies its composer's physical frailty and youth.

Conducted by yet another Boulanger pupil, Igor Markevitch, the performances have a unique vigor and authority and the recorded sound retains an astonishing presence and weight. For anyone anxious to make the acquaintance of this fascinating and tragic figure, this is the only place to begin.

Bowen, York (1884–1961)

Piano Music

Hough, piano. Hyperion CDA 66838 [CD].

London-born and trained, York Bowen is one of those shadowy figures of modern music for whom the compact disc revolution might have been designed. Thanks to Stephen Hough's inspired advocacy—both in the playing itself and in his thoughtful program notes—we can finally make the acquaintance of a charming and utterly distinctive musical personality, whose captivating miniatures have the same sort of endearingly quirky individuality as Peter Warlock's songs. Like many before him, Bowen produced a cycle of twenty-four *Preludes,* some of which compare more than favorably with those of Chopin and Rachmaninoff. The only complaint is that Hough presents only thirteen of them—the rest, one hopes, will appear on a second album. Bowen's powerful Fifth Piano Sonata suggests that he was equally comfortable in larger forms, making one very curious to hear what his three piano concertos, *Symphonic Fantasia,* and Symphony in E might be like. All that Frederick Delius needed to get his gentle ball rolling was one inspirational interpreter like Sir Thomas Beecham; in Stephen Hough, Bowen may have found *his* man.

Boyce, William (1711–1779)

Symphonies (8)

English Concert, Pinnock. Deutsche Grammophon 419631-2 [CD].

William Boyce found himself in the unenviable position of being a native-born English composer at a time when the English musical scene was completely dominated by a Saxon immigrant named George Frederic Handel. Like his near contemporary Thomas Augustine Arne, the composer of a masque named *Alfred* that contained a fairly memorable ditty called "Rule Britannia," Boyce spent his career in Handel's immense shadow, apparently without bitterness or regret. A friend said of him, "A more modest man than Dr. Boyce I have never known. I never heard him speak a vain or ill-natured word, either to exalt himself or to deprecate another."

Thanks to the '60s Baroque Boom, the eight tiny "symphonies" that Boyce composed have enjoyed a considerable vogue on records. All are gems in their way, full of wit, emotion, and imagination and—if nothing else—they prove that *something* was happening in homegrown English music between Purcell and Elgar apart from *The Beggar's Opera* and Gilbert and Sullivan.

The period instrument recording by Trevor Pinnock and the English Concert is an undiluted joy. The Symphonies emerge not only as the work of an important talent, but also as that of an uncommonly healthy, intensely likable man. The best of them are as full of life as Handel's better concerto grossos, and if you have yet to make the acquaintance of the good Dr. Boyce, here is an ideal opportunity.

Brahms, Johannes

(1833–1897)

Alto Rhapsody, Op. 53; *Begräbnisgesang*, Op. 13; *Nänie*, Op. 82; *Gesang der Parzen*, Op. 89

> Hodgson, mezzo-soprano; Bavarian Radio Chorus and Orchestra, Haitink. Orfeo C-025821 [CD].

The *Alto Rhapsody*, the best-loved of Brahms's choral works after the *German Requiem*, was easily the most peculiar wedding present ever given to anyone. The composer bestowed this fretful, stygian work on Julie Schumann, the daughter of Robert and Clara, a girl he himself had hoped to marry but, of course, never would. (Brahms was never able to maintain anything approaching a normal romantic relationship: from his youth, spent playing the piano in the bordellos of Hamburg's red-light district, he developed that lifelong dependence on prostitutes that made love with "ordinary" women impossible.)

This handsome Orfeo recording combines an eloquent version of the *Rhapsody* with three beautifully sung performances of other Brahms choral pieces, including the rarely heard *Song of the Fates* and the *Funeral Ode*. The British mezzo Alfreda Hodgson has a voice whose sable resonance frequently recalls that of her great compatriot Kathleen Ferrier. Bernard Haitink, for years a superlative Brahmsian, brings his usual virtues to all the performances: the emotions are carefully controlled but never bullied; there is passion aplenty but nothing is overstated or overdone. Now that he has been succeeded as music director of the Royal Concertgebouw Orchestra of Amsterdam by Riccardo Chailly—who is as accomplished as the average truck driver, except for the fact that he can't drive a truck—let's hope Haitink will assume the post of Permanent Guest Conductor of the world.

Chorale Preludes, Op. 122

> Bowyer, organ. Nimbus NI 5262 [CD].

Composed not long after the *Four Serious Songs*, the eleven *Chorale Preludes* are Brahms's final works: a series of mellow, incomparably autumnal miniatures that sound like Bach drenched in the richest imaginable chocolate. (Those who know me understand the *depth* of that compliment; as Dr. Johnson insisted, "When a butcher tells you *that his heart bleeds for his country*, he has, in fact, no uneasy feeling.") In his splendid Nimbus survey of the complete organ works, Kevin Bowyer applies precisely the right amount of interpretive fudge to these dusky masterworks, just as he brings an abundant virtuosity to the youthful *Preludes and Fugues*. The bright, clear sound of the instrument of the Odense Cathedral made me considerably less restive than usual and the organist's notes are both witty and astute.

Piano Concerto No. 1 in D Minor, Op. 15

> R. Serkin, piano; Cleveland Orchestra, Szell. CBS MYK-37803 [CD], MYT-37803 [T].

Brahms's early D Minor Piano Concerto has always seemed to many less a concerto than a large, turbulent orchestral work with a very significant piano *obbligato* appended almost as an afterthought. The feeling, for those who have it, is more than understandable, for the concerto actually grew out of discarded materials for a projected D minor symphony that the composer could not bring himself to complete. (For more than half of his creative life, Brahms was constantly on the lookout for ways of making symphonic noises without actually having to produce that dreaded First Symphony. Sadly, his morbid fear of the inevitable comparison with Beethoven delayed its composition until he was well past forty.)

For more than twenty years no recording has fought more ferociously for the Concerto's identity *as* a concerto than the explosive and poetic performance of Rudolf Serkin and George Szell. Serkin's playing in this famous recording is magisterial, delicate, and shatteringly powerful—qualities that made him as effective in the music of Mozart as he was in the works of Franz Liszt.

George Szell, in one of the best of his Cleveland recordings, provides a muscular and exciting backdrop for his old friend. The playing of the Cleveland Orchestra is above criticism, and the digitally remastered sound is superb.

Piano Concerto No. 2 in B-flat Major, Op. 83

> Gilels, piano; Chicago Symphony, Reiner. RCA Victor 60536-2 [CD], 60536-4 [T].

For most of his distinguished and rewarding career, the late Emil Gilels was known unfairly as "The Other Russian," a man condemned to live out his entire professional life under the enormous shadow cast by his great contemporary, Sviatoslav Richter. While Gilels may have lacked his friend's charisma—a short, stocky, unpretentious man, he was the very image of a third assistant secretary of the Ministry of Textiles—he was a formidable musician whose playing matched Richter's in its depth and intensity, even if it lacked the last fraction of a percentage point of that unapproachable technique.

While Gilels's final recording of the Brahms B-flat Major Concerto, made with Eugen Jochum and the Berlin Philharmonic in the 1970s, is in every way exceptional, it is the Chicago recording, made a decade before, that captures his immense talents at their absolute best. As in all of his finest and most characteristic performances, Gilels's interpretation, while completely unmannered, is also possessed of a unique power and panache. No recorded performance of the *Scherzo* communicates half of this one's driven assurance or feverish pain, and the *Finale* is played with such a natural and unaffected charm that for once it is not the anticlimax that it can frequently be. Fritz Reiner proved to be an ideal partner in this music: generous, sensitive, and deferential, yet never afraid of showing off a little power and panache of his own. And if even in its sonic face-lift, the recorded sound remains a trifle thin and shrill, this is a trivial flaw in one of the most flawless concerto recordings ever made.

Concerto in D Major for Violin and Orchestra, Op. 77

Perlman, violin; Chicago Symphony, Giulini. Angel CDC-47166 [CD].

Kreisler, violin; Berlin Philharmonic, Blech. (Recorded 1929).
   Pearl GEMM PEA 996 [CD].

When I am packing up the trunk of recordings to haul off to that mythic desert island—though, since my mother didn't raise a fool, the island I'll probably pack myself off to is Maui—Fritz Kreisler's 1929 version of the Brahms Concerto (coupled with classic Kreisler recordings of the Beethoven, the Mendelssohn, the Mozart Fourth, and the Bach Double) will probably be put close to the top of the stack. While not the most perfect recording the Concerto has ever received, this is far and away the noblest and most inspiring. In the sweep of its patrician phrasing, melting lyricism, and hell-bent-for-leather audacity, this is as close as we will ever come to a Brahms Violin Concerto from the horse's mouth. (It should be remembered that for a time in the 1880s one of Kreisler's Viennese neighbors was the composer himself.)

Among modern recordings of the Concerto, none is more completely engaging than Itzhak Perlman's version with Carlo Maria Giulini and the Chicago Symphony. Perlman is a spiritual descendant of Fritz Kreisler: a wonderful exponent of Kreisler's own music, he also plays with that indescribable, untranslatable quality that the Viennese call, in its closest but very approximate English equivalent, "beautiful dirt." This is a dark, luxurious Brahms Concerto cut from the same cloth as Kreisler's, but one in which the modern preoccupation with technical perfection also makes itself felt. In short, it sounds very much like the kind of performance that one would give almost anything to hear: one in which Heifetz's iron fingers were guided by Kreisler's golden heart.

Concerto in A Minor for Violin, Cello, and Orchestra, Op. 120

Oistrakh, violin; Rostropovich, cello; Cleveland Orchestra, Szell. EMI
Classics CDM 64744 [CD].

The classic Angel recording by Oistrakh, Rostropovich, George Szell, and the Cleveland Orchestra was one of the final commercial recordings that George Szell would ever make. While Szell and Rostropovich never got along either personally or musically, they managed to overlook their differences in a performance of tremendous sweep and overwhelming power, with violinist David Oistrakh also close to the peak of his mature form. Unfortunately, instead of coupling it with the magnificent recording of the Violin Concerto that Oistrakh and Szell made at the same time, we're saddled with the rather overblown version of Beethoven's *Triple Concerto* with Sviatoslav Richter and the Berlin Philharmonic conducted by Herbert von Karajan. Still, it's a small compromise to make for one of the great Brahms recordings of the century.

Ein deutsches Requiem, Op. 45

Schwarzkopf, Fischer-Dieskau, Philharmonia Chorus and Orchestra,
Klemperer. Angel CDC-47238 [CD].

In one of the first of his incontestable masterworks, Brahms produced what remains the most gently consoling of all the great Requiems: a work that seems to tell us, with the utmost civility and compassion, that dying is neither the most frightening nor the most terrible thing a human being can do.

Since it was first released in the 1960s, Otto Klemperer's otherworldly recording has cast all others in the shade. Along with the characteristic breadth and depth he brings to the interpretation, the frail but indomitable conductor also projects such a moving degree of fragile tenderness that the performance will quietly, but firmly, tear your heart out by the roots. Neither of the soloists ever made a more beautiful recording, and the singing of the Wilhelm Pitz-trained Philharmonia Chorus remains an enduring monument to the greatest choral director of his time.

*H*ungarian Dances (21)

> Vienna Philharmonic, Abbado. Deutsche Grammophon 410615-2
> [CD], 410615-5 [T].
>
> Budapest Symphony, Bogár. Naxos 8.550110 [CD].
>
> Katia and Marielle Labèque, pianos. Philips 416459-2 [CD].

After he settled permanently in Vienna in 1862, Brahms's life was completely uneventful. Aside from several concert tours and summer holidays to the Austrian lakes and to Italy, his daily routine consisted of composition and those twice-daily trips to the Red Hedgehog, a coffeehouse where he caroused with his artistic cronies and from which he would set off for his regular assignations with the city's ladies of the night. He had no hobbies, and his idea of relaxation consisted of making arrangements of German folk songs for various combinations of voices and turning out trifles like the popular *Hungarian Dances.*

Abbado's zestful Vienna Philharmonic recording makes a welcome return to the catalog after a long absence. The composer's hometown band has had this music in their bones for more than a century and they play it with the same charm and authority that they bring to Strauss waltzes. (Fritz Reiner's shockingly schmaltzy recordings of eight of them on London 448568-2 [CD] are also irresistible, especially at the bargain price.)

If the Budapest Symphony under István Bogár may lack the Vienna Philharmonic's deep-pile richness and finesse, then any minor technical shortcomings are swept aside by their sheer enthusiasm and idiomatic response to the stylized gypsy idioms. These are sly, ingratiating performances with just the right dose of teasing rubato.

For the *Dances* as they were originally written for piano four hands, the version by the Labèque sisters is without equal. The Labèques are so glamorous and have been hyped so mercilessly that we tend to forget what absolutely thrilling musicians they are.

In his first recording as music director of the North German Radio Orchestra (Deutsche Grammophon 437506-2 [CD]) Sir John Eliot Gardiner—perhaps best known for his consistently imaginative and exciting recordings of early music—proves that he is just as comfortable on the well-worn Romantic path. In nine of the *Hungarian Dances* and in the Dvořák, *Symphonic Variations* and *Czech Suite,* there is a feeling of unflagging enthusiasm and a sense of constant discovery. The North German Radio Orchestra sounds almost unbelievably fine—in fact, like a real rival of the Berlin Philharmonic—and the recorded sound is superb. Had they recorded all of the *Hungarian Dances,* they would have easily swept the field.

The arrangements for violin and piano made by the composer's Hungarian-born friend Joseph Joachim feature some hair-raising virtuoso writing, none of which seems the least bit troubling to the Kazakhstani violinist Marat Bisengaliev. His Naxos recording (8.553026 [CD]) is full of thrills and chills (and no serious spills), though for warmth and gypsy charm, Aaron Rosand's Biddulph album (LAW 003 [CD]) has a magic all its own.

Liebeslieder Waltzes

> Guzelimian, Herrera, pianos; Los Angeles Vocal Arts Ensemble. Elektra/Nonesuch 79008-2 [CD].

One of the few musical issues upon which Brahms and Wagner were in perfect agreement was their admiration for the music of Johann Strauss. The irresistible lilt of the Waltz King's music may have actually influenced Wagner in the seductive Flower Maidens scene from *Parsifal* and it can certainly be felt in the two sets of *Liebeslieder Waltzes* that Brahms composed under the spell of his famous Viennese neighbor.

No recording of these irresistible but formidably difficult works has ever captured more of their freshness or sheer inventiveness than the version by the Los Angeles Vocal Arts Ensemble. Musically and vocally, the performances are all but flawless, with the singers missing none of the music's joy or romance (and few of its nuances) and the pianists offering some exceedingly deft support.

Piano Music

Two Rhapsodies, Op. 79; *Three Intermezzi,* Op. 117; *Six Pieces,* Op. 118; *Four Pieces,* Op. 119

> Lupu, piano. London 417599-2 [CD].

When the Rumanian pianist Radu Lupu first arrived on the scene in the late 1960s, I must admit that I heaved an enormous yawn at the prospect of yet *another* oppressed victim of Communism seeking artistic freedom—to say nothing of a few bucks here and there—in the West. These were the days when overzealous press agents were hailing that ham-fisted oaf Lazar Berman as the "new Horowitz"—a process that has continued even into the age of *glasnost* with that storm of nonsense generated over the very modestly equipped Vladimir Feltsman.

Lupu, as everyone quickly discovered, was something quite different: an inquisitive, deeply "spiritual" pianist whose playing reminded many of that other incomparable Rumanian, Dinu Lipatti. Although over the last two decades, he has made comparatively few commercial recordings, each of them has been something of a milestone: witness that extraordinary series of late Brahms piano works that were originally recorded in 1971.

No living pianist—and only a handful from the past—can rival either the depth or the intensity of Lupu's performances. When he is at his best, as he clearly is here, there is also a wonderfully paradoxical quality in the playing that suggests that every detail has been worked out ahead of time *and* that he is making it all up as he goes along: a kind of "interpretation" that frequently crosses that thin dividing line into active creation, without doing any disservice to the composer or his work.

No one who loves Brahms or great piano playing will fail to be moved.

Piano Quartet in G Minor, Op. 25; Piano Quartet in A Major, Op 26; Piano Quartet in C Minor, Op. 60

Domus. Virgin Classics VC-790709-2 [CD] (Op. 25 and 60); VC 790739-2 [CD] (Op. 26).

With his first two Piano Quartets, the twenty-eight-year-old Brahms introduced himself to Viennese musical society in 1861. The debut was auspicious and, for the composer, rather unnerving: on the strength of these pieces, one of the city's leading critics dubbed him "Beethoven's heir," an honor and a curse that would haunt him for the rest of his life. The early Piano Quartets were Brahms's first important chamber works and, with the stormy C Minor String Quartet that would follow three years later, remain pillars of Romantic chamber music.

The group that calls itself "Domus" is one of many young ensembles that adds fuel to the argument that as far as chamber music performance is concerned, we may in fact be passing through a new Golden Age. Technically, they are completely seamless, as we have automatically come to expect; musically, they show as much poise and savvy as any of the finest chamber groups in the world today. In the tempestuous *Finale* of Op. 25, for instance, they play with a wild, fearless abandon, yet in the more somber moments of Op. 60, they probe the rueful depths of the composer's heart in a way that would make a thoracic surgeon gasp.

Coupled with the very Brahmsian Piano Quartet Movement that the teenage Gustav Mahler composed during his Vienna Conservatory days, these two generously packed CDs set a standard in this music that's going to be very difficult to match.

Piano Quartet in G Minor, Op. 25 (orchestrated by Arnold Schoenberg)

London Symphony, Järvi. Chandos CHAN 8825 [CD]; ABTD 1450 [T].

Suddenly, and for no apparent reason—other than the obvious explanation that conductors and recording companies are belatedly discovering what a tremendously entertaining and marketable work it is—there are now *five* excellent modern versions of Arnold Schoenberg's inspired orchestration of Brahms's

G Minor Piano Quartet. Arguing that in all of the performances that he had ever heard, the piano part always overbalanced the strings, Schoenberg produced what has been called with some justification "The Brahms Fifth": an imaginative and, for the most part, utterly faithful adaption of one Brahms's most colorful chamber works.

With the brilliant version by Simon Rattle and the City of Birmingham Symphony now out of print, Neeme Järvi's fine London Symphony recording is the best currently available. Although not quite as sensitive as Rattle's in the arrangement's subtler niceties, it is very nearly as exciting in the finale, where all hell breaks loose.

For the most convincing reading of the Quartet as it was actually composed, the Virgin Classics recording by Domus continues to lead the field. (I blush to confess that since I first learned of the Quartet through Robert Craft's old Chicago Symphony recording of the Schoenberg orchestration, the original version has always seemed slightly pale. In fact, the *Finale* never sounds completely right without that wildly incongruous xylophone.)

Piano Quintet in F Minor, Op. 34

Ashkenazy, piano; Cleveland String Quartet. London 425839-2 [CD].

Before Brahms's friend Robert Schumann did it, no major composer had ever written a work for piano and string quartet. True, Luigi Boccherini *did* toy with the form a half century earlier, but those experiments were lost in that avalanche of quintets he produced for other combinations of instruments. Like the Schumann, with which it is frequently paired on recordings, Brahms's F Minor Quintet is one of his strongest chamber works—this in spite of a lengthy, structurally tricky finale that in many performances can seem to ramble.

With the wonderful Naxos recording by Jenö Jandó and the Kodály Quartet unaccountably withdrawn—and it's probably a dubious but inevitable measure of the maturity of this young and scrappy company that they, too, have finally discovered the irritating joys of the nefarious deletions ax—the London recording with Vladimir Ashkenazy and the Cleveland Quartet is the most satisfying reasonable alternative, especially since it is fleshed out with a richly overripe version of the composer's Clarinet Trio. Among the *un*reasonable alternatives (i.e., those featuring less than state-of-the-art recorded sound), the Testament recording by Victor Aller and the Hollywood String Quartet (SBT 3063 [CD] and see page 356, under Hollywood String Quartet) is unsurpassable in its power and superhuman perfection, while a live 1945 Library of Congress recording with George Szell and the Budapest Quartet (Bridge BRI 9062 [CD]) offers a fascinating pendant to a great conductor's career.

Quintet in B Minor for Clarinet and Strings, Op. 115

D. Shifrin, clarinet; Chamber Music Northwest. Delos DE-3066 [CD].

Although the two Clarinet Sonatas, the *Four Serious Songs,* and the *Chorale Preludes* for organ were Brahms's actual valedictory, no composer ever wrote a more breathtakingly beautiful farewell than the slow movement of the B Minor Clarinet Quintet. In it, Brahms's celebrated mood of "autumnal melancholy" can be heard at its most wistful.

The haunting recording by Chamber Music Northwest has a fair claim to being the best currently available. In the opinion of many, David Shifrin might well be the finest clarinetist alive. His fingers are as nimble as anyone's and he plays with a tone the size of four-bedroom house. His musical personality is a combination of heroic swagger and melting sensitivity, both of which are heard to special advantage in this great work.

Among the available tapes, the recording by Thea King and the Gabrieli Quartet for Hyperion (KA 66107) is very nearly as fine.

Serenade No. 1 in D Major, Op. 11; Serenade No. 2 in A Major, Op. 16

London Symphony, Kertesz. London 412628-2 [CD].

This is Brahms at his most relaxed, joyous, and lyrical in performances that will wash over you like the first spring rain. Superlatives fail me. *Buy* this one.

Sonatas (2) for Cello and Piano

Rostropovich, cello; Serkin, piano. Deutsche Grammophon 410510-2 [CD].

One of the highlights of Rudolf Serkin's not entirely successful series of Indian Summer recordings for Deutsche Grammophon were the versions of the Brahms Cello Sonatas he made with Mstislav Rostropovich. What on paper looked like a very odd pairing proved to be an inspired and mutually beneficial one, with Serkin losing some of his characteristic reserve and Rostropovich gaining an added measure of emotional discipline and control. Still, each remained very much his own man and the occasional friction served the music very well, especially in the febrile F Major Sonata, which has rarely sounded so intense. The youthful E Minor is also exceptional and the recorded sound is superb.

Sonatas (2) for Clarinet and Piano

Stolzman, clarinet; Goode, piano. RCA 60036-2-RG [CD].

The self-taught German clarinetist Richard Mühlfeld was not only one of Richard Wagner's favorite musicians—he was the principal clarinettist at every

Bayreuth Festival from 1884 to 1896—but he was also responsible for Brahms's last great love affair, the composer's completely *requited* passion for the clarinet.

Like Mozart, who was born at about the same time the instrument was and wrote its first great pieces, Brahms was utterly taken by its richly burnished, deeply melancholy voice. Between 1891—the year they met—and 1894, Brahms wrote for Mühlfeld those four towering works that constitute the instrument's New Testament, and his own farewell to chamber music: the clarinet trio and quintet, and the two late sonatas.

Richard Stolzman is at his most natural and unaffected in his superb recording with Richard Goode. Although there is a pervasive gentleness in the interpretations, whenever the music demands it there is plenty of power, too. Rarely, for instance, has the opening movement of the F Minor seemed as portentous, just as the finale of the E-flat Major has rarely sounded so blithely unbuttoned. Although the players are rather closely miked, the recorded sound is excellent.

For those interested in the composer's own transcription for viola and piano, the often wayward but always compelling Deutsche Grammophon recording (437248-2 [CD]) by Pinchas Zukerman and Daniel Barenboim should more than fill the bill.

Sonatas (3) for Piano

Richter, piano. (Nos. 1 and 2) London 436457-2 [CD].

Perahia, piano. (No. 3) Sony Classical SK 47181 [CD].

At the time Brahms composed his youthful piano sonatas, he was already demonstrating what an unusual Romantic he was. Few of the composers of his generation concerned themselves with anything as cumbersome and outmoded as the sonata: for the young Romantics, the short, lyrical "musical moment" was the favored form of communication. Schumann first recognized the yearning for symphonic expression inherent in these turbulent works, calling them "veiled symphonies," and it was the composer's performance of one of them that led to the famous entry in Schumann's diary, "Brahms to see me, a genius."

With Krystian Zimerman's commanding recording for Deutsche Grammophon out of print but presumably awaiting medium-price reissue, the best available versions are a pair of live performances of the First and Second from the late 1980s featuring the great Sviatoslav Richter and Murray Perahia's Sony Classical recording of No. 3. Although Richter was in his midseventies and reportedly not in the best of health when the recordings were made, he still towers above almost every living pianist. If his technique is not as overwhelming as it once was, then his grasp of the music's architecture and spiritual implications remain as acute as ever. Perahia is also at his most profound and revealing in the F Minor Sonata, a performance whose subtlety and scale rivals that of any recording ever made.

Sonatas (3) for Violin and Piano

>Osostowicz, violin; Tomes, piano. Hyperion CDA 66465 [CD]; KA
>66465 [T].

If in the symphony Brahms came closest to approximating the achievement of his hero and idol Beethoven, then in the apparently less demanding realm of the violin sonata he may have actually surpassed him. Each of Brahms's three works in the form is a mature masterpiece: the earliest of them, the so-called "Rain" Sonata, Op. 78, is at least the expressive equal of Beethoven's "Kreutzer" Sonata, while the final two were written when the composer was in his mid-fifties and at the zenith of his powers.

If they are not as well known as some of the others who have recorded these great works, then Krysia Osostowicz and Susan Tomes yield to none of them in terms of imagination, temperament, or technique. These are carefully thought-out, beautifully executed performances that also seem completely spontaneous and utterly fresh. The lovely give-and-take of the conversation is captured by one of Hyperion's warmest recordings.

Songs

>Ameling, soprano. Deutsche Harmonia Mundi 74321-26617-2 [CD].
>
>Ferrier, contralto; Spurr, piano. Danacord DACOCD 301 [CD].
>
>Fischer-Dieskau, baritone; Höll, piano. Bayer 100006 [CD].
>
>Kipnis, bass. Pearl 89204 [CD].
>
>Norman, soprano; Parsons, piano. Philips 416439 [CD].
>
>Price, soprano. RCA 09026-60902-2 [CD].

With Schubert, Schumann, and Hugo Wolf, Brahms was one of the four undisputed masters of German lieder and the only one, ironically, who did not succumb to what might almost be called "The Song-Writer's Disease." (Given his lifelong dependence on prostitutes, it was the purest luck that he never contracted the tertiary neurosyphilis that claimed the other three.) Brahms's two hundred songs form one of the loveliest and most important facets of his output, from the eternal little *Wiegenlied* to the *Vier ernste Gesänge* (Four Serious Songs), one of the last and greatest of all his works.

Spiritually, musically, and vocally, no two singers were more perfectly suited to the Brahms lieder than were the German bass Hans Hotter and the English contralto Kathleen Ferrier. Recorded live at the 1948 Edinburgh Festival, Ferrier's performances with Bruno Walter at the piano are among the most deeply moving she would ever give. It's unlikely that any female singer—even the composer's friend Ernestine Schumann-Heink—could have gotten more pathos out of dark meditations like *Immer leiser wird mein Schlummer,* and Walter's accompaniments are similarly heartbreaking. (That this famous recording has been allowed to slip out of print is a scandal; Danicord's reissue of a wrenching collection of songs recorded with Phyllis Spurr suggests just how badly we need to hear *this* voice in this music.) By that same token, except for the recording by the Russian bass Igor Kipnis, there has never been a version of the *Four Serious Songs* to compare with the depth and wisdom of Hotter's. This is musical and human communication the like of which has not been heard in the recording studio for a generation, and its deletion is shockingly insensitive, even by EMI's standards.

Among recent recordings, the reissue of Elly Ameling's early recordings is most welcome. Although recorded at the very beginning of her career when the voice was at its most irresistibly girlish, the performances are already full of the knowing artistry that would characterize the soprano's work throughout her long and glorious prime.

Dietrich Fischer-Dieskau's Bayer anthology is not quite as ideal as the deleted Orfeo recording of a 1958 Salzburg Festival recital; still, intelligence and canny musicianship are evident everywhere, even in the thoughtful and probing accompaniments.

Like the famous recordings that Alexander Kipnis made for the Hugo Wolf Society in the 1930s, his recordings for the Brahms Society represent some of his finest work as a lieder singer. The highlights of those 1936 and 1940 recording sessions have been gathered together in an indispensable collection from Pearl.

Among collectors of great lieder recordings—among collectors of great twentieth-century singing—Kipnis's version of the *Four Serious Songs* is often spoken of with hushed reverence, for reasons that become instantly obvious. Beginning with the chilling hopelessness he conjures in the first song—and his delivery of the famous line from Ecclesiastes that "all is vanity" is positively sepulchral in its yawning despair—continuing with the dignified suffering of the second, the calm resignation of the third, as the speaker moves from an acceptance to a longing for death, and culminating in the intensely noble utterance of the final song (this of the famous passage from First Corinthians, which begins, "Though I speak with the tongues of men and of angels, and have not charity, I am become as sounding brass, or a tinkling cymbal"), the utterance becomes so intensely noble that the tongue does seem far more angelic than human.

Jessye Norman's Philips recital offers songs whose moods and range seem especially chosen to show off the sable richness of her middle and lower registers. The performances also feature the typically sensitive and imaginative work of the late Geoffrey Parsons, perhaps the finest accompanist since Gerald Moore.

The RCA album from Dame Margaret Price is also cleverly chosen to mix serious items (six Heine settings) with some of the delightful *Volkslieder*. The recital concludes with a *Zigeunerlieder* full of fireworks and gypsy abandon.

String Quartets (3)

Gabrieli Quartet. Chandos CHAN 8562 [CD].

As with the Symphonies, the relative dearth of Brahms String Quartets was the direct result of his festering Beethovenophobia, that debilitating fear of following his god and hero into any form that Beethoven had made his own. The C Minor Quartet—cast, significantly, in the same key as Brahms's First Symphony—was not completed until sixteen years after it was first sketched. As with the Second Symphony, the A Minor Quartet followed almost immediately, and the series ended abruptly a few years later with the B-flat Major Quartet, Op. 67. Like the Symphonies, each of the Quartets is the work of a mature and confident master, and no two are even remotely alike: the somber, turbulent First Quartet; the tender, graceful, elegiac Second; and the whimsical, good-natured Third.

Although finer individual interpretations may exist—the Emerson Quartet's tumultuous recording of the C Minor (Book-of-the-Month Club Records 21-7526 [CD], 11-7525 [T]) is especially gripping—the Gabrieli Quartet gives unusually satisfying accounts of all three, particularly the Opus 51. Although the recording is a bit reverberant, the musicians' wonderful precision keeps the textures admirably transparent and clean.

String Sextets (2)

Raphael Ensemble. Hyperion CDA 66276 [CD], KA 66276 [CD].

Given their scope, charm, and elegance, it has always been a little surprising that Brahms's two wonderful String Sextets have not been more popular. They are among the most ingratiating and symphonic of all his chamber works and inspired a largely self-taught twenty-six-year-old composer named Arnold Schoenberg to write a string sextet of his own called *Verklärte Nacht*.

The Sextets have probably never been served more handsomely than by this beautiful recording by the Raphael Ensemble. While no subtlety of surface detail or inner voicing escapes their attention, it is their response to the romantic sweep of the music that ultimately carries the listener away.

On another Hyperion recording (CDA 66804) the Raphaels are equally engaging in the two Quintets, mixing vitality with languorousness in the wondrous F Major Quintet—which Brahms considered one of the most beautiful things he had written up to that time—and projecting precisely the right note of wistful exuberance that characterizes the G Major, which he fully intended to be his vale-dictory work (and it might very well have been, had he not met an extraordinary clarinetist named Richard Mühlfeld, for whom he produced the Clarinet Quintet, Trio, and Sonatas).

Symphony No. 1 in C Minor, Op. 68

Columbia Symphony, Walter. CBS Odyssey MBK-44827 [CD].

Even though Otto Klemperer's titanic recording from the early 1960s has returned on an Angel compact disc (CDM-69651), Klemperer still faces some formidable competition from his old friend Bruno Walter, whose final recording of Brahms's First Symphony was made at about the same time.

Walter's 1936 Vienna Philharmonic recording was one of the great glories of the 78 era: lithe, sinewy, and intensely passionate, it was every bit the dramatic equal of Arturo Toscanini's famous interpretation, while investing the music with an expressive freedom of which the Italian maestro scarcely could have dreamed.

Although Walter was well past eighty when the Columbia Symphony recording was made, there is no hint of diminished concentration in the performance; if anything, the first movement unfolds with such searing intensity that we are almost forced to wonder what the elderly conductor had for breakfast that day. Although as usual, Walter is without peer in the Symphony's gentler passages, the great theme of the final movement rolls out with an unparalleled sweetness and dignity, and the performance concludes in a blaze of triumph.

Among the available tapes, the powerful and athletic recording by George Szell and the Cleveland Orchestra (CBS MYT-37775) is far and away the best.

Symphony No. 2 in D Major, Op. 73

Vienna Philharmonic, Bernstein. Deutsche Grammophon 410082-2 [CD].

Recorded live in Vienna in 1983 as part of a larger Brahms cycle, Leonard Bernstein's performance of the composer's sunniest symphony is the most invigorating since Sir Thomas Beecham's. The general mood is one of relaxed expansiveness, and while tempos tend to be on the leisurely side, the phrasing and rhythms never even threaten to become lethargic or slack. Which is not to say that the familiar Bernstein fire is not available at the flick of a baton: the *Finale* crackles with electricity and ends with a deafening roar of the incomparable Vienna Philharmonic trombones.

As a bonus, the recording includes a performance of the *Academic Festival Overture,* whose sly humor and rambunctious good spirits are all but impossible to resist. Among the current crop of tapes, George Szell's hyperkinetic CBS recording (MYT-37776) is a clear first choice.

Symphony No. 3 in F Major, Op. 90

Columbia Symphony, Walter. CBS MK-42022 [CD], CBS Odyssey YT-32225 [T].

Cleveland Orchestra, Szell. CBS MYK-37777 [CD], MYT-37777 [T].

All of the qualities that made Walter's recording of the First so special can be heard in even greater abundance in his version of Brahms's most concise and original symphony. If you have the chance to audition the recording before you buy it, listen to the last three minutes. For in this daring *coda*—which marked the first time that an important symphony ended on a quiet note—Walter is so ineffably gentle that those three magical minutes should be more than sufficient to make the sale. An equally warmhearted account of the *Variations on a Theme by Haydn* fills out this unusually generous and irresistibly attractive compact disc.

George Szell's stunning Cleveland Orchestra recording runs Walter a very close second. The recorded sound and playing are both superior, and the performances shine with the typical Szell gloss.

Symphony No. 4 in E Minor, Op. 98

Royal Philharmonic, Reiner. Chesky CD-6 [CD].

Vienna Philharmonic, Carlos Kleiber. Deutsche Grammophon 400037-2 [CD].

In spite of formidable competition from Bernstein, Walter, Klemperer, and the always provocative Carlos Kleiber—whose stunning Deutsche Grammophon recording is perhaps the most impressive of those that are relatively easy to find—this recent release from the small Chesky Records label preserves one of the loveliest Brahms symphony recordings ever made. Available for a time on Quintessence, the performance was originally recorded for—are you ready for this?—one of those omnibus, great-music-for-just-plain-folks collections produced by the *Reader's Digest.*

At the playback that followed the recording sessions, Reiner was quoted as saying, "This is the most beautiful recording I have ever made," and many have been tempted to agree. Wisely, Reiner chose to capitalize on the particular strengths of the Royal Philharmonic, without trying to turn them into a British carbon copy of his own Chicago Symphony. From a string section that produced a sound that was at once darker and less perfectly homogenized than what he was used to in Chicago, Reiner coaxed the aural equivalent of a carpet made of Russian sable. While their playing in the second movement is especially memorable, the contributions of the woodwinds and brass are equally outstanding. (At the time the recording was made, the orchestra was still, in essence, Sir Thomas Beecham's Royal Philharmonic, which is to say as fine a collection of individual soloists as any orchestra in Europe could boast.)

As an interpretation, this Brahms Fourth is vintage Reiner: tautly disciplined yet paradoxically Romantic. The outer movements are brisk and wonderfully detailed, and the recording of the energetic third movement is probably the most viscerally exciting yet made.

On tape, Szell and the Clevelanders (CBS MYT-37778) once again virtually have the field to themselves.

Trio in E-flat Major for Horn, Violin, and Piano, Op. 40

Tuckwell, horn; Perlman, violin; Ashkenazy, piano. London 414128-2 [CD].

Boston Symphony Chamber Players. Nonesuch T-79076 [T].

Like Aubrey Brain and his brilliant but tragically short-lived son, who was killed in his favorite sports car while rushing home from a concert at the 1957 Edinburgh Festival, Barry Tuckwell, for more than a quarter of a century, has been living proof of the unwritten law that says that the world's foremost horn player must, almost of necessity, be an Englishman—or, in Tuckwell's case, a transplanted Australian. As the long-time principal horn of the London Symphony, and throughout an equally distinguished solo career, Tuckwell has proven to be the only horn player of the last thirty years whose artistry has been compared favorably with that of the legendary Dennis Brain.

This impeccable recording of the Brahms Horn Trio dates from 1969, or from roughly that period when Tuckwell began his ascendancy as the preeminent horn player of his time. From a purely technical standpoint, the playing is as flawless as horn playing can possibly be. Add to that a rich, singing tone, a musical personality that is a winning blend of sensitivity and swagger, and the immaculate performances of his two famous colleagues, and we're left with a recording of the Brahms Horn Trio that will probably not be bettered for a generation.

The fine performance on Nonesuch by members of the Boston Symphony Chamber Players can be considered competitive *only* if you have failed to acquire a compact disc player.

Trios (3) for Piano, Violin, and Cello

Golub, piano; Kaplan, violin; Carr, cello. Arabesque Z-6607/8 [CD].

When Clara Schumann heard Brahms's B Major Trio for the first time, she found fault with everything, especially the opening movement. Bursting with confidence as usual, the composer withdrew the piece, revising it entirely thirty-seven years later. If Brahms—or anyone else, for that matter—ever wrote a more beautifully poignant theme than the one that begins the Trio, it has yet to be heard. All three of the Trios, for that matter, are full of extravagantly lovely moments, in which a youthful enthusiasm vies with a mature resignation in that mood of ineffable sadness that was this composer's alone.

The Trios have enjoyed some superb recordings over the years, by the Beaux Arts and Borodin Trios, and by an *ad hoc* dream ensemble made up of the late American pianist and Brahms specialist Julius Katchen, cellist Janos Starker, and violinist Joseph Suk, whose London recording of the First and Second Trios (421152-2 [CD]) remains singularly moving. And yet for all the wonders contained in those and other famous interpretations—Rubinstein, Szeryng, Fournier; Fischer, Schneiderhan, Mainardi; Istomin, Menuhin, Casals—the Arabesque recording by three young American kids shoots to the very top of the list.

Individually, pianist David Golub, violinist Mark Kaplan, and cellist Colin Carr are all world-class virtuosos poised on what will undoubtedly be major solo careers; as a trio, they have few—if any—equals. As in their superlative recording of the Schubert Trios (see page 646), they demonstrate that they have already learned the secret of great chamber-music playing: the ability to function as a single well-oiled unit without losing any of their individual identities. The performances themselves are fresh, warm-hearted, audacious, lyrical, and dramatic, depending on the demands of the piece, but, above all, they are supremely musical, without so much as a single false or unnatural-sounding step.

This one is not to be missed.

Variations on a Theme by Handel, Op. 24; *Variations on a Theme of Paganini*, Op. 35

Katchen, piano. London 440612-2 [CD].

Brahms's most challenging sets of piano variations are played with tremendous technical assurance by Julius Katchen, the brilliant American pianist who died of cancer in 1969 at the age of forty-three. The performances on this London "double decker" are taken from the pianist's complete cycle of the composer's piano music, which was not only Katchen's finest individual achievement but also one of the most significant Brahms recordings of the stereo era. While the principal attractions here are the bravura accounts of the *Handel* and *Paganini*

Variations, the pianist's accounts of the two piano concertos are no less thrilling, especially the version of the B-flat Major, which remains one of the most impassioned ever recorded. If the sound occasionally betrays its age—there *is* some edginess in the recording of the D Minor Concerto with the London Symphony and Pierre Monteux—then this is a *very* minor drawback in an otherwise splendid reissue.

Variations on a Theme by Haydn, Op. 56a

Vienna Philharmonic, Kertesz. London 448197-2 [CD].

This is not only a superlative performance of the *Variations on a Theme by Haydn* but also an intensely moving human document. Shortly before setting off on that ill-fated trip to Israel in the spring of 1973, Istvan Kertesz had recorded the entire *Haydn Variations* except for the finale. When the members of the Vienna Philharmonic learned that the young Hungarian conductor had drowned in the Mediterranean off the coast of Kfar Seba, they approached English Decca with an unusual and touching proposal: Might they be allowed to record the final variation as a tribute to their young friend?

Hearing this incomparable orchestra perform the closing moments of the piece without a conductor is an eerie and heartrending experience. Played with tremendous warmth and conviction, the finale fits the rest of the performance so seamlessly that one almost senses Kertesz's presence on the podium. The theme's hushed, heartbreaking return in the closing bars is one of the great moments in modern recording.

The best available performance of the composer's version for two pianos is the Teldec CD (92257-2) by Martha Argerich and Alexandre Rabinovitch.

Braunfels, Walter (1882–1954)

Die Vögel

Kwon, Holzmair, Gorne, Krause, Wottrich, Berlin Radio Chorus,
Berlin German Symphony, Zagrosek. London 448679-2 [CD].

Of all the numerous important recordings in London's admirable and courageous "Entartete Musik" series—a series devoted exclusively to that "degenerate music" banned by the Nazis—none is more enchanting than this one. Based on *The Birds* by Aristophanes, Braunfels's second opera was introduced to great acclaim in a Munich production conducted by Bruno Walter in 1920. Like Weinberger's *Schwanda the Bagpiper*, it enjoyed a tremendous popular success throughout Europe until 1933, when its composer was condemned. Braunfels managed to survive the war, living in seclusion on Lake Constance; in the late '40s he reorganized the Cologne Hochschule, retiring as professor emeritus in 1950.

Die Vögel contains music of ethereal beauty and disarming simplicity—not the simplicity of Carl Orff but that of Engelbert Humperdinck. There is warmth and magic everywhere, with wonders of vocal writing and orchestration to take the breath away. A successful revival in Karlsruhe in 1970 and this stunning London recording prove that the opera could easily hold the stage anywhere. In what is surely one of the great coloratura roles of modern opera, Helen Kwon is astounding as the Nightingale, mixing fireworks with a melting femininity; the rest of the cast is no less compelling, as is Lothar Zagrosek's inspired conducting.

This is the kind of revelatory performance of a buried treasure that makes the cancellation of the "Entartete Musik" series so poignant.

Brian, Havergal (1876–1972)

Symphony No. 1, "Gothic"

> Soloists, Slovak Philharmonic Chorus, Slovak National Opera Theater
> Chorus, Slovak Folk Ensemble Chorus, Lucnica Chorus, Bratislava
> Chamber Chorus and Children's Chorus, Youth Echo Chorus,
> Czech Radio Symphony, Slovak Philharmonic, Lenárd. Marco Polo
> 8.223280/281 [CD].

The jury is still out on Havergal Brian and is likely to remain so for quite some time. Even in England, where eccentricity is as commonplace as scandal sheets and fog, he's considered a very odd fish: the crackpot composer of grandiose, increasingly puzzling symphonies whose rare performances were usually undertaken by amateur or student groups—the first recordings were made by the Leicestershire Schools Orchestra in 1972, the year Brian died at the age of ninety-six—but whose quixotic determination (he wrote thirty-two symphonies) and undeniable originality make him one of the fascinating characters of twentieth-century music.

As the list of performers might suggest, Brian's *Gothic* Symphony (1919–1927) is neither a shy nor retiring work. Awkward, unruly, craggy, unpredictable, and undisciplined (the final movement alone lasts more than seventy minutes) yet shot through with genuine inspiration and startling beauty, it provides the ideal introduction to Brian's unusual world, especially in such a fine performance as this. While no one is ever likely to make a flawless recording of so vast and complex a score, Lenàrd's courageous Slovak forces sing and play with obvious devotion.

The second volume in the Marco Polo Brian Cycle (8.223447/81 [CD]) brings together the hectoring Fourth Symphony, *Das Siegeslied* (Song of Victory), the powerful and relatively concise Symphony No. 17, and the valedictory Symphony No. 32, in which the ninety-two-year-old composer writes his own funeral march. Adrian Leaper and the National Symphony of Ireland are every bit as persuasive as Lenàrd's bunch, and the recorded sound is very fine.

Bridge, Frank (1879–1941)

The Sea

Ulster Orchestra, Handley. Chandos CHAN-8473 [CD].

To the present day, this gifted English composer is principally (and unfairly) known as the teacher of Benjamin Britten. In fact, for decades after his death his name was largely kept alive by that famous pupil's act of homage, the *Variations on a Theme of Frank Bridge*. As the world has belatedly begun to recognize, Bridge was one of the most individual English composers of his generation, a Nature poet whose finest inspirations rank with those of Frederick Delius. His voice, if not always unique, is utterly distinctive: clear-headed, manly, subtle, with few obvious echoes of any music other than his own.

His most celebrated orchestral score, *The Sea,* is not only one of the most vividly colorful ever produced by an Englishman but is also one that can be favorably compared with *La Mer* by Debussy. Handley and the Ulster Orchestra give it a thrilling and sumptuous send-off, and the album is rounded out by two other splendid British seascapes: Britten's *Sea Interludes* from *Peter Grimes* and *On the Sea Shore* by Sir Arnold Bax.

Among Bridge's other more readily approachable works, the enchanting children's opera *The Christmas Rose* easily deserves to become a seasonal classic and very well might, were it given the kind of loving performance that the Chelsea Opera Group delivers on a recent Pearl CD (SHE CD 9582). The charming miniatures *Sir Roger de Coverley, There Is a Willow Grows Aslant a Brook,* and *An Irish Melody*—an exquisite arrangement of the Londonderry Air—are beautifully served by William Boughton's English String Orchestra on Nimbus NI 5366 [CD].

Part of the explanation for Bridge's slow absorption into the mainstream of modern music—and he died as long ago as 1941—is that most of *his* music, like that of his near contemporary Arnold Schoenberg, is uncompromising in the extreme. Any time spent coming to terms with his more thorny and demanding scores more than repays the investment, especially the four String Quartets, which, in the devoted performances by the Brindisi Quartet on two Continuum CDs (CON 1035/6), reveal Bridge as the most breathtakingly daring English composer of his era.

Britten, Benjamin (Lord Britten of Aldeburgh)   (1913–1976)

Albert Herring

> Fisher, Cantelo, Rex, Pears, Noble, Brannigan, English Chamber Orchestra, Britten. London 421849-2 [CD].

Acquired tastes have a curious habit of becoming enduring passions—at least, such has been *my* experience with *Albert Herring*. In spite of the fact that Britten's first comedy was derived from a short story by Guy de Maupassant, it is probably the most English of his operas, with a colorful cast of quasi-Dickensian character types whose very names—Lady Billows, Florence Pike, Mr. Gedge, Mr. Upfold, Albert himself—give them away and whose droll misadventures drew from the composer one of his wittiest, liveliest scores. Among its many glories are a series of inspired Victorian musical parodies, a hiccup on a high C-flat, and perhaps opera's great nonet (a lugubrious threnody with the cheerful refrain, "In the midst of life is death").

The composer's 1964 recording reveal the high jinks and hidden depths of *Albert Herring* as no recorded performance ever will. Dramatically and vocally, Sir Peter Pears's performance in the title role is a tour de force, while several members of the large and brilliant cast are no less impressive, particularly Sylvia Fisher as the imposing Lady Bellows. Britten's conducting is a model of its kind and the recorded sound remains phenomenally realistic.

Billy Budd

> Pears, Glossop, Shirley-Quirk, Luxon, Langdon, Brannigan, Ambrosian Opera Chorus, London Symphony, Britten. London 417428-2 [CD].

Even counting *Death in Venice,* with its explicitly homoerotic theme, *Billy Budd* is in many ways the most daring of Benjamin Britten's operas. For one thing, Herman Melville's parable of good and evil on the high seas would seem far too top-heavy with symbolism to make for successful dramatic—to say nothing of *operatic*—treatment; for another, since it *is* set on a British man-o'-war, the cast is confined entirely to men. Asking an audience to sit through what might have been a waterlogged, black-and-white morality play is one thing; asking them to sit for more than two hours without hearing a single female voice is quite another.

In spite or perhaps because of these limitations, what Britten delivers with *Billy Budd* might just be his most important opera after *Peter Grimes:* a kind of all-male English *Otello* with the mood and scent of Wagner's *Flying Dutchman*. Among the other stage works, only *A Midsummer Night's Dream* can rival its musical inventiveness and imagination, and in Captain Vere, the essentially good and decent man trapped in an impossible moral dilemma, Britten may have created his single most memorable character.

As Vere, the late Sir Peter Pears gives one of the great performances of his career in this not-to-be-missed recording. But then again, under the composer's sharply disciplined yet sympathetic leadership, virtually everyone in the cast is ideal: from Peter Glossop's naive, heroic Billy to the Iago-like darkness of Michael Langdon's Claggart. As this was the last operatic project that the legendary English producer John Culshaw was to undertake, the recording is a model of clarity, vividness, and realism. The CD transfer could not have been more effective, especially in the barely audible closing lines of Captain Vere's final monologue.

And as if all this—a major modern opera, brilliantly performed and produced—weren't enough, there's more. The first CD begins with two of Britten's finest song cycles featuring the composer accompanying the singers for whom they were written: Pears's last and most moving recording of the *Holy Sonnets of John Donne* and Dietrich Fischer-Dieskau's version, in almost impeccable English, of the witty, hard-edged, frequently bitter *Songs and Proverbs of William Blake*.

A Ceremony of Carols; Hymn to St. Cecilia; Jubilate Deo!; Missa Brevis; Rejoice in the Lamb

> **Choir of King's College, Cambridge, Willcocks, Ledger. EMI Classics CDC 47709 [CD].**

For some, it wouldn't be Christmas without *Miracle on 34th Street* and Nat King Cole singing the *Christmas Song*; for others, it wouldn't be Christmas without throbbing headaches, swollen credit card balances, and those obnoxious relatives they've spent the entire year successfully managing to avoid. If Britten's *Ceremony of Carols* hasn't yet taken its place beside plum pudding, Alistair Sim's Scrooge, *The Nutcracker,* and the other seasonal favorites, it certainly should.

The sweet-voiced King's College Choir are nearly perfect in this most appealing confection, as well as giving first-rate performances of a generous selection of Britten's other soft-sell sacred works.

God bless them, every one.

Folk Song Arrangements

> **Anderson, soprano; MacDougall, tenor; Martineau, piano. Hyperion CDA 66941/42 [CD].**

Like virtually every other important English composer of the century, Britten was an enthusiastic arranger of English folk songs, primarily for use as encores in his many recitals with Peter Pears. In a famous recording from the

1960s that surfaced briefly on a London CD, the two old friends recorded many of the best of them, from the exuberant setting of "The Minstrel Boy" to that grimly disjunctive setting of "The Miller of Dee" that recalls some of the penny-dreadful ballads of Schubert. Neither Pears nor Britten ever made a more enjoyable recording, and its prompt reissue is an urgent priority.

The handsome two-CD set from Hyperion brings together *all* of the Britten folk-song arrangements, including that unusually fine sequence adapted from the French, in appealingly fresh-voiced and unpretentious performances by sopranos Lorna Anderson and Regina Nathan and tenor Jamie MacDougall. Malcolm Martineau is superb throughout in the frequently challenging accompaniments; in fact, he is as successful as the composer himself in capturing both their subtlety and astounding variety. As ever, Hyperion's recorded sound and documentation are beyond reproach.

*G*loriana

Barstow, Jones, Langridge, Ainsley, Summers, Shirley-Quirk, Terfel,
Welsh National Opera Chorus and Orchestra, Mackerras. Argo
440213-2 [CD].

Falling between two masterpieces, *Billy Budd* and *The Turn of the Screw, Gloriana* was the great disaster of its composer's career. Written to help celebrate the coronation of the young Queen Elizabeth II in 1953, Britten's study of her aging namesake's public and private life—including a death scene, by heavens!—was savagely attacked by the popular press as being insultingly dark and pessimistic. Needless to say, given the embarrassing developments in the latter part of the second Elizabethan age, *Gloriana*'s vision of an essentially helpless monarch caught at historical cross-purposes cuts uncomfortably close to home.

Forty years after the premiere, Sir Charles Mackerras's brilliant recording—the opera's first—triumphantly proves that far from being a failure, *Gloriana* is one of Britten's most complex and probing scores, an *Aida*-like fusion of pageantry and private drama that fully engages the senses, the emotions, and the mind.

The performance itself is absolutely splendid, from Josephine Barstow and Philip Langridge as the Virgin Queen (sic) and her doomed lover Essex, to the extravagant casting of smaller roles covered by singers like the ageless John Shirley-Quirk and the young Bryn Terfel. Yet the real hero of *Gloriana*'s transfiguration is Sir Charles Mackerras, who makes certain that his superbly drilled Welsh forces miss none of the splendor or searing drama. From the famous set-pieces, the *Choral* and *Courtly Dances,* to the tiniest transitional detail, the performance is shaped with passion and intelligence—the very qualities this restored masterpiece possesses in regal abundance.

A *Midsummer Night's Dream*

Brannigan, Harwood, Veasey, Watts, Pears, Deller, Shirley-Quirk, London Symphony Orchestra and Chorus, Britten. London 425663-2 [CD].

After Verdi's *Otello* and *Falstaff*, Britten's *Midsummer Night's Dream* may very well be the most completely successful Shakespeare setting in all of opera. Using a skillful digest of the play that loses little of its essence, Britten responded to the challenge with one of his most brilliantly imagined scores. The scenes with the four befuddled lovers have genuine romance and urgency, the fairy music is on a par with Mendelssohn's, and the play within the play—wherein the rustics put on their botched version of Pyramis and Thisbe—is a wickedly funny parody of the conventions of bel canto opera. While not overloaded with memorable tunes—pregnant lines like "The course of true love never did run smooth" are frequently tossed off like afterthoughts—*A Midsummer Night's Dream* can be an authentic crowd-pleaser, as recent productions by Glyndebourne and the Los Angeles Opera clearly prove.

The composer's own recording is a wondrous one, with the ethereal Oberon of the late countertenor Alfred Deller and the coarsely amusing Bottom of Owen Brannigan among the standouts of the large and accomplished cast. The London Symphony is in spectacular form and the recording, which features many examples of John Culshaw's sonic wizardry, is one of London's very best.

Peter Grimes

Pears, Watson, Brannigan, Evans, Chorus and Orchestra of the Royal Opera House, Convent Garden, Britten. London 414577-2 [CD].

Along with *Classics Illustrated*—a vivid collection of comic-book versions of *Robinson Crusoe, Frankenstein,* and *Moby Dick* that got me through many a high-school book report—and the not-to-be-missed and invariably memorized latest issue of *Mad Magazine*, one of my most cherished bits of boyhood reading matter was a book called *A Pictorial History of Music.* I still own the book and leaf through it from time to time.

The pictures are as entertaining as ever and the text, which I never bothered to read as a boy, becomes increasingly fascinating. In all seriousness, the author—Paul Henry Lang—blithely informs us that not one of Gustav Mahler's works achieves "true symphonic greatness." (I wonder if Bernstein, Solti, Haitink, Tennstedt, and others realize they've been wasting their time all these years.) He further explains that the symphonies of Anton Bruckner are not really symphonies at all. Instead, they are massive "organ fantasies" (liver? pancreas?), all of which are indistinguishable from one another. (At least that puts Bruckner in fairly good company: except for that "organ" business, Igor Stravinsky said almost the same thing about every concerto Antonio Vivaldi ever wrote.) Of Benjamin Britten, Dr. Lang was even less flattering. While duly noting his native facility, he eventually dismissed him as a pleasant but shallow and irretrievably minor composer, a kind of late twentieth-century English version of Camille Saint-Saëns.

These days, of course, we tend to take a decidedly different view of Lord Britten of Aldeburgh, not only as the foremost English composer of his generation, but also as the man who virtually singlehandedly roused English opera from a three-century sleep. The most significant English opera since Purcell's *Dido and Aeneas, Peter Grimes*—which the man who commissioned it, that inveterate mauler of the English language, Serge Koussevitzky, called "Peter und Grimes" until the end of his life—is one of the handful of twentieth-century operas that have found a substantial audience. And with good reason. For *Peter Grimes* is not only gripping theater but also a powerful and consistently rewarding musical work.

In terms of authority and understanding, the composer's own recording from the late 1950s cannot, almost by definition, be approached. The recording featured many of the singers who had created these parts, chief among them Sir Peter Pears, for whom the demanding and complex title role was written. In its compact disc reissue, this famous recording becomes more vivid and atmospheric than ever. The well-known *Sea Interludes* have an especially wonderful color and mystery, and the stature of the individual performances only grows with the passage of time.

The Prince of Pagodas

London Sinfonietta, Knussen. Virgin Classics 59578 [CD].

The richly exotic orchestration of Britten's only full-length ballet was inspired in part by the composer's visit to Bali in 1956. Along with the stylized imitation of Balinese gamelan music, the score also owes a considerable structural debt to Tchaikovsky's *The Sleeping Beauty*, which Britten kept in his bed during the time he was composing his ballet. For his assistant Colin Matthews wrote, *"The Prince of Pagodas* is the best Britten opera. It's such uninhibited music—something which, of course, isn't possible when you have to worry about voices."

Oliver Knussen's brilliant recording is the first to offer the work in its entirety, opening up the forty-odd cuts that the composer made to fit his own performance onto two tightly packed LPs. Not only is the Knussen version more complete than Britten's, but it also offers playing and recorded sound that is even more dazzling; both, in fact, are of demonstration quality.

The Rape of Lucretia

Baker, Pears, Harper, Luxon, Shirley-Quirk, Drake, English Chamber Orchestra, Britten. London 425666-2 [CD].

Written under the one of the tightest deadlines he had ever set for himself ("Excuse brief scrawl," a letter of the period concludes, "but Lucretia is patiently waiting to be raped—on my desk"), *The Rape of Lucretia* is both the most rigorously organized of Britten's operas and the most seductively lyrical. Using a pair of narrators as Male and Female Chorus to prepare, comment upon, and heighten the action—*and* give his long-time companion Peter Pears something to do in such an irretrievably heterosexual drama—Britten and his librettist Ronald Duncan transformed the ancient legend into a powerfully immediate two-act drama, shot through with moral ambiguity and sexual tension. The culminating funeral march in the form of a *chaconne* ranks with the closing moments of the *War Requiem* as one of the composer's most deeply moving inspirations.

As impressive as the recent Chandos recording led by Richard Hickox certainly is, the composer's own version is even more so. In addition to Pears and Heather Harper as the matchless Chorus, the performance captures the incomparable Dame Janet Baker at the height of her powers. While Lucretia was created by the legendary Kathleen Ferrier, it is Baker who will be most inextricably associated with the role. London's shrewd decision to couple *Lucretia* with her equally commanding reading of *Phaedra,* Britten's last major vocal work, more or less makes the set *permanently* unapproachable.

Serenade for Tenor, Horn, and Strings, Op. 31

Pears, tenor; Tuckwell, horn; London Symphony, Britten. London 417153-2 [CD].

With the possible exception of the marriage of Robert and Clara Schumann, the long-time relationship of Benjamin Britten and Peter Pears was the most productive love affair in the history of music. It was Pears's plaintive and eccentric voice that Britten heard in his mind whenever he composed, and for the great artist who possessed it, that some of the most important vocal music of the twentieth century was written.

Nowhere is Pears's intimate understanding and complete mastery of the idiom heard to greater effect than in this last of his three recordings of the *Serenade for Tenor, Horn, and Strings,* a work that in the fullness of time may very well prove to be Britten's masterpiece. There is no subtle inflection, no nuance, no hidden meaning in either the words or the music that escapes Pears's attention. The composer's conducting is as warm and witty as can possibly be imagined, and the almost insolent grace with which Barry Tuckwell negotiates the formidable horn part must be heard to be believed. With equally impressive performances of two other magnificent Britten song cycles, *Les Illuminations* and the *Nocturne,* this generously packed compact disc is not to be missed.

Sinfonia da requiem, Op. 20; *An American Overture,* Op. 27; *The Building of the House,* Op. 79; *Canadian Carnival,* Op. 19; *Diversions* for Piano (left hand) and Orchestra, Op. 21; *Occasional Overture,* Op. 38; *Praise We Great Men; Quatre Chansons françaises; Scottish Ballad* for Two Pianos and Orchestra; *Suite on English Folk Tunes (A Time There Was . . .); Young Apollo* for Piano, String Quartet, and Orchestra, Op. 16

> **Soloists, City of Birmingham Symphony, Rattle. Angel CDCB 54270 [CD].**

Apart from the *Sinfonia da requiem,* here given one of its most powerful recent interpretations, and *Diversions,* the brilliant piano concerto he wrote on a commission from the one-armed Austrian pianist Paul Wittgenstein, this invaluable two-CD collection brings together largely unknown Britten works in performances that are not likely to be bettered any time soon. While there may not be any long-lost masterpieces lurking here, there is plenty of rewarding, enjoyable music, from the jaunty *Canadian Carnival* and *American* overtures—the latter was the *Occasional Overture,* but was re-named by the present conductor—to the surprisingly dark and substantial *Suite of English Folk Tunes (A Time There Was . . .).* With polished, infectiously enthusiastic performances by Rattle's superb forces, this must be counted one of the most significant Britten releases in a decade.

Spring Symphony, Op. 44

> **Armstrong, Baker, Tear, St. Clement Danes School Boys Choir, London Symphony Orchestra and Chorus, Previn. EMI Classics CDM 64736 [CD].**

What a completely enchanting, endlessly inventive work the *Spring Symphony* is! And like the incidental music that Sir Edward Elgar composed for the *Starlight Express*—an orchestral song cycle that concludes with a richly Edwardian peroration on the familiar Christmas carol "The First Noël"—the *Spring Symphony* ends with one of the most cleverly sprung and completely appropriate surprises in English music. For as the tenor soloist is busy trying to conclude a magnificent setting of Rafe's address to London from Beaumont and

Fletcher's *The Night of the Burning Pestle,* the chorus and orchestra come crashing in with a lusty quotation of the bawdy medieval lyric, "Sumer is icumen in."

Like most of us who love this great work, I was introduced to the *Spring Symphony* by the superb London recording made by the composer in the mid-1960s. Yet as fine as that performance certainly was, Previn's, I think, is finer still.

The key to Previn's greatness as a Britten conductor lies in his stubborn refusal to present the music as Britten the *conductor* did and in constantly finding ways to shed new light on this marvelous music—thus, as all great interpreters must, making it wholly and unmistakably his own.

His approach to the *Spring Symphony* is altogether more relaxed and expansive than the composer's. In the great moments—most noticeably in the mezzo-soprano's languorous delivery of Auden's "Out on the Lawn I Lie in Bed" —Previn tends to shy away from the faster tempos the composer favored, thus allowing more time for the mood and special character of each of the work's individual sections to unfold. Of course, he is materially aided, in "Out on the Lawn" and elsewhere, by the ravishing work of Dame Janet Baker, to whom even the admirable Norma Proctor—Britten's soloist—cannot begin to compare. The London Symphony, as always, outdoes itself for this conductor (have they ever played as well for anyone since Pierre Monteux?), and the singing of both the adult and children's choir only serves to remind us why London is, far and away, the Choral Capital of the World.

*T*he Turn of the Screw

Lott, Secunde, Hulse, Cannan, Langridge, Pay, Aldeburgh Festival Ensemble, Bedford. Collins Classics COL 7030 [CD].

Although operas that have improved their mediocre literary sources are far too numerous to mention, those that equal (or even surpass) the achievement of great works of literature are understandably rare. Verdi's *Otello* is one such opera, *The Turn of the Screw* is another. Like the classic ghost story by Henry James upon which it is based, Britten's chamber opera is a miracle of atmosphere and organization. Although the ghosts in the original story were ominously mute, in the opera they are naturally obliged to sing; it is a measure of Britten's genius that this not only fails to do serious injury to Henry James's intentions but also clarifies and deepens them simultaneously. *The Turn of the Screw* is also the most rigorously economical of Britten's stage works: the music consists of a series of increasingly tense variations on a twelve-note "screw" theme, while the incredible range and variety of orchestral effects is managed by an ensemble of only thirteen players. Finally, not all the ghosts in the opera appear on stage: the theme of innocence threatened by external corruption is one that haunted this troubled composer throughout his life, giving *The Turn of the Screw* an added emotional resonance.

While nothing would make me part with the composer's own tensely atmospheric recording (London 425672-2 [CD]—mono only), the recent Collins version conducted by Steuart Bedford is in every way a worthy successor. Having led most of the Britten recordings after the composer became too ill to do so, Bedford manages to seem as authoritative as his mentor but in state-of-the-art recorded sound. The cast is an exceptionally strong one—especially Philip Langridge as Quint and Felicity Lott as the governess—and the playing of the all-star Aldeburgh Festival Ensemble is generally phenomenal.

*W*ar Requiem, Op. 66

Vishnevskaya, Pears, Fischer-Dieskau, Melos Ensemble, Bach Choir, Highgate School Choir, London Symphony Chorus and Orchestra, Britten. London 414283-2 [CD].

Harper, Langridge, Shirley-Quirk, Choristers of St. Paul's Cathedral, London Symphony Chorus and Orchestra, Hickox. Chandos CHAN 8983/4 [CD], DBTD 2032 [T].

Along with Elgar's *Dream of Gerontius* and Sir Michael Tippett's *Child of Our Time,* Britten's *War Requiem* is one of the three most important large-scale choral works written by an English composer since the time of Handel. A poignant, dramatic, and ultimately shattering experience, the *War Requiem* is an inspired fusion of the traditional Latin mass for the dead and the poems of Wilfred Owen: those starkly horrifying visions from the trenches of the Western Front that are now universally regarded as the greatest poems on the subject of war yet produced in the English language.

In retrospect, it's hardly surprising that the *War Requiem,* like *The Dream of Gerontius,* was a failure at its world premiere. Its interpretive problems are so daunting, the performing forces so enormous and complex, that only with the release of this pathbreaking recording can the *War Requiem*'s deeply universal appeal properly be said to have begun.

As a performance, it remains one of Benjamin Britten's greatest achievements. The playing and singing are consistently urgent, vivid, and immediate, and the composer controls the *War Requiem*'s quickly shifting textures, from the chamber episodes to the most aggressive mass eruptions, like the undeniably great conductor he eventually trained himself to be.

The only serious flaw remains the contribution of soprano Galina Vishnevskaya. While she is undeniably impressive in the more declamatory moments, with repeated hearings the straining and bellowing become increasingly grating—like trying to sit still in the presence of a wobbly air raid siren with feet.

On the other hand, the interpretations of the composer's other close friends, Sir Peter Pears and Dietrich Fischer-Dieskau, will probably never be bettered.

Their performance of "Strange Meeting" is all the more moving when we remember not only who, but also *what* the singers were: a lifelong British pacifist and a former foot soldier of the Wermacht, who actually spent time in an Allied prisoner-of-war camp.

Musically, emotionally, and historically, this a milestone in the history of recording.

But so, too, is the more recent recording from Chandos. Never has a version of the *War Requiem* come so close to matching the communicative power of the composer's own, while, in terms of execution and recorded sound, it actually surpasses it. The soloists are superb and the London Symphony Chorus and Orchestra perform prodigious feats for Richard Hickox, who now joins Simon Rattle, Jeffrey Tate, and John Eliot Gardiner as one of the outstanding English conductors of his generation. Similarly, the Chandos engineers respond with one of the most thrilling digital recordings yet made, a wonder of clarity, depth, immediacy, and physical presence.

No one who loves this great work can afford to be without either recording.

Young Person's Guide to the Orchestra (Variations and Fugue on a Theme of Purcell), Op. 34

Royal Philharmonic, Previn. Telarc CD-80126 [CD].

From almost the moment it was first heard in the British documentary film *The Instruments of the Orchestra,* Britten's *Young Person's Guide to the Orchestra* has remained his most popular and frequently recorded work. Over the last forty years, there has been no dearth of first-rate recordings of the *Guide,* including the one I grew up with: a long-vanished but thoroughly electrifying performance made for one of those small music appreciation–type labels featuring an anonymous pick-up orchestra conducted by George Szell. (As with my youth, I have been searching for a copy of that recording for years. To anyone who can locate it for me, I'm willing to trade any ten Herbert von Karajan recordings and what's left of my once-complete collection of 1957 Topps baseball cards.)

A narrated recording is probably redundant at this late date, unless, of course, you have an impressionable kid you'd like to hook as I once was. Among the recordings in which the *Guide* is allowed to speak for itself, which, of course, it does with great eloquence, André Previn's recent Royal Philharmonic performance is to be preferred above all others, including, rather incredibly, the composer's own. While Benjamin Britten brought a keen wit and insight to his famous London recording (417509-2 [CD]), Previn brings even more. The personalities of the various instruments are painted in broad, yet wonderfully subtle, strokes. Rarely, for instance, have the bassoons sounded quite as buffoonish, nor has anyone ever made the percussion *cadenza* seem as ingenious or as musical.

The Royal Philharmonic, especially in the Fugue, plays with a hair-trigger virtuosity, and the recorded sound could not have been bettered.

Brouwer, Leo (1939–)

Guitar Music

Beer, Draper, Ljungstrom, Patterson. Koch Schwann 3-1174-2 [CD].

Few contemporary composers write more imaginatively for the guitar than Leo Brouwer, who studied the instrument in his native Havana and studied composition with Vincent Persichetti and Stefan Wolpe in New York. From the evocative *Preludios Epigrammaticos,* each inspired by a line of poetry by Miguel Hernandez, to the *Cuban Landscape with Rain,* which makes use of minimalist and aleatoric techniques, Brouwer's adventurous, superlatively crafted music explores the limited resources of the instrument in ways that are constantly idiomatic, ingenious, and surprising.

The Koch Schwann album called *Cuban Landscape—The Music of Leo Brouwer* offers a generous and intelligently chosen cross section of the composer's output, including the *Musica incidental campesina* and *Four micropiezas* for guitar duet, the popular *Elogio de la danza,* and the vivid *El Decameron Negro,* redolent with the rich scents and languorous mood of the Cuban evening. Guitarist Robert Beer and his colleagues John Draper, Carl Ljungstrom, and Steven Patterson are sensitive and enthusiastic guides to this fascinating repertoire, while the recorded sound is natural and clear.

Julian Bream has made several important recordings of Brouwer's music, including the neo-Romantic *Concerto elegiaco,* with its cyclical structure and Afro-Cuban rhythms (RCA 7718-2-RC [CD]), and the Sonata in Three Movements, heard on a thought-provoking EMI Classics anthology of twentieth-century guitar works (CDC 54901 [CD]), which also includes Britten's *Nocturnal,* Lutostawski's *Melodie ludowe,* Frank Martin's *Quatre pièces brèves,* and Takemitsu's *All in Twilight*—one of the finest albums of its kind.

Bruch, Max (1838–1920)

Violin Concerto in G Minor, Op. 55

Perlman, violin; London Symphony, Previn. EMI Classics CDC 47074 [CD].

Chung, violin; London Philharmonic, Tennstedt. EMI Classics CDC 54072 [CD].

In 1906, toward the end of his long career, the Hungarian violinist Joseph Joachim, for whom Brahms and Dvořák had written their violin concertos, left what still remains a fair assessment of the central European history of the form:

> The Germans have four violin concertos. The greatest, the one that makes the least concessions, is Beethoven's. The one by Brahms comes closest to Beethoven's in its seriousness. Max Bruch wrote the richest and most enchanting of the four. But the dearest of them all, the heart's jewel, is Mendelssohn's.

To date, the richest and most enchanting recording of Bruch's G Minor Violin Concerto is the first of the two that Itzhak Perlman has made so far for EMI Classics. Unlike Perlman's digital remake with Bernard Haitink and the Amsterdam Concertgebouw Orchestra—a strangely inert and calculated performance from two such warmhearted musicians—the Previn recording finds Perlman at his most irresistibly boyish and romantic. There is an appealing improvisatory feeling in the playing, and the rhapsodic support that Previn supplies could not have enhanced the interpretation more.

Kyung-Wha Chung is also very fresh and spontaneous-sounding in her second recording of the concerto, which is even more daring and expressive than her first. Anne-Sophie Mutter plays astonishingly well in her Deutsche Grammophon recording (400031-2), but Herbert von Karajan's cloying, manipulative, utterly sterile accompaniment drowns an otherwise lovely performance in a vat of rancid strawberry jam.

Although not quite on a par with his masterpiece, Bruch's Second Violin Concerto is more than worth investigating, especially when paired with the popular *Scottish Fantasy* and given swaggering, lyrical performances by Itzhak Perlman at the top of his form (EMI CDC-49071).

Bruckner, Anton (1824–1896)

Symphony No. 5 in B-flat Major

Vienna Philharmonic, Furtwängler. Arkadia CDWFE 360 [CD].

Symphony No. 7 in E Major

Berlin Philharmonic, Furtwängler. Arkadia CDWFE 362 [CD].

Symphony No. 8 in C Minor

Berlin Philharmonic, Furtwängler. Arkadia CDWFE 356 [CD].

Symphony No. 9 in D Minor

Berlin Philharmonic, Furtwängler. Music and Arts CD 730-1 [CD].

More than those of any other great composer—and be assured that this squat, homely, diffident man ranks with the greatest composers of the Romantic era—the symphonies of Anton Bruckner need all the help they can get. Unlike the virtually foolproof music of Beethoven, Tchaikovsky, or Brahms, which can resist all but the most rankly incompetent mauling, for the Bruckner symphonies to emerge as the great works they so obviously are, nothing less than *great* performances will do. While they contain much that is immediately appealing, including some of the most heroic brass writing in all of music, their greatest moments tend to be private and internal: the deeply spiritual utterances of an essentially medieval spirit who was completely out of step with his time.

For the interpreter, the single most pressing problem in performing Bruckner is trying to maintain the level of concentration that these often mammoth outbursts require. If the intensity relaxes for a moment, the vast but terribly fragile structures will almost inevitably fall apart. In short, it's altogether possible that many who are persuaded they dislike Bruckner are confusing the composer with the *performances* of his music that they've heard. Indifferent, good, or even *very* good interpretations, which in recent years is about the best the composer can expect, simply will not do.

Wilhelm Furtwängler was unquestionably the greatest Bruckner interpreter of whom we have an accurate record. All that is best and most characteristic in the composer's music—its drama, grandeur, mysticism—is revealed more powerfully and clearly in Furtwängler's recordings than in those of any other conductor. Although the recorded sound in these performances from the late 1940s and early '50s ranges only from good to barely adequate, several books could easily be written on each of the individual interpretations: from the apocalyptic holocaust that Furtwängler conjures up in the last movement of the Eighth Symphony to his unutterably beautiful performance of the *Adagio* from the Fifth, in which we become a party to one of the most moving spiritual journeys ever undertaken by a nineteenth-century composer. While the point could be belabored indefinitely, suffice it to say that if you have yet to experience these astounding recordings, it's unlikely that you've ever really *heard* the Bruckner symphonies at all.

For collectors who are unable (or unwilling) to come to terms with Furtwängler's intensely personal conceptions, or for those who grow impatient with less than state-of-the-art recorded sound, a handful of recent recordings can be recommended as reasonable, if not completely satisfying, alternatives. In the Fourth ("Romantic") Symphony, Eliahu Inbal's recording of the original 1874 version (Teldec 9031-77597-2 [CD]) is as persuasive as it is fascinating, including, as it does, an entirely different *Scherzo* than the one that is usually heard. The most completely satisfying account of the more familiar edition is by Eugen Jochum and the Berlin Philharmonic on Deutsche Grammophon (427200-2 [CD]). Among modern recordings of the Fifth, Günther Wand leads the Berlin Philharmonic in a thrillingly majestic live performance for RCA (09026-68503-2 [CD]) and for the closest thing we have to a Furtwängler Seventh and Ninth in stereo sound, Bruno Walter's handsomely remastered recordings from the early 1960s (CBS MB2K 45669 [CD], MBK-44825 [CD]) come surprisingly close to filling the bill. Anyone looking for recordings of all the symphonies who also want the convenience of a boxed set will find Eugen Jochum's admirable cycle for Deutsche Grammophon (429079-2) an authentic bargain. The performances, by either the Berlin Philharmonic (Nos. 1, 4, 7, 8, and 9) or the Bavarian Radio Symphony (Nos. 2, 3, 5, and 6), are for the most part admirably direct and intensely noble, while the recorded sound rivals all but today's best.

Those wishing to explore the composer's more problematical but frequently inspiring output of sacred music should investigate the sumptuous three-disc set from Hyperion (CDA 44071 [CD], which features, as its centerpiece, the three mass settings from the mid-1860s in devoted, meticulously prepared performances by the Corydon Singers and Orchestra conducted by Matthew Best. Their versions of the *Te Deum* and Psalm settings are also extremely accomplished, as is the work of the Hyperion engineers.

Finished in 1893 during one of the several long pauses the composer took during the composition of the Ninth Symphony, the secular cantata *Helgoland* is an exciting, inexplicably neglected near-masterwork, given a suitably rousing performance by the gentlemen of the Ambrosian Chorus and a London pick-up orchestra led with obvious enthusiasm by Wyn Morris. This unusual and extremely attractive IMP recording (IMP 1042 [CD]) is made all the more so by pairing it with a Wagner rarity, *Das Liebesmahl der Apostel* (The Love-Feast of the Apostles), an early work from 1843, the same year as *The Flying Dutchman*.

Buck, Dudley (1839–1909)

Festival Overture on the American National Air, "The Star-Spangled Banner"

London Symphony, Klein. Albany TROY 235 [CD].

Once, before a Boston Symphony concert at which he planned to play his own curious arrangement of the national anthem, Igor Stravinsky was informed by two of the city's finest that if he proceeded to do so he would be placed under arrest and formally charged with "defacing national property," as the song had recently become. "The Star-Spangled Banner," tone-deaf Francis Scott Key's bellicose poem whose first stanza was grafted onto the melody of an eighteenth-century English pub song, became the national anthem only in 1931—yet another triumph of the Hoover administration.

Fortunately, at the time Dudley Buck, the Hartford organist, teacher, and composer, got his hands on it, the thing was still fair game. Buck's *Festival Overture* is not only an unqualified hoot and a first-rate party record, but it also happens to be an ingenious and tremendously exciting piece. When the famous melody makes its initial appearance in the horns or returns for its spectacular apotheosis at the end, it's virtually impossible *not* to feel a surge of national pride, however unpatriotic one might happen to be. This picturesque Albany CD—a reissue of a fondly remembered EMI album—also features important music by some of Buck's near contemporaries, including the *Prelude* from the darkly atmospheric incidental music that John Knowles Paine wrote for *Oedipus Tyrannus* and John Alden Carpenter's percussive, visionary ballet *Skyscrapers.*

Neither the performances nor the recording could be improved.

Burleigh, Harry T. (1866–1949)

Songs

McConnell, soprano; Cordovana, piano. Centaur CRC 2252 [CD].

As a student at the National Conservatory of Music in New York, Harry T. Burleigh sang Negro spirituals for Antonín Dvořák on so many occasions that the composer credited the young American baritone as a significant factor in the composition of the *New World Symphony.* Although Burleigh is best remembered for his popular arrangements of spirituals for the concert platform and his landmark publication *Jubilee Songs of the USA*, he was also the composer of more than one hundred art songs. While he often set verses by Paul Lawrence Dunbar, James Weldon Johnson, Langston Hughes, and other important African-American writers of the day, there is little in Burleigh's gentlemanly late-Romantic idiom to suggest the composer's ethnic origins; the principal influence running through these appealing, well-made miniatures is the music of Burleigh's friend Victor Herbert.

Regina McConnell's invaluable collection of twenty-three Burleigh songs offers a representative cross section of his work from 1907 to 1934. The settings are invariably resourceful and imaginative, their level of melodic inspiration extraordinarily high. The performances are devoted and respectful (perhaps a little too much so, at times) and the recorded sound is excellent.

A Northeastern CD (NR 252) offers a selection of Burleigh's still matchless spiritual arrangements in fine performances by bass-baritone Orel Moses.

Busoni, Ferruccio

(1866–1924)

Piano Concerto, Op. 39

**Ogdon, piano; John Alldis Choir, Royal Philharmonic, Revenaugh.
EMI Classics CDH 69850 [CD].**

Unlike his friend Gustav Mahler, Ferruccio Busoni is a composer whose time has not yet come. Best remembered for his arrangements of the music of Bach, as an inspired and influential teacher, and as one of history's consummate keyboard virtuosos—those who heard them both insisted that his playing was superior even to Liszt's—Busoni was an odd combination of Italian Romantic composer and North German philosopher-mystic who was one of the major musical heroes of his age and *could* be one of ours. Perhaps the best introduction to this absorbing and endlessly complex personality is the titanic Piano Concerto he composed between 1902 and 1904, one of the most involved and entertaining concertos ever written for the instrument and—at seventy minutes—the longest.

John Ogdon's historic first recording of the work will undoubtedly be that troubled English pianist's most enduring memorial. With the help of the Royal Philharmonic at the peak of their post-Beecham form and some knowing and sensitive support from Daniell Revenaugh, Ogdon negotiates the Concerto's monumental difficulties with such deceptive ease that you wonder why no one bothered to tackle it before. And if there are any lingering doubts that Ogdon's is anything less than one of the great recordings of the century, then simply compare it to any of the well-intentioned but wholly earth-bound versions that followed. It makes him seem—in Jean Shepherd's endearing phrase—"like a puff-adder among the garden worms."

String Quartets (2)

Pelligrini String Quartet. CPO CPO999 264-2 [CD].

Given the fact that memorable Italian strings quartets are hardly a lira a dozen, it's frankly amazing that these youthful wonders by the seventeen- and twenty-one-year-old Ferruccio Busoni have languished in obscurity for so long. These are emphatically *not* the works of a student or talented journeyman but fully formed, elegantly argued statements by a master craftsman, full of a sly and endearing wit, bracing themes, and seemingly inexhaustible ingenuity.

With performances by the Pelligrini Quartet that are as warm and immaculate as the recorded sound, this easily counts as one of the most surprising (and rewarding) chamber music albums in years.

Butterworth, George

(1885–1916)

The Banks of Green Willow; 2 English Idylls; A Shropshire Lad

English String Orchestra, Boughton. Nimbus NI 5068 [CD].

Like the poets Edward Thomas, Isaac Rosenberg, and Wilfred Owen, George Butterworth was of that tragic English generation decimated in the trenches of the Western Front. He enlisted during the week World War I began and was killed at the battle of Pozières two years later. During his brief career, he was an inveterate collector of English folk songs, helped Vaughan Williams arrange material for *A London Symphony,* and composed a handful of inspired miniatures that suggest that he might have become one of the most significant English composers of his time.

The four bewitching works found on this gorgeous Nimbus CD represent Butterworth at his most beguiling. If you are touched by the folk-inspired music of Delius, Holst, and Vaughan Williams, then you will probably find Butterworth irresistible. And once you find yourself in his gentle, vice-like grip, don't fail to investigate a Unicorn-Kanchana recording of his Housman song cycle, *Six Songs from "A Shropshire Lad,"* in the winning performance by baritone Brian Rayner Cook and pianist Clifford Benson.

Buxtehude, Dietrich (1637–1707)

Organ works

Alain, organ. Erato 12979-2 [CD].

All that most people know about this Swedish-born organist and composer is that the young Johann Sebastian Bach walked the two hundred miles to Lübeck—where Buxtehude served as organist at St. Mary's Church for forty years—simply to hear him play. What is less well-known is that the young Handel also made the journey (albeit by coach) from Hamburg in 1703, not to hear Buxtehude but to apply for the retiring master's job. When he discovered that custom required him to marry the daughter of his predecessor, Handel discreetly decamped.

Marie-Claire Alain's two-disc survey makes for an ideal introduction to Buxtehude's brilliant and majestic organ music, which helped to develop and codify the chaconnes, choral preludes, passacaglias, toccatas, fugues, and other basic forms of organ music more decisively than that of any other previous composer. The Schnitger-Ahrend organ in Groningen seems a perfect choice to reveal both the intricacy and grandeur of the writing, with the organist offering her customary blend of impeccable scholarship and imaginative musicianship.

Byrd, William (1543–1623)

The Great Service

The Tallis Scholars, Phillips. Gimmell CDGIM-011 [CD].

One of the giants of Renaissance sacred music, William Byrd was probably the first incontestably great English composer. Unlike his probable teacher, Thomas Tallis—only hearsay evidence suggests a link between the two men—

Byrd wrote distinguished music in virtually every form, from keyboard works and madrigals to music for High Anglican worship.

Peter Phillips and the Tallis Scholars give an inspired performance of Byrd's stirring masterpiece *The Great Service,* a work that might have been designed for people who think they don't like older sacred music. Almost as moving is an Argo recording (430164-2 [CD]) of the *Masses for 3, 4, and 5 Voices,* elegantly sung by the Choir of Winchester Cathedral led by David Hill.

Cadman, Charles Wakefield

(1881–1946)

From the Land of the Sky-Blue Water

Müller, piano. Marco Polo 8.223715 [CD].

Charles Wakefield Cadman's exquisite miniature based on an Omaha love song is only the first and best-known selection on a fascinating Marco Polo anthology called *The American Indianists,* featuring twenty-seven miniatures by nine composers based on the chants of various North American Indian tribes. Inspired by Dvořák's *American* Quartet, which modeled its themes on Indian ("Native American," to be politically correct; "Siberian American," to be anthropologically accurate) melodies, a group of American composers led by Arthur Farewell (1877–1952) produced a substantial body of authentic-sounding Indian music, much of it written in collaboration with surviving tribes.

The works contained on this intriguing album range from relatively simple transcriptions like the *Lyrics of the Redman* by Harvey Worthington Loomis (1865–1930) to brilliantly imaginative fantasies like *American Indian Rhapsody* by Preston Ware Orem (1865–1938). The Swiss pianist Dario Müller plays with considerable skill and a zealot's infectious enthusiasm, helping to make the album as enjoyable as it is unusual. Fine, realistic recorded sound.

Following up on the success of Müller's first album, Marco Polo has wisely issued another (8.223738 [CD]), which, along with more spirited music by Cadman (the *Thunderbird Suite* and *Idealized Indian Themes*) and others, features the most celebrated American work inspired by Indian sources, the *Woodland Sketches* of Edward MacDowell.

Cage, John (1912–1992)

Third Construction

Amadinda. Hyperion HDC 12991 [CD].

Perhaps more than any other figure of his generation, the late John Cage became the incarnate image of the wild-eyed, ultra avant-garde composer. A pupil of Adolf Weiss, Arnold Schoenberg, and Henry Cowell, Cage developed the technique of playing directly onto the strings in his various works for "prepared piano," which called for the placement of rubber bands, wooden pegs, coins, screws, and other objects inside the instrument's mechanism. From physics, he applied the principle of indeterminacy to music, thus assuring that no two performances of any work could be exactly alike (in some works, the actual selection of the components to be used is determined by rolling dice). In the process, Cage evolved a highly individual method of musical notation, abandoning traditional procedures in favor of bizarre and frequently beautiful pictorial representations. His quest for freedom of musical expression often led to outlandish experiments such as *4'33"*, a work in three movements in which no sounds whatever are to be produced (the composer's only instruction to the performers is "tacet, any instrument or combination of instruments") and *Imaginary Landscape* for twelve radios, twenty-four tape players, and conductor, in which the various "instruments" are turned on and off and occasionally knocked to the floor.

Composed in 1941, *Third Construction* is widely regarded as the climax of the early period of Cage's work. Written for an ensemble of four percussionists, the piece calls for a bewildering variety of instruments, from tin cans and tom-toms of various sizes, to claves, cowbells, Chinese cymbals, lion's roar, tambourine, quijadas (a Latin rattle originally made from the jawbone of an ass), cricket callers, conch shell, tin can with tacks, and ratchet. Amadinda's performance of the work—like those of *Amores* and *4'33"*—sounds definitive.

Those wishing to further explore the world of this irreplaceable loon might begin with Maro Ajemian's CRI recording (CD 700 [CD]) of the watershed *Sonatas and Interludes for Prepared Piano* or the Wergo recording (WER 6247-2 [CD]), *The 25-Year Retrospective Concert of the Music of John Cage.*

Caldara, Antonio

(c. 1670–1736)

Christmas Cantata (Vaticini di Pace)

Soloists, Arcadia Baroque Ensemble, Mallon. Naxos 8.553772 [CD].

Here's the perfect work for that inevitable moment during the holiday season when the mere thought of another *Messiah* or *Christmas Oratorio* can make you want to scream: a lively, sweetly allegorical sequence of fourteen arias by an Italian contemporary of Handel and Bach that ends in a vision of the infant Christ. Caldara's affecting sincerity and genuine melodic gifts will appeal to believers and nonbelievers alike, especially in such a bright and fresh-scrubbed performance as this one from a fine young Canadian period-instrument ensemble.

For those wishing to explore further, Caldara's *Maddalena ai Piedi di Cristo* (Mary Magdalene at the Feet of Christ), though an earlier work, is even more impressive, made up of some twenty-eight richly contrasted *da capo* arias, many requiring exceptional control and skill. The Harmonia Mundi performance (HMC 905221/22 [CD]) led by René Jacobs is superbly sung, especially by the brilliant countertenor Andreas Scholl as Heavenly Love.

Canteloube, Joseph

(1879–1957)

Songs of the Auvergne

Te Kanawa, soprano; English Chamber Orchestra, Tate. Volume 1: London 410004-2 [CD]. Volume 2: London 411730-2 [CD].

Upshaw, soprano; Lyon Opera Orchestra, Nagano. Volume 1: Erato 96559-2 [CD]; Volume 2: Erato 17577 [CD].

For much of his life, the indefatigable French composer Joseph Canteloube devoted himself to collecting and arranging the charming, haunting, and frequently scintillating folk songs of the Auvergne region of central France. Although none of his original works ever succeeded in making much of an impression, the four-volume *Songs of the Auvergne* are well on their way to becoming modern classics. Beginning with the pioneering recordings of Natania Davrath and Victoria de los Angeles in the late 1950s and early '60s (out now on Vanguard, OVC 8001/02 [CD]; and Angel, CDM 63178 [CD]), famous singers have been drawn almost irresistibly to these minor masterworks, not only because they are so vocally and musically rewarding but also because any album with "Songs of the Auvergne" on its cover is almost guaranteed to sell.

Dame Kiri Te Kanawa, in some of her finest work in the recording studio to date, has so far recorded two excellent collections and her ravishing, peaches-and-cream instrument serves the music very well.

With Frederica von Stade's Sony Classical recordings temporarily unavailable, Dawn Upshaw's Erato albums make for an appealing alternative. In fact, some might actually prefer the sense of rapt innocence that the soprano conjures in her voice, to say nothing of the sparkling wit she brings to the brighter numbers. Kent Nagano's accompaniments miss none of the color or charm of Canteloube's ingenious orchestrations, nor do the Erato engineers.

Carter, Elliott (1908–)

Piano Sonata (1945–46; revised 1982)

Lawson, piano. Virgin Classics 59008 [CD].

During the last four decades, Elliott Carter has become the most uncompromising and, for many, one of the most forbidding of modern American composers. Igor Stravinsky was quoted as saying that Carter's *Double Concerto* of 1961 was the first true American masterpiece, and in the increasingly complex music he has written since then—from the astonishing *Concerto for Orchestra* to the mysterious *Enchanted Preludes* for Flute and Cello—he has proven to be, with Milton Babbitt, the most consistently challenging composer of his generation.

The Piano Sonata, finished in 1946 and revised substantially in 1982, is probably the greatest piano sonata yet written by an American. Composed toward the middle of Carter's neo-Classical phase, it is a rich, serious, elegantly made work that includes, among its many wonders, one of the finest fugues since Beethoven. Peter Lawson's electrifying Virgin Classics album will allow you to judge if it really *is* the Great American Piano Sonata, since, with the exception of the magnificent Piano Sonata of Charles Tomlinson Griffes, it includes the only other possible contenders: the piano sonatas of Samuel Barber and Aaron Copland, in equally authoritative performances.

This is easily one of the most important recordings of American piano music yet released.

An equally exciting recording of three of Carter's most significant orchestral scores features Oliver Knussen leading the London Sinfonietta in revelatory performances of the *Concerto for Orchestra,* the Violin Concerto, and *Three Occasions* (Virgin Classics CDC-59271 [CD]). In Knussen's capable hands, even the thorniest of Carter's inspirations emerge with a new lucidity and emotional depth. Although nothing will ever transform this aristocratic composer into a man of the masses, this is easily—to use a particularly vile mass-market phrase—the most "user-friendly" Carter album yet.

Finally, to hear the starting point from which Carter's extraordinary journey began, CRI has reissued the Symphony No. 1 from 1942 (CD-552 [CD], ASC-6003 [T]). One of the most exuberant and handsomely turned-out American orchestral scores of the 1940s, the Symphony is a very far cry indeed from the endlessly fascinating minefield of late Carter. The language is no more threatening than that of the symphonies of Hanson, Harris, and Diamond, and the musical rewards are just as immediate and considerable.

Carwithen, Doreen (1922–)

Orchestral Works

London Symphony, Hickox. Chandos CHAN 9524 [CD].

The widow of the English composer William Alwyn and the driving spirit behind the superlative Chandos Alwyn series, Doreen Carwithen is also a distinctive and accomplished composer in her own right, if this eye-opening collection is any indication. While the two overtures—*ODTAA* ("One Damned Thing After Another"), based on the John Masefield novel, and *Bishop Rock,* inspired by the stormy, westernmost outcropping of the British Isles—have an exhilarating, Waltonesque rhythmic bite, the four-movement *Suffolk Suite,* drawn from a film about East Anglia, is a colorful, richly evocative work in the best English Pastoral tradition. The most significant work, the Concerto for Piano and Strings, is full of strength and character, with a brooding slow movement that seems nearly a match for the haunting *Adagio* of her husband's *Sinfonietta.* Howard Shelley is *more* than a match for the brilliant virtuoso writing, while the always sympathetic Richard Hickox again creates the distinct impression that he might have written the music himself.

Castelnuovo-Tedesco, Mario (1895–1968)

Guitar Concerto No. 1

Kraft, guitar; Northern Chamber Orchestra, Ward. Naxos 8.550729 [CD].

Born into a Jewish family that had lived in the Tuscan hills near Florence for four centuries, Mario Castelnuovo-Tedesco always claimed to have inherited his musical gifts from his paternal grandfather, a devout and private man who in his youth made sketches in a little notebook for possible musical settings of various Hebrew prayers. These themes eventually became the basis of one of his grandson's final works, *Prayers My Grandfather Wrote.*

In addition to a number of major works on sacred subjects, including the *Sacred Service for the Sabbath Eve,* the opera *Saul,* and a series of Biblical oratorios including *The Book of Ruth, The Song of Jonah,* and *The Song of Songs,* Castelnuovo-Tedesco composed prolifically—always in ink and never at the piano—in virtually all musical forms. After fleeing Hitler's Europe in 1939, the composer settled in Beverly Hills where he produced a great deal of music for films, largely under pseudonyms. The final two decades of his life were devoted primarily to teaching.

Castelnuovo-Tedesco was one of the first important twentieth-century composers to write extensively for the guitar, producing more works for the instrument than almost any other non-guitarist composer. His two guitar concertos rank with those of Rodrigo and Villa-Lobos in terms of quality and only slightly behind them in terms of popularity, and the familiar D Major Concerto has never had a finer recording than this splendid version from Naxos. Norbert Kraft proves an ideal guide through this spirited, colorful music, while Ward and his alert ensemble offer top-notch support.

Itzhak Perlman's EMI Classics recording (CDC 54296 [CD]) of the composer's Second Violin Concerto is also very special. Written for Heifetz and subtitled *I Profeti* (The Prophets), each of its three movements—Isaiah, Jeremiah, Elijah—overflows with Jewish melody, all of it instantly memorable and much of it deeply moving. Both *I Profeti* and the Violin Concerto of Paul Ben Haim draw staggering playing from the soloist, with the concert setting adding additional excitement to the occasion.

Catalani, Alfredo (1854–1893)

La Wally

Tebaldi, Marimpietri, del Monaco, Cappuccilli, Turin Lyric Chorus,
Monte Carlo Opera Orchestra, Cleva. London 425417-2 [CD].

Even before interest in its hit tune was re-awakened by the 1981 French film
Diva—and one wonders what became of its alluring star, Wilhelmenia Wiggins
Fernandez?—Catalani's sappy melodramatic potboiler had the reputation of
being a one-aria opera. This is selling the thing considerably short. For in addition to "Ebben? Ne andro lontana"—admittedly, one of the loveliest arias ever
written by anyone—*La Wally* can also boast what may well be the *stupidest* story
in Italian opera. After the heroine arranges to have the hero murdered because
she believes he insulted her—now *that's* touchy, even by soprano standards—she
changes her mind and rescues him. On the mountain top they confess their love
and are promptly swept away by an avalanche.

The great Renata Tebaldi was never more irresistibly feminine than she was
here, in one of her last complete opera recordings. The voice is at its most melting—the big aria is a wonder of passionate abandon and effortless control—and
the characterization is so enthralling that you nearly forget what utter nonsense
La Wally is. Although Mario del Monaco reminds us, gloriously, what the now
nearly extinct *tenore da forza* could be, and Fausto Cleva's old-fashioned blood-
and-thunder conducting defines *verismo* at its best, this is very much Tebaldi's
show and she steals it magnificently.

Chabrier, Emmanuel

(1841–1894)

Bourrée fantastique; España; Dance Slave; Gwendoline: Overture; Joyeuse Marche; Suite Pastorale

> Detroit Symphony, Paray. Mercury Living Presence 434303-2 [CD].

Gustav Mahler once shocked the members of the New York Philharmonic by calling Emmanuel Chabrier's *España* "the foundation of modern music." Precisely what Mahler meant by that we'll probably never know, but he certainly put his baton where his mouth was: during his two-year stay in America he programmed it half a dozen times, always in performances in which he took the liberty of quadrupling all the wind parts.

Although we now tend to think of *España* as not much more than the foundation of many a pops concert, there was a time when the reputation of its abrupt, lively, immensely likable composer was far more imposing than it is today. No less a figure than the American musicologist Gilbert Chase once wrote, "He was the direct precursor of Debussy and Ravel, whose most daring effects he anticipated"; for their part, Debussy and Ravel always admitted their fondness for the music of this late-blooming composer and celebrated salon wit. (Chabrier's caustic sense of humor was legendary. He once said, "There are three kinds of music: the good, the bad, and that of Ambroise Thomas.")

Paul Paray's wonderful Chabrier recordings from the late 1950s cannot be welcomed back into the catalogue too warmly. In this repertoire—in French music, in general—Paray had few rivals among the major conductors of his generation and he invests each of the pieces with an abundance of life and a character uniquely its own. The Detroit Symphony has rarely sounded as sensuous or alert, and the original Mercury Living Presence recording has been revived with astonishing vividness.

Piano Music

> Rabol, Dugas, pianos. Naxos 8.553009 [CD]; 8.553010 [CD]; 8.553080 [CD].

Naxos continues to demonstrate what a record label *ought* to be doing with this much-needed survey of the enchanting piano music of Emmanuel Chabrier. From the endlessly colorful *Dix pièces pittoresques* (four of which were later orchestrated as the *Suite pastorale*) to the melting *Valses romantiques,* this is the most entertaining French piano music of the mid-nineteenth century and the most important written between Chopin and Debussy. The level of inspiration and invention remains remarkably high, which is hardly surprising from a mercilessly self-critical composer whose motto was "It will be good or it will not be at all."

If the performances never threaten to efface the memory of those magical ones on a long-deleted CBS CD by Robert Casadesus, then they are alert, sensitive, and uniformly pleasurable, giving excellent value for the dollar. As they have so often, Naxos deserves our thanks and support.

Chadwick, George Whitefield (1854–1931)

Symphonic Sketches; Symphony No. 2 in B-flat, Op. 21

Detroit Symphony, Järvi. Chandos CHAN 9334.

Like John Knowles Paine and Edward Burlingame Hill—other proper New Englanders who insisted on using their given, Christian, *and* middle names— George Whitefield Chadwick was a talented member of that generation of American composers known as the "Boston Classicists": men whose names and music have all but vanished in the ever-expanding shadow cast by their Hartford contemporary Charles Ives.

Prior to Ives, there had been nothing particularly "American" in American music for, like the poetry of Holmes, Lowell, Whittier, and Longfellow, it was fashioned almost entirely on European models. After the obligatory period of study in Germany, Chadwick returned to teach at the New England Conservatory in Boston, where for years he turned out polite, albeit superbly crafted, music on themes derived from Greek antiquity *(Thalia, Euterpe)* and local folk legend *(Rip van Winkle).* It was in 1895, after completing the last of his three symphonies, that Chadwick produced the first two installments of his masterpiece, the *Symphonic Sketches.* While the work owes much to Antonín Dvořák, whose recently completed "New World" Symphony had made him America's musical hero, it also contains many unmistakably nationalistic gestures and is, with one or two possible exceptions, the most deftly orchestrated work by an American composer of the nineteenth century.

The performance by Neeme Järvi and the revitalized Detroit Symphony is so full of dash, bravado, and genuine sentiment that it nearly puts Howard

Hanson's classic Mercury Living Presence recording (434337-2 [CD]) in the shade. In addition to superb digital sound, the newer recording also offers a handsome reading of Chadwick's Second Symphony, whose lovely slow movement this conductor once impulsively pronounced "the most beautiful ever written." In Järvi's hands, it sounds dangerously close to being just that. Those who respond to these magnificent anachronisms will also want to investigate the composer's Third Symphony (CHAN 9253 [CD]) without delay.

Chaminade, Cécile (1857–1944)

Piano Works

> Jacobs, piano. Hyperion CDA 66584 [CD]; CDA 66706 [CD].
>
> Parkin, piano. Chandos CHAN 8888 [CD].

At the height of her fame in the decades immediately before and after the turn of the century, Cécile Chaminade was—and perhaps still is—the most successful female composer in musical history. Born in Paris in 1857, she studied piano with the celebrated Félix Le Couppey, theory with Augustin Savard—teacher of the American Edward MacDowell—and composition with Benjamin Godard. Much in demand as a concert pianist, Chaminade was also a prolific composer who wrote innumerable piano works for her own use. Although she also produced a fair number of more obviously serious works, including a symphony called *Les Amazones* and a *Concertstück* for piano and orchestra that served as the vehicle for her American debut in 1908, she was known primarily for her attractively turned-out salon pieces: romantic, potted-palm miniatures with titles like *Les Sylvains, La Lisonjera,* and *Six airs de ballet,* which enjoyed a considerable vogue in France, England, and America. These endearingly quaint pieces are little time machines for transporting us to an age of vanished elegance and gentility, the perfect accompaniment to sipping an elderly sherry or reading Edith Wharton.

In their splendid collections, Peter Jacobs and Eric Parkin release the still-heady bouquets of these faded wallflowers without the slightest hint of embarrassment or condescension, and both pianists benefit from exceptionally lifelike recorded sound.

Charpentier, Gustave

(1860–1956)

Louise

Cotrubas, Barbié, Domingo, Sénéchal, Baquier, Ambrosian Opera
Chorus, New Philharmonia Orchestra, Prêtre. Sony Classical S3K
46429 [CD].

Gustave Charpentier was nearly forty when, after a decade-long gestation, *Louise* was first mounted at the Opéra-Comique on February 2, 1900. At its fiftieth anniversary performance, the composer, nearing ninety, conducted the final scene of the opera, after which he was made a Grand Officer of the Legion of Honor by the President of France. In between those two historic events, Charpentier did precious little other than compose a dismal sequel called *Julien* in 1913 and ponder the mysteries of *Louise*'s phenomenal success. Part of that success had to do with the novelty of the opera's working-class setting and socialist leanings, part with the fact that an unknown singer named Mary Garden took over the title role two months into the production and created a sensation. But *Louise* has other, more durable charms, including a touching and turbulent love story and a vivid evocation of turn-of-the-century Paris, which almost becomes another character in the drama.

The Sony Classical recording makes the strongest possible case for this frequently compelling work. If Ileana Cotrubas isn't perfectly suited, vocally, to the title role—"Depuis le jour," for instance, is not ideally soaring and effortless—then her dramatic reading of the little seamstress is very affecting, as is the singing of Placido Domingo as Julien. The rest of the cast is uniformly excellent and Georges Prêtre delivers some of the most sensitive conducting of his career. All in all, it's a recording that proves that *Louise* is something considerably more than a French *La Bohème*.

Charpentier, Marc-Antoine

(1645–1704)

Messe de minuit pour Noël

> **Choir of St. John's College, Cambridge, City of London Sinfonia, Guest. Chandos CHAN 8658 [CD].**

One of my first serious duties after acquiring a driver's license was to transport my paternal grandmother to Midnight Mass on Christmas Eve. (My grandmother was a devout, eight-mass-per-week Catholic, my grandfather an orthodox atheist; they agreed to split the difference and raise my father as a Protestant.) Although I never attended the services at St. Mary's of the Lake myself, had they offered Charpentier's joyous *Messe de minuit pour Noël* as the centerpiece of the evening I might well have signed up for the duration. One of the loveliest and most sweet-spirited of all Christmas works draws an especially endearing performance from George Guest's excellent forces, and instead of one of Charpentier's other major works, the album wisely pairs it with Francis Poulenc's gorgeous *Motets pour Noël*—with his *Salve Regina* and *Motets pour un temps de pénitence* thrown in for good (and very generous) measure.

Chausson, Ernest (1855–1899)

Poème for Violin and Orchestra, Op. 25

> **Chung, violin; Royal Philharmonic, Dutoit. London 417118-2 [CD].**

One of the most provocative of all "What if?" musical speculations concerns the effect on the subsequent development of French music had Ernest Chausson been as accomplished a bicyclist as he was a composer. His premature death, from injuries sustained when he drove his bicycle into a brick wall in 1899, robbed French music of the most distinct and original voice it had produced between those of Hector Berlioz and Claude Debussy.

With the Symphony in B-flat, the best German symphony ever written by a Frenchman—Charles Munch's glorious Boston Symphony recording has recently returned on a Victor CD (09026-60683-2)—and the sumptuous orchestral song cycle *Poème de l'amour et de la mer*—best represented these days by Linda

Finnie's haunting Chandos recording (CHAN 8952 [CD]—the *Poème* for Violin and Orchestra is one of the finest and most justly popular of all Chausson's works: a finished masterpiece by an already established master, and a tantalizing, heartbreaking suggestion of what might have been.

The greatest performance the *Poème* has ever received on, or probably off, records, was that rich and passionate recording the tragically short-lived French violinist Ginette Neveu made in the late 1940s. Kyung-Wha Chung's London recording resembles Neveu's in its emotional depth and technical facility. Only Itzhak Perlman, in his superb Angel recording (CDC-47725 [CD]), can create the similar illusion that this extremely thorny work is so childishly simple to play. As usual, the support that Charles Dutoit gives Ms. Chung is as imaginative as it is sensitive, not only in the *Poème*, but also in Saint-Saëns's *Habañera* and *Introduction and Rondo Capriccioso*, and Ravel's *Tzigane*, the other popular violin showpieces that round out this extremely appealing release.

Chávez, Carlos   (1899–1978)

Symphonies (6)

London Symphony, Mata. Vox CDX 5061 [CD].

When Carlos Chávez died on August 2, 1978, at the age of seventy-nine, he was not only the most universally admired Mexican composer of his generation but was also a national hero: a brilliant conductor whose work with Mexican orchestras brought them to a new level of prominence and an educator whose efforts as head of the National Conservatory and director of Mexico's Department of Fine Arts influenced three generations of Mexican musicians. His importance in the musical life of his country was recognized as long ago as 1936 by the critic Herbert Weinstock, who perceptively wrote: "Carlos Chávez is a Mexican. His coming-of-age coincided almost exactly with the breathing space, that period of summation and expression, which the Mexican Revolution entered about 1921. He belongs with Diego Rivera, José Clemente Orozco, and other men who, through painting, writing, and education, have brilliantly expressed the renascent culture of a country challenging social experimentation."

Much of what is best and most characteristic in Chávez's music can be found in the six symphonies he composed between 1933 and 1961. These are raw, exotic, highly colorful works that blend primitive musical materials with a highly sophisticated grasp of the modern orchestra. The late Eduardo Mata never made a more powerful or heartfelt recording than this 1981 cycle, an excellent, inexpensive introduction to the music of his old teacher. The individual character of each work comes up in brilliant relief, aided by the fearless contributions of the London Symphony and the yeoman efforts of the Vox engineers.

Cherubini, Luigi (1760–1842)

Medea

Callas, Scotto, Pirazzini, Picchi, La Scala Opera Chorus and Orchestra, Serafin. Angel CDMB-63625 [CD].

Although *Medea* has always had its admirers—Beethoven, for one, Leonard Bernstein for another—and while its place in the history books as "the first modern opera" is more or less assured, its fortunes as a piece of living theater have always relied on its ability to attract extraordinary sopranos to its formidable title role. (The first Medea, Madame Scio, was said to have died of consumption brought on by singing the role once too often. But that's hardly credible, since if sopranos were to die from simply singing the wrong thing once too often, then there'd be no sopranos left.)

No singer in living memory made more of the part than Maria Callas, either in her very fine studio recording from Angel or in any of the several live performances that have been preserved. Her chilling portrait of mythology's most famous mom is imposing and overwhelming, a musical characterization cut from the same sublime cloth as her unforgettable Norma. If *Medea* is not a great opera, then you certainly couldn't prove it from this.

Chopin, Frédéric (1810–1849)

Piano Concerto No. 1 in E Minor, Op. 11; Piano Concerto No. 2 in F Minor, Op. 21

> Zimerman, piano; Los Angeles Philharmonic, Giulini. Deutsche
> Grammophon 415970-2 [CD].

In addition to being central works in the concerto literature for the instrument, the Chopin piano concertos go a long way toward dispelling several myths that continue to cling to one of history's most popular composers. There are those who still insist that Chopin was essentially an incomparable miniaturist who was uncomfortable with—and, indeed, incapable of sustaining—larger-scaled forms. These are the same people, no doubt, who are convinced that this first important composer to write piano music that was constructed entirely in *pianistic* terms, was thoroughly incapable of writing gracefully and idiomatically for other instruments—which is to say, for the nineteenth-century orchestra. Hogwash. Both as larger forms, and as concerted works for piano and orchestra, these two concertos are as masterful as those that any composer of the Romantic era produced.

One or the other of these two exceptional Deutsche Grammophon recordings probably introduced most of the world to the great young Polish pianist, Krystian Zimerman. As a general rule, I am extremely suspicious of the phrase "great young" when applied to anyone, but in Zimerman's case, it most assuredly *does* apply. He has instinct, technique, and temperament to burn, together with a maturity and insight that many pianists twice his age would be hard-pressed to match. Zimerman's performances of the Chopin concertos are as nearly perfect as any that have been heard in a generation. In them, poetry and youthful impetuosity are combined with a highly disciplined musical intelligence, and the results are an unalloyed delight for both the heart and the mind. The backdrops provided by Giulini and the Los Angeles Philharmonic could not have been more suave or sympathetic, and the recorded sound has a warm and natural bloom.

It is vigorously recommended.

Solo Piano Works

> Ballades (4); Scherzos (4). Rubinstein, piano. RCA Victor RCD1-7156
> [CD].
>
> Mazurkas (35). Rubinstein, piano. RCA Victor 5614-2-RC [CD].

Nocturnes (21). Rubinstein, piano. RCA Victor 5613-2-RC [CD], CRK2-5018 [T].

Polonaises (17). Rubinstein, piano. RCA Victor 5615-2-RC [CD].

Waltzes (19). Rubinstein, piano. RCA Victor RCD1-5492 [CD], CRK2-5018 [T].

Although this phenomenally popular body of music has attracted almost every important pianist of the last 150 years, it's unlikely that Frédéric Chopin ever found, or will ever find, a more ideal interpreter than Artur Rubinstein. To be sure, pianists like Josef Hoffman, Leopold Godowsky, and Vladimir Horowitz gave infinitely more brilliant performances of the music. Even some of the brighter lights of the younger generation, Dinu Lipatti in the 1950s and Maurizio Pollini in our time, managed to find an intellectual and spiritual depth in Chopin that Rubinstein, for much of his career, never did. Yet on balance, these remain the definitive recordings of Chopin's piano music, as authoritative and unapproachable in their way as Furtwängler's recordings of the Bruckner symphonies or the music of Frederick Delius led by Sir Thomas Beecham.

The key to Rubinstein's greatness as a Chopin interpreter was a combination of his utter naturalness as a performer and his enormously sophisticated musical mind. Nothing ever seems forced or premeditated; there are no sharp edges or sudden flashes of insight. In fact, the illusion that the performances create is one of the music flowing, without benefit of a human intermediary, directly from the printed page to the listener's heart. Of course, only the greatest artists are able to create such illusions, and then only after a lifetime of study, experience, self-examination, and back-breaking work.

At almost every moment in these classic recordings, Rubinstein discovers some wonder of color or phrasing, brings out a beautiful inner voice that it seems we've never heard before, and, in general, creates the impression of a man for whom playing this often fiendishly difficult music is no more difficult than breathing or making love. In short, Rubinstein's great and completely unaffected humanity breathes such life into these performances that they will continue to move, enlighten, and inspire for as long people require such things from recorded music.

With the Rubinsteins as the backbone of any Chopin collection, there are some superb second opinions that really should be consulted, too. Most important of all are the recordings of the Czech pianist Ivan Moravec, who is probably to the present generation of Chopin interpreters what Rubinstein was to his. With playing of an almost otherworldly refinement and purity, Moravec's Elektra/Nonesuch recording of the Nocturnes (79233-2 [CD]) may well be the loveliest Chopin recording ever made. His 1976 Supraphon recording of the Preludes (11 0630-2 [CD]) is both more technically impressive than Rubinstein's and probes even deeper beneath the surface, while his recent Dorian recording of the Scherzos (DOR-90140 [CD]) offers insight and excitement in virtually equal amounts.

Krystian Zimerman's Deutsche Grammophon recording of the Ballades (423090-2 [CD], 423090-4 [T]) features playing that is as fresh as it is powerfully dramatic, while Maurizio Pollini on another DG recording (431221-2 [CD]) demonstrates that he is still the undisputed master at solving the formidable technical and musical problems of the Études. (The set of three bargain CDs also comes with his impeccable versions of the Preludes and Polonaises.)

Dinu Lipatti's unutterably moving recording of the Waltzes, made in the last year of his tragically abbreviated life, can be found on an EMI Classics CD (CDH 69802) and an Odyssey tape (YT-60058E). At almost no time since they were first issued in the early 1950s have these miraculous performances been out of print, and with good reason. In their unfailing eloquence and deceptive simplicity, they are not only touchstones in the history of recording but are also among the enduring triumphs of human communication.

Finally, Testament has reissued the complete Chopin recordings made between 1932 and 1946 by the English pianist Solomon. These are clearly among the greatest Chopin recordings ever, as pure and poised as Lipatti's and delivered with an even more breathtaking technique: the 1942 version of the *Berceuse*, for instance, is one of the most nearly perfect piano recordings ever made. With splendid transfers from the original 78s and a revealing appreciation of Solomon's art from Bryce Morrison, this is one of the most important Chopin CDs yet released.

Sonata No. 2 in B-flat Minor, Op. 35; Sonata No. 3 in B Minor, Op. 58

Kapell, piano. RCA Victor 5998-2 [CD].

Here is some very persuasive evidence for the case that insists that William Kapell was the finest pianist America has ever produced. Only thirty-one at the time of his death in a plane crash in 1953, he was already a performer of epic abilities. His technique was the most formidable of any pianist of his generation, and his powers of communication were broadening and deepening to the very end. With the Romantics he was dashing and fearless, with Bach he was dignified and self-effacing, and his Mozart impressed the dreaded Claudia Cassidy, the virtually un-impressible critic of the Chicago *Tribune*, as the purest, most effortless music making she had ever heard.

Kapell's versions of the two popular Chopin sonatas—one recorded in the studio, one taken from a concert given in the last months of his life—make for an exhilarating, exhausting, ennobling experience. The playing is that of one of the century's towering instrumentalists: powerful, confident, poetic, and introspective, with just the right combination of an immediately recognizable personality and absolute fidelity to the spirit of the text. One of the acid tests of any performance of this music is the ability to listen to the well-known Funeral March from the B-flat Minor Sonata with a perfectly straight face. Kapell invests it with such heartrending pathos that we are left in pieces on the floor.

Rounded off with Kapell's brilliant recordings of ten of the Mazurkas, this may be the single most valuable Chopin album on the market.

Les Sylphides (ballet; orchestrated by Douglas)

> Philadelphia Orchestra, Ormandy. Sony Classical SBK 46551 [CD], SBT 46551 [T].

If Igor Stravinsky meant it as no compliment when he called Eugene Ormandy "the ideal conductor of Strauss waltzes," then that much-maligned musician was a nearly perfect interpreter of the Chopin-inspired ballet *Les Sylphides*. Recorded at a time when the Philadelphia Orchestra boasted some of the finest first-desk players of their time, the performance not only capitalizes on the wonders of the famous Philadelphia strings but also features some fabulous solo display. In addition to that inspired Chopin travesty, the budget CD comes with equally memorable versions of the suites from Delibes's *Coppélia* and *Sylvia* and a rather disappointing *Nutcracker Suite*, in which the conductor makes some exceedingly vulgar "improvements" in Tchaikovsky's orchestration.

Cilea, Francesco (1886–1950)

Adriana Lecouvreur

> Sutherland, Bergonzi, Nucci, Welsh National Opera Chorus and Orchestra, Bonynge. London 425815-2 [CD].

Like Umberto Giordano, Alfredo Catalani, and Riccardo Zandonai, Francesco Cilea was one of those second-rung figures of the *verismo* movement who had about one really good opera in him. *Adriana Lecouvreur* is an extremely good opera, and not simply because of its unforgettable money tune, the ravishing "Io son l'umile ancilla." Adriana herself—an actress at the Comédie Française in early eighteenth-century Paris—is almost as fine a character as Puccini's Tosca and in the hands of a great singing-actress will hold the stage nearly as well.

As in her surprising recording of Puccini's *Turandot* (see page 556), Joan Sutherland scores another major hit in what is hardly a "Sutherland role." With few opportunities for the dizzying bel canto display that made her famous, the Great Dame sings with enormous power and expressiveness throughout. The rest of the cast—especially the indestructible Carlo Bergonzi—is excellent and Richard Bonynge turns in some of the most richly imaginative conducting of his career.

Clarke, Jeremiah (c. 1674–1707)

The Prince of Denmark's March

Canadian Brass. RCA 09026-68257-2 [CD]; 09026-68257-4 [T].

There are several theories explaining the death of this English composer who shot himself during a deranged moment in 1707. According to some contemporary broadsheets, including *A Sad and Dismal Account of the Sudden and Untimely Death of Mr. Jeremiah Clarke,* the proximate cause of his demise was a failed love affair; a more likely explanation was his understandable despair that even during his lifetime the most famous of all his works was attributed to someone else. Purcell's "Trumpet Voluntary" was in fact Jeremiah Clarke's *The Prince of Denmark's March,* first published in *A Choice Collection of Ayres for the Harpsichord* in 1700 and given its current celebrity by the arrangement for trumpet, organ, and percussion by Sir Henry Wood. The fact that in recent decades Clarke's stirring tune has become a favorite processional at yuppie weddings would have done little to improve the composer's morale.

The Canadian Brass perform the march with customary flair on their attractive "Fireworks!" album, which contains other baroque favorites, including "The Arrival of the Queen of Sheba" from Handel's *Solomon* and the famous *Young Person's Guide to the Orchestra* rondeau from *Abdelazer; Or, the Moor's Revenge,* which is *definitely* the work of Henry Purcell.

Clarke, Rebecca (1886–1979)

Sonata for Viola and Piano; Trio for Piano, Violin, and Cello

Roscoe, piano; Endellion String Quartet members. ASV 932 [CD].

This accomplished English violist and composer is a fascinating, vaguely tragic figure of midcentury music. Born in England, she studied composition with Sir Charles Villiers Stanford at the Royal College of Music, where she met another Stanford pupil, the composer James Friskin, whom she eventually married. She began composing seriously after her arrival in America during World War I, producing the two astounding chamber works upon which her reputation will rest: the Viola Sonata of 1919 and the Piano Trio of 1921. Both are vital, romantic, deeply original works that show not only a keen awareness of the major modern trends from impressionism to atonality but also enormous strength of character and a fully formed musical personality. Unfortunately, she would write little of significance for the remainder of her long life.

Pianist Martin Roscoe and members of the Endellion String Quartet give meticulous, passionately committed performances of both works, convinced—as they clearly seem to be—that each is a masterpiece. Even a cursory glance at either will convince you they're absolutely right.

Coates, Eric (1886–1957)

Orchestral Music

Czecho-Slovak Radio Symphony (Bratislava), Leaper. Marco Polo
8.223445 [CD].

London Symphony, Mackerras; Royal Liverpool Philharmonic,
Groves; City of Birmingham Symphony, Kilbey. Classics for
Pleasure CFPD 4456 [CD].

Admittedly, there are people who cannot abide the music of the English composer Eric Coates. But then, too, there are people who enjoy pulling the wings off butterflies and pushing little old ladies into manure spreaders.

With his near contemporary, the long-time Boston Pops arranger Leroy Anderson, Coates was one of indisputable masters of "light music." In his familiar suites and bracing marches, Coates was a man who not only knew the value of a good tune but was also singularly successful in producing them over the years, from the unforgettable "Knightsbridge March" from the *London Suite* to that equally memorable inspiration from *The Three Elizabeths* that served as the signature tune of Public Television's *The Forsythe Saga*. It is music that never tries the patience, overstays its welcome, or ever fails to amuse, entertain, and delight.

On the two generously packed, reasonably priced, and very aptly named Classics for Pleasure CDs, two splendid Coatesians, Sir Charles Mackerras and Sir Charles Groves, bring the music so vividly alive that you suspect it will last an eternity, while the contributions of the City of Birmingham Symphony under Reginald Kilbey—what a perfect name for a Coates conductor!—are hardly less enjoyable.

The Coates album from Marco Polo's British Light Music series is, if anything, even more so. The playing of the Slovakian musicians is so thoroughly idiomatic it's difficult to believe they haven't known and loved this music since birth, while Adrian Leaper's consistently fresh and spontaneous interpretations make even the most familiar items seem as though they were dashed off yesterday. The recorded sound and notes are also exemplary.

Rather incredibly, the Coates is not necessarily the most valuable installment in this already memorable series. The album of Sir Edward German's music—including the irresistible *Gipsy Suite*—restores a shamefully neglected composer to the catalogue (8.223419 [CD], while those devoted to Frederic Curzon (8.223425 [CD], Robert Farnon (8.223401 [CD]), Ernest Tomlinson (8.223413 [CD]), and Haydn Wood (8.223402 [CD]) are no less thoroughly delightful.

If you have the willpower—or simply the cussedness—to resist these collections, you have my admiration and sympathy.

Songs

Cook, baritone; Terroni, piano. ASV CD WHL 2081 [CD].

It should come as no surprise to anyone familiar with Coates's irrepressibly tuneful orchestral music that he was also an accomplished song composer. Over the years, he published more than 130 songs of various kinds, from rustic West Country parodies like *Stonecracker John* to those sophisticated ballads that were eagerly championed by John McCormack, Peter Dawson, and Dame Nellie Melba. From the polite rowdiness of *Reuben Ranzo* to the aching nostalgia of *The Green Hills o' Somerset*, the best of these rank with the finest popular songs of the period between the World Wars: a heartening and—when compared with the offal being disgorged today—sobering reminder of how bloody *good* popular music used to be. Brian Rayner Cook sings with real understanding and affection, while Rafael Terroni's accompaniments are urbane and stylish.

Coleridge-Taylor, Samuel

(1875–1912)

Scenes from the Song of Hiawatha

> Field, Davies, Terfel, Welsh National Opera Chorus and Orchestra,
> Alwyn. Argo 430356-2 [CD].

Composed in 1898 and sold to the publishers for a few miserable pounds, Samuel Coleridge-Taylor's *Scenes from the Song of Hiawatha* had a tremendous vogue in oratorio-mad England during the early years of the twentiethth century; by some accounts, it was performed more frequently in its first decade than Handel's *Messiah* and made the name of its Anglo-African composer revered throughout the black world. In America, a Coleridge-Taylor Society was formed as early as 1904, and by the time of his premature death in 1912 he had become a cultural hero on the order of Paul Dunbar, Booker T. Washington, and W. E. B. DuBois. Part I, called *Hiawatha's Wedding Feast,* is still a fixture at choral festivals in England, and although the inspiration levels off considerably in Parts II and III—*The Death of Minnehaha* and *Hiawatha's Departure*—the entire score is still more than worth hearing, especially in such a completely winning performance as this. Helen Field and Bryn Terfel sing with passionate enthusiasm, while Kenneth Alwyn's direction is pointed and idiomatic, with a fine instinctive grasp of the music's shape and dramatic flow. As both a historic document and living music, *Hiawatha* continues to deserve our attention.

Second only to *Hiawatha* in popularity, the *Petite Suite de Concert* is available on a splendid Marco Polo album (8.223516) of the composer's lighter works, including the *Four Characteristic Waltzes* (which the composer used to court his wife), the slightly arch but colorful *Gipsy Suite,* and some of the incidental music for a Herbert Beerbohm Tree production of Shakespeare's *Othello.* The performances by Dublin's RTE Concert Orchestra led by Adrian Leaper are excellent.

Copland, Aaron (1900–1990)

Appalachian Spring

> Los Angeles Philharmonic, Bernstein. Deutsche Grammophon 431048-
> 2 [CD].

> St. Paul Chamber Orchestra, Davies. Pro Arte CDD-140 [CD], PCD-
> 140 [T].

Aaron Copland was, in many ways, the most dramatic musical manifestation of the "melting pot" genesis of American history. For the composer who, in his most popular works, seemed to capture the very essence of Middle America and the Western frontier, was in fact born in a working-class Jewish neighborhood of Brooklyn and received his principal musical training with Nadia Boulanger in Paris.

Appalachian Spring, a ballet composed for the celebrated American dancer Martha Graham, is probably the composer's masterpiece. All of the best qualities of Copland's "Enlightened Populist" style are heard to their best advantage. Bracing, wide-open harmonies, folksy and unforgettable melodies, are bound together with Copland's expressive idiom that mixes tenderness, exuberance, sentimentality, and sophistication, in roughly equal amounts.

Like the exhilarating recording that Leonard Bernstein made with the New York Philharmonic in the 1960s, this newer version with the Los Angeles Philharmonic is an unqualified triumph. The orchestra plays with great delicacy and conviction, and the special excitement that all of Bernstein's live performances generate can be felt throughout.

For a somewhat less compelling, but thoroughly satisfying, look at the ballet in its original version for chamber orchestra, the performance led by Dennis Russell Davies handily defeats all other contenders, including the recording by the composer himself.

Billy the Kid; Rodeo (complete ballets)

> St. Louis Symphony, Slatkin. Angel CDM 64315 [CD], 4DS-37357
> [T].

For more years than anyone can remember, Leonard Bernstein, one of the composer's oldest and closest friends, virtually owned this music. For nearly a quarter of a century his CBS recordings of Copland's immensely appealing cowboy ballets—both of which quote more actual frontier tunes than a typical Zane Grey novel—have been all but unapproachable in their dramatic flair and authority. That is, at least, until now.

Leonard Slatkin, who in the last decade has galvanized the St. Louis Symphony into becoming one of America's finest orchestras, leads a pair of performances that are even more successful than Bernstein's. The rhythms are tighter and more infectious, the phrasing is consistently more alert and imaginative, and the playing of this great young ensemble sounds every bit the equal of any orchestra in the world. Along with demonstration-quality sound, the recording has the further advantage of presenting both ballets note-complete. While this represents only a few extra minutes of actual music, it makes what is already an immensely attractive recording virtually irresistible.

Concerto for Piano and Orchestra; *Symphonic Ode; Appalachian Spring*

Hollander, piano; Seattle Symphony, Schwarz. Delos DE 3154 [CD].

While first-rate recordings of *Appalachian Spring* have become a commonplace, the same cannot be said of the Piano Concerto and the *Symphonic Ode.* Once savagely reviled—following the premiere in 1928, the Boston *Evening Transcript* called it "a harrowing horror from beginning to end"—the Piano Concerto is now widely regarded as the most successful of the composer's jazz-inflected scores, "the best roar from the roaring twenties," in Lawrence Gilman's singularly apt phrase. Copland himself considered the *Symphonic Ode* of 1929 one of the most important of all his scores, claiming he "had been striving for something grand and dramatic in this work," and achieving that and more.

Both of these criminally neglected works are brilliantly served by Gerard Schwarz and the Seattle Symphony. Lorin Hollander, whose appearances in the recording studio have become much too rare, proves an ideal soloist in the Concerto, responding with equal enthusiasm to its jazzy surface and rigorous internal logic. If anything, the version of the *Symphonic Ode* is even more valuable, easily eclipsing the composer's own recording and revealing it as the neglected masterpiece it clearly is. Even without the excellent *Appalachian Spring* that fills it out, this would be one of the most important Copland albums in years.

Fanfare for the Common Man; Danzón Cubano; El Salón Mexico; Appalachian Spring

New York Philharmonic, Bernstein. CBS MYK-37257 [CD], MYT-37527 [T].

The advantage of this particular coupling—and CBS is repackaging Bernstein's hugely marketable Copland recordings in a variety of combinations—is that it brings together all but definitive performances of three of the composer's shorter works and a version of *Appalachian Spring* that is second only to the conductor's Los Angeles Philharmonic recording for Deutsche Grammophon.

If the *Fanfare* is slightly compromised by the wobble of the Philharmonic's principal trumpet, the performance as a whole is gloriously gutsy. (Be warned, though: this is not the original version of the score but instead an extract from its memorable appearance in Copland's Third Symphony.) On the other hand, the two Latin items are unapproachable, especially *El Salón Mexico*, which here becomes a triumph of salsa and swank.

Film Music

> St. Louis Symphony, Slatkin. RCA 09026-61699-2 [CD], 09026-
> 61699-4 [T].

No American composer of more obviously "serious" music worked in Hollywood films with greater enthusiasm or success than Aaron Copland. Beginning with the music for the 1939 documentary *The City*, Copland produced a small but distinguished body of scores that are rightly considered screen classics: from the adaptations of John Steinbeck's *Of Mice and Men* and *The Red Pony* to *The Heiress*, William Wyler's version of Henry James's *Washington Square*, which earned Copland and Olivia de Havilland the Academy Award. More recently, his music was used to wonderful effect in Spike Lee's *He Got Game*.

In this valuable RCA recording, Leonard Slatkin leads vivid, splendidly cinematic interpretations of the best of Copland's film music, including the moving music from Thornton Wilder's *Our Town* and (rather unbelievably) the first commercial recording ever of music from *The Heiress*. Also included is another rarity, the *Prairie Journal*, featuring radio music from 1937. Slatkin is equally impressive in the *Music for a Great City*, Copland's adaptation of his final film score, *Something Wild*, used as a filler for his fine recording of the composer's Third Symphony (RCA 60149-2-RG [CD], 60149-4-RC [T]).

Grogh; Hear Ye! Hear Ye!; Prelude

> Cleveland Orchestra, London Sinfonietta, Knussen. Argo 443203-2
> [CD].

Forget the folksy charms of *Appalachian Spring* or the stirring populism of *Fanfare for the Common Man*: the early ballet *Grogh* is Copland's most violent, disturbing score. Composed in Paris under the watchful eye of Nadia Boulanger and inspired in part by the 1921 German silent film *Nosferatu*, *Grogh* is part *Miraculous Mandarin*, part *Petrushka*, part soft-core pornography, and a tantalizing suggestion of where Copland's art might have gone had he remained an expatriate for a few more years. After the music from *Grogh* was later cannibalized for the *Dance Symphony*, the full score was lost until the 1980s, when Oliver Knussen discovered it, misfiled, in the Library of Congress. Knussen leads the Cleveland Orchestra in a suitably hair-raising performance, with brilliantly detailed recorded sound to match. With first recordings of two other rarities, this is obviously a release no Copland lover should miss.

Lincoln Portrait

Stevenson, narrator; Philadelphia Orchestra, Ormandy. Sony Classical SBK 62401 [CD]; SBT 62401 [T].

Among the many memorable narrators chosen to speak Abraham Lincoln's stirring lines—from the poet and Lincoln biographer Carl Sandburg to General Norman Schwarzkopf to *On Golden Pond* co-stars Henry Fonda and Katharine Hepburn—none ever delivered the text with more character and depth of feeling than the two-time presidential candidate and United Nations ambassador Aldai Stevenson. Supported by one of Eugene Ormandy's finest recorded performances, this is a *Lincoln Portrait* that will fill any American with patriotic pride and thrill the most cost-conscious collector. For along with Ormandy's awesome version of the *Fanfare for the Common Man*, this bargain "Essential Classics" CD also returns to circulation André Previn's brilliant St. Louis Symphony recording of a suite from *The Red Pony* and a spirited version of the four dance episodes from *Rodeo* with the Cleveland Orchestra conducted by Louis Lane.

Piano Music

Smit, piano. Sony SM2K 66345 [CD].

Apart from the Piano Sonata of 1941, Copland's piano music is virtually unknown—an astonishing fact, given its quality and importance. From early works like *The Cat and Mouse,* written when he was twenty, through *Proclamation,* finished when he was eighty-two, the piano music reveals a consistently high level of inspiration and invention and clearly deserves to be much better known.

Copland's long-time friend Leo Smit is the perfect guide to this music, as evidenced by the fact that he is the dedicatee of *Midsummer Nocturne* and the jazzy *Four Piano Blues.* The performances are incomparably lively and authoritative, delivering enormous pleasure and insight despite the rather cramped recorded sound.

Symphony No. 3; *Quiet City*

New York Philharmonic, Bernstein. Deutsche Grammophon 419170-2 [CD].

Among the candidates for that musical equivalent of the Great American Novel, the Copland Third has always ranked very high on most people's lists. I have never been persuaded that this is, in fact, the Great American Symphony—my own nominee is the Roy Harris Third—nor am I usually inclined to think of it as a great American *anything*. The gritty, affably belligerent *Scherzo* is prime Copland, the incorporation of the *Fanfare for the Common Man* is clever, exciting, and all of that, but for the most part the Symphony has always seemed to me a melancholy victory of manner over matter: one of the major *shallow* masterpieces of American music—except when it is being conducted by Leonard Bernstein.

His most recent version—taken from a live New York Philharmonic performance—proves once again that this composer has never had a more eloquent advocate. No other recording of the work, including the two that the composer made himself, can begin to match this one in its nervous tension and sustained energy. Moreover, what can seem merely rhetorical in other hands, in Bernstein's is miraculously transformed into deeply felt emotion; no one, for instance, has ever made the *Fanfare*'s final apotheosis seem more inevitable or just.

With one of the loveliest of all versions of *Quiet City* as the welcome filler, this would seem to be a recording that no Copland lover could afford to pass up.

The Tender Land

Soloists, Chorus and Orchestra of Plymouth Music Series, Brunelle. Virgin Classics 59207 [CD].

Copland never wrote more a gently affecting piece than his only full-length opera, *The Tender Land*. While the touching little story of a farm girl and a drifter has no big arias and no big scenes, it is suffused with the same folksy richness that animates *Appalachian Spring*. In fact, the opera's most memorable moment, the Act I finale called "The Promise of Living," is based on "Zion's Walls," the same tune Copland used in one of the *Old American Songs*.

The performance by the Plymouth Music Series is as accomplished as it is affectionate. The soloists—especially Elizabeth Comeaux and Dan Dressen as the young lovers—all seem perfectly cast, while Philip Brunelle allows the undeniable charm of the opera to quietly unfold. An equally moving performance of the orchestral suite features the composer in one of his earliest recordings as a conductor leading the Boston Symphony on RCA Victor (6802-2-RG [CD], 6802-4-RG [T]).

Corelli, Archangelo

(1653–1713)

Concerti Grossi, Op. 6 (12)

> English Concert, Pinnock. Deutsche Grammophon ARC-423626-2
> [CD].

Along with being one of the finest violinists of the Baroque era and a man who did as much as anyone to codify the form and substance of the sonata and concerti grossi, the penurious Archangelo Corelli was far and away the most tight-fisted cheapskate in the history of music. He refused to buy new clothes until the old ones literally disintegrated on his back, and although he was an avid collector of paintings and sculpture, he never went to public galleries on days when admission was charged.

Yet for all his personal idiosyncracies, Corelli was as admired by his contemporaries as he is largely unappreciated today. The richly inventive collection of Op. 6 Concerti Grossi were among the most influential works of the High Baroque. In addition to the well-known "Christmas" Concerto—which is about as Christmas-y as a Fourth of July Parade—the eleven other works in the set contain one felicitous idea after another. Along with the innovative melodic and harmonic thinking, the craftsmanship is of an order that would not be surpassed until Handel's own Opus 6 collection, which owes Corelli's an incalculable debt.

Trevor Pinnock's enthusiastic period-instrument performances make an exceptionally strong case for these works. The interpretations are as bracing and articulate as the music itself, and the recorded sound is wonderfully lifelike and clear.

Sonatas for Violin and Continuo

> S. Kuijken, violin; W. Kuijken, cello; Kohnen, harpsichord. Accent
> ACC 48433 [CD].

Perhaps even more important than the Opus 12 Concerti Grossi was Corelli's Opus 5 collection of violin sonatas from 1700, in which the violin sonata itself first emerged as a distinct musical form. These tremendously influential works also went a long way toward standardizing writing and playing for the instrument and were among the first instrumental works to introduce the two-theme (or binary) form that would become a standard feature of the subsequent Classical sonata.

Sigiswald and Wieland Kuijken give spirited period-instrument interpretations of five of the twelve sonatas, including the famous one that concludes with a series of variations on the eighteenth-century pop tune "La Folia." There is nothing remotely stuffy or academic in any of the performances, which reveal the strength and felicity of Corelli's invention with a disarming ease.

Corigliano, John (1938–)

Symphony No. 1

Chicago Symphony, Barenboim. Erato 2292-45601-2 [CD].

Unlike Henryk Gorecki's vapid Symphony No. 3 (see page 291), John Corigliano's Symphony No. 1 might have been a similarly opportunistic exercise in political correctness were it not for the fact that it is as genuinely moving as it is sincerely felt. Written in memory of friends of the composer who have died of AIDS, the Symphony is a gruff, angry, impassioned, lyrical, and—best of all—deeply personal outburst. For it is the composer's seething indignation that makes it such an intensely wrenching experience. Whether it will prove to be a '90s equivalent of Luciano Berio's *Sinfonia* or something more enduring, only time will tell.

Barenboim and the Chicago Symphony give a suitably shattering performance, which is captured to perfection by Erato's engineers.

Cornelius, Peter (1824–1874)

The Barber of Bagdad

Schwarzkopf, Hoffman, Gedda, Unger, Czerwenka, Philharmonia Orchestra and Chorus, Leinsdorf. EMI Classics CDMB 65284 [CD].

Shy, generous, amusing Peter Cornelius once insisted, "I can quietly lay claim to one good thing—what little I have is my own property." In spite of his friendship with Liszt and his passion for the music of Wagner, Cornelius managed to produce one of the few wholly original German operas of the nineteenth century, the witty, tuneful *Der Barbier von Bagdad*. Adapted from a story in *A*

Thousand and One Nights, the composer's libretto is nearly as intricate and agile as the music, which has much of the exotic charm of *The Abduction from the Seraglio* and some of the Romantic sweep of *Lohengrin.*

While it is neither note-complete nor ideally cast, this fine EMI Classics recording has much to recommend it, from the delicious Margiana of Elisabeth Schwarzkopf to the spirited conducting of Erich Leinsdorf. With Busoni's fizzing one-act comedy *Arlecchino* as a generous and rewarding bonus, this is a set to acquire immediately before the deletions ax falls.

Couperin, François (le Grand) (1668–1733)

L'Apothéose de Lully; Dans le goût théatral; Le Parnasse (L'Apothéose de Corelli)

English Baroque Soloists, Gardiner. Erato 2292-4511-2 [CD].

As a sage English philosopher once insisted, "Murder, like talent, seems occasionally to run in families," especially if talent, like murder or anything else, *also* happens to be the family business. His title "le Grand" (the Great) was as much a means of identification as an accolade, for François Couperin was merely the most illustrious member of a family that for two centuries produced illustrious professional musicians, beginning with the offspring of Charles Couperin, a merchant and organist of Chaumes in the province of Brie, whose eldest son, Louis, became organist of St. Gervais in Paris in 1653 and was succeeded in that post—without interruption—by other members of the family and its descendants until the line became extinct in 1826 with the death of Gervais-François, grandson of François "le Grand's" cousin Nicolas.

These three engaging works by the first great French composer of instrumental music are given nearly ideal performances by Gardiner and his superb ensemble. Even those of us who are not usually drawn to the stately pronouncements of the French Baroque should readily respond to both the magnificent music itself and the equally magnificent performances.

By that same token, Kenneth Gilbert's monumental recording of Couperin's complete *Pièces de clavecin* on four densely packed boxed sets of CDs from Harmonia Mundi (HMA-190351/53, HMA-190354/56, HMA-190375/58, HMA-190359/60) sets a standard for scholarship and enthusiasm that will probably not be approached for the remainder of the century.

In a far less comprehensive release from Deutsche Harmonia Mundi (77219-2-RC), Skip Sempé demonstrates why he is one of the most talked-about harpsichordists in the world today, with the kind of imaginative, impassioned playing that is rare enough among pianists.

Creston, Paul (1906–1985)

Symphony No. 2, "Three Mysteries"; *Invocation and Dance; Out of the Cradle;* Partita for Flute, Violin, and String Orchestra

Seattle Symphony, Schwarz. Delos DE 3114 [CD].

The late Paul Creston once insisted, "I make no special effort to be American. I conscientiously work to be my true self, which is Italian by parentage, American by birth, and cosmopolitan by choice." Born Giuseppe Guttoveggio in New York City in 1906, the son of an immigrant housepainter, the future composer began his musical studies on a ten-dollar piano and would remain almost entirely self-taught. After changing his name in high school—"Creston" from a school play in which he appeared, "Paul" because he liked the sound—he worked at a variety of jobs while studying music at night. In 1934, Henry Cowell invited him to play *Seven Theses* at a composer's forum at the New School for Social Research; in 1938, the year he received his first Guggenheim Fellowship, Fritz Reiner premiered his *Threnody* in Pittsburgh; in 1941, his First Symphony won the New York Music Critics' Circle Award. In all, Creston composed five symphonies, two ballets, two violin concertos, and numerous choral, chamber, and instrumental works, as well as some memorable scores for the CBS television series *The Twentieth Century.*

The four works contained in Volume 1 of the Delos Creston series show this vital, stubbornly unfashionable composer at something close to his best. While the new recording of the profound (and profoundly moving) Third Symphony is most valuable of all, the shorter works are equally welcome. For the conductor, the orchestra, and the Delos engineers, this was clearly a labor of love.

Volume 2 (Delos DE 3127 [CD]) is no less distinguished, with equally loving and vital performances of the *Choreographic Suite,* the intense, conflict-riddled Fifth Symphony, and the brilliant *Toccata for Orchestra* from 1957.

Even when the Delos Creston series gets around to recording what may well be the composer's masterpiece, the enthralling Second Symphony—which its composer described as "an apotheosis of the two foundations of all music: song and dance"—they will be hard-pressed to match the dramatic point and surging energy of Neeme Järvi's recording with the Detroit Symphony (Chandos CHAN 9390 [CD]), the companion piece to their slightly over-civilized reading of the Ives Second Symphony.

Crumb, George (1929–)

Vox balaenae (Voice of the Whale) for Electric Flute, Electric Cello, and Electric Piano

Mueller, flute; Sherry, cello; Gemmell, piano. New World NW 80357-2 [CD].

One of the most admired and widely discussed composers of his generation, George Crumb was born into a musical family in Charleston, West Virginia, on October 24, 1929. After earning degrees at the University of Illinois and the University of Michigan, he studied with Boris Blacher at Berlin's prestigious Hochschule für Musik. To date, Crumb has proven to be one of the most colorful of modern American composers, a grand and imaginative eccentric in the classic tradition of William Billings and Charles Ives.

The late Nicolas Slonimsky supplied an inimitable précis of the composer's methods and techniques:

> In his music he preserves the external formalities of traditional music, suggesting Baroque procedures, but he makes revolutionary changes in his technical resources, demanding from the performer an exceptional precision and subtlety of interpretation, exploiting the extreme instrumental registers and making use of outlandish effects in the vocal part, including tongue clicks, explosive shrieks, hissing, and whispering, as well as singing fractional intervals. In his *Makrokosmos I* for piano he instructs the pianist to shout at specified bars of the music. His musical notation often emulated the symbolic designs of the Middle Ages and the Renaissance; particularly intriguing is his use of spiral staves for recurring motives, as exemplified in *Makrokosmos* and *Star-Child*.

Scored for amplified flute, amplified cello, amplified piano, and rattles, *Vox balaenae* (Voice of the Whale) was written in 1972. In a preface, the composer instructs each of the players to perform in a black half-mask throughout, because— he argues—"the masks, by effacing a sense of human projection, will symbolize the powerful impersonal forces of nature." Cast in three movements—*Vocalise* (for the beginning of time), *Variations on Sea-Time* (sea theme), and *Sea Nocturne* (. . . for the end of time)—Voice of the Whale has been heard as both a virtuoso evocation of various marine images and an angry protest against mankind's treatment of the sea's most majestic inhabitants.

The performance on this invaluable New World album is both wild and definitive, as are the versions of two other key Crumb works: *An Idyll for the Misbegotten* for amplified flute and three percussionists and the *Madrigals* on texts by Garcia Lorca, lovingly sung by the late Jan DeGaetani. The adventurous will also want to explore the Kronos Quartet's dumbfounding performance of *Black Angels* (Elektra/Nonesuch 79242-2-P [CD], 79242-4-H [T]), that chilling and disorienting work for string quartet and electronic sounds that has serious claims as the composer's masterpiece.

Crusell, Bernhard Henrik

(1775–1838)

Clarinet Concertos (3)

> Johnson, clarinet; Royal Philharmonic, Herbig (No. 1); English Chamber
> Orchestra, Groves (No. 2) and Schwarz (No. 3). ASV 784 [CD].

Hearing any of the attractive concertos or chamber works that this brilliant Finnish virtuoso composed for his own use when one *could* be listening to the clarinet music of Mozart, Weber, or Brahms can leave some people with a curious and slightly disquieting feeling: a feeling not unlike that oddly unsatisfying one that follows sex with a pretty but shallow woman—or the male equivalent. No one makes the experience (with Crusell's music) seem more significant than Emma Johnson, who along with the undoubted charm, vigor, and merriment in the music also finds an unexpected depth and substance. All three of her partners fall in with her plans perfectly, and the remastered recorded sound is as bright and lively as the music itself.

On Bis (741 [CD]) Osmo Vänskä proves he is as exceptional a clarinetist as he is a conductor, with delightful performances of Crusell's three Clarinet Quartets, all of them cut from the same entertaining cloth as the Concertos.

Dahl, Ingolf (1912–1970)

Concerto for Saxophone and Wind Orchestra; *Hymn; Music for Brass Instruments; The Tower of Saint Barbara*

The New World Symphony, Thomas. Argo 444459-2 [CD].

Born in Hamburg of Swedish parents, Ingolf Dahl was a member of that distinguished community of emigré composers who settled in Southern California in the years immediately before the beginning of the Second World War. For a time, his Los Angeles neighbors included such diverse and potent talents as Igor Stravinsky, Arnold Schoenberg, Darius Milhaud, Ernst Krenek, and Mario Castelnuovo-Tedesco. A fastidious craftsman whose music is as distinctive for its intellectual integrity as for its emotional depth, Dahl—like his near contemporary Paul Hindemith—was fascinated by the problems of dissonant counterpoint and constantly strove to connect the music of the twentieth century with the great Austro-German contrapuntal tradition: the very titles of works like the *Symphony Concertante* and the *Sonata Seria* suggest his fondness for the forms and procedures of the past. Appointed to the faculty of the University of Southern California in 1945 and a member of the composition department of the Berkshire Music Center at Tanglewood during the summers of 1952 through 1955, Dahl remained an inspired and inspiring teacher until his death in August of 1970. One of his best-known pupils is Michael Tilson Thomas.

Thomas leads his superb New World Symphony in a bracing and revealing program of Dahl's works, from the well-known *Music for Brass Instruments* (whose breezy *Intermezzo* went on to enjoy a life of its own as the signature tune of the popular WQXR radio series "Music at First Hearing") to the mystical *Tower of Saint Barbara,* a close cousin to Hindemith's *Nobilissima Visione.* It goes without saying that the conductor brings a unique enthusiasm and depth of understanding to this rewarding music, while his young players respond with prodigious virtuosity.

Danzi, Franz (1763–1826)

Woodwind Quintets

Berlin Philharmonic Wind Quintet. BIS CD 592 [CD].
Albert Schweitzer Wind Quintet. CPO 999180 [CD].

Just as the name of the Beethoven pupil Carl Czerny won't mean much except to piano students who have slogged their way through his innumerable volumes of exercises, this amiable German composer (born in Mannheim of Italian parents) is principally beloved of wind players who have studied and performed his entertaining woodwind quintets. Although firmly rooted in the eighteenth century, Danzi's music was also touched by the spirit of early Romanticism, thanks largely to his friendship with his one-time pupil Carl Maria von Weber.

The quintets featured on these two volumes are all extremely enjoyable works with perky, intelligently crafted *allegros* and singing, italianate slow movements that remind us that Danzi made his initial reputation as an operatic composer. The Berlin Philharmonic and Schweitzer Quintets play them all with obvious relish, while the recorded sound on both discs is excellent, if a bit distantly focused, on the CPO.

The four Danzi flute concertos are no less ingratiating, particularly in the stylish performances by flutist András Adorján and the Munich Chamber Orchestra conducted by Hans Stadlmair on Orfeo 003812 [CD]. None are pieces of real substance but are ideal as background for sipping martinis at the end of especially trying days.

Debussy, Claude (1862–1918)

La Boîte à joujoux; Jeux

Montreal Symphony, Dutoit. London 444386-2 [CD].

Becoming a father for the first time late in life changed Debussy dramatically, both as a man and as a musician. In writing the *Children's Corner Suite* for his three-year-old daughter—the dedication comes "with her father's apologies for what follows"—Debussy finally allowed a measure of humor to creep into his work. The tender feelings an increasingly doting father felt for his only child would also manifest themselves in the charming ballet for children, *La Boîte à joujoux*, composed in 1913.

So fine a performance as the one led by Michael Tilson Thomas makes the neglect of the work all the more inexplicable, as is Sony Classical's decision to withdraw the recording. The conductor found precisely the right combination of sophistication and wide-eyed innocence in Debussy's toy box ballet, as Charles Dutoit nearly does in his excellent London recording. He is also very suave and charming in André Caplet's orchestral version of *Children's Corner Suite* and the early *Printemps* from 1887. As always for Dutoit's recordings of French music, the recorded sound is a model of atmosphere and clarity.

Children's Corner Suite; Images for Piano, Books I and II

Michelangeli, piano. Deutsche Grammophon 415372-2 [CD].

Without much question, Arturo Benedetti Michelangeli was the most completely exasperating musician of his generation. A monstrously gifted pianist and a wholly unique musical personality, Michelangeli's name could have become a household word had he only been a little more interested in playing the piano. A cult figure with a small but fanatical following, his public appearances were likened to the sightings of a rare and exotic bird. Michelangeli played whenever he felt like it (which wasn't often) and recorded even less.

This Debussy collection, taped in the early 1970s, reveals just what kind of spellbinder this fabulous oddball was in his prime. The playing itself is largely unbelievable, and the interpretations have an almost promethean originality. Only Ivan Moravec could find such wondrous charm in the familiar *Children's Corner Suite,* and even the great Walter Gieseking would have been hard-pressed to wring more color or individuality from the bewitching *Images.*

What a pity that one of the accomplished musicians of modern times should have been such a thoroughgoing spook.

La Chute de la maison Usher (two scenes, after Poe)

Soloists, Monte Carlo Philharmonic, Prêtre. EMI Classics CDM 64687 [CD].

Like that of most Frenchmen, Debussy's enthusiasm for Edgar Allan Poe was based on the brilliant translations of Charles Baudelaire, who transformed his gloomy American contemporary into a French literary phenomenon. Toward the end of his life, Debussy began a one-act opera based on the *Fall of the House of Usher,* whose sketches disappeared until the 1970s, when the Chilean composer Juan Allende Blin put some four hundred bars into performing shape.

Even in its fragmentary form, *La Chute de la maison Usher* is a startling work, freer in its harmonic expression than almost anything Debussy had written up to that time and uniquely sensitive to the brooding intensity of its source. While the cast in this 1983 recording is uniformly excellent, baritone Jean-Philippe Lafont is especially compelling as Roderick Usher, with Georges Prêtre lending his typically enthusiastic support. With equally fine accounts of André Caplet's *Conte fantastique* for harp and strings after Poe's *Masque of the Red Death* and Florent Schmitt's twelve-minute Poe fantasy *Le Palais hanté,* this is a singularly attractive and unusual album that should be snatched up quickly before it vanishes.

La Damoiselle élue; L'Enfant prodigue

Cotrubas, Norman, Carreras, Fischer-Dieskau, Stuttgart Radio Symphony and Chorus, Bertini. Orfeo 012821 [CD].

On his third attempt to win the prestigious *Prix de Rome,* Debussy finally succeeded with the cantata *L'Enfant prodigue* in 1884. Debussy consciously tailored the music to the tastes of the conservative members of the jury; the strategy paid off handsomely, since one of the judges, Charles Gounod, pronounced it a work of genius.

Debussy left for Rome—and the three-year residence at the Villa Medici—in January of 1885. He despised the city, the food, the people, and resented having to regularly send back musical *envois* to the *Prix de Rome*'s judges. His final *envoi,* the cantata *La Damoiselle élue,* so disturbed the *Prix de Rome* judges that they refused to allow it to be performed.

While neither of these early works offers many clues as to the composer Debussy would become only a few years later, both are richly romantic, beautifully scored, and handsomely served on this Orfeo recording. The soloists are all first-rate—especially Jessye Norman, who sings the best-known moment in either score, the *Air de Lia* from *L'Enfant prodigue,* with exceptional refinement—and Gary Bertini coaxes some meltingly Gallic playing from his fine Teutonic forces. The recorded sound is excellent.

The orchestral fragments from another intriguing Debussy choral work, *Le Martyre de Saint Sébastien,* can be heard to memorable advantage in the classic Boston Symphony performance conducted by Charles Munch, available now on a medium-priced RCA Victor CD (09026-60684-2).

Danses sacrée et profane for Harp and Orchestra; *Fantaisie* for Piano and Orchestra; *Première Rhapsodie* for Clarinet and Orchestra; *Rapsodie* for Saxophone and Orchestra

> **Soloists, Ulster Orchestra, Tortelier. Chandos CHAN 7018 [CD].**

Two of the greatest works ever written for the harp, Debussy's *Danses sacrée et profane* and Ravel's *Introduction and Allegro,* were composed as the result of a commercial rivalry between two French harp-making firms: Erald, whose pedal harp was introduced in about 1810 by its founder Sébastien Érald, and Pleyel, whose new chromatic harp was brought out in 1897. Despite the fact that it abandoned the cumbersome pedal mechanism entirely by substituting a string for every semitone, in its first years of production the chromatic harp showed no sign of displacing its pedaled rival. In 1904, Pleyel commissioned Debussy to write a work to show off the chromatic harp's potential; in the following year, Erald responded by commissioning a similar work from Ravel.

One of Debussy's most ethereal works is given a suitably dreamy performance by harpist Rachel Masters and Yan-Pascal Tortelier's astonishingly Gallic Ulster Orchestra, this from a now indispensable Chandos recording—culled from their superb Debussy cycle—that contains the composer's entire output for solo instrument and orchestra: the youthful piano *Fantaisie* of 1889; the *Première Rapsodie* for clarinet (a *deuxieme* never followed), composed as a entrance examination piece for the Paris Conservatory; and the *Rapsodie* for Saxophone and Orchestra, written for a Boston dowager named Mrs. Richard J. (Elisa) Hall, whose unmitigated gall was matched only by her husband's swollen bank account. All are performed with surpassing tonal beauty and finesse, as are the delightful fillers, which include the composer's witty, cimbalom-laced arrangement of *La Plus que lent,* Ravel's brilliant orchestration of the *Sarabande,* and Lucien Caplet's heart-tugging version of *Clair de lune.*

A companion album (CHAN 7017 [CD]) features Caplet's equally skillful translation of the *Children's Corner Suite,* Ravel's orchestration of the *Tarantelle styrienne,* and one of the finest of all Debussy arrangements, the version of the *Petite suite* made by the venerable Paul-Henri Büsser, who led the third performance of *Pelléas et Mélisande* in 1902 and died in Paris in 1973 at the age of 101.

Images for Orchestra

> **Montreal Symphony, Dutoit. London 425502-2 [CD].**
>
> **Chicago Symphony, Reiner. RCA 60179-2-RG [CD] (Ibéria only).**

Claude Debussy both despised and distrusted the term *Impressionism* whenever it was applied to his own music, largely because he did not want anyone to think that he had merely created a slavish aural imitation of the paintings of Monet and the poetry of Stéphane Mallarmé. Of course, the composer had a point. For his music represents one of the great turning points in the history of music: a rethinking of musical color and texture so complete that its influence would rival that of Wagner's harmonic upheaval or the rhythmic revolution that began in Igor Stravinsky's *Rite of Spring*.

As in their near-historic series of Ravel recordings, Dutoit and his fabulous orchestra turn in performances of the *Images* that are all but unapproachable in their sensitivity to the almost infinite variety of Debussy's orchestral sound. Not only are these brilliantly lit and colored performances, but they are also remarkable for their rhythmic acuity and dramatic flair: with one exception, *Ibéria* has never sounded so richly various in a commercial recording.

The exception is the legendary Reiner version, which has a fair claim to being the finest recording that often sadistic perfectionist ever made. As in his version of *La Mer* (see below), there seems to be no detail of Debussy's complex orchestration that escaped his hooded, hawklike glare. Yet along with the wondrous details comes a grasp of form and a projection of life that after four decades continue to make the performance unique. Coupled with equally compelling versions of Ravel's *Alborada del gracioso, Pavane for a Dead Princess, Rapsodie espagnole,* and *Valses nobles et sentimentales,* this is one of the great French orchestral collections.

La Mer

> **Chicago Symphony, Reiner. RCA Victor 09026-60875-2 [CD];**
> **09026-60875-4 [T].**

The final test of any performance of *La Mer* is the extent to which it makes you see, taste, and smell the sights and sounds of the sea. The wonderful recording that Fritz Reiner made with the Chicago Symphony in the late 1950s still does that more effectively than any other. In the compact disc reissue, the range of color in this virtuoso performance is as incredibly rich and varied as ever, and the drama that Boulez's otherwise fine interpretation lacks, Reiner finds in abundance. Listen, for instance, to the electrifying playing in *La Mer*'s final bars, where the conductor whips up such visceral excitement that you might almost suspect you're listening to the finale of a Tchaikovsky symphony.

Originally, and rather incongruously, coupled with Reiner's final and finest recording of Strauss's *Don Juan,* the digitally remastered CD now offers the sexiest of all commercial recordings of Rimsky-Korsakov's *Scheherazade* (see page 593).

Nocturnes for Orchestra; Jeux

Concertgebouw Orchestra of Amsterdam, Haitink. Philips 438742-2
[CD],

I blush to confess that it took me far too long to see the light on the subject of Bernard Haitink. As an ardent admirer of his great predecessor in Amsterdam, Eduard Van Beinum, and an absolute *fanatic* on the subject of Van Beinum's predecessor, Willem Mengelberg, for years Haitink seemed to me little more than a competent journeyman, a talented but rather anonymous figure who could be relied upon for polite and handsomely organized performances but little more. For the last two decades, with the release of every new Haitink recording, I have eaten what amounts to Brobdingnagian helpings of crow. In almost every recording that Haitink has made, recordings that cover an unusually broad range of repertoire, he combines intelligence, passion, craftsmanship, and utter professionalism more thoroughly than any other conductor before the public today. If Haitink, like Felix Weingartner and Pierre Monteux before him, may not be the most glamorous conductor of his generation, he is probably the most consistently satisfying.

Naturally, he faces formidable competition in one of the most popular of all Debussy's major works, yet no other modern recording of the *Nocturnes* can begin to match the effortless perfection of this one. The interpretation of "Nuages" is a masterpiece of mood and texture, "Fêtes" crackles with electric excitement, and "Sirens" is so seductively alluring that you begin to understand why countless ancient mariners were more than willing to crack up on these dangerous ladies' reefs. On the other hand, Haitink's interpretation of *Jeux* is nothing less than a major revelation. Whereas other conductors have made this strange tennis-court ballet seem an interesting work at best, Haitink dares to suggest that it may actually be an unjustly neglected masterpiece.

Pelléas et Mélisande

Alliot-Lugaz, Golfier, Henry, Carlson, Cachemaille, Thau, Montreal Symphony and Chorus, Dutoit. London 430502-3 [CD].

From its disastrous premiere in 1902 to the present day, *Pelléas et Mélisande* has never been a popular opera. Although the first-night disturbances were organized by friends of the playwright Maurice Maeterlinck, who disowned the project when he was told that his mistress Georgette Leblanc would *not* be cast as the heroine, there is more than enough in *Pelléas* to irritate the more conservative opera lover, beginning with a virtual absence of memorable arias. Moreover, there are no big scenes, no dramatic outbursts—in the entire score there are only four *fortissimos*—and the whole work can seem to move in a hazy, ill-defined half light.

It is also an opera that overflows with the most subtle musical invention, offers ample dramatic challenges—*Pelléas* made Mary Garden a star—and creates an expressive universe wholly and unmistakably its own. Its adherents insist that it is the one indisputably great French opera after *Carmen,* a claim that its finest recording to date would seem to substantiate.

With this triumphant new recording, Charles Dutoit proves yet again that he is the most resourceful and sensitive conductor of French music before the public today. Although almost without exception the cast of superb singers does everything that is asked of it and more—Colette Alliot-Lugaz and Didier Henry are both radiant and utterly believable as the lovers, while Gilles Cachemaille is probably the most three-dimensional villain since the legendary Martial Singher—it is ultimately Dutoit's wondrous conducting that will make a *Pelléas* to dominate the catalogue for years to come.

The fine Naxos recording (8.660047-9 [CD]) offers a surprisingly competitive super-budget price alternative, an excellent transfer—with minimal foot-shuffling and audience participation—of a series of live performances staged by the Lille Opera. Lovingly (and at times languorously) conducted by Jean-Claude Casadesus, whose generally philosophical tempos cause the opera to spread out over three CDs instead of the usual two, the production features in Mireille Delünsch and Gérard Théruel two young singers who really sound like the lovesick kids they're supposed to be. With outstanding contributions from Armand Arapian as an unusually ardent Golaud and Gabriel Bacquier as the aged Arkel, the set may actually prove a credible first choice for the cost-conscious buyer.

Piano Music (complete)

Gieseking, piano. EMI ZDHD 65855 [CD].

Born in Lyons of German parents who never allowed their son to attend French public schools—"At the age of five, I discovered I could read and write," he said, "I never needed to learn anything after that"—Walter Gieseking was and remains a controversial figure. He was the century's peerless interpreter of the piano music of Debussy and Ravel but was also a very unsavory human being, an early and active supporter of the Nazi movement who signed all of his correspondence with the words "Heil Hitler!"

Restored on four brilliantly remastered CDs, the famous Debussy recordings Gieseking made in London between 1951 and 1954 remain a source of wonder and despair not only for other pianists but also for anyone who feels that listening to them presents a serious moral dilemma. Almost every individual item in the collection offers some laser-like insight into how a particular phrase should be shaped, a chord voiced, a note shaded. These are the most subtly colored, delicately nuanced, supremely sensitive of all piano recordings, and if the man who made them didn't literally have blood on those magical hands, then he kept horrifically close company with those who did.

As the tormented American poet John Berryman wrote in the introduction to his *Sonnets,* "The original fault was whether wickedness was soluble in art." This is a question these priceless recordings continue to ask.

Preludes for Piano, Books I and II

Jacobs, piano. Nonesuch 73031-2 [CD].

The American pianist Paul Jacobs has the tragic distinction of having been the first well-known musician to have died of AIDS. A versatile performer who brought a special fire and distinction to the music of the twentieth century, he was one of the most persuasive advocates of modern American piano music, and his recordings of the music of Arnold Schoenberg (Nonesuch 71309-4 [T]) were among the few that could be mentioned in the same breath with those of the composer's friend and pupil Eduard Steuermann.

Even though he faces formidable competition in this popular repertoire, Jacob's recordings of the Debussy Preludes are second to none. His humanely analytical approach and meticulous attention to detail serve all of the music—especially the better-known pieces—extremely well. Like the restorers of the Sistine Chapel, he scrapes the decades of accumulated interpretive treacle off favorites like "The Girl with the Flaxen Hair" yet manages to do so without robbing it of any of its essential tenderness and charm. There are also healthy helpings of passion and fireworks whenever they are required, together with a sly and knowing wit. In all, this is one of the most satisfying of all Debussy albums and a suitable memorial to a fine and talented man.

A far more individual vision of these marvelous works can be found in Krystian Zimerman's multiple award–winning recording from Deutsche Grammophon (435773-2 [CD]). The playing is staggering in its tonal variety and dramatic range, with some of the pieces—*Ce qu'a vu le vent d'Ouest* is a notable example—threatening to disintegrate in the blaze of the pianist's intensity. On the other hand, virtuoso staples like *Les Collines d'Anacapri* and *Feux d'artifice* are dispatched with frightening ease. It might not be everybody's Debussy, but it *is* very impressive.

Mitsuko Uchida's recording of the twelve Études for Philips (422412-2 [CD]) gives the lie to the notion that she is solely a Mozart specialist. Her command of color and suggestion is as phenomenal as her manual dexterity, and the recorded sound is almost unbelievably real. While the sound of Ivan Moravec's incomparable interpretations of the three *Estampes* has clearly begun to fade, the performances never will. Not even Gieseking managed such a controlled dynamic shading in these sublimely subtle works; with the most pianistically sophisticated recording of the *Images* for Piano now available, this bargain Vox Box (5103) is some bargain indeed.

Prelude to the Afternoon of a Faun

London Philharmonic, Baudo. EMI Classics for Pleasure CDEMX 9502 [CD].

Although the term *Impressionism* would forever be associated with the revolution launched by Claude Debussy's *Prélude à l'après-midi d'un faune* in 1894, it was not the paintings of Monet, Degas, or Renoir that inspired the work but the poetry of Stephane Mallarmé. For years, Debussy had been a fixture at those Tuesday night gatherings at Mallarmé's modest apartment on the unfashionable rue de Rome. And it was during those endless, animated discussions with the most challenging poets and painters of the time that Debussy become resolved to accomplish in music what his friends were accomplishing with pigments and the printed word.

The marvelously ambiguous language of Mallarmé's poem found a perfect parallel in Debussy's musical treatment of the misty, half-conscious recollections of the faun as he attempts to recall either the experience or a dream—he can't be certain which—of an encounter with two beautiful nymphs. The result was a music more languorously suggestive, more subtly erotic than any music had ever been. That gentlest of music's major revolutions begins with a winding, deliberately vague and unsettled melody in the solo flute. "The flute of the *Faun*," Pierre Boulez suggests, "brought new breath to the art of music. What was overthrown was not so much the art of development, but the very concept of form itself."

Rarely has a performance captured more of the *Prélude*'s wonder and delicate mystery than Serge Baudo's beautiful version with the London Philharmonic, available now on a medium-priced import with equally memorable versions of *La Mer* and *Jeux*. Sensual and erotic, the performance shimmers with precisely the right degree of afternoon heat. Of course, for the absolute last word in atmosphere and orchestral perfection, one needs to consult another Serge: Koussevitzky's 1944 Boston Symphony recording, from the historic sessions of November 22 that also yielded those astonishing versions of Berlioz's *Roman Carnival Overture* and Tchaikovsky's Fifth Symphony (BSO Classics BSO 441122 [CD]).

Quartet in G Minor, Op. 10

Guarneri Quartet. RCA Victor 60609-2 [CD], 60909-4 [T].

While a relatively early work, it was the last piece Debussy would compose in an identified key and to which he assigned an opus number. The G Minor String Quartet is nonetheless the finest of the composer's chamber works and a cornerstone of the modern quartet literature.

For years, the most meltingly beautiful of all its many recordings was a version by the Guarneri Quartet for RCA Victor, now reissued on a dirt-cheap, no-frills (such as program notes) compact disc. While the Guarneri has been perhaps the most maddeningly inconsistent of the world's great quartets, they are at their absolute best in both the Debussy and its inevitable companion piece, the F Major Quartet of Maurice Ravel. The playing has such a natural ease, sensitivity, and unanimity of frankly Romantic purpose that the recording easily sweeps a very crowded field.

Sonatas (3) for various instruments

Chung, violin; Lupu, piano; Melos Ensemble of London. London 421154.

Debussy was already in the final agonizing stages of rectal cancer when he began writing that curiously anachronistic series of works with which he would conclude his career: three instrumental sonatas modeled on eighteenth-century forms. While occasionally they might suggest a diminished concentration—especially in the Violin Sonata, his final piece—the Sonatas contain an abundance of intriguing ideas and ripe invention: the Cello Sonata seems, for the most part, to be deliberately written *against* the instrument's principal strengths, while the Sonata for Flute, Viola, and Harp is so ethereal it seems the work of an inhabitant of another world.

Even with the convenient Chandos recording that offered consistently excellent performances by the Athena Ensemble *in*conveniently withdrawn, Kyung-Wha Chung's London recording (421154-2) of the Violin Sonata with Radu Lupu remains in a very special category, with similarly breathtaking versions of the Sonata for Flute, Viola, and Harp, the Franck Violin Sonata, and Ravel's *Introduction and Allegro*. While there is no current recording of the Cello Sonata to match Chung's performance, Frans Helmerson's BIS recording (CD 28 [CD]) is unfailingly intelligent and musical, as are the accompanying versions of *Syrinx* and several of the composer's songs, including the *Chansons de Bilitis*.

Debussy's early Piano Trio from 1880 is made to seem richer and more substantial than usual in a first-rate Arabesque recording (Z 6643 [CD]) by the Golub/Kaplan/Carr Trio, which also offers trios by Saint-Saëns and Ravel.

Songs

Ameling, Command, Mesplé, Souzay, von Stade; Baldwin, piano.
Angel CDMC-64095.

This elegant collection on three medium-priced CDs gathers fifty-five of Debussy's eighty-plus songs in performances that represent some of the best Debussy singing ever captured in a recording studio. With the always sensitive and resourceful Dalton Baldwin as the common denominator, the series traces Debussy's growth as a composer of *chansons* from the very beginning to the very end of his career. Elly Ameling, Frederica von Stade, and Gérard Souzay are all but incomparable in this repertoire, with readings that teem with insight and surge with life. The recorded sound from the early- to mid-1970s is warm and natural, and although English translations of the texts would have been a helpful touch, this is a minor drawback to an absolutely indispensable release.

Suite bergamasque; Estampes; Images oubliées; Pour le piano

Kocsis, piano. Philips 412118-2 [CD].

Given that Debussy was responsible for some of the most original and popular piano music produced after Chopin, there is a surprising, one is tempted to say *scandalous,* dearth of first-rate recordings now in print. (Perhaps we are simply going through one of those predictable droughts, during which the major recording companies are gearing up to reissue the Debussy piano treasures in their vaults as compact discs.) Whatever the explanation, virtually none of the definitive recordings made by that arch-poet Walter Gieseking are readily available, and Debussy's greatest living interpreter, the Czech pianist Ivan Moravec, is currently represented by only a few tantalizing bits and pieces.

This generous and brilliantly played collection by the Hungarian pianist Zoltán Kocsis is one of the few genuine treasures in a shockingly barren field. Kocsis, who obviously possesses an important technique, plays with great subtlety and refinement. The *Suite bergamasque* is particularly successful, offering considerable wit, admirable control, and an attractively understated account of the famous *Clair de lune* (which the incomparable Victor Borge, before all of his inimitable performances, invariably introduced by saying, "English translation: Clear the saloon"). The recorded sound, especially in compact disc format, offers one of the most realistic recreations of piano timbre that has yet been heard.

DeLalande, Michel-Richard (1657–1726)

Symphonies pour les soupers du roi (complete)

> La Simphonie du Marais, Reyne. Harmonia Mundi HMC 901337/40 [CD].

Along with the food, the girls, and the reasonably decent accommodations—Versailles, Fontainbleau, plus the miscellaneous getaway spots in the country—one of the very best things about being Louis XIV was the dinner music. In all, the Sun King's court composer Michel-Richard DeLalande wrote an even dozen suites of pieces to aid His Majesty's digestion, recorded now in their entirety for the very first time.

The Simphonie du Marais under Hugo Reyne give unusually vivid and lively performances of these unfailingly attractive works, with no hint of routine evident anywhere on the four tightly packed CDs. To those for whom this might be a bit too much of a very good thing, an album of highlights is available (HMC 901303 [CD]; HMC 401337 [T]).

Delibes, Léo (1836–1891)

Lakmé

> Sutherland, Vanzo, Bacquier, Monte Carlo Opera Chorus and Orchestra, Bonynge. London 425485-2 [CD].

In the days when the glamorous Lily Pons was its most famous exponent, Delibes's tuneful and exotic *Lakmé* was known primarily for its tinkling "Bell Song," which the famous soprano typically sang with great abandon and a quarter step flat. (Her pitch was always a problem: Once, while working on a film with Max Steiner, she tearfully confessed on the sound stage that she could not sing properly "without *l'amour*." When Steiner picked up her then husband André Kostelanetz at the airport the next day, he said, "André, do you think you could pump her up a half step or two?") Recently, thanks to some TV airline ads and its use in a peculiar film called *The Hunger*, the melting Act I duet "Dôme épais, le jasmin" has gone on to enjoy a similar life of its own.

For anyone interested in getting to know the rest of *Lakmé*—and what a lovely and fascinating opera it is—the London recording provides a near-ideal introduction. Although Joan Sutherland's reading of the title role is something of a wash, dramatically, her work in the "Bell Song" and "Dôme épais" is breathtaking. The rest of the cast is excellent, as is the recorded sound and Richard Bonynge's conducting.

Those not content with the fine Ormandy/Philadelphia Orchestra recording of the suites from *Coppélia* and *Sylvia* (Sony Classical SBK 46551 [CD], SBT 46551 [T]) will find Bonynge's versions of the complete ballets equally delightful. The electrifying performance of the familiar "Procession of Bacchus" from *Sylvia*—listen especially to the swagger of the National Philharmonic brass—is almost in itself worth the price of the album (London 425475 [CD]), while the recording of *Coppélia* (414502-2 [CD], 414502-4) presents the ballet's finest recording ever and some of Bonynge's most pointed and imaginative work to date.

Delius, Frederick *(1862–1934)*

Concerto for Cello and Orchestra; Double Concerto for Violin, Cello, and Orchestra; Paris—The Song of a Great City

Little, violin; Wallfisch, cello; Royal Liverpool Philharmonic, Mackerras. EMI Classics for Pleasure CDEMX 2185 [CD].

There aren't many Delius albums more accomplished or valuable than this one, which brings together three neglected major works in performances that have a fair claim to being the finest ever recorded. The Cello Concerto, which was the composer's favorite among his four instrumental concertos, is given a ripely committed reading by Raphael Wallfisch, who proves its most forcefully individual exponent since Jacqueline du Pré.

With the gifted Tasmin Little as an ideal partner, Wallfisch is no less compelling in the normally problematical Double Concerto, which here emerges as one of the composer's most cogently argued larger works. In both scores, Sir Charles Mackerras confirms his reputation as one of the great living Delians, and the sweeping yet delicately detailed reading of the magnificent travelogue *Paris—The Song of a Great City* is easily the best since Beecham's.

Florida Suite; Idylle de printemps; Over the Hills and Far Away; La Quadroone; Scherzo; Konanga: Closing Scene

> Soloists, English Northern Philharmonia Orchestra, Lloyd-Jones. Naxos 8.553535 [CD].

For Delius lovers on a budget, the first installment of the new Naxos Delius series is cause for considerable excitement, particularly because the recording would be exceptionally worthwhile at whatever the price. The performances of some of Delius's earliest works are so insightful and hypnotic that we tend to forget for the moment just *how* inexperienced the young composer was at the time; this *Florida Suite* is especially subtle and understanding, rivaling any on the market today, while the version of *Over the Hills and Far Away* is the most incandescent since Beecham's. Add the equally magnetic interpretations of three genuine rarities—the vernal *Idylle de printemps,* which proves fresh as its name, and the dance-like *La Quadroone* and *Scherzo,* the only movements that survive from a projected suite—and its value and importance become all the more obvious. David Lloyd-Jones reveals himself throughout as a major Delius conductor and thus future installments in his series should be anticipated with the keenest excitement.

A Mass of Life; Requiem

> Rodgers, Rigby, Robson, Evans, Coleman-Wright, Waynflete Singers, Bournemouth Symphony Chorus and Orchestra, Hickox. Chandos CHAN 9515 [CD].

Begun not long after his marriage to Jelka Rosen in 1903, *A Mass of Life* is not only one of the most ambitious of all Delius's works but is also one of the most heartfelt and exuberant. Bursting with love, confidence, and gratitude, with a text drawn from Jelka's copy of Nietzsche's *Also sprach Zarathustra,* it was a perfect reflection of his buoyant feelings at the time, feelings best summarized in the final lines of the text: "All joy wants eternity,/Wants deep, profound eternity."

In this overwhelming recording, Hickox and his superbly drilled forces effortlessly capture both the swelling exultation of the piece and its more reflective joyousness. As in no other previous recording, the structure of the work is revealed in all its strength and integrity, with equal attention paid to its gorgeous surface details. The choruses, so central to *A Mass of Life*'s meaning and impact, come off with a thrilling, full-throated magnificence, while every detail of the often intricate orchestration emerges with a startling clarity and vividness.

The performance of the darker, far more concentrated *Requiem*—completed in 1916 on texts from Nietzsche and Ecclesiastes—is also exceptional, revealing a once-maligned and still neglected work as the masterpiece it is.

Over the Hills and Far Away; Sleigh Ride, Marche caprice; Brigg Fair—An English Rhapsody; Florida Suite; Dance Rhapsody No. 2; Summer Evening; On Hearing the First Cuckoo in Spring, Summer Night on the River; A Song Before Sunrise; Intermezzo from Fennimore and Gerda; Prelude to Irmelin; Songs of Sunset

> Forrester, contralto; Cameron, baritone; Beecham Choral
> Society, Royal Philharmonic Orchestra, Beecham. Angel
> CDCB-47509 [CD].

With the possible exception of the amoral, egomaniacal, virulently anti-Semitic, and treacherous Richard Wagner, who repaid the unswerving loyalty of at least two of his most ardent supporters by sleeping with their wives, Frederick Delius, of all the great composers, was probably the most thoroughly unpleasant human being. Cruel, ruthless, pathologically selfish, and a self-styled reincarnation of Nietzsche's idealized Nordic superman, Delius fought his long, lonely struggle for recognition, while making the lives of everyone around him (especially that of his devoted, long-suffering wife, Jelka) absolutely miserable. As much as his apologists, his amanuensis Eric Fenby and the Australian composer Percy Grainger, have tried to pardon his unpardonable behavior, Delius, to the day he died—a blind and paralyzed victim of tertiary neurosyphilis—was a complete and thoroughgoing beast.

And yet contained within this difficult, often despicable man was one of the most original and rarefied talents in musical history. At its best, Delius's music is among the most delicate and ineffably gentle ever produced by an English composer, and as one of the last of the late-Romantic Nature poets, he remains unique.

For those of us who are hopelessly addicted to his admittedly limited but irresistibly appealing art, or for those perfectly sensible, though sadly misguided, souls who gag at the very mention of his name, this recent Angel recording is the most valuable single release since the introduction of the compact disc. For contained on these two tightly packed and handsomely remastered compact discs are all the stereo recordings of Delius's music that his greatest champion, Sir Thomas Beecham, ever made.

In Beecham's hands—though, alas, in few others' since the conductor's death—the music of Delius clearly emerges as that of a major composer. Almost every bar of these famous performances is shot through with Beecham's special interpretive wizardry. *On Hearing the First Cuckoo in Spring* very nearly says as much as the whole of Beethoven's "Pastoral" Symphony, and the legendary version of *Brigg Fair* sounds not only like the finest Delius recording ever made but also preciously close to the most magical fifteen minutes in recording history.

For dyed-in-the-wool Delians, this is an invaluable release; for the unconverted, it's an ideal invitation to join us.

Sea Drift; Songs of Farewell; Songs of Sunset

Soloists, Bournemouth Symphony Orchestra and Chorus, Hickox. Chandos CHAN 9214.

A partial setting of Walt Whitman's moving poem "Out of the Cradle Endlessly Rocking"—which is also said to have inspired the cradle scenes in D. W. Griffith's screen classic *Intolerance*—*Sea Drift* not only has a fair claim to being Delius's masterpiece but is also one of the few indisputably great choral works of the twentieth century. Whitman's tale of a child's coming to terms with the terror and beauty of death struck a resonant chord in the composer; not only is the poignant little drama of the sea bird losing and mourning its mate captured to perfection, but so, too, are the scents and sounds of the sea, which Delius evokes as magically as any composer ever has.

At the beginning of his career, Richard Hickox made a thrilling recording of this great work for English Decca, available until recently on a London compact disc. Happily, the new version for Chandos is in every way more sumptuous and refined. Hickox coaxes committed and rapturous performances from his alert forces and Chandos's engineers—as they usually do for this conductor—respond with their very best sound. Coupled with versions of the *Songs of Farewell* and *Songs of Sunset* to rival those Fenby and Beecham, this is the finest album of Delius choral music now available.

Sonata for Cello and Piano; Sonatas for Violin and Piano (3)

Welsh, cello; Graham, Barantschik, violins; Margalit, piano. EMI Classics CDC 55399 [CD].

The Cello Sonata is one of Delius's strongest chamber works: long-breathed and lyrical, with a structural coherence that gives the lie to the preposterous notion that its composer was rarely more than an inspired miniaturist. Similarly, the three Violin Sonatas are all as tightly argued as they are intensely felt, especially the final one, which the blind composer was forced to dictate note by painful note to Eric Fenby.

Until Unicorn restores Fenby's historic recordings with Ralph Holmes, these excellent modern versions by members of the London Symphony will continue to remind people just how fine these vastly underappreciated works really are. Moray Welsh's performance of the Cello Sonata is as warm and sympathetic as any ever recorded, with all four given rich and present recorded sound.

Two Aquarelles; Caprice and Elegy; Fantastic Dance; Prelude to Irmelin; "La Calinda" from Koanga; Cyrana; Idyll; A Late Lark; A Song of Summer; Songs of Farewell

Soloists, Ambrosian Singers, Royal Philharmonic, Fenby. Unicorn-Kanchana UK 2072; 2076 [CD].

These recordings by Eric Fenby, who took dictation and abuse from Delius during the composer's final years, would be invaluable for their historic value alone. To hear the molten *Song of Summer* led by the man who actually wrote it down, note by note, makes for a slightly eerie experience. For that matter, Delius's ghost hangs almost palpably over these proceedings, as well it should, since they are overseen by someone who knew him—both as man *and* musician—as intimately as anyone.

Beyond their documentary interest, these are absolutely marvelous performances, as loving and individual as Beecham's, which they complement but in no way supplant. While the versions of *A Song of Summer,* the *Irmelin* Prelude (which Fenby arranged), and the little known *Fantastic Dance* (a piece Delius dedicated to Fenby) are understandably authoritative, it is the conductor's handling of the larger works that makes the recording so priceless. The extended love scene called *Idyll* has a Puccini-like redolence, and the *Songs of Farewell,* in Fenby's hands, emerges as one of the composer's most singular and unforgettable works.

The sensitive, devoted contributions of the soloists, the Ambrosian Singers, and the great Royal Philharmonic only help to prove that for this composer, there *is* life after Beecham.

A Village Romeo and Juliet

Soloists, Royal Philharmonic, Beecham. EMI Classics ZDMB 64386 [CD].

A Village Romeo and Juliet, the fifth of Delius's six operas, is easily his most successful work for the stage. The familiar, matzo-thin plot—centered around a feud between a pair of Swiss families and the two children who are tragically caught in between—drew from the composer some of his most ravishing music, including the unspeakably touching "Walk to the Paradise Garden."

Recorded as long ago as 1948, Sir Thomas Beecham's classic interpretation has lost none of its freshness or immediacy. In fact, in terms of placing the listener in the center of the drama, it is even more engrossing than the far more recent versions led by Meredith Davies and Sir Charles Mackerras, both unfortunately withdrawn. Beecham's unique way with Delius's fragile textures is evident throughout this magical recording, as is the devotion of all the soloists, who are clearly inspired to give their very best. As a bonus, the set is topped off by the most intensely moving of Beecham's three recordings of *Sea Drift*.

Violin Concerto; *Légende for Violin and Orchestra*; Suite for Violin and Orchestra

Holmes, violin; Royal Philharmonic, Handley. Unicorn UK CD 2072 [CD].

The Delius Violin Concerto is one of several works that give the lie to the notion that the composer was essentially a miniaturist uncomfortable with the larger musical forms. True, the architecture and underlying organization of Delius's most ambitious instrumental work may not be as obvious as in the more traditional concertos of Elgar and Walton, but with some help from an inspired soloist and an insightful conductor, the Delius can seem to emerge as the equal of either.

Ralph Holmes is a meticulous and passionate advocate of the Concerto, a musician who spares no effort to illuminate the music without a hint of self-serving display. In addition to the warmth and beauty of the playing, the natural flow of the musical argument has never been captured more convincingly. In this, the soloist is aided and abetted by one of the great Delians of modern times. Like Beecham, Vernon Handley has an instinctive grasp of the composer's highly individual idiom, all the more obvious in the far weaker—but thoroughly agreeable—*Légende* and Suite that round out the disc.

Perhaps even more impressive is Handley's recording with the Ulster Orchestra for Chandos of two major Delius scores, the *North Country Sketches* and the *Florida Suite* (CHAN-8413 [CD]). Again like Beecham, Handley makes the youthful suite by the twenty-five-year-old composer seem far more forward-looking and original than it probably is, while the much later *North Country Sketches* is revealed again as one of the composer's supreme achievements.

Dello Joio, Norman (1913–)

Air Power (Symphonic Suite)

Philadelphia Orchestra, Ormandy. Albany TROY 250 [CD].

Like most healthy warmongering American males growing up in the 1950s, my initial contact with the music of this gifted composer came via the Sunday afternoon broadcasts of the CBS television series *Air Power*. And just as the kids on my block tended to be divided into two warring and irreconcilable camps on the subject of American Flyer versus Lionel trains—a snobbish purist even then, I, of course, preferred the infinitely more realistic two-rail American Flyers to the oafish, over-sized *three*-rail Lionels—I was an *Air Power* type while most of my friends preferred *Victory at Sea,* largely, I suspect, because of Norman Dello Joio's wonderful score. After more than forty years, it still seems to me the most distinguished score ever broadcast on American television: from the moving and unforgettable main title through the powerful drama of the War Scenes—on the air, I played the heart-dissolving "The Lonely Pilot's Letter Home" on the first night of Desert Storm—this is also substantial, memorable music that can stand brilliantly on its own.

Reissued as part of Albany's indispensable "American Archive" series, Eugene Ormandy's Columbia recording sounds more vivid and colorful than ever and will call up countless images for those with fond memories of the series. As a bonus, the album comes with equally definitive performances of a pair of splendid and shamefully neglected works by Dello Joio's near contemporary John Vincent: the *Symphonic Poem after Descartes* and his "Festival Piece in One Movement," the Symphony in D.

Another Dello Joio masterpiece, the passionately argued *Meditations on Ecclesiastes*—which won the 1957 Pulitzer Prize for music—is given a fiercely eloquent reading by the Oregon Symphony conducted by James DePreist (Koch International Classics KIC 7156), while on another Koch CD (KIC 7243) James Sedares leads the New Zealand Symphony in very fine performances of *The Triumph of St. Joan Symphony* (a powerfully dramatic three-movement work cannibalized from his unsuccessful 1949 opera) and the three symphonic dances, *Variations, Chaconne,* and *Finale.*

Diamond, David (1915–)

Symphony No. 2; Symphony No. 4; Concerto for Small Orchestra

> Seattle Symphony, New York Chamber Symphony, Schwarz. Delos DE 3093 [CD].

In the work of David Diamond, a particular species of American symphony may have reached its most polished and exuberant form of expression. During the late '40s and early '50s, Diamond became one of the principal purveyors of the neo-Classical American symphony, a composer whose finest works in the form rival the best brought forth upon this continent.

The three works presented in the first volume in Delos's Diamond Series show the composer at his most characteristic and attractive. If the Schwarz performance of the wonderful Symphony No. 4 doesn't completely efface the memory of Leonard Bernstein's pioneering recording from 1958, then it is still a superb reading, with warmth, energy, and individuality to burn. Here, as in the other pieces, Schwarz continues to reveal himself as the most sympathetic and significant champion that American music has had since the death of Howard Hanson.

The subsequent installments in the Diamond Series have proven no less valuable. The powerful Symphony No. 3, together with the elegant *Romeo and Juliet,* the moving *Psalm,* and the eloquent *Kaddish* for Cello and Orchestra, fill the second volume (DE 3103 [CD]), while the Symphony No. 1, Second Violin Concerto, and the fascinating tone poem based on e. e. cummings's *The Enormous Room* make up Volume 3 (DE 3119 [CD]).

Anyone responding to Diamond's fresh and bracing idiom will certainly want to investigate the music of his near contemporary Harold Shapero. The sparkling *Symphony for Classical Orchestra,* together with the snappy *Nine-Minute Overture,* are brilliantly served by André Previn and the Los Angeles Philharmonic (New World NW-80373-2 [CD]).

Dittersdorf, Carl Ditters von

(1739–1799)

Symphonies (6) on Ovid's Metamorphoses

Failoni Orchestra, Gmür. Naxos 8.553368 (Nos. 1–3);
8.553369 [CD].

This gifted man with the wonderful name wrote some of the finest and most entertaining symphonies of the early Classical period, including a series of twelve—six of which have survived—based on various sections of Ovid's *Metamorphoses.* With titles like *Transformation of the Lycian Peasants into Frogs,* these are obviously vividly pictorial works, with much of the wit, melodic richness, and endless surprise of the best middle-period Haydn symphonies. The faster movements bristle with life and energy, while the *adagios* are among the most moving of the period: for instance, the slow movement of *The Fall of Phaeton,* with its liquid flute solo, bears a close family resemblance to Gluck's "Dance of the Blessèd Spirits."

If fractionally less stylish than the superb Chandos recording by Adrian Shepherd and Cantilena (CHAN 8564/65 [CD]), then the spirited set by the Failoni Orchestra of Budapest under the young Swiss conductor Hanspeter Gmür offers comparable pleasure at considerably less than half the price. The interpretations are as wry, tender, and imaginative as the works themselves, while the warm acoustics of the Festetich Castle seems ideal.

Dohnányi, Ernst von   (1877–1960)

Capriccio in F Minor; *Variations on a Nursery Song,* Op. 25

Wild, piano; New Philharmonia Orchestra, Dohnányi.
Chesky CD-13 [CD].

Until relatively recent times, the smart money insisted that Ernst von Dohnányi was the greatest Hungarian composer of the twentieth century. A late-Romantic whose painstaking craftsmanship earned him the sobriquet "The Hungarian Brahms," Dohnányi would eventually be overtaken and almost completely overshadowed by his younger, more radical contemporaries, Béla Bartók and Zoltán Kodály. In fact, the extent to which Dohnányi's reputation is now in eclipse may be gathered from the fact that there are only a handful of available recordings of his most popular piece, the witty and ingratiating *Variations on a Nursery Song.*

Why the American pianist Earl Wild is not better known has always been something of a mystery. Technically, he is one of the most formidably equipped pianists of his generation. Though he is a musician of considerable taste and refinement, he is also among the more viscerally exciting musicians of our time. As in his superb set of the Rachmaninoff Concertos (see page 563), this recording from the mid-1960s finds him at the peak of his form. The interpretation is as fiery as it is playful, featuring a combination of a thunderous pianism that recalls the legends of the old barnstorming days and an ability to spin out the music's delicate filigree that is almost unheard of today.

Christoph von Dohnányi is a predictably sympathetic advocate of his grandfather's music, in both his best-known piece and the virtually unknown *Capriccio* in F Minor that accompanies it. Another Wild performance—in both senses of the phrase—rounds out this bargain release: the old *Reader's Digest* recording of the Tchaikovsky Concerto that could stand a cue ball's hair on end.

Volume 6 of the Romantic Piano Concerto Series from Hyperion (CDA 66684 [CD]) is devoted to Dohnányi's two rarely heard piano concertos. While the Second is a lushly mature work, the youthful E Minor Concerto is a good deal more fun. It's a long, sprawling, dreadfully serious piece with a lot of melodramatic gestures and *fin-de-siècle* lily-gilding. Yet the very overwritten earnestness of the thing makes it so endearing, especially in its long and unintentionally amusing coda, which seems a virtual catalogue of late-Romantic concerto clichés. Martin Roscoe's playing is refined and dashing throughout and is admirably supported by Fedor Glushchenko and the BBC Scottish Symphony.

Piano Music

Jandó, piano. Koch SCH 311812 [CD]

The tireless Jenö Jandó—who apparently eats and sleeps at the recording studio—is a predictably idiomatic guide to his countryman's charming and imaginative piano music, offering the best single-volume collection currently available. *Ruralia hungarica* emerges with abundant national feeling but without the slightest hint of picture-postcard cheapness, while the four *Rhapsodies* of 1911 are made to seem the most significant such works since Brahms. The recording is good, if slightly reverberant.

Piano Quintets (2); *Serenade in C*, Op. 10

Schubert Ensemble of London. Hyperion CDA 66786 [CD].

When the manuscript of the C Minor Piano Quintet by the eighteen-year-old Dohnányi was sent to the aging Johannes Brahms, the composer arranged to have it performed at his summer retreat in Bad Ischl and later engineered the Vienna premiere with the young Dohnányi at the piano. It is an amazingly confident if slightly derivative work—Brahms undoubtedly detected signs here and there of a sincere and touching hero-worship—while its E-flat Minor companion piece, written two decades later, is the work of the fully mature master whose *Variations on a Nursery Song* had just begun its triumphant conquest of Europe. Both are given beautifully detailed performances by the excellent Schubert Ensemble of London, three of whose members also acquit themselves handsomely in what is probably the finest (and is *certainly* the most entertaining) of the composer's chamber works, the much-recorded *Serenade in C*. This enchanting string trio from 1902 also served as the vehicle for the greatest of all

Dohnányi recordings: the incomprehensibly brilliant 1941 RCA recording by Jascha Heifetz, William Primrose, and Emanuel Feuermann, currently available in an immaculate transfer from Biddulph (LAB 074 [CD]).

Symphony No. 2, Op. 40; *Symphonic Minutes*, Op. 36

BBC Philharmonic, Bamert. Chandos CHAN 9455 [CD].

With the delicious Suite in F-sharp, Op. 19—currently represented by a fine, if hardly spine-tingling, reading by the Budapest Symphony conducted by Tamás Vásáry (Hungariton HCD 31637 [CD])—the charming *Symphonic Minutes (Szimfonikus percek)* was once the most popular and frequently performed of Dohnányi's purely orchestral scores, a work championed and recorded during the 78 era by Sir Henry Wood and Oswald Kabasta, the gifted, guilt-ridden Austrian conductor whose close association with the Nazis caused him to commit suicide a few months after the end of World War II. Matthias Bamert leads this fine Manchester orchestra in a performance so fresh and invigorating that you begin to suspect the piece could easily return to general circulation, given advocacy like this. The sprawling Second Symphony is a more problematical work, finished in 1944 during the German occupation of Budapest. Except for a quotation in the final movement of the Bach chorale *Komm, süsser Tod*, there are few hints in the fifty-minute work of the turbulent times in which it was composed: impeccably mannered and beautifully crafted, it is a poised and passionate work that seems to grow in stature on repeated hearings. As in the *Symphonic Minutes*, neither the performance nor the recorded sound could possibly be improved.

Violin Concerto No. 2 in C Minor, Op. 43

Kaplan, violin; Barcelona Symphony, Foster. Koch International Classics KIC 7387 [CD].

Finished in 1950, Dohnányi's Second Violin Concerto could have easily been written a half century before, so intensely Romantic are its vocabulary and gestures and so vividly Straussian are its orchestral colors. The spirit of Dohnányi's beloved Brahms also hovers benignly over the proceedings, as do the shades of Ysaÿe, Sarasate, and Kreisler. In short, this is a big, high-cholesterol virtuoso display piece containing a lot of lush and exciting music that deserves to be far better known.

Mark Kaplan proves the ideal advocate of this virtually unknown work, playing it with all the passionate abandon one usually brings to an established repertory work. Lawrence Foster and his excellent Barcelona Symphony are equally convincing partners—both here and in the Bartók Violin Concerto that accompanies it—and the recorded sound is fine.

Donizetti, Gaetano (1797–1848)

Arias

Caballé, soprano. RCA 09026-60941-2 [C].

Hvorostovsky, baritone; Philharmonia Orchestra, Marin. Philips 434912-2 [CD].

Jo, soprano; English Chamber Orchestra, Carella. Erato 17580 [CD].

Kasarova, mezzo-soprano; Munich Radio Symphony, Haider. RCA 09026-68522-2 [CD].

If the arias that grace Donizetti's operas are not quite as instantly memorable as those of Rossini, Verdi, and Puccini—and after all, the most famous moment in his entire output is the *Sextet* from *Lucia di Lammermoor*—then they are nonetheless the springboard for some of the most thrilling moments in bel canto opera: collections of incredibly daunting vocal obstacles that tend to appeal to only the most courageous (or foolhardy) singers.

Gathered from her famous "Rarities" collections—and works like *Belisario, Gemma di Vergy, Parisina d'Este,* and *Torquato Tasso* certainly count as *that*—Montserrat Caballé's singing is so technically dazzling and physically beautiful throughout that she makes you wonder why the works that contain such miracles aren't as popular as *Carmen* and *La Bohème.*

Similarly, Dimitri Hvorostovsky and Sumi Jo offer the highest standards of modern bel canto singing on their respective collections, the baritone a model of suave virility, the soprano remarkably fresh and girlish, yet thoroughly adult.

Perhaps most exciting of all is the debut recording by the Bulgarian mezzo Vasselina Kasarova, who is already, clearly, the most exciting female singer to have emerged from that tiny country since Ljuba Welistch. Hers is a large, wide-ranging, and colorful voice, managed with passion and a deceptive effortlessness. The big scene from *Anna Bolena*—Jane Seymour's "Per questa fiamma indomita"—is breathtaking in its secure authority, promising some very exciting things to come.

Don Pasquale

Mei, Bruson, Allen, Bavarian Radio Chorus, Munich Radio Orchestra, R. Abbado. RCA 09026-61924-2 [CD].

There are many who would argue that *Don Pasquale*—the last successful opera Donizetti completed before his mental breakdown in 1844—is the composer's masterpiece: the freshest, most sparkling of all his comedies and thus one of the finest *opera buffas* of all time. Along with a flashing musical wit that rivals anything in Rossini, there are moments of tender sentiment—particularly Ernesto's Act III serenade "Com' è gentil"—in which the flowing lines of Donizetti's vocal writing help explain what *bel canto* really means. If *Don Pasquale* is not his finest opera, then it is certainly his most lovable.

The recent RCA recording is the most satisfying since the classic—and now retired—1964 London recording with Fernando Corena. In addition to Roberto Abbado's crisp, unforced conducting, it affords Renato Bruson his most memorable outing since the Giulini *Falstaff:* he postures and blusters with the best of them, but he also *sings* the role. With stylish support from Thomas Allen as an unusually suave Malatesta, Frank Lopardo as the ardent, Schipa-like Ernesto, and Eva Mei as the Norina you'd like to take home to meet the folks, this is not only the best *Don Pasquale* but also one of the strongest Donizetti recordings currently available.

L'elisir d'amore

Sutherland, Pavarotti, Malas, Cossa, Ambrosian Singers, English Chamber Orchestra, Bonynge. London 414461-2 [CD].

As one who is not invariably carried away by Dame Joan Sutherland, and who cordially—well actually, *virulently*—despises what Luciano Pavarotti has become, even *I* can recognize one of the great Donizetti recordings when I hear it. As a comedienne, Sutherland is deliciously effective: coy, girlish, warmly and irresistibly human. Pavarotti, too, is tremendous fun as the lovesick Nemorino, and his singing of the show's hit tune, "Una furtiva lagrima," contains some of the best work of his career. Spiro Malas's Dr. Dulcamara is wonder of transparent, W. C. Fields–like hokum, and Richard Bonynge's touch is as light-fingered as a pickpocket's.

The same team is responsible for an equally engaging recording of Donizetti's *Daughter of the Regiment* (London 414520-2 [CD])—indeed, the *very* recording in which Pavarotti pops all of those ringing high Cs, while Sutherland is at her most imposing in the 1987 recording of *Anna Bolena* (London 421096-2 [CD]), with Samuel Ramey leading the excellent supporting cast.

As long as the credit card is out, get the clerk to play Sutherland's frightening imprecation "Vil bastarda!" from Donizetti's Elizabethan potboiler *Maria Stuarda* (425410 [CD]); if that doesn't make the sale, then the menacing Elizabeth I of Huguette Tourangeau—this was the Catholic perspective on the idiot Mary Queen of Scots—certainly will. While the Great Dame is no less formidable in the title role of *Lucrezia Borgia* (421497-2 [CD]), it is Marilyn Horne who steals the show in the trouser role of Count Orsini. Her version of the famous brindisi, "Il segreto per esser felici," popularized by Ernestine Schumann-Heink, is the most hair-raising since Sigrid Onegin's. (This is also a moment that gives the lie to all of those terrible tenor jokes—including the favorite one of the Chilean tenor Ramon Vinay, who asked, "Did you hear the one about the tenor who was *so* stupid that even the other tenors noticed?"—since it's a *contralto* who's dim-witted enough to raise a glass of wine in an opera called *LUCREZIA BORGIA!*)

If in the London *La Favorita* (430038-2 [CD]) the glorious Fiorenza Cossotto is somewhat past her prime, then even in decline she is more impressive than any of her recorded rivals. And as though any compensation were needed, Pavarotti as Fernando turns in one of his most beautiful and intelligent recorded performances.

For those who *really* want to go off the deep end, almost all of the several Opera Rara recordings of genuinely obscure Donizetti are more than worth investigating. *L'assedio di Calais* (OR 9 [CD]) is an exciting, shockingly neglected work with superb choruses and a sextet nearly as good as *Lucia*'s; *Emilia di Liverpool* (OR 8 [CD]) is far from the practical joke the ridiculous title might suggest: this lively *opera buffa* is engaging early Donizetti, as is the revised *L'eremitaggio di Liverpool*, also included in the set; *Maria Padilla* (ORC 6 [CD]) seems at times like a dress rehearsal for *Lucia*, with the bizarre notion of a Mad Scene for the tenor.

Lucia di Lammermoor

> Callas, Tagliavini, Cappuccilli, Ladysz, Philharmonia Orchestra and Chorus, Serafin. Angel CDCB 56284 [CD].

More than any other of Gaetano Donizetti's sixty-odd operas, which were often produced at the mind-boggling rate of eight to ten per year—a contemporary caricature shows the composer seated at a desk, his famous mop of hair askew, writing with two hands simultaneously—*Lucia di Lammermoor* is the archetypal representative of all that is best *and* most ridiculous in *bel canto* opera. As theater, it is both grippingly effective and utterly absurd. The famous *Sextet* is one of the high-water marks of nineteenth-century ensemble writing, the long and demanding *Mad Scene*, a silly and thinly veiled excuse for a twenty-minute coloratura concert. (Of course, it could be argued that Lucia's lengthy conversation with an equally energetic flute is no more preposterous than that goofy scene that the recently stabbed Gilda, fresh from her gunnysack, is asked to deliver at the end of Verdi's *Rigoletto*, or that equally exhausting vocal and dramatic tour de force that the consumptive Violetta uses to conclude that same composer's *La Traviata*.) But then again, loving opera has always been dependent on a healthy disregard for common sense. And *Lucia di Lammermoor*, with the proper attitude and, more important, the proper cast, can be as rewarding an experience as the opera house has to offer.

Vocally, the most impressive Lucia of modern times was the young Joan Sutherland, whose 1959 London recording recalled the exploits of the almost mythic Luisa Tetrazzini, the great turn-of-the-century diva who is today best remembered for the recipe for chicken and spaghetti that still bears her name. (Tetrazzini's astonishing artistry is now conveniently preserved on a set of five handsomely produced Pearl CDs—GEMM CDS-9220—that contain all the singer's known recordings from 1903 through 1922. As examples of vocal legerdemain, many have never been surpassed and the set is required listening for anyone interested in opera, singing, or the possibilities of the human voice.) Dramatically and emotionally, the Sutherland Lucia was a rather different matter, and in her far less impressive remake with her husband, Richard Bonynge, what were once merely Sutherland eccentricities had already become annoying clichés.

What the opera *should* be, as both a dramatic and vocal experience, is still best suggested by the classic recording made by Maria Callas. Like the Callas *Norma*, it is an exceedingly rich and beautiful characterization. It contains some of the finest singing that Callas would ever deliver in a recording studio. The famous *Mad Scene,* for once, is not the unintentionally uproarious joke it usually is but a riveting piece of theater cut from the same cloth as Shakespeare's scene on the blasted heath from *King Lear.* The rest of the cast, even the aging tenor Ferruccio Tagliavini, are more than adequate. And the veteran Tullio Serafin gives us countless thrilling moments that confirm his reputation as one of the last of the great blood-and-thunder opera conductors. For Callas fans, or for anyone interested in making the rare acquaintance of *Lucia di Lammermoor* as convincing musical drama, this one is an absolute must.

Dowland, John (1563–1626)

Lute Music

Lindberg, lute. BIS CD 722-24 [CD].

John Dowland was not only the greatest of the Elizabethan lutenists, but he was also—by a comfortable margin—the gloomiest. Numerous pieces have the word *lachrimae* somewhere in the title, and one of his most famous lute works, *Sempre Dowland, sempre dolens,* seems to say it all. Yet as melancholy as much of Dowland's music certainly tends to be, it is also surpassingly eloquent and fabulously inventive—especially in its harmonic thinking, which in many cases seems centuries ahead of its time.

If obtaining Jakob Lindberg's four-CD set of the "complete" solo lute music—a designation that is certainly open to debate—might seem rather extravagant to all but the most interested parties, then the music is so lovely and the playing so accomplished that in time the album will more than repay the investment. For the unconvinced, an attractive highlights album (824 [CD]) is also available.

On two superb Harmonia Mundi albums (HMC 90244 [CD], HMC 90245 [CD]), countertenor Alfred Deller offers a pair of imaginative and highly enjoyable collections of Dowland's consort music.

Doyle, Patrick (1953–)

Henry V

City of Birmingham Symphony, Rattle. CDC 49919-2 [CD], 4DS 49919 [T].

The most astonishing thing about this utterly astonishing score is *not* how favorably it compares (and it compares *very* favorably indeed) with one of the greatest film scores of all time—the classic score that Sir William Walton supplied for Sir Laurence Olivier's 1944 screen version of Shakespeare's stirring *History*. What is most astonishing about Patrick Doyle's score for Kenneth Branagh's critically acclaimed *Henry V* is that it was the very first he ever composed. As subsequent scores from *Dead Again* to *Sense and Sensibility* have proven, Doyle is one of the most gifted practitioners of this difficult and demanding craft: in addition to a seemingly inexhaustible supply of memorable tunes, the music has character, personality, and an unfailing dramatic sense that has materially enhanced every film in which it has appeared. Many of the cues are already classics of their kind, from the intricate and resourceful *St. Crispin's Day—The Battle of Agincourt* to the ravishing, justly famous setting of *Non nobis, Domine*. The recording is further distinguished by a masterful performance by Sir Simon Rattle and the City of Birmingham Symphony.

No less memorable is Doyle's exuberant score for Branagh's second Shakespeare film, *Much Ado about Nothing,* with its soaring Overture and haunting setting of "Sigh No More, Ladies," available on Epic EK 54009 [CD], ET 54009 [T].

Dufay, Guillaume   (c. 1400–1474)

Missa, "Se la face ay pale" for four voices; "Se la face ay pale" (ballade) for three voices; *Gloria ad modum tube*

> Early Music Consort of London, Munrow. Virgin Classics CDM 61283 [CD].

Missa, "L'Homme armé"; Motet: *Supremum est mortalibus bonum*

> Oxford Camerata, Summerly. Naxos 8.553087 [CD].

Described by his near contemporary Loyset Compère as "the moon of all music and the light of all singers," Guillaume Dufay was the great master of the Burgundian school of polyphony, a prolific and influential composer whose *chansons,* motets, and masses are among the principal glories of fifteenth-century music.

The late David Munrow's stunning recording of the Mass "Se la face ay pale," and the *chanson* upon which it was based, was initially released to help commemorate the five-hundredth anniversary of the composer's death in 1974. This brilliant and troubled musician proves an ideal guide to this visionary music, not only in his infectiously enthusiastic direction of the Early Music Consort but also in his astonishing performance on the alto shawm. Virgin Classics cannot be commended too warmly for acquiring the rights to these classic recordings for their "David Munrow Edition" from the chronically deletions-happy EMI Classics. (They've performed a similar noble service for Sir Roger Norrington's recordings of the Beethoven symphonies with the London Classical Players.)

The performance by Jeremy Summerly and the Oxford Camerata of the Missa, "L'Homme armé"—this from a *chanson* that begins with the wise observation "The armed man should be feared"—is also exceptionally fine, with movements of the Mass alternating with suitably austere plainchant.

Dun, Tan   (1957–   )

Symphony 1997

Although he was speaking about weddings, Goethe said something that clearly applies here: "One should only celebrate a happy *ending;* celebrations at the outset exhaust the joy and energy needed to urge us forward and sustain us in the long struggle." And if he was correct in adding, "And of all celebrations a wedding is the worst; no day should be kept more quietly and humbly," then what is one to make of *celebrating* the fact that the world's most vibrant city was returned to the tender care of the people who brought us the Tiananmen Square Massacre? As far as it goes, Tan Dun's *Symphony 1997* is colorful and cleverly made and is further enhanced by memorable appearances by Yo-Yo Ma and twenty-four-hundred-year-old ceremonial bells. As one who loves Hong Kong passionately, I'm afraid can't listen to this admittedly skillful hackwork without an involuntary shudder, wondering what might actually be celebrated a few years from now.

Dukas, Paul (1865–1935)

The Sorcerer's Apprentice

New York Philharmonic, Bernstein. Sony Classical SMK 47596 [CD].

Don't let any of those slightly smug and self-important music lovers who are going through that inevitable, pseudo-sophisticated "Trashing the Warhorses" phase of their development fool you. In spite of the fact that *The Sorcerer's Apprentice*, in that otherwise turgid and self-conscious classic *Fantasia, did* serve as the backdrop for one of Mickey Mouse's greatest performances, it is still one of the most dazzlingly inventive tone poems in musical history.

Of the twenty of so versions of *L'Apprenti sorcier* that are currently available, the winner and still champ is Leonard Bernstein's early CBS recording. The conductor earns high marks for both wit and drama, and the performance also has a visual acuity that makes the playing extremely cinematic in the best possible sense of the word.

For those who might find the thirty-year-old recorded sound a trifle muddy—and it was not, even in its day, one of Columbia's more impressive sonic efforts—Mariss Jansons's EMI Classics recording with the Oslo Philharmonic (CDD-64291 [CD) is one of the most spectacular-sounding in years.

The best available version of Dukas's "other" work, the ballet *La Péri,* is the gleaming Chandos recording (CHAN 8852 [CD] by the Ulster Orchestra led by Yan Pascal Tortelier. During his tenure in Belfast, this gifted conductor somehow managed to transform a bunch of Irishmen into one of the world's most responsive French orchestras, with a wonderfully supple string tone and that characteristic Parisian tang in the double reeds. As in the classic Ansermet recording, Tortelier manages to give the famous *Fanfare* its magnificent due without letting it completely wag the rest of the dog. As a bonus, the album offers a *Sorcerer's Apprentice* that is second only to Jansons's, as well as superb modern versions of Chabrier's *España* and *Suite pastorale.*

If anything, the same forces are even more persuasive in Dukas's hugely underrated Symphony in C (CHAN 9225 [CD]), a superbly crafted, frequently inspired work that deserves to be far better known. The generous and usual filler is the *Polyeucte Overture,* a quarter-hour introduction to a play by Corneille that contains some of the loveliest music that Dukas would ever produce.

Duparc, Henri (1843–1933)

Songs

Te Kanawa, soprano; Orchestra of the Royal Opera House, Covent Garden, Pritchard. EMI Classics CDR 69802 [CD].

By any conceivable standard, Henri Duparc was a very peculiar man. The composer of no more than a dozen or so mature *mélodies,* on which his reputation as one of the great song composers continues to rest, Duparc (like Rossini before him) stopped composing in his late thirties and for the remaining half century of his long life did absolutely nothing of note. A lifelong hypochondriac who was also frequently and seriously ill, he once actually took a pilgrimage to Lourdes, hoping for a miraculous cure. He was also disarmingly honest: "It is frightful to be as neurotic as I certainly am," he wrote. "The least little thing finishes me." Before the nerve-wracking prospect of writing an opera based on Pushkin's *Russalka* finished his career for good, Duparc managed to produce a tiny group of art songs whose almost superhuman perfection would never be surpassed by any other French composer.

Rarely has Dame Kiri Te Kanawa used her lovely voice to more bewitching effect than in her EMI Classics recording of seven of the best-known songs, including *L'Invitation au voyage* on a sea-haunted text by Baudelaire and the exquisite *Chanson triste,* whose punning title makes reference to the composer's ardent reaction to his discovery of the music of Wagner. If the performances might not be the last word in a subtle penetration of the text, then their physical beauty is so seductive that after the first few sentences it hardly matters.

Duruflé, Maurice (1902–1986)

Requiem, Op. 9

**Bonney, soprano; Larmore, mezzo-soprano; Hampson, baritone;
Ambrosian Singers, Philharmonia Orchestra, Legrand. Teldec
90879 [CD].**

Like his teacher Paul Dukas, the talented French organist and composer
Maurice Duruflé seems destined to be remembered for a single work, the sweetly
beautiful *Requiem* composed in 1947. Consciously modeled on the *Requiem* of
Gabriel Fauré, Duruflé's masterpiece is similar in its structure, thematic content,
and its gently consoling message, although the similarities, on repeated hearings,
prove increasingly superficial. The Duruflé stands on its own as a sincerely felt,
quietly moving work with more real religious feeling than many Requiems three
times its age and twice its size.

The performance led by the French film composer Michel Legrand—he of
The Summer of '42 and *The Umbrellas of Cherbourg*—is the finest in years,
mixing subtlety and passion in a way that seems appropriately cinematic. He
certainly has the best team of soloists in living memory, with Jennifer Larmore's
contribution to the *Pie Jesu* especially moving. How fine the entire performance
really is may be gathered from the fact that alongside the excellent version of
the Fauré *Requiem* with which it is paired, the Duruflé in no way suffers in
comparison.

A fine budget-priced alternative is the recent Naxos recording (8.553196
[CD]) by the Ensemble Vocal Michel Piquemal and the Orchestre de la Cité.
Piquemal proves a natural and sensitive Duruflé conductor, while the marvelous
acoustics of the church of Saint-Antoine des Quinze-Vingts in Paris bathe everything in warm, late-afternoon glow. A second volume (8.553197 [CD]) offers the
gorgeous, shamefully neglected *Messe: Cum Jubilo,* plus two of the composer's
most significant organ works, the *Suite,* Op. 5, and the *Prélude, Adagio et Choral
varié sur le thème du Veni Creator,* splendidly played by Eric Lebrun.

Dussek, Jan Ladislav (1760–1812)

Piano Sonatas (3)

Marvin, piano. Dorian DIS 80110 [CD].

The Czech-born Jan Ladislav Dussek was not only the first of the great touring keyboard virtuosos but was also the first important pianist in musical history to perform at a ninety-degree angle to the audience. In his youth, Dussek was a singularly vain man, excessively proud of his heroic nose and handsome profile. Alas, he also has the melancholy distinction of being the only significant musician who ever *ate* himself out of a career: during his years of dissolute service as household music director for Talleyrand in Paris, he became so immense that his pudgy little fingers could no longer reach the keyboard.

In addition to being the first great champion of the Beethoven sonatas, Dussek composed over forty of his own, the best of them ranking with the finest of the entire late-Classical period. Decorous, melodically inspired, and brilliantly made, they also anticipate many of the harmonic innovations of composers from Schubert to Brahms; in short, Dussek's was an aristocratic voice touched by the early Romantic spirit, with a personality wholly and unmistakably its own.

Dorian has begun to reissue those superb recordings that Frederick Marvin originally made for Genesis in the mid- to late-'70s. The performances are both sophisticated and spontaneous-sounding, with a sense of discovery and eager anticipation in every bar. Compare Marvin's performance of the best known of the sonatas—the F Minor, known as "L'invocation"—with the superb Vox recording by the late Rudolf Firkušný (CDX 5058 [CD]). As fine as the great Czech pianist's version is, Marvin's is finer still. Not only does he play the notes with elegance and obvious affection, but he also brings them to life as no pianist on recordings ever has. Those who respond to the civilized and attractive works on Volume 1 should acquire Volume 2 (DID 80125 [CD]) without delay.

Dutilleux, Henri (1916–)

Symphonies (2)

BBC Philharmonic, Tortelier. Chandos CHAN 9194 [CD].

Over the years the French composer Henri Dutilleux has maintained a consistently lower profile than his far more celebrated near contemporary Olivier Messiaen. For one thing, Dutilleux has tended to work in more traditional forms, thus earning him the undeserved reputation of being an "academic" composer; for another, he tends to produce music that is utterly free of the sort of gimmickry—from catchy, politically correct subjects and titles to that tiresome Left Bank mysticism—that helped Messiaen to catch on. Although posterity will, of course, be the judge, I tend to suspect that when the smoke clears in the middle of the next century, Dutilleux will emerge as the far more significant voice.

One of the best ways to make the acquaintance of this highly individual composer is through the fascinating First Symphony, written in 1951 to portray the birth and death of a dream. In the composer's words, "The music emerges from the shadow in the first movement only to return whence it came in the very last ones. Thus there is established a transition between the real and imaginary world. It is a little like the inception and unfolding of a dream." The music is suitably fanciful and mysterious, with an astonishing range of orchestral color and texture and no mean emotional clout. If anything, the Second Symphony is even more arresting, with a physical sound that is almost impossibly refined.

Although the electrifying recording by Yan Pascal Tortelier and the BBC Philharmonic won a *Gramophone* engineering award, the performances are even more sensational, with playing so cultivated and fearless that this Manchester ensemble must now be counted among the finest in Europe.

Those who respond to the Symphonies should waste no time investigating the stunning *L'Arbre des songes*, one of the most beautiful of contemporary violin concertos, written in 1985 for Isaac Stern (Sony Classical MK-42449 [CD]), or the darkly poetic string quartet *Ainsi la nuit*, available on IMP Masters MCD 17 [CD].

Dvořák, Antonín (1841–1904)

Concerto in B Minor for Cello and Orchestra, Op. 104

Fournier, cello; Berlin Philharmonic, Szell. Deutsche Grammophon 429155-2 [CD].

Feuermann, cello; Berlin State Opera Orchestra, Taube. Enterprise ENT QT 99328 [CD].

Du Pré, cello; Chicago Symphony, Barenboim. Angel CDC 47614.

The events that led to the composition of this greatest of all cello concertos are movingly documented in Josef Skvorecky's magnificent 1987 novel *Dvořák in Love* (Knopf), probably the finest fictional treatment of the life of any composer. The concerto's second movement was written as an elegy for the composer's sister-in-law, the only woman with whom Dvořák was ever in love. In fact, embedded in this poignant outpouring of grief is a quotation from an early song that Dvořák wrote for Josephine Cermáková, a few years before he married her sister Anna.

For more than half a century, the Dvořák Cello Concerto has been brilliantly served in the recording studio, beginning in 1929 with what remains the most spellbinding realization of the solo part. In that classic recording by cellist Emanuel Feuermann, the recorded sound is fairly dismal even by the standards of the time, and the Berlin State Opera Orchestra under Michael Taube was barely equal to the task. Still, it is this recording, more than any other, that demonstrates so conclusively why Feuermann, and not Pablo Casals, was the great cellist of the twentieth century. The combination of bravado, patrician phrasing, and flawless technique that Feuermann brought to the Concerto has never been duplicated. Hearing it makes us realize anew what the world lost when Emanuel Feuermann died during a routine operation in 1942, a few months short of what would have been his fortieth birthday.

The modern recording that comes closest to approaching the brilliance and passion of Feuermann's is that pointedly dramatic interpretation by Pierre Fournier and George Szell, recorded in Berlin in the 1960s and now available on Deutsche Grammophon. Fournier plays the solo part with fire, subtlety, and conviction, and Szell, who led the Czech Philharmonic in Casals's famous recording from the 1930s, gives what is arguably his most intense and involving recorded performance. (Now, for a Feuermann-Szell recording in up-to-date sound, I would willingly trade my priceless baseball autographed by Mickey Mantle, 10 percent of my annual income, and my firstborn male child.)

The late Jacqueline du Pré's Angel recording with Daniel Barenboim and the Chicago Symphony is also very special. It is a red-blooded, slightly (but

always persuasively) wayward interpretation in which the playing may owe something to that of her teacher Mstislav Rostropovich but that fortunately lacks his tendency to vulgarity and self-indulgence. The cellist's husband, Daniel Barenboim, offers a sweepingly romantic yet sensitive accompaniment, and both the orchestra and recorded sound are absolutely first-rate.

Concerto in A Minor for Violin and Orchestra, Op. 53

Perlman, violin; London Philharmonic, Barenboim.
Angel CDC 47168 [CD].

Somewhere between that Mount Everest of Cello Concertos and the foothills of his likable but hopelessly minor Piano Concerto lies the concerto that Dvořák wrote for violin, a work that has never quite managed to challenge the popularity of the Bruch or Tchaikovsky Concertos, though, in terms of quality, it is easily the equal of either.

Written for Brahms's great friend, the Hungarian-born virtuoso Joseph Joachim, the piece cost its composer an unusual amount of time and anguish. The maniacally fastidious Joachim kept the score for nearly two years and finally returned it with so many suggestions for "improvements" that Dvořák all but rewrote the solo part. The result—which Joachim never got around to actually playing—is one of the most broadly rhapsodic of nineteenth-century violin concertos, a lush, yearning, quintessentially Romantic work rounded off by a spirited rondo-finale whose principal theme, once heard, is all but impossible to forget.

Despite some fine recent releases—especially the swashbuckling Deutsche Grammophon recording by Schlomo Mintz (419618-2 [CD])—Itzhak Perlman's Angel recording from the 1970s still comfortably dominates the field. The most striking thing in the Perlman interpretation is the ease with which he evokes the "Bohemian" elements in the score. The playing, in fact, is so idiomatic that one wonders if he might not have more than a few drops of Czech blood in his veins. Daniel Barenboim is an alert and able partner, and the remastered recorded sound more than holds its own with the best today.

In spite of its weaknesses, the Dvořák Piano Concerto has never gone begging for first-rate recordings, the most memorable of which features the late, great Rudolf Firkušný on RCA (09026-60781-2 [CD]). Recorded in Prague at the concert that marked his return to his homeland after an exile of nearly half a century, Firkušný's performance is not only full of warmth and character but is also remarkably vibrant and technically secure for a pianist who was approaching eighty at the time. As a historic document it is also undeniably moving, as touching in its way as the recordings of concerts that another Prodigal Son, the conductor Rafael Kubelik, gave at about the same time.

Hymn for Chorus and Orchestra, "The Heirs of the White Mountain"

Prague Philharmonic Choir, Czech Philharmonic Orchestra, Neumann.
Supraphon SUP 3281 [CD].

For the first ten years of his career as a composer, only his closest friends knew that Dvořák was writing music. He supported himself by teaching and playing the viola, a time he would later describe as being full of "hard study, occasional composing, much revision, a great deal of thinking, and very little eating." In 1872, he wrote a cantata for mixed chorus and orchestra on a patriotic poem by Vítězslav Hálek that expressed the undying love of the Czechs for their country. The work drew from the thirty-two-year-old composer a passionate musical expression he had never ventured before. First performed by the three-hundred-voice Prague Hlahol Choral Society on March 9, 1873, *The Heirs of the White Mountain (Dídicové bílé hory)* was a tremendous critical and popular success, the first of Dvořák's career. This unknown but exciting work is given a bracing, authoritative interpretation by Václav Neumann and his forces, a performance enhanced by the lush but detailed recorded sound.

On a fine Telarc recording (80287 [CD]) Robert Shaw and the Atlanta Symphony Chorus and Orchestra give a stirring performance of another Dvořák choral work of considerable historic significance. It was this piece that Dvořák used to introduce himself to America at a Carnegie Hall concert of October 21, 1892.

Overtures

Ulster Orchestra, Handley. Chandos CHAN 8453 [CD].

Czech Philharmonic, Ančerl. Supraphon 11 0605-2 [CD].

Although they usually turn up as filler in recordings of the symphonies, the three overtures that Dvořák composed in 1891 were conceived—and should be presented—as a single, indissoluble work with the general title *Nature, Life, and Love.* The "Life" section—the *Carnival* Overture—became an instant sensation and still overshadows the evocative *In Nature's Realm* and what is, by far, the greatest panel of the trilogy, the searing Shakespearean fantasy *Othello.*

While *Carnival* has had more brilliant and daring performances—those by Kubelik, Kertész, Szell, and Fritz Reiner are not easily forgotten—the excellent Ulster Orchestra under Vernon Handley brings more than enough moxie to that pops concert favorite and offers the strongest versions of *Othello* and *In Nature's Realm* currently in print. *In Nature's Realm* is the verdant nature tone poem that the composer intended, and *Othello* seems the stuff of genuine tragedy, without once flirting with melodrama or hysterics. The interpretation of the *Scherzo capriccioso* that fills out the album is also top drawer, as is the orchestral execution and recorded sound.

Considerably less well recorded are the classic interpretations from the 1960s by the Czech Philharmonic led by Karel Ančerl. In addition to the late trilogy, the CD also offers brilliantly idiomatic readings of the *Hussite* and *My Home* Overtures played as only this orchestra can. The quality of the music making and the reasonable price more than make up for the distant, slightly fuzzy recorded sound.

Piano Music

Firkušný , piano. Vox CDX 5058 [CD].

Dating from the early 1970s and available now as part of a two-CD set that also features rarely heard piano works by Smetana, Benda, Dussek, Tomásek, and Voříšek, Rudolf Firkušný's performances of some of the most important of Dvořák's solo piano music are the most distinguished yet recorded. In addition to the Mazurkas, Op. 56, and the Opus 101 Humoresques—his version of the famous one in G-flat is a model of disarming simplicity—the *Poetic Tone Pictures* are played with a tenderness and affection that are all but impossible to resist.

Among the other works featured on this treasurable recital is a most famous sonata by the great keyboard virtuoso of the late Classical period, Jan Ladislav Dussek. As Frederick Marvin's splendid cycle on a series of Genesis LPs clearly proved, Dussek's sonatas were second only to Beethoven's in terms of quality and depth. Firkušný's poised yet fiery performance of "L'invocation" will leave you anxious to hear more.

Quintet for Piano and Strings in A Major, Op. 81; Quartets (2) for Piano and Strings; *Bagatelles*

Firkušný, piano; Juilliard String Quartet. Sony Classical SBK 48170 [CD], SBT 48170 [T].

By any definition, these two dirt-cheap Odyssey CDs constitute an incredible bargain. Though not as well known, perhaps, as the "American" Quartet or the "Dumky" Trio, the A Major Piano Quintet is among the most attractive and accomplished of Dvořák's chamber works, which places it with the greatest chamber music of the Romantic era. The Piano Quartets are hardly less appealing, while the delectable *Bagatelles*, scored for the unusual combination of strings and harmonium, make a haunting physical sound unique in nineteenth-century music.

That dean of Czech pianists, Rudolf Firkušný, was obviously an ideal exponent of an idiom that had flowed through his veins since childhood. (As a very young boy, he played some of Janáček's music for the aging composer, who was mightily impressed.) The Juilliard String Quartet prove to be perfect accomplices in an enterprise that will steal your heart without leaving you broke.

*R*equiem, Op. 89

> **Soloists, Ambrosian Singers, London Symphony Orchestra, Kertész. London 448089-2 [CD].**

At the height of his European fame in 1884 Dvořák made his first trip to England, where, like Mendelssohn a generation earlier, he was treated as a conquering hero. From his first appearance in London in March of 1884, leading a performance of the *Stabat mater* at the Albert Hall, the English took Dvořák to their hearts, just as he took them to his. It was for the oratorio-mad English that Dvořák, would write some of his most ambitious scores: the cantata *The Spectre's Bride*, the epic oratorio *St. Ludmilla*, and the devout and haunting *Requiem*. If not quite the equal of the those by Verdi and Brahms, the Dvořák *Requiem* is one of the most moving such works of the late-Romantic era, especially in a performance as intensely involved and involving as this. István Kertész again reveals his natural affinity for Dvořák's music with an interpretation that disguises the *Requiem*'s weaker moments while emphasizing the stronger ones. The powerfully dramatic ebb and flow of Kertész's interpretation is captured in vintage London late-'60s sound; with magnificent versions of Kodály's *Hymn of Zrinyi* and *Psalmus Hungaricus* as the generous filler, this medium-priced two-CD set is a not-to-be-missed bargain.

*R*omantic Pieces for Violin and Piano, Op. 75; Sonata in F for Violin and Piano, Op. 57; Sonatine in G for Violin and Piano, Op. 100

> **G. Shaham, violin; O. Shaham, piano. Deutsche Grammophon 449820-2 [CD].**

By the fall of 1886, the interest in Dvořák's music had become so widespread that the composer was finding it difficult to keep up with the demand for new works. Still hoping to capitalize on the enormous success of the first set of *Slavonic Dances*, Dvořák's publisher Simrock kept urging him to orchestrate the second set. The composer had been procrastinating for months and bitterly complained that it would be "an accursed job"; once he actually began, his enthusiasm for the project returned and he could report with pride that "they sound like the devil."

Shortly after the completed Opus 72 collection was dispatched, the composer wrote to Simrock: "Just imagine: I am writing small 'bagatelles' for two violins and viola. I enjoy the work as much as when I write a big symphony—but what do you say to this? They are intended mainly for amateurs, but didn't BEETHOVEN and SCHUMANN express themselves with quite modest means?"

The amateur musicians for whom Dvořák wrote the delightful *Terzetto*, Opus 74, was his mother-in-law's lodger, a chemistry student named Josef Kruis, and Kruis's violin teacher, Jan Pelikán. When the music proved beyond Kruis's abilities, Dvořák wrote a simpler work that all three of them could play, quickly arranging his new terzetto into the *Four Romantic Pieces* for Violin and Piano, Opus 75. As simple in structure as they are direct in expression, the *Four Pieces* have much of the color and romance of the *Slavonic Dances,* from the rich passion of the opening *Allegro moderato* through the quiet poetry of the concluding *Larghetto.*

Gil Shaham and his sister Orli prove ideal advocates of this enchanting music and are equally persuasive in the more challenging Sonata and Sonatine. A lifetime of mutual love and understanding shines through all of the performances, given warm and brightly lit recordings by the DG engineers.

*R*usalka

> Beňačková, Soukupová, Ochman, Novák, Prague Philharmonic
> Chorus, Czech Philharmonic Orchestra, Neumann. Supraphon 10
> 3641 [CD].

On his return home after his protracted stay in America, where he was both deeply homesick and phenomenally productive, Dvořák entered what would prove to be the most nationalistic phase of his career. In the last years of his life, he devoted himself entirely to symphonic poems and operas based on Czech folk stories: from that series of orchestral ballads based on poems by Karel Jaromir Erben (see page 230), to that fairy-tale opera in which a water sprite confesses to the moon that she has fallen in love with a prince and now wishes to become human.

The last but one, and by far the most successful, of Dvořák's thirteen operas, *Rusalka* received its first performance in March of 1901, five months before the composer would celebrate his sixtieth birthday. Although, like all of Dvořák's operas, it has had some difficulty holding the stage over the years—I once saw a wonderful performance at the National Theater in Prague that, in spite of the brilliant production and glorious singing, seemed about a half-hour too long—*Rusalka*'s dramatic shortcomings are barely noticeable in this spellbinding recording that features the reigning Czech diva of our time and the incomparable Czech Philharmonic in the pit. Gabriela Beňačková's performance of the molten "Mesicku na nebi hlubokem"—the love theme from *Driving Miss*

Daisy—is ravishing, as is the work of the orchestra throughout. All in all, this is a performance that finally begins to suggest the greatness of one of Dvořák's most beautiful scores.

Serenade for Strings in E Major, Op. 22; Serenade in D Minor, Op. 44

Academy of St. Martin-in-the-Fields, Marriner. Philips 400020-2 [CD].

There has never been a day so wretched, a problem so insoluble, a night so long, a winter so bleak, a toothache so painful, that one or the other of these enchanting works couldn't cure. On those days when I walk in the door exhausted, disgruntled, disillusioned, full of contempt for all things human, and beating down an insane desire to kick the cat, I put on one of the Dvořák Serenades, make for the nearest chair, and within a few minutes a dippy grin—the external manifestation of a mood of avuncular forgiveness and beatific peace—invariably steals over my face. If only this inexhaustibly charming music were a little better known, many of the nation's psychiatrists would have to start looking for honest work.

Sir Neville Marriner's glowing Philips recording contains the most radiant performances of both Serenades on the market today. The string tone in the Op. 22 is the aural equivalent of a morning in early June, while the wind playing in the Op. 44 is a marvel of individuality and character. (The thin, nasal twang of English oboes has never been one of my favorite sounds; here, I hardly notice.)

Slavonic Dances, Op. 46 and Op. 72

Cleveland Orchestra, Szell. Sony Classical SBK 48161 [CD], SBT 48161 [T].

Royal Philharmonic, Dorati. London 430735-2 [CD].

Matthies, Köhn, piano. Naxos 8.553138 [CD].

Once, during the interval of a Cleveland Orchestra rehearsal at Severance Hall, a member of the orchestra greeted a visiting friend by saying, after carefully looking over his shoulder to see who might be listening, "Welcome to the American home of Bohemian Culture." And throughout his tenure with the orchestra, George Szell was an enthusiastic champion of the music of Dvořák, Smetana, and that Moravian giant, Leoš Janáček. Although born in Budapest, Szell had considerable Czech blood in his veins; he studied in Prague and early in his conducting career was a familiar fixture in the Bohemian capital.

Szell's recordings of Dvořák's most popular works, the *Slavonic Dances,* are the only ones that bear favorable comparison with Václav Talich's unsurpassable versions from the late 1940s, available now on Supraphon SUP 111897 [CD]. (Talich's pioneering recording from 1935, whose sound probably makes it a "collectors only" item, has surfaced on Music and Arts CD 658-1 [CD]). The playing of the Cleveland Orchestra is a wonder of brilliance and flexibility, and the conductor, while demanding the last word in virtuoso execution, never overlooks the music's wealth of subtle color and irrepressible charm.

From a somewhat less dizzying height, Antal Dorati's London recording is also very satisfying, especially if nearly flawless recorded sound is an absolute must. On the other hand, Dorati's recording of the ingratiating *Czech Suite* is the finest currently available (London 443015-2 [CD]), particularly since it comes with the delicious *Prague Waltzes* and Dvořák's hypnotic Wagnerian experiment, the *Nocturne for Strings.* Dorati's recording of the *American Suite*—a made-to-order curiosity that nonetheless has its moments of charm—is also excellent (430702-2 [CD]), coupled with Kiril Kondrashin's expansive Vienna Philharmonic recording of the *New World Symphony.*

In the original version for piano, four hands, the team of Silke-Thora Matthies and Christian Köhn, are poised and entertaining in their excellent Naxos recording. If not quite as charming as the Kontarsky brothers on their long-deleted Deutsche Grammophon recording, then the young pianists still have a fine instinctive grasp of Czech dance rhythms and a genuine talent for communicating their enthusiasm for the music. The sound is as warm and transparent as the performances themselves.

Songs

Beňačková, soprano; Firkušný, piano. RCA 09025-60823-2 [CD].

For a composer with such an effortless gift of melody, it's rather surprising that song should have accounted for such a relatively unimportant part of Dvořák's total output. Although written at virtually every stage of his career—from a small 1865 collection of four items published as his Opus 2 through the *Biblical Songs* of 1895—the songs tend to be charming rather than significant: poetic, delightful, and decidedly minor works.

In their generous and well-chosen collection, interspersed with songs by Janáček and Martinů, Gabriela Beňačková and Rudolf Firkušný offer one of the finest recitals of Dvořák songs ever recorded. Whether expressing the aching sorrow of the darker *Biblical Songs* or the robust joys of the *Gypsy Songs,* these two great artists seem ideally suited to both the material and each other.

*S*tabat Mater; *Biblical Songs*

Soloists, Westminster Symphonic Choir, New Jersey Symphony, Macal. Delos DE 3161 [CD].

Few works have ever represented a more personal outpouring of grief than Dvořák's setting of the *Stabat mater,* the Latin poem of the thirteenth-century Franciscan Jacopone da Todi that presents a vision of Mary's contemplation of the crucifixion of her Son. Dvořák began to sketch the work following the death of his infant daughter in the fall of 1875 but put it aside for other projects until the following year when his second daughter, during an unguarded moment, drank a bottle of phosphorus solution used for making matches. Barely a month later, his three-and-a-half-year-old son Ottokar contracted smallpox and died on his father's birthday. Having thus buried all three of his children within the space of two years, Dvořák returned to the abandoned *Stabat mater* sketch and in a single cathartic outburst of activity completed the full score in less than six weeks.

The recent Delos recording is one of the most poignant this great work has yet received. In addition to being a wholly idiomatic interpretation of genuine stature, it further benefits from the intensity of a live performance and Delos's typically flawless recorded sound. The *Biblical Songs* are also done quite beautifully, and at what amounts to two CDs for the price of one, this is a major bargain.

*S*tring Quartet in F Major, Op. 96, "American"

Smetana Quartet. Testament SBT 1074 [CD].

Written during a few days of the summer vacation that the composer spent in the amiable, hard-drinking Czech colony of Spillville, Iowa, where he also completed the "New World" Symphony, Dvořák's "American" Quartet is only the most famous and colorful of those fourteen works that, taken together, constitute the most important contribution a nineteenth-century composer would make to the form after the death of Franz Schubert. Like the "New World" Symphony, the "American" Quartet was inspired by Dvořák's passionate love affair with the sights and sounds of America, although like the Symphony it does not contain, as has been so frequently suggested, a *single* American folk tune. (The subtitle, incidentally, was not the composer's but instead the idea of a discreet publisher who sought to correct the brazen stupidity of an unforgivably insensitive time. Shamefully, on the original title page, the F Major Quartet was called "The Nigger.")

Dating from 1961, the recording by the Smetana Quartet remains quite special. Few ensembles of the time—and even fewer since—could match the range and subtlety of their tonal production or the sheer perfection of their technique.

From the incomparable richness of the first movement's opening viola solo through the magical bounce of the finale, this is among the most finished and resourceful of all Dvořák recordings. Paired in the Testament reissue with a version of the Piano Quintet in A Major, in which Pavel Stepán proves the equal of either Firkušný or Sir Clifford Curzon plus that unapproachable version of Janácek's *Kreutzer Sonata,* this is a must for all chamber music lovers.

The Prague String Quartet is warmly appealing in their Deutsche Grammophon recording, available only as part of their sumptuous nine-CD cycle of the complete string quartets (429193-2 [CD]). The music making throughout is of the highest possible caliber, with playing that is both superbly idiomatic and technically unimpeachable. Few recorded performances are more consistently satisfying or give more genuine pleasure, especially in what can often seem the long-winded early quartets and in the enchanting *Cypresses,* arranged from some of the composer's youthful songs. The recorded sound is as welcoming as the performances themselves.

String Quartet No. 10 in E-flat, Op. 51; Quartet No. 12 in F Major, Op. 96, "American"; Quartet No. 13 in G Major, Op. 106; Quartet No. 14 in A-flat Major, Op. 105

> Panocha String Quartet. Supraphon 11 0581-2 [CD] (Nos. 10 and 12);
> Supraphon 11 1459-2 [CD] (Nos. 13 and 14).

If they stay together and stay healthy—to use an indispensable sportscaster's cliché—then the young Panocha String Quartet should become one of the dominant chamber ensembles of the next quarter century. On the basis of the recordings they have so far made, and some firsthand experience hearing them on their last American tour, I am convinced they are already one of the finest quartets around.

Paradoxically for a quartet, their principal strength—aside from a highly evolved musicality and very sophisticated technique—is their unwillingness to forget their own individual identities for the sake of that mushy, pasteurized uniformity that so many groups seem obsessed with these days. If they have a counterpart among the older outfits, it is the Borodin Quartet: another collection of rugged individualists who are not only instantly recognizable *as* individuals but who also add up to an even more appealing whole.

There are no better versions of these late Dvořák quartets currently available. The performances are understandably fresh and youthful but are also—to coin a phrase—"mature beyond their years." Only the Talich Quartet digs into this music with such abandon, authority, and finesse.

If this is the beginning of a cycle of *all* the Dvořák quartets, be prepared to drop some serious cash. You won't regret it.

Symphonic Poems (complete)

Scottish National Orchestra, Järvi. Chandos CHAN 8798/99 [CD].

Although they are not as consistently inspired as his symphonies and overtures, Dvořák's symphonic poems are mature, colorful settings of some of the wonderfully gruesome folk ballads collected by K. J. Erben: stories rife with murder, betrayal, dismemberment, and assorted mayhem—something for the whole family.

While not quite as magical as the recently withdrawn Kubelik set or the legendary recordings that Václav Talich made in the early 1950s, the performances by the Scottish National Orchestra under Neeme Järvi are nonetheless very fine. Like Kubelik, Järvi is a natural and arresting storyteller who leads the listener through the gory plots so graphically that one need not necessarily know what's going on to enjoy them. (People with sensitive stomachs would probably not *want* to know.) As always, the Scottish National Orchestra under Järvi sounds like one of the best in Europe and, as always, the Chandos recording is ideal.

Symphonies (9)

Scottish National Orchestra, Järvi. Chandos CHAN 9008 [CD].

Fifty or even twenty-five years ago it would have been nearly impossible to convince the average music lover that there were really nine, as opposed to only *three,* Dvořák symphonies. Ironically enough, the composer himself became the principal culprit in the misunderstanding, since he considered the F Major Symphony of 1874 his first mature work in the form and preferred to forget the rest. (He quite literally forgot a couple of the early works, neither of which would be performed during his lifetime.)

These days, perhaps there as many as five Dvořák symphonies that have wormed their way into the general awareness: in addition to the final three, the D Major (No. 6) has begun showing up in concerts with increasing frequency, as has the exuberant, rowdy F Major (No. 5), which finally seems to be shaking off the dust of more than a century of neglect.

The unique value of any complete recording of the Dvořák Symphonies is the extent to which it demonstrates that the early pieces were not merely apprentice works or dry runs for what was to follow but important, attractive, often inspired stages in the evolution of a great Romantic symphonist. The Second, Third, and Fourth Symphonies contain a wealth—sometimes an almost *embarrassing* wealth—of ingenious melodic ideas, and even the gabby, frequently clumsy "Bells of Zlonice" often seems the creation of a sleeping giant who is just on the verge of waking up.

Neeme Järvi's Chandos cycle has several attractive qualities, not the least of which are the sumptuous digital sound and the bargain price (six CDs for the price of four). While none of the performances may be the preferred versions, the set as a whole has considerable individuality and character, with excellent orchestral execution and a definite point of view. Moreover, for those wanting the convenience of a boxed set, this is currently the only choice. If and when any of the wonderful cycles by Kubelik, Kertész, or Rowicki are reissued, the situation will change dramatically.

Symphony No. 1 in C Minor, "The Bells of Zlonice"; *Legends,* Op. 59, Nos. 1–5

Symphony No. 2 in B-flat, Op. 4; *Legends,* Op. 59, Nos. 6–10

Slovak Philharmonic, Czechoslovak Radio Symphony, Gunzenhauser. Naxos 8.550266 [CD] (No. 1); 8.550267 [CD] (No. 2).

Here, for less than you'd pay for a single full-priced CD, are vibrant, thoroughly idiomatic readings of the first two Dvořák symphonies, both written when the struggling composer was earning a tenuous living playing the viola in Smetana's Provisional Theater Orchestra. The young American conductor Stephen Gunzenhauser leads the most satisfyingly cogent interpretation of the sprawling "Bells of Zlonice" since Kubelik's, while his relaxed and easy-going approach to its B-flat Major companion piece makes this usually problematic work all but irresistible. As an unusually attractive bonus, the recordings come with the complete Opus 59 *Legends,* enchanting miniatures that are very nearly as appealing as the composer's *Slavonic Dances.*

Gunzenhauser's recordings of the Third (8.550268 [CD]) and Fourth (8.550269 [CD]) Symphonies are similarly commendable, although he faces formidable competition (see pages 232–233) in the Sixth and Eighth (the works with which they are coupled). Nonetheless, the performances of the early works are so refreshingly natural that, at Naxos prices, the albums are still a steal.

Symphony No. 5 in F, Op. 76; *Othello Overture,* Op. 93; *Scherzo Capriccioso,* Op. 66

Oslo Philharmonic, Jansons. EMI Classics CDC 49995 [CD].

With its inspired writing for the flute and clarinet and echoes of the *Forest Murmurs* from Wagner's *Ring,* the woodsy F Major was once regarded as Dvořák's answer to Beethoven's "Pastoral" Symphony. A key work in its late-blooming composer's early maturity and his first fully confident work in the form, the Symphony was one of a flood of works that followed his winning of the Austrian State Stipendium in 1874. The gorgeous slow movement and rollicking Scherzo rank with Dvořák's finest achievements as a symphonist, and as the outer movements are also strong and original, its failure to enter the standard repertoire remains a perplexing mystery.

With his celebrated Chandos set of the Tchaikovsky symphonies (see pages 734–735), this glorious EMI recording is one of the finest Mariss Jansons has made to date. The interpretation unfolds with a glowing warmth and unforced exuberance that not even the fine recordings of Kertész and Kubelik can match. With performances of the *Othello Overture* and *Scherzo capriccioso* that are hardly less extraordinary, the album clearly flirts with the Desert Island category.

Symphony No. 6 in D Major, Op. 60; *The Wood Dove,* Op. 110

Czech Philharmonic, Bělohlávek. Chandos CHAN 9170 [CD].

Jírí Bělohlávek has the melancholy distinction of being not only the first man to have been dismissed as principal conductor of the Czech Philharmonic but also the first to make way for a non-native replacement: the German Gerd Albrecht, who has since (to the relief of most observers) resigned. Whatever personal or political difficulties Bělohlávek may have had with the orchestra—like the Berlin Philharmonic, they elect their own conductor—the problem could *not* have been his musical abilities, if his many brilliant recordings are any indication.

His recording of Dvořák's Sixth Symphony is one of the most rewarding since Václav Talich's pioneering version from the 1930s. While the interpretation fully acknowledges this sunny work's structural debt to the D Major Symphony of Dvořák's idol, Johannes Brahms, it also pays homage to its intensely Czech melodic and rhythmic language in the most perfectly natural way. *The Wood Dove* is equally memorable and the recorded sound is suitably rich and clear.

Symphony No. 7 in D Minor, Op. 70; Symphony No. 8 in G Major, Op. 88; Symphony No. 9 in E Minor, Op. 95, "From the New World"

Cleveland Orchestra, Dohnányi. London 452181-2 [CD].

Czech Philharmonic, Talich. Koch Historic KIC 7007 [CD] (No. 7); Supraphon SUP 11 1898 [CD] (No. 8); Supraphon SUP 111899 [CD] (No. 9).

Unlike his recording of the Dvořák Seventh—which, admittedly, has been enthusiastically, even ecstatically praised elsewhere—it was this recording of the Eighth, more than any other, that confirmed the Cleveland's reemergence as one of the world's great orchestras. Although during Lorin Maazel's unsettled and unsettling tenure as the orchestra's music director, standards were never allowed to slip, the orchestra nevertheless played as though their hearts weren't quite in it. At the very least, the old Szell electricity was clearly gone.

Their splendid recording of the most amiable and openhearted of Dvořák's mature symphonies proves, triumphantly, that the Cleveland Orchestra's spirit, under Christoph von Dohnányi, has been thoroughly revived. Not since Szell has the orchestra given another conductor such awesome precision. But the healthiest indication that Dohnányi's was not to be a caretaker regime can be heard in the work of the middle and lower strings, who play with an even darker, more sensual quality than they did under Szell. The interpretation itself reminds me more than anything of Bruno Walter's immensely rewarding CBS recording, though one in which the Walter charm is matched by a Szell-like bite and point. For instance, in the rousing coda of the final movement, Dohnányi makes a point that many conductors seem to miss: namely, that this three minutes of unbridled enthusiasm is nothing more than a thinly veiled *Slavonic Dance*.

On the other hand, if recorded sound is not an issue, then the Talich recording will probably remain without equal in both this world and the next. Listen to only two minutes of the third movement and the ineffably sorrowful yet impish thing that he makes of it, and you'll understand why Talich has always been regarded as the greatest Dvořák conductor of all time.

The same qualities that characterize both conductors' recordings of the Eighth Symphony can be heard in their very different versions of the "New World." Dohnányi, in the best modern tradition, is completely unforced and natural, with rhythms that nonetheless have plenty of snap and execution that is hair-raising in its perfection. Talich allows himself far more rhythmic liberties and the result is an approach to phrasing that at times seems to mirror the inflections of speech. It is one of the most deeply communicative versions of the "New World" ever recorded and something perilously close to representing Talich at the zenith of his art.

Trios for Piano, Violin, and Cello (4)

Solomon Trio. IMP 6600247 [CD].

While the "Dumky" is undoubtedly Dvořák's best-known work in the form, the strangely neglected Trio in F Minor, Op. 65, is a masterpiece, one of the most concise and dramatic of all the composer's mature chamber works. The early B-flat Major and G Minor trios are also extremely rewarding works whose chronic absence from concert programs is equally puzzling. Made up of three vastly experienced English musicians (pianist Daniel Adni, violinist Rodney Friend, and cellist Raphael Sommer), the Solomon Trio offers a series of unaffected, spontaneous-sounding interpretations whose most telling characteristic is the evident joy in the music making. While the lightly sprung dance movements are especially engaging, little of the warmth or vitality of these wonderful works is lost on these canny musicians. The recorded sound is ideal.

Trio No. 4 in E Minor, Op. 90, "Dumky"

Borodin Trio. Chandos CHAN 8445 [CD].

The liner notes that tell you that a *dumka*—of which *dumky* is the plural—is a kind of Czech dance (and I've never read a liner note that didn't) haven't got it quite right. A *dumka* isn't a dance at all, and the word isn't Czech but Russian. It means—literally—a "passing through," as in "this vale of tears," which Dvořák understood as meaning something essentially *sad*. (He may have associated it in his mind with an ancient form of song or poem that brooded—as lugubriously as possible—on the heroic deeds of a long-vanished past. This particular kind of brooding has always been a key element in the Czech national character: witness the ruminations of that Moravian neurologist Siegmund Freud or the jovial fictions of Prague's foremost novelist, Franz Kafka.) As a matter of fact, Dvořák was never really certain *what* the word meant, but that's beside the point. What is important is that he was in the mood to write something *excessively* melancholy and the "Dumky" Trio became just that.

Coupled with Smetana's equally disturbing Piano Trio in G Minor, a work written in response to the death of the composer's eldest daughter, this Borodin Trio recording is probably not the sort of thing you'd want to give to someone with even the mildest suicidal tendencies. Yet for deeply felt forays into two of the darker corners of Romantic chamber music, it possesses a rare and sinister beauty that no other recording of either piece ever has. In the "Dumky," they come to terms with the frequent mood swings of the piece with the sensitivity of three adept psychiatrists, while their performance of the Smetana unfolds as a long, unbroken cry of grief.

While the playing may be "too intense for younger audiences," for the more experienced, it should prove uncommonly rewarding.

Dyson, Sir George (1883–1964)

Concerto da camera for String Orchestra; Concerto da chiesa for String Orchestra; Concerto leggiero for Piano and Orchestra

> Parkin, piano; City of London Sinfonia, Hickox. Chandos CHAN 9076 [CD].

Sir George Dyson was always something of an outsider, one of the few composers of his generation whose work remained virtually untouched by the English folk song movement. Best known for his sacred music and *The Canterbury Pilgrims,* a cantata based on a modern translation of extracts from Chaucer's classic work, Dyson was also the composer of some powerfully individual instrumental music, as this revelatory Chandos album proves. In addition to the engaging *Concerto Leggiero* for piano and orchestra, in which Erik Parkin performs with his usual effortless panache, the *Concerto da camera* and *Concerto da chiesa* are clearly works to be mentioned in the same breath with Elgar's *Introduction and Allegro* and Vaughan Williams's *Tallis Fantasia.* Lovers of modern English music owe Richard Hickox their gratitude for unearthing yet another series of neglected masterworks. The performances by the City of London Sinfonia could not have been more alert or sympathetic and the recorded sound is impeccable.

Overture at the Tabard Inn; The Canterbury Pilgrims

> Soloists, London Symphony Chorus and Orchestra, Hickox. Chandos CHAN 9531 [CD].

Geoffrey Chaucer has probably inspired less important music than any other major English poet; largely, one suspects, because of the language barrier. Middle English is a tough nut to crack for readers as well as composers, although the late Lester Trimble did so magnificently in his *Four Fragments from the*

Canterbury Tales. In 1931, Sir George Dyson wisely opted for a standard modern translation and the result is one of modern English music's most instantly lovable works. While still popular at British choral festivals, *The Canterbury Pilgrims* is a virtually unknown commodity throughout the rest of the world; Chandos therefore deserves even more gratitude than usual for bringing such a richly rewarding work to light. In addition to the imaginative orchestral writing and vivid evocation of individual pilgrims—and Yvonne Kinney, Robert Tear, and Stephen Roberts all sing with a real sense of discovery and fun—*The Canterbury Pilgrims* features a series of wonderful choruses steeped in the grand English oratorio tradition. It's impossible to imagine anyone coaxing more color, drama, and wonderment from the score than Richard Hickox, who here delivers one of his most inspired recorded performances. *In Honor of the City,* the spirited setting of the poem by William Dunbar that in 1928 helped establish Dyson's reputation, is given a similarly engrossing performance, while the Chandos recorded sound and documentation are close to ideal.

Elgar, Sir Edward   (1857–1934)

The Black Knight; From the Bavarian Highlands

> **London Symphony Chorus and Orchestra, Hickox. Chandos CHAN 9436 [CD].**

Although both of these early works have been recorded before—*The Black Knight,* memorably, by the late Sir Charles Groves—these are the performances that persuade us of their importance beyond the tantalizing hints they offer of the composer who would soon write the *Enigma Variations.* Elgar's first big choral work, *The Black Knight,* was written shortly after the decisive event in the composer's life: his marriage to Caroline Alice Roberts, the extraordinary woman who not only fulfilled his every need but also made it possible for him to become a great composer. Like the music that Schumann wrote shortly after *his* marriage, *The Black Knight* is bursting with big tunes and a barely containable enthusiasm, this in spite of the rather gruesome story (adapted from Longfellow) that makes it a Victorian cousin of Mahler's *Das klagende Lied.* The enchanting *From the Bavarian Highlands* was also inspired by Alice Elgar, who provided her husband with a series of verse souvenirs of their Bavarian summer holidays of 1893 and 1894.

Richard Hickox—and certainly there should be a "Sir" in his near future—conducts with his customary vigor and affection, while the Chandos engineers bathe it all in their very best late-summer sound.

The same team is very impressive in *The Light of Life* (CHAN 9208 [CD]), Elgar's last major warm-up for *The Dream of Gerontius*. Along with a shimmering version of the famous "Meditation," Hickox extracts the usual impeccable singing from the London Symphony Chorus and the recorded sound is ideal.

Concerto in E Minor for Cello and Orchestra, Op. 65; *Sea Pictures*

Du Pré, cello; Baker, mezzo-soprano; London Symphony, Barbirolli. EMI Classics CDC 56219 [CD].

Anyone who has ever been sprung from an institution of higher learning has understandable feelings of affection and gratitude to Sir Edward Elgar for his best-known work. It is usually to the stirring strains of the *Pomp and Circumstance March* No. 1 in D Major, also known in England as "Land of Hope and Glory," that most high school and college inmates make their final, glorious escape. While the average music lover still persists in thinking of him as little more than the stuffy, official musical voice of Edwardian England, Sir Edward Elgar was one of the last of the incontestably great Romantic composers. Finding one's way into Elgar's rich and occasionally overripe world certainly isn't easy. I should know. For only after years of my mulish resistance did Elgar finally became one of my greatest musical passions.

I can think of no better way of introducing Elgar to People Who Don't Think They Like Elgar than this hauntingly beautiful EMI Classics recording of two of the composer's loveliest and most important works. The Cello Concerto, the only work in the literature that can be compared with Dvořák's, has never been better served than by the young Jacqueline du Pré, who made this ardent, rhapsodic recording at the beginning of her fame in 1965. Sir John Barbirolli, that most impassioned of Elgarians, captures both the aching melancholy and the searing tragedy of this great work more thoroughly than any conductor ever has. In the ravishing orchestral song cycle *Sea Pictures* he lays down a thrillingly sumptuous carpet of sound for the wonderful Janet Baker, who here gives one of the finest performances of her long and memorable career.

Concerto in B Minor for Violin and Orchestra

Kennedy, violin; London Philharmonic, Handley. EMI Classics CDM 63795 [CD].

Like the symphonies of Anton Bruckner, this longest and, many would say, *noblest* of all violin concertos has one minor flaw: In spite of its incomparably majestic length, it is still *much* too short. Originally composed for the Viennese violinist Fritz Kreisler, the Concerto dates from one of the most fertile periods of

Elgar's creative life. Written during the waning years of the Edwardian era—a period that also saw the composition of the composer's two symphonies—the Violin Concerto was one of several key works in which Elgar tried to confine his flood of melodic invention and naturally expansive temperament within the limits of more rigid musical forms.

Apart from the sheer enormity of the work—and in most performances, the Concerto requires nearly fifty minutes to play—it presents other challenging interpretive problems, chief among which is an immense (and immensely original) accompanied cadenza in the final movement. In his 1932 recording with the sixteen-year-old Yehudi Menuhin, the composer demonstrated that the Concerto's difficulties are trivial when compared to its enormous rewards, and fortunately, after years of neglect, a new generation of violinists is beginning to agree.

The modern performance that most closely approximates the depth and authority of Sir Edward's classic interpretation can be found on an EMI Classics CD by the English violinist Nigel Kennedy, recorded several years before that gifted young musician went all weird. With a purity of tone and toothsome sweetness of spirit, Kennedy surmounts the Concerto's formidable problems in much the same way that young Menuhin had before him: by tossing them off as though they were, quite literally, child's play. Yet the real star of the show is the conductor, Vernon Handley, whose ability to highlight a wealth of striking local detail without ever losing sight of the work's overall sweep and architecture only confirms his reputation as one of the preeminent Elgarians of our time.

The Dream of Gerontius (oratorio), Op. 38

Palmer, Davies, Howell, London Symphony Chorus and Orchestra, Hickox. Chandos CHAN 8641/42 [CD], DBTD-2014 [T].

When Elgar wrote "This is the best of me" in the score of his setting of Cardinal Newman's mystical poem, he might also have written "This is not only the best work written by an English composer in three centuries, but also the greatest oratorio written since the days of Handel."

To date, *The Dream of Gerontius* has had three unassailably great recordings: an impassioned account led by Sir John Barbirolli that was available briefly on CD and then maddeningly withdrawn, the heroic version by Sir Adrian Boult that is now available in England on a pair of EMI Classics CDs (47208-8), and a fascinating interpretation by Benjamin Britten in which one great English composer pays homage to another; this one, in the last couple of years, also flitted in and out of the catalogue on a pair of London CDs.

The modern interpretation that comes closest to approaching them in stature is the recent Hickox recording for Chandos. Although his trio of soloists is not quite as memorable as some from the past—Sir Peter Pears's vulnerable and deeply human Gerontius in the Britten recording was unforgettable, while Dame Janet Baker's performance as the Angel in the Barbirolli set is as close as we'll ever come to hearing it done by the real thing—Hickox has the undeniable advantage of a spectacular modern recording that makes the big moments like "Go in the Name of Angels and Archangels" irresistibly thrilling. The performance also has enormous warmth and depth, with perhaps the finest choral contribution of any *Gerontius* yet.

The other panels of Elgar's sacred triptych, *The Apostles* and *The Kingdom*, are currently available in the best recorded performances they have ever received, also led by Hickox. In marked contrast to the Boult recordings, which took their own sweet (albeit noble) time in allowing these "sublime bores" to make their points, the Chandos recordings invest the music with passion, urgency, and, above all, dramatic life. *The Apostles* (CHAN 8875/76 [CD]) smolders with a sacred fervor that recalls the Verdi *Requiem*, while *The Kingdom* (CHAN 8788 [CD]) perfectly captures the mood of rapt piety mixed with opulent late-Victorian decadence.

In the most recent recording in his Elgar series, Hickox leads a stirring account of the closest thing we have to an Elgar opera, the dramatic cantata *Caractacus* (CHAN 9156 [CD]). Although nearly hamstrung by its impossible libretto, Elgar rose to the occasion with wonderful set pieces like the "Sword Song" and "Triumphal March" (in truth, a triumphal chorus), as well as some of his most inspired orchestration. Hickox and his forces respond triumphantly, as do the Chandos engineers. The marvelous *Severn Suite* in its version for full orchestra is the extremely attractive bonus.

*E*nigma Variations, Op. 36; *Falstaff* (symphonic study), Op. 68

**City of Birmingham Symphony, Rattle. EMI Classics
CDC 55001 [CD].**

With the passing of Sir John Barbirolli and Sir Adrian Boult, many admirers of Elgar's music feared that it would suffer the same fate that Frederick Delius's did following the death of Sir Thomas Beecham. Of course, there was never any serious danger of that: unlike the rarefied, specialized genius of his younger contemporary, Elgar was always the far more important and universal composer. Alas, while no major Delius conductor has emerged to take the place of the inimitable baronet, the Elgar tradition continues to grow and flourish in the hands of a brilliant new guard of sympathetic advocates, whose brightest lights are now clearly André Previn, Vernon Handley, Richard Hickox, and Sir Simon Rattle.

Rattle's electrifying version of the *Enigma Variations* is the most distinguished since Barbirolli's and may in fact be the finer performance: an interpretation that mixes flashing brilliance, yearning sentiment, and transcendent nobility in a very heady amalgam. As in Previn's fine Philips recording, each of these inspired and inventive portraits of the composer's friends—including his own self-portrait, the majestic "E. D. U." that concludes the work—emerges in vivid relief, while the episodic quality that sabotages so many performances is nowhere to be found.

Perhaps even more exciting is the performance of the sadly neglected *Falstaff,* which Rattle places firmly among the composer's most inspired creations. As in the *Enigma Variations,* there is both resourcefulness and spontaneity in the interpretation, coupled with a compelling dramatic urgency. The orchestral execution is again a model of brilliance and finesse, while the recorded sound is as refined as the playing.

Froissart Overture, Op. 19; *In the South* (concert overture), Op. 50; *Coronation March,* Op. 65; *Light of Life: Meditation*

Royal Philharmonic, Butt. ASV ASV 619 [CD].

Say what you will about the great French chronicler Jean Froissart, whose *Chronicles of England, France, and Spain* contain some of the most invaluable source material for the daily goings-on of the late-fourteenth-century European nobility: the man knew on what side his *brioche* was buttered. He can belabor indefinitely the precise genealogy of some wealthy patron, but for the principal event of the Middle Ages—the Black Death—he had a single casual phrase: "A third of the world died." Elgar's swashbuckling overture—pronounced FROY-sart in the typically perverse English way with anything foreign—brilliantly captures the spirit of chivalric romance, just as the exuberant, Straussian *In the South* is his ecstatic love note to Italy.

With the Royal Philharmonic and the ASV engineers at their most responsive, Yondani Butt leads wonderfully swaggering performances of both works—an ideal choice for anyone who doesn't already have one or both as fillers for some other Elgar recording. Butt's fillers—the stirring *Coronation March* and the ethereal *Meditation* from *The Light of Life*—are equally memorable. (The greatest performance of *In the South*—or, indeed, any Elgar overture—ever recorded, Constantine Silvestri's miraculous version with the Bournemouth Symphony from the late 1960s, was recently in and out of the EMI catalogue faster than a politician can lie.)

*I*ntroduction and Allegro for Strings, Op. 47; *Serenade for Strings,* Op. 20

> **London Chamber Orchestra, Warren-Green. Virgin Classics CUV 61126 [CD].**

The debut recording of the resurrected London Chamber Orchestra presents virtually ideal recordings of two of Elgar's most appealing shorter works. Completed in 1892, the *Serenade for Strings* was the most substantial piece that the late-blooming Elgar had written up to that time. Prior to his marriage in 1889, the largely self-taught composer had busied himself with popular and functional music; it was his intelligent, supportive wife who urged him to become more serious and ambitious and the *Serenade* was one of the happy results.

In 1904, the recently knighted Sir Edward Elgar was approached to write a new work to help celebrate the founding of the London Symphony Orchestra. The composer's closest friend, the music editor A. J. Jaeger—"Nimrod" in the *Enigma Variations*—suggested "a real bring-down-the-house torrent of a thing such as Bach would write." What Elgar delivered was a sophisticated updating of the eighteenth-century concerto grosso, the *Introduction and Allegro for Strings,* Op. 47.

The small (seventeen-member) London Chamber Orchestra performs both works with phenomenal precision under Christopher Warren-Green. Yet in addition to the near-perfect execution, the performances are bustling with Elgarian energy: the "devil of a fugue" in the *Allegro* is tossed off with a supremely insolent swagger, while the opening theme of the *Serenade* is amiability itself. With equally inspired accounts of Vaughan Williams's *Lark Ascending, Greensleeves,* and *Tallis Fantasia,* this is a recording that no lover of English string music can afford to be without.

*P*artsongs

> **Finzi Singers, Spicer. Chandos CHAN 9269 [CD].**

Elgar composed partsongs throughout most of his creative life, from 1889's "O Happy Eyes," his first work on a text by his wife Alice, to a 1933 setting of Charles Mackay's "The Woodland Stream," virtually the last music he ever wrote. Although concise in form, these miniatures contain some of Elgar's most sweepingly romantic music and some of his most charming, from the hauntingly remote *There Is Sweet Music* in which the men and women sing in two separate keys, to the magnificent eight-part setting of *Go, Song of Mine*, with its Wagnerian chromaticism and suffering. If nothing else, they refute the preposterous suggestion that Elgar was uncomfortable writing for voices and/or in smaller forms.

The Chandos album by the Finzi Singers is an extravagantly beautiful one that allies an almost inhuman precision to an uncanny understanding of the meaning *and* implications of each song. One wonders if things like *Weary Wind of the West* have ever been sung with such real understanding or affection, or if the *Five Partsongs from the Greek Anthology* has ever been more vivid in its rapidly shifting contrasts and ornamental details. Both the Chandos recorded sound and Michael Kennedy's informative notes are superb.

*P*omp and Circumstance Marches (5); *Cockaigne Overture; Crown of India* (suite)

Scottish National Orchestra, Gibson. Chandos CHAN 8429 [CD].

This is the confident, public, tub-thumping Elgar, a man far removed from the thoughtful, melancholy Romantic who produced the Cello Concerto or the visionary mystic of *The Dream of Gerontius*. The supremely stirring *Pomp and Circumstance* Marches and the jingoistic *Crown of India* are the musical high noon of the British Empire, the perfect reflection of a self-satisfied society celebrating the fact that it had stolen half the world fair and square.

Sir Alexander Gibson rouses his Scottish musicians to great heights of eloquence and enthusiasm in the Marches and the Suite, while *Cockaigne*—a cognate of "Cockney," not a homonym for a vile, illegal substance—crackles with working-class London life.

In another and possibly even finer Chandos recording (CHAN 6574 [CD]), the same forces (together with excellent soloists and a top-notch chorus) are equally persuasive in Elgar's *Coronation Ode*, in which the great striding tune of the D Major March first became "Land of Hope and Glory." Another masterwork of Elgarian occasional music, the wartime cantata *The Spirit of England*, is offered as a generous bonus.

*S*onata in E Minor for Violin and Piano, Op. 82; *Canto popolare; Chanson de matin; Chanson de nuit; Mot d'amour; Salut d'amour; Sospiri; Six Easy Pieces in the First Position*

Kennedy, violin; Pettinger, piano. Chandos CHAN 8380 [CD].

During World War I, Elgar joined the Hampstead Division as a special constable and also enlisted his music in the war effort, producing a series of patriotic works culminating in *The Spirit of England* in 1917. Within a few weeks of the Armistice, he turned from public pronouncements to three of his most intimate pieces (and only mature chamber works): the Violin Sonata, String Quartet, and Piano Quintet. Elgar's chamber music year began with the arrival of a piano at Brinkwells, his isolated cottage in the woods of Sussex. He was soon afflicted with "a rabid attack of music writing" and produced the Violin Sonata within a month. For his wife, Alice, the Sonata contained "wonderful new music, different from anything else of his" and was full of "wood magic, so elusive and delicate."

As in his superb recording of the Violin Concerto, Nigel Kennedy has the full measure of the piece, investing it with passion, scale, and significance. The salon pieces that round out the album are all exquisitely done.

String Quartet in E Minor, Op. 83; Quintet in A Minor for Piano and Strings, Op. 84

Roberts, piano; Chillingirian Quartet. EMI CDC 65099 [CD].

These are warmly idiomatic interpretations of two of Elgar's most elusive works, written at a time when the aging composer, stung by the horrors of the Great War, turned inward with a growing sense of melancholy and disillusionment. The elegiac mood of the Cello Concerto is already evident in the Piano Quintet's slow movement, one of the most moving Elgar would ever compose. Yet for his friend George Bernard Shaw, the Quintet's principal glory was its turbulent opening movement, "the finest thing of its kind since *Coriolan*."

Bernard Roberts and the Chillingirian Quartet are by turns restrained and powerful in their fine EMI recording, capturing the shifting moods of this richly various work with consummate mastery. Their view of the String Quartet emphasizes its essential gentleness—how raptly hushed the beautiful slow movement is!—although the outer movements have considerable character and strength. The recorded sound is excellent, if a touch reverberant.

Peter Donohoe and the Maggini Quartet offer an excellent second opinion on Naxos (8.553737 [CD]) and at a super-bargain price. While the performances cook at a slightly lower level, what they lack in intensity they make up for in refinement and intelligence.

Symphonies (2)

Philarmonia Orchestra, Hallé Orchestra, Barbirolli. EMI Classics CDM-64511 [CD] (No. 1); EMI Classics CDM 64724 [CD] (No. 2).

With the dark and dramatic Symphony No. 1 in A-flat, whose brooding principal theme was used to such memorable effect in *Greystoke: The Legend of Tarzan*, Elgar's E-flat Major Symphony is one of the absolute summits of late-Romantic symphonic thought. With *The Dream of Gerontius,* it also represents much of what is best in Elgar: from the striding confidence of the opening movement through the ineffably poignant closing bars of the *Finale,* a sort of gentlemanly *Götterdämmerung* of the entire Edwardian era. As a matter of fact, the composer was already at work on the Symphony's emotional heart, the devastating *Largo,* when word reached him that the man who gave the age its name had died. This beautifully painful elegy for Edward VII is one of the great farewells of music.

The recordings that Sir John Barbirolli made in the early 1960s are among that conductor's greatest achievements, and no recorded versions before or since have captured quite so much of the passionate, red-blooded side of these magnificent scores. For instance, the finale of the A-flat Major seethes with a barely containable power, while the outpouring of grief in the *Largo* of the Second is all but insupportable. Listen, too, to the mood of feverish delirium the conductor conjures up toward the end of that Symphony's Scherzo or the triumphant grandeur with which he invests its final march. For all the special insights of the composer's own recordings (EMI Classics CDCC 54560 [CD]), to say nothing of those by Boult, Solti, or Slatkin, this pair of performances continues to persuade us that these *are* the great English symphonies to date. Given EMI's shameful record of allowing Barbirolli's classic Elgar recordings to slip out of print, snatch these up without delay.

For the bargain-hunter, a pair of Naxos recordings can now be recommended among the most desirable digital versions, regardless of price. George Hurst leads the BBC Philharmonic in an unusually pointed version of the First Symphony (8.550634 [CD]), in which the generally brisk tempos only add to the sense of urgency without missing any of the grandeur. The same orchestra under Sir Edward Downes is more ripely expansive in the Second (8.550635 [CD]), yet here the generally *slower* tempos do nothing to compromise the dramatic thrust.

The Wand of Youth Suites; Nursery Suite

Ulster Orchestra, Thomson. Chandos CHAN 8318 [CD].

All of the basic musical material for these enchanting works came from the composer's boyhood sketchbooks. As Elgar wrote of the second *Wand of Youth* Suite in 1908, "The music is now presented for the first time as imagined by the author: & in adapting to a modern orchestra these juvenile ideas the suggested instrumentation has been carried out as nearly as possible. Occasionally an obviously commonplace phrase has been polished out but on the whole the little pieces remain as originally planned." In truth, the composer was having some fun at his readers' expense: only the boyhood tunes remained, while their harmonic and contrapuntal treatment was clearly that of a mature composer in his prime.

The late Bryden Thomson's recordings of these endearing miniatures rank with his very best, capturing the vigor and abiding innocence of the music as no recordings ever have. One of the conductor's final Elgar recordings (Chandos CHAN 9022 [CD]) features the exquisite *Sea Pictures* and the rarely heard *Music Makers* in sumptuous readings by the London Philharmonic. With the classic Baker/Barbirolli version of *Sea Pictures* presently unavailable, this lovely performance with contralto Linda Finnie is now the one to own. Similarly, Thomson and company make the strongest possible case for *The Music Makers,* a work in which Elgar liberally quotes Elgar, including a rapt choral setting of *Nimrod* from the *Enigma Variations.*

Music from another engaging reworking of Elgarian juvenilia, *The Starlight Express*—which is not to be confused with Andrew Lloyd Webber's witless abomination of that same name—together with a suite from the incidental music for the play *Arthur,* a modern adaptation of Malory's famous romance *Morte d'Arthur,* can be found on another delightful Chandos recording (CHAN 6582 [CD]) in glowing performances by the Bournemouth Sinfonietta conducted by George Hurst.

Ellington, Edward Kennedy ("Duke") (1899–1974)

The River (suite)

Detroit Symphony, Järvi. Chandos CHAN 9154 [CD].

One of the giants of American jazz, Edward Kennedy "Duke" Ellington was also a prolific composer of jazz-influenced concert music, beginning with the *Creole Rhapsody* of 1931. Composed in 1970 when Ellington was finishing his *New Orleans Suite, The River,* with choreography by Alvin Ailey, was introduced in the following year as "Seven Dances from a Work in Progress Entitled 'The River.'" According to the composer's son Mercer, "the idea for *The River* had been kicking around for several years, ever since Stanley Dance had suggested an extended work depicting the natural course of a river." In Mercer Ellington's view, *The River* can also be viewed as a "religious allegory," as his father's thoughts had been turning increasingly to spiritual matters in his later years. In a preface to the score, the composer writes "of birth . . . of the wellspring of life . . . of reaffirmation . . . of heavenly anticipation of rebirth."

Neeme Järvi's Detroit Symphony recording is colorful and completely understanding, with a gentle "swing" that suggests a long familiarity with its composer's own performing style. The recording of Ellington's tone poem *Harlem* is just as convincing (CHAN 9226 [CD]) and comes with much-needed new recordings of William Grant Still's rarely heard Second Symphony and the endearing *Negro Folk Symphony* by William Levi Dawson.

Enescu, Georges (1881–1955)

Romanian Rhapsody No. 1

RCA Victor Symphony, Stokowski. RCA Victor 09026-61503 [CD].

Although the most important of all Romanian composers produced symphonies, an opera, and numerous elegantly crafted chamber works, Georges Enescu remains best known for a single score, the indestructible *Romanian Rhapsody No. 1,* which offers folksy melodies and gypsy passions decked out in spectacular orchestral garb.

Rarely has the old warhorse seemed as spry as in that mercurial performance from Leopold Stokowski's *Rhapsodies* album, now reissued in Victor's "Living Stereo" series. Even though Stoky couldn't resist the temptation of tinkering with Enescu's inspired orchestration—nothing personal: he routinely meddled with the work of master orchestrators like Rimsky-Korsakov, Stravinsky, and Ravel—the performance surges with life. From the coy opening to the wild gypsy finish, this is vintage Stokowski, as are the versions of Liszt's *Hungarian Rhapsody No. 2,* Smetana's *Vltava,* and excerpts from Wagner's *Tristan und Isolde* and *Tannhäuser,* which includes perhaps the most unabashedly pornographic version of the *Venusberg Music* ever put on tape.

For those wishing to meet the other Enescu, a Hyperion recording (CDA 66484 [CD]) offers two of the composer's violin sonatas—he was also a brilliant violinist—in fiercely committed performances by the Romanian virtuoso Adelina Oprean, accompanied by her brother Justin. While the Second Sonata is an appealing early piece, the Third is one of the finest such works produced in this century.

Although Enescu's setting of the Sophocles story has been completely overshadowed by Stravinsky's *Oedipus Rex,* his lyric tragedy *Oedipe* may actually be the finer work. It is a vivid and powerfully compelling score, as the startling new EMI Classics recording (CDCB-54011 [CD]) makes blindingly clear. With a nearly perfect cast headed by José van Dam in the title role and inspired conducting from Lawrence Foster, *Oedipe* is finally revealed as one of the major stage works of modern times.

Falla, Manuel de (1876–1946)

El amor brujo (complete)

**Price, soprano; Chicago Symphony, Reiner. RCA 09026-62586-2
[CD], 09026-62586-4 [T].**

Between its heyday in the high Renaissance until the last quarter of the nineteenth century, serious Spanish music all but disappeared: a mysterious hibernation whose depth and length was matched only by the three-century sleep of English music from the death of Henry Purcell to the emergence of Sir Edward Elgar. It was with the colorful, evocative, intensely nationalistic music of Isaac Albéniz and that of his younger contemporary Enrique Granados that Spanish music finally began to reassert itself, a music that would reach its most sophisticated expression in the works of Manuel de Falla.

Born in the port city of Cadíz in 1876 and educated in Madrid, de Falla moved to France in his early thirties. The seven years that he spent in Paris would prove the decisive period in his musical development; not only was he befriended by numerous famous French musicians, absorbing important technical influences as he went, but he also began to gain a crucial new perspective on the music of his own country. It was in Paris that he first applied the lessons he learned from Debussy, Ravel, and Dukas to the idioms of his native Spain, in effect viewing unmistakably Iberian melodies, harmonies, and rhythms through the sophisticated refracting lens of French musical Impressionism.

In addition to containing de Falla's most famous work, the once ubiquitous *Ritual Fire Dance,* the one-act ballet *El amor brujo* (Love, the Magician) was the most significant work of the Spanish nationalist movement since Albéniz's *Iberia.* Reiner's smoldering 1958 recording remains an exceptionally vivid evocation of this colorful slice of gypsy life, with Leontyne Price incomparably seductive in her throaty middle register. This classic recording has been reissued with Reiner's celebrated "Spain" album, containing equally brilliant, erotic, idiomatic readings of the *Three Dances* from *The Three-Cornered Hat,* the *Interlude and Dance* from *La vida breve,* the *Intermezzo* from *Goyescas* by Granados, and in the skillful orchestrations by Enrique Fernández Arbós, three excerpts from *Iberia*—including a version of *Triana* so magical in its sexy refinement that it alone is worth the price of the album.

Harpsichord Concerto

**Kipnis, harpsichord, New York Philharmonic members, Boulez. Sony
Classical SBK 53264 [CD], SBT 53264 [T].**

At a New York rehearsal of this beguiling work Sir Thomas Beecham made his immortal assessment of the instrument's sonic characteristics. After an initial run-through of the first movement, the conductor put down his baton and was heard to mutter, "Sounds like a pair of bloody skeletons fornicating on a tin roof."

Written to thank Wanda Landowska for taking part in the premiere of *Master Peter's Puppet Show,* the Harpsichord Concerto is one of the wittiest of de Falla's creations and—in spite of its brevity—one of his most elaborate: an intricate, loving evocation of the dense contrapuntal-style Baroque *concerti grossi.*

Igor Kipnis was in brilliant form for his 1975 recording. His playing has subtlety, energy, and tremendous humor and is impeccably matched by the principal desk players of the New York Philharmonic. The performance can be found in one of two contexts: as part of Sony Classical's "Boulez Edition," coupled with a rather thin-lipped *Three-Cornered Hat* but a marvelous version of Paul Dukas's *La Péri* (SMK 68333 [CD]), or in the preferred form listed previously, which features dazzling performances of solo harpsichord music by Blasco de Nebra, Scarlatti, and Soler.

The composer's own recording, made in Paris in 1930 with some of the most distinguished French musicians of the day, is currently available on an invaluable four-CD set from Almaviva (0121 [CD]) that also features other performances by the composer and his friends, interspersed with modern recordings made as late as 1973.

Nights in the Gardens of Spain

De Larrocha, piano; London Philharmonic, Frühbeck de Burgos. London 430703-2 [CD].

When she first walks out on stage, Alicia de Larrocha looks like nothing so much as a slightly plump but demurely elegant Barcelona housewife—which, when she is not off on one of her concert tours, is precisely what she happens to be. Yet the moment she begins to play, we are instantly ushered into the presence of one of the great pianists of modern times. While her Mozart shimmers with crystalline purity and inner strength and her Liszt is an exhilarating amalgam of volcanic intensity and urbane sophistication, it is with the colorful, evocative music of her fellow countrymen that de Larrocha remains unique. It's unlikely that Isaac Albéniz, Enrique Granados, or Manuel de Falla ever had a more sympathetic or persuasive interpreter of their piano music, and, barring some unforeseen miracle, they will probably never have one of this quality again.

In her most recent recording of de Falla's exquisitely dreamy *Nights in the Gardens of Spain,* de Larrocha plays with all the sensitivity and profound understanding that makes her new London version of Albéniz's *Iberia* one of the classics of recent recording history. Unlike many pianists who are unable to resist the temptation of cheapening the *Nights* by trying to flood it with too much local Spanish color, de Larrocha is able to approach it with the ease and assurance of one who speaks its musical language fluently. Never has the music seemed more natural or more naturally indebted to the piano music of Ravel and Debussy, nor has there ever been another performance so utterly spontaneous that it creates the illusion that the soloist is simply making all this up as she goes along. Rafael Frühbeck de Burgos provides her with some richly idiomatic support, and the recorded sound is breathtaking in its dynamic range and presence. Clearly, this is the recording of the *Nights* that will dominate the catalogues for years to come.

The Three-Cornered Hat; El amor brujo

Philharmonia Orchestra, Tortelier. Chandos CHAN 8904 [CD].

In its intoxicating rhythms and harmonic language, its color, wit, and distinctive, highly original use of the resources of the modern orchestra, Manuel de Falla's *Three-Cornered Hat*—originally composed for Sergei Diaghilev's Ballets Russes—is the most important large-scale orchestral work ever written by a Spanish composer. All of its freshness and overt, provocative sensuality have remained intact for nearly seventy years, and with that masterpiece by a great French tourist, Bizet's *Carmen,* the ballet remains one of the most vivid of all musical distillations of the sights and sounds of Spain.

While *The Three-Cornered Hat* has never gone begging for first-rate recorded performances—Ernest Ansermet, who gave the work its world premiere in 1919, left a commandingly vivid interpretation in 1961, only to be superseded by an even finer Angel recording by André Previn and the Pittsburgh Symphony two decades later—Charles Dutoit's recent effort for London captures more of the ballet's drama and atmosphere than any other recording. Alas, that recording has been temporarily withdrawn, presumably to reappear as a London Jubilee mid-price reissue.

Yet even if and when the Dutoit returns, it will face serious competition from the superb Tortelier recording. Along with an interpretation that is as full of dramatic character as one could wish, the Chandos recorded sound is exceptional: bright, airy, warm, and brilliantly detailed but with everything kept in a perfectly natural perspective. The only minor quibble is with the filler, which, instead of another important de Falla work, consists of five movements from Albéniz's *Iberia*—in admittedly stunning performances.

La vida breve

De los Angeles, Rivadeneyra, Cossutta, Higueras, Orfeon Donostiarra Chorus, National Orchestra of Spain, Frühbeck de Burgos. Angel CDM-69590 [CD].

It is often suggested that the reason that de Falla's colorful two-act opera has never really caught on has to do with weaknesses in the story. One suspects that there's more to it than that, since if weaknesses in the story were *ever* a serious consideration, then half of the most popular operas ever written would never have caught on. It probably has something to with the fact that *La vida breve* (The Short Life) is such an intensely Spanish opera that non-Spanish companies are reluctant to give it a try. Which is a pity, since in terms of its musical inspiration it ranks not that far behind the early Puccini operas or with the very best Massenet.

Victoria de los Angeles was an ideal exponent of Salud, the gypsy girl who collapses and dies of a broken heart at the wedding of her treacherous lover (OK, so it's not Ibsen). She breathes an irresistible life and color into the role and has rarely been more impressive vocally, while Frühbeck de Burgos's conducting could not have been more sympathetic or resourceful. On a single medium-priced CD, this neglected masterpiece has never been easier to investigate.

De los Angeles is also very compelling in her classic 1951 recording with pianist Gerald Moore of the *Siete canciones populares espagñolas* (usually translated as *Seven Popular Spanish Songs,* but more properly *Seven Songs of the Spanish People*) (EMI Classics CDH 64028-2 [CD]). It is the one recording of the cycle that comes closest to the electrifying 1928 version made by the composer's friend Maria Barrientos with Manuel de Falla himself at the piano, now available from Opal (CD 9852 [CD]). As in her great predecessor's interpretation, de los Angeles's singing is alternately pure, suave, insinuating, and *very* unladylike.

Farrar, Ernest (1885–1918)

Orchestral Works

Shelley, piano; Philharmonia Orchestra, Mitchell. Chandos CHAN 9586 [CD].

Like his fellow Royal College of Music graduate George Butterworth, Ernest Farrar was killed in the trenches of the First World War, leading his men into action at the Battle of Epéhy Ronssoy on September 18, 1918, two days after arriving at the front. In spite of the many tributes from friends and contemporaries—his teacher Sir Charles Stanford wrote, "He was very shy, but full of poetry, and I always thought very high things of him as a composer," his friend Frank Bridge dedicated his Piano Sonata to his memory, while his pupil Gerald Finzi wrote the *Requiem da camera* "in memory of E. B. F."—Farrar's music vanished almost without a trace following his death and has not really been heard anywhere until now.

The five works receiving their recording premieres on this Chandos album reveal Farrar as a promising and accomplished composer who might have developed into something considerably more had he lived. While the spirits of Elgar, Brahms, and Wagner hover over the proceedings, there is much here that is fresh and appealing, especially in the *English Pastoral Impressions,* a charming example of the tradition exemplified in the music of his friend Ralph Vaughan Williams. Most poignant of all—and the clearest possible indication of what Farrar might have become—is the eight-minute *Heroic Elegy* from May of 1918. With a second subject based on the familiar Agincourt Hymn and a quotation on the title page from Shakespeare's *Henry V*—"Free from vainness and self-glorious pride"—this dark and dignified work is the closest a composer of the Great War ever came to expressing the desolate mood of the battlefield.

Everything about the Chandos recording, from the attentive, carefully prepared interpretations to the packaging and recorded sound, gives every indication of a labor of love. In his illuminating program notes, Bernard Benoliel argues: "The opening of the *Heroic Elegy,* the fifth of the *Variations for Piano and Orchestra,* and the *Pastoral Impressions* suggest perhaps a musical Thomas Hardy in the making." These haunting works support the argument eloquently.

Fauré, Gabriel (1845–1924)

Ballade for Piano and Orchestra, Op. 112; *Dolly Suite,* Op. 56 (orch. Rabaud); *Elégie* for Cello and Orchestra, Op. 24; *Fantaisie* for Flute and Orchestra, Op. 79; *Masques et bergamasques,* Op. 112; *Pavane,* Op. 50; *Pénélope* (prelude)

> Davis, flute; Dixon, cello; Scott, piano; BBC Philharmonic, Tortelier.
> Chandos CHAN 9416 [CD].

This is easily the best single-volume collection of Fauré's most popular shorter works currently available. From the haunting stillness of the celebrated *Pavane,* through the melting charm of the *Dolly Suite,* to the antique austerity of the late *Masques et bergamasques,* Yan Pascal Tortelier finds the elusive heart of each of these fragile works, revealing them in all their delicate grace and tender beauty. The concertante pieces are all handsomely served, with memorable solo contributions from flutist Richard Davis, cellist Peter Dixon, and pianist Kathryn Scott.

On an earlier Chandos album with the Ulster Orchestra (CHAN 8950 [CD]) Tortelier leads similarly impeccable performances of the incidental music from *Pélleas et Mélisande* and the choral version (with the Renaissance Singers doing wonders for the sentimental gibberish that goes with it) of the *Pavane.* The album comes with excellent performances of two works by Ernest Chausson: the sumptuous *Poème de l'amour et de la mer,* superlatively sung by Linda Finnie, and the *Poème* for Violin and Orchestra, which Tortelier plays very stylishly as he conducts from (and possibly with) the bow.

Piano Music

> **Barcarolles (13). Crossley, piano. CRD 3422 [CD].**
>
> **Impromptus (5). Crossley, piano. CRD 3423 [CD].**
>
> **Nocturnes (13). Crossley, piano. CRD 3406/7 [CD].**

As with his *mélodies,* Fauré produced piano music throughout his entire creative life, from the *Trois romances sans paroles* written when he was eighteen, to the B Minor Nocturne composed nearly sixty years later. Like the songs, many of these miniatures are among his most characteristic and nearly perfect creations. In fact, given all the wonders they can contain, they are "miniatures" only in terms of duration, for they are also microcosms of the man's emotional life and expressive art.

As in his superb Poulenc and Ravel series (see page 580), Paul Crossley maintains a consistently high level of inspiration throughout his admirable Fauré project, as evidenced in the complete recordings of the *Barcarolles, Impromptus,* and *Nocturnes.* For anyone not wishing to make quite so substantial an investment, the French pianist Pascal Rogé is also polished and insightful on an attractive London recital (425606-2 [CD]) that offers some of the best of the above together with the *Valse caprice* and the *Trois romances sans paroles,* while the historic recordings of the composer's friend Marguerite Long are finally available on a Pearl CD (GEMM CD 9927).

Quartets (2) for Piano and Strings

> **Domus. Hyperion CDA 66166 [CD].**

The two Fauré piano quartets are among the most completely civilized chamber works ever written. For many, the conversation can become *too* civilized and introspective, often degenerating into elegant small talk; for others, they are the most cultivated and musically rewarding works in the form since those of Mozart.

The members of Domus obviously share the second opinion, and their immensely accomplished performances are among the most rewarding Fauré ever recorded. Their playing is not only extraordinarily refined, but it also captures the music's warmth and subtle passions as few other modern recordings have. With their versions of the Brahms Quartets (see page 119), these are Domus's most distinguished recordings to date.

Predictably, the Domus recording of the two Piano Quintets (CDA 66766 [CD]) is just as inspired, with wondrously insightful readings of these rich and subtle works, particularly in the autumnal C Minor Quintet, which reveals that Fauré, like Verdi, was still brilliantly inventive well into his seventies.

Unfortunately, the best available recording of the ethereal String Quartet in E Minor—finished during the final summer of Fauré's long life when the then totally deaf composer had just turned seventy-nine—can only be gotten as part of a two-disc set from EMI (ZDMB 62548 [CD]) with other versions of the Piano Quartets and Quintets. While not as consistently inspired as the Domus recordings, the performances all feature supremely musical and civilized playing, especially from the Perrerin Quartet.

Another superb Hyperion recording (CDA 66277 [CD]) features Domus's pianist Susan Tomes and violinist Krysia Osostowicz in lovely performances of the glorious Violin Sonatas, with the two gifted young musicians handily outperforming many far more famous teams.

*R*equiem, Op. 48

>Ashton, soprano; Varcoe, baritone; Cambridge Singers, City of London Sinfonia, Rutter (1893 version). Collegium COL-101, COLCD-109 [CD], COLC-109 [T].

>Battle, soprano; Schmidt, baritone; Philharmonia Orchestra and Chorus, Giulini (1900 fully orchestrated version). Deutsche Grammophon 419243-2 [CD].

>Beckley, soprano; Gedge, baritone; Oxford Camerata, Oxford Schola Cantorum, Summerly. Naxos 8.550765 [CD].

While the French consider Gabriel Fauré the consummate musical embodiment of their culture—and certainly no French composer ever produced a more cultivated body of chamber music, piano works, and songs—for most non-French ears, Fauré, to use the tired metaphor, is the classic example of a rare, virtually priceless wine that simply refuses to travel. Outside of his native country, his discretion, restraint, and natural reticence are still insufficiently appreciated. But then again, to expect anything but an educated Gallic audience to respond to the subtle delicacies of a song cycle like *La bonne chanson* is a little like expecting a non-German listener to fully grasp the more thorny lieder of Hugo Wolf.

Along with the melancholy and sinuously beautiful pops concert staple, the *Pavane,* one of the rare Fauré works that has enjoyed considerable popularity in

the rest of the world is that gentlest and most reserved of the great nineteenth-century Requiems. As in all of his important music, the Fauré *Requiem* makes its subdued points without so much as wrinkling an inch of its immaculately polished surface. From first note to last, the music flows in an inevitable, unhurried way, offering not only quiet spiritual consolation but also an extraordinary and original sonic beauty.

The recent Collegium recording—the first to present the work in the composer's original chamber music instrumentation—makes the strongest case for the *Requiem* that has yet been made. In fact, the reduced scale of the performing forces is such a perfect complement to the intimate nature of the music that one wonders why no one ever thought of recording it before. Both the singing and playing are engagingly fresh and youthful, and Collegium's spacious but detailed recording captures every nuance of an extremely subtle interpretation.

For those who prefer a Fauré *Requiem* with a little more meat on its bones, Carlo Maria Giulini's iridescent Angel recording of the 1900 orchestration, while maintaining the restrained poise of a fine chamber music performance, still overflows with old-fashioned romanticism and warmth.

Finally, the Naxos recording by the Oxford Camerata and Jeremy Summerly makes for an outstanding bargain, and not simply for the lovely performance of the *Requiem*. In addition to the *Andantino* for organ by Louis Vierne and the gorgeous *Tantum ergo* by Déodat de Séverac, the album offers two Fauré gems: the three movements of the *Messe basse* that he wrote in 1882 with André Messager (whose two movements aren't included) and the throat-lumping *Cantique de Jean Racine,* which movie-goers will immediately recognize as the music Farmer Hoggett (James Cromwell) was listening to just before the power outage in *Babe.*

Songs

Ameling, soprano; Souzay, baritone; Baldwin, piano. Angel CDMD-64079 [CD].

Nowhere is the exquisite refinement of Gabriel Fauré's art more evident than in his *chansons,* which taken as a whole represent the greatest contribution to the art of song made by any French composer. From his earliest song, "Le Papillon et la fleur," written on a text by Victor Hugo when he was twenty, through the cycle *L'Horizon chimérique,* composed only two years before his death, Fauré's lifelong devotion to the form produced some of the most nearly perfect fusions of words and music in musical history, from early miracles such as "Après un rêve," through mature masterpieces like "Au cimetière," "Chanson d'amour," "Clair de lune," and the greatest of his cycles, *Le bonne chanson.*

This historic set from EMI gathers all of the songs together on four CDs in performances by two incomparable Fauré interpreters, Elly Ameling and Gérard Souzay. If Souzay's voice is not quite as fresh as it was in his earlier Philips recordings, then his sheer musicality and depth of understanding more than make up for any minor vocal imperfections. On the other hand, the indestructible Elly Ameling is girlish and radiant throughout, with an instinctive grasp of Fauré's rarefied idiom to match Souzay's own. Dalton Baldwin, as always, is an ideal partner for both and the recorded sound remains very fine.

Feldman, Morton (1926–1987)

Rothko Chapel; Why Patterns?

Abel, viola; Rosenak, celeste; Winant, percussion; UC Berkeley
Chamber Chorus, Brett. New Albion NA039CD [CD].

In 1971, when the late American composer Morton Feldman was in Houston for the opening of a chapel for which the American painter Mark Rothko (1903–1970) painted fourteen enormous canvases, he was asked to write a musical tribute to the painter to be performed in the chapel the following year. The result is one of the most original and starkly hypnotic works ever written by an American. Scored for chorus, viola, celesta, and percussion, *Rothko Chapel* has an astonishing effect on listeners whenever we put it on the air, especially among those who are convinced they can't stand contemporary music. In addition to being a thoroughly spellbinding piece, it is also a very moving and spiritual one, with a number of personal references in the score, including a haunting soprano melody written on the day of Stravinsky's funeral and, in the composer's words, "Certain intervals [that] have the ring of the synagogue."

The UC Berkeley Chamber Chorus and company give *Rothko Chapel* a suitably rapt and ethereal performance in its second commercial recording, with the flawless digital sound adding immeasurably to the sense of purity and limitless space. If *Why Patterns?* from 1978 seems less convincing and original, then that's probably because *Rothko Chapel* was such a once-in-a-lifetime inspiration.

Ferguson, Howard (1908–)

Overture for an Occasion; Partita for Orchestra; Two Ballads for Baritone and Orchestra; The Dream of the Rood

Soloists, London Symphony Chorus and Orchestra, Hickox. Chandos CHAN 9082 [CD].

After establishing his reputation in the mid-1930s with a series of stubbornly romantic works, Howard Ferguson continued to produce a small but distinguished body of music until the late 1950s, when he decided he had said all he was going to say as a composer and cheerfully turned his attention to other things. Beginning with the Violin Sonata of 1931, Ferguson forged a highly personal style that shared something of the rhythmic vitality of Walton and the classical poise of Lennox Berkeley, while being somewhat less distinctive than the former and considerably more virile and energetic than the latter. His colorful *Partita* of 1936 is one of the most bracing English orchestral scores of the interwar period, while his final important work, the brooding, intensely romantic *Dream of the Rood*, would clearly seem to rank with the major British choral works of the twentieth century. Richard Hickox leads superlative performances of both pieces, together with the early *Two Ballads for Baritone and Orchestra* and the invigorating *Overture for an Occasion*, written to celebrate the coronation of Queen Elizabeth II in 1952.

Another important Chandos album (CHAN 9316 [CD]) offers a generous selection of the composer's chamber music, highlighted by the two Violin Sonatas—gripping works from 1931 and 1946 that have tremendous personality and strength of character—in exhilarating performances by Lydia Mordkovich and Clifford Benson. The *Four Short Pieces* for clarinet and the *Three Sketches* for flute are charming works, as are the delightful songs and song cycles that round out the album.

John Mark Ainsley is typically poised and musical in the *Discovery* cycle and the *Three Medieval Carols*, but the pick of the litter is probably the *Five Irish Folksongs*, sung with suitably Gaelic panache by mezzo-soprano Sally Burgess.

Beecham once said, "Music first and last should sound well, should allure and enchant the ear; never mind the inner significance." He might have been speaking of the music of Howard Ferguson.

Fibich, Zdeněk   (1850–1900)

Symphonies (3)

**Detroit Symphony, Järvi. Chandos CHAN 9230 [CD] (No. 1);
CHAN 9328 [CD] (Nos. 2 and 3).**

At the time of his sudden death at the age of forty-nine, Zdeněk Fibich was revered by his fellow countrymen with a devotion second only to his near contemporaries Smetana and Dvořák. His tone poem *Zábov, Slavoj a Luděk*, the first to be written on a Czech subject, was the direct inspiration of Smetana's *Ma Vlast* (a fact Smetana acknowledged by quoting Fibich in the cycle's opening movement, *Vyšehrad*) and his *Toman a lesní panna* (Toman and the Wood Nymph) inspired the later narrative tone poems of Dvořák. Yet for all his devotion to the ideals of a Czech national music, his German training and sympathies—together with his cultivated, cosmopolitan outlook—made him seem decidedly less "Czech" at a time when musical nationalism was reaching its height. Fibich's reputation declined alarmingly in the decades after his death and has yet to fully recover. Even in his native country, he is viewed—unfairly—as a composer singularly out of step with his time, a sort of Czech Taneyev.

The best place to meet this most thoroughly trained of nineteenth-century Czech composers is in his three symphonies, all of which are full of engaging ideas and all of which are exceptionally well made. If Fibich's musical personality is not as instantly recognizable as Smetana's or Dvořák's, then it is nonetheless a colorful and agreeable one that becomes even more so on repeated hearings.

It is doubtful that Fibich has had a more impassioned or eloquent champion than Neeme Järvi, whose recordings of the symphonies are by far the most persuasive ever made. Where the works are strongest—usually in the slow movements and Scherzos—he is content to let the music speak for itself; where they need the most help—typically in the first movement developments—he gives it in greater measure than any conductor on records ever has. The Detroit Symphony plays the music as though it had it in its bones and the Chandos sound is superb.

Field, John   (1782–1837)

Piano Concertos (2)

> O'Conor, piano; Scottish Chamber Orchestra, Mackerras.
> Telarc CD 80370 [CD].

Along with being the first significant Irish composer, John Field remains best known for having invented the *Nocturne*. An orchestral version of one of his loveliest works in the form—the B-flat Major Nocturne—serves as the slow movement of the pleasantly rhapsodic Third Piano Concerto, one of two Field concertos brilliantly played by John O'Conor on this stunning Telarc CD. The Concerto No. 2 in A-flat is also a fey and delicate work with a gentle *Adagio* and ingratiating rondo finale. With Mackerras and the Scottish Chamber Orchestra in superlative form, O'Conor makes a convincing case that these are among the finest piano concertos written between those of Beethoven and Chopin.

This gifted Irish pianist is also very persuasive in his companion album devoted to Field's *Nocturnes* (CD 80199 [CD]). Not only do these enchanting works emerge in more vivid relief than in any previous collection, but also the enormous influence they exerted on Chopin, Liszt, and Mendelssohn is made abundantly clear.

Fine, Irving   (1914–1962)

Blue Towers; Diversions for Orchestra; Music for Piano (orch. Spiegelman); Symphony (1962); *Toccata Concertante*

> Moscow Radio Symphony, Spiegelman. Delos DE 3139 [CD].

Irving Fine was already one of the most accomplished and promising composers of his generation when he died in his native Boston on October 23, 1962, at the horribly unfair age of forty-seven. With his colleagues David Diamond and Harold Shapero, he was a leading exponent of the style of American neo-Classicism that flourished in the years immediately following the end of the Second World War. Early in his career, his affinity for the music of Hindemith and Stravinsky was clearly apparent: the complexity of his contrapuntal thinking drew him naturally to the music of the astringent German-born master, just as his love of vibrant, decisive rhythmic formulas quickly brought him under Stravinsky's spell. Yet even in a youthful work like the Partita of 1948—a piece that has a fair claim to being the finest wind quintet yet written by an American—Fine also displayed a refinement of expression and lyric warmth that was unique among American composers of his era.

From the spanking *Toccata Concertante* with its propulsive Stravinskian rhythms to the tart *Music for Piano*, written to celebrate Nadia Boulanger's sixtieth birthday, the performances by the Moscow Radio Symphony conducted by the composer's pupil Joel Spiegelman bubble with excitement. The version of Fine's major work, the Symphony of 1962, is even more assured and idiomatic than Erich Leinsdorf's superb account with the Boston Symphony (Phoenix PHCD-106 [CD]).

In spite of fierce competition from a recent Chandos recording by the Reykjavik Wind Quintet, the best recording of the *Partita* can be found on a superlative album of the composer's chamber music from Elektra/Nonesuch (79175-2 [CD].)

Finzi, Gerald (1901–1956)

Clarinet Concerto; Five Bagatelles for Clarinet and Piano

Johnson, clarinet; Royal Philharmonic, Groves. ASV DCA 787 [CD].

Gerald Finzi is not one of the better-known twentieth-century British composers. His output was relatively modest—made all the more so by his death from leukemia at the age of fifty-five—and he tends to be at his best in the music he wrote for the human voice, which is hardly the way to guarantee *any* composer's popularity. The recent ripple of interest that has been shown in his music—he was never popular enough to enjoy a "revival"—has led to no fewer than four recordings of the 1948 Clarinet Concerto, one of Finzi's loveliest and most characteristic works.

Anyone—especially clarinetists themselves—who complains that too few important works have been written for the instrument, really does need to hear the Finzi Concerto, which easily ranks with those of Carl Nielsen and Aaron Copland as one of the finest produced in this century. In fact, repeated exposure to its lush, almost Brahmsian opening movement, its deeply expressive *Adagio*, and its unbuttoned but unhurried *Finale* has persuaded me that it may well be *the* Clarinet Concerto of modern times.

In her brilliant ASV recording, Emma Johnson assumes the mantle of the great Reginald Kell, taking her rightful place among the world's great clarinetists. Her breath control and command of dynamic shading are both little short of astonishing, revealing possibilities of expression and color that no recording of the Finzi Concerto ever has. She also offers a similarly inspiring account of the gorgeous *Five Bagatelles,* the second of which movie buffs will immediately recognize as John Barry's inspiration for the Big Tune from *Dances with Wolves.*

Those who respond to either of these unique works should waste no time investigating the composer's Cello Concerto in the Chandos recording (CHAN 8471 [CD]) by Raphael Wallfisch and the Royal Liverpool Philharmonic conducted by Vernon Handley. If anything, it is an even more ambitious and important work than the Clarinet Concerto: an alternately dark and exhilarating piece, performed here with intelligence and passion.

Dies natalis for Tenor and Orchestra, Op. 8; *Intimations of Immortality* for Tenor, Chorus, and Orchestra, Op. 29

> Ainsley, tenor; Corydon Singers and Orchestra, Best. Hyperion CDA 66876 [CD].

Finzi's *Dies natalis* is one of those rare Christmas works that can be heard in the middle of summer without the slightest discomfort. A meditation on Christ's nativity by the seventeenth-century metaphysical poet Thomas Traherne drew from Finzi some of his most profoundly beautiful music, placing *Dies natalis* beside Elgar's *Sea Pictures* and Britten's *Serenade for Tenor, Horn, and Strings* as one of the century's finest English song cycles. The *Intimations of Immortality,* after the poem by Wordsworth, is even more ambitious: a cantata of enormously wide expressive range in which Wordsworthian exuberance vies with the bucolic geniality of the English pastoral tradition.

Matthew Best leads beautifully focused performances of both works, with John Mark Ainsley a musical and probing soloist. If Richard Hickox's EMI recording of *Intimations* (CDM 64720 [CD]) is more impulsively dramatic, then Best's reserved, almost chamber-like approach seems equally valid, while the work of his fine chorus and orchestra is above reproach.

Songs

> Hill, tenor; Varcoe, baritone; Benson, piano. Hyperion CDA-66161/62 [CD].

> Varcoe, baritone; City of London Sinfonia, Hickox. Chandos CHAN-8743 [CD].

Here is the compelling evidence for the argument that Gerald Finzi was among the most important song composers of the twentieth century. The Hyperion set offers five of Finzi's cycles based on the poetry of Thomas Hardy, a total of forty-three songs that present an astonishing range of musical and emotional expression: from the roistering charm of "Rollicum-Rorum" through the heart-tugging wistfulness of "Childhood among the Ferns" to the *Winterreise*-like desolation of "At Middle-Field Gate in February," completed only a few months before the composer's death. With richly imaginative support from pianist Clifford Benson, tenor Martyn Hill and baritone Stephen Varcoe are ideal guides to this hugely rewarding repertoire. Although the piano sounds a bit distant, the balance is otherwise very natural.

Perhaps an even more attractive introduction to Finzi's vocal music is the Chandos recording of *Let Us Garlands Bring,* five of the most inspired of all modern Shakespeare settings. While Finzi's versions of "O Mistress Mine" and "It Was a Lover and His Lass" are every bit the equal of the far more familiar settings of Peter Warlock, the beautiful centerpiece of the cycle, "Fear No More the Heat o' the Sun" from *Cymbeline* ranks with the very greatest of English songs. Varcoe is again the perfect exponent of this material, with Hickox lending his typically impeccable support. With equally inspired performances of other items by Butterworth, Elgar, Ireland, Quilter, and Vaughan Williams, this is one of the loveliest albums of English vocal music now available.

Flagello, Nicolas (1928–1994)

The Passion of Martin Luther King

Bazemore, bass; Portland Symphonic Choir, Oregon Symphony, DePreist. Koch International Classics KIC 7293 [CD].

As a composer, Nicolas Flagello remained intensely and unabashedly romantic to the end of his life, with the fondness for traditional musical forms and soaring lines that characterizes the work of other Italian-American composers, from Walter Piston to John Corigliano. Written in 1968, *The Passion of Martin Luther King* was one of the first musical reactions to Dr. King's assassination and remains one of the best. The title of the piece draws the inevitable parallel to the Passions of Bach, in which the suffering and death of Christ are told in narrative form, with commentary and meditations from the Chorus. In place of the New Testament story, Flagello's narrative consists of excerpts from Dr. King's speeches and writings; in place of the old German chorales that Bach employed, Flagello uses his own settings of various Latin liturgical texts.

Joseph Schwantner's *New Morning for the World ("Daybreak of Freedom")* was composed in 1982 on a commission from the American Telephone and

Telegraph Company. As in Copland's *Lincoln Portrait*, the orchestra and speaker carry an equal narrative burden, with Dr. King's words supported and illuminated by an orchestral fabric of unusual variety and flexibility.

Both of these riveting works are given deeply committed readings by James DePreist and his splendid Oregon Symphony, which on the basis of this and other recent recordings must now be considered one of the very finest in the country.

This is an important and intensely moving recording.

Floyd, Carlisle (1926–)

Susannah

Studer, Hadley, Ramey, Chorus and Orchestra of the Opéra of Lyon, Nagano. Virgin Classics CDCB 45035 [CD].

Carlisle Floyd was only twenty-nine when his opera *Susannah* was introduced in 1955. In transporting the Apocryphal story of Susannah and the Elders to rural Tennessee, the composer succeeded in producing a resonant, heady mixture of verismo, Grand Guignol, and mid-century American realism, a kind of *Cavalleria Rusticana* meets *Wozzeck* meets *Elmer Gantry*. While other Floyd operas would follow *Susannah*, none have begun to approach its popularity: with its amalgam of vivid characters, folksy Coplandesque tunes, and B-movie melodrama, it has become one of the most frequently staged contemporary operas, chalking up more than 700 performances in some 150 productions.

For those of us who have long admired *Susannah* (and collected one or more of its several pirated versions), the first commercial recording is almost everything we had hoped it would be. Although Cheryl Studer fell ill shortly before the recording sessions and was forced to dub in her performance at a later date, nothing is remotely patchwork-sounding: the ensembles have a very natural give-and-take and her version of "The Trees on the Mountains Are Cold and Bare" steals the show, as it always does. Although Samuel Ramey as Olin Blitch doesn't quite efface the memory of Norman Treigle, he is suitably gripping in the role of the itinerant preacher, while Jerry Hadley is equally convincing as Sam. Kent Nagano squeezes every ounce of lyricism and tension from the score and the recorded sound is close to ideal. In short, if this *Susannah* doesn't convince you, then you can't be convinced.

Foote, Arthur (1853–1937)

Suite in E Minor, Op. 53

> **Boston Symphony, Koussevitzky. Pearl PEA 9492 [CD].**

With its echoes of Dvořák, Grieg, and Brahms, the charmingly old-fashioned Suite in E Minor by Arthur Foote is the least "American" work—not counting Harl McDonald's *San Juan Capistrano*—on this invaluable Pearl reissue called "Koussevitzky Conducts American Music." Along with that still peerless version of Copland's *El Salón Mexico,* here are those classic recordings of the First and Third Symphonies of Roy Harris, whose brilliance and intensity have never been approached on records and probably never will. If there is any doubt that the Boston Symphony under Koussevitzky was the great American orchestra of its time, then any of these spellbinding performances should quickly convince all but the most rabid Philadelphia Orchestra or NBC Symphony fan. The transfers are all excellent.

Foss, Lukas (1922–)

Time Cycle; Song of Songs; Phorion

> **Addison, soprano; Tourel, mezzo-soprano; Columbia Symphony, New York Philharmonic, Bernstein. Sony SMK 63164 [CD].**

Once, in an unguarded moment during a break in a long interview on a totally unrelated subject—the life and music of Arnold Schoenberg—Lukas Foss made an extraordinary pronouncement on Mahler's setting (in his Third Symphony) of "O Mensch, gib Acht" from Nietzsche's *Also sprach Zarathustra.* With disarming candor, he said (in a stage whisper), "I like my setting better." I said I agreed, and I still do. It comes at the end of one of the most fascinating large-scale works of midcentury music, *Time Cycle,* which had its historic first performance on October 20, 1960. On that occasion, the composer's old friend Leonard Bernstein made an unprecedented offer: "My colleagues on the stage and I think so highly of Lukas Foss's *Time Cycle* that we would like to make a proposal: If you wish, we will repeat the whole piece for you . . . And if there are only twelve people in this house who want to hear it again, we will play it for those twelve." *Time Cycle* was in fact repeated, making it the first work the New York Philharmonic ever played twice at its premiere.

With its combination of twelve-tone, nontonal, and "chance" techniques, *Time Cycle* remains one of the key works of the period: not only a watershed in this composer's career, but also one of the first works to seriously attempt to fuse the modern avant-garde with the actual improvisational techniques of jazz. Bernstein's 1961 recording still makes for a mind-boggling experience, tempered by the more traditional beauties of the neo-Classical *Song of Songs* and the fun of *Phorion*—the first of the composer's *Baroque Variations,* whose title is a Greek word meaning "stolen goods"—which makes wacky sport of the Prelude from the E Major Violin Partita of Bach.

The CD transfers are all one could have hoped.

Foster, Stephen Collins   (1826–1864)

Songs

DeGaetani, soprano; Guinn, baritone; Washington Camerata, Kalish.
Nonesuch 79158-2 [CD]; 71333-4 [CD].

Hampson, baritone; Fiddle Fever. Angel CDC 54621 [CD];
4DS-54621 [T].

Gregg Smith Singers, New York Vocal Ensemble, Smith, Beegle. Vox
Allegretto ACD 8167 [CD]; ACS 8167 [T].

With John Philip Sousa, Stephen Collins Foster was the only American composer of the nineteenth century whose music remains an indelible part of our national experience; Henry Clay Work—*Grandfather's Clock; Father, Come Home; Marching through Georgia*—may have been more topical and accomplished, but with the passage of time, it is the best of Foster's 189 songs—*Old Folks at Home, Jeanie with the Light Brown Hair, Come Where My Love Lies Dreaming, Camptown Races, Oh! Susanna, Beautiful Dreamer*—that have *become,* in the popular mind, the nineteenth-century American experience.

The late Jan DeGaetani was one of the first important modern singers to take Foster seriously, treating the songs not as saccharine embarrassments but as important compositions worthy of attention and care. The Nonesuch albums she made with baritone Leslie Guinn and pianist Gilbert Kalish are models of affection and respect, magically recreating the spirit of the time and place in which they were composed. Using arrangements based on Foster's own, Fiddle Fevers offer engaging accompaniments to Thomas Hampson, who clearly identifies with Foster's emotional idiom and emotes magnificently throughout. Finally, the Vox album by the Gregg Smith Singers and the New York Vocal Ensemble offer pointed and stylish appraisals of some lesser known and generally lighter Foster works *(The Merry, Merry Month of May; The Great Baby Show; If You've Only Got a Moustache)* that prove there was much more to the man than sentimental hearts and flowers.

The rather corny but endearing *Stephen Collins Foster: A Commemoration Symphony* that the composer's native city of Pittsburgh commissioned from Robert Russell Bennett to help celebrate its bicentennial has been reissued with Bennett's *A Symphonic Story of Jerome Kern,* in the invigorating performances by the hometown band conducted by William Steinberg (Everest EVC 9027 [CD]). As in virtually all of the recordings that company made during the period, the sound that emanates from the original 1960 tapes is phenomenal.

Foulds, John (1880–1939)

Le Cabaret Overture; April—England; Pasquinade Symphonique No. 2; Hellas, A Suite of Ancient Greece; Three Mantras

London Philharmonic, Wordsworth. Lyrita SCRD.212 [CD].

Here is an invaluable representative sampling of the music of John Foulds; he began his career as a composer of fashionable "light" music—as in the overture to a French comedy, *Le Cabaret*—and ended as a musical seer and mystic whose final scores are among the most individual and fascinating ever written by an Englishman. From *April—England,* with its occasional echoes of Delius and Vaughan Williams, to the *Three Mantras,* the only surviving music from his Sanskrit opera *Avatara* (he spent the last years of his life as the Director of European Music for All-India Radio, dreaming of a final fusion of the music of West and East), Fould's music is daring, exhilarating, and utterly distinctive, in its way as individual and challenging as that of his near contemporary Frank Bridge.

Barry Wordsworth leads the London Philharmonic in performances that are as carefully prepared as they are spontaneous sounding—no mean feat in music as difficult and unfamiliar as this. The *Three Mantras,* with their exotic harmonies and tricky cross-rhythms, are most impressive, but so is the poised, neo-Classical serenity of *Hellas,* Foulds's exquisite experiment in the modes of ancient Greece.

Clearly, he is a man you should get to know

Françaix, Jean (1912–1997)

L'Horloge de Flore for Oboe and Orchestra

DeLancie, oboe; London Symphony, Previn. RCA Victor 7989-2 [CD].

As they do with most right-thinking people, the perky, tuneful, mercilessly cheerful excretions of Jean Françaix—the A. A. Milne of French music—usually fill me with an irresistible urge to rip out daisies by the roots and hurl bricks at the nearest chirping bird. Except for *The Flower Clock.*

Written for John deLancie, the former principal oboist of the Philadelphia Orchestra, *L'Horloge de Flore* is one of the most ingratiating and gratefully written of all modern oboe concertos and forms the centerpiece of an album that no lover of the instrument—or of elegant French music—can afford to be without. With suave and stylish accompaniments by Previn and the London Symphony, de Lancie turns in equally definitive performances of the Ibert *Symphonie concertante* and the ethereal *Gymnopédie* by Erik Satie.

As a bonus, the CD reissue includes a 1987 recording of the Strauss Oboe Concerto, a work the elderly composer was prompted to write thanks to a chance conversation with an American GI named John deLancie. Although one could wish that the oboist had recorded it in his prime, it is easily the finest now available and a historic document of considerable significance.

Franck, César (1822–1890)

Le Chasseur maudit

Toulouse Capitole Orchestra, Plasson. EMI Classics CDC 55385 [CD].

A fondness for Franck's splendidly gruesome *Le Chasseur maudit* (The Accursed Huntsman) usually accompanies similar passions for B horror pictures of the 1940s (usually the ones with Rondo Hatton, Martin Kosleck, or both) or reading the unabridged memoirs—if indeed they exist—of President Grover Cleveland. Actually, the tone poem is one of the key works in an honorable line of black-schlock masterpieces that stretches back to Bach's *Mein Herze schwimmt im Blut* and looks forward to the Shostakovich Eighth.

Michel Plasson leads his fine Capitole de Toulouse Orchestra in a powerfully dramatic performance that fully exploits the more grotesque elements in the music without missing its occasional subtleties. The performance comes as part of an attractive anthology of French tone poems, including Dukas's *The Sorcerer's Apprentice*, Saint-Saëns's *Danse macabre*, and two rarities by Henri Duparc—*Aux étoiles* and *Léonore*—all vividly performed and recorded.

Piano Quintet in F Minor

Aller, piano; Hollywood String Quartet. Testament SBT 1077 [CD].

Like the Janáček string quartet called "Intimate Pages," Franck's F Minor Piano Quintet was inspired by a passion the older composer conceived for a much younger woman, in this case, one of Franck's students. In addition to the boiling emotions—and in no other work by this master of form and gesture are the emotions in more imminent danger of boiling *over*—there is more than a touch of mysticism in this otherworldly piece, its composer's first unqualified masterpiece.

Recorded in 1953, the towering performance by pianist Victor Aller and the Hollywood String Quartet has never really been equaled, even by the splendid (and recently withdrawn) London recording by Sir Clifford Curzon and members of the Vienna Octet. There is a ferocious sense of commitment in the playing, coupled with the group's typically maniacal attention to detail. The actual recording sessions involved unusually long takes requiring little editing, which helps account for the feeling of an actual performance as opposed to a polite and careful studio job. Reissued with a performance of the Shostakovich Piano Quintet that is every bit as authoritative, this is the version that handily sweeps the field, monophonic sound and all.

Prélude, choral et fugue

Hough, piano. Hyperion CDA 66918 [CD].

Enthusiasm for Franck's piano music waxes and wanes over the decades, this in spite of its obvious beauty and importance. In one of the most important such collections in years, Stephen Hough manages to acknowledge its obvious structural debts to the piano music of Liszt—particularly in the *Prélude, choral et fugue*—while simultaneously underscoring the individuality of its rich harmonic language. From relatively early works like *Les Plaintes d'une poupée* of 1865 through the astonishingly neglected *Prélude, aria et final,* finished three years before the composer's death, the music maintains a phenomenally high level of inspiration and invention. Thoughtful, spontaneous-sounding, and poetic, Hough's performances are among the most perceptive and persuasive ever recorded.

Psyché (symphonic poem) for Orchestra and Chorus

BBC Welsh National Chorus and Orchestra, Otaka. Chandos CHAN 9342 [CD].

The most one usually hears from Franck's last symphonic work is the brief final section, *Psyché et Eros,* a favorite of conductors from Toscanini and Mengelberg to Giulini and Barenboim. Given how ravishing the rest of *Psyché* is—and yes, indeed, the inherently erotic subject matter drew from Franck some of the sexiest music of his career—the paucity of complete recordings has always been a mystery. If the text by the composer's son Georges set new standards for bourgeois banality, then the glorious music redeems and transfigures it at every turn.

Tadaaki Otaka leads his Welsh forces in a performance that is so alert and sympathetic that you almost begin to believe poor *Psyché* must have been the victim of some bizarre conspiracy all these years. While the chorus—sopranos, altos, tenors—is predictably gorgeous (what Welsh chorus is *not?*), the orchestra is as lithe and flexible as a fine French ensemble, without the nasal double reeds and crooning horns. Obviously, if *Psyché* is not César Franck's masterpiece, then you couldn't tell it from a recording like this.

Sonata in A Major for Violin and Piano

Perlman, violin; Ashkenazy, piano. London 414128-2 [CD].

Like the Moravian composer Leós Janáček, who did not begin to produce his greatest music until he entered his seventh decade of life, the Belgian-born César Franck was a classic late-bloomer among the major composers. He produced some shockingly dreadful music early in his career—*Hulda,* for instance, has a better than average claim to being the worst French opera of the nineteenth century, and *that's* saying something—and yet, toward the end, he found his own distinct voice in a tiny handful of masterworks that will probably endure forever.

Franck's Violin Sonata in A Major—known in some irreverent corners of the classical music radio trade as "The Frank Sinatra"—stands with those of Brahms and Schumann as one of the finest violin sonatas after those of Beethoven. As in all of Franck's most powerful and characteristic music, the Sonata represents a conscious attempt to contain Romantic sentiment within formal classical structures, a tendency that his French critics lambasted mercilessly, charging the composer with an unseemly and almost treasonous fondness for German formalism. (As preposterous as it might seem, many of those same critics took George Bizet's *Carmen* to task for being so obviously and slavishly "Wagnerian.")

Although I still have the fondest memories of a long-vanished Decca interpretation by the fabulously musical Viennese violinist Erica Morini, Itzhak Perlman's London recording from the mid-1970s easily surpasses all currently available recordings of the work. While poised and elegant throughout, the playing of both the violinist and pianist is also shot through with a wonderful sense of dramatic urgency and immediacy. In their hands, for instance, the turbulent second movement emerges as one of the composer's greatest creations.

Symphony in D Minor

Chicago Symphony, Monteux. RCA Victor 6805-2-RG [CD].

There are people whose friendship I value and whose musical opinions I respect who absolutely cannot *abide* Franck's D Minor Symphony. (Curiously enough, they tend to be the same people who have an inexplicable revulsion for the music of Frederick Delius. Consequently, I never argue either subject with them but instead tend to look their way with a mixture of benign sorrow and genuine confusion.) For if truth be told, what's *not* to like in this tuneful, brilliant, melancholy, triumphant work? It has something for everyone: despair, adventure, exuberance, romance, and an English horn solo in the second movement for which anyone who ever played the instrument, myself included, would cheerfully sell his grandmother to the gypsies.

For students of English horn playing, the legendary Laurence Thorstenberg gives one of the greatest performances of his incomparable career in this 1961 RCA Victor recording. For those whose interests are a bit less parochial, Larry's luscious playing can be heard in what also happens to be the greatest recorded performance that the Franck D Minor Symphony has ever been given.

If further proof was needed that Pierre Monteux was one of the most consistently satisfying conductors of the twentieth century, this stunning performance goes a long way to underscoring the point. With the youthful impetuosity that only this ageless octogenarian could muster, he levitates Franck's often problematical symphony almost to the level of those of Johannes Brahms. The first movement seethes with a barely containable intensity, the slow movement is a seamless diaphanous love song, while the finale becomes a Tchaikovskian explosion of exuberance and romance. With his London Symphony *Daphnis and Chloé* and Boston Symphony version of Stravinsky's *Rite of Spring*—two works that Pierre Monteux introduced to the world—this is one of the principal monuments of a unique and irreplaceable talent.

To make the reissue all the more attractive, RCA has coupled the performance with two Boston Symphony recordings led by Charles Munch: a scintillating account of Berlioz's Overture to *Béatrice et Bénédict* and what remains the most distinguished available recording of d'Indy's *Symphony on a French Mountain Air.*

With the classic recording by Sir Clifford Curzon of Franck's other great orchestral score, the Symphonic Variations, no longer available, most of the better alternatives—Bolet, Entremont, Firkušný—mean getting stuck with yet *another* recording of the Symphony in D Minor. Which therefore leaves the field to Artur Rubinstein (RCA 09026-61496-2 [CD], 09026-61496-4 [T], who, in addition to a pleasantly brooding interpretation of the Franck, offers a beautifully atmospheric version of de Falla's *Nights in the Gardens of Spain* and possibly the finest ever recording of the Second Piano Concerto of Camille Saint-Saëns.

Frankel, Benjamin   (1906–1973)

Symphony No. 2, Op. 38; Symphony No. 3, Op. 40

> Queensland Symphony Orchestra Brisbane, Albert. CPO 999241-2 [CD].

Born in London of Polish-Jewish parents, Benjamin Frankel began his career as a jazz pianist and arranger/musical director of shows in London's West End. He is still best known as a film composer, having written more than one hundred scores, including *The Seventh Veil, The Importance of Being Ernest,* the Alec Guinness classics *The Prisoner* and *The Man in the White Suite, Night of the Iguana,* and *Battle of the Bulge.* On the evidence of this electrifying CPO recording, posterity might also come to regard him as one of the most important symphonists of the second half of the twentieth century.

From 1958 to 1972, Frankel produced a series of eight symphonies that led William Mann to call him "doubtless our most eloquent symphonist" in *The Times* of London. Except for the First Symphony, all of his works in the form were written during a period of ever-worsening health dating from the first of his heart attacks in 1959. Dedicated to the memory of his wife and prefaced by quotations from Wordsworth, the Second Symphony of 1962 is a shattering work: large, eventful, adult, full of searing anguish and a singularly virile despair. In marked contrast, the Third Symphony written two years later is a generally optimistic work in which the composer temporarily abandons his highly personal (and always intensely *human*) serialism for the bracing joys of the diatonic.

Werner Andreas Albert and his fine Australian orchestra play with obvious skill and devotion, while each performance is prefaced by a brief but illuminating talk by the composer. When complete, the Frankel cycle may prove to be one of the key recordings of the decade.

Frescobaldi, Girolamo (1583–1643)

Madrigals

Concerto Italiano, Alessandrini. Opus 111 OPS 30-133 [CD].

One of Bach's most important predecessors as a composer of organ music—as a performer, his exploits led one contemporary to call him "the marvel of the age"—Frescobaldi was also a precocious madrigalist, as the astonishingly fresh and inventive items of *Il primo libro de madrigale* clearly demonstrate. Published in Antwerp in 1608 when their composer was only twenty-five, they tend to confine themselves to traditional Renaissance themes—love, loss, unrequited passions of various kinds. They invite (in fact, require) a startlingly Romantic freedom of expression—in the composer's words, "according to the emotions aroused or the meaning of the words that are sung."

Even for those who don't normally respond to the rarefied pleasures of early vocal music, Concerto Italiano's rapt, expressive performances will be difficult to resist. Their purity of tone and voicing is combined with an extraordinary musical and emotional range, so essential to these richly various pieces.

Friedhofer, Hugo (1911–1981)

The Best Years of Our Lives

London Philharmonic, Collura. Varèse Sarabande VSD 70470 [CD], VSC 70470 [T].

Along with being one of the major American film composers, Friedhofer was also a legendary Hollywood misanthrope. Once, when a young admirer's praise began getting out of hand, Friedhofer silenced it, famously, by saying: "Kid, I'm a fake giant among real pygmies."

After years as one of Hollywood's top arrangers—the inspired orchestration of *Casablanca* and countless other classic scores are his—Hugo Friedhofer came into his own as a composer with *The Best Years of Our Lives.* On the advice of a misguided assistant, the director William Wyler—whose knowledge and appreciation of music were primitive at best—was nearly persuaded to throw out the score until the composer's friend David Raksin intervened. He not only pointed out that it was one of the finest film scores ever written but also prophesied that it would win the Academy Award, which it eventually did.

The studio recording by the London Philharmonic conducted by Frank Collura clearly demonstrates why *The Best Years of Our Lives* has remained one of the best-loved of all film scores. In addition to perfectly complementing the moving story of three returning World War II servicemen, the tender, dramatic, Coplandesque music also stands brilliantly on its own. This is wonderful music, superbly played and recorded.

Fucík, Julius (1872–1916)

Marches and Waltzes

Czech Philharmonic, Neumann. Orfeo C-147861 [CD].

In many of the more benighted corners of the planet, the Czech composer Julius Fucík is known as "The John Philip Sousa of Bohemia." Those of us who know better refer to the March King as "The American Julius Fucík." Best known as the composer of the immortal circus march, *The Entry of the Gladiators,* Fucík was also the composer of many tunefully appealing waltzes that, if they don't exactly eclipse those of Johann Strauss II, then are at very least cut from the same entrancing cloth.

Václav Neumann proves to be an enthusiastic advocate of his countryman's music, and, with the great Czech Philharmonic at its most precise and congenial, Fucík emerges as a composer with genuine character, originality, and charm. Besides, without a first-rate recording of his imperishable masterwork, what will you do if you suddenly acquire an elephant?

Gabrieli, Giovanni (ca. 1557–1612)

Canzoni for Brass Choirs

> Chicago Symphony Brass Ensemble, Cleveland Orchestra Brass
> Ensemble, Philadelphia Orchestra Brass Ensemble. Sony Classical
> Masterworks Heritage MHK 62353 [CD].

Canzoni for Brass Choirs; 7 Intonazioni d'organo; 7 Motets; 3 Mass
Movements; Sonata in the 9th Tone for 8 Parts

> Biggs, organ; Gregg Smith Singers, Texas Boys' Choir, Edward Tarr
> Brass Ensemble. Sony Classical SBK 62426 [CD], SBT 62426 [T].

Canzoni for Brass Choirs; *Sacre symphoniae* for Instrument and Chorus

> His Majesties Sagbutts and Cornetts, Roberts. Hyperion
> CDA 66908 [CD].

When the stunning recording by the Chicago, Cleveland, and Philadelphia
brass ensembles was originally released in the late 1960s, a review in a respected
English magazine insisted that it was a great pity that no one who really knew the
"proper" way of playing this glorious music was present at the recording sessions. By that I suppose the reviewer meant one of those terminally serious period-instrument types who would have found the lush and full-throated
excitement generated by some of the world's finest brass players *too* stimulating
for his or her refined and etiolated tastes. Thank goodness, no such creature
could be found.

No doubt the performances contained on this famous recording—brilliantly
remastered and sounding better than ever on CD—*are* woefully anachronistic by
purists' standards. Imagine the gall of playing older music on modern instruments,
and playing it in such a way that the magnificent music of a sixteenth-century
composer becomes instantly—and irresistibly—accessible to twentieth-century
ears. Tsk, tsk. The only pity is that the recording was followed up by only a single
sequel (of sorts): an album featuring thirteen *canzoni* played by the Canadian
Brass, aided by the first-desk players of the Boston Symphony and New York
Philharmonic.

The handsome collection called "The Glory of Venice—Gabrieli in San
Marco"—made quite a noise when it was first released in 1967 and it still sounds
pretty spectacular today. Recorded in the incomparable acoustics of St. Mark's
Cathedral, the original venue in which most of these pieces were first heard,
Gabrieli's antiphonal writing has never seemed more affecting, nor were many of
the participants ever moved to more joyously inspired work. Hearing these

thrilling performances, you almost believe they had just read the Biblical injunction to "make a *joyful* noise unto the Lord."

As if to prove that period-instrument Gabrieli can also be tremendously exciting, His Majesties Sagbutts and Cornetts make some marvelously rude noises on their excellent Hyperion album. While neither as dramatic nor as "present" as their modern-instrument counterparts, they play with both fervor and precision and are extremely well recorded.

Gade, Niels (1817–1890)

Symphonies (8)

> Stockholm Sinfonietta, Järvi. BIS CD 339 [CD] (Nos. 1 and 8);
> CD 335 [CD] (Nos. 2 and 7); CD 338 [CD] (Nos. 3 and 4);
> CD 356 [CD] (Nos. 5 and 6).

Born in Copenhagen in 1817, the only son of an impoverished instrument maker, Niels Vilhelm Gade was the first significant Scandinavian composer and the single most important figure in nineteenth-century Danish music. When in 1842 his First Symphony was not accepted for performance in Copenhagen, Gade sent it to Mendelssohn, who performed it with great success in Leipzig. Yet in spite of Gade's enthusiasm for the Germanic school, distinctly Danish themes and harmonies color his work: at his best—as he tends to be in his eight symphonies—he is a composer of genuine charm and considerable substance, with a pronounced gift for inventing fresh and endearing melodies and sufficient craft to make them to do interesting, often surprising, things.

Neeme Järvi's Gade cycle for BIS is one of the very best things this much-recorded conductor has ever done. The Stockholm Sinfonietta plays with total conviction while the recorded sound is warm and brilliantly focused. If this is definitely *not* music with which to plumb the depths or storm the heights, then it will make you feel a good deal better at the end of a rotten day.

Gay, John   (1685–1732)

The Beggar's Opera

Soloists, Pro Arte Chorus and Orchestra, Sargent. Classics for Pleasure
CFP CFPSD 4778 [CD].

Soloists, Broadside Band, Barlow. Hyperion 66591/92 [CD].

Few works had a more decisive impact on the development of musical theater than *The Beggar's Opera*, first staged by the dour John Rich at London's
Lincoln's Inn Fields in 1728. Writing at the suggestion of Jonathan Swift, John
Gay concocted a lurid story set in the Newgate underworld and a series of new
lyrics set to the tunes of popular folk songs and ballads of the day, with musical
arrangements supplied by Dr. John Christopher Pepusch. The success of this first
"Ballad Opera" was so immediate and overwhelming that it not only "made Gay
rich and Rich gay" but also spelled the beginning of the end of Italian opera in
England, bankrupting George Frederic Handel in the process and forcing that
composer to turn his attentions elsewhere. Thus, in addition to being the proximate cause of *Messiah* and the other Handel oratorios, *The Beggar's Opera* was
also the distant ancestor of the Savoy operas of Gilbert and Sullivan, the Viennese
operetta, and the modern Broadway musical and is the *direct* inspiration for
Bertolt Brecht's modern updating, *The Threepenny Opera*.

Sir Malcolm Sargent—called "Flash Harry" by his colleagues—never made
a finer, more entertaining recording than this one. (Once, when Sir Thomas
Beecham learned that Sargent was about to conduct a series of concerts in Tokyo,
he quipped, "Ah!—Flash in Japan." Later, when Beecham heard the rumor that
Sargent had been kidnapped in China, he said, "My dear fellow, I had no idea the
Chinese were so musical.") Sounding almost impossibly fresh and sonically up-
to-date in its Classics for Pleasure reissue, the 1955 EMI recording has lost none
of its pith and vinegary charm. Aided by a splendid cast of actors speaking the dialogue and some of the most colorful English singers of the period—including
Owen Brannigan, Monica Sinclair, and Elsie Morrison—Sargent leads a vital,
wonderfully theatrical performance that seems to bring the action directly into
the listener's living room. With the premiere recording of Britten's *Young Person's
Guide to the Orchestra* and his two delectable series—from the '30s and '50s—of
Gilbert and Sullivan recordings, this is the key item in the Flash's discography.

The Hyperion recording is also a very fine one. If not quite as much fun as
the Sargent or as Richard Bonynge's outrageous (and outrageously entertaining)
modern version—complete with saxophones—starring Dames Joan Sutherland
and Kiri Te Kanawa (surely a prime candidate for reissue in London's Duo series),
then the period-instrument reading with the Broadside Band still captures much of
the flavor and punch of the original without being needlessly stuffy or pedantic.

Geminiani, Francesco   (1687–1762)

Concerti Grossi (6), from various collections

    Tafelmusik, Lamon. Sony Classical SK 48043 [CD].

Concerti Grossi (6), Op. 2; Concerti Grossi (6), Op. 3

    Capella Istropolitana, Kreček. Naxos 8.553019 [CD].

Concerti Grossi (12), Op. 5 (after Corelli)

    I Musici. Philips 438766-2 [CD].

Concerti Grossi (6), Op. 7

    Academy of St. Martin-in-the-Fields, Brown. ASV ASV 724 [CD].

The more you get to know Francesco Geminiani—pupil of Corelli and Alessandro Scarlatti, purportedly the finest violinist of his time, author (at first anonymously) of *The Art of Violin Playing* (written in English), the first how-to treatise ever published on the subject—the more you like him. Early in his career he was relieved as leader of a Neapolitan orchestra, apparently because his performances were too interesting. His "unexpected accelerations and relaxations of measure" proved too much for his colleagues and he was moved to a place among the second violins. In 1714, at a time when George Frideric Handel was out of favor with his Hanoverian masters, he was invited to play at the English court but refused to do so unless Handel appeared as his accompanist. In 1728, he was offered the highly lucrative (and largely ceremonial) post of Music Master for the State of Ireland but indignantly refused because it required him to renounce his Catholicism.

If Geminiani's instrumental music seldom breaks new ground or rarely equals the finest achievements of Bach, Handel, Vivaldi, or his teacher Corelli, then his various sets of concerti grossi are lively, entertaining, and highly addictive—as any of the collections listed here will readily prove.

The brilliant period-instrument recording by Tafelmusik offers an exciting introduction to the highly inventive Opus 2 set, together with two of those twelve engaging items from Opus 5, which are essentially imaginative arrangements of Corelli's Opus 5 Violin Sonatas. The non-period recordings by Jaroslav Kreček and the Capella Istropolitana are the first two installments in a projected series to record all of Geminiani's concertos. The fresh, unpretentious, consistently enjoyable performances bode very well for the project's future.

The ASV album by Iona Brown and the Academy maintains the same high standard as their recordings of the Handel Concerti Grossi; in fact, few recorded performances draw a more obvious and appropriate parallel to those master-pieces of the form. I Musici are both scintillating and warmly expressive in their version of the complete Corelli concertos, which reveals Geminiani as a master of Baroque texture and color.

Gerhard, Roberto (1896–1970)

La Peste (after *The Plague* by Albert Camus)

Lonsdale, narrator; Spanish National Youth Orchestra, BBC Symphony Chorus, Colomer. Montaigne MO 782101 [CD].

There are a handful of works so overwhelming in their content and devas-tating in their impact that they can only be heard a few times during the course of any well-adjusted lifetime: Shostakovich's Fourteenth Symphony is one, Roberto Gerhard's *The Plague* is another.

Born in Catalonia and trained by Granados and Pedrell, Gerhard moved to Vienna in 1923 to study with Arnold Schoenberg. Following the Fascist victory in the Spanish civil war, Gerhard moved to England and became a research fellow at Cambridge, where he remained for the rest of his life. His was a complex, highly charged expansion of Schoenberg's twelve-tone technique—from the early 1950s onward, rhythmic texture and orchestral color began replacing melody and harmony as the center of his musical organization—and only during the last years of his life did his music begin to speak in its own powerfully original voice.

Based on Albert Camus's celebrated novel, *The Plague* is a melodrama for speaker, chorus, and orchestra that has no real precedent in modern music, except perhaps for Schoenberg's *A Survivor from Warsaw*. Working from his own skillful condensation of Camus's story, Gerhard fashioned a drama of astonishing strength and jarring immediacy that holds the listener spellbound in its grip. If not quite as musically accomplished as the premiere recording with Alec McCowen and the National Symphony conducted by Antal Dorati, then this first volume in Montaigne's Roberto Gerhard edition is nonetheless extremely impressive, with Michael Lonsdale a superbly understated narrator and the young Spanish orchestra playing on the edge of their chairs.

Gerhard's 1947 opera based on Sheridan's play *The Duenna* had to wait forty-five years for its first production and even longer for a first recording, both under the auspices of England's adventurous and energetic Opera North. The sparkling Chandos recording (CHAN 9520 [CD]) reveals *The Duenna* as one of the most important and attractive of modern operas, a brilliant, fast-moving *ersatz*-eighteenth-century comedy in which the Spanish elements of Gerhard's music were at their most potent and appealing. Neither the performance nor the recording could be improved.

Gershwin, George (1898–1937)

An American in Paris; Concerto in F; *Rhapsody in Blue*

Golub, piano; London Symphony, Miller. Arabesque Z 6587 [CD].

At the very *least*, this is the greatest single Gershwin recording ever made. Where it ranks among the great classical recordings of the last twenty-five years only time will tell, though my suspicion is that it will rank very high. Among so many other things—peerless oboist, television star, and recording executive whose list of discoveries reads like a Who's Who of American popular music— Mitch Miller is also one of the most revealing and exciting conductors in the world today. This recent Arabesque recording of music by his friend George Gershwin may well be the crowning achievement to date in a long and colorful career.

What Miller brings to Gershwin's music is an unusual combination of freshness and authority. But paradoxically, the freshness comes from simply playing the music as the composer intended: intentions that Miller discovered firsthand while playing in the orchestra for the composer's 1934 American tour and in the original production of *Porgy and Bess*. Working from scores that Miller carefully marked from Gershwin's own interpretations and instructions, the performances emerge from this astonishing Arabesque recording sounding like no others you've ever heard before. While infinitely more lyrical, expansive, and direct in their emotional expression, they are also more intricate and subtle than any other Gershwin recording on the market today. The important, but rarely heard, inner voices are coaxed out of the background with a startling clarity, and the jazz inflections, for once, are not simply tossed in as cheap effects but can clearly be heard for what they were all along: part of the natural organic structure of the music itself.

The playing of the London Symphony ranges from the merely sensational to the absolutely terrifying—at times, the LSO brass section wails with the electrifying unanimity of purpose of the old Count Basie Band—and the technically spellbinding, yet intelligent and poetic, playing of David Golub suggests that he is clearly one of the finest pianists before the public today.

For Gershwin lovers, the recording is an obvious necessity; for those who have never been able to warm to the composer's more obviously "serious" music, this is an excellent opportunity to hear it—quite literally—for the very first time.

Piano Music

Bolcom, piano. Nonesuch 79151-2 [CD].

The major qualitative difference between the songs of Franz Schubert and those of George Gershwin is that, by and large, Gershwin worked with better texts. The best of the songs that he wrote to lyrics by his brother Ira *are* the enduring lieder of the twentieth century. Often, all that separates works like "An die Musik" and "The Man I Love" is their harmonic language and emotional content; as to their ultimate merit, five hundred years from now the connoisseur of art songs will probably be hard-pressed to choose between them.

In addition to the "Gershwin Song Book"—arrangements of eighteen songs that were made by the composer himself—this inviting Nonesuch recording gathers together most of Gershwin's music for solo piano in performances that are as stylish as they are unaffected.

An eclectic and frequently arresting composer in his own right, William Bolcom speaks Gershwin's musical language without any discernible accent: the frequently recorded *Three Preludes* sound more mysterious and rhythmically intriguing than they ever have before, and the *Rialto Ripples* are tossed off with a typically Gershwin-esque wise-guy smile.

Porgy and Bess

Haymon, Blackwell, Clarey, White, Baker, Evans, Glyndebourne
Festival Chorus, London Philharmonic, Rattle. Angel
CDCC 56220 [CD].

Although many of its arias have long since become popular standards—is there anyone who can forget their first encounter with "Summertime"?—Gershwin's last great achievement, *Porgy and Bess*, remains a neglected classic. Its initial run, while more than respectable for an opera, was disastrous by the standards of a Broadway musical, and ever since its ill-fated first production, *Porgy and Bess* has had the undeserved reputation of being a hard-luck show.

The handsome RCA Victor recording by the Houston Grand Opera—the same adventurous company that recently brought us John Adams's *Nixon in China*, whether we wanted it or not—proved conclusively that Gershwin knew precisely what he was about. For with the proper care and dedication—which does not necessarily mean the services of world class voices or an internationally famous conductor—*Porgy and Bess* can clearly be heard as the closest thing we have to the Great American Opera. Not since the pathbreaking Columbia recording that Goddard Lieberson produced in 1950 has any recorded version of the opera made such a convincing case for *Porgy and Bess's* greatness. What a pity that RCA had the shortsightedness to withdraw it from circulation.

Having spent considerable time re-listening to the Angel recording led by Simon Rattle, I must confess that I've warmed to it considerably. The singers are every bit as good as the Houston group—Harolyn Blackwell's version of "Summertime" seems to get sexier every time you hear it—while Rattle's sense of pacing and attention to detail become increasingly impressive. I'll still miss the Houston *Porgy*, but perhaps just a little less.

Gesualdo, Carlo, Prince of Venosa (1560–1613)

Madrigals and Sacred Music

Consort of Musicke, Rooley. L'Oiseau-Lyre 410128-2 [CD].

Hilliard Ensemble. EMI Classics 78118-21215-2 [CD];
  78118-21215-4 [CD].

Oxford Camerata, Summerly. Naxos 8.550742 [CD].

Let the feminists, civil libertarians, and right-to-lifers say what they will about Don Carlo Gesualdo, Prince of Venosa: the man was *not* infirm of purpose. In 1590, having discovered his wife (and first cousin) *in flagrante delicto* with her lover, the Prince had the miscreants murdered and ordered their corpses placed on public display. In the remaining twenty-three years of his life, he devoted himself to the composition of some of the most harmonically adventurous music produced during the entire Renaissance, a music whose tortured dissonances and shocking chromaticism still have an astonishingly modern ring. Among his most passionate admirers was Igor Stravinsky, whose *Tres Sacre Cantiones* and *Monumentum pro Gesualdo* helped spark the modern revival of interest in Gesualdo's unusual, often ravishing art.

Each of the three albums listed here offers excellent introductions to the various facets of Gesualdo's music. Anthony Rooley and the Consort of Musicke are perfect guides to the tormented eroticism of the secular madrigals, while Jeremy Summerly and the dozen gifted singers of the Oxford Camerata are equally polished in the equally expressive sacred motets. For the fully persuaded, the two-CD set by the Hilliard Ensemble of the complete Responses for Holy Week offers the finest realization yet of Gesualdo's masterpiece, a work in which radical musical expression and depth of emotion are fused in perfect equilibrium.

Gibbons, Orlando (1583–1625)

Choral Music

> **Cummings, organ; Oxford Camerata, Summerly. Naxos
> 8.553130 [CD].**

From the opening bars of *O Clap Your Hands,* it's clear that this is one of the most inspired and inspiring recordings of early sacred music in years. Gibbons wrote some of the most intensely moving vocal works of the Tudor era, including those magnificent verse anthems that capture a distinctively English nobility and optimism. The expressive range of these beautifully made pieces is exceptional, from the stark dignity of *See, See, the Word Is Incarnate* to the soaring grandeur of *Hosanna to the Son of David.*

The Oxford Camerata under Jeremy Summerly perform the music with all the obvious devotion it deserves. Their singular purity of tone is especially helpful in revealing Gibbons's often intricate voicing, while the slightly reverberant acoustic infuses everything with an appealing glow. One hopes that their next order of business is an album of the composer's madrigals.

Gilbert, Sir William S. (1836–1911), and Sullivan, Sir Arthur (1842–1900)

H. M. S. Pinafore

> D'Oyly Carte Opera Company, Sargent (recorded 1930).
> Pro Arte CDD 598 [CD].

Iolanthe

> D'Oyly Carte Opera Company, Godfrey. London 414145-2 [CD].

The Mikado

> D'Oyly Carte Opera Company, Nash. London 425190-2 [CD].

Patience

> D'Oyly Carte Opera Company, Godfrey. London 425193-2 [CD].

The Pirates of Penzance

> D'Oyly Carte Opera Company, Godfrey. London 425196-2 [CD].

Like their inedible cuisine (and who but they would even consider *looking* at such emetic delights as "Steak and Kidney Pie" and "Beans on Toast"?) or their public monuments (are there any structures in the civilized world quite as ugly as the Albert Memorial or the facade of Euston Station?), another of the great and presumably imperishable English National Monuments are those fourteen operas written by two of the strangest and most unlikely bedfellows in theatrical history, W. S. Gilbert and Arthur Sullivan. (By the way, the myth that the two were close, inseparable friends is precisely that. From beginning to end, the relationship was characterized by mild mutual respect, tempered by constant suspicion, distrust, and frequently open, albeit gentlemanly, contempt. In fact, all the two men had in common was an unshakable belief that each was prostituting his sacred talent for the sake of making money.)

Those of us who are hopelessly drawn to the Gilbert and Sullivan operas tend to treat the affliction as any other incurable disease. For except among ourselves, to admit a passion for Gilbert and Sullivan is a bit like admitting to something of which one should be slightly ashamed. For instance, that we might be—to quote Sheridan Whiteside in *The Man Who Came to Dinner*—"the sole support of a two-headed brother."

For anyone similarly smitten or for those who are thinking of taking the ghastly plunge for the very first time, the recordings listed here represent a fair cross section of the D'Oyly Carte Opera Company's finest achievements. While the *Iolanthe, Mikado, Patience, Pirates,* and Godfrey-led *Pinafore* recordings are among the very best that the late and greatly lamented company founded by Gilbert and Sullivan themselves would ever make—John Reed, the last in the unbroken line of Savoy patter comics is especially delightful, while the late Donald Adams is an incomparable Dick Deadeye and Pirate King—the 1930 *Pinafore* remains in a class by itself. The principal attraction here, aside from the buoyant conducting of the young Malcolm Sargent, is one of the few complete recorded performances left by the greatest Savoyard of all. After a career spanning more than fifty years, Sir Henry Lytton was the only Gilbert and Sullivan performer ever knighted for his services. Even the great Martyn Green could not approach the horrible perfection of Lytton's Sir Joseph Porter, KCB. Dramatically, it is a triumph of bumbling incompetence and unbridled lechery. Musically, it is absolutely glorious, thanks in no small part to an inimitable "voice" that can best be described as a cross between a soggy Yorkshire pudding and a badly opened beer can.

Ginastera, Alberto (1916–1983)

Concerto for Harp and Orchestra

   Masters, harp; City of London Sinfonia, Hickox. Chandos CHAN
   9434 [CD].

Unlike the artfully disheveled and intensely poetic-looking Brazilian Heitor Villa-Lobos, the Argentinean Alberto Ginastera never quite *appeared* to be what he so clearly was: one of the two most significant composers that South America has so far produced. Described by one friend as having "all the rakish personal charm of a bank teller," Ginastera was a modest, unprepossessing man whose ballet *Panambi* had made him a national figure at the age of twenty. Nowhere was that contrast more obvious than in Ginastera's most celebrated work, the opera *Bomarzo,* which in 1967 made him internationally famous. Centered around the rather excessive experiences of a sixteenth-century hunchbacked Italian duke, *Bomarzo* combined violence (torture, murder, suicide) and sex (nudity, voyeurism, narcissism, homosexuality) into a heady brew that astonished, excited, revolted, and scandalized practically everyone who attended its first performance in Washington, D.C., or who saw the even more sensational production mounted by the New York City Opera in the following year. The president of Argentina personally banned its scheduled premiere in Buenos Aires. One wonders why the old Columbia recording has not been reissued and shudders to think what could be done these days with the cover art.

The Harp Concerto from 1956 is one of the most attractive and readily digestible of Ginastera's works and clearly one of the most important ever written for the instrument. Rachel Masters and Richard Hickox respond sympathetically to its bright colors and infectious rhythms, which the Chandos engineers capture to perfection.

Some of the composer's most significant piano music is handsomely served by Alberto Portugheis on a handsome ASV CD (ASV 865) that runs the gamut from the charming, listener-friendly *Piezas infantiles* to the thorny, explosive *Toccata*. A companion album (ASV 865 [CD]) features the mercurial, endlessly fascinating Cello Sonata (with Aurora Natola-Ginastera, the composer's wife and the work's dedicatee) and the powerful First Piano Sonata in equally authoritative performances

Giordano, Umberto (1867–1948)

Andrea Chénier

> Caballé, Pavarotti, Nucci, National Philharmonic, Chailly. London
> 410117-2 [CD].

The actual moment that probably won Tom Hanks the Academy Award for his performance in *Philadelphia* was the scene in which he explained to Denzel Washington what Maria Callas was singing about in the big Act III aria, "La mamma morta," from *Andrea Chénier*. Actually, it's the tenor who has the lion's share of the great moments in Giordano's impassioned love story set during the French Revolution, from the molten *Improvviso* to the melting "Come un bel dì di maggio." In its sustained inspiration, dramatic power, and wealth of melody, Giordano's third opera is one of the high-water marks of the verismo movement, and its title role has been a favorite of tenors from Zanatello and Gigli to Pavarotti and Domingo.

With Placido Domingo's soaring RCA recording currently unavailable—a European pressing (74321-39499-2 [CD]) has been on the market there for some time; what's keeping BMG from releasing it here?—the London recording is the best stopgap and, indeed, has many qualities that for some will make it preferable to the Domingo. For one thing, Pavarotti's voice is at its most imposing throughout; for another, Montserrat Caballé is vocally superior to Renata Scotto—how typically thrilling those floated *pianissimos* are!—although in dramatic terms she is less than overwhelming. Riccardo Chailly manages to move things along effectively, drawing virtuoso playing from the National Philharmonic. The recorded sound, too, is extremely impressive: vivid, brilliantly detailed, shattering in the big climaxes.

The real reason to acquire the 1969 London recording of Giordano's "other" opera, *Fedora* (433033-2 [CD]), is the singing of the storied Magda Olivero, who in one of her all-too-rare studio recordings confirms all the legends, especially in the heroic company of Mario del Monaco. Lamberto Gardelli's conducting is as incisive as always, while the vivid, lifelike recorded sound demonstrates why the London engineers were once the envy of the industry.

Giuliani, Mauro   (1781–1829)

Guitar Music

> P. Romero, guitar; Academy of St. Martin-in-the-Fields, Marriner.
> Philips 454262-2 [CD].

Universally regarded as the incomparable guitarist of his generation—Beethoven was so enthralled with his playing that he wrote a few pieces for his concerts in Vienna, and the English were so excited by his first visit to London that a special magazine called *The Giulianiad* was launched to report his activities—Mauro Giuliani wrote more than two hundred works for his chosen instrument, most of them pleasant ephemera full of virtuoso fireworks and catchy Italianate tunes. An artist with extraordinary gifts can make the music seem far more significant and memorable than it really is—a guitarist such as Mauro Giuliani was reputed to be, or one such as Pepe Romero clearly is.

This tightly packed Philips Duo collects what sound like definitive performances of Giuliani's major works: the three Guitar Concertos, the *Grand Sonata Eroica* (the title is the publisher Ricordi's wishful thinking), and several sets of variations including the *Variazioni Concertanti*, a late work for two guitars that is probably Giuliani's masterpiece. Pepe Romero's playing is breathtaking in its dazzling bravura and effortless grace, while the accompaniments by Marriner and the Academy could not have been more enchanting. An ideal album for relaxed, uncomplicated listening and a must for guitar fans.

Glazunov, Alexander (1865–1936)

Concerto in A Minor for Violin and Orchestra, Op. 82;
The Seasons, Op. 67

**Shumsky, violin; Scottish National Orchestra,
Järvi. Chandos CHAN-8596 [CD].**

Of all the well-known composers, Nikolai Rimsky-Korsakov had, by far, the most hideous wife. And considering the dispositions of women like Frau Haydn and the dread Pauline Strauss, that's saying something.

At her husband's funeral in 1908, Madame Rimsky-Korsakov, with an atypical rush of human feeling (to say nothing of a completely unprecedented flash of perception) noticed that the deceased's prize pupil, a young man named Igor Stravinsky, was utterly disconsolate. In an effort to comfort him, the woman put her arm on Stravinsky's shoulder and said, "Don't despair. We still have *Glazunov.*"

Although we now tend to think of him primarily as Rimsky's acolyte and as the teacher of Dmitri Shostakovich, such was the extent of Alexander Glazunov's reputation at the turn of the century. That he did not quite become what everyone thought he would—the towering giant of Russian music—came as a shock to everyone, except, perhaps, to the composer himself.

But then, too, neither was he the cut-rate Tchaikovsky that he was widely regarded as being only a generation ago. In the last few years, the musical world—and especially the recording companies—have begun to reassess this minor but immensely attractive musical personality with some extremely gratifying results.

Not surprisingly, that indefatigable Estonian recording machine, Neeme Järvi, is in the vanguard of the current Glazunov revival. While neither recording of the composer's two most enduring achievements—the Violin Concerto and the ballet *The Seasons*—is the last word in delicacy or excitement, both are the best available versions of these once-popular works and might help steer the listener in the even more interesting direction of the Glazunov symphonies.

With the Bamberg Symphony and Bavarian Radio Orchestra, Järvi has recorded all eight of the completed symphonies for Orfeo—a ninth exists as a fragmentary single movement—and almost without exception, both the pieces themselves and the performances are sources of undiluted pleasure. For those who'd prefer to begin slowly rather than investing in the entire set, the best place to begin is at the beginning, with the youthful, invigorating Symphony No. 1. Coupled with the brashly heroic Symphony No. 5 (Orfeo C-093101 [CD], M-093101 [T]), this is an excellent introduction to a body of work that deserves to be far better known.

Glière, Reinhold   (1875–1956)

Symphony No. 3 in B Minor, "Ilya Murometz," Op. 42

BBC Philharmonic, Downes. CHAN 9041 [CD].

Best known for the ballet *The Red Poppy* and its—try as you will—*unforgettable* "Russian Sailor's Dance," Reinhold Glière was the Norman Rockwell of Soviet Socialist Realism, a man whose native musical conservatism (he was in fact irretrievably reactionary) fitted in perfectly with what the tone-deaf Joseph Stalin thought a "revolutionary" society ought to hear.

Glière's most important work, a mammoth programmatic symphony celebrating the life of a legendary Russian hero, is also his most controversial. The debate centers on just *how* bad the "Ilya Murometz" Symphony is.

Heavily edited, as it was in a famous recording by Leopold Stokowski, it was merely awful; given an uncut and committed performance—as it is here—it is *obscene*. Vulgar, vapid, *stupid* beyond description, it is a pathetic mélange of bathos, bombast, and empty, knuckle-headed gestures. It is also terribly loud and terribly long.

If you love "Ilya" as helplessly as I do, you will acquire this splendid, virtually note-complete recording without delay. On the other hand, you might want to hold up on acquiring the other installments in the series. Coupled with the tone poem *The Zaporozhy Cossacks* (whose frightful title says it all), Glière's Second Symphony is rather like a bad steak in that the more you chew it, the bigger it gets (CHAN 9071 [CD]), while the youthful First Symphony is even worse, with—to push the unfortunate metaphor even further—the unsavory texture of (in Neil Simon's phrase) either very old meat or very new cheese. To make matters even worse, the album forces you to endure the *whole* of *The Red Poppy* (CHAN 9160 [CD]). For Glière in a substantially smaller and infinitely more palatable dose, his attractive Harp Concerto from 1938 (going on 1880) sounds sweeter than ever in another recent Chandos recording (CHAN 9094) from the City of London Sinfonia and Richard Hickox.

Glinka, Mikhail (1804–1857)

A Life for the Tsar

Pendachanska, Toczyska, Merritt, Martinovich, Sofia Festival
Orchestra and National Opera Chorus, Tchakarov. Sony Classical
S3K 46487 [CD].

No less an authority on the subject than Igor Stravinsky once said of Mikhail Ivanovich Glinka, "All music in Russia stems from him." What Stravinsky meant, of course, was not that Russia had been a musical wasteland prior to Glinka: Its traditions of liturgical and folk music had been established for centuries before Glinka was born on June 1, 1804. But Glinka was the first composer to write serious music that was as unmistakably Russian as was the poetry of his friend Alexander Pushkin.

Both men had been swept up in the tide of Romantic nationalism that spread across Europe in the early decades of the nineteenth century. In fact, it was during endless St. Petersburg coffeehouse discussions about a national poetry and literature with Pushkin, Gogol, Zhukovsky, and other young writers that Glinka first conceived the notion of a Russian national music based on the modalities of Russian folk song. His first important work to do so was the opera *Ivan Sussanin,* based on the true story of a seventeenth-century peasant who sacrificed himself to save Michael Feodorovich, first of the Romanovs. To the arias and ensembles of Italian opera, Glinka added a group of thrilling choruses based on the old *slavsia* (songs of praise), while other melodies are derived from folk tunes and old Russian church music. Tsar Nicholas himself attended one of the early rehearsals and was so enthusiastic that the grateful composer renamed his opera *A Life for the Tsar.*

The best thing in this live performance from the Sofia National Opera is the conducting of the late Emil Tchakarov, a man who clearly understood the peasant underpinnings of Glinka's music and inspired his company to some hugely satisfying feats of red-blooded singing and playing. The soloists, too, seem to revel in the down-to-earth lyricism, and unlike the incredibly intrusive Sofia audience in Sviatoslav Richter's famous 1960 hack-and-sneeze recording of Mussorgsky's *Pictures at an Exhibition*, you'd hardly know *this* bunch of Bulgarians was there.

Russlan and Ludmilla

**Gorchakova, Diadkova, Bogachova, Netrebko, Masurin, Ognovenko,
Kirov Opera Chorus and Orchestra, Gergiev. Philips 456248-2 [CD].**

The text of Glinka's second and final opera was born under an evil star. Based on an early poem of Pushkin, the libretto was to have been fashioned by the poet himself; his untimely death in a duel forced Glinka to turn the project over to no fewer than five collaborators, each of whom did his utmost to make an already muddled story even more confusing. The first production in December of 1842 was not a success—the powerful critic Alexander Serov considered it "the last aberration of lamentably warped genius"—and by the time it was revived triumphantly in 1859, Glinka had been dead for two years.

Whatever dramatic limitations continue to afflict this fairy tale of a Russian princess who is kidnapped by an evil magician and must be saved by one of three suitors, none are obvious in this riveting live performance from the Kirov Opera. Vladimir Ognovenko and Anna Netrebko are suitably fresh and ardent in the title roles while the rest of the large cast is no less excellent, particularly Larissa Diadkova in the trouser role of Ratmir, the oriental prince. Valery Gergiev inspires some stunning work from both the orchestra and chorus—especially as the "voice" of the giant head the hero battles in Act II—and although taped at a series of actual performances, the recorded sound remains focused and true throughout.

Recordings of the scintillating *Russlan and Ludmilla* overture are many and varied. The one that captures maximum excitement without turning it into a breathless horse race is a 1959 RCA recording (09026-68363-2 [CD]; 09026-68363-4 [T]) with Fritz Reiner and the Chicago Symphony. Feodor Chaliapin's famous 1938 version of the hilarious, tongue-twisting *Farlaf's Rondo* is available on two indispensable Pearl CDs (PEA 9920), which also feature this greatest of all Russian singers in arias from *Boris Godunov, A Life for the Tsar, Russalka* (Dargomizhsky's, not Dvořák's), *Prince Igor, Sadko, The Demon,* and *Aleko.*

Gluck, Christoph Willibald (1717–1787)

Orfeo ed Euridice

Horne, Lorengar, Donath, Chorus and Orchestra of the Royal Opera House, Covent Garden, Solti. London 417410-2 [CD].

Listening to this best-known of Gluck's "Reform" Operas today, it is all but impossible to understand the violent passions it unleashed more than two centuries ago. In Paris, where Gluck had set up shop in 1773, the composer's insistence that drama, instead of florid singing, should be the true focus of the operatic stage generated heated public debates. As a matter of fact, it even provoked a number of private duels, in which many of his partisans and those of his principal rival, Niccolò Piccinni, were killed. Today, of course, Gluck's revolutionary operas seem rather tame and timid stuff, largely because the reforms he inaugurated have long been accepted as elementary tenets of how opera should behave.

After Purcell's *Dido and Aeneas, Orfeo ed Euridice* is the earliest extant opera that is performed with any frequency today. While the action is generally static, and the characters are little more than cardboard cut-outs, *Orfeo* has some beautiful moments that still have the power to move us deeply, including the celebrated "Dance of the Blessèd Spirits" and the haunting aria "Che farò senza Euridice."

With Dame Janet Baker's Glyndebourne Festival recording currently unavailable, the Solti recording is an acceptable, if not wholly satisfying, alternative. Vocally, Marilyn Horne makes an impressive hero: her deep, throaty sound and virile delivery are both positive assets in the role of Orfeo. If Pilar Lorengar, as Euridice, has seen better days—the characterization is surprisingly tentative and the sound is insecure and unfocused—then Sir Georg Solti, who would seem to be rather out of his element in this staid and stately music, gives one of the better recorded performances of his career. The conducting is as tasteful as it is pointed, and rarely—as in "The Dance of the Blessèd Spirits"—has this music conveyed more genuine feeling or quiet charm.

Goldmark, Karl (1830–1915)

Rustic Wedding Symphony

Royal Philharmonic, Butt. ASV CD DCA 791 [CD].

The son of an impoverished synagogue cantor born in the small Hungarian town of Keszthely, Karl Goldmark would eventually become one of the most popular and respected composers of his generation, thanks largely to a group of three works dashed out in short order between 1875 and 1878, beginning with the exotic and tuneful *The Queen of Sheba*. Three years later, Goldmark produced one of the most instantly appealing of all late-Romantic violin concertos, which has never sounded more like the standard repertoire item it clearly deserves to be than in Itzhak Perlman's sumptuous now-deleted EMI Classics recording or a fine recent Delos album (DE 3156 [CD]) by Nai-Yuan Hu, the Seattle Symphony, and Gerard Schwarz, which imaginatively couples the work with the rarely heard D Minor Concerto of Max Bruch.

Goldmark's masterpiece, though, is the delightful *Rustic Wedding Symphony* of 1876, which Brahms described as "clear-cut and faultless" and the young Mahler obviously admired, too. The ASV recording by the Royal Philharmonic led by Yondani Butt is the most impressive since Leonard Bernstein's New York Philharmonic version from the late 1960s. Like Bernstein, Butt resists the temptation of making the bucolic and purposefully naive music sound more sophisticated than it was intended to be; the result is a wholly natural, spontaneous-sounding performance that contains not the slightest hint of strain or condescension. In place of the more familiar Overture *Im Frühling*, the slightly windy (eighteen-minute) but generally charming *Sakuntala Overture* is the generous fill.

Górecki, Henryk (1933–)

Symphony No. 3, "Symphony of Sorrowful Songs"

Upshaw, London Sinfonietta, Zinman. Nonesuch 79382-2 [CD], 79319-4 [T].

There are some bits of bitter, pessimistic wisdom that you desperately hope aren't true—from Voltaire's glib assertion that "Marriage is a dull meal at which dessert is served at the beginning" to Dostoyevsky's rueful suggestion that "I believe the best definition of man is the ungrateful biped."

Yet amid the darkest ruminations of the poets and philosophers—from Chamfort's "Whoever is not a misanthrope at forty can never have loved mankind" to Diane de Poitier's "To have a good enemy, choose a friend: he knows where to strike"—some of the most disturbing of all are the ones that question our capacity for wisdom itself: from "There's one born every minute" to that horrendous possibility proposed by the archiconoclast H. L. Mencken, who blithely insisted, "No one ever went broke underestimating the intelligence of the American people."

The Third Symphony of the Polish composer Henryk Górecki is almost enough to make you believe the most cynical curmudgeons may actually have a point. In a recent *Record Shelf* called "Flim-Flams, Frauds, and Floozies"—an angry look at some of the more blatant of recent musical frauds—the Górecki Third was the featured work, after due consideration was given to: Zamfir, undisputed master (since who else in their right mind would want to bother?) of the ridiculous pan flute; the cocktail piano Puccini of John Bayless; the "Three Tenors Concert," which offers a lot of shouting, bellowing, and generally second-rate singing; Paul McCartney's kitschy and excruciating *Liverpool Oratorio;* that sophomoric, amateurish, misbegotten swill called "The Juliet Letters" by Elvis Costello; the aptly named "Low" Symphony (adapted from the music of David Bowie) by Philip Glass; and Górecki's most serious competitor, the sleazy and oafish Leslie Garrett, a soprano of transcendentally modest accomplishment whose willingness to display herself on the album covers in various degrees of sexual arousal has earned her a fortune.

In a two-page ad taken out in *The Gramophone,* that most important and influential of English Classical Music magazines, Elektra/Nonesuch, the publishers of Górecki's Third Symphony, reproduced a sampling of the witheringly negative reviews the piece had received, from *The Evening Standard*'s abrupt "A load of gloomy piffle," to Michael Kennedy's admonition "Why this really rather dreary symphony has sent all those people to the record shops baffles me." On another page, they offered statistics in place of opinions—including the most important one of all from their point of view, "Over 300,000 copies sold."

The implication is obvious: How can that many satisfied customers be wrong? To answer that purely rhetorical question, they can be wrong as easily as all those people who bought another surprising classical best-seller of a generation ago, a dull exercise in tone clusters that, had it been called "Etude No. 2," would have gone completely unnoticed but that created a sensation because it was called "Threnody for the Victims of Hiroshima."

Based on various sacred and secular laments—including one inscribed on a wall at Gestapo headquarters in Warsaw—the politically correct Third Symphony is equally dull, but dull in a slightly different way. For the concentrated dullness of Penderecki's "Threnody" is merely diluted in Górecki's Symphony.

As Dr. Johnson said of Thomas Gray, "He was dull in a new way, and that made many people think him great." Or, even more to point, as the good Doctor said of Sheridan: "He is dull, naturally dull; but it must have taken him a great deal of pains to become what we now see him. Such an excess of stupidity, Sir, is not in nature."

Over 300,000 copies sold. The mind reels.

Gottschalk, Louis Moreau (1829–1969)

Music of Gottschalk

Various artists. Vox CDX 5009 [CD].

America's first great matinee idol, Louis Moreau Gottschalk was one of the most colorful figures of nineteenth-century music: a spellbinding pianist whose concerts generated the same hysteria as those of Franz Liszt, a legendary womanizer whose affair with a student at the Oakland Female Seminary escalated into a national scandal that forced him to flee the country, and the first American composer whose music reflected the richness of Creole, Afro-Hispanic, and other recognizably American idioms, clearly pointing to the eventual emergence of ragtime and jazz.

This generously packed two-CD set from Vox is a nearly ideal introduction to Gottschalk's always vivid, frequently vulgar world. Although the two "symphonies" *A Night in the Tropics* and *A Montevideo* have sounded more idiomatic (especially in the memorable Vanguard recording of the former by the Utah Symphony and Maurice Abravanel—OVC 4051 [CD]), the works for piano and orchestra have never had a more persuasive exponent than the late Eugene List, who more than anyone else sparked the modern Gottschalk revival. His witty, overripe, wonderfully stylish recordings of the solo piano music are also available from Vanguard (OVC 4050 [CD]).

Gould, Morton (1913–1996)

Fall River Legend (suite); *Declaration* (suite); *Interplay* for Piano and Orchestra; *Latin American Symphonette* (selections)

Morton Gould Orchestra, Gould. RCA 09026-61651-2 [CD].

The music of Morton Gould has always been so readily approachable, so lucid, entertaining, and supremely well made, that it has been understandably neglected in some modern music quarters—especially those that insist that New Music must be obscure, difficult, mindless, unpleasant, or all of the above. Beginning with the first of the *American Symphonettes* in 1933, and continuing through works like the *Spirituals for Orchestra,* the *Cowboy Rhapsody,* and the ballet *Fall River Legend,* Gould was always keenly interested in American themes and the unmistakable inflections of popular American music. "Whatever newness there might be in my music," he said in an interview in the mid-1950s, "is not so much a radical departure as an integration and crystallization of influences in our native American scene. It is a distillation of the heavy and light—not necessarily one or the other."

Here, in classic recordings, are four of the works that helped establish Morton Gould as one of the most popular and frequently performed of American composers. Gould's own version of the suite from *Fall River Legend* is so gripping that you realize why many have compared the work favorably to Copland's *Appalachian Spring,* while the *Tango* and *Guaracha* from the *Latin American Symphonette* are irresistible.

Gould's most celebrated work, *American Salute*—a scintillating four-minute series of variations on "When Johnny Comes Marching Home"—is still brilliantly represented by Arthur Fiedler's recording with the Boston Pops (RCA 6806-2-RD [CD], 6806-4-RG6 [T]), part of an uncommonly attractive American album featuring works by Bernstein, Copland, Gershwin, Grofé, and Richard Rodgers.

Gounod, Charles (1818–1893)

Roméo et Juliette

Malfitano, Kraus, Quilico, Van Dam, Bacquier, Capitole de Toulouse Chorus and Orchestra, Plasson. Angel CDCC-47365 [CD].

Poor Charles Gounod has fallen on decidedly hard times. But then again, it's rather difficult to work up any real sympathy for one of the luckiest musicians who ever lived. It was a major miracle that the man who was perhaps the tenth-best French composer of his generation parlayed a gift for sugary melody into one of the greatest successes in the history of the operatic stage. His opera *Faust* was once performed with such monotonous frequency that a turn-of-the-century wag recommended that the Metropolitan in New York be renamed the "Faustspielhaus."

That *Faust* may finally be losing its vicelike grip on the world's affections is suggested by the fact that while there are currently about a dozen available recordings of the opera, only one of them really works: the recent (and magnificently sung) Angel recording with Cheryl Studer, Richard Leech, Thomas Hampson, José van Dam, and the Capitole de Toulouse Orchestra led by Michel Plasson (CDCC 54228 [CD]).

In marked contrast to the composer's immensely lucrative Goethe travesty, his setting of Shakespeare's *Romeo and Juliet* is a far less presumptuous, and probably far finer, work. With the proper cast, this genuinely touching but sadly neglected opera can make a very moving impression, as this superb Angel recording easily proves. While the two principals don't exactly efface the memory of the legendary performances that Jussi Björling and the Brazilian soprano Bidù Saÿao gave at the Metropolitan Opera shortly after the end of the War, both are exceptionally fine: Catherine Malfitano is a melting, delectably innocent Juliette, and the Romeo of the aging but always canny Alfredo Kraus is a triumph of interpretive savvy and consummate musicianship over a voice that has clearly lost its bloom. As in his *Faust* recording, Michel Plasson's conducting is consistently sensitive, supportive, and richly romantic. The orchestra plays wonderfully, and the recorded sound is first rate.

Grainger, Percy (1882–1961)

Composer, conductor, pianist, ethnomusicologist, linguistic theorist—he thought his true mission in life was to purge the English language of its corrupting Latin influences; hence, in his scores he eschewed words such as *crescendo* in favor of toothsome phrases like "louden lots"—the Australian-born Percy Grainger was one of the certifiable madmen of twentieth-century music.

He experimented in polyphony plus electronic and "chance" music well in advance of almost everyone and was married before a cheering crowd of fifteen thousand during an intermission at a Hollywood Bowl concert in 1928—at which he conducted the premiere of *To a Nordic Princess*, written for his bride. He maintained that the three greatest composers in history were Bach, Frederick Delius, and Duke Ellington, and following the example of the English philosopher Jeremy Bentham—who left his entire fortune to the University of London on condition that his corpse be present at all subsequent meetings of the Board—stipulated in his will that his remains be stuffed and placed on display at the Grainger Museum at the University of Melbourne. (Alas, cooler heads prevailed.)

In addition to be being an irrepressible zany, Grainger was one of the most distinctive musical talents of his generation: a great pianist in an era of great pianists, a fearlessly quirky and individual composer, and perhaps the most inspired arranger of folk music who has ever lived.

His evergreen *Lincolnshire Posy* is available again in the classic recording by the Eastman Wind Ensemble led by Frederick Fennell (Mercury Living Presence 423754-2 [CD]), whose equally memorable versions of Grainger standards like "Country Gardens," "Mock Morris," and "Handel in the Strand" can be found on another Mercury Living Presence CD (434330-2). Kenneth Montgomery leads the Bournemouth Sinfonietta in a Chandos anthology (CHAN 6542 [CD]) that is every bit as enjoyable (the version of "Blithe Bells," a "free ramble" on Bach's "Sheep May Safely Graze" is alone worth the price of the album), while the Michigan State University Symphonic Band steps off very smartly on a Delos album (DE 3101 [CD]) called "To the Fore!"

The music that Grainger "dished up for piano" is brilliantly realized by Nimbus albums (NI-5220-2 [CD], NC-5220 [T]; NI 7703 [CD]). Jones's playing is as fresh and imaginative as the music itself and there isn't a single less than intriguing performance (or piece, for that matter) in the entire collection. The arrangements for piano four-hands are also delectably served by the duo piano team of Thwaites and Lavender on a pair of Pearl CDs (SHE CD 9611 [CD], 9623 [CD], 9631 [CD]), while Richard and John Contiguglia have recorded those inspired Gershwin arrangements on a beautiful album for MCA (MCAD-6626 [CD], MCAC-6626 [T]).

On an intriguing Chandos album called "Themes of Grainger" (CHAN 9346 [CD]), the Academy of St. Martin-in-the-Fields Chamber Ensemble offer delectable performances of nine Grainger standards, including "Molly on the Shore," "Handel in the Strand," "Mock Morris," and the "Irish Tune from County Derry," together with Kenneth Leighton's *Fantasy Octet on Themes of Grainger,* a severe and beautiful work that proves a real find.

Having clearly established his credentials as a major Graingerian with his stunning Deutsche Grammophon recording (445860-2 [CD] of *The Warriors,* that magnificently outlandish "Music to an Imaginary Ballet," John Eliot Gardiner's Philips recording of folksong and other arrangements (446657-2 [CD]) is one the most important and entertaining Grainger releases since Benjamin Britten's shamefully withdrawn *Salute to Percy Grainger.* In addition to "I'm Seventeen Come Sunday," "Brigg Fair," "Scotch Strathspey and Reel" (a raucous, eight-minute meditation on "What Shall We Do with the Drunken Sailor?"), and the *Bolero*-like "Lost Land Found," there are some real off-the-wall items like *Tribute to Foster* and the *Love Verses from the Song of Solomon,* all performed with deep affection and high zest.

Sir Simon Rattle's EMI collection (CDC 56412 [CD]) is no less exhilarating than Gardiner's. One of Grainger's most challenging works, the suite *In a Nutshell,* is given its most penetrating recorded performance, while the *Lincolnshire Posy* seems positively new-minted. Most intriguing of all are two dazzling French arrangements—Debussy's *Pagodes* (from *Estampes*) and Ravel's *La Vallée des cloches*—both in performances of surpassing subtlety and skill.

In what is easily the most exciting news Grainger-lovers have ever heard, Chandos has announced its intention to record every single note of the man's music in a coordinated integral series that when complete will run to some twenty-five CDs. At press time, the first five volumes (CHAN 9554 [CD], 9499 [CD], 9549 [CD], 9503 [CD], 9584 [CD]) have proven to be almost everything that the most fanatical Grainger devotee could have wished. The quality and infectious enthusiasm of the performances, the recorded sound and notes, even the handsome packaging that color-coordinates the albums by general category—music for orchestra, songs for baritone, works for band—is in every way exemplary. Under Richard Hickox's spirited direction, the albums for chorus and orchestra are full of zest and color—the Kipling setting *The Widow's Party* is an ear-popping delight—and the first of the wind ensemble issues with the Royal Northern College of Wind Music Orchestra led by Timothy Reynish and Clark Rundell is the snazziest since Fennell's.

Finally, Grainger's own extraordinary gifts as a pianist are on abundant display in a Pearl recital (GEMM CD 9957 [CD] that features music of Bach, Chopin, Schumann, Grieg, Debussy, and Grainger in recordings made between

1923 and 1948. The playing is among the most individual and incandescent ever captured in a recording studio and the transfers are superb. His famous interpretation of the Grieg Piano Concerto can be sampled on a Music and Arts CD (MUA 1002) that features a live 1946 Hollywood Bowl performance conducted by Leopold Stokowski. If the performance might sound wayward and idiosyncratic to modern ears, then keep in mind that Grainger was the composer's favorite interpreter of the work. Also invaluable is the version from piano and orchestra of *In a Nutshell,* dished up with consummate zaniness and authority.

Granados, Enrique (1867–1916)

Goyescas

De Larrocha, piano. EMI Classics CDMB 65424 [CD].

When the SS *Sussex* went down in the English channel, torpedoed by a German U-boat in the second year of the Great War, she took with her one of the most original talents that Spain had ever produced, the forty-nine-year old composer Enrique Granados. Although the composer was actually pulled out of the water by a British lifeboat, he dove back in to save his wife and both were drowned.

With his friend Isaac Albéniz, Granados reawakened serious music in Spain with a group of colorful, electric, rhythmically vibrant reactions to the etchings and paintings of Francisco Goya. The suite for piano, *Goyescas,* not only helped to establish the vocabulary and parameters of modern Spanish music but also has remained a pianistic tour de force to be undertaken only by the most fearless virtuosos. (Granados would later adapt the music into an opera by the same name, adding an orchestral *Intermezzo* that would eventually become his most familiar work.)

As in her most recent recording of *Ibéria,* Alicia de Larrocha is literally incomparable in this music. Other pianists have certainly tried to invest *Goyescas* with this kind of wit, passion, and insouciance but none has ever come close. She makes it all sound so natural and preposterously *easy* that we need only sit back, relax, and enjoy the spells cast by one of the most beguiling sorceresses in living memory.

Until a complete recording of the opera surfaces—breath-holding is definitely *not* encouraged—Victoria de los Angeles's 1950 recording of bits and pieces has resurfaced on EMI (CDH 64028-2 [CD]), together with her classic versions of songs by de Falla and Turina. The one—the only—recording of the famous *Intermezzo* remains Fritz Reiner's (RCA 09026-61608-2 [CD], 09026-61608-2 [T]), from that indispensable anthology of Iberian favorites called *Spain*.

The same virtues that make de Larrocha's *Goyescas* so memorable can also be heard in her stunning recording of the *Danzas espagñolas* available on another EMI CD (CDM 64529) with the *Allegro di concierto* and *Danza lenta*. The '60s recorded sound remains clear and faithful.

Guitar Music

Bream, guitar. RCA 09026-61608-2 [CD], 09026-61608-4 [T].

What Alicia de Larrocha's recordings are to the piano music of Granados, Julian Bream's are to the music for guitar. While all of these works began life as piano pieces, Bream's performances are so completely idiomatic and redolent with flamenco feeling that they make it seem as though they couldn't have been written for anything else. While the *Valses poeticos* are particularly astonishing in both their grace and Spanish flavor, all of the performances are little short of miraculous, as is the immediacy of the recorded sound.

Montserrat Caballé's recording of songs (RCA 09026-62539-2 [CD]) is one of the most valuable Granados albums ever issued, not only because of the quality of the performances but also because of the exceptional value of the *canciones* themselves. The best of them—"Mira que soy niño," "El mirar de la maja," and "L'Ocell profeta"—are as fine as almost any of the far more familar songs of Manuel de Falla, and all certainly deserve to be much better known.

Gregorian Chant

Nova Schola Gregoriana. Naxos 8.550711 [CD]; 8.550952 [CD].

Schola Hungarica. Hungariton HCD 12048 [CD]; HCD 12559; HDC 12889 [CD]; HCD 31086 [CD]; HCD 31168 [CD]; HDC 903031 [CD].

Only a few years ago, no rational person could have predicted the sudden, inexplicable popularity of this ancient music, much less the elevation to pop icon status of the monks of the Monasterio Benedictino de Santo Domingo de Silos, whose *Chant* albums for EMI Classics have out-sold those of many a rock star. Whatever the reason for this surprising turn of events, it would seem to have less to do with some brilliant marketing ploy—as in the fetching cover art adorning an RCA recording that is already being called the "cleavage" *Carmina Burana*—and still less with any real appreciation of the subtle intricacies of its inspired monotony, than a conscious, completely understandable attempt to turn the "mood-altering" characteristics of this hypnotic serenity into a convenient quick-fix cure for the ills of an increasingly savage (and noisy) society. In short, it would seem that chant has become for the '90s what the sitar was for the '60s.

Those wishing to move beyond the best-selling *Chant* (CDC 4DS-55138 [CD]; 2435-55138-4 [T]) and *Chant Noël* (CDC 55206 [CD]; 4DS 55206 [T]) should begin with the two lovely Naxos albums, which in addition to being very inexpensive are very well produced; hard-core addicts are directed to any of the several stunning albums by the Budapest-based Schola Hungarica, who not only sing with uncommon clarity and passion but also enliven the texture with boy trebles and women.

Grieg, Edvard   (1843–1907)

Piano Concerto in A Minor, Op. 16

> **Perahia, piano; Bavarian Radio Orchestra, Davis.**
>   **CBS MK-44899 [CD].**
>
> **Andsnes, piano; Bergen Philharmonic, Kitayenko.**
>   **Virgin Classics 59613 [CD].**

One of the most apt but not completely flattering descriptions of the music of Edvard Grieg came from Claude Debussy, who called the diminutive Norwegian composer "a bonbon filled with snow." The implication, of course, is that along with the bracing Nordic freshness of his music, Grieg was essentially a miniaturist, a composer of delicious little trifles and nothing more. For more than a century one of the most popular of all Romantic piano concertos has given the lie to the suggestion that Grieg was only at his best when he was thinking small. True, his finest work *does* tend to come in smaller packages, but this enduring classic also demonstrates that he was perfectly comfortable in large-scale forms as well.

From a recording made at an actual concert, Murray Perahia and Sir Colin Davis turn in a performance of uncommon dramatic power and interpretive finesse: one of those rare recordings in which everyone concerned seems to walk the tightrope between Romantic anarchy and modern control. The disciplined and completely unobtrusive German audience almost forgets to breathe, and the recorded sound is supremely transparent and warm.

The Virgin Classics recording by the young Leif Ove Andsnes is the finest in a generation, with an easy brilliance of execution allied to the most probing poetic insight. The sense of utter spontaneity is also remarkable, as though in the more rhapsodic passages the pianist is simply making it up as he goes along. A second Grieg collection (CDC 59300 [CD]) containing equally marvelous versions of some of the *Lyric Pieces, Poetic Tone Pictures,* and the normally elusive E Minor Piano Sonata suggests that Andsnes may be the most interesting young pianist to have arrived on the scene since Krystian Zimerman.

If sound is not a major consideration, then no recording has ever duplicated the poetry and insight of Dinu Lipatti's eternal 1947 recording, now available on a lovingly remastered Angel CD (CDH-63497) or on an Odyssey tape (YT 60141).

Holberg Suite, Op. 40

Orpheus Chamber Orchestra. Deutsche Grammophon 423060-2 [CD].

Written for the bicentennial of the birth of Ludvig Holberg, the patriarch of Danish literature, the *Suite from Holberg's Time* is, after *Peer Gynt* and the Piano Concerto, the most popular and most frequently recorded of Grieg's larger works.

The recording by the Orpheus Chamber Orchestra finds that brilliant conductorless ensemble at the top of its form, in both the *Holberg Suite* and the *Two Elegiac Melodies* that accompany it. It's a pity that in place of the very fine version of the Tchaikovsky *Serenade for Strings,* they couldn't have recorded another major Grieg work. Better yet, perhaps DG could graft their performances onto an exceptional Grieg recording by Neeme Järvi and the Gothenberg Symphony. That strenuously recommended release (419431-2 [CD]) brings you the finest available versions of the *Lyric Suite,* the *Norwegian Dances,* and the *Symphonic Dances,* Op. 64. It's not only a great Grieg bash but also a great buy.

Lyric Pieces

Gilels, piano. Deutsche Grammophon 449721-2 [CD].

Here are some of the most bewitching piano miniatures ever, in performances that are not likely to equaled, much less surpassed. Emil Gilels might seem to be well off his regular beat in this music, but his recording remains a standard against which all others will be judged. The playing reaches stratospheric heights, and the mixture of the familiar with the scarcely known works makes this one of the most desirable Grieg recordings ever made.

Anyone *seriously* devoted to this composer's piano music will find all of it—yes, *all* of it—on a monumental set of ten Bis compact discs (BCD-104-113) that feature the gifted and apparently indefatigable Eva Knardahl. If her playing cannot really compare with either Gilels's or Gieseking's, then it is not to be taken lightly, either. The interpretations are for the most part balanced, idiomatic, and unobtrusive yet are not lacking in fire and individuality whenever the spirit moves her or the music demands. Not the least of the innumerable attractions of this gallant undertaking is the recorded sound. As we might expect from Bis— Robert von Bahr's small but maniacally perfectionist Swedish label—this is as close to being in a room with an actual piano as modern technology has come.

The Hungarian pianist Balázs Szokolay's recordings for Naxos (8.550450 [CD], 8.550577 [CD], 8.550650 [CD]) are very distinguished indeed. There is an unforced natural charm in Szokolay's playing, together with a feeling of utter spontaneity that places the best of his performances on the same rarefied heights as Gilels's. They are among the most enjoyable Grieg recordings currently available and, at a mere six bucks a pop, represent a rather incredible bargain

Peer Gynt (incidental music), Op. 23

Hollweg, soprano; Beecham Choral Society, Royal Philharmonic, Beecham. Angel CDM 64751 [CD].

Carlsen, Hanssen, Bjorkoy, Hansli, Oslo Philharmonic Chorus, London Symphony, Drier. Unicorn UKCD-2003/04 [CD].

Like Tchaikovsky, who thoroughly despised his *Nutcracker* Suite, and Sergei Rachmaninoff, who often became violently nauseous at the prospect of having to give yet another performance of his C-sharp Minor Prelude, Edvard Grieg was not especially fond of his most frequently performed work. In a famous letter written to the playwright Henrik Ibsen, he had this to say of the soon-to-be world-famous *In the Hall of the Mountain King:* "I have written something for the hall of the Troll king which smacks of so much cow dung, ultra-Norwegianism, and self-satisfaction that I literally cannot bear to listen to it." In that, of course, Grieg has always been a minority of one. For the score he composed for a production of Ibsen's poetic drama *Peer Gynt* contains some of the best-loved moments in all of music.

For anyone who cut their musical teeth on the evergreen chestnuts from the two *Peer Gynt* Suites, the world premiere recording, from Unicorn, of the complete incidental music will come as a major and unfailingly delightful surprise. (Incidentally, all the other recordings that claim to contain the "complete" incidental music are stretching the laws of truth in advertising. With Neeme Järvi's recent, and slightly less successful, Deutsche Grammophon recording, there are now precisely *two.*) Containing nearly an hour of unknown *Peer Gynt* music, the performance led by the fine Norwegian conductor Per Drier makes for an enlightening experience, to say the very least. While the "heavy hits" are all done to near-perfection, the cumulative impact of the other, completely unfamiliar episodes creates the more indelible impression. Far from being the lightweight collection of saccharine lollipops it can often become, the *Peer Gynt* music for once emerges as vivid and powerful drama. Drier leads his forces with great individuality, charm, and authority; the Norwegian cast and chorus are consistently brilliant and idiomatic; and the playing of the London Symphony is above reproach.

The only serious flaw in this otherwise flawless recording is one that none of these dedicated performers could possibly control. For all its professionalism and devotion, it is simply *not* in the same stratospheric league with that vocally klutzy, harshly recorded source of wonder and despair that Sir Thomas Beecham perpetrated a generation ago. In its new compact disc incarnation, this ageless performance seems even more magnetic and unsurpassable than ever. *Anitra's Dance* contains some of the most graceful playing ever captured in a recording studio, the *Death of Aase* becomes a muffled outcry of insupportable grief, and *Morning* dawns with a sylvan freshness that suggests the first morning of the world. Yet it is in *The Hall of the Mountain King* that Beecham really makes us wonder what the composer's whining "cow dung" letter was all about. Unless, of course, Beecham read it, too, and took that as his cue to do his best, in this macabre and terrifying performance, to scare a similar substance out of his listeners.

Sonatas for Violin and Piano (3)

Dumay, violin; Pires, piano. Deutsche Grammophon 437525-2 [CD].

Grieg completed only five mature chamber works during his career, all of which continue to refute the suggestion—as the Piano Concerto already had—that Grieg was incapable of sustaining inspiration over lengthier musical forms. In the three Violin Sonatas composed between 1865 and 1887, the manipulation of the thematic material is masterful and highly original, with the themes themselves pouring forth in inspired profusion. Augustin Dumay and Maria João Pires are consistently fresh and persuasive in all three, reveling in the melodic richness of the music while revealing the solid architecture underneath.

Grieg was especially proud of his only completed String Quartet, finished in the summer of 1878. "It strives toward breadth, soaring flight, and above all resonance for the instruments for which it was written." And so it certainly does in the classic 1938 recording by the Budapest Quartet, coupled in a Biddulph reissue (LAB 098 [CD]) with their equally unapproachable versions of Sibelius's *Voces intimae* Quartet and Hugo Wolf's *Italian Serenade*. A fine modern alternative is the Olympia recording (OLY 432 [CD]) by the Raphael Quartet, which also features a reconstruction by Julius Röntgen of the two movements from the unfinished F Major Quartet of 1891 and the *Andante con moto* for Piano, Violin, and Cello.

Dedicated to the composer's cello-playing brother John and containing a theme in the second movement that bears a striking resemblance to the "Homage March" from *Sigurd Jorsalfar,* the Cello Sonata of 1883 is a boldly imaginative work, given a richly inventive performance by Steven Isserlis and Stephen Hough on their RCA album (09026-68290-2 [CD]) called "Forgotten Romance."

The lyrical, plain-spoken Cello Sonata No. 1 by Anton Rubinstein and a sequence of Liszt miniatures round out this extremely desirable collection.

Songs

Von Otter, mezzo-soprano; Forsberg, piano. Deutsche Grammophon 437521-2 [CD].

From Jenny Lind and Olive Fremstad to Jussi Björling and Birgit Nilsson, tiny Sweden has produced an exceptional collection of first-rate singers, including the delicious mezzo-soprano Anne Sophie von Otter. With a voice of extraordinary range and color guided by a commanding musical intelligence, she is not only one of the great Mozart singers of her generation but also, arguably, its most accomplished and daring lieder specialist.

To date, she has not made a finer album than this inspired Grieg recital, which was *Gramophone*'s Record of the Year in 1993. The composer's most important cycle, *Haugtussa* (The Mountain Maid), has never had a more pointed or richly various recording, while the individual items are similarly done to perfection. Amid the flood of recordings issued to mark the composer's sesquicentennial, this one still stands out.

As does the massive, three-CD collection from Simax (PSC 1810), which features an astonishing roster of Golden Age singers, including Chaliapin, Destinn, Farrar, Flagstad, Galli-Curci, Lehmann (Lilli, not Lotte), Rethberg, Slezak, Tauber, and Tetrazzini in nearly eighty songs. Although there is considerable repetition—eleven versions of *Jag elsker Dig* (I Love Thee) and sixteen *Solveig's Songs*—and the recorded sound is very much of the period, this is an invaluable lesson in Grieg interpretation from artists who were, for the most part, his contemporaries. Most moving of all is a noisy fragment recorded in 1889 by Nina Grieg, the composer's wife.

For those who don't need quite this much historic Grieg, a fine RCA collection (09026-61827-2 [CD]) offers many of the same singers (together with Melchior, Traubel, and the radiant Lucy Isabelle Marsh) in a far more manageable form.

Griffes, Charles Tomlinson (1884–1920)

The Kairn of Koridwen

Ensemble M, deCou. Koch 3-7216-2 [CD].

Prior to his death at the age of thirty-five, Charles Tomlinson Griffes was the most gifted and original American composer of his generation and quite possibly the most significant musical talent America had yet produced. His *Poem for Flute and Orchestra, The White Peacock,* and *The Pleasure Dome of Kubla Khan* are among the most physically beautiful musical works of the period, while his extraordinary Piano Sonata of 1917–1918 still has a fair claim to being the greatest such work yet written by an American.

Composed in 1916 during Griffes's most richly productive period, *The Kairn of Koridwen,* subtitled "A Druid Legend," is a forty-five-minute ballet scored for eight players and his most ambitious single work. Drawing inspiration from Debussy, Scriabin, Stravinsky, and others, though speaking in a voice clearly and unmistakably his own, Griffes would also anticipate voices as remote as those of Messiaen and Shostakovich in this mysterious and exhilarating score.

Rather unbelievably, this Koch CD represents the world premiere recording of *The Kairn of Koridwen* (*kairn* = "sanctuary," *Koridwen* = the Druid goddess of the moon). The young American conductor Emil deCou leads a lithe and shapely performance that more than suggests the importance of the work; in fact, it's difficult to think of a *more* important Griffes recording, ever.

Gerard Schwarz and the Seattle Symphony remain the last word in the *Bacchanale, The Pleasure Dome of Kubla Khan,* and *The White Peacock* on Delos (DE 3099 [CD]), while Peter Lawson's heroic traversal of the Piano Sonata has been repackaged with music by Ives and Sessions on Virgin Classics CDC 59316 [CD]. Phyllis Bryn-Julson, Seiji Ozawa, and the Boston Symphony prove ideal guides to the ravishing *Three Poems of Fiona McLeod* (New World NW 273-2 [CD]), while seventeen of the composer's exquisite songs on German texts can be found on a thrilling Teldec recital (9031-72168-2 [CD]) by baritone Thomas Hampson and pianist Armen Guzelimian.

Grofé, Ferde (1892–1972)

Grand Canyon Suite

Cincinnati Pops, Kunzel. Telarc CD-80086 [CD], CS-30086 [T].

There is a special category of quasi-Classical pieces—one resists the phrase "semi-Classical" since it immediately conjures up images of the "101 Strings" and Montovani—of which the *Grand Canyon Suite* seems to be the most stubborn survivor of all. Other examples include *Victory at Sea,* the *Warsaw Concerto,* the *Red Shoes* Ballet (conducted in the movie by Sir Thomas Beecham), and one that never received anything like the attention it deserved: the suite from the music that Norman Dello Joio composed for the CBS News series *Air Power,* which was recorded (and how!) by Eugene Ormandy and the Philadelphia Orchestra. For want of a term both more succinct and more descriptive than "semi-" and/or "quasi-Classical," let's call this stuff "Music That Serious Music Lovers Wouldn't Be Caught Dead Admitting That They Liked, Even If They Did."

Apart from its intrinsic merits—which are considerable—Ferde Grofé's celebration of the world's most inspiring ditch was given enormous credibility by the advocacy of Arturo Toscanini, who loved this brilliantly effective tour of his favorite spot on earth. (Since it was also the vehicle of one of the Maestro's few palatable NBC Symphony recordings, one wonders why Victor didn't issue it, instead of those dreadful Beethoven, Brahms, and Verdi catastrophes, as part of the first installment of the Complete Toscanini on CD.)

Among modern recordings of the *Grand Canyon Suite,* none is more spectacular than Erich Kunzel's Cincinnati Pops outing for Telarc. Part of the gimmick—and who doesn't love a good gimmick, when it works?—is a second version of the *Cloudburst* movement that includes a frighteningly realistic recording of an actual desert thunderstorm captured by Telarc's engineers. The performance itself is an exceptionally fine one: the orgasmic climax of *Sunrise* is beautifully built, and *On the Trail* lopes along with just the right touch of innocent humor.

Grosz, Wilhelm (1894–1939)

Afrika Songs, Op. 29; *Bänkel und Balladen,* Op. 31;
Rondels, Op. 11; Songs

> **Soloists, Matrix Ensemble, Ziegler. London 455116-2 [CD].**

After studies at the Vienna Music Academy with Richard Heuberger and Franz Schreker, Wilhelm Grosz conducted for a single season (1920–1921) at the Mannheim Opera before returning to Vienna to establish his reputation as one of the city's most admired pianists and composers of music for the stage and concert hall. He was forced to flee the Nazis in 1934, taking refuge in England and later America. It was as Will Grosz—later Hugh Williams—the composer of popular songs that he enjoyed his greatest fame, producing a string of hits that included *Isle of Capri, Red Sails in the Sunset,* and *Harbor Lights.*

Some of his most famous songs, together with more obviously serious works from the 1920s and early '30s, make for an unusually poignant installment in London's recently canceled *Entartete Musik* series. Grosz's *Afrika Songs* (1924) is one of the first serious works by an Austrian composer to employ jazz elements, while the satirical *Bänkel und Balladen* shows a fine sense of the grotesque. Along with conducting the Matrix Ensemble and an excellent collection of singers—Cynthia Clarey, Kelly Hunter, Andrew Shore, and Jake Gardiner—Robert Ziegler has arranged the popular items with an appropriate period decadence. Indeed, the entire album is a haunting evocation of that exciting and tragic era.

Haas, Pavel (1899–1944),
and Krása, Hans (1899–1944)

String Quartets

> **Hawthorne Quartet. London 440853-2 [CD].**

This album of chamber music by two gifted young Czech composers may be the most heartrending installment yet in London's laudable and adventurous *Entartete Musik* series, devoted entirely to that "degenerate music" by Jews, Communists, and their sympathizers that was once banned by the Nazis. Born within five months of each other (Haas on June 21 in Prague, Krása on November 30 in Brno), both had begun to establish impressive reputations when the outbreak of war led to their internment in Theresienstadt concentration camp; each continued to compose until almost the very end, which came on the same day at Auschwitz in October of 1944.

While both of the Haas quartets occasionally reveal the influence of his teacher Janáček, each is also the work of a clear and distinctive voice: the charming Second Quartet, "From the Monkey Mountains," with its vivid evocations of country landscapes and the Third Quartet, whose exultant final movement was inspired by a 1938 rally organized as a protest against Hitler and the Nazis. Krása is no less impressive in his ravishing String Quartet of 1921, a work whose subtle decadence bears the stamp of *his* teacher, Alexander Zemlinsky.

These silenced voices could have no more eloquent advocate than the Hawthorne Quartet, whose sensitive, passionate performances suggest just how important these three forgotten works are. In short, this is an album to both excite you and break your heart.

Hadley, Patrick (1899–1973)

The Trees So High

Philharmonia Orchestra and Chorus, Bamert.
Chandos CHAN 9181 [CD].

This is precisely what recording companies *ought* to be doing: not wasting our time with yet another meaningless Beethoven symphony cycle or Chopin recital but introducing us to unfamiliar (but fascinating) works by obscure (yet worthy) composers like the Englishmen Patrick Hadley and Philip Sainton.

While Hadley's 1931 symphonic ballad *The Trees So High* owes something of its harmonic language to the composer's friend and mentor Ralph Vaughan Williams, this lengthy four-movement meditation on the Somerset folk song "The Trees They Grow So High" is a work of stark and astonishing beauty quite unlike any large-scale English choral work of the period.

Similarly, the 1942 tone poem *The Island* by Philip Sainton is a vivid evocation fully worthy of comparison with far more famous seascapes by Bax, Bridge, and Britten. Sainton's command of the orchestra—try listening to the opening trumpet calls without getting goose bumps—is as finely honed as his dramatic instinct, which is hardly surprising from the man who supplied the memorable score for John Huston's 1956 screen version of *Moby Dick*.

A second volume devoted to their music (CHAN 9539 [CD]) is equally valuable, featuring Sainton's charming miniature ballet *The Dream of the Marionette* and the shattering *Nadir*, a symphonic elegy written after the composer witnessed a child being killed in a 1942 air raid. Hadley's austere *Lenten Meditations* and Keats's setting *La belle dame sans merci* are also very fine works, full of conviction and personality, as is the enchanting *One Morning in Spring*, written for his friend Ralph Vaughan Williams's seventieth birthday.

The sumptuousness of the performances led by Matthias Bamert is matched by the Chandos recorded sound. Even for the most jaded collector of English music, these will be thrilling discoveries.

Hahn, Reynaldo   (1874–1947)

Piano Concerto in E

> Coombs, piano; BBC Scottish Symphony, Ossonce.
> Hyperion 66897 [CD].

Songs

> Lott, soprano; Bickley, mezzo-soprano; Bostridge, tenor; Varcoe,
> baritone; Johnson, piano; London Schubert Chorale, Layton.
> Hyperion CDA 67141/2 [CD].

Born in Caracas of a Venezuelan mother and a German Jewish father, Reynaldo Hahn was taken to Paris at the age of three. He was playing the piano at five, composing at eight, and at thirteen wrote what would remain his most famous song, a setting of Victor Hugo's *Si mes vers avaient des ailes*. Pupil of Massenet, close friend of Sarah Bernhardt, and lover of Marcel Proust—who used him as the model for the poetic genius in his unfinished early novel *Jean Santeuil*—Hahn was a brilliantly gifted pianist, conductor, writer, and salon wit, and a composer with flashes of genius. During his lifetime, he was most admired for a series of sparkling operettas in which his melodic gift and comic charm made him the natural successor of Jacques Offenbach and André Messager.

Issued in Volume 15 of Hyperion's Romantic Piano Concerto series, Hahn's Piano Concerto in E from 1931 is a thoroughly ingratiating work, full of memorable tunes, facile invention, and touches of the mercurial wit for which its composer was so famous. The intelligently chosen companion piece is the Piano Concerto of Jules Massenet, an equally delightful (and completely uncharacteristic) piece written late in its composer's career. Stephen Coombs brings a light and unaffected touch to both works, with Jean-Yves Ossonce and the fine Scottish orchestra lending unusually adroit support.

The two-CD set from Hyperion's French Song Edition provides an ideal introduction to Hahn's songs and works for the stage, including a pair of items—*Y a des arbres* and the celebrated duet *Nous avons fait un beau voyage* ("We've had a lovely trip")—from his masterpiece, the 1923 operetta *Ciboulette*. Everything about the album is a model of what such things should be, including pianist Graham Johnson's brilliant and voluminous notes:

> The distinguishing marks of Hahn's style are all there: an accompaniment which undulates in the background like a slow unfurling of a skein of sumptuous material, a background of seemingly little import which nonetheless shapes the melody as if the accompanist wielded the lightest hands on a potter's wheel; a vocal line which is derived from the intimacy of speech but which contains in it the seeds of a wonderful melody truly to be sung; the use of unexpected intervals and cadences (the leaps are sometimes large) which transport us suddenly from a conversational tone in the middle of the stave to the swoon-inducing delight of a cunningly placed mezza voce. Right from the beginning Hahn was writing for singers who could cast sensual spells."

To quote the American poet Randall Jarrell, "Baby doll! What prose!"

Handel, George Frideric (1685–1759)

Arias

Augér, soprano; Mostly Mozart Orchestra, Schwarz.
  Delos DCD 3026 [CD].

Battle, soprano; Academy of St. Martin-in-the-Fields, Marriner.
  EMI CDC 49179 [CD].

Hunt, soprano; Philharmonia Baroque Orchestra, McGegan.
  Harmonia Mundi HMU 907056 [CD], HMU 907149 [CD].

Stutzmann, soprano; Hanover Band, Goodman.
  RCA 09026-61205-2 [CD].

Terfel, baritone; Scottish Chamber Orchestra, Mackerras. Deutsche
  Grammophon 453480-2 [CD].

As his forty-odd operas were all devised to appeal to the prevailing tastes of a period in which plot, characterization, and anything approaching dramatic realism took a distant backseat to those impossibly difficult display vehicles that showed off the talents of the public's favorite singers, Handel's arias are therefore among the most challenging and (for the devoted singer) rewarding ever written.

The Delos recording by Arleen Augér is one of the loveliest things this much-missed artist left. While she brings a heady agility to virtuoso items like "Let the Bright Seraphim" from *Samson,* her simple yet elegant directness is even more appealing, making the luscious "Lascia ch'io pianga" from *Rinaldo* the highlight of the collection.

Kathleen Battle's pure, light soprano is also ideally suited to her shrewdly chosen EMI anthology. For all the abundant fireworks, there is a sweet innocence in the voice that is utterly disarming—and apparently completely at odds with this aptly named singer's personality.

Mezzo-soprano Lorraine Hunt's Harmonia Mundi collection is a reminder of her many memorable collaborations with Nicolas McGegan. Used with great taste and intelligence, the voice is rich, feminine, and distinctive—as are the conductor's crisply imaginative accompaniments.

On her sumptuous RCA recording Nathalie Stutzmann actually begins to stir memories of the late Kathleen Ferrier, so rich and warmly appealing is the young French contralto's voice. There is also musicianship and temperament to burn, obvious in stirring martial items like "Fiammi combattere" from *Orlando* and in the tragic pain of "Ombra cara di mi sposa" from *Radamisto.* She is clearly an artist to watch.

Bryn Terfel approaches the height of his powers in his thrilling collection from Deutsche Grammophon. In both the florid items and the more expressive things, his command of the material (and himself) is consistently amazing. His version of "O Ruddier Than the Cherry" from *Acis and Galatea* is the most infectiously sprung since Malcolm McEachern's incomparably nimble version from the 1930s, while his intensely moving "Ombra mai fù" from *Serses* is the equal of anyone's—including Caruso's.

*C*handos Anthems (11)

Soloists, The Sixteen, Christophers. Chandos CHAN 0554 [CD].

The eleven anthems that Handel composed while in the service of the Duke of Chandos are among the most magnificently eclectic of all the Great Chameleon's works, uniting Italian lyricism, German complexity, and the grandeur of Purcell's England into a uniquely satisfying foretaste of the great oratorios to come. The invention is consistently fresh and imaginative while the scoring is necessarily resourceful, as "Princely Chandos" maintained a very small band of musicians who were also expected to perform other tasks. (One was hired because "He shaves very well & hath an excellent hand on the violin & all necessary languages.")

In their complete recording for (ironically enough) Chandos, The Sixteen under Harry Christophers seem as inspired as the music itself; the singing has both passion and precision and is enveloped in a warm but detailed recorded sound. Those hesitant to acquire the full-priced four-CD set might want to sample Volume 1 first, with its glorious versions of *O Be Joyful in the Lord, In the Lord Put I My Trust,* and *Have Mercy Upon Me.* In addition to the glowing contributions of The Sixteen, soprano Lynne Dawson and tenor Ian Partridge are extraordinary—especially the latter, who has a fair claim to being the most musical tenor to have emerged from those islands since John McCormack.

Concerti Grossi (12), Op. 6

I Musici de Montréal, Turovsky. Chandos CHAN 9004/6 [CD].

English Concert, Pinnock. Deutsche Grammophon ARC-410898-9-1 [CD].

I somehow manage to shock people when I tell them that I have always preferred the music of George Frideric Handel to that of Johann Sebastian Bach. I find Handel not only the far more appealing composer but also the far more interesting man. Aside from assiduously devoting his energies to prayer, the production of music, and twenty-odd children, Bach seems to have been a classic seventeenth-century Lutheran homebody, whose life story makes for singularly boring reading. Handel, who was an internationally famous figure while Bach was still a provincial kapellmeister, was a mass of fascinating contradictions. In spite of his many physical and psychological afflictions—he was nearly felled by several major strokes, went blind at the end of his career, and for more than sixty years exhibited many of the classic symptoms of manic depression—Handel was nevertheless one of the healthiest composers in the history of music, a man whose many enthusiasms and vigorous love of life can be heard in virtually every bar of music he ever wrote.

Nowhere is the essence of Handelian exuberance and inventiveness more clearly in evidence than in these dozen concerti grossi he composed, largely for money, in 1749. (Dr. Johnson might have actually had Handel in mind when he framed one of the most irrefutable of all his aphorisms: "No man but a blockhead ever wrote except for money.") While much of the thematic material was purloined from the works of other composers—and Handel never stole more imaginatively than from Handel himself—the collection is full of an utterly original and irresistible beauty. The dance movements are as infectious as any written by a baroque composer, the slow movements are often poignant and invariably memorable, and the slap-dash, good-natured fugues remain as impressive as any that Bach ever wrote.

With Iona Brown's scintillating Philips recording temporarily out of circulation—presumably it will return in one of the company's budget Duo collections—the recent version by Yuli Turovsky's superbly drilled I Musici de Montréal is another of those ideal compromises that involves modern instruments observing period performance practices, in this case, the use of generally brisk tempos and very little vibrato. The results are fresh, pointed, and invariably musical, materially abetted by the rich but airy recorded sound.

For the Baroque Authenticity Purists, Trevor Pinnock's only slightly less desirable Deutsche Grammophon recording offers a fine period-instrument alternative.

No recording of the delightful Opus 3 Concerti Grossi—sometimes called the "oboe" concertos because of the prominent role the instruments play—has ever surpassed Sir Neville Marriner's London recording (430261-2 [CD]) from the late 1960s. Under the watchful eye of that least pretentious of Handel scholars, the late Thurston Dart, the performances bloom irresistibly, each a model of energy, enthusiasm, and wit. Marriner and the Academy never made a more joyous recording and its reappearance in the medium-priced "Serenata" series is cause for serious rejoicing.

The three *Concerti a due cori* feature some of Handel's most inspired brass writing and stirring tunes, as befits works that undoubtedly began life as instrumental interludes for patriotic cantatas like *Judas Maccabaeus* and *Joshua*. Trevor Pinnock's Deutsche Grammophon recording (447280-2 [CD]) responds admirably to the demands of these enthralling pieces, especially in the exciting give-and-take of the antiphonal brass writing. While the performance of the accompanying *Coronation Anthems* lacks the fullness and bite of Marriner's (see page 315), the concertos alone are more than worth the price of the album.

Concerto in B-flat for Harp and Orchestra, Op. 4, No. 6

Laskine, harp; Toulouse Chamber Orchestra, Auriacombe.
EMI Classics CDK 65335 [CD].

Here is a perfect illustration of how composers of the High Baroque managed to be so incredibly prolific. They *stole*. Actually, in the case of his popular Harp Concerto, Handel *recycled* it from an equally popular organ concerto (or perhaps it was the other way around).

Lily Laskine gives a warm and thoughtful performance on an attractive EMI collection of various Handel concertos recently reissued at medium price.

Oboist Heinz Holliger is electrifying in the three surviving concertos that Handel wrote for the instrument of his youth (Philips 426082-2 [CD]). While the ornamentation might seem excessive to some tastes, it is undeniably exciting. (For some *real* thrills, Sony Classical should reissue that old Columbia LP called

"The Baroque Oboe," in which Harold Gomberg's terrifying virtuosity sends all subsequent practitioners to school.) As ever, Raymond Leppard proves a master Handelian and the physical sound is impeccable.

Concertos (16) for Organ and Orchestra

Nicholson, organ; Brandenburg Consort, Goodman.
Hyperion CDA 67291 [CD].

As a boy, my idea of ultimate torture—along with watching the deeply detested Chicago Cubs *win* the occasional game—was being made to sit still while someone was playing the organ. It undoubtedly had something to do with spending Sunday mornings languishing in a hot, stuffy Premethepiscobapterian church that smelled of dust and peppermint, while a sweet but hopelessly inept matron fumbled her way through hymn after ghastly hymn. To this day, it takes a lot to make me listen to the organ; Ton Koopman almost makes it a pleasure. Of course, he has a bit of help here from George Frederic Handel.

Handel's organ music could not be further removed from either the horrifying experiences of my youth or the leaden, insufferably self-righteous outpourings of many of the other baroque masters. (Legend has it that Bach walked two hundred miles to hear Dietrich Buxtehude play; I would have *run* several miles in the opposite direction to have avoided it.) Even in the least of these works—and the general level of quality is phenomenally high—imagination and exuberance are to be found on every page.

The Hyperion collection is one of the most impressive released in years. Paul Nicholson plays magnificently on an instrument that Handel himself used while in the service of the Duke of Chandos; Roy Goodman leads the Brandenburg Consort with his typical wit and scholarly enthusiasm. The set also comes with Frances Kelly's sterling account of the popular Harp Concerto, marginally preferable to the Laskine version listed above.

The classic recordings by E. Power Biggs and the London Philharmonic conducted by Sir Adrian Boult make the three-CD set on Sony Classical's fire-sale Odyssey label a very compelling bargain (MB3K 45825 [CD]). While Biggs's playing (on the Aylesford organ at Great Packington) is admirably crisp and insightful, Boult's alternately lively and noble conducting steals the show. In spite of its age, the recorded sound remains pleasantly natural, if a trifle bright.

Coronation Anthems (4)

Academy and Chorus of St. Martin-in-the-Fields, Marriner. Philips 412733-2 [CD].

If, until very recently, the House of Windsor has seemed one of the least interesting and most dim-witted of Britain's royal families, then the Windsors have been like rocket scientists compared to the ill-starred and unlamented Hanoverian kings. George I, the founder of the line, not only refused to learn English during his reign but also succeeded in enraging his British subjects even more by refusing to trade in his German mistresses for English ones. His unstable grandson, George III, who suffered from recurrent bouts of madness throughout his life, was responsible for the loss of the nation's American colonies. In fact, the only significant accomplishment the entire dynasty can point to with pride was its employment of the Saxon composer George Frideric Handel, who produced for them some of the greatest ceremonial and occasional music ever written.

The magnificent *Coronation Anthems* are all that survive from the thoroughly bungled coronation of George II in 1727. At their first performance, the sequence of the hymns, together with most of the actual ceremony, was somehow thrown completely out of whack, thereby making it a typically Georgian event. Still, the anthems that Handel provided are so stirring in their grandeur, so rich in their invention and execution, that upon hearing them, even the most tenaciously republican of her former colonists might almost be tempted to ask Her Majesty to take us back.

Neville Marriner's Philips recording offers suitably grand, though never grandiose, performances of these imposingly noble works. The interpretation of the seven-minute *Zadok the Priest,* with its mysteriously hushed opening and thundering final fugue on the word "Alleluia," is in itself worth more than the price of the recording. For anyone addicted to eighteenth-century pomp and circumstance or who simply wants to be convinced that there *will* always be an England, this is a recording that cannot be passed up.

The Faithful Shepherd; The Gods Go a' Begging; Amaryllis Suite; The Great Elopement; Origin of Design

London Philharmonic, Beecham. Dutton DUT 8018 [CD].

Rather than step out in the alley and try to settle *this* one again, suffice it to say that anyone who admires the works and pomps of that marvelous hybrid composer Handel-Beecham (a close relative of Handel-Harty) will love these delectable confections in the historic recordings served up by the source. None of the several orchestras that Sir Thomas founded ever played any better than the London Philharmonic, and here they routinely offer miracles of virtuosity and finesse. As we have come to expect from Dutton Laboratories, the transfers are impeccable, making sound that was excellent in its day (1933–1945) seem even better.

All that was needed to propel us baroque low-brows into ersatz-Handel heaven was the triumphant EMI Classics reissue (CDM 63374 [CD]) of Beecham's stereo recording of his masterpiece in the form, *Love in Bath*, which includes— among its numerous wonders—a trombone quotation of "Rule Britannia" and an *allegro* setting of the famous *Largo*.

Giulio Cesare in Egitto (Julius Caesar in Egypt)

Sills, Forrester, Wolff, Treigle, Malas, New York City Opera Chorus and Orchestra, Rudel. RCA 6182-2-RG [CD].

This is the actual recording that helped spark the modern revival of interest in Handel's forty-plus operas by giving the lie to the notion that they are far too stilted, stylized, and static to hold the modern stage. The City Opera *Julius Caesar* succeeded not by attempting to update Handel's stately creation but by pushing its stylized conventions to an almost surrealistic extreme; it also helped that the company's two most glamorous singers were simultaneously reaching the top of their thrilling forms.

Handel purists might object to a bass in the title role, but when the bass is Norman Treigle *any* objection is idiotic. As the surprisingly successful art-house movie *Farinelli* reminded us, such roles were written for *castrati*; therefore, *any* modern performance is by definition impure. (Incidentally, the principal flaw in that generally unpleasant movie was its wildly distorted portrait of Handel. The superb German actor Armin Müller-Stahl—who is also an excellent violinist—actually turned the part down because it made the composer look like such a ruthless, humorless jerk.) In any event, Treigle is in glorious form, as is Beverly Sills as Cleopatra. The other roles are covered with great distinction and Rudel's conducting is invariably stylish and to the point.

For those wanting a *Giulio Cesare* that reflects more up-to-date performance practices, the Harmonia Mundi recording (HMC 901385/87 [CD], HMC 401385/87 [T]) is an exceptionally fine one, with Jennifer Larmore riveting from first to last in the title role and Barbara Schlick a very sexy Cleopatra. As the performance is uncut and René Jacobs's tempos are even more stately than Rudel's, the opera requires three full-priced CDs and spills over onto an eighteen-minute fourth, which is thrown in free of charge.

Another splendid Harmonia Mundi recording (HMU 907063/65 [CD], HMU 407063/65 [T]) offers the slyly amusing *Agrippina*—yes, indeed, the Emperor Claudius's final wife—in a fetching, beautifully sung performance led by Nicholas McGegan, whose recording of highlights from the disarming pastoral *Il Pastor Fido* (Hungariton 31193 [CD]) is also enchanting.

McGegan and company are similarly persuasive in *Giustino* (HMU 907130/32 [CD]), a work that vanished after its 1737 premiere and would not resurface until 1967. While the story based on the life of the Roman emperor Justinian has an usually high "oh, come now" quotient, it drew from Handel some thrilling music, as this 1994 Göttingen Festival production clearly shows. McGegan's splendid version of *Radamisto* (HMU 907111/13 [CD]) finally allows us to hear what comes with the famous "Ombra cara." It turns out to be one of Handel's greatest operas and one of the most psychologically penetrating.

What a pleasure it is to see London's 1962 recording of *Alcina* restored to circulation (433723-2 [CD]). The tangled action concerns a sorceress who lives on an enchanted island and who, for reasons of her own, takes great pleasure in transforming brave knights into alien forms: animals, vegetables, and, occasionally, the odd mineral. Yet in spite of the ridiculous story, *Alcina* contains some of Handel's richest and most inspired music, thanks largely to two women, the soprano Anna Strada and the French ballerina Marie Sallé. While Dame Joan Sutherland occasionally goes a little mushy in the more reflective passages, her singing in the florid *da capo* arias is often frightening in its daring and precision.

The Erato recording of *Amadigi di Gaula* (2292-45490-2 [CD]) is graced by a fabulous performance by contralto Nathalie Stutzmann. The virtuoso contributions of Bernarda Fink are no less memorable, as is the pointed conducting of Marc Minkowski. His version of the long-neglected *Teseo* is perhaps even more impressive (2292-45806-2 [CD]), largely because the second opera the composer wrote for London is a not entirely comfortable amalgam of *opera seria* and the French *tragédie lyrique* and needs all the inspired architectural finagling it can get. Minkowski's conducting is again a model of period stylishness and the young cast is excellent, particularly the countertenors Derek Lee Ragin and Jeffrey Gall.

Xerxes—or *Serse,* to use the original Italian title—was the forty-third of Handel's operas and one of his last great successes. While the level of inspiration never quite rises to the level of the opening aria, "Ombra mai fù"—the famous *Largo,* which is the hero's impassioned apostrophe to a shade tree—*Serse* contains much engaging music, including some tunes adapted from London street cries for Elvira's song to the messenger. In the fine Sony Classical recording (SM3K 36941 [CD]) Jean-Claude Malgloire keeps the action moving nicely and the cast is uniformly first-rate, featuring a sympathetic Carolyn Watkinson in the title role.

*M*essiah

Marshall, Robbin, Rolfe-Johnson, Hale, Brett, Quirke, Monteverdi Choir, English Baroque Soloists, Gardiner. Philips 411041-2 [CD].

While his dramatic oratorios *Jephtha* and *Theodora* are probably finer works—Handel considered the chorus "He Saw the Lovely Youth" from

Theodora his absolute masterpiece—*Messiah* has more than earned its status as the best-loved sacred work of all time. Its level of inspiration is astronomically high, and its musical values are phenomenally impressive, given that the whole of the oratorio was dashed off in something under three weeks.

Although there are nearly two dozen *Messiah* recordings currently available, Sir Thomas Beecham's famous recording of the stunning arrangement by Sir Eugene Goossens remains unique. And until you've heard *Messiah* with Jon Vickers's singing, Beecham's racy tempos, and an orchestra that includes trombones, tubas, tam-tams, cymbals, snare drums, and gong, you haven't *really* lived (RCA 09026-61266-2 [CD]).

The wonderful version of that greatest *Messiah* arrangement of all has also turned up on ASV 960 [CD]: Sir Charles Mackerras's loving interpretation of Mozart's German edition, in which the ingenious wind parts that were grafted onto Handel's string torso make for such an intoxicating amalgam of Christ and *Don Giovanni*. Perhaps the most beautifully played and sung of all *Messiahs* is Sir Colin Davis's Philips recording with the London Symphony, now reissued (438356-2 [CD] on the company's medium-priced Duo series and *not* to be confused with his disappointing digital remake with the Bavarian Radio Orchestra.

Sir John Eliot Gardiner's triumphant period-instrument version can be confidently mentioned in the same breath with any of the great *Messiah* recordings of the past. In fact, in many ways, it is the most completely satisfying *Messiah* ever released. Using the reduced performing forces and older instruments that are common to almost every *Messiah* recording of the last decade, Gardiner nevertheless succeeds in projecting almost all of the oratorio's size and significance in a performance that is still very intimate in its physical dimension and sound. The soloists are all intelligent and musical, the chorus—in which Gardiner has wisely opted for sopranos instead of the more "authentic" choice of boys—sings with joy and devotion, and the English Baroque Soloists, while they play with great precision and high-minded intensity, still give the unmistakable impression that they're all having an enormous amount of fun. While nothing will ever make me part with my well-worn copies of the Davis, Beecham, and Mackerras recordings, the exultant new Gardiner version now joins that select circle of *Messiahs* I cannot do without.

Music for the Royal Fireworks

Cleveland Symphony Winds, Fennell. Telarc CD 80038 [CD].

London Symphony, Szell. London 417694-2 [CD], 417694-4 [T].

It was through the arrangement for modern orchestra by the gifted Ulster composer and conductor Sir Hamilton Harty that Handel's *Music for the Royal Fireworks* and *Water Music* first became accessible to twentieth-century audiences. And although that curious hybrid composer Handel-Harty is now *persona non grata* in most musical circles, George Szell's gorgeous London recording from the mid-1960s proves just how ridiculous such snobbery is. The arrangements, while admittedly anachronistic, are as tasteful as they are exciting, and if you can bear the scorn of the baroque purist crowd, this recording will offer you countless hours of undiluted pleasure and delight.

Thanks to the classic series of recordings he made with the Eastman Wind Ensemble for Mercury Living Presence, the name of Frederick Fennell is far more closely associated with Sousa Marches than with Baroque Authenticity. Nevertheless, on this brilliant Telarc recording he leads the finest "authentic" performance of the *Royal Fireworks Music* currently available. Since, as its title implies, the work was originally intended for performance in the open and soon to be sulfur-clogged air, Handel's original scoring called for instruments that had a fighting chance of making themselves heard above the ruckus: a huge wind band dominated by oboes and bassoons. Fennell's forces make a spectacular noise on this high-tech Telarc recording. You can almost hear every buzzing vibration in that forest of double reeds, and the brass are so emphatic and lively, you can nearly smell the valve oil. For audiophiles, Handel lovers, and anyone who has ever spent time in a high school band, this is an absolutely essential recording.

Ode for St. Cecilia's Day

Lott, Rolfe-Johnson, English Concert and Chorus, Pinnock. Deutsche Grammophon 419220-2 [CD].

Like his Oratorio *Israel in Egypt*—which can be heard on a superb Philips recording led by John Eliot Gardiner (432110-2 [CD])—Handel's setting of Dryden's "A Song for St. Cecilia's" day is at once one of his most brilliant and shameful works: brilliant, because it finds Handel, the composer of choral music, at the absolute summit of his powers; shameful, because all of the *Ode for St. Cecilia's Day,* as with most of *Israel in Egypt,* was cribbed from other sources. Actually, unlike the oratorio, which drew its "inspiration" from several directions, the thematic material of the *Ode* was purloined in its entirety from a collection of harpsichord pieces published by Handel's older contemporary, Georg Muffat.

Of course, it is what Handel *made* of Muffat's melodies that matters, and with the *Ode to St. Cecilia's Day* he fashioned the finest of his smaller-scaled vocal works. While several of the arias that celebrate the patron saint of music are among the most exceptional Handel would ever produce—the gently insinuating "What Passion Cannot Music Raise and Quell!" and the hectoring "The Trumpet's Loud Clangor" are only two—in its choruses the *Ode* rises to its full greatness. For instance, the final fugue on Dryden's couplet "The dead shall live, the living die/ And Music shall untune the sky" is among the principal treasures of baroque music.

What Trevor Pinnock's period instrument performance may lack in sumptuousness of sound, it makes up for in stylishness and vigor. The reflective passages are brought off with the utmost sensitivity, while the more boisterous items have an admirable snap and bustle.

Devotees of Handel's later Dryden Ode, *Alexander's Feast,* will find it elegantly realized on a Philips recording (422053-2) in a performance led—surprise! surprise!—by Sir John Eliot Gardiner. *And* as long as you're browsing through the Handel section of your favorite store, you might just as well pick up Gardiner's exciting, illuminating, incorruptible versions of *L'Allegro, Il Penseroso ed il Moderato* (Erato 2292-45377-2 [CD]), *Dixit Dominus* (Erato 2292-45136-2 [CD], 2292-45136-4 [T], *Saul* (Philips 426265-2), *Semele* (Erato 2292-45982-2 [CD], and *Solomon* (Philips 412612-2 [CD]) and save yourself some extra trips.

Judas Maccabaeus is currently best served by the 1979 Vanguard recording (OVC 4071/72 [CD]), featuring a sterling quartet of soloists (Harper, Watts, Young, and Shirley-Quirk) with the English Chamber Orchestra and Amor Artis Chorale conducted by Johannes Somary, who is even more impressive in that late masterpiece *Theodora* (OVC 4074/5 [CD], which contains the composer's own favorite of all his works, the magnificent chorus "He Saw the Lovely Youth."

Sonatas for Flute and Continuo

L'École d'Orphée. CRD 3373 [CD].

Given that Handel was such an accomplished oboist in his youth, it's hardly surprising that his sonatas for various wind instruments should contain some of his most inventive and entertaining music. The first volume of L'École d'Orphée's complete traversal of the composer's chamber music is an unalloyed delight, with spirited performances of all seven of the more or less authenticated flute sonatas, including the three marvelous "Halle" Sonatas first published in 1730. Played on the limpid baroque flute, Stephen Preston's performances are unfailingly musical and full of insight, while the continuo realization is both imaginative and discreet.

The volume devoted to the oboe sonatas is equally enjoyable (CRD 3374 [CD]), with David Reichenberg's plangent instrument honking and snarling magnificently whenever the music demands.

The trio sonata album (CRD 3375 [CD], CRD 3376 [CD]) is somewhat more problematical, not for any failure of taste or musicianship but because of the aggressively harsh scraping of L'École d'Orphée's violins. Unfortunately, since the superlative Philips recording by the Academy of St. Martin-in-the-Fields Chamber Ensemble (446563-2 [CD]) has yet to appear domestically, no really adequate version for modern instruments is currently available.

L'École is back in business with a stunning version of the recorder sonatas (CRD 3378 [CD]), with Philip Pickett and Rachel Beckett proving themselves to be among the most accomplished recorderists in the world today.

Suites for Harpsichord

Gould, harpsichord. Sony Classical SMK 52590 [CD].

Even by *his* standards, this is pretty nuts. Having whipped up something approaching a Holy War over playing Bach on the modern piano, for his one and only Handel recording Gould insisted on the harpsichord. As sorely tempted as one is to quote the frequently misquoted Emerson ("A *foolish* consistency is the hobgoblin of little minds"), Emerson's friend Walt Whitman was probably closer to the mark: "Do I contradict myself? Very well then I contradict myself, (I am large, I contain multitudes)."

Predictably, *harpsichordist* Glenn Gould's versions of the Handel suites are as full of life and distinctive musical insights as any of his other recordings. He obviously relishes the music and at every turn manages to remind us how wonderful these tiny miracles are. The 1972 recorded sound remains close but realistic.

The extraordinary recordings made by Sviatoslav Richter and Andrei Gavrilov at the 1979 Tours Festival have finally appeared on a two-CD set from EMI (CDFB 69337 [CD]). The playing is breathtaking in its confidence and authority: effortlessly brilliant in the outer movements, meltingly tender in the slower ones. The slightly close ambience of the Château de Marcilly-sur-Maulne complements the performances beautifully.

The Water Music

Los Angeles Chamber Orchestra, Schwarz. Delos DCD 3010 [CD].

My unremitting enthusiasm for the recording by the Los Angeles Chamber Orchestra has absolutely nothing to do with civic pride. The only Southern California cultural institutions for which I have a blind and uncontrollable passion are the Dodgers and Disneyland. This is, quite simply, the most thrillingly played of all recorded performances of Handel's popular score and, by a comfortable margin, the craziest. The insanity, here, consists largely of what might best be described as virtuosity gone berserk. In a performance that features nearly as many added ornaments as notes in the score, Gerard Schwarz leads his brilliant ensemble through one of the great recorded bravura exercises of the last decade. The playing is dumbfounding in its swaggering effortlessness: listen especially to the LACO oboes and horns for some of the most breathtaking technical legerdemain to be heard on recordings today.

Among available tapes of the complete *Water Music,* Trevor Pinnock's affable period-instrument recording for Deutsche Grammophon (410525-4) is easily the preferred version.

Hanson, Howard (1896–1981)

Symphony No. 2, Op. 30, "Romantic"

Seattle Symphony, Schwarz. Delos DCD-3073 [CD].

One of the most embarrassing of the numerous embarrassing moments I have suffered during my radio career occurred at a small station in upstate New York, shortly after I introduced this moltenly beautiful symphony as being a work by "the late Howard Hanson." Midway through the first movement, the "late" Dr. Hanson phoned the station and proceeded to point out, in the most unimaginably charming way, that my information was not entirely accurate.

For anyone who attended the National Music Camp at Interlochen, Michigan, the principal theme of the "Romantic" Symphony has many powerful associations. Since the late 1930s it has served to conclude every concert as the "Interlochen Theme" and was, for years, the signature theme of the camp's weekly NBC broadcasts. (More recently, Jerry Goldsmith used it to memorable effect at the end of his score for Ridley Scott's sci-fi thriller *Alien.*)

The Delos recording by Gerard Schwarz and his superbly trained Seattle Symphony is not only the finest recording of the "Romantic" that we are likely to hear for the rest of the century but is also an interpretation whose sweep and energy rivals that of the several recordings that the composer made himself. The playing is as full of genuine sentiment as it is totally lacking in mawkish sentimentality, and the rhythmic tingle that Schwarz wires into the jazzy sections of the final movement is a delight to hear. With equally convincing performances of the gorgeous "Nordic" Symphony and the rarely heard but deeply touching *Elegy in Memory of My Friend Serge Koussevitzky,* this is an important, exciting recording.

If anything, the subsequent releases in Delos's Hanson series have proven even more valuable. The greatest of the symphonies, the Third, together with the *Fantasy-Variations on a Theme of Youth* and the Symphony No. 6, are all given a gripping performances on Delos DE 3092 [CD]; the most personal work in the canon, the Fourth—called the "Requiem," since it was written in memory of his father, and the first symphony ever to be awarded the Pulitzer Prize—is paired on Delos DE 3105 [CD] with the outrageously beautiful *Lament for Beowulf,* one of the finest and most deeply moving choral works ever written by an American, and the exciting suite from the composer's opera *Merry Mount*. The Fifth and Seventh, the two symphonies with texts by Walt Whitman, are coupled with the colorful *Mosaics* for Orchestra on Delos DE 3130 [CD].

In terms of repertoire, Volume 5 (DE 3160 [CD]) may be the most interesting of all. In addition to the first recording of the orchestral version of *Dies natalis,* an inspired series of variations on an old Lutheran chorale, the CD offers three premieres: the youthful *Lux aeterna;* two masterworks from Hanson's vigorous old age, his powerfully dramatic setting of Whitman's *The Mystic Trumpeter* (with a predictably engrossing narration by James Earl Jones); and the ethereally beautiful *Lumen in Christo,* a meditation on various biblical pronouncements on the subject of light.

The only possible way to improve this brilliant series would be a complete version of *Merry Mount,* together with a Schwarz-led survey of early Hanson works like the *Symphonic Legend,* the tone poems *Before the Dawn* and *Exaltation,* to say nothing of the Organ and Piano Concertos.

Harbison, John (1938–)

Concerto for Double Brass Choir and Orchestra; *The Flight into Egypt; The Natural World*

> Soloists, Cantata Singers, Los Angeles Philharmonic, Los Angeles
> Philharmonic New Music Group, Previn, Harbison. New World
> NW 80395-2 [CD].

One of the most admired and widely performed composers of his generation, John Harbison was born in Orange, New Jersey, on December 20, 1938. A shrewd practical musician whose music manages to be as emotionally accessible as it is intellectually challenging and impeccably made, Harbison has also devoted much of his time to performing, as conductor of ensembles like the Cantata Singers and the Los Angeles Philharmonic New Music Group.

The Los Angeles Philharmonic brass section offers a gripping traversal of Harbison's powerful Concerto for Double Brass Choir, while the performance of the lyrical and engrossing *Flight into Egypt* goes a long way to explaining why the work won the Pulitzer Prize for music in 1987. Also arresting is the song-cycle *The Natural World,* a setting of the widely disparate Nature poetry of Robert Bly, Wallace Stevens, and James Wright.

Herbert Blomstedt leads the San Francisco Symphony in immaculate, deeply committed performances of two other major Harbison works, the Second Symphony of 1987 and the Oboe Concerto of 1990, the latter having a fair claim to being the most important such work yet written by an American (London 443376-2 [CD]). As a bonus, the album is rounded out by the Second Symphony of Harbison's teacher, Roger Sessions. Premiered by the San Francisco Symphony and Pierre Monteux in 1947, the Second is among the most rewarding of all its composer's works, with an austerely moving *Adagio* written in memory of Franklin Delano Roosevelt.

The exotic *Mirabai Songs* are sung bewitchingly by the wonderful Dawn Upshaw on a Nonesuch anthology (79187-2 [CD], 79187-4 [T]) that also includes Samuel Barber's *Knoxville: Summer of 1915* and arias from Stravinsky's *The Rake's Progress* and Menotti's *The Old Maid and the Thief.* Upshaw is equally captivating in another intriguing Harbison cycle, *Simple Daylight,* as is baritone Sanford Sylvan in *Words from Paterson,* on texts drawn from William Carlos Williams's major long poem.

Harris, Roy (1898–1979)

Symphony No. 3

New York Philharmonic, Bernstein. Deutsche Grammophon 419780-2 [CD].

If the late Roy Harris was not the most original and important symphonist America has so far produced, then the only other possible candidate for that distinction was the late William Schuman. This superb recording of two live New York Philharmonic performances of what are probably the finest symphonies that both men composed, affords us an excellent opportunity to make up our minds.

On balance, the Harris Third, which had a tremendous vogue during the 1930s and '40s, still seems the fresher and more startling work. And in its day, this concise, dramatic, and often soaringly lyrical work attracted more than the usual New Music Crowd audience. On a regular basis, Harris received fan mail from all sorts of people, including cab drivers, politicians, and baseball managers. The Schuman Third, while it may lack the Harris Symphony's apparent ease of inspiration, is nonetheless a starkly proud and powerful statement by a keen and frequently astringent musical mind. It may also be the better-made of the two works, which, given Harris's fanatical approach to craftsmanship, is saying a very great deal.

Leonard Bernstein's invigorating interpretations of both symphonies will provide an ideal introduction to anyone who has yet to become familiar with these seminal works in the development of American symphonic thought. While the conductor made some very fine studio recordings of both symphonies during his years with Columbia, the excitement of these concert performances easily outstrips the earlier versions.

Serge Koussevitzky commissioned Harris's masterpiece, and his uniquely powerful interpretation—together with a live 1934 recording of the *Symphony 1933* (Symphony No. 1)—is now available on a Pearl anthology of classic Koussy recordings of American music with works by Copland and Arthur Foote (PEA 9492 [CD]). Although it's good to have Vladimir Golschmann's vigorous performance of the *Folksong Symphony* (No. 4) back in circulation (Vanguard OVC 4076 [CD]), it would have been better still to have Maurice Abravanel's even more stirring account reissued by EMI Classics. If the reissue on Albany (AR 012-2 [CD]) of Robert Whitney's businesslike Louisville recording of the Fifth is little more than a stopgap until something better comes along—perhaps (be still, my heart!) a Harris cycle from Schwarz and the Seattle Symphony?—then Keith Clark's brilliant realization with the Pacific Symphony of the *Gettysburg* (No. 6) is one of the most exhilarating Harris recordings in years (Albany TROY 064 [CD]).

Harrison, Lou (1917–)

Suite for Violin, Piano, and Small Orchestra

Stoltzman, violin; Jarrett, piano; Chamber Ensemble, Hughes. New World NW 80366-2 [CD], NW 80366-4 [T].

One of the most stubbornly individual of American composers, Lou Harrison was born in Portland, Oregon, in 1917. After studying with Henry Cowell at San Francisco State College, Harrison attended classes at UCLA where he studied composition with Arnold Schoenberg. In 1945, he became a music critic for the *New York Herald Tribune*—forming a friendship with the hugely influential critic and composer Virgil Thomson that would continue until Thomson's death—while supporting himself with a variety of jobs, ranging from dance accompanist to florist. Harrison was one of the earliest champions of the music of Charles Ives, and, after helping to prepare the composer's Third Symphony for publication, he conducted its first performance in 1947. Since 1954, he has lived in Aptos, a small town two hours south of San Francisco, where he has written some of the most wildly distinctive, widely admired American music of his generation.

The Suite for Violin and Small Orchestra from 1951 reflects Harrison's abiding fascination with the music of the Far East, including Chinese classical music, the court music of Korea, and Javanese gamelan. Calling himself a "Pacific Rim" composer, he has said with his typically good-humored candor: "As a West Coast American living in Pacifica, close to Asia, while East Americans live in Atlantica and are more attached to Europe. Europe is part of Asia, too, the Northwest part." Violinist Lucy Chapman Stoltzman and pianist Keith Jarrett are wonderfully sensitive to the Suite's quirky rhythms and subtly shifting moods, while Jarrett is also a brilliant advocate of Harrison's 1985 Piano Concerto.

The *Koncherto por la Violono kun Perkuta Orkestro*—the composer prefers the original Esperanto title of the Concerto for Violin and Percussion Orchestra—is probably Harrison's most frequently performed work. "When it was first played," he later recalled, "much of the press was bewildered by the combination of a fluidly singing instrument and the accompanying ensemble of varied sounds of percussion. This has not baffled the general public but seems to have become a source of pleasure." That pleasure is communicated irresistibly on a Crystal recording (CD 850 [CD]) by violinist Eudice Shapiro and the Los Angeles Philharmonic New Music Ensemble conducted by William Kraft.

Written on a commission from the 1982 Cabrillo Music Festival, the Third Symphony is among the most ambitious and approachable of the composer's recent works. Cast in six colorful movements of varying length, it opens with a virile, vigorously confident *Allegro*, followed by three self-explanatory acts of homage to friends: the vivid, sprightly *Reel in Honor of Henry Cowell*, the languorous *Waltz for Evelyn Hinrichsen*, and *An Estampie for Susan Summerfield*, with its infectious cross-rhythms and vivid percussion writing. Concluding with a hypnotic *Large Ostinato* and an exuberant, exhilarating *Allegro*, the Third Symphony demonstrates—as so many of this composer's recent works have— that those who think contemporary music has little to say to them have yet to hear the humane and willfully *human* music of Lou Harrison. Dennis Russell Davies—who led the world premiere—leads a predictably enthralling performance on Music Masters 7073-2-C [CD].

Hartmann, Karl Amadeus   (1905–1963)

Symphony No. 2, "Adagio"; *Sinfonia tragica; Gesangsszene*

    Bamberg Symphony, Richenbacker. Koch Schwann 312952 [CD].

Symphony No. 5, "Symphonie concertante"; Symphony No. 6; Symphony No. 8

    Berlin Radio Symphony, Herbig; Leipzig Radio Symphony, Kegel.
      Berlin Classics BER 9048 [CD].

Part of the proof that the central European symphony did not die with Gustav Mahler can be found in these gripping, eloquent works by Karl Amadeus Hartmann, a German composer who began late and died young. With Hitler's rise to power in 1933, the young Hartmann completely withdrew from the musical life of the nation; following the end of World War II, he founded the "Musica Viva" concerts in Munich for the promotion of new music and with the Darmstadt premiere of his *Symphonische Ouvertüre* of 1947, his international reputation began to spread. Although several important strands of late-Romantic and modern music come together in Hartmann—from Bruckner, Mahler, and Reger to Hindemith, Bartók, Boris Blacher, and his teacher Anton Webern—the composer's mature voice is both powerful and utterly distinctive and is certainly worth getting to know.

If not as powerfully charismatic as the inexplicably deleted EMI Classics readings led by Ingo Metzmacher, then the recordings listed here still clearly indicate that Hartmann was not only a major twentieth-century symphonist but also a wizard of the modern orchestra—in this, the Symphony No. 5 for Wind Instruments, Cellos, and Double Basses is particularly resourceful and endlessly surprising. These are dense, visionary, unmistakably important works that only seem to become more important on repeated hearings.

Harty, Sir Hamilton   (1879–1941)

Irish Symphony; A Comedy Overture

Ulster Orchestra, Thomson. Chandos CHAN 7034 [CD].

The Ulsterman Sir Hamilton Harty is best known for being half of one of history's most celebrated hyphenated composers. Harty's joyous and accomplished arrangements for modern orchestra of Handel's *Royal Fireworks* and *Water Music* introduced the composer to several generations of music lovers before the snotty and pedantic Period Instrument Movement made such "tampering" unfashionable. In addition to elevating the Hallé Orchestra of Manchester to the very front rank of European ensembles, Harty was a charming and resourceful composer whose best works evidence a profound understanding of the possibilities of the modern orchestra and an abiding passion for his native Ireland.

An examination of Bryden Thomson's admirable cycle of Harty recordings should begin with the *Irish Symphony,* a beautifully made potpourri of traditional Irish airs, and the sparkling *Comedy Overture.* The performances by the Ulster Orchestra are so bracing and affectionate that most people will want to investigate other recordings in the series, beginning with the sturdy and tuneful *Violin Concerto*—intelligently repackaged with the lushly romantic Piano Concerto (CHAN 7032 [CD]—and the thoroughly charming *Variations on a Dublin Air,* now available with the gorgeous Keats setting *Ode to a Nightingale* and the ineffably moving *Children of Lir* (CHAN 7033 [CD]).

Harty's genius as an arranger is made abundantly clear on yet another Chandos album (CHAN 6583 [CD]), which brings together his famous version of Handel's *Water Music* with *A John Field Suite*—based on his countryman's piano music—and a version of *The Londonderry Air* (a.k.a. "Danny Boy") that rivals the most heartrending of Percy Grainger's several versions.

Haydn, Franz Joseph   (1732–1809)

Concertos (2) for Cello and Orchestra

Kanta, cello; Capella Istropolitana, Breiner. Naxos 8.550059 [CD].

For reasons that are not that easy to explain, Haydn's D Major Cello Concerto has never been the basic staple of the cellist's rather limited solo repertoire that it certainly deserves to be. Witness the fact that the C Major Concerto, which was not discovered until the 1960s in Prague, is nowadays heard almost as frequently. Perhaps it has something to do with the fact that neither concerto is a crowd-pleasing whiz-bang display piece and that if orchestras are going to hire big-name players, they generally want more drawing power than these modestly elegant eighteenth-century works are likely to supply.

In spite of formidable competition from older, far better-known performers—and Jacqueline du Pré's joyous recording with Sir John Barbirolli of the C Major Concerto really *does* remain in a class by itself (EMI Classics CDC 47840 [CD]—Ludovit Kanta's Naxos recording is as fine as any currently available. The playing is fresh, intelligent, and hugely accomplished, as are the accompaniments from this brilliant central European orchestra.

Add a delightful performance of the Boccherini Cello Concerto and this is *quite* a bargain.

Concertos (3) for Piano and Orchestra

Ax, piano; Franz Liszt Chamber Orchestra.
Sony Classical SK 48383 [CD].

Haydn was never the virtuoso performer his friend Mozart was; therefore his output of keyboard concertos was comparatively sparse. The most celebrated one of all, in D Major, dates from the end of 1783, the same year as the well-known cello concerto written in the same key. Although Emanuel Ax makes little attempt to place the concertos in a sort of historical perspective—for that, he would have used a fortepiano or a harpsichord, not a modern Steinway—he gives a refined, lively, and suitably chamber-sized performance of the work and is similarly successful with the roughly contemporaneous F Major Concerto and the much later Concerto in G. The Franz Liszt Chamber Orchestra is superbly responsive throughout and the recorded sound is nearly ideal.

Sadly, Teldec has withdrawn the excellent versions of the Haydn horn concertos that the group made with the Chicago Symphony's great principal horn, Dale Clevenger. Fortunately, Barry Tuckwell is comparably exciting in his 1966 London recording with Sir Neville Marriner and the Academy (430633-2 [CD]), this on a medium-priced reissue in the "Serenata" series that comes with Mstislav Rostropovich's slightly overripe version—with Benjamin Britten and the English Chamber Orchestra—of the D Major Cello Concerto and a very fine performance of the Trumpet Concerto with Marriner accompanying Alan Stringer.

Concerto for Trumpet and Orchestra in E-flat Major

Marsalis, trumpet; English Chamber Orchestra, Leppard. CBS MK-37846 [CD], MK 39310 [T].

While he was the literal father of the Classical symphony and string quartet (the nineteenth century didn't call him "Papa" for nothing), few of the numerous operas, keyboard sonatas, or instrumental concertos that Haydn composed throughout his life have ever been very popular, with the exception of the delightful and justly famous Trumpet Concerto. Along with its abundance of memorable melody and virtuoso fireworks, the E-flat Major Concerto is also a work of considerable historical significance. It was the first work by a major composer written for a newfangled contraption that was several generations ahead of its time: the first, but not completely practical, incarnation of the *valved* trumpet.

When Wynton Marsalis's now famous recording was first released a few years ago, it was accompanied by an enormous amount of ballyhoo and hype. As the first Classical recording by one of the finest jazz musicians of the younger generation, it promised little more than Barbra Streisand's ill-starred venture into art song or the wonderful Cleo Lane's horrendous Frankenstein-Meets-the-Wolfman encounter with Schoenberg's *Pierrot Lunaire*. What it delivered, on the other hand, was one of the most stylish and spellbindingly brilliant recordings that this popular work has ever received.

While Marsalis faces formidable competition from Gerard Schwarz on Delos and a majestic (and, alas, now-deleted) Deutsche Grammophon recording by the recently retired principal trumpet of the Chicago Symphony, Adolf Herseth, this CBS recording continues to set the standard for both lyric expressiveness and bravura display. In fact, the cadenzas that Marsalis supplies are so electrifying that the playing would make the hair on a bald man's head stand on end.

Concertos (2) for Violin and Orchestra; Sinfonia Concertante in B-flat for Oboe, Bassoon, Violin, Cello, and Orchestra

Wallfisch, violin; Orchestra of the Age of Enlightenment. Virgin Classics CDC 59266 [CD].

Even more than those for the cello, the Haydn violin concertos are among the most strenuously ignored of all his works. Admittedly, neither of these youthful scores is a masterpiece, but each contains a lovely slow movement and a typically bubbly Haydn finale and both are bound to give considerable pleasure, especially in performances as enthusiastic as these. The Orchestra of the Age of Enlightenment is equally persuasive in the graceful, much-harder-than-it-sounds Sinfonia Concertante and the recorded sound is both warm and refined.

Although of doubtful authenticity, the C Major Oboe Concerto is an unfailingly delightful work (*whoever* wrote it), particularly in the Deutsche Grammophon recording (431678-2 [CD]) by Paul Goodwin and the English Concert led by Trevor Pinnock. In addition to a very stylish version of the D Major Klavier Concerto, the recording also comes with a version of Haydn's greatest concerto played on the keyed trumpet, the instrument for which it was composed. Sounding like a cross between a maladjusted steam valve and a saxophone with very bad adenoids, the noises it produces are a sheer delight.

*T*he Creation (Die Schöpfung)

Augér, Langridge, D. Thomas, City of Birmingham Symphony and
Chorus, Rattle. Angel CDCB-54159 [CD].

One of the absolute high-water marks in the sacred music of the Age of Enlightenment, *The Creation* is an innocent, dramatic, unaffected, and beautifully made celebration of the God of whom Haydn said so frequently, "When I think of Him, my heart leaps with joy." Even for those who do not typically respond to lengthy religious works, *The Creation* overflows with such a wealth of inspired melodic and theatrical invention that only the most adamant of pagans are able to resist its glories. For instance, the choral outburst on the words "Let there be light" must certainly rank with the most exultant moments in all of music.

For the last thirty years, *The Creation* has led a charmed life on records. With the exception of Herbert von Karajan's most recent effort—a performance recorded at the 1982 Salzburg Festival that is so sinister in its calculation that it would warm the cockles of a Darwinian's heart—there has really never been a *bad* recording of *The Creation*. Even Karajan's 1969 Deutsche Grammophon version has much to recommend it, especially the unbelievably moving singing of tragically short-lived Fritz Wunderlich, captured in one of the final commercial recordings that that incomparable tenor would make.

The most consistently rewarding recent version of the oratorio was Sir Neville Marriner's masterful interpretation for Philips, now withdrawn but presumably awaiting resurrection on one of the company's popular Duo sets. Sir Simon Rattle's English-language version is also an exceptionally fine one, notably in its highlighting of the naive programmatic effects that so delighted Beethoven. In its bluff, Handelian confidence and humor—together with its recourse to the English text of which the composer readily approved—it is the kind of performance that only proves that Haydn, if not the Lord Himself, *must* have been an Englishman.

Masses (14) (complete)

Soloists, Choir of Christ Church Cathedral, Oxford; Choir of St. John's College, Cambridge; Academy of Ancient Music; Academy of St. Martin-in-the-Fields, Willcocks, Guest, Preston. London 448518-2 [CD].

While Haydn composed masses throughout his career—the earliest surviving example is a *Missa brevis* that he wrote in 1749 while still in his teens—it is the series of six majestic works written between 1796 and 1802 that ensure his reputation as one of the great composers of sacred music. Informed by all the orchestral experience he had gained with more than a hundred symphonies and obviously influenced by the richly various choral writing of the Handel oratorios that had so impressed him on his visits to London, the Haydn masses contain some of the most sublime music he would ever write and bear eloquent testimony to his willingness to learn and grow.

London's complete cycle of the masses remains one of the company's proudest achievements. Crammed onto seven medium-priced CDs, the set represents an exceptional bargain, with singing, playing, and recorded sound maintaining an extraordinary level of excellence. The heart of the collection is that group of recordings made in the 1960s of the *Heiligmesse, Mass in Time of War, Theresienmesse, Creation Mass,* and *Harmoniemesse* by George Guest and his spirited Choir of St. John's College, Cambridge. The interpretations are as exhilarating as they are unaffected, with impeccable work from the Academy of St. Martin-in-the-Fields and a distinguished collection of soloists, particularly from the lovely April Cantelo and that most musical of English tenors, Ian Partridge. The period-instrument recordings from the late '70s are no less enjoyable, with Simon Preston leading the Academy of Ancient Music and the Christ Church Cathedral Choir in performances that wear both their piety and scholarship very lightly.

Mass No. 11 in D Minor, "Nelson Mass"

Lott, Watkinson, Davies, Wilson-Johnson, English Concert, Pinnock. Deutsche Grammophon 423097-2 [CD].

Blegen, Killibrew, Riegel, Estes, Westminster Choir, New York Philharmonic, Bernstein. Sony Classical SM2K 47563 [CD].

The period-instrument performance of the "Nelson Mass" led by Trevor Pinnock is among the most successful that this accomplished musician has yet made. The performance is one of high drama, soaring lyricism, and unflagging energy, all captured in state-of-the-art recorded sound.

Leonard Bernstein's powerful CBS recording from the 1970s has been reissued with an equally successful version of the *Mass in Time of War* as part of

Sony Classical's "Royal Edition," the ones with all those painfully ordinary watercolors by H. R. H. The Prince of Wales on the album covers. The interpretations are both sensitive and highly charged, with brilliant, deeply committed playing and singing from everyone involved. If anything, Bernstein's recording of the *Harmoniemesse* is even more inspired. The performance is only available on a pair of Sony Classical CDs (SM2K 47560), coupled with the conductor's very fine recording of *The Creation*, providing an excellent German complement to Sir Simon Rattle's outstanding English version.

String Quartets (6), Op. 76

> **Kodály Quartet. Naxos 8.550314 [CD]; 8.550315 [CD];
> 8.550129 [CD].**

With that historic collection published as his Opus 20, Haydn, in effect, invented the single most important vehicle of Western chamber music, the modern string quartet. In all of the works he had written previously, the function of the viola, second violin, and cello was to support and embellish the first violin's solo line; with Opus 20, all four instruments became the equal partners that they have remained ever since.

Of the eighty-two string quartets—from many of his earliest published compositions to the unfinished D Minor fragment he was working on at the time of his death—none have proven to be more popular than the Op. 76 collection, which contains the "Quinten," the "Sunrise," and the "Emperor," three of the most familiar of all string quartets.

At any price, the recordings by the Kodály String Quartet on the super-budget Naxos label would be the ones to own. The performances are shot through with a sense of wonder and discovery, without a single routine or ill-considered phrase. There are few recordings—few live performances, for that matter—that seem as fresh, spontaneous, and openhearted as these, except, perhaps, for their equally memorable versions of the Opus 54 (8.550395 [CD]) and Opus 55 (8.550397 [CD]) collections, their first installment of the early quartets from Opus 1 and 2 (8.550399 [CD]), or the moving versions of the unfinished Opus 103 fragment coupled intelligently with *The Seven Last Words of Christ on the Cross* (8.550346 [CD]). When complete, their cycle of all the quartets should prove as valuable and important as Dorati's historic recording of the symphonies. Thus far, it has been an undiluted joy.

The Tátrai String Quartet play with a warm, idiomatic grasp of the material in their cycle for Hungariton, with interpretations that manage to remain straightforward without ever sounding impersonal or dull. Their recording of the pivotal Opus 20 collection is highly recommended (Hungariton HCD-11332/3 [CD]), as are their versions of the colorful Opus 33 set, which includes "The Joke" and "The Bird" (Hungariton HCD-11887/8 [CD]).

The Seasons (Die Jahreszeiten)

Bonney, Rolfe-Johnson, Schmidt, Monteverdi Choir, English Baroque Soloists, Gardiner. Deutsche Grammophon 431818-2 [CD].

Compared to *The Creation*, Haydn's final oratorio has always remained far less popular for reasons that are hardly a well-kept secret. The subject matter is the heart of the problem, for how can the mere turning of the year compare with the relatively dramatic acts recounted in *Genesis*? For many since Haydn's time, the bucolic joys of *Die Jahreszeiten* have offered about as much excitement as watching the grass grow.

Like Sir Thomas Beecham, who made a gripping recording of the oratorio in the early days of stereo, Sir John Eliot Gardiner couldn't disagree more. He finds drama and excitement aplenty throughout the score—*Die Jahreszeiten*'s storms were Beethoven's model for the "Pastoral Symphony"—together with abundant lyrical grace and an earthy, Bruegel-like humor. The soloists are exceptionally eloquent and Gardiner's chorus and orchestra respond with their usual sensitivity, enthusiasm, and prodigious skill.

Sonatas for Keyboard

McCabe, piano. (Complete) London 443785-2 [CD].

Bilson, fortepiano. Nonesuch 78018-2 [CD].

Jandó, piano. Naxos 8.550657 [CD], 8.553127[CD], 8.553128 [CD].

Pletnev, piano. Virgin Classics CDC 45254 [CD].

Gould, piano. CBS M2K-36947 [CD].

They turn up, occasionally, as opening works on recitals—not being terribly demanding, they give the performer a chance to warm up—and they are heard on the radio from time to time, usually as a palate-cleanser after a Mahler symphony. Haydn's keyboard sonatas—and he composed more than sixty—have never had the popular appeal of Beethoven's or even Mozart's, although the best of them are a constant source of astonishment.

Dating from the mid-1970s and available now on a dozen specially priced CDs, the complete London cycle by John McCabe offers an unfailingly intelligent and resourceful overview of this still-neglected repertoire with playing that is as impeccably mannered as it is bracingly refreshing. The recorded sound and voluminous notes (by McCabe himself) are wholly worthy of such an important project.

Malcolm Bilson is one of those rare period-instrument specialists who gives the impression that he is following the lonely road of the fortepianist out of choice, rather than of necessity. He is a personable, magnetic performer who persuades us—as long as he is playing—that those tinny, tinkly sounds really *are* the only appropriate ones for the keyboard music of the period. His Haydn recordings are lively and entertaining and only make us wish that more were generally available.

Jenö Jandó's ongoing series for Naxos easily matches the overall quality of his fine Beethoven and Mozart series, although it begins to beg the question, When does this tireless Hungarian ever sleep? In general, the interpretations tend to be more straightforward than McCabe's except in the finales, where Jandó typically flashes more wit and impish humor.

In what may well be the most distinguished single-CD collection currently available, Mikhail Pletnev gives incomparably authoritative performances of three of the finest sonatas—No. 33 in C Minor, No. 60 in C, and No. 62 in E-flat—and the *Andante and Variations in F Minor*. Although this is Haydn on the grand scale, the interpretations miss none of the music's Classical grace and delicacy.

If not quite as perverse as his infamous Mozart recordings, the Gould interpretations of the late sonatas are completely insane. A bizarre stylistic amalgam of Bach and Prokofiev, Gould's Haydn is a strange and strangely appealing invention, proving that these underrated works—like all important music—are open to an almost limitless variety of points of view.

Symphonies (104) (complete)

> Philharmonia Hungarica, Dorati. London 425900-2 [CD] (1-16);
>   425905-2 [CD] (17-33); 425910-2 [CD] (34-47); 425915-2
>   [CD] (48-59); 425920-2 [CD] (60-71); 425925-2 [CD] (72-83);
>   425930-2 [CD] (84-95); 425935-2 [CD] (96-104).

Listening to any of his 107 works in the form—in addition to the 104 numbered pieces, there are three others that we now know with some certainty were his—one is invariably tempted to paraphrase Will Rogers: "I never heard a Haydn symphony I didn't like." In no other body of work can one hear such a consistently high level of invention and craftsmanship, or a greater delight in the sheer act of creativity, than in that marvelous series of symphonies that history's finest professional composer produced throughout his career.

In both its scope and level of accomplishment, Antal Dorati's justly famous cycle of the complete Haydn symphonies is one of the supreme achievements in the history of recorded music. Under the watchful eye of that greatest of Haydn scholars, H. C. Robbins Landon, Dorati and his musicians turned in a series of performances that were remarkable for their vigor, imagination, and consistency. The familiar symphonies reveal themselves with a wonderful sense of discovery and life, while the more obscure ones all tend to sound like preposterously neglected masterworks. The recorded sound from the 1970s is still exceptionally clear and warm, and Robbins Landon's program notes are among the most literate and enjoyable ever written. For offering so much enjoyment and enlightenment in such an attractive and economical package, London deserves everyone's heartfelt thanks.

Symphony No. 6 in D *(Le Matin)*; Symphony No. 7 in C *(Le Midi)*; Symphony No. 8 in G *(Le Soir)*

Northern Chamber Orchestra, Ward. Naxos 8.550722 [CD].

The turning point in Franz Joseph Haydn's artistic life came in the spring of 1761 when Prince Paul Anton Esterházy heard him conduct a concert at the palace of Count Ferdinand Maxillian von Morzin. When financial difficulties forced the Count to disband his orchestra, Esterházy engaged Haydn as his vice kapellmeister, thus beginning a period of service with the family that would last some thirty years.

The first works that Haydn composed for his new employer were three programmatic symphonies (and his only symphonic cycle) to which he gave the French titles *Le Matin* (Morning), *Le Midi* (Afternoon), and *Le Soir* (Evening). (It is widely assumed that the Prince himself made the suggestion of writing works about the various times of the day, following a Gallic conceit that was then especially fashionable.) As the final form of the Classical symphony was far from fixed in the early 1760s, these youthful works are a curious amalgam of divertimento, concerto, suite, and symphony. In that they often make use of a small group of solo instruments playing against the larger string body, they also look back to the traditions of the baroque *concerti grossi*.

The performances by Manchester's Northern Chamber Orchestra conducted by Nicholas Ward are so fresh and enthusiastic that they almost make one forgive Deutsche Grammophon for withdrawing Trevor Pinnock's splendid period-instrument recording. In any event, the use of modern instruments will probably appeal to more listeners, as will the super-bargain price.

Symphony No. 22 in E-flat, *The Philosopher*; Symphony No. 29 in E; Symphony No. 60 in C, *Il Distratto*

Northern Chamber Orchestra, Ward. Naxos 8.550724 [CD].

The French academics who chastised César Franck for the revolutionary idea of including an English horn in his D Minor Symphony had obviously forgotten about (or had never heard) Haydn's *Philosopher* Symphony, which uses not one English horn but *two*. Their studied ruminations at the beginning of the

E-flat Major Symphony are one of the cleverest of Haydn's early inspirations, offering the orchestra some wonderful opportunities for tongue-in-cheek gravitas.

Similarly, the antics in *Il Distratto* (literally, "the distracted one") are among the most hilarious in Haydn's output, including that side-splitting moment in the finale when the violins collectively realize that their lowest string is tuned to an F instead of a G: the music stops dead in its tracks to allow them to tune up. In both of these works and the fine E Major Symphony from 1765, Nicholas Ward and his superb Manchester musicians respond brilliantly to the amusing demands of the music, as well as to its elegance and energy.

A companion album (8.550721 [CD]) devoted to three more middle-period symphonies (No. 26 in D Minor, *Lamentatione*, No. 35 in B-flat, and No. 49 in F Minor, *La Passione*) is almost as satisfying, except that a change in recording venue has led to somewhat less focused sound.

Symphony No. 41 in C; Symphony No. 42 in D; Symphony No. 43 in E-flat, *Mercury*

Tafelmusik, Weil. Sony Classical ("Vivarte" series) SK 48370 [CD].

On the evidence of the first few installments in the new Sony Classical series presided over by H. C. Robbins Landon, Bruno Weil and Tafelmusik are already well on their way to the most satisfying period-instrument Haydn cycle yet recorded, marginally preferable to the excellent Hyperion recordings by Roy Goodman and the Hanover Band. For one thing, Tafelmusik's playing is more consistently imaginative and spontaneous-sounding; for another, the beautifully balanced recorded sound keeps things in a slightly truer perspective. Those who respond to Weil's lithe and invigorating interpretation of the *Mercury* Symphony should immediately investigate the other installments in the series so far: Sony Classical SK 48371 [CD] (No. 44 in E Minor, *Trauer*, No. 51 in F-sharp Minor, No. 52 in C Minor); SK 53986 [CD] (No. 45 in F-sharp Minor, *Farewell*, No. 46 in B, No. 47 in G); and SK 53985 [CD] (No. 50 in C, No. 64 in A, No. 65 in A).

Symphony No. 45 in F-sharp, *Farewell*; Symphony No. 48 in C, *Maria Theresia*; Symphony No. 102 in B-flat

Capella Istropolitana, Wordsworth. Naxos 8.550382 [CD].

As in their cycle of recordings by the Kodály String Quartet, the ongoing Naxos series of the symphonies with Barry Wordsworth and the Capella Istropolitana represent another heartening refutation of my grandmother's staunchly held maxim that "There's no such thing as a bargain and *everything* costs more than it's worth." For a little less than six dollars, or about two bucks per symphony, we're offered warm, witty, and generally well-executed performances in very fine modern sound. While there are unquestionably versions of the B-flat Major Symphony with more punch and flavor, Wordsworth's interpretations of the *Farewell* and the *Maria Theresia* yield to none in terms of geniality and warmth. Similarly, even if buying his equally satisfying versions of the *Trauer, London,* and 88th Symphonies (8.550287 [CD]) or *La Reine, Oxford,* and the *Drum Roll* (8.550387 [CD]) involves some duplication, then at these prices, who should care?

Symphony No. 53 in D, *L'Impériale;* Symphony No. 73 in D, *La Chasse;* Symphony No. 79 in F

Orpheus Chamber Orchestra. Deutsche Grammophon 439779-2 [CD].

One of the few unarguably positive cultural by-products of the anarchic, self-righteous, drug-besotted '60s is the Orpheus Chamber Orchestra, an organization founded by a group of free-spirited individuals whose questioning of authority took the singularly healthy form of creating an orchestra that refused to have a conductor. To this day, their rehearsals are lively (and frequently lengthy) examples of collective bargaining at its best: genuinely collaborative exercises in which each member of the ensemble is entitled (and expected) to have a say.

Nowhere are the fruits of that process more telling than in their delightful recordings of various Haydn symphonies, now apparently being reissued three to the CD instead of the original two. The performances gathered here not only are hugely accomplished but also are so full of purpose and individuality that they eloquently support the Orpheus's long-held contention that the cheapest instrument in any orchestra is the conductor's baton.

Symphony No. 64 in A, *Tempora mutantur;* Symphony No. 84 in E-flat, *In Nomine Domini;* Symphony No. 90 in C

Nicolaus Esterházy Sinfonia, Drahos. Naxos 8.550770 [CD].

As in the other excellent issues in the Naxos Haydn Symphony series led by Nicholas Ward and Barry Wordsworth, those entrusted to Béla Drahos and the Nicolaus Esterházy Sinfonia couldn't have been placed in better hands. These are all high-quality performances that seem to revel in both the human warmth and the dazzling technical variety of Haydn's invention. Every detail of texture and phrasing unfolds in the most natural and musical way, while the rich acoustics of Budapest's Reformed Church bathe everything in the aural equivalent of late afternoon sunshine. The other Drahos installments are comparably enjoyable: Symphony No. 69 in C, *Laudon* (named for the Austrian *Feldmarschall* who finally freed Eastern Europe from the dreaded Turks), No. 89 in F and No. 90 in C (8.550769 [CD]) and No. 72 in D, coupled with two of the "London" Symphonies, Nos. 93 in D and 95 in C Minor (8.550797 [CD]).

Symphonies 82–87, the "Paris Symphonies"

New York Philharmonic, Bernstein. Sony Classical SM2K 47550 [CD].

One of Leonard Bernstein's first recordings after being appointed music director of the New York Philharmonic in 1958 was a version of Haydn's "London" Symphony, originally paired with Mendelssohn's "Italian" on a Columbia LP. I vividly remember everything about the album because it was the very first premium I got as a member of the Columbia Record Club, which I joined in the seventh grade. The Club's fliers would follow me through graduate school and beyond, with something approaching the tenacity of *The Watchtower* and *Awake.* (These days, when door-to-door evangelists try to interest me in whatever it is they're selling, I simply tell them: "No, thank you, I'm a Druid and I've been washed in the blood of a tree." That usually stops them cold.)

From that excellent "London" Symphony, Bernstein went from strength to strength as a Haydn conductor, reaching his early peak in these versions of the "Paris" Symphonies, recorded between 1962 and 1967. In addition to their grace and virility, the level of humor in these colorful interpretations is extraordinarily high: from oboist Harold Gomberg's inspired clucking in "The Hen" to the droll grumbling of the basses in the finale of "The Bear." The remastered sound is excellent.

Symphony No. 88 in G; Symphony No. 95 in C Minor; Symphony No. 101 in D, "The Clock"

"Fritz Reiner Orchestra," Chicago Symphony, Reiner. RCA 09026-60729-2 [CD].

The recordings of the C Minor and "Clock" Symphonies were the very last that Fritz Reiner made. As a great conductor's swan song, it is, of course, tempting to read a little something more into these performances—which are wonderful enough on their own. Still, there is a warmth and charm, a genial wisdom in the playing unique among Reiner recordings. For instance, the version of the 88th Symphony—which originally appeared as side four of the conductor's recording of Mahler's *Das Lied von der Erde*—is vintage Reiner: precise, witty, beautifully controlled. The others, recorded with a New York pickup orchestra, are simply among the most gracious and ethereal Haydn recordings ever made. Don't pass them up.

Nor can any Haydn lover afford to do without Wilhelm Furtwängler's celebrated 1951 version of the G Major Symphony, reissued on Deutsche Grammophon (447439-2 [CD]) with that equally famous recording (also made in Berlin's Jesus-Christus Kirche) of Schubert's "Great C Major" Symphony. The Haydn is an astonishing amalgam of strength and affability, with Romantic scale and expression allied to eighteenth-century poise. Once you hear the incredible pause Furtwängler inserts toward the end of the finale and the electrifying avalanche he makes of the final *stretto,* no other performance—Reiner's included—will ever sound exactly right again.

Symphonies 93–104, the *"Salomon* (or London) *Symphonies"*

Royal Philharmonic, Beecham. EMI Classics ZDMB 64389 [CD] (Symphonies 93–98).

Royal Concertgebouw Orchestra, Davis. Philips 442611-2 [CD], 442614-2 [CD] (Symphonies 93–104).

Cleveland Orchestra, Szell. Odyssey MB2K-45673 [CD] (Symphonies 93–98).

London Philharmonic, Jochum. Deutsche Grammophon 437201-2 [CD].

Here, in four reasonably priced box sets, are the most popular of the Haydn symphonies in performances that represent the very highest standards of modern Haydn conducting. While the Szell interpretations are phenomenally precise, with hair-trigger attacks and releases and crisply immaculate phrasing, they also bubble over with an infectious good humor: the bassoon belch in the slow movement of the 93rd must rank with the funniest musical effects ever recorded, while the famous slow movement of the "Surprise" Symphony has rarely sounded as mischievous. A minor hitch is the remastered recorded sound, in which all the original tape hiss continues to fizz away and the upper strings are made to sound uncharacteristically brittle and dry.

On the other hand, the Philips engineers lavished some of their most richly detailed sound on the Davis performances, which remain some of the most successful Haydn recordings ever made. Although generally straightforward, all of the interpretations have this conductor's stamp of intelligence and gentlemanly passion, while the Concertgebouw Orchestra ensures that they are among the best-played versions on the market today.

The spirit of boyish playfulness that Sir Thomas Beecham managed to preserve into his eighties bubbles over in these spirited recordings of several of his signature works. Once, at one of those rehearsals that some canny engineers were wise enough to preserve on tape—it may well have been a rehearsal of the *Drum Roll* Symphony—Sir Thomas asked his timpani player whether the score didn't possibly call for cymbals and side drum, too. When told it didn't, all he said was, "What a pity," but in a pouty tone of voice reminiscent of a small boy who has just been told he can't go out and play. As always, the Royal Philharmonic plays so alertly for the old imp that we can see the tongue placed high in cheek when he uttered his famous pronouncement: "There are two golden rules for an orchestra:

start together and finish together. The public doesn't give a damn what goes on between."

Finally, there are no more enjoyable Haydn symphony recordings than those Eugen Jochum made with the London Philharmonic in the early 1970s. The outer movements crackle with energy and wit—the finales tend to be unusually fleet—while one of the supreme Bruckner conductors of his generation was enough of a Romantic to make all the slow movements sing. Rarely has an orchestra seemed to enjoy itself as palpably as the London Philharmonic does in these incandescent performances, and the recorded sound doesn't seem to have aged a day.

Symphony No. 94 in G Major, "Surprise"; Symphony No. 96 in D Major, "Miracle"

Academy of Ancient Music, Hogwood. L'Oiseau-Lyre 414330-2 [CD].

While the story of how the "Miracle" Symphony earned its name is probably apocryphal—allegedly, the audience that heard the world premiere in London was so moved by the music that the people rushed up *en masse* to congratulate the composer a few seconds before a massive chandelier crashed into their recently vacated seats—and while every Haydn symphony is a "surprise" symphony in one way or another, in this delicious Oiseau-Lyre recording two of the composer's most popular works more than earn their subtitles. The playing of Christopher Hogwood's spirited Academy of Ancient Music really *is* quite miraculous in both symphonies, and the revelations in texture and balance that these period instrument performances afford *are* a source of endless surprise. The winds play with such individuality and character that you begin to suspect that the conductor must have swallowed an entire bottle of Sir Thomas Beecham pills, and Hogwood himself provides innumerable subtle comments from his chair at the fortepiano. The familiar slow movement of the 94th Symphony has rarely seemed as sly or tensely dramatic as this, and the finale of the "Miracle" Symphony rushes off with such a flurry of unbridled high spirits and good humor that we can easily believe that the old chandelier story might, after all, have been true.

Symphony No. 100 in G, "Military"; Symphony No. 103 in E-flat, "Drum Roll"

Orchestra of St. Luke's, Mackerras. Telarc CD-80282 [CD].

For a single disc pairing of these two popular symphonies giving splendid performances in up-to-date sound, you can't do much better than this. As in his wonderful Mozart recordings with the Prague Chamber Orchestra, Sir Charles

Mackerras proves that he also has the full measure of that other master of the Classical symphony, with performances overflowing with charm and good humor—not unlike the readings that another musical knight, Sir Thomas Beecham, used to give. The versions of the "Clock" and "London" Symphonies are no less desirable (CD-80311 [CD]).

Trios for Piano, Violin, and Cello Nos. 24–31

Beaux Arts Trio. Philips 454098 [CD].

Along with Antal Dorati's magnificent cycle of the complete Haydn symphonies for London, one of the major accomplishments of recent recording history was the Beaux Arts Trio's go-round of all forty-three of the Haydn piano trios. As valuable as the Dorati recordings certainly were—fully half of them remain the finest individual performances that the symphonies have yet received—the Beaux Arts's may have been even more so, for how many of us are familiar with even the best known of these inexplicably neglected works? Why history has treated the Haydn trios so shabbily is a perplexing mystery, since the best of them seem every bit as inventive and beautifully made as the finest of the composer's quartets.

Although still difficult to track down in this country, the complete recording has recently been issued in Europe on nine jam-packed CDs. Listening to this incredible wealth of treasure over a period of a few weeks will only strengthen your conviction that Haydn was the finest professional composer who ever lived.

Haydn, Michael (1737–1806)

Symphonies (5)

London Mozart Players, Bamert. Chandos CHAN 9352 [CD].

If his brother Franz Joseph was indisputably the Father of the Classical Symphony, then Michael Haydn was clearly one of its many uncles. Largely self-taught as a composer, the younger Haydn was appointed court musician and *Konzertmeister* to the Archbishop of Salzburg in 1762, holding the post to the end of his life. In spite of important commissions from the Spanish court and the Empress Maria Teresia—the so-called *Theresienmesse* of 1801—Haydn's reputation (and influence) remained local and limited throughout his career; for reasons that remain unclear, he consistently turned down offers of publication from Breitkopf and Härtel, and although other courts vied for his services, he preferred to remain in provincial Salzburg. One of the important voices in the early evolution of the classical symphony, he was also a distinguished teacher whose many celebrated pupils included Antonín Reicha and Carl Maria von Weber.

Released as part of Chandos's "Contemporaries of Mozart" series, the elegant, warmhearted performances by Matthias Bamert and the London Mozart Players reveal what a thoroughly competent and frequently charming professional the younger Haydn was. If there is little here that seems new or challenging, then this is still attractive, handsomely made music—perfect for those admittedly infrequent moments when Mozart or the elder Haydn seem to require too much work.

Headington, Christopher

(1931–1996)

Concerto for Violin and Orchestra (1959)

Xue-Wei, violin; London Philharmonic, Glover. ASV ASV 780 [CD].

Prior to his untimely death in a Swiss skiing accident, Christopher Headington was an unusually versatile pianist, author, broadcaster, and frequent contributor to *Gramophone* magazine. As a composer, Headington owed much to the teaching of Sir Lennox Berkeley and even more to the example of Benjamin Britten. His Violin Concerto of 1959 is one of the most appealing of the last half century, with a rich vein of soaring lyricism and a masterly control of texture and form. Xue-Wei plays it like the standard repertoire item it might yet become, while Jane Glover and the London Philharmonic match his obvious understanding and excitement. Coupled with the most persuasive version yet of the youthful Violin Concerto of Richard Strauss, this is an unusual and valuable release.

A companion album (ASV 969 [CD]) features Headington's fluent, warmly appealing Piano Concerto, the elegant Serenade for Cello and Orchestra, and his moving *The Healing Fountain (In Memoriam Benjamin Britten)*, a half-hour setting for tenor and orchestra of verses by poets from Shelley to Auden, with telling quotations from Britten's works. Recorded in the presence of the composer nine days before his death, the performances have a special air of poignant authority.

Hely-Hutchinson, Victor
(1901–1947)

Carol Symphony

Pro Arte Orchestra, Rose. EMI Classics CDM 64131-2 [CD].

Born in Cape Town, South Africa, the youngest son of Sir Walter Hely-Hutchinson, the last governor of the Cape Colony, Victor Hely-Hutchinson was educated in England, where he spent the bulk of his professional life teaching and serving, from 1944 until the time of his premature death, as the music director of the BBC. Although he wrote a fair amount of more obviously serious music—a string quartet, a piano quintet, and sonatas for the piano and viola—he was best known for his endearing settings of the nonsense verse of Lewis Carroll and Edward Lear and the seasonal favorite, *A Carol Symphony*, written in the late 1920s. A skillful, quietly moving, frequently witty arrangement of popular English Christmas carols, Hely-Hutchinson's work is a minor classic that receives a first-rate performance from Pro Arte Orchestra. Coupled with Vaughan Williams's *Fantasia on Christmas Carols* and other seasonal fare by Roger Quilter, Ernest Tomlinson, and Peter Warlock, this is among the most charming albums of "classical" Christmas music currently available.

Henze, Hans Werner (1926–)

Symphony No. 7

For much of the last half century, Hans Werner Henze has been the most successful German composer of his generation, as well as the most maddeningly inconsistent. His embrace of radical left-wing politics in the late 1960s led to tiresome embarrassments like *Versuch über Schweine* and *Der Floss der Medusa* (The Raft of the Frigate *Medusa*)—a cantata dedicated to Che Guevara that has the distinction of being the most gruesomely meretricious modern German score after Carl Orff's *De temporum fine comoedia*. Yet when not spouting the Party line in works that have the taste and texture of ground glass soaked in vinegar, Henze has also managed to produce two of the most intriguing (and entertaining) modern operas, *Elegy for Young Lovers* and *Der junge Lord* (whose peculiar upper-crust English hero proves to be an ape), in addition to seven brilliant symphonies.

Henze's lengthiest and most serious symphony to date—the Seventh—is given a shattering live performance by Sir Simon Rattle and the City of Birmingham Symphony (EMI Classics CDC 54762 [CD]), as is the elegiac *Barcarola*, a twenty-minute memorial to his friend and fellow communist, the German composer Paul Dessau.

Herbert, Victor (1859–1924)

Cello Concerto

Ma, cello; New York Philharmonic, Masur. Sony Classical SK 67173 [CD].

A contemporary critic of this fabulously successful composer once insisted that Victor Herbert wrote the kinds of melodies that people whistled on their way *into* the theater. Although he would achieve lasting fame as the composer of more than forty operettas, including *Babes in Toyland, The Fortune Teller, Naughty Marietta, The Red Mill,* and *Sweethearts,* the Dublin-born Herbert was a thoroughly trained classical musician who began his career as a cellist. Following the death of his father, Herbert's mother married a German physician who enrolled his fifteen-year-old stepson at the Stuttgart Conservatory; after graduation, Herbert joined the Stuttgart court orchestra. In 1886, Herbert and his wife—a singer in the court opera—left for the United States, where both were engaged by the Metropolitan Opera. In addition to performing, Herbert taught at the National Conservatory of Music, where he became friendly with its director, Antonín Dvořák. It was Herbert's performance of his own E Minor Concerto with the New York Philharmonic in March of 1894 that inspired Dvořák to compose his B Minor Cello Concerto in the following year.

Recorded at another New York Philharmonic concert more than a century later, Yo Yo Ma gives a predictably suave and dashing account of the Herbert Concerto, the unusual but wholly appropriate filler for his latest version of the Dvořák. If it obviously pales in comparison to its great companion piece, then it is nonetheless an exceedingly tuneful and friendly work that deserves to be far better known. Masur and the orchestra prove able accomplices and the recorded sound is fine.

Herrmann, Bernard (1911–1975)

Film Music

Marnie; North by Northwest; Psycho; The Trouble with Harry; Vertigo

> London Philharmonic, Herrmann. London 443895-2 [CD].

The Day the Earth Stood Still; Fahrenheit 451; Gulliver's Travels; Journey to the Center of the Earth; The Seventh Voyage of Sinbad

> London Philharmonic, Herrmann. London 443899-2 [CD].

The Devil and Daniel Webster (suite); *Welles Raises Kane; Obsession* (suite)

> National Philharmonic, Herrmann. Unicorn-Kanchana
> UK CD 2065 [CD].

On Dangerous Ground; Citizen Kane; Beneath the Twelve-Mile Reef; Hangover Square; White Witch Doctor

> National Philharmonic, Gerhardt. RCA 0707-2-RG [CD],
> 0707-4-RG [T].

Torn Curtain; Taxi Driver; North by Northwest; Marnie; The Man Who Knew Too Much; Vertigo; Fahrenheit 451; Psycho

> Los Angeles Philharmonic, Salonen. Sony Classical SK 62700 [CD],
> SM 62700 [T].

With his friends Alfred Newman and David Raksin—who called him "a virtuoso of unspecific anger"—the mordant and explosive Bernard Herrmann was one of the first generation of great native-born American film composers, part of that second wave of talent that built upon, and often dramatically expanded, the traditions established by the European Max Steiner, Erich Wolfgang Korngold, and Franz Waxman. Thanks in part to his extraordinary association with Alfred Hitchcock, but largely due to the scope, variety, and sheer quality of the music itself, Herrmann has acquired almost mythic status among students of film music: a man frequently mentioned as the greatest single practitioner of this difficult and demanding craft.

The composer's London recordings offer an invaluable introduction to ten of his most characteristic scores, the first volume devoted to five of the Hitchcock collaborations, the second concentrating on his work in science fiction and fantasy. Needless to say, the performances have a special authority, even though tempos tend to be the characteristically slow ones Herrmann the conductor favored. The original, rather gaudy "Phase 4 Stereo" sound has been tamed admirably for the CD reissue.

The Unicorn collection offers extended excerpts from his first score and only Academy Award winner, *The Devil and Daniel Webster;* music from his most celebrated score—in addition to music from *Citizen Kane,* the *Welles Raises Kane* suite also draws on material from the ill-starred *The Magnificent Ambersons;* and a poignant glimpse at his swan song, Brian de Palma's *Obsession,* for which Herrmann received his final Oscar nomination. Rather surprisingly, the *Kane* suite makes use of practically none of the film's more gloomy, atmospheric music, while *Obsession*—licensed from the London recording made shortly before the composer's death—shows that Herrmann remained powerfully inventive to the very end.

Along with performances and recorded sound in the best tradition of RCA's superlative "Classic Film Scores" series, the principal reason to acquire the Gerhardt recording is the inclusion of two bits of "serious" music from the films: excerpts from the opera *Salammbô* that the tyrannical Kane forces his second wife to sing (an understandably humiliated Dorothy Commingore in the film, the immaculate Dame Kiri Te Kanawa here), and the *Concerto Macabre* from *Hangover Square,* the Edwardian grue-and-horror thriller about a tormented composer (Laird Creger, who forced himself to lose a dangerous amount of weight for the role and died shortly after filming was completed) obsessed with murdering attractive women because they had driven his genius brother to suicide.

Esa-Pekka Salonen's Los Angeles Philharmonic anthology features superb playing, idiomatic interpretations, and music from Martin Scorsese's *Taxi Driver*—the Anglophilic Herrmann at his jazziest and most American—and part of the unused score for *Torn Curtain* that Hitchcock angrily threw out because Herrmann ignored his order to produce a marketable hit tune. One only hopes that the success of the album will lead to a sequel, including—please—music from the 1944 version of *Jane Eyre* (with a screenplay cowritten by Aldous Huxley) and extended excerpts from what Herrmann himself considered his finest score, the 1947 romantic fantasy *The Ghost and Mrs. Muir.*

Symphony No. 1

Phoenix Symphony, Sedares. Koch 3-7135-2 [CD].

Although best known for his classic film scores, Herrmann was also the composer of more obviously serious music, such as this fine symphony written in 1941. If somewhat long-winded and occasionally derivative, then the Herrmann Symphony also reflects its composer's superb sense of mood and atmosphere: this is evocative and dramatic music, full of character and incident, which is also "cinematic" in the best possible sense.

While it may not be quite as authoritative as the composer's own recording made not long before his death, James Sedares and his superbly trained Phoenix Symphony give a handsome, utterly convincing account of the work. Those who respond to the Symphony will want to investigate what may well be an even finer piece, the cantata *Moby Dick,* given a stunningly effective performance under the composer's direction (Unicorn-Kanchana UKCD 2061 [CD]).

Hildegard of Bingen (1098–1179)

Hymns and Sequences

Gothic Voices, Page. Hyperion CDA-66039 [CD], A-66039 [T].

Cleric, mystic, poet, playwright, naturalist, musician, and composer, Hildegard—later Saint Hildegard—of Bingen was one of the most fascinating characters of the Middle Ages. In addition to writing extensively on theology and natural history, she maintained a voluminous correspondence with several popes and Holy Roman Emperors; she published a collection of her mystical visions in 1151 and wrote the morality play *Ordo virtutum,* which was accompanied by some eighty-seven plainsong melodies of her own devising.

As one of the first composers of either sex of whom we have an accurate record, Hildegard's historical significance goes without saying. Yet she was also a creative musician of genuine abilities, as this astonishing Hyperion recording of some of her Hymns and Sequences clearly shows.

For people who place listening to plainsong close to the bottom of their list of things to do—and how aptly named this numbingly dull stuff has always seemed—Hildegard's rare and hypnotic talent will come like a splash of cold water in the face. In the exquisite, innocent singing of the Gothic Voices, the simple melodies with their static drone accompaniments seem infinitely more varied, subtle, and resourceful than they have any right to be. They also possess an emotional and spiritual tranquillity whose calming spells are almost impossible to resist. (This from someone who respectfully gags on almost any form of early sacred music.)

This is an unqualified, and—for a pagan like me—completely surprising winner.

Hindemith, Paul (1895–1963)

Kammermusik (complete)

> Members of the Royal Concertgebouw Orchestra of Amsterdam, Chailly. London 433816-2 [CD].

In the generation since his death, Paul Hindemith's reputation has declined alarmingly. Once considered a leading voice of the twentieth-century avant-garde, a composer whose thorny, elegantly crafted experiments in dissonant counterpoint caused many to liken him to a modern Bach, Hindemith has now been unfairly dismissed as a stiff "academic" composer who has little to say to a generation brought up on the mindless delights of minimalism.

While much of his music *can* seem rather dry and forbidding, musicians love Hindemith, since he never wrote a piece of music that wasn't at least as much fun to play as it was to hear. Witness the *Kammermusik* (Chamber Music), a series of concertos composed in the 1920s as a deliberate twentieth-century equivalent of the *Brandenburg Concertos* of Bach. In addition to the delightful *Kammermusik* No. 1 with its irrepressible "Finale: 1922," the other concertos in the collection (one each for piano, cello, violin, viola, viola d'amore, and organ) find Hindemith at his most inventive and appealing. The performances by members of the Royal Concertgebouw Orchestra of Amsterdam are both precise and flamboyant, representing Riccardo Chailly's most impressive work with the orchestra so far.

Among other recordings of the composer's chamber music, none is more valuable than that two-CD set from Sony Classical (SM2K 52671) containing Hindemith's sonatas for brass instruments (alto horn, horn, trumpet, trombone, and tuba) with the then principal brass players of the Philadelphia Orchestra and pianist Glenn Gould. The Canadian's pianist's well-known passion for Hindemith's music is evident in every bar and the brass playing is close to perfection.

*M*athis der Maler

Koszut, Schmidt, Wagemann, Cochran, Grobe, King, Fischer-Dieskau, Feldhoff, Malta, Meven, Kreile, Bavarian Radio Symphony Chorus and Orchestra, Kubelik. EMI Classics CDCC 55237 [CD].

Apart from the three-movement Symphony that the composer extracted from the score prior to its celebrated nonpremiere in 1934—the Nazis were not especially fond of Hindemith to begin with, and when they discovered that his inflammatory new opera touched on the sixteenth-century Peasants Revolt, the Berlin State Opera production announced by Furtwängler was personally banned by Hitler—*Mathis der Maler* remains the century's most famous unknown opera. After Furtwängler's impassioned defense of the composer in "The Hindemith Case," the conductor was stripped of all his official posts, Hindemith fled the country, and *Mathis der Maler* slipped into revered neglect.

Rafael Kubelik's 1977 version is a milestone in the history of opera on record, a performance that finally allows a twentieth-century masterpiece to emerge in almost all its glory. As Matthias Grünewald, the visionary painter who sides with the peasants against the power of the Church, Dietrich Fischer-Dieskau gives the most commanding operatic performance of his career, an interpretation with all the subtle penetration of his finest lieder performances but with none of the overemphasis and barking that frequently marred his work in the opera house. The other men in the cast are nearly as impressive, with James King heroically imposing as the Archbishop and Donald Grobe suitably menacing as the Cardinal. If the women are consistently disappointing, then their roles are far less critical anyway; moreover, any sins would be forgiven in light of the magnificent work of the chorus and orchestra, which Kubelik inspires to the same levels of fanatical devotion displayed a decade earlier in that phenomenal recording of Wagner's *Die Meistersinger* (see page 773). All in all, a red-letter day for Hindemith and the cause of modern opera.

*S*tring Quartets (6)

Kocian String Quartet. Praga PR 250088 [CD].

While Hindemith composed a half-dozen string quartets between 1919 and 1945, only the Third from 1922 has made any serious inroads into the repertoire. As the famous 1952 recording by the Hollywood String Quartet reveals, it is a powerful and dramatic work that embraces both the radical expressionism of the early '20s and the neo-baroque gestures that would soon become a hallmark of Hindemith's work. The most important contribution of the Kocian Quartet's outstanding budget-priced set is the eloquent case it makes for the other quartets in the cycle, each of them serious, brilliantly made, and—on repeated hearings—

possessed of considerable character and individuality. The two delightful bonus items are in themselves worth the price of the album—the hilarious, endearing *Minimax* and one of the funniest of all musical parodies, whose title, in translation, says it all: *Overture to "The Flying Dutchman"' as Played at Sight by a Second-Rate Concert Orchestra at the Village Well at Seven O'Clock in the Morning.*

Symphonia serena; Symphony *(Die Harmonie der Welt)*

BBC Philharmonic, Tortelier. Chandos CHAN 9217 [CD].

Both of these magnificent symphonies were written during Hindemith's final years in America, an unusually fertile period in the composer's career that also saw the composition of a flood of masterworks from the *Symphonic Metamorphosis on Themes of Carl Maria von Weber* to *When Lilacs Last in the Dooryard Bloom'd.*

Titularly the third of Hindemith's six symphonies, the *Symphonia Serena* of 1947 has far more in common with Béla Bartók's *Concerto for Orchestra,* which Hindemith greatly admired. As Hindemith's title makes abundantly clear, the *Symphonia serena* was not designed as an especially profound or probing work but instead as a good-natured exploration of the resources of the modern orchestra by one of its most accomplished modern masters.

Like the *Mathis der Maler* Symphony, *Die Harmonie der Welt* is a three-movement orchestral score adapted from an opera whose hero is the mathematician and astronomer Johannes Kepler.

While the composer himself recorded both works and each has had its notable champions—historic versions of *Die Harmonie der Welt* can be had conducted by Wilhelm Furtwängler (EMI Classics ZDMB 65353 [CD]) and Evgeny Mravinsky (Originals ORISH 815 [CD])—the gleaming new versions by Yan Pascal Tortelier and the BBC Philharmonic are major additions to the Hindemith discography. If anything, the performance of *Sinfonia serena* is even more amiable than the composer's own, while Tortelier's *Die Harmonie der Welt* suggests much of the vastness of Furtwängler's. As is usually the case with their Manchester recordings, the Chandos recorded sound is of demonstration caliber.

Symphonic Metamorphosis on Themes of Carl Maria von Weber; Mathis der Maler (symphony); *Trauermusik for Viola and String Orchestra*

San Francisco Symphony, Blomstedt. London 421523-2 [CD].

The bulk of Paul Hindemith's reputation now rests on a scant handful of works, including the two that Herbert Blomstedt and the San Francisco

Symphony have recorded so successfully for London. Among available versions of the Symphony drawn from that most famous of all *unknown* twentieth-century operas, *Mathis der Maler*—the first production was canceled by the Nazis in 1934, causing Wilhelm Furtwängler to resign in protest—only the last commercial recording that Jascha Horenstein ever made (Chandos CHAN 6549 [CD] is clearly superior. On the other hand, Blomstedt has no serious competition in the gravely eloquent *Trauermusik,* written for the funeral of King George V.

George Szell's incomparable version of the *Symphonic Metamorphosis* has resurfaced on a budget Sony Classical release (SBK 53258 [CD], SBT 53258 [T]), coupled with the wonderful *Variations on a Theme by Hindemith* of Sir William Walton and a rather lackluster *Mathis der Maler* Symphony from Eugene Ormandy and the Philadelphia Orchestra. Szell's performances of both the *Symphonic Metamorphosis* and the Walton are quite sensational, giving the impression of a cross between a perfectly tuned Ferrari and an elegant Swiss watch.

James DePreist leads spotless versions of the *Four Temperaments* and *Nobilissima visione,* the haunting ballet based on the life of St. Francis of Assisi (Delos DCD-1006 [CD]), and the deeply felt requiem on a text by Walt Whitman, *When Lilacs Last in the Dooryard Bloom'd,* is given a moving performance led by Robert Shaw, the man who commissioned the work (Telarc CD-80132 [CD]).

The composer's own superlative versions of the Clarinet Concerto, Concert Music for Strings and Brass, *Nobilissima visione,* and *Symphonia serena* have been repackaged with Dennis Brain's definitive recording of the Horn Concerto and the electrifying version of the String Trio with Szymon Goldberg and Emanuel Feuermann on a must-have two-CD set from EMI Classics (ZDCB 55032). Although it means duplicating *Mathis* and the *Metamorphosis* (in excellent performances led by Paul Kletzki and Claudio Abbado, respectively), David Oistrakh's 1962 recording of the Violin Concerto with the composer conducting the London Symphony (London 433081-2 [CD]) is very possibly the greatest Hindemith recording yet made. The late Russian violinist makes it seem like one of the most passionately beautiful of all violin concertos, and the recorded sound remains astoundingly fresh and alive.

Hoffnung Music Festivals

Various artists, Hoffnung Festival Orchestra, various conductors. Angel 63303-2 [CD].

It's all here, on a pair of shiny compact discs: Chopin on the tubas, "Let's Fake an Opera," Dennis Brain playing Mozart (albeit Leopold) on a garden hose, the *Leonore* Overture No. 4, the "perfectly straight" excerpt from Walton's *Belshazzar's Feast* conducted by the composer, as well as those two *magna opera*—the *Concerto Populaire,* brilliantly pieced together from dozens of well-known piano concertos, and the *Horrortorio,* in which Dracula's daughter is wed to "that freak, that zombie, that unnatural growth," Frankenstein.

With all due respect to P. D. Q. Bach, it was the series of three musical festivals inspired by the incomparable and tragically short-lived English cartoonist Gerard Hoffnung that set a standard for "murdering the classics" that only Spike Jones, at his most inspired, could begin to approach. With a typically English combination of parchment-dry wit coupled with unbridled lunacy, the Hoffnung concerts made loving fun of virtually everything musical that could be made fun of and did it with a touch that could be both extremely sophisticated and phenomenally crude.

Hoffnungians—those of us who have long since committed every note and nuance of this transcendental nonsense to memory—will be delighted at the quality of the CD transfers, which captures the sense of occasion far better than the old recordings did. For those who have never experienced this divine madness, I envy you your virgin run. Cherish it: for like your first romance, it is an experience that will never come again.

Holdridge, Lee (1944–)

Violin Concerto No. 2; *Lazarus and His Beloved* (symphonic suite)

Dicterow, violin. London Symphony, Holdridge. Citadel CTD 88104 [CD].

In addition to being one of the busiest and most accomplished film composers of his generation—along with the scores for *Splash, Old Gringo, 16 Days of Glory* (Bud Greenspan's documentary of the 1984 Los Angeles Olympics), and the cult classic *The Beastmaster,* he also wrote the unforgettable themes for the TV series *Beauty and the Beast* and *Moonlighting*—Lee Holdridge is also the composer of an impressive list of concert works, including the Violin Concerto, written in 1978 for Glenn Dicterow, then concertmaster of the Los Angeles Philharmonic, and the one-act opera *Lazarus and His Beloved,* composed in 1974.

While the *Lazarus* suite contains much lovely music, the Violin Concerto seems to me one of the most appealing modern works written for the instrument. The thematic material is haunting and instantly memorable, the harmonic language is lush and intricate, while the dramatic gestures and orchestration are decidedly cinematic—in the best possible sense of that word. In short, this is old-fashioned, large-scaled, emotionally charged music written by a man with a lot on his mind and even more in his heart. The performances, it goes without saying, are definitive.

A Varèse Sarabande album called "Symphonic Hollywood" (VSD 5329 [CD]) offers, among other things, the enchanting *Scenes of Summer* and a "Film Themes Suite" that includes the main title music for *East of Eden, 16 Days of Glory,* and the ravishing *Beauty and the Beast.*

Hollywood String Quartet

Felix Slatkin and Paul Shure, violins; Paul Robyn, viola; and Eleanor Aller Slatkin, cello

> Schoenberg: *Verklärte Nacht;* Schubert: Quintet in C, D. 956 (with Alvin Dinklin and Kurt Reher). Testament SBT 1031 [CD].
>
> Prokofiev: String Quartet No. 2; Hindemith: String Quartet No. 3; Walton: String Quartet in A Minor. Testament SBT 1052 [CD].
>
> Ravel: Introduction and Allegro; Debussy: *Danses sacrée et profane;* Turina: *La oración del torero;* Villa-Lobos: String Quartet No. 6; Creston: String Quartet No. 8. (with Ann Mason Stockton, Arthur Gleghorn, and Mitchell Lurie). Testament SBT 1053 [CD].
>
> Tchaikovsky: String Quartet No. 2; Borodin: String Quartet No. 2; Glazunov: Five Novelettes. Testament SBT 1061 [CD].
>
> Brahms: Piano Quartets 1–3, String Quartet No. 2; Schumann: Piano Quintet in E-flat, Op. 44. (with Victor Aller). Testament SBT 3063 [CD].

Formed at the end of the Second World War by four of the top Los Angeles studio musicians who simply missed the joys of performing chamber music, the Hollywood String Quartet gave its first public concert in 1946 and quickly passed into legend. Over the next fifteen years, they made a series of albums that are now widely regarded as the greatest chamber music recordings in the history of the medium: recordings in which a flawless technique and glorious physical sound are allied with interpretations of uncommon depth, range, and subtlety. In what will become—by definition—the single most important series of chamber music recordings since the invention of the compact disc, the English label Testament will reissue all of their recordings, many of which have not been available for decades.

The first installment—which won a richly deserved *Gramophone* Award— brings together two of their most famous recordings: with cellist Kurt Reher, a performance of the Schubert Cello Quintet whose slow movement glimpses the eternities, and the first recording of the sextet version (with Reher again and violist Alvin Dinklin) of Schoenberg's *Verklärte Nacht,* which not only earned the composer's imprimatur (on a picture sent to them, he wrote: "To the Hollywood String Quartet for playing my *Verklärte Nacht* with such subtle beauty") but also was the only recording of his music for which he supplied a program note (reprinted in full in the Testament booklet).

Volume Two offers three twentieth-century works by Prokofiev, Hindemith, and Walton, all in the finest recordings they have ever received. Especially hairraising is the version of Sir William Walton's demonically difficult A Minor Quartet. When he first heard it, the composer was bowled over by the recording, finding it impossible to believe that four Americans whom he had never met could have grasped his intentions with such uncanny accuracy: "I hope no one ever records my Quartet again," he told them, "because you captured so exactly what I wanted and yet we were six thousand miles apart." Listen to the almost superhuman playing in the final *Allegro molto* and you'll understand what he meant.

Volume Three consists largely of shorter works, including exquisite versions of Ravel's Introduction and Allegro and Debussy's *Danses sacrée et profane.* Although the interpretations of the quartets by Paul Creston and Heitor VillaLobos will probably always remain unsurpassable—the irrepressible Brazilian coached them in the Slatkins's living room while putting away the better part of a quart of Scotch—the playing in the brief *La oración del torero* by Joaquin Turina is so affecting in its simple eloquence that it alone (to coin a phrase) is worth the price of the album.

Volume Four—the Russian album—gives all the players ample opportunity to show off their Russian heritage (all were the children of Eastern European Jews who had emigrated to America at the turn of the century), and they show plenty: from the expressive warmth of the early Tchaikovsky Quartet—including the most moving recorded performance of the famous *Andante cantabile* in *any* of its versions—to the vivid colors of the Borodin Quartet, which features some particularly enthralling contributions from the cellist. Best of all, though, may be the rarely heard *Five Novelettes* by Glazunov, which draws playing of indescribable refinement, geniality, and wit.

In the three-CD Brahms-Schumann box, the players are joined by the cellist's brother, pianist Victor Aller, for the three Brahms Piano Quartets and the Piano Quintet by Schumann. No higher praise can be paid Aller's playing than to say it blends in perfectly with that of his colleagues: these are grand, adult, viscerally exciting performances in which nothing is done for personal glory or show. For instance, while other ensembles have drawn more gaudy gypsy color from the finale of the G Minor Quartet, none has ever infused it with such frightening intensity.

The central European album (SBT 1072 [CD]) includes their pointed and colorful version of Dvořák's "American" Quartet and that searing account of Smetana's "From My Life," in which the pain and horror of the final movement is made almost palpable. The bonus is their unapproachable version of the Second Quartet of Zoltán Kodály, one of the group's rare stereo recordings.

Neither of the piano quintets of César Franck or Dimitri Shostakovich (again with Victor Aller) has ever had more committed, thoroughly convincing recorded performances (SBT 10177 [CD]), nor, for that matter, has Schubert's "Death and the Maiden," the Third Quartet of Ernst von Dohnányi, or Hugo Wolf's *Italian Serenade* (SBT 1081 [CD]).

An album of unpublished live recordings taped while the Quartet was on tour in London (SBT 1085 [CD]) reveals that there was little to distinguish their studio recordings from their actual performances. Their versions of Haydn's "Quinten," Mozart's "Hunt," and a quartet by Johann Nepomuk Hummel are all predictably thrilling.

Perhaps the crowning glory of the cycle is the three-CD album devoted to the Late Quartets of Beethoven (SBT 3082 [CD]), in which the performances are as full of mystery, adventure, and a ready grasp of the infinities as the miraculous works themselves.

While it goes without saying that you should acquire all the albums, as a hedge against the deletions ax and those friends who will never return them if you're silly enough to lend them out, you might consider doing what I've done and will continue to urge all my friends to do: get at least *two* copies of each.

Holmboe, Vagn (1909–1996)

Symphony No. 2, Op. 15; *Sinfonia in memoriam*

Aarhus Symphony Orchestra, Hughes. BIS CD 605 [CD].

The most significant Danish symphonist since Carl Nielsen, Vagn Holmboe's early work reflected his obvious enthusiasm for his compatriot's music, together with that of Hindemith, Stravinsky, and his teacher Ernest Toch.

In a career that spanned seven decades—he finished the last of his thirteen symphonies when he was well into his eighties—Holmboe remained a composer of uncommon strength and uncompromising integrity, indifferent to fashionable trends, deaf to praise and criticism, inflexibly determined to go his own thoughtfully original way.

Finished in 1939 and awarded a national prize later in the year, Holmboe's Second Symphony established his reputation in Denmark and offers an excellent passport into his work. The Symphony has a Nielsen-like breadth of gesture and a Stravinskian neo-Classicism, together with a rugged inner vitality uniquely its own. The *Sinfonia in memoriam* was written in 1954 on a commission from the Danish Radio to celebrate the tenth anniversary of the liberation from Nazi oppression. It's a powerful, darkly craggy score full of deeply felt conviction. Under Owain Arwel Hughes, the Aarhus Symphony give both works what seem like definitive performances and the recorded sound is startling in its range and realism.

Any of the other installments in the Bis Holmboe Symphony cycle can be recommended with equal enthusiasm. Holmboe's music changed remarkably little over the years, except to become more confident, accomplished, and profound. Bis CD 605 [CD] offers the brief First Symphony with the outgoing *Sinfonia rustica* (No. 3) and the subtle, powerful Tenth, written for the Detroit Symphony.

The Fifth Symphony is among the most exuberant in Holmboe's output, a work with bracing rhythms and clear-cut neo-Classical lines. It is coupled on Bis CD 572 [CD] with the *Sinfonia sacra* (No. 4), an intensely moving six-movement choral work written in memory of his brother who died in a Nazi concentration camp.

The Sixth and Seventh Symphonies (Bis CD 573 [CD]) are probably the most recognizably Scandinavian installments in the series, with a somber intensity—especially in the one-movement Seventh—that recalls the Seventh Symphony of that other brooding Norseman, Jean Sibelius.

From its richly atmospheric opening movement through its insistent, powerfully assertive finale, the Eighth Symphony is more clearly than any of the symphonies that preceded it the work of a full-fledged master, as is the glowing, flawlessly argued Ninth (Bis CD 618 [CD].

The final volume (Bis CD 728 [CD]) offers the Eleventh, Twelfth, and valedictory Thirteenth Symphony, a work whose undiminished vitality bears inspiring testimony to a creative fire as unquenchable as Verdi's or Janáček's.

Holmès, Augusta (1847–1903)

Andromède (symphonic poem); *Ouverture pour une comédie; Irlande* (symphonic poem); *La Nuit et l'amour; Pologne* (symphonic poem)

> Rheinland-Pfalz Philharmonic, Davin, Friedmann. Marco Polo 8.223449 [CD].

Born in Paris of Anglo-Irish parents—it was widely rumored that her godfather, the poet Alfred de Vigny, was her actual father—Augusta Holmès (Holmes) was a captivating, multitalented figure who dominated the intellectual salons of her day, intriguing men as various as Liszt, Wagner, Vincent d'Indy, and Stéphane Mallarmé. A gifted composer, painter, and writer, she inspired her teacher César Franck to write his *Piano Quintet* and Camille Saint-Saëns to propose marriage, this in spite of the latter's sexual ambiguity and reservations about her "noisy" orchestration.

This fascinating Marco Polo album tends to confirm the view of her near contemporary Dame Ethel Smythe that Holmès's music was full of "jewels wrought by one who was evidently not among the giants, but for all that knew how to cut a gem." While the range and technical facility are limited—she was denied entry to the Paris Conservatory because of her sex—the music has abundant charm and character, most evident in the agreeably Lisztian tone poem *Andromède*. The performances and recorded sound are very fine.

Holst, Gustav (1874–1934)

Beni Mora (oriental suite); *Brook Green Suite; Egdon Heath; The Perfect Fool* (ballet music); Psalms 86 and 148 for Tenor, Organ, String Orchestra, and Chorus; *Short Festival Te Deum* for Chorus and Orchestra

> BBC Symphony, Sargent; Partridge, tenor, Downes, organ, Purcell Singers, English Chamber Orchestra, I. Holst; London Symphony Chorus, London Symphony Orchestra, Groves. EMI Classics CDC 49784 [CD].

This is an invaluable anthology of some of the composer's finest shorter works, including *Egdon Heath,* that brooding meditation on the somber setting of Hardy's *Return of the Native,* which many consider Holst's masterpiece. In one of his best recordings of British music, Sir Malcolm Sargent draws a shattering performance from the BBC Symphony and is no less effective with the exotic wonders of *Beni Mora* or the roistering humor of *The Perfect Fool* ballet. The composer's daughter Imogen leads authoritative performances of the two superb Psalm settings from 1912, while Sir Charles Groves rounds out the collection with a stirring version of the *Short Festival Te Deum*.

Although a brilliant Chandos album (CHAN 9420 [CD]) by the City of London Sinfonia conducted by Richard Hickox duplicates *Egdon Heath* (in a performance marginally finer than Sargent's), it offers the best available recorded performances of *Capriccio* (the *Jazz-Band Piece* of 1932 arranged by his daughter), the *Scherzo* of 1934 (his last completed orchestral work), the *Fugal Overture, Somerset Rhapsody*, and the composer's own orchestration of his great band piece, *Hammersmith*.

Among recordings of the *Hammersmith* Prelude in its original version, Frederick Fennell's classic performance with the Eastman Wind Ensemble is more or less permanently unassailable, particularly in the company of other phenomenal performances of Robert Russell Bennett's *Symphonic Songs*, Gordon Jacob's *William Byrd Suite*, Walton's *Crown Imperial*, and Clifton Williams's *Fanfare and Allegro* (Mercury Living Presence 432009-2 [CD]).

Brook Green Suite; A Fugal Concerto; Lyric Movement for Viola and Small Orchestra; *Morris Dances; St. Paul's Suite*

New Zealand Chamber Orchestra, Braithwaite. Koch 3-7058-2 [CD].

Along with the rarely heard *Fugal Concerto* and *Lyric Movement*, two impeccably crafted and instantly rewarding concerted works, this extremely appealing Koch album is devoted to music that reflects the composer's abiding love for English folk song, including the lovely *Brook Green Suite* and the jaunty *St. Paul's Suite*, both written for the orchestra of the St. Paul's Girls' School in London where Holst was music master for nearly thirty years.

Founded as recently as 1987, the brilliant New Zealand Chamber Orchestra plays with a sense of style and unanimity of purpose that completely belies their youth. Much of the credit for these exhilarating performances must go to Nicholas Braithwaite, who as a Holstian seems as deeply steeped in the idiom as Sir Adrian Boult or the composer's daughter Imogen, whose recordings do not seem any more authoritative than these. The recorded sound is also quite exceptional.

Choral Music

Finzi Singers, Spicer. Chandos CHAN 9425 [CD].

Holst Singers. Hyperion 66705 [CD].

As both of these delectable recordings clearly prove, Holst's partsongs are every bit as addictive as those of Elgar and Vaughan Williams. The Chandos collection combines some of Holst's finest individual items—including "This Have I Done for My True Love," which he considered his best partsong—with some of Vaughan Williams's most ravishing Shakespeare and folk-song settings. As we have come to expect from Paul Spicer's brilliant ensemble, the performances are exquisite.

The Hyperion anthology by the Holst Singers is, if anything, even more enjoyable, including as it does the Six Choral Folksongs of 1916—"I Sowed the Seeds of Love," "There Was a Tree," "Matthew, Mark, Luke, and John," "The Song of the Blacksmith," "I Love Thee," "Swansee Town"—and the Twelve Welsh Folk Songs from 1931. Both the performances and recorded sound are beautifully judged.

The Cloud Messenger; The Hymn of Jesus

London Symphony Chorus and Orchestra, Hickox. Chandos CHAN 8901 [CD].

These gorgeous choral works define the two radically disparate poles of Gustav Holst's spiritual life: the Anglican humanism of his youth that reached its culmination in his sacred masterpiece *The Hymn of Jesus,* and the preoccupation with Eastern mysticism in the years immediately before the First World War that led to works like the opera *Savitri* (beautifully realized in another Hickox-led performance on Hyperion CDA-66099 [CD]), the ethereal *Choral Hymns from the Rig Veda* (performed magically by the Holst Singers on Hyperion CDA-66175 [CD], KA-66175 [T]) and the ravishing *Cloud Messenger,* based on ancient Sanskrit texts.

Richard Hickox leads the London Symphony Chorus and Orchestra in performances that make both pieces—particularly *The Cloud Messenger*—seem like two of the forgotten masterworks of modern choral music. The level of inspiration in both the singing and playing is unusually high, and the Chandos recording captures the complex textures perfectly. Even for devoted Holst fans, this should prove an important discovery.

*T*he Planets (suite for large orchestra)

London Philharmonic, Boult. Angel CDM 64748 [CD].

**Philharmonia Orchestra, Gardiner. Deutsche Grammophon
    445860-2 [CD].**

Every conductor who has ever tried to come to terms with this phenomenally popular score has had to do so under an enormous shadow. Even the composer himself, who made his own recordings during the 78 era, was no match for the man who led the world premiere of *The Planets* in 1918, and during the next six decades, Sir Adrian Boult would record the work no fewer than *seven* times.

Over the years, the legendary Boult interpretation changed very little. In fact, the tempos remained so consistent that the variance in timings from one recording to another amounted to no more than a few seconds—except, that is, in his final version, which the conductor recorded in his ninetieth year.

The conductor's last look at *The Planets* is one of the great modern orchestral recordings. Beginning with a *Mars* of such weight and menace that all other performances seem positively pacifist in comparison, Boult somehow manages to find new expressive possibilities that even he had previously overlooked. *Venus* is more subtle and dreamy, *Jupiter* roars with a Falstaffian good humor, and *Uranus* lumbers along with a wit and rhythmic point that no other recording can really begin to match.

From the opening bars of the unusually slow and menacing version of *Mars*—certainly the slowest and probably the most menacing since Boult's—it's obvious that the new Deutsche Grammophon recording by Sir John Eliot Gardiner and the Philharmonia Orchestra is going to be something very special. By the final fade-out of *Neptune, the Mystic*, it's clear that it is *very* special indeed. It is one of those rare recordings that seems to do absolutely everything right. The interpretation is one of genuine stature, which not only leaves no detail of Holst's massive score to chance but also projects a measure of color, passion, and drama that only a handful of recordings ever have.

The recorded sound is a wonder of warmth and brilliance—both revealing and utterly natural by turns—while the generous and unusual filler is Percy Grainger's stunning "imaginary ballet" *The Warriors*. In short, it is in every way a triumph—proof that a musician who made his initial reputation with period-instrument performances of early music has clearly become one of the most compelling and versatile conductors of our time.

Suites (2) for Military Band

Cleveland Symphonic Winds, Fennell. Telarc CD-80038 [CD].

Among old bandsmen—and whether or not they give it the more snooty name of "Wind Ensemble," a band is still a band—the name of Frederick Fennell has been the stuff of legend for more than thirty years. An old bandsman himself—whose principal instrument, believe it or not, was the bass drum—Fennell's classic series of Mercury Living Presence records with the Eastman Wind Ensemble were probably the finest band recordings ever made. They not only forced the classical music establishment to take the "Wind Ensemble" more seriously but also, along with their celebrated, spit-and-polish Sousa albums, gave many of the first recorded performances of some absolutely wonderful music.

While Fennell's Eastman versions of these first great classics of the modern band repertoire were indispensable in their day, his latest recording of Holst's magnificent Suites for Military Band is even finer still. The Cleveland Symphonic Winds play with the same gusto and precision as the old Eastman crowd, and Fennell's interpretations, if anything, have become even more suave and energetic with the passage of time. If these marvelous performances fail to raise the hair on the back of your arms (or possibly even a lump in your throat), all that proves is that you've never experienced the indescribable thrill of sidestepping horse droppings at a brutal 120-beat-per-minute cadence during a Memorial Day parade.

Honegger, Arthur (1892–1955)

Symphonies (5)

Czech Philharmonic, Baudo. Supraphon 11 1566-2 [CD].

Of that group of a half-dozen rebellious young composers who in the 1920s banded together, with the mercurial Jean Cocteau as their spokesman, into a loose but like-minded confederation called *Les Six,* only three went on to achieve lasting recognition as major composers. If Darius Milhaud possessed the most robust and prolific talent and Francis Poulenc the most rarefied and individual gifts, then the most powerful and versatile voice in the group belonged to Arthur Honegger.

His best music is characterized by a neo-Classical formal economy in which driving rhythms, astringent harmonies, and a facile, often very moving, Gallic lyricism are thrown together, forming a very heady and original brew. His oratorio *Le Roi David* is one of the most significant sacred works of the twentieth century, and his five symphonies constitute one of the last largely undiscovered treasure troves of modern orchestral thought. Given Erato's inexplicable decision to withdraw the superb Honegger Symphony series led by Charles Dutoit, Serge Baudo's excellent cycle from the 1960s is clearly the one to have. The performances have plenty of subtlety as well as punch—No. 5 is unusually fine—and the recorded sound has been dramatically improved. As a bonus, the set comes with equally memorable performances of the *Mouvement symphonique No. 3*, *La Tempête* (a prelude to Shakespeare's *The Tempest*), and Honegger's most famous work, *Pacific 231*.

Erato has partially redeemed itself by reissuing Dutoit's powerfully dramatic 1970 recording of *Le Roi David* on its mid-priced Hommage series (2292-45800-2 [CD]) in a performance that uses the composer's original chamber-like scoring. Vanguard has also reissued Maurice Abravanel's 1964 Utah Symphony recording of the opera-oratorio *Judith* (OVC 8088 [CD]), one of Honegger's most imaginative and richly expressive works. Deutsche Grammophon has yet to make Seiji Ozawa's French National Orchestra recording (429412-2 [CD]) of *Jeanne d'Arc au bûcher* available domestically, though it can be ordered from stores that specialize in European imports. This is a totally committed performance of Honegger's powerfully haunting setting of the dramatic poem by Paul Claudel and is far superior to the well-intentioned Polish performance from Koch.

Music and Arts has made available all the commercial recordings that Honegger made of his own music (MUA 767 [CD]), including clear-cut, predictably authoritative versions of *Pastorale d'été*, *Pacific 231*, and the Third Symphony, all in perfectly serviceable sound.

Hovhaness, Alan (1911–)

Symphony No. 2, "Mysterious Mountain," Op. 132

Chicago Symphony, Reiner. RCA 09026-61957-2 [CD].

One of history's most prolific composers (it has been suggested that *profligate* might be a better description of his output), Alan Hovhaness is generally known for only two of his hundreds of mature works: *And God Created Whales*, which incorporated taped recordings of actual whale song, and "Mysterious Mountain," which became famous through Fritz Reiner's Chicago Symphony recording. I have had an enormous affection for the piece from the first moment I heard it, and for reasons that are not entirely musical.

I was playing the record one day when my paternal grandmother wandered in and asked what I was listening to. I had barely said "Hovhaness" when she fled screaming from the room, appalled not only at my rudeness, but also by the sort of language I was allowed to use. The composer's name bears a resemblance—made all the closer by my grandmother's imperfect English—to an exceedingly vulgar Czech word for the by-product of a basic bodily function.

The misty heights of the Symphony still exert a powerful allure, especially in the sublimely peaceful opening movement. The performance is even more perfect than it seemed to me as a boy, and coupled with Reiner's glistening accounts of Stravinsky's *Song of the Nightingale* and the Divertimento from *The Fairy's Kiss*—the recordings that may have led the composer to pronounce the Chicago Symphony, under Reiner, "the most precise and flexible orchestra in the world"—the CD represents an outstanding bargain.

In the first recording of their new Hovhaness series for Delos (DE 3137), Gerard Schwarz and the Seattle Symphony make elegant work of the composer's "City of Light" (No. 22) and "Mount St. Helens" (No. 50) Symphonies. If both pieces are somewhat structurally amorphous and repetitive, then you could scarcely tell it from the brilliantly focused, superbly atmospheric performances.

Volume 2 (DE 3157 [CD]) offers a version of "Mysterious Mountain" only slightly less distinguished than Reiner's, coupled with various shorter works— *Alleluia and Fugue, Prayer of St. Gregory,* and *Prelude and Quadruple Fugue*— and the best version yet of *And God Created Whales,* which rises to an imposing, perfectly judged climax. The humpbacked whale song is both haunting and eerily present, as though the beasts had stationed themselves somewhere among the violas.

Delos DE 3158 offers three symphonies for concert band—No. 20, "Three Journeys to a Holy Mountain"; No. 29 for Horn and Orchestra; and No. 53, "Star Dawn," together with some of the incidental music for Clifford Odets's *The Flowering Peach*—in exciting performances by the Ohio State University Concert Band conducted by Keith Brion.

The actor Michael York joins Schwarz and the Seattle Symphony for one of the most unusual and successful of all Hovhaness's works, the *Rubáiyát* for narrator, accordion, and orchestra (DE 3176 [CD]), an album also featuring the understandably colorful *Fantasy on Japanese Woodprints* for xylophone and chamber orchestra, and the Symphony No. 1, "Exile," from 1937.

Howells, Herbert (1892–1983)

Hymnus Paradisi; An English Mass

> Soloists, Royal Liverpool Philharmonic Choir and Orchestra, Handley.
> Hyperion CDA 66488 [CD].

A younger contemporary of Ralph Vaughan Williams and Gustav Holst, whom he succeeded as music master at St. Paul's Girls' School in 1936, Herbert Howells has remained far less well known for two obvious reasons: his musical personality is not as instantly recognizable or immediately appealing as theirs, and he devoted the bulk of his creative energies to church music. Composed after the death of his nine-year-old son, Howells's gravely beautiful *Hymnus Paradisi* ranks with the great sacred works of the twentieth century, an impassioned but dignified outpouring of grief that becomes increasingly moving and powerful on repeated hearings.

Vernon Handley leads a performance that is so committed and compassionate that you soon begin to wonder why this great work has not yet entered the standard repertoire. With an equally compelling performance of another Howells masterpiece, the quieter, less ambitious *English Mass,* the recording makes an ideal introduction to a preposterously neglected talent.

On Hyperion CDA-66139 [CD] the group called Divertimenti give a glowing performance of the evocative String Quartet No. 3, "In Gloucestershire," coupled with the gripping *Three Rhapsodies for String Quartet* by Howells's friend Sir George Dyson.

Hummel, Johann Nepomuk

(1778–1837)

Concerto in E-flat for Trumpet and Orchestra

> Hardenberger, trumpet; Academy of St. Martin-in-the-Fields, Marriner.
> Philips 420203-2 [CD]; 420203-4 [T].

Mix equal parts water and Beethoven and the result is Johann Nepomuk Hummel, possessor of the best composer's name since Carl Ditters von Dittersdorf and, with his contemporary Jan Ladislav Dussek, the largest composer's paunch. (A gaping concave indentation had to be cut into his dining room table, both at home and at court). While Hummel's music may lack the personality and emotional depth of Beethoven's—the two were on-again, off-again friends—at its best it is graceful, aristocratic, and elegantly turned out, with many hints of the humor and warmth that characterized the man himself.

In terms of quality, Hummel's brilliant and tuneful Trumpet Concerto is not that far removed from Haydn's. There is real charm and character in the writing, together with ample opportunity for virtuoso display. The young Swedish phenomenon Håkan Hardenberger glides over its technical pitfalls as though they didn't exist, with Marriner and the Academy lending their typically stylish support. Coupled with equally bravura accounts of the Haydn and the obscure but worthy concertos of Johann Wilhelm Hertel and Carl Stamitz, this amounts to a trumpet-lover's dream.

Humperdinck, Engelbert

(1854–1921)

Hänsel und Gretel

> Schwarzkopf, Grümmer, Felbermayer, Ilosvay, Philharmonia Orchestra, Karajan. Angel CDMB 69293 [CD].

Now that this best-loved of all children's operas has finally made its debut on compact disc, how appropriate that it should be in that magical recording from 1953 that captures more of the wonder and wide-eyed innocence of *Hänsel und Gretel* than any other performance ever has or ever will. Elisabeth Schwarzkopf and Elisabeth Grümmer are unsurpassable as Humperdinck's immortal tykes, and Herbert von Karajan's warm and glowing conducting provides a depressing reminder of what a chilling, arrogant wretch that once superlative musician became. The supporting cast sings with immense character and devotion, and the original recorded sound has been made to seem extraordinarily fresh and alive.

Jeffrey Tate leads an outstanding modern *Hänsel und Gretel* on EMI Classics (CDBC 54022 [CD]) that frequently approaches the Karajan in terms of mystery and wonder. Although Barbara Bonney and Anne Sofie von Otter are not quite as magical as their famous rivals, they sing with exceptional freshness and beauty and the recorded sound is thrillingly alive.

Königskinder

> Moser, Schellenberger, Henschel, Schmiege, Kohn, Bavarian Radio
> Chorus and Orchestra, Luisi. Calig 50968/70 [CD].

No one would ever suggest that *Königskinder* is a great opera, except perhaps for Nicholas Meyer, the brilliant director (*Time after Time, Star Trek II: The Search for Spock, The Day After,* etc.) and author of *The Seven-Per-Cent Solution,* who among other things has collected every single recording of *Carmen* ever made and will, upon request at social gatherings, shatter the legendary Savoyard C. H. Workman's all-time speed record in "The Nightmare Song" from Gilbert and Sullivan's *Iolanthe.*

While this tale of the Goosegirl and the handsome Prince was a triumph at its New York premiere in 1910, *Königskinder* has fallen on hard times since. If Humperdinck's second fairy-tale opera is clearly not the equal of *Hänsel und Gretel,* then it is nonetheless a work full of genuine charm, soaring lyricism, and better-than-average tunes. Fabio Luisi leads a good cast in a performance that emphasizes the richness of Humperdinck's writing while minimizing the weaknesses of a frequently chaotic libretto.

As usual in their opera recordings, the Bavarian Radio Chorus and Orchestra perform superbly and the recorded sound is distant but well focused.

Shakespeare Suites (2)

> Bamberg Symphony, Rickenbacher. Koch Schwann SCH 311972 [CD].

If Humperdinck never duplicated the success of *Hänsel und Gretel,* then he still wrote a good deal of engaging music during the remaining years of his life, much of it for the great German director Max Reinhardt. Composed for various productions of *The Tempest, The Winter's Tale,* and *The Merchant of Venice* between 1905 and 1907, the *Shakespeare Suites* collect the best moments from the incidental music into a pair of very satisfying entertainments: the melodic invention is of a very high order, the orchestration consistently inspired, the dramatic range unusually broad. The CD is rounded out by the early Mendelssohnian *Humoresque* and the sparkling *Die Heirat wider Willen* (Marriage against Their Will) Overture. Karl Anton Rickenbacher leads the Bamberg Symphony in some deftly imaginative performances—the Procession of the Shepherds from *The Winter's Tale* (the only Shakespeare play set partially in Bohemia, "A desert country near the sea") is especially magical—and the recorded sound is distant but good.

Those who enjoy this illuminating foray into unknown Humperdinck will want to investigate a lovely companion album by these same forces on Virgin Classics (59067 [CD]): the orchestral suites from *Hänsel und Gretel, Der blaue Vogel, Königskinder,* and *Dornröschen* in equally sympathetic performances and marginally superior sound.

Husa, Karel (1921–)

Music for Prague 1968

Eastman Wind Ensemble, Hunsberger. CBS MK-44916 [CD].

If you've become convinced that Contemporary Music now means either minimalist drivel or incomprehensible noise, you have yet to hear the music of Karel Husa, the major musical voice to have emerged from Czechoslovakia since Bohuslav Martinů, and one of the most powerful and original composers of our time. While his idiom is thoroughly, and often aggressively, modern, Husa is essentially a conservative: a composer who believes that music must carry enormous emotional and expressive burdens above and beyond the notes on the printed page. With his String Quartet No. 3, which won the 1969 Pulitzer Prize and is now available on a Phoenix CD (PHCD 113) in the spellbinding performance by the Fine Arts Quartet, Husa's most celebrated work to date has been *Music for Prague 1968,* which has so far amassed the astonishing total of more than seven thousand performances.

Written in reaction to the tragic events that engulfed the Czech capital in the fall of that year, *Music for Prague 1968* is a furious, brutally dramatic, and hauntingly beautiful evocation of a city and a people who, in the last ten centuries, have known precisely twenty years of political freedom. With its vivid colors, brilliant craftsmanship, and searing intensity, it is one of the handful of authentic large-scale masterworks of modern times.

The Eastman Wind Ensemble performance, while a fine one, lacks the sweep and passion of the composer's own on a now-deleted Golden Crest recording. On the other hand, the recording to wait for is of a performance that was given on February 13, 1990, when Husa, at the invitation of President Václav Havel, introduced it to the city for which it was written.

I once devoted a program to Husa's music that bore the purposefully provocative title "The Greatest Living Composer?" I should now confess what I *really* think. Lose the question mark.

Ibert, Jacques (1890–1962)

Escales (Ports of Call)

French National Orchestra, Martinon. EMI Classics CDM 64276 [CD].

Several decades after his best-known work had become firmly entrenched in the standard repertoire, the dapper French composer Jacques Ibert ruefully told a reporter: "I have written twenty important works since *Escales,* but always when they speak of Ibert, they talk about *Escales.*" Based on impressions the composer collected on a Mediterranean cruise he had made while serving in the French Navy during World War I, *Escales,* with its unforgettable evocation of the port cities of Palermo, Tunis, Valencia, and Nefta, is like a technicolor version of Debussy's *La Mer:* an obvious but highly skillful swatch of local color that deserves all the popularity it has enjoyed.

With Paul Paray's classic 1962 interpretation on Mercury Living Presence (432003-2 [CD]), Jean Martinon's 1974 recording is the finest ever made: vivid, atmospheric, and, in the languorous second movement, supremely erotic. It also has the advantage of being coupled with two rarely performed Ibert works (Paray's comes with a Ravel collection): the shallow but engaging *Ouverture de fête,* and the uneven but fascinating *Tropismes pour des amours imaginaires,* his last completed score.

The obstreperous *Divertissement,* the only other Ibert score to begin to match *Escales* in popularity, is given a suitably boisterous performance by the Ulster Orchestra under Yan Pascal Tortelier (Chandos CHAN 9023 [CD]), while the delightful *Trois pièces brèves* is given an excellent performance by the Frösunda Wind Quintet in a superb Bis anthology (CD 136 [CD]) of twentieth-century wind music.

d'Indy, Vincent (1851–1931)

Symphony No. 2 in B-flat, Op. 57; *Souvenirs*

Monte Carlo Philharmonic, DePriest. Koch 3-7280-2 [CD].

Camille Saint-Saëns once startled a room full of his admirers by proclaiming his arch-enemy, Vincent d'Indy, "The Johann Sebastian Bach of French Music." He was quick to add: "Of course, you realize that we composers say the exact *opposite* of what we think." It was probably a combination of personal animus and professional jealousy that led Saint-Saëns to so dislike the music of his younger contemporary: for what d'Indy lacked of Saint-Saëns's melodic gift and native facility, he made up for with his penetrating intelligence, spiritual depth, and consummate craftsmanship.

Completed in 1903 when its composer was fifty-two, d'Indy's Second Symphony is probably the best French work in the form since the D Minor Symphony of d'Indy's teacher César Franck. Meticulously planned, elegantly argued, and beautifully scored, the B-flat Major Symphony is alternately noble, playful, and darkly subdued—the slow movement may have been an elegy for his friend and fellow Franck pupil Ernest Chausson—and one of the most physically beautiful scores ever produced by a Frenchman.

Amazingly, the Koch recording by James DePriest and the Monte Carlo Philharmonic is only the third that the symphony has ever received—fortunately. Not only does it easily eclipse the only other modern recording (with the Capitole de Toulouse Orchestra conducted by Michel Plasson), but it also compares more than favorably with the classic 1942 Victor recording by the San Francisco Symphony conducted by Pierre Monteux. The reading has a natural, unforced eloquence, as does the performance of the touching *Souvenirs,* which d'Indy composed in 1906 as a memorial to his wife.

First choice among recordings of d'Indy's most celebrated work, the *Symphony on a French Mountain Air,* continues to be Charles Munch's 1958 RCA recording (09026-62582-2 [CD]). Although the recorded sound has become a trifle brittle, both the orchestra and pianist Nicole Henriot-Schweitzer play with intelligence and fervor. The performance has been recently repackaged with Munch's kinetic recording (with William Primrose) of Berlioz's *Harold in Italy.*

Ippolitov-Ivanov, Mikhail

(1859–1935)

Orchestral Works (including *Caucasian Sketches*)

National Symphony Orchestra of the Ukraine, Fagen. Naxos 8.553405 [CD].

Like that other luckless part-of-a-work composer, the prolific Henry Litolff, whose slender posthumous fame rests entirely on the quicksilver Scherzo from the Concerto Symphonique No. 4, all that history seems to remember of Mikhail

Mikhailovich Ippolitov-Ivanov is that pops concert favorite "The Procession of the Sardar" from the first set of *Caucasian Sketches*. A pupil of Rimsky-Korsakov, from whom he inherited a love of exotic, quasi-oriental melodies and vivid orchestration, Ippolitov-Ivanov remained a devoted and frequently inspired craftsman for more than half a century, unburdened by the need to express any real individuality or do much to advance his musical thinking or style. There is an almost comforting sameness in his output, with little to distinguish music written in the 1880s from that written in the 1920s or '30s.

With few really distinguished versions of the *Caucasian Sketches* currently available—Maurice Abravanel's stylish but indifferently recorded performance with the Utah Symphony for Vanguard (OVC 5010 [CD]) is the best of all—this Naxos anthology offers an excellent, cost-efficient introduction to the composer's work. Along with both sets of *Caucasian Sketches,* the disc offers genuine rarities like *Turkish Fragments*—a kind of *Caucasian Sketches* gone south. The performances are enthusiastic and skillful, with perfectly serviceable recorded sound.

Ireland, John (1879–1962)

A London Overture; Epic March; The Holy Boy; Greater Love Hath No Man; Vexilla Regis

> **Soloists, London Symphony Chorus and Orchestra, Hickox. Chandos CHAN 7074 [CD].**

Although the colorful and incisive *London Overture* has enjoyed memorable recordings by Boult, Barbirolli, and Sargent, most of the music of this lonely, elusive composer has languished in undeserved obscurity. Full of jazzy wit and unabashed lyricism, Ireland's Piano Concerto of 1930 is one of the richest and most individual ever written by an Englishman, while the pagan tone poem *The Forgotten Rite* is every bit the equal of the finest such works by his younger contemporary, Sir Arnold Bax. Given the slightest encouragement, the enchanting *Downland Suite* could become a pops concert staple, while the Second Violin Sonata, the Cello Sonata, and the Fantasy-Sonata for clarinet and piano rank with the most significant English chamber music of the century.

Richard Hickox leads typically sympathetic and perceptive performances in the first of his Ireland collections, from a richly atmospheric version of *A London Overture* to a deeply committed performance of the moving choral work *These Things Shall Be,* written for the coronation of George VI. Most exciting of all, though, may be the aptly named *Epic March,* which is as memorably stirring as anything by Walton or Elgar. An excellent second volume (CHAN 8994 [CD]) is devoted to equally impressive versions of *The Forgotten Rite* and Ireland's last important work, the score for Harry Watt's engrossing 1946 film about Australian cattle drovers, *The Overlanders*.

Eric Parkin gives a first-rate performance of the Piano Concerto with Bryden Thomson and the London Philharmonic on an attractive Chandos recording that also features the lovely *Legend for Piano and Orchestra* and the tone poem *Mai-Dun* (CHAN 8461 [CD]).

Lastly, Ireland's beautifully made Cello Sonata of 1923 has received what sounds like a definitive recording from cellist Raphael Wallfisch and pianist John York on Marco Polo 8.223718 [CD]. The passion and intelligence of this splendid work are evident throughout the performance; the versions of the sonatas by Moeran and Rubbra that round out the album are no less fine.

Ives, Charles

(1874–1954)

Songs

> DeGaetani, soprano; Kalish, piano. Nonesuch 71325-2 [CD], 71325-4 [T].
>
> Hampson, baritone; Guzelimian, piano. Teldec 9031-72168-2 [CD].

Like virtually everything else he ever wrote, the 114 songs that Charles Ives produced between 1884 and 1921 could not have been written by anyone else. Alternately serious, nostalgic, cranky, spontaneous, ridiculous, patriotic, cynical, feather-headed, and sentimental, they cover an astonishing range of musical and emotional expression and represent, with those of Ned Rorem, the most significant body of art songs yet produced by an American.

With her flawless intonation and uncanny rhythmic sense, the late Jan DeGaetani was an ideal interpreter of this highly individual repertoire, capturing the quirky charm of "Ann Street" and the tender beauty of "A Christmas Carol" to perfection. As part of a fascinating recital of American songs on German texts, Thomas Hampson's performances are as intelligent as they are deeply musical.

String Quartets (2)

Emerson String Quartet. Deutsche Grammophon 435864-2 [CD].

The Ives String Quartets are the great Jekyll-and-Hyde act of American chamber music. The First, a work that wouldn't offend your grandmother, was written when the composer was a twenty-one-year-old Yale undergraduate, still very much under the influence of Horatio Parker; the Second dates from the years 1907 to 1913, the very heart of his most forbidding, dad-blamed cussedest manner. As the title page describes the work: "SQ for four men—who converse, discuss, argue (in re 'politics'), fight, shake hands, shut up—then walk up the mountainside to view the firmament." That just about says it.

Although it would be delightful to have the old Columbia recording by the Juilliard String Quartet returned to circulation, the newer version by the Emersons is also very impressive. If things are kept a little too sedate and homogenized in the First Quartet, then they really let the Second rip: this is Ives at his most original and explosive, with most of the bark left on. A lovely performance of the Barber Quartet comes as the aptly chosen filler.

Symphony No. 2; Symphony No. 3, "The Camp Meeting"; *The Unanswered Question*

New York Philharmonic, Bernstein. Sony Classical SMK 47568 [CD].

Amsterdam Concertgebouw Orchestra, Thomas. (Second Symphony only) Sony Classical SK 46440 [CD].

Leonard Bernstein's famous Columbia recording of the Second Symphony almost singlehandedly sparked the Ives revival of the 1960s. Prior to the release of that classic recording by the man who had led the work's world premiere more than a half century after it had been composed, Ives had been an obscure figure with a small but knowledgeable following. Within a few years, he was to become an American Original, a cult phenomenon, a composer who, in Bernstein's words, was "the Washington, Jefferson, and Lincoln of our music."

Now that the hoopla that surrounded the Ives centennial in 1974 has begun to fade into the distance like one of the those crack-brained parades that haunt his music, a more balanced guess at the importance of his achievement can finally begin to be made. Like another insurance executive who was also a diligent weekend artist, the Hartford poet Wallace Stevens, Ives possessed an important, original, and peculiarly American talent. And if, as his admirers claim, he was one of the most forward-looking composers of his generation—and he *did* anticipate many of the most important trends in twentieth-century music, years and often decades before anyone else—there was also, in Ives, a good deal of the archetypal American Crank, a kind of musical Rube Goldberg raised to the nth degree.

The Second Symphony remains his most approachable and instantly like-able work. In fact, it's difficult *not* to like a work whose principal themes include "Bringing in the Sheaves" and "Where, O Where, Are the Pea Green Fresh-men?"—a Yale student song that sounds like an impossibly civilized version of "Dixie"—and which concludes with a fabulous peroration on "Columbia, Gem of the Ocean," flanked by reveille and the most spectacular orchestral raspberry (an eleven-note chord cluster) that anyone ever wrote.

In its compact disc reissue, Bernstein's performance sounds more joyous, committed, and spirited than ever, and his versions of the "Camp Meeting" Symphony and the intriguing *Unanswered Question* should still be considered the definitive performances of both works. While very fine, the conductor's more recent Deutsche Grammophon recording lacks some of the bite of the old Columbia outing.

Michael Tilson Thomas's more recent digital recording is also a tremendous amount of fun. While the performance may lack the last measure of Bernstein's savvy and gusto, this is the first commercial recording of the critical edition of the Symphony, and the playing of the Concertgebouw Orchestra, as playing, per se, can't really be approached.

Washington's Birthday, Decoration Day, Fourth of July, Thanksgiving and/or Forefather's Day ("Holidays" Symphony); *Central Park in the Dark; The Unanswered Question*

Chicago Symphony Orchestra and Chorus, Thomas.
CBS MK 42381 [CD].

From the off-kilter barn dance in *Washington's Birthday* to the spendthrift use of an entire chorus to intone a single verse of "God! Beneath Thy Guiding Hand" in *Thanksgiving and/or Forefather's Day,* Ives's "Holidays" Symphony contains some the composer's most characteristic and supremely eccentric inspi-rations.

While all of the pieces have had superb individual performances, this eye-opening recording by Michael Tilson Thomas and the Chicago Symphony finally persuades us that the "Holidays" are not only arresting parts but also an even more satisfying whole. (Ives himself indicated that he didn't care if they were per-formed separately or as a unit; but then, too, the only thing that Bernard Shaw would ever tell his actors was, "Speak the lines clearly and have a good time.") Never have the tempos and textures of the four pieces seemed so interconnected and interdependent, nor has any performance—at least in my experience—created the feeling of such an inevitable musical *and* dramatic flow.

The playing of the orchestra—from the barely audible opening of *Washington's Birthday* to the raucous march in *Decoration Day,* where the Chicago brass sound like the old Sousa band—is quite phenomenal, as is the recorded sound. With equally atmospheric performances of *Central Park in the Dark* and *The Unanswered Question,* this may be the most important single Ives recording yet made.

The finest recording of Ives's masterpiece, the *Three Places in New England*—one of Thomas's first—is now out on a Deutsche Grammophon compact disc (423243-2.) To get it, you have to put up with Seiji Ozawa's rather lackluster walk-through of the Fourth Symphony, but the *Three Places* are done so magically that they're more than worth the price.

Jacob, Gordon (1895–1984)

Music for Clarinet and Strings

> Russo, clarinet; Premier Chamber Orchestra, Gilbert. Premier PRCD 1052 [CD].

Best known for his orchestral version of Vaughan Williams's *English Folksong Suite* and his imposing *William Byrd Suite*—available again in the classic recording by Frederick Fennell and the Eastman Wind Ensemble (Mercury Living Presence 432009-2 [CD]), coupled with electric versions of Holst's *Hammersmith,* Walton's *Crown Imperial,* and Robert Russell Bennett's *Symphonic Songs*—Gordon Jacob was one of the most charming and accomplished English composers of his generation and one of the most durable, as the four splendid works on this handsome Premier album clearly prove. The Clarinet Quintet of 1942 is a moltenly lyrical work, every bit the equal of the far more familiar quintet by Sir Arthur Bliss; the Mini-Concerto for Clarinet and String Orchestra, written when Jacob was in his mid-eighties, shows he had lost none of his legendary craftsmanship or sparkling wit. Charles Russo performs them both with sensitivity and flair and is equally persuasive in the Clarinet Trio of 1969 and the Concertino for Clarinet and String Orchestra, skillfully arranged from keyboard sonatas by Giuseppe Tartini.

For Jacob at his most irresistible, the Irish harmonic virtuoso Tommy Reilly gives an enchanting performance of the *Divertimento for Harmonica and String Quartet* on Chandos CHAN 8802 [CD].

Janáček, Leoš (1854–1928)

Capriccio for Piano (left hand) and Winds; Concertino for Piano and Chamber Orchestra

> **Firkušný, piano; Czech Philharmonic, Neumann. RCA Victor 09026-60781-2 [CD].**

As in his recording of the composer's solo piano music (see page 380), Rudolf Firkušný was all but unapproachable in this repertoire. Completed in 1925, the *Capriccio* for Piano (left hand) and wind instruments was written for Ottokar Hollman, who, like the Austrian pianist Paul Wittgenstein, lost his right arm during the First World War. Originally called *Defiance,* undoubtedly as a tribute to Hollman's stubborn courage, the *Capriccio* contrasts wind writing of unusual richness and complexity with piano writing of a deceptive and elegant simplicity. The Concertino, written the year before, is a less obviously demanding but no less original work.

Made in Prague after an exile of nearly fifty years, Firkušný's recordings have an insight and authority that no others will ever match. His old teacher, Leoš Janáček—with whom he studied composition, not piano—would have been proud.

The Cunning Little Vixen

> **Popp, Jedlička, Randová, Vienna Philharmonic, Mackerras. London 417129-2 [CD].**

Had Leoš Janáček died at the same age as Beethoven, he would be remembered today—if at all—as a very minor late Romantic composer, conductor, and organist, whose name would occasionally turn up in the more complete biographies of his friend Antonín Dvořák. It was not until 1904, at the age of fifty, that he began to produce, apparently from out of nowhere, that startling series of works upon which his reputation as one of the most powerfully original twentieth-century composers now rests. Janáček's sudden and mysterious transformation from a provincial nobody into a modern giant is without precedent in the history of music. In the other arts, only William Butler Yeats's relatively late emergence as the great English-language poet of the twentieth century offers a similar example of such mysterious and wonderful growth.

The cornerstone of Janáček's achievement is that series of nine operas that are slowly being recognized as some of the most important works of the modern operatic stage. Their general acceptance was understandably delayed by the difficulty of the Czech language itself, and by the fact that they are by definition untranslatable, since Janáček's musical language was intimately connected with the rhythms and inflections of Czech speech. And then, too, their subject matter is often so peculiar that theaters outside of Czechoslovakia once thought them to be all but impossible to produce. For instance, the heroine of *Věc Makropulos* (*The Makropulos Case*—though a more correct translation would be *The Makropulos Thing*), is a three-hundred-year-old opera singer; *Z mrtvého domu* (*From the House of the Dead*) is set in a Tsarist prison camp; and the cast of characters in *Příhody lišky Bystroušky* includes a dog, a badger, a cricket, a grasshopper, and a group described simply as "the various vermin." In spite of its profound and delightful eccentricity, *The Cunning Little Vixen* is neither nonsense nor simply another children's story, but one of the most bewitching and enchantingly beautiful operas ever composed.

Sir Charles Mackerras's grasp of the special power, charm, and expressive potential of Janáček's music is without equal in the world today. As a student, he studied the scores with the man who gave many of them their world premieres, the composer's friend Václav Talich. At this late date it is absurd to ask if Mackerras, an American-born Englishman of Australian parentage, can possibly speak Janáček's language as idiomatically as a native; it is doubtful that any Czech conductor, except for Talich, has ever begun to speak it half as well.

Sir Charles's version of *The Cunning Little Vixen* is one of the greatest in an already triumphant series of Janáček recordings. He leads the Vienna Philharmonic through the difficult, delicate score as though it were no more challenging than an early Haydn symphony. The predominantly Czech cast is largely wonderful, especially since most of them drop the wobbly, intrusive vibrato that so many Eastern European singers are apparently taught from birth. Most wonderful of all, however, is the exquisite Vixen of Lucia Popp, one of the most hugely gifted sopranos of the last half century. Her passion, precision, and the extraterrestrial beauty of her physical sound make this one of the great characterizations of the last twenty years and further make an already invaluable recording a completely indispensable one.

The orchestral suite that Václav Talich arranged from his friend's opera is available again in the conductor's inspired recording with the Czech Philharmonic (Supraphon SUP 111905 [CD].

The Excursions of Mr. Brouček

Přibyl, Švejda, Maršik, Jonášova, Novák, Krejčik, Czech Philharmonic Chorus and Orchestra, Jílek. Supraphon SUP 112153 [CD].

No opera ever written covers more ground than *Výlety Pàně Broučkovy*— literally. Cast in two parts, *The Excursions of Mr. Brouček* is based on a pair of fantastic tales by the poet Svatopluk Čech: *The Excursion of Mr. Brouček to the*

Moon from 1887 and *New, Sensational Excursion of Mr. Brouček, This Time into the Fifteenth Century,* published in the following year. The hero—whose name means "small beetle"—was intended to represent all that was most stolid and unimaginative in the Czech middle class, a man who is as maladroit in outer space as in the remote past. While once thought to be digestible only by Czech audiences, *The Excursions of Mr. Brouček* is in fact one of Janáček's most completely approachable creations: funny, compassionate, wildly original, and delightfully off-center.

Resisting the considerable temptation to turn the character into a caricature, the stalwart Vilém Přibyl is in superb form as Brouček: subtle in his elaboration of the character's comic side while finding a surprising depth elsewhere. Jana Jonášová is similarly appealing in the dual role of Malinká/Etherea, as is the versatile Vladimir Krejčik who does yeoman service in no less than seven smaller parts. Under Frantíček Jílek's unfailingly lively and insightful leadership, the great Czech Philharmonic plays the challenging score as no other orchestra could and the 1982 recorded sound remains first-class in every way.

Jenůfa

Söderström, Popp, Randová, Dvorský, Ochman, Vienna Philharmonic, Mackerras. London 414483-2 [CD].

Jenůfa was the first of Janáček's great operas and it remains the most popular and instantly approachable. It is also, by a comfortable margin, the most conventional of all his works for the stage. Set in a sleepy Czech village, the direct but not-so-simple story of jealousy, vengeance, violence, and redemption is a dramatic amalgam of Smetana's *The Bartered Bride* and Mascagni's *Cavelleria Rusticana*. Musically, however, *Jenůfa* is an entirely different matter—a fresh, tuneful, and powerfully dramatic score in which one of history's major operatic composers first found his distinct and utterly original voice.

Like all of the recordings in Sir Charles Mackerras's historic cycle of the Janáček operas, this is the *Jenůfa* that will probably dominate the catalogues until well into the next century. It is also one of those rare studio recordings that has all the immediacy and excitement of a live performance. Elisabeth Söderström—is there a finer Janáček heroine in the world today?—is both ineffably tender and witheringly powerful in the title role, and the rest of the cast, together with the orchestra and conductor, are all captured at the very top of their forms.

If you are one of those people who are convinced, perhaps with good reason, that opera came to a screeching halt with the death of Giacomo Puccini, give *Jenůfa*—especially this *Jenůfa*—a try.

Kát'a Kabanová

Söderström, Kniplová, Dvořský, Jedlička, Krejčik, Svehla, Vienna Philharmonic, Mackerras. London 421852-2 [CD].

Kát'a Kabanová is the most powerful of the Janáček operas, a work that, when done properly, can leave an audience as shattered as Berg's *Wozzeck* or Strauss's *Elektra*. As anyone who saw Rafael Kubelík's now legendary San Francisco Opera production in the late 1970s knows, the combination of a potent dramatic soprano and a conductor who knows his business can make *Kát'a* an overwhelming experience, as it certainly is here. Elisabeth Söderström sings as memorably for Mackerras as she did for Kubelík, and although this is a studio recording, the dramatic power and subtlety of the characterization fairly bursts from the speakers. It, too, is destined to become the stuff of legend: a piece of operatic history to be mentioned in the same breath with the Lehmann Marschallin or the Callas Tosca.

As the first installment of his Janáček cycle, Sir Charles Mackerras inspired the Vienna Philharmonic to capture both the strength and the intricacy of the often difficult writing while responding with a wonderful sense of atmosphere and mood. With excellent to inspired contributions from the all-Czech supporting cast, this is the recording that argues most persuasively that *Kát'a Kabanová* is indeed the composer's masterpiece.

Nursery Rhymes

Caramoor Festival Chorus and Orchestra, Rudel. Phoenix PHCD 109 [CD].

Janáček never wrote a more enchanting work than *Říkadla,* a series of brief settings of some droll nursery rhymes that appeared in the newspaper *Lidové noviny*. With *Youth,* Janáček had returned to the world of his boyhood; with *Říkadla,* he reentered the world of childhood. Scored for chorus and a tiny instrumental ensemble (including ocarina), *Nursery Rhymes* is as fresh and innocent as Schumann's *Kinderszenen* and as amusing as Leopold Mozart's *Toy Symphony.*

It's good to have Julius Rudel's lively performance back in circulation, especially coupled with such fine versions of *Youth, Capriccio,* and the Concertino for Piano and Chamber Orchestra. If some of the rhymes lose something in translation ("Our poor doggie broke his tail off./ He stuck it in the fence/ How could he be so dense?"), then your kids—for whom they were written, after all—will probably have an easier time in English than in Czech.

Piano Music

Andsnes, piano. Virgin Classics CDC 59639 [CD].

As with his operas and orchestral scores, Janáček's piano works are the products of a wholly original musical mind. In all of the pieces on his Deutsche Grammophon recital as well as the more recent RCA remake—both unaccountably withdrawn—the late Rudolf Firkušný demonstrated why he was the foremost Janáček pianist that history has so far known. The playing had a seamless perfection and an evocative magic that made this entrancing music spring to life in practically every bar: *In the Mists* will probably never have a more refined and poetic performance, while the Piano Sonata emerged with an uncommon sense of unity and depth.

Leif Ove Andsnes is the first pianist in a generation to mount a serious challenge to Firkušný's absolute supremacy and the appearance of his Virgin Classics recital helps take some of the sting out of the recent deletions. The pervasive melancholy of *In the Mists* is beautifully shaded, while the elusive miniatures of *On an Overgrown Path* emerge in sharply delineated relief. If the performances lack the final ounce of his great predecessor's idiomatic authority, then that is only because Andsnes never had the opportunity to study the music bar by bar with Janáček himself, as the young Firkušný did.

Sextet for Winds, *Mládi* (Youth); *Idyll* for String Orchestra

Los Angeles Chamber Orchestra, Schwarz. Nonesuch 79033-2 [CD].

No work more dramatically illustrates Janáček's phenomenal growth as a composer than the youthful *Idyll* for String Orchestra, written when he was twenty-four. It is a charming, wholly derivative late-Romantic piece with echoes of Dvořák, Smetana, Brahms, and Wagner—the young Janáček was at least admirably catholic in his tastes—and one that gives not the slightest indication of the twentieth-century dynamo its composer would later become. The brilliantly inventive wind sextet *Mládi* (Youth), a youthful product of the composer's fertile old age, is a perfect complement to the earlier score. Ironically, the Sextet seems like the work of an impetuous twenty-year-old, the *Idyll* that of a tired old man.

Gerard Schwarz and the Los Angeles Chamber Orchestra give rousing performances of both, especially *Mládi,* which features some of the most adroit wind playing in years.

Sinfonietta; Taras Bulba

Vienna Philharmonic, Mackerras. London 410138-2 [CD].

Beginning with George Szell's stunning Cleveland Orchestra recording from the 1960s, Janáček's most popular orchestral work, the blazingly heroic *Sinfonietta,* has had some wonderful recordings. As both an interpretation and a recording of demonstration quality, Sir Charles Mackerras's Vienna Philharmonic performance will be difficult to better for the foreseeable future. As usual, not even the most subtle detail of Janáček's complex language escapes this conductor's attention. The occasionally intricate rhythms and always complicated inner voicing are invested with a drive and clarity they have never been given before. The last time that the Vienna Philharmonic brass, augmented for the occasion by a dozen extra players, were heard to play with such ferocious bite and mind-boggling unanimity was in Sir Georg Solti's famous recording of Wagner's *Ring,* made two decades ago.

The *Sinfonietta*'s inevitable companion work, the orchestral rhapsody *Taras Bulba,* is given an equally memorable performance. In fact, Mackerras invests it with such surging life and drama that some will be persuaded—as I must admit that I always *have* been—that *Taras* may in fact be the more important and rewarding piece.

Although not quite on the same level, the performances by the Slovak Radio Symphony under Ondrej Lenárd on Naxos (8.550411 [CD]) are very fine indeed and come with the best available version of the enchanting *Lachian Dances,* all for less than it costs to take yourself to a bad movie.

Slavonic Mass (M'sa Glagolskaja)

Söderström, Drobková, Livora, Novák, Czech Philharmonic Chorus and Orchestra, Mackerras. Supraphon 10 3575 [CD].

Kiberg, Stene, Svensson, Cold, Danish National Radio Chorus and Orchestra, Mackerras. Chandos CHAN 9310 [CD].

To call Janáček's *Slavonic Mass* one of the great sacred works of twentieth-century music is as accurate as it is slightly misleading. Written in the composer's seventy-second year, the *Slavonic Mass* was originally thought to be a final act of contrition by a lifelong agnostic. When a Prague music critic described it as being the work of a "pious old man," the composer immediately shot back a postcard with the single line, "Neither old nor pious, *young* man."

The unshakable faith that the *Slavonic Mass* expresses with such moving tenderness and medieval grandeur has to do less with the composer's religious convictions, which were all but nonexistent, than with his almost messianic belief in the survival of the Czechoslovak Republic, whose tenth anniversary in 1928 *M'sa Glagolskaja* was written to celebrate.

The Mackerras recording is one of the most successful in his brilliant Janáček series: the playing of the Czech Philharmonic is as vivid and emphatic as it has ever been on records; the soloists are exceptional; the chorus, alert and powerful; and the recorded sound is shattering in its realism and impact.

Using musicologist Paul Wingfield's careful reconstruction, Sir Charles's Chandos recording is the very first that the *Mass's* original version has ever received, and the result is a hair-raising revelation. In preparation for the first performance, the composer smoothed out many of the work's rougher rhythmic edges but even more dramatically abandoned the idea of having the concluding brassy *Intrada* also introduce the piece. With all of Janáček's initial ideas restored, the *Slavonic Mass* becomes a far more elemental, dangerous-sounding experience. Mackerras revels in the new-found power of the score, releasing its pent-up barbaric energy with a vengeance. After this withering interpretation, all other versions seem almost house-broken in comparison.

String Quartet No. 1, "The Kreutzer Sonata"; String Quartet No. 2, "Intimate Pages"

> Smetana Quartet. Testament SBT 1074 [CD] ("Kreutzer Sonata");
> Testament SBT 1075 [CD] ("Intimate Pages").

To the end of his long and unusual life, Leoš Janáček was a man whose vigor and appetites remained exorbitantly intact. Taking its cue from Smetana's famous E Minor Quartet, "From My Life," the quartet subtitled "Intimate Pages" is one of music's most extraordinary autobiographical works. In it, the aging composer confessed the pangs and torments of a hopeless love he had conceived for a much younger woman. (In truth, with his honeyed tongue and twinkling eye, Janáček had little or no trouble during what remains, in certain scandalized quarters of Bohemia and Moravia, a legendary erotic career.) With the equally individual "Kreutzer Sonata," based on the Tolstoy novella, "Intimate Pages" is one of the most highly charged and original of twentieth-century chamber works. In the proper hands, both can easily seem to rank with the finest quartets of Bartók and Schoenberg.

With the Smetana Quartet, they are in just such hands. No more committed or impassioned performance of either work has ever been recorded, except by the Smetana Quartet itself. The intensity of the playing is such that you often suspect that one or all of the performers is constantly on the verge of snapping a string or breaking a bow. This is thoroughly adult music for a thoroughly adult audience; if you qualify, enjoy.

For their superbly produced reissue, Testament has wisely spread these classic 1965 recordings over two CDs, each coupled with popular chamber works by

Dvořák: "The Kreutzer Sonata" with the "American" Quartet and Opus 81 Piano Quintet; "Intimate Pages" with the A-flat Major Quartet (No. 14) and the enchanting *Terzetto*. In all the recordings, the Smetana confirms its reputation as perhaps the most brilliantly accomplished string quartet of its time.

Janequin, Clément (c. 1485–c. 1560)

Chansons

A Sei Voci. Astrée E 8571 [CD].

Subtitled "An Orchard of Music" and decorated with a detail from a fifteenth-century Italian painting called *The Garden of Love,* this delectable album is devoted largely to the racier *chansons* of Clément Janequin, creator and principal exponent of the new sixteenth-century polyphonic *chanson* and one of the most wonderfully bawdy composers prior to the Restoration. Although the anthology includes a couple of those lengthy, complex, onomatopoeic works for which Janequin was justly famous—*La Guerre* and *Le Chant des oyseaux,* each of which lasts about six minutes—most are of the shorter, Rabelaisian variety, including *Tétin refaict plus blanc,* a three-and-a-half minute celebration of the breast, and *Ung Jour que madame,* which begins: "One day while Madame was sleeping, Monsieur was jiggling with the chambermaid. . . . "

The performances by A Sei Voci are delightfully knowing and lewd, full of high wit and low humor and plenty of prurient interest. All *you* need add is candles, a good Bordeaux, and someone you like.

Jarre, Maurice (1924–)

Lawrence of Arabia

London Symphony, Jarre. Varèse Sarabande VSD 5263 [CD], VSC 5263 [CD].

For four decades one of the most prolific of film composers, the French-born Maurice Jarre—who studied composition with Honegger and played percussion in Pierre Boulez's Renaud-Barrault theater orchestra—will always be best remembered for the scores he produced for Sir David Lean's last four films, three of which—*Lawrence of Arabia, Doctor Zhivago,* and *A Passage to India*—won the composer richly deserved Academy Awards.

The composer's Varèse Sarabande recording of music from *Lawrence of Arabia* is not his first. Although the film's main title credited Sir Adrian Boult leading the London Philharmonic, every note of the singularly exciting and evocative score was conducted by Jarre himself. Not only does the music do what all great film music must—create aural images so vivid in their visual associations that they automatically set the film going in the mind's eye of the listener—but it also stands remarkably well on its own.

Jobim, Antonio Carlos (1927–1994)

*W*ave; *Samba do Aviäo*

Garcia, guitar. Naxos 8.550226 [CD].

Best known as a jazz musician and one of the pioneers of *bossa nova,* Antonio Carlos Jobim is one of eight composers represented on guitarist Gerald Garcia's *Brazilian Portrait—Villa-Lobos and the Guitar Music of Brazil,* the single most alluring album of guitar music I know. Along with nine items by Villa-Lobos, including one of the most appealing, utterly natural recordings ever of the five *Preludes,* this beautifully planned and executed recital includes two works by Luis Bonfá (the man who wrote and performed the soundtrack of the classic film *Black Orpheus),* as well as equally seductive miniatures by Isaias Savio, Joao Pernambuco, Laurindo Almeida, Roberto Baden-Powell, and Celso Machado—composers who might be little more than names in a book for most people but who will become treasured friends after this.

Jongen, Joseph (1873–1953)

*S*ymphonie Concertante for Organ and Orchestra, Op. 81

Murray, organ; San Francisco Symphony, de Waart. Teldec CD 80096 [CD].

For anyone who ever fervently wished that Camille Saint-Saëns had written another Organ Symphony, Joseph Jongen's *Symphonie Concertante* from 1926 comes as a partially answered prayer. Born in Liège, this prolific Belgian was thirteen and already composing by 1886, the year Saint-Saëns produced his master-piece. Jongen's mature music—including the *Symphonie*—would be influenced by a striking variety of voices, from Franck, Brahms, and Wagner to Debussy and Ravel. In an effort to keep up with the latest trends in European music, Jongen even experimented briefly with atonality, as certain passages of the *Symphonie Concertante* clearly reveal.

Michael Murray, Edo de Waart, and the San Francisco Symphony offer the finest account ever of this lush, dramatic hodge-podge of conflicting—yet oddly satisfying—styles. If the *Symphonie Concertante* is not as thematically memorable or emotionally rewarding as the *Organ Symphony*, then it makes an even more imposing sound, closing with a rafter-rattling *Toccata* that will shake any loose putty from the windows and terrify the cat. The Teldec engineers rise magnificently to the challenge with one of the great demonstration albums on the market today.

Joplin, Scott (1868–1917)

Rags

> Rifkin, piano. Nonesuch 979159 [CD]; EMI Classics CDM 64668-2 [CD], EG 64668-4 [T].

Well before the composer's music was belatedly made into a national institution in the hit movie *The Sting,* I had already become hopelessly addicted to Scott Joplin's piano rags, thanks entirely to Joshua Rifkin. Rifkin's path-breaking series of Nonesuch recordings all but introduced the world to the subtle, infectious, endlessly inventive music of a man who, in essence, transformed the musical wallpaper of turn-of-the-century bordellos into a high, and distinctively American, art. In his Angel recording—all but one of the Nonesuch albums have been foolishly withdrawn—Rifkin's self-effacing, yet enormously colorful and individual, interpretations are still the definitive solo piano versions of these works.

For the serious Joplin lover, the Houston Opera production of the composer's rather quaint but utterly engaging ragtime opera *Treemonisha,* in a warm and thoroughly captivating performance led by Gunther Schuller (Deutsche Grammophon 435709-2 [CD], is vigorously recommended.

Josquin des Prés (c.1440 to 1450–1521)

Missa "Pange lingua"; Missa "La sol fa re mi"

Tallis Scholars, Phillips. Gimell CDGIM-009 [CD], 1585T-09 [T].

Though not normally an enthusiastic consumer of "monk music"—perhaps I saw the movie *Beckett* once too often or read too many cheerful books about the Spanish Inquisition as a boy—I must confess (so to speak) to an abiding admiration for the music of the greatest of the Flemish contrapuntists, Josquin des Prés. I feel a deep personal connection with him, not because he was one of the most venerated and influential composers of his era, but because he had a name that was as frequently mangled as mine.

In the *Baker's Biographical Dictionary of Musicians,* the late Nicolas Slonimsky lists "Després," "Desprez," "Deprés," "Depret," "Deprez," "Desprets," "Dupré," "Del Prato," "a Prato," "a Pratis," and "Pratensis" as a few of the ways it was most commonly spelled, while "Josquin"—from the Flemish "Jossekin," the diminutive of Joseph—was apparently mauled just as often.

The fabulous Tallis Scholars give loving performances of two of Josquin's finest masses for Gimell—a small but exceptionally fussy English label that consistently produces some of the best-sounding recordings anywhere. The *Missa "Pange lingua"* is the more familiar of the two, but the *Missa "La sol fa re mi"*—which was *not* the basis for that wretched song in *The Sound of Music*—is equally captivating.

Joyce, Archibald (1873–1963)

Orchestral Works

RTE Concert Orchestra, Penny. Marco Polo 8.223694 [CD].

Apart from the novels of E. M. Forster, there are few works that bring the Edwardian era alive more vividly than the waltzes of Archibald Joyce. In their day, works like *Songe d'automne, Dreaming,* and *A Thousand Kisses* (and how can you *not* love a man who could come up with a title like that?) earned Joyce the title "The English Waltz King," and this fetching Marco Polo album proves that it was more than deserved. Moreover, irresistible items like *Brighton Hike* and *Frou-Frou* (which is anything but) suggest that he might have been called "The English Polka King" as well.

As in all their albums in the British Light Music series, Andrew Penny and the RTE Concert Orchestra play with grace and love, while the notes and recorded sound would be difficult to improve.

Kabalevsky, Dmitri (1904–1987)

The Comedians (symphonic suite)

St. Louis Symphony, Slatkin. RCA Victor 09026-60968-2 [CD].

Unlike most of the Stalinist hacks who disgorged reams of musical slop in support of the political and social programs of the then Soviet Union—an early and inspiring example of political correctness in action—Dmitri Kabalevsky was a Bolshevik with talent. Although he wrote his fair share of crap, with titles like *Requiem for Lenin, My Great Fatherland, People's Avengers, Leninists,* and *Before Moscow,* an opera celebrating the defense of the city in 1942, followed in 1951 by *The Family of Taras,* another opera describing the heroic struggle against the Fascist invaders, Kabalevsky also produced pages of genuine charm and substance, especially those in the Second Cello Concerto, the opera *Colas Breugnon,* and the incidental music he wrote in 1938 from the children's play *The Inventor and the Comedians.*

The ten brief movements that Kabalevsky gathered into an orchestral suite called *The Comedians* has remained the composer's most popular work, especially the infectious little *Galop* that was used as the signature tune—and wouldn't Stalin have been proud!—for *Masquerade Party,* a popular program on Capitalist-Imperialist television during the McCarthy Era. Leonard Slatkin and the St. Louis Symphony give a scintillating performance of the Suite on their attractive "Russian Album," which also features first-rate readings of popular works by Khachaturian, Mussorgsky, Prokofiev, and Stravinsky.

Kalinnikov, Vasily (1866–1901)

Symphonies (2)

Royal Scottish National Orchestra. Järvi. Chandos CHAN 9546 [CD].

The life of the Russian composer Vasily Kalinnikov reads like one of the more poignant short stories of Anton Chekhov. As a matter of fact, the two men were neighbors for a time at one of those Black Sea spas in the Crimea where both had gone to die of tuberculosis. Chekhov would be remembered as one of the giants of Russian literature, while Kalinnikov became one of the great "what ifs" of Russian music, a composer of tremendous talent and promise whose name is almost completely forgotten today.

After studying bassoon at the Music School of the Moscow Philharmonic Society—he was forced to leave the more prestigious Moscow Conservatory because he was unable to pay the tuition—Kalinnikov managed to eke out a meager living playing in the city's theater orchestras. Living most of his life in the squalor of the proverbial garrets and composing assiduously, a combination of overwork and undernourishment undermined his health; he died at Yalta two days before what would have been his thirty-fifth birthday.

While the Second Symphony of 1898 is a lovely work, the earlier G Minor Symphony, written when he was twenty-nine, remains his masterpiece. Lyrical, exuberant, and utterly haunting—once heard, its principal themes will not be forgotten quickly—the symphony is one of the jewels of Russian late-Romanticism, a work to be mentioned in the same breath with any of the early symphonies of Glazunov, Tchaikovsky, or Rachmaninoff.

If the fine Järvi recordings are not quite as exciting as the now-deleted versions by the USSR State Symphony conducted by Yevgeny Svetlanov, the playing of the Royal Scottish National Orchestra is both disciplined and intensely committed, while the fabulous Chandos digital recording is a dramatic improvement over the harsh late-Bolshevik sound accorded the Russian performances. Still, for all their flaws, the Svetlanovs really *do* need to be reissued, as they contain some of the most electrifying orchestral playing ever to have emerged from the late and unlamented Soviet Union.

Kern, Jerome (1885–1945)

Showboat (original score)

> Soloists, Ambrosian Singers and Opera Chorus, London Sinfonietta,
> McGlinn. EMI Classics A23 49108 [CD].

Given the tuneless, insipid joke that the Broadway musical has recently become, it's both disconcerting and a little disheartening to experience the first great musical in its uncut, original form. In its melodic and dramatic richness, *Showboat* remains the classic American musical comedy, especially in the original stage version, which is far more complex and rewarding than any of the familiar movie treatments. Listening to Kern's astonishingly sophisticated settings of Oscar Hammerstein's classic lyrics, one wonders how anyone can settle for the musical and emotional dishwater that Andrew Lloyd Webber keeps ladling out.

The highest praise that can be heaped upon this landmark EMI Classics recording is to suggest that it is in every way worthy of its subject. With superb performances from Frederica von Stade, Jerry Hadley, Teresa Stratas, and especially Bruce Hubbard, whose *Ol' Man River* is vocally more impressive than Paul Robeson's ever was, John McGlinn leads a perfectly paced reading that lingers lovingly where it should and gets on with it when it must. Although an album of highlights is available (ZDC 49847 [CD]), one really needs to hear it all.

Ketèlbey, Albert (1875–1959)

Orchestral Works

> Czech-Slovak Radio Symphony (Bratislava), Slovak Philharmonic
> Male Chorus, Leaper. Marco Polo 8.223442 [CD].

If the English composer Albert Ketèlbey didn't necessarily *invent* musical kitsch, then with treacly horrors like *In the Mystic Land of Egypt, In a Chinese Temple Garden,* and the once ubiquitous *In a Persian Market* he raised it to the greatest heights it would reach prior to the arrival Liberace. Beginning with *In a Monastery Garden* in 1915, he produced a series of works—"narrative music," he called it—whose sentimental melodies and gaudy orchestration made him the most popular English composer of his time. And if at his worst—from the maudlin *Sanctuary of the Heart* to the relentlessly cutesie-poo *The Clock and the Dresden Figures*—Ketèlbey can still induce the gag reflex and/or insulin shock, then at his best *(Wedgwood Blue, In the Moonlight, Cockney Suite)* he is a composer of disarming sweetness and irresistible charm whose once phenomenal popularity was clearly no accident.

Adrian Leaper and his dedicated Slovak forces approach these iron butterflies with a complete lack of condescension. Even the nonsense lyrics of *In a Persian Market*—"bak sheesh, Allah, empshi"—are delivered with lusty enthusiasm, while the orchestra and conductor revel in the often tacky orchestration rather than treat it as a cause for embarrassment. As with all the installments of Marco Polo's *British Light Music* series, the recorded sound and program notes are excellent.

Khachaturian, Aram (1903–1978)

Gayane (suite); *Spartacus* (suite)

Royal Philharmonic, Temirkanov. EMI Classics CDC-47348 [CD].

One can only hope that wherever that happy-go-lucky music lover Joseph Stalin is roasting these days, he is exposed to a continuous dosage of the ballet *Gayane*, Aram Khachaturian's subtle celebration of the joys of Collective Farming. Of course, it's easy to chortle at *Gayane* and its pile-driving "Sabre Dance," or to point out—with a chill—that this is what the Soviet government once hailed as ideal proletarian music, when Shostakovich and Prokofiev were catching hell. (Actually, Khachaturian himself also came under fire at the infamous Zhdanov Conference in 1948.)

For the most part, *Gayane* is good clean Socialist Realist fun, with hummable tunes, plenty of local color, and a kind of childlike innocence that retains its freshness and seems immune to all manner of cynical trashing after nearly half a century of wear and tear. If Yuri Temirkanov's interpretations of the ballet's heavy hits—to say nothing of a blissfully truncated suite from the truly macabre *Spartacus*—are neither the most theatrical nor the most imaginative ever recorded, they are easily the best on the market today. The recording that Kiril Kondrashin made of *Gayane* and Kabalevsky's *The Comedians* is all but *screaming* for a CD reissue from RCA Victor's vaults.

David Oistrakh's definitive interpretation of the Violin Concerto can now be found on EMI Classics CDC 55035 [CD], in a thrilling live performance from 1947 with Rafael Kubelik and the Prague Radio Symphony, while one of the most electrifying Khachaturian recordings ever made has appeared in the form of a live performance of the Piano Concerto with William Kapell and the NBC Symphony from a 1945 broadcast (VAI Audio VAIA/IPA 1027 [CD]), which makes the thing seem infinitely more musical and important than it can possibly be.

Knussen, Oliver (1952–)

Where the Wild Things Are (opera)

Hardy, King, Harrington, Rhys-Williams, London Sinfonietta, Knussen. Arabesque Z-6535 [CD].

Needless to say, it's a bit too soon to tell what history—the Great Aesthetic Trash-Compactor—will make of *Where the Wild Things Are*. My own suspicion is that it will prosper as one of the enduring children's operas, if not *precisely* the late-twentieth-century equivalent of *Hänsel und Gretel,* then at least something very close to it.

Knussen's setting of Maurice Sendak's tale of the archetypal Bad Kid and the Horrible (i.e., thoroughly lovable) Monsters is not only magnetic theater but also highly inspired music making. Knussen packs more mystery, enchantment, and pure fun into his forty minutes than many another operatic composer has been able to draw out of an entire evening; the soloists—especially Rosemary Hardy as the incorrigible Max—all seem ideal in their parts, and the composer-conducted performance is undoubtedly definitive.

If you have any little wild things running around underfoot, sit them down in front of the speakers and see that they think. This aging Bad Kid loved it.

Kodály, Zoltán (1882–1967)

Dances of Galanta; Dances of Marosszék; Variations on a Hungarian Folksong (Peacock Variations)

Philharmonia Hungarica, Dorati. London 425034-2 [CD].

It was Kodály's discovery of Hungarian folk music in the early 1920s that transformed him into an internationally famous composer. Beginning with the folk opera *Háry János,* Kodály combined the unmistakable flavors of Hungarian folk song with a technique that owed much to Debussy and Ravel and created some of the most refreshingly distinctive and original music of the twentieth century.

Dorati's London recording of these popular works, together with a very fine *Háry János Suite,* is one of the most accomplished and generous Kodály albums now available, offering seventy-six minutes of world-class music making on a single medium-priced CD. If the performances of *Galanta, Marosszék,* and *Háry János* might lack the final ounce of magic the conductor squeezed out of his famous Minneapolis Symphony recordings for Mercury Living Presence (now reissued on 432005-2 [CD]), then they are still full of charm, panache, and gypsy fire and are certainly *not* to be missed.

Háry János

> Takács, Sólyom-Nagy, Gregor, Hungarian State Opera Chorus and
> Orchestra, Ferencsik. Hungaroton HVD-12837/38 [CD].

Háry János Suite

> Cleveland Orchestra, Szell. Sony Classical SBK 48162 [CD], SBT
> 48162 [T].

While the Suite that Zoltán Kodály extracted from his 1925 folk opera *Háry János* remains his most universally loved and frequently recorded work, the opera itself is one of the treasures of the modern lyric theater. Its fantastic plot is a series of tall tales told by a retired Hussar from the village of Abony Magna— the irrepressible Háry János—who, after defeating Napoleon and his legions sin-glehandedly, has nearly as much trouble fending off the attentions of Napoleon's ardent wife.

Fortunately, the only recorded performance of the complete opera is an ex-tremely attractive one. Beautifully played and, for the most part, beautifully sung, the performance projects much of the opera's unique and unmistakable color. Since much of the humor is lost on non-Hungarian listeners, one can only hope that London will some day reissue István Kertész's dazzling recording from the early 1970s, which not only included all of the opera's musical numbers but also featured the inspired Peter Ustinov in all the speaking roles.

For those who feel they don't really need to go beyond the popular *Háry János Suite,* George Szell's tender, flamboyant, meticulous, and uproarious CBS recording has never been equaled.

Sonata for Unaccompanied Cello

Starker, cello. Delos DCD 1015 [CD].

On greeting visitors to his impressive European estate, Janos Starker has often been heard to say, "Welcome to the house that Kodály built!" Thus far, the great Hungarian-born cellist has recorded the Sonata four times, the most recently in Japan in 1970. There are many—the present writer included—who would rank the Sonata alongside the *Peacock Variations* and *Psalmus Hungaricus* as one of Kodály's supreme achievements, thanks in no small part to Starker's classic interpretation. He not only makes the work's frightening difficulties seem inconsequential but also invests the music with an incredibly broad emotional range, from quiet despair to reckless excitement to everything in between. A splendid version of the Duo for Violin and Cello with Joseph Gingold is handsome and appropriate filler.

Koechlin, Charles (1867–1950)

Seven Stars Symphony (1922)

Monte Carlo Philharmonic, Myrat. EMI Classics CDM 64369 [CD].

Best remembered as a teacher (of Francis Poulenc and Germaine Tailleferre) and theorist (*Traité d'harmonie* and other valuable manuals), Charles Koechlin was a delightfully batty man and composer who once described his life as "a series of happy chances under a cloud of general misfortune."

One of the happiest of those chances was Koechlin's discovery of the cinema, which eventually led to more than a hundred miniatures inspired by Lilian Harvey (including eight scored for flute, ondes martenot, harpsichord, and piano), the *Danses (5) pour Ginger* [Rogers], the *Epitaphe de Jean Harlow,* and his most famous work, the *Seven Stars Symphony* of 1933. Less a symphony than a series of character sketches, the *Seven Stars* is an imaginative, enormously individual celebration of Douglas Fairbanks, Harvey (of course), Greta Garbo, Clara Bow, Marlene Dietrich, Emil Jannings, and Charlie Chaplin, whose concluding movement—like the star himself—is the most intricate and complex. Both the performance and the recording are fully worthy of a forgotten offbeat masterpiece that deserves a serious reappraisal.

Koechlin spent more than forty years responding to stories from Kipling's *Jungle Book,* beginning with *Trois Poèmes du "Livre de la Jungle"* from 1899. In his brilliant RCA recording with the Berlin Radio Symphony (09026-61955-2

[CD]), David Zinman attaches the settings of "Seal Lullaby," "Night-Song in the Jungle," and "The Song of Kala" to the extraordinary four-movement symphonic poem that captures so much of the charm, power, and exotic wonder of the book. If anything, *The Jungle Book* seems even more ripe for a revival than *Seven Stars*. Although the addition of the songs necessitates a second CD, RCA decently offers both for the price of one.

Korngold, Erich Wolfgang

(1897–1957)

Concerto in D Major for Violin and Orchestra, Op. 35

> Heifetz, violin; Los Angeles Philharmonic, Wallenstein. RCA Victor 7963-2-RG [CD].

> Perlman, violin; Pittsburgh Symphony, Previn. EMI Classics CDC 47846 [CD].

As a child prodigy whose accomplishments were compared to those of Mozart by no less an authority than Gustav Mahler, or as the man who first brought genuine symphonic music to Hollywood films, Erich Wolfgang Korngold was one of the most fascinating musical figures of the twentieth century. His opera *Die tote Stadt* (The Dead City), begun when he was only nineteen, made him world famous, and his frightening abilities even convinced Richard Strauss that Korngold would inevitably supplant him as the century's foremost composer of German opera. Erich Leinsdorf's generally gorgeous recording, save for the wobbly singing of the hero, has once again been withdrawn by RCA, demonstrating why the late conductor always referred to that organization as his *bête noire*. Personally, I'm tempted to call them something a bit less polite, since they've also withdrawn their several invaluable recordings of Korngold's film music.

Forced to flee Europe after Hitler's annexation of Austria, Korngold eventually settled in Hollywood. There, with the scores for *Anthony Adverse, King's Row, The Adventures of Robin Hood, The Sea Hawk,* and other classic Warner Brothers films of the 1930s and '40s, he established the grammar and syntax of an entirely new musical language, whose influence can still be clearly and distinctly heard in the scores of John Williams and countless other film composers.

The Korngold Violin Concerto, whose thematic material was derived from several of his movie themes, is one of the most startlingly beautiful works in the instrument's repertoire. Sentimental, exciting, and unabashedly Romantic, it is as instantly approachable as it is impossible to forget. Although the work was written for the Polish violinist Bronislaw Huberman, Jascha Heifetz gave it its world premiere and made the first commercial recording. Technically, of course, the playing is flawless; yet here, Heifetz invests the music with a warmth and humanity that almost none of his other recordings possess. Itzhak Perlman's Angel recording is also exceptionally lovely. If in the quicksilver finale the violinist lacks the last measure of Heifetz's dizzying abandon, he milks the molten slow movement like the wonderfully shameless Romantic he has always been.

Film Music

> Warner Brothers Orchestra, Korngold. Rhino Movie Music
> R2 72243 [CD].
>
> National Philharmonic, Gerhardt. RCA 0185-2-RG [CD], 0185-4-RG
> [T]; 60863-2 [CD], 60863-4 [T].

Whichever Hollywood pseudo-sage insisted that the greatness of a film score was directly proportional to the extent that you *didn't* notice it was obviously an imbecile. One might just as well say that an actor's greatness may be measured by the extent to which you can't understand his lines. From almost the moment movies learned to talk, music has been an integral part of the twentieth-century's most characteristic art form. While a score can't save an awful picture, it can ruin a good one. On occasion—witness *Laura*, for instance—it can turn a fine film into a great one.

Here, on two generously packed CDs, are selections from sixteen Korngold scores—*Captain Blood, The Green Pastures, Anthony Adverse* (Academy Award, 1936), *The Prince and the Pauper, The Adventures of Robin Hood* (Academy Award, 1938), *Juarez, The Private Lives of Elizabeth and Essex, The Sea Hawk* (perhaps his greatest score), *The Sea Wolf, King's Row, The Constant Nymph, Devotion, Between Two Worlds* (his favorite score), *Of Human Bondage, Escape Me Never,* and *Deception*—in performances conducted by the composer from the original soundtracks. While the recorded sound is understandably variable, the thrill of hearing the composer's incomparably authoritative way with his own music more than makes up for any sonic limitations.

The RCA collections are drawn from the company's phenomenally successful "Classic Film Scores" series, the brainchild of the composer's son, the late George Korngold. In addition to an expanded version of music from *The Sea Hawk*, which includes the spine-tingling chorus "Strike for the Shores of Dover" and in many ways is the musical equal of a Strauss tone poem, Volume 2 contains the famous *King's Row* fanfare, the germ from which seemingly half of all the film music written afterward would grow. The National Philharmonic under

Charles Gerhardt plays with fire and devotion, and the original analogue sound remains in the demonstration category. Get out your handkerchiefs and prepare to swash those buckles.

Orchestral Works

> **Northwest German Philharmonic, Albert. CPO 999 037-2 [CD]**
> **(The Snowman: Incidental Music; Dramatic Overture; Sin-**
> **fonietta); 999 046-2 [CD] (Symphonic Overture; Much Ado About**
> **Nothing: Incidental Music; Piano Concerto); 999 077-2 [CD]**
> **(Baby-Serenade; Cello Concerto; Symphonic Serenade for String**
> **Orchestra); 999 146-2 (Straussiana; Symphony in F-sharp; Theme**
> **and Variations).**

The first comprehensive recorded examination of Korngold's orchestral music from the small European label CPO provides the ideal means of better understanding this unique composer's achievement, and on the basis of the evidence contained on these four handsome CDs, the achievement was considerable. Even in the earliest works, produced when Korngold was not yet out of kneepants, one immediately detects the presence of a distinct, confident, and fully formed musical personality; in mature works like the Symphony in F-sharp—which Dimitri Mitropolous called "the perfect modern score"—one hears the heir of Mahler and Richard Strauss at the peak of his late-Romantic powers.

While there have been finer performances of individual works—the Violin Concerto is very well served by two classic recordings (see page 394), and the compelling debut recording of the Symphony, with the Munich Philharmonic led by Rudolf Kempe, has resurfaced on Varèse Sarabande (VSD 5346 [CD]—the series, as a whole, is a major triumph, offering carefully thought-out, wholly sympathetic performances in beautifully rich recorded sound.

Das Wunder der Heliane

> **Tomowa-Sintow, Welker, De Haan, Berlin Radio Symphony Chorus**
> **and Orchestra, Mauceri. London 436636-2 [CD].**

To the end of his life, Korngold considered *Das Wunder der Heliane* his masterpiece. The mysterious, overheated tale that owes something to the operas of Franz Schreker bears a striking resemblance to Szymanowski's *King Roger*: a Dionysus-like stranger is imprisoned in a country ruled by a tyrant whose wife, the chaste Heliane, befriends him. At his request, she reveals her body to him, whereupon the king—who has yet to enjoy her favors—condemns them both to death.

Now that *gratuitous* nudity has become a commonplace of modern operatic production, one longs to see one that *requires* it for seven pages of score. While *Das Wunder der Heliane* may lack *Die tote Stadt*'s big hit tune—Heliane's "Ich ging zu ihm" is the closest thing to *Marietta's Lied*—at well over two-and-a-half hours it is a generous, generally gorgeous work with many memorable moments, plus a few here and there that are less so. The lyricism and lush orchestration are vintage Korngold, while the overt eroticism matches anything in Szymanowski or Strauss.

Mauceri leads a commanding performance in the opera's recording premiere, marred only by a somewhat rough-edged villain. Anna Tomowa-Sintow's vulnerable, girlish Heliane represents her best work in the recording studio to date, while John David de Haan is clearly a heroic tenor to watch. As always in one of London's main line opera productions, the recorded sound is wondrous.

Kraft, William (1923–)

Concerto for Percussion and Chamber Ensemble (1993); *Contextures I: Riot—Decade '60*

Los Angeles Philharmonic, Mehta. London 448580-2 [CD].

In his entry on William Kraft in the *Baker's Biographical Dictionary of Music and Musicians,* the late Nicolas Slonimsky offers a typically apt summation: "As a composer, he explores without prejudice all genres of techniques, including serial procedures; he develops the rhythmic element to the full."

That Kraft's music should be among the most rhythmically vital and imaginative ever written by an American is hardly surprising: after study with the New York Philharmonic's storied Saul Goodman, he became a percussionist with the Los Angeles Philharmonic in 1955 and its timpanist in 1962, later becoming its assistant conductor and composer-in-residence. In addition to its rhythmic life, Kraft's music is also remarkable for its mixture of the most experimental techniques with a musical personality that is at once challenging and surprisingly accessible, making it some of the most *enjoyable* modern music now being written. In short, Kraft is that great rarity: an avant-garde Humanist.

With Luciano Berio's *Sinfonia*—whose recording by the Swingle Singers and the New York Philharmonic conducted by Pierre Boulez is in urgent need of reissue—*Contextures I* is one of the most gripping of serious works to actually address the political problems of the troubled 1960s, particularly urban racial problems and the war in Vietnam. It is a tribute to the inherent power of the piece that it remains a vivid emotional experience decades after the events it describes. Like the composer's Timpani Concerto, the Concerto for Four Percussion Soloists and Orchestra is one of the most electrifying ever written for these instruments: a stunningly imaginative and resourceful exploration of sounds that this composer literally knows from the inside out.

On a Cambria CD (CBM 1071), Kraft's own interpretation is tremendously exciting, as are the performances of two of his most intriguing and adventurous chamber works: the Double Trio for Piano, Prepared Piano, Amplified Guitar, Tuba, and Percussion and *Games: Collage No. 1 for Brass.*

Kramář, František (a.k.a. Franz Krommer) (1759–1831)

Octet-Partitas for Winds (4)

Sabine Meyer Wind Ensemble. EMI Classics CDC 54383 [CD].

The Moravian composer František Kramář was one of innumerable musicians of the eighteenth century whose sheer numbers led the rest of the continent to call Bohemia-Moravia "The Conservatory of Europe." Like most of the talented musicians from that part of the world, Kramář Teutonicized his name to find employment in the German-speaking world: as Franz Krommer he held a number of important court posts, including imperial kapellmeister in Vienna.

While he wrote symphonies, concertos, and a fair amount of sacred music, Kramář is best remembered for some of the most accomplished and engaging wind music of the entire Classical period, including the four irresistible Octet-Partitas heard on this delightful EMI Classics recording. The performances by the Sabine Meyer Wind Ensemble are flawless, as is the playing of clarinetist Sabine Meyer herself: if you can listen to her dizzying noodling on the final band of the album and *not* have to suppress a giggle (or a least a smile), then you have my admiration and deepest sympathy. The performance has warm, remarkably life-like recorded sound.

In what one can only hope will be the first Kramář installment in Chandos's "Contemporaries of Mozart" series (CHAN 9275 [CD]), Matthias Bamert leads persuasively enthusiastic performances of two of the composer's mature symphonies, No. 2 in D Major from 1803 and No. 4 in C Minor, written toward the end of his career. Although there are echoes of other voices in both works—

Mozart and Beethoven in the first, Schubert and Hummel in the second—this is interesting, enjoyable music, beautifully played and recorded.

Three of the composer's major works for clarinet—the Concerto in E-flat, Op. 36, and the two Double Concertos—are available on a fine Naxos CD (8.553178) that showcases the considerable talents of the Japanese clarinetists Kaori Tsutsui and Tomoko Takashima. The second Double Concerto is an unusually appealing work, with a beautifully spun-out *Adagio* that might have come from a moonlit scene of a Weber opera. The clarinet duo has topflight support from the Nicolaus Esterházy Orchestra under Kálmán Berkes and from the Naxos engineers.

Kreisler, Fritz (1875–1962)

Violin Pieces and Arrangements

Perlman, violin; Sanders, piano. EMI Classics CDC 47467 [CD].

In addition to being one of the great violinists of history whose recordings of the Beethoven, Brahms, and Mendelssohn concertos remain unsurpassed in their Romantic daring and philosophical depth—all of which can now be found on an indispensable two-CD set from Pearl (PEAS 9362)—Fritz Kreisler was also the composer of some of the most enchanting music ever written for the instrument. Evergreen classics like *Caprice Viennoise, Liebesfreud,* and *Schön Rosmarin* were the apotheosis of turn-of-the-century Viennese charm and helped make their creator an immensely rich and famous man.

Nowhere does Itzhak Perlman reveal himself more clearly as Kreisler's natural heir than in this delectable recording of Kreisler miniatures and arrangements. While less free and arbitrary than the master (whose celebrated recordings from the 1930s and '40s keep slipping in and out of print), Perlman brings huge reserves of sensitivity and schmaltz to the proceedings, always drawing the fine but inviolable line between sentiment and sentimentality. Samuel Sanders is a wholly sympathetic partner and the mid-'70s recorded sound remains ideal.

Kurka, Robert (1921–1957)

The Good Soldier Schweik (suite)

Music for Westchester Symphony, Landau. Allegretto ACD 8191 [CD].

With the late Ernst Krenek's *Jonny spielt auf* and Jaromir Weinberger's *Schwanda the Bagpiper,* Robert Kurka's *The Good Soldier Schweik* has for years been at the top of my list of once-famous-twentieth-century-operas-that-nobody-ever-mounts-these-days that I would most like to see. Completed shortly before Kurka's death from leukemia at the age of thirty-six, *Schweik* is a setting of Jarolav Hasek's celebrated antiwar novel, which introduced one of the classic characters of modern literature, a seemingly "feebleminded" Everyman who endures the lunacies of modern warfare with indestructible optimism and triumphant good humor.

On the basis of the brilliant six-movement Suite that the composer extracted from the opera, Kurka—himself of Czech descent—captured the very essence of Hasek's darkly hilarious vision. With the stunning Koch CD by the Atlantic Sinfonietta under Andrew Schenck unaccountably withdrawn, it's good to have the old Turnabout recording from 1974 back in circulation. Here, as in the Schenck version, it emerges as one of the unique works of modern American music: a memorable, tuneful, colorfully dramatic score—this in spite of the fact that the instrumentation calls for winds and percussion only.

Now then, it's high time for Delos, Schwarz, and Seattle to launch their Kurka series, beginning with *Schweik,* the Serenade for chamber orchestra, and the exhilarating Second Symphony.

Lalo, Édouard (1823–1892)

*Symphonie espagnole f*or Violin and Orchestra, Op. 21

Perlman, violin; Orchestre de Paris, Barenboim. Deutsche Grammophon 429977-2 [CD].

One of the most individual and restlessly inventive of all nineteenth-century French composers, Édouard Lalo is now known for only two apparently indestructible works: the D Minor Cello Concerto and the *Symphonie espagnole,* which is not, in fact, a "symphony" at all but rather a form of the composer's own devising that incorporates the structural elements of the concerto and the suite. As one of the most inspired of all French musical tourist works, *Symphonie espagnole* is to the brighter elements of Spanish musical culture what Bizet's *Carmen* is to the darker side: a virtuoso evocation of a specific time and place that few other works can match.

With some vivid, expressive support from Daniel Barenboim and the Orchestre de Paris, Itzhak Perlman here gives one of his most buoyant and colorful recorded performances. Along with its fabulous dexterity, the playing combines a bracing rhythmic vitality with tasteful schmaltziness in a way that only Perlman, these days, seems able to do.

Lalo's only other well-known piece, the Cello Concerto in D Minor, is now admirably served by a half-dozen first-rate recordings, the most impressive of which is the Sony Classical version (MK 35848 [CD] with Yo Yo Ma and the National Orchestra of France conducted by Lorin Maazel. This is one of the most refined and beautifully detailed of Ma's many recordings, with the cellist investing tremendous amounts of thought and discreet passion in seemingly every bar. As an accompanist, Maazel has made no finer recording to date, with the orchestra following the soloist's every move with an uncanny ease. The performance of the Saint-Saëns Cello Concerto No. 1 is every bit as gripping, making this in every way an outstanding release.

Lambert, Constant (1905–1951)

Concerto for Piano and Nine Instruments; *Horoscope* (ballet suite); *The Rio Grande* for Contralto, Piano, Orchestra, and Chorus

> **Soloists, English Northern Philharmonia, Lloyd-Jones. Hyperion 66565 [CD].**

As a droll and perceptive English friend put it recently, "In mid-twentieth-century British music, there were two major schools of composition: drunken and homosexual." Constant Lambert was one of the most brilliant and tragic representatives of the former. Having achieved early fame with *The Rio Grande*, that formally indescribable jazz-inflected piano concerto *cum* cantata on a near-nonsense text by Sacheverell Sitwell, Lambert was never able to repeat its success; he turned increasingly to drink and music criticism, becoming the most engaging British music critic since George Bernard Shaw and the author of the classic *Music Ho! A Study of Music in Decline*, which should become required reading for anyone having anything to do with the profession. He died in 1951 at the age of forty-six.

In addition to a spirited performance of *The Rio Grande,* this indispensable Hyperion recording offers a major work inspired by the death of Lambert's friend Peter Warlock, the ambitious *Summer's Last Will and Testament,* a setting of some disturbing plague lyrics by the Elizabethan poet Thomas Nashe that may very well be Lambert's masterpiece. The album is rounded out by the touching *Aubade Héroïque,* inspired by memories of Holland prior to the Nazi invasion.

Another Hyperion anthology (CDA 66754 [CD]) features four more endlessly fascinating Lambert scores, beginning with the witty and acerbic Concerto for Piano and Nine Instruments, another work written in Warlock's memory. Based on a Russian fairy tale, *Mr. Bear Squash-You-All-Flat* is an engaging early work by the teenage Lambert, with a spoken part delivered memorably by Nigel Hawthorne. The powerful Piano Sonata of 1929 is performed with great flare and authority by Ian Brown, while the exquisite *Eight Poems by Li-Po* are sensitively sung by Philip Langridge.

Larsson, Lars-Erik (1908–1986)

Pastoral Suite

Swedish Radio Symphony, Westerberg. Swedish Society SCD 1020 [CD].

Like his exact contemporary Dag Wirén, the Swedish composer Lars-Erik Larsson would remain best known for a single work of his youth: the delicious *Pastoral Suite* composed in 1938, the year after Wirén brought out his *Serenade for Strings.* An outgrowth of those "lyrical suites"—poetry readings interspersed with music—designed for broadcast on Swedish Radio, the *Pastoral Suite* is an attractive fusion of Larsson's early Nordic Romanticism with the cooler forms of neo-Classicism; after more than half a century the three brief movements, *Overture, Romance,* and *Scherzo,* retain an astonishing freshness and charm.

With the entrancing Naxos anthology called "Swedish Orchestral Favorites" currently unavailable—and perhaps it is an inevitable sign of its growing maturity that that wonderful young company has finally discovered the deletions ax—the older Swedish Society recording by the Swedish Radio Symphony led by Stig Westerberg offers a performance as expert and suitably unpretentious as the one led by Okko Kamu.

Among Larsson's more substantial works, the Violin Concerto of 1952 ranks with the most approachable and engrossing modern works in the instrument's literature, with moments of rare lyric beauty contrasted with a very

Swedish, almost Bergmanesque angst. While another Swedish Society recording (SDC 1004 [CD]) conducted by Westerberg is an unusually fine one, a historic 1955 broadcast by the work's first great champion, the late Louis Kaufmann, presents the far more compelling vision of the piece (Music and Arts CD 667-1 [CD]).

A God in Disguise, one of the Swedish Radio productions that mixes poetry and music, has an endearingly innocent, folklike aura and is handsomely served on a 1978 Bis recording (CD 96 [CD]) that also features the composer's rarely heard Third Symphony. Another Bis recording devotes two CDs (CD 473/74) to the twelve Concertinos for various instruments that Larsson composed between 1954 and 1957. Designed for performance by amateur ensembles, these are ingeniously crafted examples of Hindemith's *gebrauchsmusik* (practical or functional music, but more popularly, "music for use") played here with enormous professional skill.

Lassus, Orlande de (Orlando di Lasso) (1532–1594)

Choral Music

Concerto Italiano, Alessandri. Opus 111 OPS 30-94 [CD].

While it was his masterly sacred music that made Orlande de Lassus the last and greatest exponent of the Flemish contrapuntal school, it is his delightfully risqué secular music that keeps his name alive. From the famous, uproarious "Matona mia cara," a parody of a German trying to sing an Italian serenade, with many embarrassing mispronunciations, to the zany "Zanni-piasi, patro?"—a heated exchange between a master and his drunken servant—Lassus was a virtuoso of the salacious wink and the sexually charged innuendo: neither as vulgar nor as overt as Janequin (see page 383) but every bit as funny.

Concerto Italiano sing the naughty stuff with high zest and bring a genuine depth of feeling to the several (largely boring) serious items, presumably tossed in as a sop to Renaissance Purists and nuns. You'll quickly learn which ones to avoid and program your CD player accordingly.

Lauridsen, Morten (1943–)

Lux Æterna; Les Chansons des Roses; Ave Maria; Mid-Winter Songs; O Magnum Mysterium

> Los Angeles Master Chorale and Sinfonia, Salamunovich. RCM 19705 [CD].

This hypnotically beautiful album might almost be characterized as contemporary vocal music for people who don't think they *like* contemporary vocal music, for the first recording of the ravishing *Lux Æterna* by the Los Angeles-based composer Morten Lauridsen demonstrates that it *is* possible for important contemporary music to speak directly to the heart.

Composed in 1997 for the Los Angeles Master Chorale—who, not surprisingly, perform the work as though it had been written for them—*Lux Æterna* is a rich, complex, intensely moving piece that people will be listening to for a long time to come. While the idiom is no more threatening than that of the English composer John Rutter, the music itself is of far greater substance and depth. The other works on the album are no less lovely, especially *Les Chansons des Roses,* which has a fair claim to being the finest Rilke setting yet made by an American composer. Paul Salamunovich extracts brilliant performances from his superbly drilled forces and the recorded sound is superb.

If you think that modern music is largely confined to the mindless delights of minimalism or incomprehensible noise, then this wonderfully *human* music will prove how wrong you are.

Leclair, Jean-Marie (1697–1764)

Violin Concertos (12)

> Standage, violin and conductor; Collegium Musicum 90. Chandos CHAN 0551 [CD]; CHAN 0589 [CD].

Often called the "French Corelli," Jean-Marie Leclair has the melancholy (and rather surprising) distinction of being the only important composer murdered by his spouse. Although the guilt of his estranged wife Louise has never been proven, Nicolas Slonimsky assembled an impressive circumstantial case in "The Murder of Leclair" from *A Thing or Two about Music:* the composer was murdered in his home, stabbed three times (in the shoulder, stomach, and chest) by someone he obviously knew, robbery was not a motive, and his wife was furious that Leclair had refused to take his nephew (who was also her lover) into the Duke of Gramont's orchestra. Besides, the only other suspects—the nephew, the gardener (who had a criminal record), and the gardener's mistress—were subsequently exonerated. As Thoreau reminds us, "Some circumstantial evidence is very strong, as when you find a trout in the milk."

Whoever killed Leclair was certainly not a music lover, for the dozen concertos he published between 1737 and 1744 represent the zenith of the baroque violin concerto in France, works that clearly move the form he inherited from Corelli and Vivaldi toward the more advanced, intricately developed structures of the classical era. Simon Standage and Collegium Musicum 90 prove adroit and enthusiastic guides to this bracingly inventive music, with crisp tempos, transparent textures, and an instantly appealing *joie de vivre*. The recorded sound is typical of the Chandos "Chaconne" series: medium-distant, natural-sounding, and very flattering.

Lees, Benjamin (1924–)

Violin Sonatas (3)

Orner, violin; Wizansky, piano. Albany TROY 138 [CD].

Born of Russian parents in Harbin, China, Benjamin Lees was brought to America when still a child. Like his teacher George Antheil, Lees has never belonged to any particular movement or school: in a deliberate attempt to remain aloof from the many contradictory trends sweeping serious American music in the 1950s, he lived and worked in Europe. His essentially traditional yet stubbornly original music has been performed by most of the major American orchestras and has long been admired for its finish, individuality, and strength.

With many of his major orchestral scores inexplicably absent from the catalogue, this Albany recording of the three Violin Sonatas offers an excellent introduction to Lees's ruggedly powerful idiom. Composed between 1953 and 1989, these are large, important, virile works—among the most significant yet written by an American. The performances seem absolutely definitive, with close, immediate recorded sound.

The Violin Concerto of 1958 is one of the strongest works of the period, an enthralling virtuoso exercise that is even more importantly an eminently serious work bursting with personality and integrity. Ruggiero Ricci's commanding 1976 recording has been reissued on a very desirable two-CD Vox Box (CDX 5158

[CD]) called "American Concertos," which also includes William Bergsma's Violin Concerto (1966); Michael Colgrass's *Concert Masters* for Three Violins and Orchestra (1976); Lou Harrison's Concerto for Violin and Percussion Orchestra (see page 326); Meyer Kupferman's Concerto for Cello, Tape, and Orchestra (1974); Walter Piston's Concertino for Piano and Orchestra (1937); and Robert Starer's Concerto for Viola, Strings, and Percussion (1958).

There are few modern works for the instrument that can match the musical depth and visceral excitement of Lees's 1991 Concerto for Horn and Orchestra. It is given a thrilling performance by William Caballero, Lorin Maazel, and the Pittsburgh Symphony on a New World CD (NW 80503-2) that also features the *Lament from the Earth* for Oboe and Orchestra by Leonardo Balada and the 1993 Bassoon Concerto by Ellen Taaffe Zwillich. While the Lees piece is obviously the prize of the collection, the other soloists, oboist Cynthia Koledo DeAlmeida and bassoonist Nancy Goeres, are no less impressive than Mr. Caballero.

Le Flem, Paul (1881–1984)

Symphony No. 4 (1978); Film Music *(Le Grand Jardinier de France)*; *Pièces enfantines; Pour les morts*

Rhenish Philharmonic, Lockhart. Marco Polo 8.223655 [CD].

On the one hand, there are those tiny pieces—an *andante* and an *allegro*—that Mozart wrote when he was five; on the other, the incredible Symphony No. 4 by Paul Le Flem, finished when its composer was ninety-seven. Born in Brittany, educated in Paris—where his teachers included Vincent d'Indy and Albert Roussel—Le Flem spent the bulk of his long career as a teacher, critic, and choral conductor. While his own music was clearly influenced by that of his teachers and Claude Debussy, it also has a uniquely melancholy charm inspired by the storm-tossed coast of his native province. The Fourth Symphony is a powerful, expertly argued, impeccably crafted work: a major achievement for a composer of any age, a scarcely believable one for a composer of his. The earlier pieces, from 1912 through 1942, reveal a remarkable consistency of purpose and quality. Although the performances occasionally seem tentative and ill-prepared, they nonetheless give inspiring testimony to a creative talent unprecedented in its durability.

Lehár, Franz (1870–1948)

*T*he Merry Widow

**Schwarzkopf, Steffek, Gedda, Wächter, Philharmonia Orchestra and
Chorus, Matačič. EMI Classics CDCB 47177 [CD].**

While he never quite scaled the golden heights of Strauss's *Die Fledermaus,
The Gypsy Baron,* or *A Night in Venice*—the primary reason why his music has
since been designated the summit of the Viennese operetta's "Silver Age"—Franz
Lehár was a charming and entirely individual composer whose stage works represented the final, bittersweet sunset of one of the most endearing of all musical
forms. While *Giuditta* and *The Land of Smiles* are probably finer works, it was
the effervescent and eternally glamorous *Die lustige Witwe* that became the only
operetta in history—short of the Savoy Operas of Gilbert and Sullivan—to
mount a serious popular challenge to the absolute supremacy of *Die Fledermaus.*

Even if Viennese operetta in general, or Lehár operettas in particular, are
not exactly your cup of *Kaffee mit Schlag,* I guarantee you will find this ageless
recording one of the most thrilling musical experiences of your life. Elisabeth
Schwarzkopf, the greatest Marschallin and Mozart singer of her time, gives what
may well be the performance of her career as Hanna: regal, witty, sentimental,
and unbelievably sexy, the characterization all but leaps into your living room. As
a matter of fact, there have been only two or three other operatic recordings in
history that begin to match the uncanny sense of presence that this one generates
from its very first notes. The admirable Nicolai Gedda and Eberhard Wächter
also turn in something close to the performances of *their* careers, and under the
inspired leadership of Lovro von Matačič, who casts what amounts to a magical
spell over the proceedings, this *Merry Widow* effortlessly swirls its way into the
ranks of the greatest recordings of all time.

For those who absolutely *insist* on more up-to-date sound, the recent
Deutsche Grammophon recording (439911-2 [CD]) is the first to offer serious
competition to the Matačič in more than a generation. Along with the sumptuous
sonics—detailed, intimate, yet warmly enveloping—the album's principal glories
are John Eliot Gardiner's incandescent conducting and the playing of the Vienna
Philharmonic, here recording *Die lustige Witwe* (believe it or not) for the very
first time. The cast is a strong one, with Cheryl Studer fetchingly girlish in the
title role, yet the poor woman is up against *Schwarzkopf* after all, which in this
role means Motherhood and the flag.

The Telarc Lehár series is one of the most exciting projects the company has
ever launched, featuring sparkling English-language performances conducted by
Richard Bonynge, who, with some judicious cuts that only the most devoted

Lehárian would notice, manages to cram almost all the music from each of the operettas onto a single CD. *The Land of Smiles* (CD 80419 [CD]) or *Giuditta* (CD 80426 [CD]) would be a good place to start, but *Paganini* (CD 80435 [CD]) and *Der Zarewitsch* (CD 80395 [CD]) are just as delectable. The casts are fresh and uniformly excellent—Jerry Hadley especially so in the all-important Tauber roles—with the flawless digital sound constantly revealing some new felicity of Lehár's orchestration. As a kind of German-language pendant to the series, Hadley and Bonynge offer a generous selection of tenor arias—splendidly sung— for RCA (09026-68258-2 [CD]) on an album called "Jerry Hadley in Vienna," which also unearths delightful rarities by Edmund Eysler, Leo Fall, Emmerich Kálmán, and composer Richard Tauber (the swooning "Du bist die Welt für mich" from *Der singende Traum*).

Lovers of Lehár's highly addictive melodies should take note that many of the best of them, in recordings from 1934–1942 led by the composer himself, are available on an album called "Lehár conducts Lehár" from Preiser (90150 [CD]). In addition to the voices of Lehár specialists Esther Rethy, Maria Reining, and the late, exquisite Jarmilla Novotna, the album features the incomparable recordings of the composer's friend Richard Tauber, the great Austrian tenor for whom many of these roles were written.

On a very attractive Angel CD (47020), Willi Boskovsky leads the Vienna Johann Strauss Orchestra in a program of Lehár waltzes.

Leifs, Jón (1899–1968)

Symphony No. 1, Op. 26, "Saga Symphony"

Iceland Symphony, Vänskä. BIS CD 730 [CD].

One might reasonably expect something rather unusual from a work whose orchestration includes iron and wooden shields, replicas of Bronze Age horns, anvils, skinless drums bashed with enormous mallets, and—believe it or not— tuned rocks! And a *most* unusual work the "Saga Symphony" by the Icelandic composer Jón Leifs assuredly is. Written in the early 1940s as a protest against what this fiercely nationalistic composer considered Richard Wagner's "detestable" perversion of the Icelandic sagas in *Der Ring des Nibelungen,* this astonishing and terrifying work is one of the most wholly original outbursts of mid-twentieth-century music: a wild, atavistic evocation of five characters from the ancient sagas that seems less a modern orchestral score than something dark and nameless that emerged out of the rocks and trees. Try listening to this stuff in a completely darkened room late at night; if you can last more than ten minutes without bolting for the door, then you're a lot tougher cookie than me.

In short, the "Saga Symphony" is not only for those who thought they'd heard it all, but also—and perhaps especially—for those who've lost their capacity for amazement.

Lekeu, Guillaume (1870–1894)

Sonata for Violin and Piano

Y. Menuhin, violin; H. Menuin, piano. Biddulph LAB 058 [CD].

Although the gifted Belgian composer Guillaume Lekeu did not begin serious musical studies until his mid-teens and died of typhus at twenty-three, he produced an impressive body of first-rate music during his brief lifetime, including the Violin Sonata commissioned by his famous fellow countryman Eugène Ysaÿe, who had also introduced the A Major Sonata by Lekeu's teacher César Franck. Surprisingly, this youthful masterpiece owes little to Franck's example or to that of Lekeu's other important teacher Vincent d'Indy. Overflowing with fresh ideas that are presented in a surprisingly mature manner, the Sonata invariably has a powerful effect on listeners—not merely for what it is, but also for what it suggests its young composer might have become.

In nearly sixty years, no recorded performance has begun to approach the passion and finish of the famous 1938 HMV recording that Yehudi Menuhin made at roughly the same age that Lekeu was when he wrote the piece. With his sister Hephzibah a perfect foil, Menuhin's playing is by turns rhapsodic and aristocratic, effortlessly adapting itself to the shifting demands of the piece. Although obviously dated, the recorded sound in Biddulph's meticulous transfer remains focused and true. With equally memorable versions of the Franck Sonata and the Chausson *Poème,* this is a key item in Lord Menuhin's discography and an album that no lover of great violin playing can afford to live without.

Lekeu's most celebrated work, the molten *Adagio for Strings,* is beautifully played by the Ensemble Musique Oblique on a valuable Harmonia Mundi album (HMC 901455 [CD]) on which the major work is the eloquent Piano Quartet, whose unfinished second movement was wrestled into performing shape by d'Indy. An equally intriguing Koch Schwann recording (CD 310060 [CD]) offers a devoted reading of the ambitious Piano Trio of 1890, in which the young composer works out his youthful enthusiasm for Franck and Wagner while still speaking in his own unmistakable voice.

Leoncavallo, Ruggero (1857–1919)

I Pagliacci

Callas, Di Stefano, Gobbi, Panerai, La Scala Chorus and Orchestra, Serafin. EMI Classics CDCC 47981 [CD].

Since the days that Enrico Caruso virtually adopted Canio's histrionic Act I aria "Vesti la Giubba" as his signature tune, Leoncavallo's *I Pagliacci,* with its inseparable companion piece, Mascagni's *Cavalleria Rusticana,* has remained a staple of the operatic repertoire. Based on an actual case that the composer's father, a local magistrate, tried when Leoncavallo was a boy, *I Pagliacci* is one of the two quintessential works of the slice-of-life *verismo* school of Italian opera: a work in which the uncontrollable passions of ordinary people result in a delightful mosaic of jealousy, betrayal, and violent death.

The famous La Scala recording from the early 1950s is more earthy and blood-curdling than ever in its recent compact disc reincarnation. Titto Gobbi is a wonderfully sly and malevolent Tonio, and the Nedda of Maria Callas is unapproachable in its vulgar animal magnetism and dramatic intensity. Still, *I Pagliacci* has always been the tenor's show, and this recording, perhaps more than any other, demonstrates what Giuseppe di Stefano *might* have been. As it stood, his career was probably the most brilliant of any of the postwar Italian tenors; had it been managed with greater intelligence and care, it might have been *the* career since Caruso's. His Canio is painted in very primary colors and, for the most part, is very beautifully sung; still, for all its power, we can hear the unmistakable signs that his incredible instrument had already seen its best days.

Of the more recent *Pagliaccis,* RCA has wisely reissued the 1971 recording with Monserrat Caballé, Placido Domingo, and Sherrill Milnes (09026-60865-2 [CD]), all in peak condition, supported by some stylish, blood-and-thunder conducting from Nello Santi. The recording also benefits from vintage early '70s recorded sound and the inclusion of the frequently cut Nedda-Silvio duet.

For the *really* adventurous opera lover, the Orfeo recording of Leoncavallo's *La Bohème* (023822 [CD]) is an intriguing oddity. Over lunch one day Leoncavallo told his friend Giacomo Puccini that he was at work on an opera based on Henri Murger's *Scènes de la vie de Bohème;* Puccini thought it was a splendid idea and immediately set to work on the same text. For some reason, Leoncavallo never forgave him. Listening to the Leoncavallo *La Bohème* in light of the Puccini makes for a fascinating experience, rather like meeting your father's long-lost (and far less interesting) brother. Nothing sounds quite right or good enough, although on its own terms and in such a devoted performance, it emerges as a most attractive score.

Liadov, Anatol (1855–1914)

Orchestral Music

> **Russian National Orchestra, Pletnev. Deutsche Grammophon 447084-2 [CD].**
>
> **Slovak Philharmonic, Gunzenhauser. Naxos 8.550328 [CD].**

The history of modern music might have been entirely different had Anatol Liadov *not* been the most pathologically lazy composer since Gioacchino Rossini. In 1910, Liadov so dithered and dawdled over an important ballet commission that a frantic Sergei Diaghilev was forced to take a chance on a young and completely unproven composer named Igor Stravinsky. In retrospect, Liadov would probably not have been able to write *The Firebird*, even if he had been able to muster the requisite gumption. He was by nature a miniaturist, as his modest output of enchanting little masterworks clearly shows. The best of them, like the *Eight Russian Folksongs* or the tone poem *Kikimora*, with its unforgettable English horn melody and concluding piccolo tweak, are among the most perfectly crafted gems of late-Romantic Russian music, an aural equivalent of the Fabergé Easter eggs.

Pletnev and the Russian National Orchestra are superbly atmospheric in *The Enchanted Lake, Baba Yaga, and Kikimora,* with virtuoso playing brilliantly captured in DG's warmest, most revealing recorded sound. While the performances on Naxos are only slightly less magical, there *is* that bargain-basement price tag. Both are guaranteed to delight, and perhaps enthrall.

Liebermann, Lowell (1961–)

Piano Concertos (2)

> **Hough, piano; BBC Scottish Symphony, Liebermann. Hyperion 66966 [CD].**

Born in New York City in 1961, Lowell Liebermann studied composition with David Diamond and Vincent Persichetti at Juilliard and has since received an impressive list of honors and commissions, including a Flute Concerto for James Galway and an opera based on Oscar Wilde's *The Picture of Dorian Gray* for the Monte Carlo Opera.

The Piano Concertos are colorful, communicative scores whose unusually friendly musical vocabulary embraces a variety of influences from Prokofiev to Diamond though it has a charm and exuberance uniquely its own. Accompanied by the composer, Stephen Hough gives thrillingly committed performances of both works.

Those who admire Liebermann's exact contemporary Michael Torke should investigate immediately.

Ligeti, György (1923–)

Bagatelles (6) for Wind Quintet

Ensemble Wien-Berlin. Sony Classical SK 48052 [CD].

Concerto for Cello and Orchestra; Concerto for Thirteen Chamber Instruments; Concerto for Piano and Orchestra

Perényi, cello; Wiget, piano; Ensemble Modern, Eötvös. Sony Classical SK 58945 [CD].

The music of the Hungarian composer György Ligeti first began to reach a wider audience in 1969 when Stanley Kubrick included it in his film *2001: A Space Odyssey*. An influential member of the European avant-garde from the mid-1950s onward, Ligeti's experiments have included works like *Atmosphères,* which abandoned specific intervals and rhythms, and even more radical departures such as *Poème symphonique,* a work scored for one hundred metronomes, all running at different speeds.

From 1949, the year of his graduation from the Budapest Academy of Music, Ligeti—Bartók and Kodály before him—became deeply interested in the folk music of Hungary and Romania, a passion that led to numerous folk song arrangements and various folk-inspired works like the *Bagatelles.* Ensemble Wien-Berlin plays this attractive, inventive music with style and flair on an album of twentieth-century wind music that also includes Samuel Barber's *Summer Music,* Luciano Berio's *Opus Number Zoo,* and the wind quintets of Helmut Eder and Jean Françaix.

The three concertos were written between 1966 and 1988 and all are thoroughly representative of Ligeti's mature style. These are thorny, brilliantly colorful, endlessly intriguing works that challenge both the mind and ear; Perényi,

Wiget, and company play them with obvious skill and devotion, while Sony Classical's recorded sound captures every nuance to perfection.

Liszt, Franz (1811–1886)

Années de pèlerinage

Berman, piano. Deutsche Grammophon 437206 [CD].

Liszt's sprawling three-volume collection of musical impressions of Switzerland and Italy contains some of his most inspired and characteristic music, from the shimmering magic of *Les Jeux d'eau à la Villa d'Este* to the thunderous power of the *Dante Sonata*. As the *Years of Pilgrimage* also features a fair amount of aimless wandering, the obvious challenge to the performer of the complete twenty-six-piece cycle is to not only give the famous set pieces their due but also to enliven the dull bits without being *obvious* about it.

Lazar Berman's justly famous 1977 recording is so unshakable in its conviction that *Années de pèlerinage* is a masterpiece in which not a single note is wasted that the pianist convinces *us* at virtually every step along the way. Along with passion and brilliance, the playing has tremendous intellectual depth and emotional refinement: while often exciting and spontaneous-sounding in the extreme, nothing seems to be done arbitrarily or merely for show. It was this recording, more than any other, that led many to hail Berman as a second Sviatoslav Richter. While *that* was largely a public relations fantasy, this *Années de pèlerinage* remains an incredible achievement.

Piano Concerto No. 1 in E-flat Major; Piano Concerto No. 2 in A Major

Richter, piano; London Symphony, Kondrashin. Philips 446200-2 [CD].

Composer, conductor, philosopher, ascetic, charlatan, religious mystic, prodigious sexual athlete, and, in all probability, the greatest pianist who has ever lived, Franz Liszt was the epitome of the Romantic musician: a restless bundle of ambition, nervous energy, and insatiable appetites whose influence on the development of nineteenth-century music was so enormous that it still remains difficult to assess. As a composer, he all but invented the tone poem, one of musical Romanticism's most enduringly popular forms. His experiments in thematic transformation were decisive in the leitmotif technique perfected by his son-in-law Richard Wagner. And in churning out endless reams of fiendishly difficult piano music for use on his innumerable concert tours, he helped provide gainful employment for virtuoso pianists from his day to our own.

Liszt's Piano Concertos have long been staples of the concert repertoire, and each is a revealing glimpse at the two mutually complementary, and often contradictory, sides of the composer's essential makeup: the brash, outgoing, self-indulgent E-flat Major Concerto and the moody, poetic, introspective Concerto No. 2 in A Major.

No modern interpretations have ever captured more of the Concertos' poetry and barnstorming excitement than that sensational Philips recording by Sviatoslav Richter. On a purely technical level, they are among the most hair-raising piano recordings ever made. Yet along with the phenomenal virtuosity, Richter brings such a measure of grandeur and profundity to the music that those who are tempted to dismiss it as empty-headed bombast will never be tempted to do so again.

Among recordings with more up-to-date recorded sound, the Deutsche Grammophon version (423571-2 [CD]) by the Polish pianist Krystian Zimerman is extremely impressive. While Zimerman's playing, per se, can't quite match the depth or brilliance of Richer's, the interpretations are both poised and adult and Seiji Ozawa and the Boston Symphony are admirable accomplices. They also combine for a suitably spooky performance of the always-tasteful *Totentanz,* a work that should never be listened to in a dark room or after having just consumed a pizza.

*D*ante Symphony

> **Berlin Radio Women's Choir, Berlin Philharmonic, Barenboim. Teldec 77340 [CD].**

If the *Dante Symphony* is neither as ambitious nor as consistently inspired as *A Faust Symphony,* then it is still one of Liszt's most powerfully argued works. The opening vision of the Gates of Hell is one of the composer's most horrific creations, while the music associated with Francesca da Rimini is as fine as anything in Tchaikovsky's far more familiar tone poem. Had the rather placid *Purgatorio* maintained the *Inferno*'s frenzied level of inspiration—a tall order, given the subject matter—then the *Dante Symphony* might well have become Liszt's masterpiece.

Daniel Barenboim's intensely committed recording is by far the most successful the work has ever received. The genuinely demonic energy he wrings from the *Inferno* is exhilarating, as is the ardor he finds in the frequently anticlimactic *Magnificat* that concludes the work. An appealingly theatrical version of the *Dante Sonata* by pianist Daniel Barenboim rounds out a most satisfying disc.

A Faust Symphony

Riegel, tenor; Tanglewood Festival Chorus, Boston Symphony Orchestra, Bernstein. Deutsche Grammophon 447449-2 [CD].

Except for the final movement of Gustav Mahler's "Symphony of a Thousand," *A Faust Symphony* is probably the most inspired of all musical treatments of Goethe's great philosophical poem. It may also be Franz Liszt's masterpiece. Each of its three movements is an elaborate character sketch of the play's three central figures: a brooding, heroic, poetic movement devoted to Faust himself; a lyrical second movement called "Gretchen"; and a finale devoted to Mephistopheles, in which Liszt, like Milton before him, could not resist giving the Devil all of the best lines. One of the lengthiest and most challenging symphonies written up to that time, *A Faust Symphony* still makes tremendous demands on its interpreters, and the recording that was most successful in solving the work's innumerable problems was the one recorded in the mid-1950s by Sir Thomas Beecham: lyrical, pensive, impetuous, and shot through with a demoniacal wit, its only serious drawback was the rather shrill and harsh recorded sound, which the compact-disc remastering brilliantly managed to correct.

With the Beecham recording now withdrawn from circulation, it is an even greater pleasure to welcome Leonard Bernstein's back. Both the recorded sound and the orchestral execution are marginally better than in Beecham's and the interpretation is vintage Bernstein, featuring—among its many glories—the most shamelessly licentious version of the lovely "Gretchen" movement so far recorded, and playing in "Mephistopheles" that will curl your tail. While not the *most* pornographic of Bernstein's recordings, it will certainly do, and I, for one, welcome it back with open arms.

Hungarian Rhapsodies (19)

Szidon, piano. Deutsche Grammophon 453034-2 [CD].

Close to the top of my "whatever became of" list, just behind the Italian conductor-*wunderkind* of the 1950s, Pierino Gamba, is the Brazilian pianist Roberto Szidon, who made a couple of recordings in the early 1970s and then seemed to vanish without a trace.

It took a certain amount of bravado to choose as one of his first recordings these popular works that everyone and his mother has been recording since time began. The results came as quite a jolt to *HR* collectors: not only were they among the most exciting performances heard in a generation, but they also brought a refined musicality to these frequently flogged warhorses that is almost never heard. While a few individual performers (Cziffra, Kapell, and Horowitz in his maniacal transcription of No. 2) have outscored Szidon at various points, no more satisfying interpretation of the entire cycle has ever appeared. The playing has authentic poetry and finesse, plus electrifying moments of out-on-a-limb derring-do. This was clearly a major career in the making, and we can only wonder again what happened.

For those willing to put up with some rather variable recorded sound—which is hardly shocking, given that the recordings were made between 1926 and 1994—VAI Audio has put together an intriguing two-CD anthology (VAIA/IPA 1066-2) that offers some of the most memorable recordings these works have ever received. While the level of playing and individuality is extraordinarily high, the versions of No. 6 by Mischa Levitzky (surely the only one ever to rival William Kapell's), No. 7 by the great Leschetizky pupil Mark Hambourg, and No. 15 by the incomparable English pianist Solomon stand out in a most distinguished field.

Among recordings of the orchestral version of the *Rhapsodies,* Antal Dorati's Mercury Living Presence recording with the London Symphony (432015-2 [CD]) has dominated the catalogues for more than a generation. The colorful interpretations are bursting with gypsy fire and energy, the playing is a model of daring, edge-of-the-seat virtuosity, the recorded sound remarkably full and detailed for its age.

Sir Georg Solti's London recording (443444-2 [CD]) of the *Second Rhapsody* is very special, even compared to Dorati's. With the breathtaking playing and flawless digital sound, the performance communicates an endearing sense of almost boyish enjoyment unique among this conductor's later recordings. Indeed, the entire album—aptly named "Mephisto Magic"—is one of the most completely enjoyable Solti would ever make, including similarly enthralling readings of the first *Mephisto Waltz,* Bartók's *Hungarian Sketches* and *Rumanian Folk Songs,* Kodály's *Háry János Suite,* and *Prinz Csongor und die Kobolde* by Fritz Reiner's childhood friend Leó Weiner.

Piano Music

The late Jorge Bolet was a fabulous Liszt player, as one of his few surviving London recordings (425689-2 [CD]) readily proves. An attractive grab-bag culled from several of his Liszt recitals, it features a *Liebestraum* of intense nobility and a *Les Jeux d'eau à la Villa d'Este* to stand your hair on end.

While Claudio Arrau was another pianist who brought an ample measure of Latin American fire to Liszt, he was also one of the most thoughtful, instantly recognizable performers of the modern era: mannered and finicky if you didn't like him, heroically individual if you did. His Philips recording (416458-2 [CD]) of the *Transcendental Études* combines an imposing technique with an interpretive vision so adult and profound that the *transcendental* of the title is *clearly* the word.

Jean-Ives Thibaudet's London recording of opera transcriptions (436736 [CD]) is one of the most exciting Liszt albums in years. Along with the more familiar (and rafter-rattling) *Rigoletto, Faust,* and *Eugene Onegin* paraphrases are four far more serious reactions to the music of his future son-in-law Richard Wagner. Throughout, Thibaudet's passage-work is phenomenal, recalling that of Josef Hofmann in his prime.

For many, the century's most distinctive Liszt was Alfred Cortot's. Unlike the playing of some of the Liszt pupils, many of whom lived to make commercial recordings, it was not the conventional, fire-raising, barnstorming, pound-the-piano-till-it-collapses-in-a-heap Liszt. While it had its share of fire and grandeur, it was also suave, genial, elegant, and charming—which is to say, very French. Two invaluable collections restore some of his classic 78 recordings to circulation: a Music and Arts album (CD 662-1 [CD]) that features that phenomenal B Minor Sonata and those impossibly eloquent versions of the two Chopin songs, plus a treasure chest from Pearl (PEA 9396 [CD]) that includes wonders like *St. François de Paul marchant sur les flots* and perhaps the most bloodcurdling *Second Hungarian Rhapsody* ever recorded.

An Enterprise CD (ENT PL 222) brings together several of Egon Petri's imposing recordings from the 1920s and '30s, including the 1937 *Paraphrase on Rigoletto* and two elegant versions of Schubert transcriptions *(Auf dem Wasser zu singen* and *Die Forelle)* from 1929.

While Liszt himself left no commercial recordings, of course, many of his best-known students did. On another Pearl album called "The Pupils of Liszt" (PEAS 9972 [CD]), Conrad Ansorge (1862–1930), Eugen d'Albert (1864–1932), José Vianna da Motta (1868–1948), Arthur de Greef (1862–1940), Arthur Friedheim (1859–1932), Frederic Lamond (1868–1948), Moriz Rosenthal (1862–1946), Emil von Sauer (1862–1942), and Josef Weiss (1864–1945) reveal an approach to Liszt at once wilder, freer, and far more serious than that generally taken by pianists today.

Piano Sonata in B Minor

Curzon, piano. London 452306-2 [CD]

Richard Wagner was especially fond of his father-in-law's only piano sonata. Shortly after Liszt sent him the manuscript, Wagner wrote back, saying, "It is sublime, even as yourself." While Johannes Brahms was also particularly keen to hear it performed, at the private concert that Liszt arranged in his honor Brahms showed his gratitude by falling asleep. If much of Liszt's piano music is little more than gaudy ephemera, then his B Minor Sonata, with those of Schubert and Chopin, remains the Romantic Era's most enduring contribution to the form, and one of that tiny handful of nineteenth-century piano sonatas that is every bit the equal of any that Beethoven ever wrote.

Recorded in Vienna in 1963, Sir Clifford Curzon's version is one of the great piano recordings of the century, a performance of astonishing confidence, subtlety, and power. No recording has ever had a surer grasp of its complex structure, nor has any been quite as successful revealing its incredible wealth of ornamental detail. The emotional range of the playing is also staggering, from the pits of despair to soaring ecstasy to everything in between. The beautifully remastered sound captures every sigh and explosion to perfection, in both the Sonata and all the shorter works—the *Berceuse, Gnomenreigen, Liebestraum in A-flat,* and *Valse oubliée No. 1*—that round out the album.

Les Préludes (Symphonic Poem No. 3)

London Philharmonic, Solti. London 417513-2 [CD].

Of the thirteen works with which Franz Liszt all but invented the tone poem, only *Les Préludes* is heard with any frequency today. Listening to Bernard Haitink's heroically ambitious cycle for Philips—now available on a pair of Philips Duo albums (438751-2 [CD], 438754-2 [CD])—will quickly show you why. For despite the best of intentions and some of the best recorded performances that any of these works are ever likely to receive, most of the Liszt tone poems are unmitigated junk. (It *is* difficult to think of another great composer whose ratio of trash to masterworks was quite as high as his.) While often as schlocky and bombastic as the rest, *Les Préludes* is saved in the end by its grandiose gestures, flood of memorable melody, and utter sincerity. Schlock it most certainly *is*, but of a wonderfully urgent and lovable variety.

Sir Georg Solti's recording with the London Philharmonic is one of that conductor's most completely successful recordings. While the playing is undeniably exciting, rarely has *Les Préludes* been invested with such power and genuine nobility. Coupled with equally riveting and dignified performances of the rarely heard *Tasso* and *Prometheus*, this is probably the strongest case for the Liszt tone poems that any single recording has ever made.

Llobet, Miguel (1878–1938)

Nine Catalan Folksongs

Williams, guitar. Sony Classical SK 48480 [CD].

For many who heard them both, the Catalan guitarist Miguel Llobet was a more refined and accomplished artist than his younger contemporary Andrés Segovia. He was certainly the far more admirable human being. Called "the gentle Llobet," his kindness and sensitivity were legion; it was said that he died of a broken heart at the sight of Spain being destroyed by civil war.

Llobet's love of his country and its most characteristic instrument glows warmly in the tender, ineffably touching *Nine Catalan Folksongs*, the centerpiece in John Williams's wonderful *Iberia* album. Throughout the Llobet, as well as his own transcription of Granados's *Valses poéticos* and Steve Gray's tasteful orchestration of three excerpts from Albéniz's *Iberia,* Williams's playing is clearly that of the greatest guitar technician of whom we have an accurate record, with every nuance captured to perfection by Sony Classical's engineers.

Lôbo, Duarte (c. 1565–1646)

Requiem, *Missa pro defunctis*

Oxford Schola Cantorum, Summerly. Naxos 8.550682 [CD].

Maestro de capilla of the Lisbon Cathedral from 1594 until a few years before his death, Duarte Lôbo was the foremost Portuguese composer of his time, eventually publishing six volumes of enormously accomplished sacred music that combines a ready grasp of the intricacies of Renaissance polyphony with that special emotional ardor that characterizes the Iberian music of the period. The *Missa pro defunctis* is a richly inventive, gravely beautiful work that bears favorable comparison with the best work of Palestrina and Victoria—especially in such an ardent, deeply sensitive performance as this one. Coupled with another splendid *Missa pro defunctis* by Lôbo's exact contemporary Manuel Cardoso (c. 1566–1650), the album fills an important gap in our appreciation of Portuguese music and marks another triumph for Jeremy Summerly's exceptional Oxford Schola Cantorum.

On a full-priced Gimell album (CDGIM 028 [CD], 1585T-28 [CD]), Peter Phillips and the Tallis Scholars give predictably flawless performances of two more important Lôbo works: the *Requiem for Six Voices* and the *Missa Vox clamantis.*

Locatelli, Pietro (1695–1764)

L'arte del violino (12 concertos and 24 caprices) for Violin, Strings, and Continuo, Op. 3

> **E. Wallfisch, violin; Raglan Baroque Players, N. Kraemer. Hyperion CDA 66721/3 [CD].**

The contemporaries of Pietro Locatelli spoke of his playing with hushed awe: one went so far as to claim that his performance of a sonata by his teacher Corelli would have made a canary fall from its tree in a swoon of pleasure. One can only imagine its effect on the female members of his large and adoring public. Locatelli brought the art of violin playing to a new level of virtuosity, and in works like *L'arte del violino,* published in Amsterdam in 1733, he helped codify various elements of standard usage, including double stops, high positions, and the written-out cadenza.

Elizabeth Wallfisch makes child's play of Locatelli's demanding writing—especially in the fiendishly difficult solo caprices that come two to a concerto—in performances that wear both their virtuosity and their scholarship very lightly. Nicholas Kraemer's Raglan Baroque Players offer suitably zestful accompaniments. The same players are equally effective in Locatelli's twelve *Concerti grossi,* Op. 1 (CDA 66981/2 [CD]), even if the general level of inspiration is a cut or two below that of the Opus 3 concertos.

The six *Introduttioni teatricali* contain some of Locatelli's most inspired writing, vividly projected by Thomas Hengelbrock and the enthusiastic young Freiburg Baroque Orchestra (Deutsche Harmonia Mundi 05472-77207-2 [CD]). Both the works themselves and the performances are exhilarating, making it all the antithesis of baroque "sewing machine" music.

Loeffler, Charles Martin (1861–1935)

A Pagan Poem

> **Houston Symphony, Stokowski. EMI Classics CDM 65074 [CD].**

At a New York Philharmonic rehearsal of a piece by this Alsatian-born composer, Gustav Mahler was heard to mutter, "Das ist *Buttermilchmusik.*" With all due respect, this is nonsense.

After settling in the United States in 1881, Loeffler—the son of German parents who spent his youth in Alsace, the Ukraine, Hungary, Berlin, and Paris—produced a small but impressive body of works distinguished by their impeccable craftsmanship and their composer's cosmopolitan experience. French, German, and Russian influences can be heard throughout his work, as can elements of Irish and Spanish folk music and the rhythms of American jazz.

Based on a poem by Virgil that tells the story of a distraught young woman who tries to win back a faithless lover through sorcery, *A Pagan Poem* is among the most dramatically sensual scores ever produced in America and one of the most brilliantly orchestrated, with some especially thrilling writing for the English horn and brass. Stokowski's late-'50s recording is a classic one: committed, sinuous, and flawlessly overripe.

The lovely *Rhapsodies* (*L'Étang* and *La Cornemuse,* after poems of Maurice Rollinat) for oboe, viola, and piano are played with passion and finesse by oboist Alan Vogel on an intriguing Delos album (DE 3161 [CD]) that also offers distinguished performances of the Nielsen and Prokofiev Quintets. The work many regard as Loeffler's masterpiece, the *Music for Four Stringed Instruments,* written in memory of the American flyer Victor Chapman who was killed in France in 1917, is given a moving performance by the Kohon String Quartet on a Vox Box called "The Early String Quartet in the U.S.A" (CDX 5057 [CD]), which includes a piano quintet by Henry Hadley; string quartets by George Whitefield Chadwick, Arthur Foote, and Daniel Gregory Mason (the Quartet "Based on Negro Themes"); together with the *Two Sketches on Indian Themes* by Charles Tomlinson Griffes and a delightfully primitive suite of dances attributed to Benjamin Franklin.

Loewe, Carl (1796–1869)

Songs and Ballads

> Prey, baritone; Endres, piano. Capriccio 10759 [CD].
>
> Mathis, soprano; Garben, piano. CPO 999334-2 [CD].
>
> Moll, bass; Garben, piano. CPO 999306-2 [CD].

Among lovers of German lieder, the songs of Carl Loewe have always commanded enormous affection and respect. Wagner actually preferred his setting of Goethe's *Erlkönig* to Schubert's, and his masterful settings of the old Scots ballad *Edward,* Ferdinand Freiligrath's vainglorious *Prinz Eugen,* and the Goethe ballad *Der Zauberlehrling* (which also inspired Dukas's *The Sorcerer's Apprentice*) have been prized by great recitalists from Slezak and Kipnis to Fischer-Dieskau and Prey.

Hermann Prey's Capriccio anthology features a collection of Goethe settings recorded in 1995. While the sixty-six-year-old voice shows some understandable signs of wear and tear, the consummate artistry remains unaffected. The performance of *Erlkönig* is so gripping that you begin to suspect that Wagner may have actually had a point, while the two *Wanderers Nachtlieder* are made to seem as resourceful and moving as the far more famous settings of Schubert, Schumann, and Wolf.

The CPO recitals by Edith Mathis and Kurt Moll are intelligently chosen and generally very well sung, though each makes one even more anxious for the prompt reissue of the superb Deutsche Grammophon recordings by Brigitte Fassbänder and Dietrich Fischer-Dieskau.

Yet best of all, in the midst of this appalling Loewe drought, is a two-CD set from Preiser (PRE 89230) that features an incomparable roster of Golden Age singers, including Elisabeth Rethberg, Leo Slezak, Franz Völker, Hans Hotter, and Richard Mayr doing something like complete justice to these marvelous, incomprehensibly neglected songs.

Lully, Jean-Baptiste (1632–1687)

Atys

Soloists, Les Arts Florissants, Christie. Harmonia Mundi HMC 901257/59 [CD].

Not counting Felix Mottl and Joseph Keilberth, who each suffered a heart attack during Wagner's *Tristan und Isolde,* Jean-Baptiste Lully, the Italian-born inventor of French opera, was the only important musician who literally conducted himself to death. While beating vigorous time with a heavy walking stick during a performance of his *Te Deum,* he repeatedly stuck himself in the foot and was eventually carried off by the resulting gangrene. According to legend, his final opera *Achille et Polyxène* so offended his confessor that the good cleric demanded the dying Lully give orders to burn the score in order to obtain absolution; Lully readily complied, secure in the knowledge that a second copy was concealed in his desk.

First staged in January of 1675, *Atys* employs many of the structural innovations Lully brought to French opera, including ballet, pastoral scenes, and a refined species of recitative that lent itself admirably to the graceful flow of French poetry. The historic Christie recording—the first ever of a complete Lully opera—continues to prove that while frequently static, the action can hold the listener's attention throughout the opera's five-act, three-hour span. The performance lends a bracing life to the best numbers, minimizes the stodginess of the weaker ones, and in general proves that if Lully can no longer hold the stage, then he can certainly command the living room.

Lumbye, Hans Christian (1810–1874)

Waltzes, Polkas, Marches, Mazurkas, Galops, and so forth

> **Odense Symphony, Guth. Unicorn-Kanchana DKP 9143 [CD].**
>
> **Danish National Radio Symphony, Rozhdestvensky. Chandos CHAN 9209 [CD].**

Anyone who has been to the famous Tivoli Gardens in Copenhagen has heard the music of Hans Christian Lumbye, who, with that other storyteller Hans Christian, has long been a Danish national hero. After first hearing the music of Josef Lanner and the elder Johann Strauss in 1839, Lumbye formed his own orchestra in the following year; when Tivoli opened in 1843, he became its music director, serving in that post until 1872 and establishing the traditions that are still in force today. At its best, from the stirring *My Salute to St. Petersburg* march to the poetic *Dream Pictures Fantasia* to the utterly disarming *Copenhagen Steam Railway Galop,* with its unforgettable portrait of a wheezing little engine that could, Lumbye's music is a worthy rival to that of Johann Strauss II: bracing, effervescent, hauntingly tuneful music full of wit, sentiment, and high spirits galore.

Both of the only available Lumbye collections offer much to treasure, with Gennady Rozhdestvensky frequently whipping up the Danish National Radio Symphony into a froth of excitement—the *Copenhagen Steam Railway Galop* seems at times a portrait of a runaway train—and Peter Guth taking a more relaxed and natural approach with the superlative Odense Symphony. After sustained exposure to the "Johann Strauss of the North," you'll begin to realize why the Danes think of the Waltz King as "The Lumbye of the South."

Lutoslawski, Witold (1913–1994)

Concerto for Orchestra

Cleveland Orchestra, Dohnányi. London 425694-2 [CD].

The easiest way of entering the challenging world of Poland's major contemporary composer is through the brilliant *Concerto for Orchestra* of 1954, a work that owes something to Bartók's great work of that same name but that also reveals an important new voice on the verge of finding itself. If Lutoslawski's score lacks the depth and universality of Bartók's, then it is still a dramatic, restlessly inventive work—and a singularly exciting one, given the right kind of performance.

Dohnányi's is easily the finest recorded performance the *Concerto* has received since Seiji Ozawa's fondly remembered Angel recording with the Chicago Symphony. Not only does he capture the color and dynamism of the piece, but he also underscores the fact that the similarities to the Bartók really *are* skin deep. Why else would Dohnányi confidently pair both works on the same CD? The Cleveland Orchestra has not sounded quite this frightening since the final, glorious years of the Szell regime and the recorded sound is in the demonstration league.

Those wishing to follow the later changes in Lutoslawski's style are directed to Esa-Pekka Salonen's incomparable Los Angeles Philharmonic recording (Sony Classical SK 66280 [CD]) of the Third and Fourth Symphonies, in which these thorny, complex, uncompromising works are made to seem more sensuous, luminous, and approachable than they might actually be. Anne-Sophie Mutter, the BBC Symphony, and the composer are predictably stimulating guides to *Chain II* for Violin and Orchestra (Deutsche Grammophon 423696-2 [CD]), one of the most successful of those later pieces that mix written sections with extended periods of improvisation.

Lyatoshynsky, Boris (1895–1968)

Symphony No. 2, Op. 26; Symphony No. 3 in B Minor, Op. 50

> Ukrainian State Symphony Orchestra, Kuchar. Marco Polo 8.223540 [CD].

A pupil of Reinhold Glière—which certainly shouldn't be held against him—and friend of Dmitri Shostakovich, who not only admired his music but also considered him the finest composition teacher of his generation, Boris Lyatoshynsky is revered in his native Ukraine as the nation's greatest composer. Although echoes of other voices can clearly be heard—Glière, Rachmaninoff, and Sibelius early on, Prokofiev and Shostakovich toward the end—there is also a strong, instantly identifiable personality at work throughout: a dark, craggy, frequently explosive presence with a penchant for dense counterpoint and gaudy orchestration.

Most musical Ukrainians cite the Third Symphony as Lyatoshynsky's masterpiece and a formidable piece it certainly is. At its first performance in 1951 it ran afoul of the Soviet censors, who forced the composer to provide a new finale if he expected to hear it performed again. If in the revised 1954 version the optimistic finale *does* sound rather tacked on, then there is still plenty to admire here. Listen, if you can, to the striking opening movement, which features a mysterious secondary theme cut from the same cloth as the medieval *Dies irae* and some of the most imposing brass writing to have ever emerged from the Soviet Union.

Led by the gifted young American conductor Theodore Kuchar, the Ukrainian State Symphony plays with obvious relish and pride, as they do in the darker, leaner Symphony No. 2. Those who catch the bug will also want to explore the Fourth and Fifth Symphonies on Marco Polo 8.223541 [CD].

MacDowell, Edward (1860–1908)

Piano Concertos (2)

> Amato, piano; London Philharmonic, Freeman. Olympia OLY 353 [CD].

The work of Edward MacDowell, the foremost American composer of the nineteenth century unless one counts the gifted Stephen Foster, is the musical equivalent of the poetry of Longfellow, Holmes, and Whittier, for it is "American" only in the sense that it was produced by a musician born in this country. After studying in Germany with Joachim Raff and Franz Liszt, MacDowell began turning out a series of pleasant works on European models, including the two Piano Concertos with their echoes of Mendelssohn, Schumann, and (not surprisingly) Liszt.

Donna Amato, the London Symphony, and Paul Freeman are eloquent advocates of both works. While Van Cliburn's eternally fresh and glittering interpretation of the D Minor Concerto remains something very special (RCA 60420-2-RG [CD], 60420-4-RG [T]), the newer recording makes an even stronger case for the musical merits of these pieces. Without minimizing the influences on MacDowell's music, they emphasize its peculiar strengths: its open-hearted melodic thinking, its manliness and warmth. Amato's playing offers abundant lyricism and dash, while Freeman's accompaniments are both sensitive and brilliant.

Machaut, Guillaume de (c. 1300–1377)

La Messe de Nostre Dame

Oxford Camerata, Summerly. Naxos 8.553833 [CD].

Among the many cables and letters of condolence that Igor Stravinsky's widow received in the days following her husband's death in 1971, one of the most telling came from the American composer George Perle: "This is the first time since Guillaume de Machaut that the world has been without a great composer." Stravinsky himself would have relished the compliment. The music of this giant of the Middle Ages had a decisive influence on the austere work of Stravinsky's final years. And just as the *Rite of Spring* did more than any other single work to symbolize the music of the twentieth century, so Machaut's *Messe de Nostre Dame* was the defining work of the fourteenth: the earliest known setting of the ordinary of the mass—*Kyrie, Gloria, Credo, Sanctus,* and *Agnus Dei*—and a work of almost otherworldly purity and remarkable expressive power.

Recorded at the Reims Cathedral, where the *Messe* was first performed at the coronation of Charles V in 1364, the performance by the Oxford Camerata led by Jeremy Summerly not only captures the mystic serenity of the piece but also easily accommodates its startling harmonic adventurousness. Machaut's extraordinary gifts as a poet and composer of secular *chansons* are attractively displayed in a sequence *of ballades, rondeaux,* and excerpts from the brief cycle *Le Livre du Voir dit,* inspired by a passionate love affair with Machaut's adolescent admirer Péronne d'Armetières. The performances are both passionate and beautifully controlled.

MacMillan, James (1959–   )

Veni, Veni, Emmanuel

> Glennie, percussion; Scottish Chamber Orchestra, MacMillan. RCA
> Catalyst 09026-61916-2 [CD].

Devoutly Catholic, passionately leftist, intensely proud of his Scottish heritage, James MacMillan is a genuine phenomenon in contemporary music: a profoundly serious young composer with an extraordinary gift for speaking directly to ordinary people. The gap between the modern composer and the popular audience has grown so cavernous in the past few decades that a work like MacMillan's electrifying percussion concerto *Veni, Veni, Emmanuel* will come as a shock to most people. Without compromising its challenging, highly personal idiom, it manages to carry enormous expressive and theological burdens in a way that is both immediate and instantly comprehensible. Inspired by the ancient Latin plainsong from which it derives its name, the work is a musical reaction to the period between Advent and Easter, concluding with a thrilling vision of the Resurrection. While the array of textures and colors is spellbinding, the depth of its emotional power is even more so. Evelyn Glennie performs with numbing virtuosity, as does the Scottish Chamber Orchestra. While the brief companion pieces are worthy works one and all, *Veni, Veni, Emmanuel* will help define the decade, musically.

Madetoja, Leevi (1887–1947)

Symphony No. 1 in F Major, Op. 29; Symphony No. 2 in E-flat Major, Op. 35

Iceland Symphony, Sakari. Chandos CHAN 9115 [CD].

Although the Finnish composer Leevi Madetoja was the principal pupil of Jean Sibelius, he also spent several years studying with Vincent d'Indy in Paris. This combination of influences—Scandinavian darkness leavened by French clarity—is in part what makes Madetoja so appealing. While the first two symphonies are very much in the Sibelius tradition, they are also the product of a proud and highly individual talent. These are expert, beautifully crafted pieces that hold up very well on repeated hearings and become increasingly distinct and memorable over time.

The Finnish conductor Petri Sakari and his brilliantly trained Icelanders make the strongest possible case for these extremely attractive works, as they do in a companion album (CHAN 9036 [CD]) devoted to the masterful Third Symphony, suites from *Okon Fuoko* and the opera *The Ostrobothnians,* and the bracing comedy overture *Huvinäytelmäalkusoitto*—which is clearly no joke to pronounce. The recorded sound, liner notes, and cover art are all close to ideal.

Mahler, Gustav (1860–1911)

Das Lied von der Erde

King, tenor; Fischer-Dieskau, baritone; Vienna Philharmonic, Bernstein. London 417783-2 [CD].

The popularity that Gustav Mahler's music now enjoys would have been all but unthinkable a generation ago. Most of the symphonies remained unrecorded, and of those that were, many featured mediocre to wretched performances that could only begin to hint at the greatness contained in these noble, neurotic, enervating, and uplifting works. Today, recordings of the Mahler symphonies are nearly as common as those of Beethoven's, which is as it should be. For just as the Romantic symphony was born in that series of nine works that Beethoven produced at the beginning of the nineteenth century, its convulsive, extravagantly beautiful death can be heard in the works that Mahler wrote at the beginning of our own.

For many of his eighty-five years, Bruno Walter—Mahler's disciple and protégé—was the composer's most impassioned and indefatigable champion. It was Walter who led the world premieres of the Ninth Symphony and *Das Lied von der Erde* and left what remain some of the most telling and authoritative of all Mahler recordings.

His famous 1952 version of the great symphonic song cycle *Das Lied von der Erde* is not only one of Walter's greatest recorded performances but also one of the most intensely moving Mahler recordings ever made. While the credit for this must be shared with the incomparable Kathleen Ferrier, whose haunting, richly sabled singing of the concluding "Abschied" has never been matched, and the superb Viennese tenor Julius Patzak—whose thin, leathery voice and consummate musicianship recall the art of another leather-voiced Viennese magician, Richard Tauber—it is the conductor's gentle intensity that makes this one of the major triumphs in the history of the gramophone. All the passion and subtlety of this brilliantly executed interpretation can be heard with remarkable clarity in London's remastered recording. The compact disc was especially miraculous in the way it made the original 1952 recording seem as though it had been made the day before yesterday. Shamefully, it has now been withdrawn.

In its absence, Leonard Bernstein's Vienna Philharmonic recording—one of his very first with the orchestra—remains a noble and engrossing, if not entirely convincing, experiment. James King sings well enough and the orchestra goes out of its mind; the problem may lie in hearing a baritone sing the contralto's songs. Fortunately, the baritone is Dietrich Fischer-Dieskau at his most reserved, penetrating, and dignified. The principal selling point is Bernstein's rather unbelievable conducting, which he would certainly equal on records but never surpass.

Songs of a Wayfarer; Kindertotenlieder; Rückert Lieder

Baker, mezzo-soprano; Hallé Orchestra, New Philharmonia Orchestra, Barbirolli. EMI Classics CDC 47793 [CD].

Even in a career as long and memorable as Dame Janet Baker's, the performances captured on these recordings stand out as pinnacles of her vocal art. Never have the *Songs of a Wayfarer* sounded as Schubertian in their refinement, and *Kindertotenlieder,* while devastating in its sorrow, is both tenderly consoling and totally lacking in self-pity.

Sir John Barbirolli was not only a great Mahler conductor but also a perfect partner for the mezzo-soprano; they seem to sense each other's needs and desires, not simply bars but literally *pages* ahead of time, and yet move together so naturally that it sounds as though it were all being made up on the spur of the moment. (If this seems suspiciously like a description of fantastic sex, that—in a sense—is precisely what it is.)

Dame Janet's Hyperion recording of the piano version (with Geoffrey Parsons) of *The Songs of a Wayfarer* plus some early Mahler rarities is recommended just as highly (CDA 66100 [CD]).

Symphony No. 1 in D Major

Concertgebouw Orchestra of Amsterdam, Bernstein. Deutsche Grammophon 427303-2 [CD].

Few composers have ever been more obviously the composers they would eventually become in their first major orchestral works than Gustav Mahler was in his First Symphony. Completed when Mahler was only twenty-eight, the D Major Symphony—still known, in spite of the composer's violent objections, as the "Titan"—contains many of the key compositional ingredients of the mature Mahler style. Its Olympian length, the sheer size of the performing forces, the gentle Viennese charm, the obsession with death in the gallows humor of the funeral march, and the ecstatic, almost hysterical triumph of its closing bars are all significant portents of what was to come.

While there are nearly two dozen versions of the D Major Symphony currently in print, none can come within shouting distance of that overwhelming and endlessly inventive recording that Jascha Horenstein made with the London Symphony in the late 1960s, now shamefully withdrawn. Available for a time on the Nonesuch label and then on a Unicorn CD, it was one of the few studio recordings that managed to convey the on-the-spot sense of creation that we encounter in only the most gripping live performances. A triumph of excess, exaggeration, and personality—and certainly no conductor ever made the final ten minutes seem more exultant or monumental—it was the Mahler First of a lifetime, and one we shouldn't have expected to be bettered any time soon.

Leonard Bernstein's latest version *is* a recording of a gripping live performance—although "stupefying" would be far closer to the point. While the first two movements sound more serene and bucolic than usual—the *Ländler* is an amusing country bumpkin affair—the Funeral March is straight out of Edgar Allen Poe (or possibly Alfred Hitchcock) and the *Finale* is one of those apocalyptic firestorms that threatens to incinerate everything in sight.

Symphony No. 2 in C Minor, "Resurrection"

Schwarzkopf, soprano; Rössl-Majdan, mezzo-soprano; Philharmonia
Chorus and Orchestra, Klemperer. EMI Classics CDM 69662 [CD].

Augér, soprano; Baker, mezzo-soprano; City of Birmingham
Symphony and Chorus, Rattle. EMI Classics CDCB 47962 [CD].

When Leonard Bernstein's final recording of the "Resurrection" Symphony was first released, most of the critics pounced all over it for its alleged self-indulgence and exaggerations. Of course, to say that of *any* performance of this inherently self-indulgent and exaggerated work would have been a bit like busting a Sodom and Gomorrah city councilman for indecent exposure. In fact, the recordings of the "Resurrection" that fail most decisively—those by Kubelik, Maazel, and Sinopoli, for example—are those that try to make the Symphony more polite, coherent, and civilized than it can possibly be. To his great credit, Bernstein simply yanks out all the stops and allows this paradoxical hodgepodge of pathos, bathos, banality, and nobility to speak eloquently—and unforgettably—for itself.

Unfortunately, Bernstein's recording can only be had as part of Deutsche Grammophon's thirteen-CD set of the complete symphonies (435162-2). Although this may represent a daunting investment to the average collector, each of the performances is full of the conductor's special insights and manic authority, making his versions of the First, Third, Sixth, and Ninth uniquely satisfying (see below).

As a young pianist and aspiring conductor, Otto Klemperer used his piano reduction of the "Resurrection" Symphony's *Scherzo* as a means of impressing the composer; Mahler *was* duly impressed, and after writing a glowing recommendation to the director of Prague's German Opera, subsequently engaged Klemperer as an assistant to lead the off-stage orchestra. After Bruno Walter, no one had a longer or more distinguished association with the Mahler symphonies than Klemperer, and with his Job-like succession of physical and emotional calamities, who was better qualified to understand a work called "Resurrection"? Digitally remastered onto a single CD, Klemperer's performance remains an overwhelming experience: titanic, transcendent, and—in its closing bars—bathed in a blinding, heavenly light.

Among more recent recordings, Sir Simon Rattle's glowing version is as impressive as his exceptional recording of the Seventh (see below). The playing and singing constantly flirt with the superhuman, while the stunning recorded sound captures both the grandeur of the interpretation and its phenomenal wealth of detail.

Symphony No. 3 in D minor

Procter, mezzo-soprano; Wandsworth School Boys Choir, Ambrosian
Singers, London Symphony, Horenstein. Unicorn-Kanchana
UKCD-2006/07 [CD].

Ludwig, mezzo-soprano; Brooklyn Boys Choir, New York Choral
Artists, New York Philharmonic, Bernstein. Deutsche Grammophon
423328-2 [CD].

Baker, mezzo-soprano; London Symphony Orchestra and Chorus,
Thomas. CBS M2K 44553 [CD].

The longest symphony ever written by a major composer—and because of
that, one of the few classical works that earns a place in the *Guinness Book of
World Records*—the Third is obviously one of the more challenging Mahler symphonies to perform. In concert, it can make for a long and uncomfortable evening
if the conductor has not done his homework; in the living room, it can offer
countless excuses to turn off the receiver and see what's on TV.

And yet for all its daunting challenges, the Third has probably accounted
for more important recordings than any other Mahler symphony, led by the three
listed here. As extravagant as it may sound for such a work—the Mahler Third
is hardly the Beethoven Fifth—I would suggest buying all three recordings: not
only because I am unable to distinguish a clear-cut winner, but also because I
would be unwilling—wild horses notwithstanding—to be dragged away from the
other two.

The oldest of the three, Jascha Horenstein's famous utterance of a generation ago, only seems to grow in stature over the years. Both in terms of sweep and
detail, he hardly misses a trick. The first movement marches in with a beautiful
relentlessness, and the *Finale,* taken at a dangerously slow pace, more than justi-
fies Horenstein's courage: here it sounds like the greatest single movement in all
of Mahler.

The Bernstein recording, taped at a live performance, is also overwhelming.
(Mark Swed, the critic I trust more than any other, was present at the concert and
came away talking to himself.) The relatively dry acoustics can't compromise either the lush romance or the cumulative power of the performance; it is—as it
should be—a thoroughly exhausting experience.

If Michael Tilson Thomas does not yet have the reputation of being a great
Mahler conductor, then his version of the Third should change that immediately.
Huge in scale, meticulous in its ornamentation, and bursting with energy, it more
than holds its own with those of his older colleagues—which is to say, with the
finest Mahler recordings ever made.

Again, each of these triumphant releases is an unqualified winner. If you
must narrow it down to only one, I suggest you toss a three-headed coin.

Symphony No. 4 in G Major

Raskin, soprano; Cleveland Orchestra, Szell. Sony Classical SBK 46535 [CD]; SBT 46535 [T].

It is with this most concise, charming, and popular of the Mahler symphonies that most people find their way into the composer's music: the Mahlerian equivalent of Bruckner's "Romantic" Symphony. Yet like that other Fourth Symphony, the Mahler G Major is probably the composer's least characteristic work. Genial, untroubled, and—except for a few dark moments in the third movement—completely lacking in any neurotic symptoms, the Fourth is as happy as Mahler can become and still remain Mahler. Even the inevitable presentiment of death in the *Finale* is a singularly trusting and innocent vision of heaven provided through the eyes of a child.

George Szell's classic 1965 interpretation remains one of the most completely successful Mahler recordings ever made. With a charm and glowing humanity that many of his enemies rarely accused him of possessing, Szell handles the music with a deceptively relaxed but always exceedingly firm grip. Climaxes—even the shattering one at the end of the third movement—merely seem to happen, and in fact the entire performance creates the illusion of unfolding by itself, without the intervention of human will.

The late Judith Raskin gives one of the most engrossingly spontaneous performances of her brilliant career in the final movement; the Cleveland Orchestra has never been better; and in spite of some slightly intrusive hiss from the original analogue tapes, the compact disc restoration is remarkably fine.

Symphony No. 5 in C-sharp Minor

Chicago Symphony, Solti. London 414321-2 [CD]; 433329-4 [T].

Chicago is a still a town that suffers from its age-old "Second City" complex and is hence a place where superlatives tend to get thrown around more casually than anywhere else. The local Republican newspaper, the *Chicago Tribune*, calls itself "The World's Greatest Newspaper" on the masthead, hence the call letters of its television and radio stations WGN. WLS, its Sears-owned competitor, is a reminder of "The World's Largest Store." Only in Chicago would things like the World's Tallest Building (the Sears Tower) or the World's Busiest Airport (O'Hare International) be pointed to as objects of civic pride, and only in Chicago would the city's orchestra, fresh from its first European tour, be cheered by a crowd who had probably not, for the most part, ever set foot in a concert hall, with banners proclaiming it (what else?) the World's Greatest Orchestra.

I was there in Orchestra Hall when Sir Georg Solti led an absolutely spell-binding performance of the Mahler Fifth during his first season as music director of the Chicago Symphony. The recording that was made several weeks later not only captured much of the overwhelming excitement of the interpretation but also served to announce that the orchestra, after its stormy association with Solti's predecessor Jean Martinon, was at last back on form. They *do* sound very much like the World's Greatest Orchestra in one of the first recordings they made with their new music director. The woodwinds and brass negotiate this difficult music with supreme confidence and bravado, and the strings—both in the famous, gentle *Adagietto* and in the whirlwind *Finale*—give Solti everything he asks for, which here amounts to the last word in excitement and finesse. Along with the playing itself—and this is, by a comfortable margin, the best-played Mahler Fifth ever released—Solti's interpretation is a subtle yet powerfully dramatic one, and the somewhat harsh sound of the original recording has been improved considerably.

Warning! Do not confuse this recording with the conductor's far less compelling 1990 remake (433329-2 [CD], 433329-4 [T]), in which all concerned seem to be doing little more than going through the motions.

Symphony No. 6 in A Minor, "Tragic"

Vienna Philharmonic, Bernstein. Deutsche Grammophon
427697-2 [CD].

The Sixth Symphony occupies a unique position in Mahler's output as perhaps the most paradoxical work that this endlessly paradoxical composer would ever produce. It is simultaneously the most objective and deeply personal of all his symphonies, the most rigorous in its formal organization, and the most devastating in its emotional effect. It is the only one of his ten completed works in the form—including *Das Lied von der Erde*—which, in its original version, adhered to the traditional format of the classical symphony, and the only one that ends on a note of catastrophic, inconsolable despair.

Bernstein's DG version of this dark masterpiece easily eclipses his earlier CBS recording, which in its day was the most compelling recorded performance available. Although the conductor's tempo in the first movement might seem a shade brisk to some, his shaping of the problematical *Finale* is nothing short of masterly. The music rises heroically after each of the catastrophes signaled by one of those famous "hammer blows of fate," while the desolation he conjures in the final bars gives you the chilling feeling that someone has just walked on your grave. Thomas Hampson's beautifully sung *Kindertotenlieder* is the extremely attractive bonus.

Symphony No. 7 in E Minor

City of Birmingham Symphony, Rattle. EMI Classics CDC 54244 [CD].

The Seventh is easily the most difficult of all the Mahler symphonies to approach and, finally, to love. In the mysterious *Scherzo,* flanked by two movements called *Nachtmusik,* the composer wrote some of his most harmonically adventurous, forward-looking music. And if the opening movement presents more than its share of structural problems, the *Finale* has always seemed, in comparison, utterly fragmented and frightfully banal.

In a pirated tape of a live London Symphony concert that has had a vigorous circulation in the underground market, Jascha Horenstein proved conclusively that the symphony's many problems are only surface deep. Not only was the conductor's grasp of the subtle, complex atmosphere of the three central movements amazing, but he was also able to make the usually thin-sounding, patchwork *Finale* seem as cogent and triumphant as the finale of the Mahler Fifth.

Simon Rattle makes the point even more dramatically. Recorded in concert at the Aldeburgh Festival, the performance is one of the most thrilling that *any* Mahler symphony has ever been given on records. In addition to an opening movement of incomparable thrust and power, the central movements are so brilliantly characterized that the *Scherzo* and especially the second *Nachtmusik* for once don't seem too long. Yet it is in the final movement that Rattle moves from the ranks of the very good Mahler conductors to those of the great. The tempo relationships are so brilliantly judged that at no point is the movement's forward momentum allowed to flag, thereby creating a unique feeling of rightness and inevitability. The playing is not only phenomenally accurate but also burns with a fierce conviction and that sense of excitement that only a live performance can provide. If you have any lingering doubts about Mahler's problem child, then this is the performance to clear them up.

Symphony No. 8 in E-flat Major, "Symphony of a Thousand"

Augér, Harper, Popp, Minton, Watts, Kollo, Shirley-Quirk, Talvela, Vienna State Opera Chorus, Vienna Singverein, Vienna Boys Choir, Chicago Symphony, Solti. London 414493-2 [CD].

Sir Georg Solti said in print that he considered the Eighth the greatest of the Mahler symphonies, and from this stupendous Chicago Symphony recording, taped in Vienna, even the most rabid admirers of the Sixth and Ninth would be tempted to agree. Produced on a singularly tight recording schedule—and the tension, at times, is almost palpable—Solti unleashes the greatness of the music in a way that even Leonard Bernstein, in his famous London Symphony recording, is not quite able to match.

The performance of the opening movement, a setting of the medieval hymn *Veni creator spiritus,* is almost withering in its joyous excitement, and the lengthy setting of the closing scene from Part I of Goethe's *Faust* is wonderfully operatic, in the best possible sense of the world. Solti loses no opportunity to exploit either the high drama or the endless color of the score, from the hushed and sinister opening bars of the second movement to the vast and vastly moving chorus with which the symphony concludes. The massed choruses sing with tremendous accuracy and enthusiasm, and the performance boasts the strongest collection of soloists of any Mahler Eighth on the market today. Yet it is the superhuman playing of the Chicago Symphony that tips the scales—perhaps forever—in Solti's favor. Rumor has it that members of the Vienna Philharmonic who attended the recording sessions were deeply shaken by what they heard. Many left the hall speechless, while others were heard mumbling incoherently to themselves.

Symphony No. 9

Amsterdam Concertgebouw Orchestra, Bernstein. Deutsche Grammophon 435378-2 [CD].

Even before that historic series of concerts in May of 1920, when Willem Mengelberg presided over the first important festival of his friend's music, the Amsterdam Concertgebouw Orchestra has enjoyed the longest unbroken Mahler tradition of any of the world's major orchestras. The composer himself was a frequent guest conductor in Amsterdam, and in addition to Mengelberg's famous interpretations, those of his successors, Eduard van Beinum and Bernard Haitink, have gone a long way toward cementing the Concertgebouw Orchestra's reputation as the finest Mahler orchestra in the world. Fortunately, in recent years, the greatest living Mahler conductor has begun to appear with them on a regular basis, and this live performance of the Ninth Symphony must now be counted with the three or four greatest Mahler recordings yet made.

In the two decades since his New York Philharmonic recordings became the principal impetus for the modern Mahler revival, Leonard Bernstein's approach to the composer's music has both deepened and grown more extreme. The surface drama has become increasingly turbulent—his detractors have called it "self-indulgent" and "overwrought"—while its deeper implications have been plumbed with an understanding that is ever more lucid and profound.

This live Concertgebouw performance of the composer's most shattering work is a triumph of extremes. Where other conductors have been intense in this music, Bernstein is almost savagely so; where others have heard the final movement as Mahler's poignant farewell to life, Bernstein transforms it into the stuff of universal tragedy, a farewell to *all* life, possibility, and hope. In essence, the conductor's most recent version of this great work is as much Bernstein's Ninth as it is Gustav Mahler's. Besides, during the final years of Lenny's life, the distinction really *had* begun to blur.

Symphony No. 10 (unfinished; performing edition prepared by Deryck Cooke)

Bournemouth Symphony, Rattle. EMI Classics CDC 54406 [CD].

As controversial as the "finished" Tenth Symphony continues to be, there is little question that Deryck Cooke's performing version amounts to the most impressive piece of musical detective work in recent history or that this particular recording is the most convincing ever made commercially available. (A live performance by Jean Martinon and the Chicago Symphony, burning with ferocious conviction and long a legend among Mahler collectors, could be gotten for a time as part of an album celebrating the orchestra's one-hundredth anniversary.) In addition to a devastating performance of the opening *Adagio*—the only movement Mahler lived to complete—Rattle is so persuasive in the reconstructed movements that any objections must be filed on grounds of principle, which famous Mahlerians like Bernstein, Horenstein, and Solti clearly had.

Similarly, Rattle's version of the youthful *Das klagende Lied* is the most satisfying yet recorded, effortlessly bringing out all the delightfully gruesome joy of this penny-dreadful tale of murder and supernatural revenge. If at this early stage in their collaboration, the City of Birmingham Symphony was not quite the brilliantly disciplined instrument it would soon become, the playing has tremendous energy and character, as does the singing of the chorus and soloists, especially that of the late Alfreda Hodgson.

Marcello, Alessandro (1684–1750)

Concerto for Oboe and Strings

Holliger, oboe; I Musici. Philips 420189-2 [CD].

If far less celebrated as a composer than his younger brother Benedetto—a poet, painter, mathematician, and philosopher, the elder Marcello composed under the pseudonym Eterio Stinfalico after his election to the Arcadian

Academy—then the most famous work either would write was the Oboe Concerto in D Minor once attributed to Benedetto (and initially to Vivaldi) but now definitely known to be the work of Alessandro Marcello. Among its many admirers were Johann Sebastian Bach, who transcribed it as his Harpsichord Concerto, S. 974, and practically every important oboist who has recorded it since the '60s Baroque Revival.

Heinz Holliger gives a characteristically meticulous and exciting performance accompanied by I Musici, this from an unusually desirable Philips anthology of popular baroque oboe concertos. In addition to works by Albinoni, Lotti, and Sammartini, the album offers the popular Oboe Concerto that the Australian composer Arthur Benjamin adapted from four harpsichord sonatas of Domenico Cimarosa.

Marek, Czeslaw (1891–1985)

Méditations for Orchestra, Op. 14; *Sinfonia for Orchestra*, Op. 28; *Suite for Orchestra*, Op. 25

Philharmonia Orchestra, Brain. Koch Classics KDC 6439 [CD].

Like Jean Sibelius and the Englishman Howard Ferguson, the Polish-born composer Czeslaw Marek was one of those rare composers who simply gave up composition in mid-life. As pathologically modest as he was independently wealthy, Marek wrote nothing after 1940 and, for the remaining forty-five years of his life, steadfastly refused to allow public performances of his works, much less commercial recordings.

This first in a projected series of recordings of Marek's entire output presents a finely honed late-Romantic sensibility guided by an appealing individuality and love of meticulous craftsmanship, already obvious in the brilliantly scored *Méditations for Orchestra*, composed when Marek was twenty-two. While the *Suite* from 1926 is even more finished and imaginative, the *Sinfonia* of 1928 is clearly the work of an emerging master: confident, resourceful, and succinctly argued, with its many disparate elements beautifully balanced and controlled. (One wonders what would have happened to Marek's career had the *Sinfonia* not been barely beaten out by Atterberg's Symphony No. 6 in the 1928 Schubert Centenary Competition.)

Gary Brain and the Philharmonia Orchestra offer passionately enthusiastic, stunningly recorded performances of all three works, making the adventurous listener very eager for more.

Martin, Frank (1890–1974)

Concerto for Seven Wind Instruments, Percussion, and Strings; *Petite Symphonie Concertante; Six Monologues from Jedermann*

Soloists, L'Orchestre de la Suisse Romande, Jordan. Erato 2292-45694-2 [CD].

It's both astonishing and inexplicable that the music of Frank Martin, the greatest composer that Switzerland has ever produced and one of the most distinctive musical voices of the twentieth century, isn't far better known. Like the work of any truly major composer, Martin's music creates and inhabits a unique sonic world, with a refined sense of color and texture, an emotional range and depth, and a rigorous—though by no means rigid—internal logic and order unmistakably its own. Although he was touched by most of the major twentieth-century movements, from the Impressionism of Debussy through the French neo-Classicism of the 1920s to Schoenberg's twelve-tone techniques, Martin remained an utterly distinctive voice in modern music and one whose present neglect is a perplexing mystery.

Each of the works contained on this superb Erato recording has a fair claim to being Martin's masterpiece, from the *Six Monologues from Jedermann,* a setting of excerpts from Hugo von Hoffmansthal's dark and despairing *Everyman* that ranks with the greatest twentieth-century song cycles, to those two dazzling reinterpretations of the *Sinfonia concertante* that established Martin's early reputation in the 1940s. The performances are all sympathetic and compelling—the *Petite symphonie concertante* particularly so—and the recording is ideally warm, detailed, and spacious.

Yet even more exciting for admirers of Martin's music is the brilliant new cycle of recordings recently launched by Chandos. It was with his series of *ballades* for various solo instruments and orchestra that Martin's mature style first began to crystallize in the late 1930s. Matthias Bamert's integral recording with the London Philharmonic (CHAN 9380 [CD]) is therefore not to be missed, especially since in the case of the *Ballade for Alto Saxophone and Orchestra,* the *Ballade for Cello and Orchestra,* and the meditative *Ballade for Viola, Winds, Harpsichord, and Harp*—written when the composer was eighty-two—there are no other available recordings. Yet even where Bamert faces serious competition—in the *Ballade for Flute, String Orchestra, and Piano,* the *Ballade for Piano and Orchestra,* and the *Ballade for Trombone and Orchestra*—his meticulous yet freshly imaginative interpretations are to be preferred to all others.

Two other installments in the series are equally valuable: the first recording (CHAN 9312 [CD]) of the haunting, impressionistic Symphony from 1937, coupled with the *Symphonie concertante*—an arrangement for full orchestra of the

Petite symphonie concertante—and the 1962 orchestration of the powerful *Passacaglia* for organ. Another album (CHAN 9465 [CD]) brings together two unassailable masterworks: the intensely moving *In terra pax,* commissioned by Radio Geneva in 1944 to be ready for performance on the day World War II ended, and the magically scored *Les quatre éléments,* composed in 1967 for the eightieth birthday of his old friend Ernest Ansermet.

Martinů, Bohuslav (1890–1959)

The Epic of Gilgamesh

> **Soloists, Slovak Philharmonic Chorus and Orchestra, Kosler. Marco Polo 8.223316 [CD].**

With the work of his Polish near contemporary Karol Szymanowski, the music of the Czech composer Bohuslav Martinů remains one of the last largely undiscovered treasure troves of twentieth-century music. Like Szymanowski, Martinů was a restless eclectic whose music nevertheless spoke with a unique and thoroughly original voice. In all of the more than four hundred works he eventually produced, one can hear the same quality that so impressed Igor Stravinsky in the music of Sergei Prokofiev—an elusive commodity that Stravinsky called "the instant imprint of personality."

Nowhere is that personality heard to more original or powerful effect than in the vast *Epic of Gilgamesh,* based on the Babylonian poem—thought to be civilization's oldest—that Martinů set to music in 1954. Like the music that Szymanowski composed for the cathedral scene in his opera *King Roger,* Martinů's choral writing is infused with an eerie, almost medieval grandeur that serves the ancient tale exceedingly well. The performers respond to this hypnotic and mysterious score with enthusiasm and devotion, as do the Marco Polo engineers. Admirers of Honegger's *Le Roi David* or Walton's *Belshazzar's Feast* will find *Gilgamesh* no less compelling.

Frescos of Piero della Francesca; Double Concerto for Two String Orchestras, Piano, and Timpani

> **Soloists, Prague Radio Symphony, Mackerras. Supraphon SUP 3276 [CD].**

The Swiss conductor Paul Sacher commissioned Martinů's *Double Concerto* for his Basel Chamber Orchestra in 1938, two years after he introduced Bartók's *Music for Strings, Percussion, and Celesta.* While considerably less well-known than Bartók's masterpiece, the *Double Concerto*—unleashed by the composer's anguish over the recently signed Munich Pact that allowed the Nazi occupation of the Sudentenland—is every bit its equal. Concentrated, sweepingly dramatic, and vibrantly alive, it is one of the most powerfully inventive orchestral scores of the twentieth century. By that same token, the *Frescos of Piero della Francesca*, written following a motor tour of Italy in 1955, is one of Martinů's most accessible and physically beautiful scores.

Sir Charles Mackerras here proves that he speaks Martinů's distinctive language as fluently as he speaks Janáček's. As in his brilliant—though alas, now-deleted—recording of the colorful ballet *Špaliček*, there seems to be no detail of the often complex texture that he doesn't clarify or make even more beautiful. The Prague Radio Symphony has never sounded better and the recording, while somewhat reverberant, is nonetheless well focused and clear.

Nonet; *La Revue de cuisine*; Trio in F Major for Flute, Cello, and Piano

The Dartington Ensemble. Hyperion CDA 66084 [CD].

In addition to bringing us some of the finest performances of Martinů's chamber music that have yet been made, this invaluable Hyperion recording by England's Dartington Ensemble also provides a representative cross section of the three major phases of Martinů's creative life. *La Revue de cuisine* is a sassy, jazzy ballet produced during the composer's nineteen-year stay in Paris, while the Trio in F, composed during Martinů's American exile in 1944, is one of the most Czech and ebullient of all his works. Yet the gem of the collection is the bright and deceptively simple-sounding Nonet, composed five months before the composer's death in 1959. In its serenity, melodic inventiveness, and structural elegance, it is easily one of the most nearly perfect and instantly enjoyable chamber works written since the end of the Second World War.

A stunning Supraphon recording by the Panocha String Quartet (SUP 110994 [CD]) features the seven string quartets that Martinů composed between 1918 and 1947. While the level of inspiration might not be quite as consistently high as it is in the composer's symphonies, the best of them—especially the Fifth and Sixth—rank not far behind those of Bartók and Schoenberg. The performances are excellent, as is the recorded sound.

Piano Concertos 2–4

Firkušný, piano; Czech Philharmonic, Pešek. RCA 09026-91634-2 [CD].

It's difficult to imagine a more fitting or moving tribute to the late Rudolf Firkušný than this recording made in Czechoslovakia during the summer of 1993, when the pianist returned home to a hero's welcome after an absence of more than forty years. As Firkušný had introduced all three of these concertos and was the dedicatee of the Third, it goes without saying that the performances are definitive; the music itself is extremely rewarding, especially the Fourth Concerto, called *Incantations,* one of the most probing and inventive works of Martinů's final period.

For those of us who were lucky enough to know this lovely gentleman, this seems an ideal memorial.

La Revue de cuisine; Sonatine for Clarinet and Piano; *Pastorals (Stowe);* Quartet for Clarinet, Horn, Cello, and Side Drum

> **Zukovsky, clarinet; Bohemian Ensemble of Los Angeles. Summit DCD 214 [CD].**

Except for *La Revue de cuisine,* all of the works on this enchanting album are virtually unknown. Composed in 1956 when a dejected Martinů was living in New York, the Sonatine for Clarinet barely conceals its composer's intense longing for home; the oddly scored Quartet dates from 1924 and clearly shows the influence of his Parisian neighbors Igor Stravinsky and Arthur Honegger. Most interesting of all, though, is the *Pastorals (Stowe),* here receiving its first commercial recording. It was written in 1951 in Stowe, Vermont, for the same Trapp Family that would soon become the subject of Rodgers and Hammerstein's *Sound of Music.* Scored for five recorders, clarinet, two violins, and cello, it is one of Martinů's most disarming and loveable works.

Led by Michele Zukovsky, principal clarinet of the Los Angeles Philharmonic, the Bohemian Ensemble of Los Angeles—liberally peppered with other members of the orchestra—give such sparkling performances of all four works that one only hopes this will be the first in a series.

Symphonies (6)

> **Bamberg Symphony, Järvi. Bis CD-362 (Nos. 1 and 2); Bis CD-363 (Nos. 3 and 4); Bis CD-395 (Nos. 5 and 6).**

Neeme Järvi, the conductor of the Detroit Symphony (among other ensembles) is, to say the very least, an enigma. One of the most frequently recorded of contemporary conductors, he has plugged more holes in the catalogue than a hundred little Dutchboys could. In repertoire that is either unknown or well off the beaten track, the burly Estonian tends to be vigorous, imaginative, and persuasive.

Some of his most valuable contributions to date are the recordings of the six Martinů symphonies made for the Swedish label, Bis. The decision to use the

Bamberg Symphony—as opposed to his Gothenberg Orchestra—was a wise one. The idiomatic, intensely committed playing of the orchestra may have something to do with the fact that the Bamberg Symphony was originally founded after the communist take-over in 1949 by Czechoslovakian refugees.

Since Martinů did not produce a symphony until he was already fifty-two, all six are the products of a fully mature musical personality. The First, a gleaming, rhythmically ingenious work commissioned by Serge Koussevitzky, was followed by the relaxed and rustic Second, Martinů's "Pastoral" Symphony. The Third is a brooding, violent, often desperate commentary on the events of World War II, while the Fourth, written in the spring of 1945, mixes joy, hope, and idyllic tenderness, with a *largo* whose depth and complexity rivals the somewhat more familiar *Largo* from Dvořák's "New World" Symphony. The Fifth is another of the composer's obstinately life-affirming statements, and the Sixth, the *Fantaisies symphoniques,* is the most ambitious and far-reaching of all his orchestral scores.

With playing and recorded sound that are both nearly perfect, this constitutes an ideal introduction to a major symphonic talent.

Martucci, Giuseppe (1856–1909)

La Canzone dei ricordi; Notturno

Madalin, mezzo-soprano; English Chamber Orchestra, Bonavera.
Hyperion CDA 66290 [CD].

Born in Capua in 1856, Giuseppe Martucci was the most important of those late-nineteenth-century Italian composers who consciously turned their backs on the nation's long-standing operatic tradition in favor of a return to instrumental music. After an early career as a touring keyboard virtuoso, his appointment as professor of piano at the Naples Conservatory in 1880 marked the beginning of a new phase in his artistic development. His impassioned advocacy of Brahms and Wagner—he led the Italian premiere of *Tristan und Isolde* in 1888—had a marked impact on the evolution of his own music: Brahms, in his love for clearly defined forms; Wagner, in his enthusiasm for vivid orchestration and adventurous chromatic harmonies. Among Martucci's most devoted admirers was his friend Arturo Toscanini, whose refusal to perform the Fascist anthem at an all-Martucci memorial concert in 1932 prompted the riot that hastened the conductor's self-imposed exile from Mussolini's Italy.

One of the few Italian song-cycles of the Romantic period, *La Canzone dei ricordi* (The Song of Remembrance) was begun in 1886 and completed in the following year. A setting of seven nostalgic poems by E. E. Pagliara, the cycle is one of the most physically gorgeous ever composed, full of an autumnal late-Romantic heartbreak tempered by an uncommon delicacy of expression. The young American mezzo Carol Madalin brings both a keen understanding and a sumptuous instrument to the proceedings, while Alfredo Bonavera provides some knowing and sensitive support. *La Canzone dei ricordi,* coupled with the ravishing *Notturno* and one of the best-available recordings of *Il Tramonto* by Martucci's pupil Ottorino Respighi, makes the album all the more desirable.

Mascagni, Pietro (1863–1945)

Cavalleria Rusticana

> **Milanov, Björling, Smith, Merrill, Robert Shaw Chorale, RCA Victor Symphony, Cellini. RCA Victor 6510-2-RG [CD].**

Long before he died in abject poverty and disgrace—like Giacomo Puccini, he had been one of Mussolini's most ardent supporters—Pietro Mascagni was one of the most tragic figures in operatic history. At the age of twenty-six, *Cavalleria Rusticana* made him world famous, and for the next fifty-six years he was condemned to live out his life haunted by an overwhelming early success that he was never able to repeat. "I was crowned before I was King," was the composer's own rueful assessment of his career, and history has been forced to agree.

While this lurid tale of betrayal and revenge has very little to do with "Rustic Chivalry," the literal translation of its title, *Cavalleria Rusticana* has remained the most justly popular one-act opera ever written. Like Leoncavallo's *I Pagliacci,* with which it is usually paired, Mascagni's masterpiece is the central work of the Italian *verismo* school. Like *"Pag," "Cav"* explodes with vivid drama and raw emotions, though it also boasts a musical subtlety and sensitivity to character that only the best of Puccini's mature operas can begin to match.

The recording that captures more of the opera's finesse and earthiness than any other is that classic RCA Victor recording from the mid-1950s, which has recently been released on compact disc. Zinka Milanov was one of the century's great Santuzzas. Passionate, vulnerable, immensely feminine, she was also equipped with a voice that was as physically impressive as those of Leontyne Price and Rosa Ponselle. This recording catches her at something past her prime, but with her temperament and most of her instrument still intact, the interpretation still makes for an overwhelming experience. With the insouciant and spectacularly well-sung Turiddu of Jussi Björling, and the sensitive, yet richly powerful and garlic-laden, conducting of Renato Cellini, this remains *the* recording of the opera to own.

With that other fine RCA recording with Renata Scotto, Placido Domingo, and the National Philharmonic conducted by James Levine currently unavailable, there is currently no modern recording of the opera that merits a serious recommendation.

Luciano Pavarotti is at his most appealing in the EMI Classics recording (CDCB-47905 [CD]) of Mascagni's "other" opera, *L'Amico Fritz,* which is as gently amusing and charming as *Cavalleria Rusticana* is seething and passionate. If there are no other moments in the score to match the famous "Cherry Duet," then the opera still holds up well to repeated use, especially in this warmly affecting 1969 recording that also offers the young Mirella Freni at the beginning of her career.

Mason, Daniel Gregory (1873–1953)

Quartet in G Minor (Based on Negro Themes)

Kohon Quartet. Vox CDX 5057 [CD].

Like his grandfather Lowell Mason, Daniel Gregory Mason was one of America's most distinguished music educators, teaching at Columbia University from 1910 to 1942 and authoring numerous books on musical subjects. As a composer, he is best remembered for the *Chanticleer* Overture—enthusiastically played by the Albany Symphony on New World 80321-2 [CD]—and the haunting Quartet in G Minor (Based on Negro Themes). As the subtitle suggests, each of the work's three movements contains material developed from black spirituals, including a richly harmonized version of *Deep River* that dominates the beautiful slow movement.

The Kohon String Quartet give the work a spirited performance on a Vox Box called *The Early String Quartet in the U.S.A,* which also includes capable performances of quartets by Chadwick, Loeffler, Foote, and Griffes (his *Two Sketches Based on Indian Themes*) and the Piano Quintet by Henry Hadley. The *real* oddity of the collection is a tiny quartet for open strings attributed to Benjamin Franklin. While none of the works are deathless masterpieces (except, perhaps, for the Griffes and Loeffler), they offer vigorous proof that the form was alive and very well during America's musical coming of age.

Massenet, Jules (1842–1912)

Manon

De Los Angeles, Legay, Dens, Borthayre, Berton, Chorus and
Orchestra of the Opéra-comique, Monteux. EMI Classics CDMC-
63549 [CD].

At the time of his death in 1912, the suave and urbane Jules Massenet was
one of the wealthiest composers who ever lived. His impeccably crafted, gently
sentimental operas are among the finest and most popular ever written by a
French composer. Audiences love them for their directness, dramatic realism, and
inexhaustible flow of lovely melody. Singers love them because they are so carefully and gracefully written that even the most demanding Massenet role will invariably make even a fair or barely adequate singer sound exceptionally good.

With the reappearance of the classic Monteux *Manon,* one of the great operatic recordings returns to the catalogue. Even those who normally do not respond to Victoria de los Angeles's singing—one opera-loving friend still insists on
referring to her as "an air-raid siren with feet"—cannot fail to be bowled over by
the freshness and sheer dramatic ingenuity of the performance. Monteux's conducting is a wonder of panache and aching sensitivity, the rest of the cast is splendid, and the only real drawback is the rather fierce recorded sound.

For those who absolutely must have more up-to-date sound, Beverly Sills is
at her most attractive in a fine EMI Classics recording conducted by Julius Rudel
(CDMC 69831 [CD]), while Sir Colin Davis's utterly memorable version of
Werther on Philips (416654-2) remains, with the Monteux *Manon,* one of the
most completely satisfying Massenet recordings ever made.

Chérubin, the composer's enchanting "sequel" to Mozart's *Marriage of
Figaro*—this time, the over-sexed Cherubino is in hot pursuit of the king's favorite dancer—is given a delectable performance by a starry cast that includes
Frederica von Stade, Samuel Ramey, June Anderson, and Dawn Upshaw on RCA
(09026-60593-2 [CD]), while the ingratiating *Don Quichotte,* which became one
of Feodor Chaliapin's great star vehicles, is brilliantly served by Nikolai
Ghiaurov, Gabriel Bacquier, and Régine Crespin on London (430636-2 [CD]).

Joan Sutherland and Richard Bonynge prove an irresistible combination
in the exotic *Le Roi de Lahore* (433851-2 [CD]), with its celebrated saxophone
waltz.

Mathias, William (1934–1992)

Dance Overture; Divertimento for String Orchestra; Invocation and Dance; Laudi; Prelude, Aria and Finale; Sinfonietta; Vistas

> **Various orchestras, Atherton, Davison. Lyrita SRCD 328 [CD].**

Born in Whitland, Carmarthenshire, educated at University College, Aberystwyth, William Mathias has a fair claim to being the most significant composer of serious music Wales has yet produced. Although occasionally influenced by Hindemith, Stravinsky, Walton, Tippett, and his teacher Lennox Berkeley, Mathias was also a diligent, often strikingly inventive craftsman who remained stubbornly determined to go his own way. The seven works included in this Lyrita anthology cover a period of roughly two decades, from the cheery *Divertimento for String Orchestra* from 1958, through the mystical *Vistas* of 1975, inspired by a trip to the United States. Most immediately appealing are the infectious *Dance Overture* of 1961 and the buoyant, jazzy *Sinfonietta,* written for a youth orchestra in 1967. The National Youth Orchestra of Wales plays the latter with obvious skill and enjoyment, while David Atherton leads various London orchestras in the rest with his customary insight and enthusiasm. This anthology is highly recommended for those on the lookout for new and exciting friends.

Maxwell Davies, Sir Peter (1934–)

Eight Songs for a Mad King; Miss Donnithorne's Maggot

> **Eastman, speaker; Thomas, mezzo-soprano; Fires of London, Davies.**
> **Unicorn DKPCD 9052 [CD].**

On first hearing *Eight Songs for a Mad King,* most people are flabbergasted. As well they should be, since it is the most frighteningly original musical work produced by an Englishman in this century.

Employing some of King George III's actual demented ruminations, the piece is so grotesque, poignant, ridiculous, touching, stupid, and powerful that it defies description. Julius Eastman, who "interprets" the role of the King, is quite unbelievable: his repertoire of sighs, shrieks, howls, and moans is astounding, as is his ability to draw us into the "mind" of the character and make us feel genuine compassion and concern.

Miss Donnithorne's Maggot, a similarly unhingeing tribute to the actual eccentric who provided Dickens with his model for Miss Havisham in *Great Expectations,* while it has many intriguing moments, pales in comparison to the *Songs.*

I should admit that when I first heard this dizzy work, I was convinced that everyone concerned with the project—composer, performers, recording company executives—was in *desperate* need of serious psychiatric care. I'm now fairly certain that *Eight Songs for a Mad King* is a major twentieth-century masterpiece.

An Orkney Wedding, with Sunrise

BBC Philharmonic, Maxwell Davies. Collins Classics 10952 [CD].

If it's difficult to think of this leading figure of the avant-garde as a composer of pops concert staples, then that is precisely what *An Orkney Wedding, with Sunrise* might one day become. A "picture postcard" of a traditional wedding on the Orkney island of Hoy, the thirteen-minute work includes a series of band tunes that build to an inebriated climax, after which the sun rises in the magnificent blaze of highland pipes. No less entertaining are the scintillating *Ojai Festival Overture,* the touching *Lullaby for Lucy*—celebrating the first birth in the Orkney valley of Rackwick in thirty-two years—and the "Foxtrot for orchestra on a pavan by John Bull," *St. Thomas Wake.*

Medtner, Nikolai (1880–1951)

Piano Concertos (2)

Demidenko, piano; BBC Scottish Symphony, Maksymiuk. Hyperion CDA 66580 [CD].

Like his near contemporary Sergei Rachmaninoff, the stubbornly old-fashioned Russian composer Nikolai Medtner was also a formidable pianist, as his own recordings of the last two of his three piano concertos, made in his late sixties, clearly attest. As exemplary as those famous recordings are, not even they can stand up to the searing energy of Nikolai Demidenko, who with this single album moved into the very front rank of the major young pianists of our time. His playing is so fiercely intense, the feats of pianistic legerdemain so breathtaking, that what can often seem like discursive, heavily padded scores emerge as the important Romantic piano concertos they probably aren't. If Jerzy Maksymiuk and the BBC Scottish Symphony can't quite match his protean brilliance, then it's difficult to think of anyone who could.

Demidenko's album of Medtner's solo piano music (CDA 66636 [CD]) is no less memorable, with immensely sophisticated performances of some of the composer's finest works, including the impassioned *Sonata Tragica* and the imaginative *Theme and Variations,* Op. 55. The superb playing is further enhanced by the luxurious acoustics of the Maltings, Snape.

Mendelssohn, Felix (1809–1847)

Piano Concerto No. 1 in G Minor, Op. 25; Piano Concerto No. 2 in D Minor, Op. 40

Perahia, piano; Academy of St. Martin-in-the-Fields, Marriner. CBS MK 42401 [CD].

While far less familiar than the justly ubiquitous Violin Concerto, Mendelssohn's Piano Concertos are full of memorable ideas and exquisite surface detail. And while they are easy on the ear and psyche, they are by no means powder puffs: the stormy opening movement of the G Minor is as substantial as anything in Mendelssohn and the slow movements of both concertos are superbly crafted and richly felt.

It's hardly surprising that such a fine Mozart pianist as Murray Perahia should be such a cunning advocate of these works, which so clearly have their roots in the eighteenth century. Their essentially Classical poise and structure is not lost on him, nor does he ignore that breath of early Romanticism that makes all of Mendelssohn's music what it is. Marriner, as always, is a witty and generous partner, and the CD version comes with equally impeccable performances of the Prelude and Fugue, Op. 35/1, the *Rondo capriccioso,* and the *Variations sérieuses.*

This is a must for Mendelssohn lovers or Perahia fans.

Violin Concerto in E Minor, Op. 64

Menuhin, violin; Berlin Philharmonic, Furtwängler. EMI Classics CDC 69799 [CD].

This fresh, buoyant, eternally sweet-spirited work is probably the best-loved violin concerto ever written. And in spite of the apparent effortlessness of its invention, the E Minor Concerto had an unusually long and painful gestation: from first sketch to finished score, it occupied the usually deft and facile composer's attention for the better part of six years.

While every important violinist of the century has recorded the work, and many of them more than once, there is still something very special in Sir Yehudi Menuhin's 1954 recording with Wilhelm Furtwängler and the Berlin Philharmonic. Unlike their monumental interpretation of the Beethoven Concerto, which fills out this unusually generous compact disc, the performance of Mendelssohn is a marvel of quiet intimacy and elfin grace. Menuhin's playing—which in recent years has been seriously compromised by a neurological disorder—was never more poignantly innocent than it is here, and the conductor, who had only a few months left to live, turns in one of the freshest and most impetuous of all his recorded performances.

With Cho-Liang Lin's inspirational Sony Classical recording unaccountably yanked from circulation, Itzhak Perlman's sparkling early recording with André Previn and the London Symphony has been reissued with an even finer version of the Bruch G Minor Concerto on EMI Classic's medium-priced "Red Line" series (CDR 69863 [CD]), making for an outstanding bargain.

Elijah, Op. 70 (oratorio)

Plowright, Finnie, Davies, White, London Symphony Orchestra and Chorus, Hickox. Chandos CHAN-8774/75 [CD].

From its startling opening recitative, which actually begins before the dirge-like overture, through such powerfully dramatic choruses as "Hear Our Cry, O Baal," *Elijah* is one of the great *de facto* Romantic operas: a gripping, lyrical, wonderfully theatrical work that, with a little lighting and makeup, could hold the stage as easily as the early Wagner operas.

The glowing performance led by the ever-imaginative Richard Hickox transforms *Elijah* into something very far removed from the sanctimonious Victorian monstrosity that Shaw used to complain about. This is vivid, utterly committed music making as well as compelling theater: Mendelssohn's inspiration shimmers in every bar and the drama is made to seem consistently immediate and real. Hickox's team of soloists is exemplary and the exhilarating work of the London Symphony Chorus only confirms his growing reputation as the preeminent European choral director since the legendary Wilhelm Pitz.

For those in whom the Old Testament grandeur of *Elijah* strikes a responsive chord, Mendelssohn's New Testament oratorio, *St. Paul,* can be found on Erato 45279-2 [CD] in a devout and moving performance led by Michel Corboz.

A *Midsummer Night's Dream* (incidental music), Op. 21 and 61

Watson, Wallis, London Symphony Chorus and Orchestra, Previn. EMI Classics CDC 47163 [CD].

The famous overture that Felix Mendelssohn composed for Shakespeare's Festive Comedy, *A Midsummer Night's Dream,* has a fair claim to being the greatest single musical work ever written by a teenager. Only Mozart and Schubert produced music of similar quality at a comparable age. The remainder of the incidental music that Mendelssohn would write over the next twenty years was also of a very high caliber, including the finest example of a form he would make forever his own, the quicksilver *Scherzo,* and one of the most famous five minutes in all of music, the stirring and, for many, bloodcurdling *Wedding March,* to whose famous strains countless freedom-loving people have trooped off to join the ranks of the Living Dead.

On records, André Previn has established a hard-earned reputation as one of the finest interpreters of the music of the major modern English composers and of other mainline twentieth-century figures from Rachmaninoff and Prokofiev, to Debussy and Ravel. That he is equally comfortable in the mainstream of the Austro-German tradition is amply documented by a recording like this one, in which he proves, quite conclusively, I think, that he is the finest Mendelssohn conductor in the world today.

All of the familiar moments—the *Overture, Scherzo, Intermezzo, Nocturne,* and the *Wedding March*—are invested with an exhilarating freshness and immensely individual character, while the less familiar set pieces and linking passages are given a weight and significance that no other recording can begin to match. The spooky menace and rhythmic point of *You Spotted Snakes* is alone worth the price of the recording.

Octet in E-flat for Strings, Op. 20

Academy of St. Martin-in-the-Fields Chamber Ensemble. Philips 420400-2 [CD].

When I was sixteen, I read something from the second volume of George Bernard Shaw's *Dramatic Opinions and Essays* that struck a painfully responsive chord:

> With the single exception of Homer, there is no eminent writer, not even Sir Walter Scott, whom I can despise so entirely as I despise Shakespeare when I measure my mind against his. It would positively be a relief to me to dig him up and throw stones at him.

At a time when I was wasting my life fighting acne and the oboe, yelling at girls, and trying to beat out three other guys for one of the two defensive end spots on my high-school football team, Felix Mendelssohn was composing his miraculously inspired E-flat Major Octet. After weeks of excruciating soul-searching, leavened by the then major triumphs of making the team, and thereby attracting the attentions of an exceedingly cute cheerleader, I resolved to stop hating Mendelssohn by simply facing the irrefutable facts. I was a perfectly normal Midwest high-school kid; he was a genius.

Nowhere is Mendelssohn's youthful brilliance revealed more felicitously than in the finest single work ever composed for this particular combination of instruments. The level of melodic inspiration and richness of ornamental detail is so phenomenal that the Octet is obviously the work of a mature master, not a boy of sixteen. This superlative recording captures almost all of the Octet's melting warmth and blindingly brilliant inspiration.

Overtures

Bamberg Symphony, Flor. RCA 07863-57905-2 [CD].

With Weber, Berlioz, and Rossini, Mendelssohn was one of the supreme early-Romantic masters of the concert overture, as this delightful RCA collection readily proves. In addition to the familiar warhorses *Midsummer Night's Dream* and *Fingal's Cave*—which has not had a more atmospheric, darkly mysterious performance since Furtwängler's in the early '30s—*Calm Sea and Prosperous Voyage* and *Ruy Blas* are marvelous works, while *Athalia* and the overture to his first opera, *The Marriage of Camacho,* will come as delightful surprises.

Claus Peter Flor and the Bamberg Symphony have yet to make a finer recording than this one. There is a freshness and sense of discovery in the playing, coupled with an aristocratic control that makes it difficult to imagine that any more completely satisfying recordings will be showing up any time soon. Like the performances, the recorded sound is immaculate.

Piano Music

Frith, piano. Naxos 8.550939 [CD]; 8.550940 [CD].

Listening to these first two volumes in Naxos's series of Mendelssohn's complete piano music, one wonders again why this marvelous music is so little played. Apart from the *Variations sérieuses* and the occasional *Song without Words,* most of the composer's elegant, consistently engaging piano works are unfamiliar to the majority of listeners for reasons that remain unfathomable. From the composer's youthful E Major Sonata of 1826—the year of the

Midsummer Night's Dream Overture—to his most substantial Bach homage, the six Preludes and Fugues, Op. 35, this is generally top-drawer Mendelssohn: tuneful, capricious, exceedingly well-made music.

As fine as Martin Jones's admirable Nimbus cycle certainly is, the new one by the young British pianist Benjamin Frith promises to be finer still. His playing has an endearing wit and newly minted freshness, together with a complete technical security not always obvious from his rival. Even the thorniest of the Fugues are tossed off with a relaxed abandon, while the *Scherzo in B Minor* and *Perpetuum mobile in C* sparkle with fairy dust. Add first-rate recorded sound and the super-budget price, and Naxos gives us yet another reason for rejoicing.

Songs without Words

Barenboim, Piano. Deutsche Grammophon 423931-2 [CD].

Along with being able to hear the *William Tell Overture* without immediately thinking of the Lone Ranger, one of the acid tests of the true music lover is the ability to listen to Mendelssohn's "Spring Song" without breaking into fits of convulsive laughter. With the second *Hungarian Rhapsody,* it was pilloried in more cartoons of the 1940s and '50s than any other musical work, and its unaffected innocence *can* degenerate into saccharine ditziness if the performer fails to treat it like the delicate blossom that it is.

Unlike so many performances of the *Songs without Words* that have treated these magical, fragile miniatures like Victorian potted palms, Daniel Barenboim's reveal the wondrous little tone poems that lay buried beneath the decades of calcified interpretive treacle. While obviously affectionate, the interpretations have just enough twinkle of wit to prevent things from getting mushy. And even when the pianist does turn on the ooze, he does so with a charming old-world graciousness—which is a pretty neat trick for a musician born in 1942.

String Quartets (complete)

Coull String Quartet. Hyperion CDS 44051/3 [CD].

The comparative neglect of the Mendelssohn quartets in both the concert hall and recording studio remains a perplexing mystery: from the early pair, written when the precocious composer was still in his teens, to the masterful trio published as his Opus 41, these rank with the finest chamber works produced during the entire Romantic era.

Like the Melos Quartet before them—whose recently deleted Deutsche Grammophon cycle is slated, one hopes, for a medium-priced reissue—the Coull Quartet prove ideally suited to this wonderful collection, with playing that is as fresh, ardent, and carefully thought out as the music itself. Interpretively, their identification with the idiom seems absolutely complete, from the mercurial wit of the Scherzos to the gentlemanly romance of the slow movements. Not surprisingly, the recorded sound, notes, and packaging are fully worthy of the performances themselves.

Symphonies (12) for String Orchestra

English String Orchestra, Boughton. Nimbus NI 5141/43 [CD].

Mendelssohn's String Symphonies scarcely sound like what they are: the apprentice work of a composer not yet out of knee pants. Written for concerts in the comfortable family home on the fashionable Neue Promenade in Berlin, the earliest were composed when Mendelssohn was only twelve, the latest when he was fourteen. They show such an astonishing confidence and a fertility of invention that it's easy to hear why the aging Goethe, on meeting Mendelssohn during this period, accepted the frail boy on terms of absolute equality.

The performances by the English String Orchestra under William Boughton are as full of youthful enthusiasm as the works themselves. No attempt is made to inflate the music beyond its inherent limits or to make it seem more significant than it is. The result is playing of the utmost naturalness and grace, which lets these precocious little charmers speak for themselves.

Symphony No. 1 in C Minor, Op. 11; Symphony No. 5 in D, Op. 107, "Reformation"

Bamberg Symphony, Flor. RCA 09026-60391-2 [CD].

With his youthful C Minor Symphony, Mendelssohn first conquered England. Following its world premiere in London on March 31, 1824, the composer endeared himself to both the orchestra and the audience by personally shaking hands with every member of the London Philharmonic. In spite of its late-sounding opus number, the "Reformation" Symphony is also an early work. In it, Felix Mendelssohn enthusiastically quotes Martin Luther's *Ein' feste Burg ist unser Gott* (although one can only wonder what the composer's philosopher grandfather Moses—the "Jewish Plato"—would have made of his grandson's homage to a man who was so notoriously anti-Semitic).

As in their recording of Mendelssohn overtures, the performances by Claus Peter Flor and the Bamberg Symphony are fresh and inventive in addition to being immaculately played, making this one of the most attractive Mendelssohn recordings now available.

Symphony No. 3 in A Minor, Op. 56, "Scottish"

London Symphony, Maag. London 433023-2 [CD].

Chicago Symphony, Solti. London 414665-2 [CD].

It is no accident that in Great Britain, Felix Mendelssohn is revered as one of the most important of all composers. In addition to writing the incidental music for Shakespeare's *Midsummer Night's Dream,* he supplied the oratorio-mad English with *Elijah,* one of the greatest nineteenth-century examples of their favorite form of musical entertainment. And with the *Hebrides Overture* and the "Scottish" Symphony—the latter dedicated to Queen Victoria—he wrote two of the best and most popular of all musical travelogues based on British themes.

Since it was first released more than thirty years ago, no recording of the "Scottish" Symphony has come within hailing distance of that astonishingly vivid and spontaneous performance by the London Symphony led by the Swiss conductor Peter Maag. Impulsive yet highly polished, beautifully detailed yet sweepingly cinematic, the interpretation remains one of the great glories of the stereo era. Coupled with Sir Georg Solti's brilliant Israel Philharmonic recording of the "Italian" Symphony—and you simply will not believe the ferocious pace of the *Finale*—this is one of the major bargains now on the market. Solti's slightly driven, yet compellingly dramatic, Chicago Symphony recording is the best alternative if something like state-of-the-art sound is an absolute necessity. With thrilling playing and dazzling recorded sound, this would actually be the first choice among all "Scottish" Symphony recordings, were it not for the once-in-a-lifetime combination of freshness and poetry that Peter Maag found in the score so long ago.

Symphony No. 4 in A Major, Op. 90, "Italian"

Cleveland Orchestra, Szell. Sony Classical SBK 46536 [CD], SBT 46536 [T].

More than any other work, it is the colorful, impeccably crafted "Italian" Symphony that best fixes Mendelssohn's place in the development of Western music. Essentially a Classicist who was touched by the first winds of the Romantic movement, Mendelssohn reconciled eighteenth-century structural decorum with nineteenth-century emotionalism more comfortably than any other composer of his time. The "Italian" Symphony is one of the great transitional works of the early Romantic era, a piece whose formal organization is as tightly knit as the symphonies of Haydn and Mozart, but whose expressiveness clearly points the way to Berlioz, Chopin, and Schumann.

The performance that most successfully projects both sides of the "Italian" Symphony's essential character is that immaculate and exciting CBS recording by the Cleveland Orchestra and George Szell. Along with the highly buffed playing of the finest Mozart orchestra of modern times, Szell finds countless ways to remind us that this is also an intensely Romantic work. The Pilgrim's March, even at a rather brisk tempo, has a wonderfully melancholy grandeur, and in the concluding *tarantella*, taken at a break-neck clip, there are many dark and disquieting moments lurking beneath the swirling, giddy surface.

With equally lucid and revealing performances of the best-known moments from the *Midsummer Night's Dream* music, this is one of the classic Mendelssohn recordings of the stereo age.

Trios (2) for Violin, Cello, and Piano

Kaplan, violin; Carr, cello; Golub, piano. Arabesque Z-6599 [CD].

With the phenomenal Octet for Strings, the two Piano Trios represent Mendelssohn's major achievement as a composer of chamber music. With their singing slow movements, sparking Scherzos, and powerfully dramatic finales, both of these passionate, elegantly wrought works rank with the finest chamber music of the Romantic era.

Although for years the recordings by the Beaux Arts set the standard in both of the Trios, the newer versions by this brilliant trio of young Americans handily surpasses them. There is not only a freshness in the approach but also an effortlessness in the execution that makes the performances seem both utterly natural and thoroughly alive.

Mennin, Peter (1923–1983)

Concertato for Orchestra, "Moby Dick"; Symphony No. 3; Symphony No. 7

Seattle Symphony, Schwarz. Delos 6164 [CD].

Dapper, urbane, with the polished look of a successful businessman (or an actor who specialized in businessman roles), Peter Mennin was something of an anomaly among the major American composers of his generation. Stubbornly unfashionable, his considerable gifts as a music administrator—he was the longtime president of the Juilliard School of Music—allowed him to write only the sort music that *he* wanted to write. Unlike many American composers of Italian descent—from Walter Piston (Pistone) to Paul Creston (Giuseppe Guttovegio)—

an Italianate lyricism was not a defining factor in Mennin's art. His music is also remarkably free of humor and charm, nor is it especially sensual or colorful in any conventional way; his orchestration, while skillful and efficient, deliberately avoids any color or effect that might get in the way of the musical argument. Rugged, virile, intellectually uncompromising, Mennin's art, at its best, has a driven energy and concentrated power unique in American music.

The three works on this Delos recording offer an ideal introduction to Mennin's challenging and rewarding world, from the austere power of the Third Symphony—the composer's Eastman School of Music doctoral dissertation that established his reputation in the late 1940s—through the rigorous complexities of the "Variation Symphony," written for George Szell and the Cleveland Orchestra. Although both have been recorded before, the Schwarz easily outstrips the previous recordings by Mitropolous and Martinon in terms of brilliance of execution and a natural, instinctive grasp of Mennin's wholly American idiom. An equally compelling version of the *Concertato*, "Moby Dick"—which has little direct connection to the Melville novel—makes an already extremely attractive package even more so.

Menotti, Gian Carlo (1911–)

Amahl and the Night Visitors (orchestral excerpts); *Sebastian*

New Zealand Symphony, Schenck. Koch 3-7005-2 [CD].

For several years now, no commercial recording of the Christmas classic *Amahl and the Night Visitors* has been available. It's bad enough that MCA withdrew its lovely modern Covent Garden production; it's *scandalous* that RCA dropped the original soundtrack recording. Perhaps there really *is* a Grinch. *Amahl* fans can console themselves with the beguiling three-movement set of orchestral excerpts *(Introduction, March,* and *Shepherd's Dance)* on this attractive Koch recording that also includes the fetching suite from the composer's ballet *Sebastian.* The performances are both pointed and refreshing.

Another Koch recording (3-7156-2 [CD]) of *Apocalypse* is a good deal more than that. This beautiful, mysterious work may well be Menotti's masterpiece—or so it certainly seems in the gleaming performance by James DePriest and the Oregon Symphony. Far from being the somber (or chilling) work the title might imply, Menotti's first nontheatrical orchestral score is full of shimmering beauties and mystical visions, all of them deeply felt. Coupled with Norman Dello Joio's powerful *Meditations on Ecclesiastes,* this is one of the most important albums of American music in years.

Mercadante, Saverio (1795–1870)

Flute Concertos (3)

Galway, flute; I Solisti Veneti, Scimone. RCA 09026-61447-2 [CD].

An exact contemporary of Gioacchino Rossini, who was fulsome in his praise of many of the man's sixty-plus operas, Saverio Mercadante is the most important Italian operatic composer of the nineteenth century whose operas are no longer performed. While blessed with a sizable lyric gift and a rare appetite for work, Mercadante was such a fussy craftsman that he tended to write any semblance of dramatic life out of his scores; from the rare revival—*Il Bravo* or *Il Giuramento*, both available in live performances from Nuova Era—it would seem that the typical Mercadante opera is serious of purpose, impeccably made, and dead.

Not so the instrumental music, if these charming flute concertos are any indication. Bursting with good ideas, lyrical charm, and infectious humor, they are among the most attractive solo works in the instrument's literature, several of the movements suggesting miniature operatic scenes (from which they may, in fact, have grown). Throughout, Galway plays with fire and wit, with Claudio Scimone and I Solisti Veneti providing the elegant backdrops.

Messiaen, Olivier (1908–1992)

Turangalîla Symphony; Quartet for the End of Time

City of Birmingham Symphony, Rattle. EMI Classics CDCB-47463-2 [CD].

To give credit where credit is due, Olivier Messiaen is the only composer of serious music whose work has ever made me throw up. *Literally* throw up. I was listening to a new recording of *Vingt regards sur l'Enfant Jésus*—which one announcer of my acquaintance always translates on the air as "Give my regards to Jesus"—when I felt that unmistakable feeling and made it to the restroom just in time. True, I was running a fever of 102 degrees; true, there was a particularly virulent form of intestinal flu making the rounds, and true, I *had* consumed an inhumanly large and greasy cheeseburger not an hour before. Nevertheless, I firmly believed that it was *Messiaen* who made me puke, and I still believe it today.

There are numerous respected musicians—and a fair-sized public—who take Messiaen's mumbling mysticism and interminable bird calls seriously, so he can't be dismissed out of hand. Recently, for sins too horrible to mention, I assigned myself the penance of listening to Simon Rattle's recording of the endless *Turangalîla Symphony*. If you're drawn to this gibberish, you'll find the interpretation all you could possibly hope for: like André Previn's deleted Angel recording, the performance may even be far too good for the piece.

An older recording of that other Messiaen favorite, the knee-slapping *Quartet for the End of Time*—which was composed in a concentration camp and *sounds* like it—rounds out what is, for my taste, a far too generous release.

Piano Music

Cheng-Cochran, piano. Koch International Classics KIC 7267 [CD].

I am the first to admit a virtually impenetrable blind spot when it comes to this composer. David Raksin, composer of *Laura* and one of the most shameless punsters God made, insists that it has something to do with my distaste for the Frenchman's slovenly personal habits: "She must have been a lousy housekeeper—why else would they call her 'messy Anne'?" (But I digress.)

Recently, however, I have begun to see a glimmer of light, thanks to Michael Kieran Harvey's electrifying performance of some of the *Preludes* in the finals of the Ivo Pogorelich International Solo Piano Competition and to this superb Koch recital by the brilliant Los Angeles-based pianist Gloria Cheng-Cochran. Prepared with the cooperation of the composer's widow, this is the single most attractive Messiaen recital in my experience. Even at its thorniest—in the explosive *Cantéyodjaya* or the insanely difficult *Études de Rhythme*—Cheng-Cochran brings an almost classical poise and refinement of expression to the music, which only serves to underscore its less-than-obvious links to the later piano music of Debussy and Ravel. The album also features the recording premiere of the two-page *Pièce pour le tombeau de Paul Dukas,* first published in a Paris magazine in 1935.

Clearly, this is an album that could be called *Messiaen for People Who Think They Hate Messiaen*—and believe me, I should know.

Meyer, Edgar (1960–   )

Quintet for String Quartet and Double Bass

Meyer, double bass; Emerson String Quartet. Deutsche Grammophon
298 453 506-2 [CD].

In the grand tradition of Giovanni Bottesini and Serge Koussevitzky, Edgar Meyer is something more than the foremost double bass player of his generation. Along with being the first bassist awarded the Avery Fisher Career Grant and a founding member of the progressive bluegrass band Strength in Numbers, he is a versatile and accomplished composer who premiered his Bass Concerto in 1993 with Edo de Waart and the Minnesota Orchestra and took part in the celebrated *Appalachia Waltz* tour with Yo Yo Ma and Mark O'Connor.

The Quintet, written in 1995 for the Emerson String Quartet, is a resourceful and entertaining work with memorable themes and a wry sense of humor—rare qualities in a contemporary chamber work. Although the Meyer Quintet is undoubtedly intended as the principal draw, its companion piece is even more impressive.

Composed in 1994, the Fourth Quartet by Ned Rorem is a series of ten brief interrelated movements inspired by paintings of Pablo Picasso. It is a strong, richly various, fabulously colorful work that proves that one of America's most distinctive composers continues to improve with age.

Meyerbeer, Giacomo (1791–1864)

Les Huguenots

Sutherland, Arroyo, Tourangeau, Vrenios, Cossa, Bacquier, Ghiuselev,
Ambrosian Opera Chorus, New Philharmonia Orchestra, Bonynge.
London 430549-2 [CD].

Like Felix Mendelssohn, Jakob Liebmann Beer was the son of a wealthy Berlin banker. His maternal grandfather bestowed an immense legacy on the boy, with the sole stipulation that he add his grandfather's name to his own. After his early success as a composer of Italian opera, he Italianized his given name, and as Giacomo Meyerbeer, through a career that spanned more than half a century, did more than anyone else to establish the grammar and syntax of what would come to be known as Grand Opera.

While they have largely fallen out of favor—in part because they were tailor-made to the gaudy tastes of the midcentury Parisian public, and in part because there are so few singers capable of performing them today—Meyerbeer's operas were among the most successful written during the entire nineteenth century. In fact, Richard Wagner's hysterical, lifelong anti-Semitism was only inflamed by his envy of Meyerbeer; in the revolting pamphlet *Jewry in Music,* begun shortly after he attended a Paris performance of Meyerbeer's *Le Prophète,* he argued that Jews had no place in German life and art—arguments that would later have a profound influence on Wagner's ardent admirer Adolf Hitler.

Les Huguenots, Meyerbeer's epic treatment of the St. Bartholomew's Day Massacre of 1572, is one of the composer's most impressive works. Even Wagner considered its beautiful Act IV love duet one of finest moments in all of opera, while the powerful Viennese critic Eduard Hanslick—and Wagner's model for the narrow-minded town clerk Sixtus Beckmesser in *Die Meistersinger*—insisted that a failure to appreciate the dramatic power of *Les Huguenots* suggested serious deficiencies in the listener's critical faculties. In addition to its splendor and spectacle, the opera also offers a love story of genuine depth and feeling, together with an almost embarrassing wealth of memorable set pieces and highly singable tunes.

Except for Dame Joan Sutherland, the level of singing on this fine London recording from 1970 is not quite what one imagines it was on those evenings at the turn of the century when *Les Huguenots* was used as the vehicle for those "nuits des sept étoiles." Although the other six stars here range from the very good to the barely adequate, much of the opera's appeal and power still manages to come through, thanks largely to the brilliant conducting of Richard Bonynge, who has never been more passionately persuasive. For anyone wondering what all the shouting was about in the middle of the last century, this recording will offer many clues.

Miaskovsky, Nikolai (1881–1950)

Symphony No. 21 in F-sharp Minor, Op. 51

New Philharmonia Orchestra, Measham. Unicorn-Kanchana UK CD 2066 [CD].

A pupil of Liadov and Rimsky-Korsakov and the teacher of Khachaturian, Kabalevsky, and many others, Nikolai Miaskovsky remains a shadowy figure outside his native Russia. International recognition came late with the appearance of the twenty-first of his twenty-seven symphonies, written in 1940 on a commission from Frederick Stock and the Chicago Symphony. It remains the most frequently performed of Miaskovsky's works, a compact, beautifully crafted score tinged with a mood of nostalgic melancholy that seems to be its composer's most characteristic emotional state.

David Measham and the New Philharmonia Orchestra give a deeply sympathetic performance of the work in what is easily the best recording of any Miaskovsky symphony currently available. Thus far, the Marco Polo Miaskovsky series has been a very mixed bag. Although Sir Edward Downes leads the BBC Philharmonic in a glowing version of the bright, untroubled Fifth of 1918—Miaskovsky's "Pastoral" Symphony—coupled with the persuasively argued Ninth of 1927 (8.223499 [CD]), the installments entrusted to Robert Stankovsky and the Czech-Slovak Radio Symphony have so far been extremely variable, with frequent evidence of insufficient planning, study, and rehearsal time.

Miaskovsky's Cello Concerto is a radiantly beautiful work, full of the same dignified sorrow that characterizes the Elgar Concerto, written a quarter century before. The recording that Mstislav Rostropovich made with Sir Malcolm Sargent and the Philharmonia Orchestra in 1956 is one of the Russian cellist's most eloquent (EMI Classics CDM 65419 [CD]), a performance mercifully free of any hint of mannerism or exaggeration. The ideal coupling is Sergei Taneyev's *Suite de concert* for Violin and Orchestra, another mysteriously neglected gem given an equally memorable performance by David Oistrakh and the Philharmonia conducted by Nicolai Malko.

Milhaud, Darius (1892–1974)

Les Choëphores

Soloists, Schola Cantorum, New York Philharmonic, Bernstein. Sony Classical MHK 62352 [CD].

Written in 1915 on a text adapted by Paul Claudel from the *Oresteia* of Aeschylus, *Les Choëphores* is Milhaud's most radical, startlingly original work. An extended experiment in polytonality subtitled "harmonic variations," the action is advanced by a female narrator—the ballerina Vera Zorina, in a tour de force of single-minded intensity and concentration—who declaims the text in strict synchronization to a huge battery of percussion instruments, punctuated by the whistles, groans, and shrieks of the chorus. In a performance like this one, issued as part of Sony Classical's Masterworks Heritage series, *Les Choëphores* seems one of the elemental outbursts of modern music, a departure as terrifying in its power as Stravinsky's *Rite of Spring* or Schoenberg's *Pierrot lunaire.* The album is rounded out with stunning performances of works closely associated with Bernstein's mentor, Serge Koussevitzky: the Third Symphony of Albert Roussel and Arthur Honegger's *Rugby* and *Pacific 231.*

La Création du monde

> **National Orchestra of France, Bernstein. EMI Classics**
> **CDC 47845 [CD].**

One of the most prolific and entertaining composers that history has known, Darius Milhaud was also one of the largest. In fact, to find a composer of comparable girth, one has to go back to the late-eighteenth century Bohemian composer and keyboard virtuoso Jan Ladislav Dussek, who became so obese toward the end of his career that his hands could no longer reach the keyboard of his piano. (Fortunately for posterity, Milhaud never learned to play the instrument and thus was free to compose all of his music while seated at a desk.)

La Création du monde (The Creation of the World), the jazz ballet written after the composer's encounter with American jazz in 1923, is probably Milhaud's finest and most characteristic work. It is given racy, vibrant performances in both of the recordings listed here, and a choice between them will depend largely on your preference of format. The Bernstein compact disc also includes spirited interpretations of Milhaud's *Saudades do Brasil* and *Le Boeuf sur le toit*—the equally jazzy and surrealistic ballet whose scenario, by Jean Cocteau, calls for (among other things) a Paris gendarme to be decapitated by an overhead fan. This is my kind of ballet.

Piano Music

> **Madeleine Milhaud, narrator; Tharaud, piano. Naxos 8.552442 [CD].**

> **Sharon, piano. Unicorn-Kanchana DKP 9155 [CD].**

For a man who never learned to play the piano, Milhaud composed an enormous amount of extremely idiomatic music for the instrument. The three works on this winning Naxos recital represent the composer at something close to his best: the *Saudades do Brazil* from 1921, a suite of a dozen colorful dances, each bearing the name of a district of Rio de Janiero; *La Muse ménagère* (The Household Muse), fifteen miniatures written in honor of his hard-pressed wife; and *L'Album de Madame Bovary,* adapted from the score for Jean Renoir's 1933 film of the Flaubert novel. In addition to the pert and highly musical performances of the young French pianist Alexandre Tharaud, the album affords us the pleasure of hearing Madame Milhaud introduce each section of *La Muse ménagère* with the utmost charm, followed by her accomplished reading of favorite passages from Flaubert.

The Unicorn-Kanchana recital by the Israeli pianist Boaz Sharon is no less enjoyable. Although there is some duplication—*Saudades* and three dances from *Bovary*—the pianist's highly spiced playing more than makes up for the added cost. Best of all are the jazzy *Trois Rag-caprices*, the 1957 suite *Les Charmes de la vie*, and the familiar-sounding *Tango des Fratellini*, adapted from the themes from *Le Boeuf sur le toit*.

Moeran, E. J.   (1894–1950)

Symphony in G Minor; *Overture to a Masque*

Ulster Orchestra, Handley. Chandos CHAN 8577 [CD].

It is frankly astonishing that a work as fine as Moeran's G Minor Symphony should be so completely unknown outside of Britain. Brilliantly argued and crafted, with its roots firmly planted in British folk song, it is a work to be mentioned in the same breath with most of the Vaughan Williams symphonies and one that would undoubtedly attract a large following were it simply to be played more often.

Given an unusually pointed and powerful performance by Vernon Handley and the fine Ulster Orchestra, the Symphony has a moiling, craggy intensity that recalls late Sibelius, although it has more than enough character and personality of its own. With an equally smashing account of the rambunctious *Overture to a Masque*, this is both an ideal introduction to an important, strangely neglected composer and an absolute must for lovers of modern British music.

Moeran's Cello Concerto is no less fine a work and is given a sumptuous performance by Raphael Wallfisch and the Bournemouth Sinfonietta led by the late Norman Del Mar, who is equally persuasive with the refreshing *Sinfonietta* (Chandos CHAN 8456 [CD]). Another superb Chandos album (CHAN 8807 [CD]) features the lovely Violin Concerto with its many references to Irish folk song, handsomely played by Lydia Mordkovich and the Ulster Orchestra conducted by Vernon Handley.

Finally, two collections of Moeran partsongs, *Songs of Springtime* and *Phyllis and Corydon*, contain some of the composer's most moving inspirations.

Exquisitely performed by the Finzi Singers (Chandos CHAN 9182 [CD]), they seem among the finest vocal works produced by an Englishman in this century.

Molter, Johann Melchior (1696–1765)

Trumpet Concertos (3)

Touvron, trumpet; Württemberg Chamber Orchestra, Faerber. RCA 09026-61857-2 [CD], 09026-61857-4 [T].

Unlike the brilliant Bohemian composer and virtuoso Pavel Vejvanovský, who died three years before this prolific German's birth, Johann Melchior Molter was not a trumpet player, in spite of everything that his dazzling, wholly idiomatic works for the instrument might suggest. Few composers of any era wrote more naturally for the trumpet, fewer still produced display pieces that were quite so satisfying in both musical and virtuoso terms.

Guy Touvron is a formidably equipped player who tosses off these daunting concertos with what almost amounts to an insolent ease. The durable Jörg Faerber and his trusty Württemberg Chamber Orchestra are as graceful and enthusiastic now as they were in their recording heyday during the 1960s, while the recorded sound is both warm and splendidly detailed.

Mompou, Federico (1893–1987)

Piano Music

Hough, piano. Hyperion CDA 66963 [CD].

There is an endearing, artless simplicity in the music of this Spanish composer who was so pathologically shy and retiring that a concert career was completely out of the question. Like his older contemporary Manuel de Falla, he was profoundly influenced by French music, particularly the miniatures of Erik Satie. Mompou's own music—and he confined himself almost entirely to brief works for the piano—has something of the same childlike quality but without Satie's archness or sophistication. In its innocence and purity, Mompou's is a small but unique voice of twentieth-century music, with many lovely and individual things to say.

This generous Hyperion anthology is an ideal introduction to Moupou's oddly appealing world. Stephen Hough responds admirably to the moody, improvisatory nature of the music with both affection and finesse. His work is not a major discovery, perhaps, but an increasingly haunting one.

Monteverdi, Claudio (1567–1643)

L'Incoronazione di Poppea

> McNair, Von Otter, Hanchard, Chance, English Baroque Soloists, Gardiner. Deutsche Grammophon 447088-2 [CD].

Just as Nathaniel Hawthorne's most famous novel might be subtitled "How Hester Won Her Letter," so the last and greatest of Monteverdi's operas literally demonstrates "What Poppea's Willing to Do to Get Crowned." *L'Incoronazione di Poppea* has an element of sexual frankness that would be unique in an opera of any period, much less for one produced by a seventy-five-year-old composer in 1642.

The recording conducted by Sir John Eliot Gardiner is easily the finest the opera has ever received. With Sylvia McNair predictably alluring in the title role and Anne Sophie von Otter breathtaking as Ottavia, wife of the faithless Nero, Gardiner molds the complicated action into a powerfully convincing whole; not a single member of the cast is less than excellent, and the excitement of a live performance—recorded at Queen Elizabeth Hall in London—only adds to the dramatic effect.

Precisely how well these old operas can hold the stage was driven home for me recently by the Los Angeles Opera's astounding production of Monteverdi's *Il ritorno d'Ulisse in patria*, which proved to be the surprise hit of the season and one of the hottest tickets in town. If not quite as memorable as Frederica von Stade and Thomas Allen, then Bernarda Fink and Christoph Prégardien sing superbly for René Jacobs in his Harmonia Mundi recording (HMC 901427/29 [CD]). Although *The Return of Ulysses* contains little action and even less in the way of arias—only the occasional fleeting whip of a tune that ends almost before it begins—it makes for a thoroughly engrossing experience, even in the comfort of one's living room.

Madrigals

Consort of Musicke, Rooley. Virgin Classics 59621 [CD].

Though possibly not the most representative of the Consort of Musicke's irreproachable series of recordings of the Monteverdi Madrigals—more balanced collections include their versions of the complete Book 2 (Virgin Classics 59282 [CD]), Book 3 (Virgin Classics 59283 [CD]), or Book 6 (Virgin Classics 59605 [CD]—none is more uplifting than this anthology of works on frankly erotic themes. As in Elizabethan poetry, the use of the phrase "to die" (and its many cognates) as a euphemism for achieving sexual climax was an honored convention among the Renaissance madrigal composers. Needless to say, there is nearly as much dying here—often accompanied by the most funky, salacious harmonies—as there was in the Papal Wars.

Rooley's singers make one feel like an honored guest at an immensely civilized orgy, and the rich but cozy recorded sound is close to ideal. Recommended only for those who are willing to practice safe listening.

L'Orfeo

Rolfe-Johnson, Baird, Dawson, Von Otter, Argenta, Robson, Monteverdi Choir, English Baroque Soloists, Gardiner. Deutsche Grammophon 419250-2 [CD].

While Jacopo Peri's *Dafne* predates it by about a decade, Monteverdi's *L'Orfeo* is now generally regarded as the first genuine opera, as the word is commonly understood today. While *L'Orfeo* is an extended vocal work that *does* attempt to tell a continuous, coherent story, it is not "operatic" in the same sense that *Carmen* and *Aida* are. The action, as in most operas before those of Mozart, tends to be static to the point of stagnation, and the characters are often less than two-dimensional. As a matter of fact, to the untrained ear, *L'Orfeo* can seem little more than a sequence of one- and two-part madrigals (if that's not a contradiction in terms), thrown together with exquisite imagination and taste.

John Eliot Gardiner's interpretation is every bit as persuasive as the recently deleted Angel version led by Nigel Rogers. As always, this most spirited of antiquarians finds the perfect balance between the demands of textual authenticity and the needs of human communication. The story unfolds crisply and cleanly, yet with ample amounts of drama and color, making it seem a far more modern and digestible experience than it usually is. All of the soloists, especially the virtuoso tenor Anthony Rolfe-Johnson, are exceptional, and Gardiner's Monteverdi Choir and English Baroque Soloists turn in their usual flawless performance.

Vespro della Beata Vergine (1610)

Soloists, Monteverdi Choir and Orchestra, Gardiner. Deutsche Grammophon 429565-2 [CD].

G. K. Chesterton once insisted that "It is the test of a good religion whether you can make a joke about it." By that same token, the test of any performance of Monteverdi's *Vespers* of 1610 is how many of the faithful remain awake at the end of the experience. Unlike *Messiah,* which contains many "hit tunes" to cling to and can thus be sampled in pieces, like so many sacred chocolates, the *Vespers* must be swallowed and digested—all two hours of it—as a complete and indissoluble whole.

Unlike his earlier version for London recorded in 1974, which used modern instruments, John Eliot Gardiner's newer and even finer Deutsche Grammophon recording uses period instruments and the incomparable acoustics of the Basilica of St. Mark's in Venice, and the music emerges with a sweep and grandeur that none of the more scholarly recordings can begin to match. For anyone unfamiliar with this glorious score, here is the perfect introduction.

Moore, Thomas (1779–1852)

Irish Melodies

Invocation. Hyperion CDA 66774 [CD].

Friend of Byron, lion of the London salons, author of a notorious collection of erotic verse published under the pen name "Thomas Little," Thomas Moore, the son of a Dublin grocer, has the distinction of being the first Catholic ever admitted to Trinity College. Although he became an overnight literary sensation in 1799 with the publication of his *Odes to Anacreon,* his posthumous fame would rest on the ten volumes of *Irish Melodies* he published between 1807 and 1834. Based on melodies collected by Edward Bunting in *The Ancient Music of Ireland,* Moore supplied new English lyrics to the old tunes that were then arranged by the Dublin composer John Stevenson.

Anyone who enjoys the Haydn or Beethoven arrangements of Irish folk music will be enchanted by this lovely Hyperion album. The period-instrument performances by an ensemble called Invocation are models of their kind. In fact, the Broadwood grand and single-action harp provide such a perfect accompaniment to the voices that it all magically conjures up the Regency parlors of Moore's time to an astonishing degree. Everything about the Hyperion production—from the cover art to the recorded sound—is so impeccable that it makes you hope that this is only the first of many such albums to come.

Moross, Jerome   (1913–1983)

Symphony No. 1; *Last Judgment* (ballet suite); *Variations on a Waltz*

London Symphony, Falletta. Koch International Classics
KIC 7188 [CD].

Educated at Juilliard and New York University, Jerome Moross spent his journeyman years in Hollywood, arranging and orchestrating film music that included classics like Aaron Copland's *Our Town* and Hugo Friedhofer's *The Best Years of Our Lives*; his own eclectic, highly accomplished scores include *The War Lord*, *Hans Christian Anderson* (for which he supplied a ballet for "The Little Mermaid," based on themes from Liszt), and *The Big Country*, for which he was nominated for an Academy Award.

The most important of his works for the concert hall is the Symphony No. 1, finished in 1942 and introduced in Seattle by Sir Thomas Beecham. It is one of the strongest and most immediately appealing American symphonies of the period, a work with much of the folksy charm and wide-open grandeur of Copland and Harris but with a personality distinctly its own. JoAnn Falletta leads the London Symphony in an invigorating performance and is equally successful in the rugged *Last Judgment* and the resourceful and entertaining *Variations on a Waltz*. A second Koch album (7367 [CD]), with Falletta conducting the New Zealand Symphony, features the Concerto for Flute and String Orchestra, music from the jazzy ballet *Frankie and Johnny*, and the droll *Tall Story* for orchestra.

Moross's finest film score, *The Big Country*, is handsomely served on a recent release from Silva America (SDD 1048 [CD]), while a companion album (SDD 1049 [CD]) offers suites from the scores for *The Adventures of Huckleberry Finn*, *The Sharkfighters*, *The Mountain Road*, *Rachel Rachel*, *The Warlord*, *Five Finger Exercise*, and *The Valley of Gwangi*.

Moscheles, Ignaz   (1794–1870)

Sonate caractéristique

Marvin, piano. Genesis GCD 109 [CD].

Born into a wealthy Jewish family in Prague, Ignaz Moscheles moved to Vienna in 1808 to further his studies but largely to be near his idol, Beethoven. As a pianist, Moscheles himself became a hero to the younger generation—Litolff, Thalberg, and others adored his playing and benefited from his tutelage—and one of Mendelssohn's first acts after founding the Leipzig Conservatory was to appoint his old friend principal professor of piano. As a composer, he confined himself largely to studies and salon music, saving his most serious thoughts for his piano sonatas, which Schumann considered among the finest of the period.

Frederick Marvin's superb 1974 recording of the *Sonate caractéristique* only confirms Schumann's high opinion. It is a strongly appealing late-Classical work with a Beethoven-like size and concentration, yet one that is also clearly touched by the early Romantic spirit. Marvin projects both qualities admirably and is perhaps even more persuasive in *Sonata-Pathétique* of Ludwig Berger, another of Mendelssohn's teachers whose own music was also deeply influenced by Beethoven. Although Berger's sonata borrows both the key and subtitle from Beethoven's Op. 13, it is a work of considerable charm and individuality, especially in its maddeningly unforgettable finale.

Mozart, Leopold   (1719–1787)

Toy Symphony; Musical Sleigh Ride; Symphonies (2)

Munich Chamber Orchestra, Stadlmair. Tudor TUD 737 [CD].

After his son Wolfgang Amadeus, Leopold Mozart's most celebrated composition was the charming *Toy Symphony*, long erroneously attributed to Haydn. "Symphony" is also a misnomer, being in fact a three-movement *cassation* for two violins, double bass, penny trumpet, quail call, rattle, cuckoo, screech-owl whistle, toy drum, and triangle. With its sleigh-bell effects, *Die musikalische Schlittenfahrt* is a similarly endearing work whose musical virtues far outweigh the novelty of its sound effects.

We might have suspected that the man who gave us such inspired performances of the Albrechtsberger Jew's Harp Concertos (see page 6) would prove a perfect interpreter of these delightful works. Without the slightest condescension, exaggerated slapstick, or cuteness, Stadlmair simply lets the music speak for itself. The two brief symphonies that round out the album are also handsomely done, although more appropriate companions might have been the Trumpet Concerto in D (thrillingly played by Wynton Marsalis on Sony Classical SK 57497 [CD], ST 57497 [T]) or the *Sinfonia pastorella* for alphorn and strings, manfully negotiated by Michel Garcin-Marrou on Dale Clevenger's recording of the Mozart horn concertos (Sony Classical SBK 62639 [CD], SBT 62639 [T]).

If the Tudor album proves difficult to find, then Antonio Janigro's spirited 1958 recording has been reissued on Vanguard Classics (OVC 5005 [CD]) with a fine version of Tchaikovsky's *Nutcracker Suite* conducted by Maurice Abravanel and a very memorable reading of Prokofiev's *Peter and the Wolf* from Boris Karloff.

Mozart, Wolfgang Amadeus (1756–1791)

Once, when filling out an application for a summer job, on that line next to "other" in which the employer asks the prospective employee to list his or her religion, I wrote the word "Mozart." The personnel officer was *not* amused, but then again, I hadn't intended it as a joke. For there was a time when I was absolutely convinced that Mozart was at least as divinely inspired as Moses, Christ, the Buddha, Lao-tse, or Mohammed, and I suppose I still am. For in no other works of the human imagination can the divine spirit be heard more distinctly than in the *literally* miraculous music that this often vulgar, unpleasant, and difficult man produced during his pathetically brief thirty-five years. Were this book to do him any justice, the section devoted to Mozart's music would take up more than half of this total book. What follows, therefore, is a painfully compressed selection.

The Abduction from the Seraglio (Die Entführung as dem Serail)

> Orgonasova, Sieden, Olsen, Peper, Hauptmann, Minetti, Monteverdi Choir, English Baroque Soloists, Gardiner. Deutsche Grammophon 435857-2 [CD].

> Hollweg, Marshall, Simoneau, Unger, Frick, Beecham Choral Society, Royal Philharmonic, Beecham. EMI Classics CDHB 63715 [CD].

As we learned from Milos Forman's *Amadeus*—a stylized, brazenly inaccurate account of Mozart's life that I have only seen 128 times—it was with *The Abduction from the Seraglio* that he made his initial splash in Vienna and through which he met the soprano Katharina Cavalieri (the original Constanze), with whom he may or may not have had a brief but toasty affair. (If true, that would have placed the soprano in some not terribly select company, for the composer of *Don Giovanni* certainly knew whereof he wrote.) In *Die Entführung*, Mozart transformed the decidedly low-brow entertainment called *singspiel* into a high art, a form to which he would return a decade later in *The Magic Flute*. In the process, he produced the first great opera of the German language and the earliest opera in *any* language that still commands a place in the standard repertoire.

With Karl Böhm's scintillating Deutsche Grammophon recording currently unavailable, the choice now boils down to Sir John Eliot Gardiner's sparkling period-instrument performance and the classic Beecham recording, handsomely restored on EMI Classics. In addition to the superior sound, the Gardiner offers the excitement of a nearly live performance—recorded under studio conditions following a series of successful London concerts—and the dazzling Konstanze of Luba Orgonasova, who uncorks one of the most thrilling versions of *Martern aller Arten* in living memory. The Beecham boasts the special insights of a magical Mozart conductor and the uproarious, magnificently sung Osmin of Gottlob Frick. While the recording is obviously not the equal of Gardiner's, the remastered sound is warmer and much less edgy than the original LPs.

Both would do honor to any collection and either can be bought without reservation.

Arias

Anthologies of Mozart arias typically come in one of two varieties—and on occasion, as a mixture of both: those devoted to excerpts from the composer's operas and those that feature the free-standing concert arias for which he reserved some of his most brilliant writing for the human voice.

A good place to begin sampling the latter is with Elisabeth Schwarzkopf's EMI Classics recording (CDH 63702 [CD]), which couples four of the best-known arias—including *Ch'io mi scordi di te?* the most brutally difficult of all—with sixteen of the singer's famous Mozart lieder recordings made with pianist Walter Gieseking (see page 498). With little duplication, the voice of Dame Kiri Te Kanawa is captured at its most seductive on London (440401-2 [CD]). For the more serious collector, all fifty-seven of the concert arias—together with alternative arias and duets from the operas plus other odds and ends—can be found on Volume 23 of Philips's Complete Mozart Edition (422523-2 [CD]), in generally superlative performances from the company's frontline singers.

Among the recordings of the operatic arias, start with a Nimbus anthology (NI 7822 [CD]) called "Great Singers in Mozart," which offers twenty Golden

Age recordings from 1906 to 1938 whose variety and sheer excellence boggle the mind: here, for instance, is Richard Tauber's flawless 1922 German-language version of *Dalla sua pace* from *Don Giovanni* (pity they couldn't include John McCormack's 1916 *Il mio tesoro* and thus have *both* of the most nearly perfect Mozart recordings ever made), the imposing Sarastro of Alexander Kipnis, Lotte Lehmann's unforgettable Countess, and that most musical of Papagenos, Gerhard Hüsch.

Though not as famous for her Mozart as her Verdi, Leontyne Price proves a ravishing guide to the standard soprano arias plus a number of rarities on an RCA album (09026-61357-2 [CD], 09026-61357 [T]), recorded when the voice was in its glorious prime. While Cecilia Bartoli nearly lives up to the claims of her extravagant publicity in her highly musical, technically dazzling London collection (443452-2 [CD], 443452-4 [T]), the lovely Jennifer Larmore is even more impressive in her solo debut album on Teldec (4509-96800-2 [CD]). Not only is the voice larger, sexier, and more compelling, but the program is also much more interesting, including little known items from *La finta giardiniera*, *La finta semplice*, and *Mitridate, rè di Ponto*. The album is rounded out with a sequence of brutally taxing Handel arias, all sung with such insolent ease and real dramatic flair that by the end you might almost be tempted to ask yourself—as I nearly did—Cecilia *who?*

Ballet and Theater Music

Netherlands Chamber Orchestra, Academy of St. Martin-in-the-Fields, Berlin Radio Symphony, Zinman, Marriner, Klee. Philips 422525-2 [CD].

Volume 25 of Philips's Complete Mozart Edition may prove to be the most irresistible of all. The ballet *Les Petits Reins*, composed during Mozart's frustrating visit to Paris in 1778, and the incidental music written at about the same time for T. P. Gelber's play *Thamos, König in Ägypten* contain much wonderful music, as does the ballet he was obliged to provide for the Paris premiere of *Idomeneo*. The two-CD set is rounded out by Franz Beyer's orchestration of the pantomime *Pantalon und Colombine* and Eric Smith's brilliant reconstruction of an unfinished *Intermezzo*.

All of the performances are exceptionally fine, especially Bernhard Klee's spirited *Thamos*. This is an ideal gift for the Mozart collector who has practically everything.

Cassations (3) for Winds and Strings

Salzburg Chamber Orchestra, Nerat. Naxos 8.550609 [T].

By the middle of the eighteenth century, a new kind of musical entertainment had become common throughout Austria and Germany; while given various names—*cassation, notturno, divertimento, serenade*—the character and purpose of such works was always the same. Most of the serenades of this period—including the chamber pieces and nine large-scale orchestral works that Mozart produced during his Salzburg years—were specifically conceived as light background music for festive social occasions, most for his detested employer, the Prince Archbishop of Salzburg.

If the three youthful *cassations* on this enchanting Naxos album are not absolutely top-drawer Mozart, then they are still ideal for any sort of background listening (studying, pleasantly pretentious cocktail parties, the less strenuous sorts of romantic interludes, etc.)—the purpose for which they were designed. The Salzburg Chamber Orchestra plays all three with abundant warmth and finesse, while the sumptuous recorded sound only adds to the pleasure of a thoroughly delightful disc.

La clemenza di Tito

Baker, Minton, Burrows, Popp, von Stade, Lloyd, Chorus and Orchestra of the Royal Opera House, Covent Garden, Davis. Philips 422544-2 [CD].

Mozart's final opera was one of the final examples of *opera seria*, a once-popular form that was already dying while Mozart's ink was still wet on the page. And although most representatives of the species do tend to be unendurably static and stultifying—it was *opera seria* that Tom Hulce, as Mozart, was castigating in *Amadeus* when he complained that the characters were so remote and lofty that they "shit marble"—*La clemenza di Tito* is a sublime masterpiece, though one that is perhaps better suited to the living room than to the operatic stage.

Davis and his unbelievably fine cast make a very strong case for the work. Dame Janet Baker has never seemed more agile or noble, while even the smallish roles are covered by singers of the stature of Frederica von Stade. The Covent Garden forces respond as enthusiastically as they ever have on records and the remastered sound is exceptionally vivid.

It is heartily recommended.

Concerto in B-flat Major for Bassoon and Orchestra, K. 191; Concerto in C Major for Oboe and Orchestra, K. 314; Concerto in A Major for Clarinet and Orchestra, K. 622

> Turnovsky, bassoon; Gabriel, oboe; Ottensamer, clarinet; Vienna Mozart Academy, Wildner. Naxos 8.550345 [CD].

Although these concertos may have had more distinguished individual performances—the bewitching and shamefully deleted EMI Classics recording of the Bassoon Concerto with Gwydion Brooke, the Royal Philharmonic, and Sir Thomas Beecham, or John deLancie's limpid account of the Oboe Concerto, now available only as part of a three-CD set of the complete wind concertos in the rather uneven performances conducted by Eugene Ormandy (Sony Classical SM3K-47215 [CD])—this handsome Naxos CD offers performances that rank with the very best available, not to mention up-to-date sound *and* a superbudget price. Best of all is Stepan Turnovsky's droll reading of the Bassoon Concerto, although oboist Martin Gabriel and clarinetist Ernst Ottensamer also have some pointed and very stylish things to say. As with so many Naxos releases, this is an incredible bargain.

Concerto in A Major for Clarinet and Orchestra, K. 622; Sinfonia Concertante in E-flat Major for Violin, Viola, and Orchestra, K. 364

> Marcellus, clarinet; Druian, violin; Skernick, viola; Cleveland Orchestra, Szell. Sony Classical SBK 62424 [CD], SBT 62424 [T].

This is one of the most nearly perfect Mozart recordings ever made. Robert Marcellus, the Cleveland Orchestra's principal clarinetist, gives a flawless, dramatic performance of the late and strangely uneven Clarinet Concerto, with some customarily precise and enthusiastic support provided by his colleagues under George Szell, and the gleaming version of the great Sinfonia Concertante is probably Szell's finest Mozart recording. Instead of big name soloists, the conductor wisely chose to place the Cleveland's immensely accomplished concertmaster and principal violist in the spotlight. The result is an interpretation of such total generosity and uncanny unanimity of purpose that even after thirty years, it must still be heard to be believed. For much of the time, the soloists seem like a single player with two sets of arms. Each of the beautifully wrought phrases is shaped with precisely the same dynamic shading and inflection, and even the tiniest details are never left to chance. For instance, the trill at the end of the second movement cadenza is a miracle of timing and expressiveness. Szell's accompaniment is as energetic as it is patrician, and at the time the recording was made, the orchestra, as a Mozart ensemble, had no rival in the world.

Concerto in C Major for Flute, Harp, and Orchestra, K. 299; Flute Concerto No. 1 in G Major, K. 313

Galway, flute; Robles, harp; Academy of St. Martin-in-the-Fields, Marriner. RCA 09026-68256-2 [CD].

For most people, the choice of a recording of the finest work that Mozart composed for an instrument he thoroughly detested will boil down to which of the various versions of the Flute and Harp Concerto that James Galway or Jean-Pierre Rampal has so far made. Given the fact that yuppiedom's once insatiable appetite for flute music has apparently begun to be sated—and why should this basically cold and inexpressive instrument have gotten so hot all of a sudden?—there are only *two* Galway versions listed in the current catalogue and only *one* for Rampal.

While a far more theatrical virtuoso than his French colleague, Galway has also been a consistently finer player—wide vibrato, syrupy phrasing, penny-whistle antics and all. In his RCA Victor recording, the brilliant Marisa Robles more than holds her own, as do Sir Neville Marriner and the Academy, who provide their typically stylish support.

Concertos (4) for Horn and Orchestra

Brain, horn; Philharmonia Orchestra, Karajan. EMI Classics CDC 56231 [CD].

Tuckwell, horn and conductor; Philharmonia Orchestra. Collins Classics 11532 [CD].

Written for a man named Ignaz Leutgub (or Leutgeb), one of the most delightfully vulgar of his Salzburg cronies and the favorite butt of many of the composer's practical jokes, the four Horn Concertos are among the most enchanting of all of Mozart's works. From the evidence of the difficult solo parts, Leutgub must have been a virtuoso of considerable accomplishment. For as taxing as they are even for the modern performer, the concertos were originally written for the *waldhorn,* an instrument without valves.

In their recent compact disc reissue, the classic recordings from the mid-1950s made by the legendary Dennis Brain are a moving, inspiring reminder of a man who was not only the century's greatest horn player but also one of its finest musicians. The secret of Brain's art lay in the fact that his approach to the instrument was that of a great vocalist. His phrasing, command of dynamics, and dramatic coloration rivaled those of the finest Mozart singers of his generation. In fact, the slow movements of the Concertos become, in effect, hauntingly beautiful arias without words.

The modern recording that comes closest to duplicating Brain's achievement is the most recent of the four recordings made thus far by Barry Tuckwell, in which the great Australian-born virtuoso gives the liveliest and most technically accomplished performances that have been heard on records since Dennis Brain's death. If they lack the final measure of depth and tenderness that Brain brought to his famous recordings, then they are still a magnificent accomplishment in their own right and are vigorously recommended.

Concertos (25) for Piano and Orchestra

Perahia, piano and conductor; English Chamber Orchestra. Sony Classical SX12K-46441 [CD].

Brendel; Academy of St. Martin-in-the-Fields, Marriner. Philips 442269-2 [CD]; 422571-2 [CD].

With the possible exceptions of his operas and last half dozen symphonies, it is in the series of piano concertos that he wrote throughout his career that the full scope of Mozart's achievement can best be understood. From the earliest of these pieces, some of which were merely arrangements of the music of his teacher Johann Christian Bach, through the towering masterworks of his final years, the concertos also offer the most dramatic evidence of Mozart's evolution from the most celebrated child prodigy in the history of music to the greatest composer who has ever lived.

Each of these triumphant sets of the complete piano concertos is a milestone in the recent history of recording, and, since Murray Perahia and Alfred Brendel are among the most compelling Mozart performers of the last three decades, a choice between them will have to be made on personal, rather than musical, grounds. For those who respond to the "intellectual" approach to Mozart, Brendel's thoughtful, always self-possessed and disciplined playing serves almost all of the concertos exceptionally well. Like his teacher Edwin Fischer, Brendel is always acutely aware of the shape and architecture of the music. Everything is calculated—in the best possible sense of the word—to make the individual details subordinated to the needs of the greater whole. Which is not to say that Brendel's playing is in any way academic or lacking in emotion. Whereas other pianists—including Murray Perahia—can never resist the temptation of letting an especially grateful episode pass them by without embellishing it with the stamp of their own personality, Brendel always does. The result are many of the most satisfying and natural-sounding Mozart recordings available today.

Sir Neville Marriner's accompaniments are invariably invigorating, refined, and stylish, and the recorded sound, primarily from the 1970s, is both as brilliantly detailed and as warmly unobtrusive as the performances themselves.

Like Daniel Barenboim and the late Géza Anda before him, Murray Perahia serves as his own conductor in his consistently fascinating CBS set. As it turns out, the decision was a sound one, not only because the arrangement helps to underscore Perahia's essentially chamber-like approach to the concertos, but also because his ideas are so firm, and intensely personal, that the presence of another musical "personality" would have simply gotten in the way.

If in the most general and oversimplified terms, the Brendel recordings represent the modern Classical vision of Mozart, then Perahia's are a bold and generally successful attempt to rethink the Romantic approach taken by the great pianists of a half century ago. In virtually all of the recordings, Perahia always finds something fresh and personal to say, especially in the slow movements, which are drawn out almost to the point of languorousness. The phrasing is consistently imaginative and spontaneous, and the physical sound of both the soloist and the orchestra, while decidedly hedonistic, also has a wonderful feeling of openness and inevitability. While many will find the performances a trifle precious and fussy, as many others will hear them as an endless source of discovery and delight.

A clear-cut choice between these two superb cycles is not an easy one to make. And needless to say, either of them—especially given the current highway-robbery pricing of compact discs—represents a substantial investment. The wise collector should probably just bite the bullet (or perhaps persuade one of the kids to take a part-time job at McDonald's) and acquire them both.

Piano Concerto No. 19 in F Major, K. 459; Piano Concerto No. 20 in D Minor, K. 466

> Serkin, piano; Cleveland Orchestra, Szell. CBS MYK-37236 [CD], MYT-37236.

Why the nineteenth century tended to take a rather dim view of Mozart remains one of music's most perplexing historical mysteries. Of course, that it chose to venerate its own, far lesser figures at his expense was nothing particularly unusual or new. The wholesale dismissal of the accomplishments of preceding ages was already a time-honored institution by the late fifteenth century: "The Dark Ages"—and for that matter, "Renaissance"—were both terms that Renaissance propagandists coined.

Even so, how the Romantic era could have dismissed Mozart as that rococo lightweight with the powdered wig is all but impossible to fathom, especially in light of works like the D Minor Piano Concerto, which, with *Don Giovanni,* the 40th Symphony, and the G Minor String Quintet, is one of the darkest outpourings of tragedy in all of music.

Having known each other since their student days, George Szell and Rudolf Serkin—an especially formidable combination in the music of Mozart, Beethoven, and Brahms—always managed to communicate with each other as if by some mysterious musical telepathy. Their performance of the D Minor Concerto is one of the most profound and deeply serious ever recorded. Serkin's playing seethes with a brooding, impassioned intensity, and Szell's contribution, as usual, is a model of cooperative understanding that still maintains a distinct and potent personality of its own. The interpretation of the F Major Concerto is just as impressive, lending to what is often tossed off as a far lighter work an unexpected and startlingly novel significance and weight.

Piano Concerto No. 21 in C Major, K. 467

Jandó, piano; Concentus Hungaricus, Ligeti. Naxos 8.550202 [CD]
    (with concertos nos. 12 and 14)

Since its memorable appearance in Bo Widerberg's lovely 1967 film *Elvira Madigan,* the C Major Piano Concerto, or at the very least its ravishing second movement, has become one of the most popular of all Mozart's works, with recordings for every conceivable taste in every price range. Listening to Wilhelm Kempff's relaxed and elegant interpretation from the early 1960s, one can readily believe the legend that that great German pianist was never once nervous before a performance. (Kempff came from a town called Jüterborg where his father and grandfather before him had been the local kapellmeisters; the young Kempff was thus apprenticed to the family business with no more fuss or fanfare than was accorded the son of any other tradesman.) His playing, as always, is full of life and wisdom, as are Ferdinand Leitner's insightful accompaniments. It's a pity they haven't yet been transferred to CD.

When completed, Jenö Jandó's Mozart cycle may well prove to be as distinguished as Perahia's or Brendel's and, at Naxos's prices, might even be more desirable. The performance of the C Major Concerto is an exceptional one, with an extraordinarily beautiful slow movement and a finale that crackles with wit. Coupled with equally memorable versions of the 12th and 14th Concertos, this is quite a bargain even by Naxos standards.

Piano Concerto No. 22 in E-flat Major, K. 482; Piano Concerto No. 23 in A Major, K. 488

**Uchida, piano; English Chamber Orchestra, Tate. Philips
420187-2 [CD].**

There are few musicians these days who are more disquieting to watch than the brilliant Japanese pianist Mitsuko Uchida. Her array of tics, grimaces, and other facial contortions is as impressive in its way as Glenn Gould's repertoire of grunts, sighs, and off-pitch moans. Fortunately, those antics apparently never get in the way of her playing and on a recording, of course, they matter not at all.

Uchida's versions of these two popular concertos are not only among the most musically satisfying these works have yet received, but they are also among the most rewarding Mozart concerto recordings now available. Rarely has the A Major Concerto seemed so luxuriant yet precise, while its great companion piece is superbly graceful and majestic. The accompaniments by the English Chamber Orchestra led by Jeffrey Tate are full of character, with the warmth and clarity of the performances matched by the recorded sound.

Piano Concerto No. 23 in A Major, K. 488; Piano Concerto No. 25 in C Major, K. 503

**Moravec, piano; Czech Philharmonic, Vlach. Supraphon SUP
3076 [CD].**

It was probably no accident that when the producers of *Amadeus* were casting about for a pianist to supply the music for the picture, they should have settled on Ivan Moravec. For a quarter of a century, this unassuming Czech musician has been one of the great Mozart interpreters of the modern era. His versions of these two popular concertos are graced with a unique poetry and insight. The playing is so effortless that we are constantly reminded of the composer's advice to future pianists, "Make it flow like oil." Joseph Vlach and the Czech Philharmonic provide exceedingly civilized settings for these gem-like performances, and the recorded sound remains admirably focused and warm.

Piano Concerto No. 24 in C Minor, K. 491; Piano Concerto No. 21 in C Major, K. 467

Casadesus, piano; Cleveland Orchestra, Szell. CBS MYK-38523 [CD].

The ideal companion piece to the stormy C Minor Concerto is the equally troubled D Minor Concerto, K. 466. In that coupling, the single-disc repackaging from Alfred Brendel's complete cycle for Philips is extremely desirable, especially at medium price and with the delectable D Major Rondo thrown in as a bonus.

On the other hand, as a *performance* of the D Minor Concerto, none has yet to seriously challenge that classic recording by Robert Casadesus and George Szell. On the face of it, the Casadesus-Szell partnership—and they recorded many of the Mozart concertos together—must have seemed to many a rather peculiar one. On the one hand, there was Szell, the fanatical perfectionist; on the other, the frequently inspired Frenchman whose approach to technical niceties could be shockingly cavalier. Yet somehow, together, their differences always seemed to cancel each other out.

Their version of the D Minor Concerto is as poised and turbulent as any Mozart concerto recording ever made. While the soloist's contribution is not the last word in mechanical perfection, the playing communicates a sense of tragic grandeur that no other performance does. Szell, as he did so often, rises not only *to*, but frequently *above* the occasion. The conducting is so quick to pick up the music's dark and shifting moods, so tightly coiled in its pent-up intensity, that we can only wonder what kind of unspeakably shattering experience a Szell recording of *Don Giovanni* might have been.

The other recordings in the Casadesus-Szell Mozart series have been repackaged on a set of three medium-priced Sony Classical CDs (SM3K 46519), which offer incredible value for the dollar. Except for the 25th Concerto, which Szell recorded with his protégé Leon Fleisher (and which appears as filler in their box of the Beethoven concertos), all the concertos Nos. 21–27 are here, together with a version of the Double Concerto in E-flat with the pianist's talented wife Gaby and the Philadelphia under Ormandy. The level of inspiration and execution is phenomenally high, and the slightly thinning, late '50s–early '60s recorded sound remains more than adequate.

Piano Concerto No. 25 in C Major, K. 503; Piano Concerto No. 26 in D Major, K. 537, "Coronation"

Ashkenazy, piano and conductor; Philharmonia Orchestra. London 411810-2 [CD]

If conclusive proof was ever needed for the case that an artist's work need not necessarily reflect the circumstances of the artist's life, it is to be found in the final two piano concertos that Mozart composed during the last year of his life. By any standard, 1791 was a nightmare for the composer. His spendthrift wife was seriously ill, and the always fickle Viennese public had clearly grown tired of his music. He was living in abject penury, and his health—which had been frail to begin with—was slowly succumbing to at least a dozen potentially fatal diseases. Depressed, discouraged, and racked by what amounted to continuous pain, he nevertheless produced two of the greatest and most buoyantly extroverted of all his piano concertos during this period: the magisterial "Coronation" Concerto, and the irrepressibly optimistic B-flat Major Concerto, K. 595.

As both soloist and conductor, Vladimir Ashkenazy is close to the top of his form in his recordings of both works. The performance of the "Coronation" Concerto, while capitalizing fully on the work's overtly ceremonial elements, makes it seem far more personal and significant than it usually is. On the other hand, Ashkenazy's interpretation of the B-flat Major is an irresistible explosion of gaiety and sunshine, made all the more brilliant by the lustrous playing of the Philharmonia Orchestra and the equally gleaming recorded sound.

Piano Concerto No. 27 in B-flat Major, K. 595; Concerto No. 10 in E-flat Major for Two Pianos, K. 365

> Gilels, piano; Vienna Philharmonic, Böhm. Deutsche Grammophon
> 429810-2 [CD]

Emil Gilels never made a more completely winning recording than this version of Mozart's last great piano concerto. There is that Olympian ease in the playing that comes only after an artist fully understands both the music and himself, and Gilels's grasp of the B-flat Major Concerto is both effortless and profound. By that same token, Karl Böhm brings the same qualities to his accompaniments that he brought to his famous recording of *Così fan tutte:* here, as there, wisdom and humor pervade every bar.

The version of the delightful Double Concerto is no less enjoyable, joining the versions by Perahia-Lupu on Sony Classical and Brendel-Klein on Prieser as one of the very best available. The communication between Gilels and his daughter Elena is predictably natural and intimate, with Böhm again lending glowing support.

Concertos (5) for Violin and Orchestra

> Perlman, violin; Vienna Philharmonic, Levine. Deutsche Grammophon
> 415958-2 [CD] (No.1 plus Adagio and Rondos); 415975-2 [CD]
> (Nos. 2 and 4); 410020-2 [CD] (Nos. 3 and 5).
>
> Nishizaki, violin; Capella Istropolitana, Wildner, Gunzenhauser.
> Naxos 8.550414 [CD] (No. 1 and 2); 8.550418 [CD] (Nos. 3 and
> 5); 8.550332 [CD] (No. 4 and Sinfonia Concertante, K. 364).

Of all the incredible stories that combine to make the Mozart legend, one of the most far-fetched also happens to be absolutely true. Mozart was never taught how to play the violin. One day at the age of seven, he simply picked it up and that was that. Within a year he was performing in public on a half-size instrument—on one momentous occasion, before the Empress Maria Theresa herself. (Although he once sat on her voluminous lap, Mozart never thought very highly of the controversial monarch, who was said to be the real-life model for *The Magic Flute*'s sinister Queen of the Night; for her part, Maria Theresa dismissed the entire Mozart family as "useless people, running around the world like beggars.") Written in Salzburg in 1775 when the nineteen-year-old composer was resting between concert tours, the five violin concertos are not only an arresting amalgam of the Italian, French, and German traditions he had absorbed during his travels but are also, in their proud bearing and graceful melodic invention, a perfect reflection of late-rococo tastes.

In his brilliant recording for Deutsche Grammophon, Itzhak Perlman occasionally creates the impression that he is trying to disguise his own virtuosity, as if to suggest that too much technique might rob these youthful works of their freshness and charm. For the most part, he succeeds admirably, except in moments like the "turkish" episodes from the *Finale* of the A Major Concerto, when the sleeping volcano simply *must* blow its top. Levine is an unassuming but never anonymous accompanist, and the Vienna Philharmonic is on its very best behavior—which is saying something in a city that consistently boasts the most dreadfully sloppy Mozart playing in the world.

Takako Nishizaki's Naxos cycle is an excellent budget alternative and for some might be the preferred version, regardless of price. There is a refreshing openness and sense of discovery in the playing that brings the tiniest details of these youthful masterworks to life; the outer movements are invariably crisp and exciting, the slow movements full of lyrical warmth. The bonus items are no less enjoyable, especially a first-rate version—with violist Ladislav Kysélák—of the Sinfonia Concertante, K. 364, and the *Andante in F,* Camille Saint-Saëns's touching arrangement of the slow movement from the Piano Concerto in C Major, K. 467, better known as the Love Theme from *Elvira Madigan.*

Così fan tutte

Schwarzkopf, Ludwig, Steffek, Kraus, Taddei, Berry, Philharmonia Chorus and Orchestra, Böhm. EMI Classics CDMC 69330 [CD].

Caballé, Cotrubas, Baker, Gedda, Ganzarolli, Van Allen, Chorus and Orchestra of the Royal Opera House, Covent Garden, Davis. Philips 422542-2 [CD].

While it has never attained the popularity of *Don Giovanni, The Marriage of Figaro,* and *The Magic Flute,* the effervescent *Così fan tutte* certainly belongs in the company of the greatest operas that Mozart—which is to say, anyone—ever wrote. Its lightweight but enchanting plot about the ever-present danger of female infidelity (the best approximation of the title is "So do they all" or "They're all like that") is not as male chauvinist as it might seem, and Lorenzo da Ponte's witty and ingenious libretto drew from Mozart some of the most inspired music he would ever write for the stage.

Since, as characters, the two romantic couples are as purposefully interchangeable as the four ditzy lovers in Shakespeare's *Midsummer Night's Dream,* and since the old misogynist Don Alfonso and the scheming maid Despina merely exist to move the delightfully complicated plot along, *Così fan tutte* is of necessity an ensemble opera, and probably the finest ever composed. While it has its share of memorable arias, its greatest moments are the duets, trios, and quartets in which operatic polyphony reached heights of inventiveness it would never again approach.

Among all the recordings the opera has ever received, none can equal the wit, unanimity, and astonishingly generous give-and-take that can still be heard in the historic Angel recording from the early 1960s. While vocally and dramatically all of the principals are dazzling, Elisabeth Schwarzkopf and Christa Ludwig, as the sisters Fiordiligi and Dorabella, give two of the most delectable performances ever put on record, and the elfin, yet ruefully world-weary Don Alfonso of Walter Berry is one of the great comic portrayals of modern times.

The more recent and extremely entertaining Philips recording offers some particularly captivating singing from Monserrat Caballé and Dame Janet Baker and spirited conducting from Sir Colin Davis, together with a tape option and more modern recorded sound.

Divertimentos (complete)

New York Philomusica, Johnson. Vox CDX 5049/51 [CD].

Here, on three tightly packed budget-priced Vox Boxes, is the greatest aural wallpaper ever produced: the miraculous Divertimentos that Mozart composed as background music for the various social gatherings of his tin-eared employer, the Prince Archbishop of Salzburg. Even in the slightest of these pieces, Mozart's genius blazes forth in every bar: in the melodic invention, the harmonic ingenuity, the sheer delight in the act of music making, these endlessly enchanting works could not possibly have been written by anyone else.

Recorded in the early 1970s by some of the finest studio musicians in New York, the performances by the New York Philomusica are as full of life as the music itself. If there are still lingering doubts that American wind playing is the standard of the world, then these recordings should silence them. And the freshness of the playing is matched by the recorded sound, which in its warmth, transparency, and presence remains in the demonstration class. All in all, this is one of the best Mozart buys on the market today.

Don Giovanni

> Sutherland, Schwarzkopf, Sciutti, Alva, Wächter, Cappuccilli, Frick, Philharmonia Chorus and Orchestra, Giulini. EMI Classics CDCC 56232 [CD].

> Vaness, Ewing, Allen, Gale, Van Allan, Lewis, Glyndebourne Festival Chorus, London Philharmonic, Haitink. EMI Classics CDCC 47036 [CD].

Since the Giulini *Don Giovanni* was first released in 1963, there have no doubt been a few people who've waited for a finer recording of the greatest opera ever written. Good luck to them, and to those who await the Great Pumpkin, the Tooth Fairy, honest politicians, and anything worth hearing from Philip Glass.

While, in the title role, Eberhard Wächter may not have had the animal magnetism and dramatic savvy of a Cesare Siepi or an Ezio Pinza, his performance was nevertheless exceptionally musical and intelligent, and very beautifully sung. And Wächter was the *weakest* link in the chain. All the other roles are represented by what still remain their finest recorded performances: from the suave, sweet-spirited Don Ottavio of Luigi Alva—who, for once, makes the character seem like something other than the mealy-mouthed chump he probably is— to the horrifying Commendatore of Gottlob Frick. Yet it is that incomparable trio of ladies, Elisabeth Schwarzkopf, Joan Sutherland, and Graziella Sciutti, together with the phenomenally inspired direction from the man in the pit, that levitates this *Don Giovanni* onto a plane shared by only a handful of operatic recordings.

Bernard Haitink's handsomely recorded, richly dramatic interpretation is the obvious second choice for those who need more up-to-date sound, while Roger Norrington's endlessly fascinating period-instrument performance, which features both the Prague and Vienna versions wherever the two are substantially different, offers (EMI Classics CDCB 54859 [CD] an eye-opening alternative.

Exsultate, jubilate (motet); Ave verum corpus; Kyrie in D Minor; Vesperae solennes de confessore

> Te Kanawa, soprano; London Symphony, Davis. Philips 412873-2 [CD].

As a Freemason and lifelong free-thinker, Mozart was not always at his most inspired in the church music that he wrote at virtually every stage in his career; when the spirit genuinely moved him, the results could be overwhelming, as they are in the four works collected here. From Dame Kiri Te Kanawa's glowing realization of the youthful *Exsultate, jubilate* (with that most famous of "Alleluias"), to the heartbreaking *Ave verum corpus,* finished less than six months before the composer's death, all the performances here rank with the finest currently available. For those wanting all four together, this reasonably priced anthology should be an answer to their prayers.

Those wanting even more are directed to Volume 20 of Philips's Complete Mozart Edition (422520-2 [CD]), a five-disc set containing all the vespers, litanies, and other sacred odds and ends—including the early *God Is Our Refuge,* written in London to an English text—given equally fine performances by the Leipzig Radio Choir and the Dresden Staatskapelle conducted by Herbert Kegel.

*I*domeneo

> **McNair, Martinpelto, Rolfe-Johnson, Von Otter, Monteverdi Choir, English Baroque Soloists, Gardiner. Deutsche Grammophon 431674-2 [CD].**

Written for the Munich carnival season in 1781, *Idomeneo* was revived only once during Mozart's lifetime and was not heard in America until 1947 in a performance at the Tanglewood Festival. Composed in part to show off the extraordinary virtuosity of the castrato del Prato, *Idomeneo* has acquired the reputation of a rather staid and static example of *opera seria* at its worst, this in spite of the great Mozart scholar Alfred Einstein's insistence that it is "one of those works that even a genius of the highest rank, like Mozart, could write only once in a life."

No recording makes Einstein's case more persuasively than this electrifying live performance conducted by John Eliot Gardiner. With his customary blend of impeccable scholarship and passionate music making, he makes the opera come alive as no other conductor ever has. Inspired by his vision of *Idomeneo* as living theater, all of the principals sing with beauty and dramatic conviction, while the fabulous Monteverdi Choir and English Baroque Soloists perform with their customary fervor and finesse. The recording includes every note of *Idomeneo* that Mozart composed, making this the lengthiest version of the opera as well. It is all done with such obvious joy that one might begin to suspect that it is still too short.

In sum, it's a revelation.

*T*he Magic Flute

> **Popp, Gruberová, Lindner, Jerusalem, Brendel, Bracht, Zednik, Bavarian Radio Chorus and Orchestra, Haitink. EMI Classics CDCC 47951 [CD].**

For Bruno Walter, *The Magic Flute,* and not the *Requiem,* was Mozart's last will and testament. For in the characters of the questing hero Tamino, the noble priest Sarastro, and the vulgar, buffoonish, bird catcher Papageno, Walter saw the three essential components of Mozart's complex and often contradictory personality. Like most of the great conductor's speculations, this one carries a certain gentle authority and, in fact, may contain more than a grain of truth. The most divinely simple of all his great operas, *Die Zauberflöte* affords some even more tantalizing grist for the speculation mill: Had he lived, would Mozart have continued the process of simplification heard here, and in other later works? And if so, what effect would this new directness have had on the infant Romantic movement?

In his recording debut as an operatic conductor, Bernard Haitink leads one of the warmest and most dramatic performances the opera has ever received. The unusually strong cast includes many of the finest living Mozart singers. Lucia Popp is an adorably sensual Pamina; Siegfried Jerusalem, a subtle yet vocally exciting Tamino; and Edita Gruberová, as the Queen of the Night, recalls the most brilliant and commanding German coloraturas of the past. In all, this is one of the great Mozart recordings of the last decade and will probably tower above the competition for years to come.

The Marriage of Figaro

Schwarzkopf, Moffo, Cossotto, Wächter, Taddei, Vinco, Philharmonia Chorus and Orchestra, Giulini. EMI Classics CDMB 63266 [CD].

The same qualities that made the Giulini *Don Giovanni* one of the classic operatic recordings of the stereo era can be heard to equally memorable advantage in his version of what is widely regarded as the greatest comic opera ever written. While the contributions of the stunning cast cannot be praised too highly—for instance, the Countess of Elisabeth Schwarzkopf is in every way as great a creation as her Marschallin in Strauss's *Der Rosenkavalier*—it is Giulini's magical conducting that seems to place a stamp of immortality on the recording.

Only Erich Kleiber, in his famous, early-stereo version for London, managed to draw as much both from the singers and from the score itself. Yet if the Kleiber performance offered an abundance of sparkling wit, vocal beauty, and effortless grace, then the Giulini offers even more. While virtually every moment of the performance offers some startling yet utterly natural insight, the ineffable purity Giulini conjures out of the Act IV *Finale* makes it one of the most ethereally beautiful five minutes ever heard on a commercial recording.

Masonic Music

Dresden State Orchestra, Schreier. Philips 422522-2 [CD].

On December 14, 1784, Mozart was inducted as an Entered Apprentice into the *Zur Wohltätigkeit* ("Beneficence") Lodge of Vienna's Freemasons. In the late eighteenth century, Freemasonry—that secret society dedicated to the exploration of life's spiritual mysteries and to "the Brotherhood of Man under the

All-Seeing Eye of God"—was becoming extremely popular throughout the Europe of the Age of Enlightenment. Attracted by its humanistic ideals, Mozart became a Master Mason and eventually persuaded his father as well as his friend Franz Joseph Haydn to join. Not only would his love of Freemasonry inform and animate *The Magic Flute,* but it also led him to compose a substantial amount of music for actual Masonic rituals. The *Mauerische Trauermusik* (Masonic Funeral Music) is one of the darkest and most shattering of all his works, while the "Little Masonic Cantata," K. 623 *(Laut verkünde unsre Freude)* written on his deathbed to a text by Emanuel Schikaneder (the librettist of *The Magic Flute*) was his last finished composition.

With the inspired London recording by István Kertész currently unavailable, Peter Schreier's accomplished Dresden recording for Philips is a perfectly acceptable substitute, *except* that it can only be had as part of a six-CD package that also includes the cantata *Davidde penitente,* cannibalized from the C Minor Mass, plus the youthful oratorios *La Betulia liberata* and *Die Schuldigkeit des ersten Gebots* (The Duty of the First Commandment), written when Mozart was only twelve. In first-class performances conducted by Sir Neville Marriner, *Davidde* and *Die Schuldigkeit* are more than worth owning, while *La Betulia liberata* is little more than a curiosity. As with all the installments in the Complete Mozart Edition, the remastered sound and documentation are the standard of the industry.

Mass in C Minor, K. 427, "The Great"

> Cotrubas, Te Kanawa, Krenn, Sotin, John Alldis Choir, New Philharmonia Orchestra, Leppard. EMI Classics CDC 47385 [CD].

With the unfinished *Requiem,* the C Minor Mass is the most important of all of Mozart's choral works and the equal to the finest of that towering series of masses that his friend Franz Joseph Haydn completed at the end of his career. Like the *Requiem,* "The Great" C Minor Mass is a dark and disturbing work, full of uncharacteristic doubts and unsettling tensions.

Raymond Leppard leads an extremely humane and civilized interpretation of the work in a performance that features both a choir and an orchestra of chamber proportions. While the soloists are all very individual and moving, Kiri Te Kanawa gives us one of her finest recorded performances. Her singing—as well as that of Ileana Cortrubas—is as physically beautiful as any to be heard on records today, and she also invests the music with a character and sense of involvement that most of her recordings rarely reveal.

Music from the Operas, Arranged for Winds

Così fan tutte; Abduction from the Seraglio (arranged by Johann Nepomuk Wendt)

> **Berlin Philharmonic Wind Ensemble. Orfeo C 260931 [CD].**

The Marriage of Figaro (arranged by Wendt); *La Clemenza di Tito* (arranged by Josef Triebensee)

> **Berlin Philharmonic Wind Ensemble. Orfeo C 238911 A [CD].**

Don Giovanni (arranged by Triebensee)

> **Athena Ensemble. Chandos CHAN 6597 [CD].**

Josef Triebensee (1772–1846) and Johann Nepomuk Went (1745–1801) were Bohemian oboists who were active in Vienna during Mozart's time: Triebensee actually took part in the premiere of *The Magic Flute* in 1791 and eventually published two sets of Harmoniemusik that featured arrangements of excerpts from Mozart operas; as second oboist of the Kaiserlich-Königliche Harmonie, Went arranged over forty ballet and opera scores for the wind ensemble, including *The Abduction from the Seraglio, Così fan tutte,* and *The Marriage of Figaro.*

For anyone looking for some of the most elegant Music Minus One albums ever released, the three listed here are an unalloyed pleasure. Not only are the arrangements themselves unfailingly entertaining and discreet, but they are also played to perfection by the Athena Ensemble and Berlin Philharmonic Winds. On those days when you want to hear the tunes but would rather do without the voices, here's the delightful solution.

Overtures

> **Royal Philharmonic, Davis. EMI Classics CDE 67777 [CD].**
>
> **Capella Istropolitana, Wordsworth. Naxos 8.550185 [CD].**

Here, for less than it costs to take a spouse and two-and-a-half children out for frozen yogurt (not counting gas and parking) are a pair of super-budget recordings offering no fewer than twenty-two Mozart overtures in spirited, well-recorded performances led by a well-established Mozartean and a younger colleague who is about to become one.

Sir Colin Davis's recordings with the Royal Philharmonic were models of grace and enthusiasm a generation ago and have lost little of their appeal over the years. The stylish playing has abundant energy and wit, in marked contrast to this conductor's increasingly sedate recent efforts.

In addition to all the familiar classics—*Così fan tutte, Don Giovanni, The Magic Flute,* and *Figaro*—Barry Wordsworth's Naxos collection offers ten other items, some of which are little more than names in a book for most people: the early *opera serias Mitridate, rè di Ponto,* and *Lucio Silla* and the Intermezzo— and surely you remember it?—*Apollo et Hyacinthus seu Hyacinthi Metamorphosis,* written when Mozart was eleven. As in their recordings of the Haydn and Mozart symphonies, the performances by the Capella Istropolitana are both alert and affectionate and the recorded sound is first-rate.

Piano Sonatas (17)

Schiff, piano. London 430333-2 [CD].

No one has ever suggested that Mozart's piano sonatas are in any way comparable in stature or importance to the concertos he wrote for the instrument; with a couple of exceptions—the A Minor Sonata, K. 310, and the eternally popular A Major Sonata, K. 331—they are relatively unimportant in Mozart's output. Of course, the operative word is "relatively." In absolute terms, they are as instructive and enjoyable as any keyboard works written between Bach and Beethoven, and for undemanding, "easy" listening—a phrase we Serious Music types are supposed to deplore—they are worth five times their weight in Vivaldi concertos and virtually every note of music that Telemann ever wrote.

Since the days when only Artur Schnabel and Walter Gieseking seemed interested in playing them—Gieseking's peerless Angel set from the early 1950s has finally appeared on an eight-disc set from EMI Classics that includes all of the solo piano music (CDHH 63688 [CD])—there has been an explosion of Mozart sonata recordings, with superb complete cycles from András Schiff, Mitsuko Uchida, and Ingrid Haebler, among others, including a largely unheralded series from Peter Katin on the small Olympia label that includes some of the most enjoyable performances of all. Two outstandingly fine budget cycles have only complicated the choice further: those by Walter Klien on Vox and Jenö Jandó on Naxos (although at rock-bottom prices, both could be added to virtually any collection without busting the budget).

With Daniel Barenboim's EMI Classics cycle currently out of print, the performances that come closest to duplicating the vitality of those red-blooded interpretations are the London recordings by András Schiff. While consistently brilliant, the playing also has an unruffled grace and easy individuality, with just enough Romantic dash to remind us that if Mozart had had anything like a normal life span, he could have easily been around to advise the young Chopin. The recorded sound is free and full, in keeping with the spirit of the performances.

Piano Sonata No. 8 in A Minor, K. 310; No. 11 in A Major, K. 331; *Allegro and Andante, K. 533*

Perahia, piano. Sony Classical SK 48233 [CD], SM 48233 [T].

Here are the two most popular Mozart sonatas in performances that rank with the most subtle and musical ever recorded. While no ornamental detail or felicity of inner voicing escapes Perahia's attention, the interpretations unfold with an ease and naturalness that is thoroughly disarming. Although the catalogue is becoming crowded with first-rate cycles of the sonatas, Perahia makes one long for another.

Quartets (4) for Flute and Strings

Robison, flute; Tokyo String Quartet members. Vanguard OVC 4001.

On his old nightly radio program on WOR in New York, Jean Shepherd used to do a wonderful Music Minus One version of one of these pieces with a nose flute obligatio. Of late, America's greatest humorist has been far less visible than his fans would wish, although those who have listened to *A Prairie Home Companion* or watched *The Wonder Years* have been delighted to see how wide his influence has spread. His classic volumes of short stories, *In God We Trust, All Others Pay Cash,* and *Wanda Hickey's Night of Golden Memories, And Other Disasters,* not only rank with the best work of Shepherd's own hero, George Ade, but also with that of Mark Twain and Anton Chekhov as among the most darkly amusing visions of what is drolly referred to as the Human Experience.

After Shepherd, it is Paula Robison who has given me the most pleasure over the years in these charming works Mozart wrote for an instrument he disliked so intensely. Her playing has an almost elfin grace, coupled with an extraordinary musicality and purity of tone. The members of the Tokyo Quartet play at the top of their early form and the '60s recorded sound has held up incredibly well.

Quartet in F Major for Oboe and Strings, K. 370

Mack, oboe; Cleveland Orchestra Ensemble. Crystal CD 323 [CD], C 323 [T].

Kiss, oboe; Kodály String Quartet. Naxos 8.550437 [CD].

One of the principal glories of twentieth-century American wind playing—which by common consent is now regarded as the most vital and distinguished in the world—is the incomparable sound of the American oboe, the final stage in the evolution of an instrument that began life as the raucous business end of the medieval bagpipe. Essentially a fusion of the flexibility of the French school with the strength and solidity of the German sound, it came to final fruition in the example and precept of Marcel Tabuteau, the longtime principal oboist of the Philadelphia Orchestra and professor of music at the Curtis Institute, and in the playing of the first great native-born virtuoso, Mitch Miller.

The greatest of Tabuteau's pupils, longtime principal oboist of the New York Philharmonic, and in the opinion of many the finest player who ever drew an incredibly deep breath, the legendary Harold Gomberg recorded this alpha and omega of the instrument's chamber literature twice: once in the 1950s for American Decca and again toward the end of his career for Vanguard. Until the latter is returned to circulation—and with such a treasure at their disposal, how *could* Vanguard reissue that limp essay in the art of wobbling by André Ladrot?—lovers of the Mozart Quartet will have to make the best of a bad situation.

The finest available performance of the piece is by the Cleveland Orchestra's adroit John Mack, who plays with considerable style and finesse on a not always easy to find Crystal recording. While the performances of the Britten *Metamorphoses* and the Loeffler *Rhapsodies* are no less fine, more appropriate couplings can be found on the Naxos recording with the Hungarian oboist József Kiss. In addition to a first-rate version of the Oboe Quartet, the album offers stylish performances of Mozart's Horn Quintet and *A Musical Joke,* all at fire-sale prices.

Quartets (2) for Piano and Strings

Giuranna, viola; Beaux Arts Trio. Philips 410391-2 [CD].

As much as any of the composer's chamber works, these glorious quartets have led a charmed life in the recording studio, beginning with Artur Schnabel's 1934 recording of the G Minor Quartet with the Pro Arte, available now on Angel CDHB 63870 [CD]. While George Szell's brilliant 1946 versions with the Budapest Quartet can be found on a Sony Classical Masterworks Portrait CD (MPK 47685), those transcendent 1952 performances by Sir Clifford Curzon and the Amadeus, while in the London CD catalogue briefly, have now been withdrawn.

The modern recordings that most clearly belong in that distinguished company are those by the Beaux Arts Trio and company. The playing has sparkle and purpose and the recorded sound is admirably vivid and clear. The elegant performances by Gyula Kiss and the Tátrai Trio on White Label HRC 170 offer a fine budget-priced alternative.

Quintet in A Major for Clarinet and Strings, K. 581

Shifrin, clarinet; Chamber Music Northwest. Delos DCD 3020 [CD].

Unlike the flute and the tenor voice, the two instruments he thoroughly despised, Mozart's initial reaction to the sound of the recently invented clarinet was love at first sight. He first heard them at the court of Mannheim in the late 1770s and, during the next decade, he would compose the first great works written for the instrument: the E-flat Major Trio, K. 498, and the most popular of all his chamber works, the great A Major Clarinet Quintet.

From the recording made during the 78 era by the legendary English clarinetist Reginald Kell, to that poignant little performance with a group of captured Chinese musicians led by Major Charles Emerson Winchester III (David Ogden Stiers) in the concluding episode of *M.A.S.H.*, the Quintet has received countless memorable performances over the years and is currently represented by at least a half-dozen superlative recordings.

While less well known than his glamorous near contemporary Richard Stoltzman, David Shifrin is every bit his equal, as this sterling Delos recording clearly shows. Physically, Shifrin's sound is as large and as beautiful as any in the world today. Musically, he is one of the most imaginative and individual performers of his generation, mixing an attractive, instantly recognizable musical personality with an unerring sense of decorum and good taste. While cast on a somewhat grand and Romantic scale, Shifrin's interpretation is also superbly detailed and intimate. With sensitive and enthusiastic support from four of his Chamber Music Northwest colleagues, coupled with its dazzling recorded sound, this is easily the most appealing recording the Quintet has received in at least a dozen years.

Currently, Stolzman's recording with the Tokyo Quartet (RCA 60723-4) is the best of the available tapes.

Quintet in E-flat Major for Piano and Winds, K. 452

Perahia, piano; English Chamber Orchestra members. CBS MK 42099 [CD].

In an otherwise chatty letter written to his father around the time of the E-flat Major Quintet's premiere, Mozart said that he considered this the finest work he had written up to that time. Not the finest *chamber* work, mind you, but the finest work, *period*. As an indication of just how highly he thought of the piece, the music he had written up to that time included most of the string quartets, all the masses (save the *Requiem*), and all of the symphonies except for the last three.

Among its many admirers was the young Beethoven, who just *happened* to produce a quintet for the same combination of instruments—piano, oboe, clarinet, bassoon, and horn—in the same exact key. (Recording company executives have been eternally grateful to Beethoven for his thoughtfulness: the Op. 16 Quintet has always been the inevitable companion piece for the Mozart, as it is on this CBS release.)

Murray Perahia's bracing, eventful recording with the winds of the English Chamber Orchestra has much in common with his versions of the Mozart piano concertos. Although Perahia is clearly the leader of the band—the piano is the dominant voice, as it was certainly meant to be—the four wind players are given an unusual amount of freedom in terms of texture and phrasing, and all seem to fall in happily with Perahia's plans. Neil Black, the finest oboist the British have produced since Leon Goossens, is especially stylish and playful, but his ECO colleagues aren't far behind. With an equally spry and sensitive account of the Beethoven—which, if it can't compare with the Mozart, is still a very impressive work for a rude, uncouth kid from the Rhineland—this is one of the most enjoyable chamber music recordings in years.

Quintets (6) for Strings

Gerecz, Lesueur, Grumiaux Trio. Philips 422511-2 [CD].

Sandwiched between the C Minor Quintet, which he arranged from his unsettling Serenade for Winds, K. 388, and the Quintet in E-flat Major, his last significant chamber work completed a few months before his death, are two of Mozart's greatest compositions in any form: the sunny Quintet in C Major, K. 515, and its tormented companion piece, the Quintet in G Minor, K. 516. Cast in the composer's favorite "tragic" key, the G Minor Quintet is one music's most desperate outcries, the work—in Alfred Einstein's vivid phrase—"of a lonely man surrounded on all sides by the walls of a deep chasm."

If other recordings may have plumbed that chasm more dramatically, then none have done it with greater understanding or more sheer beauty than that accomplished ensemble led by the Belgian violinist Arthur Grumiaux. In fact, in all of these sublime works one can hear some of the purest and most responsive chamber-music playing ever recorded.

An eminent critic of my acquaintance, whenever he feels himself in danger of buying a surplus Sherman tank and giving the human race what it probably deserves, heads for a cabin in the woods armed only with mineral water and cassettes of these performances. So far, he has always returned restored and refreshed, with renewed hope for the species. Considering what even used tanks must be going for these days, this recording may be one of your shrewder long-term psychiatric investments.

*R*equiem, K. 626

> Kenny, soprano; Hodgson, mezzo-soprano; Davies, tenor; Howell,
> bass; London Symphony Chorus, Northern Sinfonia, Hickox.
> Virgin Classics CUV 61260 [CD].

In recent years, the trend in recordings of this great and terrifying work has been toward performances with faster speeds and lighter textures, as if any hint of nineteenth-century opulence and grandeur might do some irreparable harm. While the Hickox interpretation clearly falls within the parameters of that new performing tradition, it is also one that steadfastly refuses to throw out the baby with the bathwater. Although everything is clearly sung and crisply articulated, the awe and terror at the heart of the piece are projected with a frightening immediacy. The London Symphony Chorus performs with a single-minded intensity that matches their work in Hickox's stunning recording of Walton's *Belshazzar's Feast* (see page 784), while each of the soloists sings with tremendous conviction and personality. With outstanding playing from the Northern Sinfonia, and the modest price tag, this is an exceptional bargain.

For those who need the authentic snarl of period instruments, John Eliot Gardiner's Philips recording (420197-2 [CD]) is an obvious first choice. In addition to an interpretation of withering intensity and high drama, the album offers the moving but rarely heard *Kyrie in D Minor*, K. 368a, as an attractive bonus.

*S*erenade in D Major, K. 239, *Serenata Notturna;* Serenade in D Major, K. 250, "Haffner"

> Prague Chamber Orchestra, Mackerras. Telarc CD 80161 [CD].

Few people begin what Voltaire called "that dull meal at which dessert is served at the beginning" as memorably as did the offspring of one of Salzburg's most prominent families, for whose marriage Mozart composed the "Haffner" Serenade. Like most of the composer's lighter occasional works, this one contains deep and unsuspected riches: for contained within its eight diverting movements is a de facto violin concerto.

While Oldřich Vicek, the concertmaster of the Prague Chamber Orchestra, acquits himself admirably in the demanding solo part, Sir Charles Mackerras never loses sight of the essentially frivolous—albeit *divinely* frivolous—nature of the music. From first to last, this is a spirited, good-natured romp characterized by sprightly tempos, pointed rhythms, and uncomplicated emotions. As a generous bonus, the recording comes with an equally persuasive account of the *Serenata Notturna*.

Mackerras's companion version of the "Posthorn" Serenade (80108 [CD]) is also outstanding, as is the accompanying performance of "Eine kleine Nachtmusik." The Prague Chamber Orchestra again plays with a disarming naturalness, while the recorded sound is equally unaffected.

Serenade No. 10 in B-flat Major, K. 361, "Gran Partita"; Serenade No. 11 in E Major, K. 375; Serenade No. 12 in C Minor, K. 388

Chamber Orchestra of Europe, Schneider. ASV CDCOE-804 [CD]
(No. 10); ASV CDCOE-802 [CD] (Nos. 11 and 12).

Even counting the *Music for the Royal Fireworks,* the Dvořák D Minor Serenade, the Holst Suites, and that score of deathless masterworks by John Philip Sousa, these three Mozart serenades are probably the greatest music ever written for winds. In its variety, invention, and sheer humanity, the "Gran Partita" is one of the best arguments ever put forward for being alive— and at nearly an hour, it is *still* too short. The E-flat Major Serenade is all but a dictionary definition of "geniality," while its C Minor companion piece is one of the most mysterious works that Mozart ever wrote. (We know nothing about the occasion for which Mozart produced this turbulent outburst, whose complexity and depth of emotion are so at odds with what is supposed to be an essentially lightweight form. Nor can we guess how it must have been received by its first audience. While the analogy might overstate the case ever so slightly, it would be very similar to a modern audience trooping off to see a Neil Simon comedy and being treated to something on the order of *King Lear.*)

Without making too much of the May-December metaphor, the combination of the young, enthusiastic Chamber Orchestra of Europe and the sage, vastly experienced Alexander Schneider must account for some of the special chemistry of these glowing performances. The kids and the Old Man get on like a house afire, with results that are so wide-eyed *and* knowing it reminds you of one of the key lines from Masters's *Spoon River Anthology:* "Genius is wisdom and youth."

Serenade in G Major, K. 525, "Eine kleine Nachtmusik"

Columbia Symphony, Walter. CBS MK-37774 [CD], MT-37774 [T].

Recordings of this imperishable charmer come and go, but none has ever seriously challenged that miracle of freshness and amiability that Bruno Walter recorded in the final years of his career. If the strings of the Columbia Symphony are not as clean and precise as they could have been, or the remastered recorded sound still retains its tubby bottom and hissy top, what does it matter? The music unfolds with such affectionate deftness and spontaneity that you'll almost suspect that the ink was still wet on the page.

In addition to this most ingratiating of all recorded versions of the Serenade, the album also features vintage Walter interpretations of *The Impresario, Così fan tutte, The Marriage of Figaro,* and *The Magic Flute* Overtures, together with the moving, important, yet rarely heard *Masonic Funeral Music.*

Sonata in D for Piano Four-Hands, K. 381; Sonata in C for Piano Four-Hands, K. 521; Sonata in D for Two Pianos, K. 448

Argerich, Rabinovitch, piano. Teldec 91378-2 [CD].

No one ever wrote more imaginatively for two pianos or with more idiomatic grace than Mozart, whose favorite childhood musical experiences included playing duets with his sister Nannerl. Martha Argerich and Alexandre Rabinovitch project a similarly natural affinity for these works, not only in the way they reveal the uncanny skill of the voicing as the argument moves so effortlessly from one pair of hands to another, but also in the dramatic bite they bring to an important work like the D Major Sonata, K. 448. Teldec's recorded sound is as natural and effortless as the playing.

Sonatas (16) for Violin and Piano

Goldberg, violin; Lupu, piano. Decca 448526-2 [CD].

These elegant, deeply musical recordings of the mature Violin and Piano Sonatas were the fruits of a unique collaboration. The concertmaster of Wilhelm Furtwängler's Berlin Philharmonic who, despite the conductor's impassioned defense of his Jewish musicians, was forced to flee Nazi Germany in 1934, Szymon Goldberg was also, for a time, the violinist of a famous string trio whose other members were cellist Emanuel Feuermann and *violist* Paul Hindemith. At the time he recorded the Mozart sonatas in 1975 with the then young Rumanian pianist Radu Lupu, Goldberg was in his mid-sixties, a player of vast experience and understanding with almost all of his technique intact.

While other teams such as Perlman and Barenboim have brought more color and flash to these marvelous works, no recordings have ever presented the sonatas more naturally or shown as much mutual respect and affection as these. For just as the youthful pianist is inspired to play with a burnished wisdom, so the playing of the aging violinist seems infused with a spring-like glow. The result, in short, is a series of performances that are as ageless and timeless as they are undeniably beautiful.

Although the recording is not readily available in America, many of the larger stores will stock it or be able to order it through European suppliers.

Songs

Ameling, soprano; Baldwin, piano. Philips 422524-2 [CD].

Bonney, soprano; Parsons, piano. Teldec 2292-46334-2 [CD].

Schwarzkopf, soprano; Gieseking, piano. EMI Classics CDH 63702 [CD].

If Mozart's achievement as a song composer doesn't really begin to approach that of Schubert or the later masters of the form, then some of his lieder are among the freshest and most endearing ever composed: from the childlike charm of *Die kleine Spinnerin* to the more mature demands of *Abendempfindung* to the tongue-in-cheek heartbreak of *Das Veilchen*.

Elly Ameling's complete recording for Philips is the natural place to begin exploring this minor but delightful corner of a great composer's workshop. Recorded in 1977, Ameling's voice was captured at its most pristine, while the artistry of the great lieder specialist of her generation is spellbinding throughout. The two-CD set contains some enchanting rarities, like a pair of miniature songs with mandolin accompaniment.

Spellbinding, too, are the famous recordings that Elisabeth Schwarzkopf made with Walter Gieseking in 1956. While almost every item contains some jaw-dropping wonder of phrasing, dynamic coloration, or word-painting, the portrait of the pouting child in *Sehnsucht nach dem Frühling* is priceless—one of this legendary singer's greatest achievements.

That adjective may very well be applied one day to exquisite young American soprano Barbara Bonney, if she keeps making recordings like this. Her Mozart album for Teldec is in every way a worthy companion to those of her distinguished predecessors: the voice is not only strikingly pretty, but it is also guided by vast reserves of intelligence, musicianship, and interpretive savvy. The late Geoffrey Parsons was never more sympathetic and the recorded sound is excellent.

String Quartets 14–19, "Haydn Quartets"

Quartetto Italiano. Philips 422512-2 [CD].

Chilingirian Quartet. CRD 3362/64 [CD].

Juilliard String Quartet. Odyssey MB3K-45826 [CD].

Begun in 1782 after a nine-year period during which he composed no string quartets at all, the six works that Mozart wrote under the influence of, and eventually dedicated to, his friend Franz Joseph Haydn constitute one of the great summits in the history of chamber music. Haydn himself was overwhelmed by his young friend's touching act of homage. It was this music that led Haydn to tell Mozart's father, "I swear before God and as an honest man, that your son is the greatest composer known to me, either in person or by reputation."

Collectors who would like to buy the six quartets together in a convenient package now find themselves in one of those difficult quandaries that the recording companies seem to take such delight in. The most charming and completely memorable versions of the "Haydn" Quartets—those classic performances by Quartetto Italiano—are now only available as part of an eight-CD box from Philips, which also brings us superb performances of the rest of Mozart's twenty-three quartets. To be sure, this represents a substantial outlay of money, but this "medium-priced" set—and how long will it be before compact disc prices start becoming rational?—actually is a bargain in the long run. Compared to the hit-and-miss six-CD set with the Amadeus Quartet on Deutsche Grammophon, the all-important pleasure-per-dollar ratio is extremely high.

Of the recordings that feature the "Haydns" all by themselves, the lively, insightful interpretations by the Chilingirian Quartet are probably the most consistently rewarding. The Odyssey recording by the Juilliard Quartet offers brilliant playing and a budget price, along with a slightly fierce recorded sound and absolutely no documentation.

Symphonies 1–20

Academy of St. Martin-in-the-Fields, Marriner. Philips 422501-2 [CD].

Marriner's admirable set of the early symphonies, the first volume of Philips's epic Complete Mozart Edition—a 45-volume, 179-CD collection of the man's *entire* output—offers refreshingly vibrant and consistently stylish interpretations of the first twenty numbered symphonies, together with eleven other equally agreeable works. Unlike Haydn, who didn't begin exploring the form until he was well into his twenties, Mozart's early essays are clearly juvenalia—although being *Mozart's* juvenalia, virtually every scrap has something enchanting or revealing to say. Expect no hidden masterworks here, just a fascinating glimpse into the evolution of the most extraordinary genius the world has ever known.

Symphony No. 25 in G Minor, K. 183; Symphony No. 29 in A Major, K. 201; Symphony No. 38 in D Major, K. 504, "Prague"; Symphony No. 40 in G Minor, K. 550; Serenade in D Major, K. 239, *Serenata Notturna*

English Chamber Orchestra, Britten. London 444323-2 [CD].

Recorded in the embracing acoustics of the Maltings, Snape, these justly famous readings have a special authority not usually encountered in studio recordings. Most famous of all is Britten's version of the G Minor Symphony, which, by taking every possible repeat, expands the piece to "Eroica" Symphony proportions. The interpretation itself is full of drama and insight, with the English Chamber Orchestra obviously inspired by the spirit of the occasion. Similarly, Britten gives the "Little G Minor" an uncommon weight and significance, while the A Major glows with youthful warmth. Best of all, though, may be the performance of the "Prague" Symphony, which along with a joyous projection of its festive elements clearly underscores the family resemblance to *Don Giovanni*.

Symphony No. 25 in G Minor, K. 183; Symphony No. 28 in C Major, K. 200; Symphony No. 29 in A Major, K. 201

Prague Chamber Orchestra, Mackerras. Telarc CD 80165 [CD].

At an age when most teenage boys are beginning to think about whom to ask to the Junior Prom, Mozart was busy writing music like this for his boss, the reactionary Prince Archbishop of Salzburg. On hearing the "Little G Minor" Symphony for the first time, his Eminence's only comment was, "Far too modern."

This trio of youthful works—surely the greatest symphonies ever written by an adolescent—have had no finer recorded performances than those by Sir Charles Mackerras and the Prague Chamber Orchestra. Benjamin Britten's famous versions of Nos. 25 and 29 (available in the UK, though, alas, not here) were exceptionally dramatic and resilient, but Mackerras yields nothing to those classic interpretations in terms of sparkle or elegance; besides, the Brittens are now long out of print.

As in the other releases in his exceptional Mozart symphony series, Mackerras takes the middle ground between the grand opulence of a Bruno Walter or an Otto Klemperer and the desiccated stinginess of period-instrument recordings. The orchestra, using modern instruments, is one of chamber proportions, but the slightly reverberant acoustics create the impression of space and depth without sacrificing any of the detail. Tempos tend to be brisk but judicious, and the execution is as meticulous as it is exuberant. With the C Major Symphony tossed in for *very* good measure, this amounts to nearly eighty minutes of world-class music making—a best buy in anybody's book.

Symphony No. 27 in G Major, K. 299; Symphony No. 33 in B-flat Major, K. 319; Symphony No. 36 in C Major, K. 425, "Linz"

Symphony No. 34 in C Major, K. 338; Symphony No. 35 in D Major, K. 385, "Haffner"; Symphony No. 39 in E-flat Major, K. 543

> Capella Istropolitana, Wordsworth. Naxos 8.550294 [CD];
> 8.550186 [CD].

As in their marvelous Haydn symphony recordings, Barry Wordsworth and this fine Slovak ensemble prove wonderful guides to the Mozart symphonies. The performances are consistently joyous, alert, and unpretentious, unfolding with a natural ease that is a delight to hear. While all the installments in the series are excellent, the pairing of the "Haffner" Symphony with the Symphony No. 39 in E-Flat (with the Symphony No. 34 thrown in as a bonus) is the most attractive since Szell's now-deleted CBS recording. Similarly, Wordsworth's version of the "Linz" Symphony is as enjoyable as any currently available, while the same may be said of its two companions. The recorded sound is as appealing as the interpretations, offering a richly detailed yet perfectly natural perspective.

At Naxos prices, it really makes little sense *not* to acquire the other splendid offerings in the series, regardless of how many alternative recordings one might own. To date, these include Naxos 8.550113 [CD] (Nos. 25, 32, and 41, "Jupiter") and 8.550164 [CD] (Nos. 28, 31, "Paris," and 40). Symphonies Nos. 40 and 41 are also available together on 8.550299 [CD].

Symphony No. 29 in A Major, K. 201; Symphony No. 31 in D Major, K. 297, "Paris"; Symphony No. 34 in C Major, K. 388

Symphony No. 40 in G Minor, K. 550; Symphony No. 41 in C Major, K. 551, "Jupiter"

> Vienna Philharmonic, Bernstein. Deutsche Grammophon
> 431040-2 [CD].

In terms of important recordings, Leonard Bernstein's association with the Vienna Philharmonic was probably the most significant of his career. Not since Furtwängler had the orchestra fallen so completely under the spell of a single musical personality—"seduced" is the word that was bandied about in the Viennese press for years—nor did Bernstein ever seem more completely himself than when working with this unique and difficult ensemble. The most dramatic difference between the New York and Vienna Bernsteins was the ease with which the Europeans fell in with even the most willfully Romantic of the conductor's designs: for the New Yorkers, following Lenny's often wayward requests was a matter of professional pride; for the Viennese, it was doing something that was already in their blood.

Nowhere is the special magic of the Bernstein–Vienna partnership more obvious than in their versions of Mozart's final symphonies, taped—as the bulk of their recordings were—during actual concert performances. From the harrowing intensity of the opening movement to the oddly fanciful finale, Bernstein's version of the G Minor Symphony is one of the most individual ever recorded, as is his expansive, triumphant reading of the "Jupiter," a performance that simultaneously rings down the curtain on the Classical era and clears the stage for Beethoven. Reissued at medium price, this constitutes either a clear first choice or a fascinating second opinion for any collection.

Symphony No. 35 in D Major, K. 385, "Haffner"; Symphony No. 36 in C Major, "Linz"; Symphony No. 38 in D Major, "Prague"

London Philharmonic, Beecham. Dutton Laboratories DUT 5001 [CD].

At the luncheon celebrating Sir Thomas Beecham's seventieth birthday, a number of congratulatory telegrams were read, including those from Sibelius, Stravinsky, Richard Strauss, and other composers thanking the conductor for all he had done for their music. During a lull in the applause, Beecham was heard to ask: "Nothing from Mozart?"

With the possible exception of Bruno Walter, no conductor did more to revive and popularize the Mozart symphonies in the early decades of the century than Beecham, whose vigorous, stylish recordings from the 78 era are among the most exhilarating ever recorded. For Beecham, "Mozart emancipated music from the bonds of a formal age, while remaining the true voice of the eighteenth century. His new sentiment or emotion, as expressed by a matchless technique, was his supreme gift to the world. That sentiment was an intimacy, a masculine tenderness, unique—something confiding, affectionate." This is precisely what every bar of these magical recordings convey. The 1939–1940 recorded sound remains perfectly serviceable on this and a companion album (DUT 5008 [CD]), featuring similarly unique accounts of the 29th, 34th, and "Paris" Symphonies, also lovingly restored by the Dutton engineers.

Beecham once said: "If I were a dictator, I should make it compulsory for every member of the population between the ages of four and eighty to listen to Mozart for at least one-quarter of an hour daily for the coming five years." He couldn't have done better than these.

Symphony No. 35 in D Major, "Haffner"; Symphony No. 40 in G Minor, K. 550; Symphony No. 41 in C Major, K. 551, "Jupiter"

Cleveland Orchestra, Szell. CBS MYK-38472 [CD], MYT-38472 [T].

Nowhere are George Szell's considerable skills as a Mozart conductor more conspicuously on display than in his recordings of three of Mozart's greatest symphonies. From its thrilling opening flourish, the performance of the "Haffner" crackles with unfailing energy and transcendent wit, just as the G Minor bristles with nervous intensity and the "Jupiter" surges with noble power. The Cleveland Orchestra proves again that it was the finest Haydn-Mozart ensemble of its time, and the remastered sound, while slightly shrill, is perfectly adequate.

Symphony No. 40 in G Minor, K. 550; Symphony No. 41 in C Major, K.551, "Jupiter"

Philharmonia Orchestra, Klemperer. EMI Classics CDMD 63272 [CD].

With their transcendentally serene and good-natured companion piece in E-flat, the G Minor and "Jupiter" Symphonies form a trilogy that marks the absolute high-water mark of eighteenth-century symphonic thought. In these great and mysterious works—why or for what occasion Mozart wrote them has never been known—the Classical symphony reached its final stage of perfection. After Mozart, there was literally no place for the form left to go, other than through the bold and convulsive experiments of Beethoven, which signaled the beginning of the Symphony's inevitable death.

Otto Klemperer's monumental performances from the early 1960s have a fair claim to being the greatest recordings each of the last two symphonies have ever received. It is not simply the breadth of the interpretations that make them so extraordinary, for other conductors have adopted tempos in the outer movements that are nearly as slow. It is the conductor's Olympian insight—whether in probing the depths of despair in the Fortieth or the heights of the "Jupiter's" exultation—that gives the performances a sense of scale and scope that makes them unique. While there have been more turbulent recordings of the G Minor Symphony and more exciting readings of the "Jupiter," there are none that capture more of the tragedy and triumph of Mozart's farewell to the symphony than these.

If Klemperer's Mozart is to your taste—for *my* hard-earned money, his Mozart conducting ranks with Beecham's and Walter's as the greatest we are ever likely to hear—then this four-CD set combines these two recordings with versions of eight of the other late symphonies, Nos. 25, 29, 31, 33, 34, 35, 36, and 38, into one convenient, not-to-be-overlooked box.

Bruno Walter's integral recording of the last six symphonies is equally indispensable, especially in the brilliantly remastered versions from Sony Classical's "Bruno Walter Edition" (MBK 44778 [CD], SMK 64474 [CD], SMK 64477 [CD]). All the performances glow with this conductor's unmistakable warmth and humanity, while the sound of the recordings, made in the early '60s at the old Legion Hall in Hollywood, has retained much of its presence and bloom.

Trio for Clarinet, Viola, and Piano, K. 498, "Kegelstatt"

Balogh, clarinet; Konrád, viola; Jandó, piano. Naxos 8.550439 [CD].

Legend has it that Mozart composed this unusually scored trio while playing skittles, a game called ninepins by the English and *Kegel* by the Germans. If the legend is true, then it is one of the most eloquent testimonies to the man's genius—to say nothing of his powers of concentration—as the "Kegelstatt" Trio is a work of unique power, blending the sensuous voices of the clarinet and viola, Mozart's two favorite instruments, as no other chamber work ever has.

These three Hungarian musicians give a warmly sympathetic performance of the piece, with leisurely but completely satisfying tempos and an excellent feel for balances and inner details. Equally enjoyably are the performances of the two Clarinet Quartets arranged—probably *not* by Mozart—from other chamber sources but both unalloyed delights.

Trios (6) for Piano, Violin, and Cello

Beaux Arts Trio. Philips 446154-2 [CD]

In spite of the largely secondary role assigned to the cello, the best of Mozart's piano trios—those in G, K. 496; in B-flat, K. 502; and in E, K. 542—rank with the finest of all his chamber works; even when the composer's inspiration wanes (as it does in the last two trios, K. 548 and 564, written during one of the most hard-pressed periods of his life), the surface gaiety is enough to make them thoroughly entertaining experiences.

Reissued on a medium-priced Philips Duo, the Beaux Arts Trio recordings from the late 1960s give enormous pleasure, thanks in no small part to the imaginative playing of pianist Menahem Pressler. If the performances are not quite as subtle nor as handsomely recorded as their later digital version—available only as part of the five-disc Volume 14 of Philips's Complete Mozart Edition (422514-2 [CD])—then the fine performances and modest price tag offer more than adequate compensation.

Variations for solo piano (complete)

Barenboim, piano. EMI Classics CDCC 54362 [CD].

This handsome three-CD set from Angel is obviously not to be digested over the course of one or two evenings but is instead something to be indiscriminately dipped into like Boswell's *Life of Johnson* whenever the spirit needs a quick fix of civilizing charm. From famous sets like the Twelve Variations on "Ah, Vous dirai-je, Maman" to oddities like the Six Varations on "Mio caro Adone" by Antonio Salieri, Barenboim is here as consistent and imaginative as he was in his magnificent cycle of the Piano Sonatas, bringing to each set a sense of eager discovery that makes even the least of them seem utterly unique.

Mussorgsky, Modest (1839–1881)

Boris Godunov

**Valente, Gorochovskaya, Nichiteanu, Zarmeba, Lipovšek, Langridge,
Wildhaber, Fedin, Leiferkus, Kotcherga, Shagidullin, Ramey, Larin,
Nikolsky, Berlin Radio Chorus, Slovak Philharmonic Chorus,
Berlin Philharmonic, Abbado. Sony Classical S3K 58977 [CD].**

In any of its several versions—the two by the composer himself, and the famous revision made by a well-intentioned friend—Mussorgsky's *Boris Godunov* is not only the most powerful and original Russian opera ever written but also one of the most relentlessly gripping theatrical experiences of the operatic stage. Since the days that Feodor Chaliapin's famous, overwhelming interpretation made it a major box-office attraction in the West, most listeners have come to know *Boris* through Rimsky-Korsakov's brilliant arrangement. While that wizard of the late-Romantic orchestra deserves the lion's share of credit for the opera's subsequent popularity, in the composer's 1872 revision, the opera emerges as a cruder, rougher, and more starkly original piece.

Based on a series of live concert performances given in Berlin and a stage production at the Salzburg Festival, Claudio Abbado's version is the most thrilling and immediate ever recorded, handily surpassing the now-deleted Philips recording led by Vladimir Fedoseyev. Along with the dramatically intense yet beautifully sung Boris of Anatoli Kotcherga, every one of the soloists makes a vivid contribution, particularly Gleb Nikolsky as the drunken Varlam, Marjana Lipovšek as Marina and—in an especially extravagant bit of casting—Samuel Ramey as Pimen. In the massed choral scenes—and in *Boris,* as in Puccini's

Turandot, the chorus is at least as important any of the opera's other major characters—the Berlin Radio and Slovak Philharmonic Choruses sing with electrifying power and precision, while Abbado inspires his great orchestra to amazing feats of courage and virtuosity. At the time of its release, it was rumored that this was the first opera recording to cost in excess of two million dollars. Judging from the final product, it was worth every penny.

The Capture of Kars: Triumphal March; Scherzo in B-flat; St. John's Night on Bare Mountain (original version); *Khovanshchina:* Prelude and *Galitsin's Journey; The Destruction of Sennacherib; Oedipus in Athens: Chorus of the People in the Temple; Salammbô: Chorus of Priestesses*

> London Symphony Chorus and Orchestra, Abbado. RCA 09026-
> 61354-2 [CD].

When this RCA anthology came out in the early 1980s, it was the single most unusual Mussorgsky album yet released. By a comfortable margin, it still is. Apart from the familiar *Khovanshchina* Prelude, all of the items are oddities, including the original version of *Night on Bare Mountain,* which is radically different from the Rimsky-Korsakov arrangement that made it world famous: in its harmonies, structure, and orchestration, Mussorgsky's original is the far wilder and woollier piece. The remainder of the program is equally fascinating, especially the early choruses that show the genius of this most gifted of nineteenth-century Russian composers about to bloom. The playing and singing are of the highest order and the remastered recorded sound is superb.

Khovanshchina

> Borodina, Galusin, Minjelkiev, Ohotnikav, Kirov Opera Chorus and
> Orchestra, Gergiev. Philips 432147-2 [CD].

Set against the backdrop of the political turmoil that swept Russia at the time the forward-looking Peter the Great ascended to the throne in 1682, *Khovanshchina* is in many ways a more ambitious opera than *Boris Godunov* and, in most respects, far less universal. Essentially a sweeping historical panorama, it lacks the cohesiveness, to say nothing of the riveting central character, that animates Mussorgsky's masterpiece. But in its best moments—the lovely prelude "Dawn on the Moscow River," the wonderfully suggestive "Dance of the Persian Slaves," the thrilling choral passages, the deeply poignant closing scene in which the Old Believers opt for a *Götterdämmerung*-like immolation rather than renounce their faith—*Khovanshchina* clearly springs from the same source of inspiration that yielded that greatest of Russian operas.

Captured during actual performances at the Vienna State Opera, Claudio Abbado's now-deleted Deutsche Grammophon version was one of the conductor's finest recordings. Aided by an alert and sensitive cast, he infused the often episodic action with an uncharacteristic urgency and sense of purpose. Apart from the occasional cough or stomping entrance, the live recording only heightened the sense of drama and occasion. Anyone even remotely interested in Russian opera can only hope that this indispensable recording will be reissued without delay.

Until it is, the Kirov Opera production conducted by Valery Gergiev makes for an adequate earthbound alternative. While neither the singing nor the conducting matches Abbado's standards, there are many fine moments and a few genuinely exciting ones, with some particularly thrilling contributions from the chorus.

Pictures at an Exhibition

New York Philharmonic, Bernstein. Sony Classical SMK 46595 [CD],
    SM 47595 [T].

Pletnev, piano. Virgin Classics 59611 [CD].

Either in its original piano version or in the familiar orchestration that Serge Koussevitzky commissioned from Maurice Ravel in 1925, *Pictures at an Exhibition* is among the most inventive and original works ever written by a Russian composer. Beginning with the pioneering recordings by Koussevitzky and Arturo Toscanini (on RCA 60287-2-RG [CD], a performance complete with the famous unwritten tympani roll toward the end of "The Great Gate of Kiev," which suggests the Maestro's devotion to the inviolability of the score was not quite as fanatical as his legend would have you believe), the Ravel edition of the *Pictures* has probably received more great recordings than any other twentieth-century orchestral score.

One of Leonard Bernstein's earliest recordings after assuming the directorship of the New York Philharmonic in 1958 also remains one of his best. It was also the most impressive stereo recording that CBS—then Columbia—had made up to that time. Bright and richly detailed, with a particularly solid and resonant bottom end, the physical sound remains astonishingly impressive in its compact disc transfer, and Bernstein's performance, after nearly thirty years, still remains the one to beat. In no other recording do all of the individual pictures emerge with such character and clarity, from the heavy ponderousness of the oxcart section, to the delicate humor of the "Ballet of the Chicks in Their Eggs." Yet it is with the final two portraits that Bernstein leaves the competition at the museum door. The "Hut on Fowls' Legs" is a wonder of demonic fury and intensity, and the performance concludes with the most thrilling and majestic "Great Gate of

Kiev" ever put on records. The explosive version of *Night on Bald Mountain* that accompanies the *Pictures* makes it seem like a very wild evening indeed.

The arrival of Mikhail Pletnev's spellbinding Virgin Classics recording takes some of the sting out of Sony Classical's incomprehensible decision to yank the late Sviatoslav Richter's astounding 1958 recording from circulation. Pletnev manages to match his great predecessor in a number of key areas, especially in the single-mindedness of his vision and control of dynamic effects. If the overwhelming power of the Richter interpretation remains unique, then in this Pletnev is not far behind—his "Great Gate of Kiev" is wonderfully concentrated and massive—and, of course, he has the advantage of far superior recorded sound.

Songs (complete)

> Christoff, bass; Labinsky, Moore, piano; ORTF Orchestra, Tzipine.
> EMI Classics CHS 63025 [CD].

If Mussorgsky had written nothing except for the music contained in this collection, then he would still be remembered as one of history's most powerfully original composers. Like the Dostoyevsky novels or the Chekhov plays, Mussorgsky's songs create a reality that is both unmistakably Russian and thoroughly universal. With the lieder of Hugo Wolf, they are also the most disturbingly "modern" of nineteenth-century art songs: not simply because they tend to avoid the great traditional Romantic subjects of love and nature, but also because in their essentially ironic vision of human experience they anticipate the defining attribute of the twentieth-century mind.

Recorded in the late 1950s, Boris Christoff's tour of this dark, sarcastic, satiric, frequently beautiful universe is one of the major achievements in recording history. Like Feodor Chaliapin and Alexander Kipnis before him, the great Bulgarian bass is the kind of consummate singing-actor who is able to capture the full measure of the composer's range, from the black humor in the famous "Song of the Flea"—for which he produces the most menacing laugh since Chaliapin's—to the delicate nostalgia of *Sunless* and the *Nursery Songs*.

Lovers of lieder, Mussorgsky, and great singing will have replaced their worn LPs the day this three-CD set hit the stores. Everyone else should get their copies now.

Nancarrow, Conlon   (1912–1997)

Studies for Player Piano

> Nancarrow, piano. Wergo WER 6168/69-2 [CD]; 60166/67 [CD];
> 60165-50 [CD].

Let the English boast all they will about *their* eccentrics: only America could have produced a Conlon Nancarrow. After private studies in Boston with Roger Sessions, Walter Piston, and Nicolas Slonimsky, he joined the Abraham Lincoln Brigade in 1937 to fight in the Spanish Civil War. On his return, he moved to Mexico in 1940 and remained there for the rest of his life, adopting Mexican citizenship in 1956. From the beginning, Nancarrow's principal musical preoccupation was rhythm, which eventually led to a fascination with the player piano. Using a specially developed punching machine of his own devising, he evolved an elaborate technique of composing directly onto the piano roll, which in turn enabled him to create unimaginably complex rhythms and textures far beyond the limits of human performers.

The *Thirty-Seven Studies for Player Piano* (1950–1968) constitute a kind of *Well-Tempered Clavier* for the instrument and their composition was one of the most startlingly original creative acts of twentieth-century music. Taped in Mexico City in 1988, the Wergo recordings are a source of endless wonder and stupefaction, as they present nothing less than an entirely new system of organizing sound, as radical in its way as the revolutions launched by Debussy, Stravinsky, or Schoenberg. Nothing can prepare you for the experience of this incredible music or make you forget it easily, even if you try.

Newman, Alfred   (1900–1970)

Film Music

> National Philharmonic, Gerhardt. RCA 0184-2-RG [CD], 0184-4-RG
> [CD].

More than a generation after his death, Alfred Newman remains the most honored of all film composers, with a total of forty-four Oscar nominations and nine Academy Awards, which is also the most ever given to any individual in any branch of the industry. Ironically enough, Newman thought of himself primarily as a conductor and, although largely self-taught as a composer, produced something upward of three hundred scores. He was also the patriarch of what has become the Hollywood equivalent of the Bach family: Randy Newman is his nephew, his sons David and Thomas are distinguished film composers, and his daughter Maria is a gifted composer of more obviously serious music.

The Newman album from RCA's Classic Film Scores series begins appropriately with his most frequently heard work, the 20th Century Fox *Fanfare*, which has introduced all of the studio's films for more than half a century. The remaining items attest to Newman's incredible versatility, from the swashbuckling march from *Captain from Castile* to the sparkling *Street Scene* from *How to Marry a Millionaire* to the evocative mood pieces from *Wuthering Heights* and *The Song of Bernadette*. The performances and recorded sound are in keeping with the high standards of the series.

Nicolai, Otto   (1810–1849)

The Merry Wives of Windsor

> Mathis, Donath, Schwartz, Schreier, Moll, Berlin State Opera Chorus and Orchestra, Klee. Berlin Classics BER 2115 [CD].

A book on the subject of German Comic Opera might be a bit more involved than one on, say, Irish Erotic Art. But not by much. For if you discount the efforts of southern Germans (i.e., Austrians) and those that seem to capture the German wit at its rapier-like best (believe it or not, the second most frequently performed of all operas in Germany, after Weber's *Der Freischütz,* is Albert Lortzing's *Zar und Zimmermann*), there isn't a lot to be said.

Friedrich von Flotow, composer of the once ubiquitous *Martha,* was French in all the essential characteristics but birth, as was the little cellist from Cologne who moved to Paris as a boy and called himself Jacques Offenbach. Richard Strauss's *Der Rosenkavalier* has its comic moments, to be sure, but its prevailing mood is one of wistful melancholy. Schoenberg's *Von Heute auf Morgen* requires a *very* special sense of humor to appreciate its arcane drolleries, while Henze's *Der junge Lord* shares much of its humor with Alfred Hitchcock and *The Twilight Zone.*

This leaves Otto Nicolai's bubbly *Merry Wives of Windsor,* which had its first performance a scant two months before its composer's premature death. The fifth and final opera of the founder (in 1842) of the Vienna Philharmonic, *Die lustigen Weiber von Windsor* can be one of the most instantly likable of all German operas, as it certainly is here. If Kurt Moll's Falstaff doesn't really compare with one of the late Gottlob Frick's greatest creations on the now-deleted EMI Classics recording, then his performance is still excellent, as are those from the rest of the talented cast. Those spoilsports who only require the giddy Overture are directed to a Sony Classical CD (SMK 47601) of popular overtures *(The Marriage of Figaro, The Bartered Bride, Die Fledermaus,* and *Mignon)* in vintage New York Philharmonic performances led by Leonard Bernstein.

Nielsen, Carl   (1865–1931)

Choral Works *(Hymnus Amoris; Motets; The Sleep; Springtime in Funen)*

> **Soloists, Copenhagen Boys' Chorus, Danish National Radio Chorus and Orchestra, Segerstam. Chandos CHAN 8853 [CD].**

Whenever you find yourself in the midst of a romantic campaign with an object who refuses to melt, introduce him/her/it to Nielsen's *Hymnus Amoris* and relax. For years, a singularly ugly friend of mine—so ugly, in fact, that if you pushed his face in a big wad of dough, you'd get gorilla cookies—has been using the ploy with astonishing success. Just put it on and prepare to be jumped.

In addition to the heart-dissolving beauties of the *Hymn of Love,* this loveliest of all Nielsen albums offers the entrancing *Springtime in Funen,* the challenging and dramatic *The Sleep,* and the gravely beautiful *Motets.* Both the performances and the recorded sound are ideal.

Saul and David

> **Kiberg, Gjevang, Lindroos, Westi, Haugland, Klint, Danish National Radio Symphony Chorus and Orchestra, Järvi. Chandos CHAN 8911 [CD].**

Probably the only thing that keeps *Saul and David* out of the standard repertoire is the Danish language, for in all other respects Nielsen's first opera is as engrossing a score as the twentieth century can boast. In addition to portraying a central figure of genuinely tragic proportions, the music is ablaze with inspiration, offering something moving or memorable in virtually ever bar. Especially noteworthy is the choral writing, which frequently rises to the level of *Boris Godunov* and *Turandot.*

The Chandos recording, sung in the original Danish, easily supersedes the 1972 English-language recording from Unicorn, now long out of print. Neeme Järvi's conducting is even more compellingly dramatic than Jascha Horenstein's, while Aage Haugland makes for a singularly imposing Saul. At every point in the performance, the singers, orchestra, and conductor seem completely caught up in the drama and their enthusiasm is contagious. By almost any criteria, this is one of the most important operatic recordings of the decade.

Songs

Schiøtz, tenor. Pearl PEA 9140 [CD].

Nielsen is typically at his most unaffected and charming in his wonderfully tuneful songs, many of which unfold with the ease and deceptive simplicity of folk music. These famous recordings made between 1938 and 1941 by tenor Aksel Schiøtz have never been approached, much less surpassed, and remain vivid souvenirs of a courageous gentleman and very great artist. Schiøtz heroically continued performing Danish music secretly for members of the Resistance throughout the Nazi occupation, earning the sobriquet "The Voice of Denmark" in the process; at the end of the War, he was honored by a grateful King and nation. The defiant spirit of that period still rings through these eloquent performances and one need not necessarily be one of his fellow countrymen to hear them with a shiver of patriotic pride. With his 1945 recording of Schubert's *Die schöne Müllerin* (see page 641), these rank with the greatest musical and human documents of the twentieth century.

Symphony No. 3, Op. 27, "Sinfonia Espansiva"; Symphony No. 5, Op. 50

Royal Danish Orchestra, New York Philharmonic, Bernstein. Sony Classical SMK 47598 [CD].

For a time during the mid-1960s, it seemed to many that the late-Romantic Danish composer Carl Nielsen was belatedly going to join his Finnish contemporary Jean Sibelius as one of the last and most popular practitioners of modern symphonic form. While the Nielsen revival has obviously begun to lose momentum in recent years—there were once *two* complete recorded cycles of all six symphonies; today there are none—Nielsen's remains a charming, provocative, and utterly original voice, especially in this first of the three major symphonies upon which most of his future reputation would be based.

It's difficult to imagine a more inspired performance of the "Sinfonia Espansiva" than the one contained on this CBS recording, which did so much to advance the Nielsen revival. Bernstein's enthusiasm for the work is as obvious as it is infectious. The Royal Danish Orchestra catches fire in what is probably the finest performance it has given in its collective memory, from their thunderous exuberance in the swaggering opening movement, to the way they assault the normally flaccid *Finale* as though it were an undiscovered masterwork of Johannes Brahms.

Bernstein's version of the Fifth, if not quite as overwhelming, still sets a standard for commitment and intensity that has yet to be approached. In this fabulously difficult work, the New York Philharmonic responds with one of its pluckiest performances; Bernstein inspires the snare-drummer to play with the verve and individuality of an Art Blakey, and CBS's engineers almost succeed admirably in disentangling the Symphony's complex web of sound.

Symphony No. 4, Op. 29, "Inextinguishable"

San Francisco Symphony, Blomstedt. London 421524-2 [CD].

Even the bungled acoustics of its horrid new concert hall cannot obscure the fact that the San Francisco Symphony, under Herbert Blomstedt, has entered its Golden Age. In less than a decade, this unpretentious musician has so completely rejuvenated the old band that it now must rank among the world's very best: the woodwinds play with grace and character, the brass are a model of fearless solidity, and the strings play with that glowing warmth that suggests a fine German orchestra at the top of its form.

Blomstedt's new version of the Nielsen "Inextinguishable" is one of his most impressive recordings to date: an interpretation of high tension, soaring lyricism, and withering drama, thrillingly played and recorded. In fact, it is the only recent "Inextinguishable" that can be mentioned in the same breath with Jean Martinon's classic RCA recording with the Chicago Symphony. The performance of the Fifth Symphony that fills out the CD is every bit as strong.

The London recording (425607 [CD]) by the same forces of the composer's delightful First Symphony and the problematical Sixth, the not-so-simple "Sinfonia Semplice," is equally impressive in capturing the freshness of Nielsen's youthful masterpiece and the bitter irony of his swan song. As in the other recordings in the series, no praise would be too extravagant for the San Francisco Symphony's playing or the work of London's engineers.

While their version of the Second Symphony, "The Four Temperaments," is excellent, too, the performance of the "Espansiva" is really no match for Bernstein's. Thus a more attractive pairing on Bis CD 247 [CD] features a thrilling interpretation of the Symphony with the enchanting *Aladdin Suite* in near-perfect performances by the Gothenberg Symphony led by Myung-Whun Chung.

Wind Chamber Music (complete)

Bergen Wind Quintet, et al., Bis CD-428 [CD].

When he isn't busy being epic and heroic, that is, "expansive" and "inextinguishable," Nielsen is at his absolute best doing charming little things, as in his naively disarming songs (Angel has something close to a moral obligation to reissue the Danish tenor Aksel Schiøtz 's immortal recordings) and the brief masterworks contained on this treasurable Bis CD.

While the centerpiece is clearly the great Wind Quintet of 1922—with Hindemith's *Kleine Kammermusik* and the Wind Quintet of Arnold Schoenberg, surely the twentieth century's most important example of the form—the other items are no less appealing, from the *Allegretto for Two Recorders* to that inspired study in tongue-in-cheek winsomeness, the *Seranata in vano*. The Bergen Wind Quintet and their friends play this music with unquenchable enthusiasm and grace, and the Bis recorded sound—as per usual—is close to perfection.

Among recordings of the two wind concertos that Nielsen lived to complete (he had planned to compose one each for the five friends who gave the Quintet its premiere), the Bis version (CD 616 [CD]) of the unsettled and far-reaching *Clarinet Concerto* is easily the finest to date. Ole Schill's effortless handling of the all-but-impossible solo part is a marvel, as is the conducting of Myung-Whun Chung. If anything, his Bis recording of the Flute Concerto (CD 454 [CD]) is even more exhilarating, thanks to flutist Patrick Gallois, who gives the most imaginative recorded performance yet of the solo part. In such an inspired interpretation, the Nielsen sounds suspiciously like the great modern flute concerto.

(To round out a collection of all three Nielsen concertos, Cho-Liang Lin's CBS recording (MK-44548 [CD]) of the Violin Concerto is easily the most startling that has so far appeared. The playing of both the soloist and the Philharmonia Orchestra under Esa-Pekka Salonen is so fiercely committed that this curiously underrated piece seems at very *least* the equal of the far more familiar work that fills out the recording—the Violin Concerto of Jean Sibelius.)

Novák, Vítěslav (1870–1949)

Slovak Suite, Op. 32; *About the Eternal Longing*, Op. 33; *In the Tatras,* Op. 26

Royal Liverpool Philharmonic, Pešek. Virgin Classics CDC 45251 [CD].

There is a kind of piece with which everyone in classical music radio is familiar and that some of us—especially the patient, gallant people who man the switchboards—have come to dread. These are what might be called, for want of a better phrase, the "What-was-that?-Where-can-I-buy-it?-What-the-hell-do-you-mean-it's-out-of-print!" recordings; not the Pachelbel Kanons, Fauré Pavanes, and other readily obtainable (i.e., *uncontrolled*) substances that seem to affect listeners like catnip, but those odd, off-beat, out-of-the-way things that—perhaps because of their relative obscurity—have an even more dramatic effect. Morton Feldman's mesmerizing *Rothko Chapel* is one such work that will invariably light up the phone banks; the *Slovak Suite* by Vítěslav Novák is another.

A student of Dvořák whose early work was vigorously praised by Johannes Brahms, Novák—like his friend Josef Suk—was the last of the Bohemian late-Romantics, composers who were deeply influenced by Dvořák's example but who also managed to make highly individual statements of their own. Like Suk's youthful *Serenade for Strings*, the *Slovak Suite* is so warmhearted, subtle, sophisticated, and opulent that it will have the most jaded listener sighing for more. (If you can persuade someone in the store to audition the CD for you, tell them to cue up the movement called "Two in Love." If they don't sell out their stock and take another half-dozen orders for more, I would be greatly surprised.)

Libor Pešek and his fine English orchestra give a lovely performance of the work and are equally compelling in Novák's finest tone poems: the exhilarating *In the Tatras* and the impressionistic retelling of a fairy tale by Hans Christian Andersen, *About the Eternal Longing*. This is the finest single Novák recording currently available and provides an ideal introduction to this wholly singular voice.

For the absolute last word in this music—if not in recorded sound—Talich's matchless recording from the early '50s has finally resurfaced on a Supraphon CD (SUP 11 0682-2), paired with his equally incomparable versions of Janáček's *Taras Bulba* and *Cunning Little Vixen* Suite.

Those responding to Novák's gentle, enchanting idiom will find much to admire in the most ambitious of his orchestral scores, the five-movement symphonic poem *Pan,* which has finally been given a decent modern recording by the Slovak Philharmonic led by Zdenek Bílek on Marco Polo 8.223325 [CD]. Though perhaps not as consistently inspired as either of the Suites, there are some thrilling moments in this long and fascinating work. The performance of what might for most people be a major discovery is rapt and solicitous, and the sound is very good.

Similarly, *The Storm* is an amazing achievement: a vast choral work of exceeding complexity grown from a series of tiny thematic fragments heard in the opening bars of the piece. Supraphon has reissued the first stereo recording (SUP CD 3088 [CD]), a thrilling 1978 performance by the Czech Philharmonic Chorus and Orchestra conducted by Zdeněk Košler. The late Czech conductor releases so much of work's power and lyric beauty that this recording, with his magical version of Smetana's *The Bartered Bride* (see page 673), will probably remain his most enduring memorial.

Ockeghem, Johannes (c. 1410–1497)

Missa, "Fors seulement" for Five Voices; *Requiem* for Four Voices

The Clerks' Group, Wickham. ASV Gaudeamus ASV 168 [CD].

Building on the tradition of his teacher Guillaume Dufay, Johannes Ockeghem was the leading figure of the second wave of Flemish contrapuntists who dominated the serious music of the fifteenth century, an inspired composer and gifted teacher whose pupils included Josquin des Prés. Nowhere is the mysticism of the late Middle Ages expressed more hauntingly than in Ockeghem's sacred music, which is also notable for the richness of its polyphonic structure and the depth of its religious feeling.

Ockeghem's *Requiem*, the earliest known setting that exists in manuscript form, is both a moving and confusing work, with differences in style and notation from movement to movement so extreme that they suggest a pastiche of various earlier sources. The performance by The Clerks' Group under Edward Wickham is hypnotic in its precision and purity, as is their version of the three surviving movements—*Kyrie, Gloria,* and *Credo*—from the celebrated *Missa,* "Fors seulement," given with the old melody that serves as the *cantus firmus* of the piece.

The Orlando Consort, who perform one voice to a part, give a beautifully restrained performance of the *Missa,* "De plus en plus" (Deutsche Grammophon Archiv 453419-2 [CD]), together with a generous selection of Ockeghem's stunning motets and *chansons*.

Offenbach, Jacques   (1819–1880)

Gâité Parisienne (ballet, arranged by Manuel Rosenthal)

Pittsburgh Symphony, Previn. Philips 442403-2 [CD].

Like *Les Sylphides* and *La Boutique fantasque*, those ersatz ballets arranged from the piano music of Chopin and Rossini, *Gâité Parisienne*, Manuel Rosenthal's inspired adaptation of melodies from the Offenbach operettas, still tends to raise eyebrows (and many noses) among the Serious Music Lover set. While as a smug and jaded musical curmudgeon, I yield to no one in my arrogance or pickiness, I've never understood how it's *not* possible to like this dazzling confection, especially in a performance as lively and charming as this.

While the ballet has received numerous fine recordings—including one by Manuel Rosenthal himself—none can approach the urbane wit and Gallic grace of this superb Philips recording by André Previn. All of the great set pieces—the *Barcarolle* from *The Tales of Hoffman*, the "Can-Can" from *Orpheus in the Underworld*—are given the most lively and affectionate performances imaginable. In fact, the recording is a triumph of bracing rhythms, inventive phrasing, and tasteful sentimentality from beginning to end.

Overtures

Vienna Symphony, Weill. Sony Classical SK 53288 [CD].

Many of the best-loved of Offenbach's overtures—*Orpheus, La Périchole, La Belle Hélène*—are not, strictly speaking, his own work. Like Sir Arthur Sullivan, Offenbach frequently left much of the actual business of arranging and orchestrating the tunes from the operettas to others. Since the overtures were rarely more than potpourris, he would simply indicate which melodies he wanted in which order and then proceed to get on with more important things, such as writing or producing his next project or chasing after his most recent *amour*.

The Sony Classical album is a generous one, bringing together all of the well-known overtures—*Orpheus in the Underworld, La Belle Hélène*, and *Barbe-blue*—with rarities like *La Fille de tambour major, La Grande-Duchesse de Gérolstein, Monsieur et Madame Denis, La Vie pariesienne*, and *Vert-Vert*. If the performances don't completely efface the memory of Sir Neville Marriner's fizzing Philips recording (recently withdrawn), then they are nonetheless lively and committed and give a good deal of pleasure.

Although in the CD reissue, Herbert von Karajan's Deutsche Grammophon anthology sounds a bit bleached (400044-2), the performances themselves are astonishingly vivid and brilliant, making this one of the conductor's very best later recordings.

The Tales of Hoffman

> Sutherland, Domingo, Tourangeau, Bacquier, Cuénod, Chorus
> and Orchestra of Radio Suisse Romande, Bonynge. London
> 417363-2 [CD].

Throughout his long and lucrative lifetime as the father of the operetta—his astonishing output of tuneful, racy, frequently *naughty* musical satires earned him the sobriquet, "The Mozart of the Boulevards"—Jacques Offenbach dreamed of writing a single, serious opera that would be the crowning achievement of his career. With the *Tales of Hoffman,* finished a few months before the composer's death (Offenbach died while it was in rehearsal for the first production), the diminutive German-born cellist-turned-lighthearted-French-composer did precisely that. While overshadowed in popularity by Gounod's once-ubiquitous *Faust,* Offenbach's immortal adaptation of stories by E. T. A. Hoffman is the only French opera that, in the quality and consistency of its inspiration, can be mentioned in the same breath with *Carmen* and Debussy's *Pelléas et Mélisande.*

The stunning London recording from the early 1970s is still the single most satisfying recorded performance that *Hoffman* has ever received. Joan Sutherland, who undertakes all four of the opera's heroines, has never been more impressive. While Antonia and Giulietta are a trifle lacking in character, both are splendidly sung. As the doll Olympia, however, she turns in a virtuoso tour de force of such staggering dimensions that even those of us who do not count ourselves among the most rabid Sutherland fans come away in a state of slack-jawed amazement. As the opera's several villains, Gabriel Bacquier is as suavely malevolent as any singer who has ever undertaken the roles, but the gem of the production is Placido Domingo's Hoffman. For nearly two memorable decades now, Domingo's achievements have rivaled those of the greatest tenors of the century's Golden Age. Vocally and dramatically, this Hoffman is one of his most impressive creations, a performance that—if it isn't already—will one day become the stuff of legend.

Orff, Carl (1895–1982)

Carmina Burana

> Armstrong, English, Allen, St. Clement Danes Boys' Choir, London
> Symphony Chorus and Orchestra, Previn. EMI Classics CDC
> 56444 [CD], 4AM 34770 [T].

Like acne and an insatiable lust for Milk Duds, Carl Orff's *Carmina Burana* is a juvenile affliction that most people eventually outgrow. As that torrent of unspeakably dull and repetitious music clearly proved, Carl Orff was not only a one-work, but also a one-*idea* composer. That none of his subsequent pieces ever achieved a fraction of *Carmina Burana*'s popularity is hardly surprising. This astonishingly simple, musically primitive setting of some bawdy medieval lyrics can be a dazzlingly effective experience the first couple of times you hear it. It is only after repeated encounters that the vulgarity and yawning vapidity of *Carmina Burana* really begin to get on a person's nerves.

For those who have an incomprehensible affection for this trash—and I must admit that I always have—André Previn's Angel recording is one of the finest ever made. To his credit, Previn does nothing to cheapen the work further than its composer already has but, instead, constantly seeks out its humor, limited subtlety, and frequently engaging wit. Which is not to say that the performance attempts to housebreak *Carmina Burana*. For at the end, we are thoroughly convinced that this is music that a gland would write, if only it could.

Pachelbel, Johann (1653–1706)

Kanon in D

> Stuttgart Chamber Orchestra, Munchinger. London 411973-2 [CD].

What violent emotions Pachelbel's sweet little Kanon continues to provoke! While it is now one of the most frequently recorded of all classical works, there are those of us who still can't quite understand what all the shouting is about. At best, Pachelbel was a third-rate baroque nonentity who occasionally rose to the level of the second-rate in some of his organ music. And while the Kanon was composed more than a century before Napoleon showed the world what *really* heavy ordnance could do, it still unquestionably qualifies as *large bore*.

If you really *must*, then Karl Munchinger leads the Stuttgart Chamber Orchestra in a tender yet admirably disciplined performance on London. The compact disc version is especially useful, in that you can program the Kanon to repeat again and again, and thus save yourself untold thousands of dollars by putting off that frontal lobotomy you had planned.

Raymond Leppard and the English Chamber Orchestra are equally attractive on a CBS tape (MYT 38482).

Paderewski, Ignacy Jan   (1860–1941)

Piano Concerto in A Minor, Op. 17

Lane, piano; BBC Scottish Symphony, Maksymiuk. Hyperion CDA 66452 [CD].

Matinee idol, Prime Minister of Poland, film star—of the otherwise forgettable 1937 British soaper *Moonlight Sonata*—Ignacy Jan Paderewski was the most famous (and highest paid) musician of his era, the man who inspired the 1902 hit song "Since Sister Nell Heard Paderewski Play" and who was, in the words of one biographer, "the victim of a greater amount of female adulation than any pianist since Liszt." His colleagues were less enthusiastic. Following a London recital, the Liszt pupil Moritz Rosenthal summed up an attitude that would prevail among professional musicians for half a century: "Yes, he plays well, I suppose, but he's no Paderewski."

While best known for endearing miniatures like the Minuet in G, Paderewski had serious ambitions as a composer, producing a three-act opera called *Manru* and the Symphony in B Minor, introduced in Paris in 1911. The most successful of his large-scale compositions is the Piano Concerto in A Minor, finished in 1888, the year of his sensational Paris debut. It is large, colorful, exciting work in the tradition of the Chopin and Liszt concertos, with an appealing melodic personality and an abundance of creative vigor. Piers Lane gives it a refreshing face-lift in the first volume of the Hyperion Romantic Piano Concerto series: the playing has genuine grace and wit, as does the accompaniment from the BBC Scottish Symphony conducted by Jerzy Maksymiuk. If the Piano Concerto in E by Paderewski's near contemporary Moritz Moszkowski (1854–1925) seems a little threadbare in comparison, then as an indication of what was driving turn-of-the-century audiences wild, it is more than worth hearing.

Paganini, Niccolò (1782–1840)

Caprices (24) for Unaccompanied Violin, Op. 1

Perlman, violin. EMI Classics CDC 47171 [CD].

Unlike his rather lumpy and charmless violin concertos, the Paganini Caprices are among the most intriguing works ever written for the violin by the man who was, by all accounts, its greatest master. Stories of Paganini's virtuosity are legion. For a week after a concert during which he played the whole of Beethoven's "Kreutzer" Sonata on a single string, he was the talk of Paris; when his chauffeur asked for a considerable raise since his master was becoming so famous, Paganini readily agreed, provided he be driven everywhere on a single wheel.

Musically and technically, the recordings made by Itzhak Perlman in the early 1970s have yet to be bettered. The playing is as sensitive as it is audacious, and for once even the most difficult of the individual pieces emerge with a color and freshness that suggest miniature tone poems, instead of mere excuses for wanton virtuoso display.

Violin Concerto No. 1 in D Major, Op. 60

Kaplan, violin; London Symphony, Miller. Arabesque Z-6597 [CD].

Having written off this piece years ago as feeble, empty-headed fluff, I must now recant completely. But then again, I never understood that Paganini's popular D Major Concerto was in reality a miniature Rossini opera without words. At least, that's the way Mark Kaplan and Mitch Miller make it seem in their electrifying Arabesque recording.

While Kaplan is not yet as well known as some of his more highly publicized female colleagues, he proves conclusively here that he can—to badly mix a metaphor—play the pants off any of them. Technically, he is on a par with any violinist in the world today; musically, he is already a highly evolved personality, whose daring and bravado are matched only by his intelligence and wit.

Throughout the Paganini—as in the blazing performance of the Wieniawski D Minor Concerto that accompanies it—he treats this dog-eared classic as music, not simply as a convenient vehicle for showing us what he can do. With a shrewd conductor who also adopts—or perhaps inspired—that refreshing attitude, both of the tired old warhorses are up and running like colts from the opening bars.

In spite of formidable competition in both pieces, these recordings leave all others in the dust.

Paine, John Knowles   (1839–1906)

Symphonies (2)

> New York Philharmonic, Mehta. New World NW 80374-2 [CD]
> (Symphony No. 1; As You Like It: Overture); NW 80350-2 [CD],
> NW 80350-4 [T] (Symphony No. 2).

John Knowles Paine was the John Greenleaf Whittier of American music. Portland-born and Berlin-trained, Paine's music looked to European models for precept and sustenance and, except for certain titles like *Columbus March and Hymn,* is no more distinctly American music than "Maud Muller" is an especially American poem. Although formal and derivative, Paine's two symphonies—the first ever published by an American composer—are richly imagined, elegantly crafted, moving, manly, and surprisingly memorable works. While it has admittedly scant competition, Paine's Second Symphony—called "Im Frühling" as a nod to his beloved Schumann—is easily the strongest American symphony produced during the nineteenth century. If the earlier work in C minor is less determined and individual, then it is still full of clever touches and fine tunes and more than repays repeated hearings.

It is difficult to imagine more eloquent champions than Mehta and the Philharmonic, who give both symphonies and the snazzy *As You Like It* Overture top-drawer performances, captured in admirably lifelike recorded sound.

Palestrina, Giovanni   (c.1525–1594)

Missa Papae Marcelli

> Tallis Scholars, Phillips. Gimell CDGIM-339 [CD], 1585T-39 [T].

It's the gloomy winter of 1563, and the Council of Trent, concerned that the whacked-out new music they're playing in church is taking everyone's mind off the meaning of the words that are being sung, is about to outlaw the use of polyphony—music in which several voice parts are heard simultaneously. (If the old monotonous monophonic chants were good enough for Pope Gregory and the boys, then by Jesu, they should be good enough for us!)

At which point young Giovanni Pierluigi, who's from the town of Palestrina just outside of Rome (and who at thirty-eight isn't all *that* young), bursts in with the manuscript of his latest polyphonic mass, which is not only utterly gorgeous but is also so skillfully written that you can understand *every* single syllable. The Council relents, decides that polyphony is not the work of the Devil, and the subsequent history of Western music—from Bach to the Beatles—is assured.

It would make a terrific movie. In fact, it *did* make an intriguing opera: Hans Pfitzner's somewhat long-winded but errantly inspired *Palestrina*. The only problem with one of music's most dramatic stories is that it almost certainly never took place. Polyphonic music was not banned from the churches in 1563, not because the prelates were impressed with Palestrina's work, but because of the viselike pressure that was put on the Council by the music-loving Emperor Ferdinand I.

Be that as it may, the most famous mass of the Church's greatest composer has never sounded more, well, *heavenly* than it does in this transcendent performance by the Tallis Scholars. The starkly beautiful *Vox patris caelestis* by the Tudor composer William Mundy and the catchy Allegri *Miserere*—which with time may yet become the ecclesiastical Pachelbel Kanon—round out one of the best recordings of sacred music available today.

Panufnik, Andrzej   (1914–1991)

*A*rbor Cosmica; Symphony No. 3 *(Sinfonia sacra)*

Royal Concertgebouw Orchestra, New York Chamber Symphony, Panufnik. Elektra/Nonesuch 79228-2 [CD], 79228-4 [T].

One of the most respected of modern Polish composers, Andrzej Panufnik was born in Warsaw on September 24, 1914. After graduating from the Warsaw Conservatory in 1936, he continued his studies at the Vienna Academy, where one of his teachers was the conductor Felix Weingartner. (Throughout his life, Panufnik remained active as a conductor, noted especially for his meticulously prepared interpretations of contemporary music.) On the eve of World War II, he moved to Paris to study conducting with Philippe Gaubert.

Although Panufnik composed extensively throughout the period, the first of his works to display a distinctive musical personality was the *Tragic Overture,* a dark and impassioned reaction to the Nazi occupation, finished in 1942. Following the War, he began to produce a series of works in an unmistakably nationalist style, from the *Five Folk Songs* that represented Poland at the first postwar festival of the International Society for Contemporary Music (ISCM), to the *Sinfonia rustica* of 1948, which has remained his most frequently performed work.

With Panufnik's music shockingly underrepresented in the catalogue, these superb performances of two of his finest scores are particularly valuable, especially the enthralling *Sinfonia sacra* of 1963, with its brilliant ritual use of fanfares and hymns. *Arbor Cosmica* is a similarly fascinating experiment whose structure mirrors that of a tree. Both the Dutch and American players are obviously inspired by the composer's presence, and the recorded sound is excellent.

Paray, Paul (1886–1979)

Mass for the 500th Anniversary of the Death of Joan of Arc; Symphony No. 1

> **Soloists, Royal Scottish National Chorus and Orchestra, Paul.**
> **Reference RR 78 [CD].**

As his marvelous series of Mercury Living Presence recordings with the Detroit Symphony clearly attest, Paul Paray was one of the outstanding French conductors of the twentieth century. He was also one of the most courageous. In 1940, while he was serving as conductor of the Concerts Colonne, the Nazis insisted on changing the name of the orchestra since its founder had been Jewish. Paray, a devout Catholic, resigned in protest and began working for the Resistance. Following the Liberation in 1944, he returned to his old orchestra and a hero's welcome.

Composed in 1931, Paray's *Mass for the 500th Anniversary of the Death of Joan of Arc* is an unabashedly romantic work full of lovely themes, memorable invention, and deep yet unaffected religious conviction; those who admire the *Requiems* of Gabriel Fauré and Maurice Duruflé should warm to it immediately.

Although the composer's own recording (Mercury Living Presence 432719-2 [CD]) has a special authority, the new Reference version is equally compelling, with a performance that responds with equal success to the *Mass's* sweetness and grandeur—and does so in state-of-the-art, demonstration-quality recorded sound. The coupling, too, is more appropriate than Paray's admittedly stunning version of Saint-Saëns's *Organ Symphony:* Paray's own ingratiating and brilliantly scored First Symphony, performed and recorded with equal conviction.

Parry, Sir (Charles) Hubert (Hastings) (1848–1918)

Symphony No. 3 in C Major, "The English"; Symphony No. 4 in E Minor

London Philharmonic, Bamert. Chandos CHAN 8896 [CD].

It isn't *quite* true that there was no significant music produced by native-born English composers between the death of Henry Purcell in 1695 and the appearance of Elgar's first undoubted masterpiece, the *Enigma Variations,* in 1899: the Savoy operas of Gilbert and Sullivan are among the most valuable theatrical commodities ever devised by the mind of man, while the symphonies and choral works of that eminent Victorian, Sir Hubert Parry, are clearly those of an important composer, possibly even a major one.

Best known for that stirring anthem *Jerusalem,* Parry was very much a musician cut from the same cloth as his younger contemporary, Elgar. There is a stately—and occasionally self-satisfied—Victorian grandeur in his best pages, coupled with a natural vigor and deep-seated melancholy that makes him an appealing and completely approachable "private" composer as well.

Parry's Third Symphony, finished in 1889 and called "The English" because of its many folk-like melodies, is an ideal introduction to his vaguely Elgarian yet still utterly individual world. If anything, the Fourth Symphony is an even finer work, bursting with ideas and a dignified energy.

The London Philharmonic under Matthias Bamert plays these marvelous works with an ease and confidence that almost suggests they are standard repertoire items; in fact, the performances make *such* a strong case, that you almost wonder why they aren't. The other recordings released thus far in their Parry Symphony cycle are just as enjoyable: the Symphony No. 2, "The Cambridge," coupled with the resourceful *Symphonic Variations* (CHAN 8961 [CD]), and the agreeably Brahmsian Symphony No. 5 paired, appropriately, with the *Elegy for Brahms* (CHAN 8955 [CD]).

More impressive than any of the symphonies, though, are the deeply moving "sinfonia sacra," *The Soul's Ransom* and the politely sensuous *The Lotus Eaters,* on a text by Tennyson—two of Parry's greatest choral works that draw from Bamert his finest recorded performances to date. Packed into another Chandos CD (CHAN 8990) lasting nearly eighty minutes, this is a release that no one interested in choral and/or English music can afford to miss.

Pärt, Arvo (1935–)

Arbos; Pari intervallo; An den Wassern zu Babel; De Profundis; Es sang vor langen Jahren; Stabat mater

> Various soloists, Hilliard Ensemble, Hillier. ECM 78118-21325 [CD].

More than anything else, the music of the Estonian composer Arvo Pärt resembles the bumblebee: for by all the laws of aerodynamics neither should be able to fly, and yet somehow, preposterously, they do. To call Pärt a minimalist is both accurate and misleading: although he seems to adopt many of the static, lifeless procedures of Philip Glass and that crowd, his *real* source of inspiration would appear to be the hypnotic stasis of Gregorian Chant. In Pärt's music, there is little in the way of development of musical ideas—in fact, there are few *ideas* at all. Somehow, though, he manages to wring genuine substance and feeling from his stubbornly thin materials: his gravely austere setting of the *Stabat mater,* for instance, is absolutely bewitching, and the brief *An den Wassern zu Babel* has a stark grandeur that utterly belies its modest size.

The performances sound definitive.

Penderecki, Krzysztof (1933–)

Anaklasis; Capriccio for Violin and Orchestra; *Canticum Canticorum Salomonis; De Nautra Sonoris I and II; The Dream of Jacob; Fonogrammi; Threnody for the Victims of Hiroshima*

> Polish National Radio Symphony, Penderecki. EMI Classics CDM 65077 [CD].

Except perhaps for György Ligeti, whose fleeting pop-star vogue was entirely due to his unlikely appearance in Stanley Kubrick's *2001: A Space Odyssey,* it is difficult to think of another avant-garde composer who has enjoyed as wide a popular currency as Krzysztof Penderecki. To a large extent, Penderecki's success has also been based on non-musical considerations, especially his ability to pick large, sexy, politically correct subject matter and respond with appropriately dramatic music. The *Threnody for the Victims of Hiroshima* made his reputation in the early 1960s, and although many might have preferred elegies for the Bataan Death March or the Rape of Nanking, it is a powerfully effective piece of emotional and musical manipulation. The composer-led performance is presumably definitive, as are the others on this excellent introductory album, especially the shimmering *Song of Solomon* for sixteen solo singers and orchestra.

If the *Passion according to St. Luke* isn't heard these days with the same monotonous frequency it once was, then it remains a central work in Penderecki's output: a huge, imaginative, consistently gripping sacred work with the same direct emotional appeal as the Berg Violin Concerto. The composer's Argo recording (430328-2 [CD]) is suitably overwhelming.

Pergolesi, Giovanni Battista

(1710–1736)

Stabat mater

> Marshall, Valentini-Terrani, sopranos; London Symphony, Abbado.
> Deutsche Grammophon 415103-2 [CD].

It's probably no accident that those ingratiating themes from which Igor Stravinsky fashioned his ballet *Pulcinella* were long thought to be the work of Giovanni Battista Pergolesi, since most of them do resemble the lithe, endearing melodies that poured out of this gentle, sweet-spirited father of *opera buffa*. Pergolesi was already desperately ill with consumption when he began work on what would prove to be his final masterpiece, that devout and impassioned setting of the *Stabat mater,* most of which was written in a Capuchin monastery where the destitute composer had gone to seek refuge. The legend that this first great *Stabat mater* was written during the composer's last fever is made all the more believable in Claudio Abbado's singularly intense reading; Margaret Marshall and Lucia Valentini-Terrani are compelling soloists, with the London Symphony offering its highly charged support.

The Hungariton recording of a period-instrument performance of *La serva padrona* (HCD 12846 [CD]) proves that the first *opera buffa* is also an extremely entertaining show, with Jószef Gregor in rollicking form as the much put-upon Uberto and Katalin Farkas splendid as the mother of all crafty maids.

Persichetti, Vincent (1915–1987)

Music for Winds

Winds of the London Symphony, Amos. Harmonia Mundi HMU 907092 [CD].

No one ever wrote more eloquently for the modern wind ensemble than Vincent Persichetti, whose first published work was the Serenade for Ten Winds, composed when he was only fourteen. Although he would eventually write an opera, nine symphonies, a dozen piano sonatas, and numerous chamber, choral, and vocal works, he remains best known for his band music. Anyone who played in an American high school band from the mid-50s onward probably played one of his pieces, from relatively simple things like *Psalm for Band* to more challenging items like *Parable*. No matter what level your bunch was at, Persichetti's music was so cleverly constructed that it could make *any* band sound good. (During my sophomore year in high school, *Pageant* was the required test piece at the state competitions; I probably played it five hundred times and I still never tire of hearing it.)

David Amos leads the Winds of the London Symphony through a splendid series of representative Persichetti works. In addition to three recording premieres—they claim the same for *Pageant*, but David Paynter and the Northwestern Wind Ensemble recorded it years ago for New World—the anthology also includes two of his most important works, the *Divertimento* and *Masquerade for Band*. The performances are exhilarating, as is the recorded sound.

Pettersson, Allan (1911–1980)

Symphony No. 7; Symphony No. 11

Norrköping Symphony, Segerstam. Bis BIS CD 580 [CD].

Born in abject poverty and reared by an atheist father and a deeply religious mother who exposed her children early on to a steady diet of Salvation Army hymns, the Swedish composer Allan Pettersson would not enjoy his first real success until October of 1968, when Antal Dorati led the first performance of his Seventh Symphony. Given the Bergmannesque bleakness of his first half century—in addition to the generally unfavorable reviews his music received, arthritis ended his career as an orchestral violist in 1964, leaving him, in effect, without a livelihood—it's hardly surprising that the principal tenor of Pettersson's music should be resigned self-pity, leavened by outbursts of violently dissonant anger alternating with a disarming, childlike simplicity. In Sweden, Pettersson is revered as the nation's great modern symphonist; elsewhere, his music is dismissed as gloomy self-indulgence. The Seventh is a passionate, cogently argued work that recalls Mahler and Shostakovich at their darkest (and it makes both seem positively lighthearted in comparison), while the shorter, more concentrated Eleventh for the most part seems more of the same. Segerstam and the Norrköping Symphony give deeply involving performances of both works, making the strongest possible case for this dark and controversial voice.

Pfitzner, Hans (1869–1949)

Palestrina: Preludes; *Das Herz:* Love Theme; *Das Käthchen von Heilbronn:* Overture

> Orchestra of the German Opera, Berlin, Thielemann. Deutsche Grammophon 449571-2 [CD].

Like that of his near contemporary Hugo Wolf, the music of Hans Pfitzner is so intimately bound up with the subtleties of the German language that his most important works—the opera *Palestrina,* the cantata *Von deutscher Seele,* and his many beautiful lieder—have always presented serious problems for non-German listeners. While *Palastrina* has had its passionate admirers, including Thomas Mann and Bruno Walter, who led the world premiere in 1917, it has rarely been performed outside Germany and Austria, where it continues to be revered as one of the major modern operas.

The ideal way to approach *Palastrina* is through its three Preludes, which contain the thematic germs of the entire work. Christian Thielemann, the most talked-about young German conductor of his generation, leads the most impassioned and intensely musical recorded performance the Preludes have ever received. Coupled with the overture to his second opera, the love music from his last, and some elegantly turned-out Strauss rarities—orchestral excerpts from *Guntram, Feuersnot,* and *Capriccio*—this makes for an unusually interesting and valuable release.

Piazzolla, Astor (1921–1992)

Five Tango Sensations

Piazzolla, bandoneon; Kronos Quartet. Elektra/Nonesuch 79254-2 [CD].

The late Astor Piazzolla was not only history's undisputed master of the accordion-like bandoneon, but he was also the man who elevated a popular South American dance to the status of high art, doing approximately the same thing for the tango that Johann Strauss II did for the waltz. As a performer, Piazzolla's touch was magical: of the twelve-hundred-odd recordings that have been made of David Raksin's *Laura*, Piazzolla's remains far and away the composer's favorite.

The *Five Tango Sensations* that he composed for the Kronos Quartet are the perfect introduction to his sophisticated, intensely erotic art. The Kronos is inspired to one of its finest performances by Piazzolla's unbelievably seductive playing, which is also heard to memorable effect on a Milan album (73138-35758-2 [CD]) devoted to the Bandoneon Concerto from 1979 and the Three Tangos for Bandoneon and Orchestra.

The Deutsche Grammophon album *Piazzolla for Two* (449185-2) by flutist Patrick Gallois and guitarist Göran Söllscher is also irresistibly alluring, with superlative performances of *Las cuatro estaciones porteick* (The Four Seasons of Buenos Aires), *Études tanguistiques*, *Histoire du Tango*, and other Piazzolla works.

Piston, Walter (1894–1976)

Symphony No. 2; Symphony No. 6; *Sinfonietta*

Seattle Symphony, Schwarz. Delos DE 3074 [CD].

In addition to being a great musical pedagogue whose pupils included Leonard Bernstein and whose books *Harmony* and *Orchestration* remain standard texts, Walter Piston was one of the finest of all American composers. His music combines an Italianate lyricism (the family name was Pistone) with a ruggedly virile individuality that often suggests the rocky coast of his native Maine. At his best, as he is in the powerful, exquisitely crafted Second Symphony of 1943, Piston reveals himself as one of our most important symphonists and an immediately appealing, instantly recognizable voice. Gerard Schwarz and the Seattle Symphony give it a bracing and virile performance, in almost every way as satisfying as Michael Tilson Thomas's stunning—but now deleted—recording for

Deutsche Grammophon. Also excellent are the versions of the 1941 *Sinfonietta* and the Sixth Symphony from 1955, which was played on the Boston Symphony's 1956 tour of the Soviet Union, the first ever made by an American orchestra.

Schwarz's hugely successful Piston series is further highlighted by a splendid recording of the Fourth Symphony (arguably the composer's masterpiece), the *Serenade for String Orchestra,* and the *Three New England Sketches* (DE 3106), while the composer's most popular work, the suite from the ballet *The Incredible Flutist,* is now represented by a colorful, high-voltage performance by the St. Louis Symphony and Leonard Slatkin, coupled with an equally fine account of the Sixth Symphony (RCA 60798-2-RC [CD]).

Pizzetti, Ildebrando (1880–1968)

Messa da Requiem; Tre composizioni corali; Due composizioni corali

Danish National Radio Chamber Choir, Parkman. Chandos
CHAN 8964.

A contemporary of Respighi, Montemezzi, and Malipiero, Ildebrando Pizzetti was perhaps the most urbane and poetic Italian composer of his generation and the one whose current neglect is the most difficult to explain. (With Rossini and Schoenberg, he was also one of the most superstitious of all composers: in addition to decorating his scores with four-leaf clovers, he refused to begin any new work on a Tuesday and would mark the seventeenth page of each of his scores as "16 + 1.") With Montemezzi's *L'amore dei tre re,* Pizzetti's *Debora e Jaele* and *Assassinio nella Cattedrale* (a setting of T. S. Eliot's *Murder in the Cathedral*) are among the most original and effective Italian operas written after Puccini's, and his elegantly wrought choral music is among the most moving produced in this century.

Pizzetti composed what may well be his masterpiece, the intensely beautiful *Messa da Requiem,* in 1920 following the death of his first wife. (Deeply affected, he would continue to wear the black clothes of mourning even after his second marriage, and indeed wore nothing else for the remainder of his life.) Making memorable use of the medieval *Dies irae,* Pizzetti's *Requiem* is an extraordinarily simple and eloquent work that wastes not a note or a second of the listener's time. Coupled with five considerable shorter but no less striking a cappella choral works in equally gripping performances by the brilliantly drilled Danish National Radio Chamber Choir, this is the most distinguished Pizzetti recording in a generation.

String Quartets (2)

Lajtha String Quartet. Marco Polo 8.223722 [CD].

Twenty-six years and most of the important works upon which his reputation would rest separate Pizzetti's two string quartets. The first was written in 1906, when the young composer was just beginning his collaboration with Gabriele d'Annunzio via the incidental music for the radical play *La nave;* the second dates from 1933, when the fifty-three-year-old composer was being dismissed by his younger colleagues as hopelessly unfashionable and written-out.

Once again, Marco Polo deserves our heartfelt thanks for plugging yet another important gap in the catalogue. If the First Quartet is clearly a young man's work, full of youthful ardor and homages to his various musical heroes—echoes of Schubert, Verdi, and Dvořák can be heard here and there—then the Second is something altogether different: larger, darker, more important-sounding, with a brooding slow movement and richly inventive Scherzo. Yet the key to both works—and something that makes their neglect *so* inexplicable—is the wealth of entrancing, instantly memorable melody. Listen to the haunting modal opening theme of the First Quartet and then *try* to get it out of your mind.

The performances by the Lajtha Quartet are excellent, as is the recorded sound.

Ponce, Manuel (1882–1948)

Concierto del sur

Williams, guitar; London Symphony, Previn. CBS M2K 44791 [CD].

Along with giving the guitar a respectability that it had never before possessed, Andrés Segovia was also the catalyst for the most dramatic expansion of the repertoire in the instrument's history. Writing music for Segovia became a virtual cottage industry for contemporary composers, from Heitor Villa-Lobos and Joaquin Rodrigo to Roussel, Tansman, Castelnuovo-Tedesco, Mompou, Torroba, and numerous others who all came under his spell.

The Mexican composer Manuel Ponce met Segovia in 1923 and quickly wrote his *Sonata mexicana.* Over the years, he produced a considerable body of guitar music for his friend, including the work many consider his masterpiece, the

Concierto del sur of 1941. In this *Concerto from the South,* Ponce skillfully combines the three basic elements that inevitably characterize his finest music: the clear-cut neo-Classical forms that he so admired in the work of his near contemporary Igor Stravinsky; the delicate Impressionism that he absorbed from his last important teacher, Paul Dukas; and finally—and most important—the rhythms, harmonies, and melodic patterns that he adapted from the folk music of his native Mexico.

John Williams and André Previn give a sparkling, utterly winning performance of the work as part of a two-CD anthology of popular concertos by Castelnuovo-Tedesco, Giuliani, Rodrigo *(Concierto de Aranjuez),* Villa-Lobos, and Vivaldi. Some of the solo guitar music, including the vivid and haunting *Folies d'Espagne,* can be heard on an Iron Needle album (IN 1347 [CD]) featuring the young Segovia's historic recordings from the 1930s.

Ponchielli, Amilcare (1834–1886)

La Gioconda

> Callas, Cossotto, Compañez, Ferraro, Cappuccilli, Vinco, La Scala
> Chorus and Orchestra, Votto. EMI Classics CDCC 49518 [CD].

The next time you're at a party with people who really think they know a lot about opera, challenge any one of them to relate, in its simplest terms, the plot of *La Gioconda*. In retrospect, its almost impossible to fathom how the future librettist of Verdi's *Otello* and *Falstaff* and the composer of *Mefistofele,* Arrigo Boito, could have come up with such a hopelessly confusing pile of gibberish, or how Amilcare Ponchielli, a composer of limited abilities, could have fashioned from it one of the most powerful and enduring works of the Italian operatic stage. *La Gioconda* would have a decisive influence on almost every Italian opera that followed it, including the later operas of Verdi and those of Ponchielli's most celebrated pupil, Giacomo Puccini.

For more than three decades, the only *Gioconda* has been that of Maria Callas. It is one of the most gripping of all her recorded characterizations and one that seems to inspire everyone around her—from the other principal singers to every member of the chorus and orchestra—to give of his or her absolute best. The recorded sound, from 1960, is surprisingly lively and realistic in the CD transfer.

Poulenc, Francis (1899–1963)

Aubade for Piano and 18 Instruments; Concerto for Piano and Orchestra; Concerto for 2 Pianos and Orchestra

> Tacchino, Ringeissen, piano; Monte Carlo Philharmonic, Prêtre. EMI
> Classics CDM 64714 [CD].

If there was ever a composer who wrote music that bore an uncanny resemblance to the way he actually looked, then it was the tall, gangly, always slightly off-center Francis Poulenc, one of whose closest friends once described him as looking like a cross between a monk and a thug. There was a pervasive and goofy oddness in all the work that this deft, graceful, and highly original composer produced. Had he been only slightly less peculiar, he might have been as important as Debussy; as it stands, he is responsible for some of the major French art songs of the twentieth century and is, perhaps, modern France's major composer of sacred music. In addition to being an important composer, Poulenc was also a gifted pianist who was often heard in recital with his long-time companion, the incomparable French baritone Pierre Bernac.

Toward the end of Poulenc's life, Georges Prêtre was the composer's favorite conductor, as might be gathered from these saucy and authoritative recordings of three of his most delightful works. Prêtre misses none of the tenderness or the tongue-in-cheek charm of these enchanting scores, while Gabriel Tacchino—like the composer and Jacques Février before him—is a thoroughly idiomatic exponent of the solo parts.

Le Bal masqué (cantata); *Le Bestiaire*

> Allen, baritone; Nash Ensemble. CRD CRD 3437 [CD].

The twenty-year-old Poulenc composed *Le Bestiaire* in 1919 while he was still serving in the French army as a clerk-typist at the Ministry of Aviation. If the music still shows Satie's quirky influence, then it is nonetheless a surprisingly mature and confident setting of Apollinaire's witty, elusive verse. *Le Bal masqué*, written in 1932 to a text by his friend, the outlandish voice of Montmartre bohemianism, Max Jacob—"Their violence, their truculence, their whimsicality attracted me then; I found in them that 'tuppence colored' quality of the pictures in the Paris weeklies of my youth, and from there was born that odd musical carnival I've always prized greatly"—was one of its composer's favorite works, in which the raucous peasant side of his personality was given free and uninhibited reign.

Thomas Allen and the Nash Ensemble prove unusually skillful guides to both cycles: sly and whimsical in the early work, fleshy and boisterous in the later one. The Nash is also deft and charming in the Trio for Piano, Oboe, and Bassoon and the *Sextuor* for Piano and Winds. If the playing lacks the last measure of Gallic spice found in the London recording by Pascal Rogé and a fine French ensemble (see page 539), then it still serves to make an extremely attractive album even more so.

Les Biches (ballet suite)

Ulster Orchestra, Tortelier. Chandos CHAN 9023 [CD].

Impressed with the young composer's *Trois mouvements perpéuels*, the impresario Sergei Diaghilev commissioned Poulenc to write a similarly witty ballet for the 1924 season of his Ballets Russes de Monte Carlo and the result was *Les Biches* (The Does), his most ambitious score up to that time and his first major success. The practically nonexistent plot about a fashionable hostess who to tries to seduce one of her young guests at a house party drew from Poulenc a delightful score full of rhythmic vitality and elegant rakishness, all propelled by some of the composer's most pungent and memorable tunes.

Tortellier's superb Chandos recording revels in the wit, charm, and irresistible gaiety of the piece, yet without shortchanging its considerable tenderness and subtlety. The Ulster Orchestra has never seemed more French or alert, both here and in the delightful versions of the Ibert *Divertissement* and Milhaud's *Le Boeuf sur le toit* and *La Création du monde*, which fill out this unusually desirable album.

Concert champêtre; Concerto for Organ, Strings, and Timpani; Concerto for Piano and Orchestra; Concerto for Two Pianos and Orchestra; *Gloria; Sextuor* for Piano and Winds; Sonata for Two Pianos

Malcolm, harpsichord and organ; Academy of St. Martin-in-the-Fields, Brown. London 448270-2 [CD].

The principal attractions on this generously packed Double Decker set are George Malcolm's versions of the Organ Concerto and the sparkling *Concert champêtre*. The Organ Concerto of 1938 is top-drawer Poulenc, touched with a new solemnity that hints at the more serious direction his music would soon take. Composed in 1929 for Wanda Landowska, the *Concert champêtre* also represents the composer at his best, with its blend of Parisian gaiety and the antique refinement of seventeenth-century French keyboard music. Malcolm is brilliantly effective in both works, even if the recording balances *in Concert champêtre* seem to place the listener in the harpsichordist's lap.

The other concertos are performed ably—especially Pascal Rogé's account of the Piano Concerto—as is the *Gloria,* given a lush but pointed interpretation by Jésus López-Cobos.

Dialogues des Carmélites

Van Dam, Dubosc, Yaker, Gorr, Dupuy, Lyon Opera Orchestra, Nagano. Virgin Classics CDCB 59227 [CD].

Since it was introduced at Milan's La Scala on January 26, 1957, Poulenc's masterpiece, *Dialogues des Carmélites,* has been universally accepted as one of the half-dozen finest operas written since the end of World War II. Set in Paris at the time of the Revolution, it is the story of fourteen Carmelite nuns who prefer death on the guillotine to dissolving their order. Like the most inspired of Poulenc's sacred music, the opera is full of an exultant spirituality, coupled with a soaring, dignified lyricism, and a quietly shattering dramatic intensity: the final scene, in which the Prioress and her followers mount the scaffold singing the *Salve Regina,* as one by one their voices are silenced, is among the most powerful in modern opera.

If anything, the recording by the Lyon Opera led by Kent Nagano is even more impressive than their electrifying version of Prokofiev's *Love for Three Oranges.* The new version either matches or supersedes virtually everything in the pioneering EMI Classics recording led by the late Pierre Dervaux; the cast is without exception superb—the ageless Rita Gorr is particularly gripping as Madame de Croissy, as is Catherine Dubosc as the volatile Sister Blanche—and Nagano conducts as though guided by an inner light. For anyone persuaded that *Turandot* was the last great twentieth-century opera, this haunting masterpiece will come as major surprise.

Figure humaine (cantata) for A Cappella Chorus

Monteverdi Choir, Gardiner. Philips 446116-2 [CD].

Poulenc composed this cantata—the greatest of his secular vocal works—during his wartime service with the French Resistance movement. Paul Éluard's poem expresses both the suffering of the French people and their will to resist, culminating in a moving paean to liberty, all of which Poulenc projects with an electrifying immediacy and intensity. Sir John Eliot Gardiner's Monteverdi Choir captures its shifting moods to perfection on an exciting Philips anthology called "Jubilate Deo!" which includes other a cappella masterpieces by Bach, Gabrieli, Monteverdi, Purcell, Schütz, and Taverner.

Gloria in G Major; Organ Concerto

**Carteri, soprano; Duruflé, organ; French National Radio Chorus and
Orchestra, Prêtre. EMI Classics CDC 47723 [CD].**

Composed only two years before the composer's death, Poulenc's *Gloria* is one his most consistently inspired, touching, and exhilarating works. Not since Haydn had another composer set the *Laudaumus Te* quite as joyously, and the work's closing bars easily rank with the most divinely inspired moments composed in this century.

Georges Prêtre's Angel recording was not only the first to be made of this great modern sacred work, but it was also done with the composer himself in attendance. Only Leonard Bernstein—in a Sony Classical recording now available on CD (SMK-44710)—found the same immensely appealing combination of fun and devotion in the *Gloria,* although for the most part, the Prêtre interpretation is far more charming, and hence, far more French. The recording has the further advantage of having been made with the composer in attendance. It's a sensation that is impossible to explain in words, but while listening to the music, you can actually feel his presence.

Similarly, with composer Maurice Duruflé as soloist, the performance of the Organ Concerto has a full-throated authority about it, while Prêtre's accompaniment is equally incisive. Although slightly brittle around the edges, the 1960s recorded sound has held up remarkably well.

L'Histoire de Babar (le petit éléphant)

**Streep, speaker; New Zealand Symphony, Falletta. Koch International
Classics KIC 7368 [CD], KIC 7368 [T].**

Having spent my childhood devouring pictorial histories of music and the Second World War, and having no children of my own yet (of whom I'm aware), I'm a fairly recent Babar convert. A friend introduced me to Jean de Brunhoff's plucky pachyderm through a Christmas gift of the French version of *Le Roi Babar,* and I've been hooked ever since. (I can sing the *Chanson des éléphants* in my sleep—"Pata Pata, Ko Ko Ko" and so on, but enough of that.)

Although not quite a match for Peter Ustinov's scandalously deleted Angel recording, the newer version by Meryl Streep has plenty of character and charm, too. Why this modern children's classic doesn't boast at least as many recordings as Prokofiev's *Peter and the Wolf* is anybody's guess; I suppose we should be grateful to have this one.

*M*ass in G; Motets

Robert Shaw Festival Singers, Shaw. Telarc CD 80236 [CD].

Francis Poulenc once told Ned Rorem that during a performance of the *Stabat mater* led by Robert Shaw, the tempos the conductor selected were so appropriate that they seemed to match the exact pace of the blood flowing through the composer's veins. Shaw's tempos are similarly natural-sounding in the moving *Mass in G*, written in 1937 and dedicated to the memory of Poulenc's father. The singing has great tenderness and urgency and the lovely surface details are buffed to a very high gloss. The winsome *Motets pour le temps de Noël*, the gravely beautiful *Motets pour en temps de pénitence*, and the intimate *Quatre petites prières de Saint François d'Assise* are accorded similarly impeccable treatment and the Telarc recording captures it all to perfection.

Although Shaw leads an equally fine account of Poulenc's wonderful *Stabat mater* on another Telarc CD, Serge Baudo's performance on Harmonia Mundi (HMC 905149 [CD]) is marginally more expressive and has the further advantage of being part of an all-Poulenc program that also includes excellent versions of the *Salve Regina* and the austere *Litanies à la vierge noir*.

*P*iano Music

Rogé, piano. London 417438-2 [CD].

Poulenc's piano music, like his *chansons,* have attracted far too few major interpreters. In the case of the songs, that's almost understandable; the memories of performances by the composer and Pierre Bernac—Poulenc's long-time lover and the man for whom many of the best of them were written—remain indelible (EMI Classics CDC 54605 [CD]), and few singers are anxious to go up against such a vividly remembered legend. And then, too, the songs have a quivering, elusive enchantment that makes them extremely difficult to perform well, as do many of the composer's finest piano works.

For the uninitiated or the unconvinced, Paul Crossley's heroic survey of the complete piano music for CBS (M3K-44921) may prove a bit intimidating, especially when it comes time to fork over the cost of three full-priced CDs. The set is more than worth the expenditure, since Crossley is a subtle, imaginative pianist whose performances are as astute as they are enjoyable.

Pascal Rogé's London recording might prove a far more manageable introduction. In addition to including some of Poulenc's most important and characteristic piano works—the three *Mouvements perpétuels*, the *Novelettes,* and judicious sampling of the mercurial *Improvisations*—the playing is fairly sensational, full of capriciousness, sentiment, and Poulencian wise-cracking, all captured in remarkably realistic sound.

Sextuor for Piano and Wind Quintet; Sonata for Clarinet and Piano; Sonata for Flute and Piano; Sonata for Oboe and Piano; Trio for Oboe, Bassoon, and Piano

> Portal, clarinet; Gallois, flute; Bourgue, oboe; Wallez, bassoon; Cazalet, horn; Rogé, piano. London 421581-2 [CD].

Poulenc's most consistently entertaining contribution to twentieth-century music could very well be that series of fourteen instrumental chamber works that he produced at every stage of his long and colorful career: from the modest Sonata for Two Clarinets of 1918—written, in Poulenc's words, "for entertainment and without pretension"—through the magnificent Clarinet Sonata of 1962.

Here, conveniently gathered together on a single CD, are five of Poulenc's most ingratiating chamber works in performances that range from very good to near definitive. If some of these marvelous pieces have had finer individual performances—both Richard Stoltzman and Gervase de Peyer have managed to project more character in the Clarinet Sonata, while the composer's own Columbia recording of the *Sextuor* with the Philadelphia Wind Quintet cries out for a CD reissue—then the wind playing is witty, pungent, and suitably Gallic and pianist Pascal Rogé again proves his mastery of the idiom.

Praetorius, Michael   (1571–1621)

Terpsichore Dances

> London Early Music Consort, Munrow. EMI Classics CDM 69024 [CD].

When the extravagantly gifted David Munrow died by his own hand a dozen years ago, the cause of early music lost one of its most devoted and appealing advocates. While he was as committed to the "authentic" performance of renaissance and medieval music as any musician of his generation, Munrow was also a great entertainer and a compelling performer, as this stupendous 1973 recording of music by Praetorius clearly shows.

Rarely have the famous *Terpsichore Dances* sounded more lively, lovely, or utterly infectious, and the lesser-known, but stunningly beautiful, motets from *The Muses of Zion* here emerge as one of the most important vocal collections of the period.

If, like a highly respected critic and one-time tennis partner, you are usually tempted to dismiss Renaissance dance fare as "Village Idiot Music," this wonderful monument to David Munrow's towering talent will make a believer out of almost anyone.

Prokofiev, Sergei (1891–1953)

Alexander Nevsky (Cantata)

Cairns, mezzo-soprano; Los Angeles Master Chorale, Los Angeles Philharmonic, Previn. Telarc CD 80143 [CD].

The way to come to Sergei Eisenstein's *Alexander Nevsky* is *not* through a modern recording of the cantata that Prokofiev cannibalized from his score for the film. I should know. After committing Fritz Reiner's interpretation to memory but never having seen the picture itself until I entered college, I eagerly made my way to one of Ann Arbor's little revival houses in the late-1960s, fully prepared for one of the cinematic experiences of my life. And so it proved to be.

With growing incomprehension, I sat through the sloppy editing, the hammy acting, the inexcusable "humor," and the execrable sound, until the fateful moment when I turned to my date, a beaded, willowy quasi-hippie named Heather—and I still think it should be against the law for parents to name their children after anything that can be found in a field—and asked, far more loudly than I had intended, "What *is* this shit?" I was resoundingly booed by the *cognoscenti* and retired from the theater in disgrace.

To this day, I fail to understand *Nevsky*'s status as one of the milestones of cinema. An OK Stalinist propaganda orgy, sure: the scene where the comic book Teutonic Knights throw the kids in the fire is grisly and disturbing, though it would be tame stuff indeed compared to what actually happened three years later. But a great film? If so, I have no idea what the phrase "great film" could possibly mean. From the wretched soundtrack that was nonetheless unable to disguise an inept, hideously out-of-tune performance, it would be hard to tell that Prokofiev did indeed produce a wonderful score; for that we can thank the recording companies, who with various versions of the *Alexander Nevsky* Cantata have given this thrilling piece a life of its own.

As splendid as Reiner's classic recording is (RCA 09026-68363-2 [CD], 09026-68363-4 [T]), the fact that he used an English text all but cripples the performance. The words—in a perfectly accurate translation—are so irretrievably silly, and the diction of Margaret Hillis's Chicago Symphony chorus is so flawless, that even the most sympathetic listener (as I have always been) is hard-pressed not to crack up.

Among the Russian versions of *Nevsky*—in which gems like "Arise! Arise! Ye Russian folk,/In battle just to fight to death!" are mercifully blocked by the language barrier—André Previn's Telarc recording, if not quite as vibrant as his older outing with the London Symphony, is clearly the first choice. Previn's *Nevsky* has become much darker and richer over the years, and the Philharmonic's deeper voices—the lower strings and brass, and the orchestra's exceptional bass clarinettist, David Howard—respond with a wonderfully menacing rumble. Yet the performance also has its moments of blazing, flood-it grandeur: *Alexander's Entry into Pskov* will push your speaker's tweeters—to say nothing of your neighbor's patience—to their absolute limits. Christine Cairns sings her solo beautifully, and the chorus—like the orchestra—is enthusiastic, responsive, and when the score requires, very, *very* loud. As we have come to expect from Telarc, the recorded sound is miraculous.

An RCA recording by Yuri Temirkanov and the St. Petersburg Philharmonic offers the complete score recently re-recorded for the new restoration of Eisenstein's film (09026-68642-2 [CD]). While the performance itself is altogether gripping, much of the extra material comes off as little more than padding.

Much more valuable is the oratorio extracted from Prokofiev's other Eisenstein score, *Ivan the Terrible,* arranged by the late Christopher Palmer and handsomely performed by the Philharmonia Chorus and Orchestra conducted by Neeme Järvi. Like *Alexander Nevsky, Ivan the Terrible* was to be a period film with powerful political overtones. The enigmatic sixteenth-century ruler, Tsar Ivan IV, enjoyed one of the longest reigns in Russian history, thanks to a combination of intelligence, ferocity, and maniacal suspicion. Although the English translation of the title *Grozny*—"Terrible"—fails to capture the implicit awe in the Russian word, one of Ivan's most enthusiastic admirers was Joseph Stalin, who called him "a great and wise ruler, who guarded the country from the penetration of foreign influence and strove to unify Russia." While the thematic invention is considerably less memorable than in *Alexander Nevsky,* there are some thrilling choral moments—the scene in the cathedral is especially so—while the music for the Battle of Kazan is also powerfully effective.

*C*antata for the 20th Anniversary of the October Revolution

Rozhdestvensky, speaker; Philharmonia Chorus and Orchestra, Järvi. Chandos CHAN 9095 [CD].

In spite of what the title might suggest—a piece of laughable Socialist hackwork in the tradition of Shostakovich's *The Sun Shines on Our Motherland* and the stirring Chinese Communist *O How I Love to Haul Manure Up the Hill for the Collective Farm*—the *Cantata for the 20th Anniversary of the October*

Revolution is perhaps the wildest and most powerfully dramatic of all Prokofiev's works. Beginning with a moving choral hymn based on one of the most haunting of the composer's melodies—which was lifted, note for note (and without acknowledgement), by James Horner for the main title of Arnold Schwarzenegger's *Red Heat*—the *Cantata* reaches its climax with an insane central section called *The Revolution,* featuring sirens, machine-gun fire, an accordion band, and a speaker bellowing the inspirational works of Comrade Lenin.

If not quite as electric as the long vanished Melodiya/Angel recording by Kiril Kondrashin that tactfully omitted the section called *Stalin's Vow,* then Järvi's version is still a thrilling one, with brilliant contributions from the chorus, orchestra, and the Chandos engineers. Those who admire *Alexander Nevsky* can't fail to be bowled over by this one.

Piano Concerto No. 3 in C Major, Op. 26

Graffman, piano; Cleveland Orchestra, Szell. CBS MYK-37806 [CD].

The most popular of Sergei Prokofiev's five piano concertos has received numerous first-rate recordings since the composer himself left his historic account of this profound, ebullient piece in the 1930s. Incidentally, that exhilarating performance with the London Symphony conducted by Piero Coppola (grandfather of the film director) can now be found on Pearl PEA 9470 [CD]. The greatest modern performance of the Third Concerto can be found on a CBS recording that also includes equally gripping run-throughs of the audacious First Concerto and the Third Piano Sonata. This generously packed reissue includes some of the finest playing that Gary Graffman ever left in a recording studio and is further cause for lament that that brilliant career was cut short by a neurological disorder. In both of the concertos, the accompaniment that George Szell provides is spellbinding, and the late 1960s recorded sound is still more than adequate.

Concertos (2) for Violin and Orchestra

Shaham, violin; London Symphony, Previn. Deutsche Grammophon 447758-2 [CD].

No two works will better explain Sergei Prokofiev's position as one of the most popular of all twentieth-century composers than these two magnificent violin concertos, written just before and immediately after his long, self-imposed exile from the recently created Soviet Union. While the youthful D Major Concerto is one of the freshest and most original works Prokofiev had written up to that time, the G Minor Concerto is among the greatest modern works written for the instrument. Lyrical, dramatic, sardonic, and overflowing with that utterly distinctive melodic personality that makes all of Prokofiev's music so unique, the Second Concerto ranks with the finest of all the composer's mature works, which is to say, with the finest music written since the turn of the century.

Nowhere is Gil Shaham's status as Itzhak Perlman's heir apparent more obvious than in his enthralling recording of the Prokofiev concertos. Like Perlman before him, Shaham brings equal amounts of swagger and sensitivity to these richly colorful works, together with a degree of instantly recognizable personality that only the most important musicians seem able to muster. Previn's accompaniments are as alternately warm and dramatic as Shaham's playing, and the recorded sound in its richness and focus is very nearly ideal.

Eugene Onegin

> Soloists, New Company, Sinfonia 21, Downes. Chandos CHAN 9318 [CD].

At first, you're convinced it's a misprint. *Eugene Onegin* by *Prokofiev?* Composed in 1936 for a planned radio dramatization of Pushkin's poem by the Russian director Alexander Tairov, Prokofiev's *Onegin* would deliberately concentrate on scenes that had been left out of Tchaikovsky's popular opera, particularly the chapter in which the rejected Tatyana wanders in the callous Onegin's library, trying to fathom his behavior. When Tairov heard what Prokofiev had written, he immediately canceled the production; the composer later cannibalized some of the music for *War and Peace* and *Onegin* was promptly forgotten.

Part of *Onegin*'s difficulty is that it lies in that dramatic no-man's-land between conventional incidental music—brief, free-standing pieces typically used to introduce or separate scenes—and music designed to be heard during spoken dialogue, precisely like music written for film. While not always completely successful in accomplishing its mission—much of Tatyana's music, for instance, makes her seem far more gloomy than she actually is—this fascinating score contains more than an hour's worth of vintage Prokofiev, all of it worthwhile, much of it—like the St. Petersburg ballroom scene—truly memorable.

This admirable Chandos recording wisely opts for an English translation of Pushkin's poem, brilliantly read by Timothy West and his talented cast. This is matched by a superb realization of Prokofiev's score, with Sir Edward Downes flawlessly matching the music to the text. Prokofiev often said that *Eugene Onegin* was one of his favorite works in all of literature, and one "from which I could never be parted." This unusual and enthralling work might help explain why.

Lt. Kijé Suite; The Love for Three Oranges Suite; Classical Symphony

Philadelphia Orchestra, Ormandy. MBK 39783 [CD].

During the many years when he was one of the world's most frequently recorded conductors, Eugene Ormandy never made a finer recording than these versions of three of Prokofiev's most popular scores. If the interpretation of the *Classical Symphony* leaves out the final measure of sassy wit and the outer movements of *The Love for Three Oranges Suite* could use a touch more maniacal energy, then none of the pieces has ever been better played in a recording studio. At almost every turn, Ormandy's great orchestra manages some wonder of unanimity or solo display. At Odyssey prices, this is a phenomenal bargain that must not be missed.

For those who are interested in *Lt. Kijé* alone, the magic of two performances from the 1960s has never been surpassed. George Szell's Sony Classical recording (SBK 48162 [CD], SBT 48162 [T]) is coupled with that finest of all recorded performances of Kodály's *Háry János Suite,* and Fritz Reiner's dazzling RCA Victor recording (09026-68363-2 [CD], 09026-68363-4 [T]) accompanies that conductor's incomparable—though, alas, English-language—version of *Alexander Nevsky.*

Prokofiev's endlessly inventive opera has finally received an adequate recording: a sparkling French-language production of *L'Amour des trois oranges* by the Lyon Opera under Kent Nagano (Virgin Classics 59566 [CD]). Those who have long suspected from the famous Suite that *The Love for Three Oranges* must be one of the great twentieth-century operas will be heartened to discover that they were absolutely right.

Peter and the Wolf

Flanders, narrator; Philharmonia Orchestra, Kurtz. EMI Classics CDM 63177 [CD].

You have to be a pretty irretrievably crusty curmudgeon not to respond to the warmth and wonder of Prokofiev's best-known work. Like *Hänsel und Gretel, Peter and the Wolf* transcends the traditional limits of a conventional "children's work"; its simplicity can be grasped and loved by the tenderest of musical ears, while its immense wit and sophistication can appeal to the most refined of musical tastes.

For years, the most delectable of all recordings of the work has featured a wonderfully sly narration (complete with some marvelously personal sound effects) by the late Michael Flanders. Anyone familiar with his *At the Drop of a Hat* "after dinner farragos" with Donald Swann—available, finally, in a three-CD boxed set from EMI Classics (CDS 7974642) that includes *The Bestiary of*

Flanders and Swann—realizes how uniquely charming a performer he was; coupled with his equally memorable readings of Saint-Saëns's *Carnival of the Animals* and Britten's *Young Person's Guide to the Orchestra,* this *Peter and the Wolf* is an endearing memorial to an irreplaceable talent.

The first modern recording to mount a serious challenge to Swann and Kurtz features Patrick Stewart and the Lyon Opera Orchestra on Erato (97418-2 [CD], 97418-4 [T]). Unlike many of the famous actors who have recorded the part, Stewart is a natural-born storyteller who understands the subtle differences between acting on stage and reading for the microphone. His performance has both a vivid immediacy and a "once upon a time" gentleness that is very affecting, with Nagano and his French orchestra lending sensitive, colorful support. The imaginative coupling is the children's ballet *La Boîte à joujoux* that Debussy wrote for his daughter.

Quartets (2) for Strings

Chilingirian String Quartet. Chandos CHAN 8929 [CD].

Unlike Dmitri Shostakovich, whose cycle of fifteen string quartets encompassed most of his creative life and represented, after the symphonies, his finest achievement, Prokofiev was curiously indifferent to the form, producing only two quartets during his entire career. Although they have yet to enter the standard quartet repertoire, both are strong and individual pieces, redolent with Prokofiev's unmistakable melodic quirkiness and wit.

The Chilingirians make a virtually air-tight case for both works. The earlier and more difficult First Quartet of 1930 nearly comes off as the more musically incisive of the two, but the folksiness of the wartime Second Quartet casts the more appealing spell. The recorded sound is every bit as fine as we have come to expect from Chandos's adept engineers.

*R*omeo and Juliet (complete ballet)

London Symphony, Previn. EMI Classics CDFB 68607 [CD].

At the Paris premiere of his Second Symphony in 1925, Prokofiev is alleged to have turned to a companion and asked the rueful question, "Can it be that I really *am* a second-rate composer?" Any of a dozen works will answer that, including what may well be the greatest full-length ballet ever written.

Romeo and Juliet is not only a worthy successor to *Swan Lake* and *The Sleeping Beauty* but is also—in many significant respects—superior to both. The level of melodic and rhythmic invention is generally more inspired than it is in either Tchaikovsky masterpiece, and as drama it is far more immediate, cogent, and profound. It is not the path-breaking work that Stravinsky's *Rite of Spring* clearly was, but as an old-fashioned epic on the grand scale, nothing like it would emerge from twentieth-century Russia.

No performance of the complete ballet, its various suites, or other compilations has ever gotten more out of the score than André Previn's 1973 EMI Classics recording. The conductor never puts a foot wrong at any point in the interpretation: all the set pieces, from the sparkling "The Young Juliet" through the savage "Death of Tybalt" through the ecstatic love scene, are brought off with precisely the right combination of musical sensitivity and savvy theatricality, yet it is in the other, less familiar, moments where this *Romeo and Juliet* soars above the competition. For Previn, no bar of the score seems unimportant, and each is accorded its proper measure of warmth, wit, and tenderness. With the London Symphony at its most responsive—whispering at one moment, going ballistic the next—this is easily one of the finest of all Prokofiev recordings.

Among single-disc versions—although since everybody fits the entire ballet on two CDs these days, an excerpts album hardly seems worth the trouble—Joel Levi's Cleveland Orchestra recording for Telarc (CD-80089 [CD]) is the most desirable since Erich Leinsdorf's stunning but now deleted Boston Symphony anthology for Victor.

Among complete recordings of Prokofiev's other great ballet, *Cinderella*, the Cleveland Orchestra plays with even greater dash and finesse for Vladimir Ashkenazy (London 410162-2 [CD]) than they did for Lorin Maazel in their intoxicating (and sadly deleted) recording of *Romeo and Juliet*. In fact, the interpretation is so vivid and colorful that it makes *Cinderella* seem every bit as inspired.

Sonata for Piano Nos. 6–8.

Pogorelich, piano. Deutsche Grammophon 413363-2 [CD] (No. 6).

Pollini, piano. Deutsche Grammophon 419202-2 [CD] (No. 7).

Richter, piano. Deutsche Grammophon 449744-2 [CD] (No. 8).

Written between 1942 and 1944 during the darkest days of the Great Patriotic War, Prokofiev's wartime piano sonatas are not only his most important works for the instrument but are also, conceivably, the most significant contribution to the form made by a twentieth-century composer. Formidably difficult and emotionally exhausting, they place enormous burdens on both the performer and the listener. While only the most courageous virtuosos need bother to approach them, an immense technique is not enough: they all plumb depths that require a considerable expressive maturity and a degree of self-knowledge that few pianists possess.

These three recordings are among the respective pianists' finest achievements, especially Pogorelich's spellbinding version of the A Major Sonata, his most exciting single recorded performance to date. Pollini, too, proves that in addition to a rarified poetic sensibility he also possesses a thunderous technique, while Richter is simply being Richter in his astounding Deutsche Grammophon recording of the Eighth Sonata—which is to say, the greatest pianist of his time.

For those who want the less familiar works in the series, Boris Berman's Chandos cycle is absolutely first-rate. Each sonata comes with an attractive anthology of shorter works, all of them performed with wit, fire, and a seemingly instinctive grasp of the idiom. Buy any with confidence.

Sonatas (2) for Violin and Piano

Perlman, violin; Ashkenazy, piano. RCA 09026-61454-2 [CD].

Begun in 1938, shortly after his return to the Soviet Union, the fierce, brooding First Violin Sonata is one of Prokofiev's finest works, inspired—he told his wife, Mira—by some music by Handel he had heard at the summer resort of Teberda. The lighter, lyrical Second Sonata is an arrangement of the popular Sonata for Flute and Piano that the composer made for his favorite chess partner, David Oistrakh, whose classic recordings with Sviatoslav Richter are currently out of print.

Itzhak Perlman's version for RCA was one of the most successful of his early recordings, full of probing intensity in the F Minor Sonata and romantic exuberance in its D Major companion piece. The young Vladimir Ashkenazy proves an ideal partner, thoughtful or impassioned as the music requires.

Symphonies (7)

Scottish National Orchestra, Järvi. Chandos CHAN 8931 [CD].

Except for the "Classical" Symphony and the wartime Fifth, few of the Prokofiev symphonies are heard with any frequency in the concert hall these days—for reasons that aren't that difficult to understand. The Second is a bitter, dissonant work cut from the same user-unfriendly cloth as the *Scythian Suite*. The Third, cannibalized from the extraordinary opera *The Fiery Angel*, constantly betrays its operatic origins, while the Fourth, with a Scherzo drawn from *The Prodigal Son*, often seems closer to the spirit of ballet. The Sixth, with its brooding atmosphere and tragic overtones, is the most profound of the series, while the lighthearted Seventh, designed primarily for young people, also represented a dramatic retrenchment brought on by the savage attacks of the infamous Zhdanov Conference of 1948, which accused Prokofiev (among several others) of "decadent formalism" and "the negation of the basic principles of classical music."

The strongest performances in Järvi's admirable series with the Scottish National Orchestra are precisely the ones you want to be, that is, of the weaker, lesser-known symphonies. In addition to intensely committed performances of both versions of the Fourth—the original from 1930, and the rather long-winded 1947 revision—the set offers interpretations of the Second, Third, Sixth, and Seventh, which are as persuasive as any currently available. The orchestral execution is both refined and exciting throughout and is further enhanced by wonderfully natural recorded sound.

Symphony No. 5 in B-flat Major, Op. 100

New York Philharmonic, Bernstein. Sony Classical SKM 47602 [CD].

Since it first began to be known in the late 1940s, the Fifth has remained the most popular and is probably the most important of the composer's seven symphonies. Like the equally celebrated Fifth Symphony of Dmitri Shostakovich, it is the one large-scale symphonic work to emerged from the Soviet Union that seems destined to occupy a permanent place in the standard repertoire, and rightly so. For the Prokofiev Fifth, like the Shostakovich, is a big, powerful, intensely dramatic and unmistakably *Russian* composition, which will probably continue to move and inspire audiences well into the next century and beyond.

While the Prokofiev Fifth has had some memorable recent recordings—in Leonard Slatkin's amazing St. Louis Symphony version (RCA Victor 09026-61350-2 [CD]), the orchestra sounds like the Berlin Philharmonic in overdrive—Leonard Bernstein's first recording is easily the most overwhelming recorded performance that this popular work has yet received. Tempos are all on the extreme side, as is the emotional content of what can often be heard as a rather cool and sardonic work. Bernstein builds some of the most tremendous climaxes heard these days on commercial recordings: the *Scherzo* whips by with a tremendous sense of urgency, and the *Finale* contains some of the most exhilarating moments that this conductor—which is to say, *any* conductor—has so far left in a commercial recording.

*W*ar and Peace

Borodina, Gergalov, Prokina, Gregoriam, Okhotnikov, Morozov,
Kirov Theater Orchestra and Opera Chorus, Gergiev. Philips
434097-2 [CD].

There are many who insist that if *Romeo and Juliet* is not Prokofiev's masterpiece then *War and Peace* certainly is. Anyone fortunate enough to have seen one of its understandably rare productions usually comes away persuaded that it is one of the great twentieth-century operas: epic in its scope and ambitions, masterful in its delineation of character, inexhaustible in its supply of unforgettable melodies. Capable of lasting well over four hours—as it does in Rostropovich's deleted Erato recording—*War and Peace* never threatens to over-stay its welcome; in fact, like the vast, multi-part BBC series of the early 1970s (Sir Anthony Hopkins still speaks of Pierre as his finest role), in a good performance Prokofiev's opera can actually seem too short.

If, on the whole, Valery Gergiev's Kirov Opera production is not quite as electric as the Rostropovich, then at least it doesn't have to put up with the slightly embarrassing Natasha of Galina Vishnevskaya, then in her early sixties. Not that Yelena Prokina is all that much of an improvement: while the voice is clearly fresher, it tends to get squawky when pushed too hard, which the singer does fairly often. The rest of the cast is first-rate—especially Alexander Gergalov as Prince Andrei and Nikolai Okhotnikov as General Kutuzov—and Gergiev conducts brilliantly, with a strong sense of dramatic involvement and Russian feeling. Even when Rostropovich's much-praised recording is brought back into circulation, the choice won't be easy. On balance, the marginally preferable heroine and the excitement of a live performance tips the scales toward this one.

Puccini, Giacomo   (1858–1924)

Arias

> Caballé, soprano; London Symphony, Mackerras. EMI Classics CDC 47841 [CD].
>
> Callas, soprano; Philharmonia Orchestra, Serafin. EMI Classics CDC 47966 [CD].
>
> Pavarotti, tenor; various orchestras and conductors. London 425099-2 [CD]; 425099-4 [T].
>
> Price, soprano; New Philharmonia Orchestra, Downes. RCA 5999-2-RC [CD].
>
> Price, soprano; Orchestra of the Rome Opera House, Fabritiis. RCA 09026-68883-2 [CD].

Here, in a nutshell—in fact, in a series of incomparable nutshells—is the reason why Giacomo Puccini was the most important and popular Italian operatic composer after Verdi. For like Verdi, Puccini had the great gift of expressing emotion and character through the most completely memorable tunes: some of the most ravishing and unforgettable melodies ever conceived by the mind of man.

Each of these splendid aria collections represent the recent art of Puccini interpretation at something close to its best, from Maria Callas's dramatically incisive readings to the sheer sumptuous beauty of those by Montserrat Caballé. Pavarotti's London album captures the tenor at the height of his thrilling early form, while Leontyne Price demonstrates that although she was far more familiar as a Verdi heroine, her Puccini was also a model of passion, insight, and breathtaking control, both in the "Puccini Heroines" album with Sir Edward Downes and in the famous "Blue Album" from 1960, which first alerted the world to the arrival of this extraordinary singer.

La Bohème

> De los Angeles, Björling, Merrill, RCA Victor Chorus and Orchestra, Beecham. EMI Classics CDCB 56236 [CD], 4X2G 47235 [T].

This astonishing recording—certainly one of the greatest commercial recordings ever made—was thrown together at the last possible moment and, in fact, was very nearly never made at all. For more than thirty years it has remained the standard recording of Giacomo Puccini's most popular opera and will undoubtedly continue to be so for as long as recordings are made.

Along with a superlative cast (De los Angeles and Björling are especially wonderful as the lovers), most of the real magic of this most magical of all Puccini recordings comes from the pit. Several volumes could be written about the special insights, the beautifully shaped phrases, the aching tenderness, and the surging passion that Sir Thomas Beecham finds in Puccini's score. No one has ever made the love music bloom as tenderly or captured more of the high spirits or bitter tragedy of the work than Beecham did on what was an impossibly tight recording schedule. Robert Merrill, the superb Marcello, once told me that Sir Thomas caused great consternation by insisting that the duet "O Mimì, tu più non torni" be recorded again, even though time was running out and the first try had seemed to be a virtually perfect performance. Later, when the producer, who could hear no difference in the two versions, asked the conductor why he insisted on a second take, Beecham replied with characteristic glee, "Oh, because I simply *love* to hear those boys sing it!" That this very special recording *was* a labor of love from beginning to end is as obvious now as on the day it was first released.

La fanciulla del West

Neblett, Domingo, Milnes, Howell, Chorus and Orchestra of the Royal Opera House, Covent Garden, Mehta. Deutsche Grammophon 419640-2 [CD].

Many people continue to wonder why *The Girl of the Golden West,* Puccini's major effort between *Madama Butterfly* and *Turandot,* has never caught on. It certainly got off to a galloping start at its Metropolitan Opera premiere: Arturo Toscanini—temporarily on speaking terms with the composer—was in the pit, and the principals included the dream trio of Emmy Destinn as Minnie, Enrico Caruso as Dick Johnson, and Pasquale Amato as Jack Rance.

Although the opera has always had its passionate advocates—and I include myself among them—the problem is so obvious that it hardly seems worth mentioning: *La fanciulla del West,* in spite of its many wondrous beauties, is really, *really* dumb. And it's not that the action, based on a play by *Butterfly*'s author, David Belasco, is either foolish or implausible; in many ways, it is one of the better dramatic constructs that Puccini was given to work with. *Fanciulla*'s central impossibility, at least for American audiences, is the language: for how are we to credit a literal horse opera in which the miners, cowboys, and Indians all sing in Italian? (The acid test is the first scene of Act II. If you can listen to Billy Jackrabbit and his "squaw" Wowkle grunting and "Ugh-ing" at each other in between bouts of flawless Italian and not burst out laughing, then you have my undiluted admiration.)

The Deutsche Grammophon recording makes the strongest case for the opera since the magnificent 1958 London set with Tebaldi and Del Monaco, which is now available on a pair of compact discs. While still a stunner—Tebaldi's Minnie is arguably the most finely crafted of all her Puccini heroines—the older recording yields to the newer one on a pair of important points: the far more sensitive and sympathetic Johnson of Placido Domingo and the more expressive, imaginative conducting of Zubin Mehta.

Madama Butterfly

> Tebaldi, Bergonzi, Cossotto, Sordello, Santa Cecilia Academy Chorus
> and Orchestra, Serafin. London 425531-2 [CD].

That this radiant, heart-stopping opera was a fiasco at its world premiere in 1904 still seems impossible to most opera lovers today. We forget that the audience at Milan's La Scala was not exactly anxious to embrace a love story between an occidental and a fifteen-year-old Japanese girl, and that the composer—as he later admitted—had made a serious miscalculation in the structure of his new work. What we now know as the Second and Third Acts of the opera were once a single, uncomfortably lengthy act that would have tested the patience of even the most ardent of the composer's admirers.

While as one of the best-loved operas ever written, *Madama Butterfly* has had more than its fair share of memorable recordings, none was ever more radiant than this classic 1958 version, with the sumptuous Renata Tebaldi in the title role. Tebaldi's Cio-Cio-San is a marvel of dramatic evolution: from the innocent child of the opening scene, to the towering, tragic heroine of the opera's final moments. The supporting cast—especially the beautifully sung Pinkerton of Carlo Bergonzi and the vastly resourceful Suzuki of the young Fiorenza Cossotto—could not have been improved upon. Tullio Serafin's conducting is its usual admirable amalgam of sensitivity, understanding, and dramatic bite, and the original late-1950s acoustics have held up surprisingly well.

Manon Lescaut

> Callas, Di Stefano, Fioravanti, La Scala Chorus and Orchestra, Serafin.
> EMI Classics CDCB 47392 [CD].

It was no accident that on stage the Callas–Di Stefano love scenes always had the fiery ring of truth, since all of them had been rehearsed many times behind closed doors. The singers' off-stage love affair not only made good grist for the tabloid mills but also gave their moments together a magic that no other operatic duo of the 1950s could even approximate.

Manon Lescaut, Puccini's first major success as a composer, provided the vehicle for one of the best of their recorded collaborations, with Callas at her most penetrating and believable and di Stefano at his most musical and refined. (There are many who still remember the singer as a kind of bellowing, lyric tenor version of his great contemporary, the bellowing *tenore da forza*, Mario del Monaco. Here Di Stefano displays both the ardor and vocal sophistication—to say nothing of the naturally beautiful physical sound—that led many to predict a career as long and brilliant as Gigli's.)

The always reliable Tullio Serafin catches fire and turns in the best-conducted *Manon Lescaut* yet recorded, and even the mono sound proves no serious distraction: from the opening scene we are caught up in the poignant drama and are soon swept away.

*M*essa di Gloria

> Carreras, tenor; Prey, baritone; Ambrosian Singers, Philharmonia
> Orchestra, Scimone. Erato 96367-2 [CD].

The twenty-year-old Puccini was still a student at the Milan Conservatory when he completed his *Messa di Gloria* in 1880. It is an ambitious, frequently vulgar, utterly confident work that, here and there, shows unmistakable signs of the Puccini to come: the *Gratias*, for instance, which has the shape and feel of so many latter Puccini arias, and the sweet-spirited *Agnus Dei*, which would later be cannibalized for *Manon Lescaut*. The march that dominates the *Gloria* is an obvious (and stirring) homage to Verdi's *Aïda*, while the climactic fugue is an astonishing achievement for so young and inexperienced a composer.

What a pleasure it is to welcome back Claudio Scimone's version of the *Messa di Gloria*, far and away the most satisfying yet recorded. In contrast to Eliahu Inbal's recently deleted Philips recording, Scimone's is not only more vivid and faster-paced but also features José Carreras in splendid voice in the big tenor moment in the *Gratias*, clearly the germ of many Puccini tenor arias to come. Both the chorus and orchestra make heroic contributions, as do the Erato engineers.

*L*a Rondine

> Te Kanawa, Domingo, Rendall, Nucci, Ambrosian Opera Chorus,
> London Symphony, Maazel. CBS M2K-37852 [CD].

During a visit to Vienna in 1912, Puccini was asked by an enterprising Austrian publisher to write a Viennese operetta. Presumably, what the publisher had in mind was a kind of *Madama Butterfly* meets *Die Fledermaus*. The result was *La Rondine*, the lightest and least performed of the composer's mature works.

While certainly no *La Bohème, La Rondine* ("The Swallow") is just as certainly not the misbegotten disaster that its detractors have always claimed it to be. If the opera is not exactly riddled with unforgettable Puccinian melodies, then the tunes are still ingratiating enough to be worth anyone's time. Moreover, the characters are likable, the action is swift and certain, and the orchestral fabric is full of wonders from the composer's top drawer.

The CBS recording makes by far the strongest case for the piece that any version of *La Rondine* ever has. Te Kanawa's luscious voice is ideally suited to the heroine, Magda, an appealing cross between Violetta and the Merry Widow, while Domingo lavishes his usual care and intelligence on a role that is far more interesting than it might otherwise seem. Although Maazel's conducting is not ideally subtle and relaxed, he still coaxes some marvelous playing from the London Symphony as well as skilled contributions from the rest of the cast.

There are really no excuses left for not exploring this charmer.

*T*osca

**Callas, Di Stefano, Gobbi, La Scala Chorus and Orchestra, De Sabata.
EMI Classics CDCB 47174 [CD], 4AV 34047 [T].**

If there was ever such a thing as a perfect opera recording, then this is it. It features, among other things, Maria Callas, the greatest Tosca of the modern era, the most elegantly sung of tenor Giuseppe di Stefano's heroes, and a villain—the Baron Scarpia of Tito Gobbi—that will set your hair on edge. But what puts this *Tosca* on a level that will probably never be approached is the conducting of Victor de Sabata. While not as well-known as his more famous near contemporary, Arturo Toscanini, de Sabata, I think, was always the finer conductor. Like Toscanini, his dramatic sensibilities were very highly developed, yet unlike the Maestro, de Sabata had an immensely complex musical mind that not only probed the music with greater depth but also allowed it sufficient space to breathe. His conducting throughout this inspired recording is nothing less than miraculous: from the soaringly beautiful support he lends to the love music to that chillingly violent moment in the Second Act when the evil Baron finally "gets the point."

In short, this is a classic recording that no opera lover can afford to be without.

Il trittico (Il tabarro; Suor Angelica; Gianni Schicchi)

Donath, Popp, Seiffert, Panerai, Munich Radio Orchestra, Patanè.
    Eurodisc 7775-2-RC [CD] (Il tabarro); 7806-2-RC [CD] (Suor
    Angelica); 7751-2-RC [CD] (Gianni Schicchi).

De los Angeles, Barbieri, Gobbi, Prandelli, Rome Opera Chorus
    and Orchestra, Bellezza, Serafin, Santini. EMI Classics CDMC
    64165 [CD].

One hit, one near-miss, and a dud; not a bad average, unless your name happens to have been Giacomo Puccini. *Il trittico,* the composer's trilogy of one-act operas that had its premiere at the Met on December 14, 1918, has rarely been presented in that form since. *Gianni Schicchi,* the comedy, was a resounding success from the beginning and is frequently heard alone. While the melodramatic curtain-raiser, *Il tabarro* (The Cloak), is enjoyably gruesome and direct, nothing, apparently, will ever save *Suor Angelica*—the literal weak sister of the set—although some very great divas have given Puccini's Nun-with-a-past a try.

You might think that with all the big-name talent—Renata Scotto, Ileana Cotrubas, Marilyn Horne, Placido Domingo, and Tito Gobbi—the CBS recording would have the field to itself. Much of the reason that the upstart Eurodisc version knocks the giant off so easily has to do with the conducting of Giuseppi Patané. Unlike Lorin Maazel, a competent stick-waver but little more, the Italian constantly searches out—and usually finds—precisely the right color or mood that the moment demands.

In addition to the exemplary conducting, the Bavarian *Trittico* features some striking individual performances: the droll, sharply drawn Schicchi of Rolando Panerai is more than a match for Tito Gobbi's legendary characterization; and if Lucia Popp can't quite save the feckless Angelica, then she makes her an exceptionally lovely thing to hear.

The classic EMI Classics recording makes a welcome appearance on CD, with Gobbi and de los Angeles giving two of the great performances of their careers. While *Il tabarro* and *Suor Angelica* are in perfectly acceptable mono, the sound of the early stereo *Gianni Schicchi*—in many ways, the most magical ever captured in a recording studio—is superb.

*T*urandot

**Sutherland, Pavarotti, Caballé, Pears, Ghiaurov, Jon Alldis Choir,
London Philharmonic, Mehta. London 414274-2 [CD], 421320-4
[T] (highlights).**

The emergence of *Turandot* as an opera whose popularity has begun to challenge that of Puccini's other major works is a relatively recent phenomenon. For years, all that anyone ever knew about *Turandot* was the beautiful Third Act aria, "Nessun dorma," and the fact that the opera remained unfinished at the time of the composer's death. For all of its obvious flaws and inconsistencies (the unfinished love duet would have undoubtedly been the crowning achievement of Puccini's career, and the problems with the hero's character would have unquestionably been ironed out had the composer been given time to revise the score), *Turandot* is a great opera—as daring, original, and phenomenally beautiful a work as Puccini would ever write.

When it was first released in the early 1970s, this now-legendary London recording shocked the operatic world. What was Joan Sutherland, the reigning bel canto diva of her time, doing recording a role that she never had sung, and obviously never would sing on stage? Whatever the reasons, the gamble paid off handsomely. As Puccini's icy princess, Sutherland gave one of her finest recorded performances. The interpretation is full of fury, dramatic intensity, and—in the final scene—a startling warmth and femininity that have never been this singer's strongest suits. Similarly, Luciano Pavarotti—who recorded the role of Calaf before he ever sang it on stage—is brilliant as the Unknown Prince. Unlike the Pavarotti of recent years, who seems to shout and croon his way through almost every performance, this is not only an interpretation by a great tenor in his prime, but also a sad reminder of what a vulgar sot this once electrifying artist has allowed himself to become.

While I have never been Zubin Mehta's greatest fan, here he delivers one of the finest performances of his career. No detail in Puccini's astonishing orchestration is overlooked, while the conducting is as tenderly lyrical as it is compellingly dramatic. For those who have yet to make the acquaintance of what may well have become the composer's masterpiece, this is the *Turandot* for you.

Also very special is RCA's Rome recording made during the summer of 1960 (RCD2-5932 [CD]). The chief glories of this memorable performance are the molten Calaf of Jussi Björling (who manages to transform "Nessun dorma" into "Nessun-ah dorma") and the powerful Birgit Nilsson in the title role. Although the Rome Opera House forces are clearly no match for London's superbly disciplined group, Erich Leinsdorf brings a measure of soaring lyricism to the score that Mehta can't quite match.

Le Villi

Scotto, Domingo, Gobbi, Nucci, Ambrosian Chorus, National Philharmonic of London, Maazel. CBS MK 36669 [CD].

Puccini was still a student of Ponchielli at the Milan Conservatory in 1883 when he entered a competition for one-act operas sponsored by the publishing firm of Edoardo Sonzogno. Although he didn't win—as Mascagni would six years later with *Cavalleria Rusticana*—he performed a piano reduction of the opera at a house party in the following year and so impressed the publisher Giulio Ricordi and the librettist Arrigo Boito that *Le Villi* was mounted with great success at the Teatro del Verme. Ricordi promptly commissioned a second opera and the young composer's career was launched.

Based on the same legend that would animate Adam's ballet *Giselle*, the story concerns a shallow young man named Roberto who leaves his village girlfriend, Anna, when he inherits a fortune, preferring the excitement and dissipation of city life. When Roberto returns, he discovers that not only has poor Anna died, but she has also become one of those ghosts of jilted maidens *(Villi)* who return from the grave to force their faithless lovers to dance themselves to death.

Not surprisingly, *Le Villi* was seriously hampered by both the ludicrous plot and the young composer's inexperience; still, there are many thrilling hints—Anna's "Se come voi piccina," for instance—of what was soon to come, made unmistakably obvious in this exciting, wholly committed performance. Scotto, Domingo, and Gobbi all sing with passion and conviction, while Maazel molds the frequently patchwork score into an unusually satisfying whole.

Unfortunately, nothing that Scotto, Carlo Bergonzi, and conductor Eve Queler can do seems able to save *Edgar*, Puccini's ill-fated second opera that the composer himself described as *una cantonata*—a blunder. Nonetheless, there are occasional inspired moments and Puccini lovers will probably want to acquire the CBS recording (M2K 34584 [CD]), if for no other reason than completeness.

Purcell, Henry   (c. 1659–1695)

The Bell Anthem; Come Ye Sons of Art (Ode on the Birthday of Queen Mary, 1694); *My Beloved Spake* (Anthem); *Ode for St. Cecilia's Day* ("Welcome to All the Pleasures")

Deller Consort. Vanguard OVC 8027 [CD].

Although the performance of early music in general and Purcell in particular has changed considerably since the late Alfred Deller and his Consort made these famous recordings in the early 1960s, time has not diminished either their warmth or their infectious enthusiasm. Coming from this large, bearded, burly man, Deller's countertenor voice was one of the most instantly recognizable of its time: a high, reedy, plangent instrument that was used with tremendous intelligence and consummate skill. Rarely have these glorious odes and anthems seemed as fresh or expressive as they do here, and the recorded sound has kept its presence and focus to a surprising degree.

Although not quite as pungent as his early Vanguard recording, Deller's Harmonia Mundi version (HMC 90242 [CD], HMC 40242 [T]) of some of Purcell's delightfully smutty catches and glees reminds us how splendidly bawdy the Restoration was and how irresistibly naughty its greatest composer could be.

Dido and Aeneas

Norman, McLaughlin, Kern, Allen, Power, English Chamber Orchestra and Chorus, Leppard. Philips 416299-2 [CD].

More than any other recording of the last generation, this new version of *Dido and Aeneas* best demonstrates why this incredible work by the thirty-year-old Henry Purcell is the oldest of all operas that can still hold a place in the standard repertoire today. Under Raymond Leppard's inspired direction, the work leaps to life in a way that it rarely has on commercial recordings. Jessye Norman's Dido rivals those of Kirsten Flagstad and Janet Baker in its depth and intensity, and Thomas Allen is the most manly and heroic Aeneas I can remember hearing. For those who usually find this greatest of English operas too thin in its characterization or too slight in its development, this magnificent and luxuriant new version will probably change their minds.

*T*he Fairy Queen

Soloists, Monteverdi Choir, English Baroque Soloists, Gardiner. Deutsche Grammophon 419221-2 [CD].

Not an adaptation of the epic poem by Edmund Spenser—which, of course, would have made it *The Faerie Queene,* as well as something that would have had to be at least two days long—but of Shakespeare's *Midsummer Night's Dream,* this ridiculously under-performed "semi-opera" contains some of the most miraculous music that Purcell ever composed. Tuneful and fanciful, with a gossamer lightness and extraordinary rhythmic life, *The Fairy Queen* should be far more familiar, and undoubtedly would become so, were it routinely given performances as vital and engaging as this.

With his customary blend of unassailable scholarship and boyish enthusiasm, John Eliot Gardiner misses no opportunity to underline the manifold glories of the score, yet does so with a deftly unobtrusive hand. The only other Purcell recording quite like it was Gardiner's Erato version (2292-45211-2 [CD]) of *King Arthur,* the most important of Purcell's collaborations with another seventeenth-century giant, John Dryden. In both recordings Gardiner makes an extremely convincing case that *each* work is in fact the composer's masterpiece, and with both he reminds us with a renewed sense wonder and tragedy what music lost when Henry Purcell died at the age of thirty-six.

*F*antasias

Fretwork. Virgin Classics CDC 45062 [CD].

In the wrong hands—Nikolaus Harnoncourt's, for instance—Purcell's *Fantasias* for viols can become unbearably gloomy and stultifying; in the right ones, this is some of the most accomplished and adventurous instrumental music of the entire seventeenth century. With their flawless ears, seamless technique, and impeccable taste, Fretwork has precisely the right tools for this haunting, visionary music: clarifying its phenomenal contrapuntal and harmonic richness, reveling in its mystery, depth, and infinitely subtle coloration.

On a two-disc Chandos album (CHAN 0572 [CD]) the Purcell Quartet is no less compelling in the sonatas for two violins, bass viol, and continuo, written after Purcell's excited discovery of Italian music. The playing has tremendous vitality and finish, in both the sonatas and the justly celebrated *Chacony in G Minor.*

Music for the Theater

Kirkby, Nelson, Bowman, Hill, Covey-Crump, Keyte, Thomas, Academy of Ancient Music, Hogwood. L'Oiseau Lyre 425893-2 [CD].

More than six hours of the incidental music that Henry Purcell composed for various largely forgotten plays might be much too much of a good thing for most people, yet these classic recordings by the Academy of Ancient Music remain a source of unalloyed delight. Hogwood's soloists prove ideal accomplices, with vocal timbres skillfully adjusted to match the sound of the antique instruments.

Quantz, Johann Joachim

(1697–1773)

Concertos (4) for Flute and Orchestra

Galway, flute; Württemberg Chamber Orchestra, Faerber. RCA 60247-2-RC [CD].

Apart from his decision in the early 1720s to abandon the oboe for the transverse flute, the decisive event in the life of Johann Joachim Quantz occurred in the spring of 1728, when he became the teacher of the future King of Prussia. Eventually, he would enjoy a unique position at the court of the flute-playing Frederick the Great: in addition to a handsome stipend of two thousand talers a year for life, he received extra fees for new compositions and flutes (he began manufacturing instruments as early as 1739) and was the only person at court given the honor (and grave responsibility) of criticizing the King's playing. Perhaps even more important than the three hundred concertos, two hundred sonatas, and numerous other works he is known to have written for Frederick's pleasure and edification is his *Versuch einer Anweisung die Flöte traversiere zu spielen,* the first comprehensive flute method ever attempted and an invaluable source of information on late baroque performance practices.

The four concertos recorded here are all attractive and appealing works, poised stylistically between the baroque and Classical eras. Galway's performances are alert and elegant, with especially graceful readings of the flowing slow movements. Faerber and the Württemberger are able partners and the recorded sound is superb.

Quilter, Roger (1877–1953)

A Children's Overture; Where the Rainbow Ends, As You Like It, The Rake (suites); *Country Pieces; Three English Dances; Rosmé: Waltz*

Czech-Slovak Radio Symphony, Leaper. Marco Polo 8.223444 [CD].

Wealthy, well educated, frail, and generous (his acts of private charity were legion and he was a founding member of the Musicians' Benevolent Fund), Roger Quilter was the most amiable member of that group of young British composers who studied in Germany and later came to be known as the Frankfurt Group (the other members included Percy Grainger, Cyril Scott, Norman O'Neill, and Henry Balfour Gardiner, great-uncle of conductor John Eliot Gardiner). Although Quilter made his initial reputation as a song composer, he was best known for a series of light orchestral works that Sir Henry Wood introduced at his popular Promenade Concerts. *A Children's Overture,* cleverly fashioned from a sequence of English nursery tunes, became a Prom staple, while for years his score for the fairy play *Where the Rainbow Ends* was a Christmas favorite on the London stage. At its best, Quilter's music has a natural melodic grace and a plummy, slightly overripe charm; his tendency to mix the sentimental harmonies of English folk song with the mildly jazzy dissonances of the 1920s—as in the Hogarth-inspired ballet, *The Rake*—often suggests the work of an Art Deco Delius.

Marco Polo's Quilter anthology is another triumph of its adventurous British Light Music series. As usual, Adrian Leaper coaxes thoroughly idiomatic performances from his Slovakian musicians, and—as usual—the recorded sound and exhaustive annotations (by Tim McDonald) are first-rate.

While Quilter's songs are still shockingly under-represented in the catalogue, three of the his best Shakespeare settings in stylish performances by Stephen Varcoe can be heard on that indispensable Chandos anthology of English orchestral songs (CHAN 8743 [CD]), while the *Seven Elizabethan Lyrics* and *Now Sleeps the Crimson Petal* are elegantly done by Thomas Allen on Virgin Classics (59581 [CD]).

Rachmaninoff, Sergei   (1873–1943)

The Bells (choral symphony)

> Pendachanska, soprano; Kaludov, tenor; Leiferkus, baritone; Choral
> Arts Society, Philadelphia Orchestra, Dutoit. London 440355-2
> [CD].

Outside of the English-speaking world, where he has always been something of an embarrassment to the literary establishment, Edgar Allen Poe is widely regarded as a major figure of modern poetry. In France, for instance, where one sees more statues to his memory than to that of Shakespeare, his reputation is enormous, thanks largely to the passionate advocacy of Charles Baudelaire. The great Frenchman's translations are markedly superior to their models, perhaps because Poe's poetry tends to lose so much in the original. Working from an excellent Russian translation of Poe's noisiest masterpiece, Rachmaninoff fashioned a dramatic, volatile, supremely colorful cantata that easily ranks among his greatest works.

Charles Dutoit's recording is easily the best thing from his curiously uneven Philadelphia Rachmaninoff series. The aching refinement that tended to eviscerate his interpretations of the symphonies is here a positive blessing, revealing more of the subtle intricacies of Rachmaninoff's orchestration than any other recording yet has. It has the further advantages of a trio of intensely Russian soloists—baritone Sergei Leiferkus is particularly gripping in the finale—and a great orchestra with a distinguished Rachmaninoff tradition at the very top of its form. Moreover, it is the only recording that offers superlative versions of the composer's only other works for chorus and orchestra, the fresh-faced *Spring* cantata and the *Three Russian Songs* from 1926.

Caprice bohémien (Capriccio on Gypsy Themes), Op. 12; *Isle of the Dead,* Op. 29; *Prince Rostislav* (symphonic poem, after Tolstoy); *The Rock* (symphonic fantasy), Op. 7; *Scherzo for Orchestra; Symphonic Dances,* Op. 45; *Vocalise; Youth Symphony; The Bells; Russian Folksongs; Spring* [Vesna] (cantata), Op. 20

> Soloists, St. Louis Symphony and Chorus, Slatkin. Vox CD3X 3002
> [CD].

Although some of these works may be represented by finer individual performances, this three-CD Vox Box that includes all of Rachmaninoff's music for orchestra, excluding the concertos and symphonies, makes for an exceptionally attractive bargain. In general, the best performances tend to be (as one might hope) of the lesser-known works: indeed, Slatkin's polished, dramatic readings of the vivid *Caprice bohémien,* the windy but entertaining *Prince Rostislav,* the enchanting *Scherzo for Orchestra,* and the hugely underrated, Tchaikovskyesque *The Rock* are the finest now available. As the other performances are on a comparably high level and the late '70s recorded sound remains superb, even if this involves some duplication, then at these prices it should scarcely matter.

*I*sle of the Dead; Symphonic Dances

> **Amsterdam Concertgebouw Orchestra, Ashkenazy. London**
>   **430733-2 [CD].**

While he is best known for his once ubiquitous piano music, during his lifetime Sergei Rachmaninoff was equally celebrated as a composer of orchestral music and songs. The dark and richly atmospheric *Isle of the Dead,* one of the most accomplished of all his compositions, and the four *Symphonic Dances,* his last major work, have never been served more brilliantly than in this recent London recording by the Concertgebouw Orchestra, led by Vladimir Ashkenazy. While the *Symphonic Dances* were actually composed for, and dedicated to, Eugene Ormandy and the Philadelphia Orchestra—the last of their several recordings can still be found on Sony Classical SBK 48279 [CD], SBT 48279 [T]—Ashkenazy's version is in every way more colorful, rhythmically vibrant, and intense. For those who are still persuaded that the heart of Rachmaninoff's output was the Prelude in C-sharp Minor and the syrupy *Vocalise,* these wonderful performances of a pair of masterworks should come as an extremely pleasant surprise.

*P*iano Concertos (4); *Rhapsody on a Theme of Paganini*

> **Wild, piano; Royal Philharmonic, Horenstein. Chandos 8521 [CD].**

In one form or another, these thrilling recordings have remained in circulation since the mid-1960s, when they were originally recorded for *Reader's Digest.* The American pianist Earl Wild and the dapper, impulsive Russian-born conductor Jascha Horenstein had never worked together before, though it would be difficult to gather that from this finest integral recording of the Rachmaninoff concertos ever made.

The success of the project rested primarily on the almost perfect fusion of two surprisingly similar musical temperaments; for in spite of the differences in their ages and backgrounds, the youthful soloist and the aging conductor were arch-Romantics in classic mold.

Even more than the composer's own recordings with Stokowski, Ormandy, and the Philadelphia Orchestra, or Ashkenazy's cycles with Haitink and Previn, the electricity that Wild and Horenstein generated together remains unique. On records, only a handful of pianists can match Wild's thunderous impetuosity in this music, and the conductor brought the same sort of measured lunacy and passionate brinkmanship to the accompaniments that can be heard in his famous Mahler recordings.

With beautifully remastered recorded sound that completely belies its age, this is an ideal choice for anyone who wants all four concertos and the *Paganini Rhapsody* in a convenient, hugely exciting, and unusually economical package.

Piano Concerto No. 2 in C Minor, Op. 18

Richter, piano; Warsaw Philharmonic, Wislocki. Deutsche Grammophon 415119-2 [CD].

Graffman, piano; New York Philharmonic, Bernstein. CBS MYK 36722 [CD], MYT 36722 [T].

Although the composer himself—who was certainly one of the great pianists that history has so far known—left a series of famous, authoritative recordings of all of his major works for piano and orchestra, no recording of his most popular concerto has ever generated more sheer wonder or excitement than Sviatoslav Richter's famous version from the mid-1960s. Interpretively, the performance is something of a madhouse. Tempos are invariably extreme—from the slowest of *adagios* to a breakneck clip in the final movement that will leave most listeners panting on the floor. Yet as extreme as the interpretation certainly is, it is also utterly convincing, thanks to the technique and temperament of the foremost pianist of our time.

For those who prefer a cassette version of this high-cholesterol classic, Gary Graffman's version with Leonard Bernstein remains as polished as it is poetic, with one of the finest—in fact, my favorite—modern version of the *Rhapsody on a Theme of Paganini* as the extremely attractive filler.

Piano Concerto No. 3 in D Minor, Op. 30

> Horowitz, piano; New York Philharmonic, Ormandy. RCA Victor
>   09026-61564 [CD].

> Kapell, piano; Toronto Symphony, MacMillan. VAI Audio VAIA/IPA
>   1027 [CD].

Some very reliable rumors insist that Rachmaninoff stopped playing his D Minor Concerto in public shortly after he heard it performed for the first time by the young Vladimir Horowitz. And for the better part of fifty years, the Rachmaninoff D Minor was a cornerstone in what was surely the tiniest concerto repertoire that any major pianist has ever possessed. While I have always felt about Horowitz much the same way I feel about his father-in-law, Arturo Toscanini, and his near contemporary, Jascha Heifetz, give the man his due: in this particular music, no pianist of the century has ever come close. Of course, for something close to the ultimate in hair-raising piano fireworks, the 1951 studio recording that Horowitz made with Fritz Reiner and the RCA Victor Orchestra (RCA 7754-2-RG [CD], 7754-4-RC [T]) surpasses this 1978 live performance. But as a souvenir of one of the century's most phenomenal technicians, this recording belongs in almost every collection.

As does the live performance from April 13, 1948, by William Kapell. The playing from first to last is little short of stupendous—in every way in the Horowitz league. Not even the fairly muffled recorded sound or the occasionally scrappy orchestral accompaniment can obscure the genius of the greatest pianist America has yet produced.

Piano Music

> Rachmaninoff, piano; Philadelphia Orchestra, Stokowski, Ormandy.
>   RCA 09026 61265-2.

Here, on ten generously crammed CDs, are all of the commercial recordings that Sergei Rachmaninoff made for RCA Victor from 1919 to 1942, both as a pianist and as a conductor. The solo piano works and transcriptions offer convincing evidence for the argument that Sergei Rachmaninoff was one of the greatest pianists of whom we have an accurate record. For a composer of such overtly Romantic music, Rachmaninoff the pianist was strikingly modern in his outlook and technique. In all of these recordings, he takes surprisingly few liberties: the approach is generally free of rubato and other rhythmic distortions and any suggestion of nineteenth-century rhetoric is conspicuously absent. The playing itself ranges from the revelatory to the spellbinding. The famous C-sharp Minor Prelude is done in the darkest possible tones with a feeling of completely detached understatement, while the technical legerdemain in encores like the *Midsummer*

Night's Dream Scherzo will stand your hair on end. While the recordings of the Piano Concertos and *Rhapsody on a Theme of Paganini* are justly famous—the set includes the first complete reissue of the electrifying 1924 acoustical version of the Second Piano Concerto—the composer-led versions of the Third Symphony and *Isle of the Dead* reveal what an astounding conductor the world lost when Rachmaninoff decided to opt for the far more lucrative career of a touring keyboard virtuoso. Cuts and all, the tone poem has a smoldering intensity exceeded on records only by Koussevitzky, while in the Symphony he draws on playing of incredible refinement and vitality. (For those wishing to acquire them separately, a separate "Rachmaninoff Conducts Rachmaninoff" album—09026-62532-2 [CD]—is also available.) Special, too, are the recordings with Fritz Kreisler of violin sonatas by Beethoven, Schubert, and Grieg, in which two of the most distinctive musical personalities of the twentieth century take such obvious pleasure in both the marvelous music and each other's company.

This is an exciting and invaluable document.

Preludes (23) for Piano

Ashkenazy, piano. London 414417-2 [CD].

Incredibly enough, given their wealth of invention, emotional and musical variety, and fabulous melodic richness—as with a Chopin melody, a Rachmaninoff tune can be maddeningly impossible to forget—there has only been one completely successful recording of all twenty-three of these miniature miracles, the London version by Vladimir Ashkenazy. The pianist is uncannily successful in drawing out the special character of each of the individual pieces, and, in general, the playing has a wonderful audacity, mixed with a lyrical tenderness and engaging wit. While the Ashkenazy compact discs should be snapped up by anyone interested in stupendous piano playing or the music itself, Hyperion's recent set by Howard Shelley (CDA-66081/2 [CD]) offers a fascinating and distinctly *non*-Russian second opinion. While some of the interpretations might seem a bit odd—the famous C-sharp Minor Prelude lumbers along like a brontosaurus with bad knees—even the oddest of the pianist's ideas are strangely persuasive, as is Hyperion's ultra-realistic sound.

With Ashkenazy's formidable versions of the complete *Études-Tableaux* currently out of print, Shelley's incisive, technically fluent Hyperion interpretations (CDA 66091 [CD]) are the most desirable now available.

Sonata for Cello and Piano in G Minor, Op. 19

Mørk, cello; Thibaudet, piano. Virgin Classics CDC 45119 [CD].

After suffering his famous nervous breakdown at the turn of the century and undergoing hours of autosuggestion at the hands of an eminent Moscow physician named Dahl—"You will compose again . . . You will write a piano concerto. . . . You will write with great facility . . . " (the good Doctor's actual words)—Sergei Rachmaninoff broke his creative log-jam with the C Minor Piano Concerto, which he gratefully dedicated to his therapist. The same resurgence of creativity that would lead to one of Rachmaninoff's best-loved works would also produce one of his finest, the Sonata for Cello and Piano, which followed the Second Piano Concerto by only a few months.

There are those who suggest the Sonata may be Rachmaninoff's masterpiece, and it's easy to hear why. In this intimate yet turbulent work, the composer avoids most of the rhetorical pitfalls that can sabotage his other large-scale pieces; there is no hint of empty gesture or padding and no suggestion that the music has been over-composed. Instead, the Sonata's emotions—most notably, its aching melancholy—are expressed with a disarming honesty and directness.

Softening the blow of the recent deletions of recordings by Lynn Harrell and Yo Yo Ma, Virgin Classics comes to the rescue with this stunning new version by the young Norwegian cellist Truls Mørk and pianist Jean-Yves Thibaudet. Along with an elegant tone and consummate musicianship, Mørk is also a player with a genuine personality: thoughtful, passionate, and playful by turns, all of which suits the music perfectly. Thibaudet is both a sensitive and imaginative partner, not only in the Rachmaninoff Sonata but also in the intriguing filler: the Two Pieces for Cello and Piano—*Prelude* and *Oriental Dance*—from 1892, a version for cello and piano of the *Vocalise,* plus the rarely heard but hugely rewarding Cello Sonata of Nikolai Miaskovsky.

Songs

DeGaetani, soprano; Kalish, piano. Arabesque Z 6674 [CD].

**Hvorostovsky, baritone; Arkadiev, piano. Philips 442536-2 [CD];
446666-2 [CD].**

Larin, tenor; Bekova, piano. Chandos CHAN 9562 [CD].

Leiferkus, baritone; Shelley, piano. Chandos CHAN 9374 [CD].

The more than eighty songs that Rachmaninoff composed were written during the most richly productive years of his career, from his student days in the early 1890s through 1916, the year before he would leave Russia forever. With the exception of the Opus 38 collection that set the work of contemporary

Russian symbolists like Balmont, Blok, and Sologob, virtually all of the songs are settings of poems by Russian Romantics from Pushkin and Lermontov to Tyutchev and Korinfsky. The best of them—"Lilacs," "To the Children," "How Fair This Spot," "Daisies," "The Dream," and the famous, wordless *Vocalise*—are among the finest ever written by a Russian composer.

Unfortunately, the glorious series of recordings made in the late 1970s by Swedish soprano Elisabeth Söderström and pianist Vladimir Ashkenazy are not yet available domestically, though they have been reissued in Europe on a set of three Decca CDs (436920-2). Throughout, Söderström's perceptiveness and unerring musicianship are matched only by the ravishing physical beauty of her voice; Ashkenazy accompanies her as perhaps no other pianist could, with a musical resourcefulness and depth of understanding that only confirms his status as the great Rachmaninoff pianist of his generation. Keep a watchful eye on the Rachmaninoff bins of the larger stores that specialize in European imports, or on your next trip to Britain be certain to stock up, the better to scalp your friends.

Jan DeGaetani's lovely versions of eight of the most popular songs are the highlight of an unusual Russian recital that finds her well off her beaten contemporary track; the singing is exquisite, both here and in the Tchaikovsky and Mussorgsky songs that round out album.

Dmitri Hvorostovsky's two Philips collections show off his thrilling instrument to excellent advantage, especially the darker items on the "My Restless Soul" album, part of an intelligently chosen collection that also includes many captivating items by Borodin, Rimsky-Korsakov, and Tchaikovsky. The eight items on the companion album are also beautifully done, as is the disturbing contemporary cycle *Russia Cast Adrift* by Georgy Sviridov.

The Chandos recordings are the first two installments of a projected series of the complete Rachmaninoff songs. Musically, emotionally, and dramatically, Sergei Larin and Sergei Leiferkus seem perfectly attuned to the composer's darkly romantic idiom; may future installments in the series prove equally rewarding.

Suites for Piano (2); *Russian Rhapsody; Symphonic Dances* (for two pianos); *Etudes-tableaux,* Op. 33; *Variations on a Theme by Corelli*

Ashkenazy, Previn, piano. London 444845-2 [CD].

Like all of Rachmaninoff's major works, the two Suites for Two Pianos and the *Symphonic Dances* create the distinct impression of being the work of a man proudly and defiantly out of step with his time. In fact, most of Rachmaninoff's larger scores can often seem like long, important, beautifully thought-out letters that, having been written and dutifully mailed, were then delivered fifty years late.

Rachmaninoff was only twenty when the Suite No. 1, Opus 5, was published. (Hearing it again at a private recital more than forty years later, he said to his friends: "Do not judge this piece too severely. I was underage when I wrote it.") Dedicated to Tchaikovsky and showing obvious signs of that composer's influence, the Suite consists of four brief movements that are preceded in the score by quotations from four of Rachmaninoff's favorite poets, Lermontov, Byron, Tyutchev, and Khomyatov, whose verses provided the germinating ideas for the work. Nearly twenty years would separate Suite No. 1 from its successor, and as accomplished and strikingly confident as the earlier work certainly is, Suite No. 2 marked a significant advance not only in the wealth of its ornamental detail but also in the extent to which its technical facility had become completely internalized, allowing the composer's poetic sensibility free reign.

Vladimir Ashkenazy and André Previn are passionately committed in this wonderful, strangely neglected music, responding effortlessly to its brilliance, color, and romance. They are no less successful in the two-piano version of the *Symphonic Dances*—given its first performance at the Rachmaninoffs' Long Island home by the composer and Vladimir Horowitz—and the youthful *Russian Rhapsody*. As a bonus, this already appealing album also offers Ashkenazy's brilliant versions of the Opus 33 *Études-tableaux* and another preposterously underperformed masterpiece (and his final work for the piano), the *Variations on a Theme by Corelli* from 1931.

Symphony No. 1 in D Minor, Op. 13

Royal Philharmonic, Litton. Virgin Classics CDC 59547 [CD].

Rachmaninoff's First Symphony very nearly killed him. The scandalously ill-prepared first performance on March 27, 1897, was such a disaster that the composer later suffered a complete nervous breakdown; during his long and painful recovery, he contemplated suicide on more than one occasion. "There are serious illnesses and deadly blows from fate which change a man's character," he later wrote. "This was the effect of my own Symphony upon myself. When the indescribable torture of this performance had at last come to an end, I was a different man."

While certainly not the most cogent or well-behaved of Rachmaninoff's larger works, the First Symphony is a colorful and entertaining score—Monty Python fans will instantly recognize the fanfare that begins the final movement as the signature tune of one of their recurring skits—and a logical continuation of the Russian symphonic tradition established by Tchaikovsky and Borodin.

Andrew Lytton's recording with the Royal Philharmonic is one of the most impressive that the talented young Music Director of the Dallas Symphony has made thus far. Instead of apologizing for the work's Romantic excesses, this expressive, rubato-laden interpretation revels in them at every opportunity. The playing has the old-fashioned sweep of another era, while the recorded sound ranks with Virgin Classics's very best to date.

Symphony No. 2 in E Minor, Op. 27

London Symphony, Previn. RCA 60791-2-RV [CD], 60791-4-RV [T].

There are two ways of viewing Rachmaninoff's E Minor Symphony: as a late-Romantic dinosaur, completely out of step with its time, or as one of the lushest and loveliest symphonies ever written. Both views are equally correct. Compared to what was going on in music at the time it was written, Rachmaninoff's finest orchestral work was a complete anachronism, a throwback to an era when unabashed sentiment was not the cause for blushing embarrassment it would eventually become. Yet for all its old-fashioned sentimentality, the Symphony is also an utterly *genuine* expression of the essence of the Romantic spirit. For instance, if there is Romantic symphony with a lovelier slow movement than the famous *Adagio* of this one, then it has yet to be discovered.

André Previn has so far recorded the Symphony three times, and although his finest version—a London Symphony recording for Angel made in the mid-1970s—can only be found on a three-CD set from EMI Classics that includes all the symphonies (ZDMC 64530), his first outing for RCA Victor remains a more economical alternative. Aside from a few standard cuts, the performance has all the thrust, exuberance, and compassion of the later recording, and what it may lack in way of the final measure of confidence, it makes up for with youthful exuberance and panache. An equally fine interpretation of *The Rock*, one of the composer's most strangely underrated and under-played scores, is the generous filler.

Symphony No. 3 in A Minor, Op. 44; *Symphonic Dances*

St. Petersburg Philharmonic, Jansons. EMI Classics 54877 [CD].

If a helpless enthusiasm for this majestic anachronism might be inexcusable—for who, aside from the Hollywood film composers, was producing this kind of deep-pile, wall-to-wall lushness in 1936?—then I beg to be excused. The Third Symphony, like the Second, is so hopelessly likable that I've never been able to understand those who don't. I'd even go so far to suggest that people who aren't moved at least in some small way by the great subordinate theme of the first movement—the one that sounds so much like the folksong "Shenandoah"—are probably capable of *anything:* drowning puppies, eating babies, pushing little old ladies into manure spreaders, attending Philip Glass concerts . . .

The Jansons recording is the most thoroughly exciting since Leopold Stokowski's National Philharmonic recording from the mid-1970s. While markedly less idiosyncratic than Stokowski, who conducted the world premiere in 1939, Jansons leads a performance that is similarly full of life and personality: ineffably tender in the lyrical passages—how lovely the initial appearance of the first movement's "Shenandoah"-like subordinate theme is!—blazing with passion when the music ignites. Add a version of the *Symphonic Dances* that is second to none in its mystery and excitement, and this is not only Jansons's most impressive album since his electrifying version of the Tchaikovsky symphonies (see page 734) but also one of the great Rachmaninoff albums currently available.

Vespers for Contralto, Tenor, and Unaccompanied Mixed Chorus, Op. 37

Robert Shaw Festival Singers, Shaw. Telarc CD-80172 [CD].

Composed only two years before the October Revolution, Rachmaninoff's *Vespers* of 1915 was probably the last important sacred work written in Russia; soon, such impulses would be totally subsumed in a state-controlled "spirituality" that would lead to countless deathless masterworks that praised Stalin, the Motherland, and the latest hydroelectric dam.

Although we don't usually think of Rachmaninoff as a composer of sacred music, the *Vespers* contains moments of extraordinary depth and beauty: the evocation of the spirit—and often, it seems, the letter—of the Eastern Orthodox worship is uncanny, especially of those dark, unmistakably Russian services that combine awe and terror in roughly equal doses.

Although not as idiomatic as several Soviet recordings that have appeared over the years—and where else in the world can one find those rumbling, impossibly resonant basses?—the Shaw performance is the best Western recording that this singular masterpiece has yet received. Technically, Shaw's forces are predictably flawless, and they also manage to inject an unusually high percentage of the ineffable "spook element" into the score. The recording is suitably rich and warm.

The *Liturgy of St. John Chrysostom* is every bit as moving, with many moments—including a startling pure and unaffected setting of *Our Father*—of sublimely simple beauty. The EMI Classics recording (CDFB 68664 [CD]) by the Bulgarian Radio Chorus conducted by Mikhail Milkov reveals it as one of the greatest of Russian sacred works, a moving declaration full of profound mystery and imperishable faith.

Raff, Joachim   (1822–1882)

Symphony No. 5 in E, Op. 177, "Leonore"

Berlin Radio Symphony, Bamert. Koch Schwann CD 311013 [CD].

There are few more sobering musical illustrations of the cruel vagaries of fame than the career of the German composer Joachim Raff. At the time of his death, Raff's reputation was comparable to that of Wagner and Brahms; by the turn of the century he had already begun to enter that stony oblivion from which he may never fully emerge.

Like the *Rustic Wedding Symphony* of his near contemporary Karl Goldmark, a once hugely popular composer whose reputation suffered a similarly Carthaginian decline, Raff's "Leonore" Symphony is a splendid example of high-Romantic kitsch. Based on a penny-dreadful ballad about a doomed love affair—as if Romantic love affairs were anything *but*—the Symphony is full of good tunes and wonderfully cornball effects, like the unconscionably long-winded march that represents the arrival and departure of the soldier-lover's regiment. Needless to say, the hero is killed but eventually returns, only to be transformed into a skeleton during an *Erlkönig*-like night ride with his beloved. (I've been on many such dates myself.)

As fine as Bernard Herrmann's now deleted recording with the London Philharmonic certainly was, the new version by Matthias Bamert and the Berlin Radio Symphony is finer still. For one thing, Bamert's tempos tend to be more lightly sprung; for another, his textures are far more transparent. The happy result is that "Leonore" seems a much less stodgy work. Fortunately, it still emerges as the endearingly silly schlock masterpiece that it is, all bombast, bathos, and blather.

All in all, party records don't come much better than this.

Rameau, Jean Philippe   (1683–1764)

Castor et Pollux

Gens, Mellon, Cook, Corréas, Les Arts Florissants, Christie. Harmonia Mundi France HMC 901435/37.

One of the first great masters of French opera and one of the earliest significant musical theorists, Jean Philippe Rameau was both venerated and despised by his contemporaries. Tall and gaunt, with a loud, penetrating voice, Rameau was often described as resembling a pipe organ. Rude, boorish, and avaricious, he was characterized by the playwright Charles Collé as "a hard man, very difficult to get along with, as narrow and mulish as he was unjust, and was cruel even to his family." In his operas, Rameau elevated the orchestra to the status of a genuine partner in the dramatic action, while endowing the aria and recitative with an unprecedented expressiveness. These qualities—together with his unfailing gift for vivid dance music—led Voltaire to insist "Rameau has made of music a new art."

In his recording based on a series of actual performances given at the 1991 Aix-en-Provence Festival, William Christie proves how vividly alive Rameau's opera can be made to seem by a conductor who refuses to treat it as a fragile museum piece. The performance has a wonderful sense of immediacy and momentum, with splendidly dramatic contributions from every member of the gifted cast. Les Arts Florissants play with their customary verve and stylishness and the recorded sound is excellent.

For those who acquire this admittedly acquired taste—or for those who have it already—Marc Minkowski's Deutsche Grammophon Archiv recording of *Hippolyte et Aricie* (445853-2 [CD]), Rameau's first important *tragédie-lyrique*, is hardly less enjoyable, even if the drama, spread out over a prologue and five lengthy acts, is more difficult to sustain. Véronique Gens and Bernarda Fink again reveal themselves as two of the most eloquent champions of early opera, while Minkowski's conducting is full of point and obvious enjoyment.

With a plot that makes *Il trovatore* seem almost rational—the action moves from Turkey to Peru to the Amazonian jungle and includes tempests, erupting volcanoes, and the on-stage smoking of a peace pipe!—*Les Indes galantes* is tremendous fun, replete with trumpet-laden crowd scenes and infectious dance music. In his delightful 1974 Erato recording (95310-2 [CD]), Jean-François Paillard leads a richly colorful performance that becomes all the more enjoyable when you haven't the slightest idea of what's going on.

Pièces de clavicin

Christie, harpsichord. Harmonia Mundi 1901120-21 [CD]

With the exception of *La Dauphine,* all of Rameau's keyboard music was composed before he wrote his first opera in 1733. While clearly not as important as his works for the stage—the sixty-five individual works are largely stylized dances and genre pieces—the *Pièces de clavicin* contain some of the composer's freshest and most original inventions, from the impassioned *La Poule* and *Les Sauvages* to the meditative *L'Entretien des Muses* to the irresistibly charming *Tambourin,* his single most famous work.

William Christie proves as resourceful a guide to this music as he is to the operas, with playing that is unfailingly vivid, dramatic, and insightful. Another Harmonia Mundi album (HMX 2901418 [CD]) offers equally stylish versions of the *Pièces de clavicin en concert* by harpsichordist Christophe Rousset, violinist Ryo Terakado, and viola de gambist Kaori Uemura. The vitality of the performances is extremely appealing, as is the bargain price.

Le Temple de la Gloire; Näis (selections)

Philharmonia Baroque, McGegan. Harmonia Mundi HMU 907121 [CD].

Under Nicholas McGegan, the Philharmonia Baroque has become America's finest period-instrument ensemble and they prove lively guides to two of Rameau's most colorful orchestral suites. The playing has genuine bite and character and although tempos tend to be on the brisk side, none of the drama or grandeur is lost. The *Näis* suite includes some eight hundred bars of previously unknown music.

Raskin, David (1912–)

Film Music

New Philharmonia Orchestra, Raksin. RCA 1409-2-RG [CD].

Composer, conductor, arranger, teacher, raconteur, and legendary Hollywood wit, David Raksin once confessed his secret ambition to walk around disguised as a Honda. The point of the deception was to be the sign he planned to wear around his neck, "WOULD YOU BUY A USED MAN FROM THIS CAR?"

A former pupil of Arnold Schoenberg who can still do a droll imitation of his old teacher, and producer of the radio series *The Subject Is Film Music* (by common consent, the definitive oral history on the topic), Raksin and his friends Alfred Newman and Bernard Herrmann were the first of the great native-born American film composers, men whose work rivaled the quality and quantity of their European colleagues Max Steiner, Erich Wolfgang Korngold, and Franz Waxman.

One of the most successful installments of RCA's "Classic Film Scores" series, the Raksin album features the composer's own account of the immortal *Laura*—this in the arrangement he made at the request of Arthur Fiedler—together with extended excerpts from the classic *The Bad and the Beautiful* and a suite from *Forever Amber,* whose principal inspiration was neither Kathleen Windsor's period novel nor Otto Preminger's direction but the music of Henry Purcell. The performances are so compelling, the music itself so superlatively made that the distinctions between "classical," "popular," "serious," and "film" music all begin to blur.

Rautavaara, Einojuhani (1928–)

Angels and Visitations; Concerto for Violin and Orchestra; *Isle of Bliss*

> Oliveira, violin; Helsinki Philharmonic, Segerstam. Ondine ODE 881-2 [CD].

Here are three persuasive exhibits for the argument that Einojuhani Rautavaara is the most important Finnish composer to have emerged since the death of Jean Sibelius. The Violin Concerto of 1977 is a wholly absorbing, continuously fascinating work that combines ethereal mood-painting with dizzying virtuoso display (including extemporaneous contributions from the soloist), all in a space that carves out its own unique sound world. The visionary *Angels and Visitations* of 1978 moves from mysterious whisper to shattering climax, while *Isle of Bliss* (1995) is among the most rapturous, richly erotic scores of the decade. Leif Segerstam guides the Helsinki Philharmonic through what seem ideal performances, all of them captured in meticulously detailed sound.

Ravel, Maurice   (1875–1937)

Alborada del gracioso; Une Barque sur l'océan; Bolero; Daphnis et Chloé; L'Eventail de Jeanne: Fanfare; Menuet antique; Pavane for a Dead Princess; Piano Concertos (2); *Mother Goose; Rapsodie espagnole; Le Tombeau de Couperin; Valses nobles et sentimentales; La Valse*

   Montreal Symphony, Dutoit. London 421485-2 [CD].

   For anyone interested in Ravel's entire orchestral output in state-of-the-art performances and recorded sound, it would be difficult to improve upon one of Charles Dutoit's fabulous London collection. The playing of the Montreal Symphony is quite sensational: *La Valse* and *Rapsodie espagnole,* in particular, are barn burners; *Bolero* has rarely sounded so sensual *and* civilized, and the brief *Alborada del gracioso* is an unmitigated delight. The versions of the two piano concertos with Pascal Rogé are the only modern performances worthy of comparison with Alicia de Larrocha's hair-raising RCA recording with Leonard Slatkin and the St. Louis Symphony. Dutoit breathes an incredible freshness into the famous *Pavane for a Dead Princess,* which never once threatens to become the cloying wad of sentimentality it so often is. Rarely have the closing bars of the *Mother Goose* music sounded so imposing or the fabulously difficult music that begins *Le Tombeau de Couperin* been tossed off with such apparent ease. Throughout, London's engineers have provided Dutoit with demonstration-quality recorded sound, while the Montreal Symphony sounds like nothing less than one of the greatest orchestras in the world. Repackaged on four medium-priced CDs, this is one of the greatest bargains currently available.

Alborada del gracioso; Pavane for a Dead Princess; Rapsodie espagnole; Valses nobles et sentimentales

   Chicago Symphony, Reiner. RCA 60179-2-RG [CD].

   If you can listen to Reiner's recording of the *Prélude à la nuit* (the first movement of the *Rapsodie espagnole*) and *not* want to commit some indiscretion upon the person of your significant other, then it's time to make an appointment with your neighborhood endocrinologist. These are among the most erotic of all Ravel recordings, as well as some of the most nearly perfect. Even the normally chaste *Pavane for a Dead Princess* seems full of the most *un*-chaste suggestions, while the remainder of the *Rapsodie* and all of the *Valses nobles et sentimentales* ooze sensuality from every bar. Coupled with the most vivid and sophisticated version of Debussy's *Ibéria* ever recorded, this remains my desert island French album.

Boléro; Daphnis et Chloé: Suite No. 1; *Mother Goose Suite; Valses nobles et sentimentales*

Czech-Slovak Radio Symphony Jean. Naxos 8.550173 [CD].

For bargain hunters, this super-budget anthology should prove all but irresistible—as it will for spendthrift music lovers who only care about quality of performance and recorded sound. Under the gifted young American Kenneth Jean, this fine Slovak ensemble performs well above its already impressive recorded average, offering playing of enormous finesse and tonal beauty. And if the performances might lack the final measure of excitement and interpretive character—though the *Mother Goose* is nearly as fine as any on the market— then the dazzling recorded sound and inconsequential price tag provide ample compensation.

A second album (8.550424 [CD]) offers comparably enjoyable versions of the second suite from *Daphnis et Chloé, Pavane for a Dead Princess, Rapsodie espagnole,* and *La Valse.*

*C*oncertos (2) for Piano and Orchestra

De Larrocha, piano; St. Louis Symphony, Slatkin. RCA 09026-60985-2 [CD].

Ravel completed both of his piano concertos in 1931. They would prove to be his last major compositions and the composer himself considered them his most important works. (Ravel's pronouncements on his own music, like those of any composer, should be taken with a few pounds of salt. He once said, of *Bolero,* "I have written only one masterpiece. Alas, it contains no music.") The jazzy, elegant G Major Concerto, consciously written in the spirit of the Mozart concertos, and the dramatic *Concerto for the Left Hand,* produced for the Austrian pianist Paul Wittgenstein who had lost his right arm during the First World War, are certainly *among* Ravel's finest and most enduring efforts. Apart from being a brilliant solution to an impossible technical challenge, the *Concerto for the Left Hand* is an endlessly imaginative and resourceful work (who but Ravel would introduce the soaring principal theme on the contrabassoon?). In addition to its wit and gaiety, the G Major Concerto contains one of Ravel's most ethereal inspirations, a seamless love song that recalls a Bach *arioso.*

Beginning with Marguerite Long, who introduced the G Major Concerto in 1933, both works have enjoyed a singular run of first-rate female interpreters, including their greatest living exponent, Alicia de Larrocha. From her thunderous entrance in the *Concerto for the Left Hand* to those otherworldly musings in the G Major's slow movement, there is virtually nothing in either concerto that she doesn't do better than anyone else. Leonard Slatkin's accompaniments are both polished and stylish, as is RCA's recorded sound.

Daphnis et Chloé (complete ballet)

> Montreal Symphony, Dutoit. London 400055-2 [CD].
>
> London Symphony, Monteux. London 448603-2 [CD].
>
> Boston Symphony, Munch. RCA 09026-61846-2 [CD].

In many ways, the initial installment in Dutoit's already fabulous Ravel series is still the most impressive. The dynamic range of both the performance and the recording is phenomenal, from the most delicate whispers in Ravel's diaphanous orchestration, to the thunderous outbursts in the orgiastic final scene. Dutoit's command of the idiom is as complete and masterly as that of any of the greatest Ravel conductors of the past, and the playing of his impeccable orchestra cannot be praised too extravagantly. Clearly, this is already one of the milestones of the early digital era.

Pierre Monteux's celebrated 1959 recording was one of the very best that the ageless French conductor ever made. Having led the world premiere in 1912, he brings a unique authority to the interpretation, and not simply because it bears the composer's imprimatur. There is a warmth and spontaneity in the performance unlike any other, together with a sensitivity to the diaphanous textures that remains unique. For its latest CD incarnation, London has added his otherworldly 1962 recording of the *Pavane for a Dead Princess* and the shimmering version of *Rapsodie espagnole*.

When Charles Munch made his first recording of the ballet for RCA Victor in 1955, the Boston Symphony was still very much Serge Koussevitzky's orchestra. The playing has both the suave sophistication and the electric energy that characterized the best Koussevitzky recordings of the 1930s and '40s but is here treated to infinitely superior recorded sound. The sheer virtuosity is breathtaking from beginning to end, especially when the music is at its most impossibly complex and demanding. From the disappointing remake of barely a half dozen years later, it's obvious that as much of the credit for this magical recording belongs to Koussevitzky as to Munch.

L'Enfant et les sortilèges

**Soloists, French National Radio Orchestra and Chorus, Bour.
Testament TESSBT 1044 [CD].**

Ravel never wrote a more magical work than this haunting study of child-hood and its fantasies—surely the *most* nearly perfect and childlike work of history's most childlike composer. And *L'Enfant et les sortilèges* never had a more magical recording than this one—the opera's first—recorded with a distinguished French cast in Paris in 1948. Although subsequent versions by Ansermet, Maazel, and Previn—all slated for CD reissue—would offer dramatic improvements in recorded sound, none would ever capture the same bewitching amalgam of inno-cent wonder and utter sophistication in quite this same degree. In Testament's brilliant transfer, the recorded sound is remarkably fresh and lifelike.

A hearty welcome back, then, to one of the great recordings of the century.

Among modern versions of the opera, André Previn's EMI Classics for Pleasure recording (CDEMX 2241 [CD]) easily dominates a not terribly crowded field. Along with an excellent cast, the London Symphony performs wonders with Ravel's infinitely subtle score, with every trill, shout, and nuance flawlessly captured in top-of-the-line analogue sound.

Introduction and Allegro for Harp, Flute, Clarinet, and String Quartet

**Allen, harp; Wilson, flute; Shifrin, clarinet; Tokyo String Quartet. EMI
Classics CDC 47520 [CD].**

Although this album is essentially a showcase for the talent of the lovely American harpist Nancy Allen, the highlight is the performance of Ravel's *Introduction and Allegro*, surely one of the composer's most finespun inspira-tions and one of the most beautiful of twentieth-century chamber works. Allen and flutist Ransom Wilson are especially effective in mining the *Introduction*'s dreaminess and gaiety, with excellent support from the rest of the high-powered talent. The Ravel and Debussy miniatures that fill out the album are also hand-somely done.

While I generally disapprove of using serious music as background noise, aural wallpaper, or for any other nonmusical purpose (such as a sleeping pill or an aphrodisiac), this is one of those recordings that, when slipped on after a par-ticularly miserable day, will make almost anyone human again.

Piano Music (complete)

Crossley, piano. CRD 3383/4 [CD].

As in his witty, sensitive survey of Poulenc's complete piano music for CBS, Paul Crossley's Ravel omnibus is one of the most engaging recordings of French piano music to have been released in years. While several individual performances might be preferred—the spellbinding *Gaspard de la nuit* from Ivo Pogorelich on Deutsche Grammophon (413363-2 [CD]) or Vlado Perlemuter's technically suspect but uniquely authoritative *Miroirs* for Vox (CDX2 5507 [CD])—each of Crossley's polished, stylish, refreshingly self-effacing interpretations ranks with the very best available today.

As a colorist, Crossley has much in common with that master of Impressionistic understatement Walter Gieseking; as a technician, his performances recall the pure, unobtrusive beauty that Alicia de Larrocha brought to her Ravel recordings. *Le Tombeau de Couperin* has an almost Mozart-like poise and elegance, though in the gnarlier moments of *Valses nobles* and *Miroirs* the pianist has plenty of ready technique at his disposal. CRD's recorded sound is as pristine and luminous as the performances themselves.

String Quartet in F Major (see Debussy: Quartet)

Trio for Violin, Cello, and Piano

Borodin Trio. Chandos CD 8458 [CD].

Amid Ravel's scant output of chamber music, the Trio for Piano, Cello, and Piano is second in importance only to the great String Quartet. In many ways, the Trio is the more complex and interesting work and one whose built-in austerity and restraint can make it far more elusive.

The Borodin Trio bring an unaccustomed passion to the music that ultimately serves it very well: this is far and away the most intensely emotional of all its recordings; even those who might find it slightly overheated won't fail to respond to its undeniable eloquence. While versions of the Ravel sonatas might have been far more welcome, the performances of Debussy's Cello and Violin Sonatas are superb, as is the warm and focused recorded sound.

Among available recordings of the Ravel Violin Sonata, Dmitri Sitkovetsky and his mother, Bella Davidovich, offer a brilliant performance as part of an extremely attractive Ravel recital on Orfeo (C 108841 A [CD], M 108841 A [T]), which also offers intelligent, virtuoso accounts of the *Berceuse sur le nom de Fauré*, the *Sonate posthume* from 1897, and the popular *Tzigane*.

Rawsthorne, Alan (1905–1971)

Piano Concertos (2); Concerto for 2 Pianos and Orchestra

> Tozer, Cislowski, piano; London Philharmonic, Bamert. Chandos
> CHAN 9125 [CD].

Symphonies (3)

> London Philharmonic, Pritchard (No. 1); Braithwaite (No. 2); BBC
> Symphony, Del Mar (No. 3). Lyrita SCRD 291 [CD].

Like Albert Roussel, this gifted and prolific English composer came to music surprisingly late, having originally intended to become a dentist. After studies at the Royal Manchester College of Music and with the German pianist Egon Petri in Berlin, Rawsthorne devoted himself to composition from the mid-1930s onward, producing a body of work remarkable for its quality and consistency, whether in large-scale orchestral works like the three Symphonies and *Improvisations on a Theme by Constant Lambert*—Rawsthorne married his friend's widow in 1954—or in rigorously crafted chamber pieces like the Clarinet Quartet or scores for numerous films, including most notably *The Man Who Never Was*. There is a contrapuntal density and rugged strength in the best of Rawsthorne's music that allows it wear extremely well on repeated hearings; with increased familiarity comes increased affection for the often vulnerable man beneath the tough-guy façade.

The Chandos recording of the piano concertos is an excellent introduction to Rawsthorne's witty, hard-edged world. The First—an arrangement of an earlier work with string and percussion accompaniment—is particularly exhilarating (especially the hearty *chaconne* written in homage to Bach), but the others are no less so, offering an abundance of strength, humor, and imaginatively worked-out musical ideas coupled with an obvious and intimate knowledge of the instrument itself.

The Symphonies are also challenging but exceptionally appealing, especially the Second, called "Pastoral," which includes a delightfully bucolic Scherzo and a wistful setting of a poem by the Earl of Surrey that meditates briefly on the changing seasons. As in the Concertos, all the performers involved play with the evident pride of people who are convinced they're helping to promulgate neglected music of real quality. The remastered analogue recorded sound is equally exceptional.

Reger, Max (1873–1916)

Variations on a Theme of Hiller, Op. 86; *Variations on a Theme by Mozart,* Op. 132

New Zealand Symphony, Decker. Naxos 8.553079 [CD].

Cantankerous, excitable, generous, impulsive, physically repellent—a friend once described him as "a swollen myopic beetle with thick lips and a sullen expression"—Max Reger once said that composers, like pigs, could be enjoyed only *after* their deaths. If since his own death from a heart attack in 1916, Reger has given the general public little to enjoy, then musicians from Arthur Nikisch to Paul Hindemith revered this most scholarly composer of his generation, applauding his quixotic attempt to bring the contrapuntal techniques of Johann Sebastian Bach into the Romantic era.

Given the slightest encouragement, Reger's *Hiller* and *Mozart Variations* could easily become standard repertory items: both are bursting with ideas, humor, and ingenious solutions to difficult problems, including two of the most impressive double fugues since the High Baroque.

If the performances by the New Zealand Symphony under Franz-Paul Decker are not quite the last word in either polish or excitement—for *that,* one should consult an Orfeo recording of the *Hiller* (C 090841 A [CD], M 090841 A [T]) and a long-deleted Philips version of the *Mozart,* both conducted by Sir Colin Davis—then this is still an attractive and inexpensive way to begin exploring some wonderful music by a composer who is far more approachable than his reputation would make him seem.

Reger's last completed work, the Quintet for Clarinet and Strings, was until recently ably represented by a top-notch recording from the Muir String Quartet and the great American clarinetist Mitchell Lurie on the small EcoClassics label (ECO-CD-005 [CD]). Lurie's playing is so supple and intensely musical that you quickly begin to understand why he was Fritz Reiner's favorite clarinetist; the fine Muir String Quartet provide able support, as they do in the equally engaging Clarinet Quartet by Paul Hindemith, which rounds out this generous and unusual disc. Some of the larger stores may still have copies in stock; if not, the best alternative is the Koch Schwann recording (SCH 3115020 [CD]) by Pierre Woudenberg and the Schoenberg String Quartet.

Finally, two of Reger's most enjoyable scores, the *Suite in the Olden Style* and *the Serenade in G,* receive gracious, spirited performances from Horst Stein and the Bamberg Symphony on Koch 3-1566-2 [CD]. Either might easily enter the standard repertoire if conductors, orchestras, and audiences weren't so lazy.

Reich, Steve (1936–)

Drumming (1970–1971)

Steve Reich Ensemble. Elektra/Nonesuch 79170-2 [CD], 79170-4 [T].

Tehillim for Winds, Strings, Percussion, and Voices (1981)

Steve Reich and Musicians. ECM New Series 78118-21215-2 [CD], 78118-21215-4 [T].

While Steve Reich is most closely identified with what is usually called the minimalist movement, his music defies easy categorization, perhaps because his enthusiasms—like his talent and education—have been so exceptionally diverse. In addition to formal study with such disparate teachers as Hal Overton, Darius Milhaud, and Luciano Berio, Reich has also been influenced by jazz, the Balinese masters of the gamelan, and the African drummers of Ghana, where he went to study in 1970.

In 1966, he organized a performing group called Steve Reich and Musicians, which introduced the works that first brought him international attention, including *Drumming,* a mesmerizing seventy-minute tour de force scored for drums, marimbas, glockenspiels, piccolo, whistler, and two female voices. *Tehillim,* a setting of Psalms 18 and 19, adds a quartet of voices—high soprano, two lyric sopranos, contralto—together with clapping and infectious syncopations. As in *Drumming,* the now familiar Reichian hallmarks are all conspicuously on display: the hypnotic, unvarying pulse above which the most subtle rhythmic patterns are built, together with an equally imaginative exploration of dynamics, textures, and colors.

It goes without saying that the performances are definitive.

Reicha, Anton (1770–1836)

Wind Quintets

Albert Schweitzer Wind Quintet. CPO CD 999022-2 [CD].

A friend and exact contemporary of Beethoven, Antonín Rejcha—better known by the teutonicized version of his name, Anton Reicha—was born in Prague in 1770. Although he produced works in virtually every musical form and would become one of the early nineteenth century's most significant theorists and teachers—his many pupils included Berlioz, Liszt, Franck, and Gounod—Reicha is best remembered as the father of the woodwind quintet.

Reicha's two dozen works in the form are invariably charming, elegant, tuneful, and challenging (even on modern instruments, the agile contrapuntal writing presents serious technical difficulties): nothing profound or even very significant, certainly, but ingratiating, well-made music that is always easy on the ear and eager to please.

In their ten-volume survey, the Albert Schweitzer Quintet acquits itself admirably, playing with vigor, polish, and an infectious enthusiasm that never seems to flag. Begin with Volume 1 (listed here), then add others as the need arises. This is ideal music to use while studying for finals or as background at pretentious cocktail parties.

Respighi, Ottorino (1879–1936)

Ancient Airs and Dances for the Lute (3 sets); *Gli uccelli* ("The Birds")

Australian Chamber Orchestra, Gee. Omega OCD 1007 [CD].

Although the Sydney and Melbourne Symphonies—to name the two ensembles that are probably best known "Up Over"—have each made fine recordings, I'm not so sure that this isn't the *finest* orchestral recording to have come out of Australia. If their recordings of Schubert symphonies with Sir Charles Mackerras and an album of Strauss and Stravinsky with the present conductor suggested they were a top-notch outfit, then this version of four popular Respighi works proves that the Australian Chamber Orchestra is one of the great chamber orchestras of the world.

The competition in both *The Birds* and the popular *Ancient Airs and Dances* suites is ferocious. Sir Neville Marriner's recordings with the Academy of

St. Martin-in-the-Fields and the Los Angeles Chamber Orchestra, to say nothing of the late Antal Dorati's classic version with the Philharmonia Hungarica, have set a standard in the *Ancient Airs* that many of us thought would never be approached. Similarly, wonderful recordings of *The Birds* have appeared and vanished, including a surprisingly nubile interpretation from Eugene Ormandy that CBS really can't afford *not* to reissue.

So along comes this recording by Christopher Lyndon Gee and his plucky Aussies that blithely mops up the floor with all of them. Not only are the performances extremely sophisticated—especially in the subtly shifting colors of the *Ancient Airs*—but they also manage to convey a sense of discovery, wonderment, and enthusiasm that few recordings by professional musicians ever do. The recorded sound, like the playing itself, is absolutely impeccable; so much so that further Omega releases by the ACO can be awaited with the keenest possible interest.

Nearly as skillful as the *Ancient Airs and Dances* are Respighi's technicolor orchestrations of the music of the giant of the German Baroque, some of which are now available on a stunning Delos album called "Symphonic Bach" (DE 3098 [CD]). The arrangements themselves are generally more idiomatic and tasteful (!) than the more famous transcriptions by Leopold Stokowski, while the performances by Gerard Schwarz and the Seattle Symphony are everything a Baroque Romantic could hope for, with some especially thrilling contributions from the SSO brass.

Belfagor Overture; Fantasia slava for Piano and Orchestra; *Tre corali; Toccata* for Piano and Orchestra

BBC Philharmonic, Downes. Chandos CHAN 9311 [CD].

Sir Edward Downes's Respighi series continues with the first really distinguished recording of the *Toccata* for Piano and Orchestra, which the composer introduced to New York in 1928. Written at about the same time as *Roman Festivals*, the *Toccata* is one of the most original and appealing of Respighi's scores and easily his finest work for piano and orchestra. As always, Downes is such a completely sympathetic advocate that you begin to suspect he may own stock in Respighi's publishing company, while Geoffrey Tozer dispatches the challenging solo part with fire and imagination. While less inherently rewarding, the other pieces are given the same devoted treatment and the recorded sound is excellent.

Perhaps even more valuable is the album devoted to Respighi's major works for violin and orchestra, the *Concerto gregoriano* and the *Poema autumnale*. The former, with its haunting use of the modes of Gregorian chant, is one of Respighi's most refined and eloquent works, as is the lovely *Autumn Poem*, with its darkly meditative lyricism. Best of all, though, may be the *Ballata delle Gnomidi* (The Ballad of the Gnomes), which is so full of wit, color, and magical orchestral effects that its present obscurity is impossible to fathom. Violinist Lydia Mordkovitch is as commanding as Tozer in the piano works, while Downes draws the last drop of finesse and excitement from the BBC Philharmonic.

La Boutique fantasque, (ballet, after Rossini)

Boston Pops, Fiedler. RCA 09026-61847-2 [CD], 09026-61847-4 [T].

Like those other classic pastiche ballets, Stravinsky's *Pulcinella* and Vincenzo Tommasini's adaptation of some Scarlatti sonatas called *The Good-Humored Ladies*, Respighi's *La Boutique fantasque* is a startlingly successful fusion of two distinct styles and centuries. And nowhere is the orchestral genius of Ottorino Respighi more clearly evident than in this fizzing, luxurious concoction arranged from the melodies of Rossini.

Arthur Fiedler's recording is one of the very best that the long-time conductor of the Boston Pops ever made. Behind the avuncular, Santa-minus-the-beard facade, Fiedler was a tough disciplinarian who got astonishing results with next to no rehearsal time. (His public image, like that of Robert Frost, was a carefully manicured fabrication to disguise the soul of a true curmudgeon and misanthrope; he was *not* a beloved figure among orchestral players, but then again, what truly competent conductor ever is?) His interpretation of *La Boutique fantasque* twinkles with an impish wit from beginning to end yet misses little of the ballet's considerable charm and warmth. The version of the Offenbach pastiche *Gaîté parisienne* is possibly even finer, with snapping rhythms, whiplash attacks, and a glowing sentimentality—especially in the famous *Barcarolle*—that would melt an India rubber ball.

Three other—and far less familiar—*pastiche* ballets by Respighi have surfaced on an attractive CD from Marco Polo (8.223346 [CD]), which seems intent on recording the man's entire output. Like the *Ancient Airs, Sèvres de la vieille France* draws its inspiration from seventeenth- and eighteenth-century models, while *Le astuzie di Colombina* makes use of popular Venetian melodies. Best of all, though, is *La pentola magica*, which rifles through some fairly unfamiliar (albeit undeniably charming) Russian works by Gretchaninov, Arensky, Anton Rubinstein, and Vladimir Rebikov. The Slovak Radio Symphony plays with skill and obvious relish, while Marco Polo's engineers respond with warm—if somewhat distant—recorded sound.

Brazilian Impressions; Vetrate di chiesa ("Church Windows")

Philharmonia Orchestra, Simon. Chandos CHAN 8317 [CD].

Although neither is as memorable or as cogently argued as the Roman tone poems, both the *Brazilian Impressions* and *Church Windows* make some spectacularly colorful noises, especially the exotic souvenir of the composer's visit to South America. The thrilling performances by Geoffrey Simon and the Philharmonia Orchestra are further enhanced by one of the finest of all Chandos recordings, a demonstration-quality effort with the widest imaginable dynamic range and most natural-sounding balances.

The Fountains of Rome; The Pines of Rome; Roman Festivals

Philadelphia Orchestra, Muti. EMI Classics CDC 47316 [CD].

How unfortunate for this tremendously gifted composer that he was also a man with virtually no musical conscience or taste. (I have always thought that it was no accident that the word "pig" can actually be found within his name.) A wizard of the modern orchestra, and Italy's only significant non-operatic composer of the prewar era, Ottorino Respighi is best remembered for that triptych of tone poems that celebrates the sights and sounds of his beloved Rome. Respighi's command of orchestration rivaled that of any composer who has ever lived, which is largely why these three pieces of unadulterated trash rank with the most popular orchestral showpieces of the twentieth century. (And like everyone else who has ever fallen under their vulgar spell, I love all three to distraction.) While nothing will ever make me give up my cherished RCA Victor recording of the *Fountains* and *Pines* by Fritz Reiner and the Chicago Symphony (RCA 09026-68079-2 [CD]), the performances contained on Riccardo Muti's Angel recording are very much in that same rarefied league. In addition, he also gives us a spine-tingling run-through of the grisly *Roman Festivals*, my own nomination as the greatest single piece of musical schlock produced by anyone in the last hundred years. (The only other possible contender, Richard Addinsell's *Warsaw Concerto*, was written for a movie and only accidentally went on to a macabre life of its own.) As in so many of their recent recordings, the actual playing of the Philadelphia Orchestra really must be heard to be believed. The last vestiges of Eugene Ormandy's "Philadelphia Sound" have been all but eradicated by his dynamic successor. And while Muti may not be the most consistently profound or interesting conductor before the public today, he certainly deserves enormous credit for having revitalized a great American orchestra.

Metamorphoseon modi XII; Belkis, Queen of Sheba (Suite)

Philharmonia Orchestra, Simon. Chandos CHAN-8405 [CD].

One of the marks of true genius is its infinite capacity to renew, rejuvenate, and surpass itself. Although *Metamorphoseon* is an academic, agreeably turgid series of variations on a medieval tune, the music from *Belkis, Queen of Sheba* is something very special, even for Respighi.

Compared to *Belkis, Roman Festivals* is the *Saint Matthew Passion*. The suite from this 1934 biblical ballet (and what wouldn't one give to hear the whole thing!) is so smarmy, so brazenly crude, so ineluctably vile, that "schlock" is a poor and trifling word to describe it. At this stratospheric level, trash ceases being mere trash, and *Belkis* is a kind of final apotheosis of Respighian vulgarity. It's hardly surprising that the composer died only two years later. What was left to be done?

It goes without saying that I love every millisecond of it, especially in Geoffrey Simon's resolutely wanton interpretation. The Philharmonia Orchestra comports itself like a band of shameless harlots and the Chandos engineers capture every grunt and groan to perfection.

Sinfonia drammatica

BBC Philharmonic, Downes. Chandos CHAN 9213 [CD].

Say what you will about Respighi's *Sinfonia drammatica*: it's definitely *not* the sort of thing you want to meet some night in a dark alley. Completed shortly before the outbreak of the First World War and only a couple of years before the *Fountains of Rome* would make him famous, Respighi's only symphony is, on the surface, a long, noisy, irresponsible pastiche of Franck, Rimsky-Korsakov, and Richard Strauss, in which one overblown climax follows another until the composer finally throws in the towel with what can only be described as a lumbering, quasi-biblical tango! Yet for all its goofiness and pomposity, the *Sinfonia drammatica* is the work of a man with something important to say who is desperately trying to find a way of saying it. There is a dark, almost endearing urgency in the best pages of the score, together with the composer's soon-to-be-legendary genius for manipulating great waves of orchestral sound.

The work's third commercial recording has indeed proven to be a charm, with the BBC Philharmonic under Sir Edward Downes playing as though their lives depended upon it. Unlike the rival performance on Marco Polo, there is a passionate intelligence at work here, which not only gives the *Dramatic Symphony* more shape and substance than it has ever had before, but also infuses it with a genuine seriousness of purpose and something approaching real respectability. The recording, like the performance, is in the demonstration class.

Il tramonto (cantata, after Shelly); *Trittico Botticelliano; Gli Uccelli* ("The Birds"); *Adagio con variazione* for Cello and Orchestra

Finnie, mezzo-soprano; Wallfisch, cello; Bournemouth Sinfonietta, Vásáry. Chandos CHAN 8913 [CD].

Even the most gleeful Respighi-basher—and I blush to confess, I *have* been one in my time—cannot fail to be moved by *Il tramonto* ("The Sunset"), a hauntingly beautiful setting of an Italian version of a poem by Shelley that ranks with the loveliest moments in Puccini. By that same token, the *Three Botticelli Pictures* find Respighi at his most sensitive and refined, especially in the melting second movement with its sinuous oboe solo.

Linda Finnie gives one of the finest of all her recorded performances in *Il tramonto,* with her large, feminine, richly expressive instrument easily eclipsing all the current competition. Cellist Raphael Wallfisch is similarly convincing in the youthful *Adagio con variazione,* while Tamas Vásáry proves an ideal exponent of this evocative music, missing none of its subtle color or dramatic point. More recordings like this one and we won't have Respighi to kick around any more.

Revueltas, Silvestre   (1899–1940)

Orchestral Works

Various orchestras and conductors. Catalyst 09026-62672-2 [CD].

With his sometime friend and exact contemporary Carlos Chávez, the brilliantly gifted, tragically self-destructive Silvestre Revueltas, who drank himself to death at the age of forty, remains the most celebrated composer that Mexico has yet produced. Although from the outset Revueltas's music concerned itself with the sights and sounds of his native Mexico—he made extensive use of native percussion instruments and possessed a profound natural understanding of Mexican music—he had no real interest in Mexican or Indian folklore and never actually quoted musical folk material. An impulsive, instinctive composer with little use for study or systems, Revueltas insisted, "Music that makes one think is intolerable, excruciating. I adore music that puts me to sleep." Nonetheless, his music is redolent with unmistakably Mexican melodies, harmonies, and rhythms that, in his own words, "are reminiscent of other rhythms and sonorities, just as building material in architecture is incidental with any building material, but it serves for constructions that are different in meaning, form, and expression."

This RCA Catalyst CD is easily the single most valuable Revueltas anthology currently available, including the composer's most popular work, the spellbinding snake-killing ritual *Sensamaya,* the suite from the 1939 film *La noche de los Mayas,* and the moving *Homenaje a Federico García Lorca.* The performances range from the very fine to the exceptional, as does the recorded sound.

Riegger, Wallingford (1885–1961)

Dance Rhythms; Movement; Music for Brass Choir; Music for Orchestra; Nonet for Brass; Romanza; Symphony No. 3

Various orchestras, ensembles, conductors. CRI 572 [CD].

In death, as in life, the Georgia-born Wallingford Riegger remains a classic American outsider. Like his near contemporaries Charles Ives, Carl Ruggles, and Henry Cowell, this gentle, good-humored man belonged to no established school or tradition, developed slowly (and largely in isolation), adapted various modern procedures—most notably, Cowell's cluster technique and elements of Schoenberg's twelve-tone method—into his own intensely personal idiom, producing music in a distinct variety of styles that the composer described at various times as "non-dissonant (mostly)," "impressionist," "partly dissonant," and "dissonant."

With so little of Riegger's music currently available, this CRI anthology provides an invaluable introduction to one of the most original and important American composers. Riegger's most celebrated work, the enchanting, delicately syncopated *Dance Rhythms,* is given a lithe and graceful performance by the Oslo Philharmonic conducted by Antonio Antonini, the long-time conductor of the CBS Symphony who worked tirelessly on the documentary series *Air Power, The Twentieth Century,* and *World War I.* While the various works for brass are competently handled by the National Orchestra Alumni Association, the gem of the collection is Howard Hanson's recording of the spare and powerful Third Symphony, which won the New York Music Critics' Circle award in 1948.

Even a passing acquaintance with the least of these works will make you wonder how music of this quality and obvious importance has remained neglected for so long. It's high time that some enterprising conductor and recording company—Schwarz and Delos?—begin the systematic and long overdue examination of Riegger's work.

Riley, Terry   (1935–)

The Heaven Ladder, Book 7; The Walrus in Memoriam

Cheng-Cochran, piano. Telarc CD-80513 [CD].

One of the leading voices of the minimalist movement, Terry Riley first attracted international attention in 1964 with *In C,* a daring experiment in improvisational monotony in which each member of a group of unspecified performers plays through a sequence of fifty-three tiny melodic motifs over an unvarying C major pulse an unspecified number of times. The entire "score" was printed on the jacket of the original Columbia LP (reissued on CBS MK 07178 [CD]), and I remember following along in baffled fascination, in which state I continue to remain.

The five pieces of *The Heaven Ladder, Book 7,* are "the first entirely written-out piano works" that Riley has produced since 1959. In their charm *(Misha's Bear Dance),* mystery *(Simone's Lullaby),* and startling complexity *(Ragtempus Fugatis),* they offer a dramatic contrast to the composer's typical minimalist efforts, as does *The Walrus in Memoriam,* one of a number of works written on a commission from EMI celebrating the music of the Beatles.

In her new Teldec recording, Gloria Cheng-Cochran—for whom the piece was written—suggests that *The Heaven Ladder, Book 7,* is one of the most important American piano works of the last quarter century. The playing is so intelligent, probing, and physically beautiful that you begin to wonder how much of that impression is the result of the performance, how much of the music itself. John Adams's *Phrygian Gates*—a key work of this "minimalist bored with minimalism"—receives a comparably definitive reading.

Rimsky-Korsakov, Nikolai (1844–1908)

Capriccio Espagnol

New York Philharmonic, Bernstein. Sony Classical SMK 47595 [CD], SM 47595 [T].

CBS didn't exactly make the bargain hunters ecstatic with this skimpy release, which combines Rimsky's Spanish travelogue with Tchaikovsky's *Capriccio Italien.* Even in the long-vanished LP days, that kind of "radical cheap" packaging would have been ballsy; given today's CD and tape prices, it took—as my grandmother used to say—"some *real* stones." As if to make amends, Sony Classical has repackaged them both with *Capriccio Espagnol*'s original LP coupling, the Ravel orchestration of Mussorgsky's *Pictures at an Exhibition.*

The performances are vintage early Bernstein and are thus, in terms of sheer animal excitement, extremely difficult to surpass. *Capriccio Espagnol* is as seductive and vibrant as ever; the solo display—most notably from oboist Harold Gomberg—matches anything from the rival Philadelphia Orchestra's heyday, and the closing bars flash by in a blinding swatch of local color. From the tender oboe duet to the orgiastic finale, *Capriccio Italien* is also brimming with character, and the remastered sound of both is excellent.

Sadko

Galusin, Tsidipova, Tarassova, Minjelkiev, Gergalov, Grigorian, Kirov Opera Chorus and Orchestra, Gergiev. Philips 442138-2 [CD].

For those who really know and love them—Neeme Järvi, for one, who has long owned the scores and parts for *all* of them and has offered to conduct any of them anywhere on a moment's notice—Rimsky-Korsakov's fifteen operas are not only his most important and original contribution to serious music, but are also the greatest sustained achievement of Russian opera. If none of them can quite match the individual accomplishment of *Boris Godunov* and *Prince Igor*—neither of which would have found a public without Rimsky's inspired arrangement and orchestration—then as a whole they represent one of the most consistently inspired imaginative acts of nineteenth-century music, the creation of a make-believe world in which, to quote the composer's English biographer Gerald Abraham, "reality was inextricably confused with the fantastic, naivete with sophistication, the romantic with the humorous, and beauty with absurdity."

In addition to famous set pieces like the tenor aria sung by an Indian merchant, known universally as "The Song of India," and the equally celebrated bass aria "The Song of the Viking Guest," *Sadko* is an opera bursting with vivid imagination, exotic atmosphere, and inspired invention, as this recent Kirov production makes abundantly clear. The live performance is a uniformly excellent one, with generally fine singing—especially from Vladimir Galusin in the title role and Valentina Tsidipova as the Sea Princess—and superbly evocative conducting from Valery Gergiev. This is so easily the finest recording of any Rimsky-Korsakov opera currently available—the various recordings from Capriccio, Russian Season, Arlecchino, and Koch perform little useful service for either the composer or the listener—that one hopes Gergiev and company will soon turn their attention to other scores, especially *Le Coq d'or, May Night, The Snow Maiden,* and— be still my heart!—*The Legend of the Invisible City of Kitezh.*

Scheherazade

Chicago Symphony, Reiner. RCA 09026-60875-2 [CD].

Royal Philharmonic, Beecham. EMI Classics CDC-47717 [CD].

It's difficult to think of another composer who better deserves the title of History's Greatest Minor Composer. Camille Saint-Saëns actually predicted that that is how posterity would remember him, but he forgot about the work of this Russian near-Giant. An orchestrator and teacher of genius (his brilliant edition saved his friend Mussorgsky's *Boris Godounov* from oblivion, and his best-known pupil, of course, was Igor Stravinsky), Rimsky-Korsakov never quite grasped the greatness that always seemed to be just outside of his reach. For moments, even for entire acts of dazzling operas like *Le Coq d'or, Mlada,* or *The Snow Maiden,* you can hear him on the verge of actually *doing* it, and then, inevitably, the music draws back at the very last.

By that same token, *Scheherazade,* one of history's most colorful and beautifully made orchestral scores, is also, in a sense, one of its most heartbreaking. It is a work that never quite adds up to much more than the sum of its fabulous parts: an elegant, vivid, brilliant, clever, colorful piece, but never a great one.

Among the many memorable recordings that *Scheherazade* has had over the years, none has ever made it *seem* closer to being a great piece than the performance recorded in the late 1950s by Fritz Reiner and the Chicago Symphony. In spite of formidable competition from Sir Thomas Beecham, whose legendary interpretation recorded at about the same time remains the last word in individuality, charm, and staggeringly inventive solo display, Reiner's combination of near-perfect execution, finesse, and unadulterated sex, makes this—by a whisker—*the* performance of *Scheherazade* to own. While the original recorded sound has been dramatically improved, it is most spectacular in the compact disc, which, as a bonus, includes that most electrifying of all recordings of Debussy's *La Mer.*

Suites from the Operas *(Christmas Eve; Le Coq d'or; Legend of the Invisible City of Kitezh; May Night (Overture); Mlada; The Snow Maiden; Tsar Saltan)*

Scottish National Orchestra, Järvi. Chandos CHAN 8327 [CD].

As Dmitri Shostakovich may or may not have pointed out in *Testimony*— the authorship of the controversial memoirs is still in question—for more than a decade Rimsky-Korsakov suffered from a debilitating emotional disease called

Piotr Ilyich Tchaikovsky. "Tchaikovsky kept Korsakov from composing, interfered simply by existing," Shostakovich may or may not have observed. "For ten years, Rimsky-Korsakov couldn't write an opera and after Tchaikovsky's death he wrote eleven operas in fifteen years. And it's interesting to note that this flood began with *Christmas Eve*. As soon as Tchaikovsky died, Korsakov took a theme already used by Tchaikovsky and rewrote it his way."

Whoever proposed the theory, it does have a dreary and peculiarly Russian ring of truth; for with the passing of his arch-antagonist, Rimsky-Korsakov did enter the most fruitful period of his creative life, producing the bulk of the music upon which his reputation—at least, in Russia—continues to rest.

Why his operas have never gained a significant toehold in the West remains a baffling mystery. Some, like *Le Coq d'or*, are as masterly as any Slavic opera short of Smetana's *The Bartered Bride* and Mussorgsky's *Boris Godunov*, and many of them—as this gorgeous series of recordings from Chandos will show— contain some of his most distinctive and original music: from the eerie mystery of the *Invisible City of Kitezh* to the delightful *Christmas Eve*, whose stirring Polonaise is alone worth the price of admission.

This is possibly the best—and certainly one of the most valuable—of the many recordings that the rather overexposed Neeme Järvi has made. Honed to a fine edge, the Scottish National Orchestra cuts through the formidable difficulties of this music with ease, and the conductor has a genuine knack for revealing both its obvious and hidden treasures. Folks with a sweet tooth for *Scheherazade* will have a fine time gorging themselves on these equally tasty goodies; the more shameless gluttons will also want to explore Dmitri Kitayenko's skilled and idiomatic recordings with the Bergen Symphony of the composer's three symphonies, this on a pair of medium-pieced Chandos Enchant CDs (CHAN 7029), released just in time to replace Järvi's recently withdrawn Deutsche Grammophon recording.

Rodrigo, Joaquín   (1901–)

Concierto de Aranjuez for Guitar and Orchestra

> Williams, guitar; English Chamber Orchestra, Barenboim. CBS MK
> 33208 [CD].

> Angel Romero, guitar; London Symphony, Previn. EMI Classics CDC
> 47693 [CD].

With the possible exception of the dippy Pachelbel Kanon, Joaquín Rodrigo's *Concierto de Aranjuez* has become the great "hit" classical piece of the last dozen years, and its popularity is richly deserved. Written with the great Andrés Segovia in mind, Rodrigo's *Concierto* is easily the finest such work ever written for the instrument: a work that not only exploits virtually all of the rather limited expressive possibilities of the guitar, but also provides us with one of the most haunting of all musical evocations of the sights and sounds of Spain.

To date, the great John Williams has recorded the *Concierto* no fewer than four times, and it is his version with Daniel Barenboim and the English Chamber Orchestra that is still the most completely satisfying recording the piece has ever received. Technically, Williams is without equal among living guitarists, and here, as in all of his recordings, he tosses off the *Concierto*'s formidable difficulties as though they didn't even exist. Yet unlike his other versions, there is a freshness and spontaneity in this performance that no other recording can begin to match. Thanks, no doubt, to Daniel Barenboim's rich and flexible accompaniment, Williams is allowed to phrase and emote with a freedom he has rarely shown on records before or since. On the EMI Classics CD, Angel Romero's playing is nearly as brilliant and refreshing as Williams's, and instead of the Villa-Lobos Guitar Concerto that comes with the Williams recording, this one offers the more conventional (and desirable) coupling of Rodrigo's equally enchanting *Fantasía para un gentilhombre*.

Concierto madrigal for Two Guitars and Orchestra; *Concierto Andaluz* for Four Guitars and Orchestra

> The Romeros, guitars; Academy of St. Martin-in-the-Fields, Marriner.
> Philips 400024-2 [CD].

It has been suggested that with the *Concierto de Aranjuez* of 1939, Rodrigo stumbled upon a formula so successful that he was content to build a career out of rewriting the piece indefinitely. Even if this were perfectly true—which it isn't, quite—then who could possibly care? Only the naive or the very young tend to prefer the *idea* of originality to the reality of cleverness, since the latter is a precious, hard-won skill and the former, for all practical purposes, simply doesn't exist. Besides, if an idea is a good one and the market will bear it, then by all means, use it again. Bach, Handel, Rossini, Stravinsky, and numberless other lesser figures never felt any qualms about recycling their own, as well as other, composer's ideas, and the composer of *Star Wars* and other hugely successful film scores has grown wealthy and famous by scrupulously avoiding *any* musical idea that might even remotely be called his own. (The list of composers and specific works that have "inspired" him is a long and eclectic one and would make a fascinating little book; at the very least, it might be turned into documented monograph that the "powers that be" at ASCAP might be interested to read.)

If they *are* warmed-over versions of *Concierto de Aranjuez,* then *Concierto madrigal* and *Concierto andaluz* prove what every mother knows, to wit, that leftovers can often be every bit as delicious—if not more so—than the original meal. These gracefully melodious and instantly assimilable works are thoroughgoing delights, especially in performances such as these. The gifted, extrovert Romeros play the concertos as if they had been written specifically for them—which, as a matter of fact, they were. Marriner's accompaniments and Philips's recorded sound are worthy of both the soloists and the music itself.

Guitar Music

A. Romero, guitar. RCA 09026-68767-2 [CD].

Rodrigo's solo guitar music is much less well known than his concertos, but much of what makes the *Concierto de Aranjuez* and *Fantasía para un gentilhombre* so popular—the catchy tunes, piquant harmonies, lively rhythms, and effortlessly idiomatic command of the instrument—is in ample evidence here. Predictably, Angel Romero is an ideal interpreter of these engaging miniatures, from colorful genre pieces like *Por los campos de Espay* to more substantial items like the *Sonata giocosa.* For lovers of Rodrigo and/or the guitar, the album is bound to give enormous pleasure.

Music of Rodrigo

Various soloists; London Symphony, Mexico State Philharmonic, Royal Philharmonic, Bátiz. EMI Classics CDZD 67435 [CD].

If the performances of the *Concierto de Aranjuez, Fantasía para un gentilhombre, Concierto madrigal,* and *Concierto andaluz* included in this four-CD anthology don't quite eclipse those listed above, then they are all certainly worth having in this extensive Rodrigo collection, which gathers all of the composer's instrumental concertos—except for the *Concierto para una fiesta* and the

Concierto como un divertimento—in one convenient box. Fortunately, the best performances are of the less familiar works: the Vivaldi-inspired *Concierto de estío* (Summer Concerto) for violin, the *Concierto serenata* for harp (seductively played by Nancy Allen), the *Concierto pastoral* (which draws nearly as memorable a performance from flutist Lisa Hansen as it did from James Galway, its dedicatee), and the concertos for cello and piano—*Concierto en modo galante* and *Concierto heróico*—in bracing, characterful performances by Robert Cohen and Jorge Osorio. Enrique Bátiz is wholly attuned to Rodrigo's colorful idiom, both in the stylish accompaniments he provides in all the concertos and in the rarely heard orchestral pieces, including the tone poem *A la busca del más allá;* the enchanting quartet of lullabies, *Música para un jardin;* and the equally charming *5 Piezas infantiles,* plus assorted miniatures.

Roger-Ducasse, Jean-Jules Aimable (1873–1954)

Le Joli Jeu de furet; Marche français (Symphonic poem); *Nocturne de printemps; Orphée* (excerpts); *Petite Suite*

> Rhineland-Palatinate State Philharmonic, Segerstam. Marco Polo
> 8.223501 [CD].

Au Jardin de Marguerite (excerpts); *Epithalame; Prélude d'un ballet; Suite française*

> Rhineland-Palatinate State Philharmonic, Segerstam. Marco Polo
> 8.223641 [CD].

A pupil of Gabriel Fauré, and Paul Dukas's successor as professor of composition at the Paris Conservatory, Jean-Jules Aimable Roger-Ducasse remains a shadowy figure of modern French music, this in spite of the distinctiveness of his style, the refinement of his musical thinking, and the elegance of his orchestration. While there are occasional echoes of Fauré, d'Indy, Debussy, and Ravel, his best music reveals an approach to melody, harmony, rhythm, and counterpoint that in the aggregate suggests the work of no one else. At first hearing, it is immediately intriguing; on repeated contact, it inspires increasing affection and respect.

The Marco Polo recordings are the most important that Roger-Ducasse's music has ever received, finally allowing this fascinating talent to step out of the shadows. From the earliest work presented here, the Fauré-like *Petite Suite* of 1898, the first of his works to be performed in public, through the witty and meticulously crafted *Suite française* with its allusions to Chabrier, the shimmering post-Impressionist textures of *Nocturne de printemps,* and the boisterous humor of *Epithalame,* this is music of exceptional interest and quality that will reward any listener willing to stray from the well-worn paths. Leif Segerstam and his German orchestra provide intelligently thought-out, superbly executed interpretations, captured in first-rate recorded sound.

Roman, Johan Helmich
(1694–1758)

Drottningholmsmusiquen

> Drottningholm Chamber Orchestra, Westerberg. Swedish Society SCD 1019 [CD].

> Stockholm National Museum Chamber Orchestra, Génetay. Proprius PRCD 9047 [CD].

Called at various times "The Father of Swedish Music" and "The Swedish Handel," Johan Helmich Roman was the first composer of real significance that his country had ever produced. Although widely traveled—he spent five years in England (1716–1721), where he studied with Dr. Pepusch and came under the spell of Handel—it was Roman's comparative isolation that probably helps account for the pleasant individuality of a style characterized by its harmonic quirkiness, rhythmic imagination, and passion for that emerging "modern" form, the symphony.

Roman's most famous work, the *Drottningholmsmusiquen,* is an extensive orchestral suite written in 1744 for the marriage of the Crown Prince Adolphus Frederik to Lovisa Ulrika of Prussia, sister of Frederick the Great. If this consistently fresh, charming, and inventive music is not on a par with the best of Handel, then it easily matches the finest Telemann and is clearly worth getting to know.

Both of these fine Swedish recordings present the music in the most favorable imaginable light: Stig Westerberg's spirited look at the standard suite and Claude Génetay's version of the *Lilla Drottningholmsmusiquen,* seventeen further dances that are every bit as delectable.

Those wishing to know this appealing personality even better are directed to a Bis recording (BIS CD 284 [CD]) that offers three of the authenticated violin concertos and a trio of his more than thirty *sinfonias*. Violinist Nils-Erik Sparf and the Stockholm Philharmonic's Orpheus Chamber Orchestra take obvious pleasure in this delightful music, as will you.

Rorem, Ned (1923–)

Songs

Rees, soprano; Rorem, piano. Premier PRCD 1035 [CD]

Nantucket Songs (cycle); *Some Trees* (cycle); *Women's Voices* (cycle)

Curtin, soprano; Wolff, contralto; Gramm, baritone; Rorem, piano.
CRI CD 657 [CD].

Gramm, bass-baritone; Istomin, piano. Phoenix PHCD 116 [CD].

It is both astonishing and shameful that the most accomplished American composer of art song should be currently represented in the catalogue only by recorded collections. As these superb anthologies demonstrate, however, Ned Rorem's songs are imaginative, memorable, and uniquely sensitive to their texts, perhaps more so than those of any other American composer. Until some enlightened and enterprising recording company begins a systematic examination of his amazingly rich and varied output, these collections will have to hint at what treasures lie awaiting discovery. On a more positive note, the performances with the composer—himself a skilled and seductive pianist—are definitive, as are those of the *War Scenes* and other Whitman settings by Donald Gramm and Eugene Istomin.

Rorem's enormous gifts as a composer of nonvocal music are obvious in his Pulitzer Prize–winning *Air Music* (Albany TROY 047 [CD]) and in the magical *Summer Music* he composed for the Beaux Arts Trio, this from a recently deleted Philips recording that may still be found in some cut-out bins. Robert Shaw and the Atlanta Symphony give meticulous, highly sympathetic performances of *Eagles*, the ravishing *String Symphony*, and *Sunday Morning* (New World NW 353-2 [CD]), while Gary Graffman plays the entertaining and endlessly inventive *Concerto for the Left Hand* (New World 80445-2 [CD]) as though it were written for him, which in fact it was.

Rosenberg, Hilding   (1892–1985)

Symphony No. 4, "The Revelation of St. John" (1940)

Hagegård, baritone; Rilke Ensemble, Pro Musica Chamber Choir,
  Swedish Radio Chorus, Gothenberg Symphony, Ehrling. Caprice
  CAP 21429 [CD].

This wholly extraordinary score, which exists somewhere between symphony and oratorio, goes a long way to explaining why many of his fellow countrymen regard Hilding Rosenberg as the major Swedish composer of the twentieth century. Drawing its text from the Bible and the deliberately archaic verses of the Swedish poet Hjalmar Gullberg, *Johannes uppenbarelse* is divided into eight large sections whose choral-orchestral movements often suggest a fusion of Mahler and the Bach *Passions* (with a series of a cappella choruses that harken all the way back to Palestrina) but whose linking baritone recitatives reflect the composer's earlier enthusiasm for the music of Schoenberg, Stravinsky, and Hindemith. The result is a strikingly original, powerfully dramatic amalgam that bears favorable comparison with any of the most important large-scale choral works of the century.

Sixten Ehrling's recording is probably the finest of his career, a performance blazing with purpose and conviction. Håken Hagegård negotiates the demanding solo part with easy confidence, while the orchestra and choruses seem completely inspired by the important task before them. For the jaded music lover badly in need of rejuvenation, this astonishing work might seem heaven-sent.

Rossini, Gioacchino (1792–1868)

Arias

Anderson, soprano; Teatro Communale de Bologna Chorus and
Orchestra, Gatti. London 436377-2 [CD].

Bartoli, mezzo-soprano. London 436075-2 [CD]; 425430-2 [CD].

Horne, mezzo-soprano; Turin Radio Symphony, Zedda. CBS MK
44820 [CD].

Jo, soprano; English Chamber Orchestra, Carella. Erato 17580 [CD].

Von Stade, mezzo-soprano. Philips 420084-2 [CD].

Even more than those of Bellini or Donizetti, the arias of Gioacchino Rossini define the true parameters of bel canto singing, for they include some of the most limpidly beautiful (and murderously difficult) vocal passages ever written: passages that in requiring an entirely new system of breath distribution helped lay the foundations for modern vocal technique.

June Anderson's London recital only enhances her reputation as Dame Joan Sutherland's logical successor as the reigning queen of bel canto. Not only is she possessed of a technique that rivals Sutherland's, but she is also a far more convincing actress: in these dazzling interpretations, both the notes *and* the characters leap off the page.

In terms of sheer vocal opulence, Marilyn Horne's famous London recital, until recently available on the medium-priced Gala series, remained in a class by itself. As an extended and breathtaking essay in technical virtuosity, singing of this caliber is rivaled only by Tetrazzini, McCormack, and a handful of the greatest singers of the past. Her later CBS recording, if not quite as frighteningly impressive, still suggests that in this repertoire the great mezzo remains in a class by herself.

Both of Cecilia Bartoli's Rossini anthologies have gotten some fairly ecstatic press and for very good reason: in addition to an extraordinary command of the idiom, the projection of character is comparable to the sorts of things that Maria Callas used to do. This is a big, important voice used with tremendous skill and intelligence: one of the voices that will no doubt set the limits of the art for years to come.

Sumi Jo's silvery, beautifully controlled voice is a delight to hear on her Erato recital, not only in the Rossini arias from *Semiramide* and *Tancredi* but also in some fabulously difficult moments by Bellini, Donizetti, Ricci, and Verdi. The singing is as impressive for its personality as for its technical command, suggesting that one of the most important vocalists of the early twenty-first century is already on the scene.

Of course, when it comes to personality, none is more attractive than that of the lovely Frederica von Stade, whose Philips recording of Rossini rarities is part of a well-judged collection that also includes arias by Haydn and Mozart. No singer of the last half century has combined warmth, taste, femininity, and supreme musicality in such a completely winning package and this is one of her most attractive recordings to date.

The Barber of Seville

> Callas, Alva, Gobbi, Philharmonia Chorus and Orchestra, Galliera.
> EMI Classics CDCB 47634 [CD].

Despite some formidable competition from the beautifully sung and brilliantly recorded Philips recording led with high and obvious zest by Sir Neville Marriner (Philips 411058-2 [CD]), this imperishable Angel recording, for all its flaws, remains the most enchanting and infectious recorded performance of the world's most popular *opera buffa*. While the supporting cast is consistently excellent—especially the late and irreplaceable Tito Gobbi and the exceptionally suave Almaviva of Luigi Alva—the star of the show is clearly Maria Callas, who, in one of her rare comic roles, proves that she was every bit as successful a comedienne as she was a tragic heroine. Listen, especially, to the way she teases the phrases in "Una voce poco fa," and you'll begin to understand why we Callas cuckoos immediately begin to salivate at the mere mention of the woman's name. Although there are niggling cuts throughout the performance and the recorded sound is not up to today's standards, there is a sparkling, good-natured sense of fun in this famous interpretation that will probably never be captured in a recording studio again.

La Cenerentola

> Bartoli, Costa, Banditelli, Matteuzzi, Corbelli, Dara, Pertusi, Chorus
> and Orchestra of the Bologna Teatro Comunale, Chailly. London
> 436902-2 [CD].

Rossini's daffy retelling of the Cinderella story is proof positive that there was always more to the composer than a handful of overtures and *The Barber of Seville*. Until the bel canto revival of the 1950s and '60s, it certainly might have seemed that way, for the simple reason that the florid vocal writing in works like *La Cenerentola* is so daunting that most singers simply opted for the better part of valor. To compound the problem, the title role in *Cenerentola*—like that of Isabella in *L'Italiana in Algeri*—is written for a *coloratura* contralto, which is about as common these days as articulate vice presidents or two-headed sheep.

(For that matter, *true* contraltos of any kind are an all but extinct species. If you don't believe it, then dig out any of Ernestine Schumann-Heink's old recordings and try to find even the *vaguest* approximation of that sort of instrument today.)

If Cecilia Bartoli is the principal drawing card for the London recording, then she is only one of the many sparkling elements in a thoroughly dazzling recording. In addition to her vividly imaginative interpretation of the heroine, the rest of the cast is nearly as fine, with William Matteuzzi a suavely polished Prince and all the important bass roles impressively covered. Riccardo Chailly keeps the action hopping while London's recorded sound creates a wonderful sense of in-your-face immediacy.

In *L'Italiana in Algeri,* an even funnier opera—not witty, not amusing, but bust-a-gut-laughing *funny*—Agnes Baltsa and Ruggero Raimondi are even more impressive than in their recently withdrawn Deutsche Grammophon recording, while Claudio Abbado's conducting is an essay in the art of comic timing. The sense of presence in this Deutsche Grammophon recording (427331-2 [CD]) is exceptional, as is the playing of the Vienna Philharmonic.

Le Comte Ory

J. Sinclair, M. Sinclair, Oncina, Roux, Glyndebourne Festival Chorus and Orchestra, Gui. EMI Classics CDMB 64180 [CD].

Few Rossini operas are more entertaining than this dizzy vaudeville that follows the fortunes of the lecherous Count Ory and his unsuccessful attempts to have his way with the Countess Adèle, whose brother has lately set off for the Crusades. During the course of Count Ory's crusade, he dons the disguise of a hermit and, when this meets with disaster, dresses up as a Mother Superior, with his men pretending to be nuns. With help from some of the better moments from his *Il Viaggio a Reims,* Rossini concocted a brilliant French farce admired by critical Frenchmen from Hector Berlioz to Darius Milhaud.

Recorded in conjunction with performances at the 1956 Glyndebourne Festival, Vittorio Gui's stunning recording confirms all the legends in its CD reincarnation. This is one of the most infectiously funny opera recordings ever made, bubbling over with wit, naughtiness, and irresistible slapstick, and all of it very beautifully sung. Not even the mid-'50s monophonic sound presents much of a problem, for the performance so crackles with life that after a few minutes you hardly notice.

Overtures

London Symphony, Abbado. Deutsche Grammophon 431653-2 [CD].

London Classical Players, Norrington. Angel CDC-54091 [CD], 4DS-54091 [T].

Orpheus Chamber Orchestra. Deutsche Grammophon 415363-2 [CD].

Philharmonia Orchestra, Giulini. EMI Classics CDM 69042 [CD].

Chicago Symphony, Reiner. RCA 60387-2-RG [CD], 60387-4-RG [T].

For anyone seriously interested in many of the most famous and scintillating orchestral miniatures ever written, Sir Neville Marriner's four-CD set from Philips of all the surviving Rossini overtures was an excellent investment. The performances of the more familiar pieces were among the best available, and even the least interesting of the unfamiliar works were more than worth a hearing. Besides, you never know when you might receive a request for the overture to *Demetrio e Polibio,* and wouldn't it be nice to be prepared? In any event, each of the performances is bursting with vitality—the gallop from *William Tell* rushes by like the wind—and an unmistakably Rossinian sense of humor. While temporarily withdrawn, the recording is simply too important to vanish entirely and will undoubtedly turn up on a couple of Philips's Duo sets.

Humor and vitality also characterize the performances by the Orpheus Chamber Orchestra. In what may still be their finest recording to date—and given their list of outstanding releases, that's saying a very great deal—they demonstrate fairly conclusively that a conductor's baton is the cheapest instrument there is.

Among recordings made by Italian conductors, those by Abbado and Giulini are the most appealing. Aside from being superbly idiomatic—in both, you can just about smell the garlic frying—each brings out the lovely singing quality of the music and more than a little of its whiplash excitement. For instance, the Giulini *William Tell* goes out in such a spectacular cloud of dust that a colleague of mine—after a stunned pause of several seconds—announced on the air: "And just think, he was originally going to call it *Pavane for a Dead Princess.*"

Roger Norrington and his plucky London Classical Players offer a series of hair-trigger performances on period instruments that manage to sound neither pedantic nor stodgy. The conductor's tempos have an exhilarating bite and lift, while the orchestral fabric has a wonderfully piquant edge.

Finally, as performances or recordings, no versions of these popular works have ever superseded the scintillating recordings that Reiner and the Chicago Symphony made in 1958. The brass play with an awesome grandeur and solidity, the strings are rich yet nimble, and the woodwinds have all the personality of characters straight out of *commedia dell'arte.* This is a gifted conductor and the great American orchestra of its time, captured at the height of their powers in phenomenally remastered recorded sound.

La scala di seta

> Ringholz, Provvisionata, Massa, Vargas, Corbelli, Carolis, English
> Chamber Orchestra, M. Viotti. Claves 50-9218/20 [CD].

Here is easily the most successful installment in the rather spotty Claves series of the one-act Rossini operas, this one about a lady who has to keep her marriage secret from a *buffo* guardian and thus lowers the silken ladder of the title to allow her husband access to the house. Along with the sparkling playing of the English Chamber Orchestra under the imaginative Marcello Viotti, Teresa Ringholz makes a delectable heroine, especially in her sly exchanges with Ramon Vargas, firm and gently heroic as the husband. Alessandro Corbelli is an excellent *basso buffo*, long on characterization and vocal control, while mezzo-soprano Francesca Provvisionata as the meddling cousin nearly steals the show.

Equally engaging is the Deutsche Grammophon recording of *Il Signor Bruschino* (435865-2 [CD]), featuring a glittering cast headed by Samuel Ramey in a rare (and brilliant) *buffo* turn as the old tutor Guadenzio. The aptly named Kathleen Battle sings with an abundance of rhythmic vitality and girlish charm, Frank Lopardo is a boyishly ardent lover, and in an extravagant bit of casting, Jennifer Larmore is predictably enticing as the maid.

The English Chamber Orchestra plays as splendidly for Ion Marin as it does for Viotti and the recorded sound could hardly be improved.

Semiramide

> Sutherland, Horne, Serge, Rouleau, Malas, Ambrosian Singers,
> London Symphony, Bonynge. London 425481-2 [CD].

In spite of Gustav Kobbé's grim prognosis in his celebrated *Complete Opera Book* that *"Semiramide* seems to have had its day," this rather preposterous tale of love, sacrifice, murder, betrayal, and redemption—obviously another of those "something for everyone" evenings—may actually be the most musically rewarding of all Rossini's more obviously serious operas. It certainly contains some of his most rewarding and technically challenging duets, the best of which require a soprano and mezzo of extraordinary technical accomplishment.

Recorded in 1966 when both singers were reaching the peak of their forms, the London *Semiramide* is probably the most brilliant of the many Sutherland-Horne collaborations. Dame Joan is both phenomenally agile and endearingly human as the murderous Queen of Babylon—who only murdered her *husband,* after all—while Marilyn Horne in the trouser role of Prince Arsace gives one of her most commanding performances in or out of the recording studio. Richard Bonynge manages to keep things moving nicely while remaining sensitive to the score's many felicitous details, while London's recorded sound remains ideally warm, focused, and brilliantly detailed.

Gustav, *says you*.

Sonatas (6) for Strings

Orchestra of the Age of Enlightenment (members). Hyperion CDA 66595 [CD].

The question of how one of the laziest composers in history managed to accomplish so much in such little time—after the premiere of *William Tell*, he retired to a life of unprecedented indolence at the age of thirty-seven—is answered in part by these six miraculous little works: he got a *very* early start. Composed when Rossini was only twelve, the String Sonatas, like the equally precocious Wind Quartets, reveal a talent that was almost as highly evolved as Mozart's was at a comparable age.

If you have a youthful musical underachiever in your household, then these sparkling performances on period instruments by members of the Orchestra of the Age of Enlightenment (whose performances are as refreshingly unassuming as their name is embarrassingly pretentious) might just do the trick: the *wunderkind* will either be spurred on to greater efforts by the young Rossini's example or will be discouraged completely. Either way, you can't lose.

Stabat mater

Field, Jones, Davies, Earle, London Symphony Chorus, City of London Sinfonia, Hickox. Chandos CHAN 8780 [CD].

From the time he finished *William Tell* in 1829 until his death in 1868—like another celebrated musical triskaidekaphobe, Arnold Schoenberg, the deeply superstitious Italian also died on the thirteenth of a month—Rossini wrote little other than a pair of enchanting sacred works and those delectable miniatures he published in the thirteen (!) volumes of *Péchés de vieillesse* (Sins of Old Age).

With the *Petite messe solennelle* of 1863—best represented these days by an affectionate EMI Classics performance with Lucia Popp, Brigitte Fassbaender, Nicolai Gedda, Dimitri Kavrakos, the Labèque sisters, and the Choir of King's College, Cambridge, conducted by Stephen Cleobury (CDFB 68658 [CD]), Rossini's setting of the *Stabat mater* is one of the most thoroughly disarming sacred works ever written. Like the sacred music of Haydn and Poulenc, the *Petite messe* doesn't have a sanctimonious bone in its lusty, yea-saying body: everything is high spirits and joyful noise, with one irrepressible Rossini tune after another.

Even more than the late István Kertész in his out-of-print London recording, Richard Hickox understands the sublime goofiness of the piece, allowing it to go its merry way with little or no editorial comment, while still demanding the most alert and enthusiastic singing and playing. The result will warm the hearts of believers and make most heathens think twice.

*T*ancredi

> Jo, Lendi, Di Micco, Podles, Olsen, Spagnoli, Demeyere, Baert, Coryn,
> Collegium Instrumentale Brugense, Capella Brugensis, Zedda.
> Naxos 8.660037 [CD].

Even by Naxos standards, this is a fairly incredible bargain. Not only does it offer a substantially complete performance of one of the most exciting of the lesser-known Rossini operas on a pair of super-budget CDs but also does it with a performance that easily outshines its only rival on three *full-priced* CDs from RCA. If the Bulgarian mezzo Vesselina Kasarova is pretty thrilling in the title role, then her Naxos counterpart Ewa Podles is no less so; in every other category, the Naxos is clearly superior, with Sumi Jo blindingly brilliant as the heroine and Stanford Olsen reviving memories of that most suave of Rossini tenors, Tito Schipa. Alberto Zedda conducts with real deftness and understanding, while the recorded sound has an extremely lifelike depth and presence. The only minor drawback—or defect of a virtue, take your pick—is an Italian libretto with no English translation. Many will find that the helpful synopsis that *is* included tells them more than they need to know about the opera's ridiculous action.

*W*illiam Tell

> Caballé, Mesplé, Burles, Gedda, Bacquier, Howell, Ambrosian Opera
> Chorus, Royal Philharmonic, Gardelli. EMI Classics CDMD 69951
> [CD].

Shortly after its triumphant first production at the Paris Opera in 1829, *William Tell* began falling victim to the editor's blue pencil. Within the year, performances were being cut ever more drastically. There is a famous story that has one of the composer's ardent admirers telling him, "I heard Act II of *William Tell* at the opera last night." "What?" Rossini is alleged to have replied. "The whole of it?" The whole of this uneven work that Rossini consciously intended to be his masterpiece can last upward of five hours in the theater. It is far more easily—and profitably—digested in the comfort of one's living room, especially in as compelling a production as this one.

Not long after London withdraws its recording with Pavarotti, Freni, and Milnes (presumably for a medium-price reissue), along comes EMI—dare I say, Lone Ranger-like?—to the rescue. On balance, this is actually the far more satisfying performance, with Montserrat Caballé effortlessly outpointing her rival in the impossibly difficult coloratura role of Mathilde and Nicolai Gedda ardent and tasteful as Arnold, the lady's suitor. Yet the real stars of the show are Gabriel Bacquier, who offers a formidable musical and dramatic portrait of the famous freedom fighter, and Lamberto Gardelli, who with his customary skill gives the great set pieces their full due—with the Ambrosian Opera Chorus honed to a fine cutting edge, the choral passages are particularly thrilling—while making the weaker moments seem much stronger than they really are. In spite of the fact that he isn't a masked man, you'll still want to thank him.

Rota, Nino (1911–1979)

La strada (ballet suite); *Il gattopardo* (dances); Concerto for Strings

La Scala Philharmonic, Muti. Sony Classical SK 66279 [CD].

Like Alfred Newman and Franz Waxman before him, Nino Rota died in harness before his time. In addition to the Oscar-winning score for *The Godfather* and the haunting main title for Zeffirelli's *Romeo and Juliet,* he wrote the music for virtually all of Fellini's films through *Casanova.* His music for *La strada* is not only archetypal Rota but is also one of the great film scores: poignant, sweetly ironic, and completely indissoluble from the images on the screen—listen for ten seconds, and the movie begins playing itself in your head.

Commissioned by La Scala in 1966, the ballet Rota fashioned from the *La strada* music is a distinguished work in its own right, with the film's fondly remembered themes recast by a master of movement and dramatic point. Muti and the La Scala Philharmonic give the suite the most sophisticated performance it is ever likely to receive and the recorded sound is ideal. Combined with the equally vivid dances from Visconti's *The Leopard* and an attractive concert work, the Concerto for Strings, this makes for an irresistible introduction to Rota on his own—where he certainly has the talent to be.

Rott, Hans   (1858–1884)

Symphony in E

Norrköping Symphony, Segerstam. BIS CD 563 [CD].

If listening to Hans Rott's incredible Symphony from 1880 puts one in mind of the early Mahler symphonies, then it's not because Rott was inspired by Mahler but the other way around. A pupil of Bruckner and a close friend of Mahler, the brilliant but unstable Rott was one of the most promising young composers of his generation. Shortly after completing his only Symphony, he went to Brahms to seek his advice but was turned away. Later that month, while on a train bound for Mühlhausen, Rott began behaving erratically, waving a pistol and insisting that Brahms had placed dynamite in the train. Committed to an asylum, he destroyed many of his works by using them as toilet paper, insisting, "That's all the works of men are worth."

As in the pioneering recording by Gerhard Samuel and the Cincinnati Philharmonic, Leif Segerstam and his Swedish orchestra make a very persuasive case for this fascinating work. Although Wagner and Brahms take an important part in the proceedings—the latter is actually quoted in the finale—it is the foreshadowing of Mahler that makes the Symphony so intriguing. One clearly hears the genesis of several ideas that would turn up in Mahler's roughly contemporaneous First Symphony, as well as a Mahlerian grandeur in its extraordinary scale. The individuality and sheer abundance of the themes and the exceptional skill with which they are manipulated make Rott one of the most intriguing "what-ifs" of late-Romantic music. Even if you buy the Symphony as a guess-who-wrote-this party record, you'll find much to admire after the novelty wears off.

Rouse, Christopher   (1949–)

Symphony No. 1

Baltimore Symphony, Zinman. Meet the Composer 79230-2 [CD],
79230-4 [T].

Like most composers with significant autodidactic experience, Christopher Rouse possesses a resolutely independent musical personality that, in spite of contact with such potent forces as George Crumb, Karel Husa, and Robert

Palmer, has remained fiercely determined to go its own way. His music has been performed by orchestras in Berlin, New York, Chicago, Stockholm, and Boston and has been commissioned by soloists and ensembles as diverse as Yo Yo Ma, the late Jan deGaetani, and the Society for New Music.

Completed on August 26, 1986, Rouse's Symphony No. 1 was written on commission from the Baltimore Symphony as part of the Meet the Composer Orchestra Residencies Program. Cast in a single movement and taking the form of an "*adagio* of considerable proportions whose overall language is largely tonal in its orientation" (quoting the composer), the Symphony was written as a conscious act of homage to the symphonic *adagios* of Shostakovich, Sibelius, Hartmann, Pettersson, Schuman, and Bruckner, whose Seventh Symphony is quoted in both its original form and by a quartet of Wagner tubas. With colors "of the blackest night" and a mood that is "somber, even tragic," the Symphony is one of the most powerfully communicative of the last quarter century, daring in its design and execution, overwhelming in its emotional impact. David Zinman and the Baltimore Symphony perform the work with the dedication of zealots.

Three more important Rouse works are featured on an RCA recording (09026-68410-2 [CD]) that includes devoted performances by the excellent Colorado Symphony conducted by Marin Alsop. The Trombone Concerto, written in memory of Leonard Bernstein and awarded the 1993 Pulitzer Prize, is a richly dramatic work, featuring a provocative series of references to Mahler, Copland, Shostakovich, and Bernstein's *Kaddish* Symphony. *Gorgon* is a shattering companion piece to the First Symphony, with an expressive language (and dynamic range) that owes much to the composer's enthusiasm for rock music. The more reserved *Iscariot* is one of Rouse's most intensely felt pieces, played here with absolute conviction.

Roussel, Albert   (1869–1937)

Bacchus et Ariane; Le Festin de l'araignée (suite)

BBC Philharmonic, Tortelier. Chandos CHAN 9494 [CD].

Among the major composers—and a major twentieth-century composer is what this punctilious Frenchman is now, belatedly, thought to be—Albert Roussel is virtually unique. After preparing himself for a naval career, he did not begin to study music seriously until he was in his midtwenties, at roughly the same age a Polish sea-faring man who would become the novelist Joseph Conrad set himself the task of learning English. In spite of what should have been an impossibly late start for a life in music, Roussel slowly evolved into one of the most arresting composers of his generation, a figure only slightly less potent and individual than his near contemporaries Debussy and Ravel.

As an introduction to Roussel's stubbornly original idiom, this recording of his two most popular ballets is ideal. While the sly, poetic *Festin de l'araignée* (The Spider's Feast) is the better known work, it is *Bacchus et Ariane* that can be mentioned in the same breath with Ravel's *Daphnis et Chloé* and Debussy's *Jeux* as one of the most important of modern French ballets.

Even if Georges Prêtre's admirable EMI Classics recording had not been withdrawn, Tortelier's newer Chandos version would easily surpass it. Whatever Prêtre did especially well—releasing the subtle wit of *Le Festin* or the pent-up sexual energy of *Bacchus*—Tortelier does better, with the further advantage of state-of-the-art orchestral execution and recorded sound. This single recording establishes him as the finest Roussel conductor of his generation, who should now turn his attention to the symphonies, the operas, and anything else he might feel like recording.

Chamber Music

Divertissement for Piano and Wind Quintet; Op. 6; Piano Trio, Op. 2; Violin Sonata No. 1, Op. 11

Trio for Flute, Viola, and Cello, Op. 40; String Quartet, Op. 45; *Andante and Scherzo* for Flute and Piano, Op. 51; String Trio, Op. 58; *Music from Elpénor*

> Verhey, flute; Roerade, oboe; Van der Brink, clarinet; De Lange, bassoon; Jeurissen, horn; Kantorow, violin; Stengenga, cello; Röling, piano; Schoenberg Quartet. Olympia OLY 458 [CD]; OLY 460 [CD].

Roussel's chamber music is far less well known than his orchestral music, though most of it is every bit as distinctive and all of it as beautifully made. The important early works, the Piano Trio, Violin Sonata, and *Divertissement,* show the pervasive influence of Roussel's rigorous teacher, Vincent d'Indy, while the mature ones—the Flute Trio, String Quartet, and String Trio, his last completed score—are clearly those of a fully formed master whose least inspiration (as Stravinsky said of Prokofiev) "bears the instant imprint of personality."

This fine pair of Olympia recordings—a third, containing the *Serenade* for Flute, Violin, Viola, Cello, and Harp, has yet to be issued domestically—offers first-rate performances by a group of obviously dedicated Dutch musicians who play with enthusiasm and understanding. Fortunately, that superb recording of the *Serenade* by harpist Osian Ellis and the Melos Ensemble has just been reissued on a medium-priced London album, (452891-2 [CD]) with their breathtaking readings of Debussy's Sonata for Flute, Viola, and Harp and the *Introduction and Allegro* by Ravel.

Symphonies (4)

French Radio Philharmonic, Janowski. RCA 09026-62511-2 [CD].

If saying that the composer's final two works in the form are among the greatest symphonies ever written by a French composer would seem to be damning them with the faintest of faint praise, then put it another way: Roussel's Third and Fourth Symphonies are among the finest such works produced by any composer, French or otherwise, in this century. If in his early works, especially the haunting *Poem of the Forest,* Roussel's distinctive brand of musical impressionism is heard to lovely, often exquisite effect, then the later scores, particularly the lean and fiercely driven G Minor Symphony of 1930, are among the key works of modern neo-Classicism, works whose finest passages place them on a nearly equal footing with Stravinsky's Symphony in Three Movements and Symphony in C.

With Charles Dutoit's superb Erato recordings inexplicably withdrawn— for sheer irresponsibility in wielding the deletions ax, Erato is rapidly approaching the gory standards of EMI Classics—and the early stereo versions of the Third and Fourth that Dutoit's mentor Ernest Ansermet recorded in 1956 also unavailable, the fine new cycle by the French Radio Philharmonic conducted by Marek Janowski is a welcome edition to the catalogue. If Leonard Bernstein's Sony Classical recording (MHK 62352 [CD]) is the most vividly characterized of available recordings of the Third, then Janowski's isn't far behind, with biting rhythms, brisk tempos, and a real sense of the work's importance and individuality. While the Fourth is also excellent, the versions of the two early symphonies are even better, especially of the First—*La Poème de la forêt*—which not only firmly places this enchanting work in the *fin-de-siècle* tradition, but also underscores the telling hints of the major composer who was about to emerge. The playing of the Orchestre Philharmonique is impeccable throughout, as is the recorded sound.

Paul Paray's incomparable version of the piquant and energetic *Suite in F* has finally been reissued on a Mercury Living Presence CD (434303-2), coupled with a stunning Chabrier program (see page 159).

Rózsa, Miklós (1907–1995)

Film Music

National Philharmonic, Gerhardt. RCA 0911-2-RG [CD], 0911-4-RG [CD].

Despite being one of the most versatile and honored practitioners of a difficult and demanding craft, the Hungarian-born Miklós Rózsa was not one of those film composers who "vanished" into his scores; whatever the requirements of a specific picture—he worked in every genre from film noir to biblical epic to historical romance to comedy *(Dead Men Don't Wear Plaid)*, winning a total of three Academy Awards (for *Spellbound, A Double Life*—also the title of his 1982 autobiography—and *Ben-Hur*), his powerful musical personality always made itself felt, largely through the distinctive modal harmonies that he made unmistakably his own.

Charles Gerhardt's Rózsa album was one of the most successful installments in RCA's "Classic Film Scores" series and any collection of Rózsa's film music should properly begin here. James Sedares leads the New Zealand Symphony in extended excerpts from *Double Indemnity, The Lost Weekend,* and *The Killers* (Koch International Classics KIC 7375 [CD]), Bruce Broughton conducts the Sinfonia of London in a stunning version of the score from *Ivanhoe* (Intrada ITD 7055 [CD]), while the composer himself can be heard on a soundtrack recording of *Ben-Hur* on a two-disc set from Rhino (R2 72197 [CD]).

Symphony in Three Movements; *The Vintner's Daughter*

New Zealand Symphony, Sedares. Koch 7244-2 [CD].

Although best known for his work in film, Rózsa had also been a diligent composer of more obviously serious music throughout his long career. His youthful *Theme, Variations, and Finale* from 1933 was one of the works on the famous New York Philharmonic broadcast concert in 1943 that catapulted Leonard Bernstein to national celebrity, and a work like the Sonata for Solo Violin from 1985 suggests that the composer had lost none of his zest for life or music after entering his seventies.

Written in 1930 when the composer was only twenty-two, Rózsa's Symphony is an entertaining and energetic work, with a lovely slow movement and an exhilarating, hell-bent-for-leather *perpetuum mobile* finale. If the language occasionally suggests his older compatriots Bartók and Kodály, then it is still one of the most distinctive and substantial European symphonies from the era between the World Wars: a big, tuneful, user-friendly score that anyone with an interest in twentieth-century music should snap up immediately.

As in their earlier Koch recording of Rózsa's *Hungarian Sketches, Notturno ungherese, Overture to a Symphony Concert,* and the *Theme, Variations, and Finale* (KIC 7191 [CD]), James Sedares and the New Zealand Symphony are wonderfully eloquent exponents of Rózsa's music, as an enthusiastic testimonial from the composer printed on the album cover clearly attests. The playing is both refined and vital, a perfect complement to this youthful but precocious piece.

Although the gorgeous Violin Concerto that Rózsa composed for Jascha Heifetz was recently reissued (along with the violinist's equally definitive recordings of concertos by those other film composers Erich Wolfgang Korngold and Franz Waxman) and has already been withdrawn, the Viola Concerto—which may actually be the finer piece—is handsomely served by the brilliantly gifted American violinist/violist/composer Maria Newman on Varèse Sarabande VSD 5329 [CD].

Rubbra, Edmund (1901–1986)

Symphony No. 3; Symphony No. 4; *Resurgam* (concert overture)

Philharmonia Orchestra, Del Mar. Lyrita SRCD 202 [CD].

That Edmund Rubbra has remained one of the least well known of modern English symphonists isn't difficult to explain. There is a seriousness of purpose and a ferocious integrity in Rubbra's music that made it all but immune to fashionable modern trends. His orchestral palette tends to be serviceable to the point of austerity, with scarcely a bar or an instrument going to waste—in his Sixth Symphony, for instance, he requires a xylophone for only a single bar of the Scherzo, after which it is not heard from again—while his essentially conservative musical language has no other purpose than to serve his frequently profound, frequently mystical, richly polyphonic musical thought.

The late Norman del Mar's superlative recordings of the Third and Fourth Symphonies provide an excellent introduction to Rubbra's uniquely intense and noble world. Written immediately before and during the Second World War, neither work betrays much of the dark turbulence of the era; each is persuasively argued and beautifully made, reflecting a personality that, in spite of some superficial resemblances to Sibelius and his teachers Vaughan Williams and Gustav Holst, is at once wholly admirable and wholly its own.

The initial releases in Richard Hickox's Rubbra series with the BBC Welsh National Orchestra for Chandos already suggest a project that might prove even more important than his admirable Alwyn series. The first installment (CHAN 9401 [CD]) offers much-needed new recordings of the powerfully concentrated Tenth and Eleventh symphonies, plus a version of the serenely beautiful Fourth that matches del Mar's in matters of interpretive insight and actually exceeds it in terms of orchestral execution and recorded sound. Subsequent volumes have proven equally rewarding, especially the one devoted to the first really adequate commercial recording of the mystical, deeply felt Ninth *(Sinfonia sacra)* inspired by a painting of Donato Bramante and tracing, roughly, the Passion of Christ (CHAN 9441 [CD]. Coupled with the nobly moving *The Morning Watch* on a text by Henry Vaughan, this marks not only a turning point in the Rubbra revival but also a red-letter day for modern English music.

Rutter, John (1945–)

*G*loria; Anthems

> Cambridge Singers, Philip Jones Brass Ensemble, City of London Sinfonia, Rutter. Collegium COLCD 100 [CD], COLC 100 [T].

*R*equiem

> Ashton, Dean, Cambridge Singers, London Sinfonia, Rutter. Collegium COLCD 103 [CD]; COLC 103 [T].

Although undeniably modest, the gifts of the English composer John Rutter are also undeniably genuine: he knows how to fashion a memorable tune, how to write for the human voice, how to engage the listener's emotions, and how not to overstay his welcome. And if his music never really scales the heights or plumbs the depths, then it doesn't pretend to be anything other than the quietly moving, gently comforting, refreshingly unassuming experience that it is.

It's unimaginable that warmer or more deeply committed recordings than those made under the composer's expert direction will ever be made again. Once locked in the firm but loving coils of the exuberant *Gloria* or the tenderly consoling *Requiem*, the listener is a goner, thanks to the fact that the performances, like the music itself, know more than a thing or two about the mysteries of human communication.

Sæverud, Harald   (1897–1992)

Peer Gynt Suites; Symphony No. 6 *(Sinfonia dolorosa); Galdreslåtten; Kjampeviseslåtten*

> Stavanger Symphony, Dmitriev. BIS CD 762 [CD].

Harald Sæverud was ten years old when Edvard Grieg died in 1907 and survived him by nearly eighty-five years. Apart from an inspired use of their country's wealth of folk music, the two Norwegian composers could not be more dissimilar. Although Sæverud began in the late-Romantic tradition, by the early 1930s he was experimenting with various non-tonal and expressionist procedures; the Nazi invasion of Norway in 1940 led to his embrace of an intense, highly personalized form of Norwegian nationalism that led to works like the *Sinfonia doloroso,* an impassioned memorial to a friend who died in the Resistance. In addition to this sixth of Sæverud's nine symphonies, this Bis album also offers the powerfully indignant *Kjampeviseslåtten (Ballad of Revolt),* inspired by a Nazi barracks built near the composer's home in Bergen, as well as the music for a profoundly anti-romantic postwar production of Ibsen's *Peer Gynt.* Sæverud's *Peer Gynt* music is craggy, outlandish, and hilariously grotesque, offering a fascinating contrast to the familiar Grieg setting. Alexander Dimtriev and the Stavanger Symphony present the music with evident pride, as do the Bis engineers.

Saint-Saëns, Camille   (1835–1921)

Carnival of the Animals

> New York Philharmonic, Bernstein. CBS MYK-37765 [CD], MT-37765 [T].

Ironically enough, it was for a work he refused to have performed in public during his lifetime that the vastly prolific and once enormously popular Camille Saint-Saëns remains best known today. While much of his tuneful, ingratiating, always impeccably crafted music has apparently begun to lose its grip on the modern imagination, the ageless *Carnival of the Animals* has never gone begging for first-class recorded performances.

I have some very vivid memories of a Leonard Bernstein Young Person's Concert in which it was first explained to me that the cuckoo was represented by the clarinet, the swan by the cello, and so forth. I bought the Bernstein recording soon afterward (one of the first records in my collection that did *not* have an erotic cover) and have cherished the performance ever since. Bernstein brings an obvious and unmistakable enthusiasm to both his narration and the music. The soloists and the orchestra play with passion and devotion, and the early 1960s recorded sound is still very serviceable. In its most recent incarnation, the performance comes with an equally memorable—and when the horns get wound up, terrifically scary—interpretation of Prokofiev's *Peter and the Wolf*.

Concertos (5) for Piano and Orchestra

Rogé, piano; London Philharmonic, Philharmonia Orchestra, Royal Philharmonic, Dutoit. London 443865-2 [CD].

To use an unusually disagreeable contemporary phrase, the five Saint-Saëns piano concertos are very "user-friendly" works, meaning, among other things, that they are very easy "to access." (This is the process—the gradual pollution of the language through daily wear and tear—that the French poet Paul Valéry was thinking about when he was asked what poets really *did*. "That's simple," he said. "Each night you have to take a ten-franc whore and try to turn her into a virgin.")

Pleasant, shallow, unstintingly professional, and as easy on the mind as they are on the ear—for a man like Saint-Saëns, requiring his listeners to *think* simply wouldn't have been civilized—they rank with the Tchaikovsky suites and the Vivaldi concertos as some of the greatest elevator music ever written.

Pascal Rogé releases all of their genuine charm without trying to turn them into something they're not. For instance, in the popular Second Concerto—which pianists are often tempted to inflate into something larger than it can really become—he maintains a decidedly laissez-faire interpretive touch that compromises neither its essentially lighthearted character nor its moments of virtuoso display. Charles Dutoit is an equally level-headed advocate of this music, providing accompaniments that give the composer and the listener precisely what they want. Among recordings of Saint-Saëns's other instrumental concertos, Yo Yo Ma is at his most elegant in his version of the A Minor Cello Concerto (CBS MK 35848 [CD]), while Itzhak Perlman's Deutsche Grammophon recording (429977-2 [CD]) of the Third Violin Concerto is typically refined and exciting, paired with an unusually colorful version of Lalo's *Symphonie espagnole*.

Danse macabre; Le Rouet d'Omphale; Phaéton; Carnival of the Animals

Philharmonia Orchestra, Dutoit. London 414460-2 [CD], 414460-4 [T].

What would have made this an even more welcome addition to the catalogue would have been a recording of the last of Saint-Saëns's four tone poems, *La Jeunesse d'Hercule,* instead of the surprisingly lackluster run-through of *Carnival of the Animals* that accompanies the other three. But no matter, for these are the most articulate and individual versions of *Danse macabre* and *Omphale's Spinning Wheel* in a generation, and even the slightly stuffy *Phaéton,* in Dutoit's tactful face-lift, seems fresher than it ever has before.

Havanaise for Violin and Orchestra; Introduction and Rondo Capriccioso for Violin and Orchestra

Perlman, violin; New York Philharmonic, Mehta. Deutsche Grammophon 423063-2 [CD].

With Sarasate's *Carmen Fantasy* and Ravel's *Tzigane,* Saint-Saëns's pair of virtuoso spellbinders are among the most popular shorter works in the violin's literature. All four, together with Chausson's ravishing *Poème,* are given typically hair-raising accounts in Itzhak Perlman's most recent recordings, performances that mix phenomenal virtuosity with poetic insight, making them the most exciting *and* musical versions now available. As always, Mehta is an adroit and savvy accompanist and the recorded sound is very good.

Samson et Dalila

Domingo, Obraztsova, Bruson, Lloyd, Thau, Chorus and Orchestre de Paris, Barenboim. Deutsche Grammophon 413297-2 [CD].

After *Carmen* and *Faust, Samson et Dalila* has been the most enduringly popular of all French operas, this in spite of the fact that it took a surprisingly long time to catch on. When a single act was given in Paris in 1875, two years prior to the Weimar premiere, critics chided it for its lack of memorable melody and mundane orchestration. Of course, in addition to its lavish spectacle, exotic orientalisms, and moving human drama, it is *Samson's* wealth of unforgettable, luxuriantly scored melody that has kept it alive all these years.

Of the available recorded *Samsons,* the Barenboim version is by far the best compromise. Domingo makes an imposing, gloriously sung hero, while Barenboim's conducting misses none of the score's grandeur (the big choral scenes are especially thrilling) and very few of its more subtle details. The problem is Elena Obraztsova, who is curiously sexless as the Philistine sexpot. Rita Gorr, on the competing Angel set, makes a sensationally vivid Dalila, but that performance is seriously marred by Georges Prêtre's unimaginative conducting. The long-rumored Dutoit version may change the picture completely, but until then, this generally exciting (and moderately priced) effort will do.

Symphony No. 3 in C Minor, Op. 78, "Organ"

Hurford, organ; Montreal Symphony, Dutoit. London 430720-2 [CD].

Zamkochian, organ; Boston Symphony, Munch. RCA 09026-61500-2 [CD].

The last symphony, and only one of the *five* that Saint-Saëns actually composed that is ever performed these days, owes much of its current popularity to the recording industry. In the mid-1950s, when the record companies were casting about for "sonic spectaculars" to show off the revolutionary wonders of stereo, the "Organ" Symphony began to enjoy a new lease on life. Along with Paul Paray's wonderful Mercury Living Presence recording with the Detroit Symphony, Charles Munch's classic Boston Symphony recording dominated the catalogues for decades. The recording had fire, a healthy measure of Munchian madness, stupendous playing from the orchestra, and recorded sound to raise the roof—which it still does in its compact disc reissue. In fact, the Munch recording would remain the obvious first choice were it not for the even more extraordinary interpretation led by Charles Dutoit.

What makes the Dutoit such a great performance is as easy to hear as it is difficult to describe. In its simplest terms, this is the one recording of the "Organ" Symphony that actually makes the piece sound like what it most assuredly is *not*: a great work. The conductor captures most of the Symphony's color and dramatic gestures, but for once the gestures seem internal and natural, as opposed to the empty, bombastic postures that they probably are. In short, along with its freshness, intelligence, and subtlety, this is the only version of the "Organ" Symphony in my experience in which we seem to be hearing music of genuine grandeur, instead of something that is merely grandiose.

Although none of his earlier works in the form begin to approach the achievement that is the "Organ" Symphony, they all make for appealing listening in the recordings that Jean Martinon and the French National Radio Orchestra recorded in the mid-1970s, available now on a pair of EMI Classics CDs (CDMB 62643 [CD]). While the Second Symphony is the strongest of these unknown scores, with an effervescent Scherzo and a wild, *tarantella* finale, even the juvenile A Major Symphony, written when Saint-Saëns was only fifteen, is not that far removed in quality from Bizet's Symphony in C. The performances are both affectionate and highly accomplished while the recorded sound scarcely betrays its age.

Sallinen, Aulis (1935–)

Symphony No. 2 for Percussion and Orchestra; Symphony No. 6, "From a New Zealand Diary"; *Sunrise Serenade*

Malmö Symphony, Kamu. BIS CD 511 [CD].

If this Finnish composer has devoted much of his time in recent years to opera—*The King Goes Forth to France, Kullervo,* and most recently *Palatsi*—then like Jean Sibelius before him, Aulis Sallinen is best approached through his symphonies. This Bis recording of the Second and Sixth symphonies provides an excellent introduction to his unique world. Subtitled "Symphonic Dialogue for solo percussion player and orchestra," the Second is a startling and dramatic work that manipulates huge masses of sound with skill and imagination. The Sixth, "From a New Zealand Diary," is altogether larger and more significant: a vast, impressionistic vision of the country and the sea that surrounds it that reveals Sallinen as a Nature poet of the first rank. The opening movement is reminiscent—but in no way derivative—of the opening movement of Debussy's *La Mer,* while the slow movement, *Kyeburn Diggings,* is a haunting evocation of an abandoned gold mine district. "In the music you can hear the glorious past coming through in dance music melodies," the composer has written, "everything being surrounded by a majestic though rather sad landscape." The *Finale,* which follows without pause, is prefaced by lines from a poem by Allen Curnow: "Simply by sailing in a new direction, you could change the world." This is heady, powerfully evocative stuff that draws intensely committed performances from Okku Kamu and the Malmö Symphony.

Those wishing to explore further are urged to try Kamu's equally compelling versions of the First and Third symphonies (Bis CD 41 [CD]) or James De Preist's even finer versions of the Fourth and Fifth (Bis CD 607 [CD]).

Sarasate, Pablo de   (1844–1908)

Carmen Fantasy for Violin and Orchestra, Op. 25; *Zigeunerweisen,*
Op. 20

>Josefowicz, violin; Academy of St. Martin-in-the-Fields, Marriner.
>   Philips 454440-2 [CD].

Born in Pamplona—where he never once ran with the bulls—Pablo de
Sarasate was one of the most widely admired violinists of the last quarter of the
nineteenth century, a man for whom Saint-Saëns, Lalo, and Max Bruch all wrote
concertos and who produced a fair amount of music himself. Unlike the barnstorming virtuosos of the Paganini school, the key to Sarasate's art was its subtlety, charm, and purity of tone. Before his death in 1908, he made a number of
commercial recordings; even through the grit and swish of those decaying antiques, a great violinist clearly emerges. As a composer, Sarasate wrote exclusively
for the violin, with his own strengths and limitations in mind. (While powerful
and supple, his hands—like Chopin's—were unusually small, which helps explain
the absence of the wide stretches and extravagant stopping that characterizes
much of the virtuoso violin music of the time.) His music also reflects the rhythms
and colors of his native Spain, even when refracted through the mind of a gifted
Frenchman.

Long a favorite of virtuosos, Sarasate's *Carmen Fantasy* is one of a number
of fantasias, caprices, and Liszt-like paraphrases he wrote on themes from popular operas. It is based on five numbers from Bizet's masterpiece (including the
Habanera and *Seguidilla*), all of which are given tasteful but technically demanding treatment, especially the fiery *Chanson Bohème* that brings the *Fantasy* to its
hair-raising conclusion. The teenage American violinist Leila Josefowicz—whose
great heroes are Fritz Kreisler and Bronislaw Huberman!—gives it and the
equally colorful *Zigeunerweisen* a thrilling performance on her "Bohemian
Rhapsody" album, a lovely collection that also features pointed and precocious
versions of the Chausson *Poème*, Ravel's *Tzigane*, Saint-Saëns's *Introduction and
Rondo Capriccioso*, Wieniawski's *Polonaise*, and the *Méditation* from Massenet's
Thaïs.

Among recordings of Sarasate's many works for violin and piano, none is
finer than the Arabesque collection (Z 6614 [CD]) by violinist Mark Kaplan and
pianist Bruno Canino. The playing responds brilliantly to both the technical and
musical demands of these challenging pieces, consistently refusing to treat them
as mere excuses for virtuoso display. The result is as illuminating as it is entertaining, raising our opinion of the composer and his music in the process.

Satie, Erik   (1866–1925)

Piano Music

Rogé, piano. London 410220-2 [CD], 410220-4 [T].

Whether the arch-eccentric Erik Satie was an important composer or merely a fascinating crank is really beside the point. Since the 1960s he has attracted an ever-widening public, and for the time being he should be taken as seriously as the relatively brisk sales of Satie recordings would seem to demand. Aside from the famous crackpot titles ("Desiccated Embryos," "Flabby Preludes for a Dog," and "Sketches to Make You Run Away" must be the choicest), the celebrated publicity stunts (for the premiere of his ballet *Parade,* Picasso painted a huge sign on the curtain that read, "Erik Satie is the greatest composer in the world. Anyone who disagrees with this statement is kindly asked to leave") and the unquestioned influence he had on younger French composers, Satie was essentially a gifted, if largely unlettered, dilettante whose most inspired creation was his own bizarre public image.

Pascal Rogé's recital of some of the composer's best-known works will go a long way to making at least partial believers out of the more devout Satie skeptics, like me. The beautifully austere and justly popular *Gymnopédies* are given serenely rapt performances, and the versions of the six *Gnossiennes, Embryons desséchés* (which isn't quite as good as its title), and miniatures like *Je te veux* and the "Bureaucratic Sonatine" are hardly less inspired. A second volume (421713-2 [CD]) in what presumably will be an ongoing Satie series is just as memorable, though in the case of this composer, more can quickly turn out to be much, *much* less.

For those who really *do* need more, EMI Classics has reissued Aldo Ciccolini's pioneering Satie recordings in five separate volumes (CDC 49702 [CD] "First and Last Works"; CDC 49702 [CD] "Mystical Works"; CDC 49713 [CD] "Etudes"; CDC 49760 [CD] "Whimsical Works"; CDC 49760 [CD] "Music for the Dance"; and in a single, tightly packed two-CD package (CDZB 67282) running to over two and a half hours that contains many of the most familiar items, including the *Gymnopédies, Gnossiennes, Sarabandes,* and the three *Mouvements en forme de poire.* If the performances are not quite as sophisticated as Rogé's, then they are nonetheless infectiously enjoyable, while the recorded sound remains immediate and well-lit.

Antal Dorati's Mercury Living Presence recording of *Parade* makes a welcome return to the catalogue (434335-2 [CD]) as part of a scintillating anthology of the twentieth-century French music that also includes the *Ouverture* by Georges Auric, Paul Fetler's *Contrasts* for Orchestra, the Françaix Piano Concertino, and Milhaud's *Le Boeuf sur le toit.* The ballet's "cubist" procedures, use of ragtime rhythms, and bizarre scoring—including sirens, typewriters, guns, and airplane engines—was all pretty heady stuff in 1916 (Satie sent an insulting letter to one of the nastiest critics and was sentenced to eight days in jail for "public insults and defamation of character," a sentence that was later suspended) and in Dorati's rambunctious performance, it still is.

Scarlatti, Domenico (1685–1757)

Keyboard Sonatas

Kipnis, harpsichord. Chesky CD 75 [CD].

Pinnock, harpsichord. Deutsche Grammophon ARC-419632-2 [CD].

Pinnock, harpsichord. CRD CD-3368 [CD].

Pogorelich, piano. Deutsche Grammophon 435855-2 [CD].

Pletnev, piano. Virgin Classics 45123-2 [CD].

An exact contemporary of George Frideric Handel and Johann Sebastian Bach—1685 was one of the great vintage years in the history of music—Domenico Scarlatti was to the harpsichord what Chopin would later be to the piano: the first important composer to study the special characteristics of his chosen instrument and then write music specifically designed to show off its individual character and peculiar strengths. His output of keyboard music was as prodigious as it was inspired. In 1971, a facsimile edition of the complete music for keyboard was published in eighteen densely packed volumes. (The truly devoted and/or demented can now acquire all 555 works on a set of thirty-four Erato compact discs [2292-45309-2], wheelbarrow not included.)

It's a great pity that all the recordings featuring the father of modern Scarlatti scholarship, the late Ralph Kirkpatrick, are now out of print. His book *Scarlatti*, published in 1953, not only instantly became the standard work written about the composer but also helped clear up the centuries-old muddling of the order of composition of Scarlatti's numerous works. Kirkpatrick's performances were predictably enthusiastic and sympathetic, as are those of Trevor Pinnock, whose several recordings for Deutsche Grammophon and CRD are also models of modern baroque scholarship and musical sensitivity.

Reissued on the audiophile Chesky label, Igor Kipnis's scintillating interpretations from a quarter of a century ago continue to demonstrate why he has been one of the most joyously entertaining of all Early Music specialists. The performances have a distinctive wit and passion unlike those of any other player, while the sound remains phenomenally good.

Among the most predictably personal of all recent collections, Ivo Pogorelich's Deutsche Grammophon anthology makes no attempt to place the music in any sort of historical context but instead offers a uniquely individual—and exceedingly musical—view of the sonatas as formative building blocks of modern keyboard technique. The playing is both patrician and very moving.

As it is on the sumptuous two-CD set from Mikhail Pletnev. The range of color and emotion the pianist draws from the music is consistently amazing: listen to the breathtaking brinkmanship in his performance of the A Major Sonata, K. 24, or the astounding delicacy of its F-sharp Minor companion piece. If occasionally the pieces become distorted under the pressure of Pletnev's immense personality, then the peccadillos and perversions are invariably thrilling and always in the service of the *spirit* of the score.

Scharwenka, Xaver (1850–1924)

Piano Concerto No. 4 in F Minor, Op. 82

Hough, piano; City of Birmingham Symphony, Foster. Hyperion CDA 66790 [CD].

The Polish-born Xaver Scharwenka was one of the great pianists of his time, who regularly performed his music with Joachim, Richter, and Mahler. Though as a composer he was best known for the empty-headed but entertaining Piano Concerto No. 1 in B-flat Minor (doesn't *that* have a familiar ring!) and a little encore piece called *Polish Dance,* which he came to thoroughly despise, the F Minor Concerto—his fourth—is an entirely different matter. One of the most fiendishly difficult piano concertos ever written, it is also one of the most lithe and charming. With an ease that suggests one of the most formidable techniques in the world today (or one of the most adroit tape editors), Stephen Hough tosses it off with a blend of wit and arrogance that must be heard to be believed. The E Minor Concerto by the Liszt pupil Emil von Sauer is an equally eye-opening discovery, full of captivating melodies, infectious rhythms, and old-fashioned, barnstorming panache.

In short, Hyperion's Romantic Piano Concerto series scores another double hit.

Schiff, David (1945–)

Divertimento from *Gimpel the Fool; Scenes from Adolescence;* Suite from *Sacred Service*

Chamber Music Northwest. Delos DE 3058 [CD].

Of all the younger American composers whose music consciously tries to mix serious and popular styles, David Schiff may be the most consistently successful. In a note written for this delightful Delos recording, he explains: "To me, the interesting thing is to write a klezmer piece not using klezmer instruments, a rock/bebop piece not using rock instruments, or synagogue tradition combined with classical form."

While the most striking piece here is the Divertimento from Schiff's opera based on the Isaac Bashevis Singer story *Gimpel the Fool*—it has real claims to being the single most entertaining American chamber work of the last quarter century—the Bop- and Motown-inspired *Scenes from Adolescence* is also very ingratiating, as is the lovely *Sacred Service.* Chamber Music Northwest plays the music as though it had been written for them—the Divertimento actually *was*—and the recorded sound ranks with Delos's best.

Schmidt, Franz (1874–1939)

Symphony No. 4

Vienna Philharmonic, Mehta. London 440615-2 [CD].

The Viennese have a deep and abiding affection for the music of Franz Schmidt, an Austrian composer who was an exact contemporary of Arnold Schoenberg and a spiritual descendant of Bruckner and Mahler. While studying in Vienna with Hans Swarowsky, Zubin Mehta came to love Schmidt's music, and his interpretation of the composer's mighty Fourth Symphony might make you love it as well.

Although echoes of Schmidt's predecessors can be heard from time to time in this late-Romantic masterpiece, it presents a personality and point of view very much its own. More closely argued than Bruckner, less neurotic than Mahler, the Fourth is a work of tremendous sweep and power that commands the listener's attention from beginning to end. Mehta inspires the Vienna Philharmonic to play the piece as no other orchestra in the world possibly could, and the recorded sound is both sumptuous and beautifully detailed. For the medium-price reissue, the performance is coupled generously (and appropriately) with Mehta's refined and powerful version of Mahler's "Resurrection" Symphony, another of this conductor's very best recordings.

Those who find themselves responding to this strangely overlooked composer—as those who respond to Bruckner, Mahler, and early Schoenberg undoubtedly will—should waste no time investigating two other superb Schmidt symphony recordings: Neeme Järvi's Chandos versions of the Second (CHAN-8779 [CD]) and Third (CHAN-9000 [CD]), both of live concert performances with the great Chicago Symphony in full cry.

The full-fledged convert will want to explore the composer's masterpiece, the oratorio *Das Buch mit sieben Siegeln* (The Book with Seven Seals) in the legendary 1959 Salzburg Festival performance conducted by Dimitri Mitropoulos on Sony Classical SM2K 68442 [CD]. Although the sound on this and a recent Sony Classical reissue is fairly limited, the interpretation itself blazes with life. Aided by a dream team of soloists—Hilde Gueden, Ira Malaniuk, Anton Dermota, Fritz Wunderlich, and Walter Berry—as well as the Vienna Philharmonic at its most awesome, Mitropoulos reveals this towering masterwork as a glowing, late-Romantic sunset worthy to be mentioned in the same breath with Schoenberg's *Gurrelieder* or Pfitzner's *Von deutscher Seele*.

Schmitt, Florent (1870–1958)

Danse d'Abisag; *Habeyssée* for Violin and Orchestra; *Rêves*; Symphony No. 2

> H. Segerstam, violin; Rheinland-Pfalz State Philharmonic, Segerstam. Marco Polo 8.223689 [CD].

Best known for the voluptuous *Tragédie de Salomé*—available in the classic performance by Paul Paray and the Detroit Symphony as part of a Mercury Living Presence anthology (434336-2 [CD]) of music dealing with death—Florent Schmitt was a wizard of the post-Wagnerian orchestra. At its best, the music creates a unique and exceedingly beautiful sound world, with effects as subtle and striking as anything in Debussy or Ravel. Furthermore, while Schmitt was a pupil of Fauré and Massenet and an ardent supporter of Stravinsky, Schoenberg, Satie, and the younger French composers, he never belonged to any particular group or school. In short, he was a gifted original badly in need of a serious re-evaluation.

There is much to admire and enjoy in this lovely Marco Polo collection, from the erotic *Danse d'Abisag,* based on the biblical tale of the young Shunamite virgin who tries unsuccessfully to rouse the aging King David (she did a *much* better job on me) to the startlingly impassioned and inventive Symphony No. 2, composed when Schmitt was eighty-seven. This is heady, wholly individual music superbly played by Segerstam's well-drilled orchestra. Given the extent and quality of Schmitt's output, one hopes this is the beginning of a much-needed series.

Schoenberg, Arnold (1874–1951)

Cabaret Songs

Bryn-Julson, soprano; Oppens, piano. Music and Arts CD 650-1 [CD].

Arnold Schoenberg was forced to do many less than inspiring things to make ends meet at the turn of the century, including working for a time as an arranger at Berlin's Überbrettl Theater. The *Cabaret Songs*—or *Brettl-lieder*—were not actually written for its stage but were instead a series of stylized reactions to the popular music of the period. These are emphatically *not* precursors of the Berlin cabaret songs of the '20s, but instead sweetly playful trifles in the manner of the comic lieder of Hugo Wolf.

Though they lack the final measure of bittersweet magic heard on the classic RCA Victor recording by Marni Nixon and Schoenberg's friend Leonard Stein (and when can we expect the CD?), the performances by Phyllis Bryn-Julson and Ursula Oppens are stylish and intelligent and are clearly preferable to the rather overripe musings of Jessye Norman on Philips. Their versions of *The Book of the Hanging Gardens* and the important Opus 2 collection—which contains the masterpiece "Schenk mir deinen Goldenen Kamm"—are even finer, making this the most rewarding Schoenberg song anthology currently available.

Concerto for Cello and Orchestra (after Harpsichord Concerto of Georg Matthias Monn)

Ma, cello; Boston Symphony, Ozawa. CBS MK 39863 [CD].

As much as I am tempted to ride this personal hobby-horse into the ground, I will resist making any emotional (and they would be thoroughly heartfelt) appeals on behalf of the music of Arnold Schoenberg, the most significant composer of the twentieth century, and probably the *best* composer since Johannes Brahms. The Schoenberg debate will continue to rage long after all of us are gone and forgotten (why is it that in writing of Schoenberg one always, and almost automatically, slips into such cheerful images and turns of phrase?) Perhaps because this melancholy figure remains the most thoroughly misunderstood composer in history. In fact, the great boogeyman of the early twentieth-century avant-garde, the man whose experiments with atonality, serialism, and the twelve-tone technique "destroyed" music as we know it, was in fact the most conservative composer since Bach: an arch-Romantic who realized—correctly—that if Western music were to go on at all, it needed an entirely new language. (The five-hundred-year-old system of triadic tonality that had made such music possible had simply worn out.)

Even if you shudder at the mere mention of Arnold Schoenberg's name, then you probably won't be able to resist the Cello Concerto, a work so puppy-dog friendly that even the most musically shy five-year-old can embrace it with pleasure. Beginning with a happy little tune that bears a striking resemblance to "Rule Britannia," Schoenberg's adaptation of a harpsichord concerto by the eighteenth-century Austrian composer Georg Matthias Monn is one of his most impressive essays in virtuoso orchestration: bells tinkle, the woodwinds jabber, and the solo instrument is all but asked to stand on its head. Although the cello part is allegedly one of the most difficult ever written for the instrument, Yo Yo Ma glides through it with ease and obvious relish and Ozawa's contribution could not have been more sympathetic or alert.

A more substantial but equally unthreatening work, the Concerto for String Quartet and Orchestra, presents Schoenberg the pedagogue showing Handel, in one of his occasionally slip-shod Opus 6 Concerti Grossi, how the thing *really* ought to have been done. Listening to one great master gently wagging his finger at another—and producing a free-standing masterpiece in the process—is a delightfully amusing experience, particularly in the witty, openhearted performance by the American String Quartet and the New York Chamber Orchestra led by Gerard Schwarz (Nonesuch 79145-2 [CD]).

Concerto for Piano and Orchestra; Chamber Symphony No. 1, Op. 9; Chamber Symphony No. 2, Op. 38

> Brendel, piano; Southwest German Radio Symphony, Gielen. Philips
> 446683 [CD].

The late Clara Steuermann, widow of the foremost interpreter of Schoenberg's piano music, once said the opening of the Piano Concerto should be played "as though it were a Mendelssohn *Song Without Words*." Which is precisely the tack that Alfred Brendel takes in the latest and best of his three recordings of this magnificent work. His lyrical, rhapsodic approach to music places it firmly within the great Romantic tradition where it properly belongs, while his meticulous approach to the details constantly reveals hidden miracles of the composer's craftsmanship. As his fondly remembered Philips recording of *Moses und Aron* proved, Michael Gielen is a passionate and understanding Schoenberg interpreter, evident here in both the Concerto and the two Chamber Symphonies. No finer recording of either work exists, with the warmth and brilliance of the performances matched by the recorded sound.

Although the GM recording (2006 [CD]) of Louis Krasner's live performance of the Schoenberg Violin Concerto with Dimitri Mitropoulos and the West German Radio Symphony is an invaluable historical document—especially coupled with a live performance of the Berg Violin Concerto, which he also commissioned—no really adequate modern version is currently available. From tapes of various live performances, Viktoria Mullova's interpretation is clearly an altogether astonishing one and should be recorded commercially without delay.

Choral Music

Shirley-Quirk, narrator; BBC Singers, London Sinfonietta, BBC Symphony, Boulez. Sony Classical S2K 44571 [CD].

For a man who not all that long ago wrote the deliberately provocative (and ultimately asinine) diatribe *Schoenberg est mort*, Pierre Boulez has become one of the composer's most ardently committed interpreters. This two-CD collection of Schoenberg's choral music contains some of Schoenberg's most inspired creations, from the withering *Survivor from Warsaw,* which in seven minutes accomplishes nearly as much as *Schindler's List* did in three and a quarter hours, to the great—and, as the composer came to think of it—*accursed* motet *Frieda auf Erden.* (Because the deeply superstitious Schoenberg assigned his Opus 13 to a work called "Peace on Earth," he later became convinced that that was the actual *cause* of World War I. Nor was this breathtaking lack of modesty without its amusing side. Once, when some of his students took a sample of his script to a handwriting analyst and were told, "This man thinks he's at very least the Emperor of China," the composer asked in all innocence, "But did she say if I was justified?")

Not only are these the most powerful and meticulous recorded performances these works have yet had, but they are also the most physically beautiful. As much as anyone, Boulez fully understands the deeply Romantic underpinnings of Schoenberg's art, projecting it as gloriously as anyone ever has.

This is an alluring, indispensable album.

Five Pieces for Orchestra, Op. 16

City of Birmingham Symphony, Rattle. EMI Classics CDC 49857 [CD].

After leading the American premiere of the *Five Pieces for Orchestra* in Boston, the misanthropic German conductor Karl Muck announced with his customary tact, "I can't tell you whether we've played *music,* but I assure you we've played every one of Schoenberg's notes, just as they were written." Curiously, there are still those who entertain similar doubts about this modern masterpiece, more than eighty years after it was composed. With *Pierrot lunaire,* the monodrama *Erwartung,* and the closing moments of the Second String Quartet, the *Five Pieces* represent the summit of Schoenberg's experiments with nontonal—he detested the word "atonal"—music: a work of stupefying originality and beauty that should be heard as frequently as the "Eroica" Symphony or *The Rite of Spring.*

Like the superb but recently withdrawn Deutsche Grammophon recording by James Levine and the Berlin Philharmonic, Sir Simon Rattle leads a subtle, powerful, superbly colored performance of this early Schoenberg masterpiece, in which the musical argument becomes very nearly as lucid as anything in the music of Schoenberg's favorite composers, Mozart and Brahms. With equally loving and perceptive versions of Berg's *Lulu Suite* and Webern's *Six Pieces,* Opus 6, this is now the best single-disc collection of orchestral music by the three giants of the Second Viennese School.

Now then, if the same forces would only move on to one or two other Schoenberg items, like *Verklärte Nacht* and *Pelleas und Melisande,* the Violin Concerto (with Mullova or Perlman), the Piano Concerto (with Pollini), *A Survivor from Warsaw,* the brief but delectable *Begleitungsmusik zu einer Lichtspielszene,* and the rarely heard *Suite in G* for Strings, then I could die a happy man.

Gurrelieder

Norman, Troyanos, McCracken, Klemperer, Tanglewood Festival Chorus, Boston Symphony Orchestra, Ozawa. Philips 412511-2 [CD].

Jerusalem, Dunn, Fassbaender, Hotter, St. Hedwig's Cathedral Choir, Düsseldorf Municipal Choral Society, Berlin Radio Symphony, Chailly. London 430321-2 [CD].

Gurrelieder, Schoenberg's magnificent orchestral song-cycle/oratorio, is both the perfect introduction to the composer's early style and one of the last great masterpieces of Romantic music. If you are one of those people who turn up their noses at the mere mention of Schoenberg's name, then *Gurrelieder* might just be the medicine to cure you of a most unfortunate ailment.

While this Philips recording is not the ideal *Gurrelieder*, it is, for the most part, a very good one. It is also the only one on the market today. The strongest things in the performance are the Tove of Jessye Norman, the speaker of Werner Klemperer, the playing of the Boston Symphony, and the excitement that a live performance always generates. While the late tenor James McCracken struggles heroically with one of the most difficult parts ever written, this is not an especially comfortable or attractive performance, and the usually reliable Tatiana Troyanos is unexpectedly wobbly as the Wood Dove. Ozawa, as usual, leads an interpretation that scores very high marks for the beauties of its physical sound and the attention to detail but that nevertheless tends to gloss over the more profound elements in the music. Yet in spite of its flaws, this recording belongs in every collection, especially since *Gurrelieders* from Carlos Kleiber or Klaus Tennstedt are *not* on the horizon and probably shouldn't be expected any time soon.

Although the London performance has much to recommend it, too—preeminently, the singing of the most impressive of recorded Waldemars, Siegfried Jerusalem, as well as demonstration-quality recorded sound—Riccardo Chailly's conducting seems efficient but superficial, as it usually does. Still, of all recorded *Gurrelieders* it makes the most impressive noise.

*M*oses und Aron

> Pittman-Jennings, Fontana, Naef, Graham-Hall, Lindskog, Merritt,
> Lorenz, Devlin, Polgár, Netherlands Opera Chorus, Zaans Youth
> Choir, Waterland Music School, Royal Concertgebouw Orchestra,
> Boulez. Deutsche Grammophon 4499174-2 [CD].

There will always be a special place in hell for the well-known foundation (name withheld to prevent all right-thinking people from sending them several letter bombs per day) that turned down Arnold Schoenberg's modest request for sufficient funds to complete his oratorio *Die Jakobsleiter,* and one of the great unfinished works in musical history, *Moses und Aron.* (This same foundation, by the way, regularly doles out hefty grants to feckless boobs who, to quote my grandfather, if they had to take a trip on brains wouldn't have to pack a lunch.) Be that as it may, even without the music of its Third Act (the composer did complete the moving text), *Moses und Aron* easily ranks with the most intriguing and important of all twentieth-century operas. Were it given performances like this one on a regular basis, it might become, if not another *La Bohème,* then at least a work that would be performed with something approaching the frequency it deserves.

The late Sir Georg Solti, in one of the finest recordings he made since the completion of London's Vienna *Ring,* placed both the opera and Schoenberg where they properly belong. It has often been suggested that Schoenberg only wanted to re-write the music of Johannes Brahms for the twentieth century. The suggestion is ludicrous, of course, but it contains at least a grain of truth. For Schoenberg, even in the most advanced of his twelve-tone works, remained an arch-Romantic to the very end. Solti clearly recognized the romantic elements in this rich and moving opera and made them work. Rarely, for instance, has the most famous moment in the score, "The Dance Around the Gold Calf," sounded more lurid—in fact, the entire scene is a triumph of prurient interest, as the composer intended—and never had the difficult principal roles been more effortlessly or beautifully sung. The Chicago Symphony, as always, was miraculous in its poise and execution, and the recorded sound was stunning in its warmth and detail. If for no other reason than to honor the man who did so much for their company, London should offer a medium-priced reissue of the performance without delay.

Until they do, Pierre Boulez's second recording is a dramatic improvement over his first, which was pretty impressive to begin with. Based on a series of live performances, both the playing and singing may be even more consistently beautiful than in the Solti recording—if any orchestra in the world can out-play the Chicago Symphony, then it's the Royal Concertgebouw Orchestra—largely because Boulez takes an even more romantic view. Incredibly enough, given his recent (and execrable) Mahler recordings, Boulez seems totally immersed in this decadent, intensely emotional idiom. The performance surges with a raw but superbly controlled power that even Solti is hard-pressed to match. This is also the *Moses und Aron* that has the imprimatur of the composer's son Larry, who recently suggested it is not only the opera's best recorded version but is also one of the finest Schoenberg recordings ever made.

Be warned, *Moses und Aron* is no *Aida;* still, it is a very great work that will repay in abundance any investment of time and energy the listener is willing to make.

Pelleas und Melisande

Houston Symphony, Eschenbach. Koch International Classics KIC 7316 [CD].

During the last decade or so, Christoph Eschenbach has transformed himself from a fine pianist (which, of course, he still is) into one of the most interesting and consistently exciting conductors of his generation; he has restored much of the prestige of the once ailing Houston Symphony and his name increasingly pops up on speculative short lists of candidates for various soon-to-be-vacant posts, including those of Cleveland, New York, and Philadelphia.

Eschenbach's recording of Schoenberg's elusive early tone poem might suggest why. In addition to being a lushly romantic interpretation full of dramatic incident and beautifully observed detail, the orchestral execution is ravishing, recalling the orchestra's glory days under Leopold Stokowski.

An RCA album of Schoenberg orchestrations is equally thrilling (09026-68658-2 [CD]), with stunning versions of the Brahms G Minor Piano Quartet, the Bach Chorale Preludes, and the *Saint Anne* Prelude and Fugue.

Piano Music (complete)

Pollini, piano. Deutsche Grammophon 423249-2 [CD].

I suspect that the reason that Schoenberg's piano music turns up so rarely on recitals has less to do with the resistance of the audience than it does with the perfectly understandable unwillingness of pianists to play it. There is nothing about this important, serious music that could possibly attract a shallow or self-serving performer, and pianists—bless them—are no more profound or altruistic as a group than are any of the rest of us.

With the composer's friend and long-time champion Eduard Steuermann—whose old Columbia recordings were among the great documents of modern music making—Maurizio Pollini is one of those rare performers who is able to grapple with the music on its own uncompromising terms and yet make it seem as though he were doing it out of love and not some misplaced sense of duty. The performances are as sensitive and dramatic as his interpretations of Beethoven, Schubert, and Chopin, and should win these passionate, rarefied, uniquely lyrical works many friends.

Pierrot Lunaire, Op. 21

**DeGaetani, speaker; Contemporary Chamber Ensemble, Weisberg.
Nonesuch 79237-2 [CD], 71251-4 [T].**

With Stravinsky's *The Rite of Spring*, Schoenberg's *Pierrot lunaire* is one of the two great watersheds of modern music, a piece of such staggering originality and inventiveness that it still seems as though it might have been written yesterday, instead of in the year 1912.

This classic recording, with the late Jan DeGaetani and Arthur Weisberg's Contemporary Chamber Ensemble, is still alive and well on Nonesuch and *still* the closest thing we have yet had to an ideal realization of *Pierrot lunaire*. Ms.

DeGaetani, who made her formidable reputation by singing the most impossibly difficult contemporary music as though it had been written by Stephen Foster, weaves her way through Schoenberg's eerie, mysteriously beautiful *Sprechstimme* as though she were telling us stories from Mother Goose (which, after all, is not that far removed from what the *Pierrot* speaker is supposed to do). The highest praise that can be lavished on the accompaniment she receives from Weisberg and company is that it is altogether worthy of this legendary modern performance.

Quartets (5) for Strings

LaSalle Quartet. Deutsche Grammophon 419994-2 [CD].

As with so many of his major works, Schoenberg's quartets have been shrouded in misunderstanding and neglect for so many decades that coming to them for the first time can make for both a bewildering and an exhilarating experience. The early D Major Quartet of 1897, with its echoes of Dvořák and Schubert, is among the most buoyant and approachable of all Schoenberg's works, and, while the first and fourth of the numbered quartets have much to recommend them, the middle two rank with the masterworks of modern chamber music. The Second Quartet, in whose final movements Schoenberg first abandoned traditional harmony, is among his most boldly original works—in addition to the non-tonal experiments, there is a haunting part for soprano voice—and the Third Quartet, one of his finest twelve-tone scores, erupts with a passionate intensity not far removed from the smoldering mood of *Erwartung*.

It is good to have the sensitive, impassioned recordings by the LaSalle Quartet back in circulation, for as performances they have even more to communicate on a human level than the more technically dazzling versions by the Juilliard Quartet, no doubt slated for CD reissue by Sony Classical. In addition to the Schoenbergs, this four-CD box offers the major works for string quartet by Berg and Webern, including what is probably the finest *Lyric Suite* since the old Dial recording by the Kolisch Quartet.

Speaking of whom, those still-definitive recordings that Alfred Newman had made on the sly at a United Artists sound stage in 1936 are available on a pair of handsomely remastered CDs from Archiphon (ARC 103/4). No ensemble had a more profound understanding of this music than the quartet founded by Schoenberg's brother-in-law, Rudolf Kolisch. In addition to having an ease and warmth of expression that suggest that Schoenberg is no more difficult than Brahms (which he isn't), they played all of this music from memory, except for the recently completed Fourth Quartet. Along with the incomparable performances, the album comes with the touching speeches made by Schoenberg and members of the quartet, together with an absorbing liner note by Fred Steiner.

Variations for Orchestra, Op. 31; Chamber Symphony No. 1; *Erwartung*

Bryn-Julson, soprano; Birmingham Contemporary Music Group; City of Birmingham Symphony, Rattle. EMI Classics CDC 55212 [CD].

The *Variations for Orchestra* is a work of such astounding musical richness and historical significance—Milton Babbitt once insisted that it's *at least* as important as the "Eroica" Symphony—that one continues to be baffled by its present neglect. True, the composer's first orchestral twelve-tone work is probably never going to be a pops concert item, but given the right kind of performance it can have staggering visceral impact, as it certainly does here.

Not since Hans Rosbaud—whose pathbreaking 1961 concert performance of the *Variations* is now available on a Music and Arts CD (CD 627)—has this music been made to seem more accessible or more physically ravishing than in the superlative recording by Sir Simon Rattle and the City of Birmingham Symphony. The secret of Rattle's success—apart from a responsive, carefully drilled orchestra—is his attitude toward the music. Far from seeing Schoenberg as an avant-garde boogeyman, he sees him as Schoenberg saw himself: a late-Romantic composer who sprang from the same lush source as Brahms. With equally sumptuous accounts of the First Chamber Symphony and the monodrama *Erwartung,* this is not only the most important Schoenberg album of the decade but is also one of the most beautiful, ever.

Verklärte Nacht

Ensemble InterContemporain, Boulez. Sony Classical ASMK 48465 [CD].

Santa Fe Chamber Music Ensemble. Nonesuch D4-79028 [T].

The early *Verklärte Nacht,* written by a largely self-taught twenty-six-year-old composer, is one of the most amazing works in the history of nineteenth-century music. (And as with Brahms, the composer he admired most of all, the percentage of masterworks to lesser pieces in Schoenberg's output is extraordinarily high.) The lush sonorities, the wealth of ornamental detail, the advanced harmonic thinking, and the expressive confidence of the work completely belie the composer's youth and relative lack of experience. Had Schoenberg never written another note of music, he would still be remembered, for this piece alone, as one of the most fascinating voices of the entire late-Romantic era.

Among recordings of the orchestral version of *Verklärte Nacht,* Pierre Boulez's is an almost ideal fusion of Romantic ardor and modern clarity in which both the passions and the architecture of Schoenberg's early masterpiece emerge in the sharpest possible relief. Coupled with equally impressive versions of the pivotal *Variations for Orchestra* and the fascinating one-act opera *Die glückliche Hand,* this clearly is the *Verklärte Nacht* to own.

Among recordings of the original version of the piece, the Nonesuch version recorded at one of the Santa Fe Chamber Music Festivals remains unapproached. In fact, the only significant drawback in this otherwise virtually perfect recording (which is coupled with a blazing account of a late Schoenberg masterpiece, the great String Trio), is that it has yet to be issued on compact disc.

Schreker, Franz (1878–1934)

Chamber Symphony for 23 Solo Instruments

Berlin Radio Symphony, Gielen, Rickenbacher. Koch Schwann CD 311078 [CD].

Among all the shadowy, half-forgotten figures of late-Romantic German music, Franz Schreker is the one who most deserves the major revival. The most widely performed operatic composer of his generation, Schreker's music was banned by the Nazis in 1933 and the composer died the following year. In the catalogue that accompanied the 1938 exhibition of *Entartete Musik,* the Nazis noted: "Franz Schreker was the Magnus Hirschfield of opera composers. There was no sexual-pathological aberration he would not have set to music."

As a spate of new recordings have begun to reveal, Schreker was a composer of unique and extraordinary abilities: a master of the voluptuous, post-Wagnerian orchestra and of the rarefied, fin-de-siècle decadence that would reach its climax in works like Strauss's *Rosenkavalier.* His was a singularly complex and sophisticated voice and—as one gets to know it—an utterly distinctive one. Those who enjoy Mahler, Strauss, and early Schoenberg should make its acquaintance without delay.

The Koch recording of the stunning Chamber Symphony for 23 Instruments provides an ideal introduction to Schreker's uniquely beautiful world; the command of color and texture is as deft as anything in Debussy, while the companion pieces—*Nachtstück, Prelude to a Drama,* and *Valse lente*—have a pleasantly overripe charm.

Those wishing to make the big leap into the Schreker operas should try the London recording (444442-2 [CD]) of *Die Gezeichneten* ("The Branded" or "The Stigmatized"), which had its triumphant first performance in 1918. This haunting tale of a beautiful, gravely ill painter who realizes she could not survive the strain of physical love drew from Schreker a score of unparalleled opulence, all of it brilliantly captured by Lothar Zagrosek and his superb cast.

Perhaps even more important to the burgeoning Schreker revival is the composer's first major biography, *Franz Schreker, 1878–1934: A Cultural Biography* by Christopher Hailey (Cambridge University Press, 1993). Not only is this likely to remain the definitive scholarly study of the composer's dramatic life, but it is also so engaging and elegantly written that it reads like a first-rate novel.

Schubert, Franz (1797–1828)

Impromptus (8) for Piano

Perahia, piano. CBS MK 37291 [CD].

With Mozart and Mendelssohn, Franz Schubert was one of the authentic miracles of Western art. At sixteen, he composed the first great German *lied,* "Gretchen am Spinnrade," and in the remaining fifteen years of his tragically brief life he became not only the undisputed master of German art song (he wrote more than seven hundred) but also the most important composer of symphonies, chamber music, and piano sonatas after his hero and idol, Beethoven. Though the two men lived in Vienna for years, the almost pathologically modest and self-effacing Schubert never screwed up the courage to meet the older man. He did serve as a pall-bearer at Beethoven's funeral in 1827, which took place a scant twenty months before his own. No other composer, including Mozart, had a greater or more facile gift for melody, and none—even the indefatigable giants of the baroque era—was more prolific.

The two sets of Impromptus are among the most charming and characteristic of Schubert's piano works, and all have been served handsomely on records since the 78 era. On the basis of his CBS recording, Murray Perahia must be considered one of the great Schubert interpreters in the world today. The playing has a light, direct openness that is genuinely refreshing but also has plenty of *Schwung* and sinew whenever the music demands. In fact, these popular works have probably not been in better hands since the days of Artur Schnabel and Edwin Fischer.

Mass No. 4 in C Major; Mass No. 5 in A-flat Major; Mass No 6 in E-flat Major

Soloists, Bavarian Radio Chorus and Orchestra, Sawallisch. EMI Classics CDM 69222 [CD] (Nos. 4 and 5); CDM 69223 [CD].

If Schubert's six mass settings don't typically contain his most inspired music, then they still serve to remind us that the mediocre music of a master is preferable to the masterpieces of a mediocrity, or as Charles Caleb Colton so cheerfully put it, "Love is a spaniel that prefers even punishment from one hand to caresses from another." Which is not to say that Schubert's masses are in any way second-rate: they contain a wealth of lovely melody and sincere religious feeling, and if they lack the sustained dramatic impact of Haydn's or Beethoven's sacred music, then they are nonetheless fresh and engaging pieces that deserve to be far better known.

In these two medium-priced collections, Wolfgang Sawallisch and his brilliant forces make exceptionally strong cases for three of the composer's finest settings, especially the richly moving Mass in A-flat from 1828. Both the chorus and orchestra are warm and responsive, while the fact that some of the soloists—Helen Donath, Brigitte Fassbaender, Dietrich Fischer-Dieskau, and the late Lucia Popp—were and are major Schubert lieder specialists is evident in every phrase.

Octet in F Major for Strings and Winds, D. 803

Academy of St. Martin-in-the-Fields Chamber Ensemble. Chandos CHAN 8585 [CD].

This sublimely entertaining chamber work, which in some performances can last very nearly as long as Beethoven's Ninth Symphony, is as much fun as eight musicians can have with all their clothes on. (Rumors of an Octet au naturel given at a well-known music festival in Southern California continue to prove groundless. The festival's director told me in confidence that while they were certainly open to the idea, it was not only impossible to find a clarinetist who was willing to appear in that condition but also—and even more to the point—one that relatively normal people would be willing to look at.)

As in their Philips recording made in the late 1970s, the Academy of St. Martin-in-the-Fields Chamber Ensemble gives a performance for Chandos in which both the simplicity and sophistication of Schubert's great score are given full reign. Mechanically, the playing is all but flawless; yet it is the sheer *enjoyment* we hear in the playing that makes the recording stand out. For years, Angel's recording with the Melos Ensemble—now available in England on an EMI Classics compact disc—set a standard that I thought would never be approached. This one joins it at the very top of any list.

Piano Sonata in C Minor, D. 958; Piano Sonata in A Major, D. 959

Pollini, piano. Deutsche Grammophon 427327-2 [CD].

While Schubert produced some twenty piano sonatas over the course of his career, he was never really comfortable with the form. It was only with the last three sonatas, written during the final year of his life, that Schubert, the incomparable miniaturist of the *Impromptus* and *Moments musicaux,* produced a trio of large-scale piano works whose depth and quality rival any that his admired Beethoven ever wrote. Not since Artur Schnabel—who once said, "I play Beethoven to make my living; Schubert I play for love"—have these works had a more probing or poetic interpreter than Maurizio Pollini. If other performances of the C Minor Sonata have unleashed a more torrential strength, then Pollini stands virtually alone in evoking the bitter tragedy of the A Major. While both interpretations are full of the special insights (his detractors would call them "mannerisms") that have made Pollini the most deeply personal keyboard artist of his generation, the occasional eccentricities are far outweighed by the extraordinary depth and beauty of this set.

First choice among recordings of the great B-flat Major Sonata, D. 960, boils down to Sir Clifford Curzon's beautifully detailed London recording (448578-2 [CD]) or Stephen Kovacevich's probing and poetic interpretation for EMI Classics (CDC 55359 [CD]). For those who love this most sublime of Schubert's piano works, the decision will probably hinge on a preference for the companion pieces. Curzon offers thrilling performances of Brahms's Piano Sonata No. 3 and a pair of *Intermezzi,* while the Kovacevich comes with some delightful Schubert trifles: the *Allegretto* in C Minor and *Twelve Ländler,* D. 760, all charmingly done.

For those wanting to explore the entire cycle, Wilhelm Kempff's magisterial recordings from the mid- to late-1960s have been reissued on a set of seven medium-priced Deutsche Grammophon CDs (423496-2). As in the pianist's two separate versions of the Beethoven sonatas, the level of inspiration is extraordinarily high, with a freshness of insight and sense of discovery that prevents the slightest hint of the perfunctory or the routine. This is a classic recording and an outstanding bargain.

Quintet in A Major for Piano and Strings, D. 667, "Trout"

Curzon, piano; Vienna Octet. London 448602-2 [CD].

Like his near contemporary Solomon, Sir Clifford Curzon was one of the most unprepossessing of the great modern pianists. Looking like a cross between a Talmudic scholar and an Oxford don, Curzon possessed a blazing technique and a temperament to match. His penchant for canceling appearances eventually became legendary, and in my own personal experience only the highly strung Byron Janis backed out on more concerts for which I had tickets in hand. (A musical wit once suggested that the pianist's management should announce, "Mr. Curzon is available for only a limited number of cancellations this season.")

Nonetheless, when Curzon came to play—as he did in this celebrated 1958 recording of the "Trout" Quintet—all grumbles about his personal quirks were silenced. The playing is both completely relaxed and supremely magisterial, with a bracingly vigorous account of the Scherzo to keep the listeners on their toes. Combined with a loving account of the *Death and the Maiden* Quartet, this is a bargain that few can afford to pass up.

Quintet in C Major for Strings, D. 956

Ma, cello; Cleveland String Quartet. CBS MK-39134 [CD].

From works like the sublime and serene C Major Quintet, it would be impossible to deduce that the last eighteen months of Franz Schubert's life were an inexpressible nightmare. Dying of tertiary neurosyphilis, the composer was nonetheless able to churn out a body of work of such unearthly beauty and purity that the only thing like it was that equally astonishing annus mirabilis of the English poet John Keats.

While the great C Major Cello Quintet has had many distinguished recordings over the years—beginning with an unforgettable account by the old Hollywood Quartet dating from the mid-1950s, now available on a Testament CD (SBT 1031 [CD]), coupled with their equally memorable version of Schoenberg's *Verklärte Nacht*—no recorded performance has been more sensitive or moving than this CBS release by cellist Yo Yo Ma and the brilliant Cleveland String Quartet. One of the most impassioned and committed of all the Quintet's recent recordings, this is also one of the most polished and meticulous. The attentive and generous contribution made by the "fifth wheel" of the performance offers further evidence that Ma is the most breathtakingly complete cellist of his generation, and with good playback equipment, the amazingly lifelike recorded sound will almost persuade you that the players are in your living room.

Rosamunde (incidental music)

Von Otter, soprano; Chamber Orchestra of Europe, Abbado. Deutsche Grammophon 431655-2 [CD].

Once on the air, in introducing a work by Anton Rubinstein, I addressed the old Romantic legend that that fiery Russian composer and pianist, because of his astonishing physical resemblance to Beethoven, was in fact the great man's illegitimate son. I pointed out that since Beethoven had died in 1827 and Rubinstein was born in 1829 this would have been extremely difficult, given that in the 1820s there were no sperm banks in the city of Vienna, other than Helemina von Chézy. Not only would this giftless clown supply the transcendentally stupid libretto that would completely scuttle *Euryanthe,* the grandest of Carl Maria von Weber's operas, but she would also supply Franz Schubert with the material for one of his worst theatrical disasters, a play called *Rosamunde,* which closed after only two performances.

Claudio Abbado's masterful recording of the *Rosamunde* incidental music is a sheer delight from beginning to end. The Chamber Orchestra of Europe plays this enchanting music with just the right combination of youthful zest and mature gentility, while the soprano and chorus are utterly delectable. Given wonderfully lifelike sound by the Deutsche Grammophon engineers, this is easily one of the best Schubert recordings of the decade.

Die schöne Müllerin, D. 795

Fischer-Dieskau, baritone; Moore, piano. Deutsche Grammophon 415186-2 [CD].

Unlike his half-dozen operatic projects that came to nothing or ended in total disaster, Schubert's setting of twenty interrelated lyrics by the irretrievably minor poet Wilhelm Müller is one of the most successful music dramas ever written. In this simple, loosely structured tale of a wandering young miller who falls in love, is spurned by the "title character" (the Miller's Beautiful Daughter), and finally commits a Romantic suicide by drowning himself in a brook, Schubert fashioned history's first great song cycle and one of the two supreme masterpieces in the form.

Although there have been some memorable recordings of *Die schöne Müllerin* over the years—in many ways, the famous 1941 recording by the Danish tenor Aksel Schiøtz has never been surpassed (Danacord DAN 452 [CD]), and that other celebrated wartime recording by Julius Patzak is now available on a Preiser CD (93128)—Dietrich Fischer-Dieskau's several recordings are all impressive, most notably the now-withdrawn 1962 version for EMI Classics, followed closely by this 1972 remake for Deutsche Grammophon.

Unlike some of the baritone's later recordings that are ruined by archness and a host of exasperating mannerisms, his third version of the cycle still finds the voice at its freshest and fullest—thereby eliminating the need to posture, primp, and snort—and captures one of the greatest musical storytellers since John McCormack was in his prime. The unerringly perceptive, quietly inventive accompaniments of the great Gerald Moore are the stuff of which legends are made.

Songs

While the major recording companies now seem intent on reissuing *everything* on CD, this pleasantly profligate policy does not seem to extend to lieder, which continues to appeal to a relatively small but rabid crowd. Unbelievably, not *one* of Hermann Prey's Schubert recordings, other than some late recordings of the cycles and two versions of *Winterreise,* is to be had anywhere at any price. Apparently, no one at the several recording companies that have dealt with the baritone over the years has heard that he is—no kidding, guys—one of the greatest Schubert singers in history and, in the opinion of many of us, the foremost lieder specialist to have emerged since the end of the War.

If the Prey situation is surprising, then the Hotter is a scandal. It is as if that noblest German bass of his generation—whose recordings of Schubert came closest to sounding the ultimate depths and most profound stillnesses of the composer's heart—simply never existed. The wonderful Austrian company Preiser, which specializes in historic vocal reissues, has released one album (93145 [CD]), but again, for an artist of Hotter's stature, this is inexcusable. By that same token, the wonderful and still vigorously active Dutch soprano Elly Ameling remains woefully underrepresented: only one of her Philips recordings has made the jump to CD (420870-2), although there is an attractive collection from Deutsche Harmonia Mundi (74321-26617-2 [CD] offering radiant performances of nine songs recorded early in the singer's career.

On the brighter side, things on the Fischer-Dieskau front are definitely looking up. In addition to that ageless *Die schöne Müllerin,* two other Angel recordings from the 1950s and '60s have also resurfaced: a dandy *Schwanengesang* with Gerald Moore (CDMC-63559 [CD]), and two lovely recitals of some of the best-known songs (CDM-69503 [CD] and CDMB 63566 [CD]), in which the singing is so effortless and unaffected that those who only know the barking, hammy "Fisch" of recent years will hardly believe it's the same singer. Deutsche Grammophon has issued the first two volumes of their massive Schubert Lieder series, which features Fischer-Dieskau and Moore in more than four hundred songs spread out over eighteen discs (437215-2 [CD], 437225-2 [CD]). Recorded in the late 1960s, the voice is as firm and steady as in the EMI recordings, with both the singer and the pianist paragons of perception and good taste.

Among recent historic reissues, a recital from Preiser (89017 [CD]) documents the phenomenal artistry of the German baritone Gerhard Hüsch, whose insight, musicianship, and sheer manliness have rarely been equaled before or since. Elisabeth Schwarzkopf is finally represented on two CDs from EMI Classics: her classic recordings made in 1952 with the great Swiss pianist Edwin Fischer (CDH 64026) and the more recent ones with Gerald Moore and Geoffrey Parsons (CDM 63656). In both, incomparable musicianship, perception, and sex are combined in an irresistibly heady brew. Although never as glamorous as her famous friend and colleague, Irmgard Seefried was every bit as fine a lieder singer as Schwarzkopf, as an Ades collection of popular songs clearly proves (ADE 203102 [CD]). Although he died before his gifts as a lieder singer had fully matured, the uniquely beautiful voice of tenor Fritz Wunderlich is preserved on a pair of CDs from Deutsche Grammophon (449747-2) and Acanta (CD 43529), along with exquisitely lovely versions of songs by Beethoven and Schumann. The great Russian bass Alexander Kipnis is represented on a two-CD set from Music and Arts (661-2 [CD]) that features among its many glories his incomparable version of *Erlkönig*. The suave German baritone Heinrich Rehkemper can be heard in twenty-one songs from the mid-1920s on a superb Preiser recital (89058 [CD]).

Of the newer collections, Margaret Price's Orfeo album (C 001811 A [CD]) features some captivating singing and perhaps the finest available version of *Der Hirt auf dem Felsen* (The Shepherd on the Rock), while the late Arleen Augér's Virgin Classics recital with fortepiano (59630 [CD]) is as beautifully sung as it is intelligently conceived.

Four of the brightest young stars of the lieder world are currently represented by splendid collections. Barbara Bonney's exquisite voice and knowing manner are brilliantly showcased on a Teldec recital (90873 [CD]) that features some of the most joyous Schubert singing since Seefried. Cecilia Bartoli is predictably charming in a collection of the composer's Italian settings (London 440297-2 [CD]), which also includes some lovely and rarely heard items by Haydn, Mozart, and Beethoven. Thomas Hampson and Bryn Terfel continue to suggest that they are to the current generation what Prey and Fischer-Dieskau were to theirs: Terfel in a wide-ranging Deutsche Grammophon recital of popular favorites (445294-2 [CD]), Hampson in a fascinating Hyperion album devoted to songs inspired by ancient Greece.

Finally, Hyperion's quixotic and largely successful series, which will attempt to record *all* of the songs, has already yielded several clear winners. Volume 1 (CDJ-33001 [CD]) finds Dame Janet Baker at the height of her mature interpretive powers and the voice showing only the slightest signs of wear and tear; Volume 2 features a rousing collection of men's songs from baritone Stephen Varcoe (CDJ 33002 [CD]) that concludes with a stunningly effective performance of the massive *Der Taucher* (The Diver), which lasts nearly half an hour and here goes by like the wind; Volume 3 (CDJ-33003 [CD]) offers the lovely mezzo-soprano Ann Murray in beautiful voice, while on Volume 4 (CDJ-33004 [CD]) her husband, Philip Langridge, continues to demonstrate that he is one of the most intelligent and musical Schubert singers in the world today. Volume 5 (CDJ 33005 [CD]), centered around the theme of Schubert and the countryside, draws some delectable singing from soprano Elizabeth Connell, while Anthony Rolfe-Johnson's album of nocturnal musings (CDJ 33006 [CD]) includes a pair of ravishing items—*Jagdlied* and *Zur guten Nacht*—with male chorus. The recently retired Brigitte Fassbaender offers a delightfully gruesome collection of songs about death (CDJ 33011 [CD]), and Thomas Allen is at his most perceptive and eloquent in an anthology of Schiller settings (CDJ 33016 [CD]), including a giddy version of the same *An die Freude* that drew a very different response from Beethoven in the final movement of the Ninth Symphony.

All in all, things could be worse.

String Quartet No. 13 in A Minor, D. 804; String Quartet No. 14 in D Minor, D. 810, "Death and the Maiden"

Alban Berg Quartet. EMI Classics CDC 47333 [CD].

As in its recordings of the Beethoven Quartets, Vienna's Alban Berg Quartet is all but impossible to better in these performances of the last, save one, of the great quartets Schubert would compose. The ensemble's almost obscenely beautiful physical sound has never been captured to more thrilling effect (the hushed yet paradoxically full-bodied *pianissimos* of which they are capable continually remind me of the high notes that only Leontyne Price in her prime could pop out with such bewitching ease), but as always in their recordings, the Bergs offer us considerably more than a collection of pretty sounds. The "Death and the Maiden" Quartet—so called because one of its movements is a set of variations on Schubert's song of that name—has rarely sounded this dark and disturbing (there are, of course, ample doses of light and life as well), and the great A Minor Quartet explodes with a dramatic intensity that no other recording can match.

The sound that EMI's engineers have supplied is as opulent as the performances they capture. For Schubert lovers, or simply for anyone interested in three of the greatest string quartets written after those of Beethoven, these are absolute musts.

Symphony No. 3 in D Major, D. 200; Symphony No. 5 in B-flat Major, D. 485; Symphony No. 6 in C Major, D. 589, "Little C Major"

Royal Philharmonic, Beecham. EMI Classics CDM 69750 [CD].

Like her near contemporary and one-time Prague neighbor Franz Kafka, my grandmother held a fairly dark view of the human condition, which my arrival did little to brighten. For instance, she was persuaded that virtually all useful wisdom was contained in the old Czech beatitude "Blessèd are they who expect nothing, for they shall not be disappointed." She was also a devout believer in the Czech time payment plan (100% cash down, and *no* easy monthly payments) and was firmly convinced that there was no such thing as a "bargain." She lived to be 94.

Had she lived to be 109—as well she might have, had it not been for that final pile-up on her fully paid-for (though, as she often complained, ridiculously overpriced) Harley-Davidson motorcycle—she might have admitted that bargains *do* exist. For here are three of Schubert's most endearing early symphonies in the finest recorded performances they are ever likely to receive on one "medium-priced" compact disc.

As far as Sir Thomas Beecham was concerned, early Schubert was merely an extension of Mozart and Haydn—which, to a large extent, it was—and he treats the music with the same easy wit and amiability. Which is not to say that he sees them as warmed-over versions of the "Surprise" and "Haffner" Symphonies. Never forgetting for a moment that even as a boy Schubert was one of the great masters of melody, Beecham caresses the glorious tunes with an affection and knowledge of breath that suggest a great lieder specialist. As always, the Royal Philharmonic gives the impression they would do anything for their unpredictable founder, and the recorded sound from the late-1950s is fine. Alas, the recording is becoming difficult to find, domestically. If necessary, it is definitely worth the time and expense to import it directly from any of the large English mail order houses. (Addresses can be found in any copy of *The Gramophone* magazine.)

Anyone hunting for comparable versions of the other early symphonies will find that the Deutsche Grammophon recordings by Claudio Abbado and the Chamber Orchestra of Europe come closest to approximating the Beecham spell. The relaxed yet buoyant romps through Nos. 1 and 2 are especially enjoyable (423652-2), while the performance of the "Tragic" (No. 4) is both weightier and more supple than those we usually hear. Although this disc (423653-3) comes with the best modern recording of the Third Symphony, the Beecham remains in a universe by itself.

Symphony No 8 in B Minor, D. 759, "Unfinished"

Columbia Symphony, Walter. Sony Classical SMK 64487 [CD];
Odyssey YT 30314 [T].

The most surprising thing about Bruno Walter's famous recording of the best-loved unfinished *anything* in Western art (unless you count *The Canterbury Tales*) is the searing intensity he unleashes in the powerful opening movement. There are those who insist that in the urgency of its drama and breadth of conception, the first movement of the "Unfinished" Symphony equals anything in Beethoven, and this is one of those performances that goes a long way to making the point. Walter's ferocious—and not always perfectly controlled—explosion is one of the most exciting moments of the early stereo era, and with a second movement that casts a spell of otherworldly purity and beatific peace, this is still—by a wide margin—*the* recording to own.

Symphony No. 9 in C Major, D. 944, "The Great C Major"

Berlin Philharmonic, Furtwängler. Deutsche Grammophon 447439-2 [CD].

Vienna Philharmonic, Solti. London 400082 [CD].

Schubert's final completed symphony can be a very problematic work. Since the *Great* of the sobriquet refers as much to its massive length as to the divinity of its melodic inspiration, the C Major Symphony can—and often has—degenerated into nothing more than a collection of Sunday School tunes. Wilhelm Furtwängler's eternal recording from the winter of 1951 is the one version of the piece that makes it seem as structurally sound, and dramatically inevitable, as the Beethoven Ninth. The performance is a triumph of Furtwänglerian brinkmanship at its most magical. The unwritten, yet electrifying, *accelerando* that leads out of the Introduction to the first movement's principal theme, the spring in the *Scherzo*'s rhythm, and the headlong forward thrust of the *Finale* make this one of the most exciting orchestral recordings ever made.

The same qualities that made his version of the "Unfinished" so successful can be heard in Sir Georg Solti's recording of the Great C Major, an unforced yet vivid interpretation that is both beautifully played and recorded.

Trio No. 1 in B-flat Major for Piano, Violin, and Cello, D. 898; Trio No. 2 in E-flat Major for Piano, Violin, and Cello, D. 929; Nocturne in E-flat Major, D. 897; Sonata Movement in B-flat Major, D. 28

Golub, piano; Kaplan, violin; Carr, cello. Arabesque Z 6580-2 [CD].

This divine music has had more than its fair share of outstanding recordings, beginning with a still electrifying (if technically and interpretively wayward) performance of the B-flat Major by the *always* electrifying and wayward Thibaud-Casals-Cortot Trio. A decade later, an even more fabulous HMV version of the E-flat Major appeared, featuring violinist Adolf Busch, his cello-playing brother Hermann, and his son-in-law-to-be, Rudolf Serkin. Since then, all of the leading groups—Beaux Arts, Suk, Borodin—have come to terms with these cornerstones of the trio literature, as have some superb ad hoc ensembles like Heifetz-Feuermann-Rubinstein and Rubinstein-Szeryng-Fournier.

That these recent recordings by the Golub-Kaplan-Carr Trio are so superb will come as no surprise to anyone familiar with their versions of the Brahms Trios; what *might* be surprising is how easily these three young musicians place all previous recordings in the shade. Mechanically, the playing is impeccable, as is the individual and collective musicianship. Yet it is the unusual combination of wisdom and freshness—qualities so central to the music itself—that makes the interpretations such revelations.

In addition to the two rarely heard miniatures, the performance of the E-flat Major Trio concludes with two fourth movements: the finale as it was published and is usually performed, together with the original version that contains one hundred bars of very worthy music that Schubert persuaded himself to cut.

Wanderer Fantasie, D. 760

Rubinstein, piano. RCA Victor 6257-2-RC [CD].

Even when Sviatoslav Richter's overwhelming Angel recording from the early 1960s is released domestically—it can be found in Europe on an EMI Classics compact disc—Artur Rubinstein's startling performance from the same period won't have to yield an inch. While not known as a Schubert specialist, Rubinstein was uniquely equipped to probe one of the most influential and forward-looking of the composer's works. For in his rhapsodic, possibly *overly* romantic performance, Rubinstein draws the obvious parallel to the music that can trace its roots back to this pathbreaking composition: the piano music of Schumann, Liszt, and his beloved Chopin.

The performances of the B-flat Major Sonata and the last two Opus 90 *Impromptus* are also superb, but it's this *Wanderer*—possibly the *Wanderer* of a lifetime—that counts.

Winterreise, D. 911

Fischer-Dieskau, baritone; Moore, piano. Deutsche Grammophon 415187-2 [CD].

Hotter, bass; Moore, piano. Angel CDH-61002 [CD].

There aren't too many vocal works that can make Mahler's *Kindertotenlieder* or the Shostakovich 14th Symphony seem cheerful in comparison, but that greatest of all song cycles, Schubert's *Winterreise,* is one of them. In the entire lieder repertoire, nothing can match the heartbreaking despair of this "Winter Journey" based on twenty-four poems by Wilhelm Müller; even the relatively bright moments, like "Der Lindenbaum"—which has almost acquired the status of a folk song—are shot through with desolation and foreboding. And yet, like *King Lear, Winterreise* is neither self-pitying nor self-deluding. It is an unflinchingly courageous look at a horrible truth and, as such, a central musical catharsis of the Western imagination.

Hermann Prey's interpretation of *Winterreise* has been a classic of the recital platform for more than a quarter of a century. On stage, he typically performs it by itself, without preamble or encores and often without taking any bows. It is a mature and completely selfless conception, dark without being dour, tragic with no hint of lugubriousness, effortless yet never glib. While none of his several recordings manages to fully capture the kind of devastating experience that this *Winterreise* can be in the concert hall, the most recent version from Denon—now inexplicably withdrawn—came perilously close. Until one of the Preys is returned to circulation, Fischer-Dieskau's Deutsche Grammophon version from the early 1970s is the most satisfying modern recording, mixing insight, musicianship, and beauty of singing in precisely the right amounts.

Hans Hotter's classic recording is indispensable, but only for those who are willing to look directly into the black heart of absolute despair. More than any other singer, Hotter elevates this music to the shattering heights of Greek tragedy. This is one of the most chilling vocal recordings ever made and one of the most courageous.

Schulhoff, Erwin (1894–1942)

The Flames (Plameny)

> **Eaglen, Höhn, Lindsley, Schudel, Vermillion, Berggold, Borris, Dressen, Westi, Prein, Wolf, RIAS Chamber Choir, Berlin German Symphony, Mauceri. London 444630-2 [CD].**

Of all the important artists murdered by the Nazis, none was more interesting or accomplished than the Prague-born Erwin Schulhoff, who died in the Wülzbourg concentration camp in 1942. A brilliant pianist and teacher, he was one of the first performers to champion the quarter-tone music of his friend Alois Hába; he was also an enthusiastic jazz pianist, adapting jazz idioms to his more obviously serious music from the mid-1920s onward. Expressionism, Impressionism, neo-Classicism, Socialist Realism, and most of the other important trends of his turbulent era would inform Schulhoff's music, which nonetheless maintained a distinctive character all its own.

Finished in 1928 and first staged in Brno four years later, the two-act opera *Plameny* (*Flammen*, in German) is probably Schulhoff's masterpiece. A fantastic, richly imaginative re-telling of the Don Juan legend, the score is astonishingly complex and exotic, with echoes of Korngold, Mahler, and late Richard Strauss, yet with many individual touches, primarily in the extended—and extremely impressive—orchestral interludes.

The performance is one of the strongest in London's much-lamented *Entartete Musik* series, with Jane Eaglen—the most exciting dramatic soprano of her generation—assuming all but one of the female roles. Iris Vermillion is equally persuasive as Death, with Kurt Westi a probing and vocally exciting Don Juan. John Mauceri coaxes Herculean efforts from the chorus and orchestra, making this fabulously difficult score seem no more taxing than a repertory item like *La Bohème,* while the London engineers respond with a recording of incredible realism, presence, and depth.

Schuller, Gunther (1925–)

Seven Studies on Themes of Paul Klee

> **Minneapolis Symphony, Dorati. Mercury Living Presence 434329-2 [CD].**

Gunther Schuller began his career as a French horn player, eventually becoming principal horn of the Cincinnati Symphony and Metropolitan Opera Orchestra. By 1959, he had given up a playing career for composition and has since remained one of the most versatile and provocative voices of his generation, an entirely self-taught composer whose music draws on an unusually wide range of influences, from serialism and aleatoric techniques to folk music and Third Stream jazz. *The Seven Studies on Themes of Paul Klee* from 1959 is his most frequently performed work for reasons that become obvious at once. From the sweltering heat of *Arab Village* to the delicious humor of *The Twittering Machine* to the haunting atmosphere of *An Eerie Moment* to the rhythmic subtleties of the *Pastorale,* this is one of the most colorful and evocative of modern American orchestral scores. In their famous Mercury Living Presence recording, Dorati and the Minneapolis Symphony play the piece as though it had been written for them (which it was) and the recorded sound remains astonishingly vivid and alive.

Schuller's highly developed gifts as a conductor are obvious in his own recording of three of his provocative instrumental concertos—for bassoon, horn, and piano (GM 2044 [CD]); a fourth (for organ) and two of his most compelling recent orchestral works, *Of Reminiscences and Reflections* (1992) and *The Past Is in the Present* (1994), are available on New World NW 80492-2 [CD].

Schuman, William (1910–1992)

New England Triptych; *Judith* (choreographic poem); *Variations on "America"* (orchestration of organ work by Charles Ives); Symphony No. 5

Seattle Symphony, Schwarz. Delos DE 3115 [CD].

The music that William Schuman produced over a period of more than fifty years represented the fusion of an essentially late-Romantic temperament, a commanding modern intellect, and perhaps the most highly evolved sense of craftsmanship of any American composer of his time. One of his greatest advocates, the late Leonard Bernstein, provided a succinct summary of Schuman's art: "Vitality, optimism, enthusiasm, long lyrical line, rhythmic impetuosity, bristling counterpoint, brilliant textures, dynamic tension." All of these qualities can be heard in the four works contained on what may very well be the most completely successful Schuman recording yet released.

In the capable hands of Gerard Schwarz and his finely honed Seattle Symphony, the *New England Triptych* and the orchestration of Ives's *"America" Variations* emerge with a point and presence they have rarely enjoyed in the recording studio, while the rarely heard choreographic poem *Judith* and the magnificent Fifth Symphony are revealed as the modern American masterworks that they clearly are. For anyone interested in American music, this is a cause for serious rejoicing.

Symphony No. 3; Symphony No. 5, "Symphony for Strings"; Symphony No. 8

New York Philharmonic, Bernstein. Sony Classical SMK 63163 [CD].

These are the works—and perhaps the performances—upon which Schuman's reputation as a symphonist will probably rest. The Third and Fifth symphonies, both commissioned by Koussevitzky, are among the strongest ever written by an American; the Eighth was composed in the early 1960s for Leonard Bernstein and the New York Philharmonic to help open the Lincoln Center for the Performing Arts. No recorded performances have ever responded as fully to the power, relentless energy, and intellectual depth of Schuman's music, nor with a more obvious or instinctive grasp of its unique idiom. For their CD debut, the sound of these famous recordings has been improved dramatically, especially in the earlier works, which once seemed uncomfortably close. No one with the slightest interest in American music can afford to be without this album.

Schumann, Robert   (1810–1856)

Carnaval, Op. 9; Fantasiestücke, Op. 12; Waldscenen, Op. 82

Rubinstein, piano. RCA Victor 5667-2-RC [CD].

Nowhere is the genius of this purest and most tormented of the German Romantics heard to better advantage than in his works for solo piano. Beginning with *Carnaval*, which in 1834 announced the arrival of a major new composer, Schumann began to evolve an entirely novel form of piano music: a large structure made up of many smaller parts that were tied together by a single, unifying poetic idea. Within this loose-knit "literary" framework that allowed for the widest possible range of musical expression, Schumann produced the most fanciful, wildly imaginative piano works written up to that time. Compared to Schumann, Liszt—aside from the great B Minor Sonata—was a purveyor of empty bombast, and Chopin was a broken record stuck in the same gloomy groove, a mood that H. L. Mencken aptly described as "Two embalmers doing a postmortem on a minor poet; the scent of tuberoses; autumn rain."

Until that most phantasmagorical of all *Carnaval* recordings returns to circulation—a version from the early 1950s by the English pianist Solomon—Artur Rubinstein's Victor recording from the mid-1960s will probably remain unchallenged for years. The playing has ample color and sentiment, and just the right amount of rhythmic flippancy to make the individual pieces leap into life. The "Chopin" section is particularly lovely in its quiet restraint, and the final March of the Davidsbündler (Schumann's society of young, iconoclastic champions of the highest ideals in life and art) against the Philistines (represented by a mean-spirited little waltz) is unusually exciting.

Another Rubinstein recording (RCA 09026-61264 [CD]) that features the pianist's unforgettable interpretations of *Kreisleriana* and the *Fantasia in C* is, if anything, even more successful, while two CBS recordings by Murray Perahia offer subtle, spontaneous, and richly expressive versions of the *Davidsbündlertänze* and the Opus 12 *Fantasiestücke* (MK 32299 [CD]), together with performances of *Papillons* and the *Études symphoniques* (MK 34539 [CD]) in which poetry drips from every bar.

Concerto in A Minor for Cello and Orchestra, Op. 129

**Du Pré, cello; New Philharmonia Orchestra, Barenboim. EMI Classics
CDM 64626 [CD].**

Until Sir Edward Elgar unveiled his masterpiece in the form in 1919, this soaring work by Schumann had the field to itself as "The World's Second-Best Cello Concerto." Even now, the choice of which of these very different works should be ranked just behind the B Minor Concerto of Antonín Dvořák is largely a matter of personal taste: whether one prefers the passionate lyricism of the Schumann or the Elgar's depth and starkly beautiful despair.

For years, the glowing early recording by the young Jacqueline du Pré stood alone among all versions of the Schumann Concerto, and its return to the catalogue cannot be welcomed too warmly. With her performance of the Elgar Concerto, this winsome, ebullient interpretation will remain one of her most enduring monuments, a fitting memorial to a great and tragically short-lived talent.

Concerto in A Minor for Piano and Orchestra, Op. 54

**Vogt, piano; City of Birmingham Symphony, Rattle. EMI Classics
CDC 54746 [CD].**

With Edvard Grieg's A Minor Concerto, a work with which it is almost invariably paired on recordings, the Schumann Piano Concerto represents something close to the finest such work that the Romantic era produced in the form. Moody, sensual, and heroic, it was also one of Schumann's greatest achievements with music cast on a larger scale. Like his admired Chopin, Schumann is still accused of being a miniaturist who was completely incapable of sustaining extended forms; works like the Piano Concerto and the four symphonies triumphantly lay *that* nonsense to rest.

With the inspired but slightly insane version by Sviatoslav Richter and Lovro von Matačić currently unavailable and the exhilarating Philips recording by Stephen Kovacevich and Sir Colin Davis recently withdrawn, first choice among the many modern recordings of the concerto is the fine EMI Classics version by Lars Vogt and Sir Simon Rattle, in which the alternately impulsive and introspective young pianist is given refined and red-blooded support by that most consistently imaginative of English conductors. Solomon's classic recording from the 1950s has resurfaced on a two-disc set from EMI Classics (CDCZB 67735 [CD]), paired with equally memorable versions of the Grieg Concerto and the First and Third concertos of Beethoven. In its combination of poetic insight and flawless pianism, Solomon's interpretation of the Schumann Concerto remains unapproached; buy yours quickly before the EMI deletions ax falls.

Dichterliebe, Op. 48; *Liederkreis,* Op. 39

Fischer-Dieskau, baritone; Brendel, piano. Philips 416352-2 [CD].

When in 1840 a cigar-chomping, beer-guzzling, foul-mouthed womanizer named Robert Schumann settled down to the joys of what his near contemporary Friedrich Engels called "that leaden boredom known as domestic bliss," not only the composer's life, but also the history of art song would be altered forever. After a protracted legal struggle with his bride's domineering father, Schumann's marriage to Clara Wieck unleashed an astonishing outburst of creativity, that "Year of Song" in which he wrote most of the works that established him as Schubert's first great successor as one of the undisputed masters of German lieder. Even more than Schubert, Schumann's sensitivity to the infinite shades of meaning in any text was extraordinary, helped no doubt by the fact that the composer, in his youth, had intended to become a poet. At his best, only Schubert and Hugo Wolf are his legitimate peers; even Brahms, Mahler, and Strauss—as important as their songs most certainly are—cannot really begin to approach the scope or quality of Schumann's achievement.

This Philips recording by Dietrich Fischer-Dieskau, like his now-deleted Deutsche Grammophon version with Christoph Eschenbach, is one of the best introductions to this tender, turbulent universe, offering superlative recordings of Schumann's most important cycles, the frequently bitter and desperate *Dichterliebe* ("A Poet's Love") and the marvelous Opus 39 *Liederkreis* (literally, "Song Cycle") on poems of Joseph von Eichendorff.

While Schumann is also being seriously affected by the protracted and frustrating lieder drought we're passing through, a spate of fine recent recordings suggests that relief may finally be in sight. EMI Classics has restored Dame Janet Baker's incomparable version of Schumann's great female cycle, *Frauenliebe und -leben* (CDFB 68667 [CD]). While feminists have taken some undoubtedly warranted exception to this anthropologically accurate by-product of mid-nineteenth-century male chauvinism—the text, by a *man,* wouldn't you know it, says, in essence, that a woman's purpose is to love and serve her husband—the sweetly sentimental songs are so entrancing that you wind up not caring what the wretched words say.

Elly Ameling's equally persuasive way with Schumann is captured on a single Edito Classica CD (77085-2), while one of the rising lieder stars of the current generation, Thomas Hampson, is featured in a pair of carefully chosen, superbly executed collections from EMI Classics (CDC 55147 [CD]) and Teldec (2292-44935-2 [CD]).

*K*inderszenen, Op. 15

Brendel, piano. Philips 434732-2 [CD].

Moravec, piano. Nonesuch 79063-4 [T].

As a performance of Schumann's greatly beloved suite of childhood recollections, the Nonesuch recording of *Kinderszenen* by Ivan Moravec is probably the most beautiful ever made. Its wide-eyed innocence is matched only by its technical perfection, and it is one of several recordings that makes the convincing case that as a tonal colorist, Moravec is the late-twentieth-century equivalent of the legendary Walter Gieseking. Listen, especially, to the utterly unaffected, yet gently devastating performance of the famous "Träumerei" or the ambling miracle he makes of the celebrated opening bars of the piece, which have been pressed into service in recent films from *My Brilliant Career* to *Sophie's Choice*.

Alfred Brendel's recording from the early 1980s is wonderfully natural and unaffected and comes with thoroughly persuasive versions of the Opus 12 *Fantasiestücke* and *Kreisleriana*. Throughout, the playing is consistently thoughtful and imaginative and the recorded sound is excellent.

*Q*uartet for Piano and Strings in E-flat Major, Op. 47; Quintet in E-flat Major for Piano and Strings, Op. 44

Rhodes, viola; Bettelheim, violin; Beaux Arts Trio. Philips 420791-2 [CD].

In addition to the three string quartets that popped out within a few weeks' time, both of these vibrant works date from 1842, which musicologists—for reasons known only to themselves—have called "The Year of Chamber Music," possibly (but only *possibly*) because Schumann produced more important chamber music in 1842 than at any other time of his life. (At college, my astronomy professor, the distinguished Hazel Losh—the only woman, at the time, to have been elected to membership in the Royal Astronomical Society—once amazed us all by pointing out the big red spot that can be seen in Jupiter's southern hemisphere and saying, with a perfectly straight face, "Now this is what we professional astronomers call 'The Big Red Spot of Jupiter.'")

While the Quartet is a spectacularly fine piece, the Quintet is Schumann's greatest chamber work. Not only is it one of the most fruitful and compelling of all his compositions—I've never met anyone yet who could keep their feet from tapping in the dynamic final movement or their jaws from going slack during its incredible double fugue—but also one of the most surprisingly original. For oddly enough, prior to 1842, no one had ever written a significant work for piano and string quartet.

The Beaux Arts Trio and company are meticulous and enthusiastic in both works, and the recordings are vivid and warm. It could be argued that the playing doesn't have the abundance of "character" that Glenn Gould brought to his wildly peculiar collaboration with the Juilliard Quartet, available on a Sony Classical CD (SMK 52684). On the other hand, the "Beaux-o's" performances are recognizably those by musicians from planet Earth.

Romances for Oboe and Piano; *Fantasiestücke,* Op. 73 (arrangement for oboe and piano); Violin Sonata in A Minor (arrangement for oboe and piano); *Stücke im Volkston* (arrangement for oboe and piano)

> **Kiss, oboe; Jandr oboe and piano. Naxos 8.550599 [CD].**

German Romanticism has little to offer in the way of significant solo music for the oboe; these delightful Schumann miniatures are just about it. The Hungarian oboist Josef Kiss proves as good as his name in these gently caressing performances, while the indefatigable Jenö Jandó is as musical and supportive as always.

What a charmer!

Der Rose Pilgerfahrt, Op. 112

> **Soloists, Danish National Radio Chorus and Orchestra, Kuhn. Chandos CHAN 9350 [CD].**

The Pilgrimage of the Rose is a late work, written during the spring of 1851 when Schumann's shortcomings as a conductor were first beginning to be noticed by the amiable city fathers of Düsseldorf. None of the professional problems that were plaguing the composer are evident in this charming, folk-like score, which glows with inspiration from beginning to end. Gustav Kuhn leads an interpretation that emphasizes the cantata's lyrical magic while responding admirably to the colorful set pieces, especially the lusty drinking song and chorus of elves, which draw precise, full-throated performances from the brilliantly trained chorus. Chandos again deserves our heartfelt thanks for bringing a neglected masterpiece to light.

Sonatas (2) for Violin and Piano

Kremer, violin; Argerich, piano. Deutsche Grammophon 419235-2 [CD].

Adolf Busch, the greatest German violinist of his generation, would occasionally program Schumann's A Minor Violin Sonata, but for the most part musicians have tended to ignore it and its D Minor companion piece, for reasons that are difficult to explain. Although the Sonatas were written in 1851 at a time when Schumann was becoming increasingly nervous and irritable as well as gradually losing his powers of concentration, both are unusually fresh and powerful works, showing no sign of the mental disorders that would soon completely envelop him.

Like Adolf Busch, Gidon Kremer is a serious musician with little time for idle virtuosity and he proves to be an ideal exponent of these richly romantic works. With able support from Martha Argerich, he places these brilliant, brooding works where they properly belong: among the masterpieces of the instrument's literature.

Symphonies (4)

Cleveland Orchestra, Szell. Sony Classical MH2K 62349 [CD].

The long-awaited compact disc debut of these famous recordings from 1958 and 1960 is one of the most exciting issues yet in Sony Classical's Masterworks Heritage series. While Szell's recordings of the "Spring" and No. 4 were available for a time on a budget-priced CBS CD, the C Major and "Rhenish" have not been in circulation since the original LPs were discontinued.

Szell's interpretations are models of meticulous preparation and thrilling execution, with some of the most electrifying playing in the history of this storied partnership. Tempos in the outer movements tend to be brisk but never rushed, while the slow movements unfold with an unparalleled warmth and nobility. Although Szell prefers the various "improved" versions of Schumann's orchestration, adding a few discreet touches of his own, the result is an unprecedented clarity of texture and inner line that makes Schumann seem as transparent as Haydn or Mozart. Yet what makes the performances so arresting is their bracing sense of freshness and life; this is high Romantic music making filtered through a great Classical imagination and the results are irresistible.

Schütz, Heinrich (1585–1672)

Christmas Oratorio

Soloists, Oxford Camerata, Summerly. Naxos 8.553514 [CD].

Few tellings of the Nativity story are more quietly moving than the *Weinachtshistorie* by this great German composer of the seventeenth century. The purity of Schütz's setting casts a hypnotic spell from the opening bars, yet given its limited resources the expressive range of the piece is quite extraordinary, proving again why Schütz is the key figure in German music between the Renaissance and the emergence of Johann Sebastian Bach. Even for those of us who consider early sacred music a surefire soporific, the *Christmas Oratorio* is a moving, starkly beautiful work.

Like the now-withdrawn EMI Classics recording by Andrew Parrott and his superb Taverner Consort, Jeremy Summerly and the Oxford Camerata perform the piece with all the simple dignity it deserves, with every subtle nuance—and how subtle they are!—captured to perfection.

Scriabin, Alexander (1872–1915)

Symphonies (5)

Philadelphia Orchestra, Muti. EMI Classics CDC 54251 [CD].

Even by the transcendentally self-indulgent standards of late-Imperial Russia, Alexander Scriabin was an extravagant figure: a musician, poet, philosopher, and mystic who sought to unite music, poetry, drama, and dance into a new visionary work of art he called the "Mystery." Less an aesthetic principle than a theological one, Scriabin intended the "Mystery" to be an all-embracing new Gospel into which all of human experience would be subsumed, a kind of artistic equivalent of Einstein's elusive Unified Field Theory.

Needless to say, no one—including Scriabin himself—was precisely certain what any of this mumbling mumbo-jumbo meant, yet in the process it led to some of the most interesting and understandably decadent music to have emerged from the final years of the Romanov dynasty. Scriabin is at his intensely overwrought best in those final three symphonies, which were naturally given the excessively dramatic subtitles of "Divine Poem," "Poem of Ecstasy," and "Prometheus, the Poem of Fire." While they are not the most completely persuasive recordings that these problematical works have ever received—another conductor of the Philadelphia orchestra, Leopold Stokowski, left some hair-raising interpretations during the 78 era—Riccardo Muti's performances are alert, sensuous, and wholly sympathetic. The two early symphonies come off equally well—no finer recording of either has ever been made—and the playing of the orchestra is a wonder at every turn.

Those who respond to Scriabin's rarefied, deeply personal vision will also want to acquire Vladimir Ashkenazy's brilliant and knowing accounts of the ten Piano Sonatas, now crammed on a pair of medium-priced London CDs (425579-2). If not the ideal performances of all of these challenging works, then they still present a balanced, musical, and immensely well-played vision of an exceptionally interesting body of work.

Shakespeare, William (1564–1616)

Songs, Dances, and so forth, from the Plays

English Serenata. Meridian CDE 84301 [CD].

Along with having inspired more important music than any other writer, Shakespeare was, of course, an incomparable lyricist, as composers from Elizabethan times to the present have discovered to their advantage. This Meridian album, called *Sweet Swan of Avon,* collects thirty-two songs, dances, and instrumental excerpts from actual theatrical productions staged at Stratford-on-Avon over the years, from a pair of mid-eighteenth-century pieces by the "Rule, Britannia" composer, Thomas Augustin Arne, to music for productions as recent as 1986.

When the CD arrived, I initially intended a cursory sampling of two or three items and wound up listening to the entire album at a single sitting. *Twice.* This is easily the most imaginatively planned, beautifully executed Shakespeare anthology in my admittedly vast experience, a collection of largely unknown but unfailingly delightful works that cannot fail to entertain, enchant, and otherwise knit up the ravel'd sleeve of care. So absolutely certain am I that you'll love the album, I'll actually guarantee it. If not completely satisfied (and if you had the misfortune of buying it at a store without a no-questions-asked return policy), then simply send me the CD and the sales receipt (c/o KUSC, Los Angeles, CA 90007) and *I'll* take it off your hands. I plan to give plenty away as presents in the next few years and can always use some extras.

Fat chance you'll want to part with it, though. This one is magic.

Shchedrin, Rodion (1932–)

Carmen Ballet (after Bizet) for Strings and Percussion

Bolshoi Theatre Orchestra, Rozhdestvensky. Melodyia 74321-369008-2 [CD].

In the pre-*glasnost* 1960s some imaginative press people on both sides of what used to be called "The Iron Curtain" were trying to pass Rodion Shchedrin off as the latest incarnation of the classic Russian *enfant terrible,* whose predecessors included Sergei Prokofiev and Dmitri Shostakovich. And there actually may have been people in positions of power who *might* have been shocked by Shchedrin's music—but only those would have been shocked by the music of Lawrence Welk.

The "New Shostakovich" was in reality an irremediably conventional, extremely well-behaved composer—if not a Party hack like Koval, Chulaki, or Khrennikov, then still a man whose music was unlikely to offend the most reactionary *apparatchik*'s grandmother. (How subversive could someone be who in 1969 produced a cantata called—and surely you can whistle its principal themes, can't you?—*Lenin in the People's Heart?*)

The *Carmen Ballet,* Shchedrin's most "original" work to date, is a cutesy, though frequently inspired, arrangement for strings and a ridiculously overstocked percussion section of familiar themes from the Bizet opera. After a half-dozen exposures its charm begins to wear a little thin, but it's fun to hear every couple of years or so. In spite of the fairly harsh recorded sound, Gennady Rozhdestvensky's barn-burner of a performance is to be preferred to the inexplicably sedate and straightlaced readings by Arthur Fiedler on a Victrola cassette or the Angel CD by Gerard Schwarz.

Shostakovich, Dmitri (1906–1975)

Ballet Suites (5); Festive Overture; Katerina Ismailova (suite)

Royal Scottish National Orchestra, Järvi. Chandos CHAN 7000 [CD].

Shostakovich's *Ballet Suites* consist largely of material drawn from earlier works that ran afoul of the official censors. Listening to this entertaining, generally unthreatening music, one marvels again at what totalitarian ears found offensive and rejoices afresh at the collapse of the Soviet Union and its particular form of Political Correctness. Järvi and his fine Scottish orchestra have the full measure of these brilliant, frequently ironic scores, which are treated to a typically rich, wide-ranging Chandos recording. The far more serious *Katerina Ismailova* Suite consists of the entr'actes from the banned opera *Lady Macbeth of Mtsensk* and is also stunningly performed, as is the rowdy *Festive Overture*.

Piano Concerto No. 1 in C Minor, Op. 35; *Chamber Symphony;* Preludes

Kissin, piano; Moscow Virtuosi, Spivakov. RCA 60567-2-RC [CD].

Yevgeny Kissin is one of the latest in that seemingly inexhaustible line of gifted young pianists with which the Soviet Union has peacefully bombarded the world since a diminutive firebrand named Vladimir Ashkenazy burst on the scene in the mid-1950s. Kissin, who like all of his predecessors seems to have unlimited reserves of technique and temperament, is extremely well suited to both the wiseacre exuberance and the unexpected tenderness of Shostakovich's most familiar concerto. Vladimir Spivakov and the more or less aptly named Moscow Virtuosi give the kid admirably pointed support.

For those who believe in the Shostakovich Cello Concertos, the Norwegian cellist Truls Mørk offers a gripping new look at both of them on a Virgin Classics recording (CDC 45145 [CD]) with the London Philharmonic conducted by Mariss Jansons.

Concerto for Violin No. 1 in D Major, Op. 19

**Vengerov, violin; London Symphony, Rostropovich. Teldec
4509-92256-2 [CD].**

Even in an era when prodigiously gifted young violinists are a dime a dozen, Maxim Vengerov stands out. Technically, there seems to be nothing he can't do; temperamentally, he has charm and personality to burn; musically, there is a depth and maturity in his playing that suggests that of the young Oistrakh.

These performances of concertos by Prokofiev and Shostakovich shoot close to the top of the list of readily available recordings. Only Oistrakh brought more conviction and authority to the music, and Vengerov was barely into his twenties when the recordings were made. His subsequent recording of the Tchaikovsky and Glazunov concertos with Abbado and the Berlin Philharmonic (4509-90881-2 [CD]) proves that this award-winning album was certainly no fluke, and future installments should be awaited with the keenest anticipation.

Lady Macbeth of Mtsensk

> Vishnevskaya, Finnilä, Gedda, Petkov, Haugland, Ambrosian Opera
> Chorus, London Philharmonic, Rostropovich. EMI Classics CDCB
> 49955 [CD].

The success of the first Moscow production of *Lady Macbeth of Mtsensk* was such that in January of 1936 the opera-loving Joseph Stalin went to the Bolshoi to find out what all the shouting was about. He didn't like what he heard, as *Pravda* explained in the infamous article, "Muddle instead of Music." In the first of the composer's public denunciations, *Lady Macbeth* was accused of "modernism," "leftism," and "discordance," thus forcing the dazed Shostakovich to cancel the upcoming premiere of the *really* discordant Fourth Symphony and begin planning his great public "apology," the Fifth.

As usual, Joe got it dead wrong. *Lady Macbeth* is not only one of the most powerful twentieth-century stage works but is also a Russian opera whose originality and intensity places it in the company of Mussorgsky's *Boris Godunov*. As the murderous heroine, Galina Vishnevskaya gives one of her most thrilling recorded performances, this in a role where her customary hooting and bellowing actually add to the characterization (a Vishnevskaya Norma or Mimi—perish the thought—would be an entirely different matter). The conducting of her sometime husband, Mstislav Rostropovich, is also more impressive than it has ever been before, with moments of singular beauty alternating with moments of shattering power. The supporting cast is uniformly excellent and the recorded sound will stand your hair on end.

String Quartets (15)

> Borodin String Quartet. Melodiya 74321-40711-2 [CD].

If there was ever the slightest question that the fifteen string quartets of Dmitri Shostakovich rank not only with the major chamber works of the twentieth century but also with the most significant works in the form since Beethoven, then this triumphant recording by the Borodin String Quartet should lay all remaining doubts to rest. Begun in 1935, when the composer already had four symphonies to his credit, the quartets eventually became—as they had for Beethoven before him—the vehicle for expressing his most private thoughts and emotions. (Nevertheless, Shostakovich vigorously discouraged any suggestion that the symphonies were the public statements of the "official" Shostakovich and that the quartets were the ruminations of the introverted, painfully shy man within.

However, given that some of the early quartets are genuinely symphonic in their structure and expression, and some of the later symphonies are almost chamber-like in their size and proportions, the over-simplified generalization seems to fit.)

For a time, a superb series of all fifteen quartets in performances by England's Fitzwilliam Quartet was available domestically on Oiseau-Lyre, and they have recently resurfaced on a set of London compact discs. As fine as those interpretations certainly were, they have now been superseded by the incredible, and probably historic, version by the Borodin Quartet. Having studied with the composer extensively (they were his favorite chamber ensemble after the celebrated Beethoven Quartet, which gave most of these quartets their world premieres), the Borodins bring an incomparable authority and understanding to the music that no other ensemble can begin to rival. They also possess one of the most individual physical sounds in the musical world today: a sound that is at once rich and sparse, pointed and flexible, from a collection of clearly defined individuals who work as a completely unified, indissoluble whole.

With the exception of the autobiographical Eighth Quartet—with its programmatic allusions to the Second World War and quotations from many of the composer's previous works—none of these extraordinary pieces has yet to enter the standard chamber repertoire, nor are they likely to do so any time soon. Still, they represent as individual and uncompromising a body of work as has been produced so far in this century: from the formal complexity of the early works, to the wrenching, often lugubrious death throes of the final works in the series. The Quartet No. 15, for instance, is a series of six unrelentingly gloomy *adagios,* all cast in the key of E-flat minor. In short, while this is certainly not a series of recordings that will appeal to admirers of the *1812 Overture* and *Victory at Sea,* it represents one of the most daring and significant projects in recent recording history.

Symphony No. 1, Op. 10

London Philharmonic, Haitink. London 414667-2 [CD].

There is a case to be made that Dmitri Shostakovich never wrote a more audaciously original work than this youthful masterpiece, composed as a graduation exercise from the Leningrad Conservatory when he was only nineteen. In it, many of the Shostakovich hallmarks—the sardonic humor, the grand gestures, the often brilliantly eccentric orchestration—are clearly in evidence, together with a freshness and almost palpable joy in the act of composition that none of his fourteen subsequent symphonies would ever really recapture. (Within several years of its premiere, the Symphony had made Shostakovich a world-famous figure and hence, from the mid-1920s onward, a man that Soviet officialdom would try to keep on an increasingly tighter leash.)

Bernard Haitink's excellent London recording is easily the first choice among all versions on compact disc. While less immediate and personal than the Bernstein recording on Deutsche Grammophon, it is nevertheless a powerful, deeply committed reading, and one that is exceptionally well played and recorded.

Symphony No. 4 in C Minor, Op. 43

City of Birmingham Symphony, Rattle. EMI Classics CDC 55473 [CD].

In the wake of the scandal that surrounded the *Pravda* attack on *Lady Macbeth of Mtsensk,* Shostakovich wisely canceled the scheduled premiere of the Fourth Symphony, refusing to let it be seen or heard until the modest "thaw" in Soviet artistic policies during the early 1960s. And it's a good thing he did. The Fourth is perhaps the most aggressively modern of the composer's major scores: mysterious, bitter, frequently brutal—the single loudest thing I've ever heard at a concert was a performance Bernard Haitink conducted at Carnegie Hall—it offers many fascinating suggestions as to where Shostakovich's career might have gone had politics not intervened.

If Sir Simon Rattle's eloquent recording might not persuade you that the Fourth deserves to be a pops concert staple, then it offers the most potent argument yet that it deserves to be heard a bit more frequently than it is. Without shortchanging any of the Symphony's angry power, the interpretation makes more of its expressive refinement than any recording ever has. Coupled with Benjamin Britten's roughly contemporaneous and rarely heard *Russian Funeral Music for Brass and Percussion,* this is an intriguing and important release.

Symphony No. 5, Op. 57

**New York Philharmonic, Bernstein. CBS MYK-37218 [CD],
MYT-37218 [T].**

Not to be confused with their second recording of perhaps the most famous twentieth-century Russian symphony—a performance taped on tour in Tokyo in 1979—this is the celebrated recording that Bernstein and the Philharmonic made two decades earlier, after returning from a highly publicized tour of the Soviet Union. The reasons why this remains the most satisfying of all recordings of the Shostakovich Fifth—a work that Bernstein's mentor, Serge Koussevitzky, found as indestructible and universal as the Fifth Symphony of Beethoven—are as clear today as they were when the recording was first released a quarter of a century ago.

The success of Bernstein's interpretation rests on the fact that he refuses to view the Symphony as an ironic or paradoxical work but rather as one that marks the culmination of the nineteenth-century Russian symphonic tradition. Which is not to say, exactly, that he treats the work as though it might have been written by a harmonically advanced Tchaikovsky, but that *does* seem to be the overall impression he wants the Symphony to make. From the crushing opening statement of the principal theme, through the unusually expansive (and expressive) *Adagio,* through the giddy, helter-skelter *Finale,* this is a Shostakovich Fifth that is as direct, vibrant, and openhearted as any large-scale orchestral work that any Russian ever composed.

And if, in light of some of the more recent performances of the work, Bernstein's view might seem a bit *too* Romantic and literal, then it should be remembered that the composer often said that Bernstein was his favorite American interpreter. The New York Philharmonic plays as well as they ever have in their history, and the recorded sound—especially in the compact disc version—barely shows its age.

Symphony No. 6 in B Minor, Op. 54; Symphony No. 9 in E-flat Major, Op. 70

Oslo Philharmonic, Jansons. EMI Classics CDC 54339 [CD].

Even though the B Minor Symphony has no subtitle, this profoundly pessimistic work could easily be called "Music to go out and shoot yourself by." The *Largo* of the Sixth—regarded by some as the greatest slow movement in Shostakovich—is so full of angst and unrelieved anguish that the two slight and apparently lighthearted movements that follow it come off as a sinister, horribly un-funny joke. On the other hand, Stalin and his musical flunkies considered the Ninth Symphony another kind of very bad joke. Following the conclusion of the Great Patriotic War, he expected some grandiose paean of thanksgiving (with Stalin the principal honoree), not one of the lightest and most amusing of all Shostakovich's works.

The Riga-born, Leningrad-trained Mariss Jansons leads compellingly idiomatic performances of both symphonies, each cut from the same cloth as, but by no means slavishly imitative of, those of his teacher Evgeny Mravinsky. The playing of the Oslo Philharmonic is refined and sophisticated, as is the recorded sound.

Symphony No. 7 in C Major, Op. 60, "Leningrad"

Chicago Symphony, Bernstein. Deutsche Grammophon 427632-2 [CD].

Thanks to conductors like Bernard Haitink, Paavo Berglund, Mariss Jansons, Gennady Rozhdestvensky, and Neeme Järvi—all of whom have made dignified, searching, musical, or illuminating recordings of the composer's most controversial symphony—the once wildly lionized, once savagely pilloried "Leningrad" seems well on the way to a general "rehabilitation," to use an expression from the bad old post-Stalinist days. While it can never recapture the phenomenal popularity it enjoyed as a symbol of Soviet resistance during the Second World War, the "Leningrad" is being widely accepted now as a serious, substantial, worthwhile work.

Don't believe it for a moment.

Béla Bartók, who parodied the famous first movement march theme so mercilessly in his *Concerto for Orchestra*, was absolutely right: the "Leningrad" is seventy minutes of understandably shallow, grossly manufactured, spur-of-the-moment junk that no amount of interpretive devotion can redeem.

Leonard Bernstein, in this live recording with the Chicago Symphony, refuses to take the revisionist view of the "Leningrad" Symphony, with predictably enjoyable results. The only *enjoyment* to be had in this bellicose nonsense lies in accepting it for the trash it is and having a good, messy wallow. In a performance even more agreeably vulgar and theatrical than his old New York Philharmonic recording, this is precisely what Bernstein allows us to do.

Symphony No. 8 in C Minor, Op. 65

Leningrad Philharmonic, Mravinsky. Russian Disc RDCD 10917 [CD].

Completed only two years after the windy and prolix "Leningrad" Symphony, the Shostakovich Eighth—with the single possible exception of the Tenth—is undoubtedly the masterpiece among the composer's mature orchestral works. Beginning with one of the greatest symphonic *adagios* written after Mahler, the Eighth is a dark, sprawling, grotesque, and enervating work, a combination of a stark outcry against the terrors of the Second World War and the soundtrack for some unimaginable Hollywood horror movie that, fortunately for everyone, was never made. The reactions that this great and controversial work continues to provoke are perhaps more extreme than those caused by all of Shostakovich's other works put together: Koussevitzky considered it the greatest orchestral work written in this century; Stalin—as well as other infinitely more civilized listeners—considered it unpleasant, irredeemable trash.

The live recording of a performance led by Yevgeny Mravinsky—the Symphony's dedicatee—is certainly worth owning, not only as a souvenir of a great musician but also as an incomparable interpretation. Although as always, Mravinsky's tempos tend to be on the brisk side, these in no way lessen the cumulative impact of the performance: at its conclusion, you do feel very much as though you'd been squashed by a tank, which is precisely the effect the composer intended. It is a great interpretation and one that suggests why the composer entrusted this man with the premieres of so many of his works.

Symphony No. 10 in E Minor, Op. 93

Leningrad Philharmonic, Mravinsky. Erato 2292-45753-2 [CD].

If we are to believe Shostakovich in his posthumously published *Testimony,* then the Tenth Symphony was the composer's rueful, bitter, sardonic reflections on the Stalin years. In fact, the composer even went so far as to tell us that the diabolical *Scherzo* of the work was a portrait of that murderous psychopath himself. Whatever the immediate source of the Tenth Symphony's inspiration, it is one of the greatest symphonies of the twentieth century and one of the most compelling works that a Russian composer has so far produced.

In the late 1960s, Herbert von Karajan, in one of his last palatable recordings (Deutsche Grammophon 439036-2 [CD]), left a staggeringly brilliant account of the Tenth, which has since been superseded by one of his typical smooth-shod monstrosities that is to be avoided at all costs. On the other hand, Bernard Haitink's sober, sobering, yet ultimately triumphant and inexplicably withdrawn London recording showed what an ego of discernably human proportions coupled with an immense talent can do. The performance had a sense of dogged decency about it, as if the conductor felt the need to keep the work as far removed from the obscenity that inspired it. It also had moments of snarling rage and dizzy excitement and was exceedingly well played. One can only hope that it, as well as Haitink's other fine Shostakovich recordings that have fallen under the deletions ax, will reappear on one of London's budget labels soon.

On a medium-priced Erato recording, Mravinsky leads a typically fierce and withering interpretation in very acceptable modern sound. To be sure, it is not a note-perfect performance—toward the end, a few technical chinks finally began to appear in the old knight's armor—but in the main, it is an exhausting and exhilarating experience and one not to be missed.

Symphony No. 11 in G Minor, Op. 103, "The Year 1905"

Helsinki Philharmonic, DePreist. Delos DCD 3080 [CD].

Shortly after completing his Second Piano Concerto in February of 1957, Dmitri Shostakovich began work on a new symphony written to mark the fortieth anniversary of the October Revolution. The actual programmatic content of the Eleventh Symphony would be the pre-revolutionary events of 1905, especially those of "Bloody Sunday," January 9th, when the troops of Tsar Nicholas II opened fire on a crowd of unarmed civilians demonstrating in front of the Winter Palace in St. Petersburg. Although Soviet officials pointed to the Eleventh Symphony as another triumph of Socialist Realism—the Party musicologist Boris Asafiev called it a prime example of "musico-historical painting," a fact that led some to accuse the composer of having meekly toed the Party line—others, like the composer's friend Lev Lebedinsky, heard something entirely different: "True, Shostakovich gave it the title '1905,' but it was composed in the aftermath of the Soviet invasion of Hungary. What we heard in this music was not the police firing on the crowd in front of the Winter Palace in 1905, but the Soviet tanks roaring in the streets of Budapest. This was so clear to those 'who had ears to listen,' that his son, with whom he wasn't in the habit of sharing his deepest thoughts, whispered to Dmitri Dmitriyevich during the dress rehearsal, 'Papa, what if they hang you for this?'"

As in his superb Delos recording of the Tenth (DE 3089 [CD]), James De Preist leads a performance of tremendous power and authority that is also thrillingly recorded and played. While it faces stiff competition from Stokowski's legendary Houston Symphony version (EMI Classics CDM 65206 [CD]), DePreist's is in fact the finer interpretation: more dramatic, more incisive, and—incredibly enough—more colorful. That an American conductor of this stature is not presently at the helm of a major American orchestra—especially when three of the old "Big Five" are in the hands of kapellmeisters—constitutes something approaching a national scandal.

Symphony No. 12 in D Minor, Op. 112, "The Year 1917"

Leningrad Philharmonic, Mravinsky. Erato 2292-45754-2 [CD].

Although Shostakovich had conceived the idea for a symphony dedicated to Lenin's memory as early as 1924 and actually made sketches for a large-scale Lenin memorial for soloists, chorus, and orchestra in 1938, it was not until more than two decades later that the formal plan of the Twelfth Symphony finally took shape. As the composer explained in a radio address given in October of 1960: "In 1957 I wrote the Eleventh Symphony ('The Year 1905') devoted to the first Russian Revolution. Even then, as I was finishing the Eleventh, I was beginning to think of its continuation. This was how the plan of the Twelfth Symphony, which will be dedicated to the Great October Revolution, came about. Naturally, when you are working on a composition about the October Revolution, the first thing that comes to mind is the image of Vladimir Ilyich Lenin. Therefore, the Symphony will be dedicated to both the Great October Revolution and to the memory of Vladimir Ilyich."

Although the temptation to dismiss this most controversial of the composer's later symphonies as banal propaganda is usually enormous—I remember one performance from the 1970s that actually drew laughter from the audience—Mravinsky's searing interpretation is the sort that effectively silences all criticism and banishes all doubts. The playing of the Leningrad Philharmonic in this live 1984 concert performance is so withering in its intensity that the Symphony emerges as one of the composer's most heartfelt (if misguided) utterances, free of any hint of his usual sarcasm and irony. As in the Philips version of the Eighth, the recorded sound is among the best this great conductor ever received.

Symphony No. 15 in A Major, Op. 141

London Symphony, Rostropovich. Telarc 9031-74560-2 [CD].

Even for those of us who consider Shostakovich the most important symphonist of the twentieth century, the Thirteenth and Fourteenth Symphonies are difficult pills to swallow. As great as they clearly are, they are also unspeakably depressing. "Babi Yar," a setting of Yevtushenko's powerful poem on the subject of an infamous Nazi atrocity, and its haunted successor—which is less a symphony than a cycle of orchestral songs on the subject of death—are too painful to be heard more than once or twice in a lifetime.

For those who are inclined to approach them more frequently, Bernard Haitink's Philips recordings are unlikely to be superseded. The performance of "Babi Yar" bristles with anger and savage indignation (417261-2 [CD]), and the exhausting interpretation of the Fourteenth (417514-2 [CD]) is marked by the unusual but highly effective novelty of presenting each of the poems by Garcia Lorca, Apollinaire, Rilke, and the rest in their original languages instead of the run-of-the-mill Russian translations that were sung in earlier recordings. If the purpose was to make this death-obsessed work even more universal, then it succeeded admirably.

If with its peculiar quotations of the *William Tell* Overture and a motif from Wagner's *Götterdämmerung*, the Fifteenth Symphony would seem to be a far less serious work, then it was Haitink's recording that finally demonstrated that the quirks and clowning were only skin deep. Although some of the material still sounds rather thin for a valedictory, Haitink was the first conductor to prove conclusively that Shostakovich's cryptic final symphony was not some sort of elaborate practical joke. Rostropovich, in one of the most successful installments in his Teldec cycle, adopts a similarly serious interpretive attitude with comparably gratifying effects. The playing of the London Symphony is superlative throughout, while the recorded sound is slightly distant but extremely realistic.

Trio No. 2 in E Minor for Piano, Violin, and Cello, Op. 67

Palsson-Tellefsen-Helmerson Trio. Bis CD 26 [CD].

The E Minor Piano Trio might just be the composer's chamber masterpiece; at the very least, it is one of his most powerful and deeply personal works. Written in memory of the composer's closest friend, the brilliant musicologist

Ivan Sollertinsky, who somehow survived both the Stalinist purges of the 1930s and the Nazis only to drink himself to death in 1944, the Trio is an exercise in hilarious anguish, or anguished hilarity—depending on which paradoxical designation you prefer. Its most excruciating moment is the finale, a jovial *danse macabre* that breaks the bonds of conventional gallows humor to enter a previously unexplored realm that can only be characterized as "concentration camp humor."

After more than twenty years, this remains one of the greatest of all Shostakovich recordings. The three young Swedish musicians exposed the bitter heart of the Trio more fearlessly than any ensemble ever has before. While they bring a special insight and finish to each of these problematical movements, it is their performance of the grotesque final dance that will chill you to the bone. In spite of its age, the recorded sound is still a model of warmth and intimacy.

Viola Sonata

Bashmet, viola; Muntian, piano. RCA 09026-61273 [CD].

In addition to being Shostakovich's swan song, the Viola Sonata is among the most pitiless and terrifying works of twentieth-century music: the composer's cold, steady look at his own rapidly approaching death, which he awaits with neither hope nor bitterness, nor even very much emotion. Yuri Bashmet gives a suitably devastating performance of the piece, with playing in the final bars so purposefully drained of life that you begin to wonder how he could have survived it. Although it makes for a thoroughly chilling experience—precisely as though someone had just walked over your grave—it is also strangely heroic: a great atheist's stubborn refusal to even consider the possibility of a deathbed conversion.

Sibelius, Jean (1865–1957)

Concerto in D Minor for Violin and Orchestra, Op. 47

Perlman, violin; London Symphony, Previn. RCA 07863-56520-2 [CD], 07863-56520-4 [T].

In many respects, Jean Sibelius remains the most mysterious composer of modern times. A national hero in his own country while still quite a young man, and a composer who, during his lifetime, enjoyed as much critical and popular adulation as any composer who has ever lived, Sibelius simply closed up his musical shop in the mid-1920s, writing nothing of significance for the next thirty years. (Rumors of a completed Eighth Symphony circulated for more than three decades, although no such work was found in his papers at the time of his death.)

The popular Violin Concerto dates from 1903, the period of some of his finest theatrical music *(Pelléas et Mélisande),* the tone poem *Pohjola's Daughter,* and the Second Symphony. Beginning with a famous early electrical recording by Jascha Heifetz and Sir Thomas Beecham, the Concerto has always been brilliantly represented on records: from an unforgettable performance recorded in the late 1940s by the French violinist Ginette Neveu, to the second of Itzhak Perlman's three recordings to date. Compared to his earlier recording with Erich Leinsdorf and the Boston Symphony, the newer version with André Previn and the London Symphony is at once more dramatic and more relaxed. While tempos, especially in the first two movements, tend to be on the leisurely side, there is nothing in the performance that could be considered even remotely lethargic or slack. The interpretation has a wonderful feeling of expansiveness to it, a performance cast—and executed—on the grandest possible scale. The support that Perlman receives from Previn and his forces is, as usual, exemplary, and the recorded sound is absolutely first rate.

In a fascinating recording for Bis (CD 500 [CD]), the young Greek violinist Leonidas Kavakos offers the recording premiere of the original version of the Concerto together with the final published version of 1905. A far longer, more heavily ornamented work, the early version certainly contains some interesting ideas but in general comes off as an attractive adolescent who still needs to lose some baby fat. Kavakos rises effortlessly to its formidable technical challenges, while Osmo Vänskä and the Lahti Symphony (to say nothing of the splendid Bis engineers) offer first-rate support in both versions.

En Saga, Op. 9; *Finlandia,* Op. 26; *Karelia Suite,* Op. 11; *Pohjola's Daughter,* Op. 49; *The Swan of Tuonela; Valse triste*

Philadelphia Orchestra, Ormandy. Sony Classical SBK 48271 [CD], SBT 48271 [T].

Except for *Tapiola*—which is brilliantly served on a London recording by the Philharmonia Orchestra led by Vladimir Ashkenazy (417762-2 [CD])—this reissue of material originally recorded in the 1950s and '60s represents the most complete and generous selection of Sibelius's shorter works now being offered on compact disc.

The composer himself was a great admirer of Eugene Ormandy's way with his music, and from these classic recordings it's easy to hear why. While the conductor could never be accused of being a Sibelius purist—his interpolation of the Mormon Tabernacle Choir into *Finlandia* saw to that—these interpretations are rich with drama and heavy with atmosphere, from the portentous opening of *Pohjola's Daughter* to the flashing colors of the march from the *Karelia Suite.* If this *Valse triste* might seem overblown to more refined tastes, then the sheer sumptuousness of the Philadelphia strings is very exciting, as it is in the superbly theatrical version of *The Swan of Tuonela,* the best since Stokowski's recording from the late 1940s with English hornist Mitch Miller.

At Sony Classical's "Essential Classics" prices, this may be the outstanding Sibelius bargain on the market today.

Four Legends from the Kalevalá (Lemminkäinen and the Maidens of Saari; The Swan of Tuonela; Lemminkäinen in Tuonela; Lemminkäinen's Return)

Gothenberg Symphony, Järvi. Bis CD 294 [CD].

Unfortunately, the second of this group of four tone poems based on the Finnish national epic was once so popular that many people were unaware that it was only part (and in some ways, the least interesting part) of a larger, superbly dramatic, hugely entertaining score. It has taken some time, but the *Four Legends* have finally begun to come together again into an indissoluble whole, thanks largely to the recording industry.

One of the most brilliant installments in his distinguished Sibelius series for Bis, Järvi's is easily the most impressive recording in a still uncrowded field. The richly atmospheric recorded sound is a perfect complement to these darkly brooding performances; the Gothenberg orchestra again plays its heart out for the conductor, while Järvi misses few opportunities to paint the scenes in the most vivid possible hues.

Another fine Bis collection (CD 359 [CD]) features the lushly erotic *Belshazzar's Feast,* the charming *Swanwhite* incidental music, together with the *Dance Intermezzo, The Dryad,* and *Pan and Echo* in similarly idiomatic, beautifully recorded performances. An anthology of generally lighter pieces (except for *The Bard,* given a powerfully introspective performance) is also delightful (CD 384 [CD]).

King Christian II (suite); *Pelléas et Mélisande* (suite); *Swanwhite:* Excerpts

Iceland Symphony, Sakari. Chandos CHAN 9158 [CD].

While considerably simpler and lighter than the symphonies or tone poems, Sibelius's work for the theater contains some of his most attractive and atmospheric music, from the youthful *King Christian II* and its famous "Musette" ("It should be for bagpipes and reeds," the composer said at the time, "but I've scored it for two clarinets and two bassoons. Extravagant, isn't it? We have only two bassoon players in the entire country, and one of them is consumptive. But my music won't be too hard on him—we'll see to that.") to the majestic score he provided for a 1926 Copenhagen production of Shakespeare's *Tempest*.

The performances that Petri Sakari coaxes out of the Iceland Symphony are as vivid as they are utterly natural sounding, especially in the *King Christian II* music, which includes the *Fool's Song* sung by Sauli Tiilikainen and the first recording of the *Minuet*. The *Pelléas et Mélisande* is also a strong one—moody and superbly detailed—while the five movements from *Swanwhite* make you hope that the second volume will include the rest of the music for Strindberg's play.

Admirers of *The Tempest* music—and pieces like *The Oak-Tree* and *Chorus of the Winds* are among the most enchanting Sibelius would ever write—will find much to admire in Neeme Järvi's recording with the Gothenberg Symphony, one of the most distinguished installments of his massive Sibelius cycle for Bis (CD 448 [CD]). As always, Järvi's conducting is pointed and colorful while his fine Swedish orchestra plays as if to the manor born.

Songs for Male Voice Choir (complete)

Helsinki University Chorus. Finlandia 4509-94849-2 [CD].

Since almost all of Sibelius's vocal music remains *terra incognita*—how many people know he actually wrote an opera called *The Maid in the Tower,* a pair of cantatas with the irresistible titles *Oma maa* and *Maan virsi,* and more than a hundred songs?—here is an unusually alluring invitation to wander down this completely unbeaten path. In addition to a stunning vocal setting of the hymn from *Finlandia* that will snap the goose pimples to attention, the Helsinki University Chorus offers elegant, virile performances of twenty-four other a cappella works whose quality ranges from the merely splendid to the nearly sublime.

Symphonies (7)

Boston Symphony, C. Davis. Philips 446157-2 [CD] (Nos. 1, 2, 4, and 5); 446160-2 (Nos. 3, 6, and 7).

There was a time, not so terribly long ago, when some of these seven extraordinary works were heard with the same frequency as the nine symphonies of Beethoven. In fact, for a time, during the 1930s and '40s, they were probably the most frequently performed orchestral works written during the preceding hundred years. Much of the credit for Sibelius's popularity—aside from the power and originality of the music itself—was due to a group of gifted and tireless champions, including Sir Thomas Beecham, Leopold Stokowski, and Serge Koussevitzky, men whose compelling, highly individual interpretations made the Finnish symphonist's name a household word throughout the musical world.

From Koussevitzky's time to the present, the Boston Symphony has remained one of the world's great Sibelius orchestras. And while several individual interpretations might be marginally preferable—the thrilling new EMI Classics recordings by Mariss Jansons and the Oslo Philharmonic of the First (CDC 54273 [CD]) and Second (CDC 54804 [CD]), and Simon Rattle's dazzling EMI Classics recording of the Fifth (CDM 64737 [CD]) deserves all the lavish critical praise it has received—the BSO's complete set of the symphonies under Sir Colin Davis is one of the best imaginable introductions to the music, either for the novice or for the most jaded of collectors. As a Sibelius conductor, Davis represents a golden mean between the audacity of his predecessors and the somewhat cooler approach of the modern school. All of the strength and cragginess of the music remain intact, though Sir Colin is also meticulous with textures and details. In short, these are performances that, while they remove some of the bark, leave the trees healthy and intact.

The Boston Symphony plays this music like no other orchestra in the world, and Philips's recorded sound, after nearly two decades, remains a model of clarity and warmth. As a bonus, the generously packed, medium-priced recordings include superlative performances of the ever-popular *Finlandia, Swan of Tuonela,* and *Tapiola* and an excellent version of the Violin Concerto with Salvatore Accardo and the London Symphony thrown in as a bonus. All in all, this is one of the few authentic bargains on the market today.

Smetana, Bedřich   (1824–1884)

Prodaná Nevěsta (The Bartered Bride)

Beňačková-Capova, Dvořsky, Novák, Czech Philharmonic Chorus and Orchestra, Košler. Supraphon 10 3511 [CD].

As immensely and eternally entertaining as *The Bartered Bride* certainly is, its historical importance in the development of Czech music is all but impossible to calculate. Prior to *Prodaná Nevěsta,* Bohemia had been widely known as "The Conservatory of Europe," a tiny province of the sprawling Austro-Hungarian empire that had always supplied the courts of Europe with some of their finest musicians. Yet Czech composers, before Smetana, were indistinguishable from their German and Austrian counterparts; many, in fact, in order to secure important positions, Germanized their names.

The Bartered Bride was Bohemia's musical Declaration of Independence. A work that not only was based on decidedly Czech themes but also captured the essential spirit of Czech folk music and dance, *Prodaná Nevěsta* made its difficult, irascible composer a national hero. (While it is the only Czech opera that has entered the standard repertoire of every major opera house, in Czechoslovakia it is revered as a national monument.) Without it, the master-works of Smetana's maturity are virtually unthinkable, and had it never been written, composers like Dvořák and Janáček might never have evolved as they eventually did.

While a number of fine recorded performances of the opera have been available through the years, none can begin to approach the brilliant Supraphon recording that will undoubtedly set the standard for *Bartered Brides* for decades to come. In the title role, Gabriela Beňačková-Capova—the reigning queen of Prague's National Theatre and one of the finest dramatic sopranos in the world today—will probably not be bettered for the remainder of this century. She sings with an ease, warmth, femininity, and freshness that only Elisabeth Schwarzkopf, in a few tantalizing German-language excerpts from the late 1950s, could begin to match. Peter Dvořsky is equally outstanding as the wily hero Jenik, and the rest of the cast—especially the marriage broker of Richard Novák—could not have been bettered, either on records or off.

Although the late Zdeněk Košler's interpretation is as zestful and refreshing as any the opera has ever received, the principal selling point, in a recording loaded with selling points, is the playing of the great Czech Philharmonic. They perform this music as no other orchestra possibly could, and the lusty, brilliantly trained chorus is as rowdy, rousing, and tender as anyone could wish.

Hakon Jarl; Prague Carnival; Richard III; Wallenstein's Camp

Czech Philharmonic, Kubelik. Supraphon SUP 111911 [CD].

Apart from the well-intentioned but ultimately disastrous *Festive Symphony*, which in attempting to placate Emperor Franz Joseph used Haydn's "Emperor's Hymn" as its principal theme, thus effectively consigned itself to oblivion among the freedom-loving Czechs (an adequate if hardly inspired performance of the work is available on Marco Polo 8.223120); this appealing collection offers virtually all of Smetana's significant orchestral music written before and after *Má Vlast*. The earlier tone poems *(Hakon Jarl, Richard III, Wallenstein's Camp)* are full of Romantic enthusiasm and good ideas, while the *Prague Carnival* is top-drawer Smetana, effectively argued and brilliantly scored.

Kubelik's Supraphon recordings are wholly idiomatic and persuasive, with a fine eye for detail and a benign tolerance of the composer's early tendency toward melodramatic overstatement (the wonderfully corny off-stage bugle calls in

Wallenstein's Camp are especially effective). The Bavarian Radio Symphony is at the top of its form throughout, as are DG's engineers.

Má Vlast (My Fatherland)

Czech Philharmonic, Kubelik. Supraphon 111208 [CD].

Smetana began work on what would prove to be his only major contribution to symphonic thought in the same week of 1874 that he resigned his post as Director of Prague's Provisional Theatre. At the age of fifty, the composer of *The Bartered Bride* was totally deaf. What had at first been diagnosed as a minor ear infection proved to be the first symptom of the tertiary neurosyphilis that would also claim his sanity and ultimately, his life.

Má Vlast, his magnificent, uneven, terribly moving collection of six symphonic poems, is perhaps the greatest musical love letter a composer ever wrote to his native country. While *The Moldau* has become justly famous, the entire cycle contains much of the best that the father of Czech music had to give to nineteenth-century music. It is one of the cornerstones of Romantic art, and one of the purest expressions of the nationalistic spirit ever heard in Western music.

As a performance of the cycle, no modern recording has ever managed to efface the memory of those two versions that the great Václav Talich made in 1929 and late 1954. (A third version, from 1941, is one of the rarest recordings that any major conductor has ever made.) Both versions are finally available, the earlier from Koch (3-7032-2 [CD]), the later from Supraphon (SUP 111896 [CD]), each in excellent transfers that merely serve to confirm all the legends.

Among modern recordings of *Má Vlast,* none is more highly charged emotionally than the live performance from the 1990 Prague Spring Festival, which marked Rafael Kubelik's return to his native city after an exile of more than forty years. As in the conductor's three earlier recordings of the cycle, all of which are currently available, this is a large, full-throated, yet deeply poetic reading, made all the more electric by the special circumstances of the occasion. The orchestra plays brilliantly for its old music director and the recorded sound is first rate.

Quartet No. 1 in E Minor, "From My Life"

Panocha String Quartet. Supraphon 11 1514-2 [CD].

London Symphony, Simon (orchestration by George Szell). Chandos CHAN 8412 [CD].

There is no more poignant chamber work in music than this autobiographical string quartet that Smetana completed shortly after he was engulfed by the deafness that would remain with him throughout the remaining ten years of his life. While the final movement, which contains the famous high-pitched E in the first violin—the initial symptom of what would develop into a fatal, agonizing disease—is one of the most shattering moments in nineteenth-century music, the Quartet is in fact a predominantly buoyant and cheerful work. It looks backward to the composer's youth with a charming and gentle nostalgia, and even manages to look forward to the troubled future with great dignity and courage.

The Panocha String Quartet gives a wonderfully alert and compassionate performance of this great work, with a slow movement aching with tenderness and a finale that bristles with excitement. And instead of the inevitable coupling—Dvořák's "American" Quartet—they offer Smetana's rarely heard Second Quartet, which is certainly not as memorable as the E Minor but has its undeniable charms.

George Szell's orchestration is one of the few such arrangements of a chamber piece—Schoenberg's inspired transcription of Brahms's G Minor Piano Quartet is another—that actually expands and clarifies the composer's intentions rather than obscuring them. Geoffrey Simon leads a performance full of fire and conviction, which is also as thrillingly played as the old Szell version that was once available on a 10-inch LP. The Overture and Dances from *The Bartered Bride* are also brilliantly done.

Short Orchestral Pieces

Slovak Radio Symphony, Stankovsky. Marco Polo 8.223705 [CD].

For one who used to take inordinate pride in his knowledge of Smetana's music—when prodded at parties, I can give a detailed synopsis of the arcane goings-on in *The Brandenburgers in Bohemia,* complete with musical examples—this Marco Polo album was a humbling experience. Apart from the Polka "To Our Lasses" and some of the orchestrated piano pieces, most of the twenty items on this fascinating album were completely new to me. Yet the blow to my pride was certainly worth it, since there are some marvelous things here: from the *Festive Overture* of 1848, cut from the same exuberant cloth as the ill-starred *Festive Symphony,* to the darkly amusing *Doctor Faust,* complete with a quotation from Bach's *Art of Fugue* and a very recalcitrant trombone, written for a puppet theater production of Goethe's drama. Most intriguing of all is the *Suite from Smetana's Sketch Book,* reconstructed by Jaroslav Smolka from fragments jotted down in a linen-bound volume his wife gave the composer on his thirty-fourth birthday. The CD has delectable performances and first-class recorded sound.

Smyth, Dame Ethel   (1858–1944)

Mass in D; *March of the Women; Boatswain's Mate:* Mrs. Water's Aria

Soloists, Chorus, and Orchestra of the Plymouth Music Series, Brunelle. Virgin Classics CDC 59022 [CD].

Though not, in all probability, a major composer, Dame Ethel Smyth was a classic English character in the manner of Dame Edith Sitwell and Lord Berners. After study in Germany, she returned to England where she devoted herself primarily to opera; Beecham was an enthusiastic advocate of *The Wreckers,* which he introduced to London in 1909 (the world premiere had been led three years earlier by no less a figure than Arthur Nikisch). Smyth was also a gifted writer and polemicist, as well as a passionate leader of the women's suffrage movement, with her *March of the Women* becoming its unofficial anthem. For her services to the cause she was made a Dame Commander of the British Empire in 1922.

It was Smyth's Mass in D from 1893 that established her initial reputation. It is a large, ambitious work that, if it bites off a little more than it can chew, is nonetheless full of good ideas. Philip Brunelle leads a powerfully committed performance that minimizes the work's obvious debts to Beethoven, Brahms, and Schumann, while finding as much of its original voice as there is. The aria from the comic opera *The Boatswain's Mate* is impressively done, although the *March of the Women* comes off rather tame.

Soler, Padre Antonio   (1729–1783)

Sonatas for Keyboard; *Fandango*

Cole, harpsichord. Virgin Classics 59624 [CD].

After joining the Escorial community of Jeronymite monks in 1752, Padre Antonio Soler devoted the remainder of his fabulously productive life to writing, reflection, and composition. Best known for the hundred-plus keyboard sonatas that marked a significant advance in the form he inherited from his teacher Domenico Scarlatti, Soler was also a prolific composer of sacred music and a theorist of genius, whose *Llave de la modulacíon, y antigüedades de la música en que se trata del fundamento necessario para saber modular: theórica, y práctica para el más claro conocimiento de qualquier especie de figuras, desde el tiempo de Juan de Muris, hasta hoy, con algunos cánones enigmáticos, y sus resoluciones*

described how to move from any major or minor key to any other in less time than it took to recite the book's title.

The Virgin Classics album by Maggie Cole is the most attractive single-volume Soler collection currently available, with stylish and exciting interpretations of twelve of the sonatas and the celebrated 450-bar Fandango, whose endless repetitions of an A major–D minor harmonic ostinato may have given Ravel a few hints while writing *Bolero*. The performances are so markedly superior to any from the competition that one hopes this might be the beginning of a Soler cycle.

Sor, Fernando   (1778–1839)

Guitar Music

Holzman, guitar. Naxos 8.553340 [CD], 8.553450 [CD].

Kraft, guitar. Naxos 8.553007 [CD].

With his near contemporary Mauro Giuliani, the Spanish-born Fernando Sor wrote some of the most important guitar music of the Classical era: pleasant, melodic, ingeniously crafted pieces that owed much to the example of Haydn and Mozart and treated the instrument as if it were possible for one to do something more than endlessly strum chords. While Sor wrote nothing profound nor particularly important, this is late-Classical Muzak of a very high order, the perfect accompaniment to doing homework or paying the bills.

All three of these Naxos albums are extremely enjoyable. Adam Holzman is an accomplished performer who speaks the composer's eager-to-please language fluently, both in ambitious works like the *Grand Sonatas* and in appealing trifles like *Souvenirs d'une soirée à Berlin*. Norbert Kraft is equally deft in the challenging *Études* and charming *Minuets*.

Sousa, John Philip (1854–1932)

Marches

Philip Jones Brass Ensemble, Howarth. London 410290-2 [CD], 410290-4 [T].

Eastman Wind Ensemble, Fennell. Mercury 434300-2 [CD] ("Sound Off!" and "Sousa on Review").

Concert Arts Symphonic Band, F. Slatkin. Angel 7243 5 66827-2 [CD].

John Philip Sousa and His Band. Delos DE 3102 [CD], CS 3102 [T].

What, I hear you ask, is an entry on John Philip Sousa doing in a book dealing with Official Classical Music? Has the man (myself) no standards? Is nothing sacred? The answer to both of these questions is "No."

If, like me, you find the music of the March King irresistible, then by all means snatch up four of the five finest Sousa March collections ever released. (The other is a collection led by an ace piccolo player and a top-notch bandsman in his day, the late Henry Mancini.)

The playing on this London recording is as sharp as the most demanding drum major could wish. Rhythms are crisp, the ensemble is razor-sharp, and, for a British ensemble, this group can certainly teach us a thing or two.

The first CD reissues of Frederick Fennell's storied Mercury recordings from the early 1960s are unusually welcome, not only because of the impeccable performances but also for the unusual repertoire. While the half dozen "greatest hits" are here, so are *Bullets and Bayonets, National Game, Riders for the Flag, The Pride of the Wolverines,* and other worthy rarities.

Felix Slatkin's old Capitol album, "The Military Band," was one of the joys of my boyhood and now it returns enliven my crusty middle age. The first violinist of the Hollywood Quartet was also a fabulously accomplished conductor, as these spit-and-polish Sousa performances clearly prove. Best of all, though, may be the "Salute to the Services" medley, featuring versions of *The U. S. Field Artillery March, Anchors Aweigh, Semper Paratus* (the Coast Guard march), the Marine Corps Hymn, and the U.S. Air Force Song so stirring they would make the wimpiest pacifist want to enlist.

Needless to say, Sousa's own recordings—and he made quite a few—have a special snap and authority in spite of the vintage 1917–1923 acoustical recorded sound. Together with a 1929 radio speech, the seven marches make a fascinating filler for the splendid modern recordings by Keith Brion and His New Sousa Band.

Finally, Arthur Fiedler never made a finer recording than the version of Hershey Kay's irresistible Sousa ballet *Stars and Stripes,* which is finally available on a generously crammed RCA release (09026-61501-2 [CD], 09026-61501-4 [T]) that also includes Kay's Gottschalk-inspired *Cakewalk* ballet, as well as selections from Bernstein's *Fancy Free* and Morton Gould's *Interplay.*

Spohr, Louis   (1784–1859)

Nonet in F, Op. 31; Octet in E, Op. 32

Gaudier Ensemble. Hyperion CDA 66699 [CD].

Few musical reputations declined more precipitously than that of Louis Spohr, a composer revered in his lifetime and almost completely forgotten in death, except as a kind of archetypal Biedermeier composer: sober, self-satisfied, irretrievably middle-class. As a matter of fact, poor Spohr has gotten an unfair rap. Not only was he an important innovator whose experiments in leitmotif technique profoundly affected Wagner, but he was also a composer of genuine charm and ability whose Nonet is among the most appealing chamber works of the early Romantic era. The Gaudier performs it with obvious enthusiasm, combining high zest with meticulous ensemble work and attention to detail. With a fascinating third movement that consists of a series of imaginative variations on Handel's *Harmonious Blacksmith,* the *Octet* makes an ideal companion piece and offers further compelling evidence for the argument that Spohr's reputation requires yet another second look.

Stamitz, Johann   (1717–1757)

Symphonies (5)

New Zealand Chamber Orchestra, Armstrong. Naxos 8.553194 [CD].

The early Classical symphony might have evolved quite differently had Johann Wenzel Anton Stamitz not died suddenly at the age of thirty-nine. Not only did his symphonies crystallize the structure of the form—he was one of the first composers to introduce a second theme in his allegro movements and further divide them into exposition, development, and recapitulation sections—but he also created the first great instrument to play them: the fabulous Mannheim orchestra, whose virtuosity dazzled the young Mozart and caused the English music historian Charles Burney to insist: "No orchestra in the world has ever surpassed the Mannheim in execution. Its forte is thunder, its crescendo a cataract, its diminuendo is a crystal stream babbling along in the distance, its piano a breath of spring."

The first volume in Naxos's ambitious Stamitz Symphony series—he wrote seventy-four—is an unqualified success. The young New Zealand Chamber Orchestra is a highly responsive ensemble with cultivated strings and extremely personable winds. With unaffected and enthusiastic interpretations captured in warmly lifelike recorded sound, future installments of yet another outstanding Naxos series are awaited with eager anticipation.

Stanford, Sir Charles Villiers

(1852–1924)

Irish Rhapsodies (6)

Ulster Orchestra, Handley. Chandos Enchant CHAN 7002 [CD].

If his music has always been overshadowed by that of his great contemporary Sir Edward Elgar, then no individual did more for the modern revival of serious English music than did the Dublin-born Sir Charles Villiers Stanford. A composer of considerable depth and refinement whose symphonies owed much to the example of Brahms, Stanford was a teacher of genius whose pupils included virtually every significant British composer from the generation of Vaughan Williams, Holst, Howells, and Bridge to that of Constant Lambert and E. J. Moeran.

The best entry point into Stanford's ripely romantic but well-ordered world are the six *Irish Rhapsodies* he composed between 1901 and 1916. With their inspired use of familiar and not-so-familiar Irish folk tunes—including a stirring appearance of the celebrated *Londonderry Air* in the *Irish Rhapsody No. 1*—these are all attractive, memorable works that deserve to be far better known. Originally released as filler for Vernon Handley's recordings of the Stanford symphonies, Chandos has shrewdly repackaged them on a handsome two-CD set that includes Stanford's stalwart Clarinet Concerto and the stirring *Concert Piece for Organ and Orchestra* (in fact, an ensemble made up of brass, strings, and percussion). The performances, like the recorded sound, could hardly be improved.

Those wishing to take the more daunting step into Stanford's handsomely made yet resolutely Teutonic symphonies are directed to begin their investigations with the Third, the "Irish" Symphony (CHAN 8545 [CD]), which, as the title implies, draws on the same inspiration and thematic material that informs the *Rhapsodies*.

Steiner, Max   (1888–1971)

Film Music

**National Philharmonic, Gerhardt. RCA 0136-2-RG [CD],
0136-4-RG [T].**

After studies in his native Vienna, where his teachers included Gustav Mahler, Maximillian Raoul Walter Steiner emigrated to America in 1914, working as a Broadway arranger and conductor. In 1929, he moved to Hollywood and with his early scores for *Cimarron, A Bill of Divorcement,* and preeminently *King Kong,* he invented film music. With well over three hundred scores to his credit, he was not only the most prolific composer in screen history but was also the most versatile, moving effortlessly from sumptuous Bette Davis love themes influenced by the music of his godfather, Richard Strauss, to cynical *film noir* classics for Bogart and Cagney. In his seventies, he even managed to produce a #1 Top Forty hit with the theme from *A Summer Place.*

Charles Gerhardt's RCA collection suggests the astounding range of Steiner's output, with carefully chosen excerpts from *King Kong, The Big Sleep, The Charge of the Light Brigade, The Fountainhead, Now Voyager,* and others, all performed and recorded to the usual high standards of RCA's "Classic Film Scores" series. Although Gerhardt's brilliant version of Steiner's most famous score, *Gone with the Wind,* is currently unavailable, Fred Steiner—no relation, but a hugely gifted, much-admired film composer in his own right—leads an electrifying performance of the score from *King Kong,* reissued on Label "X" ("Cinema Maestro series" LXCD 7 [CD]).

Stenhammar, Wilhelm (1871–1927)

Symphonies (2)

Gothenberg Symphony, Järvi. Bis CD 714/716 [CD].

Like his friends Jean Sibelius and Carl Nielsen, the Swedish Wilhelm Stenhammar is revered by his fellow countrymen as the first great voice of their national music, the largely self-taught composer whose hymn *Sverige* (Sweden) enjoys the status of an unofficial national anthem. Although Stenhammar began composing under Wagner's spell, he soon began to incorporate folk materials into his music; an intensive study of Beethoven led to a more rigorous formal approach in the works written from the turn of the century onward, especially evident in the once hugely popular Second Piano Concerto, the two Symphonies, and his masterpiece, the *Serenade in F.*

While the First Symphony of 1902–1903 is partially indebted to Brahms and Bruckner, it is a freshly invigorating work with plenty of Nordic character and is given a typically crisp and alert performance by Järvi and Stenhammar's old band. The Second Symphony of 1911–1915 is an even stronger piece: virile, full-throated, openhearted, with a complete lack of pretension and very few wasted notes. The welcome filler is the stirring *Excelsior!* Overture, which in terms of range, quality, and exuberant scoring, is not far removed from Elgar's *In the South.*

Yet what remains the most attractive Stenhammar recording on the market is a medium-priced EMI CD (CDM 65081) of the Second Piano Concerto and *Serenade in F* in glowing performances from the mid-1970s conducted by Stig Westerberg. Janos Solyom's swaggering, rhapsodic playing in the Concerto is breathtaking, as is Westerberg's work throughout; in fact, you soon begin to wonder why neither of these marvelous pieces has yet entered the standard repertoire. *Florez och Blanzeflor* (Flower and Whiteflower), an early Stenhammar orchestral ballad sung beautifully by Ingvar Wixell, is the enchanting filler.

Sterndale Bennett, William

(1816–1875)

Piano Concertos (4)

Binns, London Philharmonic, Philharmonia Orchestra, Braithwaite.
Lyrita SCRD 204 (Nos. 1 and 3) [CD]; SCRD 205 [CD] (Nos. 2
and 5).

Those who insist there wasn't much happening in English music between the death of Henry Purcell and the arrival of Sir Edward Elgar simply aren't familiar with the music of William Sterndale Bennett. A brilliant pianist and friend of Mendelssohn and Schumann—who praised his "simple-minded, inwardly poetic character" and dedicated the *Symphonic Etudes* to him—Sterndale Bennett abruptly stopped composing in his late twenties, ostensibly to devote himself to teaching. Over the next several decades, he became one of the driving forces in Britain's musical education, becoming Principal of the Royal Academy of Music in 1866. While he eventually returned to composition, the works of the later period never began to approach the freshness and originality of his early music.

Sterndale Bennett's five piano concertos, all written before he was twenty, present a musical voice of enormous promise and considerable accomplishment. While they owe much to the concertos of Mozart and Mendelssohn, they are also astonishingly confident and individual works, full of grand gestures, cracking good tunes, and an abundance of youthful exuberance.

Given able support by both the London Philharmonic and the Philharmonia Orchestra conducted by Nicholas Braithwaite, Malcolm Binns proves an ideal guide to these charming and attractive works. He plays with equal amounts of sensitivity and brilliance, and seems to have an uncanny knack of getting at the individual character of each piece.

Unfortunately, the two CDs together will run you nearly fifty dollars and they won't be available everywhere. For these and other difficult-to-find items you can't do much better than the New York Tower Records (1-800-648-4844), which always seems to have at least two copies of everything.

Still, William Grant (1895–1978)

Afro-American Symphony

> **Detroit Symphony, Järvi. Chandos CHAN 9154 [CD].**

Revered for decades as the "Dean of Afro-American composers," William Grant Still was one of the first musicians to incorporate elements of his African heritage into the symphonic mainstream of European music. His extraordinary and shamefully neglected *Afro-American Symphony* of 1931 was a milestone in the history of American music, and not simply because it was the first modern symphony by an American composer of African decent. In its best pages, it ranks with the finest symphonic works written by *any* American and has finally gotten the first-rate modern recording it has long deserved. Neeme Järvi's performance is both skillful and committed, with a seemingly instinctive feel for Still's jazz-inflected idiom and a firm grasp of the Symphony's sometimes elusive architecture. The Detroit Symphony plays the piece as though they own it and are equally persuasive in the music from Duke Ellington's vivid ballet *The River.*

Still never had a more tireless or eloquent champion than the wonderful American violinist the late Louis Kaufman, whose pioneering recordings are now finding their way into compact disc (Music and Arts CD 638). While the recorded sound of these performances, many of them taken from radio air checks, is understandably variable, the interpretations themselves are marvels of fire, color, and finesse, especially those involving Kaufman's gifted wife, Annette. Either as music by an important American composer or as souvenirs of a great American violinist, the recording is indispensable.

Stokowski, Leopold (1882–1977)

Transcriptions for Orchestra

> **Philadelphia Orchestra, Stokowski. Pearl PEA 9098 [CD].**
>
> **Leopold Stokowski Orchestra, Stokowski. EMI Classics CDM 66385 [CD].**
>
> **BBC Philharmonic, Bamert. Chandos CHAN 9259 [CD].**

Over the years, Leopold Stokowski's high-cholesterol arrangements of the music of Bach and other composers have tended to divide humanity neatly into two warring camps: stuffy, narrow-chested people with names like P. Carter Frandit and Ruth Arlington Phipps, who pamper small dogs, smell of mint, and *despise* them from the opening bars, and the fun-loving, two-fisted, red-blooded rest of us who know a really good thing when we hear it. Designed to introduce concert audiences to music they might not otherwise hear, Stokowski's Bach transcriptions were controversial even in the 1920s; with the advent of the Baroque Authenticity movement four decades later, they became about as fashionable as shaven legs or *pro*-Vietnam War rallies. By that same token, the recent revival of interest in these magnificent anachronisms is also perfectly understandable, since they sound terrific and are a tremendous amount of fun.

The natural place to begin any exploration is with Stokowski's own recordings with the Philadelphia Orchestra from that historic partnership's glory days. The performances collected on a superbly mastered two-CD set from Pearl (PEA 9098) range from the astounding to the frankly unbelievable, as is most of the recorded sound. Demonstration recordings in their day—1927 through 1940—they're pretty impressive even now.

The EMI collection, a reissue of recordings made for Capitol in the late 1950s, also sounds pretty spectacular, especially in the starkly simple arrangement of *Ein feste Burg ist unser Gott* that rises to a magnificently brassy climax. The lush, unmistakable string textures he coaxes out of this fine pick-up orchestra proves again that the celebrated "Philadelphia Sound" was in truth the "Stokowski Sound."

Matthias Bamert, who served as one of Stoky's assistant conductors during his American Symphony days, has even *more* fun in his splendid album from Chandos. The readings of the famous Bach pieces—the *Toccata and Fugue in D Minor*, the "Little" Fugue, and especially the *Passacaglia and Fugue in C Minor*—have a scale and point reminiscent of Stokowski's own, without being carbon copies. The BBC Philharmonic is irreproachable, as are the Chandos engineers.

Finally, Stokowski's RCA recordings have been reissued as part of the thirteen-CD "Stokowski Stereo Collection" (09026-62599-2 [CD]), which includes some of the greatest recordings the conductor ever made. Here, for instance, is the glorious final version (from 1973) of Dvořák's *New World* Symphony—an interpretation bursting with color, character, and dramatic intensity—and that magnificent (and surprisingly straight-forward) reading of Mahler's *Resurrection* Symphony. Here, too, are those astonishingly fine-sounding early stereo versions (with Toscanini's NBC Symphony) of excerpts from Menotti's ballet *Sebastian* and Prokofiev's *Romeo and Juliet*. Badly overloaded in their original LP format, the Chicago Symphony recordings of Shostakovich's Sixth Symphony and Khachaturian's Third have been dramatically cleaned up for the CD, as has the Chicago version of Rimsky-Korsakov's *Russian Easter Overture*, paired now with that quasi-pornographic Royal Philharmonic *Scheherazade*. Even at medium price, thirteen CDs represent a substantial investment. For the amount of entertainment, illumination, and inspiration these provide, it's money well and wisely spent.

By all means, self-indulge.

Stradella, Alessandro (1644–1682)

L'anime del purgatorio

Soloists, Consort of Musicke, Rooley. Musica Oscura MOS 70984 [CD].

Why Hollywood has never filmed the life of Alessandro Stradella remains a puzzling mystery, given that compared to the lives of those who were portrayed in the vapid *Farinelli*, the laughable *Immortal Beloved* (a science fiction cum Harlequin Romance Beethoven biography), or even the marvelous *Amadeus*, Stradella's brief but turbulent history is infinitely more dramatic. From about 1669 onward, his life was a seemingly unbroken series of legal, political, and sexual scandals that would have made his eighteenth-century counterpart Giovanni Jacopo Casanova blush; following an especially embarrassing escapade with a lady of Genoa's powerful Lomellini family, the incorrigible thirty-seven-year-old libertine was murdered in the Piazza Bianchi.

With its strong rhythmic presence, virtuoso writing for both voices and strings, and fondness for harmonic and dramatic surprise, Stradella's music is very nearly as interesting as he was; what a pity so little of it is available domestically. Far and away the best of the easily obtainable recordings is Anthony Rooley's version of *L'anime del purgatorio*—and who was better qualified on *that* particular subject than this notorious cad?—performed with the Consort of Musicke's typically stylish zest.

One hopes that Erato might be persuaded to release their recording of Stradella's astonishing oratorio *San Giovanni Battista* in America (Erato/Warner 2292 45735-2 [CD]), a retelling of the tale of John the Baptist and the Princess Salome that yields little in terms of sexual intensity to the far more familiar version by Richard Strauss.

Straus, Oscar (1870–1954)

Waltzes, Polkas, Marches, and so forth

Budapest Strauss Orchestra, Walter. Marco Polo 8.223596 [CD].

What always looks like a misprint is nothing of the kind, given the fact that in spite of all his waltzes, polkas, and operettas, Oscar Straus—with a single "s"—was not related to the famous Viennese family of composers bearing a similar name. It was Johann Strauss II who advised the young Straus to learn his trade in the provinces, which he did by conducting in smaller theaters, gradually moving on to Brno, Mainz, Hamburg, and eventually Berlin, where he found work as a pianist and arranger in the same Überbrettl cabaret where his contemporary Arnold Schoenberg was so unhappily employed. On returning to Vienna, Straus began to compose a series of increasingly successful operettas, culminating in 1907 with *Ein Waltzertraum,* one of the central works of the Viennese Operetta's "Silver Age" that seriously rivaled the popularity of Franz Lehár's *The Merry Widow.* True to form, Vienna had little use for its immediate successor *Der tapfere Soldat,* which as *The Chocolate Soldier* eventually conquered the world.

Anyone with a taste for Strauss and Lehár will love this Marco Polo album of Straus's waltzes, marches, and polkas. In addition to the famous waltz from *Waltzertraum,* the anthology includes the original German version *(Komm, komm, Held meiner Träume)* of "Come, Come, My Hero" from *The Chocolate Soldier,* endearingly sung by Veronika Kincses. If anything, Alfred Walter conducts with even more obvious affection than in his many fine Strauss albums and the recorded sound is among the most beautiful Marco Polo has yet offered.

Strauss, Johann II (1825–1899)

Die Fledermaus

Gueden, Köth, Resnik, Zampieri, Wächter, Kmentt, Berry, Kunz,
Vienna State Opera Chorus, Vienna Philharmonic, Karajan. London
421046-2 [CD].

More than a century since the first production of *Die Fledermaus,* it is difficult to imagine how Vienna could have been so cool to the greatest operetta ever written—that is, of course, unless you know and love the Viennese. The fact that they were overwhelmingly indifferent to the original production of *Die Fledermaus* in 1874 places it in some very good company. The city was also unqualified in its scorn of Mozart's *Don Giovanni,* Beethoven's *Fidelio,* and countless other new works—proving that although it was at one time the musical capital of the world, Vienna was as reactionary as its brutally despotic emperor, Franz Joseph.

Die Fledermaus has never had a more effervescent recording than London's "Gala" production of the late 1950s. In addition to memorable "star turns" from many of the finest singers of the day in the Act II party scene (Leontyne Price's version of Gershwin's "Summertime" is especially haunting), the rest of the production is an unqualified triumph. As in her earlier London recording from the late 1940s, the scrumptious Hilde Gueden was and remains the ideal Rosalinde—wise, wily, sexy—and captured here in wonderful voice. The supporting cast, led by Regina Resnik as the marvelously dissolute Prince Orlovsky, and the ageless Erich Kunz as the drunken but irrepressible Frosch, is one of the best ever mustered in a recording studio. The Vienna Philharmonic plays *Fledermaus* as only *they* can play *Fledermaus,* and Herbert von Karajan, in one of his last successful recordings, conducts with tremendous joy, delicacy, and verve.

The classic London recording from the early 1950s with the Vienna Philharmonic led by Clemens Krauss has a special magic that no subsequent version has ever really equalled. With Gueden even more fresh-voiced and alluring than in the Karajan recording and an incomparable supporting cast made up of Staatsoper stalwarts Julius Patzak, Anton Dermota, Wilma Lipp, Kurt Preger, Sieglinde Wagner, and Herr Doktor Alfred Poell—who began his career as a voice doctor and ended it as one of Vienna's best-loved baritones—this is a *Fledermaus* that fizzes and bubbles in every bar.

Waltzes, Polkas, and so forth

Vienna Philharmonic, Boskovsky. London 443473-2 [CD].

Vienna Johann Strauss Orchestra, Boskovsky. EMI Classics CDC 47052 [CD]; CDE 67788 [CD].

Boston Pops, Fiedler. RCA 09026-61688-2 [CD], 09026-61688-4 [T].

Chicago Symphony, Reiner. RCA Victor 09026-68160-2 [CD], 09026-68160-4 [T].

The next time you hear a serious music snob say something demeaning about the waltzes and polkas of Johann Strauss, tell them they're full of crap. Or even better, haul off and kick them in the shin. Johann Strauss II was admired by Brahms, Wagner, and almost every other important musician of his time. His waltzes are every bit as important, and even more memorable and entertaining, than those of Chopin, and to dismiss them as "light music" or mere pops concert fare is to miss the point entirely. Almost all of them are brilliantly made, ingeniously crafted little tone poems that will undoubtedly survive long after most of the serious music of that era is forgotten.

The recordings listed here have much to offer both the beginning and experienced collector. All of the many recordings made by the long time concertmaster of the Vienna Philharmonic, Willi Boskovsky, are graceful, stunningly played, and close to the last word in idiomatic grace. The generous RCA Victor compact disc of recordings made by Fritz Reiner and the Chicago Symphony in the late 1950s is a bargain that no Strauss lover can afford to resist. The interpretations are full of Viennese lilt and schmaltz, and the performances are more zestful and precise than any others I know. Arthur Fiedler's recently restored Living Stereo collection is similarly indispensable: one of the very best recordings the long-time Boston Pops conductor ever made. These are performances brimming with sex and sentiment, the incomparable Symphony Hall ambiance flawlessly captured in excellent early stereo sound.

Although too massive to discuss in any detail, the Marco Polo series, which intends to record every single scrap of music by the entire Strauss family, is already one of the most astonishing in recording history. While the level of inspiration in the music itself and the quality of the performances are understandably variable, any of the numerous installments can be bought with complete confidence. Each volume tends to mix well-loved favorites and novelties in no particular order; in fact, the slightly haphazard nature of the enterprise is one of its most endearing characteristics. The readings by the various Eastern European orchestras are never less than polished and enthusiastic and are frequently a good deal more than that. In listening—at a guess—to more than half the CDs in the series so far, I've yet to come across one that failed to be both surprising and enjoyable. Would that the same could be said for the usual blind date.

Strauss, Josef (1827–1870)

Polkas, Waltzes, Quadrilles, and so forth

Slovak Radio Symphony, Dittrich. Marco Polo 8.223564 [CD].

Many, including his older and far more ambitious brother Johann, considered Josef the most naturally talented of all the Strausses. Plagued from childhood by ill health—he suffered from a rare neurological disorder that caused excruciating headaches and frequent fainting fits—Josef Strauss nonetheless devoted himself assiduously to both performing and composing, dying a few weeks before what would have been his forty-third birthday. A brooding introvert, he produced waltzes at once more thoughtful and romantic than those of his brother or father, music that at times displays a surprising profundity and an obvious knowledge of the harmonic innovations of composers from Chopin to Wagner.

The fourth volume in Marco Polo's ongoing Josef Strauss series is the most appealing yet, with delicious performances of the *Titi, Jocky, Schlarffen,* and *Wiener Leben* polkas, as well assorted waltzes and quadrilles. Michael Dittrich secures some vivacious playing from the Slovak Radio Symphony and the recorded sound is wonderfully rich and natural.

Volume 5 (8.223565 [CD] is also a clear-cut winner, with Christian Pollack and the Slovak State Philharmonic giving convincingly Viennese performances of charmers like the *Marketenderin* Polka—one of music's rare tributes to a prostitute, the "camp follower" of the title who peddles her favors to soldiers—and *Dynamiden,* one of the finest waltzes by any Strauss.

Volume Six (8.223566 [CD]) finds the Slovak State Philharmonic playing with infectious energy for John Georgiadis, especially in *Nilfluthen* (Nile Waters), written for the opening of the Suez canal and *Causerie* (Chatting), a polka celebrating the Viennese passion for gossip.

Strauss, Richard (1864–1949)

Die ägyptische Helena

Jones, Kastu, Hendricks, White, Rayam, Finnilä, Detroit Symphony, Dorati. London 430381-2 [CD].

The Egyptian Helen, the second of the Strauss-Hofmannsthal "Greek" operas that continues the story of Helen of Troy and her betrayed husband, Menalaus, in the aftermath of the Trojan War, was originally intended as an Offenbach-like comedy and, indeed, the first act contains some of the most light-hearted music that Strauss ever composed. Alas, in Act II his moody collaborator became increasingly serious and philosophical, with an end result that never quite hangs together. Whatever the opera's dramatic limitations, it drew some lovely, brilliantly scored music from the composer, as Antal Dorati's ravishing London recording triumphantly proves. Although Gwyneth Jones has her rocky moments as Helen and the Finnish heldentenor Matti Kastu is not ideally steady as Menalaus, Dorati and the ailing orchestra he restored to health and national prominence are in splendid form from beginning to end, becoming the real stars of a flawed but fascinating show.

Eine Alpensinfonie, Op. 64

Bavarian Radio Symphony, Solti. London 440618-2 [CD].

Probably the best thing that can be said about *An Alpine Symphony* is that it is not quite as embarrassing as the *Sinfonia domestica,* which had been written eleven years before. Unlike the homerically vulgar and, in its bedroom sequence, blatantly pornographic *Domestic Symphony,* this loud and aimless hike through the Alps is merely overblown, over written, and dumb. For all practical purposes, there is only one viable theme—a rising, slightly menacing fanfare—which the composer beats to death.

Pervert that I am, I have collected almost every recording of this magnificent trash that has ever been made, beginning with an amazing performance led by the half-mad Oskar Fried that was crammed onto a set of acoustical 78s. Among versions in which you can hear something more than the trumpet and an occasional violin, Sir Georg Solti's outing with the Bavarian Radio Symphony is pretty thrilling, especially in the richly ferocious playing he draws from the orchestra's brass. Along with the fabulous execution and recorded sound—one of London's finest analogue efforts from the late '70s—this version has one more thing in its favor. Since Solti's tempos tend to be brisker than usual, he gets it over with quicker than almost anyone else. The performance has been repackaged on one of London's medium-priced Double Decker albums with Solti's high-voltage Chicago Symphony readings of *Also sprach Zarathustra, Don Juan,* and *Till Eulenspiegel's Merry Pranks* and a fine Vienna Philharmonic version of *Ein Heldenleben.*

*A*lso sprach Zarathustra, Op. 30

Chicago Symphony, Reiner. RCA Victor 09026-61494-2 [CD], 09026-61494-4 [T].

Since Stanley Kubrick's *2001* made it a popular hit, Strauss's tone poem after Nietzsche, *Also sprach Zarathustra,* has had dozens of recordings, most of them with some outer-space scene cleverly placed on the cover of the record jacket. (Say what you will about them, but recording companies are no dolts when it comes to marketing.)

In spite of the flood of new *Zarathustras,* the one that continues to speak most eloquently is Fritz Reiner's phenomenal 1954 recording with the Chicago Symphony. One of Victor's very first stereo recordings, and one of the first recordings that Reiner made with his new orchestra, no one could have expected quite so *great* a recording as this one. The playing remains a wonder of alertness, fire, and whiplash attacks, while the recording—as old as it may be—is as warm, detailed, and sensual as many recordings made in the 1970s. Incidentally, Fritz Reiner was one of Strauss's favorite conductors. This classic recording will show you why.

The CD comes with what remains that most sparkling of all recordings of the *Le Bourgeois Gentilhomme* Suite and Reiner's own arrangement of the *Rosenkavalier* Waltzes. The tape offers the conductor's 1962 remake of *Zarathustra,* which was not quite as superhuman as the 1954 effort nor, strangely, was it as brilliantly recorded. This *Zarathustra* (also available on CD as

6722-2 RG) is accompanied by Leontyne Price's languorous version of the *Four Last Songs* and a stunning account of the Empress's Awakening Scene from *Die Frau ohne Schatten.*

Arabella

> Donath, Varady, Fischer-Dieskau, Schmidt, Berry, Bavarian State
> Opera Chorus and Orchestra, Sawallisch. Orfeo 169882 [CD].

For the last of his operas on a text by his greatest collaborator, Hugo von Hoffmanthal, Strauss returned to the scene of his greatest triumph, the Vienna of *Der Rosenkavalier.* If *Arabella* does not begin to match the earlier opera's sustained inspiration, it has much of the same scintillating atmosphere, to say nothing of a superb libretto and many inspired touches. A fine performance can persuade you that it is the finest of the composer's later operas; a performance as good as this one might almost have you believing it's a good deal more.

Julia Varady has much of the shrewd intelligence and innate musicality that characterized the work of Vienna's first Arabella, the great Lotte Lehmann. Her singing is rich, warm, and irresistibly feminine, and she is offered able support by her real-life husband, Dietrich Fischer-Dieskau, as Mandryka. The conducting of Wolfgang Sawallisch represents his finest work in the recording studio, and the recorded sound is superb. In short, this is the one *Arabella* that seems like anything *but* a cut-rate *Rosenkavalier.*

Ariadne auf Naxos

> Schwarzkopf, Seefried, Schock, Streich, Donch, Cuenod, Philharmonia
> Orchestra, Karajan. EMI Classics CDMB-69296 [CD].

No less a Strauss authority than Sir Thomas Beecham insisted in his book *A Mingled Chime* that in the original version of *Ariadne auf Naxos,* "The musical accomplishment of Strauss attained its highest reach, yielding a greater spontaneity and variety of invention, together with a subtler and riper style, than anything that his pen has yet given to the stage. . . . "

While *Ariadne* has always skirted the edges of the standard repertoire, it has enjoyed a charmed life in the recording studio, beginning with this miraculous version taped in London in 1954. Even those who fail to respond to either the chamber dimensions—the orchestra is limited to thirty-nine players—or the studied artificiality of the play within the play cannot help but be bowled over by the singing of Rita Streich, Elisabeth Schwarzkopf, and the amazing Irmgard Seefried at the height of their powers, or the deft, imaginative conducting of Herbert von Karajan, who very nearly equals the achievement of his historic EMI *Rosenkavalier.*

Aus Italien

Slovak Philharmonic, Košler. Naxos 8.550342 [CD].

A distillation of the young composer's musical impressions of Italy, the sprawling four-movement *Aus Italien* may be early Strauss, but it also contains clear indications of the rapidly maturing style that would blossom two years later in *Don Juan*. Strauss himself always realized *Aus Italien*'s pivotal importance, calling it "the connecting link between the old and the new methods."

The Naxos recording by the late Zdenek Košler is one of the finest the work has ever received, with the Slovak Philharmonic playing with a finish and intensity rivaling that of the great Dresden Staatskapelle under Kempe on EMI. The nature painting in the slow movement is beautifully done, and even the normally prolix finale on Denza's "Funiculi, Funiculà" is much less exasperating than usual. In addition to a stylish version of the second waltz sequence from *Der Rosenkavalier*, the real bonus is the fascinating symphonic fragment Clemens Krauss arranged from the rarely heard opera *Die Liebe der Danae*.

Le Bourgeois Gentilhomme (suite); *Divertimento* (after keyboard pieces by François Couperin)

Orpheus Chamber Orchestra. Deutsche Grammophon 435871-2 [CD].

Strauss's incidental music for Molière's *Le Bourgeois Gentilhomme* and the *Divertimento* after Couperin contain some of the most refined and elegant of his musical inspirations, especially the music for the play, which includes a "dinner" sequence full of musical quotations to suggest what the guests are having (the mutton course is hinted at by a reference to the "sheep" variation from *Don Quixote*) and a fizzing final movement that contains some of the most mercurial music Strauss ever wrote.

The always meticulous, always enthusiastic Orpheus Chamber Orchestra does handsomely by both of these marvelous scores, as do DG's engineers. For the most passionate of *Le Bourgeois Gentilhomme*'s admirers, Gerard Schwarz's recording with the New York Chamber Symphony and Chorus of the complete incidental music for Pro Arte (CDD 448 [CD]) is certainly worth investigating: the performance is bright and committed, though it might prove in the end to be a little too much of an admittedly very good thing.

Capriccio

Schwarzkopf, Moffo, Ludwig, Gedda, Fischer-Dieskau, Wächter, Hotter, Philharmonia Orchestra, Sawallisch. EMI Classics CDCB 49014 [CD].

Although Strauss's final opera has had its detractors—an opera *about* opera and the relative importance of music versus poetry is nothing if not a trifle in-grown, while at two and a half hours, this "conversation piece for music," as its authors called it, can seem more than a little verbose—no modern opera has had a more persuasive recording than this one. If anything, Schwarzkopf's Countess is even more compelling than her Marschallin, a characterization bursting with life as well as infinite shades of nuance and meaning. The rest of the cast is no less ideal, as is Sawallisch's conducting. The remastered monophonic sound, which somehow seems more boomy and opaque than the original LPs, is the only minor disappointment—a very *minor* disappointment in one of the greatest operatic recordings yet made.

Concertos (2) for Horn and Orchestra

Brain, horn; Philharmonia Orchestra, Sawallisch. EMI Classics CDC 47834 [CD].

When Dennis Brain died in his favorite sports car on September 1, 1957, while rushing back to London from the Edinburgh Festival, the world lost not only the preeminent French horn player of the century but also one of its greatest musicians. In the years since his death, players of comparable technical prowess have arisen, but none has managed to combine a flawless technique with such an audacious yet aristocratic musical personality. He was, to use a hackneyed phrase, a one-of-a-kind phenomenon, and it would seem extremely unlikely that we should see his equal again.

With his famous recordings of the Mozart concertos, these versions of the two concertos of Richard Strauss constitute Dennis Brain's most lasting memorial. The actual playing, of course, is breathtaking, but so is the unerring rightness of the interpretations, from the youthful ardor he projects in the early Concerto to the mellow wisdom he finds in its successor.

The highest praise that can be heaped upon Wolfgang Sawallisch's accompaniments is to say that they are completely worthy of the soloist; as a bonus, the CD offers the definitive recording of the Horn Concerto that Paul Hindemith wrote for Brain, with the Philharmonia conducted by the composer.

The composer's overly ripe, phenomenally difficult Oboe Concerto has finally been recorded by the man whose chance remark inspired it. As a GI serving in Germany after the War, John deLancie, later the principal oboist of the

Philadelphia Orchestra, happened to ask the aging composer why he had never written a concerto for the instrument. The Concerto for Oboe and Small Orchestra was the result. Though one could only wish that deLancie had recorded the work in his prime, his 1987 recording (RCA 7989-2-RG [CD]) is a brilliant one and a significant historical document.

Strauss's *impossibly* difficult *de facto* piano concerto, *Burlesque,* is currently best served in another RCA recording featuring the phenomenal, albeit tightly wound, Byron Janis with the Chicago Symphony led by Fritz Reiner (09026-68638-2 [CD]).

Although no one has ever pretended that the composer's youthful Violin Concerto is a particularly original or significant work, someone forgot to tell the brilliant Chinese violinist Xue Wei, who, accompanied by an equally committed Jane Glover and the London Symphony, gives it the most electrifying recorded performance it has ever received (on ASV CD DCA 780 [CD]).

Daphne

> Gueden, Little, King, Wunderlich, Schoeffler, Vienna State Opera
> Chorus, Vienna Symphony, Böhm. Deutsche Grammophon
> 445322-2 [CD].

In many respects, *Daphne* is a perfect living room opera: not much happens in this stately pastoral romp, and its central event—the transformation of the heroine from a flesh-and-blood fisherman's daughter into a warbling tree—is best left to the listener's imagination. Yet strangely enough, of all the late Strauss operas, *Daphne* is also, paradoxically, the least artificial and possibly the most charming. The level of musical invention, while certainly not that of *Der Rosenkavalier,* rises well above the level of decadent, stillborn efforts like *Die Liebe der Danae* and *Friedenstag,* and the central character—in the proper hands—can be one of the most enchanting of Strauss's creations.

The incomparable Hilde Gueden gives a gleaming performance in this live 1964 recording led by the man to whom the opera was dedicated. The rest of the cast is an unusually strong one and Karl Böhm's suave, incisive conducting makes even the least inspired pages come alive.

Perhaps as a memorial to the late Lucia Popp—who never made a more affecting or physically beautiful performance on records—EMI will reissue the brilliant studio recording she made in Munich with Bernard Haitink, but don't hold your breath.

*D*eath and Transfiguration; Don Juan; Till Eulenspiegel's Merry Pranks

Cleveland Orchestra, Szell. Sony Classical SBK 48272 [CD], SBT 48272 [T].

The young Richard Strauss initially made his reputation with this trio of early tone poems, which remain the most popular and frequently performed of his orchestral works. Although there may have been finer individual recordings of each (a live Salzburg Festival recording of *Death and Transfiguration,* led by Victor de Sabata, is so white hot in its intensity that it might melt the plastic elements in your speaker system), no collection of all three has ever been more successful than this one.

The Cleveland Orchestra is honed to a fine state of perfection by George Szell, who leads them through a *Till Eulenspiegel* of enormous wit and character, a *Death and Transfiguration* of great power and grandeur, and a *Don Juan* that is a model of swagger and romance. Given the 1960s vintage, the sound is surprisingly good, although the compact disc remastering, like most of CBS's efforts with recordings from this period, tends to be on the hissy side. This is a minor drawback, though, to one of the great Strauss recordings of modern times.

*D*on Quixote, Op. 35

Tortelier, cello; Dresden State Orchestra, Kempe. EMI Classics CDZC 64350 [CD].

Not counting the shamelessly self-indulgent *Ein Heldenleben (A Hero's Life), Don Quixote* is easily the greatest of the mature Strauss tone poems. The structure—a set of variations "on a theme of knightly character"—is beautifully worked out, the orchestration, a wonder of subtle ingenuity, and the dramatic content (who can forget the final, sliding note in the cello as old Don dies?), among the most powerful and moving of all Strauss's works.

While I continue to have great affection for Fritz Reiner's Chicago Symphony recording, now available on an RCA Victor compact disc (09026-68170-2 [CD], 09026-68170-4 [T]), Rudolf Kempe's 1973 EMI version, part of his complete cycle of the composer's orchestral music, remains in a special category. Although Paul Tortelier's projection of the Knight of the Woeful Countenance is both poignant and heroic, it is the incomparable burnished copper glow of the Dresden Staatskapelle, Richard Strauss's favorite orchestra, that makes the recording unique. Kempe weaves an orchestral fabric of uncommon richness and sophistication, while the analogue recorded sound remains ideal in its warmth and clarity.

Elektra

Nilsson, Collier, Resnik, Stolze, Krause, Vienna Philharmonic, Solti.
London 417345-2 [CD].

In many ways, *Elektra* is the most successful and satisfying of all the Strauss operas. For one thing, it is loaded with all those ingredients that make an opera great (cruelty, horror, bloodshed, and revenge), and for another, it is *not* twenty minutes too long (a charge that has been leveled at every other Strauss opera, with the exception of the equally compressed and gory *Salome*).

There is only one completely acceptable recording of the opera currently available, and a very great one it is. In the title role, Birgit Nilsson gives one of her most absorbed and shattering recorded performances: from the savage confrontations with her mother, Klytemnestra, sung to chilling effect by Regina Resnik, to one of the most beautiful and moving versions of the thrilling Recognition Scene. The rest of the cast is splendid. Sir Georg Solti's conducting is vividly dramatic and intense, and the recorded sound in the compact disc format—the only one currently available—will rattle the rafters of the best-built house.

RCA Victor has issued some generous selections from the opera, together with excerpts from *Salome,* in the classic recordings made by Inge Borkh (my favorite Elektra of all time) and the Chicago Symphony conducted by Fritz Reiner. As much as I tend to dislike operas chopped up into what George Bernard Shaw used to call "bleeding chunks of meat," this recording is a very special one and shouldn't be passed up. (RCA 09026-68636-2 [CD].)

Four Last Songs

Schwarzkopf, soprano; Berlin Radio Symphony, Szell. EMI Classics
CDC 56241 [CD].

Written when Strauss was in his early eighties, the ravishing *Four Last Songs* is the work of a man who, if he was not anxious to die, then was certainly more than ready for death. There is a case to be made that Strauss was artistically dead long before his actual demise in 1949. A nineteenth-century revolutionary who lived to see himself become a twentieth-century reactionary, his music from the 1920s onward became increasingly repetitive and uninspired until he was finally reduced to such drivel as *The Happy Workshop* and the pleasant but featherweight *Oboe Concerto.* With the *Four Last Songs* Strauss dug deeply into himself and the past and became, for the final time, the great composer he had once been: the Strauss of *Der Rosenkavalier* and *Death and Transfiguration,* one of whose themes is quoted so movingly in the last of the songs.

Among all the superb interpretations of Strauss's final masterpiece by Lucia Popp, Arleen Augér, Jessye Norman, and Leontyne Price—to say nothing of the recording of the world premiere with Kirsten Flagstad and Wilhelm Furtwängler that has been slipping in and out of print for forty years—no performance has ever captured more of the serenity or melancholic intensity of the music than the one Elisabeth Schwarzkopf taped in the mid-1960s with the Berlin Radio Symphony and George Szell. Both of these superlative musicians respond to every musical nuance in the score, and the soprano brings a depth of understanding to the words that demonstrates why she was the greatest German singer since Lotte Lehmann.

A generous selection of the composer's orchestral songs rounds out what may be the finest Strauss recording available today.

*D*ie Frau ohne Schatten

Varady, Behrens, Domingo, Van Dam, Vienna State Opera Chorus, Vienna Philharmonic, Solti. London 436243-2 [CD].

Nilsson, Rysanek, Hesse, King, Berry, Vienna State Opera Chorus and Orchestra, Böhm. Deutsche Grammophon 445325-2 [CD].

There are many who consider this heavily symbolic Wagnerian fairy tale the high point of Strauss's collaboration with the doomed, brilliantly accomplished Viennese poet and playwright Hugo von Hoffmannsthal, which is to say an even greater work than *Elektra, Ariadne auf Naxos,* or *Der Rosenkavalier.* There are also those who believe that the composer always got the better end of the bargain, including Hoffmannsthal himself, who is alleged to have confessed to a friend, "How nice it would be if (Franz) Lehár had composed the music for *Rosenkavalier* instead of Strauss." (Apropos of absolutely nothing, the opera served as the basis for one of the most arcane musical bumper stickers I have ever seen. Unlike the amusing, though rather obvious "*Carmen* made Mérimée Prosper," "O Milhaud My," and "The Sugar Plum Fairy made the Nutcracker Suite," this one read "Die Frau ohne Schatten once a day." Think about it.)

Although history has not been especially kind to this most demanding and far-reaching of Strauss's creations, it has had a small but fanatically loyal following from the very beginning; and while it can be an extremely difficult nut to crack, it will more than repay any amount of time that the listener is willing to invest.

Solti's recording is among the most impressive of the conductor's career, a near-perfect fusion of superlative singing, staggering orchestral execution, and ear-popping recorded sound. Yet chief among its many glories is Solti's conducting, which, among his many disappointing recent recordings, is the one that fully recaptures the vigorously imaginative Solti of old. The interpretation is a triumph of dramatic power and psychological insight, in which an almost fanatical attention to detail is wedded to a glorious human warmth and projection of the big Straussian line.

The live 1977 performance led by the composer's old crony Karl Böhm also makes a very persuasive case for the opera. The cast is an extremely strong one, headed by the ageless Leonie Rysanek as the Empress and Birgit Nilsson as the Dyer's Wife. Still, for all the fine, frequently superlative singing, it is Böhm's warm, effortlessly dramatic, infinitely resourceful conducting that best convinces us that *Die Frau*'s admirers could be right. For a live performance, the recording is exceptionally clear and detailed, with both the foot-shuffling on stage and noises from the usually rude Viennese audience kept to a bare minimum.

Ein Heldenleben, Op. 40

Chicago Symphony, Reiner. RCA Victor 09026-61709-2 [CD], 09026-61709-2 [T].

Richard Strauss was not, by any stretch of the imagination, a lovable, or even a particularly likable, man. He collaborated openly with the Nazis from the late 1930s onward, was shamelessly mercenary throughout his life, and was probably the only composer in history whose ego could be compared with Richard Wagner's. The great German conductor Hans Knappertsbusch may have summed it up best when he said, "I knew him well. We played cards every week for forty years and he was a pig."

In spite of the fact that it is one of the most self-indulgent pieces in the history of art, *Ein Heldenleben* is a very great work. The "Hero's Life" that the tone poem celebrates is, of course, Strauss's own. And though we blush for the sheer audacity of the man, he does blow his own horn (in fact, all eight of them) magnificently.

In a heroically crowded field of superb recordings, the one by Fritz Reiner should now be regarded as the very best. Perhaps more than in any of his other Strauss recordings, the Reiner *Heldenleben* is a study in disciplined lunacy: the battle music erupts with a horrible, yet carefully studied violence and the love music is infused with a very overt yet almost gentlemanly eroticism. Like all of Victor's Reiner recordings, this one wears its age with exceptional grace.

Music for Winds (complete)

London Winds, Collins. Hyperion CDA 66731/2 [CD].

This ingratiating Hyperion collection brings together all of the music that Strauss wrote for wind ensemble, from the youthful Suite in B-flat of 1884, to the genially overripe wind symphony "The Happy Workshop" of 1944. Although none of the pieces can be considered great music or even top-drawer Strauss, there is much here that will delight admirers of this composer's music, especially in the consistently captivating performances of the London Winds. Predictably, Hyperion's recorded sound is a model of naturalness and warmth.

Orchestral Music (complete)

> Dresden State Orchestra, Kempe. EMI Classics CDZC 64342 [CD] (Volume 1: Horn Concertos; Oboe Concerto; *Duett-Concertino; Burleske; Panathenäenug; Parergon to the Symphonia domestica; Till Eulenspiegel; Don Juan; Ein Heldenleben*). EMI Classics CDZC 64346 [CD] (Volume 2: Violin Concerto; *Symphonia domestica; Also sprach Zarathustra; Death and Transfiguration; Der Rosenkavalier: Waltzes; Salome: Dance of the Seven Veils; Der Bürger als Edelmann; Schlagobers Waltz; Josephs-Legende: excerpts*). EMI Classics CDZC 64350 [CD]. (Volume 3: *Metamorphosen; Eine Alpensinfonie; Aus Italien; Macbeth; Don Quixote; Divertimento*, Op. 86).

There are several obvious advantages in acquiring Rudolf Kempe's epic cycle of the complete Strauss orchestral music, not the least of which is the budget price tag. Then, too, some of the works—the *Parergon* to the *Sinfonia Domestica* and the *Panathenäenug*, both written for the left hand of Paul Wittgenstein—have no other adequate recording.

Of course, the real reason to buy the set is that it offers nearly ten hours of glorious music in consistently inspired performances by the orchestra with the longest unbroken Strauss tradition of any in the world. Rudolf Kempe was a Strauss conductor of genuine stature, and if some of the performances are probably not first choices—notably, the somewhat underpowered *Don Juan* and the much too literal *Divertimento* after Couperin—then an astonishing percentage of the rest rank with the very best currently available. In the CD transfers, the superb mid-'70s analogue sound retains much of its opulence and only in the most hysterical climaxes begins to show its age. For anyone just beginning to build a Strauss collection, here is an ideal place to start.

Der Rosenkavalier

> Schwarzkopf, Ludwig, Stich-Randall, Edelmann, Philharmonia Chorus and Orchestra, Karajan. EMI Classics CDCC 56242 [CD], 4CDX 3970 [T].

Shortly after his new and dreadful Deutsche Grammophon recording of the loveliest of the Strauss operas was released, Herbert von Karajan, tactful gentleman that he always was, said something to the effect that he was *so* happy to have finally made a recording of *Der Rosenkavalier* with what he has called "an adequate cast." Taking nothing away from Anna Tomowa-Sintow, just what did that slime bag think he had in Elisabeth Schwarzkopf thirty years ago? Chopped liver?

The first Karajan *Rosenkavalier* has all the tenderness, charm, impetuosity, and dramatic tension that his newer recording lacks. And with Schwarzkopf, he clearly has the finest Marschallin since Lotte Lehmann was singing the role in the 1930s. From either the compact disc or the tapes, the recording emerges as what it has clearly been since it was first released: one of the great operatic recordings of the century. The LPs, alas, have recently been withdrawn, and aside from Karajan's hideous new version, no other version of the opera is available in that format.

Salome

Nilsson, Hoffman, Stolze, Kmentt, Wächter, Vienna Philharmonic, Solti. London 414414-2 [CD].

Salome, that tasteful, innocent entertainment whose first Berlin performance Kaiser Wilhelm II *personally* banned, has served as the vehicle for some of the most startling operatic creations of recent years. Montserrat Caballé, whom one would not *immediately* think of as the nubile heroine, made a dazzling recording for Victor a number of years ago that has finally resurfaced on compact disc (6644-2-RG). Vocally and visually, Maria Ewing's recent performances with the Los Angeles Music Center Opera proved a major revelation. In addition to a *Dance of the Seven Veils* in which this disturbingly beautiful soprano did *not* stop, as they usually do, with veil number six (in the original production she wore a G-string under protest; in the revival, she eschewed it, arguing that Salome herself would never have given in to something so ridiculously modest), the final scene was a musical and dramatic tour de force. If someone doesn't record it soon, it will only prove what I have long assumed—to wit, that the recording industry is nuts.

As Strauss's terrifying, oversexed adolescent, Birgit Nilsson gives one of the most powerful performances of her long and brilliant career. The closing twenty minutes, when she has that grisly "duet" with the head of John the Baptist, are among the most terrifying ever captured in a recording studio. Sir Georg Solti, here as elsewhere, lends the kind of sympathetic, though never sycophantic, support of which most singers only dream. The rest of the cast, especially Gerhard Stolze as King Herod, is overwhelming, and the remastered sound will take your breath away. In a word, heady.

*S*chlagobers

Detroit Symphony, Järvi. Chandos CHAN 9606 [CD].

Begun in 1921 as a deliberate tonic to the arcane complexities of *Die Frau ohne Schatten* and the prevailing gloom of postwar Germany and Austria, *Schlagobers* (Whipped Cream) is Strauss's *Nutcracker*: a delightfully frivolous ballet in which the sweets in a Viennese confectioner's shop come to life. The premiere in 1924 was a disaster, largely because Vienna's economy was again teetering on collapse (an earlier bust helped ruin the premiere of Johann Strauss's *Die Fledermaus*) and Strauss was just completing his unpopular tenure as co-director of the Vienna State Opera.

Schlagobers contains much charming music, the best of it extracted by the composer in 1932 for an extended suite lasting about fifty minutes. With echoes of *Le Bourgeois Gentilhomme* and the waltzes from *Der Rosenkavalier*, *Schlagobers* is an unfairly neglected work, as Järvi's witty and affectionate recording clearly attests. The dance rhythms are managed with the utmost skill, as are the felicities of the intricate scoring. As a bonus, the album offers the *München* Waltz, written in 1939 for a documentary film about old Munich that was personally banned by Hitler.

*S*ongs

Fischer-Dieskau, baritone; Moore, piano. EMI Classics CDMF 63995 [CD].

Hotter, bass; Klein, piano. Preiser 93367 [CD].

Norman, soprano; Parsons, piano. Philips 416298 [CD].

Reining, soprano; Piltti, soprano; Dermota, tenor; Strauss, piano. Preiser 93262 [CD].

Te Kanawa, soprano; Solti, piano. London 430511-2 [CD].

It was with song that Richard Strauss began and concluded his career, from a little Christmas ditty written when he was six to the serenely majestic *Four Last Songs* of 1948, composed when he was eighty-four. Although his achievement was not as consistent as that of Schubert, Schumann, Brahms, or Wolf—his choice of texts was not always ideal nor was his musical invention always at its most inspired—the best Strauss lieder rank with the most moving and sinuously beautiful ever written.

Dietrich Fischer-Dieskau's epic six-CD collection of 134 songs is the ideal place to begin investigating this generally marvelous repertoire. Recorded between 1967 and 1970, a golden era in this singer's career when the voice was at its freshest and the singing was at its least mannered, the baritone's understanding and enthusiasm prove irresistible, especially in the gorgeous early songs of Opus 10, 15, and 17.

Although the Hotter recordings were made toward the end of his singing career—in 1967, two years after his incomparable, albeit vocally woolly *Die Walküre* for London—the depth of feeling and nobility of utterance in songs like "Die Nacht" is incomparable. Incomparable, too, are the recordings that Strauss himself made with three of his favorite singers in 1942, especially those with the lovely Maria Reining, one of the composer's favorite Marshallins. The composer proves a sympathetic (and understandably authoritative) accompanist, while the wartime recorded sound is perfectly acceptable.

Among the more recent recitals, those by Jessye Norman and Kiri Te Kanawa capture two of the most impressive voices of our time in peak condition, with Norman at her most dramatically expressive and Dame Kiri at her most seductively feminine.

Symphonia domestica

Chicago Symphony, Reiner. RCA 09026-68636-2 [CD].

Say what you will about the *Domestic Symphony,* it is one of the most shamelessly vulgar musical works ever written by the man who once claimed that he could set anything to music. It traces, in gruesome detail, the singularly banal events transpiring in the Strauss household during an average day, including the composer's young son being given his bath and the composer and his wife fulfilling their conjugal obligations. Many of Strauss's closest musical friends pleaded with him not to publish the Symphony's program; he did, and ever since, the *Sinfonia domestica* has remained his most maligned work.

Fritz Reiner's classic recording from 1956 is so completely spellbinding that you can almost overlook the yawning vapidity of the work itself and simply revel in the phenomenal execution. Even the closing pages, which can seem so overwritten and overblown, have a magnificent inevitability about them, together with a brassy grandeur that will silence all criticism. The recorded sound, like the Chicago Symphony's playing, remains a marvel.

Stravinsky, Igor   (1882–1971)

Abraham and Isaac; The Flood; Requiem Canticles; Variations (Aldous Huxley in Memoriam)

> Soloists, New London Chamber Choir, London Sinfonietta, Knussen. Deutsche Grammophon 447068-2 [CD].

I vividly remember being glued to the tube for the premiere of Stravinsky's "musical play" for television, *The Flood*. Even though I was just a kid and couldn't really make heads or tails out of the music, I was terribly excited by it all and rather shocked that none of my friends at school had bothered to tune in; I even used it as the basis for a lengthy exegesis on Stravinsky at Show and Tell—an ominous foretaste of things to come.

If the excellent performance led by Oliver Knussen doesn't completely blot out my memories of Stravinsky's, then it's good to have this colorful and intriguing work in a first-rate modern performance on a single CD. Alas, the original recording, with its unforgettable contributions from Sebastian Cabot, Elsa Lanchester, and Paul Tripp, can only be had as part of the twenty-two-CD "Igor Stravinsky Edition" from Sony. The versions of the thorny *Abraham and Isaac* and the gravely beautiful *Requiem Canticles* seem both warmer and more approachable than Stravinsky's own, while Charles Wuorinen's *Reliquary for Igor Stravinsky*, based on musical materials Stravinsky was working on at the time of his death, is an interesting and worthwhile homage given an enthusiastic send-off from all concerned.

In all, this is a disc that is certain to make many friends for late Stravinsky—which needs (and deserves) all it can get.

Agon

> London Symphony, Thomas. RCA 09026-68865-2 [CD].

The major work on this attractive and important album called "Stravinsky in America" is *Agon*, the seventy-five-year-old composer's farewell to ballet. Begun in 1953 but interrupted by the composition of *In Memoriam Dylan Thomas* and the *Canticum Sacrum*, *Agon* features a group of dances in which Stravinsky applies a free adaptation of Webern's serial technique to stylized seventeenth-century French dance forms. As the serial episodes are framed by strongly diatonic movements—how exciting the opening C Major fanfares are!—this all makes for a very heady mix.

Michael Tilson Thomas leads a dramatic and beautifully alert performance, easily the finest recording *Agon* has ever received, including the composer's own.

Similarly, the thorny *Variations (Aldous Huxley in Memoriam)* has never seemed more musical and approachable. While considerably less important, the other items are thoroughly delightful, particularly the high-stepping version of the *Circus Polka* and the buoyant *Greeting Prelude,* a series of droll canons on "Happy Birthday to You," written for Pierre Monteux's eightieth birthday. Here, too, are the best available versions of the *Concertino for Twelve Instruments, Scherzo à la russe, Ode, Scènes de ballet,* and that rather funky version of "The Star-Spangled Banner" that was banned in Boston. (Following a performance on January 14, 1944, a Police Commissioner informed him of a Massachusetts law that forbade "tampering with national property," whereupon Stravinsky's arrangement was removed from the music stands.)

*A*pollo; *Orpheus*

St. John's Smith Square Orchestra, Lubbock. ASV 618 [CD].

From the early 1920s, when the Russian "primitive" was busy transforming himself into a Parisian gentleman, to the mid-1950s, when the discovery of the music of Anton Webern lured him, belatedly, into the serialism and twelve-tone procedures of the Schoenberg camp (a "defection" for which many of his closest musical friends never forgave him), the longest and most productive creative phase of Igor Stravinsky's career—the so-called "neo-Classical" phase—yielded many of the finest works that the great chameleon of twentieth-century music would produce.

The 1928 ballet *Apollon Musagète* (Apollo, Leader of the Muses) is one of the purest expressions of Stravinsky's fascination with the musical procedures and disciplines of the past. The music not only projects a cool, detached tranquillity that is perfectly attuned to its subject matter but also manifests a sweet and unmistakable sentimentality of which this tough-minded realist was very rarely accused.

John Lubbock and the strings of the orchestra of St. John's Smith Square are alternately tender and incandescent in this magnificent music and also do very handsomely by the strangely neglected *Orpheus* of 1947, which is an only slightly less inspired score. The sound of the ASV recording is unusually rich and lively.

*C*oncerto in E-flat Major, "Dumbarton Oaks"; *Pulcinella* (suite)

Orpheus Chamber Orchestra. Deutsche Grammophon 445541-2 [CD].

Stravinsky once said, with disarming honesty, "I love Mozart so much, I steal his music." And so, with *The Rake's Progress,* the great "user" of twentieth-century music made off with a complete eighteenth-century number opera modeled on *Don Giovanni*. Rossini, Tchaikovsky, American jazz, Russian folk song, Webern, and the fourteenth-century Frenchman Guillaume de Machaut were all grist for Stravinsky's incredible refracting mill, as were his two favorite baroque composers, Bach and Giovanni Battista Pergolesi. It was music attributed to the startlingly ugly, sadly short-lived Pergolesi that he arranged into *Pulcinella*, the first of his great neo-Classical ballets, and the spirit, to say nothing of the actual letter, of the *Brandenburg Concertos* of Bach that he lifted for the "Dumbarton Oaks" Concerto of 1938.

The Orpheus Chamber Orchestra give predictably polished and enthusiastic performances of the Concerto and the *Pulcinella* Suite. This is prime middle-period Stravinsky, affectionately played and handsomely recorded.

For anyone interested in the complete *Pulcinella*—and it's such a hospitable, thoroughly outgoing work that everyone *should* be interested in it—Richard Hickox's enchanting performance on Virgin Classics's dirt-cheap Virgo label (CDZ 61107 [CD]) is a phenomenal bargain that no one can afford to pass up. If anything, the playing and singing have even more comic bite and character than on Abbado's recently withdrawn Deutsche Grammophon recording, and it comes with a superb performance of the preposterously neglected *Danses concertantes* of 1942. In short, it's a steal.

As is a more recent Naxos recording of the same pairing with the Bournemouth Sinfonietta conducted by Stefan Sanderling (8.553181 [CD]). Were it not for some rather woolly singing from the baritone soloist, this would easily be the preferred recording of *Pulcinella* at any price. Tenor Ian Bostridge dispatches his duties with more flair and sensitivity than anyone who has ever recorded the part, while the work of the young conductor (son of Kurt Sanderling) is so fresh and imaginative that it clearly seems that of a major talent about to bloom.

The Fairy's Kiss

Scottish National Orchestra, Järvi. Chandos CHAN 8360 [CD].

With the possible exception of *Perséphone*, the 1934 ballet with recitation and chorus that eventually led to a bitter mudslinging match between the composer and his collaborator André Gide, *The Fairy's Kiss* is probably the most physically beautiful score that Stravinsky ever wrote. Taking Tchaikovsky's music as its point of departure—Stravinsky always claimed that about half the melodies in the ballet were by his great predecessor, half were his own—*Le Baiser* is a fetching amalgam of instantly lovable tunes (the final apotheosis on "None but the Lonely Heart" makes every audience melt), inspired instrumentation (a graduate seminar in orchestration could be devoted solely to the composer's use of the horns), and that quirky, increasingly sophisticated rhythmic thinking that characterized Stravinsky's work throughout the 1920s.

Neeme Järvi's recording of the complete ballet, which features more than twice the music of the far more familiar *Divertimento,* is a delightful one. If it's not *quite* as good as the composer's own version—and I must admit that my fondness for that recording may have something to do with the fact that it revives fond memories of a performance I once heard with Stravinsky himself and the Chicago Symphony—then it's close enough, and besides, it's the only one available. As they habitually do for Chandos, the Scottish National Orchestra sounds like a world-class ensemble in both the ballet and the fascinating "freeze-dried" arrangement that Stravinsky made of the *Bluebird pas de deux* from Tchaikovsky's *The Sleeping Beauty.*

The Firebird (complete ballet)

London Philharmonic, Haitink. Philips 438350-2 [CD].

At a fashionable party, Igor Stravinsky was once thanked by an effusive grande dame for writing her favorite work, *Scheherazade.* "But Madame, I did not write *Scheherazade,*" he tried to explain. To which the woman allegedly replied, "Oh, all of you composers are so modest."

With Igor Stravinsky's first great popular success, *The Firebird,* it's easy to hear why the poor woman was so confused. In its opulence, drama, and brilliant orchestration, *The Firebird* is a direct descendant of Stravinsky's teacher's masterwork. Only in the closing bars, with its majestic apotheosis in 7/4 time, does this early ballet give any clue to the rhythmic experimentation that eventually changed the course of twentieth-century music.

Although many great *Firebird* recordings have come and gone over the years (including another Philips recording—recently deleted—by the Amsterdam Concertgebouw Orchestra conducted by Sir Colin Davis), Bernard Haitink's London Philharmonic recording remains in a very special category, finer even than Antal Dorati's almost legendary Mercury Living Presence recording, now brilliantly transferred to CD (432012-4). Although best in the ballet's more delicate and poetic moments—surely there has never been a more mercurial performance of *The Princesses' Game with the Golden Apples* or a more tender version of the haunting *Berceuse*—the most dramatic episodes also have a splendid weight and power, including the magnificent final scene dominated by the resplendent LPO brass. Coupled with Haitink's refined and intensely musical readings of *Petrouchka* and *The Rite of Spring,* with Igor Markevitch's benchmark London Symphony recording of *Apollo* thrown in as a stunning bonus, this is *the* Stravinsky bargain on the market today.

The most exhilarating recording of the popular *Firebird Suite* comes from a rather unlikely source. George Szell's Cleveland Orchestra recording (SBK 47664 [CD], SBT 47664 [T]) is full of fire and electricity, with an icy control that must be heard to be believed—particularly in the *Infernal Dance of Kashchei's Subjects,* which would stand a lizard's hair on end. While the *Petrouchka Suite* with Ormandy and the Philadelphia Orchestra that accompanies it is pretty generic, Szell's recording of the Second Suite from Ravel's *Daphnis and Chloë* is another clear-cut winner, with finesse and sex to burn.

L'Histoire du soldat (complete)

> Lee, speaker; Scottish Chamber Orchestra, Friend. Nimbus
> NIM-5063 [CD].

The composer's old friend Lukas Foss has always insisted that *L'Histoire du soldat* was Stravinsky's most utterly original work. And as was so often the case in Stravinsky's career, the mother of originality was necessity.

Sitting out the First World War in Switzerland, cut off not only from his native roots but also from the immense orchestra of Sergei Diaghilev's *Ballets Russes,* the composer gradually abandoned both the Russian themes and the opulent scoring of his early ballets. Convinced that the impoverishment of the postwar world would require a new economy in musical settings, he produced *The Soldier's Tale,* a sparse, sinister morality play accompanied by an ensemble of only seven musicians.

For the producers of this recording to choose Count Dracula to perform all of the speaking parts was both surprising and exceptionally canny. Christopher Lee's close association with things that go bump (and suck) in the night lends an added dimension of eeriness to the supernatural tale; he is also a gifted and versatile actor who turns in a major theatrical tour de force. Lionel Friend and the members of the Scottish Chamber Orchestra prove to be worthy minions for the Count, and the recorded sound is excellent.

The best available recording of the popular Suite is the one by the Los Angeles Chamber Orchestra conducted by Gerard Schwarz for Delos (DCD 3021 [CD]). In addition to the wit and energy that characterized the composer's recently deleted Sony recording, the album offers first-rate versions of Prokofiev's *Classical Symphony* and the Piano Concerto No. 1 by Shostakovich.

*T*he Igor Stravinsky Edition

> Various soloists, choruses, orchestras, ensembles, Stravinsky. Sony
> Classical SX22K 46290 [CD].

Here, on twenty-two tightly packed compact discs, is one of the unique achievements in the history of the gramophone: the bulk of the music of one of the two major composers of the twentieth century in performances led by the composer himself.

Sony Classical's *Igor Stravinsky Edition* is essentially a CD remastering of the thirty-one-LP set originally issued in 1982. Predictably, the sound has been substantially improved, while the performances retain the special energy and insight that the ageless composer brought to his music toward the end of his life.

Aside from the obvious convenience and the handsome packaging, the principal reason to invest in this lavish collection is to acquire the recordings that are not yet available separately. For instance, more refreshing, idiomatic versions of *The Fairy's Kiss* and *Les Noces*—whose pianists were the composers Aaron Copland, Samuel Barber, Lukas Foss, and Roger Sessions—are not likely to be made. Moreover, worthy oddities like the composer's television ballet *The Flood* and his last major score, the *Requiem Canticles,* simply can't be found in any other form.

Needless to say, the investment is a substantial one. But so, too, is both the history and amount of enjoyment that this invaluable document contains.

*M*ass; Les Noces

> Soloists, English Bach Festival Chorus and Orchestra, Bernstein.
> Deutsche Grammophon 423251-2 [CD].

Written as long ago as 1917, *Les Noces,* the "Four Choreographic Scenes" for vocal soloists, mixed chorus, four pianists, and a percussion ensemble of seventeen instruments, has remained one of the most paradoxical and under-appreciated of all Stravinsky's works. An apparently guileless celebration of a Russian peasant wedding, the ballet is in fact one of the century's most audacious rhythmic experiments. It is also an unprecedented study in monochromatic orchestral color. (In addition to the "orchestra" of pianos, bells, mallet instruments, and drums, the voices, with all their barking and chanting, are almost treated as components of an extended percussion section.) Similarly, the *Mass* is a major sacred work that manages to complement without repeating the achievement of the *Symphony of Psalms,* written eighteen years before. (It was this austere yet moving piece that marked the beginning of the end of Stravinsky's association with his old friend, the conductor Ernest Ansermet. Ansermet, who led the world premiere in 1948, was tactless enough to wonder aloud how someone who pretended to be a lifelong nonbeliever—as the composer was doing at the time—could write such deeply spiritual music.)

Leonard Bernstein leads the most expressive and dramatic recorded performances that either work has ever received. *Les Noces* has a driven intensity that serves the choppy, primitive rhythms extremely well, while the passionate simplicity he reserves for the *Mass* makes it seem like one of the key sacred works of modern times.

Oedipus Rex

> Von Otter, Cloe, Gedda, Estes, Sotin, Chéreau, Eric Ericson Chamber
> Chorus, Swedish Radio Symphony and Chorus, Salonen. Sony
> Classical SK 48057 [CD].

With *Le Sacre du printemps* and *L'Histoire du soldat*, the opera-oratorio (its closest approximate formal designation) *Oedipus Rex* is one of the most staggeringly original of Stravinsky's works. Even more than *Pulcinella*, it was *Oedipus Rex*, with the "statuesque plasticity" of its Latin text, that fully engaged the composer's interest in the classical past and launched the neo-Classical phase of his career. Yet for all its stylized aloofness, *Oedipus* also possesses a ferocious power that many later works of the period would not: in spite of the remoteness of the subject matter and the use of a dead language, the emotional drama is intense and immediate, while the musical expression is among the most impassioned in Stravinsky's output.

No recording of *Oedipus Rex*, including the composer's own, has ever been more successful in capturing the paradoxical nature of the piece than the incandescent version led by Esa-Pekka Salonen. A performance of withering power and disarming tenderness, it is also flawlessly played and brilliant sung: each of the soloists easily eclipses all competitors, as do Sony's engineers. At the end, it leaves the listener exhausted and uplifted, precisely as it should.

Orpheus; Jeu de cartes

> Royal Concertgebouw Orchestra, Järvi. Chandos CHAN 9014 [CD].

Of all the fine recordings with which Neeme Järvi has established his reputation as an important Stravinsky conductor, none is more desirable than this one. Written at the height of the composer's neo-Classical phase, *Orpheus* can be an elusive and frustrating work: dry and distant in the wrong hands, or warmly expressive as it is here. Which is not to say that Järvi ever drowns Stravinsky's delicate textures in unwarranted overstatement: the interpretation strikes the perfect balance between sensuality and aloofness, with some extraordinarily deft contributions from the Concertgebouw Orchestra strings. Similarly, all the humor of *Jeu de cartes* emerges intact, without the excessively dry wit that characterized the composer's own recording. Like *Orpheus,* this still neglected "ballet in three deals" emerges as one of Stravinsky's most significant and resourceful scores.

*P*erséphone

Fournet, Rolfe-Johnson, Tiffen Boys' Choir, London Philharmonic Chorus and Orchestra, Nagano. Virgin Classics 59077 [CD].

It's almost impossible to believe that this unutterably beautiful "melodrama in three scenes" sparked one of the bitterest public debates of Igor Stravinsky's career, with the composer and his librettist, the Nobel Prize–winning novelist André Gide, trading vicious insults over the supposed inadequacies of both the music and the text. What they were bitching about is anybody's guess: Gide had in fact supplied Stravinsky with one of the loveliest—albeit purposefully old-fashioned—texts he would ever receive, while Stravinsky responded with some of his most charming, unaffected, thoroughly heartwarming music.

Compared to the composer's own recording from the 1960s, this new version is a revelation. Kent Nagano transforms it into a far more French and sensual work, with obvious musical ties to the later scores of Ravel and Debussy. Anne Fournet reads the spoken narration with far greater sensitivity than Vera Zorina did for Stravinsky, while the orchestra plays with more point and sophistication. Those who have postponed investigating an authentic Stravinsky masterpiece no longer have any excuse, especially since the recording comes with a very fine version of *Le Sacre du printemps* on a separate CD in what amounts to a two-for-one offer.

*P*etrouchka (complete ballet)

London Symphony, Abbado. Deutsche Grammophon 453085-2 [CD].

Given its first performance the year after *The Firebird* made Stravinsky an international sensation, *Petrouchka* not only confirmed the young Igor Stravinsky's remarkable gift but also proved that he was neither a flash in the pan nor a composer who was willing to simply go on repeating himself for the rest of his life. Harmonically, structurally, and, most important, rhythmically, *Petrouchka* marked a significant leap ahead of *The Firebird* and was one of his earliest works that the elderly Stravinsky professed to like. (He often said that aside from some of the orchestration, he found *The Firebird* utterly uninteresting.)

While there are at least a dozen superlative recordings of the ballet available today, the most thoroughly satisfying is Claudio Abbado's London Symphony version for Deutsche Grammophon. No nuance of texture, no quirky rhythm, no elegant phrase or ingratiating tune escapes Abbado's attention. And unlike the composer's own celebrated recording (Sony Classical MK 42433)—a more or less "revisionist" interpretation that tried to prove that the ballet was a little drier, more acerbic, and more "modern" than it actually was—Abbado refuses to deny *Petrouchka*'s Romantic roots and, in so doing, does a great service to both the listener and the work itself.

The Rake's Progress

> Raskin, Young, Reardon, Sarfaty, Miller, Manning, Sadler's Wells
> Opera Chorus, Royal Philharmonic, Stravinsky. Sony Classical
> SM2K 46299 [CD].

The culminating work of Stravinsky's richly productive neo-Classical period, *The Rake's Progress,* is also the composer's most ambitious and controversial work. Inspired by the famous series of etchings by William Hogarth and consciously modeled on Mozart's *Don Giovanni,* the piece is a full-fledged eighteenth-century number opera with arias, ensembles, and harpsichord-accompanied recitatives, a fact that naturally led to charges that the score is little more than decadent pastiche with no real style, expression, or feelings of its own. Balderdash. With a brilliantly witty text by W. H. Auden and Chester Kallman, not only is *The Rake's Progress* among the most tuneful, exuberant, and emotionally involving of twentieth-century operas, but it is also one of the most consistently entertaining.

The composer's own recording of the opera is one of the finest he would ever make, with engaging performances from all of the principals—especially Regina Sarfaty as the bearded Baba the Turk—together with lusty singing from the Sadler's Wells Opera Chorus and spirited playing from the Royal Philharmonic. The recording's principal glory, though, is Stravinsky's conducting, which releases both the lyric tenderness of the score—Anne Truelove's closing lullaby is especially touching—as well as its sparkling gaiety. The 1964 recorded sound remains lively and faithful.

Le Sacre du printemps (The Rite of Spring)

**Columbia Symphony, Stravinsky. CBS MK 42433 [CD], MGT 39015
[T].**

Philadelphia Orchestra, Muti. EMI Classics CDM 64516 [CD].

Le Sacre du printemps is one of the two seminal works, with Schoenberg's
Pierrot lunaire (first performed only a few weeks apart), that began modern
music. While *Pierrot* remains under a cloud of polite neglect, *The Rite of Spring*
has nearly become a pops concert staple. (As early as 1940, a mauled and emas-
culated edition of the ballet was used as part of the soundtrack of that tedious
Disney classic *Fantasia.*)

For one of the clearest and most provocatively objective of all the ballet's
many recordings, the composer's own is irreplaceable. As in so many recordings
of his own music, Stravinsky the conductor—though by this time, much of the
nuts-and-bolts rehearsal work was being done by his protégé and amanuensis,
Robert Craft—sought to tone down the overtly barbarous moments in the music
in favor of greater clarity and restraint. In short, he seemed intent on proving, late
in life, that stylistically there wasn't all that much separating his music from that
of Rossini, Mozart, or Bach.

The approach, needless to say, casts some fascinating light on this great
twentieth-century watershed. But for those who want a vicious, untamed, and
yet-to-be house-broken version of the ballet, Riccardo Muti's Angel recording is a
bracing tonic to the composer's own. The Philadelphia Orchestra plays as though
they were possessed, and the recorded sound will rid you of any loose putty on
the living room windows, and possibly even of the family cat.

Symphony in Three Movements; Symphony in C; Symphony of Psalms

**CBC Symphony, Toronto Festival Singers, Stravinsky. CBS MK 42434
[CD].**

If *Le Sacre du printemps* was not Stravinsky's masterpiece, then the proud,
aloof, deeply stirring *Symphony of Psalms* probably was. Written "To the Glory
of God and Dedicated to the Boston Symphony Orchestra" (Serge Koussevitzky
never forgave Stravinsky that his orchestra was given second billing), the
Symphony is one of the half-dozen great sacred works of modern music. In fact,
with a small handful of companion pieces—Poulenc's *Gloria,* Schoenberg's
Moses und Aron, Vaughan Williams's *Hodie*—it is one of the few works of this
century that has kept the divine spirit in music alive and well.

Stravinsky's own performance from the 1960s has been issued on a
generous CBS compact disc that also features the composer's somewhat Spartan
but always revealing performances of the *Symphony in Three Movements* and

Symphony in C. Here, for once, the composer's predilection for a drier sound in his music than most conductors favored, serves this particular masterpiece extremely well. The *Symphony* emerges with all of its pride, devotion, and admiration (as opposed to adoration) of the Supreme Being blissfully intact.

Subotnick, Morton (1933–)

Silver Apples of the Moon; The Wild Bull

Subotnick (computer music). Wergo WER 2035-2 [CD].

When it was first released in 1966 on a Nonesuch LP, Mort Subotnick's *Silver Apples of the Moon* enjoyed a vogue comparable to the recent success of Gorecki's *Third Symphony*. To date, *Silver Apples* is the only piece of electronic music (apart from the delightful "Switched-On Bach" series of Walter/Wendy Carlos and the oafish excretions of Isao Tomita) to have attracted a substantial popular following, and it remains, with the *Poème électronique* that Edgard Varèse created for the Philips Pavilion Brussels World Exposition—available on a Nuema CD of similar works by Milton Babbitt, Roger Reynolds, and Iannis Xenakis (450-74 [CD])—the single most distinguished work ever produced in the medium. The sheer variety and color of sounds, the range of dramatic expressiveness, and the emotional depth of the piece are little short of astonishing, and its appearance on CD with its 1967 sequel, *The Wild Bull,* gives significant aid and comfort to those who argue that avant-garde music can also be tremendous fun.

Suk, Josef (1874–1935)

Serenade for Strings in E-flat Major, Op. 6

London Chamber Orchestra, Warren-Green. Virgin Classics CDM 59607 [CD].

Josef Suk composed his most celebrated work while still a student at the Prague Conservatory. Impressed by the young man's talent but concerned that both his musical and personal outlook were far too serious, Suk's teacher, Antonín Dvořák, suggested that his grim young pupil "lighten up" with something a bit less earnest than the sternly academic music he was writing at the time. The result was the luscious Serenade for Strings in E-flat.

Although written when its composer was only eighteen and modeled quite consciously on Dvořák's famous E Major String Serenade, Suk's piece, rather incredibly, is the superior work. Although it owes much to Dvořák—the lilting Waltz, particularly, has an unmistakably Dvořákian flavor—the Serenade is also the work of a precocious master, who is melodically and rhythmically far more subtle than his teacher was when his Serenade was written and who projects a melancholy tenderness that is already very much his own.

If no recording will ever surpass the magical ones made by the composer's friend Václav Talich, whose 1938 version is now available on a LYS CD (LYS 036/39), while the 1951 remake is available from Supraphon (SUP 111899 [CD]), then the recent version by Christopher Warren-Green's brilliant London Chamber Orchestra is the best modern alternative. Not only is the Suk given a graceful, if somewhat overly animated performance, but it also comes with delectable versions of the Dvořák and Tchaikovsky serenades, therefore making it an irresistible bargain.

For the more adventurous, a far more important release is the newest version of Suk's masterpiece, the *Asrael Symphony*.

Begun shortly after Dvořák's death in 1904, the symphony was already well underway when Suk's wife, Dvořák's favorite daughter Otilia, died in the following year. The result is a powerful, crippling eruption of grief equal to the greatest requiems in music. Either Talich's pioneering recording (Supraphon SUP 111902 [CD]) or the stunning new version by Libor Pesek and the Royal Liverpool Philharmonic (Virgin Classics CDC 59838 [CD]) will serve to introduce many to a neglected but authentic late-Romantic masterwork.

Nearly as important as the *Asrael Symphony* is the vast symphonic poem *The Ripening*, a bewitching essay in hedonistic (albeit elegantly crafted) pantheism that is probably Suk's most physically beautiful score. On another invaluable Virgin Classics CD (CDC 59318 [CD]), Pesek and the Royal Liverpool Philharmonic perform with commanding skill and utter devotion, as they do in *Praga*, the colorful celebration of the Czech capital that comes as the generous filler.

Sullivan, Sir Arthur (1842–1900)

(Also see Gilbert and Sullivan)

Victoria and Merrie England

RTE Sinfonietta, Penny. Marco Polo 8.223677 [CD].

The life of that Eminent Victorian, Arthur Seymour Sullivan, is a mournful study in the seemingly endless human capacity for self-delusion. To the end, Sullivan remained unshakably convinced that he was an important composer who only wrote those flippant entertainments with W. S. Gilbert to maintain himself in a style to which few composers of *any* sort ever become accustomed. Even a passing acquaintance with Sullivan's "serious" music—the turgidly pious oratorio *The Light of the World* and his positively *lethal* opera after Sir Walter Scott's *Ivanhoe* (the mere titles of cantatas like *The Martyr of Antioch* speak for themselves)—proves conclusively that had Sullivan never met Gilbert, he would be best remembered today for his bellicose, imperialistic, loot-the-world-six-ways-from-Sunday-for-Queen-and-Christ hymn, "Onward Christian Soldiers" and that wilted hot-house flower "The Lost Chord."

Sullivan composed his only ballet as part of the celebrations that attended Queen Victoria's Diamond Jubilee in 1897. Commissioned by the Alhambra Theater in Leicester Square, a house famous for its leggy *corps de ballet* and sensational special effects (fires, shipwrecks, military maneuvers, etc.), *Victoria and Merrie England* celebrated Her Majesty's sixty years in a sweeping panorama of British history and legend, from the adventures of Robin Hood and Friar Tuck to evocations of Christmas revels in the time of Charles II. The final scene, "1897—Britain's Glory," must have been *quite* a sight, as a list of the individual numbers might suggest: "Entrance of the English, Irish, and Scottish Troops," "The Union," "Artists' Volunteers," "Colonial Troops," "Military Manoeuvres," "Sailors' Hornpipe," "Pas Redoublé," "Entrance of Britannia," "The Albert Memorial," and "God Save the Queen!"

Sullivan responded to this heady nonsense with a score bursting with patriotic fervor, catchy tunes, and High Victorian charm, all wrapped up in a fast-moving, brilliantly scored package. Andrew Penny and his alert Irish musicians obviously enjoy themselves hugely throughout—as will you.

A pair of equally engaging companion albums are devoted to Sullivan's incidental music for various plays. Marco Polo 8.223460 [CD] includes the delightful suites for Shakespeare's *The Merchant of Venice* and *Henry VIII* together with an early rarity, some of the music the twenty-five-year-old composer wrote for an 1867 Crystal Palace production of H. F. Chorley's *The Sapphire*

Necklace. If anything, the second volume (8.223635 [CD]) is even better, with the later, more accomplished scores for *Macbeth* and *The Merry Wives of Windsor,* along with five numbers for Joseph Comyns Carr's 1895 verse drama *King Arthur.* There is much here that is both beautiful and memorable, from the Mendelssohnian "Chorus of the Spirits of the Air" from *Macbeth* to the heart-tugging "May Song" from *King Arthur.* Lovers of *Iolanthe, Patience,* and *Ruddigore* will find all of it irresistible, especially with the RTE Orchestra and Chamber Choir in such winning form. Can a Marco Polo series devoted to Sullivan's serious choral music from *The Martyr of Antioch* to the *Ode for the Opening of the Colonial and Indian Exhibition* be far behind?

Three more of Sullivan's most important and engaging serious works, the delightful *Irish* Symphony and *Overture di ballo* coupled with the unpretentious 1866 Cello Concerto in Mackerras's loving reconstruction (the original score was lost in a 1964 fire), can now be sampled on an appealing EMI CD (CDM7 64726) that features the spanking performances led by the late Sir Charles Groves.

Another fine album of Sullivan going solo is Alexander Faris's recording with the Scottish Chamber Orchestra of the Overtures (Nimbus NIM-5066). Sir Malcolm Sargent's recordings—drawn from his classic series of most of the operas for EMI—are also thoroughly delightful, especially at the Classics for Pleasure bargain price (CDCFP 4529 [CD].

Suppé, Franz von   (1819–1895)

Overtures

Detroit Symphony, Paray. Mercury Living Presence 434309-2 [CD].

In some quarters, an enthusiasm for Suppé Overtures (the operas and operettas they served to introduce have long since disappeared) is looked on very quizzically. It is as though the person who professes the enthusiasm tacitly admits a fondness for cheap detective movies of the 1940s, spy novels, and long summer afternoons in front of the television, watching baseball and nursing a few long, cold beers.

I admit that, like millions of others, I am thoroughly addicted to these cornball classics. And with both of the superlative collections by Charles Dutoit and Sir Neville Marriner withdrawn by the philistines at Polygram, pride of place now goes to the suave Paul Paray's Detroit Symphony recordings, made at the dawn of the stereo era. The recorded sound is remarkably fresh and transparent for its age, the performances full of an ageless sparkle and élan.

Suppé-lovers, rejoice. Suppé-haters, in your ear.

To date, Alfred Walter's ambitious series for Marco Polo elicits more admiration than enthusiasm, as the performances rarely rise above the level of competent routine. Predictably, the quality of the interpretations seems to rise in direct proportion to the *un*familiarity of the music, suggesting that Volume 4 (8.223739 [CD]) might be the best place to start. Except for *Morning, Noon, and Night in Vienna,* none of them are exactly pops concert staples, unless the pops concerts you attend feature *Flotte Bursche, Über Berg, Über Tal, Zehn Mädchen und kein Mann,* and some *really* obscure stuff like *Mozart* and *Afrikareise* (African Journey).

Svendsen, Johan   (1840–1911)

Symphonies (2)

Gothenberg Symphony, Järvi. BIS CD 347 [CD].

The Norwegian composer Johan Svendsen had no more devoted admirer than Edvard Grieg, who once admitted that his friend had those two qualities as a composer that he himself lacked: an instinctive grasp of the larger Classical forms and a complete command of the intricacies of the Romantic orchestra. Svendsen's two symphonies are widely regarded as the most important written in Scandinavia prior to Sibelius, far more substantial in content and deft in execution than the four written by the Swedish Franz Berwald. Both were composed early in his career: the First in 1867 when he was still a student at the Leipzig Conservatory, the Second in 1876 during that fertile period when he was also conducting those concerts for Christiana's Music Society that raised Norwegian orchestral standards to unheard-of levels of excellence. Fresh, inventive, wholly distinctive works, they make one regret that within five years of finishing the Second Symphony, Svendsen would abandon composition forever, devoting the remaining years of his career to conducting.

Järvi and his excellent Gothenberg orchestra seem passionately committed to Svendsen's cause, offering playing that is as remarkable for its enthusiasm and affection as for its finesse and precision. The performance of the two *Swedish Folk Melodies* is also very lovely, responding with simple eloquence to these moving little works.

Svendsen's last and best-known piece, the *Romance in G for Violin and Orchestra,* is affectingly played by Kenneth Silito and the Academy of St. Martin-in-the-Fields Chamber Ensemble. The Chandos album (CHAN 9258 [CD]) offers as its major works Svendsen's youthful and charming *Octet,* Op. 3, and the String Quintet by Carl Nielsen, who played under Svendsen in the orchestra of the Royal Danish Opera and was deeply influenced by his music.

Sveshnikov, Alexander   (1890–?)

Russian Folk Song Arrangements

Patriarchal Choir, Moscow, Rybakova. Naxos 8.550781 [CD].

Unlike the many boisterous Red Army Chorus albums of the 1960s that often seemed more like recruiting posters than folk-song anthologies, this Naxos recording of seventeen popular items is the most musically rewardingly in my experience. Nine of them use the tasteful, always imaginative a cappella arrangements by Alexander Sveshnikov, but the others are no less attractive, including an uncredited version of *Ochni chernye* that might have been taken from an unknown Mussorgsky opera. A sterling ensemble rich in those sepulchral Russian basses, the Patriarchal Choir of Moscow sing with equal amounts of finesse and passion and the recorded sound is excellent. Given the richness of the available material, one hopes this will be the first installment in an extensive series.

Szymanowski, Karol   (1882–1937)

During the last years of his unhappy life, Karol Szymanowski lamented the fact that he ever became a composer. One can hardly blame him. Even now, more than a half century after his death, his music remains an unknown commodity to most people, this in spite of the fact that he was the only incontestably great Polish composer after Chopin and one of the giants of twentieth-century music.

To some extent, the recording industry must bear the brunt of the responsibility for the shabby treatment Szymanowski has received. Compared to his compatriots Witold Lutoslawski, whose inspiration has grown increasingly threadbare with the passage of time, and Krzysztof Penderecki, one of the founding fathers of the Grunt-and-Groan school of modern music, Szymanowski has been recorded far less frequently over the years, even though he could out-compose both of them standing on his head with one hand tied behind his back while lighting a cigarette.

King Roger, one of the most beautiful of all modern operas, is finally back in circulation on a set of Koch compact discs (CD 314014 K2). The performance by the Warsaw Opera is polished and idiomatic and the recorded sound, while less than ideal, is perfectly acceptable.

Naxos has so far issued two invaluable Szymanowski CDs. The first (8.553686 [CD]) contains the wonderful ballets *Mandragora* and *Harnasie*—the latter sounding like an impossibly profound and civilized *Carmina Burana*—while the second (8.553687) is devoted to the choral music, including a setting of the *Stabat mater* that ranks with the great sacred works of Western music.

On a recent London compact disc (436837-2), Chantal Juliet, the Montreal Symphony, and Charles Dutoit give the most shimmering performances of the two ravishing Violin Concertos ever recorded, surpassing even the classic version of the First Concerto made in 1959 by David Oistrakh, while the Carmina Quartet's Denon recording of the two quartets (CO 79462 [CD]) places them firmly among the major chamber works of the twentieth century.

The breathtaking *Myths* for violin and piano is the centerpiece of a beautiful Szymanowski recital on Chandos (CHAN 8747 [CD], ABTD 1386 [T]) featuring the bewitching violinist Lydia Mordkovitch. Carol Rosenberger's lovely Delos recording of some of the piano music (DE-1002 [CD]) only serves to underscore his position as Chopin's heir, and Howard Shelley is extremely impressive in the Symphony No. 4 for Piano and Orchestra, the "Symphonie concertante" (Chandos CHAN 9478 [CD].)

Although Antal Dorati's matchless recordings of the Symphony No. 2 in B-flat, and the Symphony No. 3, called "Song of the Night," have been recently withdrawn, a pair of equally fine performances by the Polish Radio Symphony led by Jacek Kaspryzk (try saying that three times with a load of marbles in your mouth) and Jerzy Semkow have resurfaced on a medium-priced Matrix CD (CDM 5 65082) from EMI. While the earlier work is an intriguing, if somewhat derivative, piece that clearly shows an interesting, ambitious young composer on the verge of becoming a major one, the "Song of the Night" is one of the undoubted masterworks of twentieth-century orchestral music: strange, exotic, wholly original, and once heard, never to be forgotten.

Finally, another EMI recording (CDC 55121 [CD]) of the *Stabat mater, Litany to the Virgin,* and Third Symphony is probably the finest single Szymanowski album ever released. In addition to breathtaking interpretations by Sir Simon Rattle and the City of Birmingham Symphony, soprano Elzbieta Szmytra proves an ideal soloist in the *Litany,* with the CBSO Chorus performing wonders of coloration and Polish diction throughout. In short, here's the ideal place to begin your lifelong Szymanowski addiction.

Tailleferre, Germaine   (1892–1983)

Concertino for Harp and Orchestra

> Benet, harp; Women's Philharmonic, Faletta. Koch International
> Classics KIC 7169 [CD], KIC 7169 [T].

Apart from Louis Durey, the eldest and least productive of all, Germaine Tailleferre is the most unfamiliar member of *Les Six,* that group of six young French composers who banded together in the early 1920s with Jean Cocteau as their spokesman and Erik Satie as their spiritual father. At its best—as it clearly is in the Concertino for Harp and Orchestra from 1927—Tailleferre's music has much of the freshness and wit of Milhaud, the grace of Poulenc, and the elegant finish of her teacher and friend Maurice Ravel. The performance conducted by JoAnn Faletta is a superb one, the centerpiece in a fascinating anthology of music by female composers, which includes Lili Boulanger's masterful *D'un matin de printemps* and *D'un soir triste,* an overture by Fanny Mendelssohn, and Clara Schumann's Piano Concerto.

A wonderful Elan collection (CD 82278 [CD]) by Mark Clinton and Nicole Narboni of Tailleferre's piano music is as enjoyable as it is historically valuable, including no fewer than seven recording premieres. In addition to the ballet *La Nouvelle Cythère,* left unorchestrated because of the death of Sergei Diaghilev in 1929, there are several amazing souvenirs of the composer's hale old age, including the rambunctious *Suite Burlesque,* finished when she was eighty-seven.

Takemitsu, Toru   (1930–1996)

Music of Takemitsu

> Bell, flute; Hulse, oboe; Crossley, piano; London Sinfonietta, Knussen.
> Virgin Classics CDC 59020 [CD].

Since the sensational 1967 New York Philharmonic premiere of his *November Steps*—a work for two traditional Japanese instruments, the *biwa* and *shakuhachi,* and modern Western orchestra—Toru Takemitsu was widely regarded as the foremost composer of serious music that Japan has ever produced. In 1951, he joined with a group of other young Japanese composers to form the avant-garde group called "Experimental Laboratory," which established the compositional aesthetic that has dominated Japanese music since the end of the War. It was the expressed intention of the Laboratory to write music that would be an amalgam of traditional Japanese modalities and the modernistic procedures of the West.

Takemitsu emerged as the dominant exponent of this aesthetic, not only because he followed it most closely and cleverly, but also because he was an artist of immense and genuine gifts. As early as 1957, with the composition of the *Requiem* for strings, a work that drew extravagant praise from Igor Stravinsky, he was recognized as a major voice in modern music.

Those who respond to Takemitsu's hypnotic, rarefied idiom should investigate a superb Virgin Classics anthology (CDC 59020 [CD]) in which Oliver Knussen leads definitive-sounding versions of *Rain Coming, Riverrun* for Piano and Orchestra, *Tree Line,* and *Waterways.*

Tallis, Thomas   (c. 1505–1585)

Church Music

The Tallis Scholars, Philips. Gimell GDGIM 006 [CD].

After rudely dismissing the music of his contemporary Ralph Vaughan Williams as was his wont—following a BBC broadcast of the "Pastoral" Symphony, the conductor could be heard to say quite audibly, "A city life for me!"—Sir Thomas Beecham was reprimanded by a friend, who said: "But surely you wouldn't write off that wonderful *Fantasia on a Theme by Thomas Tallis?*" "No," Beecham said, "But Vaughan Williams made the cardinal error of not including in all his compositions a theme by Tallis."

If the modern revival of interest in this colossus of Tudor music began with Vaughan Williams's haunting masterpiece, then its continuation has depended on the extraordinary quality of Tallis's music itself, including one of the most complex of all polyphonic studies, the celebrated *Spem in alium non habui,* a "Song of Forty Parts" for eight five-part choirs. In addition to the famous motet, the Tallis Scholars under Peter Philips offer some ethereally beautiful performances of their namesake's other sacred hits, including a perfectly bewitching setting of *Sancte Deus* that could be even more eloquent.

As one of the first composers to write sacred music on English texts for Henry VIII's newly founded Church of England, Tallis's English anthems are of special historic interest and can be heard on a superlative companion album (Gimell CDGIM 007 [CD], 1585T-07 [T]) in which the singing of the Tallis Scholars is equally inspired.

Taneyev, Sergei (1856–1915)

Symphony No. 4 in C Minor, Op. 12; *The Oresteia* (overture)

Philharmonia Orchestra, Järvi. Chandos CHAN 8953 [CD].

Whenever a late-Romantic composer was referred to as the "(fill in the name of the country) Brahms," it usually meant a composer resolutely out of step with his time. What was true for the "Hungarian Brahms" (Ernst von Dohnányi) was even more so for the "Russian Brahms," Sergei Ivanovich Taneyev. Like the great German master whose music he professed to dislike, Taneyev was an impeccable craftsman in love with abstract form and suspicious of all extra-musical distractions—in his case, the entire folk-inspired Russian nationalist tradition begun by Glinka. Taneyev is unique among Russian composers of the nineteenth century in that there is nothing discernibly "Russian" in his music, except in the texts of his songs and choral works. Even on those rare occasions when a Russian idea *does* appear—as in the *Overture on a Russian Theme* from 1882—its working-out is almost wholly devoid of Slavic color, flavor, and intensity.

Finished in 1898, Taneyev's Fourth Symphony is one of the finest ever written by a Russian composer. While the ideas are not as memorable as those of his teacher, Tchaikovsky, or his pupils Scriabin and Rachmaninoff, they are nonetheless developed with unerring skill; the sonata structures of the opening and closing movements are handled with a Brahms-like meticulousness, while the slow movement has a serene grandeur and the marvelous Scherzo an abundance of gentlemanly wit. Järvi leads a first-rate performance full of spirit and carefully observed details, made all the more enjoyable by the natural perspective of the Chandos recorded sound. The performance of the overture to *The Oresteia*, his ambitious opera based on the plays of Aeschylus, is equally impressive.

Tansman, Alexandre (1897–1986)

Capriccio for Orchestra; Concerto for Orchestra; Etudes for Orchestra

Moscow Symphony, De Almeida. Marco Polo 8.223757 [CD].

While the reputation of the Polish-born Alexandre Tansman plummeted precipitously in the years immediately following his death—the centennial of his birth in 1997 passed by almost unnoticed—it seems only a matter of time before his appealing and distinctive music will again receive the attention it deserves.

After winning the Polish National Music Competition in dramatic fashion in 1919—he entered two works under different pseudonyms and won both first and second prize—Tansman moved to Paris where he was befriended by Ravel, Milhaud, Honegger, and Koussevitzky, who introduced his First Piano Concerto in 1926. Although influenced early on by Ravel and Stravinsky, who became a close personal friend, Tansman had a Stravinsky-like knack for adapting his lyrical, rhythmically inventive gift to a wide variety of styles, ranging from experiments in atonality and serialism to scores written for radio and film.

The three works on this Marco Polo collection date from 1950–1962, the period of his most important and ambitious works, including the oratorio *The Prophet Isaiah,* the opera *Le Serment,* and the ballet *Resurrection.* The performances are not great ones, but they still give ample evidence of Tansman's charm, power, and inventiveness, together with his abundant gifts as an orchestrator. If nothing else, they suggest that a systematic examination of his enormous output is long overdue.

Tavener, John (1944–)

The Protecting Veil

Isserlis, cello; London Symphony, Rozhdestvensky. Virgin Classics 59052 [CD].

The most violent reaction I've ever had to a movie was to Bob Fosse's *All That Jazz.* I saw it on a Saturday night in a crowded theater on the trendy West Side of Los Angeles and, from the opening scene onward, was barely able to contain my rage; it seemed to me the most unimaginably artificial, pretentious, self-absorbed twaddle, made all the more unbearable by the Westsiders' obvious approval and delight. A week later, I was still trying to figure out why the movie should have bothered me so much. On a Wednesday afternoon, I went to a bargain matinee in an effort to find out. Not only did I cease hating it immediately, but I came away persuaded that *All That Jazz* is one of the most inspired films of all time—an opinion I hold to this day.

I bother you with this tale only because John Tavener's *The Protecting Veil* can inspire precisely the same kind of reaction. Having been assaulted in the last few years by an especially pernicious series of empty-headed Emperor's New Clothes frauds—from the Gorecki Third Symphony to the Michael Nyman Piano Concerto to virtually any of witless abominations of Philip Glass—*The Protecting Veil* might at first seem cut from the same cloth: a long, slow-moving, seemingly uneventful sequence of not particularly challenging musical ideas dominated by the modal harmonies of the string orchestra and the seemingly improvisatory, chant-like meditations of the soloist.

The title is a reference to a tenth-century celebration central to Tavener's adopted Greek Orthodox faith. "At a time of grave danger for the Greeks from Saracen invasion," the composer writes, "Andrew, the 'holy fool,' together with his disciple Epiphanios, saw the Mother of God during an all-night vigil. She was standing high up above them in the air, surrounded by a host of saints. She was praying earnestly and spreading out her Veil as a protective shelter over the Christians. Heartened by this vision, the Greeks withstood the Saracen assault and drove away the Saracen army. The Feast of the Protecting Veil is kept by the Orthodox Church in celebration of this event."

To a remarkable extent, Tavener's work not only captures the mystical serenity of the moment but also manages to seem—through the most deceptively simple means—a genuinely visionary work in its own right. Steven Isserlis, for whom the piece was written, gives a rapt and ethereal performance of the vital solo part while Gennady Rozhdestvensky weaves the delicate strands of the accompaniment into an unusually well-argued whole.

After provoking an initial *All That Jazz*-like reaction, *The Protecting Veil* now seems to me convincingly large, unique, and important.

Taylor, Deems (1885–1966)

Through the Looking Glass

Seattle Symphony, Schwarz. Delos DE 3099 [CD].

Although best known as a commentator and critic—for years he hosted the intermission broadcasts of the New York Philharmonic, and who could forget his introduction to Disney's *Fantasia* or his fascinating explanation of how the cannons and bells were recorded in Antal Dorati's early stereo version of the *1812 Overture?*—Deems Taylor was also a composer of considerable accomplishment. His operas *The King's Henchman* (on a text by Edna St. Vincent Millay) and *Peter Ibbetson* were both mounted by the Metropolitan Opera, and *Through the Looking Glass*, his five pictures from Lewis Carroll's classic, is among the most endearing orchestral scores ever written by an American. From the tender Introduction, with its heart-dissolving principal theme, through the witty "Jabberwocky," to the soaring romance of "The White Knight," *Through the*

Looking Glass is one of those magical, instantly memorable works that most listeners find impossible to forget.

Gerard Schwarz and his fine orchestra miss none of the work's color, vitality, or charm, making this a worthy successor to Howard Hanson's celebrated 1953 recording. The playing has a wonderful (albeit paradoxical) sense of relaxed intensity, with first-rate solo contributions from the orchestra's principals; nor has this conductor ever led a more sensitive, completely understanding performance. With equally evocative versions of four marvelous works by the hugely underrated Charles Tomlinson Griffes, including his masterpieces, *The Pleasure Dome of Kubla Khan* and *The White Peacock,* this cannot possibly be missed.

Tchaikovsky, Piotr Ilyich

(1840–1893)

Capriccio Italien; Marche Slave; Nutcracker Suite; 1812 Overture

Montreal Symphony, Dutoit. London 417300-2 [CD].

Although an enormous percentage of music lovers first made their way into Serious Music via the works of Tchaikovsky, many seem strangely loath to admit it. As our tastes mature and we become ever more knowledgeable and sophisticated, we tend to drop—or perhaps even be ashamed of—our youthful enthusiasms. (Who was it who said, "Don't let the young confide to you their dreams, for when they drop them, they'll drop you"?)

Although he can be extremely obvious, bellicose, cheap, and vulgar, Tchaikovsky more than earns his position as one of the three or four most popular composers. He never cheats his listeners, giving them huge doses of overwhelming (and often surprisingly complex) emotions, a keen sense of orchestral color, and one of the greatest melodic gifts that any composer possessed. In short, if you love Tchaikovsky, don't be ashamed. And don't think you're alone. Uncounted millions of us can't *all* be wrong.

This superb and unusually generous London collection brings together four of the composer's most popular works in performances that are as civilized as they are exciting, as brash and brazen as they are thoughtful and refined. Although the *1812 Overture* could be a bit noisier—as it is in the classic Mercury recording with Antal Dorati and the Minneapolis Symphony, complete with

Deems Taylor explaining how they got the bells and cannon blasts, now brilliantly transferred to CD (416448-2)—these are the performances I turn to whenever the mood strikes.

Piano Concerto No. 1 in B-flat Minor, Op 23

Cliburn, piano; RCA Victor Symphony, Kondrashin. RCA Victor 07863-55912-2 [CD], 07863-55912-4 [T].

It's no accident that this is one of the best-selling classical recordings of all time. Naturally, much of it had to do with the ballyhoo that attended Van Cliburn's winning of the Tchaikovsky competition in Moscow during one of the chilliest moments of the Cold War. (Yes, the Russians had a definite jump in the space race—remember all those films of our rockets blowing up on the pad?—but we had this long, lanky Texan who beat them, and beat them *decisively,* at their own game.)

Three decades later, in the midst of the *glasnost* thaw, it's time we started judging this recording on its own merits and not on its historical context. I have; and, simply stated, in *any* context, this is one hell of an exciting performance. Cliburn's mixture of elfin delicacy and animal ferocity has remained intact since the recording was first released. It is a poetic, explosive, lyrical, and deeply humane interpretation that no recording of the last thirty years begins to match.

Piano Concerto No. 2 in G Major; Piano Concerto No. 3 in E-flat Major

Douglas, piano; Philharmonia Orchestra, Slatkin. RCA 09026-61633-2 [CD].

The long overdue rehabilitation of Tchaikovsky's "other" piano concertos would not be long delayed if performances of them were as committed and electrifying as these. Using the composer's uncut original version, Barry Douglas is perhaps even more impressive than he was in his version of the B-flat Minor Concerto. Like Peter Donohoe in his superb but now-deleted Angel recording, Douglas transforms the Second Concerto into something as engrossing—and very nearly as exciting—as the First: with substantial contributions from the concertmaster and principal cellist, the slow movement emerges as one of Tchaikovsky's most original inspirations, while the *Finale* erupts in a blaze of Vesuvian fireworks that outshines even the startling version that Gary Graffman recorded a generation ago. Despite being a much lesser piece, the Third Concerto also responds brilliantly to Douglas's poetry and panache, while Leonard Slatkin is as quick and canny a partner as always.

Concerto in D Major for Violin and Orchestra, Op. 35

> Heifetz, violin; Chicago Symphony, Reiner. RCA Victor
> 09026-61495-2 [CD], 09026-61495-4 [T].

> Oistrakh, violin; Philadelphia Orchestra, Ormandy. Sony Classical
> SBK 46339 [CD], SBT 46339 [T].

From a purely technical point of view, there has never been a recording to match Jascha Heifetz's famous version with Fritz Reiner and the Chicago Symphony. Although the violinist was placed uncomfortably close to the microphone, which accounts for the unaccustomed rasp in his famous tone, the playing is genuinely spellbinding. Listen especially to the first movement cadenza, in which the soloist uses one of his own devising that makes Tchaikovsky's original seem like child's play.

On the other hand, if you're after the warmth, color, and abiding romance of the Tchaikovsky concerto, then David Oistrakh's meltingly lovely recording with Eugene Ormandy and the Philadelphia Orchestra is clearly the one to own. Unfortunately, the recording is currently available only on cassette.

Eugene Onegin

> Focile, Hvorostovsky, Shicoff, Walker, Arkhipova, St. Petersburg
> Chamber Choir, Orchestre de Paris, Bychkov. Philips
> 438235-2 [CD].

Of the ten operas that Tchaikovsky composed, only *Eugene Onegin* and *Pique Dame,* both based on works by Pushkin, have made any inroads into the standard repertoire. (For any Slavic opera to do so has been next to impossible, given the language barrier: to this day, Smetana's masterpiece is usually heard as *Die Verkaufte Braut,* or *The Bartered Bride*—as opposed to *Prodaná Nevěsta*— and even *Boris Godunov* didn't begin making the international rounds until the title role was taken over by a lunatic named Chaliapin.) Although it can often seem to lack sustainable dramatic interest or clearly delineated characters—part of the problem lay in the fact that the composer adored Pushkin's heroine and regarded his hero as "a cold, heartless coxcomb"—*Eugene Onegin* is full of unforgettable set pieces like Tatiana's Letter Scene, the Waltz and Polonaise, and the exquisite aria in which the doomed Lensky recalls his youth. (Like his tenor, Pushkin himself was killed in a duel only six years after completing *Onegin,* defending the "honor" of his not entirely honorable wife.)

The impassioned Philips recording with Dmitri Hvorostovsky in the title role easily supplants all previous and currently available versions of *Onegin,* including the recently deleted London version conducted by Sir Georg Solti.

Vocally and dramatically, Nuccia Focile is far more impressive than Solti's Tatiana, Teresa Kubiak, possessed as she is of an astounding command of Russian diction and Tchaikovsky's soaring line. Bychkov's conducting is as passionately committed as Solti's, but it is also far more flexible and idiomatic, capturing the music's Russian inflections to perfection. In the title role, Hvorostovsky demonstrates why he is the most exciting Russian singer of his generation, combining an abundance of old-fashioned temperament and high intelligence with a startlingly large and beautiful voice. All in all, this is an *Onegin* to set the standard well past the turn of the century.

Hamlet; Francesca da Rimini

Stadium Symphony of New York, Stokowski. Dell'Arte CDDA 9006 [CD].

This is a thoroughly impossible recording. Anyone with any taste knows that Tchaikovsky's *Hamlet* is trash, pure and simple, and that *Francesca da Rimini,* on the dreck-o-meter, isn't far behind. Moreover, anyone who has heard the Stadium Symphony of New York—a name that the New York Philharmonic minus its first-desk musicians adopted to protect the identity of its players—must suspect, as I do, that their summer evening concerts may have provided the inspiration for George A. Romero's *Night of the Living Dead.*

So here are two second-rate works performed by a third-rate orchestra under the direction of a man whose podium antics, tabloid romances, Bach arrangements, and other glitzy hokum made the word *charlatan* lose all its respectability. After more than thirty years, the results are *still* not to be believed. While *Francesca da Rimini,* through an interpretation whose sheer ferocity is matched only by its tenderness and subtlety, is transformed into what sounds like the most electrifying tone poem ever written, *Hamlet* becomes what it cannot possibly be: not only something worthy of the name, but also one of the most pointed and perceptive Shakespeare commentaries in all of music.

Add this to Stokowski's 1927 Philadelphia *Scheherazade,* and you have two of the ten greatest recordings of Russian music ever made.

Impossible, but true.

The Nutcracker (complete ballet)

L'Orchestre de la Suisse Romande, Ansermet. London 417055-4 [T].

Amsterdam Concertgebouw Orchestra, Dorati. Philips 442562 [CD].

If ever a recording deserved the designation "Imperishable," it is that triumphant early stereo version of *The Nutcracker,* which has more sheer interpretive magic than you can shake a sugar plum at. Although the sound has definitely begun to show its age, the performance never will. Ansermet's conception brings out every ounce of charm and color that this often hackneyed work offers, and does it with a touch so light and sure that we're reminded once again of what we all owe this great pioneer of the early stereo age.

Antal Dorati's Philips recording is nearly as magical, with generally finer orchestral execution and clearly superior recorded sound. For those who find the sound of the Ansermet unacceptably boxy and brittle, this is the best modern alternative.

*R*omeo and Juliet (overture-fantasy); *Francesca da Rimini*

Royal Philharmonic, Ashkenazy. London 421715-2 [CD].

London Symphony, Simon. Chandos CHAN 8310 [CD].

Vladimir Ashkenazy's Royal Philharmonic recording offers an excellent, old-fashioned *Romeo* and a topflight *Francesca*. While neither performance has the dash or drama of Leonard Bernstein's inexplicably withdrawn Deutsche Grammophon recording with the Israel Philharmonic, they do offer superior playing and recorded sound. With stellar performances of *Capriccio italien* and the *Elegy for Strings* tossed in as a bonus, it makes for an easy first recommendation.

Geoffrey Simon's Chandos recording is an entirely different matter. In this fascinating and, for Tchaikovsky aficionados, can't-live-another-day-without-it release, Simon unearths the original 1869 version of the work that put the composer on the musical map of Europe in the early 1880s. This is not simply an early version of *Romeo and Juliet* but a virtually unrecognizable piece: less finished and professional than the *Romeo* we're used to, yet one whose unvarnished enthusiasm and power are hard to resist. In addition to this proto-*Romeo*, the Simon collection offers a version of *Hamlet* that features both the Overture and the incidental music, including a mad scene for Ophelia and a lively (if that's really the right word) *Gravedigger's Song,* together with some *bona fide* off-the-wall discoveries such as the *Festival Overture on the Danish National Anthem* and, as I have now come to think of it, the absolutely indispensable *Serenade for Nikolai Rubinstein's Saint's Day.*

*T*he Seasons

Pletnev, piano. Virgin Classics CDC 45042 [CD].

Tchaikovsky composed his best-known piano work as a monthly serial for the St. Petersburg music magazine *Nuvellist*. Although neither a profound nor an important work, *The Seasons* is an engaging and imaginative collection of miniatures with a consistently high level of melodic inspiration.

Pletnev's recording is easily the most distinguished the work has ever received. A relaxed grace in the lyrical pieces is matched by an effortless panache in the more challenging ones, with the entire performance given an unmistakable Russian glow.

Although not quite as imaginative as Pletnev, the Hungarian pianist Ilona Prunyi gives a very enjoyable performance on Naxos 8.550233 [CD], in the first of two albums devoted to Tchaikovsky's piano music. If anything, Volume 2 (8.550504 [CD]) is even more appealing, with delightful miniatures like the *Humoresque in E Minor* and *Rêverie du Soir* played with unaffected charm.

In the single most valuable album of Tchaikovsky piano music now available, Sviatoslav Richter offers poetry and fabulous pianism in a 1983 recital from Olympia (OLY 334 [CD]).

Serenade in C Major for String Orchestra, Op. 48

Australian Chamber Orchestra, Pini. Omega OCD-1010 [CD].

Academy of St. Martin-in-the-Fields, Marriner. London 411471-2 [CD].

With so many first-rate recordings of the popular Serenade for Strings floating around, the final choice for many people might depend on how the piece is packaged. For those who want the traditional pairing with the Dvořák Serenade, Sir Neville Marriner's London recording isn't going to be bettered, at least until Angel bestirs itself and issues those spellbinding Barenboim/English Chamber Orchestra performances on a medium-priced CD.

For a less predictable yet far more logical coupling, the brilliant Australian Chamber Orchestra and Carl Pini offer one of the most alert and amiable performances on the market, together with an arresting version of the composer's own favorite piece, the *Souvenir of Florence*.

The Snow Maiden

Soloists, University of Michigan Musical Society Choral Union, Detroit Symphony, Järvi. Chandos CHAN 9324 [CD].

Tchaikovsky composed the incidental music to Alexander Ostrovsky's play *The Snow Maiden* during three hectic weeks of the spring of 1873. This tale of the daughter of Frost and Spring who can live only so long as her heart remains unwarmed by love obviously struck a resonant chord in the composer: "*The Snow Maiden* is not one of my best works," he confessed to Madame von Meck, but was quick to add: "It is one of my favorite offspring." With many of its principal themes derived from Russian folk-song, *The Snow Maiden* is one of the most nationalistic of Tchaikovsky's works, after the "Little Russian" Symphony: along with the famous "Dance of the Tumblers," the score abounds in memorable set pieces, including a dance for birds and a song for spring accompanied by a chorus of flowers.

Predictably, Neeme Järvi leads a vividly colorful performance that captures both the folksy elements in the score and its magical interaction between the real and supernatural worlds, all the while maintaining a strong sense of dramatic unity and forward momentum. The singing, playing, and recorded sound are all of a very high order, making this an ideal introduction to a little-known but utterly delightful work.

String Quartets (3)

Borodin Quartet. EMI Classics ZDCB 49775 [CD].

The Tchaikovsky String Quartets, with those of Alexander Borodin, are among the pivotal Russian chamber works of the nineteenth century: the first important Russian string quartets and virtually the only ones until the advent of Dmitri Shostakovich. Beginning with the early D Major Quartet of 1871, whose unforgettable slow movement is the famous *Andante cantabile,* the level of inspiration and invention remained extremely high, as these vivid, mercurial performances by the Borodin Quartet demonstrate at every turn. With the finest available recording of the sextet version of the *Souvenir of Florence* thrown in as a bonus, it is extremely unlikely this collection will ever be bettered.

Suites (4) for Orchestra

USSR Academic Symphony, Svetlanov. Melodiya 17099-2 [CD] (Suites Nos. 1 and 2); 17100-2 [CD] (Suites Nos. 3 and 4).

National Orchestra of Ireland, Sanderling. Naxos 8.550644 [CD] (Suites Nos. 1 and 2); Naxos 8.550728 [CD] (Suites Nos. 3 and 4).

Their small but devoted circle of admirers have always realized how much wonderful music is to be found in Tchaikovsky's four Orchestral Suites; now, thanks to what have to be counted as the most inspired of Evgeny Svetlanov's recordings thus far, everyone else will realize it, too. In these miraculous performances of the Third and Fourth Suites, a new insight, a fresh inspiration, an astonishing Gee-why-didn't-anyone-ever-think-of-doing-it-that-way-before? solution seems to leap out at every turn. Under Svetlanov's firm but infinitely flexible guidance, the USSR Academic Symphony performs the music with such effortless grace and joy that you're very nearly persuaded they must be making it up as they go along.

As a budget-priced alternative, the recordings by Stefan Sanderling and the excellent National Orchestra of Ireland are nearly as fine. If at this stage in his career the young conductor can't quite match Svetlanov's imagination and finesse, then the interpretations are still fresh and satisfying and are superbly played and recorded.

Swan Lake (complete ballet)

Philharmonia Orchestra, Lanchbery. EMI Classics for Pleasure CDCFP 4727 [CD].

To his everlasting credit, Tchaikovsky never gave up on the two forms that he most wanted to master but whose perplexing secrets always just eluded him. And it is his masterpiece, *Swan Lake,* that best explains why he never became the great operatic composer and symphonist he so earnestly wanted to be. For the glory of Tchaikovsky's art was neither its intellectual depth nor its grasp of structure, but its ability make melody and emotion indistinguishable from one another. In no other composer's work is melody the *meaning* of the music to the extent that it is in Tchaikovsky's, and nowhere else is his melodic genius more finely tuned than it is in *Swan Lake.* In none of his major works—except perhaps for *The Sleeping Beauty*—do we have the sense of such concentration and economy, even in spite of its formidable length; the sense that every tune is not only memorable but absolutely necessary, and that not a note or gesture is wasted. It is a unique achievement that, by itself, would refute the nonsensical suggestion that Tchaikovsky was not a great composer.

If it doesn't have all the character of some fine recordings of the recent past—Rozhdestvensky's Moscow Radio, as opposed to his BBC performance, and Previn's senselessly deleted London Symphony recording—then John Lanchbery's is an enthusiastic and completely professional job and is easily the best *Swan Lake* left in the pond. For those who might not need the entire ballet(s), Muti and the Philadelphia Orchestra offer colorful, spectacularly well-played versions of the *Swan Lake* and *Sleeping Beauty* Suites (EMI Classics CDC 47075 [CD]).

*S*ymphonies 1–6; *Manfred* Symphony

Oslo Philharmonic, Jansons. Chandos CHAN 8672 [CD].

My own introduction to the Tchaikovsky symphonies came via an RCA Victor Camden recording of the Fifth with the Oslo Philharmonic led by its long time (1931–1961) conductor, Odd Grüner-Hegge. I remember that exciting interpretation virtually note for note, not only because it was so exceptionally good, but also because, forever after, no other performance of the piece has ever sounded quite right. Grüner-Hegge, who studied conducting with Felix Weingartner, observed the whopping cuts his old teacher made in the score, including the whole of the last movement's development section. This still heads my list of must-be-reissued Tchaikovsky Fifth recordings (as it has in Europe), followed closely by the zany Paul van Kempen version made with the Amsterdam Concertgebouw Orchestra at about the same time, which includes, among *its* enthralling perversities, a pair of cymbal crashes just before the final *stretto* and an additional horn note that creates an unresolved seventh chord at that great pause before the march—undoubtedly a holdover of one of the many tricks conductors have tried in an attempt to head off the applause that customarily breaks out at that inopportune moment. (Stokowski tried to cure this "premature congratulation" by simply having the timpani keep rolling through the break, but the only time I heard him do it—with the Chicago Symphony—the unwashed and unsanctified fell in where they always do, earning a withering Stokie glare.)

But I digress.

The current conductor of the Oslo Philharmonic, Mariss Jansons, has built a considerable reputation as a Tchaikovsky conductor, thanks to his Chandos recordings, and all of them—even his game go-round with the hopeless *Manfred* Symphony, are among the finest currently available and will probably remain the standard recordings for years. The interpretations are both disciplined and spontaneous, with wonderful playing from an orchestra that sounds, for much of the time, like a junior edition of the Berlin Philharmonic. Although none of the available alternatives can begin to match them, two classic recordings should be returned to print to provide at least *some* choice: Carlo Maria Giulini's whirlwind version of the "Little Russian" for Angel and one of the most electric Tchaikovsky recordings ever made, the Deutsche Grammophon "Winter Dreams" with the Boston Symphony conducted by Michael Tilson Thomas.

For those who prefer to acquire the later symphonies singly, a few reasonable alternatives exist. Leonard Bernstein's early CBS recording of the Fourth (Sony Classical SMK 47633 [CD]) still packs plenty of wallop and highly individual pizzazz. Claudio Abbado's brooding yet exhilarating performance of the Fifth ranks with the finest recordings to date (CBS MK-42094 [CD]), while an Erato recording of a live performance of the *Pathétique* led by Jansons's old mentor Evgeny Mravinsky (2292-45756-2 [CD]) takes at least some of the sting out of Deutsche Grammophon's criminally insensitive decision to withdraw the conductor's classic studio recordings of the last three symphonies from circulation.

Variations on a Rococo Theme for Cello and Orchestra, Op. 33

Rostropovich, cello; Berlin Philharmonic, Karajan. Deutsche Grammophon 447413-2 [CD].

By common consent, Mstislav Rostropovich has all but owned Tchaikovsky's *de facto* cello concerto for a generation and this most eloquently argued of his several recordings demonstrates why. The cellist refuses to treat the piece as merely an engaging ball of cuddly virtuoso fluff but considers it a major work that requires major concentration. Which is not to say that the cellist misses any of the charm or fun of the piece. Quite the contrary. His impish enthusiasm even infects his usually grim-lipped partner, who here delivers one of the most uncharacteristically witty and humane of his later performances.

A good, though by no means exceptional, performance of the Dvořák Concerto rounds out the CD, and on cassette Rostropovich's earlier Deutsche Grammophon recording with Rozhdestvensky and the Leningrad Philharmonic is an equally obvious first choice (413161-4).

Telemann, Georg Philipp

(1681–1767)

During his lifetime, Georg Philipp Telemann completely overshadowed his near contemporary, an obscure German organist and composer named Johann Sebastian Bach. People in later centuries slowly realized that what had made Telemann so fashionable during his lifetime—the clear, uncomplicated structures, the easy-to-follow contents of a music that had nothing profound to say—ultimately gave him next to no staying power, especially in comparison with the *real* baroque giants, Handel and Bach.

While I can make no specific recommendations for recordings of the man's music (it all sounds more or less the same to me), I will offer a few general hints for the Telemann shopper: (1) Avoid any recording with a reproduction of an eighteenth-century landscape painting on the front cover. (2) Avoid any concerto for more than one instrument (anything more complicated seems only to have confused him). (3) Avoid any recording featuring Nikolaus Harnoncourt, his wife Alice, or their friend Gustav Leonhart. If you see them in the cut-out or used record bins, and I mean *anything* produced by the Telemann society, avoid them as though your life depended on it. (Several people have laughed themselves to death listening to their well-intentioned but hopelessly feeble efforts.) (4) If the temptation to buy a Telemann recording proves irresistible, make certain your cupboard is well stocked with strong, and I do mean *strong,* coffee.

Thomas, Ambroise (1811–1896)

Hamlet

Anderson, Hampson, Graves, Kunde, Ramey, Ambrosian Singers, London Philharmonic, de Almeida. EMI Classics CDCC 54820 [CD].

If the Germans have never been able to tolerate the celebrated *Faust* travesty of Charles Gounod, calling it *Marguerite* whenever it is staged there, then the English have never been particularly sanguine on the subject of the *Hamlet* setting of Gounod's near contemporary Ambroise Thomas. Yet it spite of its more obvious outrages, such as a mad scene in lilting three-quarter time and an exuberant drinking song put in the mouth of the Melancholy Dane, *Hamlet* can be an effective piece of theater, given the proper singers. The title role was one of the major star vehicles of the "Caruso of Baritones," the legendary Titta Ruffo, while Ophelia has been a favorite of coloraturas from the age of Adelina Patti to that of Joan Sutherland.

The foremost living heirs to that great tradition, Thomas Hampson and June Anderson, make the strongest possible case for the opera in this superb EMI recording, with Hampson virile yet sensitive in the title role and Anderson suitably agile and pliant in hers. While Anderson's mad scene does not completely efface the memory of Tetrazzini's or Sutherland's, it is a staggering piece of singing: accurate, fearless, and perfectly on pitch. Hampson's Brindisi, on the other hand, is every bit the equal of Ruffo's, with possibly even more fire and rhythmic dash. Antonio de Almeida does his best to keep the rest of the action from flagging and the supporting cast is first-rate.

Those with a *Faust* sweet tooth should waste no time giving this delightful confection a try.

Thompson, Randall   (1899–1984)

Symphony No. 2; Symphony No. 3

> New Zealand Symphony, Schenck. Koch International Classics
> 3-7074-2 [CD].

One of the most urbane and gentlemanly of American composers, Randall Thompson was primarily known for vocal works like the elegant *Alleluia* of 1940 and the stirring *Testament of Freedom* on a text by Jefferson, currently available on a very fine Reference CD (RR 49). He was also the composer of two of the finest of all American symphonies, both of which are memorably served on this recent Koch recording.

Although the Third Symphony of 1949 is a spirited, beautifully made work that never wears out its welcome or wastes a single gesture, the Second Symphony of 1931 is a masterpiece: virile, tuneful, seamlessly argued, and completely satisfying, it compares favorably with any American symphony written to date.

The New Zealand Symphony under Andrew Schenck makes a virtually airtight case for both works. The young orchestra plays with polish and enthusiasm, while only the occasional thinness in the upper strings reveals that they are not quite a world-class ensemble. The recording, if slightly distant, is excellent.

Thomson, Virgil (1896–1989)

Autumn (Concertino for Harp, Strings and Percussion); *The Plow That Broke the Plains* (orchestral suite); *The River* (orchestral suite)

> Los Angeles Chamber Orchestra, Marriner. EMI Classics CDM 64306
> [CD].

If it's still too soon to get a clear picture of Virgil Thomson's stature as a composer, his position as one of America's most perceptive, courageous, and bitchiest music critics is assured. During his enlightened Reign of Terror (1940–1954) as the critic of the New York *Herald Tribune*, Thomson enraged and delighted readers with countless inflammatory observations, including the then heretical suggestions that Arturo Toscanini was *not* the risen Christ and that the Second Symphony of Jean Sibelius, then at the height of his popularity, was "vulgar, self-indulgent, and provincial beyond all description."

After *Four Saints in Three Acts,* the transcendentally daffy opera that he wrote with Gertrude Stein—and that can be heard on a superbly successful Nonesuch recording (79035-2 [CD])—Thomson, the composer, is probably best represented on records these days by the music he wrote for Pare Lorentz's WPA documentary films, *The Plow That Broke the Plains* and *The River.* Like the *Symphony on a Hymn Tune,* an ingenuous portrait of the nineteenth-century American Midwest painted by a citified Parisian in the 1920s, these are folksy, openhearted, sophisticated works that immediately enfold the listener in a bear-hug embrace. The performances by Sir Neville Marriner and the Los Angeles Chamber Orchestra are even more affectionate and evocative than Leopold Stokowski's famous Symphony of the Air recordings, and the twenty-year-old recorded sound remains fertile and uneroded.

Tippett, Sir Michael (1905–1998)

A Child of Our Time (oratorio)

> **Soloists, BBC Symphony and Chorus, Rozhdestvensky. IMP ("BBC Radio Classics" Series) IMP 9130 [CD].**

Sir Michael Tippett spent most of his career in the tremendous shadow cast by his far more famous contemporary, Benjamin Britten. In many ways, Tippett was the more interesting composer (and this from someone who has always adored Britten's music). Unlike Britten, Tippett ventured down several important modern roads in the last years of his career. His idiom became increasingly harsh and dissonant, while his expression became ever more concentrated and precise. Late Tippett (from, say, the early 1970s onward) can be a very thorny, though immensely rewarding, row to hoe.

A Child of Our Time, completed in 1941, is not only one of Tippett's most accessible pieces but also one of the most shattering, yet heart-breakingly lovely, choral works of the last hundred years. Patterned consciously after the Passions of Bach, Tippett's Oratorio presents black spirituals in place of the familiar chorales at key moments in the drama. Their effect can be overwhelmingly moving and beautiful.

Obscenely, as the superb versions conducted by André Previn, Sir Colin Davis, Sir John Pritchard, and Richard Hickox have all been withdrawn, only one complete performance is currently available. Fortunately, it's a great one. If the Russian conductor Gennady Rozhdestvensky is not a name one immediately associates with English music, then like Previn before him, he speaks this specialized language like a native. If the spirituals don't have quite the same irresistible "swing" they do in the Previn version, then they nonetheless unfold with a wonderful inevitability and sense of purpose. Indeed, it is the special sense of urgency in this live 1980 performance that would give the recording a slight edge over its distinguished predecessors, even if they were available.

For Tippett admirers—and the man certainly deserves millions more than he has so far attracted—two other important recordings can also be recommended without reservation. The first is an invaluable two-CD set from EMI Classics (ZDMB 63522) that offers irreproachable versions of the Concerto for Double String Orchestra, the *Fantasia Concertante on a Theme of Corelli* (conducted by the composer), the First String Quartet, and the First and Second Piano Sonatas played by John Ogdon. The second, from London (425646-2 [CD]), features all four of the symphonies that Sir Michael has written to date, coupled with the slender but enchanting *Suite for the Birthday of Prince Charles,* in the virtually definitive performances led by Sir Colin Davis (1–3) and Sir George Solti (4, *Suite*).

*T*he Midsummer Marriage

> Remedios, Carlyle, Herincx, Harwood, Bainbridge, Burrows, Watts, Dean, Chorus and Orchestra of the Royal Opera House, Covent Garden, Davis. Lyrita SRCD 2217 [CD].

Don't bother to ask what any of it means. Instead, if you get the chance, listen to the last few minutes of Act I, beginning with King Fisher's line, "Now is this nonsense at its noon." The "nonsense" eventually reaches its climax in the swirling, ecstatic chorus "We are the laughing children," which in its driving, unstoppable, full-throated vigor is precisely what an orgasm would sound like if only it could sing. And *that's* only the end of the first Act.

When I first heard this breathtaking recording of *The Midsummer Marriage* more than twenty years ago, I was quickly persuaded that Sir Michael Tippett had written the most joyous, mysterious, exuberant, perplexing, and life-affirming of all modern operas. I still am. Recorded during a landmark revival at Covent Garden, where the 1955 premiere garnered mixed but generally baffled reviews, Sir Colin Davis's version of this giddy, puzzling fable with echoes of *Siddartha,* T. S. Eliot, *Heartbreak House,* and *The Magic Flute* is one of the finest operatic recordings ever made. In both the great set pieces—from Mark's surging "As stallions stamping" to Bella's adorable "They say a woman's glory is her hair" to the celebrated *Ritual Dances*—and in his ability to tie up all the complex thematic strands into a convincing whole, Davis has never made a better recording or a more necessary one. For he places *The Midsummer Marriage* where it clearly belongs: among the great operas of all time.

Torke, Michael   (1961–)

Color Music

> Baltimore Symphony, Zinman. Argo 433071-2 [CD].

Born in Wisconsin in 1961, Michael Torke is not only one of the most frequently performed and widely discussed composers of his generation, but he is also one of the most difficult to classify. Although at first hearing his music suggests an amalgam of serious classical music, popular music, and jazz, with procedures adapted from such disparate sources as Stravinsky and minimalism, it stands somewhat apart from any recognized style or school. Torke's harmonic language is both tonal and accessible, or as he himself has so disarmingly suggested, "Harmonic language is, then, in a sense, inconsequential. If the choice of harmony is arbitrary, why not use tonic and dominant chords—the simplest, most direct and—for me—the most pleasurable?" Yet more than his harmonic or melodic language, Torke's command of the resources of the modern orchestra has gained the most attention. His most celebrated music to date is that series of works whose very names reflect his interest in orchestral colors, from *Bright Blue Music* to *Green, Ash,* and *Purple.*

This Argo recording made Torke's international reputation—and rightly so. David Zinman leads performances that are so immediate and involving that they silence all doubts as long as you have them on. Whatever the ultimate value or staying power of *Color Music,* in the short run it's all a great deal of fun.

Tubin, Eduard   (1905–1982)

Symphony No. 5; *Kratt* (ballet suite)

> Bamberg Symphony, Järvi. Bis CD 306 [CD].

Unlike sex, politics, and television, music is always full of surprises. Until quite recently, the surprising music of Eduard Tubin was a carefully guarded secret outside of his native Estonia and adopted Sweden; now, thanks largely to the Estonian conductor Neeme Järvi and the enterprising Swedish label Bis, Tubin has at last begun to take his rightful place among the most substantial and original of mid-twentieth-century symphonists.

Each of the ten completed symphonies that Tubin composed over a half-century period—an eleventh was left unfinished at the time of his death—

manages to say something fresh and individual. Although the spirits of near contemporaries like Sibelius, Prokofiev, and Shostakovich might flit in and out of the music from time to time, Tubin is very much his own man: a rational yet emotionally intricate personality whose superbly crafted, immediately engaging music says what it has to say—which is often an earful—without wasting a moment of our time, or its.

The pairing of the neo-Classical Fifth Symphony of 1946 and a suite from the ruggedly dramatic 1961 ballet *Kratt* is an ideal introduction to Tubin's bracing, lucid, mysterious universe, and Järvi's interpretations reveal a deep and obvious affection for his countryman's music. The only serious drawback is that the recording may prove addictive, forcing you to engorge the other symphonies as quickly as possible.

Turina, Joaquín (1882–1949)

Danzas fantásticas; La procesiòn del Rocio; Ritmos; Sinfonia sevillana

Bamberg Symphony, De Almeida. RCA 09026-60895-2 [CD].

Although this immensely prolific composer worked industriously in all of the standard musical forms—his first important work was the Opus 1 Piano Quintet, purposefully modeled on those of Schumann, Brahms, and Franck, and he was the only Spanish composer of the period to produce a symphony (the three-movement *Sinfonia sevillana* of 1920)—the bulk of Joaquín Turina's reputation rests on those exotic works that make such inspired use of the harmonies and rhythms of Spanish folk music.

With his first great Spanish success, *La procesiòn del Rocio,* premiered in Madrid in 1913, and later in works like the *Sinfonia sevillana,* the *"Fantasia coreográfica" Ritmos,* and the *Danzas fantásticas,* that vivid adaptation of Andalusian dance rhythms that would become his most frequently performed orchestral score, Turina became one of the leading voices of the Spanish nationalist movement, a composer whose command of the modern orchestra was matched only by Manuel de Falla's.

This album of four of Turina's most representative works is one of the finest that the late Antonio de Almeida ever made. The German musicians play this exotic music as though the Iberian colors and rhythms were in their blood, with every nuance of the subtle orchestration captured by RCA's wide-ranging recorded sound.

Turina's most celebrated work, *La oraciòn del torero* (The Bullfighter's Prayer) is incomparably served by the Hollywood Quartet on a Testament anthology (STB 1053 [CD]) that also features matchless performances of works by Creston, Debussy, Ravel, and Villa-Lobos; the version for string orchestra is beautifully played by I Musici de Montréal led by Yuli Turovsky, this from a Chandos album (CHAN 9288 [CD]) devoted primarily to Rodion Shchedrin's *Carmen Ballet*.

Two superb examples of Turina's more "European" music are the Piano Trios from 1926 and 1933: elegant, commanding, subtly original works given predictably involving performances by the Beaux Arts Trio (Philips 446684-2 [CD]).

Varèse, Edgar (1883–1965)

Arcana; Intégrales; Ionisation

Los Angeles Philharmonic, Mehta. London 448580-2 [CD].

Ecuatorial; Déserts; Hyperprism

Ensemble InterContemporain, New York Philharmonic, Boulez. CBS Sony SK 45844 [CD].

Following a brief bout of unlikely popularity in the 1960s—due in part to the *Poeme électronique* that, when performed over four hundred speakers at the Philips Pavilion, became an unexpected hit at the 1958 Brussels World's Fair, and thanks, too, to the spirited advocacy of Frank Zappa, another unruly genius who immediately knew a kindred spirit when he heard one—Edgar (née Edgard) Varèse slipped back into the not-so-benign neglect in which he languished for most of his career.

In his entry on Varèse in *Baker's Biographical Dictionary of Musicians*, the late Nicolas Slonimsky dropped the usual one- or two-word preparatory appraisal ("distinguished conductor . . . ," "famous Bulgarian heckelphone virtuoso . . . ") in favor of this: "One of the most remarkable composers of his century who introduced a totally original principle of organizing the materials and forms of sound, profoundly influencing the direction of new music." That just about says it.

Pierre Boulez's recordings are by far the most valuable yet made of this composer's music. Predictably, the French conductor is most impressive whenever

Varèse is at his thorniest: the dense, often barbaric textures are untangled to an astonishing degree, emerging with a Mozart-like clarity coupled with a sensuousness that will remind many listeners of Debussy.

Mehta's recordings are among his most completely successful Los Angeles efforts, mixing formidable virtuosity with an almost relaxed command of the idiom, as though the orchestra were as comfortable with Varèse as they are with Brahms.

Vaughan Williams, Ralph

(1872–1958)

Fantasia on a Theme by Thomas Tallis; Symphony No. 2, "A London Symphony"

> **London Philharmonic, Boult. EMI Classics CDM 64017 [CD].**

For those who have yet to acquire the gentle addiction of Ralph Vaughan Williams's music, this superb Angel recording should do the trick. On it are two of Vaughan Williams's finest and most characteristic pieces, the ravishing *Fantasia on a Theme of Thomas Tallis* and that greatest of modern English musical travelogues, "A London Symphony."

Although both works have had marginally finer, but currently unavailable, performances (Sir John Barbirolli's version of the Symphony ranks with the great orchestral recordings of modern times), the Boult performances are excellent in every way. A close friend of the composer, Boult has unimpeachable credentials as a Vaughan Williams conductor that shine through every bar of these works. The *Fantasy* has enormous dignity, as well as sensual beauty, while the performance of the Symphony, if not quite as colorful a tour as Barbirolli's, is unforgettable. The London Philharmonic is at the top of its form in both performances and the remastered sound of the compact disc is extremely impressive.

Five Mystical Songs; Dona nobis pacem

> **Wiens, soprano; Rayner-Cook, baritone; London Philharmonic Orchestra and Choir, Thomson. Chandos CHAN 8590 [CD].**

As his Chandos cycle of the Vaughan Williams symphonies clearly proves, in the decade prior to his untimely death the gifted Bryden Thomson was just beginning to come into his own as a conductor. With a few exceptions—his rather too literal version of the highly atmospheric *Sinfonia Antarctica* was a considerable disappointment—the Thomson recordings are in most respects competitive with the far more celebrated recordings of Sir Adrian Boult and André Previn.

Dona nobis pacem and the early *Five Mystical Songs* are two of the most serious and gravely beautiful of all Vaughan William's vocal works and both are given sumptuous performances under Thomson's direction. The soloists acquit themselves admirably, as do the chorus, the orchestra, and Chandos's highly skilled engineers.

Five Tudor Portraits

> **Soloists, London Symphony Orchestra and Chorus, Willcocks. EMI Classics CDM 64722 [CD].**

Based on the crack-brained, near-doggerel verse of the Tudor poet and eccentric John Skelton, the *Five Tudor Portraits* is one of the most exhilarating and enjoyable of all Vaughan Williams's large-scale works, an affable and consistently surprising tour of Skelton's surreal and bawdy world that culminates in the roaring "Jolly Rutterkin." Sir David Willcocks leads a performance that admirably captures both the warmth and vitality of the piece, with lusty, full-throated singing from the chorus and sparkling playing by the London Symphony. Coupled with a lovely version of the radiant and rarely heard *Benedictine* for soprano, chorus, and orchestra and a very fine account of the *Five Variants of Dives and Lazarus,* this is a release than no VW lover can afford to pass up.

Folksong Arrangements

> **London Madrigal Singers, Bishop. EMI CMS5 65123-2 [CD].**
>
> **Deller Consort, Deller. Vanguard Classics OVC 8109 [CD].**
>
> **Bostridge, tenor; George, bass; Holst Singers, Layton. Hyperion CDA 66777 [CD].**

While it's the sworn policy of this *Guide* to recommend only those recordings that are readily available to North American consumers, this is a necessary exception. If you can't persuade your local store to special order the EMI CD from the UK, then wait till the air fares to London are at their most advantageous, get on a plane, make for the nearest record store, and buy it. (Those who can contain themselves can order it directly from an outfit with which I've always had very good luck: The Music Group, Dept. A, Regal Lane, Soham, Cambridgeshire, CB7 5BA, England, Tel: 01353 722223; Fax: 01353 723733.) Put as clearly and simply as possible, these Vaughan Williams settings for unaccompanied chorus are far and away the most beautiful arrangements of British folk songs ever made, and these are far and away their most beautiful recorded performances. Be warned, though: Some of the items, like the version of "Greensleeves" with its unforgettable tenor solo from Ian Partridge, will open your heart as easily as one peels a ripe banana. In addition to the ravishing Vaughan Williams items, this generously packed two-CD reissue features comparably wonderful versions of part songs by Elgar, Holst, Britten, Warlock, and others.

More readily available is the Vanguard Classics album that is also one of the loveliest that the late Alfred Deller and his Consort ever made. Included with fifteen of the a cappella settings are five in which the countertenor is accompanied by lutenist Desmond Dupré. Their gentle, ineffably touching version of "The Cuckoo and the Nightingale" is alone worth the modest price of the album.

The twenty-five items on this tightly packed Hyperion disc cover most of the composer's creative life, from a setting of *The Willow Song,* made when he was eighteen, to a version of Thomas Campion's *Heart's Music,* finished only three years before his death. The singing of the Holst Singers is joyous, tender, and unaffected throughout, with some especially memorable solo contributions from young Ian Bostridge, who is beginning to sound like the most intelligent and musical English tenor since Ian Partridge. As in many of Hyperion's choral albums, the perspective is a trifle distant, although given the superb diction and tightness of the ensemble, it hardly matters.

Job (a masque for dancing)

English Northern Philharmonic, Lloyd-Jones. Naxos 8.553955 [CD].

Vaughan Williams's biblical ballet is one of his most inspired and therefore most inexplicably neglected works. Along with a sequence of consistently engrossing set pieces—from the gravely beautiful *Saraband of the Sons of God* to the understandably demonic *Satan's Dance of Triumph*—the score coheres more effectively as a dramatic whole than almost any of the composer's other stage works. While the rhythmic inventiveness is predictably striking, the thematic inspiration is also maintained on the highest possible level.

Although this newcomer from Naxos faces formidable competition from *two* of Sir Adrian Boult's five recordings (the very first, reissued on Dutton DUT 8016 [CD] with a series of other Boult recording premieres of music by Bliss and Smyth, and the Everest recording from the late 1950s, which still sounds pretty fabulous on EVC 9006 [CD]) and from Richard Hickox's brilliantly theatrical version for EMI (CDC 54421 [CD]), David Lloyd-Jones and his spirited Leeds forces give a performance of comparable stature *and* do it at a super-bargain price. The playing is as dramatic and subtle as in any previous version, while the recorded sound is the most immediate and richly detailed yet. Coupled with a beautifully ethereal version of *The Lark Ascending,* this is a bargain that can't be missed.

*T*he Pilgrim's Progress (morality play in four acts)

Noble, et al., London Philharmonic Choir and Orchestra, Boult. EMI
  Classics CDMB 64212 [CD].

Completed in 1951 when the composer was seventy-eight, *The Pilgrim's
Progress* has strong claims to being Vaughan Williams's masterpiece. The composer called it neither an opera nor an oratorio but a Morality, whose purpose
was to examine the mystical implications of Bunyan's classic tale rather than its
limited dramatic content. Using material that also appeared in the beautiful Fifth
Symphony, Vaughan Williams fashioned a score of extraordinary beauty and
spiritual depth that ranks with Elgar's *Dream of Gerontius* as one of the central
works of modern English choral music.

Sir Adrian Boult's lifetime of devotion to his friend's music is obvious at all
points in this magnificent performance, one of the crowning glories of that venerable conductor's career. In addition to plumbing the work to its depths, Boult also
reveals its enormous variety, from the pastoral *Shepherds of the Delectable
Mountains* episode to the seductive evils of Vanity Fair. John Noble gives a
searching and resourceful performance as the Pilgrim, while the other members
of the cast are no less fine. Now if only EMI could be persuaded to reissue their
superlative recording of the composer's folksy Falstaff opera, *Sir John in Love*,
the full range of Vaughan Williams's achievement could be even better understood.

*R*iders to the Sea

Soloists, London Philharmonic, Davies. EMI Classics CDM
  64730 [CD].

Based on the masterful one-act play by John Millington Synge, *Riders to the
Sea* is Vaughan Williams's most concise and powerful stage work, a haunting,
emotionally draining study of a poor Irish woman who has lost her husband and
five sons to the sea and becomes persuaded she is about to lose her sixth. Helen
Watts is quietly shattering in the central role, while the contributions of Margaret
Price, Benjamin Luxon, and Norma Burrowes are no less fine. Meredith Davies
conducts with conviction and dignity and the atmospheric recorded sound has
held up extremely well.

Vaughan Williams's entertaining "ballad opera" *Hugh the Drover* is handsomely served on Hyperion (CDA 66901/02 [CD]) by an enthusiastic cast of
young singers headed by Rebecca Evans and Bonaventura Bottone. Conductor
Matthew Best not only projects the rustic, folksy charm of the score but also understands its underlying subtleties. In short, it is the kind of utterly winning performance that makes you wonder why this entertaining gem remains so obscure.

Serenade to Music

London Philharmonic, Boult. EMI Classics CDM 64022 [CD].

Written to a text from Shakespeare's *The Merchant of Venice,* the *Serenade to Music* may be the most bewitchingly beautiful work that Vaughan Williams ever wrote. And to say that of the man who wrote *The Lark Ascending,* the *Fantasia on a Theme of Thomas Tallis, Flos Campi,* and the folk-opera *Sir John in Love* is to say a very great deal indeed.

Although usually performed with a full chorus, Sir Adrian Boult gives a gleaming performance of the work as it was originally written. Composed for Sir Henry Wood's Golden Jubilee, the *Serenade* included solo parts for sixteen singers with whom Sir Henry had been especially close. That historic interpretation, recorded by Sir Henry and company in 1938 only a week after the *Serenade's* premiere, is now out on a Pearl compact disc (GEMM CD 9342). While obviously for specialists, it is a lovely performance and a recording of considerable historic importance.

For those who can do without history—especially the late '30s recorded sound, which isn't all that bad, by the way—the Boult interpretation remains a modern classic. Coupled with equally charming and authoritative versions of *In the Fen Country, The Lark Ascending,* the *English Folksong Suite,* the *Norfolk Rhapsody,* and the *Fantasia on Greensleeves,* this is probably the most desirable Vaughan Williams recording now available.

Songs of Travel

Terfel, baritone; Martineau, piano. Deutsche Grammophon 445946-2 [CD].

This memorable cycle on a famous text by Robert Louis Stevenson has never been sung with such complete musical understanding or depth of feeling. And it's only one of the many glories on *The Vagabond,* the finest single album of English songs now available. Gerald Finzi's wondrous Shakespeare sequence, *Let Us Garlands Bring,* displays a dramatic insight worthy of an Olivier or a Gielgud, while the poignant simplicity of Butterworth's *A Shropshire Lad* is sufficient to rend the most cynical heart; in fact, Terfel's version of the *Erlkönig*-like "Is my team plowing?" ranks with the greatest lieder recordings of the century. Like Gerald Moore before him, Malcolm Martineau's accompaniments are models of discretion and individuality, while the recorded sound—like the voice itself—is generous, round, and firm.

On EMI, Thomas Allen gives a knowing and sympathetic performance of the composer's orchestral version of the cycle, intelligently coupled with Robert Tear's insightful account of the orchestrated *On Wenlock Edge* (CDM 64731 [CD]).

Symphony No. 2, "A London Symphony"

Bournemouth Symphony, Bakels. Naxos 8.550734 [CD].

"It has been suggested that this symphony has been misnamed, it should rather be called 'Symphony by a Londoner,'" the composer wrote in 1925. "That is to say it is in no sense descriptive, and though the introduction of the 'Westminster Chimes' in the first movement, the slight reminiscence of the 'Lavender Cry' in the slow movement, and the very faint suggestion of mouth organs and mechanical pianos in the Scherzo give it a tinge of 'local colour,' yet it is intended to be listened to as 'absolute' music. Hearers may, if they like, localize the various themes and movements, but it is hoped that this is not a necessary part of the music."

Although he faces formidable competition from far better-known Vaughan Williams conductors, such as Barbirolli, Boult, Handley, and Previn, Kees Bakels's fabulous Naxos recording currently sweeps the field. In addition to an interpretation that fully exploits the Symphony's color, humor, and grandeur, the playing of the Bournemouth Symphony is staggeringly beautiful, perhaps their most refined and polished work on records since that series of recordings with Constantin Silvestri from the 1960s. With a cracking version of *The Wasps* Overture thrown in for good measure, this is yet another astounding bargain from Naxos.

Symphony No. 4 in F Minor; Symphony No. 6 in E Minor

New Philharmonia Orchestra, Boult. EMI Classics CDM 64019 [CD].

A number of years ago at the first San Francisco Symphony performance of Vaughan Williams's Sixth Symphony, the conductor a very fine conductor, who will remain nameless—decided that since the piece was bound to be unfamiliar to most of the audience, he should probably say a few words about it. He began his impromptu talk with the unfortunate sentence, "The Vaughan Williams Sixth is basically a very depressing piece . . . " Before uttering another syllable, he was abruptly cut off by a shy, retiring friend of mine (and a *full* professor of Vaughan Williams) who pointed an accusing finger at the luckless musician and said, "But that *simply* isn't true!" Stunned and speechless, the conductor broke off his comments and began the piece without further ado.

The most bleakly pessimistic of the composer's symphonies it most certainly is; yet it is no more "depressing" than Robert Lowell's poetry, Max Beckmann's paintings, or some of Ingmar Bergman's jollier films. Begun in the midst of World War Two and completed two years after its conclusion, the Sixth is an appropriately dark vision of life from the middle of the darkest century in recorded history.

Sir Adrian Boult's powerful recording is one of the best from his historic Vaughan Williams cycle. The performance is honest and unblinkingly courageous, with a final movement that rises to tragic heights reminiscent of the greatest Mahler *adagios.* Coupled with the explosive, dissonant Fourth Symphony in an equally unnerving performance, this is *not* a recording for fans of the *Greensleeves Fantasia* who are looking for more of the same.

Symphony No. 5 in D Major

London Symphony, Previn. RCA Victor 60586-2 [CD].

The Fifth is not only the most beautiful of the nine Vaughan Williams symphonies but also one of the most completely characteristic. In it, we hear an impeccable craftsman with a complex yet thoroughly humane mind—an utterly modern man who was content with stirring us deeply and who left probing the depths or shaking the heavens to others.

There are many who feel that André Previn is the most persuasive of all living Vaughan Williams conductors, and I agree. This Fifth, part of Previn's cycle of all nine symphonies for RCA, remains one of the best recordings the conductor has made so far. In general, Previn brings more life and freshness to this great work than any conductor ever has. The great themes of the first movement unfold with an ease and naturalness that not even Boult can match. For a very different view of the work and one coupled with something more substantial than the admittedly delightful *Tuba Concerto* and *Three Portraits,* Boult's Angel recording comes with perhaps the finest version of the "Pastoral" Symphony (No. 3) on EMI Classics CDM 64018 [CD].

While space, alas, does not permit a complete discussion of all nine Vaughan Williams symphonies, the other Angel recordings by Sir Adrian Boult and those by André Previn on RCA Victor can be recommended enthusiastically. The Boult interpretations have the advantage of the conductor's long friendship with the composer and his fifty-year immersion in the music. Previn, on the other hand, brings an engaging spontaneity to the music and a youthful, interpretive insight that make his recordings no less valuable. The wise collector will want them all, especially since all have been reissued on compact disc.

Vejvanovsky, Pavel Josef
(c. 1633–1693)

Sonatas and Serenades

Virtuosi di Praga, Vlček. Discover International DIC 920243 [CD].

If you're thrilled by the sound of baroque trumpets, then Pavel Vejvanovsky's your boy. A superb composer whose work had a powerful influence on the work of his younger contemporary Heinrich Ignaz Franz von Biber, Vejvanovsky was also one of the great trumpet virtuosos of his day—as may be gathered from the supremely idiomatic trumpet parts that grace the serenades and sonatas heard on this exciting disc. Best of all is the *Serenata* from 1679, with its rich harmonies and jaunty rhythms, and the brief *Sonata à 4 be mollis,* with its obvious debt to Czech folk song more than two centuries before Smetana wrote *The Bartered Bride.*

The stylish performances by the Virtuosi di Praga under Oldřich Vlček are enhanced by the magnificent acoustic of the Lobochovice castle, which bestows a medieval splendor on the proceedings. At Discover's rock-bottom prices, the thrills are cheap indeed.

Verdi, Giuseppe   (1813–1901)

Aida

Milanov, Barbieri, Björling, Warren, Christoff, Chorus and Orchestra of the Rome Opera House, Perlea. RCA Victor 6652-2-RG [CD], ALK3-5380 [T].

Price, Bumbry, Domingo, Milnes, London Symphony, Leinsdorf. RCA Victor 6198-2 RC [CD].

Verdi is unique among the great composers in that his posthumous fame is of virtually the same magnitude as that which he acquired during his lifetime. In 1842, the year of *Nabucco,* Verdi became a national hero in his own country, and within the next few years he was lionized throughout the operatic world. Although there were occasional setbacks (the famous initial failure of *La Traviata,* for instance), he enjoyed more than half a century of increasing honors and died, at the age of eighty-seven, steeped in wealth and adulation.

Aida, which was to have been his final opera, is a good indication of why Verdi, now as then, is the very heart of Italian opera. Amid all its pomp and spectacle, *Aida* is essentially a work about human conflict—the conflicting emotions of its central characters, both with each other and within themselves. Given an even half-way decent production, *Aida* easily demonstrates why its power is virtually indestructible and why it remains one of the three or four most popular works of the operatic stage.

As a performance, no recording has yet to supersede the brilliant version made in Rome in the mid-1950s, which featured what was, and remains, an ideal cast. Beginning with Zinka Milanov, who is as poignant as she is powerful in the title role, all of the parts are covered by superb choices, from the glorious Rhadames of Jussi Björling, to the menacing, ink-black Ramfis of the young Boris Christoff. The conducting of the vastly underrated Jonel Perlea is full of fire and poetry, and the recorded sound is much better than you'd expect from that era.

For the best modern version of the score, Leontyne Price's RCA recording easily sweeps the field. Although not quite as intense and probing as in her London recording with Sir Georg Solti, the singing clearly shows why Price, after Rosa Ponselle, was the greatest Verdi singer America has so far produced.

*A*rias

Caballé, soprano. RCA 09026-60941-2 [CD].

Callas, soprano. EMI Classics CDC 47730 [CD]; CDC 47943 [CD].

Caruso, tenor. RCA 09026-61242-2 [CD].

Domingo, tenor. EMI Classics CDM 66532 [CD]; RCA 09026-68446-2 [CD].

Hvorostovsky, baritone. Philips 426740-2 [CD].

Pavarotti, tenor. London 417570-2 [CD].

Ponselle, soprano. RCA 7810-2-RG [CD].

Price, soprano. RCA RCD1-7016 [CD].

Ruffo, baritone. Iron Needle IN 1356 [CD].

Rysanek, soprano. RCA 09026-68920 [CD].

Here, in the work of ten unique singers, are many of the most celebrated Verdi arias in some of the best recordings ever made. Caruso was, of course, the prototype of the modern Verdi tenor, and this intelligently chosen, superbly remastered RCA collection indicates *just* how remote the possibility is that we'll ever hear his like again. The performances are electrifying examples of his art, confirming (and then some) all the legends. The singing of "The Caruso of Baritones," Titta Ruffo, is thrillingly captured on the Iron Needle anthology, which includes the stupendous version with Caruso of the Vengeance Duet from *Otello,* arguably the most opulent vocal recording of all time.

In an interview for *Downbeat Magazine,* Nat Hentoff once asked the late Miles Davis to say a few words about the history of jazz. The garrulous trumpet player said, "I only need four: Louis Armstrong, Charlie Parker." By that same token, much of the history of modern Verdi singing can be summed up in four other words: Rosa Ponselle, Leontyne Price. Ponselle's recordings from the mid- to late-'20s capture what is still the single most glorious voice that America has ever produced. Even through the antique recorded sound, you know you're in the presence of a Niagara Falls–size natural wonder, while the famous interpretations mix fire, grandeur, and melting tenderness in a very heady brew. If Ponselle's was the century's most imposing Verdi instrument, then Price's was the most beautiful. The RCA collection captures it in its absolute prime, with singing so effortless and ravishing that you suspect its sheer physical beauty will never be surpassed.

The singing on Caballé's "Verdi Rarities" album is also very beautiful, with many intriguing items given the star treatment they deserve, while Callas recordings capture the century's foremost singing actress at the very top of her form. The late Leonie Rysanek was uncharacteristically (though understandably) pleased with her famous RCA anthology, writing, "If there is a single record with which I'm largely satisfied, it is this recital of Italian arias." Indeed, the collection does reveal her uniquely passionate singing in the most favorable possible light.

The Domingo and Pavarotti albums show off the work of the two leading Verdi tenors of modern times, with Domingo displaying that unerring taste and musicianship that make him the most satisfying lyric tenor since Björling (and the best *Otello* since Vinay) and Pavarotti the most distinctive and exciting instrument of his generation. Finally, the Philips album from Dmitri Hvorostovsky suggests that there *is* hope for the future of Verdi singing, with performances that are as interpretively commanding as they are beautifully sung.

Un ballo in maschera (A Masked Ball)

M. Price, Pavarotti, Ludwig, Battle, Bruson, National Philharmonic Orchestra, Solti. London 425529-2 [CD].

At first glance, this didn't look at all promising. (Actually, it did, but I hate to tell you exactly *what* it seemed to promise.) At the time, Pavarotti was obviously in serious vocal trouble, Margaret Price was merely getting louder and louder, and Sir Georg Solti hadn't made an operatic recording with any genuine passion in it for nearly a dozen years.

The surprising result is a milestone in recent operatic history. This *Ballo* takes off like a shot and refuses to let up until the very end. The cast could not have been better (Pavarotti sounds like the Pavarotti of old), and there is no praise too high for Solti's alert, incisive conducting. In short, this is a *Ballo* for you.

Don Carlo

Mattila, Meier, Alagna, Hampson, Van Dam, Châtelet Theater Choir,
Orchestre de Paris, Pappano. EMI Classics CDCC 56152 [CD].

The universal acceptance of *Don Carlo* as one of the greatest of Verdi's operas is a fairly recent phenomenon that was helped along by two historic productions: the 1950 revival with which Sir Rudolf Bing began his controversial but always lively tenure at the Metropolitan Opera, and Visconti's Covent Garden production eight years later, which introduced many to a brilliant new Italian conductor named Carlo Maria Giulini.

Taped in London thirteen years later, Giulini's EMI recording was not only the best *Don Carlo* we are likely to hear this century, but also one of the great Verdi recordings yet made. While the cast is one of the strongest assembled during the 1970s—Placido Domingo as the feckless hero and Ruggero Raimondi as the King are especially engrossing—it is Giulini's subtle intensity that makes the recording click. Even the problematic *Auto da fé* scene explodes with an uncommon point and veracity; many listeners, no doubt, will be tempted to bring their own weenies and marshmallows. As with most of the EMI CD restorations, the recording sounds as though it had been made last week. The recording has been withdrawn temporarily, presumably for a medium-price reissue (not even EMI, with its reckless deletions policy, could keep *this* one out of the catalogue for long).

Until it returns, the newer EMI recording is the best alternative, especially since it presents the opera in the original French. While Antonio Pappano is no match for Giulini in his prime, he conducts with subtlety and passion and is blessed with an outstanding cast headed by the sweet-voiced and expressive Roberto Alagna in the title role. The fact that the recording was made during actual performances only adds to the excitement.

Ernani

L. Price, Bergonzi, Sereni, Flagello, RCA Italiana Opera Chorus and
Orchestra, Schippers. RCA 6503-2-RG [CD].

One of *Ernani*'s harshest early critics was Victor Hugo, who considered Verdi's adaptation of his play *Hernani* a complete travesty. A century and a half later, it is this "travesty" alone that keeps the memory of that once popular play alive.

For his fifth opera, Verdi produced a score bursting with vigor, rousing tunes, and good old-fashioned moustache-twirling melodrama. By the standards of the masterworks of the 1850s, much of this can seem fairly naive and obvious stuff; yet in the right hands, the opera can pack a tremendous vocal and emotional wallop, as it does in this powerful recording from 1967.

If Leontyne Price was not at her absolute dramatic peak as the *Ernani* Elvira, then it is still her usual vocal tour de force. With suave and powerful support from the always wonderful Carlo Bergonzi and the magnetic conducting of Thomas Schippers, this is the *Ernani* to have.

Falstaff

> **Freni, Ligabue, Simionato, Elias, Krause, Evans, Merrill, RCA Italiana Opera Chorus and Orchestra, Solti. London 417168-2 [CD].**

Poor *Falstaff* has fallen on hard times of late, with the outstanding versions by Bernstein, Giulini, and Karajan (EMI, *not* DG) currently unavailable. But like Sir John himself, the opera keeps bouncing back—this time thanks to London's medium-priced reissue of a classic recording originally made by RCA. Chief among the performance's many glories is the Falstaff of the late Sir Geraint Evans, in every way the most complex and amusing of all recorded characterizations and clearly superior to his now deleted rivals (Dietrich Fischer-Dieskau, Renato Bruson, and Tito Gobbi). What the late Sir Georg Solti's conducting may lack in comic subtlety—and it doesn't lack all that much—it more than makes up for with energy and excitement.

La forza del destino

> **Tebaldi, Simionato, Del Monaco, Bastianini, Siepi, Chorus and Orchestra of the Santa Cecilia Academy, Rome, Molinari-Pradelli. London 421598-2 [CD].**

Of all the great middle-period Verdi operas (from *Rigoletto* of 1851 through *Aida*, 1871), *La forza del destino* is easily the most incredible. And by "incredible," I mean in the literal sense, as something that can barely be believed. The plot of the opera is hopelessly twisted and complicated, and the irony so extreme that it would have made Charles Dickens blush. And yet, in spite of the unintentional silliness of its goofy and frequently embarrassing plot, *Forza* is one of the greatest of Verdi's operas. And despite its great length, it is one of the most compressed of all Verdi's operas. In its musical concentration and dramatic power, *Forza* is the one early Verdi work that clearly points the way to *Aida,* and ultimately, *Otello.*

After Rosa Ponselle, Leontyne Price was probably the finest Leonore of the century. The power of her middle register, the incomparable beauty of her high notes, and the enormous strength and dignity of her characterization turned her RCA recording into the stuff of legend. While it is clearly Price's show, the rest of the cast was no less splendid. Domingo and Milnes are almost as fine as they are in their superb *Otello* (see page 759), and Levine, here, offers some of his most assured and sympathetic conducting on records. Without question, this is one of the best operatic recordings of the last three decades, which has now been inexplicably withdrawn.

Incredibly enough, there is no currently available version of *Forza* that can be recommended with complete enthusiasm. The old London recording offers Renata Tebaldi singing very beautifully—her "Madre, madre, pietosa Vergine" is heart-stopping—but neither Mario del Monaco nor Francesco Molinari-Pradelli was having one of his better days. But until the Price is reissued—and surely, that must be its destiny?—the Tebaldi will have to do.

Inno delle nazioni (Hymn of the Nations)

Peerce, tenor; Westminster Choir, NBC Symphony, Toscanini. RCA 60299-2-RG [CD], 60299-4-RG [T].

The next time you find yourself in an opera trivia match and are stuck for a question, ask your opponent to name the first of the Verdi-Boito collaborations. No, it wasn't *Otello,* but this pastiche of national anthems concocted for the London International Exhibition of 1862. For his performances during World War II, Arturo Toscanini dutifully added *The Star-Spangled Banner* as a finale and with Jan Peerce, the Westminster Choir, and the NBC Symphony all obviously caught up in the spirit of the moment, this makes for one of the Maestro's most exciting recordings.

The sound, predictably, is harsh and strained.

I Lombardi

Deutekom, Domingo, Raimondi, Ambrosian Singers, Royal Philharmonic, Gardelli. Philips 422420-2 [CD].

One of the most consistently impressive series of operatic recordings was Philips's cycle of Verdi's early "galley slave" operas in performances led by Lamberto Gardelli, most of which have now found their way onto CD. While there are no hidden masterpieces lurking here, each offers an abundance of entertaining, if not always inspired or inspiring music, together with invaluable insights into the early development of the supreme tragedian of the operatic stage. *I Lombardi,* the work that followed the extraordinary success of *Nabucco,* has much to recommend it, including the heroine's lovely "Salve Maria" (changed from "Ave Maria" to placate the Church sensors) and a villain who can be seen as an embryonic version of Iago in *Otello.* As the hero Oronte, son of the tyrant of Antioch—well, no one said that this was Checkov—Placido Domingo sings with ringing conviction, while Gardelli shapes a powerfully theatrical performance that breathes fire and pathos from beginning to end.

Those who respond to the rough but often enthralling pleasures of early Verdi should waste no time acquiring the other installments in the Philips series before they're withdrawn: a stirring *Attila* with Ruggero Raimondi giving a formidable performance in the title role (426115 [CD]); a swift and exciting *La Battaglia di Legnano* with José Carreras and Katia Ricciarelli in spectacular form (422435-2 [CD]); and Norman, Carreras, and the always wonderful Fiorenza Cossoto proving that the youthful comedy *Un giorno di regno* is not the unmitigated disaster of legend but in fact a great deal of Rossiniesque fun (422429-2 [CD].

Lamberto Gardelli leads a cracking performance of *Alzira* for Orfeo (057832 [CD]), while the CBS recording of *Aroldo* (M2K 35906 [CD]) finds Caballé in excellent form in this concert performance of the revised version of *Stifelio*.

Luisa Miller

Millo, Quivar, Domingo, Chernov, Metropolitan Opera Chorus and
Orchestra, Levine. Sony Classical S2K 48073 [CD].

Finished just before *Rigoletto* launched the composer's incomparably rich Middle Period—that canon of works upon which every opera company in the world depends for its very existence—*Luisa Miller* is very nearly a great opera. There are many who insist that it actually *is,* including Placido Domingo, who declares that the tenor's big moment is his favorite single aria. (He facetiously claims it is such because "Quando le sere al placido" actually contains his name, but it *is* an extravagantly beautiful moment, one of the finest that Verdi ever wrote.)

Domingo and almost everyone else perform magnificently in this first-rate Covent Garden production. The only exception is Aprile Millo, who, like Elena Obraztsova in Domingo's now-deleted Deutsche Grammophon recording, is not ideally steady in the punishing title role. Levine's conducting is a model of middle-period Verdi blood and thunder, while the recorded sound has a striking immediacy and presence.

Macbeth

Cappuccilli, Verrett, Ghiaurov, Domingo, Chorus and Orchestra of La
Scala, Milan, Abbado. Deutsche Grammophon 449732-2 [CD].

In many ways *Macbeth* was Verdi's *Fidelio,* the work that caused him more time and anguish than any other in his career. A comparative failure at its Florence premiere in 1847, it was revised substantially for an 1865 production in Paris, where it proved to be an even bigger flop. In spite of its comparative lack of success, it remained one of his own favorite operas for reasons that aren't difficult to explain. For along with being the finest opera of the 1840s—the decade he called his "years as a galley slave"—*Macbeth* is also the first in which we hear the unmistakable voice of the composer that Verdi would eventually become. For here, dramatic values become as important as musical ones, and the revelation of character—which Verdi sought all his life to perfect—had its first great success in the figure of Lady Macbeth, one of the most important female roles he would ever conceive.

If Shirley Verrett's voice isn't really suited to the part, then that has not prevented her from becoming the great Lady Macbeth of our time. In fact, the characterization is so menacing, eerie, and vivid—the Sleepwalking scene would chill a Sicilian's blood—that it nearly overwhelms the fine performance of Piero Cappuccilli in the title role. Abbado's sharply dramatic conducting ranks with his best on records, and the rest of the cast is excellent, as is the recorded sound.

Nabucco

Suliotis, Predevi, Gobbi, Cava, Vienna State Opera Chorus and Orchestra, Gardelli. London 417407-2 [CD].

Nabucco was Verdi's first great success and is the only one of his operas—unless one counts that anvil thing in *Trovatore*—that is best-known for a chorus: the celebrated lamentation "Va Pensiero" that immediately became the unofficial anthem of the Italian independence movement and, sixty years later, would be sung spontaneously by Milan's heartbroken masses at Verdi's funeral in 1901. While certainly not a great opera, *Nabucco* can be an entertaining and intermittently enthralling experience, especially in a performance such as the one London recorded in Vienna in the mid-1960s.

The principal attractions of this fine recording—which, in spite of its age, is to be preferred to Sinopoli's mannered and finicky outing for Deutsche Grammophon—are the Nabucco of the late Tito Gobbi, who here demonstrates why he was the most accomplished dramatic baritone of his generation, and the spirited, sensitive conducting of Lamberto Gardelli, one of the major Verdi specialists of the last half century.

For those who are interested only in "Va Pensiero," it can be heard to supremely tear-jerking effect (along with other favorite Verdi choruses) on a superb London recording (430226-2 [CD]) by the Chicago Symphony Chorus—drilled to their usual awe-inspiring perfection by Margaret Hillis—and the Chicago Symphony Orchestra led by Sir Georg Solti.

*O*tello

**Domingo, Scotto, Milnes, National Philharmonic, Levine. RCA Victor
RCD2 2951 [CD].**

The choice of a recorded *Otello* inevitably becomes a choice between the two great Otellos of modern times, Jon Vickers and Placido Domingo. On balance, I tend to favor the Domingo version, but only by a hairsbreadth. The Domingo *Otello* is a large, powerful, beautifully sung, and ultimately withering experience. While the Vickers is no less enthralling, both of his recorded versions have drawbacks: a spotty cast and strangely inert support from Tullio Serafin in the RCA Victor recording, and Herbert von Karajan's heavy hand in the more recent version for Angel.

However, the Domingo *Otello* is not without its flaws. It features the often shrill Desdemona of Renata Scotto and conducting from James Levine that is occasionally so enthusiastic that some very important singing is lost. (In the opening "Esultate," for instance, Domingo is practically drowned out.) Nevertheless, with the splendid Iago of Sherrill Milnes, this *Otello* is an outstanding performance, and we are not likely to hear a finer one any time soon.

*R*equiem; *Quattro pezzi sacri* (Four Sacred Pieces)

**Schwarzkopf, Ludwig, Gedda, Ghiaurov, Philharmonia Chorus and
Orchestra, Giulini. EMI Classics ZDCB 56250 [CD].**

This is the one recording of the Verdi *Requiem*—that magnificent opera disguised as a sacred work—that will make even the most unregenerate sinner *believe*. (If the Day of Judgment isn't as overwhelming as Verdi and Giulini make it sound, I, for one, will be extremely disappointed.) In the quarter of a century since its release, this version of the *Requiem* has dominated the catalogues in a way that no other recording has. In its compact disc format, the performance is even more thrilling than ever, and if this one doesn't spur you on to buying a compact disc player, nothing will.

If any recording on tape came within an inch of this one's instep, I'd be the first to recommend it. To date, no such recording exists. Coupled with Giulini's incomparable version of the *Four Sacred Pieces*, this is now a bargain that no Verdi lover—no music lover, for that matter—can possibly resist.

*R*igoletto

Callas, Di Stefano, Gobbi, Zaccaria, La Scala Chorus and Orchestra,
Serafin. EMI Classics CDCB 56327 [CD].

The ultimate test of any performance of *Rigoletto* is your reaction to the final scene. Are tears rolling down your cheeks, or are you laughing so hard you're afraid of committing an indiscretion on your seat? *Both* reactions, by the way, are perfectly plausible. Consider the bare bones of the scene itself. A hunchback jester opens a gunnysack, thinking it contains the corpse of the heartless rogue who deflowered his daughter. Much to his surprise, he discovers his daughter herself, who, while bleeding to death, sings one of the most demanding duets in all of opera. (If you think *singing* on your side isn't a tough trick, just try drinking a glass of beer that way.)

Whenever I hear the final duet in this historic version of Verdi's early masterpiece, I am *never* tempted to laugh. One of the most enduring of the many great recorded collaborations of Maria Callas and Tito Gobbi, this *Rigoletto* virtually defines the phrase "Grand Opera." To Callas and Gobbi, add the slightly edgy but still magnificent Giuseppe di Stefano as the Duke, and the firm yet flexible conducting of Tullio Serafin, and you have something close to a *Rigoletto* for the ages. The mid-1950s recorded sound is more than adequate, and in the compact disc transfer, its bite and clarity are amazing.

*S*imon Boccanegra

Freni, Carreras, Cappuccilli, Ghiaurov, Van Dam, Fioani, Chorus and
Orchestra of La Scala, Milan, Abbado. Deutsche Grammophon
449752-2 [CD].

With the overly long and generally uninspired *I Vespri Siciliani*—even the composer himself complained about the excessive length of his made-to-order French grand opera—*Simon Boccanegra* is the only one of Verdi's works after *Rigoletto* that has failed to become a staple of the standard repertoire. Part of the reason that this masterpiece has been so long in catching on—and a masterpiece it most certainly is—has to do with the casting of the title role.

Whenever a production is blessed with a magnetic star-caliber baritone—Victor Maurel for the premiere of the 1881 revision; Lawrence Tibbett at the Metropolitan in 1932; Warren, Gobbi, and Sherrill Milnes in more recent years—the opera usually proves to be an overwhelming success. Abbado's sensational 1977 recording with the bright, musical, though hardly heart-stopping Piero Cappuccilli proves that *Simon* is not only *not* a one-man show but also that it can stand on its own with any middle-period Verdi opera.

Most of the credit for one of the most exciting and nearly perfect of all modern Verdi recordings must go to Claudio Abbado, who has never been more impressive in the recording studio or out; the conducting is noble, poetic, subtle, and intense, with a sense of life and on-the-spot creativity that is rarely encountered in a commercial recording. The soloists, chorus, and orchestra all catch fire under Abbado's incandescent direction and DG's engineers come through with their very best recorded sound.

If, for you, *Simon Boccanegra* is still a question mark, this is the recording that will turn it into an exclamation point.

String Quartet in E Minor

Alberni String Quartet. CRD 3366 [CD].

Verdi wrote his only mature instrumental work in 1873 while supervising the Naples premiere of *Aïda*. When two of the leading singers fell ill, he "composed a quartet, in the hours when I had nothing to do." Following a private performance in the grand salon of the Hotel delle Crocelle, Verdi refused to have it performed again for several years. With typical modesty he said: "I don't know whether it is beautiful or ugly. I only know that it is a quartet." As a matter of fact, it's a very beautiful work, respectful of the chamber music traditions of Mozart and Beethoven but also unmistakably Verdian from beginning to end.

The recording by the Alberni Quartet is not only the most involving and idiomatic currently available, but it also offers the most attractive couplings: the deft, enormously appealing Quartet No. 13 by Donizetti and the lovely *Crisantemi* (Chrysanthemums) by Puccini.

La Traviata

Callas, Di Stefano, Bastianini, La Scala Chorus and Orchestra, Giulini. EMI Classics CDMB 63628 [CD].

You take the good with the bad. Unfortunately, neither Giuseppe di Stefano nor Ettore Bastianini was at his best in this 1955 recording, nor, alas, were the EMI engineers. Compared to the famous *Tosca* recorded in the same venue two years earlier, the sound was always boxy and diffused and it has *not* improved with age.

Still, for the Violetta that Verdi and God intended, one need look no further. Callas remains the ultimate modern incarnation of the star-crossed courtesan; on records, only Claudia Muzio penetrated this deeply into the character's soul. The wealth of fascinating detail and the immediacy of the singing remain astonishing;

the pathos of the final scene is so overwhelming that the recording's flaws pale to insignificance.

Among the numerous better-sounding alternatives, Dame Joan Sutherland's second recording (London 430491-2 [CD]) is easily the best. As a technical tour de force her performance is exhilarating, while Pavarotti and Richard Bonynge are both in excellent form.

Il Trovatore

Milanov, Björling, Barbieri, Warren, RCA Victor Chorus and Orchestra, Cellini. RCA Victor 6643-2-RG [CD], CLK2 5377 [T].

This (to use a phrase without which every sportscaster in America would be unable to do his job) really *is* what it's all about. Add a Leonore made of 50 percent volcano and 50 percent pathos, a gleaming, heroic Manrico (his high C in "Di quella pira" will shake you down to your socks), and a sinister, brooding, old-fashioned Azucena "whose very urine" (to use Philip Wylie's immortal phrase), "would probably etch glass," and you have one of the most electric operatic recordings ever made. The combination of Zinka Milanov, Jussi Björling, Fedora Barbieri, and Leonard Warren, the same team responsible for that greatest of all recorded *Aidas,* is all but unstoppable here. Even the occasionally phlegmatic Renato Cellini catches fire and turns in what is undoubtedly the performance of his career.

For those who are bothered by the monophonic, mid-1950s recorded sound—and if you're listening to sound instead of music, then you might want to make sure you have the *right* hobby—another fine RCA Victor release (60560-2-RG [CD], 60560-4-RG [T]) with Price, Cossotto, Domingo, Milnes, and Mehta at the top of *their* forms is the best recent alternative.

I vespri siciliani

Studer, Merritt, Zancanaro, Furlanetto, La Scala Opera Chorus and Orchestra, Muti. EMI CDCC 54043 [CD].

Tailor-made to the spectacle-loving tastes of the Parisian public, *I vespri siciliani* (The Sicilian Vespers) scarcely seems the work of the composer of *Rigoletto, Il Trovatore,* and *La Traviata,* the operas that immediately preceded it. Part of the problem was that Verdi disliked the libretto—he considered the treacherous behavior of the Sicilian patriots as insulting to all Italians—nor was he able to work comfortably within the unwieldy five-act form of French Grand Opera. Yet if it is not one of Verdi's strongest pieces, then *I vespri siciliani* nonetheless contains much marvelous music, including one of his finest overtures;

one of his finest bass arias, "O tu Palermo" from Act II; one of his most irresistible soprano *cabalettas*—Elena's Act V bolero, "Mercè, dilette amiche"; and nearly a half hour of top-notch dance music, the Ballet of the Seasons from Act III.

In this live recording from Milan's La Scala, Riccardo Muti leads a performance full of dash and sweep, with Cheryl Studer a fetching and vocally dazzling heroine. The rest of the cast is good to excellent, with recorded sound that captures the excitement of a live performance with few of its pitfalls. On balance, it is the most persuasive argument yet made for an unjustly (for the most part) neglected score.

At press time, the recording had just been withdrawn. As there is currently no viable alternative—save some pirated versions of live performances of variable quality featuring Caballé, Callas, and the formidable Anita Cerquetti—interested collectors should consult the cut-out bins or various English sources (see Vaughan Williams: Folk Song Arrangements, page 745).

Victoria, Tomás Luis de

(c. 1548–1611)

Ave Maria; Ave maris stella (hymn); *Missa vidi speciosam; Ne timeas, Maria; Sancta Maria, succérre miseris; Vidi speciosam*

> Westminster Cathedral Choir, Hill. Hyperion CDA 66129 [CD].

Officium defunctorum

> Westminster Cathedral Choir, Hill. Hyperion CDA 66250 [CD].

Tenebrae Responsories

> Westminster Cathedral Choir, Hill. Hyperion CDA 66304 [CD].

King Philip II was correct in his famous assertion that "The destiny of Spain cannot await upon the fitness of time." Alas, it *did* have to await upon the whims of that arrogant, boneheaded monarch who in a single, ill-advised stroke managed to throw away one of the greatest empires since the fall of Rome. When the Armada went down in the unforgiving waters of the English Channel in 1588, it not only marked the end of the Spanish domination of both the Old and New Worlds but also the beginning of the end of the Golden Age of Spanish Art, as epitomized by the paintings of El Greco, the fiction of Cervantes, the drama and poetry of Lope de Vega, and the music of composers like Tomás Luis de Victoria.

Nearly four centuries after his death, Victoria's music retains the ardor and spiritual daring that made it one of the purest Renaissance manifestations of Spanish mysticism, an intense, ecstatic, transcendent beauty that is projected to absolute perfection in these lovely Hyperion recordings. The committed, emotionally high-powered interpretations that David Hill draws from the Westminster Choir are far removed from the typical dry-as-dust approach to early sacred music, and the warm, enfolding acoustics of Hyperion's recording prove an ideal setting for the spirit of a very great composer and his glittering age.

Vierne, Louis   (1870–1937)

Symphonies for Organ

> Sanger, organ. Meridian CDE 84192 [CD] (Nos. 1 and 2); CDE 84176 [CD] (Nos. 3 and 4).

This extraordinary blind French organist and composer died as he always wished he might, at the organ of Notre Dame in Paris. After succeeding his teacher Charles Marie Widor at St. Sulpice and the Paris Conservatory, Vierne won the post of organist at France's most famous cathedral in 1900, where the great figures of the period—from Rodin, Clémenceau, and Sarah Bernhardt to his pupils Nadia Boulanger and Marcel Dupré—came to hear him play. His many works for organ, including six "symphonies" modeled on those of Widor, capture much of the grandeur and complexity of Notre Dame's incomparable Gothic architecture.

David Sanger seems thoroughly immersed in these highly rewarding works, playing with equal amounts of power and grace on the attractive organ of London's La Chiesa Italiana di San Pietro. The recorded sound is admirably full-throated and clear.

Vieuxtemps, Henri (1820–1881)

Concerto No. 5 for Violin and Orchestra

> Zukerman, violin; London Symphony, Mackerras. Sony Classics SBK
> 48274 [CD], SBT 48274 [T].

Given their inherent quality and sheer bravura excitement, it's frankly shocking that the six Vieuxtemps Violin Concertos have fallen on such hard times. Technically, the best of them—the First, Third, Fourth, and Fifth—are every bit the equal of those virtuoso show-stoppers by Paganini and Wieniawski, while musically they frequently have more to say and often say it with greater skill.

Pinchas Zukerman's interpretation is predictably outgoing, colorful, and full of character, and note for note is as impressively played as Heifetz's celebrated recording for RCA Victor. Speaking of whom, that violinist's electrifying 1935 recording of the Fourth Concerto with the London Symphony led by the young John Barbirolli is available in an attractive anthology of Heifetz showpieces from EMI (CDH 64251-2 [CD]).

Villa-Lobos, Heitor (1887–1959)

Bachianas brasileiras Nos. 1, 5, and 7

> Hendricks, soprano; Royal Philharmonic, Bátiz. EMI Classics CDC
> 47433 [CD].

Almost everyone who discovers the music of South America's foremost composer, the Brazilian Heitor Villa-Lobos, does so through the wordless aria from the hauntingly beautiful *Bachiana brasileira No. 5*. A startlingly imaginative transposition of the spirit of Bach to the soil of Brazil, this, and indeed, *all* of the *Bachianas* are major contributions to the music of the twentieth century, as is the work of Heitor Villa-Lobos in general.

Not since the Brazilian soprano Bidù Saÿao made her famous recording with the composer in the 1940s has there been a more heart-stopping version of the work than this gleaming EMI recording by Barbara Hendricks, who certainly has the talent, the drive, and the looks—she is a dazzlingly pretty woman—to become one of the dominant voices of the waning years of the twentieth century. This stunning Angel recording is one of her best to date. The singing has a lush yet otherworldly quality that suggests an over-sexed seraphim, and the accompaniment she receives from Enrique Bátiz is a model of sympathetic support. For something slightly off the beaten track, that is, as a gift for the collector who seems to have *almost* everything, you can't go wrong with this lovely recording, even if you simply give it as a gift to yourself.

Concerto for Guitar and Orchestra

> **Williams, guitar; English Chamber Orchestra, Barenboim. Sony M2K 44791 [CD].**

If Villa-Lobos's Guitar Concerto is not one of his most distinguished or characteristic works, then it is still one of the instrument's most attractive modern works and sounds very close to a masterpiece in the ardent, imaginative performance by John Williams. Although Sony might easily have reissued his masterful performance of the composer's Five Preludes, the Concerto comes as part of a two-CD set that also includes near-definitive readings of Rodrigo's *Concierto de Aranjuez* and *Fantasia para un gentilehombre,* together with versions of the concertos of Castelnuovo-Tedesco, Ponce, Giuliani, and Vivaldi that leave little doubt that John Williams is the great guitarist of modern times.

String Quartets (17)

> **Danubius String Quartet. Marco Polo 8.223389 [CD] (Vol. 1—Nos. 1, 8, 13); 8.223390 [CD] (Vol. 2—Nos. 11, 16, 17); 8.223391 [CD] (Vol. 3—Nos. 3, 10, 15); 8.223392 (Vol. 4—Nos 5, 9, 12); 8.332294 (Vol. 5—Nos. 2 and 7).**

Aside from the rare individual item—like the Hollywood String Quartet's classic recording of the Sixth—the string quartets of South America's greatest composer and self-confessed "string quartet addict" have been conspicuously ignored in the recording studio until now.

In their immensely impressive Marco Polo cycle of all seventeen quartets, the Danubius String Quartet reveals them as a collection of endlessly fascinating works that—like the Beethoven quartets—occupied their composer's attention throughout most of his creative life. As with the quartets of his near contemporary Dmitri Shostakovich, Villa-Lobos reserved much of what was most personal and immediate in his art for this demanding medium and through it achieved some of his greatest successes.

Volume 1 is the obvious place to begin exploring the series, since it brings together the folkloric First Quartet of 1914, with the more mature and confident Eighth Quartet of 1944 and the unsettling Thirteenth Quartet of 1951. Throughout, the Danubius Quartet performs with subtlety and passion, while the recorded sound is immediate and realistic.

All in all, this is one of the most important chamber music series in a decade.

Vine, Carl   (1954–   )

Piano Sonata (1990)

Harvey, piano. Tall Poppies TP 013 [CD].

There was a time when virtually all anyone knew about Australian music were those immortal chestnuts of Percy Grainger and perhaps John Antill's vivid 1946 ballet *Corroboree*. Times are certainly changing, if the music of Carl Vine is any indication. A formidably equipped musician with a passion for jazz and avant-garde experimentation, Vine is clearly one of the most talented young composers working anywhere. His orchestral scores, like the compressed and brilliantly inventive *Microsymphony*, define and inhabit a unique musical world, while his Piano Sonata of 1990 is one of the most significant works in the form since the great Piano Sonata of Elliott Carter.

The Australian pianist Michael Kieran Harvey, co-winner of the first Ivo Pogorelich International Solo Piano Competition, plays with the same imagination and reckless abandon that he displayed in the Competition's final round, which featured the Vine Sonata as his closing work. It is a phenomenally creative and compelling performance by the most exciting pianist I've heard in twenty years.

Vivaldi, Antonio (1678–1741)

I'm the first to admit that I have a total blind spot when it comes to this composer. Everyone loves Vivaldi, don't they? At the very least, he is the perfect yuppie composer, a man whose tuneful, relentlessly good-natured, cleverly made music turns up more frequently at cocktail parties than that of anyone else. And the music *is* inventive, distinctive, and exceedingly well made. Yet apart from the surface details (what instrument is playing, what key the work is in, and so forth), most of his music seems exactly the same to me. Stravinsky certainly had a point when he said that Vivaldi wrote the same concerto several hundred times. This explains why there are so few entries devoted to this composer. Vivaldi lovers, forgive me. Besides, isn't your BMW double-parked?

Concertos for Violin(s), Strings, and Continuo, Op. 3, "L'estro armonico"

Standage, violin; English Consort, Pinnock. Deutsche Grammophon Archiv 423094-2 [CD].

In *The Private War of Harry Frigg,* one of the most forgettable of Paul Newman's movies, one of the characters—a Nazi officer—indulges in one of the rare bits of serious music criticism ever captured in a popular film. While some extremely appealing music is playing in the background, he says, "Vivaldi is charming, of course, but Bach did that sort of thing *so* much better." Thus, even in the movies, critical opinions of Antonio Vivaldi tend to be mixed. Johann Sebastian Bach himself was one of Vivaldi's staunchest admirers and made several arrangements of his older contemporary's works; Igor Stravinsky, on the other hand, insisted that he simply rewrote the same concerto five hundred times.

The extraordinary number and variety of Vivaldi's instrumental concertos is explained by the fact that after taking holy orders in about 1703 he served, from 1709 to 1740, as violin teacher and *maestro de' concerti* at the Ospedale della Pietà in Venice, a shelter for about six thousand orphaned, illegitimate, or wayward girls. According to numerous accounts, his young charges were exceedingly gifted: a French visitor wrote "there is no instrument, however unwieldy, that can frighten them." Another visitor reported that "each concert is given by about forty girls. I assure you there is nothing so charming as to see a young and pretty nun in her white robe, with a bouquet of pomegranate in her hair, leading the orchestra and beating time with all the precision imaginable."

Vivaldi's first published collection of concertos, *L'estro armonico* (Harmonic Inspiration) consists of four solo concertos and eight concerti grossi, almost all of which are among his most inspired creations. Pinnock and the English Consort achieve affectingly intimate results playing one instrument per part. Although the readings are thus necessarily chamberlike, the interpretations lose nothing in scale or expressiveness. These are graceful *and* exciting performances, captured in first-rate recorded sound.

Sir Neville Marriner and the Academy of St. Martin-in-the-Fields take a more frankly red-blooded approach to the twelve Opus 4 concertos of *La Stravaganza* (London 430566-2 [CD]). Slow movements are invested with a lush sensuality, while the *allegros* have a wonderful lilt and rhythmic snap. The 1973 analogue sound has been beautifully repossessed, making this medium-priced reissue another exceptional bargain in London's "Serenata" series.

Iona Brown and the Academy are no less successful in the twelve concertos of Opus 9, called *La Cetra* (The Lyre), on a London Double Decker set (448110-2 [CD]). In addition to fresh and rhythmically resilient performances of the violin concertos, the set comes with equally winning versions of the Concerto in D Minor for Two Oboes, R. 535, and the delightful C Major Piccolo Concerto, R. 443.

Concertos for Cello and Orchestra

Harnoy, cello; Toronto Chamber Orchestra, Robinson. RCA 7774-2-RC [CD], 7774-4-RC [T]; 60155-2-RC [CD], 60155-4-RC [T]; 09026-61578-2 [CD], 09026-61578-4 [T]; 09026-68228 [CD].

Vivaldi has the unique distinction of being the only composer designated an official tourist attraction during his lifetime. Listed among such celebrated sites as the Grand Canal and St. Mark's Cathedral in a 1713 guidebook designed for visitors to Venice were the names of the city's most celebrated violinists, "Gian-Battista Vivaldi and his son—a priest."

Although Vivaldi's output of nearly thirty concertos for the cello was relatively modest compared to the nearly four hundred he wrote for the violin, they contain some of his darkest and most characteristic inspirations. In her distinguished series for RCA, Ofra Harnoy has no stylistic or musicological axes to grind; the playing is warm, gracious, and unaffected, constantly allowing the music to speak for itself. Rafael Wallfisch is similarly appealing in his Naxos recordings with the City of London Sinfonia and Nikolas Kraemer (8.550907 [CD]; 8.550908 [CD]; 8.550909 [CD]; 8.550910 [CD]), which, in addition to the super-budget price tag, has the further advantage of unusually realistic recorded sound.

Daniel Smith brings an abundance of intelligence and character to his ambitious ASV cycle of the thirty-seven bassoon concertos (ASV 971 [CD], ASQ 6177 [CD], ASV 973 [CD], ASV 974 [CD], ASV 975 [CD]). There is considerable warmth and humor in Smith's playing, which, while not in the superhuman category, is nonetheless completely enjoyable.

Patrick Gallois's interpretations of the Opus 10 flute concertos are imaginative and aristocratic, with typically alert support from the Orpheus Chamber Orchestra (Deutsche Grammophon 437839-2 [CD]).

The Hungarian oboist Stefan Schilli is very successful at projecting the bravura fireworks of the composer's oboe concertos for Naxos (8.550859 [CD]; 8.550860 [CD]). Béla Nagy and the Budapest Failoni Chamber Orchestra provide stylish, often witty accompaniments and the recorded sound is superb. (Incidentally, the Schilli and Wallfisch recordings are early installments in what Naxos has promised will be the first absolutely complete recorded traversal of *all* the Vivaldi concertos, however many there are.)

The Four Seasons

> Loveday, violin; Academy of St. Martin-in-the-Fields, Marriner. Argo
> 414486-2 [CD].

> Standage, violin; English Concert, Pinnock. Deutsche Grammophon
> 400045-2 [CD].

With the possible exception of Pachelbel's Kanon, nothing makes me want to start throwing things more, and I mean, *literally* throwing things, than a half dozen bars of *The Seasons*. I hate it with the same irrational intensity that I reserve for peanut butter, and for reasons that remain as difficult to explain. Like all of his other concertos, these four are exceedingly inoffensive and exceptionally graceful. In me, alas, they stimulate nothing but violence, and if allowed to go on too long, peristalsis.

The recording that I have found least offensive over the years is the Argo version by Alan Loveday and Sir Neville Marriner. The playing is as exciting as it is tidy and communicates a deep and abiding sense of enjoyment. Among period instrument recordings, the interpretation by Simon Standage and Trevor Pinnock's superb English Concert is undoubtedly the best.

Gloria in D Major, R. 589

> Nelson, Kirkby, Watkinson, Elliot, Thomas, Christ Church Cathedral
> Choir, Academy of Ancient Music, Preston. Oiseau-Lyre 414678-2
> [CD].

This is the sort of recording that almost makes one believe in miracles, for, miraculously, I managed to remain conscious to the very end.

Vořišek, Jan Václav   (1791–1825)

Symphony in D, Op. 24

> Scottish Chamber Orchestra, Mackerras. Hyperion CDA 66800 [CD].

A friend of Beethoven who sent his own physician to attend him during his final illness, the amiable Jan Václav Vořišek managed to compose only a single symphony during his brief lifetime. While Beethoven's influence is everywhere—especially in the outer movements—the music has a distinct individuality as well, particularly in the long-breathed slow movement and energetic Scherzo. In terms of quality, it is altogether comparable with some of the early Schubert symphonies, and anyone with a fondness for the music of the period should investigate it without delay.

Sir Charles Mackerras leads a typically alert and vigorous performance of the work, which is imaginatively coupled with the youthful D Major Symphony of the Spanish composer Juan Crisostómo Arriaga. For an album of offbeat though utterly worthy late-Classical symphonies, you can't do much better than this.

Wagner, Richard   (1813–1883)

Der fliegende Holländer (The Flying Dutchman)

> Silja, Burmeister, Kozub, Unger, Adam, Talvela, BBC Chorus,
>   New Philharmonia Orchestra, Klemperer. EMI Classics CDCC
>   55179 [CD].

> Haubold, Schiml, Seiffert, Hering, Muff, Knodt, Budapest
>   Radio Chorus, Vienna ORF Symphony, Steinberg. Naxos
>   8.660025/26 [CD].

It was in this, the first of his operas destined to occupy a place in the standard repertoire, that the musical world encountered the man who, after Beethoven, would become the most influential composer that history has so far known. Although much of *The Flying Dutchman* places it in the company of traditional nineteenth-century opera (the discrete arias, choruses, and other set pieces), there is much to indicate that as early as 1843, Wagner the arch-revolutionary was beginning to evolve. For one thing, *The Flying Dutchman,* in its original version, was cast in a single, continuous act. (Two and a half hours without a break was an outrageous demand to make on mid-nineteenth-century derrières.) Also, we can hear the composer flirting with odd harmonies and dissonances and an embryonic version of the leitmotif technique that would eventually lead to those vast music dramas that changed not only opera, but also the course of Western music itself.

With Sir Georg Solti's Chicago Symphony recording for London now withdrawn, EMI could not have chosen a better time to reissue Otto Klemperer's famous recording. Although the young Anja Silja may not be the most sweet-voiced or sympathetic of Sentas and Klemperer's tempos may be a bit too philosophical for some, this is still a performance of overwhelming power and intensity, with Theo Adam an admirably tortured Dutchman and the New Philharmonia working wonders of execution for the old man. All in all, this is one of Klemperer's most imposing recorded performances, a worthy companion to his celebrated version of Beethoven's *Fidelio*.

For those requiring more up-to-date sound, the Naxos recording offers state-of-the-art sonics together with a performance of extraordinary vividness and dramatic intensity. Although there are no stars in the fine ensemble cast, everyone sings with devotion and enthusiasm, while Pinchas Steinberg reveals himself as a Wagner conductor of genuine stature, coaxing stirring singing from the alert chorus and brilliant playing from the ORF orchestra. This is an astonishing bargain, especially since, for those who find Klemperer's tempos *too* philosophical, it might be a clear first choice regardless of price.

Lohengrin

> Norman, Randová, Domingo, Nimsgern, Fischer-Dieskau, Vienna State Opera Chorus, Vienna Philharmonic Orchestra, Solti. London 421053-2 [CD].

Never expect to hear a *Lohengrin* like this at your neighborhood opera house. For one thing, your local opera company couldn't afford to mount one with this caliber of singers. For another, it's not every day that you hear the likes of the great Vienna Philharmonic in the pit. The reasons why this is the finest recording of Wagner's early opera have as much to do with the conducting as with the choice of the tenor for the title role. Given the wonderful idea of casting Placido Domingo as Walter in *Die Meistersinger* a number of years ago, it's a bit surprising that no one ever thought of doing it again until now. No, Domingo is obviously *not* a Wagnerian in the grand tradition: his command of the language is questionable, and his sense of the character is at times rather sketchy. Yet what a pleasure it is to hear a world-class voice *singing* the part, instead of the usual grunting, howling, and groaning that passes for Wagnerian singing today.

For the remainder of the cast, London has put together a formidable ensemble, and Sir Georg Solti's conducting is precisely what it needs to be—neither overly measured nor uncomfortably rushed. The Vienna Philharmonic has not sounded this impressive since their epoch-making recording (also with Solti) of Wagner's complete *Ring*, and the recorded sound will send shivers down your spine.

Die Meistersinger von Nürnberg

Grümmer, Frantz, Schock, Frick, Kusche, Unger, Höffgen, Prey,
Choruses, Berlin Philharmonic, Kempe. EMI CDMD 64154 [CD].

Janowitz, Fassbaender, Kónya, Unger, Helmsey, Stewart, Krass,
Bavarian Radio Chorus and Orchestra, Kubelik. Calig CAL
50971/74 [CD].

While *Tristan und Isolde* is probably his masterpiece, and the *Ring,* taken as a whole, his most significant achievement, *Die Meistersinger* finally showed the world the human side of Richard Wagner. Given the nature of the beast that Wagner was, his human side proved to be shockingly warm, generous, and complete. In the only operatic comedy worthy of comparison with Verdi's *Falstaff* and Mozart's *Figaro,* Wagner also succeeds in showing us not only what is finest and best in the German people, but also by inference, what is finest and best in ourselves. For this one Wagner opera, cast on a completely human scale, is about friendship and trust, young love and mature wisdom, tradition and rebellion—in short, the human condition itself.

For my money, neither of the fine London recordings by Sir Georg Solti nor the extremely satisfying Deutsche Grammophon version led by Eugen Jochum can begin to match that virtually flawless 1956 mono-only EMI recording conducted by Rudolf Kempe (who stepped in at the last possible moment for Sir Thomas Beecham). Except for the lack of modern recorded sound—which *is* a factor in the riotous Act II finale and the big crowd scenes in Act III—this is a *Meistersinger* for the ages: the best conducted, the best played, and, for the most part, the best sung. Although EMI could have easily had the services of the great Hans Hotter as Sachs—a fact for which he has understandably never forgiven them—Ferdinand Frantz gives the performance of his career, as do Gerhard Unger as David and Benno Kusche as a wonderfully snide and snarling Sixtus Beckmesser. Rudolf Schock, best known for his work in operetta, is dashing and ardent as Walther, Gottlob Frick is the finest Pogner ever recorded, and the ladies are absolutely enchanting, with the radiantly girlish Eva of Elisabeth Grümmer surpassing even Elisabeth Schwarzkopf's. As in his EMI *Lohengrin,* Kempe's conducting is warm, dramatic, and utterly natural, with everything vividly alive yet completely unforced, while the Berlin Philharmonic and the superbly trained choruses are models of flexibility and responsiveness.

After decades of whispers and excited rumors, Rafael Kubelik's 1967 Bavarian Radio performance has finally been issued by the small Calig label, proving that all of the whispers and rumors were true. This is one of the greatest of all Wagner recordings, in every way worthy of comparison with the Kempe set and in some respects its obvious superior. In addition to the fabulously rich and detailed recorded sound that is actually *finer* than that of either the Jochum or the first Solti recording, the Hungarian tenor Sándor Kónya at his most heroic proves the finest Walter on records. The silvery Gundala Janowitz gives Elisabeth Grümmer serious competition as Eva, while the young Brigitte Fassbaender is a marvelous Magdalene, full of fussy fun and mischief. I kept the recording in my car's CD changer for the better part of six months, never for a moment tiring of a performance as noble, exciting, and warmly enveloping as the opera itself.

For the absolute last work in Hans Sachs, though, all of the electrical recordings of the incomparable Friedrich Schorr can now be found on a single Pearl CD (PEA 9944). Recorded between 1927 and 1931, these priceless acetates preserve one of the great characterizations in operatic history, an interpretation to be mentioned with Chaliapin's Boris Godunov or Lotte Lehmann's Marschallin.

Overtures and Preludes

For those who accept the old saw that Wagner wrote some of the most inspired minutes and some of the most tedious hours in the history of music—or for people who simply prefer to do without all that singing—the recorded selection of overtures, preludes, and the rest of what Shaw called "the bleeding chunks of meat" has always been varied and impressive, all the more so since the introduction of the compact disc.

Fritz Reiner's Chicago Symphony recording for RCA Victor (09026-61792-2 [CD]) of thrillingly played excerpts from *Meistersinger* and *Götterdämmerung* is an absolute necessity. Stokowski (London 411772-4 [T]) and Solti (London 440107-2 [CD] lead highly successful anthologies of *Ring* excerpts that are as radically different as they are extremely exciting. Sir Georg's collection of Wagner choruses, culled from his various complete recordings, is invaluable for sing-a-long types (London 421865-2 [CD]), offering singing and playing of matchless excellence.

Leonard Bernstein's dramatic, highly charged Wagner recordings have been collected on a pair of Sony CDs (SMK 47643, SMK 46744), the latter including Eileen Farrell's majestic interpretations of the Immolation Scene from *Götterdämmerung* and the *Wesendonck Lieder*. The late Klaus Tennstedt's equally individual recordings have been collected in a two-disc set from EMI's Doubleforte series (CDFB 68616 [CD]). The interpretations have a depth and scale that suggest the Wagner conducting of an earlier generation, while the Berlin Philharmonic is at its frightening best.

Among the newer collections, Mariss Jansons's EMI Classics anthology (CDR 69848 [CD]) features typically exciting playing from the Oslo Philharmonic and rafter-rattling sound. James Levine's Deutsche Grammophon recording (435874-2 [CD]) with the resurgent Met Orchestra confirms their status—with the Vienna Philharmonic—as the greatest pit band in the world, while the Philharmonia Orchestra performs with both grandeur and abandon under

Yuri Simonov on a stunning Collins Classics CD (COL 1294). The recorded sound of Lorin Maazel's seventy-minute *Ring* synthesis with the Berlin Philharmonic for Telarc is awe-inspiring in its weight and clarity (CD 80154 [CD], CS 30154 [T], as is Gerard Schwarz's Seattle Symphony album for Delos (DCD 3053 [CD]), which includes an especially gripping account of the Prelude and *Good Friday Spell* from *Parsifal*.

For something well off the beaten track, Glenn Gould's highly personal piano transcriptions of "Dawn and Siegfried's Rhine Journey" from *Götterdämmerung,* the *Meistersinger* Prelude, and the *Siegfried Idyll* are available on Sony SMK 52650 [CD]. The release also includes Gould's conducting debut (and final commercial recording), in which he leads a performance of the *Siegfried Idyll* slow enough to stop the clock and moving enough to break the heart.

Sir Roger Norrington's period-instrument anthology (EMI CDC 55479 [CD]) is probably the conductor's most fascinating experiment to date, with unusually fleet performances of the *Prelude and Liebestod* that still manage to sound remarkably passionate and intense. The most controversial performance of all—an eight-minute, twenty-second scamper through *Die Meistersinger*— is ironically the most historically justifiable: Wagner once complained that *everyone* played his music too slowly and spoke of a performance he led that lasted "a few seconds over eight minutes." The performance of the *Liebestod* is greatly enhanced by the imposing singing of Jane Eaglen, who is even more electrifying in her debut solo album for Sony (SK 62032 [CD]). In addition to the most thrilling version of the Immolation Scene since Nilsson's, this fabulous collection also includes stunning versions of various Bellini arias, including a ravishing "Casta Diva." (The pairing of Bellini and Wagner is singularly appropriate, as Wagner was a passionate admirer of the Italian composer's music and once said he hoped that *Tristan und Isolde* might some day be viewed as the German *Norma*.)

Finally, if the absence of demonstration-quality recorded sound is not the end of the world, the work of several of the most individual of all Wagnerians is still on hand to instruct, amaze, and delight. Dutton Laboratories has issued two collections featuring the highly distinctive recordings of a pair of unique English Wagnerians: the impassioned recordings that a young John Barbirolli made during his stormy tenure with the New York Philharmonic (CDSJB 1001 [CD]) and Sir Thomas Beecham's London Philharmonic recordings (DUT 7007 [CD]): interpretations of incredible strength, charm, and refinement (listen to the harps in the *Meistersinger* Prelude). Perhaps the *most* individual and underrated of the Golden Age conductors, the Russian-born Albert Coates, can be heard in some astounding recordings of excerpts from *Die Meistersinger* and *Parsifal* on a two-disc set from Claremont (GSE 785070/71 [CD]. Hans Knappertsbusch's famous Munch recordings—including the slowest performance of the *Rienzi* Overture ever attempted—are out on a pair of MCA compact discs (MCAD2-9811); two representative collections by perhaps the greatest Wagner conductor of all,

Wilhelm Furtwängler, are available from EMI (CDHB 64935 [CD]) and Enterprise (ENTLV 911 [CD]), while the work of the deeply misanthropic, profoundly spiritual Karl Muck may be sampled on a Centaur CD (CRC 2142). And in what must be counted among the most exciting Wagner releases in years, Pearl has reissued those legendary Wagner recordings that Leopold Stokowski made with the Philadelphia Orchestra in the 1930s and '40s. A marvel in its day, the recorded sound still retains an incredible clarity and presence; the interpretations are inspired and theatrical, with playing that has rarely been approached for its vividness and fearless abandon. Volume 1 includes extended excerpts from *Tannhäuser* and *Parsifal* (including Stokowski's Act III "Symphonic Synthesis") (PEA 9448 [CD]); Volume 2 features the *Lohengrin* and *Meistersinger* Preludes and some *very* steamy *Tristan* excerpts (best is an Act II *Liebesnacht* "Symphonic Synthesis") (PEA 9238 [CD]).

*P*arsifal

Ludwig, Kollo, Fischer-Dieskau, Kélémen, Frick, Vienna State Opera Chorus, Vienna Philharmonic, Solti. London 417143-2 [CD].

There used to be an ancient Metropolitan Opera curse that one still hears from old-timers. "May you be trapped in a performance of *Parsifal* without a sandwich." The implication is, of course, that *Parsifal* does tend to go on and on and on. As a matter of fact, nothing can be more thoroughly numbing than an indifferently prepared production of the opera, just as nothing can be more genuinely stirring than when all the parties involved are giving the opera all it demands, which is to say, *everything*.

Recorded live at the 1962 Bayreuth Festival, Hans Knappertsbusch's Philips recording proved more conclusively than any other that *Parsifal* was in fact a fitting conclusion to Wagner's career, containing as it does, many of the most inspired pages the composer ever wrote. With a cast that included George London, Jess Thomas, and the great Hans Hotter among others, the recording featured some of the finest Wagner singing heard on records. *Parsifal* was always the great Knappertsbusch house specialty, and he led a performance of unparalleled dignity, depth, and majesty. Although the recording was of an actual performance, the foot-shuffling, coughing, and vocal drop-outs are kept to a bare minimum, and besides, the thrill of hearing those incomparable Bayreuth acoustics more than compensates for the occasional glitch. For their "Wagner Edition," Philips has withdrawn the recording in favor of a far lesser but better-sounding 1985 version conducted by James Levine. So much for loyalty and good sense. Another Knappertsbusch *Parsifal* from 1964 is available on a rather murky-sounding Melodram set (GM 10004 [CD]), which features as its principal point of interest the thrilling singing of Jon Vickers in the title role.

Until Philips sees the error of its ways and restores the Knappertsbusch, Sir Georg Solti's London recording remains the best available modern alternative, with exceptionally fine singing from a very strong cast and conducting so intensely committed that *Parsifal*'s more static passages seem much less the stop-the-clock affairs than they can often be. The often hard-pressed René Kollo has never been more relaxed and confident; in fact, except for Siegfried Jerusalem in Daniel Barenboim's mysteriously withdrawn Teldec recording, he is the most completely satisfying of modern Parsifals.

Yet for the absolute last word in *Parsifal* recordings, Preiser offers the finest CD transfer (PRE 90270 [CD]) of Karl Muck's legendary 1928 recording of Act III, with distinguished Golden Age Wagnerians Gotthelf Pistor, Cornelius Bronsgeest, and Ludwig Hoffmann giving the performances of their careers. But it is Muck's contribution that levitates the performance onto those dizzying heights shared by Bruno Walter's 1935 *Die Walküre,* Act I, and the 1929 Leider-Melchior *Tristan* love duet. This is Wagner conducting in which transcendent spirituality and immaculate technique fuse into something eternal.

*R*ienzi

Wennberg, Martin, Kollo, Schreier, Adam, Dresden State Chorus and Orchestra, Hollreiser. EMI Classics CDMB 63980 [CD].

Rienzi, the Last of the Tribunes was Wagner's *Nabucco*. Introduced in October of 1842, only seven months after Verdi's third opera made him an overnight success, Wagner's third effort also proved to be a charm: it soon became the most popular work in the Dresden Opera's repertoire and made the twenty-nine-year-old composer's name known throughout Germany for the first time.

Although long and frequently derivative—the shadow of Giacomo Meyerbeer hangs heavily over the proceedings—*Rienzi* has many wonderful moments and the ardent Wagnerian will certainly want to give this recording a try. Unfortunately, the performance is one to admire rather than cherish. Heinrich Hollreiser's able conducting and René Kollo's sturdy interpretation of the title role are the best things in the set; the less said about the women, the better. Still, the passion and youthful enthusiasm of the music carry most of the day.

More charming and in many ways more original is Wagner's very first opera, *Die Feen* (The Fairies), written when he was only twenty. If Mendelssohn and Beethoven cast a benign shadow over the proceedings, then the young Wagner's inventiveness is often startlingly fresh and audacious, with many tantalizing suggestions of what was to come. The Orfeo recording (CO62833 [CD]) is as delightfully engaging as the work itself, with Wolfgang Sawallisch leading an unusually clear-headed yet riveting performance, and John Alexander and the young Cheryl Studer are particularly impressive among the fine cast.

Der Ring des Nibelungen (Das Rheingold, Die Walküre, Siegfried, Götterdämmerung)

Soloists, Vienna Philharmonic, Solti. London 455555-2 [CD].

Das Rheingold

Flagstad, Madeira, Svanholm, London, Neidlinger, Böhme, Vienna Philharmonic, Solti. London 414101-2 [CD].

Die Walküre

Nilsson, Crespin, Ludwig, King, Hotter, Frick, Vienna Philharmonic, Solti. London 414105-2 [CD].

Siegfried

Nilsson, Windgassen, Stolze, Hotter, Neidlinger, Vienna Philharmonic, Solti. London 414110-2 [CD].

Götterdämmerung

Nilsson, Watson, Ludwig, Windgassen, Fischer-Dieskau, Frick, Vienna Philharmonic, Solti. London 414115-2 [CD].

It is only fitting that one of the most titanic outbursts of the human imagination inspired one of the genuine cornerstones of recording history: the now legendary English Decca/London version of Wagner's *Ring*. In spite of its obvious flaws, and there are several, this will undoubtedly be our once and future *Ring*—an achievement so massively ambitious, audacious, and successful that it boggles the mind.

True, this is not the ideal performance of Wagner's sprawling fifteen-hour tetralogy. But then again, much evidence suggests that Wagner himself at last concluded that an ideal *Ring* existed only in his mind. The major flaws in the recording include a Siegfried who is barely adequate (although Wolfgang Windgassen was the best the world had to offer at the time) and the rather wobbly Wotan of the once great Hans Hotter.

In spite of these important drawbacks, the great moments far outnumber the uncomfortable ones. Here is Kirsten Flagstad, singing the *Rheingold* Fricka, a role she learned especially for this recording. Here, too, are those extravagant bits of casting, including Christa Ludwig as Waltraute and Joan Sutherland as the Forest Bird. Through it all, one still feels the spirit of the late John Culshaw (the most imaginative recording producer of his generation), who here, with Sir Georg Solti in the pit and the finest cast that could then be assembled, puts together not only his own greatest achievement but also those of many who were involved.

*T*annhäuser (Paris Version)

Dernesch, Ludwig, Kollo, Braun, Sotin, Vienna State Opera Chorus,
Vienna Philharmonic, Solti. London 415581-2 [CD].

While Sir Georg Solti recorded every Wagner opera from *The Flying Dutchman* to *Parsifal*, none of those recordings is finer than this stupendous version of the Paris edition of *Tannhäuser*. In Helga Dernesch and Christa Ludwig, he has a pair of ladies for whom any conductor would give what remains of his hair. And René Kollo, who has had serious vocal problems over the years, here sounds more free and fresh than he ever has on recordings. Nevertheless, Solti's conducting, as languorous and limpid as it is ferocious and exultant, makes this one of the great Wagner recordings of the last twenty years.

*T*ristan und Isolde

Flagstad, Thebom, Suthaus, Fischer-Dieskau, Greindl, Philharmonia
Chorus and Orchestra, Furtwängler. EMI Classics CDCD 56254 [CD].

M. Price, Fassbaender, Kollo, Fischer-Dieskau, Moll, Dresden State
Opera Chorus and Orchestra, C. Kleiber. Deutsche Grammophon
413315-2 [CD].

The famous 1952 recording of *Tristan und Isolde,* most collectors concede, is the greatest single Wagner recording yet made. In spite of a frequently negligible Tristan and an Isolde who was crowding sixty at the time, no other version of this passionate masterwork has captured as much black magic or animal intensity as this one. The legendary Kirsten Flagstad is quite literally *that* in her finest studio recording. This Isolde beguiles and terrifies with equal ease, and is more convincingly and beautifully sung than any we are ever likely to hear.

Furtwängler's conducting is similarly inspired and more than confirms his reputation as the greatest Wagner conductor of his time. The dynamic contrasts range from the merest whisper to the most shattering climaxes. Phrases are stretched out to unimaginable lengths, and in general, the performance creates a feeling that no Wagner opera ever does—that it is far too short.

The deletion of Leonard Bernstein's Philips recording leaves a serious gap among modern *Tristans,* one that is best filled by Carlos Kleiber. Like the Furtwängler, this is a performance dominated by the soprano and the conductor. Vocally, Dame Margaret Price is not only the most lusciously beautiful of the modern Isoldes, but the characterization is also the most meltingly feminine since Frieda Leider's. Kleiber's conducting is impassioned to a fault, with tempos so urgent and climaxes so highly charged that they make Bernstein's seem almost sedate in comparison. This is certainly not a relaxing *Tristan,* but then again, who would want opera's greatest paean to illicit sex to seem *relaxed?*

Die Walküre, Act I

Lehmann, Melchior, List, Vienna Philharmonic, Walter (Recorded 1935). EMI Classics CHD 61020 [CD].

So much has been said and written about this legendary recording—including the frequently repeated suggestion that it was, is, and will always be (with the possible exception of the Furtwängler *Tristan*) the greatest Wagner recording of all time—that all that really needs to be said is that the CD transfer is even better than anyone could have hoped. The voices—especially Lotte Lehmann's—have never sounded more realistic, and the orchestral detail (which was always rather phenomenal for 1935) is clearer and cleaner than ever.

That other desert island Wagner recording—the 1929 version of the *Tristan* love duet with an even younger Lauritz Melchior; that most warm and feminine of the great Isoldes, Frieda Leider; and the astonishing Albert Coates, whose conducting manages to maintain the tension and animal excitement of the scene in spite of the fact that it was recorded in two separate cities (Berlin and London), several months apart—can now be found with other historic versions of excerpts from the opera on a pair of Legato Classics compact discs (LCD-146-2).

Wesendonck Lieder

Flagstad, soprano; Moore, piano. EMI Classics CDH 63030 [CD].

Norman, soprano; London Symphony, Davis. Philips 412655-2 [CD].

Cut from the same cloth as *Tristan und Isolde,* these ravishing songs were settings of the rather feeble poetry of Mathilde Wesendonck, the pretentious wife of one of Wagner's most generous patrons and the composer's real-life model for Isolde. Characteristically, once *Tristan* was finished, Wagner completely lost interest in the woman who inspired it, leaving her to return to her understanding husband.

Although the great Kirsten Flagstad was in her mid-fifties when she recorded the songs with Gerald Moore, the voice was still in magnificent condition: supple, commanding, and phenomenally voluminous, it allowed Flagstad to explore the full range of expression inherent in these wondrous lieder as no singer has before or since. Moore, as always, is a model of ardor and discretion and the recorded sound has held up amazingly well.

For those who need modern recorded sound (to say nothing of Wagner's glorious orchestral colors), Jessye Norman's 1976 Philips recording with Sir Colin Davis is splendidly sung, if less than ideal in its projection of meanings and moods.

Waldteufel, Emile   (1837–1915)

Waltzes

Slovak State Philharmonic, Walter. Naxos 8.553956 [CD].

After the Strauss family, the Frenchman Emile Waldteufel was the most popular waltz composer of the late nineteenth century, rising from obscurity to become chamber musician to the Empress Eugénie (for whom he directed extravagant court balls) and even achieving great fame following the Revolution of 1871 by presiding over the presidential balls at the Elysée Palace and the annual galas at the Paris Opéra. He composed nearly three hundred waltzes, polkas, and galops, the best of which are instantly memorable and brilliantly scored. His most famous waltz, *Les Patineurs* (The Skaters) once rivaled *On the Beautiful Blue Danube* in popularity, with others like *Pomone* and *Mon Rêve* not far behind.

Drawn from Marco Polo's fine (and full-priced) Waldteufel series, this super-budget Naxos collection offers a generous selection of nine of the composer's most characteristic works—including *Les Patineurs, Pomone, and Mon Rêve*—in straightforward but wholly attractive performances led by Alfred Walter. In his firm tempos and discreet rubato, the conductor wisely makes a clear distinction between Waldteufel's unmistakably French inspirations and their Viennese counterparts, while the excellent Slovakian orchestra plays with skill and charm. Among the innumerable bargains Naxos has given us, none is more thoroughly delightful.

Walker, George   (1922–   )

Concerto for Trombone and Orchestra

Lindberg, trombone; Malmö Symphony, DePriest. BIS CD 628 [CD].

Born in Washington, D.C., educated at Oberlin College, Curtis, and the Eastman School of Music, George Walker established his reputation in 1946 with the elegiac *Lyric* for Strings, an arrangement of a movement from a string quartet that was first heard in 1941. Since then, his career has been marked by an increasingly prestigious series of commissions and honors, culminating in 1996 with the Pulitzer Prize for his *Lilacs* for Voice and Orchestra, the first time the award has gone to a composer of African descent.

The Concerto for Trombone and Orchestra was written in 1957 during the composer's final year at the Eastman School of Music. A virile, imaginative, instantly appealing neo-Classical work in the traditional three movements, it is understandably one of the most frequently performed of the instrument's modern concertos. Christian Lindberg and the Malmö Symphony conducted by James De Preist give what sounds like a definitive performance as part of a stunning BIS album (BIS CD-628) called "American Trombone Concertos." In spite of formidable competition from Paul Creston's *Fantasy for Trombone and Orchestra,* Gunther Schuller's delightful *Eine kleine Posaunenmusik,* and the Trombone Concerto of Ellen Taaffe Zwilich, the Walker steals the show.

The composer himself proves a formidable advocate of his own piano and chamber music on an Albany collection (TROY 154 [CD]) that offers further insight into this distinctive and important voice.

Wallace, Vincent (1812–1865)

Maritana

Cullagh, Lee, Clarke, Caddy, Smith, Hayes, RTE Concert Orchestra and Philharmonic Choir, O Duinn. Marco Polo 8.223406-2 [CD].

With Michael William Balfe's *The Bohemian Girl* and Julius Benedict's *The Lily of Killarney,* Vincent Wallace's *Maritana* was the most popular stage work produced in Great Britain since John Gay's *The Beggar's Opera.* For a half century and more, it was a key work of Victorian musical theater, with its great hit tune "Scenes That Are Brightest" retaining its phenomenal appeal well into the new century, as evidenced by famous recordings like those of Rosa Ponselle and John McCormack. Although the dramatic material is frequently thin and silly, the music is refreshingly lively and genuinely memorable, with many of the best arias and ensembles clearly pointing the way to the Savoy operas of Gilbert and Sullivan.

Proinnsias O Duinn leads an enthusiastic Irish cast in a wonderfully affectionate performance that not only revels in *Maritana*'s melodic richness but also approaches the frequently melodramatic action without the slightest trace of irony or condescension. The results are so thoroughly enjoyable that one hopes they'll move on to *The Bohemian Girl* and *The Lily of Killarney* without delay.

Wallace, William (1860–1940)

Symphonic Poems: *The Passing of Beatrice; Sister Helen; Sir William Wallace; Villon*

BBC Scottish Symphony Orchestra, Brabbins. Hyperion CDA 66848 [CD].

After studying medicine in his native Glasgow and in Paris and Vienna, William Wallace devoted the bulk of his enormous energies to music, teaching at the Royal Academy in London, writing provocative books like *The Threshold of Music,* and composing some of the first symphonic poems produced in Great Britain, all of them modeled on those of his hero, Franz Liszt. Although Wallace was largely self-taught as a composer, this Hyperion recording of four of his most significant works reveals an impressive command of this most important of late-Romantic musical forms and extraordinary gifts as an orchestrator.

The most striking work here is the tone poem dedicated to the composer's namesake, the same William Wallace who was played by Mel Gibson in the Oscar-winning *Braveheart. William Wallace, Scottish Hero, Freedom-fighter, Beheaded and Dismembered by the English*—pity that Mel couldn't have used that title, too—is a powerful and satisfying work: brooding, dramatic, darkly colorful in its use of the Scots folk song, "Scots wha' hae." *Villon,* a tribute to the fifteenth-century French vagabond poet, is no less vivid, as are *The Passing of Beatrice* and *Sister Helen,* based on Dante and Rosetti. The BBC Scottish Symphony, under the gifted young Martyn Brabbins, plays with enthusiasm and obvious pride, while the Hyperion recording, documentation, and packaging are typically top of the line.

Walton, Sir William (1902–1983)

Anon. in Love (song cycle); *Christopher Columbus* (suite from the radio play); *Songs after Edith Sitwell*; *A Song for the Lord Mayor's Table* (song cycle); *The Twelve* (anthem)

> Hill, tenor; Finnie, mezzo-soprano; Davies, tenor; Gomez, soprano; Westminster Singers, City of London Sinfonia, Hickox. Chandos CHAN 8824 [CD].

Here, on one convenient and valuable album, is much of Walton's most important music for solo voice, including the two captivating song cycles *Anon. in Love* (originally written with guitar accompaniment) and *A Song for the Lord Mayor's Table*, both heard in the composer's inspired orchestrations from 1970. Tenor Martyn Hill's readings of the anonymous sixteenth- and seventeenth-century love poems are sly and knowing, while Jill Gomez is equally appealing in the witty ceremonial cycle, written for the first City of London Music Festival in 1962. The anthem *The Twelve* was composed in 1965 to a text by W. H. Auden for the choir of Walton's old school, Christ Church, Oxford. As with the song cycles, the orchestral version marks a dramatic improvement over the version for voices and organ. The album is filled out with two brilliant arrangements by Christopher Palmer: orchestrations of four songs (three of them from *Façade*) on texts by Edith Sitwell, and excerpts from the long-forgotten incidental music to Louis MacNeice's 1942 radio play *Christopher Columbus*.

On a splendid Nimbus album (NI 5346 [CD]) the Choir of Christ Church Cathedral offer a spirited and moving collection of Walton's choral music, beginning with *A Litany*, written when the fifteen-year-old composer was still a member of the group. Here are many of the best (and best-known) of Walton's vocal works, including *Missa Brevis* and *Chichester Service*, the settings of *Jubilate Deo* and *Nunc dimittis*, and the masterful Sir Henry Wood memorial, *Where Does the Unuttered Music Go?*

Belshazzar's Feast

> Wilson-Johnson, baritone; London Symphony Chorus and Orchestra, Hickox. EMI Classics for Pleasure CFP CDEMX 2225 [CD].

Belshazzar's Feast has led a charmed life in the recording studio, beginning with the composer's first version with the Huddersfield Choral Society and Liverpool Philharmonic, an interpretation whose erotic energy and barbaric splendor have never really been surpassed. Richard Hickox leads a very similar performance in this startling 1989 recording, which has not been available in

America until now. From the tension of the opening fanfare to the orgasmic release of the final "Alleluia," this is the kind of *Belshazzar* that one always imagined but never really expected to hear. Everything is as dramatic, colorful, and highly charged as possible, with edge-of-the-seat playing from the London Symphony and full-throated incisiveness from its fabulous chorus, all of it captured in sumptuous but brilliantly defined recorded sound. As if all of that were not enough, the filler is the recording premiere of Walton's *In Honor of the City of London,* a rousing, well-made occasional piece here given a spectacular send-off.

Concerto for Cello and Orchestra; Symphony No. 1

Harrell, cello; City of Birmingham Symphony, Rattle. EMI Classics CDC 54572 [CD].

This is probably the single most exciting Walton recording ever issued. And it's not that Rattle and company don't face formidable competition in both of these towering modern masterworks: Gregor Piatigorsky's splendid creator recording of the Cello Concerto is available from RCA (09026-61498-2 [CD]), and the composer himself pronounced André Previn's first version of the Symphony the finest he'd ever heard, inside the recording studio or out.

Not only does Harrell play the Concerto with an unprecedented understanding and panache, but his incomparable tone also works wonders in the wistful coda, which is here transformed into something unspeakably poignant, with Rattle offering the most alert and sensitive accompaniment ever recorded. The conductor's version of the Symphony is frankly astounding, bringing a withering intensity to the first movement, a snarling bitterness to the Scherzo, a bleak devastation to the slow movement, and a giddy exultation in the finale, which makes this the greatest and most universal recording the piece has ever received.

Concerto for Viola and Orchestra; Concerto for Violin and Orchestra

Kennedy, viola and violin; Royal Philharmonic, Previn. EMI Classics CDC 49628 [CD].

Listening to these exceptional performances makes one fervently hope that Nigel Kennedy will some day feel like playing the violin again. Shortly before his "retirement," his live performances had degenerated into embarrassing displays that replaced sound musicianship with outlandish costumes. In the process he became a kind of British Nadja Salerno-Sonnenberg, who seems to think that exaggerated podium antics will disguise sloppy technique.

Kennedy's playing in this greatest of all viola concertos rivals the subtlety of Frederick Riddle's in the pioneering 1937 recording made with the composer (Dutton Laboratories CDAX 8003 [CD]). The concerto's bravura elements hold no terrors for him, nor do those of the Violin Concerto, which he dashes off with an insolent ease. With inspired support from Previn and the London Symphony, this is a must for any collection.

Façade

Walton, Baker, speakers; City of London Sinfonia, Hickox. Chandos 8869 [CD].

Listening to the voice of Dame Edith Sitwell, one was strangely reminded of W. H. Auden's description of his own face late in life as "a wedding cake left out in the rain." Among the major modern poets, only Dylan Thomas had a comparably individual instrument. But it was not merely Dame Edith's indescribable voice—to say nothing of her overwhelming authority—that made her second version of *Façade* so far and away the greatest recording this daffy entertainment has ever received. In the faster poems, the superhuman diction of Sir Peter Pears had to be heard to be believed, with Anthony Collins's conducting a model of crack-brained panache.

Since London has criminally withdrawn that classic recording from circulation—along with most of the other wonderful items in their medium-priced British Collection series—that leaves the recent Chandos recording featuring the composer's widow to hold the fort until it reappears. Born in Argentina, Lady Susana Walton's charming accent (and her obvious sympathy with her husband's music) add immeasurably to her infectiously enthusiastic reading, while Richard Baker is equally impressive in the virtuoso stuff, offering Peter Pears his only serious competition. In addition to the witty contributions of Hickox and company, the recording comes complete with *Façade 2:* all the poems (some of them very fine indeed) that for one reason or another failed to make the final cut.

Film Music

Bott, soprano; Gielgud, speaker; Academy of St. Martin-in-the-Fields, Marriner. (*As You Like It; Hamlet*) Chandos CHAN 8842 [CD].

Academy of St. Martin-in-the-Fields, Marriner. (*Battle of Britain; Escape Me Never; The First of the Few: Spitfire Prelude and Fugue; Three Sisters; Wartime Sketchbook*) Chandos CHAN 8870 [CD].

Plummer, speaker; Academy of St. Martin-in-the-Fields Chorus and Orchestra, Marriner. (*Henry V—A Shakespeare Scenario arranged by Christopher Palmer*) Chandos CHAN 8892 [CD].

Gielgud, speaker; Academy of St. Martin-in-the-Fields, Marriner. (*Macbeth: Banquet and March; Major Barbara: A Shavian Sequence for Orchestra; Richard III—A Shakespeare Scenario arranged by Christopher Palmer*) Chandos CHAN 8841 [CD].

Here, in four indispensable albums, is the bulk of Sir William Walton's brilliant achievement as a film composer, much of it never recorded before. The "Shakespeare Scenarios" devised by the gifted Christopher Palmer collect the bulk of the composer's two finest scores—those for Olivier's *Henry V* and *Richard III*—into compelling, virtually self-contained dramas with Christopher Plummer and Sir John Gielgud delivering cleverly chosen excerpts from the plays. (In the case of Gielgud, this is limited to Richard's "Now is the winter of our discontent" monologue, recorded with Walton's witty underscoring that went largely unheard in the finished film.) If anything, the *Hamlet* and *As You Like It* recordings are even more valuable, since the music is so little known. Gielgud is in even finer form in the "O that this too, too solid flesh" and "To be or not to be" soliloquies and Walton's invention is never less than memorable, both here and in the 1936 *As You Like It*. Volume 4 is devoted primarily to the wartime music, including the "Wartime Sketchbook" that collects the best moments from three films of the period and the famous *Spitfire Prelude and Fugue* from *The First of the Few,* the screen biography of the heroic R. J. Mitchell, whose incomparable fighter plane turned the tide in the Battle of Britain (the stirring March is a close cousin to the noble Henry Tudor theme from *Richard III*).

Marriner and the Academy are in splendid form throughout the series, with vivid interpretations that go to the very heart of this inherently dramatic music and playing that is far more polished and exciting than any that appeared in the original films. With sumptuous, superbly detailed recorded sound and illuminating notes, these are the most valuable issues yet in Chandos's wonderful Walton Series and should be snapped up at once by anyone with even a passing interest in this composer or in great film music.

Quartet for Piano and Strings; Sonata for Violin and Piano; *Bagatelles* (5) for Guitar

Margalit, Alley, piano; Graham, violin; Silverstone, viola; Welsh, cello; Kerstens, guitar. EMI Classics CDC 55404 [CD].

Outstanding recordings of Walton's scant chamber music output have never been a glut on the market, so when one as fine as this comes along, it's time to crack open the champagne. The Piano Quartet was Walton's first large-scale work, written in 1918 when the composer was a sixteen-year-old student at Oxford. Although understandably derivative—there are persistent echoes of Elgar and Vaughan Williams—the Romantic manner and harmonic language offer many tantalizing hints of what was to come. The Violin Sonata from 1949 is one of Walton's finest works, written in response to the illness and harrowing death of Lady Alice Wimborne, who became the composer's mistress in 1934. Both performances are exceptional, especially in the way each manages to clarify the overall structure of a pair of works that are frequently accused (unjustly) of lacking formal focus. As a bonus, the album includes a performance of the five *Bagatelles* by Tom Kerstens that is even more mercurial and imaginative than the one by its dedicatee, Julian Bream.

The greatest of Walton's chamber works, the String Quartet in A Minor, is still best served by the phenomenal recording made in 1950 by the Hollywood String Quartet (Testament SBT 1052 [CD]). The composer was completely bowled over by both the depth and staggering virtuosity of the interpretation, and so will you be.

Those requiring more modern sound will enjoy the spirited performance by the Coull String Quartet on Hyperion (CDA 66718 [CD]), coupled with winningly affectionate readings of the Elgar Quartet and the *Three Idylls* by Frank Bridge.

The Quest (complete ballet); *The* Wise Virgins (ballet suite)

London Philharmonic, Thomson. Chandos CHAN 8871 [CD].

Always a painfully slow worker, Walton was forced to compose the music for his 1943 patriotic ballet *The Quest* with what was, for him, blinding speed: forty-five minutes of music in slightly less than five weeks. Loosely adapted from Spenser's *The Faerie Queene*, with choreography by Frederick Ashton—given special leave from the RAF for the purpose—and a brilliant cast headed by Margot Fonteyn, Moira Shearer, and Robert Helpmann ("looking more like the Dragon than St. George," according to the composer), *The Quest* has many fine moments, as this superb performance makes abundantly clear. The late Bryden Thomson never made a finer or more valuable recording, gently but firmly buttressing the ballet's weaker moments while investing the stronger ones with all the character and dramatic intensity the score allows.

The Wise Virgins is an arrangement of Bach cantata movements selected by Constant Lambert for a 1940 production by Sadler's Wells. According to legend, one of the original season posters bore the unfortunate disclaimer *"The Wise Virgins* (subject to alteration)." Walton's treatment is both tasteful and inspired, particularly in the ineffably delicate textures of "Sheep May Safely Graze." If Thomson's performance lacks the point and thrust (to coin a phrase) of Louis Lane's old Cleveland Orchestra recording, then it is nonetheless a fine postscript to an invaluable album.

Symphony No. 2; Viola Concerto; *Johannesburg Festival Overture*

> Tomter, viola; English Northern Philharmonia, Daniel. Naxos 8.553402 [CD].

With George Szell's benchmark recording of Walton's Second Symphony currently out of print (see tirade below), this brilliant new version is most welcome, especially at the super-budget price. Paul Daniel's interpretation is both thoughtful and dramatically penetrating, with the complex textures of the fugal final movement given a Szell-like point and clarity. The performance of the *Johannesburg Festival Overture* is also very exciting, making the current neglect of this sparkling, colorful score even more difficult to explain. If this version of the Viola Concerto with the Norwegian violist Lars Anders Tomter doesn't quite displace the Kennedy recording (see page 785), then it runs a very close second, rounding out an incredible bargain.

Troilus and Cressida

> Howarth, Davies, Bayley, Robson, Opie, Thornton, Chorus of Opera North, English Northern Philharmonia, Hickox. Chandos CHAN 9370 [CD].

During an unguarded moment, Sir William Walton once confessed that in one way or another, all of his major works were "about girls." The girl who inspired the composer's only full-length opera was Susana Gil, daughter of a prominent Argentine attorney, who in 1949 became Mrs.—later Lady—Walton. Written on the Italian Isle of Ischia and dedicated to his young wife, *Troilus and Cressida* was indifferently received at its premiere in 1954; a revised version, with the heroine turned into a mezzo-soprano to accommodate Dame Janet Baker, fared little better in a 1976 Covent Garden revival, and for a time it seemed that the composer's most ambitious work was firmly set on the slippery slope to oblivion.

Based on a 1995 production by Opera North, Richard Hickox's stunning recording triumphantly proves that *Troilus and Cressida* is not only one of the great English operas of the century but also one of the great modern operas, *period*. The score overflows with memorable themes and striking set pieces, the characters are all vividly drawn, and in spite of its complicated plot—adapted from Chaucer, not Shakespeare—the action is swift and unerring. Walton handles his massive forces with the same power and sensual abandon that characterizes the best pages of the First Symphony and *Belshazzar's Feast,* yet there is also a refinement and sensitivity in the writing that he never duplicated before or since.

Although the cast of this pathbreaking Chandos recording could not have been bettered—with an ease I would have thought impossible, Judith Howarth handily surpasses both Dame Janet Baker in the complete live recording and Elisabeth Schwarzkopf in the famous disc of excerpts conducted by the composer (EMI ZDM 64199 [CD])—it is Richard Hickox who deserves most of the credit for this astonishing achievement. In both its richness of ornamental detail and dramatic sweep, this performance not only proves conclusively that a masterpiece has been languishing in almost total neglect for forty years, but it also serves notice that those days are at an end.

Not surprisingly, Hickox's recording of Walton's affable one-act "extravaganza" after Chechov, *The Bear* (CHAN 9245 [CD]), is also an unalloyed pleasure, with pointed, characterful singing from Della Jones, Alan Opie, and John Shirley-Quirk. The conductor not only makes the chamber scoring seem unusually opulent but also skillfully underscores the numerous musical parodies and comic references without allowing them to disrupt the dramatic shape of the piece. As in their version of *Troilus,* Chandos's recorded sound is ideal.

Variations on a Theme by Hindemith

London Philharmonic, Latham-König. Chandos CHAN 9106 [CD].

This is even more *bloody* infuriating than before. After issuing what was perhaps the single most valuable Walton recording then available, George Szell's incomparable Cleveland Orchestra recordings of the Second Symphony, *Partita for Orchestra* and *Hindemith Variations,* Sony withdraws and repackages the latter with Szell's admittedly unparalleled version of Hindemith's *Symphonic Metamorphosis on Themes of Carl Maria von Weber* and a mediocre *Mathis der Maler* Symphony with Ormandy and the Philadelphia. Not that the *Hindemith Variations* wasn't magnificent: it simply belonged with the other, equally magnificent Waltons, not in that cutesy-poo mix. Apparently the new motto at Sony is

"If It Ain't Broke, Break it"—or perhaps simply the tried-and-true recording company variation on *Caveat emptor: Emptor fornicatum est*—for to add even further insult to wretched injury, they've now withdrawn the whole thing.

The only other available versions of the *Hindemith Variations* each pose a problem. A highly charged live performance from 1963 featuring the BBC Symphony conducted by the composer is available on an IMP "BBC Radio Classics" album (IMP 5691782 [CD]), unfortunately paired with Sir Adrian Boult's largely inert and etiolated version of the First Symphony. Jan Latham-König leads a superbly alert performance with the London Philharmonic for the Chandos Walton series, but to get it, you have to acquire another full-priced version of the Viola Concerto. As fine as Nobuko Imai's performance certainly is, it doesn't displace the incandescent recording by Nigel Kennedy and André Previn (see page 785). Still, a first-rate performance of a Walton rarity, the *Sonata for String Orchestra*—an arrangement from the A Minor String Quartet—makes it very tempting. Of course, if Sony would only repackage and reissue the three Szell recordings, then we'd all sleep better at night.

Warlock, Peter (1894–1930)

Capriol Suite

Ulster Orchestra, Handley. Chandos CHAN 8808 [CD].

On the night of December 17, 1930, a brilliant, erratic English composer fulfilled the secret fantasy of every composer who has ever lived by actually murdering a music critic. Tragically, the composer Peter Warlock and his victim, the critic Philip Heseltine, were one and the same person. At thirty-six, Warlock was already one of the most distinctive English voices of his generation, a composer whose charming, gem-like miniatures reflected the two great passions of his life: the gentle impressionism of his friend Frederick Delius and the forms of the great English music of the Renaissance. With the publication of the composer's first major biography, Barry Smith's *Peter Warlock: The Life of Philip Heseltine* (Oxford University Press, 1994), perhaps a systematic series of recordings of the finest English songs since Purcell's might finally be attempted. Perhaps Chandos might be persuaded to do the same invaluable service for Warlock that they're currently performing for Percy Grainger.

Warlock's most popular work, the *Capriol Suite,* based on Elizabethan dances that are given an unmistakably modern yet at times surprisingly sentimental spin, is superbly represented by Vernon Handley's colorful recording with the

Ulster Orchestra. Other than the undoubted quality of the performance itself, the principal advantage of the recording is that it presents the composer's rarely heard version for full orchestra (instead of the more usual string band) and also offers Warlock's marvelous *Serenade for String Orchestra* as a bonus. The *Serenade in G* and *Nocturne*—unqualified winners both—by Warlock's contemporary E. J. Moeran round out this unusually desirable collection.

With the recent deletion of two of the finest Warlock recordings ever made—Ian Partridge's Etcetera recital and EMI version o*f The Curlew*—John Mark Ainsley's wonderful Hyperion album of Warlock songs (CDA 66736 [CD]) is especially welcome. While he lacks something of Partridge's rhythmic swagger, Ainsley brings an abundant humor and sensitivity to this large and varied collection, with Roger Vignoles providing uncommonly adroit support. While slightly distant, the recorded sound is both realistic and beautifully balanced. A second album (CDA 66938 [CD]) features the finest version of *The Curlew* since Partridge's, together with nine songs with accompaniments arranged for string quartet.

For a man who purported to detest the season, Warlock wrote an enormous amount of inspired Christmas music, much of the best of it now collected on a lovely Continuum album by Louis Halsey and the Allegri Singers called "The Frostbound Wood" (CON 1053 [CD]).

Wassenaer, Count Unico Wilhelm van (1692–1766)

*C*oncerti Armonici (6)

Brandenburg Consort, Goodman. Hyperion CDA 66670 [CD].

Although the two most famous of all musical mis-attributions have finally begun to be straightened out—rarely does one see Jeremiah Clarke's *Prince of Denmark's March* called "Purcell's *Trumpet Voluntary*" and even less frequently is Haydn credited with Leopold Mozart's *Toy Symphony*—the subtitle of Igor Stravinsky's *Pulcinella* remains "Ballet in One Act with Song after Pergolesi," although much of the music is now generally thought to be the work of an inspired Dutch nobleman and amateur composer named Unico Wilhelm, Graf von Wassenaer. Wassenaer's six *Concerti armonici*—also for years attributed to Pergolesi—are astonishingly fresh and individual works, among the most accomplished concerti grossi of the entire High Baroque. Roy Goodman and the Brandenburg Consort treat them with all the respect, vigor, and imagination they deserve.

Waxman, Franz (1906–1967)

Film Music

> National Philharmonic, Gerhardt. RCA 0708-2-RG [CD], 0708-4-RG [T].

In 1933, the same year that Max Steiner produced his epoch-making score for *King Kong*, the German composer Franz Wachsmann wrote the music for Fritz Lang's screen version of Molnar's *Liliom*. Two years later, Wachsmann had moved to Hollywood, had changed the spelling of his name to Waxman, and had written the music for *The Bride of Frankenstein,* the first of more than 180 film scores he would write during the next thirty years. Of all the major film composers, none was more accomplished and certainly none was more versatile: Waxman was as comfortable with sophisticated comedies like *The Philadelphia Story* as he was with the gothic romance of *Rebecca*; with costume swashbucklers like *Prince Valiant* (with a score written in conscious homage to Richard Strauss) and gritty war pictures like *Objective, Burma!* (directed by Raoul Walsh, of whom Jack Warner once said, "To him, a tender love scene is burning down a whorehouse").

The Waxman album from RCA's "Classic Film Scores" series provides a brilliant overview of his career, from one of the most celebrated cues in screen history, *Creation of the Female Monster* from *The Bride of Frankenstein* (which had to be painstakingly restored from the soundtrack by the conductor Charles Gerhardt, since the score and parts were lost) to a suite from *Taras Bulba*, the last film score Waxman completed before turning his full attention to more obviously serious works like the *Sinfonietta* and the song cycle *The Song of Terezin*. Along with suites from *Old Acquaintance, The Philadelphia Story, Prince Valiant,* and *Rebecca,* the anthology also contains excerpts from his two Oscar-winning scores, *Sunset Boulevard* and *A Place in the Sun.* Even by the exacting standards of this extraordinary series, the performances and recorded sound are exceptional.

Waxman's most familiar concert work, the *Carmen Fantasy for Violin and Orchestra,* adapted from the 1947 Joan Crawford/John Garfield soaper *Humoresque,* is heard to wonderful advantage in a 1946 recording featuring Isaac Stern (Garfield's ghost violinist) and the Warner Brothers Orchestra conducted by the composer. This appears in a four-disc set of Stern recordings from Sony (M4K 42003 [CD]) called "Celebration: Life with Music," which also features other Waxman arrangements, including Dvořák's *Humoresque* and Rimsky-Korsakov's *The Flight of the Bumblebee*.

Weber, Carl Maria von (1786–1826)

Concerto No. 1 in F Minor for Clarinet and Orchestra, Op. 73;
Concerto No. 2 in E-flat Major for Clarinet and Orchestra, Op. 74;
Concertino for in E-flat Major for Clarinet and Orchestra, Op. 26

> Pay, clarinet; Orchestra of the Age of Enlightenment. Virgin Classics 59002 [CD].

Midway between the Old Testament (the Concerto, Quintet, and Trio of Mozart) and the New (the late masterpieces of Brahms) fall those several appealing works that the third undisputed master of the instrument, Carl Maria von Weber, composed for the clarinet. Written for his friend, the suave Bavarian clarinetist and lady-killer Heinrich Bärmann, Weber's concertos and chamber works not only represent one of the high-water marks of early Romantic wind writing but also display the composer's talent at its freshest and most inventive.

In his period-instrument recording with the Orchestra of the Age of Enlightenment, the English clarinetist Anthony Pay strikes the perfect balance between swagger and sensitivity in his approach to the music; the playing has both bite and delicacy, as does the finely drilled (but by whom?) contribution of the conductor-less orchestra. Again, the Virgin Classics engineers prove that they are among the best in the business, with impeccably clear and detailed recorded sound.

Euryanthe

> Norman, Hunter, Gedda, Krause, Leipzig Radio Chorus, Dresden State Orchestra, Janowski. Berlin Classics BER 1108 [CD].

Apart from its swaggering overture, Weber's final opera remains almost completely unknown, thanks entirely to a libretto so absurdly incomprehensible it makes *La Gioconda* read like Ibsen. Helemina von Chézy, the witless oaf who was poor Schubert's collaborator on *Rosamunde*, is again the culprit, although to be fair, no one held a gun at Weber's head forcing him to set her gibberish. Yet for all the limitations of the drama (if it may so be called), *Euryanthe* represented a striking advance over *Der Freischütz,* not only in its richer harmonic language and more expressive use of the orchestra, but also in the way formal arias and other set pieces are blended into a larger, continuous structure, thus clearly laying the groundwork for the Wagner music dramas.

Originally recorded for EMI, this exciting performance reveals what a thoroughly arresting work *Euryanthe* really is. Jessye Norman and Rita Hunter are hugely impressive as the virtuous Euryanthe and the wicked Eglantine (leave it to Helemina to give them confusingly similar names), while Nicolai Gedda and Tom Krause make for a superb hero and villain (even when you can't quite tell them apart). Marek Janowski's conducting is consistently intelligent and resourceful, allowing the genuinely magnificent moments (and there are many) to unfold naturally, while helping the weaker ones move right along.

Der Freischütz

Seefried, Streich, Holm, Wächter, Böhme, Bavarian Radio Chorus and Orchestra, Jochum. Deutsche Grammophon 439717-2 [CD].

The next time you're trapped in a game of musical trivia and need a question that will stump everyone, ask, "What is the second most frequently performed opera in Germany today?" The totally unexpected answer is Albert Lortzing's *Zar und Zimmermann.* In fact, the work that occupies the number one spot will also come as a surprise to most people, simply because it isn't performed very often outside the German-speaking world. The reasons for the phenomenal popularity of *that* opera, Weber's *Der Freischutz,* are as obvious now as they were when it was first performed. Along with its wonderfully dark atmosphere (Germans love anything set in a forest), *Der Freischütz* boasts a succession of unforgettable arias, choruses, and other set pieces. Also, with *Der Freischütz,* Carl Maria von Weber brought Romanticism into the opera house, and thus composers as diverse as Meyerbeer, Berlioz, Wagner, and Strauss owe Weber an incalculable debt.

The splendid Deutsche Grammophon release that marked Carlos Kleiber's recording debut as an operatic conductor has been temporarily withdrawn, but what an auspicious debut it proved to be! Kleiber led the superb cast and the always impeccable Dresden State Opera forces with tremendous energy, enthusiasm, and imagination. Only in the most darkly brooding moments of the second act did hints of Weber's subtler poetry escape him. Still, it was a bracing introduction to a wonderful opera and its medium-priced resurrection cannot be awaited more eagerly.

Although Deutsche Grammophon chose to reissue their 1960 recording in preference to the Kleiber, this is hardly a tragedy, since the Jochum *Freischütz* is splendid in every way. Irmgard Seefried and Rita Streich are dazzling as Agathe and Aennchen, while the alert and enthusiastic Bavarian Radio Chorus matches its wonderful contribution to the Kubelik *Meistersinger.* In terms of pacing and attention to detail, Jochum's contribution could not be more impressive, while the recorded sound has held up remarkably well. There are some niggling cuts (primarily in the dialogue) that only the hardest-core *Freischütz* junkies will ever miss.

Rafael Kubelik's stunning version of Weber's English opera *Oberon is* available on a medium-priced DG reissue (419038-2 [CD]), with Placido Domingo a gleaming hero, Birgit Nilsson overwhelming in "Ocean, Thou Mighty Monster," and Kubelik turning in some of the most refined and pointed conducting of his career. The spoken dialogue and narration that made the ridiculous plot seem a little less so has been omitted—a minor reservation in an otherwise invaluable release.

Overtures (6) and *Invitation to the Dance*

Philharmonia Orchestra, Järvi. Chandos CHAN 9066 [CD].

There was a pressing need for a good modern recording of the six Weber overtures and the Berlioz orchestration of *Aufforderung zum Tanze;* alas, Hermann Scherchen's zestful yet scrappy interpretations (now out on an Adès compact disc) have almost outlived their usefulness, while the more recent (and already withdrawn) releases by Karajan and Sawallisch were, respectively, perverse and inert.

Neeme Järvi and the Philharmonia Orchestra were just getting to know each other at the time their Weber overture album was recorded. For the most part, the performances tend to be professional and workmanlike rather than inspired, though from time to time the music does catch fire, as in the opening flourish of *Euryanthe* or in the crisply sprung rhythms of *Peter Schmoll.* With the excellent Nimbus collection by Roy Goodman and the Hanover Band unaccountably withdrawn, Järvi has the field virtually to himself.

Wilhelm Furtwängler's incomparably Romantic interpretations of the three greatest overtures—*Der Freischütz, Euryanthe, Oberon*—can be heard on a Historic Performers album (HPS 8 [CD]), coupled with his extraordinarily Brahmsian version of the Fourth Symphony of Tchaikovsky. Except for the dingy sound, the Webers are everything that one could wish, with volcanic tempo eruptions and monsters out of the *Urwald.*

For the last word in that Berlioz-arranged charmer *Invitation to the Dance,* Fritz Reiner's witty, high-voltage recording is now available on RCA 09026-61250-2 [CD], 09026-61250-4 [T].

Symphonies (2); *Konzertstück* for Piano and Orchestra

> Tan, fortepiano; London Classical Players, Norrington. EMI Classics
> CDC 55348 [CD].

Weber's symphonies are not only important works in the development of the early-Romantic symphony, but they are also tremendous fun, brimming over with good tunes, inspired invention, and a fresh-faced *gemütlichkeit* that never seems to pale. Plugged in to any symphonic program in place of a Haydn symphony, they would never fail to surprise and delight.

Roger Norrington and the London Classical Players have not made a more entertaining recording than this one, with the pungent textures and—in the conductor's phrase—"filthy noise" of the old instruments perfectly suited to these rollicking, romantic scores. Melvyn Tan is a formidable soloist in the brilliant, programmatic *Konzertstück* in F Minor, making this one of the most thoroughly desirable Weber albums now available.

Webern, Anton   (1883–1945)

Music of Webern

> Various soloists, chamber ensembles, orchestras, Boulez. Sony Classical
> SM3K 45845 [CD].

Anton Webern was the most tragic member of the so-called Second Viennese School, whose other members were his teacher Arnold Schoenberg and his fellow pupil Alban Berg. Accidentally shot by an American soldier during the postwar occupation of Austria, Webern's tragedy had in fact begun years earlier. Both of his daughters were married to high-ranking Nazi officials, and he himself seems to have been extremely sympathetic to the cause, not because he was evil but because he was incredibly naive. On the day the Nazis marched into Vienna, Webern allegedly said, "Well, now at least we will be able to hear Mahler!" Until quite recently, this pathetic, lonely figure was one of the most influential composers of the twentieth century. In fact, "Post-Webern" became a designation that was once used as frequently as "neo-Classicism" or "New Romanticism."

Those with a serious interest in Webern's rarefied art will find the bulk of it collected on these three medium-priced Sony CDs (SM3K 45845) in those meticulous performances from the 1960s under the general supervision of Pierre Boulez. As always, the conductor's sense of reverent enthusiasm is matched only by the depth of his understanding. The orchestral performances are unfailingly refined and beautiful, while the Juilliard String Quartet and others work comparable wonders with the chamber music. It isn't often that one can encounter virtually the whole of a major composer's output in such a compact and attractively priced container.

Weill, Kurt (1900–1950)

Die Dreigroschenoper (The Threepenny Opera)

Lenya, Litz, Gunter, Mund, Markworth, Murch, Southwest German Radio Chorus and Orchestra, Brückner-Rüggeberg. CBS MK 42637 [CD].

When the gruff, foul-mouthed Marxist playwright was first introduced to the shy young composer after a performance of one of the latter's symphonies, he got right to the point: "My name is Bert Brecht," he announced, "and if you want to work with me, you're going to have to stop writing that shit stuff and come up with some *tunes*." And so began the collaboration that would culminate in *The Threepenny Opera* of 1929, the apotheosis of the spirit of Berlin in the '20s, and one of German art's last great creative gasps before the Nazi deluge.

With Kurt Weill's widow, Lotte Lenya, singing Jenny—a role she created and would eventually make world-famous—this *Dreigroschenoper* from the mid-1950s will never be superseded. With the help of an excellent supporting cast and a very canny conductor, Lenya conjures up the darkness, danger, and sense of all-pervasive corruption that hung over the Weimar Republic like a sickeningly sweet poison gas, a decadent miasma that makes a sanitized entertainment like *Cabaret* seem like the innocent child's play it is.

The best version of the *Kleine Dreigroschenmusik* (the *Threepenny Opera* Suite) is Michael Tilson Thomas's mordant and deliciously overripe recording for CBS (MK 44529 [CD]).

The more obviously serious side of Weill's character can be heard in the Philips recording of the two Symphonies (434171-2 [CD]), which are given tough, aggressive, hugely sympathetic performances by the Leipzig Gewandhaus Orchestra conducted by Edo de Waart.

Weinberger, Jaromir (1896–1967)

Schwanda the Bagpiper: Polka and Fugue

Chicago Symphony, Reiner. RCA 09026-62587-2 [CD],
   09026-62587-4 [T].

One of the most frequently performed of all twentieth-century operas—within five years of its Prague premiere it would be heard in literally thousands of performances in dozens of productions around the world—*Schwanda the Bagpiper* was given an unaccountably cool reception at the Metropolitan Opera in 1931, and two years later, with the advent of Hitler, its fate in Europe was sealed. As the first commercial recording demonstrated a few years ago, *Schwanda*'s once phenomenal popularity was obviously no fluke. In fact, it is such a tuneful, vibrant, utterly disarming work that one can only wonder why more companies don't take a chance on it today. It has fantasy, spectacle, romance, and an abundance of unforgettable set pieces: in addition to the well-known Polka and Fugue (the last is, in truth, a triumphal chorus), the First Act aria "Ich bin der Schwanda" is one of those arias that, once heard, can't be forgotten, no matter how hard you try. Produced by the late George Korngold, the recording not only deserves a medium-priced reissue but should also become mandatory listening for every director of every opera company in the civilized world, especially those now planning future seasons who can't face the prospect of yet another *La Bohème*. Surefire winners don't come along all that often, and a surefire, iron-clad, gold-plated, take-it-to-the-bank, hock-your-grandmother-and-bet-the-bundle winner *Schwanda* most certainly is. With Hermann Prey in the title role, the luscious Lucia Popp as his wife, the young Siegfried Jerusalem as the robber Babinsky, a first-rate supporting cast, and superlative conducting from Heinz Wallberg, this is one of the most thoroughly enjoyable operatic recordings ever made and it *must* be made available again without delay.

Until it is, *Schwanda* withdrawal symptoms may be partially treated with Fritz Reiner's classic recording of the Polka and Fugue, which comes as part of a wonderful Czech anthology that includes Dvořák's *New World Symphony* and *Carnival Overture* and the Overture to Smetana's *The Bartered Bride*. Constant Lambert's classic recording of Weinberger's only other substantial success, *Under the Spreading Chestnut Tree,* can now be found on Time Machine 0099 [CD].

White, Edward (1910–1994)

Puffin' Billy

RTE Concert Orchestra, Tomlinson. Marco Polo 8.223522 [CD].

While few people would recognize Teddy White's name or the actual title of his best known work, millions on both sides of the Atlantic know and love *Puffin' Billy* as the signature tune for the BBC Radio program *Children's Favorites* and as the theme from *Captain Kangaroo*.

White's amusing portrait of an antiquated steam engine on the Isle of Wight is only the best-known work on perhaps the most appealing album yet in Marco Polo's wonderful British Light Music series. A program of miniatures by seventeen different composers, the collection includes familiar gems like Arthur Benjamin's *Jamaican Rumba,* together with little discoveries like Mark Lubbock's infectious *Polka Dots* and Geoffrey Toye's lovely concert waltz, *The Haunted Ballroom.*

Ernest Tomlinson leads the RTE Concert Orchestra with his customary affection and authority and even provides the engrossing program notes. The CD has first-rate recorded sound, as usual.

Widor, Charles Marie (1844–1937)

Organ Symphony No. 5

Tracey, organ. Chandos CHAN 9271 [CD].

Like his immensely prolific near contemporary Henry Charles Litolff, Charles Marie Widor is one of history's mercifully few examples of a Part-of-a-Work Composer. For just as poor Litolff is remembered only for the mercurial *Scherzo* from his Concerto Symphonique No. 4, Widor survives almost entirely on the strength of the *Toccata* from the Organ Symphony No. 5.

Although it can be found in any number of recorded grab-bags of organ favorites, the best way to hear the remorselessly buoyant piece is in the context of the "Symphony"—actually, the extended suite—in which it originally appeared. Ian Tracey's Chandos CD offers the imposing, colorful organ of the Liverpool Cathedral and a recording with an absolutely astonishing dynamic range—the sort that might easily melt the fillings in the unwary listener's teeth if the volume is turned up to capture the gossamer *pianissimos*. Moreover, for those reluctant to invest in a full-priced CD of solo organ music, the performance comes with superlative versions of the Poulenc Organ Concerto and the rarely heard (but thoroughly ingratiating) Organ Symphony of Félix Guilmant, in which Tracey is brilliantly supported by the BBC Philharmonic conducted by Yan Pascal Tortelier.

Those feeling they can make do with the famous *Toccata* alone are directed to an unusually attractive Naxos anthology of French organ music (8.550581 [CD]) by the gifted Simon Lindley, who is also very persuasive with shorter works by Guilmant, Vierne, Charpentier, Langlais, Bonnet, and Boëllmann.

Wieniawski, Henryk   (1835–1880)

Violin Concerto No. 1, Op. 14; Violin Concerto No. 2, Op. 22

Shaham, violin; London Symphony, Foster. Deutsche Grammophon 431815-2 [CD].

In the century since his death, the Polish composer Henryk Wieniawski has been represented almost exclusively in the concert hall and the recording studio by his D Minor Violin Concerto, one of the classic late-Romantic barn burners and a piece that can still get the blood boiling when a violinist with the right equipment is in charge. As his stunning Deutsche Grammophon versions (437540-2 [CD]) of the Sibelius and Tchaikovsky Concertos demonstrated conclusively, Gil Shaham's equipment is among the most impressive of his generation, and his thundering technique and interpretive élan not only do wonders for the D Minor Concerto but are also extremely effective in its lesser-known F Minor companion piece. Lawrence Foster and the London Symphony offer pointed and ingratiating support while the recorded sound could hardly be improved.

Wilder, Alec   (1907–1980)

Concerto for Oboe, Strings, and Percussion

> Lucarelli, oboe; Brooklyn Philharmonic, Barrett. Koch International
> Classics 7187-2 [CD].

Best known for his *sui generis* Octets that fused elements of classical chamber music with jazz rhythms and melodies that suggested popular songs, Alec Wilder was one of the most diverse and difficult to classify of all American composers. Largely self-taught, Wilder produced an enormous number of works in a bewildering variety of forms from ballets and operas to tunes for his friend Frank Sinatra, all of them urbane, ingratiating, and enormously appealing.

Bert Lucarelli gives a superb account of the Oboe Concerto that Wilder wrote for Mitch Miller, together with limpidly beautiful performances of miniatures by John Corigliano and Robert Bloom. The recital opens with Wayne Barlow's ineffably haunting *The Winter's Past*, which in itself is more than worth the price of the album.

Willan, Healey   (1880–1968)

Tenebrae, Responsaries, Missa brevis

> Church of St. Mary Magdalene Choir, Hunter. Virgin Classics
> 45260 [CD].

The English-born Healy Willan spent the last forty-seven years of his long career directing music at the small High Anglican Church of St. Mary Magdelene in Toronto, producing an enormous amount of choral music for its services. From the relatively simple hymn tunes to the more elaborate settings, Willan's music has genuine strength, depth, and character: fresh, unaffected, deliberately archaic, it is among the most moving and memorable church music produced in this century. The performances by the composer's own choir are predictably polished and affectionate, with recorded sound and documentation on the same high level as the previous installments in Virgin's Willan series.

Williams, Grace (1906–1977)

Fantasia on Welsh Nursery Songs; Carillons for oboe and orchestra; *Penillion;* Trumpet Concerto; *Sea Sketches*

> London Symphony, Royal Philharmonic, Groves; English Chamber
> Orchestra, Atherton. Lyrita SCRD 323 [CD].

While her early work was written under the shadow of her teacher, Ralph Vaughan Williams, the guiding influence in the mature music of Grace Williams was the folk heritage of her native Wales. Her most popular work, the *Fantasia on Welsh Nursery Songs,* is a potpourri of skillfully arranged folk tunes, while later works like *Penillion* and *Carillons* are bursting with Welsh national feeling. The 1963 Trumpet Concerto—an example of a work in her more deliberately cosmopolitan style—is one of the most accomplished and attractive in the instrument's modern repertoire.

Culled from several LP sources, this Lyrita reissue is an excellent introduction to Williams's civilized, lyrical world. Howard Snell, then principal trumpet of the London Symphony, dispatches his challenging part with grace and aplomb, as does oboist Anthony Camden in the captivating *Carillons.* The orchestral contributions are no less distinguished, as is the surprisingly lifelike '70s recorded sound. The only serious drawback is the Lyrita price tag, which at about $25 retail is asking a lot from all but the most devoted Williams admirer.

Williams, John (1932–)

Film Music

> Cincinnati Pops, Kunzel. Telarc CD 80094 [CD], CS 30094 [T].

On listening to her old acoustical recordings toward the end of her life, the Golden Age coloratura Amelita Galli-Curci said something to the effect that when she heard them in light of what she had hoped to do, she was very humble; when she heard them in comparison to those of her colleagues, she was very proud. With the possible exceptions of Elmer Bernstein and Jerry Goldsmith, no film composer working today is more admired than John Williams. In addition to virtual star status among the public, his reputation is extraordinarily high among studio musicians, who speak of his consummate professionalism in almost reverential tones. And if he has been accused in the past of occasionally "borrowing" ideas from a variety of composers from Elgar to Korngold, almost every film composer of the younger generation now shamelessly borrows from him.

Erich Kunzel leads the Cincinnati Pops in a rousing collection of excerpts from Williams's best-known scores, including the *Star Wars* Trilogy, *Superman*—whose love theme *does* bear a striking resemblance to the resurrection motif from the Strauss tone poem *Death and Transfiguration*—*Close Encounters of the Third Kind, E.T.,* and *Raiders of the Lost Ark.* What may prove to be the finest of all his film scores, *Schindler's List,* is available on MCA MCAD 10628 [CD], MCAC 10628 [T].

Williams's considerable gifts as a composer of music intended for the concert hall can be sampled on a fine Varèse Sarabande recording (VSD 5345 [CD]) of his haunting Flute Concerto and the attractive and accomplished Violin Concerto, both in stylish performances led by Leonard Slatkin.

Wirén, Dag   (1905–1986)

Serenade for Strings

Bournemouth Sinfonietta, Studt. Naxos 8.553106 [CD].

Dag Wirén was a Swedish composer of enormously agreeable music who remains best known outside of his native country for a single work, the enchanting *Serenade for Strings* of 1937. It is an infectiously tuneful, immediately appealing work that bears more than favorable comparison with Grieg's *Holberg Suite* or Nielsen's *Little Suite for Strings,* the other major pieces on this irresistible Naxos anthology of Scandinavian music, which also includes some heart-dissolving arrangements of Icelandic, Norwegian, and Swedish folk melodies by Johann Svendsen. The strings of the Bournemouth Sinfonietta play with finesse and character and the recorded sound is close but warm.

By the way, this is a perfect recording with which to catch a reluctant object of your affections off guard. (It's worked for me; it will work for you.)

Wolf, Hugo   (1860–1903)

Songs

After Franz Schubert, there were only three incontestably great composers of German lieder: Schumann, Brahms, and Hugo Wolf. And if Schubert practically invented the form, then Wolf presided over its final, bittersweet flowering. In the work of no other composer are words and music so intimately connected, and in no other German songs do we encounter so much effortless perfection.

Among the available recordings of Wolf songs, and there are shamefully few, the EMI Classics recording (CDC 55163 [CD]) of the *Italian Song Book* with Dawn Upshaw, Olaf Bär, and pianist Helmut Deutsch is a welcome edition to the catalogue, offering interpretations as fresh and nearly as imaginative as those of the celebrated Schwarzkopf/Fischer-Dieskau recording (EMI Classics CDM 63732 [CD]) and far finer recorded sound. Bär is joined by the wonderfully resourceful Anne Sofie von Otter in an even finer version of the *Spanish Song Book* (EMI Classics CDC 55325 [CD]), in which the artistry of both young singers is magically enhanced by the late Geoffrey Parsons in one of his final recordings.

Thomas Allen's Virgin Classics recital (CDC 59221 [CD]) features performances that are both interpretively probing and handsomely sung, and although Elisabeth Schwarzkopf's enchanting *Spanish Song Book* with Fischer-Dieskau is temporarily out of circulation, her legendary 1953 Salzburg recital with Wilhelm Furtwängler is currently available (EMI Classics CDM 65749 [CD], as are two other incomparable Wolf anthologies (CDM 63653; CDM 64905) that rank with the finest recordings this unique singer ever made.

Preiser continues its laudable series of historic reissues with some of the most valuable Wolf recordings of all: fourteen songs from the pioneering Hugo Wolf Society recordings made between 1933 and 1935 by the great Russian bass Alexander Kipnis, whose depth of insight would not be matched until the arrival of Hans Hotter, whose Preiser and EMI collections have shamefully been allowed to slip out of print. While her voice is clearly not as fresh as it once was, Elly Ameling's recent Hyperion album (CDA 66788 [CD]) demonstrates that her extraordinary interpretive powers remain gloriously intact.

Among available recordings of the magical *Italian Serenade*, I Musici offers a light and witty version of the chamber orchestra version on a Philips Duo (456330-2 [CD]) that also includes first-rate performances of the Mendelssohn Octet, the Rossini String Sonatas, and Bottesini's *Gran Duo Concertant* for Violin, Double Bass, and Strings. In the string quartet version, no performance is ever likely to surpass that miracle of wicked insinuation and effortless virtuosity recorded in 1953 by the Hollywood String Quartet, reissued by Testament (SBT 1081 [CD]) as a delicious postscript to their recordings of Dohnányi's Third Quartet and *Death and the Maiden* by Schubert.

Wolf-Ferrari, Ermanno (1876–1948)

Overtures and Intermezzi

Academy of St. Martin-in-the-Fields, Marriner. EMI CDC 54585 [CD].

Granted, the "secret" of *Il segreto di Susanna* (the lady smokes cigarettes) is hardly comparable to the shock of *The Crying Game;* still, this is no reason for the current neglect of this enchanting modern variation on the eighteenth-century *Intermezzo.* Among one-act Italian comic operas, *The Secret of Susanna* is second only to Puccini's *Gianni Schicchi,* and the current lack of a first-rate recording is a minor scandal.

Sir Neville Marriner leads a fizzing performance of its famous *vivacissimo* Overture, together with lesser-known overtures and *intermezzi* on a superb Wolf-Ferrari anthology. The sheer charm and melodic inventiveness of the music—especially in the string pieces from *I quattro rusteghi* and *The Jewels of the Madonna* Suite—make you wonder how long a Wolf-Ferrari revival can be postponed. Perhaps Sir Neville would consider a much-needed recorded cycle of the operas?

Wordsworth, William (1908–1988)

Symphony No. 2 in D Major, Op. 43; Symphony No. 3 in C Major, Op. 48

London Philharmonic, Braithwaite. Lyrita SCRD 207 [CD].

Like his near contemporaries William Alwyn and Edmund Rubbra, William Wordsworth—a direct descendant of the poet's brother, Christopher—was an English symphonist at the wrong place at the wrong time. Just when he was coming into his full maturity, the English musical establishment—particularly the BBC—was turning its back on the "old-fashioned" point of view that composers like Wordsworth represented. Like many of the more traditional English composers of the period, he was treated to a benign neglect throughout what should have been the years of his greatest success.

The two symphonies on this revealing album suggest that Wordsworth was a composer of genuine stature: a stubbornly unfashionable, tough-minded voice with genuine character and integrity. The Second Symphony, with its distant echoes of Sibelius, is a powerful work full of austere beauties, while the Third is no less appealing in its craggy reserve. Nicholas Braithwaite draws intensely committed playing from the London Philharmonic and the recorded sound, which won a richly deserved *Gramophone* award, is ideal.

Wüsthoff, Klaus   (1922–   )

Die Schlehde; Voyage to Greece; Old England Suite; Street Scenes

Berlin Radio Symphony, Smola. Koch Schwann 3-1805-2 [CD].

This ingratiating German composer had a most unusual musical apprenticeship: he learned his trade in a Russian prisoner-of-war camp, where for four years he wrote music for the camp theater on hand-ruled tobacco paper. Yet unlike Olivier Messiaen, whose *Quartet for the End of Time* was written under similar circumstances, Wüsthoff developed into a composer with a singularly bright and sunny disposition, a man whose work in film, television, and other popular media has made him a kind of German Leroy Anderson.

Judging from this delectable Koch Schwann CD, Wüsthoff, the composer of "light symphonic music," is not that far removed in terms of quality from Anderson or Eric Coates. His music is crammed with engaging melodies and sparkling wit, with a distinctive—and extremely attractive—personality all its own. And like Anderson and Coates, he has an exasperating talent for writing tunes that stick in the back of your mind for days, whether you want them there or not.

From the sprightly overture to *Die Schlehde*, which in its broad, airy themes and gibbering winds closely resembles Reznicek's *Donna Diana*, to the *Voyage to Greece* and the seven-movement *Old England Suite*, there isn't a tired or unimaginative item in the entire collection—or one that overstays its welcome or *doesn't* make you want to hear more. The Berlin Radio Symphony under Emmerich Smola plays with obvious affection and the recorded sound is appropriately open and warm.

Ysaÿe, Eugène   (1858–1931)

Sonatas (2) for Solo Violin

> Josefowicz, violin. Philips 446700-2 [CD].

The hero of several generations of younger virtuosos, from Fritz Kreisler and Jacques Thibaud to Bronislav Huberman and Joseph Szigeti, the portly, amiable Eugène Ysaÿe is now widely regarded as the father of modern violin playing. Although the recordings made toward the end of his performing career, when a serious tremor afflicted his bowing arm, cannot be considered representative, according to all firsthand accounts Ysaÿe's playing was as individual as it was technically flawless, an assessment that is also borne out by the way he wrote for the violin. The Six Sonatas for solo violin, Op. 27, are among the most original and demanding ever composed for the instrument. Each is dedicated to one of Ysaÿe's many admirers, the Third to Georges Enesco, the Fourth to Fritz Kreisler.

Leila Josefowicz offers staggeringly impressive versions of both on her *Solo* album for Philips, which contains equally challenging works by Kreisler (the *Recitativo and Scherzo-Caprice*), Paganini *(Introduction and Variations on "Nel cor più non mi sento" from Paisiello's "La Molinara")* and Ernst (the *Grand Caprice for Solo Violin after Schubert's "Erlkönig"*). Yet it is the performance of the Ysaÿe Sonatas and the Bartók Sonata for Solo Violin that confirms the arrival of one of the most precocious talents since the young Yehudi Menuhin.

Zandonai, Riccardo   (1883–1944)

Francesca da Rimini

> Olivero, et al., La Scala Chorus and Orchestra, Gavazzeni. Legato
> Classics LCD 186-2 [CD].

The principal reason to acquire this live 1959 recording of Zandonai's blood-and-thunder retelling of the most famous cautionary tale from Dante's *Inferno* is the rare opportunity it affords to sample the extraordinary art of Magda Olivero. Cilea's favorite interpreter of *Adriana Lecouvreur,* Olivero was as widely admired for her superb acting as for her singing, which she continued well into her seventies. Shy of the microphones, she made only a handful of commercial recordings—including some excerpts from *Francesca* for London now available on 433033-2 [CD]—but what few there are suggest an artist of exceptional range and ability. Her singing in this 1959 La Scala production is full of fire and insight, obvious even through the murky recorded sound and despite the less than inspiring contributions of some of her colleagues. In short, this is an invaluable souvenir of a unique and mysterious talent.

Zelenka, Jan Dismas   (1679–1745)

Orchestral Works

Collegium 1704. Supraphon SUP 0009 [CD].

Among the odd fish washed up on the wave of the great Baroque Revival of the 1960s, none was odder or more interesting than that Bohemian recluse Jan Dismas Zelenka. Little is known about the man's life other than the fact that Bach was one of his most passionate admirers. He may or may not have been a mystic, a visionary, or simply a short-tempered hypochondriac (two of his works are called *The Angry Man* and *Hipocondrie*); the lack of an authenticated portrait has added fuel to the legend that he was either severely deformed or hideously disfigured.

Whatever it was that combined to make this strange and mysterious figure, he was one of the most startlingly original composers of his period, a kind of non-vocal central European equivalent of the batty Carlo Gesualdo, a man whose experiments in form, harmony, and expression were as radically daring in his time as Gesualdo's had been a century before.

If not quite as stylish as the recently deleted recordings by the Camerata Bern, these fine performances by Collegium 1704 of some of the composer's most significant orchestral works are the perfect introduction to Zelenka's peculiar and beautiful world. While some of the music is so advanced that Zelenka might sometimes seem a contemporary of Chopin and Schumann rather than of Handel and Bach, he remains—for all his apparent flirtations with Romanticism—a figure of the baroque era, and possibly a major one at that.

Zemlinsky, Alexander von

(1871–1942)

Lyric Symphony; Symphonische Gesänge

Soloists, Royal Concertgebouw Orchestra, Chailly. London 443569-2 [CD].

Until quite recently, the name of Alexander von Zemlinsky came up only in relation to his onetime pupil and brother-in-law Arnold Schoenberg. Actually, he was one of the most respected and influential teachers of his era and, as we're beginning to discover belatedly, one of its most interesting and original composers.

This stunning London recording of the *Lyric Symphony* and *Symphonic Songs* may be the single most important recording of Zemlinsky's music yet released. Both works are symphonic song cycles of extraordinary beauty cut from the same approximate cloth as Mahler's *Lied von der Erde* and Schoenberg's *Gurrelieder.* In soprano Alessandra Marc, baritone Håken Hagegård, and bass Willard White, Riccardo Chailly has an exceptional team of soloists and in the great Concertgebouw Orchestra perhaps the perfect instrument for revealing the astonishing beauty and variety of Zemlinsky's orchestration.

By any standard, this should prove a milestone in the history of the composer's long overdue rehabilitation.

Zwilich, Ellen Taaffe   (1939–)

Concerto Grosso 1985 (after Handel); Concerto for Trumpet and Five Players; Double Quartet for Strings; *Symbolon*

> Smith, trumpet; New York Philharmonic, Mehta, Zwilich. New World
>   NW 80372-2 [CD].

Born in Miami in 1939, Ellen Taaffe Zwilich is a member of that talented generation of musicians who have finally been able to shake off the designation "female composer." There was *always* something condescending and faintly preposterous in that usage; how often, for instance, does one hear the phrase, "the celebrated male composer Beethoven"?

As these recordings of four of her works from 1984 to 1988 clearly show, Zwilich is an intelligent, important composer whose music more than deserves the celebrity it has begun to receive. While the *Concerto Grosso 1985*, written for the tercentenary of Handel's birth, is the most immediately accessible piece in the collection, the others are also challenging and enjoyable, proving, if nothing else, that music is neither a "male" nor a "female" but a wholly human art.

Index

A Montevideo (Gottschalk), 293
A Sei Voci, 383
Aarhus Symphony Orchestra, 356
Abbado, Claudio, 117, 209, 210, 352, 505–507, 527, 603, 604, 640, 641, 645, 660, 707, 712, 713, 735, 757, 758, 760, 761
Abbado, Roberto, 210
Abdelazar: Or, the Moor's Revenge (Purcell), 170
Abduction from the Seraglio (Mozart), 181, 471, 489
Abendempfindung (Mozart), 498
About the Eternal Longing (Novák), 515
Abraham and Isaac (Stravinsky), 705
Abravanel, Maurice, 293, 325, 363, 371, 471
Academic Festival Overture (Brahms), 127
Academy of Ancient Music, 332, 341, 560, 770
Academy of St. Martin-in-the-Fields, 18, 29, 34, 226, 276, 285, 297, 310, 320, 332, 365, 449, 451, 473, 476, 477, 499, 535, 595, 621, 638, 720, 732, 768, 770, 787, 806
Academy of St. Martin-in-the-Fields Chamber Ensemble, 297, 320, 451, 638, 720
Accardo, Salvatore, 24, 25, 673
Adagio con variazione (Respighi), 589

Adagio for Organ and Strings (Albinoni/Giazotto), 5
Adagio for Strings (Barber), 5, 38–39
Adagio for Strings (Lekeu), 409
Adams, Donald, 283
Addinsell, Richard, 2, 587
Ade, George, 491
Adelaide (Beethoven), 59
Adni, Daniel, 234
Adolf Busch Chamber Orchestra, 21
Adorján, András, 186
Adriana Lecouvreur (Cilea), 169, 808
Adventures of Huckleberry Finn, The (Moross), 469
Adventures of Robin Hood, The (Korngold), 394
Afrika (Grosz), 307
Afrikareise (Suppé), 719
Afro-American Symphony (Still), 685
Age of Anxiety (Symphony No. 2) (Bernstein), 93
Agon (Stravinsky), 705
Agrippina (Handel), 316
Ägyptische Helene, Die (Strauss), 691
Ah, Heaven! What Is't I Hear? (Blow), 104
Aïda (Verdi), 110, 136, 467, 553, 632, 751–752, 755, 761
Ainsi la nuit (Dutilleux), 219
Ainsley, John Mark, 136, 256, 260, 792
Air Music (Rorem), 599
Air Power (Dello Joio), 203–204, 590

Airplane Sonata (Antheil), 11
Ajemian, Maro, 153
Aladdin Suite (Nielsen), 513
Alagna, Roberto, 754
Alain, Marie-Claire, 151
Alban Berg Quartet, 66, 67, 644
Albéniz, Isaac, 2–4, 246, 248, 249, 298, 419
Alberni String Quartet, 761
Albert, Eugen d', 4, 417
Albert Herring (Britten), 134
Albert Schweitzer Wind Quintet, 186, 584
Albert, Werner Andreas, 271
Albinoni, Tomasso, 5–6, 438
Alborada del gracioso (Ravel), 190, 576
Albrecht, Gerd, 232
Albrechtsberger, Johann, 6, 470
Album de Madame Bovary (Milhaud), 463
Alcina (Handel), 317
Aldeburgh Festival Ensemble, 141–142
Aleko (Rachmaninoff), 289
Aler, John, 100–101
Alexander, John, 777
Alexander Nevsky (Prokofiev), 540–542, 544
Alexander's Feast (Handel), 320
Alford, Kenneth, 14
Alfvén, Hugo, 7
Alkan, Charles-Henri Valentin, 7–8
All in Twilight (Takemitsu), 144
Allegri Singers, 792
Allegro di concierto (Granados), 299

Alleluia (Hovhaness), 364
Alleluia (Thompson), 738
Allen, Nancy, 579, 597
Allen, Thomas, 40, 210, 466, 534, 558, 561, 644, 748, 805
Aller, Victor, 120, 267, 354, 356
Alliot-Lugaz, 191–192
Almeida, Antonio De, 724, 737, 742
Alpine Symphony, An (Strauss), 691
Also sprach Zarathustra (Strauss), 199, 263, 692, 701
Alsop, Marin, 610
Altenberg Lieder (Berg), 79
Altenberg, Peter, 79
Alto Rhapsody (Brahms), 113
Alva, Luigi, 485, 602
Alwyn, Kenneth, 2, 173
Alwyn, William, 9, 156, 806
Amadigi di Gaula (Handel), 317
Amadinda, 153
Amahl and the Night Visitors (Menotti), 457
Amato, Donna, 4
Amato, Pasquale, 551
Ameling, Elly, 123–124, 196, 254–255, 498, 642, 653, 805
American Festival Overture (Schuman), 38
American in Paris, An (Gershwin), 278
American Indian Rhapsody (Orem), 152
American Overture, An (Britten), 140
American Pieces (Foss), 93
American Quartet (Dvořák), 223, 228, 229, 356, 383, 676
American Salute (Gould), 294
American String Quartet, 50, 628
American Suite (Dvořák), 227
Amico Fritz, L' (Mascagni), 445
Amor brujo, El (Falla), 246, 249
Amores (Cage), 153
Amos, David, 528
An den Wassern zu Babel (Pärt), 526
An die ferne Geliebte (Beethoven), 59
Anaklasis (Penderecki), 526
Ančerl, Karel, 222–223
Ancient Airs and Dances for the Lute (Respighi), 584
And God Created Great Whales (Hovhaness), 364
Anda, Géza, 478
Andante cantabile (Tchaikovsky), 355, 733
Andersen, Hans Christian, 515
Anderson, June, 92, 446, 601, 737

Anderson, Leroy, 10, 171, 807
Anderson, Lorna, 136
Andrea Chénier (Giordano), 284
Andromache's Farewell (Barber), 40
Andromède (Holmes), 358
Andsnes, Leif Ove, 300–301, 380
Angels and Visitationos (Rautavaara), 575
Anna Bolena (Donizetti), 209–210
Anna Magdalena Notebook (Bach), 20
Années de pèlerinage (Liszt), 413
Anon. in Love (song cycle) (Walton), 784
Ansermet, Ernest, 109, 215, 249, 440, 579, 612, 710, 730, 731
Ansorge, Conrad, 417
Antheil, George, 11, 405
Anthony Adverse (Korngold), 394–395
Antony and Cleopatra (Barber), 39, 42, 45
Antill, John, 767
Antonini, Antonio, 590
Apocalypse (Menotti), 457
Apollinaire, Guillaume, 534, 668
Apollo (Britten), 140
Apollo (Stravinsky), 706, 708
Apollo et Hyacinthus seu Hyacinthi Metamorphosis (Mozart), 490
Apostles, The (Elgar), 239
Apothéose de Lully (Couperin), 181
Appalachian Spring (Copland), 38, 174–176, 178, 294
Appassionata Sonata (Beethoven), 62, 63
Après un rêve (Fauré), 254
April—England (Foulds), 265
Arabella (Strauss), 693
Arapian, Armand, 192
Arbor Cosmica (Panufnik), 523–524
Arbos (Pärt), 526
Arbos, Enrigue, 3
Arbre des Songes, L' (Dutilleux), 219
Arcadia Baroque Ensemble, 154
Arcana (Varèse), 743
Archbishop of Salzburg, 342, 474, 484, 500
Archduke Trio (Beethoven), 73
Arensky, Anton, 12–13, 100, 586
Argerich, Martha, 32, 65, 130, 497, 656
Ariadne auf Naxos (Strauss), 693, 699
Aristophanes, 131

Aristotle, 94
Arkadiev, Mikhail, 567
Arlecchino (Cornelius), 181
Arlésienne, L' (Bizet), 98–99
Armstrong, Louis, 753
Arne, Thomas Augustine, 13–14, 112, 658
Arrau, Claudio, 416
Arriaga, Juan, 15, 771
Arrival of the Queen of Sheba (Handel), 170
Arroyo, Martina, 40, 460
Art of the Fugue, The (Bach), 21
Arte de Violino, L' (Locatelli), 420
As You Like It (Film Score) (Walton), 787
As You Like It: Overture (Paine), 522
As You Like It: Suite (Quilter), 561
Asafiev, Boris, 666
Ash (Torke), 741
Ashkenazy, Vladimir, 65–66, 120, 128, 268, 481, 482, 546, 547, 563, 564, 566, 568, 569, 658, 660, 670, 731
Ashton, Frederick, 788
Asrael Symphony (Suk), 716
Assedio di Calais, L' (Donizetti), 211
Astuzie di Colombina, Le (Respighi), 586
Athalia (Mendelssohn), 452
Athena Ensemble, 195, 489
Atherton, David, 447, 803
Atlanta Symphony, 222, 599
Atlantic Sinfonietta, 400
Attack on the Iron Coast (Schurmann), 2
Atterberg, Kurt, 16
Attila (Verdi), 757
Atys (Lully), 422
Au Jardin de Marguerite (Roger-Ducasse), 597
Aubade for Piano and 18 instruments (Poulenc), 534
Aubade Héroïque (Lambert), 402
Auber, Daniel-François-Esprit, 17
Auden, W.H., 141, 343, 713, 784, 786
Augér, Arleen, 310–311, 331, 431, 435, 643, 698
Auriacombe, Louis, 313
Aus Italien (Strauss), 694, 701
Australian Chamber Orchestra, 584, 732
Autumn (Thomson), 738
Autumn Legend (Alwyn), 9
Autumn Poem (Respighi), 585
Aux étoiles (Duparc), 267

Ave Maria (Lauridsen), 404
Ave Maria (Victoria), 763
Ave maris stella (Victoria), 763
Ave, verum corpus (Mozart), 485
Avinson, Charles, 18
Awake My Lyre (Blow), 104
Ax, Emanuel, 329

Babbitt, Milton, 18, 155, 635, 715
Babi Yar (Symphony No. 13)
  (Shostakovich), 668
Baby-Serenade (Korngold), 396
Bacchus et Ariane (Roussel),
  610–611
Bach, Anna Magdalena, 19
Bach Ensemble, 27–28
Bach, Johann Christian, 477
Bach, Johann Sebastian, 4, 5,
  19–30, 32–36, 47, 62, 74, 113,
  115, 142, 149, 151, 154, 168,
  208, 241, 261, 264, 267, 271,
  276, 296, 297, 312, 314, 321,
  335, 349, 353, 369, 438, 453,
  477, 490, 510, 523, 536, 577,
  581, 582, 585, 596, 600, 623,
  628, 633, 657, 676, 685, 686,
  707, 710, 714, 715, 730, 736,
  739, 765, 768, 789, 809
Bach, Wilhelm Friedemann, 36
Bachianas brasileiras
  (Villa-Lobos), 765
Bacquier, Gabriel, 192, 197, 295,
  446, 460, 518, 607, 608
Bad and the Beautiful, The
  (Raksin), 575
Baden-Powell, Roberto, 384
Bagatelles (Beethoven), 53
Bagatelles (Dvořák), 223–224
Bagatelles for Guitar
  (Walton), 788
Bahr, Robert von, 302
Baiser de la fée, Le (Stravinsky),
  364, 707, 710
Bakels, Kees, 749
Baker, Dame Janet, 84, 87, 91,
  139, 141, 239, 290, 429, 474,
  484, 643, 653, 789, 790
Baker, Richard, 786
Bal masqué, Le (Poulenc), 534
Balada, Leonardo, 406
Balakirev, Mily, 36–37
Baldwin, Dalton, 196, 255
Balfe, William, 782
Ballata della Gnomini
  (Respighi), 586
Ballet mécanique (Antheil), 11
Ballet Theater Orchestra, 12
Ballo in maschera, Un
  (Verdi), 753
Balmont, Constantine, 568
Balogh, Jozef, 504
Baltimore Symphony,
  43, 609, 741
Baltsa, Agnes, 603

Bamberg Symphony, 367, 442,
  452, 582
Bamert, Matthias, 208, 308, 309,
  343, 398, 439, 525, 572, 581,
  685, 686
Banfield, Raffaello de, 12
Bänkel und Balladen (Grosz),
  307
Banks of Green Willow, The
  (Butterworth), 150
Bantock, Sir Granville, 37–38
Bär, Olaf, 59, 805
Barbe-bleue: Overture
  (Offenbach), 517
Barber of Baghdad, The
  (Cornelius), 180
Barber of Seville, The (Rossini),
  103, 602
Barber, Samuel, 38, 39, 43, 44,
  93, 155, 324, 412, 710
Barbieri, Fedora, 555, 751, 762
Barbirolli, Sir John, 52, 87,
  237–239, 243–245, 329, 371,
  429, 744, 749, 765, 775
Barcarola (Henze), 345
Barcelona Symphony, 208
Bard, The (Sibelius), 671
Barenboim, Daniel, 73, 79, 122,
  180, 220, 221, 268, 400, 401,
  414, 453, 478, 490, 497, 505,
  595, 618, 652, 732, 766, 777
Barlow, Jeremy, 275
Barlow, Wayne, 802
Bärmann, Heinrich, 794
Barrientos, Maria, 250
Barry, John, 260
Barstow, Josephine, 136
Bartered Bride, The (Smetana),
  378, 511, 516, 594, 673–676,
  729, 751, 799
Bartók, Bela, 45–51, 206, 208,
  327, 351, 382, 412, 416, 424,
  440, 441, 613, 665, 808
Bartoli, Cecilia, 58–59, 473,
  601–603, 643
Bashmet, Yuri, 669
Basie, William "Count", 278
Bastianini, Ettore, 755, 761
Bátiz, Enrique, 596–597, 765
Battaglia di Legnano, La
  (Verdi), 757
Battle, Kathleen, 311, 605
Baudelaire, Charles, 22, 80, 187,
  216, 562
Baudo, Serge, 194, 362, 363, 538
Bavarian Radio Symphony, 60,
  147, 350, 675, 691, 692
Bax, Sir Arnold, 51–52, 101,
  133, 308, 371
Bayless, Richard, 292
BBC Concert Orchestra, 2
BBC Philharmonic, 208, 219, 244,
  251, 287, 351, 448, 462, 585,
  586, 588, 610, 685, 686, 801

BBC Scottish Symphony, 4, 207,
  309, 411, 448, 449, 520, 783
BBC Symphony, 277, 358, 359,
  424, 581, 629, 739, 791
BBC Welsh Symphony, 101,
  268, 615
Beach, Mrs. H. H. A., 52
Bear, The (Walton), 790
Beardsley, Aubrey, 38
Beatles, The, 33, 523, 591
Béatrice et Bénédict: Overture
  (Berlioz), 84, 87, 270
Beauclerk, Lady Diana, 72
Beaumont, Francis, 140
Beauty and the Beast
  (Holdridge), 354
Beaux Arts Trio, 12, 56, 73,
  342, 492, 493, 504, 599,
  654, 655, 743
Beckett, Rachel, 321
Beckmann, Max, 749
Beckus the Dandipratt Overture
  (Arnold), 14
Bedford, Stuart, 141–142
Beecham, Sir Thomas, 2, 16, 25,
  37, 57, 85, 90, 92, 98, 99, 112,
  126, 128, 149, 167, 198,
  199–203, 239, 247, 256, 275,
  302, 303, 306, 315, 316, 318,
  334, 340–342, 415, 469, 471,
  472, 475, 502, 503, 550, 551,
  593, 644, 645, 670, 673, 677,
  693, 723, 773, 775
Beer, Robert, 144
Beerbohm Tree, Sir Herbert, 173
Beethoven, Ludwig van, 4, 6, 35,
  53, 55–74, 81, 89, 96, 100,
  106, 114–116, 119, 123, 125,
  145, 146, 155, 165, 186, 200,
  214, 218, 223, 225, 232, 258,
  268, 285, 306, 308, 331, 334,
  335, 356, 365, 366, 376, 398,
  399, 418, 428, 432, 450, 469,
  470, 479, 481, 490, 494, 502,
  503, 521, 566, 584, 633,
  637–641, 643–646, 652,
  661–663, 672, 677, 683,
  687, 688, 761, 766, 770–772,
  777, 811
Beggar's Opera, The (Gay), 112,
  275, 782
*Begleitungsmusik zu einer
  Lichtspielszene*
  (Schoenberg), 630
Begräbnisgesang (Brahms), 113
Behrens, Hildegard, 699
Beinum, Eduard Van, 191, 436
Bekova, Eleonora, 567
Belasco, David, 551
Belfagor (Respighi), 585
Belisario (Donizetti), 209
Belkis, Queen of Sheba
  (Respighi), 588
Bell Anthem, The (Purcell), 558

Bell, Joshua, 32
Bellini, Vincenzo, 54, 75, 76, 601, 775
Bells of Zlonice, The (Dvořák), 231
Bells, The (Rachmaninoff), 231, 562, 728
Bělohlávek, Jírí, 232
Belshazzar's Feast (Sibelius), 671
Belshazzar's Feast (Walton), 91, 93, 353, 440, 495, 784, 790
Ben Haim, Paul, 77, 157
Ben-Hur (Rózsa), 613
Beňačková-Cápová, Gabriela, 673–674
Benedictine (Vaughan Williams), 745
Benet, Gillian Vivia, 722
Beni Mora (Holst), 358–359
Benjamin, Arthur, 438, 800
Bennett, Richard Rodney, 78
Bennett, Robert Russell, 265, 359, 375
Benoliel, Bernard, 251
Benson, Clifford, 151, 256, 260, 261
Bentham, Jeremy, 296
Benvenuto Cellini: Overture (Berlioz), 87
Berberian, Cathy, 83
Berceuse sur le nom de Fauré (Ravel), 580
Berg, Alban, 79–82, 797
Bergen Symphony, 594
Bergen Wind Quintet, 514
Berger, Ludwig, 470
Berglund, Paavo, 664
Bergman, Ingmar, 749
Bergonzi, Carlo, 169, 170, 552, 557, 754, 755
Bergsma, William, 405
Berio, Luciano, 83, 180, 397, 412, 583
Berkeley, Sir Lennox, 78, 82, 343
Berkes, Kálmán, 399
Berlin Philharmonic Orchestra, 67, 70, 88, 115–117, 146, 147, 186, 220, 232, 414, 449, 450, 489, 497, 505, 548, 630, 646, 660, 735, 736, 773, 774, 775
Berlin Philharmonic Wind Ensemble, 489
Berlin Philharmonic Wind Quintet, 186
Berlin Radio Symphony, 327, 393, 396, 473, 572, 630, 636, 698, 699, 807
Berlin State Opera Orchestra, 220
Berlioz, Hector, 72, 84–91, 163, 194, 270, 370, 452, 455, 584, 603, 795, 796
Berman, Boris, 547
Berman, Lazar, 118, 413

Bernac, Pierre, 534, 538
Berners, Lord, 91–92, 677
Bernhardt, Sarah, 309, 764
Bernstein, Elmer, 803
Bernstein, Leonard, 25, 38–41, 54, 60, 68, 77, 92–95, 99, 103, 126, 127, 137, 165, 174, 175, 178, 205, 215, 263, 291, 294, 324, 325, 332, 333, 339, 373, 374, 415, 428–432, 434, 436, 437, 462, 463, 501, 502, 507, 511–513, 530, 537, 548, 564, 591, 592, 609, 612, 613, 616, 617, 650, 663–665, 680, 710, 711, 731, 735, 755, 774, 779, 803
Berry, Walter, 484, 626
Berryman, John, 193
Bertini, Gary, 188
Berwald, Franz, 96, 719
Best, Matthew, 39, 54, 147, 260, 747
Best Years of Our Lives, The (Friedhofer), 271–272, 469
Bestiaire, Le (Poulenc), 534
Bettelheim, Bruno, 654
Betulia liberata, La (Mozart), 488
Between Two Worlds (Korngold), 395
Beyer, Franz, 473
Biber, Heinrich, 97, 751
Biblical Songs (Dvořák), 227–228
Biches, Les (Poulenc), 535
Bickley, Susan, 37–38, 309
Big Sleep, The (Steiner), 682
Biggs, E. Power, 273, 314
Bílek, Zdenek, 515
Billings, William, 97–98, 183
Billy Budd (Britten), 134, 136
Billy the Kid (Copland), 174
Bilson, Malcolm, 334
Bing, Sir Rudolf, 754
Binns, Malcolm, 37, 684
Birds, The (Respighi), 131, 584, 585, 589
Bisengaliev, Marat, 117
Bizet, Georges, 98–100, 249, 269, 401, 619, 621, 659
Björling, Jussi, 101, 295, 304, 444, 550, 551, 556, 751–753, 762
Blacher, Boris, 183, 327
Black Angels (Crumb), 184
Black Knight, The (Elgar), 236
Black, Neil, 494
Blackwell, Harolyn, 279–280
Blake, William, 135
Blakey, Art, 513
Blasco de Nebra, Manuel, 248
Blaue Vogel, Der (Humperdinck), 367
Blegen, Judith, 20, 332

Blin, Juan Allende, 187
Bliss, Sir Arthur, 2, 101, 375
Bloch, Ernest, 102–103
Blomdahl, Karl-Birger, 103–104
Blomstedt, Herbert, 324, 351–352, 513
Bloom, Robert, 802
Blow, John, 104
Blue Towers (Dahl), 258
Bluebeard's Castle (Bartók), 45
Bluebird pas de deux (Stravinsky), 708
Bly, Robert, 323
Boatswain's Mate, The (Smyth), 677
Boccherini, Luigi, 83, 105–106, 120, 329
Boeuf sur le toit, Le (Milhaud), 463–464, 535, 622
Bogart, Humphrey, 682
Bohème, La (Leoncavallo), 410
Bohème, La (Puccini), 91, 162, 209, 550, 554, 631, 649, 799
Bohemian Ensemble of Los Angeles, 442
Böhm, Karl, 472, 482, 696, 700
Bôite à joujoux (Debussy), 186, 545
Boito, Arrigo, 106–107, 533, 557, 756
Bolcom, William, 279
Bolero (Ravel), 3, 297, 576–577, 678, 763
Bolet, Jorge, 270, 416
Bolshoi Theatre, 1, 659, 661
Bonci, Allesandro, 76
Bonavera, Alfredo, 444
Bonfá, Luis, 384
Bonne chanson, La (Fauré), 253–254
Bonney, Barbara, 217, 334, 366, 498, 643
Bonynge, Richard, 1, 17, 76, 169, 170, 197, 198, 210, 212, 275, 407, 408, 446, 460, 461, 518, 605, 606, 762
Book of the Hanging Gardens, The (Schoenberg), 627
Borge, Victor, 196
Boris Godunov (Mussorgsky), 106, 505–506, 593–594, 729
Borkh, Inge, 698
Borodin, Alexander, 107–110
Borodin String Quartet, 108, 229, 355, 662, 733
Borodin Trio, 234, 580
Boskovsky, Willi, 408, 689
Boston Pops Orchestra, 10, 11, 108, 171, 294, 586, 689, 690
Boston Symphony Chamber Players, 128–129

Boston Symphony Orchestra, 69, 79, 80, 85–90, 93, 128, 148, 163, 178, 188, 194, 259, 263, 269, 270, 273, 305, 414, 415, 531, 546, 578, 619, 627, 630, 631, 670, 672, 673, 714, 735

Bostridge, Ian, 309, 707, 745–746

Boswell, James, 505

Bottesini, Giovanni, 110, 460, 805

Bottone, Bonaventura, 747

Boughton, William, 133, 150, 454

Boulanger, Lili, 111, 722

Boulanger, Nadia, 111, 174, 176, 259, 764

Boulez, Pierre, 48–49, 79, 82, 190, 194, 247, 248, 383, 397, 629, 631, 632, 635, 743, 797

Boult, Sir Adrian, 238, 239, 244, 314, 359, 361, 371, 384, 744–750, 791

Bour, Ernst, 579

Bourgeois gentilhomme, Le (Strauss), 694, 703

Bournemouth Sinfonietta, 245, 296, 464, 707, 804

Bournemouth Symphony, 199, 201, 240, 437, 749

Bourrée fantastique (Chabrier), 159

Boutique fantasque, La (Respighi), 517, 586

Bow, Clara, 393

Bowen, York, 111–112

Bowie, David, 292

Bowman, James, 104, 560

Bowyer, Kevin, 113–114

Boyce, William, 112

Brabbins, Martyn, 783

Brahms, Johannes, 2, 33, 52, 62, 72, 109, 113–130, 145, 146, 184, 206–208, 218, 221, 224, 232, 251, 253, 263, 268, 269, 291, 306, 354, 356, 380, 385, 398, 417, 443, 479, 513, 515, 525, 572, 610, 628, 630, 632–635, 639, 646, 653, 676, 677, 681, 683, 689, 703, 724, 742, 744, 794, 805

Brain, Aubrey, 128

Brain, Dennis, 128, 352, 353, 476, 477, 695

Brain, Gary, 438

Braithwaite, Nicholas, 359, 684, 807

Bramante, Donato, 615

Branagh, Kenneth, 213

Brandenburg Concertos (Bach), 21, 30, 34, 62, 349, 707

Brandenburg Consort, 314, 792

Brannigan, Owen, 134, 137, 275

Braunfels, Walter, 131

Brazilian Impressions (Respighi), 587

Bream, Julian, 3–4, 144, 299, 788

Brecht, Bertolt, 275, 798

Brendel, Alfred, 23, 61, 477–480, 482, 486, 628, 653, 654

Brettl-lieder (Schoenberg), 627

Brian, Havergal, 132

Bride of Blue Frankenstein, The (Waxman), 102, 793

Bridge, Frank, 133, 250, 265, 788

Bridge on the River Kwai, The (Arnold), 14

Brigg Fair (Delius), 200

Brigg Fair (Grainger), 297

Bright Blue Music (Torke), 741

Brighton Hike (Joyce), 386

Brion, Keith, 364, 679

Britten, Benjamin, 9, 21, 22, 30, 82, 94, 133–144, 238, 239, 260, 275, 297, 308, 329, 343, 344, 492, 499, 500, 545, 663, 739, 746

Broadside Band, The, 275

Bronze Horse, The: Overture (Auber), 17

Brook Green Suite (Holst), 358–359

Brooke, Gwydion, 475

Broughton, Bruce, 613

Brouwer, Leo, 144

Brown, Iona, 277, 313,

Browning, John, 43–44

Bruch, Max, 145, 221, 291, 450, 621

Bruckner, Anton, 137, 146–147, 167, 237, 327, 341, 433, 609, 610, 625, 626, 683, 798

Brückner-Rüggeberg, Wilhelm, 798

Brunelle, Philip, 178, 677

Brunhoff, Jean de, 537

Bruson, Renato, 209–210, 618, 753, 755

Bryn-Julson, Phyllis, 305, 627, 635

Buck, Dudley, 148

Buckley, William F., Jr., 27

Budapest Festival Orchestra, 7

Budapest Strauss Orchestra, 687

Buddha, 471

Building of the House, The (Britten), 140

Bullets and Bayonets (Sousa), 679

Bülow, Hans von, 74

Bundeslied (Beethoven), 57

Bunting, Edward, 468

Bunyan, John, 747

Bureaucratic Sonatine (Satie), 622

Burgess, Sally, 256

Burleigh, Harry T., 148–149

Burleske (Strauss), 701

Burney, Charles, 97, 681

Burrowes, Norma, 141, 747

Busch, Adolf, 21, 62, 646, 656

Busoni, Ferruccio, 54, 149–150, 181

Büsser, Paul-Henri, 189

Butt, Yondani, 240, 291

Butterworth, George, 150–151, 250, 261, 748

Buxtehude, Dietrich, 29, 151, 314

Bychkov, Semyon, 729, 730

Byrd, William, 151, 152, 359, 375

C.P.E. Bach Chamber Orchestra, 19

Caballé, Montserrat, 106, 209, 284, 285, 299, 410, 483, 484, 550, 556, 607, 608, 702, 752, 753, 757, 763

Cabaret Songs (Schoenberg), 627

Cabot, Sebastian, 705

Cachemaille, Giles, 85, 191, 192

Cadman, Charles Wakefield, 152

Cage, John, 97, 153

Cagney, James, 682

Cairns, Christine, 540–541

Cakewalk (Gottschalk), 680

Caldara, Antonio, 154

Callas, Maria, 75–76, 165, 211, 212, 284, 379, 410, 533, 550, 552, 554, 601, 602, 752, 753, 760, 761, 763

Calm Sea and Prosperous Voyage (Beethoven), 53, 57

Calm Sea and Prosperous Voyage (Mendelssohn), 452

Cambridge Symphony (Parry), 525

Camden, Anthony, 803

Camerata Bern, 809

Camerata Budapest, 19–20

Camp Meeting (Symphony No. 3) (Ives), 374

Campion, Thomas, 746

Camus, Albert, 277

Canadian Brass, 170, 273

Candide (Bernstein), 92–93

Candide Overture (Bernstein), 93

Canino, Bruno, 621

Cantata for the 20th Anniversary of the October Revolution (Prokofiev), 541

Cantata on the Accession of Emperor Leopold II (Beethoven), 53

Cantata on the Death of Emperor Joseph II (Beethoven), 53

Cantelo, April, 84, 134, 332

Canteloube, Joseph, 154–155
Canterbury Pilgrims, The
  (Dyson), 235, 236
Cantéyodjaya (Messiaen), 459
Canticum Canticorum Salomonis
  (Penderecki), 526
Cantilena, 14, 206
Cantique de Jean Racine
  (Fauré), 254
Canzone dei ricord, Lai
  (Martucci), 443–444
Canzone for Flute and Piano
  (Barber), 40
Capella Istropolitana, 276, 328,
  337, 482, 489, 490, 501
Capital of the World
  (Antheil), 11
Capitole de Toulouse Orchestra,
  267, 295, 370
Caplet, André, 187–189
Caplet, Lucien, 189
Cappuccilli, Piero, 76, 158, 211,
  485, 533, 757, 758, 760
Capriccio (Holst), 359
Capriccio (Strauss), 695
Capriccio Espagnol (Rimsky-
  Korsakov), 591–592
Capriccio for Orchestra
  (Tansman), 724
Capriccio for Piano, Left Hand
  (Janáček), 376
Capriccio for Violin and
  Orchestra (Penderecki), 526
Capriccio in F minor
  (Dohnányi), 206
Capriccio Italien (Tchaikovsky),
  591, 727, 731
*Capriccio on the Departure of
  His Most Beloved Brother*
  (Bach), 27
Capriccio: Prelude (Strauss), 529
Caprice and Elegy (Delius), 202
Caprice bohémien
  (Rachmaninoff), 562–563
Caprice Péruvien (Berners), 92
Caprices (24) for Unaccompanied
  Violin (Paganini), 521
Capricieuse (Symphony No. 2)
  (Berwald), 96
Capricorn Concerto (Barber), 41
Capriol Suite (Warlock), 791
Captain Blood (Korngold), 395
Captain from Castile
  (Newman), 510
*Capture of Kars, The: Triumphal
  March* (Mussorgsky), 506
Caractacus (Elgar), 239
Caramoor Festival Chorus and
  Orchestra, 379
Cardinal Newman, 238
Cardoso, Manuel, 419
Carillons for Oboe and
  Orchestra (Williams), 803
Carlos III of Spain, 105

Carlos, Walter/Wendy, 715
Carlyle. Joan, 740
Carmen (Bizet), 98–99, 101, 192,
  209, 249, 269, 367, 401, 467,
  518, 659, 699
Carmen Ballet (Bizet/Shchedrin),
  659, 743
Carmen Fantasy (Sarasate),
  618, 621
*Carmen Fantasy for Violin and
  Orchestra* (Waxman), 793
Carmen: Suites (Bizet), 99
Carmina Burana (Orff), 300,
  519, 721
Carmina Quartet, 721
Carnaval (Schumann), 651
Carnival of the Animals (Saint-
  Saëns), 545, 616, 618
Carnival Overture (Dvořák), 87,
  194, 222, 799
Carpenter, John Alden, 148
Carr, Colin, 129, 195, 456, 646
Carr, Joseph Comyns, 718
Carreras, José, 95, 188, 553,
  757, 760
Carroll, Lewis, 344, 726
Carrosse du Saint-Sacrement
  (Berners), 92
Carter, Elliott, 155, 767
Caruso, Enrico, 100–101, 311,
  410, 551, 737, 752, 753
Carwithen, Doreen, 156
Casa del diavolo, La
  (Boccherini), 105
Casadesus, Gaby, 481
Casadesus, Jean-Claude, 192
Casadesus, Robert, 65, 160, 481
Casals, Pablo, 6, 27, 33, 129,
  220, 646
Casanova, Giovanni Jacopo, 687
Cassidy, Claudia, 168
Castelnuovo-Tedesco, Mario,
  157, 533, 766
Castor et Pollux (Rameau), 572
Cat and Mouse, The
  (Copland), 177
Catalani, Alfredo, 158, 169
Caucasian Sketches (Ippolitov-
  Ivanov), 370–371
Cavalieri, Katharina, 472
Cavalleria Rusticana (Mascagni),
  262, 410, 444, 445, 557
CBC Symphony, 714
Ce qu'a vu le vent d'Ouest
  (Debussy), 193
Čech, Svatopluk, 377
Cellini, Renato, 445, 762
Cenerentola, La (Rossini), 602
Central Park in the Dark (Ives),
  374–375
Ceremony of Carols
  (Britten), 135
Cerha, Friedrich, 82
Cermaková, Josephine, 220

Cerquetti, Anita, 763
Cervantes, Miquel de, 764
Cetra, La (Vivaldi), 768
Ch'io mi scordi di te? (Mozart),
  472
Chabrier, Emmanuel, 159–160,
  216, 598, 612
Chadwick, Charles Whitefield,
  160–161, 421, 445
Chailly, Riccardo, 113, 284, 285,
  349, 602, 603, 630, 631, 810
Chain II (Lutostawski), 424
Chairman Dances (Adams), 2
Chaliapin, Feodor, 75, 106, 289,
  304, 446, 505, 508, 729, 774
Chamber Concerto (Berg), 79
Chamber Music Northwest, 121,
  493, 625
Chamber Orchestra of Europe,
  24, 496, 640, 641, 645
Chamber Symphony
  (Shostakovich), 660
*Chamber Symphony for 23 Solo
  Instruments* (Schreker), 636
Chamber Symphony No. 1
  (Schoenberg), 628, 635–636
Chamfort, Sébastien Roch
  Nicolas, 292
Chaminade, Cécile, 161
Chance, Michael, 104
Chandos Anthems
  (Handel), 311
Chansons de Bilitis
  (Debussy), 195
Chansons des Roses, Les
  (Lauridsen), 404
Chant Noël, 300
Chanticleer Overture
  (Mason), 445
Chapman, Victor, 421
Charge of the Light Brigade, The
  (Steiner), 682
Charpentier, Gustave, 162
Charpentier, Marc-Antoine,
  163, 801
Chase, Gilbert, 159
Chasseur maudit, Le
  (Franck), 266
Chaucer, Geoffrey, 235, 790
Chausson, Ernest, 163–164, 252,
  370, 409, 618
Chávez, Carlos, 164, 589
Chekhov, Anton, 388, 491, 508
Chelsea Opera Group, 133
Cheng-Cochran, Gloria,
  459, 591
Chérubin (Massenet), 446
Cherubini, Luigi, 165
Chester (Billings), 97–98
Chesterton, C.K., 468
Chézy, Helemine von,
  641, 794
Chicago Symphony Chorus, 42,
  72, 84, 540, 758

Chicago Symphony Orchestra, 31, 42, 46–49, 68, 69, 72, 73, 84, 85, 100, 114, 115, 120, 128, 180, 189, 190, 220, 246, 269, 273, 289, 329, 330, 339, 363, 364, 374, 424, 433–437, 455, 462, 513, 540, 576, 587, 593, 604, 626, 632, 664, 665, 686, 689, 692, 696–698, 700, 704, 708, 729, 735, 758, 771, 774, 799

Chichester Psalms (Bernstein), 39, 93, 95

Child of Our Time, A (Tippett), 142, 739

Children of Lir (Harty), 328

Children's Corner Suite (Debussy), 186–187, 189

Children's Overture, A (Quilter), 561

Chilingirian String Quartet, 15, 545

Chloe Found Amyntas Lying All in Tears (Blow), 104

Chocolate Soldier, The (Straus), 688

Choëphores, Les (Milhaud), 462

Choir of Christ Church Cathedral, 332, 784

Choir of King's College, Cambridge, 135, 606

Choir of Winchester Cathedral, 152

Chopin, Frédéric, 7, 37, 111, 160, 166–169, 196, 258, 297, 308, 353, 417, 455, 491, 517, 520, 566, 621, 623, 633, 647, 651, 652, 689, 690, 720, 721, 809

Choral Fantasy (Beethoven), 54

Choral Hymns from the Rig Veda (Holst), 360

Choral Symphony (Beethoven), 72

Chorale Preludes (Bach/Schoenberg), 633

Chorale Preludes (Brahms), 113, 121

Chorley, H.F., 717

Christmas Cantata (Vaticini di Pace) (Caldara), 154

Christmas Concerto (Corelli), 179

Christmas Eve: Suite (Rimsky-Korsakov), 593

Christmas Oratorio (Bach), 23

Christmas Oratorio (Schütz), 657

Christmas Rose (Bridge), 133

Christoff, Boris, 508, 751, 752

Christopher Columbus (Walton), 784

Christophers, Harry, 311–312

Chromatic Fantasy and Fugue (Bach), 23, 36

Chung, Kyung-Wha, 48, 145, 164

Chung, Myung-Whun, 513

Church Windows (Respighi), 587

Chute de la maison Usher (Debussy), 187

Ciccolini, Aldo, 622

Cilea, Francesco, 169, 808

Cimarosa, Domenico, 438

Cincinnati Philharmonic Orchestra, 610

Cincinnati Pops Orchestra, 306, 803, 804

Cincinnati Symphony Orchestra, 74, 649

Cinderella (Prokofiev), 546

Circus Polka (Stravinsky), 706

Cislowski, Tamara-Anna, 581

Citizen Kane (Herrmann), 346–347

City of Birmingham Symphony, 46, 56, 120, 140, 171, 172, 213, 239, 331, 345, 431, 435, 437, 458, 624, 630, 635, 652, 663, 721, 785

City of Light (Symphony No. 22) (Hovhaness), 364

City of London Sinfonia, 9, 163, 235, 253, 260, 283, 287, 359, 606, 615, 769, 784, 786

Clair de lune (Debussy), 189, 196

Clair de lune (Fauré), 254

Clarey, Cynthia, 279, 307

Clark, Keith, 325

Clarke, Jeremiah, 170

Classical Symphony (Prokofiev), 547

Claudel, Paul, 363, 462

Clemenza di Tito, La (Mozart), 474, 489

Cleobury, Stephen, 606

Clerks' Group, The, 516

Cleva, Fausto, 158

Cleveland Orchestra, 44, 54, 55, 61, 68, 70, 114, 116, 126, 127, 176, 177, 226, 227, 233, 273, 340, 381, 393, 424, 433, 455–457, 475, 478, 480, 492, 503, 542, 546, 656, 697, 709, 789, 790

Cleveland Orchestra Ensemble, 492

Cleveland String Quartet, 120, 640

Cleveland Symphonic Winds, 362

Clevenger, Dale, 329, 471

Cliburn, Van, 55, 426, 728

Clinton, Mark, 722

Clock and the Dresden Figures (Ketèlbey), 389

"Clock" Symphony, The (Haydn), 339, 342

Close Encounters of the Third Kind (Williams), 804

Cloud Messenger, The (Holst), 360

Coastal Command (Vaughan Williams), 2

Coates, Albert, 775, 780

Coates, Eric, 171, 807

Cockaigne Overture (Elgar), 242

Cockney Suite (Ketèlbey), 390

Cocteau, Jean, 362, 463, 722

Cohen, Robert, 597

Cohn, Harry, 60

Coin, Christophe, 106, 229, 355, 432, 789

Colas Breugnon: Overture (Kabalevsky), 387

Cole, Maggie, 677–678

Cole, Nat "King", 135

Coleridge-Taylor, Samuel, 173

Colgrass, Michael, 406

Collé, Charles, 573

Collegium 1704, 809

Collegium Musicum 90, 405–406

Collines d'Anacapri, Les (Debussy), 193

Collins, Anthony, 786

Collura, Frank, 271–272

Colomer, Edmon, 277

Color Music (Torke), 741

Colorado Symphony, 609

Colour Symphony, A (Bliss), 101–102

Colton, Charles Caleb, 638

Columbia Symphony Orchestra, 70–71, 126, 127, 263, 496, 645, 714

Combat, The (Banfield), 12

Come Ye Sons of Art (Purcell), 558

Comeaux, Elizabeth, 178

Comedians, The (Kabalevsky), 387, 390

Comedy Overture, A (Harty), 328

Commingore, Dorothy, 347

Compère, Loyset, 214

Comte Ory, Le (Rossini), 603

Concentus Hungaricus, 479

Concentus Musicus of Vienna, 22

Concert champêtre (Poulenc), 535

Concertato for Orchestra, "Moby Dick" (Mennin), 456

Concertino for 12 Instruments (Stravinsky), 706

Concerto balletta for Cello and Orchestra (Arensky), 13

Concerto da Camera (Dyson), 235

Concerto da Chiesa (Dyson), 235

Concerto elegiaco (Brouwer), 144

Concerto for Orchestra (Bartto for Orchestrara (Arensky),*Concerto for Orchestra* (Carter), 155–156
Concerto for Orchestra (Lutostawski), 424
Concerto for Orchestra (Tansman), 724
Concerto for Seven Wind Instruments (Martin), 439
Concerto Grosso 1985 (Zwillich), 811
Concerto in F (Gershwin), 278
Concerto Italiano, 271, 403
Concerto Leggero (Dyson), 235
Concerto Populaire (Reizenstein), 353
Concerto Symphonique No. 4: Scherzo (Litolff), 370, 800
Concierto andaluz (Rodrigo), 595–596
Concierto como un divertimento (Rodrigo), 597
Concierto de Aranjuez (Rodrigo), 533, 595–596, 766
Concierto del sur (Ponce), 532–533
Concierto madrigal (Rodrigo), 595–596
Conquest of the Air (Bliss), 2
Conrad, Joseph, 610
Consecration of the House Overture (Beethoven), 61
Consort of Musicke, 280, 467, 687
Constant Nymph (Korngold), 395
Conte fantastique (Caplet), 188
Contemporary Chamber Ensemble, 633
Contextures (Kraft), 397
Contiguglia, Richard and John, 296
Continental Harmonist Ballet (Billings/Smith), 98
Contrasts (Bartók), 48
Contrasts for Orchestra (Fetler), 622
Cook, Brian Rayner, 151
Cooke, Deryck, 437
Coombs, Stephen, 309–310
Cooper, Dr. Barry, 56
Cooper, Kenneth, 32
Copenhagen Steam Railway Galop (Lumbye), 423
Copland, Aaron, 11, 38, 39, 42, 111, 155, 174–178, 259, 262, 263, 294, 325, 469, 609, 710
Coppélia (Delibes), 169, 198
Coppola, Piero, 542
Coq d'or, Le (Rimsky-Korsakov), 593–594
Corbelli, Alessandro, 602, 605
Corboz, Michel, 450
Corelli, Archangelo, 179–180

Corena, Fernando, 210
Corigliano, John, 180, 261, 802
Coriolan (Beethoven), 61, 243
Corneille, Pierre, 216
Cornelius, Peter, 180, 777
Cornemuse, La (Loeffler), 421
Coronation Anthems (Handel), 313, 315
Coronation Concerto (Mozart), 482
Coronation Ode (Elgar), 242
Corréas, Jérôme, 572
Corroborree (Antill), 767
Corsaire, Le (Adam), 1
Cortot, Alfred, 417, 646
Corydon Singers, 53, 147, 260
Così fan tutte (Mozart), 482–484, 489, 490, 497
Cossotto, Fiorenza, 487, 533, 552, 762
Costello, Elvis, 292
Cotrubas, Ileana, 483, 488, 555
Coull String Quartet, 453, 788
Country Gardens (Grainger), 296
Country Pieces (Quilter), 561
Couperin, François, 181, 694
Courtly Dances from *Gloriana* (Britten), 136
Covey-Crump, Rogers, 560
Cowell, Henry, 153, 182, 325, 326, 590
Craft, Robert, 120, 714
Crawford, Joan, 793
Creation, The (Haydn), 331, 333–334
Création du Monde, La (Milhaud), 463, 535
Creatures of Prometheus, The (Beethoven), 56, 57, 61
Creatures of Prometheus: Overture (Beethoven), 61
Creger, Laird, 347
Crespin, Régine, 87, 446, 778
Creston, Paul, 182, 354, 355, 456, 743, 782
Crisantemi (Puccini), 761
Cromwell, James, 254
Crossley, Paul, 252, 538, 580, 722
Crown Imperial (Walton), 359, 375
Crown of India: Suite (Elgar), 242
Crusell, Bernhard Henrik, 184
Cuban Landscape with Rain (Brouwer), 144
Cui, César, 36
Culshaw, John, 135, 137, 778
cummings, e.e., 205, 281
Cunning Little Vixen, The (Janáček), 376–377, 515
Cunning Little Vixen: Suite (Janáček), 515
Cupid and Psyche (Berners), 92

Curlew, The (Warlock) 792
Curtin, Phyllis, 72, 599
Curzon, Frederic, 172, 492
Curzon, Sir Clifford, 229, 267, 270, 417, 418, 639, 640
Cypresses (Dvořák), 229
Cyrana (Delius), 202
Czech Philharmonic Orchestra, 222, 225
Czech Suite (Dvořák), 117, 227
Czechoslovak Radio Symphony, 231
Czerny, Carl, 186
Cziffra, György, 415

d'Annunzio, Gabriele, 532
d'Armetières, Péronne, 427
d'Indy, Vincent, 270, 358, 369–370, 406, 409, 428, 597, 611
D'Oyly Carte Opera Company, 282–283
D'un Matin de printemps (Tailleferre), 722
D'un Soir triste (Tailleferre), 722
Da Motta, José Vianna, 417
Da Ponte, Lorenzo, 484
Dafne (Peri), 467
Dahl, Dr, Nikolai, 567
Dahl, Ingolf, 185
Damnation of Faust, The (Berlioz), 84, 88
Damoiselle élue, La, (Debussy), 188
Dance Intermezzo (Sibelius), 671
Dance of the Blessèd Spirits (Gluck), 206, 290
Dance of the Sylphs (Berlioz), 84
Dance of the Tumblers (Rimsky-Korsakov), 733
Dance Overture (Mathias), 447
Dance Rhapsody No. 2 (Delius), 200
Dance Rhythms (Riegger), 590
Dance Suite (Bartók), 48
Dances of Galánta (Kodály), 391
Dances of Marosszék (Kodály), 391
Danish National Radio Chamber Choir, 531
Danish National Radio Symphony, 423, 511
Dans le goût théâtral (Couperin), 181
Danse d'Abisag (Schmitt), 626–627
Danse macabre (Saint-Saëns), 267, 618, 669
Danses sacrée et profane (Debussy), 189, 354–355
Dante, 83, 413, 414, 783, 808
Dante Sonata (Liszt), 413–414
Dante Symphony (Liszt), 414

Danubius String Quartet, 766
Danza lenta (Granados), 299
Danzas espagñolas
  (Granados), 299
Danzas fantásticas
  (Turina), 742
Danzi, Franz, 186
Danzón Cubano (Copland), 175
Daphne (Strauss), 696
Daphnis et Chloé (Ravel),
  576–578
Dargomizhsky, Alexander, 289
Dart, Thurston, 34, 313
Dartington Ensemble, 441
Das Lied von der Erde (Mahler),
  8, 339, 428, 429, 434, 810
Das Veilchen (Mozart), 498
Daudet, Alphonse, 98
Daughter of the Regiment, The
  (Donizetti), 210
Dauphine, La (Rameau), 573
Davidde penitente
  (Mozart), 488
Davidovich, Bella, 580
Davidsbündlertänze
  (Schumann), 651
Davies, Meredith, 202, 747
Davin, Patrick, 358
Davis, Bette, 682
Davis, Miles, 753
Davis, Sir Colin, 61, 72, 84,
  88–91, 300, 318, 446, 484,
  490, 582, 652, 673, 708, 739,
  740, 780
Davrath, Natania, 155
Dawn and Siegfried's Rhine
  Journey (Wagner), 775
Dawson, Lynne, 312
Dawson, Peter, 172
Day the Earth Stood Still, The
  (Herrmann), 102, 346
De Greef, Arthur, 417
DeLancie, John, 266, 475,
  695–696
De Larrocha, Alicia, 2–3, 248,
  298, 299, 576, 577, 580
De los Angeles, Victoria, 155,
  249, 250, 298, 446, 550,
  551, 555
De Luca, Giuseppe, 100–101
De Lucia, Fernando, 76
De Nautra Sonoris I and II
  (Penderecki), 526
De Palma, Brian, 347
De Peyer, Gervase, 539
De Sabata, Victor, 554, 697
De Waart, Edo, 2, 384, 385,
  460, 798
Death and the Maiden Quartet
  (Schubert), 644
Death and Transfiguration
  (Strauss), 697–698, 701, 804
Death in Venice (Britten), 134

Debussy, 81, 109, 133, 159, 160,
  163, 186–196, 246, 249, 297,
  300, 305, 354, 355, 369, 385,
  391, 406, 439, 451, 459, 509,
  518, 534, 545, 576, 579, 580,
  593, 597, 611, 612, 620, 626,
  636, 712, 743, 744
Decameron Negro
  (Brouwer), 144
Decker, Franz-Paul, 582
Declaration (Gould), 294
Decoration Day (Ives), 374–375
DeCou, Emil, 305
DeGaetani, Jan, 184, 264, 372,
  567, 568, 633, 634
Degas, Edgar, 194
Del Mar, Norman, 464, 581,
  614, 615
Del Monaco, Mario, 158, 285,
  551, 553, 755, 756
Del Prato, 486
DeLalande, Michel-Richard, 197
Delibes, Léo, 169, 197
Delius, Frederick, 52, 112, 133,
  167, 200, 239, 269, 296, 791
Deller, Alfred, 137, 213,
  558, 746
Deller Consort, 558, 745
Dello Joio, Norman, 203–204, 306
Delünsch, Mireille, 192
Demidenko, Nikolai, 448–449
Denza, Luigi, 694
DePreist, James, 78, 204, 261,
  262, 352, 369, 370, 457, 620,
  666, 667, 781–782
Der Bürger als Edelmann, Der
  (Strauss), 701
Dermota, Anton, 626, 689, 703
Dernesch, Helga, 779
Déserts (Varèse), 743
Dessau, Paul, 345
Destinn, Emmy, 304, 551
Destruction of Sennacherib, The
  (Mussorgsky), 506
Detroit Symphony Orchestra, 17,
  43, 52, 159, 160, 183, 245,
  256, 257, 357, 442, 524, 619,
  626, 685, 691, 703, 718, 732
Devereux, Robert, Earl of Essex,
  136, 395
Devil and Daniel Webster, The
  (Herrmann), 346–347
Devotion (Korngold), 395
Di Stefano, Giuseppe, 410,
  552–554, 760, 761
Diabelli, Anton, 74
Diabelli Variations
  (Beethoven), 74
Diaghilev, Sergei, 91, 249, 411,
  535, 709, 722
Dialogues des Carmélites
  (Poulenc), 536
Diamond, David, 204, 258, 411

Dichter, Mischa, 2
Dichterliebe (Schumann), 653
Dickens, Charles, 85, 448, 755
Dicterow, Glenn, 353–354
Dido and Aeneas (Purcell), 90,
  104, 138, 290, 558
Die tote Stadt (Korngold),
  394, 397
Dies natalis (Finzi), 260
Dies Natalis (Hanson), 323
Dietrich, Marlene, 393
Dinklin, Alvin, 354–355
Disney, Walt, 714, 726
Distratto, Il (Symphony No. 60)
  (Haydn), 336–337
Dittersdorf, Carl Ditters von,
  205, 365
Dittrich, Michael, 690
Diversions (Bennett), 78
Diversions for Orchestra
  (Fine), 258
Diversions for Piano (left hand)
  and Orchestra (Britten), 140
Divertimento (after keyboard
  pieces by Couperin) (Strauss),
  694, 701
Divertimento (Bartók), 48
Divertimento for Band
  (Persichetti), 528
Divertimento for Harmonica and
  String Quartet (Jacob), 375
Divertimento for String
  Orchestra (Mathias), 447
Divertimento from *The Fairy's*
  Kiss (Stravinsky), 364
Divertissement (Ibert), 100,
  369, 535
Divertissement for Piano and
  Wind Quintet (Roussel), 611
Divine Poem, The
  (Scriabin), 657
Dix pièces pittoresques
  (Chabrier), 159
Dixit Dominus (Handel), 320
Dixon, Peter, 251
Dmitriev, Alexander, 616
Doctor Faust (Smetana), 676
Dohnányi, Christoph von, 81,
  206, 233
Dohnányi, Ernst von, 206,
  356, 724
Dolly Suite (Fauré), 251
Domingo, Placido, 101, 106,
  162, 284, 299, 410, 445, 518,
  551–555, 557, 618, 699, 751,
  752–757, 759, 762, 772, 796
Domino noir, Le (Auber), 17
Domus, 119–120, 252–253
Don Carlo (Verdi), 754
Don Giovanni (Mozart), 318,
  472, 473, 478, 481, 483, 485,
  487, 489, 490, 500, 688,
  707, 713

Don Juan (Strauss), 190, 692, 694, 697, 701
Don Pasquale (Donizetti), 209–210
Don Quichotte (Massenet), 446
Don Quixote (Strauss), 694, 697, 701
Dona nobis pacem (Vaughan Williams), 744–745
Donath, Helen, 290, 510, 555, 638, 693
Donizetti, Gaetano, 209–211, 601, 761
Donne, John, 135
Donohoe, Peter, 243, 728
Dorati, Antal, 74, 103, 104, 226, 227, 277, 333, 335, 342, 391, 416, 528, 585, 622, 623, 649, 691, 708, 721, 726, 727, 730, 731
Dostoyevsky, Feodor, 291, 508
Double Indemnity (Rble IndemniDouglas, Barry, 728
Dover Beach (Barber), 40, 43
Dowland, John, 212–213
Downes, Sir Edward, 244, 462, 543, 550, 585, 588
Doyle, Patrick, 213
Drahos, Béla, 60–61, 338
Dramatic Overture (Korngold), 396
Draper, John, 144
Dream of Gerontius (Elgar), 142, 237, 238, 242, 244, 747
Dream of Jacob, The (Penderecki), 526
Dream of the Marionette, The (Sainton), 309
Dream of the Rood (Ferguson), 256
Dream Pictures Fantasia (Lumbye), 423
Dreaming (Joyce), 386
Dresden Opera, 777
Dresden Staatskapelle, 486–487, 694, 697, 701, 794
Dressen, Dan, 178, 648
Drier, Per, 302–303, 713, 715
Drottningholmsmusiquen (Roman), 598
Druce, Duncan, 96
Druian, Rafael, 475
Drum Roll Symphony (Haydn), 338, 341
Drumming (Reich), 583
Dryad, The (Sibelius), 671
Dryden, John, 104, 319, 320, 559
Du fond de l'abîme (Boulanger), 111
Du Pré, Jacqueline, 198, 220, 237, 652
DuBois, W. E. B., 173

Dubosc, Catherine, 536
Due composizioni corali (Pizzetti), 531
Duenna, The (Gerhard), 277–278
Duett-Concertino (Strauss), 701
Dufay, Guillaume, 214, 516
Dukas, Paul, 215–217, 246, 248, 267, 422, 459, 533, 597
Dumbarton Oaks Concerto (Stravinsky), 706, 707
Dumky Trio (Dvořák), 223, 234
Dun, Tan, 214
Dunbar, Paul Lawrence, 149, 173
Dunbar, William, 236
Duncan, Ronald, 139
Duparc, Henri, 216, 267
Durey, Louis, 722
Duruflé, Maurice, 217, 524, 537
Dussek, Jan Ladislav, 218, 223, 365, 463
Dutilleux, Henri, 219
Dutoit, Charles, 88, 89, 99, 163, 164, 186, 187, 189–192, 249, 363, 562, 576, 578, 612, 617–619, 718, 721, 727
Dvořák, Antonín, 52, 117, 127, 145, 148, 152, 160, 220–234, 237, 256, 257, 263, 289, 345, 356, 376, 380, 383, 443, 496, 515, 532, 634, 652, 674, 676, 686, 715, 716, 732, 736, 794, 799
Dvořák, Ottokar, 376
Dvořsky, Peter, 674
Dylan, Bob, 33

E.T. (Williams), 804
Eaglen, Jane, 648–649, 775
Eagles (Rorem), 599
Early Music Consort of London, 214
Easdale, Brian, 2
East of Eden (Holdridge), 354
Eastman, Julius, 447
Eastman Wind Ensemble, 296, 319, 359, 362, 368, 375, 679
Ecole d'Orphée, L', 320–321
Ecuatorial (Varèse), 743
Eder, Helmut, 412
Edgar (Puccini), 557
Edward Tarr Brass Ensemble, 273
Edward VII, 244
Egdon Heath (Holst), 358–359
Egmont: Incidental Music (Beethoven), 57
Egmont: Overture (Beethoven), 63
Ehrling, Sixten, 103–104, 600
Eichendorff, Joseph von, 653
Eight Poems by Li-Po (Lambert), 402

Eight Russian Folksongs (Liadov), 411
Eight Songs for a Mad King (Maxwell Davies), 447–448
1812 Overture (Tchaikovsky), 74, 662, 726–727
Ein feste Burg ist unser Gott (Bach), 454, 686
Eine kleine Nachtmusik (Mozart), 496
Eine kleine Posaunenmusik (Schuller), 782
Einstein, Alfred, 62, 486, 494
Eisenhower, Dwight D., 10
Eisenstein, Sergei, 540–541
El Greco, 764
El Salón Mexico (Copland), 175–176, 263
Elegiac Trio (Bax), 52
Elegy for Brahms (Parry), 525
Elegy for Strings (Tchaikovsky), 731
Elegy in Memory of My Friend Serge Koussevitzky (Hanson), 322
Elektra (Strauss), 379, 698, 699
Elgar, Lady Alice, 236
Elgar, Sir Edward, 55, 112, 140, 142, 203, 235–246, 251, 260, 261, 360, 372, 462, 525, 652, 681, 683, 684, 746, 747, 788, 804
Elias, Rosalind, 44, 755
Elegischer Gesang (Beethoven), 57
Elijah (Mendelssohn), 450, 455
Eliot, T. S., 740
Elisabeth Brasseur Chorale, 111
Elisir d'Amore, L' (Donizetti), 210
Elizabeth II, 136, 256
Elizabethan Dances (Alwyn), 9
Ellington, Edward Kennedy "Duke", 245, 296, 685
Ellington, Mercer, 245
Elogio de la danza (Brouwer), 144
Éluard, Paul, 536
Elvira Madigan (Mozart), 479, 483
Embryons desséchés (Satie), 622
Emerson, Ralph Waldo, 321
Emerson String Quartet, 39, 43, 50, 109, 373, 460
Emperor Quartet (Haydn), 333
Empress' Awakening Scene (Strauss), 693
En Saga (Sibelius), 670
Enchanted Lake, The (Liadov), 411
Endellion String Quartet, 40, 53, 171
Enescu, Georges, 245–246, 808

Enfance du Christ, L' (Berlioz), 85

Enfant et les sortilèges, L' (Berlioz), 579

Enfant prodigue, L' (Debussy), 188

Engels, Friedrich, 653

English Baroque Soloists, 23, 27, 31, 60, 181, 317, 318, 334, 466–468, 471, 486, 559

English Chamber Orchestra, 1, 12, 17, 21, 22, 24, 30, 56, 64, 110, 134, 139, 154, 184, 209, 210, 320, 329, 330, 358, 443, 477, 480, 493, 494, 499, 500, 520, 558, 595, 601, 605, 732, 766, 803

English Concert, 21–22, 112, 179, 312, 319, 331, 332, 770

English Folksong Suite (Vaughan Williams), 375, 748

English Mass, An (Howells), 365

English Northern Philharmonia, 37, 199, 401, 789

English Pastoral Impressions (Farrar), 251

English Serenata, 658

English String Orchestra, 133, 150, 454

English Suites (Bach), 25

Enigma Variations (Elgar), 236, 239–241, 245, 525

Enormous Room, The (Diamond), 205

Ensemble InterContemporain, 79, 635, 743

Ensemble M, 305

Ensemble Musique Oblique, 409

Entretien des Muses, L' (Rameau), 574

Entry of the Gladiators, The (Fucik), 272

Eötvös, Peter, 412

Epic March (Ireland), 371

Epic of Gilgamesh (Martinů), 440

Érald, Sébastien, 189

Erben, Karel Jaromir, 225, 230

Eremitaggio di Liwerpool, L' (Donizetti), 211

Ernani (Verdi), 754–755

Eroica Symphony (Beethoven), 57, 70, 630

Erwartung (Schoenberg), 82, 630, 634, 635

Es sang vor langen Jahren (Pärt), 526

Escales (Ibert), 369

Eskin, Virginia, 53

España, (Chabrier), 159, 216, 596

Essays for Orchestra (Barber), 39

Estampes (Debussy), 193, 196, 297

Estrella di Soria: Overture (Berwald), 96

Etang, L' (Loeffler), 421

Études de Rhythme (Messiaen), 459

Études-Tableaux (Rachmaninoff), 566, 568–569

Études tanguistiques (Piazzolla), 530

Eugen Onegin (Prokofiev), 543

Eugene Onegin (Tchaikovsky), 417, 729

Euryanthe (Weber), 641, 794–796

Evans, Rebecca, 747

Evans, Sir Geraint, 755

Ewell, Tom, 110

Ewing, Maria, 485, 702

Excelsior! Overture (Stenhammar), 683

Excursions (Barber), 40, 42

Excursions of Mr. Brouček (Janáček), 377–378

Exile Symphony (Hovhaness), 364

Exsultate, jubilate (Mozart), 485

Eysler, Edmund, 408

Façade (Walton), 92, 784, 786

Faerber, Jörg, 465, 560

Fahrenheit 451 (Herrmann), 346

Failoni Orchestra, 205, 206, 769

Fairbanks, Douglas, 393

Fairy Queen, The (Purcell), 559

Fairy's Kiss, The (Stravinsky), 364, 707, 710

Faithful Shepherd, The (Handel/Beecham), 315

Faletta, JoAnn, 469, 722

Fall, Leo, 408

Fall River Legend (Gould), 294

Falla, Manuel de, 246, 248–250, 270, 298, 299, 465, 742

Falstaff (Elgar), 239–240

Falstaff (Verdi), 137, 210, 755, 773

Fanciulla del West, La (Puccini), 551

Fancy Free (Bernstein), 94, 680

Fanfare for the Common Man (Copland), 175–178

Fantaisie espagnol (Berners), 91

Fantasia Concertante on a Theme of Corelli (Tippett), 740

Fantasia on a Theme by Thomas Tallis (Vaughan Williams), 723, 744

Fantasia on Christmas Carols (Vaughan Williams), 344

Fantasia on Greensleeves (Vaughan Williams), 748

Fantasia on Welsh Nursery Songs (Williams), 803

Fantasia para un gentilhombre (Rodrigo), 595–596

Fantasia slava (Respighi), 585

Fantasiestücke (Schumann), 651, 654–655

Fantastic Dance (Delius), 202

Fantasy Octet on Themes of Grainger (Leighton), 297

Fantasy on Japanese Woodprints (Hovhaness), 364

Fantasy-Variations on a Theme of Youth (Hanson), 322

Farewell Symphony (Haydn), 337–338

Farinelli (Carlo Broschi), 316, 687

Faris, Alexander, 718

Farkas, Katalin, 527

Farnon, Robert, 172

Farrar, Ernest, 250–251

Farrar, Geraldine, 304

Farrell, Eileen, 774

Fassbaender, Brigitte, 422, 606, 630, 638, 643, 773, 774, 779

Fauré, Gabriel, 217, 251–255, 515, 524, 580, 597, 598, 626

Faust (Gounod), 295, 618, 737

Faust Symphony, A (Liszt), 414–415

Fedora (Giordano), 285, 762

Fedoseyev, Vladimir, 505

Feen, Die (Wagner), 777

Feldman, Morton, 255, 515

Fellini, Federico, 608

Feltsman, Vladimir, 118

Femme 100 têtes, La (Antheil), 11

Fenby, Eric, 200–202

Fennell, Frederick, 296–297, 318–319, 359, 362, 375, 679

Fennimore and Gerda (Delius), 200

Ferdinand I, 523

Ferencsik, János, 393

Ferguson, Howard, 78, 256, 438

Ferrier, Kathleen, 113, 123, 124, 139, 311, 429

Festin de l'araignée, Le (Roussel), 610–611

Festival March (Alwyn), 9

Festive Overture (Shostakovich), 659–660, 676

Festive Symphony (Smetana), 674, 676

Fetler, Paul, 622

Feuermann, Emanuel, 33, 67, 208, 220, 352, 497, 646

Feux d'artifice (Debussy), 193

Février, Jacques, 534

Fibich, Zdeněk, 256–257

Fiddle Fever, 264–265

Fidelio (Beethoven), 54, 57–58, 688, 757, 772

Fiedler, Arthur, 10–11, 108, 294, 575, 586, 659, 680, 689, 690

Field, Helen, 173

Field, John, 40, 258, 328
Fields, W. C., 210
Fiery Angel, The (Prokofiev), 547
Figure humaine (Poulenc), 536
Film Themes Suite
(Holdridge), 354
Fine, Irving, 40, 258
Fink, Bernarda, 317, 466, 574
Finlandia (Sibelius), 670,
672, 673
Finnie, Linda, 164, 245, 252,
450, 589, 784
Finzi, Gerald, 250, 259–261,
360, 465, 748
Finzi Singers, 241–242, 360, 465
Firebird, The (Stravinsky), 411,
708, 709, 712
Fires of London, 447
Firkušný, Rudolf, 221, 223, 227,
229, 270, 376, 380, 441, 442
Fischer, Adam, 45
Fischer-Dieskau, Dietrich, 58–59,
116, 123, 124, 135, 142, 188,
350, 422, 428, 429, 638,
641–643, 647, 648, 653, 693,
695, 703, 755, 772, 776, 778,
779, 805
Fischer, Edwin, 35, 477,
637, 642
Fisher, Sylvia, 134
Fitzgerald, Edward, 38
Fitzwilliam Quartet, 662
*Five Bagatelles for Clarinet and
Strings* (Finzi), 259–260
Five Finger Exercise
(Moross), 469
Five Folk Songs (Panufnik), 523
Five Mystical Songs (Vaughan
Williams), 744–745
Five Novelettes (Glazunov),
354–355
*Five Partsongs from the Greek
Anthology* (Elgar), 242
Five Pieces for Orchestra
(Schoenberg), 630
Five Piezas infantiles
(Rodrigo), 597
Five Preludes (Villa-Lobos), 384
Five Tango Sensations
(Piazzolla), 530
Five Tudor Portraits (Vaughan
Williams), 745
*Five Variants of "Dives and
Lazarus"* (Vaughan
Williams), 745
Flagello, Ezio, 754
Flagello, Nicolas, 261
Flagstad, Kirsten, 304, 558, 699,
778–780
Flanders, Michael, 544–545
Flaubert, Gustave, 463–464
Fledermaus, Die (Strauss), 407,
511, 553, 688, 689, 703
Fleisher, Leon, 54–55, 481

Fletcher, John, 141
Flood, The (Stravinsky),
705, 710
Flor, Claus Peter, 452, 454
Florez och Blanzeflor
(Stenhammar), 683
Florida Suite (Delius),
199–200, 203
Flotow, Friedrich, 510
Flotte Bursche (Suppé), 719
Flower Clock, The
(Françaix), 266
Floyd, Carlisle, 262
Flying Dutchman, The (Wagner),
147, 351, 771, 779
Focile, Nuccia, 729–730
Fogel, Henry, 100
Folk Song Arrangements
(Britten), 135
Folk Song Arrangements
(Vaughan Williams), 746
Folk Songs Berio), 83
Folksong Symphony
(Harris), 325
Fonogrammi (Penderecki), 526
Fonteyn, Margo, 788
Foote, Arthur, 263, 325,
421, 445
For Children
(Bartildrenr,Forman,
Milos, 471
Forever Amber (Raksin), 575
Forgotten Rite, The (Ireland),
371–372
Forrester, Maureen, 200, 316
Forsberg, Bengt, 304
Forster, E.M., 386
Forza del Destino, La (Verdi), 755
Foss, Lukas, 93, 263–264,
709, 710
Fosse, Bob, 725
Foster, Lawrence, 208, 246, 801
Foster, Stephen, 264–265,
425, 634
Foulds, John, 265–266
Fountainhead, The (Steiner), 682
Fountains of Rome (Respighi),
587–588
Four Characteristic Waltzes
(Coleridge-Taylor), 173
Four Cornish Dances
(Arnold), 14
Four English Dances
(Arnold), 14
Four Irish Dances (Arnold), 14
Four Last Songs (Strauss), 693,
698, 703
Four Legends from the Kalevalá
(Sibelius), 671
Four Micropiezas (Brouwer), 144
4'33" (Cage), 153
Four Piano Blues (Copland), 177
Four Romantic Pieces
(Dvořák), 225

Four Sacred Pieces (Verdi), 759
Four Saints in Three Acts
(Thomson), 739
Four Scottish Dances
(Arnold), 14
Four Sea Interludes from *Peter
Grimes* (Britten), 133
*Four Seasons of Buenos Aires,
The* (Piazzolla), 530
Four Seasons, The (Vivaldi), 770
Four Serious Songs (Brahms),
113, 121, 123, 124
Four Short Pieces
(Ferguson), 256
Four Temperaments
(Hindemith), 352
Four Temperaments
(Nielsen), 513
Fournet, Anne, 712
Fournier, Pierre, 129, 220, 646
Fourth of July (Ives), 374
Fra Diavolo: Overture
(Auber), 17
Françaix, Jean, 266, 412, 622
Francesca da Rimini
(Tchaikovsky), 730–731
Francesca da Rimini
(Zandonai), 808
Francescatti, Zino, 65
Francis of Assisi, Saint, 49, 352
Franck, César, 268, 336, 356,
358, 370, 409, 584
Franco, Generalissimo Francisco,
33, 45
Frankel, Benjamin, 270–271
Frankie and Johnny
(Moross), 469
Franklin, Benjamin, 421, 445
Frantz, Ferdinand, 773
Franz Joseph I, Emperor, 674
Frau ohne Schatten, Die
(Strauss), 693, 699, 703
Frauenliebe und –leben
(Schumann), 653
Frederick the Great, 19, 29,
560, 598
Freeman, Paul, 425–426
Freiburg Baroque Orchestra, 420
Freischütz, Der (Weber), 510,
795, 796
French National Orchestra,
363, 369
French National Radio
Orchestra, 98–99, 579, 619
French Suites (Bach), 25
Freni, Mirella, 445, 608,
755, 760
Frescobaldi, Giorlamo, 29, 271
Frescos of Piero della Francesca
(Martinů), 440–441
Fretwork, 559
Freud, Siegmund, 234
Frick, Gottlob, 58, 471, 472,
485, 511, 773, 776, 778

Fried, Oskar, 692
Friedheim, Arthur, 417
Friedhofer, Hugo, 271–272, 469
Friedman, Ignaz, 65–66
Friend, Lionel, 709
Friskin, James, 171
Frith, Benjamin, 452–453
Froissart (Elgar), 240
From a New Zealand Diary
  (Sallinen), 620
From My Life Quartet
  (Smetana), 382, 675
From the Bavarian Highlands
  (Elgar), 236
*From the Land of the Sky-Blue
  Water* (Cadman), 152
From the Monkey Mountains
  (String Quartet No. 2)
  (Haas), 308
Frost, Robert, 568
Frou-Frou (Joyce), 386
Frühbeck de Burgos, Rafael,
  248–250
Fucík, Julius, 272
Fugal Concerto, A (Holst), 359
Für Elise (Beethoven), 35, 61
Furtwängler, Wilhelm, 2, 55, 56,
  68, 70, 146, 147, 167, 339,
  340, 350–352, 449, 450, 452,
  497, 501, 646, 699, 776, 779,
  780, 796, 805

Gabriel, Martin, 475
Gade, Niels, 274
Gaelic Symphony (Beach), 52
Gâité Parisienne
  (Offenbach/Rosenthal),
  517, 586
Gall, Jeffrey, 317
Galli-Curci, Amelita, 304, 803
Gallois, Patrick, 514, 530, 539, 769
Galusin, Vladimir, 506, 592
Galway, James, 32, 411, 458,
  476, 560, 597
Gamba, Pierino, 32, 415
Games: Collage No. 1 for Brass
  (Kraft), 398
Garben, Cord, 421
Garbo, Greta, 393
Garcia, Gerald, 384
García Lorca, 184, 590, 668
Garcin-Marrou, Michel, 471
Gardelli, Lamberto, 285, 607,
  608, 756–758
Garden, Mary, 162, 192
Garden of Fand, The (Bax), 51
Gardiner, Balfour, 561
Gardiner, Jake, 307
Gardiner, Sir John Eliot, 22, 23,
  28, 31, 59, 60, 68, 85, 87, 117,
  143, 297, 318, 319, 320, 334,
  361, 407, 466–468, 472, 486,
  495, 536, 559, 561

Garfield, John, 793
Garrett, Leslie, 292
Gaspard de la nuit (Ravel), 580
Gattopardo, Il (Rota), 608
Gaubert, Philippe, 523
Gaudier Ensemble, 680
Gavazzeni, Gianandrea, 808
Gavrilov, Andrei, 37, 321
Gay, John, 275, 782
Gayane (Khachaturian), 390
Gedda, Nicolai, 17, 44, 92, 180,
  407, 483, 606–608, 661, 695,
  711, 759, 794, 795
Gee, Christopher Lyndon,
  584–585, 733
Gelber, T.P., 473
Geminiani, Francesco, 276–277
Gemma di Vergy (Donizetti), 209
Génetay, Claude, 598
George I, 315
George II, 315
George III, 315, 447
George V, 352
George VI, 371
Georgiadis, John, 691
Gergalov, Alexander, 549, 592
Gergiev, Valery, 289, 506, 507,
  549, 592
Gerhard, Roberto, 277
Gerhardt, Charles, 396, 613,
  682, 793
German, Edward, 172
German Requiem, A
  (Brahms), 113
Gershwin, George, 44, 278, 279
Gesang der Parzen (Brahms), 113
Gesualdo, Don Carlo, 280,
  281, 809
Gettysburg Symphony (No. 6)
  (Harris), 325
Gezeichneten, Die
  (Schreker), 636
Ghiaurov, Nikolai, 76, 107, 446,
  556, 757, 759, 760
Ghost Trio (Beethoven), 73–74
Gianni Schicchi (Puccini),
  555, 806
Giazotto, Remo, 5
Gibbons, Orlando, 281
Gibson, Mel, 783
Gibson, Sir Alexander, 56, 87,
  88, 242, 783
Gide, André, 707, 712
Gielen, Michael, 628–629, 636
Gielgud, Sir John, 748, 787
Gieseking, Walter, 187, 192, 193,
  196, 302, 472, 490, 498,
  580, 654
Giesen, Hubert, 58
Gigli, Beniamino, 284, 553
Gilbert and Sullivan, 92, 112,
  275, 282, 283, 367, 407, 525,
  717, 782

Gilbert, Kenneth, 35, 181
Gilels, Emil, 63, 114, 301, 482
Gilman, Lawrence, 175
Gimpel the Fool: Divertimento
  (Schiff), 625
Ginastera, Alberto, 283–284
Gingold, Joseph, 394
Gioconda, La (Ponchielli),
  533, 794
Giordano, Umberto, 169,
  284, 285
Giorno di regno (Verdi), 757
Gipsy Suite (Coleridge-Taylor),
  172–173
Girl with the Flaxen Hair
  (Debussy), 193
Giselle (Adam), 1, 557
Giuditta (Léhar), 407–408
Giulini, Carlo Maria, 55–56, 60,
  71, 115, 166, 210, 253, 254,
  268, 485, 487, 604, 735, 754,
  759, 761
Giulio Cesare in Egitto
  (Handel), 316
Giuranna, Bruno, 492
Giustino (Handel), 317
Galdreslåtten (Sæverud), 616
Glass, Philip, 2, 292, 485, 526,
  570, 725
Glazunov, Alexander, 13, 107,
  286, 354, 355, 388, 660
Gleghorn, Arthur, 354
Glennie, Evelyn, 7, 427
Gli uccelli (Respighi), 584, 589
Glière, Reinhold, 287, 425
Glinka, Mikhail, 108, 288,
  289, 724
Gloria (Dufay), 214
Gloria (Poulenc), 535–537, 714
Gloria (Rutter), 615
Gloria (Vivaldi), 770
Gloria ad modum tube
  (Dufay), 214
Gloriana (Britten), 136
Glossop, Peter, 90, 134, 135
Glover, Jane, 343, 696
Gluck, Christoph Willibald, 20,
  206, 290
Glückliche Hand, Die
  (Schoenberg), 636
Glushchenko, Fedor, 207
Gluzman, Vadim, 78
Glyndebourne Festival Orchestra,
  137, 279, 290, 485, 603
Gmür, Hanspeter, 19–20,
  205–206
Gnossiennes (Satie), 622
Go, Song of Mine (Elgar), 242
Gobbi, Tito, 410, 554, 555, 557,
  602, 755, 758, 760
God in Disguise, A
  (Larsson), 403
Godard, Benjamin, 161

Godfrey, Isadore, 282–283
Godowsky, Leopold, 167
Gods Go a'Begging
  (Handel/Beecham), 315
Goeres, Nancy, 406
Goethe, Johann Wolfgang von,
  57, 214, 295, 415, 421, 422,
  436, 454, 676
Goldberg, Rube, 374
Goldberg, Szymon, 67,
  352, 497
Goldberg Variations (Bach), 2,
  26, 27, 35, 62, 74
Goldmark, Karl, 291, 572
Goldsmith, Jerry, 322, 803
Golschmann, Vladimir, 325
Golub, David, 129, 195, 278,
  456, 646
Gomberg, Harold, 25, 39, 314,
  339, 492, 592
Gomez, Jill, 784
Good Friday Spell (Wagner), 775
Good Soldier Schweik, The: Suite
  (Kurka), 400
Goode, Richard, 121–122
Goodman, Benny, 48
Goodman, Roy, 96, 314, 337,
  793, 796
Goodman, Saul, 397
Goodwin, Paul, 331
Goossens, Eugene, 318
Goossens, Leon, 494
Górecki, Henryk, 180, 291–293,
  715, 725
Gorne, Matthias, 131
Gorr, Rita, 536, 619
Gothenberg Symphony
  Orchestra, 96, 301, 513, 671,
  672, 683, 719
Gothic Symphony (Brian), 132
Gothic Voices, 348
Götterdämmerung, Die
  (Wagner), 244, 506, 668, 774,
  775, 778
Göttingen Festival Chorus and
  Orchestra, 317
Gottschalk, Louis Moreau, 293,
  680
Gould, Glenn, 25–27, 35, 321,
  349, 480, 655,
Gould, Morton, 294, 680
Gounod, Charles, 188, 295, 518,
  584, 737
Goya, Francisco, 298
Goyescas (Granados), 246,
  298, 299
Graffman, Gary, 55, 542, 564,
  599, 728
Graham, Martha, 174
Grainger, Percy, 200, 296–298,
  328, 361, 561, 767, 791
Gramm, Donald, 72, 599
Gramont, Duke of, 406

Gran Partita (Mozart), 496
Granados, Enrique, 246, 248,
  277, 298, 299, 419
Grand Canyon Suite (Grofé), 306
*Grand Caprice for Solo Violin
  after Schubert's "Erlkönig"*
  (Ernst), 808
Grand jardinier de France, Le
  (Le Flem), 406
Grande Messe des morts
  (Berlioz), 88
Grant Still, William, 245, 685
Gray, Steve, 419
Gray, Thomas, 293
Great C Major Symphony
  (Schubert), 339
Great Service, The (Byrd), 152
Greater Love Hath No Man
  (Ireland), 371
Green, Adolph, 92
Green Hills o' Sommerset
  (Coates), 172
Green, Martyn, 283
Green Pastures (Korngold), 395
Greenhouse, Bernard, 73
Greenspan, Bud, 353
Greeting Prelude
  (Stravinsky), 706
Gregg Smith Singers, 97–98,
  264–265, 273
Gregor, Jószef, 527
Gregorian Chant, 299, 526, 585
Greissle, Felix, 79
Gretchaninov, Alexander, 586
Grey, Zane, 174
Grieg, Edvard, 300–304, 616,
  652, 719
Grieg, Nina, 304
Griffes, Charles Tomlinson, 42,
  155, 305, 421, 445, 727
Griffith, D.W., 201
Grillparzer, Franz, 58
Grobe, Donald, 350
Grofé, Ferde, 294, 306
Grogh (Copland), 176–177
Gropius, Manon, 80
Grosse Fuge (Beethoven), 66
Grosz, Wilhelm, 307
Groves, Sir Charles, 172, 236,
  359, 718
Gruberová, Edita, 486–487
Grumiaux, Arthur, 31–32, 494
Grümmer, Elisabeth, 366, 774
Grünewald, Matthias, 350
Grüner-Hegge, Odd, 734–735
Guarneri String Quartet, 50,
  67, 195
Gueden, Hilde, 626, 688,
  689, 696
Guest, George, 163, 332
Guevara, Che, 344
Gui, Vittorio, 603
Guinn, Leslie, 264

Guinness, Sir Alec, 105, 270
Guiraud, Ernest, 99
Gullberg, Hjalmar, 600
Gulliver's Travels (Herrmann), 346
Gunzenhauser, Stephen, 231,
  411, 482
Gurrelieder (Schoenberg), 626,
  630–631, 810
Guth, Peter, 423
Guzelimian, Armen, 118,
  305, 372
Gwendoline (Chabrier), 159
Gymnopédies (Satie), 622
Gypsy Songs (Dvořák), 227

H. M. S. Pinafore, 282
H.R.H. The Prince of Wales, 333
Haan, Johann David de,
  396–397
Haas, Karl, 40
Haas, Pavel, 307
Hába, Alois, 648
Habañera, Al (Saint-Saëns), 164
Habeyssée (Schmitt), 626
Hadley, Jerry, 92, 262, 389, 408
Hadley, Patrick, 308
Haebler, Ingrid, 490
Haenchen, Harmut, 19
Haffner Serenade (Mozart), 495
Haffner Symphony (Mozart),
  501–503
Hagegård, Håken, 600, 810
Hahn, Reynaldo, 309–310
Hailey, Christopher, 637
Haitink, Bernard, 56, 113, 137,
  145, 191, 418, 436, 485–487,
  564, 662–664, 666, 668, 696,
  708
Hálek, Vítězslav, 222
Hallé Orchestra of Manchester,
  85, 243, 328, 429
Halsey, Louis, 792
Hambourg, Mark, 416
Hamburg sinfonias
  (C.P.E. Bach), 19
Hamelin, Marc-André, 7–8
Hamlet (Tchaikovsky), 730–731
Hamlet (Thomas), 737
Hamlet (Walton), 787
Hammerklavier Sonata
  (Beethoven), 63, 74
Hammersmith (Holst), 359, 375
Hammerstein, Oscar, 389, 442
Hampson, Thomas, 40, 43, 217,
  264, 265, 295, 305, 372, 434,
  643, 653, 737, 754
Handel, George Frideric, 5, 13,
  23, 28, 104, 112, 129, 130,
  142, 151, 154, 170, 173, 179,
  238, 275–277, 296, 297,
  310–321, 328, 332, 473, 547,
  596, 598, 623, 628, 680, 736,
  809, 811

Handley, Vernon, 37–38, 133, 203, 222, 237–239, 260, 365, 464, 681, 749, 791
Hangover Square (Herrmann), 346–347
Hanks, Tom, 284
Hanover Band, 310, 337, 796
Hänsel und Gretel (Humperdinck), 366–367, 391, 544
Hanslick, Eduard, 461
Hanson, Howard, 156, 161, 205, 321–323, 590, 727
Happy Forest, The (Bax), 51
Happy Workshop, The (Strauss), 698, 700
Harbison, John, 323–324
Hardenberger, Håkan, 365–366
Hardy, Rosemary, 391
Hardy, Thomas, 251, 260
Harlow, Jean, 393
Harmonie der Welt, Die (Hindemith), 351
Harmoniemesse (Haydn), 332–333
Harmonious Blacksmith (Spohr/Handel), 680
Harnasie (Szymanowski), 721
Harnoncourt, Nikolaus, 22, 34, 736
Harnoy, Ofra, 102–103, 769
Harold in Italy (Berlioz), 85–86, 370
Harp Quintet (Bax), 52
Harper, Heather, 30, 139, 142, 320, 435
Harrell, Lynn, 103, 567
Harris, Roy, 43, 178, 263, 324
Harrison, Lou, 325–326, 405
Hartmann, Karl Amadeus, 327, 609
Harty, Sir Hamilton, 85, 315, 318, 319, 328
Harvey, Lilian, 393
Harvey, Michael Kieran, 459, 767
Harwood, Elizabeth, 137, 740
Háry János (Kodály), 392, 416, 544
Háry János Suite (Kodály), 392, 392, 416, 544
Hašek, Jaroslav, 400
Hatton, Rondo, 266
Haugland, Aage, 511–512, 661
Haugtussa (Grieg), 304
Haunted Ballroom (Toye), 800
Havanaise (Saint-Saëns), 618
Have Mercy Upon Me (Handel), 312
Havel, Václav, 368
Havilland, Olivia de, 176
Hawthorne, Nathaniel, 466
Hawthorne, Nigel, 402

Hawthorne String Quartet, 307–308
Haydn, Franz Joseph, 15, 19, 20, 65, 69, 105, 127, 130, 172, 205, 286, 328–343, 356, 366, 377, 455, 469, 470, 488, 490, 498, 499, 501, 503, 537, 602, 606, 638, 643, 645, 656, 674, 678, 792, 797
Haydn, Michael, 342
Haydn Quartets (Mozart), 499
Headington, Christopher, 343
Healing Fountain, The (In Memoriam Benjamin Britten) (Heddington), 343
Hear Ye! Hear Ye! (Copland), 176
Heaven Ladder, Book 7 (Riley), 591
Hebrides Overture (Mendelssohn), 455
Heifetz, Jascha, 6, 65, 66, 115, 157, 208, 394, 395, 565, 614, 646, 670, 729, 765
Heiligmesse (Haydn), 332
Heirat wider Willen (Humperdinck), 367
Heiress, The (Copland), 176
Heirs of the White Mountain, The (Dvořák), 222
Heldenleben, Ein (Strauss), 692, 697, 700, 701
Helgoland (Bruckner), 147
Hellas, A Suite of Ancient Greece (Foulds), 265
Helmerson, Frans, 195, 668
Helpmann, Robert, 788
Helsinki Philharmonic Orchestra, 575, 666
Helsinki University Chorus, 672
Hely-Hutchinson, Victor, 344
Hemingway, Ernest, 11
Hempel, Frieda, 100
Hendricks, Barbara, 100–101, 691, 765
Hengelbrock, Thomas, 420
Henriot-Schweitzer, Nicole, 370
Henry, Didier, 192
Henry V (Doyle), 213
Henry V (Walton), 787
Henry V of England, 251
Henry VIII of England, 717, 723
Henschel, Sir George, 367
Hentoff, Nat, 753
Henze, Hans Werner, 344–345, 510
Hepburn, Katharine, 177
Herbert, Victor, 149, 345
Herbig, Gunther, 184, 327
Herincx, Raymond, 740
Hermit Songs (Barber), 39, 43, 44
Hernandez, Miquel, 144

Heroic Elegy (Farrar), 251
Herrera, Raul, 118
Herrmann, Bernard, 102, 346–348, 572, 574
Herseth, Adolph, 330
Hertel, Johann Wilhelm, 366
Herz, Das (Pfitzner), 529
Heseltine, Philip (Peter Warlock), 791
Heuberger, Richard, 307
Hewitt, Angela, 30
Hiawatha's Wedding Feast (Coleridge-Taylor), 173
Hickox, Richard, 9–10, 14, 15, 93, 139, 142, 143, 156, 199, 201, 235–239, 256, 260, 261, 283, 284, 287, 297, 359, 360, 371, 450, 495, 606, 607, 615, 707, 739, 746, 784, 786, 789, 790
Hildegard of Bingen, 348
Hill, David, 152, 764
Hill, Edward Burlingame, 160
Hill, Martyn, 261, 784
Hilliard Ensemble, 280, 281, 526
Hillier, Paul, 526
Hillis, Margaret, 42, 85, 540, 758
Hindemith, Paul, 49, 67, 185, 258, 327, 349–352, 354–356, 403, 447, 497, 514, 582, 600, 695, 790, 791
Hinrichsen, Evelyn, 326
Hippolyte et Aricie (Rameau), 573
Hirschfeld, Magnus, 636
Hirt auf dem Felsen (Schubert), 643
Histoire de Babar, L' (Poulenc), 537
Histoire du soldat, L (Stravinsky), 709, 711
Hitchcock, Sir Alfred, 347, 430, 510
Hitler, Adolf, 58, 157, 192, 308, 327, 350, 394, 461, 703, 799
Hobson's Choice (Arnold), 14
Hodgson, Alfreda, 30, 113, 437, 495
Hoffman, E.T.A., 518
Hoffmann, Ludwig, 777
Hoffnung, Gerard, 353
Hoffnung Music Festivals, 353
Hofmann, Josef, 417
Hofmannsthal, Hugo von, 691, 699
Hogarth, William, 561, 713
Hogwood, Christopher, 28, 341, 560
Höhn, Carola, 648
Holberg Suite (Grieg), 301, 804
Holdridge, Lee, 353–354
Holidays Symphony (Ives), 374

Höll, Hartmut, 123
Hollander, Lorin, 175
Holliger, Heinz, 5–6, 83, 313, 437, 438
Hollman, Ottokar, 376
Hollreiser, Heinrich, 777
Hollywood Bowl Orchestra, 102
Hollywood String Quartet, 120, 267, 350, 354, 355, 766, 788, 805
Holmboe, Vagn, 356–357
Holmes, Olivier Wendell, 160, 426
Holmes, Ralph, 201, 203
Holmès, Augusta, 358
Holst, Gustav, 78, 101, 151, 358–362, 365, 375, 496, 614, 681, 745, 746
Holst, Holst, 78, 360, 365, 614
Holst Singers, 101, 360, 745, 746
Holy Boy, The (Ireland), 371
Holy Sonnets of John Donne, The (Britten), 135
Holzman, Adam, 678
Homenaje a Federico García Lorca (Revueltas), 590
Homer, 451
Hone, Nathaniel, the younger, 52
Honegger, Arthur, 362–363, 383, 442, 463, 725
Hoover, Herbert, 148
Hoover, J. Edgar, 94
Hopkins, Sir Anthony, 549
Horenstein, Jascha, 352, 430, 432, 435, 437, 512, 563, 564
Horne, Marilyn, 95, 99, 210, 290, 555, 601, 605, 606
Horner, James, 542
Horoscope (Lambert), 401
Horowitz, Vladimir, 6, 42, 118, 167, 415, 565, 569
Horrortorio, 353
Hosanna to the Son of David (Gibbons), 281
Hotter, Hans, 123–124, 422, 630, 642, 647, 648, 695, 703, 704, 773, 776, 778, 805
Hough, Stephen, 111–112, 267, 268, 304, 411, 412, 465, 466, 624
Housman, A.E., 151
Houston Grand Opera, 279
Houston Symphony Orchestra, 420, 632, 667
Hovhaness, Alan, 363–364
How to Marry a Millionaire (Newman), 510
Howard, David, 541
Howarth, Elgar, 679, 789, 790
Howarth, Judith, 790
Howells, Herbert, 365, 681
Hubbard, Bruce, 389

Huberman, Bronislaw, 65–66, 395, 621, 808
Hugh the Drover (Vaughan Williams), 747
Hughes, Langston, 149
Hugo, Victor, 254, 309, 754
Huguenots, Les (Meyerbeer), 460–461
Hulce, Tom, 474
Hummel, Johann Nepomuk, 74, 356, 365, 366, 399
Humoresque in E minor (Tchaikovsky), 732
Humperdinck, Engelbert, 131, 366, 367
Hungarian Dances (Brahms), 117
Hungarian Pictures (Bartók), 49
Hungarian Rhapsodies (Liszt), 415
Hungarian Rhapsody No. 2 (Liszt), 246
Hungarian Sketches (Bartók), 46, 48, 416
Hungarian Sketches (Rózsa), 614
Hungarian State Orchestra, 47
Hunsberger, Donald, 368
Hunt, Lorraine, 311
Hunt Quartet (Mozart), 356
Hunter, Kelly, 307
Hurford, Peter, 29, 619
Husa, Karel, 368, 609
Hüsch, Gerhardt, 473, 642
Hussite Overture (Dvořák), 223
Huston, John, 308
Huvinäytelmäalkusoitto Overture (Madetoja), 428
Huxley, Aldous, 347, 705, 706
Hvorostovsky, Dmitri, 209, 567, 568, 729, 730, 752, 753
Hymn of Jesus (Holst), 360
Hymn of Zrinyi (Kodály), 224
Hymn to St. Cecilia (Britten), 135
Hymnus Amoris (Nielsen), 511
Hymnus Paradisi (Howells), 365
Hyperprism (Varèse), 743

"I Am the Rose of Sharon" (Billings), 98
I Musici, 5, 6, 13, 276, 277, 312, 313, 437, 438, 743, 805
I Musici de Montréal, 13, 312, 313, 743
I Profeti (Castelnuovo-Tedesco), 157
I quattro rusteghi (Wolf-Ferrari), 806
Ibéria (Albéniz), 2–3, 246, 248, 249, 298
Ibéria (Debussy), 189–190
Ibert, Jacques, 100, 266, 369, 535

Ibsen, Henrik, 250, 302, 616, 794
Iceland Symphony Orchestra, 408, 428, 671, 672
Ich liebe Dich (Grieg), 59
Idealized Indian Themes (Cadman), 152
Idomeneo (Mozart), 473, 486
Idyll (Delius), 202
Idyll for String Orchestra (Janáček), 380
Idyll for the Misbegotten, An (Crumb), 184
Idylle de printemps (Delius), 199
Il distratto (Symphony No. 60) (Haydn), 337
Illuminations (Britten), 140
Ilya Murometz (Glière), 287
Images for Orchestra (Debussy), 189
Images for Piano (Debussy), 187, 194
Images oubliées (Debussy), 196
Imaginary Landscape (Cage), 153
Imai, Nabuko, 85–86, 791
Immolation Scene (Wagner), 774–775
Impériale, L' (Haydn), 338
In a Chinese Temple Garden (Ketèlbey), 389
In a Monastery Garden (Ketèlbey), 389
In a Nutshell (Grainger), 297, 298
In a Persian Market (Ketèlbey), 389, 390
In Gloucestershire (Howells), 365
In Honor of the City (Dyson), 236
In Honor of the City of London (Walton), 785
In Nature's Realm (Dvořák), 222
In Nomine Domini (Symphony No. 84) (Haydn), 338
In questa tomba oscura (Beethoven), 59
In the Beginning (Copland), 39
In the Lord Put I My Trust (Handel), 312
In the Moonlight (Ketèlbey), 390
In the Mystic Land of Egypt (Ketèlbey), 389
In the Steppes of Central Asia (Borodin), 110
In the Tatras (Novák), 515
In the Fen Country (Vaughan Williams), 748
Inbal, Elijahu, 147, 553
Incantations (Piano Concerto No. 4) (Martinů), 442

Incoronazione di Poppea, L' (Monteverdi), 466
Incredible Flutist, The (Piston), 531
Indes galantes, Les (Rameau), 573
Inextinguishable Symphony (Nielsen), 513
Inn of the Sixth Happiness (Arnold), 14
Inno delea nazioni (Verdi), 756
Intégrales (Varèse), 743
Interplay (Gould), 294, 680
Intimate Pages (Janáček), 382–383
Introduction and Allegro (Ravel), 189, 195, 354, 355, 579, 612
Introduction and Allegro for Strings (Elgar), 235, 241
241*Introduction and Rondo capriccioso* (Saint-Saëns), 164, 618, 621
Introduttioni teatricali (Locatelli), 420
Invitation to the Dance (Weber), 796
Invocation (Ensemble), 468–469
Invocation and Dance (Creston), 182
Invocation and Dance (Mathias), 447
Iolanthe (Gilbert and Sullivan), 282–283, 367, 718
Ippolitov-Ivanov, Mikhail, 370–371
Ionisation (Varèse), 743
Ireland, John, 371–372
Irish Melodies (Moore), 468
Irish Melody, An (Bridge), 133
Irish Rhapsodies (Stanford), 681
Irish Symphony, An (Harty), 328, 718
Irish Tune from County Derry (Grainger), 297
Irlande (Holmes), 358
Irmelin: Prelude (Delius), 202
Iscariot (Rouse), 609
Islamey (Balakirev), 37
Island, The (Sainton), 308
Isle of Bliss (Rautavaara), 575
Isle of the Dead (Rachmaninoff), 562–563, 566
Isle of the Dead, The (Rachmaninoff), 563
Israel in Egypt (Handel), 319
Israel Philharmonic, 77, 455
Isserlis, Steven, 41, 304, 725, 726
Istomin, Eugene, 129, 599
Italian Concerto (Bach), 23
Italian Serenade (Wolf), 303, 356, 403, 805
Italian Song Book (Wolf), 805
Italian Symphony (Mendelssohn), 339, 455

Italiana in Algeri, L' (Rossini), 602–603
Ivan the Terrible (Prokofiev), 541
Ives, Charles, 42, 97, 160, 183, 305, 325, 372–375, 417, 590, 650

Jacob, Gordon, 359, 375
Jacob, Max, 534
Jacobs, Paul, 193
Jacobs, Peter, 161
Jacobs, René, 154, 316, 466
Jaccottet, Christiane, 32
Jaeger, A.J., 241
Jag elsker Dig (Grieg), 304
Jamaican Rumba (Benjamin), 800
James, Henry, 141, 176
James II of England, 104
Janáček, Leoš, 50, 226, 268, 376, 382
Jandó, Jenö, 53, 61, 62, 120, 207, 334, 335, 479, 490, 504, 655
Janequin, Clément, 383, 403
Janis, Byron, 54, 640, 696
Jannings, Emil, 393
Jansons, Mariss, 216, 232, 570, 571, 660, 664, 673, 734, 735, 774
Jargon (Billings), 98
Jarre, Maurice, 383, 384
Jarrell, Randall, 310
Jarrett, Keith, 325–326
Järvi, Neeme, 7, 43, 49, 52, 53, 96, 119, 120, 160, 161, 183, 230, 231, 245, 256, 257, 274, 286, 301, 302, 388, 442, 511, 512, 541, 542, 547, 548, 592–594, 626, 659, 660, 664, 671, 672, 683, 685, 703, 707, 708, 711, 719, 724, 732, 733, 741, 742, 796
Je te veux (Satie), 622
Jeanne d'Arc au bûcher (Honegger), 363
Jefferson, Thomas, 373, 738
Jenůfa (Janáček), 378
Jeremiah (the prophet), 157
Jeremiah Symphony (Bernstein), 93
Jerusalem, Siegfried, 487, 631, 777, 799
Jesu, Joy of Man's Desiring (Bach), 27
Jeu de cartes (Stravinsky), 711–712
Jeux (Debussy), 186, 191, 194, 611
Jeux d'eau à la Villa d'Este (Liszt), 413
Jeux d'enfants (Bizet), 100
Jewels of the Madonna (Wolf-Ferrari), 806
Jílek, František, 377, 378
Jo, Sumi, 17, 209, 601, 607

Joachim, Joseph, 117, 145, 221, 426, 560, 572, 624
Job (masque for dancing) (Vaughan Williams), 746
Jobim, Antonios Carlos, 384
Jochum, Eugen, 115, 147, 340, 341, 773, 795, 796
Johannes Uppenbarelse (Rosenberg), 600
Johannesburg Festival Overture (Walton), 789
John Field Suite, A (Harty), 328
John the Baptist, 687, 702
Johnson, Dr. Samuel, 72, 113, 293, 312
Johnson, Emma, 184, 259
Johnson, Graham, 310
Johnson, James Weldon 149
Johnson, Lyndon, 34
"Joke" Quartet (Haydn), 333
Joli jeu de furet, Le (Roger-Ducasse), 597
Jones, Della, 790
Jones, Gwyneth, 691
Jones, James Earl, 323
Jones, Martin, 453
Jones, Spike, 353
Jongen, Joseph, 384–385
Joplin, Scott, 28, 385
Josefowicz, Leila, 621, 808
Josephs-Legende (Strauss), 701
Joyce, Archibald, 386
Joyeuse marche (Chabrier), 159
Juarez (Korngold), 395
Jubilate Deo (Walton), 784
Jubilate Deo! (Britten), 135
Judas Maccabaeus (Handel), 313, 320
Judith (Honegger), 363
Judith (Schuman), 650
Jugenlieder (Berg), 79
Juilliard String Quartet, 50, 223, 224, 373, 498, 798
Juliet, Chantal, 721
Juliet Letters (Costello), 292
Jungle Book, The (Koechlin), 393
Jupiter Symphony (Mozart), 501, 503

Kabalevsky, Dimitri, 387, 390, 461
Kabasta, Oswald, 208
Kaddish (Diamond), 205
Kaddish Symphony (Bernstein), 93, 94, 609
Kafka, Franz, 234, 644
Kairn of Koridwen, The (Griffes), 305
Kalichstein, Joseph, 56
Kalichstein-Laredo-Robinson Trio, 56
Kalinnikov, Vassily, 388

Kalish, Gilbert, 264, 265, 372, 567
Kallman, Chester, 713
Kálmán, Emmerich, 408
Kammermusik (Hindemith), 349, 514
Kamu, Okko, 402, 620
Kanon in D (Pachelbel), 519
Kanta, Ludovit, 329
Kapell, William, 54–55, 168, 169, 391, 415, 416, 565
Kaplan, Mark, 32, 51, 129, 208, 521, 621
Karajan, Herbert von, 25, 60, 116, 143, 145, 331, 366, 476, 517, 666, 688, 689, 693, 701, 702, 736, 755, 759, 796
Karelia Suite (Sibelius), 670–671
Karloff, Boris, 471
Kasarova, Vasselina, 209, 607
Kaspryzk, Jacek, 721
Kát'a Kabanová (Janáček), 379
Katchen, Julius, 129–130
Käthchen von Heillbron, Das (Pfitzner), 529
Katin, Peter, 490
Kaufman, Annette, 685
Kaufman, Louis, 685
Kavakos, Leonidas, 670
Kay, Hershey, 680
Kazan, Elia, 94, 541
Keats, John, 309, 328, 640
Kegelstatt Trio (Mozart), 504
Keilberth, Joseph, 422
Kell, Reginald, 259, 493
Kempe, Rudolf, 396, 694, 697, 701, 773
Kempen, Paul van, 735
Kempff, Wilhelm, 27, 61–62, 479, 639
Kennedy, Michael, 242, 292
Kennedy, Nigel, 32, 238, 243, 785, 791
Kern, Jerome, 265, 389, 558
Kerstens, Tom, 788
Kertész, István, 45, 121, 130, 222, 224, 231, 232, 392, 488, 607
Ketèlbey, Albert, 389
Key, Francis Scott, 148
Khachaturian, Aram, 387, 390, 461, 686
Khovanshchina (Mussorgsky), 506
Khovanshchina: Prelude and Galitsin's Journey (Mussorgsky), 506
Khrennikov, Tikhon, 659
Kikimora (Liadov), 411
Kilbey, Reginald, 171–172
Killers, The (Rózsa), 613
Kincses, Veronika, 688
Kinderman, William, 74

Kinderszenen (Schumann), 654
Kindertotenlieder (Mahler), 100, 429, 434, 647
King Arthur (Purcell), 559
King Arthur (Sullivan), 718
King Christian II (Sibelius), 671–672
King, James, 350, 429
King, Jr., Martin Luther, 83, 261
King Kong (Steiner), 682, 793
King Lear (Berlioz), 88
King Roger (Szymanowski), 396, 440, 721
King Stephen (Beethoven), 57
King, Thea, 121
King's Row (Korngold), 394–395
Kingdom, The (Elgar), 239
Kinney, Yvonne, 236
Kipling, Rudyard, 297, 393
Kipnis, Alexander, 124, 473, 508, 643, 805
Kipnis, Igor, 24, 124, 248, 623
Kirkpatrick, Ralph, 623
Kirov Opera, 289, 506, 507, 549, 592
Kiss, Gyula, 493
Kiss, József, 492, 655
Kissin, Yevgeny, 660
Kjampevise-Slåtten (Sæverud), 616
Klee, Bernhard, 473, 510
Klee, Paul, 649
Kleiber, Carlos, 71, 127, 631, 779, 795
Kleiber, Eric, 487
Klein, Walter, 148, 482, 703
Kleine Dreigroschenmusik (Weill), 798
Klemperer, Otto, 58, 70, 72, 116, 126, 431, 503, 771
Klemperer, Werner, 631
Kletzki, Paul, 352
Klien, Kenneth, 490
Klimt, Gustav, 79
Knappertsbusch, Hans, 700, 776, 777
Knardahl, Eva, 302
Knoxville: Summer of 1915 (Barber), 39, 44
Knussen, Oliver, 138, 156, 176, 177, 391, 705, 722, 723
Kobbé, Gustav, 605
Kocian String Quartet, 350
Kocsis, Zoltán, 49–50, 196
Kodály String Quartet, 333, 337, 492
Kodály, Zoltán, 206, 356, 391–393
Koechlin, Charles, 393–394
Kohon String Quartet, 421, 445
Koledo DeAlmeida, Cynthia, 405
Kolisch, Rudolf, 634
Kollo, René, 435, 776, 777, 779

Koncherto por la Violino kun Perkuta Orkestro (Harrison), 326
Kondrashin, Kiril, 227, 390, 413, 542, 728
Königskinder (Humperdinck), 367
Kontarsky, Alfons and Alois, 227
Konzertstück for Piano and Orchestra (Weber), 797
Koopman, Ton, 33, 314
Kopleff, Florence, 72
Korda, Sir Alexander, 101
Korngold, Erich Wolfgang, 41, 66, 347, 394, 575, 614
Korngold, George, 395, 799
Kosleck, Martin, 266
Košler, Zdeněk, 440, 516, 673, 674, 694
Kostelanetz, André, 197
Kotcherga, Anatoli, 505
Koussevitzky, Serge, 35, 42, 44, 46, 51, 69, 77, 86, 87, 138, 194, 263, 322, 325, 443, 460, 463, 507, 566, 578, 650, 663, 665, 673, 714, 725
Kovacevich, Stephen, 53, 639, 652
Koval, Marian, 659
Kraemer, Nicholas, 420, 769
Kraft, Norbert, 157, 678
Kraft, William, 326, 397
Kramář, František, 398–399
Krása, Hans, 307–308
Krasner, Louis, 79–80, 629
Kratt (ballet suite) (Tubin), 741
Kraus, Alfredo, 295, 483
Kraus, Tom, 99, 131, 698, 794, 795
Krauss, Clemens, 689, 694, 755
Kreisler, Fritz, 2, 24, 25, 31, 66, 115, 208, 237, 399, 566, 621, 808
Kreisleriana (Schumann), 651, 654
Krejčik, Vladimir, 377–379
Kremer, Gidon, 51, 65, 656
Kreutzer Sonata (Beethoven), 65–66, 123, 521
Kronos Quartet, 184
Kruis, Josef, 225
Kubelík, Rafael, 221–222, 230–232, 350, 379, 390, 431, 674, 675, 773, 796
Kubiak, Teresa, 730
Kubrick, Stanley, 412, 526, 692
Kuchar, Theodore, 425
Kuffner, Christoff, 61
Kuijken, Sigiswald, 179–180
Kuijken, Wieland, 179–180
Kunz, Erich, 688–689
Kunzel, Erich, 74, 306, 803, 804
Kupferman, Meyer, 406
Kurka, Robert, 400

Kurtz, Efram, 544–545
Kusche, Benno, 773
Kysélák, Ladislav, 483

L'estro armonico (Vivaldi), 768
L'Invocation (Dussek), 218, 223
La belle dame sans merci
  (Hadley), 309
La Calinda from Koanga, 202
La Chasse (Symphony No. 84)
  (Haydn), 338
La Mer (Debussy), 133, 163,
  190, 194, 252, 369, 593, 620
La Péri (Dukas), 215, 248
La Reine (Haydn), 338
La Reine de France (Symphony
  No. 85) (Haydn), 338
La Scala Opera, 165, 762
La Scala Philharmonic, 608
La strada (Rota), 608
La Stravaganza (Vivaldi), 768
La Valsse (Ravel), 576, 577
Labèque, Katia and Marielle,
  117, 606
Laborintus II (Berio), 83
Lachian Dances (Janáček), 381
Ladrot, André, 492
Lady Macbeth of Mtsensk
  (Shostakovich), 660–661, 663
LaFont, Jean-Philippe, 188
Lagerlöf, Selma, 16
Lagniappe (Babbitt), 18
Lahti Symphony, 670
Lajtha String Quartet, 532
Lakmé (Delibes), 197, 198
Lalo, Édouard, 400–401,
  617, 621
Lambert, Constant, 401–402,
  581, 681, 789, 799
Lament for Beowulf
  (Hanson), 322
Lamentatione (Symphony No.
  26) (Haydn), 337
Lamond, Frederic, 417
Lanchbery, John, 734
Lanchester, Elsa, 705
Land of Smiles, The (Léhar),
  407–408
Landau, Siegfried, 400
Landowska, Wanda, 2, 27, 35,
  248, 535
Lane, Cleo, 330
Lane, Louis, 177, 789
Lane, Piers, 4, 520
Lang, Fritz, 793
Lang, Paul Henry, 137–138
Langdon, Michael, 135
Langridge, Philip, 136, 141, 142,
  331, 402, 505, 643
Lao-tse, 471
Laredo, Jamie, 56
Larin, Sergei, 505, 567, 568
Lark Ascending, The (Vaughan
  Williams), 241, 746

Larmore, Jennifer, 217, 316,
  473, 605
Larsson, Lars-Erik, 402–403
LaSalle String Quartet,
  80–81, 634
Laskine, Lily, 313–314
Lassus, Orlando de, 403
Last Judgment (Moross), 469
Late Lark (Delius), 202
Latin American Symphonette
  (Gould), 294
Laudi (Mathias), 447
Laudon (Haydn), 338
Lauridsen, Morten, 404
Laurindo Almeida, 384
Lawrence of Arabia, 2, 383, 384
Lawson, Peter, 155, 305
Layton, Stephen, 309, 745
Lazarus and His Beloved
  (Holdridge), 353–354
Le Cabaret Overture
  (Foulds), 265
Le Flem, Paul, 406
Le Matin (Haydn), 336
Le Midi (Haydn), 336
Le Roi de Lahore
  (Massenet), 446
Le Soir (Haydn), 336
Le Villi (Puccini), 557
Lean, Sir David, 51, 383
Leaper, Adrian, 132, 171–173,
  389, 390, 561
Lebedinsky, Lev, 667
Leblanc, Georgette, 191
Lebrun, Eric, 217
Leclair, Jean-Marie, 404–405
Ledger, Philip, 135
Lee, Christopher, 709
Lee, Spike, 176
Leech, Richard, 295
Lees, Benjamin, 405–406
Legend for Piano and Orchestra
  (Ireland), 372
*Legend of the Invisible City of
  Kitezh*: Suite (Rimsky-
  Korsakov), 593
Légende (Delius), 203
Legrand, Michel, 217
Lehár, Franz, 407, 408, 688, 699
Lehmann, Lilli, 75
Lehmann, Lotte, 75, 473, 693,
  699, 702, 774, 780
Leider, Frida, 777, 779, 780
Leiferkus, Sergei, 505, 562,
  567, 568
Leifs, Jan, 408
Leighton, Kenneth, 297
Leinsdorf, Erich, 73, 180, 181,
  259, 394, 546, 556, 670, 751
Leipzig Bach Collegium, 29
Leipzig Gewandhaus Orchestra,
  60, 70, 798
Leitner, Ferdinand, 479
Lekeu, Guillaume, 409

Lemminkäinen's Return
  (Sibelius), 671
Lenárd, Ondrej, 132, 381
Lendi, Lucretia, 607
Lener Quartet, 67
Lenin, Vladimir, 387, 542,
  659, 667
Leningrad Philharmonic,
  665–667, 736
Leningrad Symphony
  (Shostakovich), 665
Lenya, Lotte, 798
Leoncavallo, Ruggiero, 76,
  410, 444
Leonhardt, Gustav, 22
Leonore Overture No. 4
  (Beethoven?), 353
"Leonore" Symphony
  (Raff), 572
Leppard, Raymond, 314, 330,
  488, 520, 558
Lermontov, Mikhail, 568–569
Les Adieux (Beethoven), 63
Les Arts Florissants, 422,
  573–574
Les Préludes (Liszt), 418
Leschetizky, Theodore, 416
Let Us Garlands Bring (Finzi),
  261, 748
Leutgeb, Ignaz, 476
Levi Dawson, William, 245
Levi, Joel, 546
Levine, James, 60, 445, 630, 759,
  774, 776
Levine, Joseph, 11
Levitzky, Mischa, 416
Lewenthal, Raymond, 8
Liberace, 389
Liebe der Danae, Die (Strauss),
  694, 696
Liebermann, Lowell, 411–412
Lieberson, Goddard, 280
Liebeslieder Waltzes
  (Brahms), 118
Liebesmahl der Apostel, Des
  (Bruckner), 147
Liebestraum (Liszt), 416, 418
Liederkreis, Op. 39
  (Schumann), 653
Life for the Tsar, A (Glinka),
  288–289
Ligabue, Ilva, 755
Ligeti, György, 412, 479, 526
Light of Life, The (Elgar),
  237, 240
Lille Opera, 192
Lilly of Kilarney, The
  (Benedict), 782
Limoges Baroque Ensemble, 106
Lin, Cho-Liang, 450, 514
Lincoln, Abraham, 177, 262,
  275, 373, 509, 650
Lincoln Portrait (Copland),
  177, 262

Lincolnshire Posy
  (Grainger), 297
Lind, Jenny, 304
Lindberg, Christian, 781–782
Lindberg, Jakob, 212–213
Lindholm, Ingvar, 90, 91
Lindsley, Celina, 648
Linz Symphony (Mozart),
  501–502
Lipatti, Dinu, 118, 167, 168, 301
Lipovšek, Marjana, 505
Lipp, Wilma, 689
List, Eugene, 293
Liszt, Franz, 4, 7, 52, 74, 84, 89,
  114, 149, 180, 246, 248, 258,
  267, 293, 304, 329, 358,
  413–418, 426, 469, 520, 584,
  621, 624, 647, 651, 783
Litany to the Virgin
  (Szymanowski), 721
Litolff, Henry, 370, 470, 800
Little C Major Symphony
  (Schubert), 644
Little Fugue in G minor
  (Bach/Stokowski), 686
Little G Minor Symphony
  (Mozart), 500
Little Masonic Cantata
  (Mozart), 488
Little Russian Symphony
  (Tchaikovsky), 733, 735
Little Shimmy (Antheil), 11
Little Suite for Strings
  (Nielsen), 804
Little, Tasmin, 198
Litton, Andrew, 110, 569
Liverpool Oratorio
  (McCartney), 292
Ljungstrom, Carl, 144
Llobet, Miguel, 419
Lloyd-Jones, David, 37, 92, 199,
  401, 746
Lloyd Webber, Andrew, 245, 389
Lloyd Weber, Julian, 38
Lôbo, Duarte, 419
Locatelli, Pietro, 420
Lockhart, Keith, 406
Loeffler, Charles Martin, 420,
  421, 445, 492
Loewe, Carl, 421–422
Logue, Christopher, 42
Lohengrin (Wagner), 181, 772,
  773, 776
Lombardi, I (Verdi), 756
London Chamber Orchestra,
  241, 715, 716
London Classical Players, 69,
  214, 604, 797
London Festival Orchestra,
  105–106
London, George, 776
London Madrigal Singers, 745
London Overture, A
  (Ireland), 371

London Philharmonic Orchestra,
  14, 82, 102, 145, 194, 221,
  237, 245, 248, 265, 271, 272,
  279, 314, 315, 340, 341, 343,
  346, 361, 372, 384, 418, 425,
  439, 454, 485, 502, 525, 556,
  572, 581, 617, 660, 661, 662,
  684, 708, 712, 737, 744, 747,
  748, 775, 788, 790, 791,
  806, 807
London Sinfonietta, 138, 156,
  176, 291, 389, 391, 629,
  705, 722
London Strings, 24
London Suite (Coates), 172
London Symphony (No. 104)
  (Haydn), 338, 339, 342
London Symphony Orchestra, 9,
  14, 41, 54, 79, 84, 85, 87, 89,
  90, 92, 93, 106, 108, 119–121,
  128, 130, 134, 137, 139–143,
  145, 148, 150, 156, 164, 165,
  171, 201, 224, 235–238, 241,
  256, 266, 269, 278, 302, 303,
  318, 352, 353, 358, 360, 371,
  383, 413, 416, 426, 430, 432,
  435, 436, 450, 451, 455, 469,
  485, 495, 506, 519, 521, 527,
  528, 532, 541, 542, 545, 546,
  550, 553, 554, 570, 578, 579,
  595, 596, 604–606, 660,
  668–670, 673, 675, 696, 705,
  708, 712, 713, 725, 731, 734,
  744, 745, 749–751, 765, 780,
  784, 785, 786, 801, 803
London Winds, 700–701
Londonderry Air, The
  (Bridge), 133
Londonderry Air, The
  (Harty), 328
Long, Marguerite, 252, 577
Longfellow, Henry Wadsworth,
  160, 236, 426
Lonsdale, Michael, 277
Loomis, Harvey
  Worthington, 152
López-Cobos, Jésus, 536
Lorengar, Pilar, 57, 58, 290
Lorentz, Pare, 739
Lortzing, Albert, 510
Los Angeles Chamber
  Orchestra, 321, 380, 585,
  709, 738, 739
Los Angeles Master Chorale,
  404, 540
Los Angeles Opera, 466
Los Angeles Philharmonic
  Orchestra, 38, 71, 166, 174,
  176, 205, 323, 326, 346, 347,
  354, 394, 397, 424, 442,
  540, 743
Los Angeles Vocal Arts
  Ensemble, 118
Losh, Hazel, 654

Lost Weekend, The (Rózsa), 613
Lott, Felicity, 141–142, 309,
  319, 332
Lotti, Antonio, 438
Lotus Eaters, The (Parry), 525
Louis XIV, 197
Louise (Charpentier), 162
Love for Three Oranges, The
  (Prokofiev), 536, 544
Love for Three Oranges: Suite
  (Prokofiev), 544
Love in Bath (Handel/
  Beecham), 316
*Love Verses from the Song of
  Solomon* (Grainger), 297
Loveday, Alan, 770
Lovers, The (Barber), 42
Lovisa Ulrika of Prussia, 598
Low Symphony (Glass), 292
Lowell, Robert, 749
Lt. Kijé Suite (Prokofiev), 544
Lubbock, John, 706
Lubbock, Mark, 800
Lucarelli, Bert, 802
Lucas, Brenda, 100
Lucia di Lammermoor
  (Donizetti), 76, 209, 211, 212
Lucio Silla (Mozart), 490
Lucrezia Borgia (Donizetti),
  210–211
Ludvig Holberg, 301
Ludwig, Christa, 58, 92, 484,
  778, 779
Luisa Miller (Verdi), 757
Luisi, Fabio, 367
Lullaby for Lucy (Maxwell
  Davies), 448
Lully, Jean-Baptiste, 181,
  422, 423
Lulu (Berg), 82, 630
Lumbye, Hans Christian, 423
Lumen in Christo
  (Hanson), 323
Lupu, Radu, 118, 195,
  482, 497
Lurie, Mitchell, 354, 582
Luther, Martin, 454
Lutoslawski, Witold, 144,
  424, 720
Lutyens, Elizabeth, 78
Lux aeterna (Hanson), 323
Lux aeterna (Lauridsen), 404
Luxon, Benjamin, 20, 134,
  139, 747
Lyapunov, Sergei, 37
Lyatoshynsky, Boris, 425
Lyra Angelica (Alwyn), 9
Lyric Movement for Viola and
  Small Orchestra (Holst), 359
Lyric Pieces (Grieg), 50, 301
Lyric Suite (Berg), 80–81, 634
Lyric Suite (Grieg), 301
Lyric Symphony
  (Zemlinsky), 810

Lyrics of the Redman (Loomis), 152
Lytton, Sir Henry, 283

Ma, Yo Yo, 32, 33, 215, 345, 401, 460, 567, 610, 617, 628, 640
Má Vlast (Smetana), 256, 674, 675
Maag, Peter, 455
Maazel, Lorin, 233, 401, 406, 431, 546, 553–555, 557, 579, 775
Macal, Zdenek, 228
Macbeth (Strauss), 701
Macbeth (Sullivan), 718
Macbeth (Verdi), 757–758
Macbeth (Walton), 787
MacDougall, Jamie, 135–136
MacDowell, Edward, 152, 161, 425–426
Machado, Celso, 384
Machaut, Guillaume de, 426–427, 707
Mack, John, 492
Mackay, Charles, 241
Mackerras, Sir Charles, 102–103, 136, 171, 172, 198, 202, 258, 310, 318, 341, 342, 376, 377–379, 381, 382, 440, 441, 495, 496, 500, 550, 584, 718, 765, 770, 771
MacMillan, James, 427
MacMillan, Sir Ernest, 565
MacNeice, Louis, 784
Madalin, Carol, 443–444
Madama Butterfly (Puccini), 551–553
Maddalena ai Piedi di Cristo (Caldara), 154
Madetoja, Levi, 428
Maeterlinck, Maurice, 191
Maggini String Quartet, 243
Magic Flute, The (Mozart), 101, 472, 483, 486, 488–490, 497, 740
Magnificat (Bach), 23
Mahler, Alma, 80
Mahler, Gustav, 119, 137, 149, 159, 327, 394, 415, 420, 428, 430, 437, 682
Mai-Dun (Ireland), 372
Maisky, Mischa, 32
Makrokosmos (Crumb), 183
Maksymiuk, Jerzy, 448, 520
Malaniuk, Ira, 626
Malas, Spiro, 210, 316, 605
Malfitano, Catherine, 295
Malgloire, Jean-Claude, 317
Malko, Nikolai, 462
Mallarmé, Stéphane, 190, 194, 358
Malloch, William, 21

Malmö Symphony Orchestra, 620, 781, 782
Malory, Thomas, 245
Man Who Knew Too Much, The (Herrmann), 346
Mancini, Henry, 679
Mandragora (Szymanowski), 721
Manfred Symphony (Tchaikovsky), 734–735
Mann, Thomas, 529
Mann, William, 270
Manon (Massenet), 80, 446
Manon Lescaut (Puccini), 552–553
Mantle, Mickey, 220
Manze, Andrew, 97
Marc, Allesandra, 810
Marcello, Alessandro, 437–438
Marcellus, Robert, 475
March of the Women (Smyth), 677
Marche caprice (Delius), 200
Marche français (Roger-Ducasse), 597
Marche slave (Tchaikovsky), 727
Margalit, Israela, 788
Margiono, Charlotte, 60
Maria Padilla (Donizetti), 211
Maria Stuarda (Bellini), 210
Maria Theresa (Symphony No. 48) (Haydn), 337–338
Maria Theresa, Empress, 483
Maritana (Wallace), 782
Markevitch, Igor, 111, 708
Marnie (Herrmann), 346
Marriage of Figaro, The (Mozart), 446, 483, 487, 489, 497, 511
Marriner, Sir Neville, 2, 29, 60, 226, 313, 315, 329, 331, 477, 488, 517, 584, 602, 604, 718, 732, 739, 768, 770, 806
Marsalis, Wynton, 330, 471
Marsh, Lucy Isabelle, 304
Marshall, Margaret, 527
Martin, Frank, 144, 439
Martin, Thomas, 110
Martineau, Malcolm, 135–136, 748
Martinon, Jean, 49, 90, 100, 369, 434, 437, 457, 513, 619
Martinů, Bohuslav, 227, 368, 440–443
Marthuslav, 227,Martucci, Giuseppe, 443–444
Martyre de Saint Sébastien, Le (Debussy), 188
Marvin, Frederick, 218, 223, 470
Masaniello: Overture (Auber), 17
Mascagni, Pietro, 76, 378, 410, 444, 445, 557
Masefield, John, 156

Mason, Daniel Gregory, 421, 445
Mason, Lowell, 445
Masonic Funeral Music (Mozart), 487–488, 497
Masquerade for Band (Persichetti), 528
Masques et bergamasques (Fauré), 251
Mass for the 500th Anniversary of the Death of Joan of Arc (Paray), 524
Mass in B Minor (Bach), 27–28
Mass in C (Beethoven), 57, 59, 60, 488
Mass in G (Poulenc), 538
Mass in Time of War (Haydn), 332
Mass of Life, A (Delius), 199
Mass: A Theater Piece for Singers, Players and Dancers (Bernstein), 94
Massenet, Jules, 250, 309, 446, 621, 626
Masses for 3, 4 and 5 Voices (Byrd), 152
Masters, Edgar Lee, 496
Masur, Kurt, 60, 346
Mata, Eduardo, 164
Matačić, Lovro von, 108, 407, 652
Mathis der Maler (Hindemith), 350–352, 790
Mathis, Edith, 421–422, 510
Matteuzzi, William, 602–603
Matthews, Colin, 138
Matthies, Silke-Thora, 227
Mauceri, John, 102, 396, 397, 648, 649
Maupassant, Guy de, 134
Maurel, Victor, 760
Maxwell Davies, Sir Peter, 447
May Night (Rimsky-Korsakov), 593
Mayr, Franz, 6
Mayr, Richard, 422
McCabe, John, 334
McCarthy, Senator Joseph, 387
McCartney, Paul, 292
McCawley, Leon, 42
McConnell, Regina, 148–149
McCormack, John, 172, 312, 473, 601, 641, 782
McCowen, Alec, 277
McCracken, James, 99, 630, 631
McDonald, Harl, 264
McDonald, Tim, 561
McEachern, Malcolm, 311
McGegan, Nicholas, 310–311, 316–317, 574
McGlinn, John, 389
McNair, Barbara, 466, 486
Measham, David, 461–462
Meck, Nadezhda, von, 732

Medea (Cherubini), 165
Medea's Meditation and Dance of Vengeance (Barber), 39–40
Meditation from Thaïs (Massenet), 621
Meditations on Ecclesiastes (Dello Joio), 204, 457
Méditations for Orchestra (Marek), 438
Medtner, Nikolai, 448–449
Mefistofele (Boito), 106
Mehta, Zubin, 77, 397, 522, 551, 552, 556, 618, 625, 626, 743, 744, 762, 811
Mei, Eva, 209–210
Meistersinger, Die (Wagner), 350, 461, 772–776, 796
Melba, Dame Nellie, 172
Melchior, Lauritz, 304, 465, 777, 780
Melodie ludowe (Brouwer), 144
Melos Ensemble of London, 142, 195, 612, 638
Melos Quartet of Stuttgart, 453
Melville, Herman, 134, 457
Mencken, H.L., 11, 35, 292, 651
Mendelssohn, Felix, 96, 451, 452, 454, 455, 460
Mendelssohn, Moses, 454
Mengelberg, Willem, 191, 268, 436
Mennin, Peter, 456–457
Menotti, Gian Carlo, 324, 457, 686
Menuhin, Lord Yehudi, 55, 86, 238, 409, 450, 808
Mercadante, Servio, 458
Merchant of Venice, The (Humperdinck), 367
Merchant of Venice, The (Sullivan), 717
Mercury (Symphony No. 43) (Haydn), 337
Merrill, Robert, 101, 103, 444, 550, 551, 755
Merry Mount Suite (Hanson), 323
Merry Widow, The (Lehár), 407, 554, 688
Merry Wives of Windsor, The (Nicolai), 510
Merry Wives of Windsor, The (Sullivan), 718
Merwin, W.S., 42
Messa di Gloria (Puccini), 553
Messager, André, 254, 309
Messe de minuit pour Noël (Charpentier), 163
Messe solennelle (Berlioz), 86
Messe: Cum Jubilo (Duruflé), 217
Messiaen, Olivier, 219, 305, 458, 459, 807

Messiah (Handel), 23, 154, 173, 275, 317, 318, 468
Metamorphic Variations (Bliss), 101–102
Metamorphosen (Respighi), 588
Metamorphosen (Strauss), 701
Metropolitan Opera, 44–45, 99, 295, 345, 551, 649, 726, 754, 757, 776, 799
Metzmacher, Ingo, 327
Meyer, Edgar, 460
Meyer, Nicholas, 367
Meyer, Sabine, 399
Meyerbeer, Giacomo 460–461, 777, 795
Miaskovsky, Nikolai, 461–462, 567
Michelangeli, Arturo Benedetti, 187
Michigan State University Symphonic Band, 296
Microsymphony (Vine), 767
Mid-Winter Songs (Lauidsen), 404
Midsommarvaka (Alfvén), 7
Midsummer Marriage, The (Tippett), 740
Midsummer Night's Dream, A (Britten), 135–137
Midsummer Night's Dream, A (Mendelssohn), 451–453, 455, 456
Midsummer Nocturne (Copland), 177
Mignon: Overture (Thomas), 511
Mikado, The (Gilbert and Sullivan), 282–283
Mikrokosmos (Bartosmosnd
Milanov, Zinka, 444, 751, 752, 762
Milhaud, Darius, 185, 362, 463, 583, 603
Milhaud, Madeleine, 463
Military Symphony (No. 100) (Haydn), 341
Milkov, Mikhail, 571
Millay, Edna St. Vincent, 726
Milne, A.A., 266
Milnes, Sherrill, 101, 410, 551, 608, 751, 755, 759, 760, 762
Minimax (Hindemith), 351
Minjelkiev, Bulat, 506, 592
Minkowski, Marc, 317, 574
Minneapolis Symphony Orchestra, 392, 649, 727
Mintz, Schlomo, 221
Minuet of the Will-o'-the-Wisps (Berlioz), 84
Mirabai Songs (Harbison), 324
Miracle Symphony (No. 96) (Haydn), 341

Miraculous Mandarin, The (Bartlous Mandar*Miroirs* (Ravel), 580
Miserere (Allegri), 8, 523
Miss Donnithorne's Maggot (Maxwell Davies), 447–448
Missa, "De plus en plus" (Ockeghem), 516
Missa, "Fors seulement" (Ockeghem), 516
Missa, "Se la face ay pale" (Dufay), 214
Missa "Pange lingua" (Des Prés), 386
Missa Papae Marcelli (Palestrina), 522
Missa Solemnis (Beethoven), 59–60
Missa vidi speciosam (Victoria), 763
Missa Vox clamantis (Lôbo), 419
Mitchell, R. J., 787
Mitridate, rè di Ponto (Mozart), 473, 490
Mitropoulos, Dimitri, 44, 626, 629
Mlada: Suite (Rimsky-Korsakov), 593
Mládi (Janáček), 380
Moby Dick (Herrmann), 348
Moby Dick (Melville), 137, 308
Moeran, E.J., 372, 464, 681, 792
Mohammed, 471
Moldau, The (Smetana), 675
Molière, 694
Moll, Kurt, 422, 510
Molnar, Ferenc, 793
Molter, Johann Melchior, 465
Mompou, Federico, 465–466, 532
Monet, Claude, 190, 194
Monks of the Monasterio Benedictino de Santo Domingo de Silos, 299
Monn, Georg Mattias, 627–628
Monroe, Marilyn, 2, 110
Monsieur et Madame Denis (Offenbach), 517
Mont Juic (Britten/Berkeley), 82
Monte Carlo Philharmonic Orchestra, 78, 187, 369, 370, 534
Monteux, Pierre, 57, 90, 130, 141, 191, 269, 324, 370, 446, 578, 706
Monteverdi, 466–468
Monteverdi Choir, 23, 27, 28, 31, 59, 60, 86, 87, 317, 334, 467, 468, 471, 486, 536, 559
Montgomery, Kenneth, 296

Montreal Symphony Orchestra, 88, 99, 186, 191, 576, 578, 619, 721, 727
Moonlight Sonata (Beethoven), 62
Moore, Gerald, 124, 250, 641, 642, 748, 780
Moore, Thomas, 468
Moravec, Ivan, 62, 167, 187, 193, 196, 480, 654
Mordkovich, Lydia, 256, 464
Morini, Erica, 269
Mørk, Truls, 567, 660
Morning Watch, The (Rubbra), 615
Moross, Jerome, 469
Morris Dances (Holst), 359
Morrison, Bryce, 168
Mort de Cléopâtre, La (Berlioz), 87
Morzin, Count Fredinand Maxillian von, 336
Mosaics (Hanson), 323
Moscheles, Ignaz, 74, 470
Moscow Radio Symphony, 258, 259
Moscow Virtuosi, 660
Moser, Edda, 367
Moses, 471
Moses, Orel, 149
Moses und Aron (Schoenberg), 629, 631, 632, 714
Moszkowski, Moritz, 520
Motets pour en temps de pénitence (Poulenc), 538
Motets pour le temps de Noël (Poulenc), 538
Mother Goose Suite (Ravel), 577
Mottl, Felix, 422
Mount Saint Helens Symphony (Hovhaness), 364
Mountain Road, The (Moross), 469
Mouse, Mickey, 215
Mouvement symphonique No. 3 (Honegger), 363
Mouvements perpétuels (Poulenc), 538
Mozart, Wolfgang Amadeus, 15, 19, 20, 62, 64, 65, 69, 74, 82, 101, 114, 115, 122, 168, 184, 193, 248, 252, 304, 310, 318, 329, 334, 335, 342, 343, 353, 356, 379, 394, 399, 406, 407, 446, 449, 451, 455, 456, 467, 470–504, 518, 577, 580, 582, 602, 606, 630, 637, 643, 645, 656, 678, 681, 684, 688, 695, 706, 713, 714, 719, 744, 761, 773, 792, 794
Mravinsky, Evgeny, 351, 664–667, 735
Much Ado About Nothing (Doyle), 213

Much Ado About Nothing (Korngold) 41, 39
Muck, Karl, 630, 776, 777
Mueller, Zizi, 183
Muffat, Georg, 319
Mühlfeld, Richard, 121, 122, 126
Muir String Quartet, 582
Müller, Dario, 152
Müller-Stahl, Armin, 316
Müller, Wilhelm, 641, 647
Munch, Charles, 85, 87–90, 163, 188, 270, 370, 578, 619, 775
Münchinger, Karl, 29, 519, 520
Mundy, William, 523
Munich Chamber Orchestra, 6, 186, 470
Munich Philharmonic, Orchestra, 396
Munrow, David, 214, 539, 540
Murger, Henri, 410
Murray, Ann, 643
Murray, Michael, 384–385
Muse ménagère, La (Milhaud), 463–464
Muses of Zion, The (Praetorius), 539
Music for a Great City (Copland), 176
Music for Brass Choir (Riegger), 590
Music for Brass Instruments (Dahl), 185
Music for Prague 1968 (Husa), 368
Music for Strings, Percussion and Celesta (Bartók), 46, 440
Music for the Royal Fireworks (Handel), 318, 496
Music for Westchester Symphony, 400
Music Makers, The (Elgar), 245
Musical Offering, A (Bach), 29
Musical Sleigh Ride (L. Mozart), 470
Musik zu einem Ritterballett (Beethoven), 61
Mussolini, Benito, 443, 444
Mussorgsky, Modest, 12, 37, 107, 108, 288, 387, 505, 506, 508, 568, 592–594, 661, 720
Mustonen, Olli, 7, 8
Muti, Riccardo, 587, 608, 657, 658, 714, 734, 762, 763
Mutter, Anne-Sophie, 24, 145, 424
Muzio, Claudia, 761
My Beloved Spake (Purcell), 558
My Home (Dvořák), 223
My Salute to St. Petersburg March (Lumbye), 423
Mysterious Mountain (Hovhaness), 363, 364

Mystic Trumpeter, The (Hanson), 323
Myths (Szymanowski), 721

Nabucco (Verdi), 751, 756, 758, 777
Nachtstück (Schreker), 636
Nagano, Kent, 154, 155, 262, 536, 544, 545, 712
Nagy, Béla, 769
Näis (Rameau), 574
Namensfeier (Name-Day Celebration) (Beethoven), 61
Nancarrow, Conlon, 509
Nänie (Brahms), 113
Nantucket Songs (Rorem), 599
Napoleon, 61, 74, 392, 519
Narboni, Nicole, 722
Nash Ensemble, The, 52, 534
Nashe, Thomas, 402
Nathan, Regina, 136
National Game (Sousa), 679
National Orchestra of France, 401, 463
National Philharmonic Orchestra, 109, 198, 284, 285, 346, 395, 445, 509, 557, 570, 613, 682, 753, 759, 793
National Symphony of Ireland, 15, 132
National Symphony Orchestra, 15, 132, 277, 370
Natola-Ginastera, Aurora, 284
NBC Symphony Orchestra, 263, 306, 391, 686, 756
Ne Timeas, Maria (Victoria), 763
Neblett, Carol, 551
Negro Folk Symphony (Dawson), 245
"Nelson Mass" (Haydn), 332
Nerat, Harald, 474
Nerone (Boito), 107
Neruda, Pablo, 42
Netrebko, Anna, 289
Neumann, Václav, 222, 225, 272, 376
Neveu, Ginette, 164, 670
New England Triptych (Schuman), 97, 98, 650
New Jersey Symphony Orchestra, 228
New Morning for the World (Schwantner), 261
New Philharmonia Orchestra, 87, 162, 206, 429, 460–462, 488, 550, 574, 652, 749, 771
New Sousa Band, 679
New World Symphony (Dvořák), 148, 160, 227, 228, 234, 443, 686, 799
New World Symphony Orchestra, 185
New York Chamber Orchestra, 628

New York Chamber Symphony, 204, 523, 694
New York Philharmonic, 25, 39, 49, 54, 77, 93, 94, 103, 159, 174, 175, 178, 215, 247, 248, 263, 273, 291, 324, 332, 339, 345, 373, 397, 420, 432, 436, 462, 492, 507, 511–513, 522, 548, 564, 565, 591, 613, 616, 618, 650, 663–665, 722, 726, 730, 743, 775, 811
New York Philomusica, 484
New Zealand Chamber Orchestra, 359, 680, 681
New Zealand Symphony, 204, 457, 469, 537, 582, 613, 614, 738
Newman, Alfred, 346, 509, 574, 608, 634
Newman, David, 510
Newman, Ernest, 16
Newman, Maria, 614
Newman, Randy, 510
Newman, Thomas, 510
Nicholas II, 666
Nicholas Nickleby (Berners), 91
Nicholson, Paul, 13, 314
Nicolaus Esterházy Orchestra, 399
Nielsen, Carl, 259, 356, 357, 421, 511–514, 683, 720, 804
Nietzsche, Friedrich, 199, 200, 263, 692
Night in the Tropics, A (Gottschalk), 293
Night on Bald Mountain, A (Mussorgsky), 108, 508
Nights in the Gardens of Spain (Falla), 248, 270
Nikisch, Arthur, 70, 582, 677
Nikolsky, Gleb, 505
Nilsson, Birgit, 304, 556, 698–700, 702, 775, 778, 796
Nine Catalan Folksongs (Llobet), 419
Nine-Minute Overture (Shapero), 205
Nishizaki, Takako, 482, 483
Niven, David, 6
Nixon in China (Adams), 2, 279
Nixon, Marni, 95, 627
Nixon, Richard M., 94
Noble, John, 747
Nobilissima Visione (Hindemith), 49, 185, 352
Noces, Les (Stravinsky), 710–711
Noche de los Mayas, La (Revueltas), 590
Nocturnal (Britten), 144
Nocturne (Borodin), 108, 110
Nocturne (Britten), 140
Nocturne (Homage to John Field) (Barber), 40
Nocturne (Moeran), 792

Nocturne de printemps (Roger-Ducasse), 597, 598
Nocturne for Strings (Dvořák), 227
Nocturne in E-flat (Schubert), 646
Nocturnes (Chopin), 167 *Midsummer Nocturne* (Copland), 177
Nocturnes (Fauré), 252
Nocturnes (Field), 258 *Nocturne* (Mendelssohn), 451
Nocturnes for Orchestra (Debussy), 191
Nordic Symphony (Hanson), 322
Norfolk Rhapsody, A (Vaughan Williams), 748
Norma (Bellini), 54, 75, 76, 165, 212, 661, 775
Norman, Jessye, 79, 124, 188, 558, 627, 631, 698, 704, 780, 795
Norrington, Sir Roger, 68, 69, 214, 485, 604, 775, 797
Norrköping Symphony, 16, 528, 529, 609
North by Northwest (Herrmann), 346
North Country Sketches (Delius), 203
North German Radio Orchestra, 117
North, Nigel, 97
Northern Chamber Orchestra, 157, 336
Northern Sinfonia, 495
Northwest German Philharmonic, 396
Northwestern University Wind Ensemble, 528
Norwegian Dances (Grieg), 301
Notturno ungherese (Rózsa), 614
Nova Schola Gregoriana, 299
Novák, Richard, 674
Novák, Vítěslav, 515
Novelettes (Glazunov), 354, 355
Novelettes (Poulenc), 538
November Steps (Takemitsu), 722
November Woods (Bax), 51
Novotna, Jarmilla, 408
Now Sleeps the Crimson Petal (Quilter), 561
Now Voyager (Steiner), 682
Nuits d'été, Les (Berlioz), 87
Nun ist das Heil und die Kraft (Bach), 28
Nun komm' der Heiden Heiland (Bach), 27
Nunc dimittis (Walton), 784
Nursery Rhymes (Janáček), 379
Nursery Songs (Mussorgsky), 508

Nursery Suite (Elgar), 244
Nutcracker Suite (Tchaikovsky), 169, 302, 471, 699, 727
Nutcracker, The (Tchaikovsky), 135, 699, 730
Nyman, Michael, 725

O Be Joyful in the Lord (Handel), 312
O clap your hands (Gibbons), 281
O Duinn, Proinnsias, 782
O Jesu Christ, mein's Lebens licht (Bach), 28
O'Connor, Mark, 460
O'Conor, John, 258
O'Neill, Norman, 561
Oberfrank, Géza, 31
Oberon (Weber), 796
Objective, Burma! (Waxman), 793
Oborin, Lev, 65
Obraztsova, Elena, 757
Occasional Overture, An (Britten), 140
Ochni chernye, 720
Ockeghem, Johannes, 516
Ode on the Death of Mr. Henry Purcell (Blow), 104
Ode to a Nightingale (Harty), 328
Odense Symphony Orchestra, 423
Odets, Clifford, 364
ODTAA ("One Damned Thing after Another") Overture (Carwithen), 156
Oedipe (Enescu), 246
Oedipus in Athens: Chorus of the People in the Temple (Mussorgsky), 506
Oedipus Rex (Stravinsky), 246, 711
Oedipus Tyrannus (Paine), 148
Of Human Bondage (Korngold), 395
Of Mice and Men (Copland), 176
Of Reminiscences and Reflections (1992) (Schuller), 649
Offenbach, Jacques, 309, 510, 517, 518, 586, 691
Officium defunctorum (Victoria) 763
Ogdon, John, 100, 149, 150, 740
Ohio State University Concert Band, 364
Oistrakh, David, 65, 116, 352, 390, 462, 547, 721, 729
Oistrakh, Igor, 24
Ojai Festival Overture (Maxwell Davies), 448
Okhotnikov, Nikolai, 549
Okon Fuoko (Madetoja), 428

Old Acquaintance (Waxman), 793
Old American Songs (Copland), 178
Oliveira, Elmar, 575
Olivero, Magda, 285, 808
Olivier, Sir Lawrence, 2, 213, 219, 458, 748, 787, 807
Olsen. Stanford, 471, 607
Omphale's Spinning Wheel (Saint-Saëns), 618
On Dangerous Ground (Herrmann), 346
On Hearing the First Cuckoo in Spring (Delius), 200
On the Town (Bernstein), 94
On the Waterfront (Bernstein), 94
On Wenlock Edge (Vaughan Williams), 748
Onassis, Jacqueline, 94
Oncina, Juan, 603
One Morning in Spring (Hadley), 309
Onegin, Sigrid, 210
Opera North, 277, 789, 790
Opferlied (Beethoven), 53, 54, 57
Opie, Alan, 789, 790
Oppens, Ursula, 627
Oprean, Adelina, 246
Oprean, Justin, 246
Oración del torero (Turina), 354, 355, 743
Orchestra of St. Luke's, 341
Orchestra of the Age of Enlightenment, 330, 606, 794
Orchestra of the Royal Opera House, Covent Garden, 1, 76, 90, 216, 290, 474, 483, 551, 740
Orchestre de la Suisse Romande, L', 439, 730
Orchestre de Paris, 400, 401, 618, 729, 754
Orchestre Révolutionnaire et Romantique, 59, 68, 86
Ordo virtutum (Hildegard of Bingen), 348
Oregon Symphony, 204, 261, 262, 457
Orem, Preston Ware, 152
Orestia, The: Overture (Taneyev), 724
L' Orfeo (Monteverdi), 467
Orfeo ed Euridice (Gluck), 20, 290
Orff, Carl, 131, 345, 519
Organ Symphony (Saint-Saëns), 137, 384, 385, 524, 619
Organ Symphony No. 5 (Widor), 384, 385, 524, 800, 801
Orgonasova, Luba, 471–472

Orkney Wedding, with Sunrise, An (Maxwell Davies), 448
Orlando Consort, 516
Ormandy, Eugene, 169, 177, 198, 203, 204, 306, 352, 475, 481, 544, 563–565, 585, 587, 670, 709, 729, 790
Orpheus Chamber Orchestra, 56, 301, 338, 599, 604, 694, 706, 707, 769
Orpheus in the Underworld: Overture (Offenbach), 517
Oslo Philharmonic Orchestra, 215, 232, 302, 590, 664, 673, 734, 735, 774
Osorio, Jorge, 597
Osorio, Jorge, 597
Osostowicz, Krysia, 123, 253
Ossonce, Jean-Ives, 309, 310
Ostrobothnians, The: Suite (Madetoja), 428
Otaka, Tadaaki, 268
Otello (Verdi), 91, 134, 137, 141, 533, 753, 755, 756, 759
Othello Overture (Dvořák), 232
Ottensamer, Ernst, 475
Otter, Anne Sophie von, 23, 85, 304, 366, 466, 467, 486, 640, 711, 805
Out of the Cradle (Creston), 182
Ouverture de fête (Ibert), 369
Over the Hills and Far Away (Delius), 199, 200
Overlanders, The (Ireland), 372
Overton, Hal, 583
Overture at the Tabard Inn (Dyson), 235
Overture di Ballo (Sullivan), 718
Overture for an Occasion (Ferguson), 256
Overture on Three Russian Themes (Balakirev), 37
Overture to "The Flying Dutchman" as Played at Sight by a Second-Rate Concert Orchestra at the Village Well at Seven O'Clock in the Morning (Hindemith), 351
Overture to a Masque (Moeran), 464
Overture to a Symphony Concert (Rrture to a Ovid, 205
Owen, Wilfred, 142, 150
Oxford Camerata, 214, 253, 254, 280, 281, 426, 657
Oxford Symphony (No. 90) (Haydn), 338
Ozawa, Seiji, 79, 80, 93, 305, 363, 375, 414, 424, 627, 628, 630, 631

Pachelbel, Johann, 5, 515, 519, 523, 595, 770
Pacific 231 (Honegger), 363, 463
Pacific Symphony Orchestra, 325
Paderewski, Ignacy Jan, 520
Pagan Poem, A (Loeffler), 420–421
Paganini, Niccolò, 65, 86, 110, 129, 130, 408, 521, 563, 564, 566, 621, 765, 808
Pageant (Persichetti), 528
Pagliacci, I (Leoncavallo), 410, 444
Pagliara, E. E., 444
Pagodes (Debussy/Grainger), 297
Paillard, Jean-François, 573
Paine, John Knowles, 148, 160, 522
Palais hanté, Le (Schmitt), 188
Palmer, Christopher, 541, 784, 787
Pan (Novák), 515
Pan and Echo (Sibelius), 671
Panambi (Ginastera), 283
Panathenäenzug (Strauss), 701
Panerai, Rolando, 410, 555
Panocha String Quartet, 229, 441, 675, 676
Pantalon und Colombine (Korngold), 473
Panufnik, Andrzej, 523, 524
Papillons (Schumann), 651
Pappano, Antonio, 754
Parable (Persichetti), 528
Paraphrase on Themes from Gounod's Faust (Liszt), 417
Paraphrase on Themes from Verdi's Rigoletto (Liszt), 417
Paray, Paul, 17, 159, 369, 524, 612, 619, 626, 718
Parergon to the Symphonia domestica (Strauss), 701
Pari intervallo (Pärt), 526
Patineurs (Waldteufel), 781
Paris Conservatory Orchestra, 100
Paris Opera, 82, 607, 781
Paris Symphonies (Haydn), 339
Paris Symphony (Mozart), 501–502
Paris — The Song of a Great City (Delius), 198
Parisina d'Este (Donizetti), 209
Parker, Charlie, 753
Parker, Horatio, 373
Parkin, Eric, 161, 235, 372
Parley of Instruments, 13, 14
Parnasse, Le (L'Apothéose de Lully) (Couperin), 181
Parrott, Andrew, 657
Parry, Sir Charles Hubert H., 525

Parsifal (Wagner), 118, 775–777, 779

Parsons, Geoffrey, 58, 123, 124, 430, 498, 642, 703, 805

Pärt, Arvo, 526

Partita for Orchestra (Berkeley), 82

Partita for Orchestra (Ferguson), 256

Partita for Orchestra (Walton), 790

Partita for Woodwind Quintet (Fine), 40

Partridge, Ian, 312, 332, 358, 746, 792

Pasquinade Symphonique No. 2 (Foulds), 265

Passacaglia and Fugue in C minor (Bach/Stokowski), 686

Passacaglia for Organ (Martin), 440

Passing of Beatrice, The (Wallace), 783

Passion according to St. Luke (Penderecki), 527

Passion of Martin Luther King, The (Flagello), 261

Passione, La (Haydn), 337

Pastor Fido, Il (Handel), 316

Pastoral Fantasia (Alwyn), 9

Pastoral Suite (Larsson), 402

Pastoral: Lie strewn the white flocks (Bliss), 101

Pastorale d'été (Honegger), 363

"Pastorale" Symphony (Beethoven), 69, 71

Pastorals (Stowe) (Martinů), 442

Patanè, Giuseppe, 555

"Pathétique" Sonata (Beethoven), 62

Pathétique Symphony (Tchaikovsky), 96, 735

Patience, 282, 283, 718

Patriarchal Choir of Moscow, 720

Patterson, Steven, 144

Patti, Adelina, 737

Patzak, Julius, 429, 641, 689

Pavane (Fauré), 251–253

Pavane for a Dead Princess (Ravel), 576–578, 604

Pavarotti, Luciano, 76, 88, 210, 211, 284, 445, 550, 556, 608, 752, 753, 762

Pay, Anthony, 794

Paynter, David, 528

Peacock Variations (Kodály), 391–392

Pearl Fishers, The (Bizet), 98, 100, 101

Pedrell, Felipe, 277

Peer Gynt (Grieg), 98, 301–303

Peer Gynt (Sæverud), 616

Peerce, Jan, 756

Pelikán, Jan, 225

Pelleas und Melisande (Schoenberg), 630, 632

Pelléas et Mélisande (Debussy), 81, 189, 191, 518

Pelléas et Mélisande (Fauré), 252, 518

Pelléas et Mélisande (Sibelius), 670–672

Pelligrini String Quartet, 150

Penderecki, Krzysztof, 292, 526, 527, 720

Penillion (Williams), 803

Penny, Andrew, 15, 387, 717

Pentola magica, La (Respighi), 586

Pepusch, Dr. John Christopher, 275, 598

Perahia, Murray, 64, 123, 300, 449, 477–479, 482, 491, 493, 494, 637, 651

Perényi, Miklay, 64, *Perfect Fool, The* (Holst), 358–359

Pergolesi, Giovanni Battista, 527, 707, 792

Perle, George, 80, 426

Perlea, Jonel, 751, 752

Perlemuter, Vlado, 580

Perlman, Itzhak, 23, 55, 56, 65–67, 77, 79, 80, 93, 115, 128, 145, 157, 164, 221, 268, 269, 291, 394, 395, 398, 400, 401, 450, 482, 483, 497, 521, 543, 547, 617, 618, 630, 669, 670

Pernambuco, Joao, 384

Perrerin String Quartet, 253

Perséphone (Stravinsky), 707, 712

Persichetti, Vincent, 144, 528

Pešek, Libor, 441, 515, 716

Peste, La (Gerhard), 277

Peter and the Wolf (Prokofiev), 471, 537, 544, 545, 617

Peter Grimes (Britten), 91, 133, 134, 137, 138

Peter Schmoll: Overture (Weber), 796

Petite Suite (Borodin), 109

Petite suite (Debussy), 189

Petite Suite (Roger-Ducasse), 597–598

Petite Suite de Concert (Coleridge-Taylor), 173

Petite symphonie concertante (Martin), 439–440

Petri, Egon, 417, 428, 581, 674

Petrouchka (Stravinsky), 708, 709, 712, 713

Pettersson, Allan, 528–529

Pfitzner, Hans, 523, 529, 626

Pforzheim Chamber Orchestra, 27

Phaedra (Britten), 139

Pháeton (Saint-Saëns), 618

Philadelphia Orchestra, 29, 41, 169, 177, 198, 203, 263, 266, 273, 306, 349, 352, 492, 544, 562–565, 587, 592, 657, 658, 670, 685, 686, 696, 709, 714, 729, 734, 776

Philadelphia Story, The (Waxman), 793

Philadelphia Wind Quintet, 539

Philharmonia Baroque Orchestra, 310, 574

Philharmonia Hungarica, 335, 391, 585

Philharmonia Orchestra, 3, 49, 55, 87, 108, 109, 162, 180, 199, 206, 209, 211, 217, 249, 250, 253, 308, 361, 366, 407, 429, 438, 460, 461, 462, 476, 481, 482, 488, 503, 514, 544, 550, 553, 572, 587, 588, 604, 614, 617, 618, 652, 670, 684, 693, 695, 724, 728, 734, 749, 771, 774, 796

Philip II of Spain, 763

Philip Jones Brass Ensemble, 615, 679

Philips, Peter, 152, 419, 723

Philosopher, The (Symphony No. 22) (Haydn), 336

Phoenix Symphony Orchestra, 348

Phorion (Foss), 264

Phyllis and Corydon (Moeran), 464

Piatigorsky, Gregor, 103, 785

Piazzolla, Astor, 530

Picasso, Pablo, 460, 622

Piccinni, Niccolò, 290

Pickett, Philip, 321

Pictures at an Exhibition (Mussorgsky/Ravel), 288, 507, 592

Pie Jesu (Boulanger), 111

Pièce pour le tombeau de Paul Dukas (Messiaen), 459

Pièces de clavecin (Couperin), 181

Pièces de clavicin (Rameau), 573–574

Pierrot lunaire (Schoenberg), 330, 463, 630, 633, 714

Piezas infantiles (Ginastera), 284

Pilgrim's Progress, The (Vaughan Williams), 747

Pines of Rome (Respighi), 587

Pini, Carl, 732

Pinnock, Trevor, 21, 22, 26, 28, 34, 112, 179, 312, 313, 319–321, 331, 332, 336, 623, 768, 770

Pinza, Ezio, 485
Piquemal, Michel, 217
Pirates of Penzance, The (Gilbert and Sullivan), 282
Pires, Maria João, 303
Piston, Walter, 261, 406, 456, 509, 530, 531
Pistor, Gotthelf, 777
Pittsburgh Symphony Orchestra, 46, 249, 394, 406, 517
Pitz, Wilhelm, 116, 450
Pizzetti, Ildebrando, 531–532
Plameny (Schulhoff), 648
Planets, The (Holst), 361
Plasson, Michel, 100, 101, 266, 267, 295, 370, 668
Plato, 93, 454
Pleasure Dome of Kubla Khan, The (Griffes), 305, 727
Pletnev, Mikhail, 334, 335, 411, 507, 508, 623, 624, 731, 732
Pleyel, Ignaz, 189
Plow That Broke The Plains (Thomson), 738–739
Plummer, Christopher, 31, 787
Plymouth Music Series, 178, 677
Podles, Ewa, 607
Poe, Edgar Allen, 187, 188, 430, 562
Poell, Alfred, 689
Poem of the Forest, The (Roussel), 612
Poème de l'amour et de la mer (Chausson), 163, 252
Poème électronique (Varèse), 715, 743
Poème for Violin and Orchestra (Chausson), 163, 164, 252
Poetic Tone Pictures (Dvořák), 223
Poetic Tone Pictures (Grieg), 301
Pogorelich, Ivo, 459, 546, 547, 580, 623, 624, 767
Pohjola's Daughter (Sibelius), 670–671
Poitier, Diane de, 292
Polish Radio Symphony, 721
Polka Dots (Lubbock), 800
Pollini, Maurizio, 63, 64, 167, 168, 546, 547, 630, 633, 639
Pologne (Holmes), 358
Polovtsian Dances (Borodin), 108–109
Polovtsian March (Borodin), 109
Polyeucte Overture (Dukas), 216
Pomp and Circumstance Marches (Elgar), 237, 242, 315
Ponce, Manuel, 532, 533, 766
Ponchielli, Amilcare, 76, 533, 557
Pons, Lily, 197
Ponselle, Rosa, 75, 444, 752, 753, 755, 782

Pople, Ross, 105–106
Popp, Lucia, 376–378, 435, 474, 486, 487, 555, 606, 638, 696, 698, 799
Porgy and Bess (Gershwin), 95, 278–280
Portland String Quartet, 103
Portugheis, Alberto, 284
Posthorn Serenade (Mozart), 496
Poule, La (Rameau), 574
Poulenc, Francis, 63, 252, 362, 393, 534–539, 580, 606, 714, 722, 801
Pound, Ezra, 11
Pour le piano (Debussy), 196
Praetorius, Michael, 539
Praga (Suk), 716
Prague Carnival (Smetana), 674
Prague Chamber Orchestra, 341, 495, 496, 500
Prague Radio Symphony, 390, 440, 441
Prague String Quartet, 229
Prague Symphony (Mozart), 499–500, 502
Praise We Great Men (Britten), 140
Prayer of St. Gregory (Hovhaness), 364
Prayers of Kierkegaard (Barber), 42
Prégardien, Christoph, 466
Preger, Kurt, 689
Prelude and Liebestod (Wagner), 775
Prelude and Quadruple Fugue (Hovhaness), 364
Prelude, Aria and Finale (Mathias), 447
Prelude in C-sharp Minor (Rachmaninoff), 563
Prelude to a Drama (Schreker), 636
Prelude to the Afternoon of a Faun (Debussy), 188
Prélude, choral et fugue (Franck), 267
Preludios Epigrammaticos (Brouwer), 144
Première Rhapsodie (Debussy), 189
Preminger, Otto, 575
Pressler, Menahem, 73, 504
Preston, Simon, 32, 332
Preston, Stephen, 32, 320
Prêtre, Georges, 162, 187, 188, 534, 537, 611, 619
Previn, Sir André, 41, 140, 141, 143, 145, 177, 205, 239, 240, 249, 266, 323, 394, 450, 451, 459, 517, 519, 532, 533, 540–543, 545, 546, 564, 568, 569, 570, 579, 595, 669, 670, 734, 739, 740, 745, 749, 750, 785, 786, 791

Prey, Herrmann, 421, 422, 553, 642, 643, 648, 773, 799
Přibyl, Vilém, 377–378
Price, Dame Margaret, 125, 643, 747, 753, 779
Price, Leontyne, 39, 246, 444, 473, 550, 644, 688, 693, 698, 752, 753, 755
Primrose, William, 86, 208, 370
Prince Igor (Borodin), 107–110, 289, 592
Prince Igor: Overture (Borodin), 108
Prince of Denmark's March, The (Clarke), 170
Prince of Pagodas, The (Britten), 138
Prince Rostislav (Rachmaninoff), 562–563
Prince Valiant (Waxman), 793
Prinz Csongor und die Kobolde (Weiner), 416
Prinz Eugen (Loewe), 421
Pritchard, Sir John, 216, 581, 739
Private Lives of Elizabeth and Essex (Korngold), 395
Pro Arte Orchestra, 344
Procesie Orchestra, 344 (Turina), 742
Proclamation (Copland), 177
Proctor, Norma, 141
Prokina, Yelena, 549
Prokofiev, Mira, 547
Prokofiev, Sergei, 37, 66, 335, 354, 355, 387, 390, 412, 421, 425, 440, 451, 471, 536, 537, 540–549, 611, 617, 659, 660, 686, 709, 742
Prometheus (Liszt), 418
Prometheus, The Poem of Fire (Scriabin), 657
Protecting Veil, The (Tavener), 725–726
Proust, Marcel, 309
Provvisionata, Francesca, 605
Prunyi, Ilona, 732
Psalm for Band (Persichetti), 528
Psalmus Hungaricus (Kodály), 224, 393
Psaume 24 (Boulanger), 111
Psyché (Franck), 268
Psycho (Herrmann), 346
Puccini, Giacomo, 79, 81, 169, 202, 209, 250, 292, 378, 410, 444, 505, 531, 533, 550, 551–553, 555–557, 589, 761, 806
Puffin' Billy (White), 800
Pulcinella (Stravinsky), 527, 586, 706, 707, 711, 792

Purcell, Henry, 104, 112, 138, 143, 170, 246, 290, 311, 358, 525, 536, 558–560, 575, 684, 791, 792
Puritani, I (Bellini), 76
Purple (Torke), 741
Pushkin, Alexander, 216, 288, 289, 543, 568, 729
Python, Monty, 569

Quadroone, La (Delius), 199
Quantz, Johann, 560
Quartet for the End of Time (Messiaen), 458–459, 807
Quartetto Italiano, 67, 498, 499
Quatre chansons française (Britten), 140
Quatre petites prières de Saint François d'Assise (Poulenc), 538
Quatre pièces brèves (Brouwer), 144
Quattro pezzi sacri (Four Sacred Pieces) (Verdi), 759
Queen Mab Scherzo (Berlioz), 87
Queen of Golconda: Overture (Berwald), 96
Queen Victoria, 455, 717
Queensland Symphony Orchestra, 270
Queler, Eve, 557
Quest, The (complete ballet) (Walton), 788
Quiet City (Copland), 178
Quilico, Louis, 100, 101, 295
Quilter, Roger, 261, 344, 561
Quinten Quartet (Haydn), 333

Rabaud, Henri, 251
Rabinovitch, Alexandre, 130, 497
Rachel Rachel (Moross), 469
Rachmaninoff, Sergei, 13, 35, 47, 100, 110, 111, 206, 302, 388, 425, 448, 451, 562, 563, 565–571, 724
Raff, Joachim, 426, 572
Ragin, Derek Lee, 317
Raglan Baroque Players, 420
Raiders of the Lost Ark (Williams), 804
Raimondi, Ruggero, 603, 754, 756, 757
Rain Coming (Takemitsu), 723
Rake, The (Quilter), 561
Rake's Progress, The (Stravinsky), 324, 706, 713
Rákóczy March (Berlioz), 84
Raksin, David, 102, 272, 346, 459, 530, 572, 573
Rameau, Jean Philippe, 572–574
Ramey, Samuel, 45, 210, 262, 446, 505, 605, 737

Rampal, Jena-Pierre, 476
Rape of Lucretia, The (Britten), 139
*Raphael Ensemble, 125
Rapsodie espagnole (Ravel), 576–577
Raskin, David, 574–575
Raskin, Judith, 433, 713
Rattle, Sir Simon, 46, 120, 143, 213, 239, 280, 297, 331, 333, 345, 431, 435, 459, 630, 635, 652, 663, 673, 721
Rautavaara, Einojuhani, 575
Ravel, Maurice, 3, 89, 109, 159, 164, 189, 190, 192, 195, 246, 249, 252, 297, 354, 355, 369, 385, 391, 451, 459, 507, 576–580, 592, 597, 611, 612, 618, 621, 626, 678, 709, 712, 722, 725, 743
Rawsthorne, Alan, 581
RCA Victor Symphony, 245, 444, 728
Reardon, John, 713
Rebecca (Waxman), 793
Rebikov, Vladimir, 586
Red Pony, The (Copland), 176–177
Red Poppy, The (Glière), 287
Red Shoes Ballet (Easdale), 2, 306
Reed, John, 283
Reformation Symphony (Mendelssohn), 454
Reger, Max, 327, 582
Reher, Curt, 354, 355
Reicha, Antonín, 343, 584
Reichenberg, David, 320
Reilly, Terry, 375
Reiner, Fritz, 46, 68, 69, 72, 73, 114, 115, 117, 127, 128, 182, 189, 190, 222, 246, 289, 299, 339, 340, 363, 364, 416, 540, 544, 565, 576, 582, 587, 593, 604, 689, 692, 696–698, 700, 704, 729, 774, 796, 799
Reinhardt, Max, 367
Reining, Maria, 408, 703, 704
Rejoice in the Lamb (Britten), 135
Reliquary for Igor Stravinsky (Wuorinen), 705
Remedios, Alberto, 740
Renoir, Jean, 194, 463
Requiem Canticles (Stravinsky), 705, 710
Requiem for Six Voices (Lôbo), 419
Resnik, Regina, 44, 688, 689, 698
Respighi, Ottorino, 444, 531, 584–589
Responses for Holy Week (Gesualdo), 281
Resurgam (Rubbra), 614

Resurrection Symphony (Mahler), 83, 431, 626
Rethberg, Elisabeth, 304, 422
Réthy, Esther, 408
Return of Ulysses, The (Monteverdi), 466
Reuben Ranzo (Coates), 172
Revenaugh, Daniell, 149
Rêverie du soir (Tchaikovsky), 732
Rêves (Schmitt), 626
Revue de cuisine, La (Martinů), 441–442
Revueltas, Silvestre, 589–590
Reyne, Hugo, 197
Reynish, Timothy, 297
Reynolds, Roger, 715
Rhapsody in Blue (Gershwin), 278
Rhapsody on a Theme of Paganini (Rachmaninoff), 563, 564, 566
Rheingold, Das (Wagner), 778
Rheinland-Pfalz State Philharmonic, 626
Rhenish Philharmonic, 406
Rhenish Symphony (Schumann), 656
Rhodes, Samuel, 654
Rialto Ripples (Gershwin), 279
RIAS Chamber Choir, 648
Ricciarelli, Katia, 757
Rich, John, 275
Richard III (Smetana), 674
Richard III (Walton), 787
Richter, Sviatoslav, 35, 65, 73, 114, 116, 122, 288, 321, 413, 414, 508, 547, 564, 647, 652
Rickenbacher, Karl Anton, 367, 636
Ricordi, Giulio, 285, 443, 444, 557
Riddle, Frederick, 786
Riders for the Flag (Sousa), 679
Riders to the Sea (Vaughan Williams), 747
Riegel, Kenneth, 84, 332, 415
Riegger, Wallingford, 590
Rienzi (Wagner), 775, 777
Rifkin, Joshua, 22, 27, 28, 385
Rigoletto (Verdi), 211, 417, 755, 757, 760, 762
Rilke, Rainer Maria, 404, 600, 668
Rilling, Helmut, 22
Rimsky-Korsakov, Nikolai, 12, 37, 98, 107, 109, 110, 190, 246, 286, 371, 461, 505, 506, 568, 588, 591–594, 686, 794
Ring des Nibelungen, Der (Wagner), 408, 778

Ringeissen, Bernard, 7, 8, 534
Ringholz, Teresa, 605
Rio Grande, The (Lambert), 401, 402
Ripening, The (Suk), 716
Rite of Spring, The (Stravinsky), 49, 190, 269, 426, 463, 546, 630, 633, 708, 714
Ritmos (Turina), 742
Ritual Dances from *The Midsummer Marriage* (Tippett), 740
Rivera, Diego, 164
Riverrun (Takemitsu), 723
Rob Roy Overture (Berlioz), 88
Robbin, Catherine, 60, 317
Robbins Landon, H. C., 335–337
Robertson, Alec, 101
Robeson, Paul, 389
Robison, Paula, 491
Robles, Marisa, 476
Robyn, Paul, 354
Rock, The (Rachmaninoff), 562, 563, 570
Rockwell, Norman, 10, 287
Rodeo (Copland), 174, 177
Rodrigo, Joaquín, 157, 532, 533, 595–597, 766
Rogé, Pascal, 252, 535, 536, 538, 539, 576, 617, 622
Roger de Coverley (Bridge), 133
Roger-Ducasse, Jean-Jules Aimable, 597
Rogers, Ginger, 393
Rogers, Nigel, 467
Rogers, Will, 335
Roi David, Le (Honegger), 362, 363, 440
Roi de Lahore, La (Massenet), 446
Rolfe-Johnson, Anthony, 317, 467, 468
Roman Carnival Overture (Berlioz), 87, 194
Roman Festivals (Respighi), 585, 587, 588
Romance in G for Violin and Orchestra (Svendsen), 720
Romanesca, 97
Romanian Rhapsody No. 1 (Enesco), 245
Romantic Symphony (Bruckner), 147
Romantic Symphony (Hanson), 321–322
Romeo and Juliet (Diamond), 205
Romeo and Juliet (Prokofiev), 545, 546, 549, 686
Romeo and Juliet (Tchaikovsky), 731
Roméo et Juliette (Berlioz), 88–89
Roméo et Juliette (Gounod), 295

Romero, Angel, 595–596
Romero, George A., 730
Romero, Pepe, 105, 285
Romeros, The, 595–596
Rondine, La (Puccini), 553–554
Rondo capriccioso (Mendelssohn), 449
Röntgen, Julius, 303
Rooley, Anthony, 280, 467, 687
Roosevelt, Franklin Delano, 38, 324
Rorem, Ned, 111, 372, 460, 538, 599
Rosamunde (Schubert), 640, 641, 794
Rosand, Aaron, 118
Rosbaud, Hans, 635
Roscoe, Martin, 53, 171, 207
Rose Pilgerfahrt, Der (Schumann), 655
Rosenberg, Hilding, 600
Rosenberg, Isaac, 150
Rosenberger, Carol, 721
Rosenkavalier, der (Strauss), 487, 510, 636, 692–694, 696, 698, 699, 701–703
Rosenkavalier Waltzes (Strauss), 692
Rosenthal, Manuel, 517
Rosenthal, Moriz, 55, 417, 520
Rosetti, Dante Gabriel, 783
Rosmé: Waltz (Quilter), 561
Rossini, Gioacchino, 17, 209, 210, 216, 411, 452, 458, 517, 521, 531, 586, 596, 601, 602, 603–607, 707, 714, 805
Rostropovich, Mstislav, 65, 103, 116, 121, 221, 329, 462, 549, 660, 661, 668, 736
Rota, Nino, 608
Rothko Chapel (Feldman), 255, 515
Rothko, Mark, 255
Rott, Hans, 609
Rouet d'Omphale, Le (Saint-Saëns), 618
Rouse, Christopher, 609–610
Roussel, Albert, 406, 463, 532, 581, 610–612
Rousset, Christophe, 23, 30, 36, 574
Rowicki, Witold, 231
Royal Concertgebouw Orchestra of Amsterdam, 89–90, 113, 127, 145, 191, 340, 349, 373, 374, 430, 436, 523, 563, 632, 708, 711, 712, 730, 735, 810
Royal Danish Orchestra, 512–513
Royal Hunt and Storm (Berlioz), 88
Royal Liverpool Philharmonic Orchestra, 91, 171, 198, 260, 365, 515, 716

Royal Philharmonic Orchestra, 37, 38, 72, 98, 99, 127, 128, 143, 144, 149, 163, 184, 200, 202, 203, 226, 240, 259, 291, 302, 340, 390, 471, 475, 489, 490, 563, 569, 593, 596, 607, 617, 644, 645, 686, 713, 731, 756, 765, 785, 803
Rozhdestvensky, Gennady, 423, 541, 659, 664, 725, 726, 734, 736, 739
Rozsa, Miklós, 613, 614
RTE Concert Orchestra, 173, 386, 387, 782, 800
RTE Sinfonietta, 92, 717
Rubáiyát of Omar Khayyám (Hovhaness), 364
Rubbra, Edmund, 372, 614, 615, 806
Rubinstein, Anton, 304, 586, 640
Rubinstein, Artur, 167, 270, 647, 651
Rückert Lieder (Mahler), 429
Rudel, Julius, 106, 107, 316, 379, 446
Ruffo, Titta, 737, 752
Rugby (Honegger), 463
Ruggles, Carl, 590
Ruins of Athens, The (Beethoven), 57, 61
Rundell, Clark, 297
Ruralia Hungarica (Kodály), 207
Rus (Balakirev), 36
Rusalka (Dvořák), 225
Russell Davies, Dennis, 174, 326
Russia Cast Adrift (Sviridov), 568
Russian Easter Overture (Rimsky-Korsakov), 686
Russian Funeral Music for Brass and Percussion (Britten), 663
Russlan and Ludmilla (Glinka), 289
Russlan and Ludmilla: Overture (Glinka), 108, 289
Russo, Charles, 375
Rustic Wedding Symphony (Goldmark), 291, 572
Rutter, John, 253, 404, 615
Ruy Blas Overture (Berlioz), 452
Rybakova, Adriana, 720
Rysanek, Leonie, 699, 700, 752, 753

Sabine Meyer Wind Ensemble, 399
Sabre Dance (Khachaturian), 390
Sacher, Paul, 440
Sacred Service (Avodath Hakodesh) (Bloch), 103
Sadko (Rimsky-Korsakov), 289, 592

Sadler's Wells Opera Chorus, 713
"Saga Symphony" (Leifs), 408–409
Saint Anne Prelude and Fugue (Bach/Schoenberg), 633
Saint John Passion (Bach), 30
Saint Matthew Passion (Bach), 30, 31, 588
Saint-Saëns, Camille, 138, 164, 195, 267, 270, 358, 369, 370, 384, 385, 401, 483, 524, 545, 593, 616–619, 621
Sainton, Philip, 308–309
Sakari, Petri, 428, 671, 672
Sakuntala Overture (Goldmark), 291
Salammbô: Chorus of Priestesses (Mussorgsky), 506
Salamunovich, Paul, 404
Salieri, Antonio, 505
Sallinen, Aulis, 620
Salome (Strauss), 91, 626, 687, 698, 701, 702
Salomon Symphonies (Haydn), 340
Salonen, Esa-Pekka, 346, 347, 424, 514, 711
Salve Regina (Poulenc), 163, 538
Sammartini, Giuseppe, 438
Samson et Dalila (Saint-Saëns), 618
Samuel, Gerhard, 610
San Diego Symphony, 87–88
San Francisco Symphony Orchestra, 2, 324, 351, 370, 384, 385, 513, 749
San Giovanni Battista (Stradella), 687
San Juan Capistrano (McDonald), 263
Sancte Deus (Tallis), 723
Sanctuary of the Heart (Ketèlbey), 389
Sandburg, Carl, 177
Sanderling, Kurt, 707
Sanderling, Stefan, 707, 734
Sanders, Samuel, 398
Sándor, György, 47, 49, 773
Sanger, David, 764
Santa Fe Chamber Music Ensemble, 635
Santi, Nello, 410
Sapphic Poem (Bantock), 38
Sappho (Bantock), 37–38
Sarasate, Pablo de, 621
Sargent, Sir Malcolm, 54, 275, 282, 283, 358, 359, 371, 462, 718
Satie, Erik, 91, 266, 466, 534, 622, 623, 626, 722
Saudades do Brasil (Milhaud), 463
Sauer, Emil von, 624
Saul (Handel), 320

Saul and David (Nielsen), 511
Sauvages, Les (Rameau), 574
Savall, Jordi, 32–33
Savio, Isaias, 384
Savitri (Roussel), 360
Sawallisch, Wolfgang, 638, 693, 695, 777, 796
Saÿao, Bidù, 295, 765
Sæverud, Harald, 616
Scala di seta, La (Rossini), 605
Scarlatti, Domenico, 18, 248, 276, 586, 623, 677
Scenes from Adolescence (Schiff), 625
Scenes from the Song of Hiawatha (Coleridge-Taylor), 173
Scenes of Summer (Holdridge), 354
Scharwenka, Xaver, 624
Scheherazade (Rimsky-Korsakov), 98, 190, 593, 594, 686, 708, 730
Schelomo (Bloch), 102
Schenck, Andrew, 42, 400, 457, 738
Scherchen, Hermann, 796
Scherzo à la russe (Stravinsky), 706
Scherzo capriccioso (Dvořák), 222, 232
Scherzo diabolico (Alkan), 8
Scherzo in B-flat (Mussorgsky), 506
Schiff, András, 24, 25, 47, 58, 59, 490
Schikaneder, Emmanuel, 488
Schill, Ole, 514
Schilli, Stefan, 769
Schindler's List (Williams), 629, 804
Schiøtz, Aksel, 512, 514, 641
Schippers, Thomas, 39, 40, 754, 755
Schlagobers (Strauss), 701, 703
Schlagobers Waltz (Strauss), 701
Schlehde, Die (Wüsthoff), 807
Schlick, Barbara, 316
Schmidt, Andreas, 253, 334, 350, 693
Schmidt, Franz, 625–626
Schmiege, Marilyn, 367
Schmitt, Florent, 188, 626, 627
Schnabel, Artur, 54, 55, 61–64, 490, 492, 637, 639
Schneider, Alexander, 496
Schock, Rudolf, 4, 693, 773
Schoenberg, Arnold, 18, 21, 50, 79–82, 119, 120, 125, 133, 153, 185, 193, 263, 277, 325, 330, 354, 355, 382, 439, 441, 463, 509, 510, 514, 531, 574, 582, 590, 600, 606, 611, 625–636, 640, 676, 688, 706, 714, 797, 810

Schola Hungarica, 299, 300
Scholl, Andreas, 154
Schöne Müllerin, Die (Schubert), 512, 641, 642
"School for Scandal" Overture (Barber), 39
Schorr, Friedrich, 774
Schreier, Peter, 58, 59, 487, 488, 777
Schreker, Franz, 307, 396, 636, 637
Schubert Ensemble of London, 207
Schubert, Franz, 16, 52, 59, 62, 72, 74, 100, 123, 129, 136, 207, 218, 228, 279, 309, 339, 354–356, 399, 417, 421, 422, 438, 451, 498, 512, 532, 566, 584, 633, 634, 637–647, 653, 703, 771, 794, 805, 808
Schudel, Regina, 648
Schuldigkeit des ersten Gebots, Die (Mozart), 488
Schulhoff, Erwin, 648
Schuller, Gunther, 80, 385, 649, 782
Schuman, William, 12, 38, 97, 324, 609, 650
Schumann, Clara, 129, 139, 722
Schumann-Heink, Ernestine, 124, 210, 603
Schumann, Julie, 113
Schumann, Robert, 20, 21, 70, 120, 653
Schurmann, Gerard, 2
Schütz, Heinrich, 536, 657
Schwanda the Bagpiper (Weinberger), 131, 400, 799
Schwanengesang (Schubert), 642
Schwantner, Joseph, 261
Schwarz, Gerard, 175, 182, 204, 205, 291, 305, 310, 321–323, 325, 330, 364, 380, 400, 456, 457, 530, 531, 585, 590, 628, 650, 659, 694, 709, 726, 727, 775
Schwarzenegger, Arnold, 542
Schwarzkopf, Elisabeth, 181, 366, 407, 485, 487, 693, 699, 702, 773, 790, 805
Schwarzkopf, General Norman, 177
Scimone, Claudio, 458, 553
Scio, Julie Angélique, 165
Sciutti, Graziella, 485
Scorsese, Martin, 347
Scotch Strasthpy and Reel (Grainger), 297
Scott, Cyril, 561
Scott, Ridley, 322
Scott, Sir Walter, 451
Scottish Ballad (Britten), 140

Scottish Chamber Orchestra, 258, 310, 427, 709, 718, 770
Scottish Fantasy (Bruch), 145
Scottish National Orchestra, 87, 230, 242, 286, 388, 547, 548, 593, 594, 659, 707, 708
Scottish Symphony (Mendelssohn), 455
Scotto, Renata, 165, 285, 445, 555, 557, 759
Scriabin, Alexander, 305, 657, 658, 724
Scribe, Eugène, 17
Sea Drift (Delius), 201, 203
Sea Hawk, The (Korngold), 394–395
Sea Pictures (Elgar), 237, 245, 260
Sea Sketches (Williams), 803
Sea, The (Bridge), 133
Sea Wolf, The (Korngold), 395
Seasons, The (Glazunov), 286
Seasons, The (Haydn), 334
Seasons, The (Tchaikovsky), 731
Seattle Symphony, 175, 182, 204, 321, 322, 456, 530, 650, 726, 775
Sebastian (Menotti), 457, 686
Sedares, James, 204, 348, 613, 614
Seefried, Irmgard, 643, 693, 795, 796
Segerstam, Leif, 511, 528, 529, 575, 597, 598, 609, 626, 627
Segovia, Andres, 419, 532, 533, 595
Segreto di Susanna (Wolf-Ferrari), 806
Sei Lob und Preis mit Ehren (Bach), 28
Semele (Handel), 320
Semiramide (Rossini), 601, 605
Semkow, Jerzy, 721
Sempé, Skip, 182
Semper Paratus, 679
Sendak, Maurice, 391
Sensemaya (Revueltas), 590
Sequenza VII (Berio), 83
Serafin, Tullio, 75, 165, 211, 212, 410, 550, 552, 553, 555, 759, 760
Serenade after Plato's Symposium (Bernstein), 93
Serenade for Nikolai Rubinstein's Saint's Day (Tchaikovsky), 731
Serenade for Strings (Dvořák), 226
Serenade for Strings (Elgar), 241
Serenade for Strings (Suk), 715

Serenade for Strings (Tchaikovsky) 301, 715, 716, 732
Serenade for Strings (Wirén) 402, 804
Serenade for Tenor, Horn and Strings (Britten), 139, 260
Serenade in F (Stenhammar), 683
Serenade in G (Moeran), 792
Serenade in G (Reger), 582
Serenade to Music (Vaughan Williams), 748
Serenata Notturna (Mozart), 495, 496, 499
Sérieuse (Symphony No. 1) (Berwald), 96
Serkin, Rudolf, 21, 54, 62, 64, 74, 114, 121, 479, 646
Serov, Alexander, 289
Serva padrona, La (Pergolesi), 527
Sessions, Roger, 305, 324, 509, 710
Seven Elizabethan Lyrics (Quilter), 561
Seven Last Words of Christ on the Cross (Haydn), 333
Seven Stars Symphony (Koechlin), 393
Seven Studies on Themes of Paul Klee (Schuller), 649
Seventh Voyage of Sinbad (Herrmann), 346
Sèverac, Déodat de, 254
Severn Suite (Elgar), 239
Sextuor for Piano and Wind Quintet (Poulenc), 535, 539
Seymour, Jane, 209
Shaham, Gil, 41, 224, 225, 542, 543, 801
Shaham, Orli, 225
Shakespeare Suites (Humperdinck), 367
Shakespeare, William, 41, 95, 102, 137, 173, 212, 213, 251, 261, 295, 360, 363, 367, 451, 455, 484, 559, 561, 562, 658, 672, 717, 730, 748, 787, 790
Shapero, Harold, 205, 258
Shapiro, Eudice, 326
Sharkfighters, The (Moross), 469
Sharon, Boaz, 464
Shaw, George Bernard, 91, 243, 374, 401, 450, 451, 698, 774
Shaw, Robert, 222, 352, 444, 538, 571, 599
Shchedrin, Rodion, 659, 743
Shearer, Moira, 788
Shelley, Howard, 156, 250, 343, 566, 567, 721
Shelly, Percy Bysshe, 589
Shepherd, Adrian, 14, 206
Shepherd, Jean, 150, 491

Sheridan, Richard Brinsley, 277, 282, 293
Shifrin, David, 121, 493, 579
Shirley-Quirk, John, 30, 84, 134, 136, 137, 139, 142, 320, 435, 629, 790
Short Ride in a Fast Machine (Adams), 2
Shostakovich, Dmitri, 50, 286, 425, 545, 548, 593, 659, 661, 662, 666, 733, 766
Showboat (Kern), 389
Shropshire Lad, A (Butterworth), 150, 151, 748
Shumsky, Oscar, 41, 286
Shure, Paul, 354
Sibelius, Jean, 7, 37, 38, 51, 96, 303, 357, 425, 428, 438, 464, 502, 512, 514, 575, 609, 614, 620, 669–673, 683, 719, 738, 742, 801, 807
Siegeslied (Brian), 132
Siegfried (Wagner), 777–778
Siegfried Idyll (Wagner), 20, 775
Siepi, Cesare, 485, 755
Siete canciones populares españolas (Falla), 250
Signor Bruschino, Il (Rossini), 605
Sillito, Kenneth, 720
Silja, Anja, 81, 82, 771
Sills, Beverly, 316, 446
Silver Apples of the Moon (Subotnick), 715
Silverstone, Paul, 788
Silvestri, Constantine, 240, 749
Sim, Alistair, 135
Simionato, Giulietta, 755
Simmons, Calvin, 100
Simon Boccanegra (Verdi), 760–761
Simon, Geoffrey, 109, 587, 588, 676, 731
Simon, Neil, 496
Simonov, Yuri, 775
Simphonie du Marais, La, 197
Sinatra, Frank, 268, 802
Sinclair, Monica, 275, 603
Sinfonia da requiem (Britten), 140
Sinfonia dolorosa (Sæverud), 616
Sinfonia drammatica (Respighi), 588
Sinfonia espansiva (No. 3) (Nielsen), 512
Sinfonia in memoriam (Holmboe) 356–357
Sinfonia sacra (Panufnik), 523
Sinfonia sacra (Symphony No. 9) (Rubbra), 615
Sinfonia semplice (Nielsen), 513
Sinfonietta (Janáček), 381
Sinfonietta (Korngold), 396

Sinfonietta (Mathias), 447
Sinfonietta (Moeran), 464
Sinfonietta (Piston), 530–531
Singer, Isaac Bashevis, 625
Singher, Martial, 192
Singulière (Symphony No. 4) (Berwald), 96
Sinopoli, Giuseppe, 431, 758
Sir Peter, 135, 138, 139, 142, 239, 786
Sirènes, Les (Berners), 92
Sister Helen (Wallace), 783
Sisyfos (Blomdahl) 103–104
Sitkovetsky, Dmitri, 580
Sitwell, Dame Edith, 786
Sitwell, Sacheverell, 401
Six Monologues from Jedermann (Martin), 439
Six Songs from "A Shropshire Lad" (Butterworth), 151
Sixteen Days of Glory (Holdridge), 353
Sixteen, The, 311–312
Skelton, John, 745
Skelton, Red, 60
Skernick, Abraham, 475
Skvorecky, Josef, 220
Skyscrapers (Carpenter), 148
Slatkin, Eleanor Aller, 354
Slatkin, Felix, 354, 679
Slatkin, Leonard, 11, 40, 41, 43, 175, 176, 387, 531, 548, 576, 578, 728, 804
Slavonic Dances (Dvořák) 224–226, 231
Slavonic Mass (Janáček), 381–382
Sleep, The (Nielsen), 511
Sleeping Beauty, The (Tchaikovsky), 138, 545, 708, 734
Sleigh Ride (Delius), 200
Slezak, Leo, 304, 422
Slonimsky, Nicolas, 183, 386, 397, 405, 509, 743
Slovak Philharmonic, 132, 231, 389, 411, 440, 505, 506, 515, 694
Slovak Radio Symphony, 171, 381, 389, 462, 561, 577, 586, 676, 690
Slovak Suite (Novák), 515
Smetana, Bedřich, 12, 89, 100, 109, 223, 226, 228, 231, 234, 235, 246, 256, 257, 356, 378, 380, 382, 383, 516, 594, 673–676, 729, 751, 799
Smetana String Quartet, 228, 382
Smit, Leo, 177
Smith, Barry, 791
Smith, Daniel, 769
Smith, Eric, 473

Smith, Gregg, 97–98, 264–265, 273
Smokey Mountains Concerto (Addinsell), 2
Smola, Emmerich, 807
Smolka, Jaroslav, 676
Smythe, Dame Ethel, 358
Snow Maiden, The (Rimsky-Korsakov), 593, 732
Snowman, The (Korngold), 396
Söderström, Elisabeth, 378, 379, 381, 568
Sofia National Opera, 107, 288
Salerno-Sonnenberg, Nadja, 32, 785
Solisti Veneti, I, 458
Söllscher, Göran, 530
Solomon, 63, 64, 168, 416, 639, 651, 652
Solomon Trio, 234
Solti, Sir Georg, 31, 46–48, 84, 108, 109, 137, 244, 290, 381, 416, 418, 433–437, 455, 632, 646, 691, 692, 698, 699, 702, 703, 729, 730, 740, 752, 753, 755, 758, 771–774, 776–779
Solyom, János, 683
Sólyom-Nagy, Sándor, 392
Somary, Johannes, 12, 320
Some Trees (Rorem), 599
Somerset Rhapsody (Holst), 359
Sommer, Raphael, 234
Sonata à 4 be mollis (Vejvanovsky), 751
Sonata de concert (Alkan), 8
Sonata sauvage (Antheil), 11
Sonata tragica (Medtner), 449
Sonata-Pathétique (Berger), 470
Sonatas and Interludes for Prepared Piano (Cage), 153
Sonate caractéristique (Moscheles), 470
Sonate posthume (Ravel), 580
Song Before Sunrise (Delius), 200
Song for the Lord Mayor's Table, A (Walton), 784
Song of Bernadette, The (Newman), 510
Song of Solomon (Penderecki), 527
Song of Songs (Foss), 264
Song of Summer (Delius), 202
Song of Terezin, The (Waxman), 793
Song of the Night (Szymanowski), 721
Song of the Nightingale, The (Stravinsky), 364
Songe d'automne (Joyce), 386
Songs after Edith Sitwell (Walton), 784

Songs and Proverbs of William Blake (Britten), 135
Songs of a Wayfarer (Mahler), 429, 430
Songs of Farewell (Delius), 201–202
Songs of Springtime (Moeran), 464
Songs of Sunset (Delius), 200–201
Songs of the Auvergne (Canteloube), 154–155
Songs of Travel (Vaughan Williams), 748
Songs without Words (Mendelssohn), 453
Sonnambula, La (Bellini), 76
Sonzogno, Edoardo, 557
Sor, Fernando, 678
Sorcerer's Apprentice, The (Dukas), 215, 216, 267, 422
Soul's Ransom, The (Parry), 525
Sousa, John Philip, 264, 272, 319, 362, 375, 496, 679, 680
Souvenir d'un soirée à Berlin (Sor), 678
Souvenir of Florence (Tchaikovsky), 733
Souvenirs (Barber), 40, 42–44
Souvenirs (d'Indy), 369–370
Souzay, Gérard, 196, 254, 255
Spagnoli, Piero, 607
Spalding, Albert, 41
Spanish Song Book (Wolf), 805
Sparf, Nils-Erik, 599
Spartacus (Khachaturian), 390
Spem in alium (Tallis), 723
Spenser, Edmund, 85, 559, 788
Spicer, Paul, 241, 360
Spiegelman, Joel, 258–259
Spirit of England (Elgar), 242–243
Spitfire Prelude and Fugue (Walton), 787
Spivakov, Vladimir, 660
Spohr, Ludwig, 680
Spring Sonata (Beethoven), 66
Spring Symphony (Britten), 140–141
Spring Symphony (Schumann), 656
Springtime in Funen (Nielsen), 511
Spurr, Phyllis, 123–124
St. François de Paul marchant sur les flots (Liszt), 417
St. John's Night on Bare Mountain (Mussorgsky), 506
St. Louis Symphony Orchestra, 11, 39–41, 43, 174–177, 387, 531, 548, 562, 576, 577
St. Paul (Mendelssohn), 450
St. Paul Chamber Orchestra, 174

St. Paul's Suite (Holst), 359
St. Thomas Wake (Maxwell Davies), 448
Stabat mater (Dvořák), 224, 228
Stabat mater (Pärt), 526
Stabat mater (Pergolesi), 527
Stabat mater (Poulenc), 538
Stabat mater (Rossini), 606
Stabat mater (Szymanowski), 721
Stadium Symphony of New York, 730
Stadlmair, Hans, 6, 186, 470, 471
Stalin, Josef, 287, 387, 390, 541, 542, 571, 661, 664–666
Stallone, Sylvester, 61
Stamitz, Carl, 366
Stamitz, Johann, 366, 680, 681
Standage, Simon, 405, 406, 768, 770
Stanford, Sir Charles Villiers, 681
Stankovsky, Robert, 462, 676
Star Dawn (Hovhaness), 364
"Star-Spangled Banner, The," 148, 706, 756
Star Wars (Williams), 596, 804
Stargell, Willie, 74
Starker, János, 33, 103, 129, 393
Starlight Express (Elgar), 140, 245
Stars and Stripes Ballet (Sousa/Kay), 680
Stasov, Vladimir, 36, 109
Stavanger Symphony, 616
Steber, Eleanor, 39, 43, 44
Steiger, Rod, 31
Stein, Gertrude, 739
Stein, Horst, 582
Stein, Leonard, 627
Steinbeck, John, 176
Steinberg, William, 265
Steiner, Fred, 634, 682
Steiner, Max, 197, 347, 575, 682, 793
Stenhammar, Wilhelm, 683
Stepán, Pavel, 229
Stephen Collins Foster: A Commemoration Symphony (Bennett), 265
Stern, Isaac, 25, 41, 219, 793
Sterndale Bennett, William, 684
Steuermann, Clara, 628
Steuermann, Eduard, 193, 633
Stevens, Wallace, 323, 373
Stevenson, Adlai, 177
Stevenson, John, 468
Stewart, Patrick, 545
Stiers, David Ogden, 493
Stignani, Ebe, 75
Still, Ray, 25

Stockholm Philharmonic Orchestra, 7, 79, 103, 104, 599
Stockholm Sinfonietta, 274
Stockton, Ann Mason, 354
Stokowski, Leopold, 29, 99, 110, 245, 246, 287, 298, 420, 421, 564, 565, 570, 585, 633, 658, 667, 671, 673, 685, 686, 730, 735, 739, 774, 776
Stolze, Gerhard, 698, 702, 778
Stolzman, Lucy Chapman, 326
Stoltzman, Richard, 121, 122, 493, 539
Stonecracker John (Coates), 172
Strada, Anna, 317
Stradella, Allesandro, 687
Stratas, Teresa, 389
Straus, Oscar, 687–688
Strauss, Johann II, 118, 272, 408, 423, 530, 688, 689, 703
Strauss, Josef, 690[endash]691
Strauss, Pauline, 286
Strauss, Richard, 38, 89, 343, 394, 396, 502, 510, 588, 648, 682, 687, 695, 697, 700, 703, 793
Straussiana (Korngold), 396
Stravinsky, Igor, 27, 33, 49, 91, 137, 148, 155, 169, 185, 190, 246, 255, 258, 269, 280, 286, 288, 305, 324, 356, 364, 387, 411, 426, 440, 442, 447, 463, 502, 509, 527, 533, 546, 584, 586, 593, 596, 600, 611, 612, 626, 633, 705–714, 723, 725, 741, 767, 768, 792
Street Scenes (Wüsthoff), 807
Streich, Rita, 693, 795, 796
Streisand, Barbra, 330
String Symphony (Rorem), 599
Stringer, Alan, 329
Stücke im Volkston (Schumann), 655
Studer, Cheryl, 43, 262, 295, 407, 762, 763, 777
Studies for Player Piano (Nancarrow), 509
Stuttgart Chamber Orchestra, 29, 519, 520
Stutzmann, Nathalie, 310, 311, 317
Subotnick, Morton, 715
Suite bergamasque (Debussy), 196
Suite for the Birthday of Prince Charles (Tippett), 740
Suite from Smetana's Sketch Book (Smetana/Smolka), 676
Suite in F (Roussel), 612
Suite in F-sharp (Dohnányi), 208
Suite in the Olden Style (Reger), 582

Suite on English Folk Tunes (A Time There Was . . .) (Britten), 140
Suite pastorale (Chabrier), 159, 216
Suites (2) for Military Band (Holst), 362
Suk, Josef, 515, 715
Suk Trio, 74
Suliotis, Elena, 758
Sullivan, Sir Arthur, 282–283, 517
Summer Evening (Delius), 200
Summer Music (Barber), 40, 412
Summer Music (Bax), 51
Summer Music (Rorem), 599
Summer Night on the River (Delius), 200
Summer's Last Will and Testament (Lambert), 402
Summerfield, Susan, 326
Summerly, Jeremy, 214, 253, 254, 280, 281, 419, 426, 657
Sunday Morning (Rorem), 599
Sunrise Quartet (Haydn), 333
Sunrise Serenade (Sallinen), 620
Sunset Boulevard (Waxman), 793
Suor Angelica (Puccini), 555
Superman (Williams), 804
Suppé, Franz von, 718, 719
Surprise Symphony (Haydn), 69, 340, 341, 645
Survivor from Warsaw (Schoenberg), 277, 629, 630
Susannah (Floyd), 262
Sussex Overture (Arnold), 14
Suthaus, Ludwig, 779
Sutherland, Joan, 1, 75, 76, 169, 197, 198, 210, 212, 275, 317, 446, 460, 461, 485, 518, 556, 601, 605, 737, 762, 778
Švejda, Antoinette (Author's grandmother), 163, 337, 364, 592, 644
Svejda, Otto (Author's father), 73, 163
Švejda, Václav (Author's grand-father), 157, 163, 631
Svendsen, Johann, 719, 720, 804
Sveshnikov, Alexander, 720
Svetlanov, Evgeny, 36, 37, 388, 733, 734
Sviridov, Georgy, 568
Swan Lake (Tchaikovsky), 545, 734
Swan of Tuonela (Sibelius), 9, 670, 671, 673
Swann, Donald, 544–545
Swanwhite (Sibelius), 671–672
Swed, Mark, 432
Swedish Folk Melodies (Svendsen), 719, 804

Swedish Radio Symphony, 96, 402, 711
Swedish Rhapsody No. 1 (Alfvén), 7
Sweet Psalmist of Israel (Ben Haim), 77
Swieten, Baron Gottfried von, 19
Swift, Jonathan, 275
Swingle Singers, 83, 397
Sylphides, Les (Chopin), 169, 517
Sylvia (Delibes), 134, 169, 198, 466
Symbolon (Zwilich), 811
Symphonia Domestica (Strauss), 701, 704
Symphonia serena (Hindemith), 351–352
Symphonic Dances (Grieg), 301
Symphonic Dances (Rachmaninoff), 562, 563, 568–571
Symphonic Etudes (Schumann), 684
Symphonic Metamorphosis on Themes of Carl Maria von Weber (Hindemith), 351
Symphonic Minutes (Dohnányi), 208
Symphonic Ode (Copland), 175
Symphonic Poem after Descartes (Vincent), 204
Symphonic Serenade (Korngold), 396
Symphonic Sketches (Chadwick), 160
Symphonic Songs (Bennett), 359, 375
Symphonic Songs (Zemlinsky), 810
Symphonic Study of Jerome Kern, A (Bennett), 265
Symphonic Variations (Dvořák), 117
Symphonic Variations (Franck), 270
Symphonic Variations (Parry), 525
Symphonie espagnole (Lalo), 400, 401, 617
Symphonie fantastique (Berlioz), 86, 87, 88, 89, 90
Symphonies pour les soupers du Roi (DeLalande), 197
Symphonische Gesänge (Zemlinsky), 810
Symphony 1933 (Harris), 325
Symphony 1997 (Dun), 214–215
Symphony for Classical Orchestra (Shapero), 205
Symphony for Strings (No. 5) (Schuman), 650
Symphony in C (Bizet), 98–99

Symphony in C (Stravinsky), 612, 714, 715
Symphony in C Dukas), 216
Symphony in Three Movements (Stravinsky) 612, 613, 714
Symphony of a Thousand (Mahler), 415, 435
Symphony of Psalms (Stravinsky), 710, 714
Symphony of Sorrowful Songs (Górecki), 291
Symphony of the Air, 739
Symphony on a French Mountain Air (d'Indy), 270, 370
Symphony on a Hymn Tune (Thomson), 739
Syrinx (Debussy), 195
Szell, George, 26, 44, 46, 54, 55, 57, 61, 68, 70, 72, 114, 116, 120, 126–128, 143, 220, 222, 226, 233, 318, 319, 340, 352, 381, 392, 424, 433, 455–457, 475, 478–481, 492, 501, 503, 542, 544, 656, 675, 676, 697–699, 709, 789–791
Szeryng, Henryk, 129, 646
Szidon, Roberto, 415
Szigeti, Joseph, 46, 48, 51, 66, 808
Szimfonikus percek (Dohnányi), 208
Szmytra, Elzbieta, 721
Szokolay, Balázs, 49, 50, 302
Szymanowski, Karol, 396, 397, 440, 720, 721

Tabarro, Il (Puccini), 555
Tabuteau, Marcel, 492
Tacchino, Gabriel, 534
Tagliavini, Ferruccio, 211, 212
Tailleferre, Germaine, 393, 722
Tairov, Alexander, 543
Takashima, Tomoko, 399
Takemitsu, Toru, 144, 722, 723
Takezawa, Kyoko, 41
Tales of Hoffman, The (Offenbach), 517–518
Talich String Quartet, 229
Talich, Václav, 226, 227, 229, 230, 232–234, 377, 515, 675, 716
Tall Story, A (Moross), 469
Tallis Scholars, 151, 152, 386, 419, 522, 523, 723
Tallis, Thomas, 151, 723
Talleyrand, Charles Maurice de, 218
Talmi, Yoav, 87–88
Tamara (Balakirev), 37
Tambourin (Rameau), 574
Tan, Melvyn, 797
Tancredi (Rossini), 601, 607

Taneyev, Sergei, 256, 462, 724
Tango des Fratellini (Milhaud), 464
Tannhäuser (Wagner), 246, 776, 779
Tansman, Alexandre, 532, 724, 725
Tapiola (Sibelius), 670, 673
Tarantelle styrienne (Debussy), 189
Taras Bulba (Janáček), 381, 515
Taras Bulba (Waxman), 793
Tarpeja: Triumphal March (Beethoven), 61
Tasso (Liszt), 418
Tate, Jeffrey, 143, 154, 366, 480
Tátrai String Quartet, 333
Taub, Robert, 18
Taube, Michael, 220
Tauber, Richard, 304, 408, 429, 473
Tavener, John, 725–726
Taverner Consort, 657
Taverner, John, 536
Taxi Driver (Herrmann), 346–347
Taylor, Deems, 726, 728
Tchaikovsky, Peter Ilyich, 12, 17, 37, 47, 74, 94, 96, 109, 138, 146, 169, 190, 194, 207, 221, 232, 286, 301, 302, 354, 355, 388, 414, 471, 543, 545, 568, 569, 571, 591, 594, 617, 660, 664, 707, 708, 716, 724, 727–736, 796, 801
Tchakarov, Emil, 107, 288
Te Kanawa, Dame Kiri, 95, 154, 155, 216, 275, 347, 472, 485, 488, 553, 554, 703, 704
Tear, Robert, 84, 236, 748
Tebaldi, Renata, 158, 551, 552, 755, 756
Tehillim (Reich), 583
Telemann, Georg Philipp, 27, 105, 490, 598, 736, 737
Telemann Society, 27, 736
Tellefsen, Arve, 668
Temirkanov, Yuri, 390, 541
Tempest, The (Honegger), 363
Tempest, The (Humperdinck), 367
Tempest, The (Sibelius), 672
Temple de la Gloire, Le (Rameau), 574
Tempora Mutantur (Symphony No. 64) (Haydn), 338
Tender Land, The (Copland), 178
Tenebrae Responsories (Victoria), 763
Tennstedt, Klaus, 137, 145, 631, 774
Tennyson, Alfred, Lord, 525

Terakado, Ryo, 574
Terfel, Bryn, 136, 173, 310, 643, 748
Terpsichore Dances (Praetorius), 539
Terroni, Rafael, 172
Teseo (Handel), 317
Testament of Freedom (Thompson), 738
Tetrazzini, Luisa, 304, 601, 737
Tetrazzini, Louisa, 212
Thalberg, Sigismond, 470
Thamos, King of Egypt (Mozart), 473
Thanksgiving and/or Forefather's Day (Ives), 374
Tharaud, Alexandre, 463–464
The Art of Fugueing (Bach/Malloch), 21
The Bear (Symphony No. 82) (Haydn), 339
The Dance Around the Gold Calf (Schoenberg), 632
The English (Symphony No. 5) (Parry), 525
The Fall of Pháeton (Dittersdorf), 206
The Hen (Symphony No. 82) (Haydn), 339
The Kreutzer Sonata (Quartet No. 1) (Janáček), 382
The Past is in the Present (1994) (Schuller), 649
The Revelation of St. John (Rosenberg), 600
The Song of Terezin (Waxman), 793
The Year 1905 (Symphony No. 11) (Shostakovich), 666
The Year 1911 (Symphony No. 12) (Shostakovich), 667
Thebom, Blanche, 779
Theme, Variations and Finale (Rózsa), 613–614
Theodora (Handel), 317, 318, 320
There is Sweet Music (Elgar), 242
There Is a Willow Grows Aslant a Brook (Bridge), 133
Theresienmesse (Haydn), 332
Théruel, Gérard, 192
Thibaud, Jacques, 66, 646, 808
Thibaudet, Jean-Ives, 417, 567
Thielemann, Christian, 529
Things to Come (Bliss), 101, 102
Third Construction (Cage), 153
Thomas, Ambroise, 159, 737
Thomas, Dylan, 705, 786
Thomas, Edward, 150
Thomas, Jess, 776
Thompson, Randall, 738
Thomson, Bryden, 51, 245, 328, 372, 744, 788

Thomson, Virgil, 325, 738
Thoreau, Henry David, 405
Thorstenberg, Laurence, 269
Thousand Kisses, A (Joyce), 386
Three Botticelli Pictures (Respighi), 589
Three Compositions for Piano (Babbitt), 18
Three-Cornered Hat, The (Falla), 246, 248, 249
Three Elizabeths, The (Coates), 172
Three English Dances (Quilter), 561
Three Mantras (Foulds), 265
Three Mysteries (Symphony No. 2) (Creston), 182
Three New England Sketches (Piston), 531
Three Occasions (Carter), 156
Three Pieces for Orchestra (Berg), 91
Three Places in New England (Ives), 375
Three Poems of Fiona McLeod (Griffes), 305
Three Portraits (Vaughan Williams), 750
Three Rhapsodies for String Quartet (Dyson), 365
Three Sketches (Ferguson), 256
Threepenny Opera, The (Weill), 798
Threnody for the Victims of Hiroshima (Penderecki), 292, 526
Through the Looking Glass (Taylor), 726
Thunderbird Suite (Cadman), 152
Tiant, Luis, 74
Tibbett, Lawrence, 760
Tiefland (d'Albert), 4
Till Eulenspiegel's Merry Pranks (Strauss), 86, 692, 697
Tilson Thomas, Michael, 57, 185, 187, 374, 375, 432, 530, 705, 735, 798
Time Cycle (Foss), 263–264
Tippett, Sir Michael, 9, 51, 142, 447, 739, 740
Titan (Symphony No. 1) (Mahler), 430
Tjeknavorian, Loris, 109
Toccata and Fugue in D minor (Bach), 686
Toccata Concertante (Fine) 258–259
Toch, Ernst, 356
Todi, Jacapone, 228
Tokyo String Quartet, 491, 579
Toll, John, 97
Tolstoy, Leo, 382, 562

Tombeau de Couperin, Le (Ravel), 576, 580
Tomes, Susan, 123, 253
Tomita, Isao, 715
Tomlinson, Ernest, 172, 344, 800
Tomowa-Sintow, Anna, 396, 397, 702
Tomter, Lars Anders, 789
Torke, Michael, 412, 741
Torn Curtain (Herrmann), 346–347
Toronto Symphony Orchestra, 565
Torquato Tasso (Donizetti), 219
Tortelier, Paul, 697
Tortelier, Yan Pascal, 215, 219, 351, 369, 801
Tosca (Puccini), 169, 379, 554, 761
Toscanini, Arturo, 16, 34, 44, 68, 70, 88, 126, 268, 306, 443, 507, 551, 554, 565, 686, 738, 756
Totentanz (Liszt), 414
Tourangeau, Huguette, 210, 460, 518
Tourel, Jennie, 263
Touvron, Guy, 465
Tower of Saint Barbara, The (Dahl), 185
Toy Symphony (L. Mozart), 379, 470, 792
Toye, Geoffrey, 800
Tozer, Geoffrey, 581, 585, 586
Tragédie de Salomé (Schmitt), 626
Tragic Interlude (Alwyn), 9
Tragic Symphony (Mahler), 434
Tragic Symphony (Schubert), 645
Traherne, Thomas, 260
Tramonto, Il (Respighi), 444, 589
Transatlantic Tango (Antheil), 11
Transcendental Études (Liszt), 416
Trapp Family, 442
Traubel, Helen, 304
Trauer Symphony (No. 44) (Haydn), 337–338
Trauermusik for Viola and String Orchestra (Hindemith), 351
Traviata, La (Verdi), 211, 751, 761, 762
Tre composizioni corali (Pizzetti), 531
Tree Line (Takemitsu), 23
Treemonisha (Joplin), 385
Trees So High, The (Hadley), 308
Treigle, Norman, 106, 262, 316
Triana (Albéniz), 246
Tribute to Foster (Grainger), 297
Triebensee, Josef, 489
Trimble, Lester, 235

Triple Concerto (Beethoven), 56
Tripp, Paul, 705
Tristan und Isolde (Wagner), 75, 80, 246, 422, 443, 773, 775, 779, 780
Trittico, Il (Puccini), 555, 589
Triumph of Neptune, The (Berners), 91–92
Triumph of St. Joan Symphony, The (Dello Joio), 204
Troilus and Cressida (Walton), 789–790
Trois mouvements perpéuels (Poulenc), 535
Trois pièces brèves (Ibert), 369
Trois romances sans paroles (Fauré), 252
Tropisms pour des amours imaginaires (Ibert), 369
Trostiansky, Alexander, 13
Trouble with Harry, The (Herrmann), 346
Trout Quintet (Schubert), 639–640
Trovatore, Il (Verdi), 574, 758, 762
Troyanos, Tatiana, 95, 630, 631
Troyens, Les (Berlioz), 72, 87, 88, 90
Tsar Saltan (Rimsky-Korsakov), 593
Tsutsui, Kaori, 399
Tuba Concerto (Vaughan Williams), 750
Tubin, Eduard, 741–742
Tuckwell, Barry, 128, 139, 140, 329, 476, 477
Turandot (Puccini), 81, 169, 506, 511, 536, 551, 556
Turangalîla Symphony (Messiaen), 458–459
Tureck, Rosalyn, 27
Turina, Joaquín, 355, 742
Turn of the Screw, The (Britten), 136, 141
Turnovsky, Martin, 475
Turovsky, Yuli, 13, 312, 313, 743
Twain, Mark, 491
Twelve, The (anthem) (Walton), 784
Twelve Welsh Folk Songs (Holst), 360
Two Aquarelles (Delius), 202
Two Ballads for Baritone and Orchestra (Ferguson), 256
Two English Idylls (Butterworth), 150
Two Fanfares (Adams), 2
Two-Headed Spy (Schurmann), 2
Two Pictures (Bartók), 48
Two Sketches Based on Indian Themes (Griffes), 445
Tzigane (Ravel), 164, 580, 618, 621

Über Berg, Über Tal: Overture (Suppé), 719
UC Berkeley Chamber Chorus, 255
Uchida, Mitsuko, 193, 480, 490
Uemura, Kaori, 574
Ukrainian State Symphony Orchestra,
Ulster Orchestra, 51, 133, 189, 203, 215, 222, 244, 251, 328, 369, 464, 535, 681, 791, 792
Unanswered Question, The (Ives), 373–375
Under the Spreading Chestnut Tree (Weinberger), 799
Unfinished Symphony (Schubert), 645–646
Unger, Gerhard, 58, 180, 471, 771, 773
University of Michigan Musical Society Choral Union, 732
Upshaw, Dawn, 154, 155, 291, 324, 446, 805
USSR Academic Symphony, 733
Ustinov, Peter, 392, 537
Utah Symphony Orchestra, 293, 363, 371

Va Pensiero Chorus (Verdi), 758
Valentini-Terrani, Lucia, 527
Valéry, Paul, 289, 507, 549, 592, 617
Vallée de cloches, La (Debussy/Grainger), 297
Valley of the Gwangi (Moross), 469
Valse caprice (Fauré), 252
Valses nobles et sentimentales (Ravel), 576–577
Valses Poeticos (Granados), 299, 419
Van Dam, José, 84, 85, 246, 295, 536, 699, 754, 760
Vanessa (Barber), 44
Vänskä, Osmo, 184, 408, 670
Varady, Julia, 693, 699
Varcoe, Stephen, 253, 260, 261, 309, 561, 643
Varèse, Edgar, 271, 354, 383, 384, 396, 614, 715, 743, 744, 804
Vargas, Ramon, 605
Variations (Aldous Huxley in Memoriam) (Stravinsky), 705
Variations for Orchestra (Schoenberg), 635
Variations on "America" (Ives/Schumann), 650
Variations on a Dublin Air (Harty), 328
Variations on a Nursery Song (Dohnányi), 206–207

Variations on a Rococo Theme for Cello and Orchestra (Tchaikovsky), 736
Variations on a Theme by Corelli (Rachmaninoff), 568–569
Variations on a Theme by Haydn (Brahms), 127, 130
Variations on a Theme by Hindemith (Walton), 352, 790
Variations on a Theme by Mozart (Reger), 582
Variations on a Theme of Hiller (Reger), 582
Variations on a Theme of Tchaikovsky (Arensky), 12
Variations on a Waltz (Moross), 469
Variations sérieuses (Mendelssohn), 449, 452
Variazioni Concertanti (Giuliani), 285
Värmland Rhapsody (Atterberg), 16
Vásáry, Tamas, 208, 589
Vaughan Williams, Ralph, 2, 51, 101, 150, 151, 235, 241, 251, 261, 265, 308, 309, 344, 360, 365, 375, 464, 614, 681, 714, 723, 744–750, 763, 788, 803
Veasey, Josephine, 84, 90, 91, 137
Vega, Lope de, 764
Vejvanovsky, Pavel, 751
Vengerov, Maxim, 660
Veni, Veni, Emmanuel (MacMillan), 427
Venusberg Music (Wagner), 246
Verbit, Marthann, 11
Verdi, Giuseppe, 76, 88, 106, 107, 110, 137, 141, 209, 211, 224, 239, 253, 306, 357, 473, 532, 533, 550, 553, 601, 751–762, 773, 777
Verklärte Nacht (Schoenberg), 125, 354, 355, 630, 635, 636, 640
Vermillion, Iris, 649
Verrett, Shirley, 757, 758
Vert-Vert: Overture (Offenbach), 517
Vertigo (Herrmann), 346
Vesperae solennes de confessore (Mozart), 485
Vespers (Rachmaninoff), 571
Vespers of 1610 (Monteverdi), 468
Vespri siciliani, I (Verdi), 760, 762
Vetrate di chiesa (Respighi), 587
Vexilla Regis (Ireland), 371
Vicek, Oldrich, 495
Vickers, Jon, 58, 90, 91, 318, 759, 776

Victoria and Merrie England (Sullivan), 717
Victoria, Tomás Luis de, 764
Vida breve, La (Falla), 246, 249, 250
Vidi speciosam (Victoria), 763
Vie parisienne, La: Overture (Offenbach), 517
Vienna Johann Strauss Orchestra, 408, 689
Vienna Mozart Academy, 475
Vienna Octet, 267, 639
Vienna Philharmonic Orchestra, 57, 58, 60, 68, 70, 71, 81, 90, 117, 126, 127, 130, 146, 227, 376–379, 381, 407, 428, 429, 434, 436, 482, 483, 501, 510, 603, 625, 626, 646, 688, 689, 692, 698, 699, 702, 772, 774, 776, 778–780
Vierne, Louis, 254, 764, 801
Vieuxtemps, Henri, 765
Vignoles, Roger, 40, 792
Vingt regards sur l'enfant Jésus (Messiaen), 458
Vigny, Alfred de, 358
Villa-Lobos, Heitor, 157, 283, 354, 384, 532, 533, 595, 743, 765
Village Romeo and Juliet, A (Delius), 202
Villon, François, 783
Vinay, Ramon, 211, 753
Vine, Carl, 767
Vintner's Daughter, The (Rózsa), 613
Viotti, Giovanni Battista, 605
Virgil, 325, 421, 738
Virtuosi di Praga, 751
Visconti, Luchino, 608, 754
Vishnevskaya, Galina, 142, 549, 661
Vistas (Mathias), 447
Vivaldi, Antonio, 5, 6, 18, 138, 276, 406, 438, 490, 533, 597, 617, 766–769
Vivaldi, Gian-Battista, 769
Vlach, Joseph, 480
Vltava (Smetana), 246
Vocalise (Rachmaninoff), 562, 563, 567, 568
Vogel, Alan, 421
Vögel, Die (Braunfels), 131
Vogt, Lars, 652
Völker, Franz, 422
Voltaire, François Marie Arouet de, 291, 495, 573
Von Stade, Frederica, 84, 196, 389, 446, 466, 474, 601, 602
Voříšek, Jan Václav, 223, 770
Votto, Antonino, 533
Vox balaenae (Voice of the Whale) (Crumb), 183

Vox patris caelestis (Mundy), 523
Voyage to Greece (Wüstoff), 807

Wächter, Eberhard, 81, 407, 485, 487, 688, 695, 702, 795
Wagner, Richard, 20, 38, 70, 72, 75, 80, 89, 118, 121, 134, 147, 180, 190, 200, 216, 232, 246, 251, 350, 358, 380, 381, 385, 408, 409, 414, 417, 421, 422, 443, 450, 461, 572, 609, 610, 668, 680, 683, 689, 690, 700, 771–780, 795
Waldscenen (Schumann), 651
Waldstein Sonata (Beethoven), 63
Waldteufel, Emile, 781
Walk to the Paradise Garden (Delius), 202
Walker, George, 781
Walküre, Die (Wagner), 704, 777, 778, 780
Wallace, Sir William, 783
Wallace, Vincent, 783
Wallace, William, 37, 782
Wallberg, Heinz, 799
Wallenstein's Camp (Smetana) 674–675
Wallfisch, Elizabeth, 420
Wallfisch, Raphael, 198, 260, 330, 372, 464, 589, 769
Wally, La (Catalani), 158
Walsh, Raoul, 793
Walter, Bruno, 43, 44, 71, 72, 89, 124, 126, 131, 147, 233, 429, 431, 486, 496, 502, 504, 529, 645, 777
Walton, Lady Susana, 786
Walton, Sir William, 9, 51, 91–93, 203, 213, 256, 352–355, 359, 372, 375, 440, 447, 495, 784–791
Wand of Youth Suites (Elgar), 244
Wanderer Fantasie (Schubert), 647
War and Peace (Prokofiev), 543, 549
War Requiem (Britten), 94, 139, 142, 143
Ward, Nicholas, 336–338
Warlock, Peter, 111, 261, 344, 402, 746, 791, 792
Warlord, The (Moross), 469
Warner Brothers Orchestra, 395, 793
Warner, Jack L., 793
Warren-Green, Christopher, 241, 715, 716
Warren, Leonard, 762
Warriors, The (Grainger), 297, 361
Warsaw Concerto (Addinsell), 2, 306, 587

Warsaw Opera, 721
Warsaw Philharmonic, 564
Wartime Sketchbook (Walton), 787
Washington, Booker T., 173
Washington Camerata, 264
Washington, Denzel, 284
Washington, George, 373
Washington's Birthday (Ives), 374, 375
Wasps, The (Vaughan Williams), 749
Wassenaer, Unico Wilhelm van, 792
Water Music (Handel), 318, 321, 328
Waterways (Takemitsu), 723
Watkinson, Carolyn, 317, 332, 770
Watson, Janice, 54
Watt, Harry, 372
Watts, Helen, 747
Waxman, Franz, 102, 347, 575, 608, 614, 793, 794
Weary Wind of the West (Elgar), 242
Weber, Carl Maria von, 186, 343, 351, 641, 790, 794, 795
Webern, Anton, 81, 327, 630, 634, 705–707, 797
Wedgwood Blue (Ketèlbey), 390
Weill, Kurt, 517, 798
Weinberger, Jaromir, 131, 400, 799
Weiner, Leo, 416
Weingartner, Felix, 89, 191, 523, 735
Weinstock, Herbert, 164
Weisberg, Arthur, 633–634
Weiss, Adolf, 153
Weiss, Joseph, 417
Welitsch, Ljuba, 209
Welk, Lawrence, 659
Well-Tempered Clavier (Bach), 35, 36, 509
Weller, Walter, 56
Wellington, Arthur Wellesley, First Duke of, 56, 61, 74
Wellington's Victory (Beethoven), 56, 74
Wells, H.G., 101
Welles Raises Kane (Herrmann), 346–347
Wendt, Johann Nepomuk, 489
Werther (Massenet), 446
Wesendonck Lieder (Wagner), 774
Wesendonck, Mathilde, 780
West Side Story (Bernstein), 92, 95, 96
West, Timothy, 543
Westerberg, Stig, 402, 403, 598, 683

Westi, Kurt, 511, 648, 649
Westminster Cathedral
  Choir, 763
Wetton, Hillary Devan, 101, 102
Wharton, Edith, 161
*When lilacs last in the dooryard
  bloom'd* (Hindemith),
  351–352
*Where Does the Unuttered Music
  Go?* (Walton), 784
Where the Rainbow Ends
  (Quilter), 561
Where The Wild Things Are
  (Knussen), 391
White, Edward, 800
White Peacock, The (Griffes),
  305, 727
White, Willard, 810
White Witch Doctor
  (Herrmann), 346
Whitman, Walt, 201, 321, 323,
  352
Whitney, Robert, 325
Whittier, John Greenleaf, 160,
  426, 522
Why Patterns? (Feldman), 255
Wickham, Edward, 516
Widerberg, Bo, 479
Widor, Charles Marie, 764, 800
Widow's Party, The
  (Grainger), 297
Wieniawski, Henryk, 521, 621,
  765, 801
Wiget, Ueli, 412–413
Wiggins Fernandez,
  Wilhelminia, 158
Wild Bull, The (Subotnick), 715
Wild, Earl, 206, 563
Wilde, Oscar, 411
Wilder, Alec, 802
Wilder, Thornton, 176
Wildner, Johannes, 475, 482
Wilhelm II, 702
Willan, Healey, 802
Willcocks, Sir David, 135,
  332, 745
William Byrd Suite (Jacob),
  359, 375
William Tell (Rossini), 453, 604,
  606, 607, 668
*William Wallace, Scottish Hero,
  Freedom-fighter, Beheaded and
  Dismembered by the English*
  (Wallace), 783
Williams, Clifton, 359

Williams, Grace, 803
Williams, John (composer),
  394, 803
Williams, John (guitarist), 34,
  419, 533, 595, 766
Williams, William Carlos, 324
Wilson, Ransom, 579
Wimborne, Lady Alice, 788
Windgassen, Wolfgang, 778
Windsor, Kathleen, 575
Wingfield, Paul, 382
Winter Dreams (Symphony
  No. 1) (Tchaikovsky), 735
Winter's Past, The (Barlow), 802
Winter's Tale, The
  (Humperdinck), 367
Winterreise (Schubert), 261, 642,
  647, 648
Wirén, Dag, 402, 804
Wise, Robert, 95
Wise Virgins, The (Walton), 788
Wislocki, Stanislaw, 564
Wittgenstein, Paul, 140, 376,
  577, 701
Wixell, Ingvar, 683
Wolf-Ferrari, Ermanno, 806
Wolf, Hugo, 123–124, 253, 303,
  356, 508, 529, 627, 653, 805
Women's Voices (Rorem), 599
Wood Dove, The (Dvořák),
  232, 631
Wood, Haydn, 172
Wood, Henry, 170, 208, 561,
  748, 784
Wood, Natalie, 95
Wooden Prince, The (Bartók), 49
Woodland Sketches
  (MacDowell), 152
Woodprints (Hovhaness), 364
Wordsworth, Barry, 91, 92, 101,
  265, 337, 338, 489, 490, 501,
  806, 807
Wordsworth, William (com-
  poser), 806
Wordsworth, William (poet),
  260, 270
Workman, C.H., 367
Worthington, Harvey, 152
Wozzeck (Berg), 81, 262, 379
Wright, James, 323
Wunder der Heliane, Das
  (Korngold), 396–397
Wunderlich, Fritz, 58, 59, 331,
  626, 643, 696
Wuorinen, Charles, 705

Wussow, Klaus-Jürgen, 57–58
Wuthering Heights
  (Herrmann), 510
Württemberg Chamber
  Orchestra, 465, 560
Wyler, William, 176, 272
Wylie, Philip, 762

Xenakis, Iannis, 715
Xerxes (Handel), 317
Xue Wei, 696

Y a des arbres (Hahn), 310
Yeats, William Butler, 376
Yevtushenko, Yevgeny, 668
York, John, 372
Young Apollo (Britten), 140
*Young Person's Guide to the
  Orchestra* (Britten), 143, 170,
  275, 545
Youth Symphony
  (Rachmaninoff), 562
Ysaÿe, Eugène, 24, 208, 409, 808

Zadok the Priest
  (Handel), 315
Zagrosek, Lothar, 131, 637
Zamfir, 292
Zamkochian, Berj, 619
Zandonai, Riccardo, 169, 808
Zanuck, Darryl F., 6
Zaporozhy Cossacks
  (Glière), 287
Zappa, Frank, 743
Zarewitsch, Der (Léhar), 408
Zedda, Alberto, 601, 607
Zeffirelli, Franco, 45, 608
Zehn Mädchen und kein Mann:
  Overture (Suppé), 719
Zeitlin, Zvi, 77
Zelenka, Jan Dismas, 809
Zemlinsky, Alexander von,
  308, 810
Zhdanov, Andrei, 390, 547
Ziegler, Robert, 307
Zigeunerlieder (Brahms), 125
Zigeunerweisen (Sarasate), 621
Zimerman, Krystian, 122, 166,
  168, 193, 301, 414
Zinman, David, 43, 291, 394,
  473, 609, 741
Zorina, Vera, 462, 712
Zukerman, Pinchas, 79, 122, 765
Zukovsky, Michele, 442
Zwillich, Ellen Taaffe, 406, 782